The McGraw-Hill
ENCYCLOPEDIA OF
WORLD BIOGRAPHY

Prado
Seymour

9

AN INTERNATIONAL
REFERENCE WORK
IN TWELVE VOLUMES
INCLUDING AN INDEX

McGRAW-HILL BOOK COMPANY

NEW YORK / SAN FRANCISCO / ST. LOUIS
DUSSELDORF   NEW DELHI
JOHANNESBURG   PANAMA
KUALA LUMPUR   RIO DE JANEIRO
LONDON   SINGAPORE
MEXICO   SYDNEY
MONTREAL   TORONTO

The McGraw-Hill
ENCYCLOPEDIA OF
WORLD BIOGRAPHY

Prado
—————
Seymour   **9**

McGRAW-HILL ENCYCLOPEDIA OF WORLD BIOGRAPHY

Library of Congress Catalog Card Number: 70-37402

International Standard Book Number: 07-079633-5

The McGraw-Hill
ENCYCLOPEDIA OF
WORLD BIOGRAPHY

Prado
Seymour
9

Prado P Pythagoras

PRADO / By C. Norman Guice

The aristocratic Peruvian political leader Manuel Prado Ugarteche (1889–1967) was twice president, and although elected by conservative and centrist groups, he attempted to reduce the tensions within his nation by incorporating more popular elements.

Manuel Prado. (Bibliothèque Nationale, Paris)

Manuel Prado (pronounced prä′thō) was born in Lima on April 21, 1889. His father, Gen. Mariano Ignacio Prado, was president of Peru for two short periods in the latter half of the 19th century. Manuel Prado graduated from the National School of Engineering in 1915. In 1918 he married Enriqueta Garland, and a son and daughter were born; after 40 years the marriage was annulled, amid popular outcry, and he then married Clorinda Málaga.

After getting his engineering degree, Prado became involved in the management of his family's properties, developing as his speciality the direction of the family banking interests. He also found time for other undertakings: between 1915 and 1919 he taught mathematics at San Marcos and was, in that same period, the editor of the university's *Science Review*.

Prado also initiated his political career in those years, becoming a member of the Lima Municipal Council in 1915. He then became a member of the Peruvian Congress in 1919 and, even though he had not made himself particularly notable, was forced into exile in 1921 by the dictator-president Augusto Bernardino Leguía. Prado shared that fate with most of the reformist-minded Peruvians of his day, though he himself was hardly an enthusiast for reform. He remained in exile until 1932 and did not resume his political career until 1939.

First Term

When Manuel Prado was elected president in 1939, he had apparently been chosen because of his moderation; he did, in fact, bring a considerable degree of political peace to his nation through his attempts to smooth over divisions and to reduce tensions. He had, it was rumored, reached a secret understanding with the left-wing non-Marxist APRA (Alianza Popular Revolucionaria Americana) before the election, committing himself to the legalization of the party. He did not, in fact, grant the party a legal status, but he did reduce the pressures upon it.

Although no serious attacks were made during Prado's first administration upon the fundamental problems of Peru, he became a popular president. He also managed to stay in office for his full term, something no other civilian president had done since 1914. His administration was able to capitalize upon the defeat of an Ecuadorian force in a border war in 1942, and the diplomatic settlement gave Peru title to vast areas of Amazon territories.

In 1945 Prado cooperated with a newly emerged political force, the National Democratic Front, which represented moderates, including some elements within the APRA itself. The coalition's candidate, José Luis Bustamante y Rivero, was elected as Prado's successor; but soon there was a renewal of violence at the same time that there was a virtual stalemate in government. In October 1948 the army, led by Gen. Manuel A. Odría, deposed Bustamente, outlawed the APRA once again, and established a government which lasted until 1956.

By 1956 a change seemed to be indicated: the era of prosperity under Odría had come to an end, and with it had come the collapse of the public works projects. Also at an end was the political truce that had come into existence. To ward off the threatened renewal of violence, a patchwork coalition of moderate and conservative elements persuaded Manuel Prado to accept the presidency. He took office once again in July 1956.

Second Term

Prado had received the support of the APRA, as well as that of Odría, largely because of the threat of a new reform group, the National Front of Democratic Youth, led by Fernando Belaúnde Terry.

The years of Prado's second administration were ones of crisis. The decline in Odría's last years threatened to become an economic collapse. Government revenues fell off, and, increasingly, the effects of a government-tolerated inflation were felt. Although the Prado regime had the support of a majority, including the APRA, whose adherents were named to Cabinet posts, it still had great difficulty in governing. Some of its economic problems were solved when, in 1959, Pedro Beltrán, a leading spokesman for conservative economic doctrines, was persuaded to accept the premiership and allowed to design new fiscal policies.

These policies, however, brought great unpopularity to the government since they included the elimination of subsidies on foods, gasoline, and many other necessities, as well as the adoption of various belt-tightening reductions in public expenditures. Nationalist elements were infuriated by the allegedly greater profits of foreign-owned oil companies; conservatives were embittered by the apparent dependence of the Prado government upon the APRA and the rumored "deal" that would allow the APRA to capture the coming elections. To the clamor of these two groups was added that of the reformers, represented by Belaúnde.

The election was held in early June 1962, but none of the three principal candidates (Odría, Haya de la Torre, and Belaúnde) managed to get the majority needed. When it was reported that an agreement between the followers of Odría and the APRA had been reached, elements of the army moved upon the presidential palace in the early hours of July 18 and replaced Prado with a three-man junta representing the military services. Prado was soon allowed to go into exile and remained in Paris until his death on Aug. 15, 1967.

Further Reading

Manuel Prado is listed in the Latin America study guide (IV, M, 1, b). Víctor Raúl HAYA was the founder of the APRA. Another Peruvian president was Augusto Bernardino LEGUÍA.

There is no biography of Prado in English. For an adequate account of Peru during the years of his political prominence see Frederick B. Pike, *The Modern History of Peru* (1967).

✳   ✳   ✳

PRAETORIUS / By Edward R. Lerner

The German composer and theorist Michael Praetorius (ca. 1571–1621) was a devout Lutheran who believed that music was the "handmaiden of theology." He composed a comprehensive musical repertory for the Evangelical Church.

Born in Creuzburg (Thuringia), Michael Praetorius (pronounced prē-tō′rē-ŏŏs) was raised in Torgau, a small town famous for its Lutheran school. He studied at the University of Frankfurt an der Oder, and for part of the time he was organist of the university church. In 1595 he entered the service of Heinrich Julius, Duke of Brunswick, at the courts of Gröningen and Wolfenbüttel. At first installed as organist and subsequently advanced to music director (1604), Praetorius composed

Michael Praetorius, a print of the composer in his thirty-fifth year. (Bildarchiv)

music for all court activities until the duke's death in 1613.

During the next 7 years Praetorius had no fixed post but was employed intermittently by several north German courts (Magdeburg, Kassel, Halle, Dresden) as musical consultant and director of musical festivities. In 1620 he was recalled to Wolfenbüttel; he died the following year.

Praetorius's voluminous output only partly reveals his overall plan for a complete corpus of secular and sacred music for all occasions. Of his secular works only one volume of dances, *Terpsichore* (volume 5 of his projected *Musa Aonia*), has come down to us. Thousands of sacred pieces are extant, most constructed on Lutheran hymn texts and tunes known as chorales. The contents of his 9-volume *Musae Sioniae* (1605–1610) range from simple *bicinia*, or two-part pieces, to enormous polychoral works for as many as 12 voices.

Baroque pieces with basso continuo, concertizing instruments, and separate choirs for soloists and chorus are first noted in Praetorius's late publications *Polyhymnia caduceatrix* (1619), *Polyhymnia exercitatrix* (1620), and *Puericinium* (1621). These mature compositions underscore his importance in transmitting Italian concerted music to Germany. Although these works are modeled on examples by Giovanni Gabrieli and Claudio Monteverdi, Praetorius, ever bound to the German chorale, rarely employed the affective style favored by the Italian innovators.

As a pendant to his music, and in part to explain its performance, Praetorius wrote a three-volume treatise, *Syntagma musicum* (1615–1620), which deals with three subjects: the history of ancient sacred and secular music, the nature and construction of musical instruments, and the performance practices of his time. Especially valuable are his definitions and explanations of early-17th-century terms and practices. In the second volume, *De organographia*, he discusses the history and construction of musical instruments. Unparalleled for its time is the appendix to this volume, the *Theatrum instrumentorum*, or pictorial atlas of instruments.

Further Reading

Michael Praetorius is listed in the Music study guide (I, C, 3; I, D, 4). His late works were influenced by Giovanni GABRIELI and Claudio MONTEVERDI. Praetorius was the most important organizer of Protestant church music after Johann WALTER.

Praetorius's work is discussed in Manfred F. Bukofzer, *Music in the Baroque Era* (1947), and in the *New Oxford History of Music*, vol. 4 (1968). The background of the baroque musical style is treated in Paul Henry Lang, *Music in Western Civilization* (1941).

PRANDTAUER / By Edward A. Maser

The Austrian baroque architect Jakob Prandtauer (1660–1726) is famed chiefly for his monastic and religious buildings, notably the abbey and church of Melk.

Jakob Prandtauer (pronounced pränt′ou-ər), born in mid-July 1660 in Stanz in the Tirol, was the son of a master mason, and he too learned the trade. He also studied sculpture and architecture, however, for by the time he was 19 he was working as a sculptor in Sankt Pölten, a city in Lower Austria not far from Vienna. By 1700 he was a master builder (*Baumeister*), working on many projects in Sankt Pölten.

From 1701 until his death Prandtauer worked for the monastery of Melk on the Danube in Lower Austria, totally rebuilding the church and all the buildings of the huge monastic complex, one of the largest of its kind. Like his great contemporaries Johann Bernhard Fischer von Erlach and Johann Lucas von Hildebrandt, Prandtauer turned to Italianate forms for his inspiration, but, as did the others, he also introduced highly personal notes into his architecture. The huge church at Melk, whose towers dominate the landscape over the Danube Valley, is embedded into the structure of the whole monastery by two wings projecting forward on either side and bound together with a curved terrace; the whole ensemble juts up out of the rock over the river. Here he created one of the most thrilling examples of baroque architecture. The stately interior, a harmony of dark-red marble and gilded ornament with golden-toned frescoes by Johann Michael

Rottmayr, is reminiscent of Roman baroque examples, although Prandtauer could only have known them through engravings.

While Melk remains his most famous creation, Prandtauer also built the beautiful pilgrimage church on the Sonntagberg (1706–1728) and the monastery at Garsten near Steyr (1703–1708), and he reconstructed the monastery of Sankt Florian near Linz, taking over the works from Carlantonio Carlone. There he built the grand staircase (1706–1714) and the great hall (Marmorsaal; 1718–1724). From 1708 on he was also in charge of works at Kremsmünster, and from 1720 at Herzogenburg, both monasteries. In every case, as was usually the practice during the period, Prandtauer not only was the architect but was actually in charge of all aspects of the construction and of the exterior and interior decoration of a project, his early training as a mason and a sculptor standing him in good stead in all these enterprises.

Prandtauer is often cited as an example of the local architect who, without training in Italy, nevertheless was able to create great buildings in the baroque style, displaying a native inventiveness and imagination which brought his work to a level of quality equal to that of Fischer von Erlach and Hildebrandt, his more formally trained contemporaries.

When Prandtauer died on Sept. 16, 1726, at Sankt Pölten, most of his projects were still unfinished. They were completed by his pupil, assistant, and cousin Joseph

Mungenast, whose famous tower at Dürnstein (1721–1725) is thought to have been largely inspired by his master.

Further Reading

Jakob Prandtauer is listed in the Art study guide (III, F, 3, d). With Johann Bernhard FISCHER VON ERLACH and Johann Lucas von HILDEBRANDT, he forms the triad of architects who made Austrian baroque architecture important. The Austrian painter Johann Michael ROTT-MAYR executed frescoes for the monastery of Melk.

Information on Prandtauer can be found in John Bourke, *Baroque Churches of Central Europe* (1958; 2d ed. 1962); Nicholas Powell, *From Baroque to Rococo* (1959); and Eberhard Hempel, *Baroque Art and Architecture in Central Europe* (1965).

✳   ✳   ✳

PRASAD / By Leonard A. Gordon

Rajendra Prasad (1884–1963) was an Indian nationalist and first president of the Republic of India. He was an important leader of the Indian National Congress and a close coworker of Gandhi.

Rajendra Prasad (pronounced pră-säd′) was born in Saran District, Bihar State, eastern India, on Dec. 3, 1884, into the Kayastha, or scribe, caste. A devout Hindu, he received his early education in Bihar and then attended Presidency College, Calcutta. The Swadeshi movement and particularly the Dawn Society influenced him to become a nationalist. He continued his education, earned advanced degrees in law, and practiced law in Calcutta and then in Patna.

When Mohandas Gandhi arrived in Bihar in 1917 to assist the peasants in Champaran, Prasad soon joined in this activity, becoming a lifelong disciple of Gandhi. Following Gandhi's lead, Prasad joined the Indian National Congress and participated in the noncooperation campaigns of 1919 and 1921–1922. Forsaking his law practice almost entirely, he became principal of the National College in Bihar, edited nationalist papers, and mobilized peasant support for the movement. During the internal split in the Congress during the 1920s, he was a spokesman for the No-Changer group, which wholeheartedly supported Gandhi's constructive program, particularly the production of indigenous cloth (or khadi) by hand spinning.

In the 1930s Prasad, along with Vallabhbhai Patel and others, led the Gandhian Old Guard, which usually dominated the Congress organization. They opposed the Congress Socialists. Prasad was Congress president in 1934 and at Gandhi's request again served as president after the serious internal struggle of 1939. Prasad was a member of the Congress Parliamentary Board, which directed the election campaign of 1936–1937. While spending most of World War II in prison, he wrote his

The monastery at Melk, Austria, designed by Jakob Prandtauer. The architect worked on it from 1701 until his death. (Library of Congress)

Rajendra Prasad (left) with the Chinese foreign minister Chou En-lai. (Popperfoto)

Autobiography in Hindi (trans. 1958) and a book opposing Moslem proposals for the partition of India, *India Divided* (1946).

After serving as minister for food and agriculture in the interim government, Prasad became president of the Constituent Assembly that eventually completed the constitution of the Republic of India in 1949. He was chosen interim president of his country and was elected the first president in May 1952. Five years later he was reelected for a second term. During his presidency, he toured India and many countries of Asia. In his speeches he stressed national and communal unity, the need for a national language, the scarcity of food and the ways to increase food production, and the achievements of Indian culture. He often drew upon the words and achievements of his mentor, Gandhi, and gave importance to the need for more extensive educational programs, particularly the implementation of Gandhi's basic education scheme. The difficulties of the postindependence years were eased by the close cooperation between President Prasad and Prime Minister Jawaharlal Nehru. Prasad died on Feb. 28, 1963, in Patna.

Further Reading

Rajendra Prasad is listed in the Asia study guide (II, A, 6, c). Other leaders prominent in India's quest for independence were Vallabhbhai PATEL, Jawaharlal NEHRU, and Mohandas GANDHI.

For more detailed information on Prasad the reader should consult Prasad's own massive *Autobiography* (1957; trans. 1958). The most useful biography is Kewal L. Panjabi, *Rajendra Prasad: First President of India* (1960).

PRAXITELES / By Jerome J. Pollitt

Praxiteles (active ca. 370–330 B.C.) was one of the leading Greek sculptors of the 4th century B.C. His style, refined and graceful, greatly influenced the art of his own time and the succeeding epochs.

Praxiteles (pronounced prăk-sĭt′əl-ēz) was probably the son of Kephisodotos, an Athenian sculptor, since he named one of his own sons Kephisodotos, and the same name ran in families in

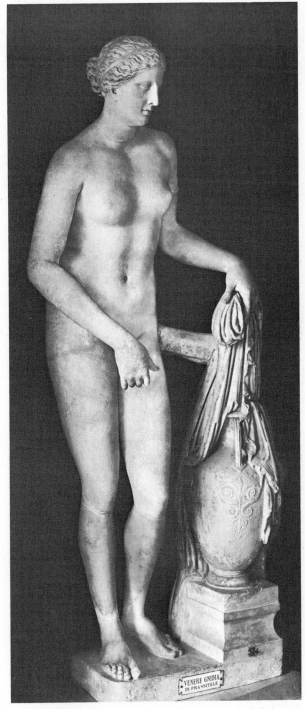

Aphrodite (Venus) of Knidos, a Roman copy of the original marble statue by Praxiteles. (Vatican Museums, Rome)

alternate generations. Pliny the Elder, in his *Naturalis historia*, places Praxiteles in the 104th Olympiad, or 364–361 B.C., and the base of a portrait statue from Leuktra bearing an inscription stating that Praxiteles the Athenian made it dates from about 330 B.C. These are the only definite dates we have regarding him.

At the beginning of the 4th century B.C. Athenian civilization had undergone profound changes. The disillusionment with civic values caused by the Peloponnesian War had turned artistic taste away from the idealism of Phidias's art toward a more humanized, personal view of the world and the gods. Praxiteles brought the gods down to a human level; he made them less majestic but gave them a consummate grace.

The marble *Hermes Holding the Infant Dionysos* was found in 1877 in the Heraion at Olympia, where Pausanias, who ascribes it to Praxiteles, had seen it in the 2d century A.D. Whether it is a Greek original, a Greek copy, or a good Roman copy, the statue is one of the finest ancient works preserved and shows the salient characteristics of the sculptor's style. Praxiteles softened the precisely articulated rendering of musculature of the previous century into a softer, fluid harmony of subtly modulated surfaces; and for the architectonically balanced composition of Polykleitos he substituted a languid S-curve. This curve, often called the "Praxitelean curve," is a hallmark of his sculpture.

In antiquity the most famous work by Praxiteles was the marble *Aphrodite (Venus) of Knidos*. His openly sensuous treatment of the nude female form was a new feature in Greek art and created an ideal type that endured until the end of antiquity. Pliny tells us that this work made the city of Knidos famous and that it was "the finest statue not only by Praxiteles but in the whole world." Athenaios adds that Phryne, Praxiteles's mistress, was the model. There are a number of Roman copies of the statue, and it is reproduced on Roman coins from Knidos.

According to Pausanias, the base of Praxiteles's statue *Leto and Her Children* at Mantinea was decorated with a scene depicting Apollo, Marsyas, and the Muses. Three slabs from the base were found in 1877 at Mantinea: two show three Muses each, lovely draped figures, and the third depicts Marsyas playing the flute and Apollo with his Phrygian slave. The base may have been executed by one of Praxiteles's students, working from the master's designs.

The *Apollo Sauroktonos* ("lizard slayer") by Praxiteles is known from Pliny's description of it, fairly accurate Roman copies in both marble and bronze (Pliny lists it with the sculptor's bronze works), and the Roman coins from Philippopolis in Thrace and Nikopolis on the Danube. Apollo is represented as a boy leaning against a tree trunk waiting to kill a lizard with an arrow. The sinuous figure of the dreamy god perhaps illustrates better than any other work by Praxiteles how his vision of the gods differed from the emotionally neutral images of his 5th-century predecessors.

Ancient authors mention many other works by Praxiteles, and almost all have been connected with anony-

Praxiteles's Hermes Holding the Infant Dionysos, *a marble statue in the Archeological Museum, Olympia, Greece. (Alinari)*

mous originals or copies in various museums. These include the famous *Eros*, which Pausanias says Phryne dedicated in her native city, Thespiai; a young satyr pouring wine, a bronze statue seen by Pausanias in the Street of the Tripods in Athens; the cult image of *Artemis Brauronia* on the Acropolis in Athens; and an image of Eubouleus, the swineherd of Eleusinian myth, at Eleusis.

Praxiteles's two sons, Kephisodotos and Timarchos, worked in the tradition of their father. The Praxitelean school profoundly influenced Hellenistic sculpture in its choice of themes and their formal realization. The soft fusion of planes and delicate expression of his style can be seen in particular in early Hellenistic sculpture and minor arts, for example, the Tanagra terra-cotta figurines.

Further Reading

Praxiteles is listed in the Art study guide (I, E, 4, a). The leading sculptors of the preceding century were PHIDIAS and POLYKLEITOS.

The best work is in Italian: G. E. Rizzo, *Prassitele* (1932). Praxiteles is discussed in all general surveys of ancient Greek sculpture, among the finest of which is Gisela M. A. Richter, *The Sculpture and Sculptors of the Greeks* (4th ed. 1970).

*   *   *

PREGL / By Hans Lieb

The Austrian physiologist and medical chemist Fritz Pregl (1869–1930) developed the methods of quantitative organic microanalysis.

Fritz Pregl. (Courtesy of Hans Lieb)

F ritz Pregl (pronounced prā′gəl) was born on Sept. 3, 1869, in Laibach, now Ljubljana in Yugoslavia, but then a provincial capital in the Austro-Hungarian Empire. After the death of his father, a bank official, he moved in 1887 with his mother to Graz, the seat of a university. There he studied medicine and obtained his medical degree in 1894.

As a student, Pregl had been interested in physiology and upon graduation became a teaching assistant in the Physiological Institute of the university. He remained in this field as he rose on the academic ladder to attain the rank of associate professor in 1904. However, he had meanwhile also been attracted to, and become quite adept in, organic chemical laboratory research, and indeed his publications from that period reveal a strong predilection for the chemical aspects of physiology as well as for the methodological. This partial switch in his research interests became complete when, after taking a long leave of absence, he transferred his activities to the Institute of Medical Chemistry in Graz. In 1910 Pregl was called to the University of Innsbruck as full professor and head of the Institute of Medical Chemistry, only to return 3 years later in the same capacity to Graz, where he remained until his death on Dec. 13, 1930.

Pregl's great contribution to chemistry and medical science was the creation, in the years 1910–1917, of the methods of quantitative organic microanalysis. This made it possible to determine quantitatively the elements and some functional groups in organic compounds in samples weighing far less (3–5 milligrams) than was required in the procedures previously in use (100–200 milligrams).

Pregl's micromethods quickly became an invaluable tool to the organic chemist and a truly indispensable one to the biochemist. The micromethods greatly aided and accelerated the elucidation of the chemical structure of

many biologically active substances of natural origin, such as hormones and vitamins, and were generally instrumental in the solution of a host of important biochemical problems. Of the many scientific honors bestowed on Pregl in recognition of this achievement, the most outstanding was the Nobel Prize for chemistry in 1923.

Pregl was an inspiring teacher who knew how to flavor his lectures with instructive experiments as well as with humor. In the 1920s chemists from all over the world flocked to his laboratory to receive instruction in microanalysis, often by him personally, in courses given practically free of charge.

Further Reading

Fritz Pregl is listed in the Science study guide (VII, D, 2). He studied under the famous German chemist Emil FISCHER.

A good profile of Pregl is in Eduard Farber, ed., *Great Chemists* (1961). There are also short biographies in Aaron J. Ihde, *The Development of Modern Chemistry* (1964), and Nobel Foundation, *Chemistry: Including Presentation Speeches and Laureates' Biographies*, vol. 2 (1966).

*   *   *

PREMCHAND / By Robert O. Swan

The Indian novelist and short-story writer
Premchand (1880–1936) was the first major
novelist in Hindi and Urdu. His writings
describe in realistic detail the political and
social struggles in India of the early 20th
century.

Premchand (pronounced prĕm-chänd′), whose
real name was Dhanpatrai Srivastava, was born in
the small village of Lamhi a few miles from
Benares. His immediate forebears were village account-
ants in Lamhi. His intimate acquaintance with village life
began here and continued when, as a schoolteacher and
subdeputy inspector of schools, he traveled extensively
for 21 years through Uttar Pradesh State.

Premchand's early writing was all done in Urdu, but
from 1915 he found that writing Hindi was more profitable. Hindi, using the Sanskrit-based script and borrowing heavily from Sanskrit vocabulary, was strongly promoted by the Hindu reform group called the Arya Samaj,
and within a few years Hindi publications numerically
outstripped those written in Urdu.

Premchand's early work in Urdu reveals the strong influence of Persian literature, particularly in the short stories. These were usually romantic love stories in which,
the course of love not being smooth, various unusual devices are used to bring lovers together again. In these
romantic stories and novels, however, also appear evi-
dences of patriotic fervor and descriptions of Indian and
foreign heroes who died bravely for their countries.
Premchand's first collection of short stories, *Soz-e-
Vatan*, brought him to the attention of the government.
The British collector of Hamirpur District called them
seditious and ordered that all copies be burned and that
the author submit future writing for inspection. Fortunately, a few copies survived, and Premchand, in order
to evade censorship, changed his name from Dhanpatrai
to Premchand.

In 1920 Premchand resigned from a government high
school and became a staunch supporter of Mohandas
Gandhi, whose influence strongly marked Premchand's
work from 1920 to 1932. With realistic settings and
events, Premchand contrived idealistic endings for his
stories. His characters change from pro-British to pro-
Indian or from villainous landlord to Gandhi-like social
servant in midstream; the frequent conversions tend to
make the stories repetitious and the characters interesting only up to the point of conversion.

Premchand's last and greatest novel, *Godan*, and his
most famous story, *Kafan* (The Shroud), both deal with
village life. However, whatever the setting, his late work
shows a new mastery. The characters appear to have tak-
en over their own world. The claims of social, moral, and
political tenets are secondary to the claims of artistry.
Premchand died from a gastric ulcer. One son, Amrtrai,
was a noted Hindi writer, and the other, Sripatrai, a talented painter.

Further Reading

Premchand is listed in the Asia study guide (II, A, 8, b).
Another Indian who wrote about village life was R. K.
NARAYAN.

Premchand's novel *Godan* was translated by Gordon
C. Roadarmel as *Gift of a Cow* (1968). *The World of
Premchand*, translated by David Rubin (1969), brings
together some of the stories. A critical study of the short
stories that includes a biographical introduction is Robert
O. Swan, *Munshi Premchand of Lamhi Village* (1969).

Premchand. (*Information Service of India, New
York*)

PRENDERGAST / By Allen S. Weller

American painter Maurice Brazil Prendergast
(1859–1924) pioneered in introducing new
directions in American painting. He was the
only true American postimpressionist of his
generation.

Maurice Prendergast was born in St. John's, Newfoundland, on Oct. 10, 1859. When his father's
grocery business failed in 1861, the family
moved to Boston. He and his younger brother Charles

finished their formal education by the time each was 14. Maurice worked in a dry-goods store, lettered show cards, and began sketching landscapes and cattle. In 1886, he and his brother worked their way to England on a cattle boat; they may have gone to Paris as well. Returning to Boston, they worked at routine jobs in order to save $1,000 for a return to Europe. Maurice went to Paris in 1891 and studied with Jean Paul Laurens at the Académie Julian. He made rapid progress in 3 years, working from the model rather than from casts. He was fascinated with the life and movement in the parks, boulevards, and cafés.

When he returned to America in 1894, Prendergast was an accomplished watercolorist and had assimilated qualities from Édouard Manet, James McNeill Whistler, Edgar Degas, Henri de Toulouse-Lautrec, Pierre Bonnard, and Édouard Vuillard and from Japanese prints. He was the first American artist to appreciate and understand the importance of Paul Cézanne. Until 1905 the Prendergast brothers lived together in Winchester, Mass., their principal means of support being a frame-making shop. Maurice's work was included for the first time in a public exhibition at the Pennsylvania Academy of Fine Arts in 1896; there was a one-man show in Boston the next year, and from this time until his death his paintings appeared in many exhibitions.

In 1898 Prendergast went to Venice, where he created some of his most enchanting watercolors. Arthur B. Davies invited him to join with other artists in the famous exhibition of "The Eight" in 1908, organized as a protest against the conservative tendencies of the National Academy of Design. Prendergast was in France again in 1909 and in Italy in 1911. The influence of Paul Signac is perhaps to be observed from this period.

The seven watercolors that were included in the cele-

Maurice Prendergast. (Courtesy Oliver Baker Associates, Dictionary of American Portraits, *Dover)*

brated Armory Show in 1913 revealed Prendergast as a major figure in American painting, probably the greatest of his generation. He was perhaps the first to deliberately abandon a primarily representational approach to art and to let the subject matter be dominated by purely artistic means.

Prendergast went to Europe for the last time in 1914. On his return he and his brother (also a painter) moved to New York, where Maurice spent his last decade working in a studio in Washington Square. During summers in New England, he painted in oil and watercolor brightly clad figures on beaches and in parks, often using a kind of pointillism which gives his work a tapestrylike quality, sometimes with almost expressionistic intensity, but relying even more on pure color, loosely applied in abrupt areas, to suggest form, movement, and texture. There is a combination of wistfulness and gaiety, a sense of elegance and innocence in his paintings. He characteristically introduces large numbers of figures; a sense of individuality is avoided, but there is always warmth and charm.

Prendergast was increasingly isolated in his later years because of deafness. He died in New York on Feb. 1, 1924.

Further Reading

Maurice Prendergast is listed in the Art study guide (IV, E, 1). Another member of "The Eight," Arthur B. DAVIES,

Carnival, a watercolor by Prendergast. (Courtesy, Museum of Fine Arts, Boston)

played an important role in promoting the modern movement in art.

Prendergast's *Sketches, 1899* was published in facsimile (1960). An excellent critical and biographical study, with numerous reproductions in color, is Hedley Howell Rhys, *Maurice Prendergast, 1859–1924* (1960). Margaret Breuning, *Maurice Prendergast* (1931), is a brief, useful picture book. Valuable material is in the comprehensive exhibition catalogs from retrospective shows at the Whitney Museum of American Art, New York, *Maurice Prendergast Memorial Exhibition* (1934), and the Phillips Academy, Addison Gallery, Andover, Mass., *The Prendergasts* (1938).

PRESCOTT / By Michael Kraus

William Hickling Prescott (1796–1859) was one of the greatest American historians. The theme that absorbed him for over 30 years was the rise and decline of the Spanish Empire.

William Hickling Prescott was born in Salem, Mass., on May 4, 1796. His father, Judge William Prescott, was a prominent Federalist. William graduated from Harvard in 1814; at college he lost sight in his left eye during a dining-hall fracas. Despite this disaster and illness (which plagued him all his life), he determined to follow a literary career. He began to contribute to the *North American Review*, the leading magazine in the country, in 1821. A former schoolmate and lifelong friend, George Ticknor, urged Prescott to devote himself to Spanish studies. Thus began a career which resulted in histories that still enchant.

Other scholars had been drawn to Spain's history before Prescott entered the field in 1826, but he gave it an unmatched sheen. At Christmas, 1837, his *Ferdinand and Isabella* (3 vols.) was published; it still holds its own as the classic of this period. He then turned to Spain's conquest of Mexico. In *The Conquest of Mexico* (3 vols., 1843) he narrated the exploits of Hernán Cortés in words never surpassed. The story, thought Prescott, was "an epic in prose, a romance of chivalry." The work was his masterpiece; its material was so drenched in an air of romanticism that it seemed difficult to treat it as sober history. But he carefully sought to distinguish fact from fiction. He had many heroes and heroines but few villains. "One likes a noble character for his canvas," he said.

Prescott next published *A History of the Conquest of Peru* (2 vols., 1847). It included important material on the civilization of the Incas. Some scholars still consider it the standard authority.

The last installment of Prescott's project was *A History of the Reign of Philip the Second* (3 vols., 1855–1858). Although he tried to be impartial, he could not overcome his bias in favor of Protestant Christianity. To him the fall

William Hickling Prescott, a daguerreotype made about 1845 by Southworth and Hawes. (The Metropolitan Museum of Art, Gift of I. N. Phelps Stokes, Edward S. Hawes, Alice Mary Hawes, Marion Augusta Hawes, 1937)

of the Aztecs was unregretted, for their civilization was inferior to that of their conquerors.

Critics dislike the excessive space Prescott gave to military affairs. But he believed his function as historian was storytelling, narrating the deeds of the chevalier, the swashbuckler, the statesman. His work, based on sound scholarship and clothed in gifted language, still entrances readers more than a century after his death in Boston on Jan. 28, 1859.

Further Reading

William Hickling Prescott is listed in the Social Sciences study guide (VI, A, 3) and the Literature study guide (I, C, 1, e). Washington IRVING was planning a history of the conquest of Mexico, but he gave up the project in 1837 when he learned Prescott was undertaking the task.

C. Harvey Gardiner edited Prescott's histories and also materials relating to Prescott in *Literary Memoranda* (2 vols., 1961) and *Papers* (1964). Roger Wolcott, ed., *The Correspondence of William Hickling Prescott, 1833–1847* (1925), provides indispensable details. The standard biography is by Prescott's friend George Ticknor, *Life of William Hickling Prescott* (1864). A modern biography is C. Harvey Gardiner, *William Hickling Prescott: A Biography* (1969). Harry T. Peck, *William Hickling Prescott* (1905), gives important analyses of

Prescott's works. William Charvat and Michael Kraus, *William Hickling Prescott* (1943), contains a biography, selections from Prescott's writings, a study of his attitudes toward history, his political ideas, and his literary style.

*   *   *

PRESTES / By Robert J. Alexander

Luiz Carlos Prestes (born 1898) was an almost mythical Brazilian guerrilla-war leader in the 1920s. He became leader of the Brazilian Communist party in the 1930s and continued in that position for almost 40 years.

Luiz Carlos Prestes (pronounced prĕ′stĭsh) first gained national prominence in 1924, when, as a young captain of engineers, he led a group of army mutineers in the state of Rio Grande do Sul against the government of President Arturo Bernardes. Hard-pressed by troops loyal to the government, Prestes led his men several hundred miles north to a juncture with another group of rebels, from the state of São Paulo, who had retreated to the area of the great Iguassú Falls on the Argentine border.

From Iguassú, the rebels began an epic march of 2 1/2 years through the interior of Brazil. They fought an almost classic guerrilla war against army and state police forces in a dozen states. Prestes was chief of staff of this rebel group, which became famous as the Prestes Column.

Exile and Travels

Soon after the rebels were finally driven into Bolivia, Prestes went to Buenos Aires, where he remained for several years. Until 1930 he remained titular head of the *Tenentes*, the former military rebels, and some civilians who had joined them to form a conspiratorial political movement.

In Buenos Aires, Prestes was courted by both Stalinist and Trotskyite Communists. Although he did not immediately join either, he did assume a much more radical position than the vague social nationalism of the Prestes Column. He opposed the revolution of October 1930—led by the former governor of Rio Grande do Sul, Getulio Vargas, and supported by the great majority of the *Tenentes*—on the grounds that it was "petty bourgeois."

In 1931 Prestes went to the Soviet Union, where he was employed on various engineering projects, became a Communist, and was elected to the Executive Committee of the Communist International. Early in 1935 Prestes returned to Brazil, where he was immediately elected to the Politburo of the Communist party. He was also named honorary president of the Alianca Nacional Libertadora (ANL), a broad left-wing opposition to President Vargas. Prestes and the Communists spoke in the name of the ANL without the authorization of its non-Communist leaders; and when the ANL was outlawed, Prestes led an attempted military insurrection in its name. When it failed, virtually all left-wing politicians were rounded up by the government. Prestes himself was captured a few weeks after the revolt, was reportedly badly tortured, and was finally sentenced to a long prison term. He remained in jail until May 1945, and his wife, a German Communist, was deported to Nazi Germany, where she died in a concentration camp.

National Politics

After Vargas had been forced to agree to end his dictatorship and had called elections for December 1945, he proclaimed a general political amnesty. It was widely rumored that before Prestes's release under this amnesty an agreement had been reached between him and Vargas. In any case, upon his release Prestes called on the Communists to support maintenance of Vargas in office until a new constitution had been written. In turn, Vargas legalized the Communist party and gave the Communists complete freedom in the labor movement.

In spite of efforts by Vargas, his supporters, and the Communists to keep him in power, he was ousted late in October 1945. In the election 6 weeks later, the Communists ran as presidential candidate Yeddo Fiuza, a former Vargas official, and presented candidates for Congress. Prestes was elected senator, and the Communists also elected 15 deputies.

Luiz Carlos Prestes in 1958. (United Press International Photo)

Between 1945 and 1947 the Communists represented about 10 percent of the national electorate and gained extensive influence in organized labor. However, early in 1947 the Communist party was outlawed by the Supreme Electoral Tribunal, and in the following year Prestes and the Communist deputies lost their seats in Congress. Prestes went into hiding for the next 11 years.

During this period, Prestes was largely out of contact with the Communist rank and file and lower leadership. However, when a strong dissident movement against the Prestes "cult of the personality" arose in 1956, after Nikita Khrushchev's denunciation of Joseph Stalin at the Twentieth Congress of the Soviet Communist party, Prestes took the lead in purging the dissidents.

In the democratic atmosphere of the Juscelino Kubitschek administration, Prestes came out of hiding, went before a court, and purged the sedition charges pending against him. During the next 5 years, he traveled widely throughout the country in his capacity as secretary general of the Communist party. When the group who had run the party while he was in hiding tried to challenge Prestes's control, they were expelled in 1961 and established a rival pro-Chinese Communist party.

During the João Goulart administration (1961–1964), the Communists made considerable headway in organized labor and general politics. Prestes on several occasions appeared on the same platform with the President at political rallies.

However, with the overthrow of Goulart on April 1, 1964, Prestes again went into hiding, leaving behind a notebook with names and addresses of many of his associates which was captured by the police. Prestes remained secretary general of the Communist party, although his control was apparently contested by elements opposed to what they conceived to be his inept leadership. He remained the principal leader of the underground Communist party.

Further Reading

Luiz Carlos Prestes is listed in the Latin America study guide (IV, C, 1, b). Though forced into exile by Getulio VARGAS, Prestes was accepted during the administrations of presidents Juscelino KUBITSCHEK and João GOULART.

Useful material on Prestes's early career is in Robert M. Levine, *The Vargas Regime: The Critical Years, 1934–1938* (1970). His later career is covered in two studies by John W. F. Dulles, *Vargas of Brazil: A Political Biography* (1967) and *Unrest in Brazil: Political-Military Crises, 1955–1964* (1970). See also the excellent study by Thomas E. Skidmore, *Politics in Brazil, 1930–1964: An Experiment in Democracy* (1967).

* * *

PRETORIUS / By A. P. J. van Rensburg

Andries Pretorius (1798–1853) was a South African political leader and general and till his death the most prominent and colorful Afrikaner figure.

In November 1838 the Voortrekker leader Pieter Retief and his companions were murdered at the kraal of the Zulu chief Dingane, and afterward the Voortrekker laagers were massacred by Zulu warriors. The first efforts of both Boer and Briton to avenge these horrors met with dismal failure, leaving the Boer emigrants in a serious plight. At this stage Andries Pretorius (pronounced prĭ-tôr′ē-əs) was invited to become their leader and command a punitive expedition against Dingane.

Andries Pretorius was born on Nov. 27, 1798, at Graaff Reinet in the Cape Colony. It is unfortunate that only the scantiest details of his early life are available. He was taught by wandering teachers but in later life could express himself well in word and writing. A female admirer wrote of him as "a handsome, tall figure of between six and seven feet, upright, friendly, and captivating." The historian Theal said of him that "his knowledge and his opinions, as well as his virtues and his failings, were those of the seventeenth, not of the nineteenth century." He had his human share of temperamental imperfections and was often quick to anger, but he had no unreasoning obstinacy.

Farmer and Voortrekker Leader

Pretorius enters the historical scene in 1837 as a prosperous townsman at Graaff Reinet; he also owned farms in the district. He does not appear to have been consulted in the early projects of the border farmers, but he soon displayed a deep interest in the emigration movement. Before he finally joined the Voortrekkers in Natal, he paid a preliminary visit to the interior. He took part in the battle of Mosega, in which Mzilikazi and his Matabele (Ndebele) warriors were put to flight. Thereafter he purchased a farm near Port Natal and returned to Graaff Reinet only to sell his property. At this stage a deputation arrived from the stricken Voortrekkers in Natal and implored him to lead an expedition against Dingane. He accepted the invitation, hastened his departure, and reached the main laager in Natal on Nov. 22, 1838.

Setting out with a commando of 464 men, from the outset Pretorius insisted on the maintenance of proper discipline, which certainly had been lacking in previous cases. Though a man of decision, he never acted without calling a council of his officers.

On December 9 the Voortrekkers took the famous "Vow." It was the desire of Pretorius that the Voortrekkers make a collective promise to God that if He granted them victory they would celebrate the day of triumph, each year, as a Holy Sabbath to the glory of His name and that they would impress this duty upon their children.

Battle of Blood River

By December 15 the commando marched up the west bank of a tributary of the Buffalo named Income (Cattle River) by the Zulu but ever since known as Blood River. Under his inspired leadership his small force put to flight the vast Zulu army of more than 10,000 men in one of the most fateful battles ever fought in South Africa.

The rejoicing which greeted the commando on its return was dampened by the grim tidings that British troops had arrived at Port Natal to occupy the territory temporarily because "of the disturbed state of the native tribes" resulting from the "unwarranted occupation" of the interior by the Voortrekkers.

Republic of Natal

The Voortrekkers remained undaunted, ignored the British, and proceeded under Pretorius to establish their own republic on the land granted by Dingane. Assisted by regiments of Dingane's brother Mpande, Pretorius in 1840 succeeded in finally overthrowing Dingane. Meanwhile the British troops had also left, and the Voortrekkers had at last achieved the independence they had been looking for. Within 3 years, however, the British were back, this time to remain. Pretorius defeated them at Congella and besieged them for over a month. After their relief, an uneasy peace followed for a year, and then Britain annexed Natal.

Differences with England

Pretorius settled near Pietermaritzburg, resigned his office, and became a British subject. In 1847 he journeyed to Grahamstown to protest before Sir Henry Pottinger, the representative of the Crown, the injustices the Natal Voortrekkers felt they had suffered. Pottinger unwisely refused to see him. This cavalier treatment infuriated Pretorius and aroused great indignation throughout South Africa.

In 1848 Sir Harry Smith, who had succeeded Pottinger, met Pretorius and a number of Voortrekkers at the foot of the Berg in Natal. The meeting was cordial, but unfortunately both men viewed the position from a totally different aspect: Smith was determined that Natal remain British, and Pretorius was adamant on the question of his people's independence. The result was that Pretorius and his followers cast off their allegiance to England.

Pretorius established himself in Rustenburg (Transvaal) and then took the bold, if unwise, step of urging burghers in Transvaal to join him in a campaign against England. Although he succeeded in evicting the British Resident from Bloemfontein, he was defeated at Boomplaats by Sir Harry Smith. He was proclaimed a rebel, and a reward of £2,000 was offered by the Cape government for his apprehension.

Sand River Convention

Meanwhile, discord ruled among the Voortrekkers in Transvaal. There were three parties, two attached to the persons of the Voortrekker leaders Pretorius and Potgieter, and that of the Volksraad, whose authority was not clearly defined. Pretorius recognized that affairs in Transvaal would never be satisfactorily settled until recognition of the independence of its people was obtained from England. At his instigation the Volksraad decided that representations should be made to the British government for peace and a permanent understanding.

In August 1851 the burghers at Winburg, who were not

Andries Pretorius. (Director of Information, South Africa House, London)

reconciled to life under British rule, invited Pretorius to take upon himself the government of the territory between the Orange and Vaal rivers. Being an outlaw from that territory, Pretorius could not accept the invitation, but he informed the British authorities that he had received it.

To prevent Pretorius from interfering outside Transvaal, his outlawry was reversed, and two commissioners were instructed to effect a settlement regarding the burghers beyond the Vaal. Acting without the blessing of the Volksraad, Pretorius met them and signed the Sand River Convention on Jan. 17, 1852, whereby England recognized the independence of Transvaal. It was ratified by the Volksraad after Pretorius and Potgieter had at last become reconciled.

After the bitterness of the Anglo-Boer struggles had died down, Pretorius frequently came into amicable intercourse with British officials, who invariably spoke of him in terms not merely of high respect but of warm friendliness. Perhaps the highest testimony to the regard in which he was universally held is the fact that, as he lay on his deathbed, several native chiefs who had heard of his illness and had come to pay their respects exhibited intense grief "as they knelt successively and kissed his hand." He died on July 23, 1853, at Magaliesberg.

Further Reading

Andries Pretorius is listed in the Africa study guide (VII, F, 3, b). Other prominent South Africans were Jan Christiaan SMUTS, James HERTZOG, and Paul KRUGER.

South African historiography lacks an objective biography of Pretorius. Gustav Preller, who had an intense admiration for Pretorius and an almost naive partisanship for the Afrikaner people, published a biography, *Andries Pretorius* (1939), but the book, meritorious for its thrilling and picturesque accounts, is far from a critical study. Recommended for general background are Sir George E. Cory, *The Rise of South Africa* (6 vols., 1910–1940); Eric Anderson Walker, *The Great Trek* (1934; 4th ed. 1960); Manfred Nathan's outstanding work, *The Voortrekkers of South Africa* (1937); and George McCall Theal, *History of South Africa*, vol. 6 (1964).

* * *

PRÉVOST / By Neal Oxenhandler

The French novelist, journalist, and cleric Abbé Prévost (1697–1763) was an adventurer who lived by his intrigues and his pen. His best-known work is the novel "Manon Lescaut."

The Abbé Prévost, an engraving dated 1746. (French Embassy Press and Information Division)

Antoine François Prévost d'Exiles, who is known as the Abbé Prévost (pronounced prā-vō′), was first exposed to conventual discipline when he entered a Jesuit school at the age of 14, following his father's death. In the years that ensued, he alternated military service, love affairs, and intense literary activity with periods as first a Jesuit and then a Benedictine novice. He was ordained a Benedictine priest in 1721 and for 8 years engaged in study, teaching, and scholarly work in a variety of Benedictine communities.

Restless and unhappy, he settled for a time at St-Germain-des-Prés in Paris, where he began to write in secret the fictional compendium *Les Mémoires et aventures d'un homme de qualité qui s'est retiré du monde*. In 1728 he threw his vow of stability to the winds and fled to London. He traveled through England, eventually becoming companion and tutor to one Sir John Eyles. *Les Mémoires* was published in part in 1728. Two years later Prévost left England for Holland, and there he worked at translating works of Samuel Richardson and also published the fifth, sixth, and seventh volumes of *Les Mémoires*.

Les Mémoires is an original work written to promote broader understanding of England in France. At a time when England was regarded by Frenchmen as a bloody and barbarous nation, Prévost had learned to love that country. Unlike most previous Frenchmen who had attempted to write about England, Prévost had learned English; he had also traveled in the provinces, gathering folklore from the peasants. His book is an impassioned plea for religious tolerance. It expresses a deep admiration for the comparative ease with which the different social classes in England mingled.

Prévost recognized that the return to nature as source and subject matter of poetry was a unique phenomenon

in English literature, and he was one of the first to introduce this essential romantic theme to France. Of all the works written about England in the 18th century by foreign travelers, *Les Mémoires* is the most complete, the most unprejudiced, and the most reliable.

Once more in England, Prévost began the publication of his serial novel, *Le Philosophe anglais ou les mémoires de Cleveland* (generally known as *Cleveland*), a task that extended from 1732 to 1739. In 1733 he also began publishing the periodical *Le Pour et le contre*. Upon his return to France and his reconciliation with the Church in 1734, he published *Le Doyen de Killerine* (1735). *L'Histoire d'une grecque moderne* and *Marguerite d'Anjou*, a historical novel, were published in 1740.

After his brief exile, Prévost produced numerous translations, most notably bowdlerized versions of Richardson's novels. He also worked on anthologies of fiction and moral essays, and he served as editor for several large publishing enterprises. In 1754 he collaborated on the *Journal étranger* and was commissioned to work on the history of the Condé family.

The seventh volume of *Les Mémoires* was published separately in France 2 years after its original publication in Holland. This highly condensed novel, *L'Histoire du chevalier des Grieux et de Manon Lescaut*, has achieved, of all Prévost's works, the most lasting success. Des Grieux, its childlike hero, is unaware of life, unaware of his own desires, when suddenly he is swept away by his passion for Manon, who is all charm and sensuality. *Manon Lescaut* is one of a handful of novels that constitute a genre uniquely French—the *roman personnel*, or personal novel. It is highly compressed, direct, sparing in style and episode; characteristically, it unfolds through a series of psychological revelations. The operas *Manon* (1884) by Jules Massenet and *Manon Lescaut* (1893) by Giacomo Puccini are based on this work.

From 1754, when Prévost was asked to write a history of the Condé family, he resided at Saint-Firmin in order to be close to the family archives in Chantilly. He died suddenly from apoplexy (or from a ruptured aorta) returning home at night through the forest of Chantilly.

Further Reading

The Abbé Prévost is listed in the Literature study guide (III, F, 1; III, G, 1). Alain René LESAGE was another French novelist of this period.

The translation of *Manon Lescaut* by Burton Rascoe (1919) is a readable version of the novel. The Modern Library translation includes a brief introduction in English by Guy de Maupassant. The best works on Prévost are in French. A useful study in English is George R. Havens, *The Abbé Prévost and English Literature* (1921).

* * *

PRICE / By John Howie

The English Nonconformist minister and political philosopher Richard Price (1723–1791), who supported the American and French revolutions, devoted his life primarily to preaching.

Richard Price was born at Tynton, Glamorganshire, on Feb. 23, 1723. The son of a dissenting minister, he himself served as Unitarian minister to congregations in London, Stoke Newington, and Hackney for about 50 years.

Price's major work in moral philosophy is *The Review of the Principal Questions in Morals* (1758). The central issue with which this work is concerned is the question: why is an action right? Right, Price argues, is a real character of actions that is discerned by the understanding rather than by a moral sense. Right and wrong are simple ideas because they are not finally definable. Like Samuel Clarke, Price held that right and wrong are immutable. Price argues, in part, that both introspection and common sense indicate that rightness and wrongness are necessary truths known through the understanding by intuition.

Price's *Four Dissertations* (1767) included a vindication of the probability of miracles in opposition to David Hume's view of a "complete impossibility of miracles." Price and Hume, evidence from letters indicates, remained good friends in spite of their differences. Price and Joseph Priestley, also good friends, although philosophical opponents, published jointly *A Free Discussion of the Doctrines of Materialism and Philosophical Necessity* (1778). This work is a group of letters in which Priestley defends materialism and philosophical necessity, while Price attacks both of them.

An outstanding mathematician, Price was chosen a fellow of the Royal Society in 1765 for his essay resolving a difficult problem concerning probability. A few years later he applied his own solution to actuarial questions in *Observations on Reversionary Payments* (1771). In this work he laid the foundation for a modern system of life insurance and pensions.

Price's contribution to financial management was also notable. At the request of William Pitt the Younger, he formulated a program for dealing with the national debt in *An Appeal to the Public on the Subject of the National Debt* (1772). His ability in this area was so widely acknowledged by his American friends, including Benjamin Franklin, that Price was asked by the U.S. Congress to advise the new government on finance in 1778.

Price's most widely read works were those supporting the American and French revolutions. His *Observations on the Nature of Civil Liberty, the Principles of Government, and the Justice and Policy of the War with America* (1776), *Additional Observations* (1777), and *The Love of Liberty* (1789), the last sermon supporting the French Revolution, were all widely read in England, the United States, and France. Price died on April 19, 1791.

Further Reading

Richard Price is listed in the Philosophy study guide (V, A, 4) and the Social Sciences study guide (V, B, 1).

Richard Price, an engraving published about 1791.
(Radio Times Hulton Picture Library)

Among his friends were David HUME and Joseph PRIESTLEY.

The most thorough analysis of Price's theories is Carl B. Cone, *Torchbearer of Freedom: The Influence of Richard Price on Eighteenth Century Thought* (1952). Also useful is Antonio S. Cua, *Reason and Virtue: A Study in the Ethic of Richard Price* (1966).

* * *

PRIDI / By David K. Wyatt

Pridi Phanomyong (born 1901) was a civilian political leader in Thailand. He was popularly associated with opposition to military dominance and was known as a proponent of parliamentary democracy.

Pridi Phanomyong (pronounced prē′dē phä-nôm′yông) was born in Ayudhya Province, the son of a prosperous Chinese farmer and merchant by his Thai wife. From local Buddhist schools he went to Bangkok to attend secondary school and the Royal Law School, from which he graduated in 1920. Awarded a government scholarship, he studied law in Caen (1921–1924) and Paris, where he gained a doctorate in 1927. In Paris he became a leader among Thai students pressing their grievances against the Thai minister. He was also strongly influenced by French socialism.

On his return to Bangkok in 1927 Pridi was made secretary to the Department for Drafting Legislation, was given the title by which he is often known, Luang Pradit Manutham, and was assigned to teach law at Chulalongkorn University. In the general discontent with royal absolutism, exacerbated by the growing economic crisis, he was drawn into the group of officials and military officers who planned and executed the coup d'etat of June 24, 1932, which abolished the absolute monarchy and established a parliamentary regime.

The intellectual leader of the group, Pridi also took a lead in drafting the first constitutions of Thailand. His national economic policy of 1933, advocating a utopian sort of state socialism, split the government and brought about his temporary exile. He returned to serve as minister of interior (1935–1936), founded the University of Moral and Political Science (Thammasat), and, as foreign minister (1936–1938), directed the renegotiation of treaties with the Western powers. He served as minister of finance under Phibun Songkhram (1938–1941) but resigned to protest against increasing collaboration with Japan and became regent for the absent boy-king Ananda Mahidol (reigned 1935–1946).

As regent during the war, when Thailand was a nominal ally of Japan, Pridi came to direct the anti-Japanese underground Free Thai movement and was responsible for the overthrow of Phibun in 1944. Pridi's work with the Free Thai gained American support, which assisted Thailand's recovery after the war. Attempting to maintain power from behind the scenes, he finally had to take leadership as prime minister in March 1946.

Pridi's radical reputation and the economic chaos of the postwar years made his task difficult, and he did not have sufficient support to weather unsubstantiated rumors that he was responsible for the unexplained death of young King Ananda in June 1946. Pridi soon had to resign, and his power evaporated with the resurgence of military rule in 1947; further attempts to regain it failed by 1951. He reappeared in Communist China in 1954, associated with a Thai underground movement there, but left China to return to France in 1970.

Further Reading

Pridi Phanomyong is listed in the Asia study guide (IV, A, 2, d). Another influential Thai political leader was PHIBUN Songkhram.

Frank C. Darling, *Thailand and the United States* (1965), provides a spirited defense of Pridi.

* * *

PRIESTLEY / By E. Scott Barr

The English clergyman and chemist Joseph Priestley (1733–1804) contributed to the foundation of the chemistry of gases and discovered the role of oxygen in the animal-plant metabolic system.

Joseph Priestley was born on March 13, 1733, at Fieldhead. His mother died when he was 6, and he was reared by an aunt. Because of ill health he was unable to go to school and was educated partly by a Nonconformist minister and partly by private study. He had a gift for languages and learned about 10. He became a minister when he was 22.

Priestley moved about the country a great deal, preaching and teaching. About 1758 he began to add experiments in "natural philosophy" to his students' activities. In 1761 he moved to Warrington to teach languages in an academy established by Dissenters. There he began to take even more interest in science in general and had an opportunity to attend a few lectures in elementary chemistry.

On a trip to London in 1766 Priestley met Benjamin Franklin, who interested him in electricity. This led to fruitful experimentation—Priestley discovered the conductivity of carbon in 1766, found that an electrical charge stays on the surface of a conductor, and studied the conduction of electricity by flames—and his *History and Present State of Electricity* (1767), which at that time was definitive.

In 1767 Priestley moved to Leeds, where he lived next to a brewery. He became interested in the gases evolved during fermentation and soon discovered that carbon dioxide was being formed. He began preparing this gas at home for study and found that it could be absorbed by

caped to London, where he encountered harassment and snubs, and in 1794 he emigrated to the United States. He was offered various positions, including that of the presidency of the University of Pennsylvania, all of which he declined, but he did pass on much of his experimental techniques to American chemists and preached from time to time. President John Adams was among those who attended his sermons, and George Washington made him a welcome visitor to his home. Priestley died at his home in Northumberland, Pa., on Feb. 6, 1804.

Further Reading

Joseph Priestley is listed in the Science study guide (V, D, 1 and 3). His "dephlogisticated air" was the gas that Antoine Laurent LAVOISIER named oxygen.

Among the biographies of Priestley are Anne Holt, *A Life of Joseph Priestley* (1931); John G. Gillam, *The Crucible: The Story of Joseph Priestley* (1954); and Frederick W. Gibbs, *Joseph Priestley: Revolutions of the Eighteenth Century* (1967). Bernard Jaffe's treatment of Priestley in his *Crucibles: The Lives and Achievement of the Great Chemists* (1930) is readable and interesting. There is also a study of Priestley in James G. Crowther, *Scientists of the Industrial Revolution* (1963).

Joseph Priestley, a painting by Rembrandt Peale. (Courtesy of The New-York Historical Society, New York City)

water. This discovery of "soda water" brought him much attention and the Royal Society's Copley Medal.

Thus stimulated, Priestley turned his attention to the preparation and study of other gases. He decided to collect them over mercury rather than water and was therefore able to prepare for the first time a variety of gases at random. His greatest discovery came in 1774, when he prepared oxygen by using a burning glass and solar heat to heat red oxide of mercury in a vacuum and collected the evolved gas over mercury. In accordance with the phlogiston doctrine, to which he remained loyal to his death, he called the new gas "dephlogisticated air," for he found that it greatly improved combustion. He realized that this gas must be the active component in the atmosphere and that the concept of air being a single substance was incorrect. Three years earlier he had discovered that plants had the capacity to restore to air the ability to support combustion after a candle had been burned in it. He could now identify oxygen as the agent involved in the animal-plant metabolic cycle.

Between 1772 and 1780 Priestley held the not very demanding post of librarian and companion to Lord Shelburne, and must of his best work was done through this patronage. Priestley then settled in Birmingham, where he became a member of the Lunar Club.

Priestley hated all oppression, openly supported the American and French revolutions, and denounced the slave trade and religious bigotry. As a result of his continued attacks on the government, public resentment rose against Priestley and in 1791 a mob sacked and burnt his house and laboratory. He and his family es-

PRIMATICCIO / By Robert Enggass

The Italian painter, sculptor, and architect Francesco Primaticcio (1504–1570) was instrumental in transplanting mannerist palace decoration from Italy to France and in giving French mannerist art its individual character.

Francesco Primaticcio (pronounced prē-mä-tēt′chō) was born in Bologna on April 30, 1504. He worked in Mantua from 1525 or 1526 until 1532 under Giulio Romano. In the Palazzo del Te, Giulio carried out one of the most elaborate programs of mannerist art in all Italy. He represented a series of mythological scenes and motifs in frescoes and stucco reliefs in a decorative style that his teacher, Raphael, had created only a few years earlier.

In 1532 Primaticcio was called to France to work on the decorations of the royal palace of Francis I at Fontainebleau. He came equipped with all the things Giulio Romano had taught him: a rich vocabulary of classical nymphs and satyrs and Roman gods and goddesses plus the fashionable new mode of paintings combined with stuccoes. Giorgio Vasari in his *Lives* (2d ed. 1568) states that "the first works of stucco done in France and the first frescoes of any account originated with Primaticcio." Together with Il Rosso, Primaticcio developed this tradition in the form that set the general direction of French palace decoration for the next 150 years.

Francesco Primaticcio, a self-portrait in the Uffizi, Florence. (Alinari)

In 1541 the King made Primaticcio one of his chamberlains. Three years later he appointed him abbot of St-Martin at Troyes, a position that carried no duties or responsibilities but an abundance of prestige and money. Meanwhile the King commissioned him to decorate one room after another at Fontainebleau with his paintings and stucco figures.

Gradually, under the influence of Parmigianino, Primaticcio's style began to change. His figures, which until now had had normal proportions, started to become fantastically elongated. Tiny heads appeared on top of long, thin, curving necks. Arms and legs tapered down to tiny hands and feet. These strange creatures lounged languidly and effortlessly in poses that were always elegant though sometimes bizarre. This figure type that Primaticcio created at Fontainebleau was endlessly repeated by French artists throughout the remainder of the 16th century and even into the 17th.

Primaticcio's works in architecture are much less well known. The most striking is the small Grotto of the Pines (ca. 1543) at Fontainebleau. Here sculptured giants appear to grow out of rough-hewn stones, and at the top of each arch the keystone seems about to slip out of place, giving the impression—quite intentionally—that the whole structure might at any moment collapse. Primaticcio designed the circular chapel for Henry II and his wife, Catherine de Médicis (ca. 1560; destroyed), at St-Denis and added a wing, the Aile de la Belle Cheminée (1568), to the palace at Fontainebleau. He died in Paris sometime between May 15 and Sept. 14, 1570.

Further Reading

Francesco Primaticcio is listed in the Art study guide (III, E, 1, c). He was influenced by PARMIGIANINO. Primaticcio and Il ROSSO introduced mannerism to France. Germain PILON executed the sculpture for the tomb of Henry II and Catherine de Médicis, at St-Denis, which was designed by Primaticcio.

The main work on Primaticcio is in French: Louis Dimier, *Le Primatice* (1928). Giorgio Vasari, *Lives of the Most Eminent Painters, Sculptors, and Architects* (many editions), contains a good although incomplete biography of Primaticcio. The best modern account is in Anthony Blunt, *Art and Architecture in France, 1500–1700* (1953).

PRIMO DE RIVERA

/ By Robert W. Kern

The Spanish general Miguel Primo de Rivera y Orbaneja (1870–1930) ruled Spain as a dictator from 1923 to 1930.

Miguel Primo de Rivera (pronounced prē′mō thä rē-vä′rä) was born in Cadiz on Jan. 8, 1870, of a middle-class family that later became landowners in the Andalusian town of Jerez. He entered the General Military Academy in Toledo in 1884 and first saw service in Africa in 1893, where he won the Cross of San Fernando. Two years later he went to Cuba as an aide to Gen. Martinez de Campos. When his uncle, Gen. Fernando Primo de Rivera, was named captain general of the Philippines in 1897, Miguel went to Manila as an aide. A major in 1898, he was prevented by the collapse of Spanish military power from becoming a lieutenant general until 1919, the interim being filled with campaigns in Morocco, a stormy military governorship of Cadiz (1915), and service as an observer at the western front during World War I.

Public notice did not come Primo's way until 1922, when, as captain general of Barcelona, he attempted to reestablish law and order at just the moment that antiwar sentiment and social unrest were pointing toward revolution. Almost by chance Primo was selected as the chief figure in the military coup d'etat that on Sept. 12, 1923, overthrew parliamentary government (possibly with the aid of King Alfonso XIII) and imposed a military dictatorship. Overnight Primo became the most important political figure in Spain.

Primo has been described as a "glorified café politician" who, though he had made no preparation for rule, nevertheless aspired to political greatness. Order was restored by suspending constitutional guarantees, dissolving the Parliament, and imposing martial law. A new party, the Patriotic Union, became Primo's political vehicle and the only legal party in the country. Aside from the King's support of it, however, it had been put together so fast that it never developed great strength. Only because Primo was able to concentrate resources and to rally the army and defeat Abd el-Krim and the Moroccans did the new regime gain some respite from political dissension. The ending of the Moroccan War in December 1925 became Primo's one solid triumph.

Internal problems, surprisingly, continued to mount. Liberals rejected Primo's local government reforms and anticentralism, and radicals, despite the addition of a Socialist, Largo Cabellero, to his Cabinet, did not feel that the regime was moving fast enough in making social reforms. University students and intellectuals, fearing that Primo was another Benito Mussolini, led the opposition from 1925 on, and one of Spain's most distinguished intellectuals, Miguel de Unamuno, went into exile. Primo in fact was far from being a Fascist like Mussolini; if anything he had a paternalistic view of the state that unfortunately was out of step with the growing ideological sensitivities of the Spaniards.

By 1928, as the revolt of the cadets at the Academy of Segovia showed, even the army was dissatisfied with Primo, mainly because law and order were breaking down. The next 2 years witnessed one act of rebellion after the other, but King Alfonso XIII delayed replacing Primo because the monarchy had used the regime to hide its involvement in a series of disastrous political and military setbacks just prior to the dictatorship. Finally,

however, Primo had no other recourse than to resign on Jan. 28, 1930, when he left for exile in Paris. He died in Paris on March 16, 1930.

Primo's son, José Antonio, frequently defended his father during the next few years of growing political bitterness, and many aspects of his father's paternalism could be found in José Antonio Primo de Rivera's much more overtly fascist philosophy. José Antonio founded the Falange party and became the martyr of the nationalist movement.

Further Reading

Miguel Primo de Rivera is listed in the European History study guide (XI, J, 1, a). He was supported by ALFONSO XIII.

Dillwyn F. Ratcliff, *Prelude to Franco: Political Aspects of the Dictatorship of General Miguel Primo de Rivera* (1957), covers Primo de Rivera's regime. Good accounts of his career are in Gerald Brenan, *The Spanish Labyrinth: An Account of the Social and Political Background of the Civil War* (1943; 2d ed. 1950), and Raymond Carr, *Spain, 1808–1939* (1966). There is also extensive material on Primo de Rivera in Charles Petrie, *King Alfonso XIII and His Age* (1963).

PROCLUS / By T. M. Robinson

Proclus Diadochus (born 410) was a Byzantine philosopher and the last of the great Neoplatonists of antiquity. His philosophy indirectly influenced Christian thought, and he directly influenced many Renaissance thinkers.

P roclus (pronounced prō′kləs) was born in Constantinople (modern Istanbul) of Lycian parentage. He received his elementary education in Xanthus and then continued his studies in Alexandria. Among his teachers were the Sophist Leonas of Isauria and the Egyptian grammarian Orion as well as a number of Roman teachers, who taught him Latin. His basic study was rhetoric, since his intention originally was to enter the legal profession. However, on a trip to Constantinople with Leonas, Proclus appears to have been "converted" to philosophy, and on his return to Alexandria he studied Aristotle and mathematics. At the age of 19 he went to the Platonic Academy in Athens, where he studied under Plutarch of Athens, founder of the Athenian school of Neoplatonism, and Syrianus, Plutarch's immediate successor.

Syrianus greatly influenced Proclus's philosophical development, and he regarded Proclus both as his pupil and as his successor at the Academy. Under Syrianus's tutelage, Proclus read widely in Plato and Aristotle, and at 28 he had produced a number of sophisticated commentaries on different dialogues of Plato, including the

Miguel Primo de Rivera, a portrait by Dibujo de Cramonal. (MAS)

monumental commentary on the *Timaeus*. When Syrianus died, the chair passed briefly to Domninus of Larissa, and it was then assumed by Proclus, who held it until his death.

According to a contemporary biographer, Proclus possessed great bodily strength and endurance and striking physical beauty. He was a practicing magician, a vegetarian, and a man of great personal asceticism. Apart from his professional teaching and writing, he must have at least occasionally spoken his mind on politics, since he left Athens at one time for a year, when political enemies were attempting to put him on trial.

In addition to his commentaries on Plato's dialogues and a commentary on Plotinus's *Enneads*, Proclus wrote important works on systematic philosophy and theology. They include the *Elements of Theology* and the *Platonic Theology*, as well as smaller treatises: *Doubts about Providence*, *Providence and Fate*, *The Continuance of Evil*, and *Conduct*. He also wrote commentaries on the Chaldean oracles, the first book of Euclid's *Elements*, and the poets Hesiod and (possibly) Homer, several astronomical treatises, a treatise on the elements of physics, and a large number of hymns to different gods.

Further Reading

Proclus is listed in the Philosophy study guide (I, C, 7). He greatly influenced Giovanni PICO DELLA MIRANDOLA. An earlier Neoplatonist was PLOTINUS.

As examples of Proclus's work the reader can examine the old Thomas Taylor translation of *The Commentaries of Proclus on the Timaeus of Plato* (1820) or E. R. Dodds's celebrated edition and translation of *The Elements of Theology* (1933; 2d ed. 1963). A detailed and sympathetic introduction to the life and work of Proclus is Laurence Jay Rosan, *The Philosophy of Proclus: The Final Phase of Ancient Thought* (1949). See also Thomas Whittaker, *The Neo-Platonists: A Study in the History of Hellenism* (1901; 4th ed. 1961).

✳ ✳ ✳

PROCOPIUS / By John W. Barker

The Byzantine historian Procopius of Caesarea (ca. 500–ca. 565), the last of the great classical Greek historians, was an eyewitness to, and prime reporter of, events in the reign of Emperor Justinian I.

Born in Palestinian Caesarea between 490 and 507, Procopius (pronounced prō-kō′pǐ-əs) was thoroughly educated and probably trained in law. In 527 he was made advisor and secretary to the young general Belisarius, then imperial commander in Mesopotamia against the Persians. In this capacity Procopius accompanied Belisarius on many of his campaigns, witnessing not only the Persian hostilities but also the suppression of the Nika Riots (532), the conquest of the

The gold medal of Justinian, commemorating his triumph over the Vandals in 534. Procopius records the wars with the Vandals in the History of the Wars. *(Trustees of the British Museum)*

Vandal kingdom of North Africa (533–534), and—after a term of service in North Africa (534–536)—the first war against the Ostrogoths in Italy (535–540). Procopius was in Constantinople in 542, where he observed the beginnings of the terrible plague that struck the empire. Presumably, Procopius did not join Belisarius on his second Italian campaign. He seems to have held government posts in the capital for the remainder of his career.

Drawing upon his experiences, Procopius began during the 540s a formal history of military and political events of his day, his *History of the Wars*, written in excellent Greek. Of its eight books, the first two narrate the empire's Persian Wars, from early in the 5th century to about 550. The next two books describe the Vandalic Wars and subsequent events in North Africa to the late 540s. Three more books describe both phases of the Ostrogothic Wars, from 535 to 551. A supplementary eighth book covers events generally between 548 and 554.

Meanwhile Procopius's attitude seems to have undergone a drastic change. Apparently cool personally to Justinian and his consort Theodora, he seems at least to have shared the aspirations of their reign's early years. The subsequent disasters and disillusionments soured him—a process increased, it is thought, by his failure to obtain all the advancements he expected. Consequently, about 550, Procopius composed *The Unpublished Sections* (*Tà anékdota*), now known as the *Historia arcana*, or *Secret History*. The *Wars*, a public and semiofficial history, had been meant for circulation. In this secret memoir, not intended for publication, Procopius poured out his frustrations in terms of ridicule and abuse of Belisarius, of his wife Antonina, of Empress Theodora, and, above all, of Justinian himself. The Emperor is depicted as malicious, rapacious, a destroyer of all established order and traditions, and, in effect, an evil demon.

Though objective and skeptical about religious matters, Procopius planned an ecclesiastical history of Justinian's reign, but this work was either lost or unrealized. In the mid-550s, however, Procopius composed an account of Justinian's architectural program entitled *On the Buildings*. Organized geographically into six books, it is incomplete as planned, lacking a section on Italy.

Procopius seems to have received some higher positions at court late in life. He is last specifically heard of in 559, and the date of his death is unknown.

Further Reading

Procopius is listed in the Social Sciences study guide (II, A, 4) and the Literature study guide (III, A, 2, b). His works describe BELISARIUS and JUSTINIAN I.

The complete works of Procopius are most readily available in the Loeb Classical Library series (7 vols., 1914–1940), with the Greek text and English translation by H. B. Dewing and G. Downey. The *Secret History* is available in paperback translations by R. Atwater (1963) and G. A. Williamson (1966). There is no comprehensive study of Procopius in English, but all major works on the age of Justinian discuss him at length. See, for example, John Bagnell Bury, *History of the Later Roman Empire from the Death of Theodosius I to the Death of Justinian* (1923).

PROKOFIEV / By Stanley D. Krebs

The Russian-Soviet composer Sergei Sergeevich Prokofiev (1891–1953) was a key figure in modern music. He was prolific in all genres and was a master craftsman. His works are probably the most played of 20th-century composers.

The accomplishment of Sergei Prokofiev (pronounced prǝ-kôf′yǝf), together with that of Dmitri Shostakovich, very nearly sums up the contribution of Soviet music in the 20th century. Although Prokofiev was a brilliant pianist and writer for piano, he sought his creative beginnings in opera. Yet very often the end product, through his lifelong habit of rewriting and recasting, was a dazzling orchestral work. His particular idiom remained distinctive although attenuated in later years under the pressure to succeed in terms not his own.

Prokofiev was born in Sontsovka (now Krasnoe) in the Ekaterinoslav Guberniya of the Ukraine, where his father managed the Sontsov family estates. Sergei's mother, a woman of considerable cultural pretension, indulged her only child's precocity. Indeed, young Prokofiev was so musically industrious that it would have been difficult to stop him. By the age of 10 he had written a number of pieces, including an opera, *Giant*. The young boy was taken to the Moscow Conservatory, and, for the next two summers, Reinhold Glière went to Sontsovka to tutor him.

At the age of 12 Prokofiev entered the St. Petersburg Conservatory. He spent the next 10 years there, and, although he later had very little good to say of the institution, its traditions, or its teachers, he received an impressive technical grounding. More important to him through the conservatory years were contacts with his fellow students Boris Asafiev and Nikolai Miaskovsky, with prominent (and rich) musical figures like Serge Koussevitsky, and with the growing body of internationally minded artists and entrepreneurs in the capital city. Prokofiev traveled to London in 1914, heard Igor Stravinsky's *Rite of Spring*, and established a liaison with the impresario Serge Diaghilev. Prokofiev was already a successful musician, published and performed, and the Diaghilev contact was the all but final stamp of Russian creative maturity in 1914.

Years Abroad

Prokofiev longed for a sustained stay and impact abroad—the Russian tradition most recently confirmed by Alexander Scriabin, Sergei Rachmaninov, and Stravinsky. But the war, Russia's faltering role therein, and the two revolutions of 1917 caused Prokofiev's Western contacts to pause. The "angels" that had financed others failed to materialize at first, and Diaghilev was not encouraging. In mid-1917 Prokofiev reached an under-

Sergei Prokofiev in 1939. (United Press International Photo)

standing with the Chicago industrialist Cyrus McCormick. By this time Prokofiev had composed a number of piano pieces, the *Scythian Suite* for orchestra (a recasting of a ballet, *Ala and Lolli*, commissioned but rejected by Diaghilev), the First (*Classical*) Symphony, the First Violin Concerto, and the First and Second Piano Concertos, the Third being in the works. With these behind him, McCormick's invitation in his pocket, and the consent of the new Soviet government, the composer left for the United States in 1918.

In 1921 Prokofiev's *Love for Three Oranges* was premiered in Chicago. The American years were fitful ones financially, not the least because of competition from other Russian émigrés. He began in America the opera *Flaming Angel*, which, though never performed in his lifetime, was to dominate his thinking for many years. In 1922 he moved to Ettal in the Bavarian Alps. Here he lived with his mother and with his first wife, Caroline Codina, working mostly on the *Flaming Angel* and on piano and vocal works. Eventually he settled in Paris with his family and made that the center of his activity until 1936.

The Western years were productive ones, and it is well to emphasize the point, since Soviet thinking insists that they were "unproductive years of rootless desperation." He completed (for Diaghilev) the ballets *Le Pas d'acier* (1925), *Prodigal Son* (1928), and *On the Dnieper* (1930); the operas *Love for Three Oranges* (1919) and *Flaming Angel* (1927); a number of vocal works; the Third, Fourth, and Fifth Piano Concertos; chamber works, including opus numbers 34, 35, 39, 50, and 56; and many other works. He worked constantly, often on more than one piece at a time, and no small part of his effort was directed toward casting works for other mediums in symphonic form. Much of his work appears in the original version and in an orchestral version or versions. This includes all the ballets, parts of the Piano Sonatas, chamber works, and even his beloved opera *Flaming Angel* (as the Third Symphony).

Return to Soviet Union

In 1927 Prokofiev visited the Soviet Union and was well received. But on a second visit in 1929 the conservative Russian Association of Proletarian Musicians (RAPM) dominated the musical press and attacked the reluctant émigré. In late 1932 he was encouraged to visit again: the RAPM had been abolished, and his friends Miaskovsky, Asafiev, and Glière were enthusiastic about creative prospects in the Soviet Union. Prokofiev still hesitated, still visited, and sought and probably got assurances from high party and government sources. He finally moved to Moscow in 1936. He had done well in the West, but he was dissatisfied: as a concert pianist he had stood in Rachmaninov's shadow; and he had failed to capture that creative leadership enjoyed by Arnold Schoenberg and Stravinsky.

Through 1938 Prokofiev continued to tour the West, but the Nazi-Soviet Pact of 1939 brought on a politically anti-international period, and he never went abroad again. He was simultaneously in the throes of separation from his wife, herself an international symbol. For these reasons his autobiographical memoirs, a substantial part of which was written during the pact, are unfortunately inaccurate in discussing the West. In his memoirs he

A scene from a 1964 production of Prokofiev's opera Flaming Angel *at the Opéra Comique, Paris. (Photo Lipnitzki-Viollet)*

characterized his own style as shaped from four main lines of development: first, the lyric, singing line; second, the classical grounding; third, the urge to seek and innovate; and fourth, a relentless, motoric, toccatalike pulse.

Prokofiev had already begun, in his Soviet period, to write movie scores (*Lieutenant Kijé*, 1934; *Alexander Nevsky*, 1938), patriotic works (*Cantata for the Twentieth Anniversary of the October Revolution*, 1937), and works of lighter genre and direct appeal (*Peter and the Wolf*, 1936). He held at this time the notion of multiple styles for the contemporary composer. In 1939 he began another opera, *Semyon Kotko*, based on a story by Valentin Kataev. The opera dealt with Germans as enemies and was difficult to mount during first a pro-German then an anti-German period. In it Prokofiev worked out a usage for those idioms and experiments too advanced for the increasingly conservative official view of art: the depiction of inimical forces. Prokofiev's coworker, the famous director Vsevolod Meyerhold, was arrested and sent to a labor camp (where he died) for creative errors. Prokofiev seemed immune to such reprimands and punishments, which were common in the late 1930s.

During World War II Prokofiev, with his second wife, Myra Mendelson, was evacuated to a series of Eastern centers. He worked on more film scores, including *Ivan the Terrible* with Sergei Eisenstein, his opera *War and Peace*, and on the Second (*Kabardinian*) String Quartet. He completed the Fifth Symphony in 1945. That year he incurred the illness, hypertension, that was finally to prove fatal, and it became clear that he was beginning to draw critical fire from official and semiofficial sources. In 1948 he was a principal target in the party and government criticism and punishment of artists. He did not live to see that criticism rescinded, as Shostakovich did. Prokofiev died on March 5, 1953.

In the works of his last 8 to 10 years Prokofiev added at least two more lines of development to those he had specified earlier. One of these was the unabashed heroic element, first used to any great extent in the Fifth Symphony. This work, with its "heroism," indicated that he had noted the combinations so successful in Shostakovich's Seventh Symphony. The other line, perhaps involuntarily developed, was that of the ingenuous—the deliberately but sincerely naive. This involved light, vulnerable, singable tunes and harmonies and showed scant trace of the caustic, irreverent treatment he often reserved for such simplicity.

In his final years Prokofiev's performances were officially limited because of his clouded political situation and were generally confined to children's concerts and children's performing groups. His last works, including the Seventh Symphony and the ballet *Stone Flower*, reflected this. He even spoke of a refreshed awareness of his own childhood. Since his death his more mature works, and especially those of his foreign period, have had increasing influence on younger Soviet composers, although many, including the *Flaming Angel*, have not been performed in the Soviet Union.

Further Reading

Sergei Prokofiev is listed in the Music study guide (I, J, 9). Other Soviet composers were Dmitri SHOSTA-KOVICH and Aram KHACHATURIAN.

The primary source on Prokofiev available in English is the *Autobiography, Articles, and Reminiscences* (trans. 1958), published by the Foreign Languages Publishing House. The autobiographical part was written in the late 1930s and early 1940s. The official biography is that of Israel Nestyev, published in English translation by Florence Jonas in 1960. This is an enlargement of an earlier book, and a comparison of the two is politically interesting. There are a number of biographies by Westerners, although the late ones in English—Lawrence and Elizabeth Hanson (1964), and Victor Seroff (1968)—are popular rather than accurate items. Malcolm Brown, *Symphonies of Prokofiev* (in press), should prove authoritative. No book on contemporary music is without its chapter on Prokofiev. A generous treatment is afforded in William Austin, *Music in the Twentieth Century* (1966); and a chapter with recent information appears in Stanley D. Krebs, *Soviet Composers and the Development of Soviet Music* (1970).

PROSSER / By Edwin S. Redkey

> Gabriel Prosser (ca. 1775–1800) was the Afro-American slave leader of an unsuccessful revolt in Richmond, Va., during the summer of 1800.

Gabriel Prosser, the slave of Thomas H. Prosser, was about 25 years old when he came to the attention of Virginia authorities late in August 1800. Little is known of his childhood or family background. He had two brothers and a wife, Nanny, all slaves of Prosser. Gabriel learned to read and was a serious student of the Bible, where he found inspiration in the accounts of Israel's delivery from slavery. Gabriel possessed shrewd judgment, and his master gave him much latitude. He was acknowledged as a leader by many slaves around Richmond.

With the help of other slaves, especially Jack Bowler and George Smith, Gabriel designed a scheme for a slave revolt. They planned to seize control of Richmond by slaying all whites (except for Methodists, Quakers, and Frenchmen) and then to establish a kingdom of Virginia with Gabriel as king. The recent, successful American Revolution and the revolutions in France and Haiti—with their rhetoric of freedom, equality, and brotherhood—supplied examples and inspiration for Gabriel's rebellion. In the months preceding the attack Gabriel skillfully recruited supporters and organized them into military units. Authorities never discovered how many slaves were involved, but there were undoubtedly several thousand, many armed with swords and pikes made from farm tools by slave blacksmiths.

The plan was to strike on the night of Aug. 30, 1800. Black men inside Richmond were to set fire to certain buildings to distract whites, and Gabriel's force from the country was to seize the armory and government buildings across town. With the firearms thus gained, the rebels would supposedly easily overcome the surprised whites.

On the day of the attack the plot was disclosed by two slaves who did not want their masters slain; then Virginia governor James Monroe alerted the militia. That night, as the rebels began congregating outside Richmond, the worst rainstorm in memory flooded roads, washed out bridges, and prevented Gabriel's army from assembling. Gabriel decided to postpone the attack until the next day, but by then the city was too well defended. The rebels, including Gabriel, dispersed.

Some slaves, in order to save their own lives, testified against the ringleaders, about 35 of whom were executed. Gabriel himself managed to escape by hiding aboard a riverboat on its way to Norfolk. In Norfolk, however, he was betrayed by other slaves, who claimed the large reward for his capture on September 25. Returned to Richmond, Gabriel, like most of the other leaders, refused to confess to the plot or give evidence against other slaves. He was tried and found guilty on Oct. 6, 1800, and executed the next day.

Further Reading

Gabriel Prosser is listed in the American History study guide (V, F, 3, a). Nat TURNER and Denmark VESEY also led black men in rebellion against slavery.

There is no full-length biography of Gabriel. There are short biographical accounts in Herbert Aptheker, *Essays in the History of the American Negro* (1945) and in Wilhelmena S. Robinson, *Historical Negro Biographies* (1968). The best account of his rebellion is in Joseph C. Carroll, *Slave Insurrections in the United States, 1800–1865* (1938). Additional information is contained in Herbert Aptheker, *American Negro Slave Revolts* (1943; new ed. 1969), and in Robert McColley, *Slavery and Jeffersonian Virginia* (1964). Arna Bontemps, *Black Thunder* (1936), is a fictionalized treatment of Gabriel and his conspiracy.

PROTAGORAS / By Donald A. Ross

The Greek philosopher Protagoras (ca. 484–ca. 414 B.C.) was one of the best-known and most successful teachers of the Sophistic movement of the 5th century B.C.

Protagoras (pronounced prō-tăg′ər-əs) was born in Abdera, the native city of Democritus, and spent much of his life as an itinerant Sophist, traveling throughout the Greek world. He was a frequent

A philosopher depicted on a red-figured amphora dating from the time of Protagoras. (Trustees of The British Museum)

visitor to Athens, being a friend of Pericles, and was said to have aided in framing the constitution for the colony of Thurii, which the Athenians established in southern Italy in 444/443 B.C. Plato said that Protagoras spent 40 years teaching and that he died at the age of 70. Stories about an indictment against Protagoras by the Athenians, the burning of his books, and his death at sea are probably fictitious.

Sophist Philosophy

Protagoras earned his livelihood giving lectures and instruction to individuals and groups. The system he taught had little to do with philosophy or the pursuit of an absolute truth; instead it imparted to its adherents the necessary skills and knowledge for success in life, especially in politics. These skills consisted mainly of rhetoric and dialectic and could be used for whatever ends a person desired. It was for this reason, for teaching people "to make the weaker cause the stronger," that Protagoras came under attack, indirectly by Aristophanes in *The Clouds* and directly by Plato in several of his dialogues.

Protagoras wrote on a wide variety of subjects. Fragments of some of his works survive, and the titles of others are known through later comments on them. His famous dictum "man is the measure of all things" is the opening sentence of a work variously called *Truth* or *Refutatory Arguments*. He also wrote *On the Gods*, a fragment of which survives. In it he says that the obscurity of the subject and the shortness of human life prevent any definite conclusions. Other works include *The Great Argument, Contradictory Arguments, On Mathematics*, and *The Art of Eristics*. The list of titles preserved in the works of the Greek biographer Diogenes Laertius may represent sections of larger works, whereas such titles as *On Ambition, On Virtues, On Human Errors*, and *Trial Concerning a Fee* almost certainly represent discussions of the common themes of Sophistic speeches. The chronology of these works is unknown.

Protagoras was a perfect example of the 5th-century Sophist. Careful thinkers could, of course, easily undermine the basis of his relative theory of knowledge; but the attractiveness of his theory and the pervasive influence of his teachings were so great that no less an opponent than Plato went to great lengths to expose the fallacies and potential evil of what he represented.

Further Reading

Protagoras is listed in the Philosophy study guide (I, A, 5). A negative Sophist was GORGIAS.

The surviving fragments of Protagoras's works are collected in H. Diels and W. Kranz, *Die Fragmente der Vorsokratiker*, translated in Kathleen Freeman, *Ancilla to the Pre-Socratic Philosophers* (1948), and discussed in her *The Pre-Socratic Philosophers* (1946; 3d ed. 1953). An excellent discussion of the Sophists and their contributions to Greek culture is in Werner Jaeger, *Paideia: The Ideals of Greek Culture*, translated by Gilbert Highet, vol. 1 (1939; 2d ed. 1945). A brief but useful account of Protagoras's importance can be found in Albin Lesky, *A History of Greek Literature* (1966).

PROUDHON / By George Weisz

The political philosopher and journalist Pierre Joseph Proudhon (1809–1864) was the greatest of the French anarchists. His insistence that a new society should be created by moral methods led to his disavowal of revolutionary violence.

Pierre Joseph Proudhon (pronounced prōō-dôN′) was born of a poor family in Besançon. His poverty, which persisted throughout most of his life, in no small measure explains his hatred of the existing economic order. At 19 he was apprenticed to a printer and a few years later supervised the printing of Charles Fourier's classic *Le Nouveau monde industriel et sociétaire*, which made a great impression on him. Lacking formal education, he taught himself Latin, Greek, and Hebrew, and, despite his loss of faith in religion, theology.

In 1838 Proudhon won a pension enabling him to devote himself to scholarship in Paris, and he began his prolific writing career. *Qu'est-ce que la propriété?* (What Is Property?), completed in 1840, won him notoriety because of his claim that owning property was theft. In fact, he was referring only to unjustly acquired property, rejecting communism because of its denial of human independence. He envisaged an anarchist society of largely agrarian small producers, bound together by free contracts.

A new element, however, was added to Proudhon's thought by his move to Lyons. He remained there for several years, learning about industry and becoming involved with the Mutualists, an illegal workers' association. In this kind of workers' association, properly organized for cooperative production and exchange of goods, he began to see, still somewhat vaguely, the force for radical societal change. He insisted in *De la création de l'ordre dans l'humanité* (1843) that economic forces were the chief motivating factors of society.

In the years before the Revolution of 1848 Proudhon made the acquaintance of the leading European leftists, including Karl Marx, but refused the latter's invitation to participate in founding an international organization because he sensed Marx's intellectual authoritarianism. He also completed one of his most interesting works, *Système des contradictions économiques* (1846), in which he claimed that contradiction and conflict were the basic characteristics of society and economics. These contradictions could never be overcome, but the different forces could be balanced, as socialism, in fact, was attempting to do, so that struggle would become construc-

Pierre Joseph Proudhon. (Archives Photographiques, Paris)

tive rather than destructive. The book placed him among the leading thinkers of French socialism, important enough to merit Marx's book *The Poverty of Philosophy*, which was directed against Proudhon's ideas.

During the Revolution of 1848, Proudhon accepted the editorship of the daily *Le Représentant du Peuple*, which became one of the most popular and controversial newspapers among workers in Paris because it criticized all parties, including the new republican government. The newspaper was suppressed, but Proudhon founded a new one which became even more popular. Finally, after a series of bitter attacks against the newly elected president, Louis Napoleon, he was sent to prison, where he spent the better part of the next 3 years.

There Proudhon continued editing his newspaper and producing books. His thoughts entered a more positive stage, and he began to give a more concrete and instructive exposition of his political ideas. In *L'Idée générale de la révolution au XIX siècle* (1851) he wrote that revolution could be brought about by workers' associations which denied the rule of governments and of capitalists and which would eventually take over industry. The new society would be regulated by contracts, and mutual undertakings would be facilitated by easy credit, available on the basis of productivity. This would effectively disperse concentrated economic power and preserve economic opportunities for the petty bourgeoisie. In *La Philosophie du progrès* (1853) he rejected all order and formula in favor of progress and continual movement.

In 1857 Proudhon completed *De la justice dans la révolution et dans l'église*, in which he attacked the Catholic Church for hindering man's freedom and for perpetuating a corrupt moral order. Prosecuted for "outraging public and religious morals," he was again condemned to prison. He fled to Belgium, where he wrote *La Guerre et la paix* (1861), in which he characterized war as a consequence of capitalism. He felt that by renewing economic equilibrium there would no longer be a necessity for war and that conflict and aggression would be transformed into constructive forces. He resolved the problem of the conflict between state and individual through his concept of federalism. The basic elements of his federalism were local units of administration, small enough to be under the direct control of the people. Larger confederal groupings would act primarily as organs of coordination among local units. Ultimately, Proudhon believed that Europe would be transformed into a federation of federations.

In the last years of his life, Proudhon continued to fight the Bonapartist regime in France. He also risked unpopularity by opposing Polish and Italian nationalism because of their concern for a national central state. Nevertheless, he wielded immense influence among French workers, urging them to separate themselves from other classes and from political parties claiming to represent them. His ideas were assimilated into the French workers' movement, and the French section of the First International followed Proudhon's program in almost every detail.

Further Reading

Pierre Joseph Proudhon is listed in the Social Sciences study guide (VI, B, 2). Later his ideas emerged in somewhat different form in the anarchism of Mikhail BAKUNIN and Peter KROPOTKIN.

Many of Proudhon's works are available in English translation. By far the best introduction to Proudhon is George Woodcock's excellent study, *Pierre-Joseph Proudhon: A Biography* (1956). S. Y. Lu, *The Political Theories of P. J. Proudhon* (1922), and Henri de Lubac, *The Un-Marxian Socialist* (1948), are somewhat dated treatments of specific aspects of Proudhon's thought. See also Denis William Brogan, *Proudhon* (1934). The essays on Proudhon in Roger Soltau, *French Political Thought in the 19th Century* (1931), and in G. D. H. Cole, *A History of Socialist Thought* (5 vols. in 7, 1953–1960), provide adequate introductions.

PROUST / By Vinio Rossi

The French novelist Marcel Proust (1871–1922) ranks as one of the greatest literary figures of the 20th century. He abandoned plot and traditional dramatic action for the vision of the first-person narrator confronting his world.

Marcel Proust (pronounced prōōst) was born to wealthy bourgeois parents on July 10, 1871, in Auteuil, a suburb of Paris. The first son of Dr. Adrien Proust and Jeanne Weil, the daughter of a wealthy Jewish financier, he was hypersensitive, nervous, and frail. When he was 9 years old, his first attack of asthma, a disease that greatly influenced his life, nearly suffocated him. In 1882 Proust enrolled in the Lycée Condorcet. Only during his last 2 years of study there did he distinguish himself as a student, attracting the interest of his philosophy professor, Marie-Alphonse Daru. After a year of military service, Proust studied law and then philosophy.

In the meantime, Proust was creating a name for himself in high society as a brilliant conversationalist with an ear for speech patterns that enabled him to mimic others with devastating ease and accuracy. His verve, dark features, pale complexion, and elegant taste fascinated the hosts and hostesses of the smart Parisian set that he eagerly courted. Although he soon earned the reputation of a snob and social climber, Proust's intimate friends saw him as generous, extremely intelligent, capable of serious thinking, and as an excellent intellectual companion. But he irritated through his eagerness to please, his intensity of emotion, and his indecisiveness. Proust was not indecisive, however, about his commitment to writing.

Early Works

In 1892 and 1893 Proust contributed a number of criti-

Marcel Proust. (Harlingue-Viollet)

cal notes and sketches and two short stories to the ephemeral journal *Le Banquet* and to *La Revue blanche*. He published his first work in 1896, a collection of short stories, short verse portraits of artists and musicians, and incidental pieces written during the preceding 6 years. *Les Plaisirs et les jours* (*Pleasures and Days*) received cursory notice in the press despite its preface by Anatole France. The book did little to dispel the prevalent notion of Proust as an effete dandy. His interest in analysis of rare and exquisite feelings, his preoccupation with high society, and his refined style were all too familiar to allow his readers to see a talented and serious writer groping for eternal truths and a personal style.

In 1895, even before he published *Les Plaisirs et les jours*, Proust had made a first attempt at a major work. Unable to handle his material satisfactorily, unsure of himself, and unclear about the manner of achieving the goals he had set, Proust abandoned the work in 1899. It appeared, under the title of *Jean Santeuil*, only in 1952; from thousands of notebook pages, Bernard de Fallois had culled and organized the novel according to a sketchy plan he found among them. As a consequence the novel is uneven; many passages announce, duplicate, or are variations of passages in Proust's masterpiece, and others are incoherent or apparently irrelevant. Some, however, are beautifully lyric or analytic. *Jean Santeuil* is Proust's first attempt to come to grips with material that later yielded so much in *À la recherche du temps per-*

du. *Jean Santeuil* is the biography of an imaginary character who struggles with himself, his family, and his environment in order to discover, justify, and affirm his artistic vocation. Through episodes and sketches Proust traced Jean Santeuil's progress toward maturity, touching upon many of the themes he later developed more fully: the impact of nature upon the sensibility; the silent work of the imagination in involuntary memory; memory bridging gaps in time; the effects of events such as the Alfred Dreyfus case upon society; the snobbery of social intercourse; the self-oriented nature of love; and the liberating power of art.

After abandoning *Jean Santeuil*, Proust returned to his studies. Although he read widely in other literatures, he was limited to translations. During 1899 he became interested in the works of John Ruskin, and after Ruskin's death (Jan. 20, 1900), Proust published an obituary of the English critic in *La Chronique des arts et de la curiosité* (Jan. 27, 1900) that established him as a Ruskin scholar. Proust's *Pélerinages ruskiniens en France* appeared in *Le Figaro* in February and was followed by several more articles on Ruskin in *Le Mercure de France* and in *La Gazette des beaux-arts*. With the help of an English-speaking friend, Marie Nordlinger, and his mother, Proust translated Ruskin's *The Bible of Amiens* (1904) and *Sesame and Lilies* (1906). Grappling with Ruskin's ideas on art and its relationship to ethics helped him clarify his own esthetic ideas and move beyond the impasse of *Jean Santeuil*.

In 1903 Proust's father died. His own health, deteriorating since 1899, suffered an even greater shock following the death of his mother in September 1905. These setbacks forced Proust into the sanatorium of Dr. Paul Sollier (in December 1905), where he entertained hopes of curing his asthma. Undoubtedly preferring his illness to any cure, Proust left, "fantastically ill," in less than 2 months. After more than 2 years of seclusion, he emerged once again into society and into print with a series of articles and pastiches published in *Le Figaro* during 1907 and 1908. From 1905 to 1908 Proust had been mysteriously working on a novel; he abandoned it, too, in favor of a new one he had begun to plan when he realized the necessity of still another dress rehearsal. He wrote pastiches of Honoré de Balzac, Gustave Flaubert, Edmond de Goncourt, Charles Sainte-Beuve, and others (February–March 1908), and this activity led Proust inadvertently to problems of literary criticism and to a clearer formulation of a literary work as an art object. By November 1908 Proust was planning his *Contre Sainte-Beuve* (published in 1954; *On Art and Literature*), a rebuttal of Sainte-Beuve, the recognized master of historical literary criticism. The true writer expresses a self, Proust felt, that is completely hidden beneath the one manifested "in our habits, in society, in our vices. If we want to try to understand that self, it is only by trying to re-create it deep in ourselves, that we can succeed." By reacting to Sainte-Beuve, Proust formulated, in terms applicable to the artist as well as to the reader, the notion that lies at the heart of *À la recherche du temps perdu*. Proust finished *Contre Sainte-Beuve* during the summer of 1909 and began almost immediately to compose his great novel.

"À la recherche du temps perdu"

Although Proust had, by 1909, accumulated and reworked most of the material that was to become À la recherche du temps perdu (Remembrance of Things Past), he still had not fully grasped the focal point that would enable him to structure and to orchestrate his vast material. In January 1909 he had a series of experiences that bore belated fruit during the early summer of that year. The sudden conjunction of flavors in a cup of tea and toast evoked in him sensations that recalled his youth in his grandfather's garden at Auteuil. Although he had had similar experiences in the past and had considered them important, he had not realized that not only were these experiences a key element in an artist's work but also they could serve as the organizing principle of his novel. They revealed the hidden self that Proust had spoken of in Contre Sainte-Beuve, a present self identical to the one in various moments of past time. This process of artistic resurrection and the gradual discovery of its effectiveness, he realized, was the focal point his novel required. À la recherche du temps perdu, like Balzac's La Comédie humaine, depicts the many facets of a whole society in a specific period of history. Political events, such as the Dreyfus case; social transformations, such as the rise of the bourgeoisie and the decline of the nobility; artistic events; evaluations in music, art, and literature; and different social milieus from the working class to bohemian circles—all found their place in Proust's panorama of French life during the decades around the turn of the century. But Proust was primarily concerned with portraying not reality but its perception by his narrator, Marcel, and its capacity to provoke and reveal Marcel's permanent self, normally hidden by habit and social intercourse. From the very first words of his predominantly first-person narrative, Marcel traces his evolution through a multiplicity of recalled experiences to the final realization that these experiences, processed and stored in his memory, reflect his inner life more truly than does his outer life, that their resuscitation in their immediacy destroys spans of elapsed time, that their telling answers his long search for an artistic vocation, and that they form, in fact, the substance of his novel. A key event in the resolution of the novel is the narrator's discovery of the powers of involuntary memory.

Proust began his novel in July 1909, and he worked furiously on it until death interrupted his corrections, revisions, and additions. In 1913, after several rejections, he found in Grasset a publisher who would produce, at the author's expense, the first of three projected volumes (Du Côté de chez Swann, Le Côté de Guermantes, and Le Temps retrouvé; Swann's Way, The Guermantes Way, and Time Regained). After the appearance of the first volume, André Gide, who had earlier rejected Proust's manuscript on behalf of Gallimard, changed his mind and in 1916 obtained the rights to publish the subsequent volumes. Meanwhile, World War I interrupted publication but not Proust's continued ex-

This bridge at Illiers inspired passages in Proust's Remembrance of Things Past. *It spans the Loire, called the Vivonne in the novel series. (Lapad-Viollet)*

pansion of his work. À l'ombre des jeunes filles en fleur (Within a Budding Grove), originally only a chapter title, appeared late in 1918 as the second volume and won the Goncourt Prize the following year. As volumes appeared, Proust continually expanded his material, inserting long sections as close to publication as the galley stage. Le Côté de Guermantes appeared in 1920; Sodome et Gomorrhe (Cities of the Plain), Part 1, appeared in 1921 and the two volumes of Part 2 in 1922. Feeling his end approaching, Proust finished drafting his novel and began revising and correcting proofs, expanding the text as he went along with what he called "supernourishment." Proust had completed revisions of La Prisonnière (The Captive) and had begun reworking Albertine disparue (The Sweet Cheat Gone) when, on Nov. 18, 1922, he died of bronchitis and pneumonia contracted after a series of violent asthma attacks. The final volumes of his novel appeared owing to the interest of his brother, Robert, and to the editorial supervision of Jacques Rivière: La Prisonnière, two volumes, 1923; Albertine disparue, two volumes, 1925; and Le Temps retrouvé, two volumes, 1927.

Further Reading

Marcel Proust is listed in the Literature study guide (III, I, 1, b; III, J, 1, a). James JOYCE and Thomas MANN were other major 20th-century novelists.

The major critical biography of Proust is George D. Painter, Proust (2 vols., 1959–1965). There are numerous critical studies of Proust's work in English. The most useful general introduction is Germaine Brée, The World of Marcel Proust (1966), which contains an extensive annotated bibliography. Other valuable studies are J. M.

Cocking, *Proust* (1956); William S. Bell, *Proust's Nocturnal Muse* (1962); and Roger Shattuck, *Proust's Binoculars: A Study of Memory, Time and Recognition in "À la recherche du temps perdu"* (1963). See also the chapters on Proust in Edmund Wilson, *Axel's Castle: A Study in Imaginative Literature of 1870–1930* (1931), and Harry Levin, *The Gates of Horn: A Study of Five French Realists* (1963). For general and historical background see Alfred Cobban, *A History of Modern France* (2 vols., 1957–1961; 3d ed., 3 vols., 1966–1967), and Barbara W. Tuchman, *The Proud Tower: A Portrait of the World before the War, 1890–1914* (1966).

PRUD'HON / By James L. Connelly

The work of the French painter Pierre Paul Prud'hon (1758–1823) stands between neoclassicism and romanticism. Best known for his allegorical paintings, he was also a successful portraitist.

Pierre Paul Prud'hon (pronounced prü-dôN′) was born at Cluny on April 4, 1758. In 1774 he went to Dijon to study painting. He was so successful as a student that in 1780 a nobleman of the district made it possible for him to go to Paris to study at the Royal Academy. In 1784 Prud'hon won the Prix de Rome, an award given by the academy to allow promising artists to study in Italy. He was in Italy until 1788.

In 1791 Prud'hon began showing his paintings in the Paris exhibitions (Salons). During the Revolutionary turmoil of the early 1790s he retreated to Burgundy, but after 1796 he resided in Paris and by 1800 was moving in the highest circles surrounding Napoleon, the new ruler of France. Prud'hon was appointed drawing master to Empress Josephine, Napoleon's first wife, and to Empress Marie Louise, Napoleon's second wife. He also enjoyed substantial patronage from the Napoleonic government for the execution of various art projects.

During Prud'hon's career, painting in France was pervaded by a severe neoclassicism and ruled by Jacques Louis David, the painter who brought the neoclassic style to its culmination and who dominated the arts in France from about 1785 to 1815. Prud'hon was well aware of the prevailing style, and one of his best friends was Antonio Canova, the leading neoclassic sculptor of the period. However, French painting was turning away from the precise draftsmanship and sculptural solidity of neoclassicism even before 1815. Within this context of shifting styles and a transitional period, Prud'hon developed an individualistic style which stands apart from the classicism of his period; his work looks back to the soft, decorative painting of the rococo and also forward to the bravura and drama of 19th-century romanticism.

In the *Union of Love and Friendship*, an allegorical work of 1793, Prud'hon makes obvious reference to clas-

sical antiquity, but the delicacy with which the graceful nude forms are rendered, the decorative composition, and the soft atmospheric tonality are very different from David's hard classicism. By 1808, the date of *Divine Vengeance Pursuing Crime*, Prud'hon had moved decisively in the direction of early romanticism. This painting, with its swooping forms, its air of desperate drama, and its shadowy lighting, links him to the romantic style which was to replace neoclassicism about 1820 and reach its height of expression in the work of Eugène Delacroix. Prud'hon was a respected portraitist, and his most famous work in this area is *Portrait of the Empress Josephine* (1805), which shows the Empress reclining languidly in a romantic, leafy glade.

The fall of the Napoleonic regime in 1815 inevitably damaged Prud'hon's artistic career, and his later years were also marred by personal unhappiness. He died in Paris on Feb. 16, 1823.

Further Reading

Pierre Paul Prud'hon is listed in the Art study guide (III, G, 1, b). The leading neoclassic artists of the period were Jacques Louis DAVID and Antonio CANOVA. Romanticism culminated in the art of Eugène DELACROIX.

There is no biography or monograph on Prud'hon in English, and reference to him must be sought in general works. Recommended surveys include Walter Fried-

Pierre Paul Prud'hon. (Cultural Services of the French Embassy)

laender, *David to Delacroix* (trans. 1952); Fritz Novotny, *Painting and Sculpture in Europe, 1780–1880* (1960); and Jean Leymarie, *French Painting: The Nineteenth Century* (trans. 1962). An excellent analysis of the complex period in which Prud'hon began working is Robert Rosenblum, *Transformation in Late Eighteenth-Century Art* (1967).

PRZHEVALSKY / By Robert E. Johnson

Nikolai Mikhailovich Przhevalsky (1839–1888) was a Russian general and traveler whose explorations were major contributions to the geography of central Asia.

Nikolai Przhevalsky. (Radio Times Hulton Picture Library)

Of Polish descent, Nikolai Przhevalsky (pronounced pər-zhə-vȧl′skĭ) was born on March 31, 1839, in Kimbory in the Smolensk district. His education was at the gymnasium in Smolensk. His military career started in 1855 with an appointment as a subaltern in an infantry regiment. In 1855 he was appointed as an officer, and in 1860 he entered the academy of the general staff. From 1864 to 1866 he taught geography at the military school in Warsaw. In 1867 he became a general officer and was assigned to Irkutsk near Lake Baikal.

Przhevalsky's first serious exploration was of the valley of the Ussuri River from its source at Lake Khanka in eastern Manchuria to its junction with the Amur River, with particular emphasis on the highlands of the Ussuri River and the foothills of the Sikhote Alin Range. The Vladivostok leg of the Trans-Siberian railway was laid out along this route.

Przhevalsky made five major expeditions. The first lasted from November 1870 to September 1873. With three men he set out from Kyakhta, south of Lake Baikal, traveled through Urga (Ulan Bator), crossed the Gobi Desert, and reached Kalgan, 100 miles northwest of Peking. On the return he explored the Ordos Plateau to the Ala Shan Range and Koko Nor and mapped parts of the upper Hwang Ho and the upper Yangtze. Finally he penetrated Tibet and reached the Drechu River.

The main objective of the second expedition (1877–1878) was to reach Lhasa through east Turkistan. Starting from Kuldja (44°N, 82°E), Przhevalsky went by way of the Tien Shan Range and Takla Makan Desert, traveling 200 miles along the foot of the Astin (Altyn) Tagh Range. He claimed to have rediscovered the great salt lake of the Chinese classical writers, Lop Nor, in the desert at 41°N, 91°E. This was one of the most interesting, yet controversial, of all his discoveries. Von Richthofen disputed the claim on the grounds that the lake was of fresh, not salt, water and that it was too far south. Sven Hedin, in two visits to Lop Nor (1895, 1900), established that Przhevalsky's lake shifts west as a result of wind and sandstorms. Hedin also found a dried salt basin, presumably the old original Lop Nor, and a number of lakes of recent origin. Kozlov dated some of these from 1750, thus agreeing with Hedin.

The third expedition tried to reach Lhasa (1879–1880). Setting out from Lake Zaysan near the northern border of Sinkiang, Przhevalsky crossed the Dzungaria region to Hami (43°N, 93°E). Thence he went south over the Astin Tagh Range and penetrated the Tsaidam swamp and the great valley of the Kyaring Tso. Reaching Nagchu Dzong, 170 miles north of Lhasa, he was turned back by order of the Lama. He went northeast, reached the upper Hwang Ho, and crossed the Gobi Desert to Kyakhta (51°N, 47°E).

Przhevalsky's fourth journey was in the mountains between Mongolia and Tibet (1883–1885). Starting from Urga, he crossed the Gobi Desert to Koko Nor and the Tsaidam region and thence to the Astin Tagh and the Shan Kunlun. He revisited Lop Nor and confirmed his previous findings of 1878 on this interesting region. He returned to Siberia by crossing the Tien Shan to Issyk Kul, a lake on the west border of Sinkiang.

Przhevalsky's fifth and final expedition was toward Lhasa (1888), a goal he always held but never reached. On Nov. 1, 1888, Przhevalsky died at Karakol on Issyk Kul. As a monument, a large cross was set up, and as a memorial, the town of Karakol was renamed Przhevalsk. It is in the Kirgiz S.S.R., 8 miles southeast of Issyk Kul.

This explorer's success depended upon small parties, moving fast. For the first expedition he chose three Cossacks. In the fourth expedition, they logged some 15,000 miles in 3 years, a tribute to their physical strength and resourcefulness in coping with severe environments, difficult terrain, and delicate relations with sometimes hostile natives.

Further Reading

Nikolai Przhevalsky is listed in the Geography and Exploration study guide (VI, A, 7, b). Another central Asian explorer was Gabriel BONVALOT.

There is no full-length biography of Przhevalsky in English. Gerald Roe Crone, ed., *The Explorers: Great Adventurers Tell Their Own Stories of Discovery* (1962), has a short discussion of Przhevalsky and a selection of his writings. His career is briefly recounted in Percy Sykes, *A History of Exploration: From the Earliest Times to the Present Day* (1934; 3d ed. 1949), and Joachim G. Leithaüser, *Worlds beyond the Horizon* (trans. 1955).

PTOLEMY I / By Jack M. Balcer

Ptolemy I Soter (367/366–283 B.C.) was a Macedonian general under Alexander the Great, founder of the Ptolemaic dynasty of Egypt, and biographer of Alexander.

Born in the upper Macedonian region of Eordaia to the Macedonian nobleman Lagos and Arsinoë, Ptolemy (pronounced tŏl′ə-mē) grew up in the royal court at Pella. In 343 he joined Alexander at Mieza and there studied for 3 years with Aristotle.

Ptolemy returned to Pella with Alexander by 340 and supported his younger friend's quarrel with his father, Philip, in 337. Alexander left Macedonia with his mother Olympias, Ptolemy, and his close friends for Epirus and Illyria but soon returned to Macedonia. Alexander remained estranged from Philip, who banished Ptolemy from the court because he considered him a dangerous adviser to his son.

Alexander's Adviser and General

In 336, when Philip was assassinated by a conspiracy of nobles, Ptolemy returned to the court and supported Alexander's claim to the feudal throne. Alexander, in turn, appointed him Companion, Life-guard, and Seneschal. Ptolemy accompanied Alexander on his campaigns to the Danube in 336 and to crush the Corinthian League's rebellion and to destroy perfidious Thebes in 335.

Ptolemy encouraged and aided Alexander's invasion of Asia Minor to liberate the eastern Greeks from the Persian Empire of Darius III and to invade Syria and conquer Persia. Ptolemy fought at Issos in 333 and, riding beside Alexander, pursued Darius into the hills; he accompanied Alexander through Phoenicia and in the siege of Tyre in 332 and marched through Jerusalem to Egypt.

In Egypt, Ptolemy aided Alexander's peaceful conquest of the country and the founding of Alexandria in the western delta, and probably accompanied his king to the temple of Zeus Ammon in Siwa. Ptolemy quickly realized the immense value of Egypt, its structure as a geographical entity, and he developed keen interests in the region.

From Egypt, Ptolemy accompanied Alexander to northern Mesopotamia and the third and final major conflict with Darius's armies, at Gaugamela in 331. During the next 6 years Ptolemy campaigned with Alexander through western India and along the Indus Valley. Ptolemy recognized Alexander's claim to the Persian throne and tiara without hesitation and revealed to Alexander the instigation of Callisthenes in the conspiracy of the royal pages to assassinate him. In India, Ptolemy fought beside Alexander and in one melée saved his king's life.

At Susa in 324, when Alexander bade his Companions marry Persians, Ptolemy dutifully married Artacama, the daughter of the Persian nobleman Artabazos. But after Alexander's death Ptolemy quickly divorced her.

Ruler of Egypt

With Alexander's death in Babylon on June 13, 323,

Ptolemy I, a portrait bust in the Louvre, Paris. (Giraudon)

Ptolemy's political and military ambitions were freed. He momentarily recognized the faulty corulership of Alexander's epileptic half brother Arrhidaeios and his posthumous son Alexander and immediately claimed Egypt as his satrapy. Ptolemy strongly opposed Perdikkas, even while Alexander lay dying, to whom Alexander gave his signet ring and the regency of the empire.

Ptolemy brought Alexander's body for burial to Memphis, though Alexander had wished to be buried at Siwa. Ptolemy built an altar there for Alexander but retained the body at Memphis until a suitable mausoleum could be built in Ptolemy's new capital, Alexandria.

Perdikkas's regency rapidly fell to violent warfare among Ptolemy, Lysimachos who held Thrace, Antigonus the "One-Eyed" in Greater Phrygia, and Seleucus who desired Syria. Until 281 the "successors" fought bitterly. In 306 Antigonus assumed the title of king and claimed all of Alexander's empire. In opposition, Ptolemy declared Egypt's independence, proclaimed himself king of Egypt, and established a dynasty which lasted until Cleopatra's suicide in 30 B.C.

After Ptolemy I divorced Artacama, he married the Macedonian noblewoman Eurydice. Unhappy with this political alliance, Ptolemy put her aside and by 317 married his widowed half sister and mistress, a niece of Eurydice, the girl Berenice (I), almost 27 years his younger. Berenice gave birth to two children, Arsinoë (II) and Ptolemy (II).

In Upper Egypt, Ptolemy I founded the city Ptolemais. As satrap of Egypt, he clashed violently with Cleomenes of Naucrates, whom Alexander in 332 had appointed financial manager of Egypt and administrative chief of the eastern delta and had entrusted with the completion of Alexandria. Cleomenes, however, had assumed the satrapship, but Alexander had pardoned him. In 321 Ptolemy charged Cleomenes with embezzlement of funds and executed him, thereby removing a political rival.

Between 306 and 286 Ptolemy concentrated on the development of his empire. He gained control of Cyrene and conquered Palestine, coastal Syria, and Cyprus. In 286 he became protector of the southern Cycladic islands and their center at Delos. Throughout his empire he established the well-constructed Ptolemaic administration: he built the legal and military organizations and the military settlements, raised mercenary armies, and conscripted native levies.

Ptolemy wrote an excellent history of Alexander and his campaigns for which he utilized Alexander's daily *Journal* and other official materials. Arrian's *Anabasis* (2d century A.D.) preserves much of Ptolemy's study.

In 285 Ptolemy abdicated in favor of his 22-year-old son, Ptolemy II. Two years later Ptolemy I died and was deified by the young king in 279 and given the title Theos Soter, "God and Savior."

Further Reading

Ptolemy I is listed in the Ancient History study guide (I, A, 7). Other successors of ALEXANDER THE GREAT were ANTIGONUS I and SELEUCUS I.

Edwyn Bevan, *The House of Ptolemy* (1927), remains the major study of Ptolemy I and Ptolemaic Egypt. Charles Alexander Robinson, Jr., *The Ephemerides of Alexander's Expedition* (1932), discusses in detail the *Journal* used in Ptolemy's biography of Alexander. A general view of the period is in W. W. Tarn and G. T. Griffith, *Hellenistic Civilisation* (1927; 3d ed. 1963). See also J. P. Mahaffy, *The Empire of the Ptolemies* (1895).

PTOLEMY II / By Margaret S. Drower

Ptolemy II (308–246 B.C.) was a king of Egypt, the second and greatest of the Lagid dynasty of Macedonian kings who ruled Egypt between 323 and 30 B.C. He was later known by the epithet Philadelphus, "Brother-loving," which he shared with his wife Arsinoë.

Ptolemy was born in Cos, the younger son of Ptolemy I by his favorite wife, Berenice. Small and slightly built and of delicate constitution, Ptolemy II succeeded his father, who abdicated in his favor in 285 B.C.; his elder brother, Ptolemy Ceraunus, was made king of Macedonia.

Consolidation of an Empire

Ptolemy inherited Palestine and resisted the attempts of Antiochus I, the Seleucid king of Syria, to wrest it from him. Ptolemy's ships controlled the eastern Mediterranean, and he was master of Cyprus, the Phoenician coast, and part of northern Syria, while his second marriage brought him possessions in the Aegean. A further Syrian war with Antiochus II ended with the marriage of the Seleucid king to Ptolemy's daughter Berenice Syra. After the defeat of Pyrrhus in 275, Ptolemy concluded a treaty with Rome to which he remained faithful during the Punic Wars.

Ptolemy II was an able administrator and a farseeing statesman. At home he had two main problems: to integrate the Greeks into the essentially alien environment of the ancient land of Egypt and to increase the kingdom's productivity and prosperity. Like his father, he took pains to make himself acceptable to the Egyptian priesthood. His marriage to his sister, which scandalized the Greeks, was in the pharaonic tradition. He founded a ruler cult, deifying members of the dynasty and instituting priesthoods in their honor.

Ptolemy encouraged learning and built the great library at Alexandria, making the city a brilliant center of art and learning; the city's lighthouse, the Pharos, became known as one of the Seven Wonders of the World. In order to promote commerce, Ptolemy established a network of trading posts on the coasts of the Mediterranean, the Red Sea, and East Africa and redug the ancient canal joining the Nile to the Red Sea.

Ptolemy also undertook great schemes of land recla-

Ptolemy II of Egypt, detail of a colossal red-granite statue dated about 260 B.C. *The statue was found at Heliopolis. (Vatican Museums, Rome)*

mation, especially in the Fayyum, where he planted Greek colonists in new towns. New methods of agriculture were introduced and the growing of vines and olives encouraged, and livestock was improved by the introduction of new breeds. Trade in many commodities became a royal monopoly, from which the Crown gained large revenues. The luxury and profligacy of his court were unparalleled in the world of his time.

Further Reading

Ptolemy II is listed in the Ancient History study guide (I, A, 7). PTOLEMY I founded the dynasty in Egypt.

There is no work devoted to Ptolemy II. The best study of the age in which he lived is M. Rostovtzeff, *The Social and Economic History of the Hellenistic World* (3 vols., 1941). For Egypt under the Ptolemies see Edwyn Bevan, *The House of Ptolemy* (1927). A less detailed treatment is H. I. Bell, *Egypt from Alexander the Great to the Arab Conquest* (1948).

PTOLEMY / By David Pingree

The Greek astronomer, astrologer, and geographer Claudius Ptolemy (ca. 100–ca. 170) established the system of mathematical astronomy that remained standard in Christian and Moslem countries until the 16th century.

P tolemy is known to have made astronomical observations at Alexandria in Egypt between 127 and 141, and he probably lived on into the reign of Marcus Aurelius (161–180). Beyond the fact that his *On the Faculty of Judgment* indicates his adherence to Stoic doctrine, nothing more of his biography is available.

The "Almagest"

The earliest and most influential of Ptolemy's major writings is the *Almagest*. In 13 books it establishes the kinematic models (purely mathematical and nonphysical) used to explain solar, lunar, and planetary motion and determines the parameters which quantify these models and permit the computation of longitudes and latitudes; of the times, durations, and magnitudes of lunar and solar eclipses; and of the times of heliacal risings and settings. Ptolemy also provides a catalog of 1,022 fixed stars, giving for each its longitude and latitude according to an ecliptic coordinate system.

Ptolemy's is a geocentric system, though the earth is the actual center only of the sphere of the fixed stars and of the "crank mechanism" of the moon; the orbits of all the other planets are slightly eccentric. Ptolemy thus hypothesizes a mathematical system which cannot be made to agree with the rules of Aristotelian physics, which require that the center of the earth be the center of all celestial circular motions.

In solar astronomy Ptolemy accepts and confirms the eccentric model and its parameters established by Hipparchus. For the moon Ptolemy made enormous improvements in Hipparchus's model, though he was unable to surmount all the difficulties of lunar motion evident even to ancient astronomers. Ptolemy discerned two more inequalities and proposed a complicated model to account for them. The effect of the Ptolemaic lunar model is to draw the moon close enough to the earth at quadratures to produce what should be a visible increase in apparent diameter; the increase, however, was not visible. The Ptolemaic models for the planets generally account for the two inequalities in planetary motion and are represented by combinations of circular motions: eccentrics and epicycles. Such a combination of eccentric and epicyclic models represents Ptolemy's principal original contribution in the *Almagest*.

"Canobic Inscription"

This brief text was inscribed on a stele erected at Canobus near Alexandria in Egypt in 146 or 147. It contains the parameters of Ptolemy's solar, lunar, and planetary models as given in the *Almagest* but modified in some instances. There is also a section on the harmony of the spheres. The epoch of the *Canobic Inscription* is the first year of Augustus, or 30 B.C.

"Planetary Hypotheses"

In the two books of *Planetary Hypotheses*, an important cosmological work, Ptolemy "corrects" some of the parameters of the *Almagest* and suggests an improved model to explain planetary latitude. In the section of the first book preserved only in Arabic, he proposes absolute dimensions for the celestial spheres (maximum and minimum distances of the planets, their apparent and actual diameters, and their volumes). The second book, preserved only in Arabic, describes a physical actualization of the mathematical models of the planets in the *Almagest*. Here the conflict with Aristotelian physics becomes unavoidable (Ptolemy uses Aristotelian terminology but makes no attempt to reconcile his views of the causes of the inequalities of planetary motion with Aristotle's), and it was in attempting to remove the discrepancies that the "School of Maragha" and also Ibn al-Shatir in the 13th and 14th centuries devised new planetary models that largely anticipate Copernicus's.

The "Phases"

This work originally contained two books, but only the second has survived. It is a calendar of the *parapegma* type, giving for each day of the Egyptian year the time of heliacal rising or setting of certain fixed stars. The views of Eudoxus, Hipparchus, Philip of Opus, Callippus, Euctemon, and others regarding the meteorological phenomena associated with these risings and settings are quoted. This makes the *Phases* useful to the historian of early Greek astronomy, though it is certainly the least important of Ptolemy's astronomical works.

The "Apotelesmatica"

Consisting of four books, the *Apotelesmatica* is Ptolemy's contribution to astrological theory. He attempts in the first book to place astrology on a sound scientific basis. Astrology for Ptolemy is less exact than astronomy is, as the former deals with objects influenced by many other factors besides the positions of the planets at a particular point in time, whereas the latter describes the unswerving motions of the eternal stars themselves. In the second book, general astrology affecting whole states, societies, and regions is described; this general astrology is largely derived from Mesopotamian astral omina. The final two books are devoted to genethlialogy, the science of predicting the events in the life of a native from the horoscope cast for the moment of his birth. The *Apotelesmatica* was long the main handbook for astrologers.

The "Geography"

In the eight books of the *Geography*, Ptolemy sets forth mathematical solutions to the problems of representing the spherical surface of the earth on a plane surface (a map), but the work is largely devoted to a list of localities with their coordinates. This list is arranged by regions, with the river and mountain systems and the ethnography of each region also usually described. He begins at the West in book 2 (his prime meridian ran through the "Fortunate Islands," apparently the Canaries) and proceeds eastward to India, the Malay Peninsula, and China in book 7.

Despite his brilliant mathematical theory of map making, Ptolemy had not the requisite material to construct the accurate picture of the world that he desired. Aside from the fact that, following Marinus in this as in much

Ptolemy. This painting, now in the Louvre, Paris, is one of a series of 28 portraits of philosophers and poets painted for the studiolo of Federigo da Montefeltro in the ducal palace in Urbino, Italy. (Giraudon)

else, he underestimated the size of the earth, concluding that the distance from the Canaries to China is about 180° instead of about 130°, he was seriously hampered by the lack of all the gnomon observations that are necessary to establish the latitudes of the places he lists. For longitudes he could not utilize astronomical observations because no systematic exploitation of this method of determining longitudinal differences had been organized. He was compelled to rely on travelers' estimates of distances, which varied widely in their reliability and were most uncertain guides. His efforts, however, provided western Europe, Byzantium, and Islam with their most detailed conception of the inhabited world.

"Harmonics" and "Optics"

These, the last two works in the surviving corpus of Ptolemy's writings, investigate two other fields included in antiquity in the general field of mathematics. The *Harmonics* in three books became one of the standard works on the mathematical theory of music in late antiquity and throughout the Byzantine period. The *Optics* in five books discussed the geometry of vision, especially mirror reflection and refraction. The *Optics* survives only in a Latin translation prepared by Eugenius, Admiral of Sicily, toward the end of the 12th century, from an

Arabic version in which the first book and the end of the fifth were lost. The doubts surrounding its authenticity as a work of Ptolemy seem to have been overcome by recent scholarship.

His Influence

Ptolemy's brilliance as a mathematician, his exactitude, and his masterful presentation seemed to his successors to have exhausted the possibilities of mathematical astronomy and geography. To a large extent they were right. Without better instrumentation only minor adjustments in the Ptolemaic parameters or models could be made. The major "improvements" in the models—those of the School of Maragha—are designed primarily to satisfy philosophy, not astronomy; the lunar theory was the only exception. Most of the deviations from Ptolemaic methods in medieval astronomy are due to the admixture of non-Greek material and the continued use of pre-Ptolemaic elements. The *Geography* was never seriously challenged before the 15th century.

The authority of the astronomical and geographical works carries over to the astrological treatise and, to a lesser extent, to the *Harmonics* and *Optics*. The *Apotelesmatica* was always recognized as one of the works most clearly defending the scientific basis of astrology in general, and of genethlialogy in particular. But Neoplatonism as developed by the pagans of Harran provided a more extended theory of the relationship of the celestial spheres to the sublunar world, and this theory was popularized in Islam in the 9th century. The *Harmonics* ceased to be popular as Greek music ceased to follow the classical modes, and the *Optics* was rendered obsolete by Moslem scientists. Ptolemy's fame and influence, then, rest primarily on the *Almagest*, his most original work, justly subtitled *The Greatest*.

Further Reading

Ptolemy is listed in the Science study guide (I, B, 2; I, C, 1). Many of his observations and techniques were derived from the works of HIPPARCHUS.

There is no comprehensive study of Ptolemy's life and works. Most of the scholarly discussion of Ptolemy is contained in critical editions of the Greek texts (there is still no critical edition of the *Geography*) and in numerous scholarly periodicals. One fairly complete bibliography is William H. Stahl, *Ptolemy's Geography: A Select Bibliography* (1953). For general background see H. F. Tozer, *A History of Ancient Geography* (1897; 2d ed. 1955); Percy Sykes, *A History of Exploration* (1934; 3d ed. 1950); James Oliver Thomson, *History of Ancient Geography* (1948); and C. Van Paassen, *The Classical Tradition of Geography* (1957).

* * *

PUCCINI / By Charles Hamm

The Italian composer Giacomo Puccini (1858–1924) was the most successful follower of Verdi, continuing the line of Italian operatic composers into the 20th century.

Born in Lucca on Dec. 22, 1858, into a family whose members had composed operas of local success for several generations, Giacomo Puccini (pronounced pōōt-chē′nē) learned the rudiments of music from the best local teachers, served as a church organist, and composed sacred choral works while still in his teens. A pension in 1880 from Queen Margherita made it possible for him to go to Milan for study at the conservatory. His most important teacher was the composer Amilcare Ponchielli, who encouraged him to write his first opera, *Le Villi*, in 1884. The work was entered in a competition sponsored by the Teatro Illustrato but received no recognition there; it was performed with such success at one of the smaller Milanese theaters that it was put on the stage at the famous La Scala opera house in 1885.

Edgar, done at La Scala in 1889, was a failure, but *Manon Lescaut*, performed in Turin in 1893, was favorably received and soon became a popular work throughout Italy and abroad. Puccini's first spectacular triumph came in 1896 with *La Bohème*, to a libretto by Giacosa and Illica, premiered in Turin. Its touching portrayal of episodes in the lives and loves of students in Paris and the simplicity and accessibility of the music in gay, romantic, and pathetic scenes excited and moved audiences from

Giacomo Puccini. (Alinari)

the first performance on, and its popularity has continued to the present day in all countries that enjoy opera.

Tosca, again to a libretto by Giacosa and Illica, which was given in Rome in 1900, was a more serious and melodramatic work, with relatively few moments of lyricism, but it was almost as successful and has also become a mainstay of the standard repertory. *Madama Butterfly*, set in Japan, was the first work in which Puccini used scales and melodies of non-Western music. It was poorly received at the first performance at La Scala in 1904 but has since become every bit as popular as *La Bohème* and probably for the same reasons: there are long passages of lush and sentimental music, tunes that are easy to remember, effective scenes of pathos, and well-calculated bits of stage business. *Madama Butterfly* was also his last completely successful work.

Welcoming the opportunity to visit America, Puccini wrote a new work for the Metropolitan Opera in New York City: *The Girl of the Golden West* (*La fanciulla del West*). The first performance, in 1910, was received with the expected enthusiasm, but the opera was not so well received later and is rarely performed today. He endeavored to capture the local color of the American West; there are scenes of gambling and saloons and an attempted lynching, and some of the tunes try to sound like American songs. But in the end the music sounds just like Puccini, and not Puccini at his best.

A comic opera, *La Rondine*, given in Monte Carlo in 1917, has not held the stage. The following year Puccini wrote three one-act operas, *Il trittico*, designed to be done together as an evening's entertainment, and premiered in New York. The first, *Il tabarro*, is melodramatic, much in the style of parts of *Tosca*; *Suor Angelica*, set in a convent and written for women's voices, is lyric and subdued; and *Gianni Schicchi*, the most successful and often done separately, is his best comic work, rapid-paced with some fine moments of contrasting lyricism.

Death took Puccini before he could complete his last work, *Turandot*. He was nearing the end of the work when he was stricken by throat cancer and taken for an operation to Brussels, where he died on Nov. 29, 1924. The opera was completed by Alfano and first performed at La Scala, conducted by Arturo Toscanini, in 1926. It has some fine lyric moments and unusually effective dramatic ones, and in some places it makes more effective use of such pseudo-Oriental devices as pentatonic scales than did *Madama Butterfly*, but the work as a whole lacks some cohesion and has not been as perennially popular as some of his earlier operas.

Puccini's strengths are his delicate and sensitive handling of both voices and orchestra in lyric and pathetic scenes and occasionally in lively scenes as well and his ability to write melodies that audiences learn quickly and apparently never tire of hearing. His best scenes are those for one or two characters; ensemble writing in his operas rarely approaches the excitement common in the works of such predecessors as Gioacchino Rossini and Giuseppe Verdi.

Music was undergoing dramatic stylistic changes in the last decades of Puccini's life with the works of such men as Igor Stravinsky, Arnold Schoenberg, and Béla Bartók. Puccini clung to the harmonic and melodic language of the late 19th century. The problem of reconciliation between radical changes of musical language and the venerable form of opera has been a thorny one, and it should be noted that the last operas to be truly successful in terms of wide acceptance by audiences and retention in the repertory are those of Puccini and Richard Strauss, two men who remained on the periphery of the widespread innovation so characteristic of the first decades of the 20th century.

Further Reading

Giacomo Puccini is listed in the Music study guide (I, I, 8). He was the most outstanding follower of Giuseppe VERDI.

The Letters of Giacomo Puccini were edited by Giuseppe Adami (1928; trans. 1931). George Marek, *Puccini: A Biography* (1951), the most extensive work in English, is a subjective and romantic treatment of the composer. Puccini's operas are discussed in Max De Schauensee, *The Collector's Verdi and Puccini* (1962), and William Ashbrook, *The Operas of Puccini* (1968). For background material Donald Jay Grout, *A Short History of Opera* (1947; 2d ed. 1965), is recommended.

PUFENDORF / By Jackson Spielvogel

The German jurist and historian Baron Samuel von Pufendorf (1632–1694) is best known for his influential writings on international and natural law. His works became standard textbooks for both juristical and historical students in the 17th and 18th centuries.

Samuel von Pufendorf (pronounced pōō′fən-dôrf) was born on Jan. 8, 1632, near Chemnitz, Saxony. The son of a Lutheran minister, he began his higher education with the study of theology at the University of Leipzig. His dislike of theological studies caused him to change to legal studies, which he pursued at the University of Jena. In 1658 he traveled to Copenhagen, where he became a tutor to the children of the Swedish ambassador to Denmark. As a result of war between Denmark and Sweden, the Swedish official and his entire retinue were arrested. Pufendorf, consequently, spent 8 months in prison. He apparently used this time to reflect on his previous legal studies, for, after his release, he went to Leiden and published in 1660 a complete system of universal law in his *Elementorum jurisprudentiae universalis libri duo* (*The Two Books of the Elements of Universal Jurisprudence*). This work was dedicated to the ruler of the Palatinate, who rewarded Pufendorf by creating a new chair of political and natural law at the University of Heidelberg. While in Heidelberg,

period of his life (1682), became the "first modern text-book in European history."

Further Reading

Samuel von Pufendorf is listed in the Social Sciences study guide (IV, B, 2) and the International Law study guide (III, B). He was influenced by Hugo GROTIUS.

There is little biographical material on Pufendorf in English. A recent study of his life and ideas is Leonard Krieger, *The Politics of Discretion: Pufendorf and the Acceptance of Natural Law* (1965). See also George Louis Bissonnette, *Pufendorf and the Church Reforms of Peter the Great* (1962). General background is in Harry Elmer Barnes, *A History of Historical Writing* (1937), and Herbert Butterfield, *Man on His Past: The Study of the History of Historical Scholarship* (1960).

＊　　＊　　＊

Samuel von Pufendorf, an engraving by Joachim von Sandrart. (Bildarchiv)

he published *De statu imperii Germanici* (*On the State of the German Empire*), a critical analysis of the organization of the Holy Roman Empire.

In 1670 Pufendorf accepted a new professorial position at the University of Lund in Sweden. There in 1672 he published his greatest work, *De jure naturae et gentium libri octo* (*The Eight Books on the Law of Nature and Nations*). A summary was published the following year, entitled *De officio hominis et civis* (*On the Duty of Man and Citizen*). In these works Pufendorf expanded upon the theories of Hugo Grotius and Thomas Hobbes. He rejected Hobbes's view of man in his natural state by maintaining that the state of nature was one of peace, not of war. Pufendorf developed a concept of secularized natural law, holding that natural law was concerned with man in this life and was derived from human reason.

In 1677 Pufendorf virtually gave up his preoccupation with law and turned to historical studies. In that year he became the official historian to the Swedish king. As a result, he wrote histories of the reigns of Gustavus II and Charles Gustavus. Called to the service of Elector Frederick William of Brandenburg and his successor, Elector Frederick III, Pufendorf completed a history of the former's reign, but he had barely begun one on Frederick III when he died on Oct. 26, 1694. Although his historical works were rather stilted, they were based on archival material and demonstrated a respect for truth. Pufendorf's general history of Europe, also written during this

PUGACHEV / By Sidney Harcave

The Russian Cossack soldier Emelyan Ivanovich Pugachev (1742–1775) led the peasant rebellion in Russia in 1773–1775.

E melyan Pugachev (pronounced pŏŏ-gə-chôf′), a Don Cossack, was born in the village of Zimoveiskaya. The main course of his life was influenced initially by the fact that, as a Don Cossack, he was subject, when of age, to duty in the Russian army. In 1770, during a Russo-Turkish conflict in which he was serving, he was given a temporary leave and, at its expiration, refused to return to his regiment. Arrested, he managed to escape, thus beginning his life as a strong-willed fugitive.

In the course of his subsequent wanderings Pugachev was struck by the bitter unrest he found among the lower classes in Russia. What he saw convinced him that the time was ripe for revolt, and being a rebel by nature and having a bent toward leadership, he took upon himself the task of directing a revolt. As a basis for appeal, he decided to assume the character of Czar Peter III, having observed that many credulous people distrusted the official report that Peter had died in 1762.

With about 80 Cossacks committed to his scheme, in September 1773 Pugachev proclaimed himself Peter III and called on the oppressed to follow him in an uprising against Catherine II (the Great). He began his campaign along the Yaik (now called the Ural) River, gathering followers among disgruntled Cossacks, fugitive serfs, released convicts, religious dissenters, Bashkirs, and Tatars. Although the force he assembled was neither well trained nor well disciplined, it was large enough to defeat local military units sent against it. To widen his campaign, Pugachev undertook the capture of Orenburg (Chkalov), the major center of government strength on the Yaik River, setting up headquarters and laying siege to the city. Meanwhile, news of the revolt prompted bloody uprisings against landlords and government officials along the Volga River and in the region east of it. Thousands left their homes to join the rebel army, and they increased its numbers to about 25,000.

Late in 1773 Catherine II, judging the revolt dangerous enough to warrant her action, sent a large force to suppress it. Pugachev was compelled to end the siege of Orenburg, but he eluded capture by the government forces. Again he marshaled a sizable following and, in July 1774, was able to resume the offensive and capture the city of Kazan. At the same time, serf uprisings took place near Nizhni Novgorod (Gorki) only 275 miles east of Moscow.

Catherine, now deeply alarmed by the nearness of the revolt, sent new contingents against Pugachev. They succeeded in destroying most of his army, near Tsaritsyn (Stalingrad), but he once again evaded efforts to capture him. Still determined, Pugachev made his way to the Yaik Cossack region, hoping that Yaik and Don Cossacks would provide him with a new army. Instead of being given support, however, he was betrayed. A group of Cossacks opposed to his aims seized him and handed him over to the authorities.

Taken in chains to Moscow, Pugachev was tried and sentenced to death. On Jan. 10, 1775, he was beheaded and quartered before a large Moscow crowd.

Further Reading

Emelyan Pugachev is listed in the European History

Emelyan Pugachev (with image of Catherine the Great), painting by an unknown artist. (Bildarchiv)

study guide (VI, I, 1). He led an uprising against CATHERINE THE GREAT.

The best account, in English, concerning Pugachev is in Philip Longworth, *The Cossacks* (1970). An excellent analysis by Marc Raeff of the causes of the Pugachev revolt is in Robert Forster and Jack P. Greene, eds., *Preconditions of Revolution in Early Modern Europe* (1971).

PUGIN / By James F. O'Gorman

Augustus Welby Northmore Pugin (1812–1852) was the most influential English ecclesiastical architect of his day and the principal theoretician of the Gothic revival.

Born in London on March 1, 1812, A. W. N. Pugin was the son of, and early assistant to, Augustus Charles Pugin, the producer of pattern books of Gothic building, such as *Examples of Gothic Architecture* (1831). The younger Pugin's conversion to Catholicism in 1834 led to a series of publications defending his chosen religion against the Established Church and advocating a correct Gothic style for its buildings. These publications had a great influence beyond the small circle of aristocratic Catholic restorationists, such as Lord Shrewsbury, who were Pugin's principal patrons.

Pugin's propaganda campaign began with the publication, at his own expense—since it was too controversial for a commercial publisher—of his intemperate *Contrasts* (1836; 2d ed. enlarged, 1841). The theme of contrast between the unity and goodness of the Middle Ages and the pluralism and degeneracy of the industrialized 19th century was common in intellectual circles of the time, but Pugin gave it architectural expression through a series of plates contrasting medieval with modern, classically inspired buildings. The final plate, in which buildings from the two periods are weighed on the scales of Truth and the modern ones "found wanting," summed up Pugin's attitude. This work established architectural criticism on an ethical basis. Only good men (that is, Christians, and more specifically, Catholics) build good buildings (that is, Gothic ones; classical buildings are pagan). John Ruskin made this a fundamental principle of architectural criticism in his popular *Seven Lamps of Architecture* (1849).

Pugin's *The True Principles of Pointed or Christian Architecture* (1841) explained the Gothic as a rational, utilitarian architectural system in stone and announced the "two great rules for design" as "1st, that there should be no features about a building which are not necessary for convenience, construction, or propriety; 2nd, that all ornament should consist of enrichment of the essential construction of the building."

In *Apology for the Revival of Christian Architecture*

A. W. N. Pugin. (National Portrait Gallery, London)

Further Reading

A. W. N. Pugin is listed in the Art study guide (III, I, 2, b). His *True Principles* heralded the rationalist theory of Eugène Emmanuel VIOLLET-LE-DUC and the functionalist theory of the early 20th century.

The older biographies of Pugin by Benjamin Ferry, *Recollections of A. N. Welby Pugin* (1861), and by Michael Trappes-Lomax, *Pugin* (1933), have been superseded by Phoebe Stanton's well-illustrated *Pugin* (1970). For a brief account of Pugin's role in English Catholicism see Denis R. Gwynn, *Lord Shrewsbury, Pugin and the Catholic Revival* (1946). His buildings are discussed in the context of the architecture of his time in Henry-Russell Hitchcock, *Early Victorian Architecture in Britain* (1954). There are good chapters on Pugin's life and work in Kenneth Clark, *The Gothic Revival* (1928), and in Alexandra Clark, *Victorian Architecture*, edited by Peter Ferriday (1963).

PULASKI / By Joseph Ernst

Casimir Pulaski (1747/1748–1779), Polish patriot and American Revolutionary War hero, fought unsuccessfully against foreign control of his native Poland and then journeyed to America to fight in the American Revolution.

in England (1843) Pugin added nationalism to religion as a justification for using Gothic forms. Christian or Gothic architecture is "the only correct expression of the faith, wants, and climate of our country . . . whilst we profess the creed of Christians, whilst we glory in being Englishmen, let us have an architecture, the arrangement and details of which alike remind us of our faith and our country." The classically inspired buildings of his contemporaries had no place in England because they were not Gothic and therefore neither Christian nor English.

The Present State of Ecclesiastical Architecture in England (1843), illustrating and describing Pugin's own church designs, pointed out his religious use of Gothic. His ornamental contributions in the English Perpendicular style to Charles Barry's Houses of Parliament (1836 onward) demonstrated the application of Gothic in the cause of nationalism.

Pugin's influence through these publications was far-reaching, but his buildings, some 70 in all, also represent an impressive achievement. They range from small parish churches such as St. Giles's, Cheadle, Staffordshire (1841–1846), to cathedrals such as St. Chad's, Birmingham (1839–1841), and from great country houses such as Alton Towers, Staffordshire (1840–1844), the seat of Lord Shrewsbury, and Scarisbrick Hall, Lancashire (after 1837), to monastic and other institutional buildings such as St. John's Hospital, Alton, Staffordshire (1840–1842). Quality varies with the budget in these works, but all are more Victorian than Gothic, and they reflect the infant state of medieval studies of the period.

Pugin died on Sept. 14, 1852, in Ramsgate, Kent, and was buried there in the church of St. Augustine, designed and built (1846–1851) at his own expense.

Born in Podolia, Casimir Pulaski (po͝o-lăs′kē) was the eldest son of Count Joseph Pulaski. After brief service in the guard of Duke Charles of Courland (now a part of Latvia), Pulaski returned home to Poland. In 1768 he joined forces with the Confederation of Bar, a movement founded by his father, in a revolt against Russian domination of Poland. The confederation, however, proved to be too small to be victorious and was decisively defeated. Pulaski's estates having been confiscated, in 1772 at the time of the first partition of Poland he fled to Turkey. Here he remained for several years in a vain attempt to provoke the Turks into an attack on Russia. Finally, penniless and destitute, he left for Paris to seek other employment.

In the spring of 1775, as the American Revolution was beginning, the American commissioners to France gave Pulaski money to make the voyage to Boston. He arrived there armed with a letter of introduction to Gen. George Washington. Shortly after a meeting with Washington in August of that same year, Pulaski became a volunteer member of the general's staff. Distinguishing himself at the Battle of the Brandywine in September, he was consequently given command of a newly created cavalry troop in Washington's army. During the winter of 1777 he and his men served at Trenton, at Flemington, and at Valley Forge, where Pulaski shared responsibility with Gen. Anthony Wayne for the provisioning of the starving Americans. But difficulties with Wayne and some of the

Casimir Pulaski, painted in 1788 by Camponeta. (Georgia Historical Society)

junior officers caused Pulaski to resign his command in March 1778.

As a result, later that same month the Continental Congress, on the advice of Washington, authorized Pulaski to raise an independent cavalry corp in the Baltimore, Md., area. Anxious for an active command, he was sent to Egg Harbor, N.J., to protect supplies there but was badly mauled by a surprise British attack on Oct. 15, 1778. He was next dispatched to Minisink on the Delaware River to prevent a repetition of an Indian massacre. The command was too tame for Pulaski's liking, however, and 3 months later he obtained orders to join in the siege of Charleston. He reached that city on May 8 and promptly directed a headlong attack on advancing British forces. Badly defeated there, Pulaski sought vainly to redeem himself. Five months later while leading another heroic charge, this time during the siege of Savannah, he was mortally wounded. He died on board the American ship *Wasp*, probably on Oct. 11, 1779.

Further Reading

Casimir Pulaski is listed in the American History study guide (III, D, 1, c). Other Europeans who fought with the American Forces in the Revolution included the Marquis de LAFAYETTE from France and Baron STEUBEN from Prussia.

Two biographical studies in English of Pulaski are Clarence A. Manning, *Soldier of Liberty* (1945), and Wladyslaw Konopczynski, *Casimir Pulaski* (trans. 1947).

PULCI / By Mark Musa

The Italian poet Luigi Pulci (1432–1484), an early Renaissance poet associated with the Medici family, wrote "Il Morgante maggiore," the first literary treatment of popular Italian romances of chivalry.

Luigi Pulci (pronounced pōōl'chē) was born in Florence on Aug. 15, 1432, of an impoverished noble family. When his father died in 1451, leaving a destitute widow and five children, Luigi worked for a time as clerk and bookkeeper. In 1453 Pulci married Lucrezia degli Albizzi, who bore him four sons. In 1461 he was introduced to the Medici and formed a close friendship with Lorenzo. He was devoted also to Lorenzo's mother, Lucrezia Tornabuoni, at whose request he began the *Morgante*, probably in 1461. Pulci's collection of *Letters* reflects his warm affection for Lorenzo and Lucrezia over many years.

Lorenzo de' Medici became ruler of Florence in 1469. Soon Pulci was entrusted with various diplomatic missions. Meanwhile the Pulci family's finances had been utterly mismanaged by Luigi's brothers Luca (who died in debtors' prison in 1470) and Bernardo.

Pulci had both friends and enemies among the men of letters in the Medici household. He profoundly respected the young poet and humanist Angelo Poliziano. His most bitter adversary was Matteo Franco, with whom he exchanged a series of fiercely polemical sonnets between 1474 and 1475. The Platonist Marsilio Ficino became his opponent, perhaps because of Pulci's interest in magic and witchcraft.

The earliest edition of the *Morgante*, published in 1478, consisted of 23 cantos. It was immediately criticized by the Florentine Platonic Academy. The first complete edition, enlarged to 28 cantos and entitled *Il Morgante maggiore*, was published in Florence in 1483. Pulci adapted two 14th-century poems: *Orlando*, which narrates Roland's adventures among the pagans in the Orient, and *La Spagna*, which relates Charlemagne's war in Spain, Roland's death at Roncesvalles, and the punishment of Gano, the traitor. Pulci, however, thoroughly transformed these popular tales. Uninterested in chivalric ideals, he took his inspiration from the humble reality of bourgeois and mercantile Florence. Gano's intrigues, instead of heroism, motivate the action. The title reveals Pulci's exuberant imagination and his lightly mocking tone. Morgante, the powerful and good-natured giant, becomes the hero of the story instead of Roland. Two characters are of Pulci's invention: Margutte, the half giant, archscoundrel, and glutton whose shrewdness contrasts with Morgante's slow wit, and Astarotte, the learned devil-theologian. Pulci's language shares the picturesque efficacy of popular Florentine speech.

Toward the end of his life, Pulci's relationship with Lorenzo de' Medici may have changed, possibly because of his antagonism toward Matteo Franco. During the last 10 years of his life, Pulci had stable employment with the

Luigi Pulci, detail from the fresco Raising of the Son of Theophilus, in the Brancacci Chapel of the church of S. Maria del Carmine, Florence. The fresco was begun in the 1420s by Masaccio and completed in the 1480s by Filippino Lippi, to whom this portrait is attributed. (Alinari)

condottiere Roberto Sanseverino. In 1484, while traveling to Venice with Sanseverino, he became ill and died in Padua in October or November.

Further Reading

Luigi Pulci is listed in the Literature study guide (III, D, 4). Marsilio FICINO and Angelo POLIZIANO were also members of the court of Lorenzo de' MEDICI.

Studies of Pulci include Lewis D. Einstein, *Luigi Pulci and the Morgante Maggiore* (1902); John Raymond Shulters, *Luigi Pulci and the Animal Kingdom* (1920); and Giacomo Grillo, *Two Aspects of Chivalry: Pulci and Boiardo* (1942).

PULITZER / By Thomas W. Wood, Jr.

Joseph Pulitzer (1847–1911), Hungarian-born editor and publisher, was instrumental in developing yellow journalism in the United States.

Joseph Pulitzer's father was a well-to-do grain dealer. Joseph was born in Budapest in April 1847. String-beanish, weak-lunged, and with faulty vision, he was unable to have an army career in

Europe. In 1864 he emigrated to America, enlisted in the Union cavalry, and became a so-so soldier. The 6-foot 2-inch red-bearded youth was among the jobless at the end of the Civil War. In St. Louis, where a large German colony existed, Pulitzer worked as mule tender, waiter, roustabout, and hack driver. Finally, he gained a reporter's job on Carl Schurz's *Westliche Post.*

A short time after joining Schurz, Pulitzer was nominated for the state legislature by the Republicans. His candidacy was considered a joke because he was nominated in a Democratic district. Pulitzer, however, ran seriously and won. In the legislature he fought graft and corruption. In one wild dispute there he shot an adversary in the leg. He escaped punishment with a fine which was paid by friends.

Newspaper Acquisitions

Industrious and ambitious, Pulitzer bought the *St. Louis Post* for about $3,000 in 1872. Next, he bought a German paper which had an Associated Press membership and then sold it to the owner of the *Globe* at a $20,000 profit. In 1878 Pulitzer purchased the decaying *St. Louis Dispatch* at a sheriff's sale for $2,700. He combined it with the *Post.* Aided by his brilliant editor in chief, John A. Cockerill, Pulitzer launched crusades

Joseph Pulitzer. (Courtesy of The New-York Historical Society, New York City)

against lotteries, gambling, and tax dodging, mounted drives for cleaning and repairing the streets, and sought to make St. Louis more civic-minded. The *Post-Dispatch* became a success.

In 1883 Pulitzer, then 36, purchased the *New York World* for $346,000 from unscrupulous financier Jay Gould, who was losing $40,000 a year on the paper. Pulitzer made the down payment from *Post-Dispatch* profits and made all later payments out of profits from the *World*.

In the 1880s Pulitzer's eyes began to fail. He went blind in 1889. During his battle for supremacy with William Randolph Hearst, publisher of the *New York Journal*, Pulitzer had to rely on a battery of secretaries to be his eyes. In New York he pledged the *World* to "expose all fraud and sham, fight all public evils and abuses" and to "battle for the people with earnest sincerity." He concentrated on lively human-interest stories, scandal, and sensational material. Pulitzer's *World* was a strong supporter of the common man. It was antimonopoly and frequently prounion during strikes.

Pulitzer in the early part of his career opposed the large headline and art. Later, in a circulation contest between Hearst and Pulitzer in the 1890s, the two giants went to ever larger headline type and fantastic "x-marks-the-spot" art and indulged in questionable practices until Pulitzer lost stomach for such dubious work and cut back. Pulitzer defended sensationalism, however, saying that people had to know about crime in order to combat it. He once told a critic, "I want to talk to a nation, not a select committee."

Pulitzer died aboard his yacht in the harbor at Charleston, S.C., on Oct. 29, 1911. In his will he provided $2 million for the establishment of a school of journalism at Columbia University. Also, by the terms of his will, the prizes bearing his name were established in 1915.

Further Reading

Joseph Pulitzer is listed in the American History study guide (VII, G, 5). Other newspaper publishers were Carl SCHURZ and William Randolph HEARST.

Biographies of Pulitzer include Don C. Seitz, *Joseph Pulitzer: His Life and Letters* (1924); James W. Barrett, *Joseph Pulitzer and His World* (1941); and Iris Noble, *Joseph Pulitzer: Front Page Pioneer* (1947). A particularly interesting book written by one of Pulitzer's secretaries is Alleyne Ireland, *An Adventure with a Genius* (1914; new ed. 1937). Julian S. Rammelkamp, *Pulitzer's Post-Dispatch* (1967), focuses on Pulitzer's early career, and George Juergens, *Joseph Pulitzer and the New York World* (1966), deals with the middle and late years and contains an excellent analysis of the appeal of the *New York World*.

PULLMAN / By Thomas B. Brewer

George Mortimer Pullman (1831–1897), American industrial innovator, developed the railroad sleeping car and built a big business with it. He was one of the last industrialists to operate a company town.

George Pullman was born on March 3, 1831, in Brocton, N.Y., but his parents soon moved to Portland, N.Y. His upbringing in the Universalist Church greatly affected his later philosophy of labor. His formal education ended at the age of 14, and in 1845 he started work in a general store. After his father died, Pullman agreed to finish his father's contracts to move some homes in the path of an Erie Canal widening. Upon completion of that work in 1855 he moved to Chicago, where he entered the business of raising buildings onto higher foundations to avoid flooding because much of Chicago's land area was only a few feet above the level of Lake Michigan.

The idea of a sleeping car for railroads was not new, and various efforts had been made to construct and operate such cars before Pullman joined the field. He formed a partnership with Benjamin Field, who had the rights to operate sleepers on the Chicago and Alton and the Galena and Union railroads. Pullman remodeled two passenger cars into sleepers, using the principle of an upper berth hinged to the side of the car and supported by two jointed arms. Business grew slowly but steadily until the Civil War. In 1862 he went to the Colorado

George Pullman. (The Smithsonian Institution)

goldfields, where he operated a trading store and in his spare time continued to develop his sleeping car.

Returning to Chicago, Pullman and Field constructed the "Pioneer" sleeping car, which became a classic in rail history. Its initial trip conveyed Abraham Lincoln's widow from Washington to Springfield, Ill. Other railroads began to use the Pullman car. In 1867, the year of Pullman's marriage, the Illinois Legislature chartered the Pullman Palace Car Company, which eventually became the world's largest such building concern. Initially, Pullman contracted for his cars; in 1870 he began construction in Detroit, although the headquarters remained in Chicago. The Pullman company always leased sleeping cars; it never sold them.

By 1880 Pullman had acquired land in the Calumet region of Chicago, where he constructed a new factory and a company town. Deeply disturbed by depressing urban conditions, he envisioned his town as a model of efficiency and healthfulness, though it was planned to return a 6 percent profit. The town cost over $5 million. A serious strike in 1894 marked the beginning of the separation of factory and town. Pullman died in Chicago on Oct. 19, 1897.

Further Reading

George Pullman is listed in the American History study guide (VII, E, 3). Involved in the famous Pullman strike were John Peter ALTGELD, President Grover CLEVELAND, and Eugene V. DEBS.

Pullman's life and work are discussed in Joseph Husband, *The Story of the Pullman Car* (1917); Stewart H. Holbrook, *The Story of American Railroads* (1947); August Mencken, *The Railroad Passenger Car* (1957); and Stanley Buder, *Pullman: An Experiment in Industrial Order and Community Planning, 1880–1930* (1967).

PUPIN / By Ralph D. Gray

The Serbo-American physicist and inventor Michael Idvorsky Pupin (1858–1935) is recognized for his contributions to telephony and telegraphy, his invention of electrical tuning, and his discovery of secondary x-ray radiation.

Michael Pupin was born on Oct. 4, 1858, at Idvor in Banat Province, a part of Austria (now of Yugoslavia) settled by Serbs in 1690. The son of illiterate but highly intelligent parents who sacrificed to give their son an education, Pupin soon left the village school to study at Pančevo and then at Prague. Following the death of his father, Pupin sailed to the United States in 1874. Arriving without funds or friends, he held farm and factory jobs, learned English, and in 1879 entered Columbia College.

Pupin subsequently became the first holder of Co-

Michael Pupin. (Library of Congress)

lumbia's Tyndall fellowship in physics. By then he was pursuing his studies abroad, at Cambridge and Berlin, studying mathematical physics and physical chemistry. Receiving his doctorate in 1889, he returned to Columbia as an instructor in its new department of electrical engineering. Pupin combined effective teaching with a program of experimental research. His preliminary work and first publications dealt with electrical charges passing through gases and then with distortions in alternating currents and a general theory of wave propagation. This work led to his development of the electrical resonator (1893), later used in radio tuning, and then to the so-called Pupin coils, inductance coils which when spaced properly along telephone circuits reinforced the vibrations and permitted long-distance calls (1894). Subsequently Pupin expanded upon this work, developing multiplex telegraphy and means to overcome static in wireless communications.

When Wilhelm Roentgen announced his discovery of x-rays in December 1895, Pupin made an x-ray tube and, within 2 weeks, discovered secondary x-radiation; he used this discovery to make short-exposure x-ray photographs, a procedure of obvious medical importance later. The Bell Telephone Company acquired the rights to his line-loading coils in 1901, as did the Siemens and Halske Company in Germany, and long-distance telephony soon became a reality.

Concern over the people in his native land led Pupin to an increasingly active role in public affairs during the Balkan War and World War I, and he headed many philanthropic and humanitarian efforts on behalf of other Serbs. He was a popular and eloquent platform speaker and a skillful interpreter of scientific learning to laymen. Pupin published approximately 70 technical articles and reports during his lifetime, obtained 34 patents, and received many awards and distinctions. He died in New York City on March 12, 1935.

Further Reading

Michael Pupin is listed in the Science study guide (VI, H, 3; VII, H, 3). His contemporary Wilhelm ROENTGEN discovered x-rays.

The best source on Pupin's life remains his charming and inspiring autobiography, *From Immigrant to Inventor* (1923), for which he received the Pulitzer Prize. His other major writings are *The New Reformation: From Physical to Spiritual Realities* (1927) and *Romance of the Machine* (1930). There is a short sketch of Pupin's work in Orrin E. Dunlap, Jr., *Radio's 100 Men of Science: Biographical Narratives of Pathfinders in Electronics and Television* (1944).

PURCELL / By Franklin B. Zimmerman

The English composer and organist Henry Purcell (1659–1695) was the only great figure of English opera until recent times. In all his works he achieved a happy merger of English traditional styles with the new baroque principles from Italy.

Henry Purcell, a painting by J. Closterman. (National Portrait Gallery, London)

Henry Purcell was probably born in Westminster, then a "city and liberty" separate from London. Son of Henry Purcell, Gentleman of the Chapel Royal and Master of the Choristers at Westminster Abbey, he learned early the fundamentals of his art. His parents lived in Great Almonry near the abbey, until his father died in 1664, at which time the family removed to nearby Tothill Street South. Young Henry was adopted by his uncle Thomas Purcell. Those proposing that Thomas was Henry's father uphold a theory that cannot be substantiated. The weight of the evidence still indicates that this Thomas was young Henry's uncle.

Very little is known of Purcell's schooling. The earliest official document bearing his name is the royal warrant for his dismissal from the Chapel Royal choir, dated Dec. 17, 1673, sometime after his voice had changed. In the Westminster School rolls a Henry Purcell, very likely the composer, is named as a scholar, *vice* Charles Purcell, a cousin or brother, in the list of "Bishop's Boys." Shortly after his dismissal from the choir, Henry was apprenticed to John Hingeston, Royal Keeper and Repairer of the Instruments. He also was paid small amounts as a copyist and for tuning the organ at the abbey. In 1677, upon the death of Matthew Locke, Purcell became a member of the Chapel Royal as composer-in-ordinary for the violins

and in 1679 succeeded John Blow as organist at the abbey.

Shortly thereafter Purcell married Frances (?) Peters, who bore him six children, only two of whom survived infancy. By then Purcell had become one of England's most promising composers. In 1677 he set a beautiful and moving elegy to Matthew Locke ("Gentle Shepherds, ye that know") for which he may also have written the text. By the end of 1680 he finished not only almost all the elegant, deeply expressive fantasias and innomines but many of the trio sonatas and early songs as well. Stylistically all these were related to England's musical traditions but owed much to French and Italian models, as Purcell acknowledged in his trio sonatas published in 1683.

On July 31, 1682, Purcell's uncle Thomas died. The following year, perhaps merely as a formality, Purcell was required to take the sacrament of the Church of England in public, an event which may point to some suspicion that he had Papist sympathies. By then, though, he was firmly established as Charles II's chief composer. Among the best-known works from this period are the incidental music for Nathanial Lee's *Theodosius*, the Service in B-flat Major, the anthems "Rejoice in the Lord" and "They that go down to the sea in ships," and the song "Bess of Bedlam."

Purcell's first compositions for James II, who ascended the throne in 1685, reflect a change in style, as may be seen in such works as the coronation anthem "My heart is inditing" and the ode "Why are all the muses mute?" Other differences in style, which in general reveal larger formal conceptions, are longer and more varied phrase constructions and evidence of greater attention to word illustrations and color contrasts. During the 3 years of James II's reign Purcell's reputation as a songwriter developed rapidly, and scarcely a collection or stage piece came out in London during this time without his participation.

Purcell was commissioned to supply music for the coronation ceremonies of William and Mary, which took place on April 11, 1689. Again a change in Purcell's music may be detected, for after the Glorious Revolution he turned to opera, to semiopera (a combined opera, stage play, ballet, and masque), and to more impressive sets of incidental music, showing a mastery of dramatic expression which no English composer ever surpassed.

Purcell began the new trend in 1689 with the opera *Dido and Aeneas*, which contains the moving lament "When I am laid in earth." He continued thereafter with at least one major dramatic composition each year. In 1690 he produced the heroic semiopera *Dioclesian* and in 1691 *King Arthur*, based on John Dryden's play; both operas relate topically to contemporary events. *The Fairy Queen* was produced in 1692, the incidental music for William Congreve's *The Double Dealer* in 1693, and the incidental music for *The Married Beau* in 1694. Purcell died while composing *The Indian Queen* in 1695, and his brother Daniel was asked to write the additional act.

During Purcell's last years he also wrote a great many other important works, including the *Ode to St. Cecilia* of 1692, six birthday odes for Queen Mary, the *Te Deum and Jubilate* in D Major, and a host of songs and dialogues. In addition, he found time to rewrite and revise portions of John Playford's *Introduction to the Skill of Music* (1694) and to carry out all his official duties as instrument repairer, organist, performer, and teacher.

Further Reading

Henry Purcell is listed in the Music study guide (I, D, 3). England did not possess another composer of his caliber until George Frederick HANDEL arrived in 1710. Thomas ARNE was a prolific composer for the stage in the 18th century.

The definitive single work on Purcell is Sir Jack A. Westrup, *Purcell* (1947), which provides a concise and perceptive account of the man and his music. A broader account of Purcell's life and times is in the projected three-volume work of Franklin B. Zimmerman, two volumes of which have been published: *Purcell's Musical Heritage: A Study of Musical Styles in Seventeenth Century England* (1966) and *Henry Purcell, 1659–1695: His Life and Times* (1967). For an analysis of Purcell's music see Zimmerman's *Henry Purcell, 1659–1695: An Analytical Catalogue of His Works* (1963). The best book on Purcell's stage music is Robert E. Moore, *Henry Purcell and the Restoration Theatre* (1961), which combines literary and musical insights in a fascinating study. For background, see Percy Young, *History of British Music* (1967).

* * *

PURVIS / By Roland C. McConnell

Robert Purvis (1810–1898) was a radical black American abolitionist and reformer as well as a prosperous gentleman farmer and businessman.

Robert Purvis was born on Aug. 4, 1810, in Charleston, S.C., of a free woman of Moorish ancestry and a wealthy abolitionist-oriented English cotton broker. In 1819 Robert's father established a school for colored children in Philadelphia at his own expense. There Robert obtained a sound education. He continued his studies at Pittsfield Academy and then at Amherst College.

Purvis became actively involved in the antislavery movement when William Lloyd Garrison, while visiting his home, unfolded plans for publishing the *Liberator*. Purvis became a regular contributor to this paper. In 1833 he was one of the founders of the American Antislavery Society and served as vice president. He also helped organize the Pennsylvania Antislavery Society, serving as president and member of the executive committee.

Only through the intercession of President Andrew Jackson did Purvis receive passports for himself and his bride to go abroad, where they met numerous opponents of slavery. Returning to the United States, Purvis single-handedly rescued Basil Dorsey from the court house in Doylestown, Pa., in 1836, just as the slave catchers appeared with the magistrate's warrant to return him to slavery. Purvis then escorted Dorsey to safety.

In 1838 Purvis published a pamphlet protesting the legislative proposal to disfranchise Pennsylvania Negroes. That year he further organized the Underground Railroad with agents, black and white, in Newbern, N.C., Baltimore, Md., and Wilmington, Del. He condemned the Dred Scott decision in the harshest terms and risked his life to publicly praise John Brown. He continually attacked the movement to colonize Negroes in Africa.

Purvis worked unremittingly to convince the U.S. government to place the Civil War on an antislavery basis and to establish a new union from which slavery would be excluded forever. He urged not only utilization of black soldiers but also appointment of black officers. He softened his antislavery stand only when Abraham Lincoln issued the Emancipation Proclamation, which Purvis felt recognized blacks as citizens. His antislavery work ceased with the passage of the 15th Amendment in 1870. In 1888 he presided at the semicentennial meeting of the Antislavery Society.

Purvis was also active in such organizations as the American Moral Reform Society, the Woman Suffrage Society, and the Committee of 100 for the Purification of Municipal Affairs in Philadelphia. As a gentleman farmer, he developed a showplace at Byberry and prizewinning livestock. He also owned a second farm and several pieces of real estate in Philadelphia, including mercantile property on Market Street. He died on April 15, 1898, in Philadelphia.

Robert Purvis (front, fourth from left) and other members of the executive committee of the Pennsylvania Antislavery Society, photographed in 1851. (Sophia Smith Collection, Smith College)

Further Reading

Robert Purvis is listed in the American History study guide (V, F, 3, e). His wife was the daughter of James FORTEN, another free black abolitionist.

Biographical sketches of Purvis appear in Richard Bardolph, *The Negro Vanguard* (1959), and Wilhelmina S. Robinson, *Historical Negro Biographies* (1967). William Wells Brown reports personal impressions of Purvis in his *The Black Man: His Antecedents, His Genius, and His Achievements* (rev. ed. 1863). For commentary on Purvis's writings see Vernon Loggins, *The Negro Author: His Development in America* (1931). James M. McPherson, *The Struggle for Equality: Abolitionists and the Negro in the Civil War and Reconstruction* (1964), and Benjamin Quarles, *Black Abolitionists* (1969), discuss Purvis.

PUSEY / By John R. Farnsworth

The English clergyman and scholar Edward Bouverie Pusey (1800–1882) was one of the major figures of the Oxford Movement, which began at Oxford in 1833 to overcome the dangers threatening the Church of England.

Edward Pusey's lineage was noble. His father had inherited the estate of Pusey, in Berkshire, where Edward was born on Aug. 22, 1800. His childhood was calm and self-assured but isolated. He accepted his mother's High Anglican teaching and moved confidently toward a clerical vocation by way of Eton and Oxford. As a student, Pusey labored endlessly, reading for as much as 17 hours a day. He won a first-class degree at Christ Church, Oxford, and then in 1823 was elected a fellow of Oriel College, where he met John Keble and John Henry Newman.

Pusey then determined "to devote my life to the Old Testament," and he studied theology and Semitic languages at the universities of Göttingen and Berlin between 1826 and 1828. On his return his father permitted him to marry Maria Barker, whom he had loved for many years, and that same year Pusey was ordained. Late in 1828 he became regius professor of Hebrew at Oxford and was appointed canon of Christ Church. He also published a critical history of German theology.

Late in 1833 Pusey gravitated toward the Oxford Movement. He wrote tracts on the advantages of fasting (1834) and on baptism (1836) in the series *Tracts for the Times*. From the standpoint of public prestige, his adhesion to the Oxford Movement, Newman said, supplied it with "a position and a name." The movement was sometimes known as "Puseyism" throughout the later 1830s.

In 1836 Pusey began his influential editorship of the *Library of Fathers*, beginning with the works of St. Augustine. Ultimately 48 volumes in this series were published, and Pusey contributed several studies of patristic works.

When Newman withdrew from the Oxford Movement, Pusey became its leader. In 1843 Pusey, who had defended Newman's Tract No. 90, was charged with preaching heresy in a sermon on the Eucharist, "The Holy Eucharist, a Comfort to the Penitent." In secret proceedings of questionable fairness he was privately suspended from preaching at Oxford for 2 years. In 1845 he assisted in the establishment of the first Anglican sisterhood, and throughout the rest of his life he assisted in establishing Anglican orders. In 1846 Pusey claimed in his sermon "The Entire Absolution of the Penitent" that the Church of England possessed the right of priestly absolution, thus inaugurating the Anglican practice of private confession.

In his remaining years at Oxford, Pusey fought for Tractarian objectives but without major successes. He opposed the increasing secularization of the university, in which intellectual life was being segregated from a moral and spiritual base. He also worked for Christian unity, but he was defeated partly by the new assertions of Roman authority under the papacy of Pius IX. His sermon "The Rule of Faith" (1851) did, however, check English conversions to Roman Catholicism.

Pusey's private life exemplified the personal holiness that marked the Tractarians' purpose. His wife died of consumption in 1839, and his only son became a chronic invalid and a cripple. Only one child survived him. For Pusey these tragedies, and the public hostility he encountered, were spurs to greater penitence, humility, and submission. He practiced simplicity, self-denial, and works of charity.

Pusey's *Eirenicon* (3 parts, 1865–1870) was an attempt to find common ground for reuniting Roman Catholicism and the Church of England. Its publication caused much controversy, being answered by Newman. Pusey died at Ascot Priory, Berkshire, on Sept. 16, 1882.

Further Reading

Edward Pusey is listed in the Religion study guide (I, P, 1, a). He was associated with John Henry (later Cardinal) NEWMAN in the Oxford Movement.

The basic biography of Pusey is Henry P. Liddon, *Life of Edward Bouverie Pusey, D.D.* (4 vols., 1893–1897). A brief panegyric by Charles C. Grafton, *Pusey and the Church Revival* (1902), is useful as an explication of Anglo-Catholic theology. Newman's comments on Pusey are in his famous autobiography, *Apologia pro vita sua* (1864). Of the large literature on the Oxford Movement generally, an early and deeply sympathetic account by a disciple is Richard W. Church, *The Oxford Movement* (1897). Among the later histories are a broad and fair treatment by Yngue T. Brilioth, *The Anglican Revival* (1933), and Geoffrey C. Faber, *Oxford Apostles* (1933), a lively work full of psychological insight but not unfriendly. A useful anthology of primary readings is Owen Chadwick, ed., *The Mind of the Oxford Movement* (1960).

✳   ✳   ✳

PUSHKIN / By Edward Wasiolek

The Russian poet and prose writer Aleksandr Sergeevich Pushkin (1799–1837) ranks as the country's greatest poet. He not only brought Russian poetry to its highest excellence but also had a decisive influence on Russian literature in the 19th and 20th centuries.

Aleksandr Pushkin (pronounced poͦosh′kĭn) is Russia's national poet. He established the norms of classical Russian versification, and he laid the groundwork for much of the development of Russian prose in the 19th century. His work is distinguished by brilliance of language, compactness, terseness, and objectivity. His poetry is supremely untranslatable, and consequently Pushkin has had less influence on world literature than on Russian literature. He may be described as a romantic in subject matter and a classicist in style and form.

Pushkin was born on May 26, 1799, the son of a family of the middle nobility. On his father's side he was a descendant of one of the oldest lines of Russian nobility, and on his mother's side he was related to an Abyssinian, Abram Petrovich Hannibal, who had been kidnaped in Africa, brought to Constantinople, and sent as a gift to Peter I (the Great). Pushkin was brought up in an atmosphere that was predominantly French, and at a very early age he became acquainted with the classic works of 17th- and 18th-century French literature. Several of the important figures of Russian literature—including Nikolai Karamzin and Vasily Zhukovsky—were visitors to the

Edward Pusey, a portrait by George Richmond. (National Portrait Gallery, London)

Pushkin home during Aleksandr's childhood.

Between 1811 and 1817 Pushkin attended a special school established at Tsarskoye Selo (later renamed Pushkin) by Czar Alexander I for privileged children of the nobility. Pushkin was an indifferent student in most subjects, but he performed brilliantly in French and Russian literature.

Early Works, 1814–1820

After finishing school, Pushkin led the reckless and dissipated life of a typical nobleman. He wrote about 130 poems between 1814 and 1817, while still at school, and these and most of his works written between 1817 and 1820 were not published because of the boldness of his thoughts on political and erotic matters. In 1820 Pushkin completed his first narrative poem, *Russlan and Ludmilla*. It is a romance composed of fantastic adventures but told with 18th-century humor and irony. Before *Russlan and Ludmilla* was published in June 1820, Pushkin was exiled to the south of Russia because of the boldness of the political sentiments he had expressed in his poems. His "Ode to Liberty" contained, for example, a reference to the assassination of Paul I, the father of Czar Alexander I. Pushkin left St. Petersburg on May 6 and he did not return to the capital for more than 6 years.

South of Russia, 1820–1824

Pushkin spent the years 1820–1823 in various places in the Caucasus and in the Crimea, and he was at first charmed by the picturesque settings and relieved to be free of the intoxications and artificialities of the life of the capital. Subsequently, however, he felt bored by the life in small towns and took up again a life of gambling, drinking, and consorting with loose women. He was always short of money, for his salary in the civil service was small and his family refused to support him. He began to earn money with his poetic works, but these sums were seldom sufficient to permit him to compete comfortably with his affluent friends. In 1823 he was transferred to Odessa, where he found the life of a large city more to his liking.

The poet's life in Odessa in 1823–1824 was marked by three strong amorous attachments. First, he fell in love with Carolina Sobansky, a beauty who was 6 years older than he. He broke with her in October 1823 and then fell violently in love with the wife of a Dalmatian merchant, Amalia Riznich. She had many admirers and gave Pushkin ample cause for jealousy. Amalia, however, inspired some of Pushkin's best poems, such as "Night" and "Beneath the Blue Sky of Her Native Land," and he remembered her to the end of his life. His third love was for the wife of the governor general, the Countess Eliza Vorontsov. She was a charming and beautiful woman. Vorontsov learned of the affair, and having no special liking for Pushkin he resolved to have him transferred from Odessa. He was aided in this endeavor by an unfortunate letter that Pushkin had written to a friend in which he had questioned the immortality of the soul. The letter was intercepted, and because of it Pushkin was expelled from the service on July 18, 1824, by the Czar and ordered to the family estate of Mikhailovskoye near

Aleksandr Pushkin's self-portrait, sketched in the album of E. N. Ushkova. The writer depicted himself in the nightcap of a monk and with a devil making fun of him. (From Wolkonsky, Alejandro Pushkin, 1947)

Pskov.

Pushkin's poetic work during the 4 years that he spent in the south was rich in output and characterized by Lord Byron's influence, which can be seen in "The Caucasian Captive" (1820–1821), "The Fountain of Bakhchisarai" (1822), and "The Gypsies" (1824). These poems are mellifluous in verse and exotic in setting, but they already show the elements of Pushkin's classic style: measure, balance, terseness, and restraint.

Mikhailovskoye, 1824–1826

On Aug. 9, 1824, Pushkin arrived at Mikhailovskoye. His relations with his parents were not good. The father felt angry at his son's rebelliousness and on one occasion spread a story that his son had attempted to beat him. The family left the estate about mid-November, and Pushkin found himself alone with the family nurse, Arina Rodionovna, at Mikhailovskoye. He lived fairly much as a recluse during the next 2 years, occasionally visiting a neighboring town and infrequently entertaining old Petersburg friends. During this period he fell in love with a Madame Kern, who was married to an old general and who encouraged the attention of many men. Also at this time the nurse told Pushkin many folktales, and it is generally believed that she imbued him with the feeling for folk life that manifested itself in many of his poems.

Pushkin's 2 years at Mikhailovskoye were extremely rich in poetic output. He completed "The Gypsies," wrote the first three chapters of *Eugene Onegin*, and composed the tragedy *Boris Godunov*. In addition he composed many important lyrics and a humorous tale in verse entitled *Count Nulin. Boris Godunov* is a chronicle play. Pushkin took the subject from Karamzin's history, and it relates the claims of the impostor Demetrius to the throne of the elected monarch Boris Godunov.

Maturity, 1826–1831

After the end of his exile at Mikhailovskoye, Pushkin was received by the new czar, Nicholas I, who charmed Pushkin by his reasonableness and kindness. The Czar placed Pushkin under a privileged tyranny by promising him that his works would be censored by the Czar himself. The practical consequences of this arrangement were that Pushkin was placed under an honorable promise to publish nothing that was injurious to the government; in time this "privileged" censorship became increasingly onerous.

Pushkin continued his dissipated life after 1826 but with less gusto. Although he was still in his 20s, he began to feel the weight of his years, and he longed to settle down. On April 6, 1830, he proposed to Nathalie Goncharova for the second time and was accepted. She came from a noble family that had fallen on hard times financially. The Goncharovs were dissatisfied with Pushkin's standing with the government and were unimpressed by his reputation as a poet. Pushkin had to ask for economic favors for the Goncharovs from the government, and he persuaded his father to settle an estate on him.

Pushkin's output in the years 1826–1829 was not so great as in the years 1824–1826, but it was still impressive. He continued to work on *Eugene Onegin*, wrote a number of excellent lyrics, worked on but did not finish a prose novel entitled *The Nigger of Peter the Great*, and wrote *Poltava*, a narrative poem on Peter the Great's struggle with Charles XII which celebrates the Russian victory over the Swedes. This poem shows the continuing development of Pushkin's style toward objectivity and austerity.

In the fall of 1830 Pushkin left the capital to visit a small estate by the name of Boldino, which his father had left him, with the intention of spending a few weeks there. However, he was blocked from returning to the capital by measures taken by the authorities because of a cholera epidemic, and he was forced to return to Boldino. During that autumn at Boldino, Pushkin wrote some of his greatest lyrics; *The Tales of Belkin*; a comic poem in octaves, "The Little House in Kolomna"; and four small tragedies; and he virtually finished *Eugene Onegin*.

Eugene Onegin was begun in 1824 and finished in August 1831. This novel in verse is without doubt Pushkin's most famous work. It shows the influence in theme of Byron's *Don Juan* and in style of Laurence Sterne's novels. It is a "novel" about contemporary life, constructed in order to permit digressions and a variety of incidents and tones. The heart of the tale concerns the life of Eugene Onegin, a bored nobleman who rejects the advances of a young girl, Tatiana. He meets her later, greatly changed and now sophisticated, falls in love with

her, and is in turn rejected by her because, although she loves him, she is married.

Pushkin's four little tragedies are models of spare, objective, and compact drama. The plays are short and vary in length from 240 to 550 lines. *The Feast during the Plague* is a translation of a scene from John Wilson's *The City of the Plague; The Stone Guest* is a variation of the Don Juan theme; *Mozart and Salieri* treats the tradition of Antonio Salieri's envy of Wolfgang Amadeus Mozart's effortless art and the injustice of Nature in dispensing her gifts; and *The Covetous Knight* has as its theme avariciousness and contains the famous monologue of the baron on his treasures.

The Tales of Belkin consists of five short stories: "The Shot," "The Snowstorm," "The Stationmaster," "The Undertaker," and "The Peasant Gentlewoman." The stories are models of swift, unadorned narration.

Marriage, Duel, and Death, 1831–1837

After 1830 Pushkin wrote less and less poetry. "The Bronze Horseman" (1833) is considered by many to be his greatest poem. The setting is the great flood of 1824, which inundated much of St. Petersburg. The theme of the poem is the irreconcilable demands of the state and the individual.

The Golden Cockerel (1833) is a volume of Russian folktales. Pushkin's masterpiece in narrative is the short story "The Queen of Spades" (1834), about a gloomy engineer who is ruthless in his efforts to discover the secret of three winning cards. Mention should also be made of his *The History of the Pugachev Rebellion* (1834) and *The Captain's Daughter* (1837), a short novel about the Pugachev rebellion.

Pushkin married Nathalie Goncharova on Jan. 19, 1831. She bore him three children, but the couple were not happy together. She was beautiful and a favorite at court, but she was also somewhat uneducated and not free of vulgarity. She encouraged the attentions of Baron George d'Anthes, an exiled Alsatian Frenchman and a protégé of the minister of the Netherlands at St. Peters-

The one-time estate of the Pushkin family in the village of Boldino. Aleksandr Pushkin, while living there during the autumn of 1830, wrote The Tales of Belkin. *(Sovfoto)*

burg. Pushkin provoked D'Anthes to a duel on Jan. 26, 1837, and the duel took place the next day. Pushkin was wounded and died on January 29. There was great popular mourning at his death.

Many of Pushkin's works provided the basis for operas by Russian composers. They include *Ruslan and Ludmilla* by Mikhail Glinka, *Eugene Onegin* and *The Queen of Spades* by Peter Ilyich Tchaikovsky, *Boris Godunov* by Modest Mussorgsky, *The Stone Guest* by Aleksandr Dargomijsky, and *The Golden Cockerel* by Nicolai Rimsky-Korsakov.

Further Reading

Alexsandr Pushkin is listed in the Literature study guide (III, G, 6). He especially influenced Mikhail LERMONTOV and Ivan TURGENEV.

Eugene Onegin is available in many translations. Recommended are those by Dorothea Prall Raddin and George Z. Patrick (1937) and by Vladimir Nabokov (4 vols., 1964); the Nabokov translation is accompanied by massive documentation. Among the excellent biographies of Pushkin are Ernest Simmons, *Pushkin* (1937), a full and readable account; Henry Troyat, *Pushkin: A Biography*, translated by Randolphe Weaver (1950), vivid and engrossing; and the most recent work on Pushkin's life, David Magarshack, *Pushkin: A Biography* (1967). Walter N. Vickery, *Pushkin: Death of a Poet* (1968), is a work on the final days of Pushkin's life.

The most readable and informative review of Pushkin's works is Prince D. S. Mirsky, *Pushkin* (1926). Mirsky's *A History of Russian Literature* (2 vols., 1927) is recommended for general historical and literary background; this same work is available in a one-volume abridgment edited by Francis J. Whitfield (1958).

PUTNAM / By Armin Rappaport

Israel Putnam (1718–1790), American soldier, was a Revolutionary War general. Although known for his courage and energy in combat, he was an incompetent commander.

Israel Putnam was born in Salem Village, Mass., on Jan. 7, 1718. He had very little education and remained nearly illiterate all his life. In 1738 he married Hannah Pope and the following year moved to Connecticut, where he bought land and farmed successfully, soon becoming a man of substance. When the French and Indian War broke out in 1756, Putnam was commissioned a lieutenant in the Connecticut militia and served throughout the conflict, rising steadily in rank until he reached a colonelcy by the time it ended in 1763. He fought in numerous engagements, earned a reputation for bravery and resourcefulness, and gained valuable military experience.

With the coming of peace, Putnam returned to farming and also operated a tavern. He took part in the develop-

Israel Putnam. (Library of Congress)

ing conflict between England and the Colonies, helping organize the Sons of Liberty in 1765. He participated in the political life of Connecticut as a representative to the General Assembly in 1766 and 1767. In 1774 he headed the local Committee of Correspondence and accepted appointment as lieutenant colonel of a regiment of Connecticut militia. When the fighting began in the spring of 1775, Putnam entered active service and in June was appointed by the Continental Congress one of the four major generals under George Washington's command. It was not a wise appointment, for although Putnam was a good soldier and an inspiring and able leader, he did not have the qualities needed for planning major operations, commanding large units, or executing grand strategy.

Putnam was at Bunker Hill, at the siege of Boston, and in New York to plan the defenses there. He was in command at the Battle of Long Island in August 1776 until Washington's arrival, and that American defeat has been blamed by one historian on "the incapacity of Israel Putnam." In subsequent assignments his performance was no better. Washington ordered him to Princeton early in 1777, but Putnam delayed. He was then sent to command an important post on the Hudson River, but in December 1777, after 7 months of inefficiency, he was removed. A court of inquiry convened to investigate his record in one action, but he was exonerated. It was clear, however, that he was unfit for a command. Washington sent Putnam to be chief of recruiting in Connecticut in 1779. In December of that year, a paralytic stroke ended his military career. He returned to his farm in Connecticut, where he died on May 29, 1790.

Further Reading

Israel Putnam is listed in the American History study guide (III, D, 1, a). Philip SCHUYLER was another of the four major generals appointed to serve under George WASHINGTON.

The best account of Putnam's career is William Farrand Livingston, *Israel Putnam, Pioneer, Ranger, and Major-General, 1718–1790* (1901). Two other biographies are useful: David Humphreys, *The Life and Heroic Exploits of Israel Putnam* (1835), and I. N. Tarbox, *Life of Israel Putnam ("Old Put"), Major-General in the Continental Army* (1877).

PUVIS DE CHAVANNES

/ By Carl Belz

Pierre Puvis de Chavannes (1824–1898) occupied a unique position in 19th-century French painting: he was one of the few academic painters whose work was deeply admired by the avant-garde artists of his day.

Born in Lyons on Dec. 14, 1824, Pierre Puvis de Chavannes (pronounced pü-vē′ də shà-vàn′) belonged to the generation of Gustave Courbet and Édouard Manet, and he was fully aware of their revolutionary achievements. Nevertheless, he was drawn to a more traditional and conservative style. From his first involvement with art, which began after a trip to Italy and which interrupted his intention to follow the engineering profession that his father practiced, Puvis pursued his career within the scope of academic classicism and the Salon. Even in this chosen arena, however, he was rejected, particularly during the 1850s. But he gradually won acceptance. By the 1880s he was an established figure in the Salons, and by the 1890s he was their acknowledged master.

In both personal and artistic ways Puvis's career was closely linked with the avant-garde. In the years of his growing public recognition, when he began to serve on Salon juries, he was consistently sympathetic to the work of younger, more radical artists. Later, as president of the Société Nationale des Beaux-Arts—the "new Salon," as it was called—he was able to exert even more of a liberalizing influence on the important annual exhibitions.

Puvis's sympathy to new and radical artistic directions was reflected in his own painting. Superficially he was a classicist, but his personal interpretation of that style was unconventional. His subject matter—religious themes, allegories, mythologies, and historical events—was clearly in keeping with the academic tradition. But his style eclipsed his outdated subjects: he characteristically worked with broad, simple compositions, and he resisted the dry photographic realism which had begun to typify academic painting about the end of the century. In addition, the space and figures in his paintings inclined toward flatness, calling attention to the surface on which the images were depicted. These qualities gave his work a modern, abstract look and distinguished it from the sterile tradition to which it might otherwise have been linked.

Along with their modern, formal properties, Puvis's paintings exhibited a serene and poetic range of feeling. His figures frequently seem to be wrapped in an aura of ritualistic mystery, as though they belong in a private world of dreams or visions. Yet these feelings invariably seem fresh and sincere. This combination of form and feeling deeply appealed to certain avant-garde artists of the 1880s and 1890s. Although Puvis claimed he was neither radical nor revolutionary, he was admired by the symbolist poets, writers, and painters—including Paul Gauguin and Maurice Denis—and he influenced the neoimpressionist painter Georges Seurat.

During his mature career Puvis executed many mural paintings. In Paris he did the *Life of St. Genevieve* (1874–1878) in the Panthéon and *Science, Art, and Letters* (1880s) in the Sorbonne. In Lyons he executed the *Sacred Grove*, the *Antique Vision*, and *Christian Inspiration* (1880s) in the Musée des Beaux-Arts. He painted *Pastoral Poetry* (1895–1898) in the Boston, Mass., Public Library. These commissions reflect the high esteem with which Puvis was regarded during his own lifetime. Among his most celebrated oil paintings are *Hope* (1872) and the *Poor Fisherman* (1881). He died in Paris on Oct. 10, 1898.

Pierre Puvis de Chavannes, a self-portrait in the Musée Galliéra in Paris. (French Cultural Services of the French Embassy)

Further Reading

Pierre Puvis de Chavannes is listed in the Art study guide (III, H, 1, g). He and Georges SEURAT explored the meaning of linear directions. The Swiss painter Ferdinand HODLER used rhythmic repetitions of lines and curves in his works.

François Crastre, *Puvis de Chavannes* (1912), and Jean Laran, *Puvis de Chavannes* (1912), are biographical studies containing some reproductions of the paintings. Frank Gibson, *Six French Artists of the Nineteenth Century* (1925), includes a chapter on Puvis. A background study which briefly discusses Puvis is Jean Leymarie, *French Painting: The Nineteenth Century* (trans. 1962).

PYM / By James E. Farnell

The English statesman John Pym (1584–1643) led the House of Commons in the opening years of the English civil war.

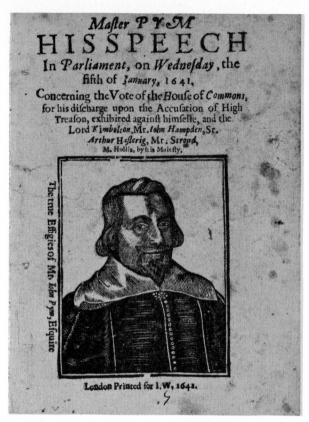

John Pym, an engraving by an unknown artist, appearing on a published speech. (National Portrait Gallery, London)

John Pym was the son of a lesser landowner of Somerset. When he was a boy, Pym's views on religion were molded by his stepfather, Sir Anthony Rous, who was a devout Puritan. The defeat of the Spanish Armada was his first memory of public events, and the Gunpowder Plot occurred when he reached his majority. These high points of foreign and domestic Catholic aggression were determinants of Pym's public career. In 1599 he entered Oxford and in 1602 took up his legal studies at Middle Temple. He entered Parliament in 1614, probably in the interest of the Earl of Bedford. The earl's family had long favored the Pyms, and the 4th earl remained John Pym's patron until the earl's death in 1641.

In the Parliament of 1614 and again in 1621, Pym was most active in the matter of enforcing penalties against Catholics. He advocated an oath of loyalty by all Englishmen. A popular defense of English liberties was also a hallmark of Pym's political life.

After Charles I dissolved Parliament in 1629, Pym became treasurer of the Providence Company, which projected colonies in Connecticut and then on Providence Island (Isla de Providencia) off the coast of Central America. Although the company had religious and economic ends, its chief importance was as a political rallying point for the opposition during Charles I's personal government.

When Charles called Parliament in 1640, Pym was the most experienced leader of the Commons, and he immediately assumed leadership of that body. In the "Short" Parliament, Pym stressed the desire of the Commons for legal security, but when Parliament was summarily dissolved by the King, Pym keynoted the "Long" Parliament with a speech which stressed that the country was in danger because of its Catholic queen and its proto-Catholic clergy. It was an inflammatory call for the widest popular support for Parliament in a mortal struggle with the King. Pym's first order of business was the impeachment of the Earl of Strafford.

Charles went to Scotland in August 1641 in order to find evidence of the complicity of Pym and others in the 1638 Scots invasion of England. When Charles returned to England in November 1641, Pym faced his greatest trial as leader of the Commons. There was a wave of support for the King, and the rebellion of the Irish in October gave Charles an excuse to raise an army which might have destroyed Parliament before it suppressed the Irish. Pym narrowly gained approval for the Grand Remonstrance, which recited the old faults of the King. Then, on Jan. 4, 1642, he maneuvered the King into making an unconstitutional entry into the House of Commons in order to arrest Pym and the other "Five Members." In that moment popular initiative returned to Pym and Parliament. They, not the King, were able to raise troops to suppress the Irish and prepare to meet the inevitable attempt of Charles to forcibly regain political mastery, which came on Aug. 14, 1642.

Pym secured the passage of the militia and assessment ordinances by Parliament despite their flagrant violation of strict legality. He also secured the passage of the unpopular excise tax to finance the parliamentary war effort and organized associations of counties to administer the war; Cromwell's Eastern Association became the most famous and effective of these. Politically, he was also able to keep persons of such diverse values as the Earl of Essex, Oliver Cromwell, and Oliver St. John steady in their combined defense of Parliament. Pym's last act was to arrange for the entry of the Scots into the war on the side of the hard-pressed parliamentary forces in September 1643. That alliance was sealed by the covenant which bound all Englishmen to support Parliament. With that final program of popular unity, Pym succumbed to cancer and was buried in Westminster Abbey on Dec. 15, 1643.

Further Reading

John Pym is listed in the European History study guide (V, A, 1, a). He opposed CHARLES I and played an important role in the impeachment and execution of Lord STRAFFORD.

Jack H. Hexter, *The Reign of King Pym* (1941), is the best study. A standard biography of Pym is Sidney Reed Brett, *John Pym, 1583–1643: The Statesman of the Puritan Revolution* (1940).

✳   ✳   ✳

PYTHAGORAS / By Donald A. Ross

The Greek philosopher, scientist, and religious teacher Pythagoras (ca. 575–ca. 495 B.C.) evolved a school of thought that accepted the transmigration of souls and established number as the principle in the universe.

Born on the island of Samos, Pythagoras (pronounced pĭ-thăg′ər-əs) was the son of Mnesarchus. He fled to southern Italy to escape the tyranny of Polycrates, who came to power about 538, and he is said to have traveled to Egypt and Babylon. He and his followers became politically powerful in Croton in southern Italy, where Pythagoras had established a school for his newly formed sect. It is probable that the Pythagoreans took positions in the local government in order to lead men to the pure life which their teachings set forth. Eventually, however, a rival faction launched an attack on the Pythagoreans at a gathering of the sect, and the group was almost completely annihilated. Pythagoras either had been banished from Croton or had left voluntarily shortly before this attack. He died in Metapontum early in the 5th century.

Religious Teachings

Pythagoras and his followers were important for their contributions to both religion and science. His religious teachings were based on the doctrine of metempsychosis, which held that the soul was immortal and was destined to a cycle of rebirths until it could liberate itself from the cycle through the purity of its life. A number of precepts were drawn up as inviolable rules by which initiates must live.

Pythagoreanism differed from the other philosophical systems of its time in being not merely an intellectual search for truth but a whole way of life which would lead to salvation. In this respect it had more in common with the mystery religions than with philosophy. Several taboos and mystical beliefs were taught which sprang from a variety of primitive sources such as folk taboo, ritual, and sympathetic magic and were examples of the traditional beliefs that the Greeks continued to hold while developing highly imaginative and rational scientific systems.

An important underlying tenet of Pythagoreanism was the kinship of all life. A universal life spirit was thought to be present in animal and vegetable life, although there is no evidence to show that Pythagoras believed that the soul could be born in the form of a plant. It could be born, however, in the body of an animal, and Pythagoras claimed to have heard the voice of a dead friend in the howl of a dog being beaten.

The number of lives which the soul had to live before being liberated from the cycle is uncertain. Its liberation came through an ascetic life of high moral and ethical standards and strict adherence to the teachings and practices of the sect. Pythagoras himself claimed to remember four different lives. Followers of the sect were enjoined to secrecy, although the discussions of Pythagoras's teachings in other writers proved that the injunction was not faithfully observed.

Mathematical Teachings

The Pythagoreans posited the dualism between Limit-

Pythagoras, an ancient sculpture in the Capitoline Museum, Rome. (Alinari)

This print, dated 1503, shows two forms of computation. Pythagoras (right) employs a counting board, while Boethius (left) uses arithmetic. (The Smithsonian Institution)

ed and Unlimited. It was probably Pythagoras himself who declared that number was the principle in the universe, limiting and giving shape to matter. His study of musical intervals, leading to the discovery that the chief intervals can be expressed in numerical ratios between the first four integers, also led to the theory that the number 10, the sum of the first four integers, embraced the whole nature of number.

So great was the Pythagoreans' veneration for the "Tetractys of the Decad" (the sum of $1 + 2 + 3 + 4$) that they swore their oaths by it rather than by the gods, as was conventional. Pythagoras may have discovered the theorem which still bears his name (in right triangles, the square on the hypotenuse equals the sum of the squares on the other sides), although this proposition has been discovered on a tablet dating from the time of the Babylonian king Hammurabi. Regardless of their sources, the Pythagoreans did important work in systematizing and extending the body of mathematical knowledge.

As a more general scheme, the Pythagoreans posited the two contraries, Limited and Unlimited, as ultimate principles. Numerical oddness and evenness are equated with Limited and Unlimited, as are one and plurality, right and left, male and female, motionlessness and movement, straight and crooked, light and darkness, good and bad, and square and oblong. It is not clear whether an ultimate One, or Monad, was posited as the cause of the two categories.

Cosmological Views

As a result of their religious beliefs and their careful study of mathematics, the Pythagoreans developed a cosmology which differed in some important respects from the world views of their contemporaries, the most important of which was their view of the earth as a sphere which circled the center of the universe. The center of this system was fire, which was invisible to man because his side of the earth was turned from it. The sun reflected that fire; there was a counterearth closer to the center, and the other five planets were farther away and followed longer courses around the center. It is not known how much of this theory was attributable to Pythagoras himself. Later writers ascribe much of it to Philolaos (active 400 B.C.), although it circulated as a view of the school as a whole.

The systematization of mathematical knowledge carried out by Pythagoras and his followers would have sufficed to make him an important figure in the history of Western thought. However, his religious sect and the asceticism which he taught, embracing as it did a vast number of ancient beliefs, make him one of the great teachers of religion in the ancient Greek world.

Further Reading

Pythagoras is listed in the Philosophy study guide (I, A, 2). PLATO eloquently acknowledged Pythagoras's immense intellectual and religious accomplishments.

Pythagoras left no written works. A first-rate technical book, J. A. Philip, *Pythagoras and Early Pythagoreanism* (1966), separates the valid from the spurious among the legends that surround Pythagoras and his views. An excellent and thorough treatment of the evidence for his life and teachings is in W. K. C. Guthrie, *A History of Greek Philosophy* (3 vols., 1962–1969). A good account of Pythagoras and his followers is in Kathleen Freeman, *The Pre-Socratic Philosophers* (1946; 3d ed. 1953), and G. S. Kirk and J. E. Raven, *The Presocratic Philosophers* (1962). Briefer treatments of the Pythagoreans and the intellectual currents of their time are in the standard histories of Greek literature, such as Albin Lesky, *A History of Greek Literature* (trans. 1966), or in accounts of Greek philosophy, such as John Burnet, *Greek Philosophy* (1914).

Quasimodo Q *Quiroga*

QUASIMODO / By Oscar Büdel

The Italian poet, translator, and critic Salvatore Quasimodo (1901–1968) was one of the chief exponents of Italian hermetic poetry.

Salvatore Quasimodo (pronounced kwä-zē-mō′-dō) was born on Aug. 20, 1901, in Modica, Sicily, where his father was a stationmaster with the Italian railroads. After several moves throughout Sicily, the family in 1908 settled in Messina, where Quasimodo finished his education and remained until 1919. Subsequently he moved to Rome to study engineering at the Politechnical Institute but did not complete his studies. For some time he worked in different jobs until he moved to Reggio Calabria in 1926 as an employee of the Civil Engineering Board. Through Elio Vittorini, his brother-in-law, he was introduced to literary circles during a visit to Florence in 1929. Among others he met Eugenio Montale and Alessandro Bonsanti, the editor of *Solaria,* which in 1930 published his first poetry.

In 1931 Quasimodo was transferred to Imperia and, after a short interlude in Sardinia, eventually was assigned to duty in Milan. There he left his job in 1938 to become editor of the weekly *Tempo* until he was named in 1941 professor of Italian literature at the Giuseppe Verdi Conservatory of Music. Quasimodo was the recipient of several literary prizes, such as the Etna-Taormina in

Salvatore Quasimodo. (Italian Cultural Institute, New York)

1953 and the Viareggio in 1958. In 1959 he was awarded the Nobel Prize for literature. Quasimodo died on June 14, 1968.

Quasimodo's poetics is characterized by a belief in the "magic of the word." Such an avowal eventually leads to the concept of an "absolute word" whose alliterative properties are stressed over its logical aspects. Quasimodo's later notion of the social potentialities of poetry does not necessarily indicate a break with his earlier manner but may be seen as a logical continuation, as he himself once said: "the words 'island' and 'Sicily' may be identified with my search for contact with the outside world." He refused to be associated with French symbolism, declaring that his work might better be seen in the tradition of "stilnovistic" poetry.

The goals of Quasimodo's poetics are already visible in his first collection of verse, *Acque e terre* (1930), in which the word no longer appears in a subordinate syntactic function but asserts its own immediate value. *Òboe sommerso* (1932), *Odore di Eucalyptus ed altri versi* (1933), and *Erato e Apòllion* (1936) are verse collections which are most characteristic of Quasimodo's hermetic approach, and it is here that his poetics of the absolute word is most clearly delineated and evident ("I divest myself by syllables," *Parola*). The themes are autobiographical, those of an odyssey and the search for a lost paradise. The almost realistic aspects of *Acque e terre* have disappeared; the technique of the analogies has become more daring; and the metaphors have become more tightened. The equilibrium between realistic and hermetic elements characteristic of the first collection is no longer existent.

Nuove poesie (1938) reiterates the old nostalgic feeling of *Acque e terre* for Sicily. Although retaining its hermetic aspects, the syntax has attained a higher degree of clarity, fusing with ease human elements with those of nature in a poised synthesis, as in the poem on Ilaria del Carretto. *Ed è subito sera* (1942), representing a stylistic and structural revision of all Quasimodo had written up to that time, arranged the poems in a chronological order and imparted the feeling of greater ease and of solutions that allowed a more detached attitude on the part of the reader.

The postwar collections *Giorno dopo giorno* (1947), *La vita non è sogno* (1949), and *Il falso e vero verde* (1956) seek a more direct relationship and dialogue with the reader, and Quasimodo himself referred to them as "poesia sociale." *La terra impareggiabile* (1958) is still oriented toward the social and dialogical approach, but it is somewhat weaker than the earlier collections.

Further Reading

Salvatore Quasimodo is listed in the Literature study guide (III, J, 3, a). Giuseppe UNGARETTI and Eugenio MONTALE also wrote hermetic poetry.

A brief biography of Quasimodo is in Nobel Foundation, *Nobel Lectures: Literature, 1901–1967,* edited by Horst Frenz (1969). For general historical background see Carlo L. Golino, ed., *Contemporary Italian Poetry: An Anthology* (1962), and Eugenio Donadoni, *A History of Italian Literature* (1923; trans. and rev. ed., 2 vols., 1969).

QUAY / By Robert C. Bannister

Matthew Stanley Quay (1833–1904) was a U.S. senator and Republican party boss in Pennsylvania. His political genius made "Quayism" a synonym for shrewd, even ruthless, politics in the "gilded age."

Matthew Quay was born on Sept. 30, 1833, in Dillsburg, Pa., the son of a Presbyterian minister. In 1850 he graduated from Jefferson College (now Washington and Jefferson) and in 1854 was admitted to the bar. He mastered several languages and boasted one of America's finest private libraries.

Quay's political career began modestly when, in 1856, he was elected prothonotary of Beaver County. His work in the gubernatorial election of 1860 gained the attention of state politicians. He served with distinction in the Civil War and won the Congressional Medal of Honor. In 1865 he was elected to the state House of Representatives.

Initially opposed to the state organization of Republican boss Simon Cameron, Quay turned from politics in 1867 to edit and publish the *Beaver Radical*. A twist in state politics brought him into the Cameron fold in 1872. The Cameron-Quay machine was as ruthless as the more famous Tweed organization of New York. As secretary of the Commonwealth of Pennsylvania (1872–1878, 1879–1881), Quay played a pivotal role in attempts to weld local organizations in Pittsburgh and Philadelphia to the state machine. An especially blatant attempt to capture Philadelphia in 1878 by making him city recorder collapsed under public protest. Although implicated in a scandal in the state treasurer's office, he was elected state treasurer by an overwhelming margin in 1885. In 1888 Quay managed the presidential victory of Benjamin Harrison but broke with Harrison over distributing patronage. Intimate knowledge of his state, control of patronage, and insistence on party loyalty made Quay supreme in Pennsylvania. Shrewdly laconic, he knew, as one observer noted, "how to keep silent in fifteen languages."

Serving in the U.S. Senate (1887–1899, 1901–1902), Quay championed the protective tariff and little else. Controversy also marked his Senate career. When the Pennsylvania Legislature failed to fill his seat in 1899, the governor appointed Quay for a third term, only to have the Senate refuse to seat him. He was reelected in 1901. His public record, as with other bosses of the period, was no measure of his great influence within the national councils of his party. He was a partisan of minority rights, defending Indian tribes and opposing Chinese exclusion.

Matthew Quay about 1895. (Library of Congress)

His brand of politics, under attack when he died in 1904, helped nationalize American politics during years of rapid industrial and social change.

Further Reading

Matthew Quay is listed in the American History study guide (VII, A, 4). William TWEED, Democratic boss of New York City, defrauded the public of millions of dollars.

In the absence of a biography, Quay's own *Pennsylvania Politics: The Campaign of 1900* (1901) provides a sampling of his oratory and ideas. John Wanamaker, *Quayism and Boss Domination in Pennsylvania Politics* (1898), is a contemporary indictment by a Philadelphia merchant, one of Quay's chief opponents. Sylvester K. Stevens, *Pennsylvania: Birthplace of a Nation* (1964), and H. Wayne Morgan, *From Hayes to McKinley* (1969), discuss Quay in the context of state and national politics respectively.

DELLA QUERCIA / By Robert A. Koch

Jacopo della Quercia (1374?–1438), an Italian sculptor and architect, was a major sculptural innovator of the Early Renaissance.

Documentation concerning Jacopo della Quercia (pronounced dāl'lä kwĕr'chä) is scant. He was born in Siena. In 1401 he entered the competition for the bronze doors of the Baptistery in Florence, along with Filippo Brunelleschi and Lorenzo Ghiberti (the winner). The panel Della Quercia submitted is lost. In 1406 he executed the marble tomb of Ilaria del Carretto in the Cathedral of Lucca, and 2 years later he was in Ferrara, where he carved the *Seated Madonna* (now in the Cathedral Museum).

The major sculptural cycle from Della Quercia's middle period is the Fonte Gaia in the square in front of the Palazzo Pubblico in Siena. (The present fountain is a replica; the dismantled marble fragments of the original are in the Palazzo Pubblico.) It was commissioned in 1409, but he did not begin work on it until 1414; it was completed in 1419. Featured in relief sculpture was the nearly life-sized Virgin and Child, Mary being the patron saint of Siena, while in niches on either side of a rectangular parapet were eight female personifications of the Virtues. The bodies no longer sit quietly, in the Gothic fashion, but twist and turn in powerful angles that show the new energy of the Renaissance.

In 1422 Della Quercia received payment for the wooden group of the Annunciation in the Pieve of S. Gimignano; the following year he finished the Trenta Altar in S. Frediano, Lucca. In 1425 he was commissioned to design the main portal of S. Petronio in Bologna, and he made trips to Verona, Venice, and Milan to acquire stone. Before the portal was completed, in 1438, the master received and executed in 1430 the commission for the bronze relief *Zaccharias Driven from the Temple* for the Baptistery font in Siena.

In 1436 Della Quercia was named master architect of the Cathedral in Siena. The next year the Signoria of the city intervened between him and the Bolognese, who claimed that the artist had not kept his promise to them. After a trip to Bologna he became ill, and he died in Siena on Oct. 20, 1438.

In the 10 well-preserved marble relief panels on either side of the portal of S. Petronio in Bologna, Della Quercia elevated the depiction of the human body, both nude and draped, to a level of inherent dignity, power, and beauty which was to be achieved by no other sculptor before Michelangelo. The panels tell the stories of the creation and fall of Adam and Eve and of Cain and Abel. Della Quercia abjured Ghiberti's delicately constructed nudes, and the voluptuous body of Eve in Della Quercia's *Temptation* was surely influenced by an ancient statue of Venus. It is clear that the noble male in his *Creation of Adam* was the prototype used by Michelangelo for his ceiling composition in the Sistine Chapel in Rome.

Further Reading

Jacopo della Quercia is listed in the Art study guide (III, B, 2). He ranks close to DONATELLO and Lorenzo GHIBERTI as an innovator. Della Quercia's heroic style appealed to MICHELANGELO, who repeatedly adopted his ideas.

Jacopo della Quercia's Original Sin, one of the reliefs on the central portal of the church of S. Petronio, Bologna. (Alinari-Anderson)

A fine scholarly study in English on the Fonte Gaia is Anne Coffin Hanson, *Jacopo della Quercia's Fonte Gaia* (1965). For general background see John Pope-Hennessy, *Italian Gothic Sculpture* (1955), and Charles Seymour, Jr., *Sculpture in Italy, 1400–1500* (1966).

QUÉTELET / By Richard C. Clark

The Belgian statistician and astronomer Lambert Adolphe Jacques Quételet (1796–1874) is considered the founder of modern statistics and demography.

Adolphe Quételet (pronounced kā-tlĕ′) was born in Ghent on Feb. 22, 1796. When he finished secondary school at the age of 17, he took a job teaching mathematics in a secondary school. A professor of mathematics at the newly established University of Ghent influenced Quételet to study mathematics. In 1819 he received his doctorate in mathematics with a dissertation in which he claimed to have discovered a new curve. The work was heralded as an important contribution to analytic geometry.

That year Quételet was appointed to the chair of ele-

mentary mathematics at the Athenaeum, and shortly thereafter he was elected to membership in the Royal Academy of Sciences and Belles-lettres of Brussels. He wrote numerous essays in mathematics and physics, founded and edited a journal, delivered lectures on science in the Brussels Museum, and published introductory works in mathematics and natural science. In 1828 he became the first director of the Royal Observatory, a position held until his death on Feb. 17, 1874, in Brussels.

In Paris gathering technical knowledge for the building of the observatory, Quételet met a number of leading French scientists and mathematicians who were actively engaged in laying the foundations of modern probability theory. Although they were working in the natural sciences and mathematics, in the course of their studies some of them had occasion to analyze empirical social phenomena. What fascinated Quételet was the possibility of using statistics as an instrument to deal with social problems.

Quételet believed that statistical theory and research could be used to determine whether human actions occur with the expected regularity. If so, it would indicate that there are social laws which are as knowable as are the laws which govern the movements of the heavenly bodies. He thought that there were such social laws. He thus developed his famous notion of the "average man."

Quételet's concept of the average man was intended to be a construct of the mind or a model which would enable social "scientists" to express the differences among individuals in terms of their departure from the

Adolphe Quételet. (Belgian Consulate General, New York)

norm. This theory led to his "theory of oscillation." According to this hypothesis, as social contacts increase and racial groups intermarry, differences between men will decrease in intensity through a process of social and cultural oscillation, resulting in an ever-increasing balance and, eventually, international equilibrium and world peace. Thus, as Quételet saw it, the task of the academic and scientific communities in the immediate future was to develop a new social science, based on empirical observation and the use of statistics. This new science of "social physics" would discover the laws of society upon which human happiness depends. Quételet's subsequent works represent an attempt to formulate this new field of social physics.

To accomplish this goal, it was necessary to refine the techniques used in the collection of statistical data, since Quételet believed that through the analysis of such data empirical regularities or laws could be discovered. He was a moving force behind many of the governmental agencies and professional organizations involved in the gathering of statistical data, and he exerted an international influence on this area. His application of quantitative methods and mathematical techniques has been judged as anticipatory of the guiding principle of contemporary social science, especially his efforts to change statistics from a mere clerical function into an exact science of observation, measurement, and comparison of results.

Further Reading

Adolphe Quételet is listed in the Social Sciences study guide (VI, D, 2). Pierre Simon de LAPLACE expounded the classical mathematical theory of probability.

Several of Quételet's major works are available in English translation. The best study in English of his significance is Frank H. Hankins, *Adolphe Quételet as Statistician* (1908), which includes a biographical sketch. See also George Sarton, *Sarton on the History of Science*, edited by Dorothy Stimson (1962), for the reasons why Sarton considers Quételet rather than Auguste Comte as the "founder of sociology," and Quételet's work *On Man and the Development of His Faculties* as "one of the greatest books of the nineteenth century."

* * *

QUEVEDO / By Francis Hayes
and Rita Houston Barlow

The Spanish poet, satirist, novelist, and wit Francisco Gómez de Quevedo y Villegas (1580–1645) ranks as one of the major writers of Spain's Golden Age.

Francisco de Quevedo, a painting attributed to Diego Velázquez, in the Instituto de Valencia de Don Juan, Madrid. (MAS)

Francisco de Quevedo (pronounced kā-vā'thō) was born in Madrid to an aristocratic family and orphaned very young. He studied the humanities at the University of Alcalá and theology at Valladolid. He learned Latin, Greek, Hebrew, and several modern languages and became a classics scholar. He published his first poem at the age of 25. In 1613 he accompanied the Spanish viceroy, the Duke of Osuna, to Italy to serve as diplomatic adviser. Quevedo became involved in a political conspiracy in Venice in 1618 and was recalled to Madrid in disgrace and kept under house arrest.

Freed but unchastened, Quevedo engaged in acrid literary and political controversies. His adverse criticism of the government soon incurred the disapproval of the Conde-Duque de Olivares, who was the royal favorite, and Quevedo was imprisoned in León from 1639 until 1643. He went to Villanueva de los Infantes, where he died 2 years later.

Quevedo's name is used as the butt of jokes throughout the Spanish-speaking world. Because he always wore nose glasses, his name in the plural, *quevedos*, came to mean pince-nez.

In its manifold variety, Quevedo's writing dazzles the intellect. Quevedo the theologian produced about 15 books on theological and ascetic subjects, such as *La cuna y la sepultura* (1612; *The Cradle and the Grave*) and *La providencia de Dios* (1641; *The Providence of God*). Quevedo the critic and literary gadfly published *La culta latiniparla* (*The Craze for Speaking Latin*) and *Aguja de navegar cultos* (*Compass for Navigating among Euphuistic Reefs*), both aimed against Gongorism—the Spanish counterpart of euphuism.

Quevedo the satirist produced profoundly melancholy buffoonery and grotesque cosmic nonsense in *Los sueños* (1627; *Dreams*). He scourged doctors, tailors, judges, Genoese bankers, barbers, bores, poets, dramatists, and every age and sort of woman, spattering them with scatological humor. His books of political theory were products of many years of earnest thought and of his own political experience. Two of the most important are *La política de Dios* (1617–1626; *The Politics of the Lord*) and *La vida de Marco Bruto* (1632–1644; *The Life of Marcus Brutus*).

Quevedo the poet produced an enormous bulk of verse, much of it extremely witty and sarcastic—no few poems based on the subjects of metaphysical anguish, the brevity of beauty, the loss of love, inexorable time, and death. Quevedo the novelist is perhaps best known through his picaresque novel *La vida del buscón* (1626; *Paul the Sharper* or *The Scavenger*), in which he followed the usual episodic pattern of the picaresque novel, intermixing sardonic wit. In this novel he sought to entertain, to ridicule, and to hold up fraud and dishonesty to scorn, but he rarely moralized directly, as did other picaresque novelists of his time.

Further Reading

Francisco de Quevedo is listed in the Literature study guide (III, E, 5). Miguel de CERVANTES and Mateo ALEMÁN were also masters of the picaresque novel.

Translations of Quevedo into English are difficult to find. A translation of *El buscón*, entitled *The Scavenger*, was done by Hugh H. Harter in 1962. This volume contains an introduction expressly for the American reader. In 1963 the University of Illinois Press reprinted *Visions—As Translated by Sir Roger L'Estrange* from Quevedo's *Los sueños*; J. M. Cohen wrote the introduction, which contains significant comments on both L'Estrange and Quevedo. Charles Duff translated selections of Quevedo's work in *Quevedo: The Choice Humorous and Satirical Works* (1926). This volume includes the work of several translators and a study by Duff of the life and writings of Quevedo, with a list of English translations, none later than 1892. Quevedo's place in Spanish literature is discussed in Gerald Brenan, *The Literature of the Spanish People* (2d ed. 1953). For general historical background see Louis Bertrand and Sir Charles Petrie, *The History of Spain* (trans. 1934; rev. ed. 1952), and John Armstrong Crow, *Spain: The Root and the Flower* (1963).

✳   ✳   ✳

QUEZON / By Epifanio San Juan, Jr.

Manuel Luis Quezon (1878–1944) was the first president of the Commonwealth of the Philippines. He prepared the groundwork for Philippine independence in 1946.

Manuel Quezon (pronounced kā′sôn) was born on Aug. 19, 1878, to Lucio Quezon and Maria Molina, both schoolteachers, in Baler, Tayabas (now Quezon) Province, in Luzon. Manuel enrolled at San Juan de Letran College, after which he was appointed lecturer at the University of Santo Tomás. There he studied law, but his studies were interrupted by the outbreak of the Spanish-American War.

Quezon was considered "bright but lazy"; but when he joined the revolutionary forces of Gen. Emilio Aguinaldo during the revolution against Spain, Quezon displayed his fearless, bold, and quick-tempered style of fighting. He was promoted from private to major until, in 1899, he surrendered to the Americans, spent 6 months in jail, and then returned to Manila.

Early Public Offices

In 1903 Quezon passed the bar examination and set up practice in Baler. He gave up private practice to assume the post of provincial fiscal of Mindoro and later of Tayabas. In 1906 he was elected provincial governor. His campaign showed his native political wisdom when he sided with popular issues in a somewhat opportunistic manner. Often he abandoned consistency for the sake of pursuing what to his enemies was nothing but plain demagoguery.

In 1907 Quezon ran successfully as candidate for the Philippine Assembly on the Nacionalista party platform. In the Assembly he was elected floor leader, and Sergio Osmeña, his archrival, became Speaker of the House. Quezon served as resident commissioner in Washington, D.C. (1909–1916), where he became notorious as a romantic dancer, playboy diplomat, and shrewd lobbyist. He was instrumental in having a law revised so that Filipinos would form a majority in the Philippine Commission, the highest governing body in the Philippines. In February 1916 he cosponsored the Jones Act, which gave the Filipinos the power to legislate for themselves subject to veto by the American governor general. With this act, Quezon returned home a hero.

In 1916 Quezon was elected to the Senate, and soon became its president. Here he began attacking Osmeña for the latter's theory of "unipersonal" leadership. Quezon's "collectivist" idea of leadership won in the 1922 election. Soon, however, the two warring factions of the Nacionalista party united in the Partido Nacionalista Consolidado, headed by Quezon, who then became president of the party.

In 1933 a bill providing for the future independence of the Philippines, the Hare-Hawes-Cutting Bill, was passed by the U.S. Senate. Quezon opposed the new law because "America would still hold military and naval bases in the Philippines even after the latter's independence, and, moreover, export duties regulated in the law would destroy both industry and trade." He was referring to what has since become the most troublesome cause of conflict between the Philippines and the United States: the right of jurisdiction over military bases and the special trade concessions given to landlords, compradors,

Manuel Quezon (right) with U.S. president Warren G. Harding, photographed in 1922. (Library of Congress)

and bureaucrat-capitalists with interests in export industries.

The real cause of Quezon's opposition to the law, apart from his objection to specific provisions, was the fact that it was identified with the Osmeña faction. Quezon led a mission to the United States to work for a bill generally similar to the Hare-Hawes-Cutting Law, the Tydings-McDuffie Law, known also as the Philippine Independence Act. This law provided for Philippine independence in 1946 and tax-free importation of Philippine products such as sugar, coconut oil, and cordage into the United States and the diplomatic negotiation of the military bases issue.

President of the Philippines

In September 1935, under the banner of a coalition party, Quezon was elected first president of the commonwealth, with Osmeña as vice president. Quezon's first act as chief executive was to push a national defense bill through the rubber-stamp unicameral legislature, which he controlled. This bill made him chairman of the Council for National Defense, with the chief of staff of the armed forces directly subordinate to him.

On Aug. 10, 1940, influenced by the growing Japanese imperialist encroachment, Quezon jammed through the National Assembly the Emergency Powers Bill, which vested him with dictatorial powers. Passed by a vote of 62 to 1, the bill gave Quezon the authority to change even the social and economic structure of the country:

he was given the authority to require civilians to render service to the government, to outlaw strikes, to commandeer shipping and other transportation, to control fuel resources, to revise the educational system, and so forth.

In November 1941 Quezon was reelected president of the commonwealth. When the Japanese forces occupied Manila in 1942, Quezon and his Cabinet fled from the Philippines and set up an exile government in Washington in May 1942. Quezon died on Aug. 1, 1944, a year before the liberation of the Philippines.

Assessment of Quezon

Although Quezon lived through the most turbulent times in Philippine history, when the peasantry—who composed 75 percent of the people—was rebelling against social injustice and age-old exploitation, he failed to institute long-lasting reforms in land tenancy, wages, income distribution, and other areas of crisis. Essentially a politician who was both tactful and bullheaded, supple and compulsive, Quezon served mainly the interest of the Filipino elite, or ruling oligarchy (about 200 families), who owned and controlled the estates and businesses.

Quezon became a popular hero when he attacked the racist policies of Governor Leonard Wood with his declaration that he preferred "a government run like hell by Filipinos to one run like heaven by Americans." Senator Claro M. Recto, a contemporary, pronounced the most balanced and acute judgment when he described Quezon as "a successful politician ... because he was a master of political intrigue. He knew how to build strong and loyal friendships even among political opponents, but he knew also how to excite envy, distrust, ambition, jealousy, even among his own loyal followers."

Further Reading

Manuel Quezon is listed in the Asia study guide (IV, C, 4). He followed Emilio AGUINALDO in his nationalist sentiments and was a strong rival of Sergio OSMEÑA.

The most authoritative source on Quezon's life is his autobiography, *The Good Fight* (1946). For his career and the historical circumstances surrounding it, the following are standard references: Carlos Quirino, *Quezon: Man of Destiny* (1935); Joseph R. Hayden, *The Philippines: A Study in National Development* (1942); Teodoro A. Agoncillo and Oscar M. Alfonso, *History of the Filipino People* (1960; rev. ed. 1967); Theodore Friend, *Between Two Empires: The Ordeal of the Philippines, 1929–46* (1965); and Teodoro A. Agoncillo, *A Short History of the Philippines* (1969).

QUINE / By Andrew J. Reck

Willard Van Orman Quine (born 1908), American philosopher, is best known for his advocacy of the logical regimentation of ordinary language.

On June 25, 1908, W. V. Quine was born in Akron, Ohio. He earned the bachelor of arts degree *summa cum laude* in 1930 from Oberlin College. At Harvard University Graduate School he concentrated on logic under the supervision of Alfred North Whitehead; he received his doctorate in 1932. He visited Vienna when the circle of logical positivist philosophers flourished, studied mathematical logic at Warsaw, and in Prague befriended Rudolf Carnap, a leader of the logical positivist movement.

Quine's *A System of Logic* (1934) contributed significantly to the development of mathematical set theory. In 1936 he joined the Harvard faculty. His essay "New Foundations of Mathematical Logic" (1937) retained in principle Bertrand Russell's theory of types (a revision of set theory) but sought to avoid its complexities. Nevertheless, Quine's new theory had drawbacks. In *Mathematical Logic* (1940) he presented a superior system. His *Set Theory and Its Logic* (1963) traced relations between his own system of set theory and others.

Two articles, "Steps toward a Constructive Nominalism" (1947) and "On What There Is" (1948), represent Quine's widely considered doctrines in ontology. Ontology—in Quine's words, "ontic" theory—consists of assertions of existence. He made clear that accepted scientific theories allow for more than one ontic theory and that it is incorrect to seek to determine that one such ontic theory is true. He proposed a method for explicating the ontic import of a theory, calling for formulation of the statements which a theory contains into symbolic expressions with existential import. The primacy of mathematical logic in Quine's ontology is evident in his celebrated definition of being: "To be is to be the value of a variable."

Quine's ontology was originally nominalistic, maintaining that only particular individuals exist and that universals or abstract entities do not exist, except perhaps as linguistic symbols. In 1947 Quine denied the existence of abstract entities and proposed the construction of logical and mathematical systems without resort to such entities. In *Word and Object* (1960) Quine abandoned his earlier nominalism by acknowledging the existence of abstract entities. He contended that language consists of dispositions, acquired by conditioning, to respond acceptably to socially observable stimuli.

Quine's main contribution to epistemology (the theory of knowledge), signaled by his article "Two Dogmas of Empiricism" (1951), was his denial of the validity of the analytic-synthetic distinction. According to this distinction, every statement in any system of knowledge is either synthetic or analytic. A synthetic statement is true or false as a matter of fact, and an analytic statement is true or false without reference to fact but with reference to meanings or formal rules within the language in which the statement is expressed. In challenging this central distinction in recent epistemology, Quine had a decisive impact on the field. He pointed out that the distinction was never made satisfactorily and, in fact, argued that it could not be made.

In 1955 Quine was appointed Edgar Peirce professor of philosophy at Harvard. President of the Association of Symbolic Logic (1953–1956), in 1957 he was elected president of the Eastern Division of the American Philosophical Association. In 1968 he inaugurated the John Dewey Lectures at Columbia University. In December 1971 he delivered the prestigious Carus Lectures before the American Philosophical Association.

Quine's philosophy at first seemed utterly fragmentary. Despite fundamental shifts in doctrine, however, his philosophy later assumed growing systematic coherence. Collections of his articles include *From a Logical Point of View* (1953), *Selected Logic Papers* (1966), *The Ways of Paradox* (1966), *Ontological Relativity and Other Essays* (1969), and *Philosophy of Logic* (1970).

Further Reading

W. V. Quine is listed in the Philosophy study guide (VII, F). The theory of sets led to paradoxes that Bertrand RUSSELL overcame by introducing his theory of types.

Quine's work is discussed in Donald Davidson and Jaakho Hintikka, eds., *Words and Objections: Essays on the Work of W. V. Quine* (1969). His importance is also analyzed in Neils Egmont Christensen, *On the Nature of Meanings: A Philosophical Analysis* (1961; 2d ed. 1965). A short biography of Quine is in Paul Kurtz, ed., *American Philosophy in the Twentieth Century* (1966).

QUINTILIAN / By Robert Dale Sweeney

Quintilian (ca. 35–ca. 99) was a Roman rhetorician and literary critic. His influence on rhetoric, literary criticism, and educational theory was profound.

Quintilian (pronounced kwĭn-tĭl′yən), or Marcus Fabius Quintilianus, was born at Calagurris in Spain, the son of a rhetorician. He studied mainly in Rome, under the orator Domitius Afer and perhaps the

W. V. Quine. (Harvard University Library)

Quintilian, a marble portrait bust in the Uffizi, Florence. (Brogi-Giraudon)

great grammarian Remmius Palaemon, among others. He then went back to Spain, probably as a teacher in his hometown, and returned to Rome in 68, the only certain date in his life. As a teacher of rhetoric, he became wealthy and famous from his lectures and was also an advocate in the law courts. Under the emperor Vespasian he was made a professor of rhetoric with a salary from the state. Among his pupils was Pliny the Younger.

At some time, probably in the early 80s, Quintilian married a very young woman. She died at the age of 18, after giving birth to two sons, who soon died as well. After 20 years of teaching, perhaps in 90, Quintilian retired and devoted himself to writing. Sometime after this, but before Domitian's death in 96, Quintilian was appointed by him as tutor to his two grandnephews; and through the influence of their father, Flavius Clemens, he received the insignia and privileges of a consul. The date of Quintilian's death is uncertain: Pliny the Younger, writing about 100, speaks of him in terms which suggest that he was already dead.

His Work

Only one work of Quintilian's has been preserved, the *Institutio oratoria* (On the Education of an Orator) in 12 books, composed about 92–96, the distillation of his long and successful career as a teacher. It treats of the education of an orator, beginning with the most elementary education. Book 1 sets the tone of the whole collection: it is moderate and practical, based on long expe-

rience with the actual behavior and psychology of children and careful attention to the smallest details of pedagogical practice. Book 2 treats of the more advanced education of the orator, and books 3 through 11 are more technical, dealing with the structure, argumentation, style, and delivery of orations.

Book 10 contains a discussion of the relative merits of the great Greek and Latin authors which has exercised a profound influence on subsequent literary criticism. Book 12 is based on a deeply moral conception of the importance of character as well as learning to the orator and of the necessity for the style to be appropriate to the subject; it rounds out the work on an impressive note of grave dignity.

A complete text of Quintilian was rediscovered in the early 15th century. His educational aims, based on Cato the Elder's definition of an orator as "a good man, skilled in speaking," and looking toward the education of literate, humane, well-rounded, and useful citizens, were congenial to the ideals of the Renaissance.

Two further works, collections of declamations, survive under the name of Quintilian, but the fantastic nature of many of their subjects, an abuse specifically attacked by Quintilian, has led most scholars to dismiss them as spurious.

Further Reading

Quintilian is listed in the Ancient History study guide (III, C, 5). His views influenced PIUS II, Philip MELANCTHON, and ERASMUS.

Two studies of Quintilian's life and work are Herbert Augustus Strong, *Quintilian, the Roman Schoolmaster* (1908), and George A. Kennedy, *Quintilian* (1969). Quintilian is discussed in John Wight Duff, *A Literary History of Rome in the Silver Age, from Tiberius to Hadrian* (1927); John W. H. Atkins, *Literary Criticism in Antiquity* (2 vols., 1934); Henri I. Marrou, *A History of Education in Antiquity* (trans. 1956); and George M. A. Grube, *The Greek and Roman Critics* (1965). See also the introductions and notes to the editions of Quintilian's *Institutio oratoria*.

QUIRINO / By Epifanio San Juan, Jr.

Elpidio Quirino (1890–1956) was the second president of the Philippine Republic. During his administration, the Philippines passed through a period of revolutionary turmoil marked by widespread corruption, demoralization, economic crisis, and political terrorism.

Elpidio Quirino (pronounced kē-rē′nō) was born on Nov. 16, 1890, in Vigan, Ilocos Sur, the son of the warden of the provincial jail. Quirino taught school while studying at Vigan High School and then went to Manila, where he worked as junior computer in the Bureau of Lands and as property clerk in the Manila police department. He graduated from Manila High School in 1911 and also passed the civil service examination, first-grade.

After graduating from the College of Law, University of the Philippines, in 1915, Quirino served as law clerk in the Philippine Commission and then as secretary to Senate president Manuel Quezon. In 1919 Quirino won the post of congressional representative from the first district of Ilocos Sur. He opposed Sergio Osmeña, the leader of the Nacionalista party, and joined Quezon's Collectivista faction of the party. In 1925 Quirino was elected to the Senate. Quezon appointed him chairman of the Committee on Accounts and Claims and of the Committee on Public Instruction and to other important congressional bodies. In 1931 Quirino was reelected to the Senate. In the controversy surrounding the Hare-Hawes-Cutting Law of 1933, he sided with Quezon.

Elpidio Quirino. (National Archives, Washington, D.C.)

In 1934 Quirino became secretary of finance. He was also one of the drafters of the constitution approved on May 15, 1935. When the Philippine Commonwealth was inaugurated on Nov. 15, 1935, he held the position of secretary of finance (1935–1936) and then became secretary of interior (1936–1938). In 1941 he was elected as senator-at-large. When World War II broke out, Quirino refused to join the puppet government of José Laurel and became an underground leader of the Filipino resistance movement against the Japanese. He was captured and imprisoned by the Japanese military police in Ft. Santiago, and his wife, two daughters, and a son were murdered by the Japanese forces.

In 1945 Quirino became the leader of the majority in the Philippine Congress and then assumed the post of president pro tempore of the Senate. On the inauguration of the Philippine Republic in 1946, he occupied the post of vice president and first secretary of foreign affairs. In 1947 Quirino (who belonged to the class of landlords, compradors, and bureaucrat-capitalists) urged the adoption of the anomalous "parity amendment," imposed by the U.S. government in exchange for independence, war damage payments, and other loans.

When President Manuel Roxas died on April 15, 1948, Quirino succeeded him as president of the republic. For his weakness in tolerating rampant graft and corruption in his party, permitting immorality in the armed forces, and neglecting the impoverished plight of the majority of Filipinos, he was very unpopular, and in 1953 he was defeated by Ramon Magsaysay.

As president, Quirino was many times justly accused by Filipino nationalists of being extremely pro-American and even subservient to alien economic interests. To maintain peace and order for the sake of national unity, he granted amnesty to the Huk guerrillas on June 21, 1948; but this measure proved futile in solving the deep-rooted social injustice and exploitation inherent in the country's semifeudal economy. Although Quirino saw the need for increasing the appeal for loans from the United States and establishing controls to protect local Filipino industries and conserve natural resources, he failed to act vigorously and sincerely in implementing drastic agrarian reforms.

Quirino was elected president in 1949, when, according to historians and newspaper reports, widespread terrorism and violation of legal electoral processes occurred. He died on Feb. 29, 1956.

Further Reading

Elpidio Quirino is listed in the Asia study guide (IV, C, 6, a). Sergio OSMEÑA and Manuel QUEZON supported different U.S. congressional bills to win independence from the United States.

Standard references on Quirino's career and achievement include Sol H. Gwekoh, *Elpidio Quirino: The Barrio School Teacher Who Became President* (1949), and Hernando J. Abaya, *Betrayal in the Philippines* (1946) and *The Untold Philippine Story* (1967).

QUIROGA / By John L. Robinson

Juan Facundo Quiroga (1788/1790–1835) was an Argentine caudillo who mastered a large part of northern Argentina for several years.

Juan Facundo Quiroga (pronounced kē-rō′gä), often known as Juan Facundo, was born into a ranching family in La Rioja Province. Although his father was moderately wealthy, Juan had little formal schooling, learning only the basics of reading and writing. He spent most of his boyhood working on the family ranch, showing qualities of leadership and shrewdness. He left home in 1806, having gambled away the proceeds from his father's cattle sale.

Quiroga spent several years in and out of military service. He joined both cavalry and infantry units but disliked the discipline and regimentation of formal military life. Finally he was discharged—or he deserted—and returned home, where he was reconciled with his father.

From 1816, when he became a captain in the provincial militia, Quiroga began his rise in political and military affairs. By 1823 he was virtual dictator of La Rioja. Skilled in battle, of unflinching courage and daring ruthlessness, he had an almost mystical ability to command the absolute loyalty of his mounted troops.

From his power base in La Rioja, Quiroga extended his sway to surrounding provinces and was soon caught up in national politics. Argentina had declared its independence from Spain in 1816, but the nation's leaders could not agree on a permanent form of government. In 1826 Bernardino Rivadavia became president and attempted to establish a unitary system of government with control emanating from Buenos Aires. Quiroga joined other provincial *caudillos* in opposition and helped force Rivadavia's resignation in 1827. After a series of seesaw battles, Quiroga finally fragmented unitary forces in the interior of the country in 1831, and the various provinces became virtually independent.

Quiroga soon moved to Buenos Aires Province, where Juan Manuel de Rosas was trying to fasten his dictatorial hold. The two were never close, for Quiroga insisted that Argentina must have a truly national government, a concept Rosas always resisted. For more than a year the backwoods *caudillo* enjoyed the delights offered by the chief city of the nation and indulged his passion for gambling. Late in 1834 Rosas persuaded him to undertake a mission as mediator between quarreling provincial governors far in the interior. While returning from this assignment in 1835, Quiroga was killed in an ambush. The

Juan Facundo Quiroga, an 1831 lithograph in the Bibliothèque Nationale, Paris. (Giraudon)

"Tiger of the Plains," champion of provincial autonomy, was a harsh man who lived in harsh times, when leadership was tested at the point of a lance and intellectual ability was valued less than raw courage. He gave northern Argentina a measure of stability in chaotic times, but he left no heritage of stable or progressive institutions, no base on which to build a greater Argentina.

Further Reading

Juan Facundo Quiroga is listed in the Latin America study guide (IV, A, 1, a). Another *caudillo* was Julio ROCA.

Domingo F. Sarmiento, *Life in the Argentine Republic in the Days of the Tyrants: or, Civilization and Barbarism* (trans. 1961), viewing Quiroga as representative of the "barbarism," recounts his life and times in a sensational and anecdotal fashion. Frederick A. Kirkpatrick, *A History of the Argentine Republic* (1931), and Ricardo Levene, *A History of Argentina*, translated and edited by W. S. Robertson (1937), place Quiroga in the larger scope of Argentina's history.

✳   ✳   ✳

Rabearivelo R *Ryle*

RABEARIVELO / By Albert S. Gérard

The Malagasy poet Jean Joseph Rabearivelo (1901–1937) was the first major French-language poet in Africa. Some of his most powerful poetry arose from the conflict between his intimacy with two cultures, Malagasy and French, and his estrangement from two societies, native and colonial.

Jean Joseph Rabearivelo (pronounced rä-bä-ə-rē′vä-lō) was born on March 4, 1901, in Tananarive (Madagascar) into a noble family which had been impoverished as a result of the abolition of slavery by the French authorities soon after the colonial conquest in 1895. He left school at 13 in order to earn a precarious livelihood as proofreader in a local printing shop.

Tananarive in the early 1920s was a focus of intense literary and journalistic activity in the vernacular, and Rabearivelo was one of the first Malagasy poets to use the French language as his medium of literary expression. His early collections, *La Coupe de cendres* (1924), *Sylves* (1927), and *Volumes* (1928), were in the romantic-academic manner of such French 19th-century poets as appeared on the school curriculum in those days. But through his friendship with Pierre Camo—a French official who was also a minor poet—Rabearivelo became acquainted with contemporary symbolist poetry and managed to free himself of the shackles of conventional

versification and diction. His best poems are to be found in *Presque-songes* (1934) and *Traduit de la nuit* (1935).

The poet's love of France, its language, and its literature was apt to take weird ritualistic forms. His wide reading in romantic and postromantic poetry had somehow driven him to the notion that poetic genius was inevitably associated with various forms of abnormality, such as reckless profligacy, chronic lack of money, almost permanent debauchery (including homosexuality), ill health (preferably tuberculosis), and suicidal proclivities. With pathetic conscientiousness, he was thus striving to ape the most futilely morbid aspects in the lives of Balzac, Baudelaire, Verlaine, and a host of other, minor, if even more wildly aberrant, writers.

This ill-advised imitation of alien models was uneasily coupled with considerable pride in the literary achievements, oral and written, of Malagasy culture, even though, as a former aristocrat and a Frenchified intellectual, he felt some contempt for the illiterate masses. He was thus rejected by his more tradition-minded or nationalistic fellow citizens. As a native, he was also rejected by the local French society of petty traders and administrators. In his bulky diaries, which have never been edited in their entirety, he described his tragic predicament as that of a Latin mind under a black skin but also as that of a proud Malagasy eager to shed the Christian and Western disguise imposed upon him. His habit of wearing the traditional robe, the *lamba*, over his Western-style clothes illustrated this duality more than it could hide—let alone solve—it.

This dual allegiance and this dual rebellion imbue

Rabearivelo's poetry. Although he mostly wrote in French, in part of his work he sought to bend the alien language to native themes, experiences, and even literary forms such as the *hainteny*. Aware of his uncommon gifts, yet confined to his underprivileged status, Rabearivelo found the best of his inspiration in an all-pervading, tragic sense of alienation, which finds adequate utterance in images of exile and death, rootlessness and sterility. He committed suicide on June 22, 1937.

Further Reading

Jean Joseph Rabearivelo is listed in the Africa study guide (X, B). Another literary figure in Francophone Africa was Léopold SENGHOR.

There is no biography of Rabearivelo in English. Information on him is in Ulli Beier, ed., *Introduction to African Literature* (1967), and in Norman R. Shapiro, ed. and trans., *Negritude: Black Poetry from Africa and the Caribbean* (1970).

RABELAIS / By Donald Stone, Jr.

The French humanist, doctor, and writer François Rabelais (ca. 1494–ca. 1553) is acclaimed a master of the comic for his creations "Pantagruel" and "Gargantua."

François Rabelais. (Bulloz)

Unfortunately there are more legends than facts about François Rabelais (pronounced răb′ə-lā). The dates of his birth and death are only scholarly guesses. No record of his activities for long periods has survived. Most certainly born in the closing years of the 15th century, Rabelais consequently experienced a time of considerable ferment in the history of France's institutions and intellectual life. Unless one grasps the issues and the attitudes in this crisis, much of Rabelais's work is meaningless or subject to misinterpretation.

Central to the problems that faced Rabelais's contemporaries were the decline of scholasticism and the rise of humanist activity. (A humanist is defined here as a scholar of the language and literature of ancient times, including biblical research.) After the constructive work of St. Thomas Aquinas and Albertus Magnus, scholastic philosophy became increasingly dominated by the nominalists, who, in distinguishing between the realm of reason and the realm of faith, placed faith firmly beyond the reach of reason. As a consequence, a scholastic education evolved into an endless exercise of rational proof that displeased many believers who felt such training failed to respond to the spiritual side of man. Humanist inquiry completed the crisis of confidence in inherited institutions by revealing the great ignorance of many scholastics and the inaccuracy of their work. At the same time, the newly studied texts, such as Plato, and the

reinterpreted texts, such as St. Paul, seemed more and more to offer the inspiration of which scholasticism had proved incapable.

During the first 30 years of the 16th century in France, the gamut of attitudes on such matters was great. Some merely studied ancient texts; others, like Lefèvre d'Étaples, brought their scholarly actions to bear on doctrinal questions without contemplating separation from the Church. Still others, like John Calvin, felt confronted by the necessity to form a new faith, a new church. All liberal minds felt disturbed by the evident disparity between, on the one hand, the sterility of scholastic pedagogy and the corruption of the Church and, on the other, the excitement in humanist studies and the vibrant faith of early Christianity.

Early Years

Rabelais's native land was the old province of Touraine, where his father, Antoine, practiced law. There is reason to believe that Rabelais was instructed according to scholastic methods. On March 4, 1521, he wrote a letter from the Franciscan monastery of Puy-Saint-Martin to Guillaume Budé, one of France's foremost humanists. Furthermore, in 1523 Rabelais's superiors confiscated his Greek books, and although the texts were returned, François soon left both his monastery and his order to become the secretary of Geoffroy d'Estissac of the Benedictines. He is next seen at Montpellier (1530), where he obtained a degree in medicine and taught the writings of Hippocrates and Galen from the original Greek text. In 1532 he settled in Lyons, where he was named physician at the Hôtel-Dieu and where, the same year, he published several works, including the first volume of his celebrated novel, *Horribles et espouventables faictz et prouesses de tres renommé Pantagruel, roy des Dipsodes.*

In addition to Rabelais's evident link with the humanists and his own scholarly accomplishments, certain critics have made much of his gradual separation from the monastery, implying that Rabelais's acts signify as well a separation from the Church (and religion). Nothing is more suspect. Rabelais wanted to study medicine, and this was not then possible if one remained a member of the regular clergy. If his books were seized, they were also returned, and the papal permission Rabelais received to change orders, too, intimates that he was far from being considered an errant atheist. Another papal authorization—this time to legitimize two children of Rabelais's (1540)—reveals that Rabelais could not recognize all the rules of monastic life, but this is not tantamount to saying that he could not recognize the tenets of the Church.

"Pantagruel" and "Gargantua"

Although *Gargantua* (1534) followed *Pantagruel* in order of publication, all modern editions place it at the beginning of the novel since the events it relates predate those of *Pantagruel*. The creation of *Gargantua*, the story of Pantagruel's father, attests to the success of the first volume. Rabelais, following the example of many medieval writers of *chansons de geste*, expands his material through a portrait of the hero's antecedents. The rapprochement with medieval literature is not gratuitous. In conception (the life and chivalric episodes of a family of giants) and execution (use of the vernacular, love of language, puns, mixture of popular and learned styles) the first two volumes of Rabelais's novel reflect practices well developed in medieval literature and known to Rabelais through the French and Italian chivalric romances, their parodies, and *Les Grandes et inestimables croniques du grand et énorme géant Gargantua.* Judging by the light and simple nature of *Pantagruel*, where traces of Rabelais's important themes are not always evident, it seems unlikely that the writer foresaw the volumes to follow or even the serious use to which his novel might be put.

It would also be incorrect to portray *Pantagruel* as devoid of any controversial material. It and *Gargantua* were signed by a pseudonym, Alcofrybas Nasier, an anagram of François Rabelais. The Sorbonne condemned both books. *Pantagruel* is not just Panurge's wild jokes or the fantastic war between the Dipsodes and Amaurotes. In portraying Pantagruel's adventures with legal cases and debating, Rabelais good-heartedly satirizes the bumbling "learned," so contemptible to the humanists. When Pantagruel visits the Library of Saint Victor, he finds such titles as *The Codpiece of the Law* and Béda's *Of the Excellence of Tripe.* If the first title is pure comedy, the second casts a satirical barb at Noël Béda, a conservative Catholic and notorious enemy of the reformers.

Contemporary religious questions keep reappearing and no doubt explain the Sorbonne's condemnation. Before a battle, Pantagruel promises God that if he is victorious, he will have God's word preached "purely, simply and wholly, so that the abuses of a host of hypocrites and false prophets will be eradicated from [his] land." Rabelais's sympathy with the reform could not be clearer. Mention should be made as well of Gargantua's letter to Pantagruel, in which the father contrasts the ignorance of his day with the new learning. It shows that the idea of a renaissance in France at this time was common among the humanists themselves.

There are striking contrasts between *Pantagruel* and *Gargantua.* Although both discuss religion and war, *Gargantua* gives these subjects an extended treatment in which Rabelais's serious thoughts direct the discussion instead of appearing sporadically as in *Pantagruel.* The reader first learns how Gargantua was taught by a (scholastic) theologian (changed in later editions to "sophist"). Gargantua studies those texts long discredited by humanist scholarship and proves his worth by learning to memorize texts backward. Under other sophists, he rises late, spends little time on studies or exercising but eats, drinks, and hears from 6 to 30 Masses. Then Gargantua receives a tutor schooled in the new humanist and religious thought. The tutor consults a doctor so that Gargantua's regime will benefit body as well as mind. The boy rises early and reads a page of the Scriptures. During the day not an hour is lost as the pupil strives to learn his lessons clearly and to absorb the great variety of skills required of a "renaissance man." There are limits to Rabelais's educational reform. He still emphasized memorization, and there can be no doubt about the continued importance of religion. His reform affects more the methods of education than its aims.

The battles against Picrochole are intended to show Rabelais's hatred of war. War is portrayed as interrupting more important pursuits, such as learning, and having an irrational basis. When Picrochole has been defeated, an entire chapter is devoted to Gargantua's treatment of the vanquished. His acts embody Christian charity. Only the King's evil minister and two instigators of the war receive a punishment (a very humanist punishment): they turn Gargantua's printing press!

The closing chapters of *Gargantua* are devoted to the Abbaye de Thélème, a utopian spot, where the motto is "Do What You Will." The phrase has been interpreted both as a frank statement of Rabelais's immorality and of his express confidence in the innate goodness of humanity. The text upholds neither interpretation. The rooms at Thélème have a chapel for worship, and Rabelais carefully enumerates those who are excluded from Thélème (hypocrites, lawyers, usurers, and jealous troublemakers) or invited (noble lords, ladies, and those who actively expound on the Scriptures). Religion is hardly absent from this abbey that also is not for everyone, and the inclusion of the aristocrat probably says more about Rabelais's association (a traditional one) of nobility of birth with nobility of soul than about his attitude toward original sin. In all three elements of *Gargantua*—education, war, Thélème—Rabelais's remarks are constructive and positive.

Later Life

Rabelais's continued association with the most able men of his time is attested to by trips he made to Rome in the party of Jean du Bellay (1534 and 1535) and by his presence at a dinner given for Étienne Dolet (1537). The same year he gave an anatomy lesson at Lyons. In 1546 he published the *Tiers livre des faictz et dictz héroïques du noble Pantagruel*, which Rabelais dared to sign with his own name and which the Sorbonne immediately condemned.

Firm traces of Rabelais now become increasingly difficult to find. The kindness of Jean du Bellay permitted him to visit Rome a third time, where he appeared definitely in 1548. That year saw published in Lyons a partial edition of the *Quart livre*. The full edition was printed in 1552. A fifth volume, called first *L'Isle sonante* in a truncated text of 1562 and then the *Cinquième livre* in a much enlarged printing of 1564, continues to bear, as it did then, the name of Rabelais, but its authenticity is yet to be confirmed. When, in January 1553, Rabelais signed

Frontispiece of the 1537 edition of Rabelais's Gargantua, *in the Bibliothèque Nationale, Paris. The print shows the infant Gargantua with his father, Grandgousier, and his mother, Gargamelle. (Photo-Hachette)*

away the rights to two ecclesiastical posts, he performed his last certain act.

"Tiers livre" and "Quart livre"

The *Tiers livre* contains much of Rabelais's most obscure writing. The romanesque battle scenes and the general hilarity of gigantic exploits no longer furnish him with a narrative line, although Pantagruel and Gargantua appear in the book. Even Panurge, the impish, amoral prankster of the first volume, shares the less funny and more disquieting quality of the *Tiers livre*, for which he provides a central theme. Panurge wonders whether he should marry and whether his wife will deceive him. The book enumerates all the efforts expended by Panurge to help him make a decision.

The complexity of the *Tiers livre* resides primarily in the portrait of Panurge. Pantagruel early states that Panurge must decide what is his will and act. If all else in life is fortuitous, man has his will and an obligation to use it. (Rabelais did not share John Calvin's views on predestination.) From this perspective the *Tiers livre* is a criticism of Panurge, who will not act and will not accept the advice given him. It has also been argued that much of the advice is open to discussion and that Panurge's final decision to consult the Dive Bouteille is a positive reaction before the need for self-knowledge. However one reads the *Tiers livre*, there is no missing its allusions to the gathering tensions in France after the reformers lost royal support.

The *Quart livre*, an account of Panurge's adventures on the voyage to the Dive Bouteille, contains the famous episode of Dindenault and his sheep, as well as Rabelais's final definition of *Pantagruélisme*: "a certain gaiety of spirit filled with contempt for fortuitous things." There is a chapter here devoted to the Papefigues (those who mocked the Pope). Their land was once rich and free. Its inhabitants are now poor, the subjects of the Papimanes (supporters of the Pope).

Later Pantagruel meets two groups of men, the Engastrimythes (ventriloquists) and the Gastrolatres (adorers of the stomach). Rabelais specifically states that Pantagruel —generally so tolerant—"greatly detested them." In both cases there is a religious overtone. The Engastrimythes are prophets who fool the simple; the Gastrolatres depict those enemies of the Cross who, in the words of St. Paul, have made Belly their God. By 1552, a mere decade before the outbreak of the religious wars, France had left far behind the optimism of the 1530s. Its evolution is well mirrored in the changing tones of Rabelais, who incorrectly but not unfortunately is remembered only as the jovial embodiment of Renaissance enthusiasm.

Further Reading

François Rabelais is listed in the Literature study guide (III, E, 2). His sense of the satiric is similar to that of LUCIAN and Jonathan SWIFT.

The most solid modern biography of Rabelais is Jean Plattard, *The Life of François Rabelais* (1930). Excellent studies of Rabelais's work include M. A. Screech, *The Rabelaisian Marriage* (1958); A. J. Krailsheimer, *Rabe-*

lais and the Franciscans (1963); and Abraham C. Keller, *The Telling of Tales in Rabelais* (1963). Aspects of Rabelais's influence are well treated in Huntington Brown, *Rabelais in English Literature* (1933).

RABI / By Roger H. Stuewer

The American physicist Isidor Isaac Rabi (born 1898) pioneered in the development of precision atomic- and nuclear-beam measurements.

Isidor Rabi. (Columbia University)

Isidor Rabi was born on July 29, 1898, in Rymanov in what was then Austria-Hungary. As an infant, he was brought to the United States, where his father engaged in the real estate business in New York City. Rabi attended Cornell University (1916–1919), obtaining a bachelor's degree in chemistry. Deciding to pursue graduate study in physics, he returned to Cornell (1922–1923) and then transferred to Columbia University, where in 1927 he obtained his doctoral degree. In 1926 he married Helen Newmark. The couple had two daughters.

Rabi studied in Europe (1927–1929), working with some of the most outstanding physicists. Otto Stern, with whom he remained for about a year, made the deepest impression on Rabi.

Work on Atomic and Molecular Beams

Immediately on his return to the United States, where he had accepted a position as lecturer in physics at Columbia, Rabi and his student V. Cohen exploited the atomic- and molecular-beam techniques Rabi had developed in Stern's laboratory. Together they proved that the sodium atom has four "hyperfine-structure" energy levels, which unambiguously fixed the "spin angular momentum" of its nucleus at a definite value, equal to 3/2 in units of $2\pi/h$. A few years later, by using beams of atomic hydrogen and deuterium, Rabi and his coworkers confirmed the surprisingly large value for the magnetic moment of the proton which Stern had found in 1933. It was during the course of this work that Rabi developed still another new method, the resonance method, that has since become the basis for all precision atomic- and molecular-beam measurements.

From the point of view of "pure physics," perhaps the most important measurements that have been made by exploiting Rabi's method have been those on the anomalous magnetic moment of the electron, the quadrupole moment of the deuteron, and the Lamb shift in hydrogen (which has become of great importance for the development of quantum electrodynamics). From the point of view of "practicality," Rabi's method has found numerous applications, for example, in the highly precise time measurements associated with "atomic clocks," in precise measurements of magnetic fields, and in the de-

velopment of the laser, an exceedingly important and versatile instrument. For his atomic- and molecular-beam work and for his discovery of the resonance method, Rabi was elected to the National Academy of Sciences in 1940 and received the Nobel Prize of 1944.

War Work and Postwar Concerns

In 1937 Rabi achieved the rank of full professor at Columbia. Three years later he became associate director of the radiation laboratory at the Massachusetts Institute of Technology, recently established to develop microwave radar and related equipment for military uses. This work, which was closely related to Rabi's past researches and which relied heavily on British contributions, was eminently successful. In 1948 he received the United States Medal of Merit and the King's Medal for Service in the Cause of Freedom for his wartime efforts.

Rabi was executive officer of the physics department at Columbia (1945–1948), during which time he increased the strength of the department, especially in high-energy and microwave physics. He was also instrumental in establishing the Brookhaven National Laboratory on Long Island in 1945, and he started the movement that resulted in the large high-energy laboratory (CERN) in Geneva, Switzerland. He was the chairman of the General Advisory Committee of the Atomic Energy Commission and served on the President's Science Advisory Committee and the United Nations Science Committee.

One of Rabi's most satisfying postwar achievements was his organization of a number of international United Nations Conferences on the Peaceful Uses of Atomic Energy. Like most physicists, he was deeply impressed by the awesome destructive power of the atomic bomb and worked unrelentingly to find means to ensure that the bomb would never be used again.

Communication is essential to understanding, and understanding is essential to unity: this was a major theme in Rabi's life, especially after the war. It applies not only to countries but also to intellectual disciplines. "What the scientist really desires," Rabi wrote, "is for his science to be understood, to become an integral part of our general culture, to be given proper weight in the cultural and practical affairs of the world. Like the poet, the scientist would rather be read than praised." According to Rabi, what people of all disciplines sorely require is wisdom: "Without it, knowledge is dry, almost unfit for human consumption, and dangerous in application. . . . Wisdom makes itself most manifest in the application of knowledge to human needs."

Granted his sincere search for unity, it is not surprising that Rabi, after holding the Higgins professorship of physics for 7 years (1957–1964), became the first university professor at Columbia. This professorship is without ties to any particular department. The last subject Rabi lectured on before his retirement in 1967 was "The Philosophical and Social Implications of 20th Century Physics."

Further Reading

Isidor Rabi is listed in the Science study guide (VII, C, 4). He studied under some of the most outstanding physicists of the period, including Wolfgang PAULI, Niels BOHR, Otto STERN, and Werner HEISENBERG.

Rabi's brief *My Life and Times as a Physicist* appeared in 1960. Although Rabi did not deliver a Nobel lecture, a short biographical sketch of him appears in the Nobel Foundation, *Nobel Lectures in Physics* (3 vols., 1964–1967). See also Tina Nellie Levitan, *Laureates: Jewish Winners of the Nobel Prize* (1960). Norman F. Ramsey, *Molecular Beams* (1956), contains detailed technical information on Rabi's contributions to physics.

RACHMANINOV / By Peter S. Hansen

Sergei Vasilievich Rachmaninov (1873–1943) was a highly successful Russian composer, an unrivaled pianist, and a distinguished conductor. "I have followed three hares," he once said. "Can I be certain that I have captured one?"

Sergei Rachmaninov (pronounced răKH-mä′nĭ-nôf) was born in Novgorod on April 1, 1873, at the estate of his aristocratic, impoverished family. His paternal grandfather gave up his career in the army so that he could practice 5 hours a day; he was an amateur because at that time it was considered demeaning for men of his social class to be professional pianists. Sergei's parents were also musical, and his mother was his first piano teacher.

When Sergei was 9, his parents separated, and the mother and children moved to St. Petersburg. This was one of the most interesting and artistic cities in the world. The musical life centered on the conservatory, where Sergei was accepted as a student. He learned little from his teachers, so in 1885 his mother sent him to Moscow, Russia's other great musical and cultural center.

Sergei Rachmaninov in 1921. (Library of Congress)

He studied piano at the conservatory with Nicolai Sverev and lived at his teacher's house.

Rachmaninov became a fine pianist, but he was more interested in composing after he entered Anton Arensky's and Alexander Taneiev's classes. In 1892 Rachmaninov graduated in piano and also received the Gold Medal in composition, the conservatory's highest honor. His final project in composition, the one-act opera *Aleko*, was considered so outstanding that it received a professional production.

Diversified Activities

During the next 3 years Rachmaninov supported himself by teaching piano at two girls' schools, an occupation he did not enjoy. Among the pieces he wrote at this time was his Prelude in C-sharp Minor, which soon became one of the most popular piano pieces in the world. Its dark, "Russian" quality was irresistible, and it did more to make his name known than any of his other accomplishments.

In 1897 Rachmaninov's First Symphony was played in St. Petersburg; it was a fiasco, and the critics' reviews were merciless. The composer was aware of the symphony's weaknesses, and he became seriously depressed and unable to compose. He accepted an offer to become assistant conductor at an opera house but resigned after a year to conduct and play in London. Still suffering from a psychological block, he sought help from Nicolai Dahl, a physician who used hypnosis and suggestion to cure mental depression. The treatments were successful. In 1901 Rachmaninov completed his Second Piano Concerto, which he dedicated to Dahl. It had an immediate success and became one of the most frequently performed of all concertos. The concerto embodied the best traits of the composer's style, from the brooding sonorities of the opening chords, and the lyricism of the slow movement, to the brilliance of the third.

In 1902 Rachmaninov married his cousin, Natalie Satin, and continued his diversified activities. He found it difficult to follow his "three hares." He neglected composition when, in 1905, he became conductor at the Grand Theater Opera, a very important post in the musical life of Moscow. He soon resigned and moved to Dresden, Germany, to devote himself to composing. Two of his best works were completed in 1907: *The Isle of the Dead*, a tone poem; and the Second Symphony, whose high emotional level and colorful orchestration show a strong Tchaikovsky influence. By the time this symphony was composed, Debussy had written *La Mer*, Richard Strauss had written *Salome*, and Scriabin had written *The Poem of Ecstasy*, but Rachmaninov remained loyal to the ideals and idioms of late-19th-century romantic music.

In 1909 Rachmaninov visited the United States. He played the first performance of his Third Piano Concerto with the New York Symphony Orchestra and conducted the Boston Orchestra, as well as the New York Philharmonic. He was offered the post of conductor of the Boston Symphony but declined.

In 1910 Rachmaninov was named vice president of the Russian Imperial Music Society, which controlled all higher music schools in the country, including the conservatories in Moscow and St. Petersburg. He concentrated on improving the smaller provincial schools and established an important one in Kiev. All the while he was composing. Among his most important works were those for piano: Thirteen Preludes (1910), Six Études Tableaux (1911), and Nine Études Tableaux (1917). He wrote over 70 songs with piano accompaniment; *The Bells*, a choral symphony for soprano, tenor, and baritone (1913); and a Vesper Mass for boys' and men's voices (1913).

The Move to America

The turning point of Rachmaninov's life was the 1917 Revolution in Russia. He was in Moscow during the early uprisings, but he realized that it would be impossible to remain and accepted an invitation to play a series of concerts in Scandinavia. His family soon joined him, and they never returned to Russia. To support his family he became a concert pianist—something he never wanted to be. He rented a house in Copenhagen and started practicing to learn recital programs; up to this time he had played his own compositions almost exclusively.

In November 1918 Rachmaninov sailed for New York and began a career as a touring virtuoso. Each season was divided between the United States, England, and the Continent. Whenever he could, he would go to his house in Lucerne, Switzerland, where he enjoyed boating, driving his car, and composing. His Fourth Piano Concerto (1927), Third Symphony (1936), and Symphonic Dances for Orchestra (1941) were not successful, but

his *Rhapsody on a Theme by Paganini* for piano and orchestra (1934) became a favorite of pianists and audiences alike and soon rivaled the Second Concerto in popularity. With the outbreak of World War II he moved to Beverly Hills, Calif. He died there on March 28, 1943.

Rachmaninov's life was not a happy one. He thought of himself as a composer, but he was never able to devote himself entirely to composition. Furthermore, although some of his compositions achieved worldwide popularity, most of the critics condemned them for being old-fashioned and reactionary, and he felt that he was out of step with the times. He hated concertizing, and his standards were so high that he was rarely pleased with his playing. His "six and a half foot tall scowl," as his friend Igor Stravinsky called it, was famous.

Further Reading

Sergei Rachmaninov is listed in the Music study guide (I, I, 6). He was influenced by Peter Ilyich TCHAIKOVSKY.

Although Rachmaninov spoke disparagingly about the book by Oscar von Riesemann, *Rachmaninov's Recollections* (1934), it contains many interesting insights. Other biographies are Victor I. Seroff, *Rachmaninoff* (1950), and Sergei Bertensson and Jay Leyda, *Sergei Rachmaninoff: A Lifetime in Music* (1956). A critical analysis of each composition is in John Culshaw, *Rachmaninov: The Man and His Music* (1950).

RACINE / By Herbert De Ley

The French dramatist Jean Baptiste Racine (1639–1699), admired as a portrayer of man's subtle psychology and overwhelming passions, was the author of 11 tragedies and a comedy. His work is the greatest expression of French classicism.

Jean Racine (pronounced rà-sēn′) was born in La Ferté-Milon and baptized there on Dec. 22, 1639. Both of his parents died within a few years, and the young Racine went to live with his paternal grandparents. There he was cared for by his grandmother and by his aunt, both of whom lived in close contact with the Jansenist convent of Port-Royal-des-Champs near Paris. Racine was educated in the schools of Port-Royal, receiving what was perhaps the best education available in his times. Sent on to the Jansenist-influenced school in Beauvais, Racine learned ancient Greek in addition to his other studies, before completing his education at Port-Royal and in Paris.

First Dramas

At some time before 1660 Racine entered the service of the Duke of Luynes in Paris, working as an assistant to a cousin who was the duke's steward. In his spare time

Racine interested himself in poetry, made the acquaintance of Jean de La Fontaine, the poet and fabulist, and wrote an official poem, *La Nymphe de la Seine* (1660). He also wrote two tragedies, both refused by the theatrical troupes of the day and now lost. Apparently discouraged, Racine spent perhaps a year in Uzés preparing to enter the priesthood, but in 1663 he returned to Paris and to literature.

Racine was approached by the great comic writer and actor Molière, whose troupe wished to commission a tragedy, *La Thébaïde*, to compete with one being put on by a rival troupe. Racine agreed to write such a tragedy according to Molière's instructions, and the play was first performed in 1664. Although it was indifferently received, Molière requested another play from Racine. Racine's *Alexandre* (1665) was his first success in the theater.

French Theatrical Situation

During this period the French theater was influenced profoundly by the famous neo-Aristotelian precepts for good literature. Playwrights observed with ever greater severity the famous "three unities" of time, place, and action, and the principles of verisimilitude and theatrical *bienséance* (seemliness). Without renouncing the influ-

Jean Racine, a drawing by his eldest son. (French Embassy Press and Information Division)

ence of Pierre Corneille, they nevertheless tended more and more to set their plays within a single stage decor, using fewer and fewer personages, simplifying their plots, and concentrating them in shorter texts. Contemporary playwrights thus presented less and less dramatic action, interesting themselves rather in the passions of their personages—and transforming the regular or "rule-conscious" theater of the 1630s and 1640s into the disciplined and passion-oriented classicist theater of the following decades. While Racine's *Thébaïde* and *Alexandre* show both Corneillian and later classical tendencies, Racine expressed more purely classicist literary ideals in his third tragedy, *Andromaque*.

"Andromaque" and La Du Parc

Between the first performances of *Alexandre* and the first performances of *Andromaque* in 1667, Racine's way of life changed considerably. Apparently dissatisfied with Molière's production of his *Alexandre*, he secretly rehearsed the play with the actors of another troupe, who played *Alexandre* in competition with Molière in December 1665. The resulting theatrical scandal gave Racine the reputation of a devious and unscrupulous young man. As if to confirm this evil reputation, an ungrateful Racine also published a pamphlet against Jansenism, attacking his former teachers of Port-Royal. One year later Racine took as his mistress a notorious actress, Thérèse du Parc. It was apparently for "La Du Parc" that Racine wrote *Andromaque*, in which she played the title role.

The action of *Andromaque* takes place some years after the conclusion of the Trojan War. The play begins with the arrival of Oreste, the son of the Greek king Agamemnon, at the court of Pyrrhus, son of the Greek hero Achilles. Ostensibly, Oreste has come as the ambassador of all the Greeks to ask for the execution of Astyanax, son of the Trojan hero Hector, whom Pyrrhus is holding prisoner. In reality, however, Oreste has come to see Hermione, daughter of Helen of Troy, with whom he is in love. Hermione, however, is in love with Pyrrhus and indeed is engaged to marry him. Pyrrhus, however, is in love not with Hermione but with Andromaque, the disconsolate widow of Hector and the mother of Astyanax.

The rest of the tragedy turns less upon the action than upon the psychological interaction of these four personages, each of whom passionately and jealously loves someone who passionately loves someone else. When Andromaque rebuffs Pyrrhus, he threatens to carry out the Greeks' request and kill Astyanax. When Pyrrhus breaks off his engagement to Hermione and prepares to marry Andromaque, Hermione persuades Oreste to kill him. But when the unfortunate Oreste and his followers succeed in doing so, she repudiates him. Oreste goes mad and Hermione commits suicide, leaving Andromaque and Astyanax to initiate another round, some day, in the Trojan War against the Greeks.

Personal Characteristics

During the following years Racine retained his reputation for deviousness, ambition, and ingratitude. Through his mistress, La Du Parc, he came to know something of the shady side of court life. He may finally have secretly married La Du Parc, and after her death in mysterious circumstances in 1668 he was accused of poisoning her. Racine subsequently was compromised with the dead La Du Parc and others in the infamous "poison affair," and he may narrowly have escaped arrest. In any case, he took as his next mistress another actress, La Champmeslé. But during this period he also consolidated his reputation as the greatest playwright of his times, writing one comedy, *Les Plaideurs* (1668), and numerous tragedies for the Parisian stage.

"Britannicus" and "Bérénice"

In his succeeding tragedies Racine continued to explore passionate love and passionate jealousy. In *Britannicus* (1669) Racine shows the young Roman emperor Néron (Nero) torn between the wise counsel of his teacher Burrhus and the influence of his domineering mother, Agrippine. Jealously in love with Junie, who loves the young prince Britannicus, Néron finally poisons the latter, revealing himself as the tyrant so well remembered in Roman history. In *Bérénice* (1670) the Roman Senate demands that the emperor Titus renounce his plans to marry Bérénice, a ruler of a foreign state and thus politically suspect. The play proceeds with no action other than successive confrontations between the various personages. With the action essentially reduced to nothing, the play relies exclusively on the beauty of Racine's verse and his analysis of the passions of his personages. Although Racine's numerous enemies attempted to conspire against the play and although the elderly Corneille wrote a *Tite et Bérénice* to compete with it, Racine's play was a remarkable success, followed by *Bajazet* (1672), *Mithridate* (1673), *Iphigénie* (1674), and *Phèdre* (1677).

Racine's Masterpiece, "Phèdre"

When it became known that Racine was preparing a play on the subject of Phèdre, the Duchess of Bouillon and other friends of the aging Corneille apparently attempted to hurt Racine's play by commissioning another playwright, Nicolas Pradon, to write one on the same subject. Apparently based on a stolen copy of Racine's text, Pradon's *Phèdre et Hippolyte* opened in Paris only 2 days after Racine's play. The two works were the occasion of a bitter literary quarrel in which insulting sonnets and other writings were exchanged, but Racine's play eventually triumphed over its rival.

In Racine's *Phèdre*, Hippolyte, son of the absent King Thésée, states his intention of leaving his palace of Trézène in order to search for his father. Although at first it appears he is ashamed of his love for Aricie, sister of some of his father's enemies, it soon becomes clear that he really wishes to avoid his stepmother, Phèdre. Phèdre is in love with Hippolyte and, in a memorable scene, declares her love for him. He at first pretends not to understand but finally can only flee her presence. When Thésée returns unexpectedly, Phèdre allows her nurse, Oenone, to accuse Hippolyte of making advances. In a rage Thésée asks the god Neptune to kill Hippolyte as he flees Trézène, hoping to marry Aricie and escape with her. Thésée learns his error too late to prevent the death

Andromaque at the feet of Pyrrhus, an engraving in the Bibliothèque Nationale, Paris, made by Chaveau for the 1676 edition of Andromaque. *(Photo-Hachette)*

of Hippolyte. Phèdre and Oenone commit suicide, leaving Thésée alone to pardon Aricie.

In *Phèdre*, as in Racine's other tragedies, critics have admired first the very refined, pure poetry of Racine's verse and second Racine's very incisive, though pessimistic, view of human psychology. A contemporary critic, Jean de La Bruyère, remarked that although tragedies on love and duty and heroic *gloire* had presented "man as he should be," Racine presented man as he really was. Man, as Racine presents him, often displays a sense of personal insecurity and self-doubt not unlike modern psychological "complexes." The Racinian character's self-doubt leads him—like Racine himself, as described by his enemies—to fight desperately and destructively to gain his ends, with inevitably tragic results. Some modern critics have ascribed this view, rather than to any Racinian observation of human nature, to the influence of Jansenism and its somber view of human helplessness before God. In any case, Racine has long been admired as one of the most perfect of French writers—that is, in another modern view, as the French writer who most successfully matches his poetic images to his psychogy, his psychology to his plot, and his plot to the structure and neo-Aristotelian view of the tragedy, giving his plays a kind of total inner coherence unequaled in France's *grand siècle*.

Later Life

Yet in spite of Racine's genius—and almost as if he had written his sublime tragedies only to gain a place in society—he stopped writing tragedies after *Phèdre*. Six months after the premiere of *Phèdre*, Racine married. In October of the same year, 1677, he accepted a post as King Louis XIV's historiographer. At the same time, he announced his return to the Jansenist faith of his childhood. During the following years Racine lived comfortably and raised a family of seven children. As director of the French Academy, he eulogized his former bitter rival, Corneille, and published a new edition of his own works, from which he had removed remarks offensive to his enemies.

Although Racine apparently intended definitively to retire from the theater, he was persuaded by Louis XIV's morganatic wife Madame de Maintenon to write two more plays, of a slightly different character than his previous works. These were *Esther* (1689) and *Athalie* (1691)—tragedies written on specifically Christian themes and without any love interest, intended to be presented by the young ladies of Saint-Cyr, a girls' establishment protected by Madame de Maintenon. More and more a respectable citizen and favorite of the King in his later years, Racine died in Paris on April 21, 1699.

Further Reading

Jean Racine is listed in the Literature study guide (III, F, 1). Pierre CORNEILLE and MOLIÈRE were other outstanding French dramatists of this period.

The best biography of Racine in English is Geoffrey Brereton, *Jean Racine: A Critical Biography* (1951). A penetrating analysis of Racine's dramaturgy, with an emphasis on structure and language, is Roland Barthes, *On Racine* (1963; trans. 1964). Other recent works in English on Racine are John C. Lapp, *Aspects of Racinian Tragedy* (1955), and Bernard Weinberg, *The Art of Jean Racine* (1963). A unique collection of critical essays is in Robert James Nelson, ed., *Corneille and Racine: Parallels and Contrasts* (1966), which includes essays from the 17th century to the present and constitutes a kind of history of literary criticism on the subject. More general studies are John Lough, *An Introduction to Seventeenth Century France* (1954), and Will G. Moore, *French Classical Literature* (1961).

✳   ✳   ✳

RADEK / By Warren Lerner

The Russian Communist leader and publicist Karl Bernardovich Radek (1885–1939) is best known for his brilliant and acerbic polemics. He was an outstanding apostle of internationalism.

Karl Radek (pronounced rǎ′dyək) was born Karl Sobelsohn in Lvov (then in Austrian Poland) to an Austrophile Jewish family. As a youth, he rejected his family's outlook and became involved in political agitation, moving to Switzerland in 1904. There he joined the left wing of Polish socialism, returning to Poland in 1905 to participate in revolutionary activity in Warsaw. After a brief prison term, Radek spent the next decade building his reputation, in both Poland and Germany, as a talented but volatile and often irresponsible journalist. His barbed comments so irritated leading Socialists that he was successively expelled from the Polish and German Socialist parties.

During World War I Radek returned to Switzerland, where he alternately collaborated with and contended with V. I. Lenin in the Zimmerwald Movement, an organization of antiwar Socialists. After the overthrow of the Czar in March 1917, Radek accompanied Lenin in the "sealed train" across Germany, but he was not allowed to enter Russia. He then spent several months in Stockholm organizing Bolshevik support among European Socialists, and after the Bolshevik coup in November 1917 he proceeded to Moscow. There he became responsible for foreign-language propaganda, accompanying Leon Trotsky to Brest Litovsk, where he propagandized Ger-

Karl Radek. (Collection Viollet)

man troops. At the end of 1918, after the collapse of the imperial regime in Germany, Radek returned to Berlin in order to help organize the German Communist party. Though he counseled against a German uprising, the "Spartacus" Putsch of January 1919 led to his incarceration for almost a year.

Upon his return to Moscow, Radek was assigned major roles in the Communist International (Comintern), where he enjoyed great influence, particularly in the German Communist party. His multilingual talents, his bizarre personal appearance—some of his contemporaries likened him to an ape—and his extraordinary sense of humor made him a great favorite of journalists in Moscow. From 1919 to 1923 Radek enjoyed considerable prominence both within and without Russia.

However, his political enemy Grigori Zinoviev used the collapse of the German revolution of 1923 to exclude Radek from the Comintern and high party posts. Under the influence of his new mistress, Larissa Reissner, Radek withdrew from party politics, and in 1925 he became rector of Sun Yat-sen University in Moscow. When Larissa died in 1926, Radek openly joined the Trotsky-ite opposition, with which he had long been identified; in 1927 he was expelled from the Bolshevik party and subsequently exiled to Siberia. In 1929 Radek renounced Trotsky and returned to Moscow to become once again a major publicist—for Stalin—although he never recovered his Comintern or party posts.

In 1936 Radek was one of the coauthors of the new Soviet constitution. However, later that year he was arrested for treason, and in a show trial in January 1937 Radek was sentenced to 10 years' imprisonment. Though rumors of his survival persisted, Radek apparently died in prison sometime in 1939.

Further Reading

Karl Radek is listed in the European History study guide (XI, O, 1). He was associated with V. I. LENIN and Leon TROTSKY.

The only biography of Radek is Warren Lerner, *Karl Radek: The Last Internationalist* (1970).

RADHAKRISHNAN

/ By Peter A. Pardue

Sarvepalli Radhakrishnan (born 1888) was an Indian philosopher, statesman, and articulate interpreter of Hindu tradition to the West.

R adhakrishnan (pronounced rä-də-krĭsh′nən) was born near Madras into a Brahmin family of orthodox Hindu persuasion. However, he was educated in Christian missionary institutions and was exposed both to routine religious criticisms of Hindu tradition and to the mainstream of Western philosophy. As his religious and philosophical sensibilities developed, he

Radhakrishnan. (Information Service of India, New York)

found himself more and more drawn to the values of the Vedanta. From the very first, he had felt himself imbued with a "firm faith in the reality of an unseen world behind the flux of phenomena." He was offended by the dogmatic and ill-informed criticisms leveled at Hindu culture by some of his teachers; and his sense of pride in his own tradition was deeply aroused by the eloquence of Vivekananda and Rabindranath Tagore.

Radhakrishnan resolved to explore his own tradition in fuller detail and wrote his master's thesis, *The Ethics of Vedanta* (1908), in part to refute the Western prejudice that the Vedanta simplistically affirmed the "illusory" (*maya*) nature of the world and lacked ethical content and power.

At the same time, Radhakrishnan found that he could not ignore the paralyzing superstitions which dominated Hindu social institutions and the life of the masses as integral features of their deepest religious commitments. He was encouraged by some of his more sensitive Western teachers to continue his research into Hindu philosophy in order to probe its innovative and universal potentials. He found much in Western philosophy—particularly in the idealists and the work of Henri Bergson—which was tangent to the Hindu and specifically Vedantic validation of mystical intuition and the spirituality of the universe.

Radhakrishnan was persuaded that philosophical enterprise must not simply provide rational verification and analysis but must give a profound and transforming insight into the spiritual content of existence in its personal and historical dimensions as an antidote to the dehumanizing values increasingly predominant in Western civilization. For Radhakrishnan, the unique strength of the Vedanta was its validation of personal spiritual striving for deeper penetration into the meaning of life itself.

Radhakrishnan combined this commitment with a humanistic focus on the need for social change and reform which he mediated in part by a reinterpretation of traditional Hindu religious forms and texts. His translation and interpretation of the *Bhagavad Gita* (Song of the Lord) strives to move traditional Hindu institutions (for instance, the caste system) in the direction of "democratic" values. He proved himself capable of performing this potentially awkward synthetic task by stressing the more profound aspects of Hindu philosophy which inherently transcend the provisional historical and social forms associated with normative Hinduism. Some of his other major works—*An Idealist View of Life* and *Eastern Religions and Western Thought*—and his scholarly commentaries on Vedantic materials are also marked by a distinctive "this-worldly" humanism uniquely imbued with Vedantic mysticism.

There is an equally powerful psychological emphasis in much of Radhakrishnan's work on the therapeutic consequences of personality integration through intuition of the essential relation of the self to the sacred force from which all phenomena spring. And this he combines with a theory of history which affirms that its most important dimension is the evolution of human spiritual consciousness. Hindu mysticism and related techniques are, therefore, not modes of withdrawal from reality but are means for strengthening personal autonomy, active capacity for love, and conscious participation in the unfolding destiny of the universe.

This evolutionary historical perspective had a marked impact on Radhakrishnan's interpretation of the traditional doctrine of *karma* (action—the law of ethical retribution). The individual is responsible not only for his own destiny within a static cosmology of personal transmigration but for the welfare of all men. Each person acts (or does not act) to promote future possibilities. In this way individual salvation is tied to the fate of mankind and the ultimate goal of the historical process itself. Although his concept of "true humanity" is deeply steeped in Vedantic teaching, he has several specific human models who embody his own commitment to reforms incorporating Western values within the deeper matrix of Hindu spirituality: they are Rabindranath Tagore, Mohandas Gandhi, and Jawaharlal Nehru. For Radhakrishnan, these paradigms of modern Indian creativity show an extraordinary ability to synthesize conflicting value systems by employing the pristine mystical and ascetic models which lie at the heart of Hinduism. It is with these men in mind that he asserts, "Man is not a detached spectator of a progress immanent in human history, but an active agent remolding the world nearer to his ideals."

Radhakrishnan's understanding of the role of the traditional *yoga* is also shaped by this commitment. Its aim is to provide a disciplined framework which facilitates the fulfillment of worldly obligations while continually reinforcing the universal search for spiritual perfection. The *yoga* renders the individual more capable of acting in the world and serving his fellowmen.

Many of Radhakrishnan's writings seem to be "apologetic"—designed for popular consumption by Western readers; and he engaged in polemics with Western theologians and philosophers who criticized Indian forms of spirituality. But the great bulk of his work is distinguished by a synthetic power clearly evident in the development of his own distinctive philosophy of life. His work as an educator and cultural ambassador to the West and his many public services to the Indian government are further evidence of his many-sided talents. He served variously as professor of philosophy and religion at the universities of Mysore, Calcutta, and Oxford, and he had many teaching engagements at major universities in the United States. From 1949 to 1952 he was ambassador to the Soviet Union, returning to India to serve for 10 years as vice president of India and chancellor of Delhi University. From 1962 to 1967 he was president of India. He combined these activities with a continuing program of productive writing and lecturing, all of which made him a living embodiment of the values which he espoused.

Further Reading

Radhakrishnan is listed in the Asia study guide (II, A, 8, a). He was strongly influenced by Rabindranath TAGORE and VIVEKANANDA.

Radhakrishnan's political writings have been collected and printed as *President Radhakrishnan's Speeches and Writings* (New Delhi, 1965). The most extensive volume on Radhakrishnan the philosopher, which also includes an autobiographical memoir, is Paul A. Schilpp, ed., *The Philosophy of Sarvepalli Radhakrishnan* (1952). Consult also C. E. M. Joad, *Counterattack from the East: the Philosophy of Radhakrishnan* (1933); S. J. Samartha, *Introduction to Radhakrishnan: The Man and His Thought* (1964); and the anniversary volume *Radhakrishnan: Comparative Studies in Philosophy Presented in Honour of His Sixtieth Birthday* (1951), edited by W. R. Inge and others.

✻   ✻   ✻

RADIN / By J. David Sapir

Paul Radin (1883–1959) was an American anthropologist and ethnographer who specialized in the ethnology of religion and mythology and the ethnography of the American Indian.

Paul Radin was born on April 2, 1883, in Łódź, Poland, and in his early childhood lived in New York City. He received his bachelor's degree in 1902 at City College and after a short period abroad went

Paul Radin. (Courtesy of Brandeis University)

The Culture of the Winnebago, as Described by Themselves (1949), and *The Trickster* (1956).

Radin never stayed at any one academic institution for more than a few years. He found the institutionalized aspect of intellectual life uncongenial and preferred to remain throughout his career an independent scholar. At various times he held posts at Berkeley, Mills College, Fisk University, Black Mountain College, Kenyon College, the University of Chicago, and, finally, Brandeis University, where he was made a Samuel Rubin professor and became head of the anthropology department. Radin died on Feb. 21, 1959.

Further Reading

Paul Radin is listed in the Social Sciences study guide (VII, E, 3). One of his fellow anthropologists under the guidance of Franz BOAS was Edward SAPIR.

An excellent biographical sketch of Radin is in Stanley Diamond, ed., *Culture in History: Essays in Honor of Paul Radin* (1960). Background studies are Robert H. Lowie, *The History of Ethnological Theory* (1937); H. R. Hays, *From Ape to Angel: An Informal History of Social Anthropology* (1958); and Marvin Harris, *The Rise of Anthropological Theory: A History of Theories of Culture* (1968).

RADISSON / By J. E. Rea

> The French explorer and soldier of fortune Pierre-Esprit Radisson (ca. 1636–1710) is the most romantic and least known of all the famous explorers of the Canadian North and West. He was one of the originators of the Hudson's Bay Company.

to Columbia University to study history and anthropology under Franz Boas, receiving a doctorate in 1911. By studying with Boas at Columbia he joined a group of young scholars that became a major influence in the subsequent 4 decades of American anthropology. He did fieldwork among the Winnebago, the Ojibwa, the Fox, the Zapotec, the Wappo, the Wintun, and the Huave. Of these, the Winnebago were his specialty and provided him with material for numerous monographs and articles as well as many extensive examples for his more general writings.

One central theme ran through the greatest portion of Radin's work—the manner by which particular individuals respond to the vicissitudes of their immediate cultural environment. This theme is particularly evident in his three major works. Thus *Primitive Man as a Philosopher* (1927) cogently argues that reflective individuals are to be found quite as readily among primitives as elsewhere. In *Primitive Religion* (1937) he demonstrates that for any given culture the degree of religiosity to be found varies from indifferent to deep, depending on the proclivities and intelligence of the individual. The position of the individual was the explicit theme of *Crashing Thunder* (1926), for here Radin obtained, translated, and edited the autobiography of a Winnebago Indian. This book was a landmark in American anthropology. It was the first and probably the best of a long line of similar autobiographical accounts of individual Indians that was published by subsequent anthropologists.

Other important works by Radin included the *The Story of the American Indian* (1927), *Social Anthropology* (1927), *The Method and Theory of Ethnology* (1933),

Pierre-Esprit Radisson (pronounced ră-dē-sōN′) was born in France, but virtually no information survives concerning his early life. When still quite young, he somehow made his way to New France, where his half sister Marguerite lived. After her husband's death at the hands of the Iroquois, Marguerite married again. Her second husband, Medard Chouart Des Groseilliers, was to share much of the adventurous life of Radisson.

From his own sketchy account of his career, it appears that Radisson was captured by the Iroquois in the early 1650s, was adopted by an Indian family, and spent some 2 years traveling and hunting with his captors. He escaped in 1654, sailed to Amsterdam, and arrived back in Three Rivers late the same year. Apparently, Radisson remained in New France for the next 4 years, except for one more trip made to the Iroquois territory near Albany.

Radisson's first trip west was undertaken with his brother-in-law in 1659. They wintered southwest of Lake Superior in Sioux country. It was probably during this trip that the two men first heard of Hudson Bay and the treasure of beaver to be found in that area. In the spring Radisson and Des Groseilliers returned to Montreal laden with furs, most of which were promptly confiscated by corrupt officials. From this point on, patriotism played little part in the adventures of Radisson.

From 1662 to 1664 the two men operated from New England and tried—unsuccessfully—to reach Hudson Bay by sea. In 1664 they were persuaded to go to London. Their ship was captured by the Dutch, with whom England was then at war. After being put ashore in Spain, the two eventually turned up in London in time to witness the great fire and the ravages of the Black Death. They were able to interest some English merchants in the exploitation of the fur trade around Hudson Bay, with the assistance of a successful trip there by Des Groseilliers. Radisson remained in London and composed his *Voyages*. On May 2, 1670, the Hudson's Bay Company was formally chartered and began its long and generally prosperous career. For the next 15 years, Radisson and his brother-in-law served the company either in the bay or in the capital.

In 1675 the two adventurers left the company, for reasons that are not at all clear, and resumed their French allegiance. It was not a rewarding transfer. Des Groseilliers settled in Three Rivers, and Radisson entered the service of the French navy and went campaigning in the Caribbean. He was back at Hudson Bay again in 1681 and was rejoined there by Des Groseilliers. They were successful in contending with the English for control of the territory around the Nelson River and in their trading ventures. But once again, they felt that rewards were unsatisfactory in the employ of the French. When his brother-in-law returned to Canada, Radisson turned up in the service of the Hudson's Bay Company once more, in 1684.

The company sent him back to the bay, where he succeeded in persuading the French at Ft. Nelson (which he had established) to abandon their allegiance and all their furs. Radisson made his last trip to Hudson Bay in late 1685 and remained there for 2 years, but he was unable to work in harmony with the other officers of the company. He returned to England and finally settled near London. Radisson married three times during his peripatetic life and was survived by several children.

Further Reading

Pierre-Esprit Radisson is listed in the Canada study guide (II, C). Other explorers of western Canada were the Sieur de LA SALLE and Louis JOLLIET.

The only reliable—and engaging—study of Radisson in English is in Grace Lee Nute, *Caesars of the Wilderness* (1943).

*   *   *

RAFFLES / By John M. Echols

Sir Thomas Stamford Raffles (1781–1826) was an English colonial administrator, historian, and founder of Singapore. A man of vision, industry, and feeling, he made incalculable contributions to the knowledge of the Malay Archipelago and to the British overseas empire.

Born on July 6, 1781, off the coast of Jamaica on board a ship under the command of his father, Benjamin Raffles, Stamford Raffles became a clerk in the office of the East India Company in London at the age of 14. In 1805 he was sent to Penang to serve as assistant secretary. Prior to his departure he married a widow, Mrs. Olivia Fancourt, who died in 1814.

On the trip out, Raffles studied the Malay language intensively, and his proficiency in this then little-known language was remarked upon by those who came in contact with him. Three years after his arrival his health broke, and he was sent to Malacca to recuperate. The East India Company was on the point of abandoning this port, but a report which Raffles prepared and in which he argued the superiority of Malacca over Penang as a potential port persuaded the company to rescind its order.

Java Annexation

Lord Minto, the governor general of India, was so impressed with the report that he called Raffles on 2

Sir Stamford Raffles. (Radio Times Hulton Picture Library)

months' leave to Calcutta. During his visit Raffles convinced Lord Minto of the necessity of annexing Java, then in French hands, and the governor general appointed him agent to the governor general of the Malay States. Raffles then returned to Malacca and participated in preparations for the attack on Java.

In August 1811 a British fleet of some 100 ships with an expeditionary force of about 12,000 men arrived off Batavia, and the city fell without a struggle. Gen. Janssens retreated to Semarang on the north-central coast of Java; in September he capitulated to the British. Lord Minto thereupon appointed Raffles lieutenant general of Java and admonished him, "While we are in Java, let us do all the good we can."

Raffles introduced numerous reforms, among which were the division of Java into 16 residencies, the introduction of a land tax, and improvements in the legal and judicial system; he also attempted to abolish slavery. He himself regarded his new land-tenure system, which prevented the native rulers from exacting feudal services, as the most solid accomplishment of his administration. The lands which were withdrawn from the control of feudal rulers were leased on a short-term basis at a moderate rental and were assessed at the value of two-fifths of the rice crop, with the remainder of the yield free of assessment and the growers exempt from personal taxes.

In spite of his excellent intentions and superb knowledge of the people, their language, and their customs, Raffles was not able to make Java a profitable enterprise. His hope of turning Batavia into the hub of a new British insular empire was dashed, and when the Netherlands regained its independence, Lord Castlereagh vigorously opposed British retention of the Dutch holdings in the East.

Raffles sent in a report explaining the great importance of Java to Britain, but his failure to make Java financially viable, together with Britain's desire to conciliate the Dutch, militated against a reversal of Lord Castlereagh's decision, and in March 1816 Raffles was removed from office and recalled. The following year he married Sophia Hull in London. His lasting contributions in Java can be seen in the fact that when the Dutch received this island back they adopted many of his reforms.

Founding of Singapore

In November 1817 Raffles, now Sir Stamford, departed England for Ft. Marlborough (or Benkoelen), in southern Sumatra, where he assumed the residentship of this town. He and Col. R. J. Farquhar, former British resident at Amboina, were on the lookout for a strategically situated way station in the Malay Archipelago which would play in the East the role Malta was playing in the West.

On Jan. 28, 1819, they landed on the island of Singapore and immediately recognized it as ideal for their purpose. They arrived at an agreement with the Sultan of Johore, and on February 6 a treaty was signed marking the establishment of Singapore as a British settlement. Farquhar was installed as its first governor under the supervision of Raffles at Benkoelen. As Charles E. Wurtzburg (1954) wrote, "It would be difficult to imagine that,

had there been no Raffles, there would have been any Singapore."

During the next 4 years four of Raffles's children died in Benkoelen; his health and that of his wife deteriorated; and in 1823 he submitted his resignation. Before leaving for England, however, he decided to pay a final visit to Singapore, where he remained 9 months. He planned the city, prepared laws, and laid the foundation of the Singapore Institution, a Malay school.

In 1824 Raffles returned to England to face a charge brought against him by the East India Company, which required him to repay to it a substantial sum for salaries and expenses that had been disbursed to him and only years later disallowed by the court of directors. Raffles was endeavoring to arrange payment when he became seriously ill again. On July 5, 1826, less than 3 months after receiving the court's letter demanding repayment, Raffles died of an apoplectic stroke.

In his short span of life Raffles had suffered numerous crushing blows which would have felled a lesser man. That he survived them in spite of a less than robust constitution can be explained, in part at least, by his tremendous interest in, and enthusiasm for, every aspect of life in the East. He was, at once, amateur natural scientist, archeologist, Oriental philologist, and reviver and active president of the Batavian Society of Arts and Sciences. An enduring monument to his knowledge and indefatigable industry is his famed *History of Java* (2 vols., 1817), which was the first comprehensive work on this subject and, although outdated, is still regarded as a classic in its field.

Further Reading

Sir Stamford Raffles is listed in the Asia study guide (IV, 5, a). Another English imperialist in Southeast Asia was Sir James BROOKE.

An intimate and contemporary account of Raffles is in Lady Sophia H. Raffles, *Memoir of the Life and Public Services of Sir Thomas Stamford Raffles* (1830; new ed., 2 vols., 1835), which contains many private letters and public dispatches. Although there is no adequate biography of Raffles, the most extensive study is Charles E. Wurtzburg, *Raffles of the Eastern Isles*, edited by Clifford Witting (1954). A very readable account, with interesting plates, is Maurice Collis, *Raffles* (1966).

The following are less valuable because they make little use of the records in the India Office Library: Demetrius C. Boulger, *The Life of Sir Stamford Raffles* (1897); Hugh Edward Egerton, *Sir Stamford Raffles: England in the Far East* (1900); J. A. Bethune Cook, *Sir Thomas Stamford Raffles* (1918); Reginald Coupland, *Raffles: 1781–1826* (1926); Emily Hahn, *Raffles of Singapore: A Biography* (1946); and Colin Clair, *Sir Stamford Raffles: Founder of Singapore* (1963). Two important studies by John Bastin deal with Raffles's policies: *Raffles' Ideas on the Land Rent System in Java and the Mackenzie Land Tenure Commission* (1954) and *The Native Policies of Sir Stamford Raffles in Java and Sumatra* (1957).

✳   ✳   ✳

RAHNER / By G. Michael McCrossin

The German theologian Karl Rahner (born 1904) was a major influence on 20th-century Roman Catholic thought. His work is characterized by the attempt to reinterpret traditional Roman Catholic theology in the light of modern philosophical thought.

Karl Rahner (pronounced rä′nər) was born on March 5, 1904, in Freiburg im Breisgau in what is now the German Federal Republic. He followed his older brother Hugo into the Society of Jesus in 1922 and pursued the Jesuits' traditional course of studies in philosophy and theology in Germany, Austria, and Holland. He was ordained a priest in 1932 and continued his studies at the University of Freiburg. After receiving his doctorate in philosophy in 1936, he taught at the universities of Innsbruck and Munich. In 1967 he was appointed professor of dogmatic theology at the University of Münster. He was a *peritus* (official theologian) at the Second Vatican Council (1962–1965), and in 1969 he was one of 30 appointed by Pope Paul VI to evaluate theological developments since the Council.

Thomism, Kantianism, and contemporary phenomenology and existentialism are the three sources of Rahner's thought. During his early years of seminary training, he studied the works of Immanuel Kant and Joseph Maréchal, along with the works of the great medieval theologian St. Thomas Aquinas. While at the University of Freiburg he came under the influence of Martin Heidegger. The overriding concern of all his work was the need to bring the best thought of the past into contact with the best thought of the present.

Often linked with Bernard Lonergan as a "transcendental Thomist," Rahner employed a method characterized by an attempt to discover the general principles underlying the various doctrines of the Roman Catholic faith. In his first work, *Geist in Welt* (1936; *Spirit in the World*), he presented his interpretation of Aquinas's doctrine of

knowledge, indicating that man's capacity to know, although rooted in the data of the senses, is nonetheless a capacity open to the infinite or to being as such. This ability to transcend particular being allows man to think metaphysically—to analyze the general structure of being necessary for the actual condition of the world known through the senses. *Spirit in the World*, in conjunction with Rahner's second major work, *Hörer des Wortes* (1941; *Hearers of the Word*), established the epistemological and speculative foundation of his later thought.

Rahner's thought is best described as a theological anthropology. Beginning with the nature of man as a being open to the infinite, Rahner's thought sees man's quest for fulfillment satisfied only in union with the God of Christian revelation, the God who became man in Jesus Christ. A proper understanding of man cannot be divorced from an understanding of God and the context of relationships uniting man and God. The fundamental fact underlying the existence of the world is that it stands in relation to God. Rahner calls this situation the supernatural existential and sees in this fundamental fact the root of all further explanations of sin, grace, and salvation.

Further Reading

Karl Rahner is listed in the Religion study guide (I, S, 2). Hans KÜNG was another modern Roman Catholic theologian.

Rahner's own writings are difficult. His *The Dynamic Element in the Church* (trans. 1964) and *Nature and Grace: Dilemmas in the Modern Church* (trans. 1964) provide good starting points for the reader interested in sampling his work. Patrick Granfield, *Theologians at Work* (1967), has an interesting interview with Rahner. The best study of Rahner in English is Louis Roberts, *The Achievement of Karl Rahner* (1967). Rahner's ideas are presented in a simplified form in Donald Gelpi, *Life and Light: A Guide to the Theology of Karl Rahner* (1966). Jakob Laubach's chapter on Rahner in Leonard Reinisch, ed., *Theologians of Our Time: Karl Barth and Others* (trans. 1964), provides a brief introduction to his thought. Sylvester Paul Schilling, *Contemporary Continental Theologians* (1966), has a critique of Rahner's work.

RAI / By Robert I. Crane

Lala Lajpat Rai (1865–1928) was an Indian nationalist leader and was well known for his many publications regarding national problems.

Lala Lajpat Rai (pronounced rī) was born in the Ferozepore district of the Punjab to a respectable Hindu family. He studied law in Lahore and in 2 years passed the first examination, which qualified him to practice. While a student, he became active in the nationalist and revivalist Arya Samaj Society of Swami

Karl Rahner. (Österreichische Nationalbibliothek, Vienna)

Lala Lajpat Rai. (Information Service of India, New York)

National Congress in 1900 he stressed the importance of constructive, nation-building activity and programs for self-reliance.

In 1905 Rai went as a Congress delegate to London, where he fell under the influence of the Hindu revolutionary Shyamji Krishna Varma. Later, in the 1905 Congress session, Rai joined Bal Tilak and Bipin Chandra Pal in support of a militant program around boycott, *swadeshi* (homemade goods), and *swaraj* (self-rule for India). In 1906 he tried to play the role of mediator between the moderates and the extremists in the Congress. The following year the Punjab government arrested and transported him without trial to Burma; he was released in time for the 1907 meetings of the National Congress, when Tilak backed him for the presidency. Rai refused to accept the office for fear of a split in the ranks of that body.

Rai lived in the United States from 1914 until 1920. He founded the Indian Home Rule League in New York City and published several important volumes on the Indian problem. Soon after his return to India he was elected president of the Calcutta session of the Congress. In 1925 he entered the Imperial Legislature as a member of the "Swarajist" group. In 1926 he broke with the leaders of the Swarajist group and formed his own "Nationalist party" within the legislature.

In 1928 Rai led the demonstrations against the Simon Commission on Indian constitutional reforms. He was injured by the police in a mass demonstration and died a few weeks later, mourned as a nationalist martyr.

Further Reading

Lala Lajpat Rai is listed in the Asia study guide (II, A, 6, c). Other prominent Indian nationalists were Jawaharlal NEHRU and Mohandas GANDHI.

Among Rai's many books see especially *Young India: An Interpretation* (1917) and *Unhappy India* (1928). Extensive selections from his writings are in the works edited by Vijaya C. Joshi: *Lal Lajpat Rai: Writings and Speeches* (2 vols., 1965–1966), which also contains information on Rai's life, and *Autobiographical Writings* (1965). N. N. Kailas, ed., *Laj Patrai: His Relevance for Our Times* (1966), contains articles on and by Rai. Works on his life and influence include P. D. Saggi, ed., *Life and Work of Lal, Bal, and Pal: A Nation's Homage* (1962), and Naeem Gul Rathore, *Indian Nationalist Agitation in the United States: A Study of Lala Lajpat Rai and the India Home Rule League of America, 1914–1920* (1966).

Dayananda. Rai joined the Samaj in 1882 and soon emerged as a prominent leader in its "Progressive," or "College," wing. He also taught at the Anglo-Vedic College, run by the Samaj; his fiery nationalism was largely the product of this involvement.

In 1886 Rai moved to Hissar, where he practiced law, led the Arya movement, and was elected to the Municipal Committee (of the local government). In 1888 and 1889 he was a delegate to the annual sessions of the National Congress. He moved to Lahore to practice before the High Court in 1892.

In 1895 Rai helped found the Punjab National Bank, demonstrating his practical concern for self-help and enterprise among Hindus. Between 1896 and 1898 he published popular biographies of Mazzini, Garibaldi, Shivajee, and Swami Dayananda. In 1897 he founded the Hindu Orphan Relief Movement to keep the Christian missions from securing custody of these children. In the

RAJAGOPALACHARI

/ **By Robert I. Crane**

Chakravarti Rajagopalachari (born 1879) was a prominent Indian nationalist leader, first Indian governor general of his country, and founder of the Swatantra party. He also wrote a popular version of the "Mahabharata."

Chakravarti Rajagopalachari (pronounced rä-jə-gō-pä′lä-chä-ryə) was born in a village in Madras and graduated from the Central Hindu College of Bangalore. He then took a law degree from the Madras Law College. In 1921 Rajagopalachari was chosen general secretary of the Indian National Congress under Mohandas Gandhi's leadership. Soon thereafter his daughter married into Gandhi's family. In subsequent years he was intermittently a member of the all-powerful Congress Working Committee, the top executive arm of the National Congress, and worked very closely with Gandhi.

In 1937, when the Congress won the provincial elections in several Indian provinces, Rajagopalachari became chief minister of Madras. He held this position until the outbreak of World War II caused all of the Congress provincial ministries to resign.

In 1942, at the time of the Cripps mission from the British Parliament to India, Rajagopalachari was among the minority of top Congress leaders who favored acceptance of the offer made by Cripps in an effort to end the political deadlock. In 1946 Rajagopalachari maintained his posture as a moderator when he advised acceptance of the Pakistan demand as the price which had to be paid for independence. Also in 1946, he became minister in the interim government which guided India in the final months up to partition and independence.

Rajagopalachari was the first Indian governor of West Bengal after independence in 1947. In 1948 he was named the first Indian governor general of India, succeeding Lord Mountbatten, the last English governor general. In 1950 Rajagopalachari was named home minister in the Jawaharlal Nehru Cabinet, and in 1952 he returned to Madras as chief minister. Soon thereafter he parted company with the Nehru Congress, and in 1959 he was instrumental in the creation of the anti-Congress Swatantra party, which became the chief proponent of the free-enterprise philosophy in the Republic of India.

Rajagopalachari played a prominent role in the international Ban-the-Bomb movement. Among other causes not popular with the Congress government was his campaign for religious instruction in the public schools. He also published a highly regarded, abridged edition of the Hindu epic *Mahabharata*. Rajagopalachari repeatedly denounced the government of India for alleged corruption, bureaucracy, inefficiency, and lack of impartiality.

Further Reading

Chakravarti Rajagopalachari is listed in the Asia study guide (II, A, 6, c). Another nationalist who rose to prominence through regional leadership was the Punjabi Lala Lajpat RAI.

An interesting but not comprehensive biography of Rajagopalachari is Monica Felton, *I Meet Rajaji* (1962). See also Nikan Perumal, *Rajaji*, edited by Duncan Greenless (1953). Interesting material on Rajagopalachari is in the official history by B. Pattabhi Sitaramayya, *History of the Indian National Congress*, vol. 2 (1947; repr. 1969).

Chakravarti Rajagopalachari. (Information Service of India, New York)

RAJARAJA I / By G. R. Welbon

Rajaraja I (reigned 985–1014) was possibly the greatest of the Cola kings of southern India. He made the Colas the paramount power in southern India, Ceylon, and the southern seas. A political and organizational genius, he was also a grand patron of religion and the arts.

Traditional Cola territories center on the fertile lands around Tanjore in southern India (about 220 miles south of Madras city). Representatives of the family seem to have been agents of the Pallavas during the period of that dynasty's great achievements and subsequently to have broken away. When Rajaraja (meaning "king of kings"; pronounced rä′jə-rä′jə) took the throne, the Colas were still suffering the conse-

The god Siva blessing a devotee, an 11th-century niche sculpture on the Brhadisavara Temple at Gangaikondacolapuram. (Photo by G. R. Welbon)

He elaborated a network of subordinate administrators and perfected a set of procedures which assured a reliable and efficient cohesion in his "empire" while allowing great autonomy to the local units. Most famous of the deeds of Rajaraja is the building of the "Great Temple," the Rajarajesvara, at Tanjore. The mighty tower (*vimana*) that surmounts the central shrine rises 216 feet to dominate the city and the adjacent land. The stone sculpture on the tower and its base is Cola art at its most vigorous. The many inscriptions at the temple provide vital information concerning the dynasty.

Rajaraja's son Rajendra I (reigned 1012–1044, initially with his father) extended the Cola sway. One military expedition reached the Ganges. The Cola navy was strengthened, and profitable campaigns were waged in Southeast Asia. Rajendra built a new capital city, Gangaikondacolapuram ("city of the Cola who brought the Ganges"), and, emulating his father, he crowned it with an exquisite "sister" temple to the Tanjore shrine.

Under Rajendra, the Cola dynasty flourished, as did art and literature. Though he surpassed his father's achievement, Rajendra owed to Rajaraja the conditions and the examples without which his own achievement would have been inconceivable.

Further Reading

Rajaraja I is listed in the Asia study guide (II, A, 3). Other early Indian leaders were HARSHA and SAMU-DRAGUPTA.

The authoritative study of the dynasty remains K. A. Nilakanta Sastri, *The Colas* (1935). Several chapters in Ghulam Yazdani, ed., *The Early History of the Deccan* (2 vols., 1960), are useful. For the general reader, K. A. Nilakanta Sastri, *A History of South India* (1955), places the Colas in the context of southern Indian history from the earliest times to the middle of the 16th century. A helpful monograph on the Rajarajesvara Temple is J. M. Somasundaram Pillai, *The Great Temple at Tanjore* (1935).

RALEIGH / By Joel M. Rodney

The English statesman Sir Walter Raleigh (ca. 1552–1618) was also a soldier, courtier, explorer and exponent of overseas expansion, man of letters, and victim of Stuart mistrust and Spanish hatred.

quences of invasions from the Deccan earlier in the century.

Rajaraja first reduced traditional Cera rivals in the southwest (present-day Kerala) and then subdued the Pandya contenders in the extreme south. Thereafter he invaded and took control of the island kingdom of Ceylon. Next, Rajaraja's armies conquered the territories in what is present-day Mysore State. In less than a decade Rajaraja had become master of southern India.

Accompanying Rajaraja's undoubted military genius was a talent for political and economic administration.

Born into a prominent Protestant Devonshire family, Walter Raleigh (or Ralegh) spent time at Oriel College, Oxford, before leaving to join the Huguenot army in the French religious war in 1569. Five years in France saw him safely through two major battles and the massacre of St. Bartholomew's Day. By 1576 he was in London as a lodger (not a law student) at the Middle Temple and saw his verses, prefixed to George

Gascoigne's *Steele Glas*, in print. His favorite poetic theme, the impermanence of all earthly things, was popular with other Renaissance poets. However, Raleigh's verse differs from theirs: for their richly decorated quality and smoothly musical rhythms, he substituted a colloquial diction and a simplicity and directness of statement that prefigured the work of John Donne and the other metaphysical poets.

After 2 years in obscurity Raleigh accompanied his half brother, Sir Humphrey Gilbert, on a voyage ostensibly in search of a Northwest Passage to the Orient but which quickly degenerated into a privateering foray against the Spanish. On their return in 1579, Raleigh and Gilbert faced the displeasure of the Privy Council. Raleigh's subsequent conduct did little to placate the Council: he engaged in several altercations and was imprisoned twice in 6 months for disturbing the peace. Once out of jail, and at the head of a company of infantry, he sailed to serve in the Irish wars.

In Ireland, Raleigh spent less than 2 years on campaign. He helped condemn one of the leaders of the rebellion, bombed a Spanish-Italian garrison into surrender, and then oversaw their massacre. After some minor but well-fought engagements, he was appointed a temporary administrator of Munster. Not satisfied, he criticized his superiors and by the end of 1581 had been sent back to London with dispatches for the Council, £20 for his expenses, and a reputation as an expert on Irish affairs.

Progress at Court

Extravagant in dress and in conduct (whether or not he spread his costly cloak over a puddle for Elizabeth to step on, his contemporaries believed him capable of the gesture), handsome, and superbly self-confident, Raleigh at first rose rapidly at court. His opinion on Ireland was sought and apparently taken by Elizabeth; when he obtained a new commission for service there, the Queen kept him home as an adviser. He received more concrete tokens of royal favor as well: a house in London, two estates in Oxford, and, most lucrative, the monopolies for the sale of wine licenses and the export of broadcloth all came from Elizabeth in 1583–1584.

Raleigh was knighted in 1584 and the next year became warden of the stannaries (or mines) in Devon and Cornwall, lord lieutenant of Cornwall, and vice admiral of the West (Devon and Cornwall). Although he was hated for his arrogance at Westminster, in Devon and Cornwall his reforms of the mining codes and his association with local privateering ventures made him very popular; he sat for Devonshire in the Parliaments of 1584 and 1586.

In 1586 Raleigh succeeded Sir Christopher Hatton (newly made lord chancellor) as captain of the Queen's Guard—his highest office at court.

Overseas Ventures

The patent under which Gilbert had led his expedition of 1578 had authorized him not merely to explore but to claim unknown lands (in the Queen's name, of course) and to exploit them as he saw fit. By 1582 Gilbert had organized a company to settle English Catholics in the Americas. Although forbidden by Elizabeth to accompany his half brother, Raleigh invested money and a ship of his own design in the venture. After Gilbert's death on the return from Newfoundland, Raleigh was given a charter to "occupy and enjoy" new lands. A preliminary expedition sailed as soon as Raleigh had his charter, reached the Carolina shore of America, and claimed the land for the court-bound empire builder.

At the same time, Raleigh sought to entice Elizabeth into a more active role in his proposed colonizing venture: not only did he name the new territory Virginia (after the Virgin Queen) but he sponsored Richard Hakluyt's *Discourse of Western Planting* and brought this great imperialistic treatise to Elizabeth's attention. Although unconvinced, she gave a ship and some funds; Raleigh remained at court and devoted his energies to financing the scheme. The first settlers were conveyed by Raleigh's cousin Sir Richard Grenville. Quarrels, lack of discipline, and hostile Indians led the colonists to return to England aboard Francis Drake's 1586 squadron, bringing with them potatoes and tobacco, both hitherto unknown in Europe.

John White led a second expedition the next year. The

Sir Walter Raleigh and his son, a painting by an unknown artist. (National Portrait Gallery, London)

Raleigh watches the Spanish governor of St. Joseph being led away captive on the island of Trinidad in 1595. The line engraving is from De Bry's Grands voyages, *published in 1599. (By Permission of the Trustees of the National Maritime Museum, Greenwich, England)*

coming of the Armada delayed sending supplies for more than 2 years. When the relief ships reached the colony in 1591, it had vanished. Raleigh sent other expeditions to the Virginia coast but failed to establish a permanent settlement there; his charter was revoked by James I in 1603.

Retirement from Court

Raleigh played a minor role in the defeat of the Spanish Armada in 1588. He organized the Devon militia and was a member of Elizabeth's War Council but did not participate in the naval battle. When he returned to court, he clashed with Elizabeth's new favorite, Robert Devereux, Earl of Essex. After the Privy Council halted an incipient duel between them, Raleigh left for Ireland, where he cultivated his estates and the friendship of his neighbor, the poet Edmund Spenser, whom he introduced to Elizabeth in 1590.

The next year Raleigh was to have gone to sea in search of the Spanish plate fleet, but again Elizabeth refused permission. Grenville, who went in his stead, was trapped by Spanish galleons, and Raleigh raised a

new fleet to avenge his cousin. At sea finally, he was immediately summoned back by Elizabeth. Upon his tardy return he was imprisoned in the Tower, for the Queen had discovered his alliance with Elizabeth Throgmorton, one of her own maids of honor. (Raleigh later married Elizabeth Throgmorton.) After the return of an enormously wealthy prize taken by Raleigh's sailors, and after Elizabeth took an inordinate share of the profits, she permitted the Raleighs to go to their estate of Sherborne in Dorset.

Forbidden access to the court, Raleigh devoted time to study and speculation about the nature of matter and the universe. During this time he sat in Parliament, joined the Society of Antiquaries, assisted Hakluyt in preparing his *Voyages,* and joined Ben Jonson and Shakespeare at the Mermaid Tavern in London.

By the end of 1594 Raleigh had regained enough of Elizabeth's favor to obtain her consent for a prospecting expedition to Guiana (Venezuela). From this he brought back many samples of gold ore and a belief in the existence of a rich gold mine.

In 1596 Raleigh and his rival Essex led a brilliantly successful raid on Cadiz, and he seemed to have finally placated Elizabeth. He was readmitted to court, continued to serve in Parliament, was given a monopoly over playing cards, held more naval commands, and became governor of the island of Jersey, where he proved again to be an excellent administrator. With Essex's execution for treason, Raleigh's place as favorite seemed secure. But the Queen herself was near death, and Raleigh's enemies lost no time in poisoning the mind of James Stuart, her heir apparent and successor, against him.

His Imprisonment

Upon James I's accession, Raleigh was dismissed as captain of the guard, warden of the stanneries, and governor of Jersey. His monopolies were suspended, and he was evicted from his London house. Soon after, he was implicated (falsely) in a plot against James and, upon being committed to the Tower, tried to commit suicide. A farcical trial before a special commission at Winchester at the end of 1603 resulted in a death sentence, followed by a reprieve and imprisonment in the Tower for 13 years.

James stripped Raleigh of all his offices and even took Sherborne on a technicality to give to his own favorite, Robert Carr. The remainder of his property was restored, and Raleigh was well treated: his family joined him in a large apartment in the Bloody Tower; his books were brought as well. Raleigh attracted the sympathy and friendship of James's eldest son, Henry, who sought his advice on matters of shipbuilding and naval defense. Raleigh dedicated his monumental *History of the World*, written during this period of imprisonment, to the prince. Henry protested Raleigh's continued incarceration but died before he could effect his release.

Last Voyage

From 1610 on, Raleigh, aware of James's need for money, sought permission to lead another search for the gold mine of his earlier Guiana voyage and at last got his way. Freed early in 1616, he invested most of his remaining funds in the projected voyage. The expedition, which sailed in June of the following year, was a disastrous failure. No treasure and no mine were found, and Raleigh's men violated James's strict instructions to avoid fighting with Spanish colonists in the area. Still worse, during the battle with the Spaniards, Raleigh's older son, Walter, was killed.

Upon his empty-handed return Raleigh was rearrested; James and Sarmiento, the Spanish ambassador, wished him tried on a charge of piracy, but as he was already under a sentence of death, a new trial was not possible. His execution would have to proceed from the charge of treason of 1603. James agreed to this course, and Raleigh was beheaded on Oct. 29, 1618.

Further Reading

Sir Walter Raleigh is listed in the European History study guide (IV, A, 1, c; IV, A, 2), the American History study guide (II, A, 2), and the Literature study guide (II, D, 2, a). Lord ESSEX was also a favorite of ELIZABETH I.

Raleigh's *History of the World*, first published in 1614, has been reissued many times. *A Report of the Truth of the Fight about the Isles of Acores* (1591) and *The Discovery of . . . the Empire of Guiana* (1596) are published in *Works of Sir Walter Ralegh* (8 vols., 1829), which also contains works published posthumously. The standard edition of Raleigh's poetry is *The Poems of Sir Walter Ralegh*, edited by Agnes M. C. Latham (1929).

There is no completely satisfactory biography of Raleigh. Edward Edwards, *The Life of Sir Walter Ralegh Based on Contemporary Documents . . . Together with His Letters* (2 vols., 1868), lacks much material that is now available. Among the most useful works are Edward Thompson, *Sir Walter Ralegh: The Last of the Elizabethans* (1935), and Willard M. Wallace, *Sir Walter Raleigh* (1959). Raleigh's role in natural philosophy and his connection with Thomas Hariot are treated in Robert Kargon, *Atomism in England* (1966). His contact with Christopher Marlowe is explored at length in M. C. Bradbrook, *The School of Night: A Study in the Literary Relationships of Sir Walter Relegh* (1936), and in Ernest Albert Strathmann, *Sir Walter Raleigh: A Study in Elizabethan Skepticism* (1951). A. L. Rowse's *The England of Elizabeth: The Structure of Society* (1950) and *The Expansion of Elizabethan England* (1955) provide a valuable general view of the period.

RAMA KHAMHAENG
/ By David K. Wyatt

Rama Khamhaeng (ca. 1239–ca. 1299) was king of Sukhothai in Thailand and the founder of Thai political power in central Indochina. He remains the Thai model of the patriarchal ruler.

Rama Khamhaeng (pronounced rä′mə käm-äng) was the third son of King Sri Indraditya, who had seized power in Sukhothai from the Cambodian empire of Angkor between 1219 and 1245. When Rama's brother, King Ban Müang, died, he inherited a small kingdom in the foothills of north-central Siam. By a combination of shrewd alliances, careful diplomacy which ensured the neutrality of rivals, and forceful military campaigns, especially in the 1290s, he extended his kingdom to Luangprabang and the Vientiane region in Laos to the north, westward to the Indian Ocean coast of Burma, and south to Nakhon Si Thammarat on the Malay Peninsula.

Apart from colorful but unreliable myth, almost all that is known of Rama Khamhaeng comes from his great inscription of 1292, the oldest known inscription in the Thai language and script. That lengthy document portrays the King as a father to his subjects, available day and night to petitioners for justice, liberal in his gifts and in his treatment of his vassals, merciful in warfare, and pious in his devotion to Buddhism. His state is depicted as happy and prosperous: "This state of Sukhothai is good. In the waters there are fish; in the fields there is rice." Implicit in this account are policies strongly in contrast to the bureaucratic complexity, impersonality, and economic rigidity of Angkor. Sukhothai under Rama Khamhaeng was a simple state with no pretensions, where justice was to be had, trade could flourish, and peace would reign. These policies, and the strong leadership of the King, were responsible for the kingdom's phenomenal success in detaching so much territory from mighty Angkor. Still experimenting with political institutions, however, Rama Khamhaeng's son and successor, Lö Thai (reigned ca. 1299–1346), was unable to hold the state together in the face of challenges from other Thai princes to the south, and the kingdom of Ayudhya (1350–1767) ultimately reduced Sukhothai to a province (1438).

The 1292 inscription, lost for many centuries, was rediscovered by King Mongkut, then a Buddhist monk, in 1834, and the image of Rama Khamhaeng, resurrected, became a powerful ideal for subsequent rulers.

Further Reading

Rama Khamhaeng is listed in the Asia study guide (IV, A, 2, a). Later Thai rulers included King MONGKUT, who began Thailand's Westernization, and King CHULALONGKORN, who continued his modernizing reforms.

The kingdom of Sukhothai, still relatively neglected by scholars, may be studied in George Coedès, *The Making of South East Asia*, translated by H. M. Wright (1966), and in Alexander B. Griswold's marvellous *Towards a History of Sukhodaya Art* (1967).

RAMAKRISHNA / By Peter A. Pardue

Sri Ramakrishna (1833–1886) was an Indian mystic, reformer, and saint who, in his own lifetime, came to be revered by people of all classes as a spiritual incarnation of God.

Born in a rural Bengal village, Ramakrishna (pronounced rä-mə-krĭsh′nə) was the fourth of five children. His parents were simple but orthodox Brahmins deeply committed to the maintenance of traditional religious piety. As a child, he did not like routine schoolwork and never learned to read or write. Instead, he began to exhibit precocious spiritual qualities, which included ecstatic experiences, long periods of contemplation, and mystical absorption in the sacred plays of the Indian epic tradition, especially with the roles of the gods Shiva and Krishna. During his formal initiation ceremony into the Brahmin caste, he shocked his high-caste relatives by openly accepting a ritual meal cooked by a woman of low caste.

Though Ramakrishna resisted orthodox priestly studies, at the age of 16 he went to Calcutta to assist his

Ramakrishna. (Courtesy of the Ramakrishna-Vivekananda Center, New York City)

brother, who was serving as a priest for a number of local families. He was disturbed by the gross commercialism, spiritual drabness, and inhumanity of the urban environment. However, when his brother was asked to become a priest at a large temple complex at Dakshineswar near the Ganges outside Calcutta, Ramakrishna found a new and ultimately permanent environment for his spiritual maturation and teaching.

Spiritual Struggles

That temple complex—one of the most impressive in the area—had been built by a wealthy widow of low caste whose spiritual ideal was the mother goddess Kali. This great deity traditionally combines the terror of death and destruction with universal motherly reassurance and is often embodied in a statue of ferocious appearance. She represents an immense spectrum of religious and human emotions, from the most primitive to the most exalted, and consequently has a symbolic universality not easily contained within conventional religious forms.

Ramakrishna was selected to serve as priest in the Kali temple, and it was in this context that he had a series of crucial religious experiences in which he felt that Kali was calling him to a universal spiritual mission for India and all mankind. His ecstatic, unorthodox, and often bizarre behavior during this period of spiritual transformation was interpreted by many as a sign of madness; but it clearly represents an aspect of his struggles to free himself from routine religious patterns and achieve a new and more profound spirituality: he imitated the actions of the god-monkey Hanuman (a sign of humility and service); he fed animals from the same food prepared for Kali (a blasphemy to the orthodox); he cleaned an outcaste's hovel with his hair (a terrible defilement for a Brahmin); he sang and danced wildly when the spirit moved; he rejected his Brahminical status, asserting that caste superiority was spiritually debasing—all of this symbolizing his inward spiritual transformation.

Spiritual Maturity

When Ramakrishna was 28, his emotional confusion subsided, and he began studying a wide variety of traditional religious teachings. His teachers were astounded at his powers of assimilation, prodigious memory, and innate spiritual skill. He was openly proclaimed a supreme sage. At the age of 33 he began to study Moslem tradition, and after a short period of instruction he had a vision of a "radiant figure"—interpreted as Mohammed himself, which confirmed his universal religious calling.

In 1868 Ramakrishna undertook an extensive pilgrimage; but despite the honors accorded him he was saddened by the poverty of the masses and took up residence with outcaste groups to dramatize their plight, insisting that his rich patrons make formal efforts to alleviate their condition. He was always a man of the people, simple, full of affective warmth, and without artificial intellectualism or religious dogma.

World Mission

By now Ramakrishna had a wide following from all classes and groups. He was not merely a great teacher; he was regarded as an embodiment of the sacred source of Indian religious tradition and of the universal ideals toward which all men strive. His spiritual vitality and magnetism were combined with a sharp sense of humor —often aimed at himself or his disciples when the hazards of pride and self-satisfaction seemed imminent.

During the last decade of his life, one of the most important events was the conversion of his disciple Vivekananda, who was destined to organize and promote Ramakrishna's teachings throughout India, Europe, and the United States. In 1886, when Ramakrishna was near death, he formally designated Vivekananda his spiritual heir.

Ramakrishna's teachings do not appear in systematic form. He wrote nothing. His disciples recorded his words only in the context of the spiritual force of his personality, and consequently in collected form these sayings have the character of a gospel—a message of salvation centered in the spiritual paradigm of his own life. He rejected all efforts to worship him personally; rather, he suggested that his presentation of man's spiritual potentialities serve as a guide and inspiration to others. Above all, Ramakrishna had a "grass-roots" appeal equaled by few others in any religious tradition, marked by his love of all men and his enthusiasm for all forms of spirituality.

Further Reading

Ramakrishna is listed in the Asia study guide (II, A, 8, a). VIVEKANANDA was his spiritual heir.

The sayings of Ramakrishna are available in several editions, such as *The Gospel of Ramakrishna* (1907) and *The Gospel of Sri Ramakrishna*, translated and introduced by Swami Nikhilananda (1942). Among the many works devoted to Ramakrishna's life and influence are Friedrich Max Mueller, *Ramakrishna: His Life and Sayings* (1898); Romain Rolland, *The Life of Ramakrishna* (trans. 1931); Christopher Isherwood, *Ramakrishna and His Disciples* (1965); and Nalini Devdas, *Sri Ramakrishna* (1966).

* * *

RAMAN / By Ainslie T. Embree

The Indian physicist Sir Chandrasekhar Venkata Raman (1888–1970) was awarded the Nobel Prize in 1930 for his work on the scattering of light and the discovery of the Raman effect, which has to do with changes in the wavelength of light scattered by molecules.

On Nov. 7, 1888, C. V. Raman (pronounced rä′mən) was born at Trichinopoly, Madras, where his father taught physics in a church college. A few years later the family moved to Vizagapatam, when

C. V. Raman, photographed outside the antiblast walls of his laboratory. In his right hand he holds a diamond and in his left an atomic model of it. (Information Service of India, Washington, D.C.)

the father was appointed as lecturer in the local college. Raman received his early education there until he entered Presidency College in Madras in 1902. He graduated with a bachelor's degree in 1904, standing first in his class and winning the Gold Medal in physics. By the time he completed his master's degree in physics in 1907, he had already done original work in optics and acoustics, but since at that time there was little scope for scientific research in India, he took the competitive examination for a post in the Finance Department of the government of India. Again he won first place and as a result was appointed assistant accountant general in the central government offices in Calcutta.

During the next 10 years, while working in the Finance Department, Raman continued his scientific researches on his own in the laboratory of the Indian Association for the Cultivation of Science. The importance of his work was recognized by his appointment in 1917 to the first endowed chair in physics at Calcutta University. He kept this post until 1933.

Raman's years at Calcutta University were marked by great creativity and intellectual excitement, although by Western standards his laboratory facilities were meager. Many honors came to him as the significance of his work was acknowledged in India and abroad, as in 1929, when he was invited to do research at the California Institute of Technology. The most tangible evidence of this recognition came in 1927, when the British government conferred a knighthood on him, and in 1930, when he was awarded the Nobel Prize.

Raman Effect

Raman's early scientific interests were centered on phenomena associated with the scattering of light, the most familiar example of which is the effect created when light enters a darkened room through a small hole. The beam of light is then clearly seen because the light is scattered by the particles of dust in the air. That scattered light contained wavelengths in different proportions from the wavelengths of the main beam of light had been known since Tyndall's experiments in 1868, but a fully satisfactory analysis of the phenomenon had not been made.

It was this and related problems that Raman was studying at Calcutta when he discovered that when an intense light was passed through a liquid and was scattered by the molecules in the liquid, the spectrum of the scattered light showed lines not in the spectrum of the incident light. This discovery was the Raman effect, which had such great influence on later work on molecular structure and radiation that Raman was recognized as one of the truly seminal minds in the history of modern physics.

After Raman retired from Calcutta University, he became director of the Indian Institute of Science in Bangalore, where he remained until 1948, when he became head of the new Raman Research Institute in the same city. Here he continued to guide research and to inspire his students and coworkers. They spoke of his intense enthusiasm and volcanic energy and of his great generosity in acknowledging the contribution of others. According to one former student, he would "give away

whole lines of research which lesser men would be tempted to keep for themselves."

Raman's attractiveness as a person was rooted in his esthetic approach to science, with his choice of subjects for investigation reflecting his love of music, color, harmony, and pattern. He told how his great discovery of the Raman effect was stimulated during a voyage to Europe in 1921, when he saw for the first time "the wonderful blue opalescence of the Mediterranean Sea" and began to think that the phenomenon was due to the scattering of sunlight by the molecules of water.

Raman influenced Indian scientific development through the *Indian Journal of Physics*, which he helped found and which he edited. He was also a gifted popularizer of modern scientific ideas, and he lectured widely to lay audiences. He died in Bangalore on Nov. 21, 1970.

Further Reading

C. V. Raman is listed in the Asia study guide (II, A, 8, c). Other Indian scientists were Homi Jehangir BHABHA and Har Gobind KHORANA.

Raman sets forth his own views on modern science in an attractive way in his *The New Physics* (1951). Some biographical details and a brief account of his scientific work are in Niels H. de V. Heathcote, *Nobel Prize Winners in Physics, 1901–1950* (1953). A more technical discussion is S. Bhagavantam, *Scattering of Light and the Raman Effect* (1940). A consideration of Raman's many-sided contribution to science is made by his students and colleagues in *Proceedings of the Indian Academy of Sciences*, vol. 28 (1949).

* * *

RAMANUJAN / By Surjit Singh Dulai

The Indian mathematician Srinivasa Ramanujan Aiyangar (1887–1920) is best known for his work on hypergeometric series and continued fractions.

Srinivasa Ramanujan (pronounced rä-mä′nŏŏ-jən), born into a poor Brahmin family at Erode on Dec. 22, 1887, attended school in nearby Kumbakonam. By the time he was 13, he could solve unaided every problem in Loney's *Trigonometry*, and at 14 he obtained the theorems for the sine and the cosine that had been anticipated by L. Euler. In 1903 he came upon George Shoobridge Carr's *Synopsis of Elementary Results in Pure and Applied Mathematics*. The book, its coverage reaching 1860, opened a whole new world to him, and he set out to establish the 6,165 theorems in it for himself. Having no contact with good books, he had to do original research for each solution. Trying to devise his own methods, he made some astounding discoveries, among them several new algebraic series.

Ramanujan became so absorbed in mathematics that when he entered the local government college in 1904 with a merit scholarship, he neglected his other subjects and lost the scholarship. Despite two later attempts, he never qualified for the first degree in arts. Ramanujan married in 1909, and while working as a clerk he continued his mathematical investigations; in 1911 he started to publish some of his results.

In January 1913 Ramanujan sent some of his work to G. H. Hardy, Cayley lecturer in mathematics at Cambridge. Hardy noticed that whereas Ramanujan had rediscovered, and gone far beyond, some of the latest conclusions of Western mathematicians, he was completely ignorant of some of the most fundamental areas. In May the University of Madras gave Ramanujan a scholarship.

In 1914 Ramanujan went to Cambridge. The university experience gave him considerable sophistication, but his mind, by this time somewhat hardened, generally continued to work according to the old pattern, in which intuition played a more important role than argument. In Hardy's opinion, if Ramanujan's gift had been recognized early, he could have become one of the greatest mathematicians of all time. In hypergeometric series and continued fractions, "he was unquestionably one of the great masters." His patience, memory, power of calculation, and intuition made him the greatest formalist of his day. But his passionate, prolific, and in some ways profound work in the theory of numbers and his work in analysis were seriously marred by misdevelopment.

In 1918 Ramanujan was elected a fellow of the Royal Society and a Fellow of Trinity College, Cambridge. He died on April 26, 1920.

Further Reading

Srinivasa Ramanujan is listed in the Asia study guide (II, A, 8, c). Other notable Indian scientists were Har Gobind KHORANA and C. V. RAMAN.

Godfrey Harold Hardy and others, eds., *Collected Papers of Srinivasa Ramanujan* (1927), and Hardy's *Ramanujan: Twelve Lectures on Subjects Suggested by His Life and Work* (1940) include biographical material. Shiyali Ramamrita Ranganathan, *Ramanujan: The Man and the Mathematician* (Bombay, 1967), is a disappointing biography. Scientific American, *Lives in Science* (1957), and James Roy Newman, *Science and Sensibility* (2 vols., 1961), have useful accounts of Ramanujan's life.

RAMEAU / By Aubrey S. Garlington, Jr.

Jean Philippe Rameau (1683–1764) was a French theoretician of music and a composer. His theoretical works provided the scientific basis for the development of traditional, functional harmony in the 18th century. His operas were the first national creations to rival those of Lully.

Jean Philippe Rameau (pronounced rà-mō′) was born in Dijon on Sept. 25, 1683, the son of a provincial organist. It is presumed that he studied with his father, no other formal training being known. He was in Italy in 1701 and then served as organist for a time at Clermont-Ferrand. In 1706 he was in Paris, where his first collection of harpsichord pieces was published. Rameau dropped out of sight for nearly a decade, returning sometime about 1715 to his former position at Clermont-Ferrand. Here he wrote his famous *Treatise on Harmony Reduced to Its Natural Principles* (1722).

In 1731 Rameau came under the patronage of one of the wealthiest, most remarkable 18th-century French aristocrats, La Pouplinière. Rameau was active as a teacher, harpsichordist, conductor, and composer in his establishment until 1753. His patron provided the necessary arrangements for Rameau to attempt his hand at opera composition.

In 1733 *Hippolyte et Aricie*, to a libretto by the Abbé Pellegrin, was presented in Paris; it was Rameau's first major public success. *Les Indes galantes* followed in 1735, and *Castor et Pollux*, generally considered to be his crowning triumph in the music theater, in 1737. These works challenged the then-prevailing taste for simpler, more tuneful diversions and entertainments, as well as the belief that Jean Baptiste Lully was the only significant composer of French operas. The ensuing

Srinivasa Ramanujan. (Information Service of India, New York)

Jean Philippe Rameau, a portrait by Jean Baptiste Chardin in the Musée de Dijon. (French Cultural Services of the French Embassy)

quarrels in French intellectual circles over the respective merits of Lully and Rameau and later over the merits of Italian versus French music assured Rameau of lasting fame. In 1745 the King awarded Rameau a lifetime pension on the basis of his pleasure with *La Princesse de Navarre,* a *comédie-ballet* (a unification of stage play and ballet) composed for the marriage of the Dauphin to Maria Theresa of Spain.

In his keyboard music Rameau followed in the steps of François Couperin. Nearly 20 years elapsed between Rameau's first publications in 1706 and a second collection of orderly, elegant pieces for the harpsichord, *Pièces de clavecin avec une méthode pour la mécanique des doigts* (1726). The *Pièces de clavecin en concert avec un violon ou une flûte et une viole ou un deuxième violon* (1741) is generally acknowledged as his master-

piece of chamber music. He died in Paris on Sept. 12, 1764.

Rameau's keyboard music is of exceptionally high quality, but he is even more widely acclaimed as a theorist. He was the only major composer who gained a reputation as a theorist before being acclaimed for composition. All his life he fought against the widely held erroneous notion that to be "scientific" in music is to be mechanical and lifeless.

Rameau's *Treatise on Harmony* established the primacy of triadic harmony as the central "law" of music. He claimed that melody must be subordinated to harmony and that harmonic considerations alone should dictate composition. He established the significant theoretical concept that the inversions of chords did not create new chords but were further manifestations of a single harmony. While Rameau's ideas were much debated and attacked, their importance for the future of theory and practice cannot be overestimated. His codification of functional harmony provided much of the theoretical basis for traditional composition well into the 19th century.

Further Reading

Jean Philippe Rameau is listed in the Music study guide (I, D, 2). His operas are the only significant milestone in the French musical theater between Jean Baptiste LULLY and Christoph Willibald GLUCK. Rameau's harpsichord music was inspired by that of François COUPERIN.

The standard biography and study of Rameau's music is Cuthbert Girdlestone, *Jean-Philippe Rameau: His Life and Work* (1957; rev. ed. 1970). See also Donald J. Grout, *A Short History of Opera* (1947; rev. ed. 1965) and *A History of Western Music* (1960).

* * *

D. **RAMSAY** / By Carl E. Prince

David Ramsay (1749–1815) was a second-line political figure of the American Revolution but a first-rate and most important contemporary historian of that epoch.

David Ramsay, a painting by Charles Willson Peale. (Independence National Historical Park Collection, Philadelphia)

David Ramsay was born in Pennsylvania on April 2, 1749, of substantial landowning parents. He graduated from the College of New Jersey (now Princeton University) and, after teaching for a while, took a medical degree from the University of Pennsylvania in 1772.

Ramsay settled in Charleston, S.C., and made it his home for the remainder of his life. The beginning of his political career coincided with the outbreak of the American Revolution. Much of that career was spent in the legislature of his adopted state, but he also served for 2 years in the 1780s in the Continental Congress, where he emerged as an early supporter of a strong federal government. After the ratification of the Constitution, Ramsay served in the upper house of South Carolina and on three occasions was named president of that body.

In these years Ramsay earned his way rather precariously by practicing medicine. He also used his ample talent as a writer to turn out occasional first-rate essays on the history of medicine. These did not pay anything, though, and Ramsay was in chronic financial need. Despite his talents, he proved a poor businessman. He speculated in land with such disastrous consequences that even a steady medical practice could not recoup his losses. He went bankrupt in 1798, having opposed leniency to debtors throughout his political career. He died in Charleston on May 8, 1815.

Ramsay is best remembered as the author of the most objective and sophisticated contemporary account of the Revolution. His *History of the American Revolution* (1789) forms the basis today for most of the multicausation theories of that epoch. Like many historians writing at this time, he relied heavily for information on the *Annual Register*, a British publication that summarized events each year; like contemporary historians, too, Ramsay was not always careful with the truth. But his interpretations were his own, and he was the first—and for a century the only—historian to suggest that a variety of motives had induced men and governments to support independence first and the Constitution later.

Ramsay emphasized the key role of "independent men" in motivating American nationalism, creating changes in the social structure, and capitalizing on expanding economic opportunity in the young republic. In approaching his assessment of the era in this sophisticated way, Ramsay, as one historian has suggested, may have "penetrated further into the essential meaning of the Revolution than the more arduous researches of twentieth-century historians have done."

Further Reading

David Ramsay is listed in the Social Sciences study guide (V, A, 3). He studied medicine with one of the leading colonial doctors, Benjamin RUSH.

There is no book-length biography of Ramsay. For a brief biographical sketch and an excerpt from Ramsay's writings see Edmund S. Morgan, *The American Revolution: Two Centuries of Interpretation* (1965).

w. RAMSAY / By June Z. Fullmer

The British chemist and educator Sir William Ramsay (1852–1916) discovered the rare gases and did important work in thermodynamics.

William Ramsay was born at Queen's Crescent, Glasgow, on Oct. 2, 1852. Both his father, a civil engineer, William Ramsay, and his mother, Catharine Robertson Ramsay, came from families noted for scientific attainment. Ramsay studied the classics, mathematics, and literature at the University of Glasgow (1866–1869) and then entered Robert Tatlock's laboratory while attending scientific lectures at the university. In 1870 he joined Robert Bunsen at Heidelberg, but he left there in 1871 to work with Rudolf Fittig at Tübingen, where he received the doctorate in 1872. On his return to Glasgow he became an assistant at Anderson's College and later an assistant in the department of chemistry at the University of Glasgow. University College, Bristol, appointed him professor of chemistry in 1880 and principal in 1881. In 1887 he succeeded Alexander W. Williamson to the chair of general chemistry at University College, London. He retired in 1912 to Hazelwood, in Buckinghamshire, where he also built a small laboratory. He had been made a fellow of the Royal Society in 1888; in 1902 he was knighted; and in 1904 he received the Nobel Prize. He died on July 23, 1916.

While Ramsay was at Glasgow, he worked as an organic chemist, synthesizing pyridine in 1877, and showing how close the relationship was between this compound and the alkaloids quinine and cinchonine. At Bristol he worked primarily as a physical chemist and, with his assistant, demonstrated the complexity of the molecular structure of pure liquids by studying the variation in their molecular surface energy with temperature. In London, Ramsay gradually shifted his attention to making very accurate determinations of the density of gases. He noted the small difference between the density of atmospheric nitrogen and that of "chemically pure" nitrogen. Together with Lord Rayleigh he disovered in 1894 a new element, christened "argon" because of its apparent chemical inertness; they announced their discovery in early 1895. Subsequently Ramsay was able to show that the gas given off when the mineral clevite was heated had a spectrum identical with that of helium.

Ramsay, now convinced that there was an entire group of elements missing from the periodic table, embarked upon a diligent search for them. In 1898, with the assistance of M. W. Travers, by careful fractional distillation of liquid air, Ramsay found three other elements: neon, krypton, and xenon. In 1903 he and Frederick Soddy announced the isolation of the final member of the series, radon, which they called "radium emanation." Ramsay also showed that the disintegration of radium proceeds with the emission of charged helium nuclei—alpha particles. For a while he believed that he had produced transmutations of copper to lithium and of thorium to carbon by exposing those materials to the products of radium

William Ramsay. (Radio Times Hulton Picture Library)

disintegration. These claims were shown to be mistaken but were, nonetheless, important, for they suggested that the energy and particles from natural nuclear disintegrations might possibly be used to effect changes in more stable nuclei.

Further Reading

William Ramsay is listed in the Science study guide (VI, D, 1). His experiments to discover the rare gases were carried out with the assistance of Lord RAYLEIGH and Frederick SODDY.

The chief sources of biographical information on Ramsay are Sir William A. Tilden, *Sir William Ramsay . . . Memorials of His Life and Work* (1918); and Morris William Travers, *William Ramsay and University College London, 1852–1952* (1952) and *A Life of Sir William Ramsay* (1956).

RAMSES II / By D. M. Dixon

Ramses II (reigned 1304–1237 B.C.) was the third ruler of the Nineteenth Dynasty of Egypt. A great warrior, he was also the builder of some of Egypt's most famous monuments.

amses (pronounced răm′sēz), or Ramesses, was the son of Seti I. Prior to his accession as sole ruler in 1304 B.C., Ramses had been coregent with his father. During the last years of Seti I the reins of government had slackened, and the first 3 years of Ramses' reign seem to have been occupied with setting in order the internal affairs of Egypt. Early in his reign he undertook the task of securing an adequate water supply for the gold-mining expeditions to and from the Wadi el-Allaqi in Lower Nubia.

Ramses' royal residence, known as Per-Ramesse, the "House of Ramses," was situated in the Delta. Its site is still a matter of debate; various scholars have identified it with the cities of Tanis and Qantir in the eastern half of the Delta. The situation of the residence in this area was convenient for a pharaoh so concerned with events in Palestine and Syria.

Hittite Campaigns

The outstanding feature of Ramses II's reign was his protracted struggle with the Hittites. An inscription of year 4 of his reign, at the Nahr el-Kalb near Beirut, records his first Asiatic campaign. In year 5 he launched a major attack on the Hittite Empire from his base in northern Palestine and Phoenicia. During the course of this offensive, Ramses at Qadesh fought the greatest battle of his career. Although neither side could claim victory, Ramses never ceased to boast on his monuments of his own part in the battle. Strategically, however, the result was a defeat for the Egyptians, who were obliged to retire homeward. The sight of the Pharaoh's army retreating encouraged many of the petty states of Palestine to revolt, and in year 6 or 7 and in year 8 Ramses was obliged to suppress uprisings in the area.

Ramses II had himself depicted four times in the seated figures on the facade of the great rock temple at Abu Simbel. The Pharaoh left other notable monuments at Karnak, Thebes, and Luxor. (Giraudon)

By year 10 Ramses was again on the Nahr el-Kalb, and the next year he broke the Hittite defenses and invaded Syria. Although he penetrated deep into Hittite territory, he found it impossible to hold indefinitely against Hittite pressure territories so far away from base, and in year 21 a treaty was concluded which terminated 16 years of hostilities between Egypt and the Hittites. After the restoration of peace, relations between the two powers became friendly, and a regular exchange of diplomatic correspondence ensued. In year 34 Ramses married the eldest daughter of the Hittite king. In addition to his wars in Palestine and Syria, Ramses vigorously combated Libyan incursions into the Delta.

No pharaoh ever surpassed the building achievements of Ramses II. Among the most famous of his constructions are his temple at Abydos, his funerary temple, known as the Ramesseum, at Thebes, and the great rock-cut temple at Abu Simbel in Nubia.

Further Reading

Ramses II is listed in the Ancient History study guide (I, A, 5). Other rulers of the New Kingdom were Queen HATSHEPSUT, THUTMOSE III, and IKHNATON.

An excellent account of Ramses II's reign is given by R. O. Faulkner in volume 2 of *The Cambridge Ancient History* (12 vols., 1924; 2d rev. ed. 1966). See also A. H. Gardiner, *Egypt of the Pharaohs* (1961).

RAMSEY / By Daniel O'Connor

The English mathematician and philosopher Frank Plumpton Ramsey (1903–1930) was recognized as an authority in mathematical logic.

rank Ramsey was born on Feb. 22, 1903. His father, Arthur Ramsey, was president of Magdalen College. Ramsey's excellent work at Winchester College won him a scholarship to Trinity College, Cambridge. He was Allen University scholar in 1924 and in the same year was elected a fellow of King's College and appointed lecturer in mathematics at the university.

Ramsey's precocious talents were legendary at Cambridge. From about his sixteenth year he was consulted by theorists in mathematics and other subjects in which mathematics is largely used. The economist John Maynard Keynes reported, "Economists living in Cambridge have been accustomed from his undergraduate days to try their theories on the keen edge of his critical and logical faculties." And indeed in his brief life Ramsey made two important contributions to economic theory: "A Mathematical Theory of Saving" and "A Contribution to the Theory of Taxation." Of the first of these, Keynes wrote that it is "one of the most remarkable contributions to mathematical economics ever made."

But Ramsey's contributions to the subject that taxed

students: "What we can't say, we can't say and we can't whistle it either."

Ramsey was widely regarded as having no equal in his generation for sheer power and quality of mind and in the originality and promise of his work. A man of large, "Johnsonian" build, he was straightforward and blunt in conversation and modest about his exceptional gifts. He died after an operation at the age of 26 on Jan. 19, 1930, survived by his wife and two daughters.

Further Reading

Frank Ramsey is listed in the Philosophy study guide (VII, F). He defended the work of Bertrand RUSSELL and Alfred North WHITEHEAD and was a friend of Ludwig WITTGENSTEIN.

Ramsey's most important essays were published posthumously by R. B. Braithwaite, *The Foundations of Mathematics and Other Logical Essays* (1931), which also contains a eulogy by G. E. Moore and a bibliography of the remaining works. Further background is in John Maynard Keynes, *Essays in Biography* (1933; rev. ed. 1951).

Frank Ramsey. (Macmillan)

the best abstract theorists of the day, the foundations of mathematics, were even more impressive. At the age of 22 he presented a brilliant defense of the mathematical theories of Bertrand Russell and Alfred North Whitehead against Continental critics. Using the *Tractatus* of Ludwig Wittgenstein, which he was among the first to appreciate, Ramsey succeeded in removing some of the most serious objections to the logicist theory. He showed how the ad hoc axiom of reducibility, one of the most vulnerable parts of *Principia Mathematica*, by Russell and Whitehead, could be eliminated, and he offered ways of improving the concept of identity used in that work.

Ramsey also made important contributions to the philosophy of science. In an effort to clarify the role played by theory in science, he introduced the important idea that scientific laws could be regarded as "inference licenses," a theme that was developed further by Gilbert Ryle and S. E. Toulmin. Taking up the work of the American philosopher C. S. Peirce on inductive logic, Ramsey sought to provide sharper criteria for the acceptability of beliefs.

On the question of whether there are important truths inaccessible to language, Ramsey went still further than his friend and colleague Wittgenstein. He gave an answer that was repeated by a generation of Cambridge

RAMUS / By David H. Stam

The French humanist logician and mathematician Petrus Ramus (1515–1572) founded the anti-Aristotelian philosophical school of Ramism.

Petrus Ramus (pronounced rā′məs) was born Pierre de La Ramée in the village of Cuth in Picardy. He worked and studied at the College of Navarre at Paris until he took his master of arts degree in 1536, having defended his thesis that "everything which Aristotle said is invented or contrived" ("quaecumque ab Aristotle dicta essent, commentitia esse"—the exact rendering in English of Ramus's dictum is still disputed, but the common translation of "commentitia" as "false" is now generally rejected). In 1543 he published his criticism of Aristotelian logic, called *Aristotelicae animadversiones*. This and further editions brought on Ramus the ire of his colleagues at the University of Paris, who accused him of heretical tendencies contrary to true religion and philosophy. Modern commentators do not see his departure from Aristotle as being as dramatic as his Parisian contemporaries did—his main differences with Aristotle are now considered to be more in pedagogical method than in logic. His case, however, was first taken before a civil magistrate, then before the Parlement of Paris, and eventually before Francis I, who in March 1544 issued a decree prohibiting Ramus's works and preventing his teaching of philosophy. Ramus left Paris and turned to mathematical studies until the decree was rescinded in 1547 by Henry II.

Ramus was a brilliant lecturer and the prolific author of more than 50 works. His adoption of Protestantism in 1561 rekindled his colleagues' hostility toward him, and he fled from Paris again in 1562. He returned in the next year, when Charles IX was able to conclude a tenuous peace with the Protestants. Ramus reclaimed his chair of philosophy and continued teaching until the religious civil wars resumed in 1567. This began a period of flight from France during which he traveled extensively and lectured at various universities throughout Europe. In August 1570 he returned to France. For 2 more years he lectured and published, but on April 24, 1572, his opponents seized the opportunity of the St. Bartholomew's Day Massacre to murder Ramus.

Ramus was a considerable influence in the humanist development of anti-Aristotelian, antischolastic, antimedieval thinking; he was a major contributor to the "new philosophy" then challenging the assumptions of the Middle Ages. His influence was especially strong (according to their own testimony) among the English and Scottish Ramists (including John Milton and Sir William Temple), in the German universities (Johann Sturm and Johann Friege), and among the Puritans of New England. Nonetheless, the controversies which he aroused in the 16th century now seem merely tendentious.

Further Reading

Petrus Ramus is listed in the Philosophy study guide (III, A) and the Literature study guide (III, E, 1). He influenced Sir Francis BACON and John MILTON.

Petrus Ramus, a print in the Bibliothèque Nationale, Paris. (Photo-Hachette)

A readable biography of Ramus is Frank Pierrepont Graves, *Peter Ramus and the Educational Reformation of the Sixteenth Century* (1912). Indispensable for a thorough study of Ramus are the works of Father Walter J. Ong, *Ramus: Method, and the Decay of Dialogue* (1958) and *Ramus and Talon Inventory* (1958). Wilbur Samuel Howell, *Logic and Rhetoric in England, 1500–1700* (1956), contains helpful chapters on the English Ramists. For Ramus's influence in colonial times see Perry Miller, *The New England Mind: The Seventeenth Century* (1939).

A. P. **RANDOLPH** / By George Meany

The American labor and civil rights leader A. Philip Randolph (born 1889), the most prominent of all Negro trade unionists, was one of the major figures in the struggle for civil rights.

The son of an itinerant minister of the African Methodist Episcopal Church, A. Philip Randolph was born in Crescent City, Fla., on April 15, 1889. He attended Cookman Institute in Jacksonville, Fla., after which he studied at the City College of New York. Following his marriage in 1914 to Lucille E. Green, he helped organize the Shakespearean Society in Harlem and played the roles of Hamlet, Othello, and Romeo, among others. At the age of 21 Randolph joined the Socialist party of Eugene V. Debs. In 1917 he and Chandler Owen founded the *Messenger*, a radical publication now regarded by scholars as among the most brilliantly edited ventures in Negro journalism.

Out of his belief that the Negro can never be politically free until he is economically secure, Randolph became the foremost advocate of the full integration of black workers into the American trade union movement. In 1925 he undertook the leadership of the campaign to organize the Brotherhood of Sleeping Car Porters (BSCP). The uphill battle for certification, marked by fierce resistance from the Pullman Company, was finally won in 1937 and made possible the first contract ever signed by a white employer with a Negro labor leader. Later, Randolph served as president emeritus of the BSCP and a vice president of the American Federation of Labor and Congress of Industrial Organizations.

In the 1940s Randolph developed the strategy of mass protest to win two significant Executive orders. In 1941, with the advent of World War II, he conceived the idea of a massive Negro march on Washington to protest the exclusion of black workers from jobs in the defense industries. He agreed to call off the march only after President Franklin Roosevelt issued Executive Order 8802, which banned discrimination in defense plants and established the nation's first Fair Employment Practice Committee. In 1948 Randolph warned President Harry

A. Philip Randolph, photographed by Gordon Parks. (Library of Congress)

Truman that if segregation in the armed forces was not abolished, masses of Negroes would refuse induction. Soon Executive Order 9981 was issued to comply with his demands.

In 1957 Randolph organized the Prayer Pilgrimage to Washington to support civil rights efforts in the South, and in 1957 and 1958 he organized a Youth March for Integrated Schools. On Aug. 28, 1963, he led the March on Washington for Jobs and Freedom, which brought a quarter million people to the nation's capital. And in 1966, at the White House conference "To Fulfill These Rights," he proposed a 10-year program called a "Freedom Budget" which would eliminate poverty for all Americans regardless of race.

The story of Randolph's career reads like a history of the struggles for unionization and civil rights in this century. He lent his voice to each struggle and enhanced the development of democracy and equality in America.

Further Reading

A. Philip Randolph is listed in the American History study guide (IX, B, 3; IX, D, 3; X, F, 1). Other civil rights leaders were Martin Luther KING, Jr., and Whitney YOUNG, Jr.

There is no full-length study of Randolph. However, his career and life are discussed in numerous books on American Negroes and the labor movement. Among the older studies are Sterling D. Spero and Abram L. Harris, *The Black Worker* (1931); Bruce Minton and John Stuart, *Men Who Lead Labor* (1937); and Edwin R. Embree, *13 against the Odds* (1944). More recent studies are Saun-

ders J. Redding, *The Lonesome Road: The Story of the Negro's Part in America* (1958); Herbert Garfinkel, *When Negroes March* (1959); Arna W. Bontemps, *100 Years of Negro Freedom* (1961); Russell L. Adams, *Great Negroes: Past and Present* (1963; 3d ed. 1969); and Roy Cook, *Leaders of Labor* (1966).

* * *

E. **RANDOLPH** / By Ralph Ketcham

Edmund Randolph (1753–1813), American statesman and lawyer, was an exceedingly influential public figure from 1780 to 1800.

Edmund Randolph's father, of a family long prominent in Virginia, was king's attorney and returned to England before the American Revolution. Edmund, however, graduated from the College of William and Mary, and influenced by his uncle Peyton who was a firm patriot, broke with his father. In August 1775 he joined George Washington's army. When Peyton Randolph (president of the first Continental Congress) died a few months later, Edmund returned to Virginia. He served in the Virginia Convention of 1776, was mayor of Williamsburg, and was attorney general of Virginia before his twenty-fifth birthday. His marriage in 1776 to Eliza-

Edmund Randolph, painting by Flavius J. Fisher after an original portrait. (Courtesy of The New-York Historical Society, New York City)

beth Nicholas, daughter of Robert Nicholas, consolidated his position in Virginia's public life.

In 1781 Randolph began serving as a delegate to the Continental Congress. There and in the Virginia Legislature he worked with James Madison to strengthen the union of the states. At the same time Randolph became one of Virginia's leading attorneys, distinguished for his learning and oratory. He was elected governor of Virginia in 1786.

Randolph's national service resumed in 1786 at the Annapolis Convention, and in 1787 he became a Virginia delegate to the Federal Constitutional Convention. Though not as thorough a nationalist as Washington or Madison, Randolph presented Madison's centralizing Virginia Plan to the Convention. He impressed the Convention with his "most harmonious voice, fine person, and striking manners," as well as with his keen sense of the dangers of tyranny. But his reservations about "energetic government," a concern for the special interests of Virginia, and a kind of indecisiveness caused him to refuse to sign the Constitution. Responding to Madison's tactful persuasion, though, he finally came out for the Constitution and played a key role at Virginia's ratifying convention.

Appointed attorney general of the United States (1789), Randolph soon became Washington's mediator in the bitter quarrels between Alexander Hamilton and Thomas Jefferson. As secretary of state (1794), he sought to maintain friendly relations with both England and France. He approved Jay's Treaty with England as well as the contradictory mission of James Monroe to conciliate republican France. Though he earned Washington's respect and gratitude, Jefferson declared him "a perfect chameleon," while Timothy Pickering aroused Washington's anger by alleging Randolph's subservience to France. Humiliated, Randolph resigned and wrote a *Vindication* of his conduct.

Randolph resumed his large law practice. In 1807 he was senior counsel for Aaron Burr in his treason trial. Randolph's health failed, however, and after writing a valuable manuscript history of the Revolution in Virginia, he died on Sept. 12, 1813.

Further Reading

Edmund Randolph is listed in the American History study guide (III, E, 4). He succeeded Thomas JEFFERSON as secretary of state.

The biography of Randolph by John J. Reardon, in progress, should become the standard work. Samuel F. Bemis, *Jay's Treaty: A Study in Commerce and Diplomacy* (1923; rev. ed. 1962), covers Randolph's career as secretary of state.

*   *   *

J. RANDOLPH / By Margaret L. Coit

John Randolph (1773–1833), half-mad, half-genius American statesman, foreshadowed

John C. Calhoun, who developed Randolph's states'-rights premises into a political philosophy.

Scion of a great Virginia family, John Randolph was born on June 2, 1773, at his grandfather's plantation in Prince George County. Through his stepfather, St. George Tucker, he was indoctrinated with a worldly wisdom beyond his years. Before he was 12 he had read widely in Shakespeare and the Greek and Roman classics. His formal education was at Columbia and Princeton, and he read law in the office of his uncle, Edmund Randolph. As a schoolboy, he witnessed the inauguration of George Washington and early sessions of the first Congress, thus igniting his interest in politics.

At the age of 25, after a "great debate" with Patrick Henry, Randolph entered the U.S. House of Representatives. His genius was soon recognized. As floor leader for his cousin Thomas Jefferson and as chairman of the Ways and Means Committee, he cracked the whip over the House members. But his eccentricities soon caught up with him. He badly muffed the impeachment trial of Judge Samuel Chase (1804), and he disqualified himself as foreman of the Aaron Burr conspiracy trial (1807) because of his long-cherished prejudices against Burr.

Randolph broke openly with Jefferson in 1806 over the attempted Florida purchase, demanding a return to the principles of 1798 and emerging as founder of the first of

John Randolph, a painting by John Wesley Jarvis.
(Courtesy of The New-York Historical Society, New York City)

America's "third" political parties, the Quids. Randolph was defeated for reelection in 1813 because of his opposition to the War of 1812. He served again in the House in 1815–1817, 1819–1825, and 1827–1829, and he also served a single term as U.S. senator from 1825 to 1827. During this time he was often ill and suffered from mental disorder.

Randolph's well-known opposition to the Missouri Compromise of 1820–1821 (though he hated slavery, he disapproved of interference with that institution), his fear of forced emancipation, and his brilliant defense of states' rights stirred the somber intellect of John C. Calhoun. Randolph was a delegate to the Virginia Convention of 1829–1830 and fiercely opposed any constitutional change. For a few months in 1830 he served as minister to Russia. He broke bitterly with Andrew Jackson over the nullification crisis of 1832 and wished that he could have his dying body strapped to his horse, Radical, and ride to the defense of South Carolina. On May 24, 1833, he died in Philadelphia.

Further Reading

John Randolph is listed in the American History study guide (IV, A, 3; IV, C, 2). John C. CALHOUN developed Randolph's defense of states' rights into the philosophy that ultimately led the South to secede from the Union.

The most comprehensive work on Randolph is William Cabell Bruce, *John Randolph of Roanoke* (2 vols., 1922). A good, brief biography is Gerald W. Johnson, *Randolph of Roanoke: A Political Fantastic* (1929), written in a popular style. Russell Kirk, *Randolph of Roanoke: A Study in Conservative Thought* (1951), a conservative view, is concerned primarily with Randolph's political principles. The 1964 edition of Kirk's work, *John Randolph of Roanoke: A Study in American Politics*, adds over 200 pages of letters and speeches by Randolph and an extensive bibliography.

*　　*　　*

RANJIT / By Surjit Singh Dulai

Ranjit Singh (1780–1839) was a ruler of the Punjab. His kingdom was so powerful that friendship with this "Lion of the Punjab" remained for 3 decades the sheet anchor of British policy in western India.

Ranjit Singh (pronounced rän′jĭt sĭn′hə) was heir to the Sukerchakia *misl*, one of the 12 *misls* which had been established by the warlike Sikhs during the 18th century and which ruled the greater part of the Punjab. Ranjit came into his own after the death of his widowed, dominating mother in 1796. Almost immediately he gathered a force of 10,000 to 12,000 horsemen.

At this time the Afghan king, Zaman Shah, was cam-

Ranjit Singh. (Victoria and Albert Museum, London)

paigning in the Punjab. The Afghans occupied but soon lost Lahore, traditionally the capital of a unified Punjab. Apparently acting in Zaman Shah's name but actually for himself, Ranjit captured Lahore in 1799. Soon he subjugated Jammu and Kasur, won the friendship of the strong Ahluwalia *misl*, the important Kanheya *misl* being already linked with him by marriage, and started on a career of expansion which by 1810 made him the supreme ruler of the Punjab north of the Sutlej.

To the south, Ranjit was checked by a treaty of mutual noninterference across the Sutlej with the British; the agreement, however, allowed Ranjit to consolidate his territories in the Punjab and systematically absorb Kashmir and much of the Punjab hills. In spite of fierce opposition from the Afghans, he also occupied areas beyond the Indus extending as far as the boundaries of Afghanistan proper, thus reversing a centuries-old pattern of military conquest in northwestern India.

Ranjit's success was primarily based on a large, loyal, well-drilled, excellently equipped, superbly led, and amazingly mobile standing army. He also pursued a wise civilian policy. He was genuinely motivated by the desire to unify the Sikhs in a Sikh state but one that would give equal participation and benefits to Sikhs and non-Sikhs.

He gave his people a government under which living conditions improved noticeably. His dedication to the cause of good government won over most of the victims of his policy of absorption, and they served him loyally.

In his foreign policy, Ranjit was extremely cautious, never alienating a neighbor unless it involved certain improvement of his own position. Perhaps he practiced this policy to an excess, appeasing the English too long. Aware that war with the English was inevitable, he might have saved his kingdom from dissolving soon after his death had he risked a conflict.

Further Reading

Ranjit Singh is listed in the Asia study guide (II, A, 6, a). A later prominent Punjabi leader was Lala Lajpat RAI.

Narendra Krishna Sinha, *Ranjit Singh* (Calcutta, 2d ed. 1945), and Khushwant Singh, *Ranjit Singh: Maharajah of the Punjab, 1780–1839* (1962), are the standard works on Ranjit. Older studies include William Godolphin Osborne, *The Court and Camp of Runjeet Sing* (1840), written by a contemporary of Ranjit, and Lepel Henry Griffin, *Ranjit Singh and the Sikh Barrier between Our Growing Empire and Central Asia* (1898). Extensive material on Ranjit is in Khushwant Singh, *A History of the Sikhs*, vol. 1 (1963). A succinct profile of Ranjit is in Ramesh Chandra Majumdar and others, *An Advanced History of India* (1946; 3d ed. 1967).

Otto Rank. (Brown Brothers)

RANK / By Robert A. Robinson

The Austrian psychotherapist Otto Rank (1884–1939) taught and practiced a form of psychotherapy based upon his own trauma-of-birth theory and will therapy.

Otto Rank was born in Vienna on April 22, 1884, into a disintegrating lower-middle-class Jewish family. His father is said to have been indifferent to the family and to have drunk. As a child, Otto found solace in the music of Richard Wagner. For intellectual nourishment he read Henrik Ibsen, Arthur Schopenhauer, and Friedrich Nietzsche. Then he discovered the early works of Sigmund Freud. They were a revelation.

When Rank was 21 he met Freud, who persuaded him to attend the gymnasium and the University of Vienna and to study psychoanalysis. Freud read a manuscript which Rank had written; with the help of Freud's criticism, Rank rewrote it. The book, *Der Künstler* (1907; *The Artist*), was well received. He followed it with *Der Mythus der Geburt des Heldens* (1909; *The Myth of the Birth of the Hero*), a work strongly influenced by Freud. In *Das Inzest-Motiv in Dichtung und Sage* (1912; *The Incest Motive in Poetry and Legend*) Rank identified many motifs from myth and poetry with the Oedipus complex.

Rank saw service during World War I. The war trans-

formed him from a shy overdeferential person to "a wiry tough man with a masterful air." He became friends with Sándor Ferenczi, and together they published *Entwicklungsziele der Psychoanalyse* (1924; *The Development of Psychoanalysis*). In *Das Trauma der Geburt* (1924; *The Trauma of Birth*) Rank maintained that all anxiety, hence neurosis, came as a result of the infant's first shock at being separated from the mother. Freud was at first impressed by this new idea of his favorite disciple, but he later cooled considerably. One report states that Freud himself had planted this new idea in the head of Rank in the first place.

In 1924 Rank tore himself away from Freud and went to America. Because Freud represented a father image, Rank suffered fear, conflict, and illness at being separated from him. By 1926 he was recognized by some Americans as a psychoanalytic leader. His therapy (which he called psychotherapy rather than psychoanalysis) consisted mainly in having the patient reexperience the birth trauma, the psychological consequences of the separation of the child from the mother's womb. This trauma had in turn caused "separation anxiety," hence neurosis. Many if not all human activities, from thumb-sucking to lovemaking, were, as interpreted by Rank, substitutions for the original pleasures of existence in the mother's womb.

Between 1924 and 1936 Rank traveled extensively between New York and Paris for teaching and practicing psychotherapy. In 1936 he settled in New York City, where he had some influence among social workers. His influence was especially strong in Philadelphia, where at the Pennsylvania School of Social Work his methods were adopted to a large extent. Rank favored a short analysis which could take weeks or months instead of years.

Later in life Rank came to a realization that knowledge is not fundamentally curative. "It is illusions that cure," he contended, "but first of all the patient must learn to get along at all—to live; and to do this he must have illusions." Psychotherapy, far from removing illusions, should help the patient to sustain them.

Rank died in New York City on Oct. 31, 1939, five weeks after Freud had passed away in London.

Further Reading

Otto Rank is listed in the Social Sciences study guide (VII, F, 2 and 3). In his early years he belonged to the charmed inner circle of Sigmund FREUD that included Ernest JONES, Alfred ADLER, and Carl JUNG.

A study of Rank's life is Jessie Taft, *Otto Rank: A Biographical Study Based on Notebooks, Letters, Collected Writings, Therapeutic Achievements and Personal Associations* (1958). Fay Berger Karpf, *The Psychology and Psychotherapy of Otto Rank* (1953), presents a three-part view of Rank: one section is devoted to his life and role in the psychoanalytic movement, one to the influences on his thought and work, and another to the essentials of his psychotherapy. An exposition of Rank's will therapy is the chapter "Rank's Will Psychology" in Lovell Langstroth, *Structure of the Ego* (1955).

RANKE / By Lothar L. Tresp

> Leopold von Ranke (1795–1886) was a German historian and one of the most prolific and universal modern historians of his time. He imparted his expertise and methodology through the introduction of the seminar as an informal but intensive teaching device.

Leopold von Ranke (pronounced räng′kə) was born on Dec. 21, 1795, in the rural Thuringian town of Wiehe, which then belonged to electoral Saxony. Although Ranke was born into the era of the French Revolution, his bourgeois, small-town, generally well-ordered, and peaceful background and upbringing did not provide much contact with the violent events of the times. After receiving his early education at local schools in Donndorf and Pforta, he attended the University of Leipzig (1814–1818), where he continued his studies in ancient philology and theology.

In the fall of 1818 Ranke accepted a teaching position at the gymnasium (high school) in Frankfurt an der Oder. His teaching assignments in world history and ancient literature, for which he disdained the use of handbooks and readily available prepared texts, as well as the contemporary events of the period, led him to turn to original sources and to a concern for the empirical understanding of history in its totality.

Making use of materials from the Westermannsche Library in Frankfurt and from the Royal Library in Berlin, Ranke produced his first work, *Geschichten der romanischen und germanischen Völker* (1824; *Histories of the Romanic and Germanic Peoples*), which earned him a professorial appointment at the University of Berlin in 1825, where he was to remain for the rest of his life except for extended research trips abroad.

Although this first work was still lacking in style, organization, and mastery of its overflowing detail, it had particular significance because it contained a technical appendix in which Ranke established his program of critical scholarship—"to show what actually happened"—by analyzing the sources used, by determining their originality and likely veracity, and by evaluating in the same light the writings of previous historians "who appear to be the most celebrated" and who have been considered "the foundation of all the later works on the beginning of modern history." His scathing criticism of such historians led him to accept only contemporary documents, such as letters from ambassadors and others immediately involved in the course of historical events, as admissible primary evidence.

With Ranke's move to Berlin, the manuscripts of Venetian ministerial reports of the Reformation period became available to him and served as the basis for his second work, *Fürsten und Völker von Süd-Europa*

Leopold von Ranke, a portrait by Julius Schrader. (Bildarchiv)

(1827; *Princes and Peoples of Southern Europe*), which was republished in his complete works as *Die Osmanen und die spanische Monarchie im 16. und 17. Jahrhundert* (vols. 35 and 36; *The Ottomans and the Spanish Monarchy in the Sixteenth and Seventeenth Centuries*).

Travels and Research

The limited collection in Berlin whetted Ranke's appetite to investigate other European libraries and archives, especially those of Italy. Armed with a travel stipend from the Prussian government, he proceeded at first to Vienna, where a large part of the Venetian archives had been housed after the Austrian occupation of Venetia. A letter of introduction brought acquaintance with Friedrich von Gentz, who, through intercession with Prince Metternich, not only opened the Viennese archives to Ranke but also brought him into immediate contact with the day-to-day politics of the Hapsburg court. During his stay in Vienna he wrote *Die serbische Revolution* (1829), republished in an expanded version as *Serbien und die Türkei im 19. Jahrhundert* (1879; *Serbia and Turkey in the 19th Century*).

In 1828 Ranke traveled to Italy, where he spent 3 successful years of study visiting various public and private libraries and archives, although the Vatican Library remained closed to him. During this period he wrote a treatise, *Venice in the Sixteenth Century* (published 1878), and collected material for what is generally considered his masterpiece, *Die römischen Päpste, ihre Kirche und ihr Staat im 16. und 17. Jahrhundert* (1834–1836; *The Roman Popes, Their Church and State in the 16th and 17th Centuries*).

Returning from Italy in 1831, Ranke soon became involved in the publication of a journal designed to combat French liberal influence, which had alarmed the Prussian government in the aftermath of the revolutionary events of 1830. Although the *Historisch-Politische Zeitschrift*, with Ranke as editor and chief contributor, contained some of the best political thought published in Germany during this time, it lacked the polemical quality and anticipated success of a political fighting journal and was discontinued in 1836. In the same year Ranke was appointed full professor and devoted the rest of his life to the task of teaching and scholarly work. A Protestant counterpart to his *History of the Popes* was published as *Deutsche Geschichte im Zeitalter der Reformation* (1839–1847; *German History during the Era of the Reformation*), which was largely based on the reports of the Imperial Diet in Frankfurt.

Last Works

With the following works Ranke rounded out his historical treatment of the major powers: *Neun Bücher preussischer Geschichte* (1847–1848; *Nine Books of Prussian History*); *Französische Geschichte, vornehmlich im 16. und 17. Jahrhundert* (1852–1861; *French History, Primarily in the 16th and 17th Centuries*); and *Englische Geschichte, vornehmlich im 16. und 17. Jahrhundert* (1859–1868; *English History, Primarily in the 16th and 17th Centuries*). Other works, dealing mainly with German and Prussian history during the 18th century, followed in the 1870s.

During the last years of his life Ranke, now in his 80s and because of failing sight requiring the services of readers and secretaries, embarked upon the composition of his *Weltgeschichte* (1883–1888; *World History*), published in nine volumes. The last two were published posthumously from manuscripts of his lectures. He died in Berlin on May 23, 1886.

The complete work of Ranke is difficult to assess. Not many of his works achieved the artistic high point of *The Roman Popes* or its appeal for the general reader. Yet there is hardly a chapter in his total enormous production which could be considered without value. His harmonious nature shunned emotion and violent passion, and he can be faulted less for what he wrote than for what he left unwritten. His approach to history emphasized the politics of the courts and of great men but neglected the common people and events of everyday life; he limited his investigation to the political history of the states in their universal setting. Ranke combined, as few others, the qualities of the trailblazing scholar and the devoted, conscientious, and innovative teacher.

Further Reading

Leopold von Ranke is listed in the Social Sciences study guide (VI, A, 2). A younger German historian was Theodor MOMMSEN.

Considerable biographical information is in T. H. Von Laue, *Leopold Ranke: The Formative Years* (1950). A comprehensive and fair study which emphasizes an evaluation of Ranke's major works and provides a useful bibliography is G. P. Gooch, *History and Historians in the Nineteenth Century* (1913; rev. ed. 1952); it also discusses Ranke's critics and pupils and provides a chapter on the Prussian school of historical scholarship that paralleled Ranke's career. An assessment critical of Ranke as historian appears in James W. Thompson, *A History of Historical Writing*, vol. 2 (1942). Historian Pieter Geyl discusses Ranke in his *Debates with Historians* (1955; rev. ed. 1958). Carlo Antoni, *From History to Sociology: The Transition in German Historical Thinking* (1940; trans. 1959), and Ferdinand Schevill, *Six Historians* (1956), contain chapters on Ranke. For general background see Georg G. Iggers, *The German Conception of History: The National Tradition of Historical Thought from Herder to the Present* (1968).

*   *   *

RANSOM / By Oscar Cargill

John Crowe Ransom (born 1888), American poet, critic, and agrarian champion, was the center of the "Fugitive" group, of the Southern Agrarians, and of the New Critics.

John Crowe Ransom was born in Pulaski, Tenn., on April 30, 1888. He took his bachelor of arts degree at Vanderbilt University in 1909. He was appointed a Rhodes scholar and was in residence at Christ Church, Oxford, from 1910 to 1913, taking the bachelor of arts degree. From 1914 to 1937 he was a member of the faculty at Vanderbilt, except for the World War I years, when he was a first lieutenant in the U.S. Army. In 1920 he married Robb Reavell; the couple had three children.

As a young instructor at Vanderbilt, Ransom assembled a group of poets, calling themselves "Fugitives"; he created and edited the magazine for their expression, the *Fugitive*. His own poetry eventually appeared in the volumes *Poems about God* (1919), *Chills and Fever* (1924), *Grace after Meat* (1924), *Two Gentlemen in Bonds* (1927), and *Selected Poems* (1945, 1963). Ransom was much influenced by the ballad poetry of the romantic revival, though he totally altered it by irony and wit. His best-known poems are "Bells for John Whiteside's Daughter," "Captain Carpenter," and "The Equilibrists." He won the Bollingen Prize in 1951 and the National Book Award for his poetry in 1964.

With the beginning of the Great Depression, Ransom joined the intellectual group of southerners, centered on Vanderbilt, who felt that the South could escape the ills of the times by rejecting the technology and financial complexities "imposed" by the North and by returning to antebellum agrarianism. Their views found expression in two symposia, *I'll Take My Stand* (1930) and *Who Owns America?* (1936).

In 1937 Ransom became Carnegie professor of poetry at Kenyon College and there founded the *Kenyon Review*, which he edited until his retirement in 1958. He also founded the unit at Kenyon that became the Summer School of Letters at Indiana University. Ransom's leaving Nashville symbolized his achievement of a larger position in American literature. From the 1920s Ransom had mixed in the healthy discussions of criticism going on in the magazines, solidifying his position in *God without Thunder* (1930), *The World's Body* (1938), and *The New Criticism* (1941). He is given credit for applying the term "New Criticism" to the dedicated search for the intrinsic in poetry, although Joel Spingarn had applied it to impressionism in 1910 and although Ransom himself, unlike the other New Critics, did not object to paraphrase in criticism. His best-known essay is "Criticism as Pure Speculation," a lecture given at Princeton in 1940.

Further Reading

John Crowe Ransom is listed in the Literature study guide (I, E, 2, e). Allen TATE was another of the southern "Fugitive" poets.

J. L. Stewart, *John Crowe Ransom* (1962), is the only study of the "whole man." Thomas Daniel Young, ed., *John Crowe Ransom: Critical Essays and a Bibliography* (1968), discusses Ransom as poet and critic. Ransom as poet is treated in Randall Jarrell, *Poetry and the Age*

John Crowe Ransom. (Kenyon College Publicity Department)

(1953). For information about the "Fugitives" see John M. Bradbury, *The Fugitives: A Critical Account* (1958), and Louise Cowan, *The Fugitive Group: A Literary History* (1959).

RAPHAEL / By Francis Ames-Lewis

The Italian painter and architect Raphael (1483–1520) was the supreme representative of Italian High Renaissance classicism.

Raffaello Sanzio, called Raphael (pronounced răf′ē-əl), was born on April 6, 1483, in Urbino. His father, Giovanni Santi, was a painter and doubtless taught Raphael the rudiments of technique. Santi died when his son was 11 years old. Raphael's movements before 1500, when he joined the workshop of Perugino, are obscure, but he evidently fully absorbed the 15th-century classicism of Piero della Francesca's paintings and of the architecture of the Ducal Palace at Urbino and the humanist tradition of the court.

During his 4 years with Perugino, Raphael's eclectic disposition and remarkable ability to assimilate and adapt borrowed ideas within a very personal style were already apparent. Many works of this period, such as the *Mond*

*Raphael, a self-portrait, in the Uffizi, Florence.
(Alinari)*

Crucifixion (1502/1503), are in stylistic detail almost indistinguishable from Perugino's gentle sweetness, but they have an inherent clarity and harmony lacking in Perugino's work. Raphael's last painting before moving to Florence, the *Marriage of the Virgin* (1504), is primarily modeled on Perugino's version of the same subject, but the compositional design is reinterpreted with greater spatial sensitivity, the figures are more accurately built, and the dramatic significance is transmitted without the artificiality of pose and gesture of the prototype.

Florentine Period

When Raphael arrived in Florence late in 1504, it must have been evident to him that his Peruginesque style was dated and provincial compared with the recent innovations of Michelangelo and Leonardo da Vinci. It was to the latter's work that he was temperamentally more attracted, and during the next 3 years he executed a series of Madonnas that adapted and elaborated compositions and ideas of Leonardo's, culminating in *La Belle jardinière* (1507). Here Raphael's own artistic personality was somewhat submerged in his fervent examination of the principles of Leonardesque design, modeling, and expressive depth. Raphael adopted Leonardo's *sfumato* modeling and characteristic pyramidal composition, yet the essential sense of clarity deriving from his 15th-century classical background was not undermined.

It was principally, however, Michelangelo's *Battle of Cascina* rather than Leonardo's companion piece, the *Battle of Anghiari*, that provided the dramatic ideas used by Raphael in his most ambitious Florentine work, the *Entombment* (1507). But perhaps unable yet to understand entirely the imaginative power of Michelangelo's works from which he borrowed, Raphael here failed to combine the figures, expressions, and emotions with the unforced balance and harmony of his later narrative works.

Stanza della Segnatura

Raphael left for Rome in 1508 and seems to have been at work in the Vatican Stanze by early 1509. Pope Julius II's enlightened patronage stimulated the simultaneous creation of the two greatest High Renaissance fresco cycles: Michelangelo's Sistine Chapel ceiling and Raphael's Stanza della Segnatura. Whereas Michelangelo's frescoes are a masterpiece of titanic creative imagination, Raphael's are the epitome of classical grandeur and harmony, disciplined in overall conception, artistic thought, and clarity of individual compositions and figures.

The theme of the Stanza della Segnatura (completed in 1511), eminently suited to Raphael's thoughtful humanism, is divinely inspired human intellect in four spheres: theology, poetry, philosophy, and law. The earliest of the principal scenes to be painted, the *Disputà* (representing Theology), shows Raphael still developing from his Florentine style in the light of the enormous challenge of the stanza: never before had he undertaken a decorative scheme on this scale. It is not until the so-called *School of Athens* (representing Philosophy), the zenith of pure High Renaissance culture, that Raphael reaches complete, independent artistic maturity.

The disposition of each figure in this great fresco is so precisely calculated as, paradoxically, to achieve the impression of absolute freedom. The ingenuity with which the grand, harmonious space is mapped out by the figures, emphasized by the superbly rich Bramantesque architecture behind, is concealed by the overall compositional balance and the monumentally calm atmosphere. The compositional lines and the distant arch focus attention on the two central figures, which set the tone of the painting in their expressive contrast: the idealist Plato points heavenward, while Aristotle, the realist, gestures flatly toward the ground. Around them are grouped many other classical philosophers and scientists, each indicating clearly by expression and gesture the character of his intellect—yet never obtrusively, for detail is throughout subordinated to the total balanced grandeur of effect.

Stanza d'Eliodoro

Divine intervention on behalf of the Church was the theme of the Stanza d'Eliodoro (decorated between 1511 and 1514). This subject gave Raphael greater scope for dynamic composition and movement, and the influence of Michelangelo's Sistine Chapel ceiling, completed in 1512, is noticeable. Compositional unity is achieved in Raphael's *Expulsion of Heliodorus* by the balance of emotional and expressive contrasts. This fresco and the *Liberation of St. Peter*, a brilliant display of the dramatic possibilities of unusual light sources, witness the beginnings in Raphael's work of expansion away from the dignity and purity of the *School of Athens*.

During the progress of the second stanza Julius II died. He was succeeded in 1513 by Leo X, who appears in the *Repulsion of Attila*, the last of the Stanza d'Eliodoro frescoes, executed primarily by Raphael's pupils. At this stage Raphael's assistants began to play an increasingly important role in the production of work to his designs, partly because Leo X's dispatch of Michelangelo to work on a Medici project in Florence left Raphael undisputedly the major artist in Rome.

Late Paintings

Commissions of all sorts poured into Raphael's workshop during the last 6 years of his life. The frescoes in the Stanza dell'Incendio (1514–1517) were based on his design but executed almost entirely by assistants, as was the fresco and stucco decoration of the Vatican loggias (1517–1519).

The monumental cartoons (in the Victoria and Albert Museum, London) depicting the lives of Saints Peter and Paul, the decoration (begun 1519) of the Villa Farnesina in Rome, and Raphael's largest canvas, the *Transfiguration* (commissioned in 1517 but incomplete at his death), all show a new dynamism and expressiveness. The cartoons were sent to Flanders to be worked into tapestries for the Sistine Chapel and were partly responsible for the dissemination of Raphael's late style, with its emphasis on gesture and movement, throughout Europe.

His Portraits

In portraiture Raphael's development follows the same pattern. His earliest portraits closely resemble those of Perugino, whereas in Florence Leonardo's *Mona Lisa* was a basic influence, as can be seen in the portraits of Agnolo and Maddalena Doni (1505). Raphael adapted Leonardo's majestic design as late as 1517 in the portrait

The School of Athens, a fresco painted by Raphael during 1509–1511 in the Stanza della Segnatura of the Vatican Palace. A number of the figures in the painting have been identified as portraits of Raphael's contemporaries. Among these are Leonardo da Vinci (Plato; center, pointing upward), Michelangelo (Heraclitus; foreground, leaning against block of stone), and Donato Bramante (Euclid; right foreground, drawing with compasses). Raphael also included a self-portrait (second figure from right in right foreground). (Alinari-Anderson)

of Baldassare Castiglione, which, like most of his finest portraits, is of a close friend. Castiglione is portrayed with great psychological subtlety, a gentle, scholarly face perfectly suited to the man, who in *The Courtier* defined the qualities of the ideal gentleman. Descriptions of Raphael's urbane good humor and courteous behavior in fact recall the very qualities that Castiglione wished to find in his perfect courtier.

His Architecture

So Bramantesque is the architecture of the *School of Athens* that it seems probable that Raphael was working with Donato Bramante as early as 1509, perhaps in preparation for his succession to the post of *capomastro* of the rebuilding of St. Peter's after Bramante's death in 1514. During the next 6 years, however, progress on St. Peter's was very slow, and his only contribution seems to have been the projected addition of a nave to Bramante's centrally planned design.

As early as the *Marriage of the Virgin* (1504), Raphael's painted architecture shows the pure classical spirit epitomized in Bramante's Tempietto at S. Pietro in Montorio, Rome (1502). This same unadorned structural clarity characterizes Raphael's first architectural work, the chapellike S. Eligio degli Orefici, Rome, designed in collaboration with Bramante (1509). The Chigi Chapel in S. Maria del Popolo, Rome (ca. 1512–1513), however, shows a much more ornate decorative idiom, although structurally it is almost identical with S. Eligio. A similar development in richness of texture and detailing can be seen between Raphael's two Roman palaces. The Palazzo Vidoni-Caffarelli is directly dependent on Bramante's so-called House of Raphael, but the richly ornamented facade decoration of the Palazzo Branconio dell'Aquila (ca. 1520; destroyed) is essentially unstructural. As in Raphael's last paintings, the tendency in these late architectural projects is toward a form of mannerism and away from the serene classicism of Bramante.

At the time of his death in Rome on Good Friday, 1520, at the age of 37, Raphael's art was developing in new directions, paralleled in his own very different way by Michelangelo in his Medici Chapel sculptures. The zenith of classical harmony and grandeur, reached about 1510, had passed, and it was left to Raphael's pupils to interpret and exploit the trends toward mannerism in the last works of their great master.

Further Reading

Raphael is listed in the Art study guide (III, D, 1, a). He, LEONARDO DA VINCI, and MICHELANGELO were the creators of High Renaissance painting. In architecture Raphael was the heir and developer of the classical style of Donato BRAMANTE. Raphael's early painting was influenced by PERUGINO and PIERO DELLA FRANCESCA. Raphael's architecture influenced Andrea PALLADIO; and the painters CORREGGIO, Annibale CARRACCI, Guido RENI, and Nicolas POUSSIN took freely from Raphael.

Studies of Raphael in English are limited. An important monograph in English is Oskar Fischel, *Raphael* (1948). John Pope-Hennessy, *Raphael* (1970), an excellent intro-

duction to Raphael's art, concentrates on his working methods and reproduces many drawings and large details. See also Ettore Camesasca, *All the Paintings of Raphael* (1963). A fine specialized study is John Shearman, *Raphael's Cartoons in the Royal Collection and the Tapestries for the Sistine Chapel* (1972). Sydney Freedberg, *Painting of the High Renaissance in Rome and Florence* (1961), is a very useful survey of the period in general.

✳   ✳   ✳

RAPP / By Louis Filler

The German-American George Rapp (1757–1847) was the founder of the "Harmonist" sect and community, the most successful utopian association in America in the 19th century, and an inspiration for comparable ventures.

Born Johann Georg Rapp in Iptingen, Württemberg, Germany, on Nov. 1, 1757, Rapp followed his well-to-do father into farming. Rapp read earnestly in religious lore, the Swedish mystic Emanuel Swe-

George Rapp. (Collection of Don Blain, New Harmony, Ind.)

denborg, among others, affecting his study of the Bible. Rapp's simple eloquence and fundamentalist views attracted followers, and by 1787 he was preaching. In a few years he counted some 300 families committed to attaining heavenly conditions on earth. Subjected to persecution by Lutheran clerics and magistrates, they looked abroad for friendlier surroundings.

In 1803 Rapp went to America and purchased 5,000 acres of unimproved land near Pittsburgh, Pa., and with additional followers prepared the site of "Harmony." By February 1805 they had organized the Harmony Society, with Rapp as leader. With a common fund, a simple and uniform style of dress and routine, and a mild approach to community offenders, the hardworking Rappites built a prosperous community.

Two years later the Rappites chose celibacy, a product of biblical interpretation. However, they enjoyed family life, food and wine (though no tobacco), art, singing, and other amenities. They did not separate men from women and emphasized cooperation rather than compulsion in most matters.

In 1814 the Rappites concluded that lack of water routes, limited space, and other conditions made moving necessary. They purchased some 38,000 acres in a southwest corner of Indiana on the Wabash River. Once again they prospered under their able leader and his adopted son Friedrich, sending wine, woolen goods, and other products as far as New Orleans.

Nevertheless, within several years they tired of the uncivilized area and early in 1825 sold their holdings to the British communitarian Robert Owen. They returned to Pennsylvania to build "Economy" on 3,000 acres on the Ohio River below Pittsburgh. Their fame as farmers and manufacturers, as well as their exemplary community life, brought distinguished visitors to view their homes and mills. Although celibacy precluded an indefinite career for the Harmonists, the group persisted even beyond its founder's death and counted 250 members as late as 1890. Rapp remained in full control of his faculties until his death on Aug. 7, 1847. In accordance with Harmonist traditions he was buried in an unmarked grave.

Further Reading

George Rapp is listed in the Religion study guide (I, Q, 1, f). Robert OWEN, a contemporary utopian, bought Rapp's midwestern holdings to build his own colony, New Harmony.

Studies of Rapp tend to be written as appendages to studies of Robert Owen and New Harmony, although Rapp's colonies were successful and Owen's were not. An exception is William E. Wilson, *The Angel and the Serpent: The Story of New Harmony* (1964). John S. Duss, *The Harmonists: A Personal History* (1943), best retains the flavor of the Rappite outlook. The treatment of Rapp in John Humphrey Noyes, *History of American Socialisms* (1870), is particularly interesting since Noyes's Oneida Community differed drastically from Rapp's colonies.

* * *

RASHI / By Malachi B. Martin

The Jewish scholar and commentator Rashi (1040–1105) wrote the greatest commentaries in Jewish exegeses on the Old Testament and the Talmud. His commentaries are still important in Jewish life.

Rashi (pronounced ră′shē) was born Shelomoh Yitzhaki in Troyes, France. The name he is known by is an abbreviation of Rabbi Solomon bar Isaac. Rashi's father died when the boy was young, and his family's circumstances did not allow him to pursue his ambition of spending his life studying at Talmudic schools in Germany. After studies at Mainz and Worms, he returned to Troyes in 1065, when he was 25 years old. Forced by economic circumstances to manage his father's vineyards, Rashi limited his scholarly activities to reading and writing. In the next years he created his famous commentaries on the Old Testament (except for a few books) and on the Talmud. These exegeses were received and read with great attention, and Rashi's reputation was established by them.

After 1096 Rashi's commentaries became even more popular because during the zeal that surrounded the First Crusade rabbinic centers of learning in the Rhineland were destroyed, their teachers killed, and their students dispersed. Students gradually were attracted to Troyes, and Rashi then opened his own academy. It rapidly became one of the most important and celebrated rabbinic centers in Europe; simultaneously it became a rallying point for Ashkenazic Jewry and a center of Jewish scholarship.

Rashi then entered the high period of his achievement. He altered several rabbinic traditions of learning; he induced his students to commit many oral traditions to writing; he developed a personal style of exegesis; and he fostered many Jewish scholars who later spread across Europe. Rashi had no sons, but his three daughters married outstanding scholars. His students of special note included two sons-in-law, Rabbi Judah ben Nathan, commentator of the Talmud, and Rabbi Meir ben Semuel; his grandson Rabbi Semuel ben Meir, known as Rasbam, also a commentator; Rabbi Shemaiah, compiler of the *Sefer ha-Pardes* (The Book of Paradise); and Rabbi Simcha, compiler of the *Mahzor Vitry*.

Rashi's commentaries and tractates spread throughout Europe and the Near East after his death at Troyes on July 13, 1105. His commentary on the Talmud has been in universal use among Talmudic students and scholars since then. The text of the Talmud is usually printed side by side with Rashi's commentary and with the tosaphist additions dating from the two subsequent centuries. Rashi's commentary on the Pentateuch (printed 1475) has enjoyed a similar popularity. It has been the subject of numerous commentaries by both Jewish and Christian scholars. Nicholas of Lyra, whose work was one of Martin Luther's main sources in composing his Bible translation, used Rashi's commentary extensively. Rashi's school at

Troyes produced custumals (collections and digests of customs and habits) and rabbinic tractates that maintained a wide influence among Jews of later generations.

Because of the wide range of Rashi's commentaries and the unique and personal character of his exegeses, he more than any other Jewish scholar has molded modern rabbinic commentary and interpretation of the Bible. He ranks as high as any ancient scholar as theologian, Bible commentator, and Talmudist.

Further Reading

Rashi is listed in the Religion study guide (II, D, 4). Isaac ABRAVANEL and NAHMANIDES also wrote commentaries on the Bible.

An older study of Rashi is Maurice Liber, *Rashi* (trans. 1906). More recent studies include Samuel M. Blumenfield, *Master of Troyes: A Study of Rashi, the Educator* (1946), and Herman Halperin, *Rashi and the Christian Scholars* (1963). Harold Louis Ginsberg, ed., *Rashi Anniversary Volume* (1941), contains biographical material and commentary on Rashi. See also Meyer Waxman, *A History of Jewish Literature*, vol. 1 (1930; rev. ed. 1943).

RASMUSSEN / By Emanuel D. Rudolph

The Danish Arctic explorer and ethnologist Knud Johan Victor Rasmussen (1879–1933) was an authority on the folklore and history of the Greenland Eskimos.

Knud Rasmussen. (Radio Times Hulton Picture Library)

Knud Rasmussen (pronounced räs′mŏŏs-ən) was born on June 7, 1879, in Jakobshavn on Disko Bay in southwestern Greenland. His father, Christian Rasmussen, was a Danish missionary who had been in Greenland 28 years and who had married a part-Eskimo girl. Knud learned both Danish and Eskimo ways and languages. He was sent to school in Copenhagen as a young man and hoped to become a writer.

In 1900 Rasmussen went as a correspondent for the *Christian Daily* on a trip to Iceland led by Ludwig Mylius-Erichsen and a year later took a trip to Swedish Lapland to gather material for literary works. He took part in Mylius-Erichsen's sledge journey to the Yap York district of west Greenland (1902–1904). Rasmussen became interested in the ethnology of the northern non-Christian Eskimos. His first book about the Eskimos was written in 1905. A book about Lapland, *People of the Polar North*, appeared in 1908, the year he married Dagmar Anderson.

Rasmussen established a trading station at North Star Bay in 1910 among the northern Greenland Eskimos, also called Polar Eskimos or Arctic Highlanders, and named it Thule, the classical word for the northernmost inhabited land. In 1912, with Peter Freuchen and two Eskimos, Rasmussen crossed the inland ice of Greenland from the Clements Markham Glacier at the mouth of Inglefield Gulf on the west coast to Denmark Fjord on the east coast in what he called the first Thule expedition.

There were seven Thule expeditions in all. Rasmussen's narrative of the fourth expedition is *Greenland by the Polar Sea* (1921). His books about the Eskimos include *Eskimo Folk Tales* (1921) and *The Eagle's Gift* (1932).

The most ambitious of the Thule expeditions was the fifth (1921–1924). It visited all of the existing northern Eskimo tribes. Several scientists accompanied the early part of the expedition to Greenland, Baffin Island, and vicinity, mapping, gathering ethnographic data, and taking movies. Rasmussen traveled across northern Canada and Alaska visiting Eskimo tribes; he always traveled and hunted as the Eskimos did. His narrative of this expedition is *Across Arctic America* (1927). On the seventh Thule expedition (1932–1933) he got food poisoning, contracted influenza and pneumonia, and died on Dec. 22, 1933, upon his return to Copenhagen.

Rasmussen was an outstanding leader. He had a unique ability for understanding the Eskimo mentality and being able to explain it to non-Eskimos. He did his ethnological studies at a critical time when it was still possible to record primitive Eskimo folklore and history. His mapping of parts of Greenland and crossing of its ice cap were valuable scientific contributions.

Further Reading

Knud Rasmussen is listed in the Geography and Exploration study guide (VII, A, 1). Other polar explorers were Robert PEARY, Sir John FRANKLIN, Roald AMUNDSEN, and Otto NORDENSKOLD.

The only biography of Rasmussen in English is Peter Freuchen, *I Sailed with Rasmussen* (1958), which treats only his early years. For general background information consult L. P. Kirwan, *A History of Polar Exploration* (1960), and Paul-Émile Victor, *Man and the Conquest of the Poles* (1962; trans. 1963).

✻   ✻   ✻

RASPUTIN / By Lester Eckman

The Russian monk Grigori Efimovich Rasputin (1872–1916) gained considerable influence in the court of Czar Nicholas II.

Grigori Rasputin (pronounced răs-py o͞o′tĭn) was born in the Siberian village of Pokrovskoe. His conduct in the village became so infamous that Bishop Anthony of Tobolsk commissioned the village priest to investigate it, with the result that the case was handed over to the civil authorities. In the meantime Rasputin disappeared into the wilderness of Russia. He wandered over all Russia, made two pilgrimages to Jerusalem, and roamed both in the Balkans and in Mesopotamia.

On Dec. 29, 1903, Rasputin appeared at the religious Academy of St. Petersburg. According to Illiodor, a student for the monkhood, Rasputin was a man who had been a great sinner but was now a great penitent who drew extraordinary power from his experiences. As such, Rasputin was welcomed by Theophan, inspector of the academy and, for a time, confessor to the Empress. Another of his early supporters was the vigorous bishop of Saratov, Hermogen. He soon had more powerful backing by one of the principal adepts of fashionable mysticism in St. Petersburg, the Grand Duchess Militsa. In St. Petersburg, Rasputin became a social favorite.

Rasputin was highly recommended to the royal family by Militsa and her sister Anastasia. It was the illness of the Czar's son, Alexis, that brought Rasputin to the palace. The date of Rasputin's entry into the palace is fixed by a note in the Czar's diary. He wrote on Nov. 14, 1905, "We have got to know a man of God—Grigori—from the Tobolsk Province."

Rasputin was able to stop Alexis' bleeding. Mosolov, an eyewitness to Rasputin's healing power, speaks of his "incontestable success in healing." Alexis' last nurse, Teglova, writes, "Call it what you will, he could really promise her [the Empress] her boy's life while he lived." Nicholas II was by no means always under Rasputin's influence. Dedyulin, at one time commandant of the palace, expressed to Nicholas his vehement dislike for Rasputin; the Czar answered him: "He is first a good, religious, simple-minded Russian. When in trouble or assailed by doubts I like to have a talk with him, and invariably feel at peace with myself afterwards." Rasputin had greater influence on Empress Alexandra. He was a holy man for her, "almost a Christ."

At his first meeting with Nicholas II and Alexandra, Rasputin addressed them as if they were fellow peasants, and his relationship to them was as if he had the voice of God. In addition, Rasputin represented for the Czar the voice of the Russian peasantry. He informed him about "the tears of the life of the Russian people." Rasputin abhorred Russian nobility and declared that class to be of another race, not Russian.

Rasputin had experienced success in several of the big salons and took a peasant's delight in enjoying this world of luxury and extravagance. He made a point of humiliating the high and mighty of both sexes. There is not an iota of truth in the easy explanation that was so often given that Rasputin became the tool of others. He was far too clever to sell himself to anyone. Rasputin was showered with presents without his asking. On many occasions he took from the rich and gave to the poor.

Rasputin had already become a concern to the chief ministers. When Stolypin's children were injured by the attempt on his life in 1906, Nicholas II offered him the services of Rasputin as a healer. At his interview with Stolypin, Rasputin tried to hypnotize this sensible man. Stolypin made a report on Rasputin to the Emperor. In

Grigori Rasputin. (Bildarchiv)

1911 Stolypin ordered Rasputin out of St. Petersburg, and the order was obeyed. Stolypin's minister of religion, Lukyanov, on the reports of the police, ordered an investigation that produced abundant evidence of Rasputin's scandalous deeds. From this time on, the Empress detested Prime Minister Stolypin. After Stolypin was assassinated, the Empress brought Rasputin back to St. Petersburg.

Beletsky, the director of the police department, reckons that "from 1913 Rasputin was firmly established." Kokovtsev states that Rasputin had no political influence before 1908 but that he was now "the central question of the nearest future." Rasputin was constantly saying to the Emperor, "Why don't you act as a Czar should?" Only the autocracy could serve as cover for him; and he himself said, "I can only work with sovereigns." The strong movement for Church reform and the call for the summons of a Church council, which had accompanied the liberal movement of 1907–1910, had been opposed by Rasputin with the words "there is an anointed Czar," a phrase which constantly recurred in the Empress's letters. Rasputin was assassinated by a group of Russian noblemen on Dec. 31, 1916, in an endeavor to rid the court and the country of his influence.

Further Reading

Grigori Rasputin is listed in the European History study guide (IX, M, 1) and the Religion study guide (I, R, 1). He was a notorious figure in the court of NICHOLAS II.

A full study of Rasputin is by René Fülöp-Miller, *Rasputin: The Holy Devil*, translated by F. S. Flint and D. F. Tait (1928). An engaging if sensational and unreliable account is by Colin Wilson, *Rasputin and the Fall of the Romanovs* (1964). Rasputin is discussed in a useful background work by Bernard Pares, *The Fall of the Russian Monarchy* (1939).

RATHENAU / By Diethelm Prowe

The German industrialist and statesman Walther Rathenau (1867–1922) pioneered the public management of raw materials in his country during World War I. As postwar foreign minister, he inaugurated a new policy of reconciliation with Germany's former enemies.

Walther Rathenau (pronounced rä′tə-nou), born in Berlin on Sept. 29, 1867, was the son of the famed German-Jewish entrepreneur Emil Rathenau (1838–1915), founder (1883) and president of AEG, the mammoth German General Electric Company. Trained as an electrochemist, he earned a doctorate in 1889. He served an apprenticeship as a researcher and manager from 1890 to 1900 before joining his father's company initially as a director, then in 1915 becoming successor to the older Rathenau as AEG president.

Walther Rathenau. (German Information Center, New York)

Vigorous and innovative as an entrepreneur associated with almost a hundred businesses, Rathenau wrote over a dozen books and many articles on philosophy, politics, and economics, in which the mechanization and suppression of modern man are overriding preoccupations. He saw the tyranny of technology and capital as fundamentally an irrational, chaotic one which he hoped would be replaced by an economy organized for the common social good without excessive politico-economic centralization (for which he believed inheritance in particular responsible) and the suppression of the working poor.

Concerned with Germany's insufficient economic preparation, Rathenau offered his services to the government at the outset of World War I and from September 1914 to March 1915 organized the German War Raw Materials Department, which was to become a crucial part of the German war effort. At the same time his inclinations and his intimate knowledge of Germany's potential made him a persistent advocate of an early, negotiated peace and a severe critic of the dominant military caste.

After the war Rathenau was brought into the government by Finance Minister Joseph Wirth in March 1920 as a member of the Socialization Committee and subsequently attended the Spa Conference on Disarmament as a technical assistant (July 1920). When Wirth became chancellor in May 1921, he appointed Rathenau to the Ministry of Reconstruction. Here Rathenau organized an extensive program of rationalization for German industry and launched his new "foreign policy of fulfillment," that is, reconciliation with the victorious powers by negotiating on the basis of the established peace treaty (Wiesbaden, October 1921; Cannes, January 1922). He became foreign minister in January 1922. The most memorable event of his brief tenure of office was a pact of peace with the Soviets, the Treaty of Rapallo, signed unexpectedly under the strain of failing reparations talks at the Genoa Conference in April 1922. The hope for international reconciliation was shattered, however, by the virulent attacks of a chauvinistic, anti-Semitic, and antirepublican right, which climaxed in the assassination of Rathenau by two young nationalists in Berlin on June 24, 1922.

Further Reading

Walther Rathenau is listed in the European History study guide (X, A, 2; XI, D, 1, a). Matthias ERZBERGER was another leading German statesman of this period.

Of Rathenau's own numerous writings, *In Days to Come* was translated by Eden and Cedar Paul (1921) and *The New Society* by Arthur Windham (1921). Several important volumes of personal writings remain untranslated. The best biographical studies of Rathenau in English are Count Harry Kessler, *Walther Rathenau: His Life and Work*, translated by W. D. Robson-Scott (1928) and by Lawrence Hyde (1930), a sensitive portrayal by a close friend; and the chapter on Rathenau in James Joll, *Three Intellectuals in Politics* (1961). An authoritative specialized study is David Felix, *Walther Rathenau and the Weimar Republic: The Politics of Reparations* (1971).

RATZEL / By T. W. Freeman

The German geographer Friedrich Ratzel (1844–1904) was the author of several books on ethnology and human and political geography in which he described his observations during extensive travels in Europe and the Americas.

The father of Friedrich Ratzel (pronounced rät′səl) was the manager of the household staff of the Grand Duke of Baden, and Friedrich was born on Aug. 30, 1844, at Karlsruhe. He went to a high school in Karlsruhe for 6 years before he was apprenticed to an apothecary in 1859. Ratzel stayed with him until 1863, when he went to Rappeswyl on the Lake of Zurich, Switzerland, where he began to study the classics. After a further year as an apothecary at Mörs near Krefeld in the Ruhr area (1865–1866), he spent a short time at the high school in Karlsruhe and became a student of zoology at the universities of Heidelberg, Jena, and Berlin. In 1868 Ratzel presented a thesis on the characteristics of worms and, a year later, a book on the work of Charles Darwin, whose *Origin of Species* had appeared in 1859. But Ratzel's work was overshadowed by Ernst Haeckel's.

Journalist and Geographer

Partly by good fortune Ratzel had the opportunity of traveling with a French naturalist, and he wrote up his experiences for a Cologne newspaper. Ratzel's travel and journalism were interrupted by a short but distinguished army career in the Franco-Prussian War of 1870–1871. In 1871 he went through the Hungarian plains, where he was fascinated by the signs of recent agricultural settlement, and the Carpathians, where he found German-speaking communities. In 1874 he went to North and Central America, where he once again saw successful German settlers. In 1876 he published a thesis on Chinese emigration, partly from his own experience in America, and in 1878 and 1880 he published two large books on North America.

In 1875 Ratzel joined the staff of the Technical High School in Munich, and in 1886 he moved to the University of Leipzig. Always an avid journalist, he also published several large books during these years, including *Völkerkunde* (2 vols., 1885–1888; Ethnology), *Anthropogeographie* (2 vols., 1882–1891; Human Geography), *Politische Geographie* (1897; *Political Geography*), and *Die Erde und das Leben* (2 vols., 1901–1902; Earth and Life).

Some of Ratzel's work was of uneven quality, for example, in the world survey of ethnology, but much of it was based on acute observation in his wide travels. He was anxious to interpret the observed movements of plant and animal life—and of people—to settle and establish themselves in a new environment, and he saw in biogeography the essential link between scientific and human phenomena. Immensely industrious throughout his life, he died of a stroke on Aug. 9, 1904, while on holiday with his wife and daughters in Ammerland, Bavaria.

Friedrich Ratzel. (Österreichische Nationalbibliothek, Vienna)

Further Reading

Friedrich Ratzel is listed in the Geography and Exploration study guide (VI, B). Earlier German geographers were Karl RITTER and Alexander von HUMBOLDT.

A terse biography of Ratzel is Harriet Wanklyn, *Friedrich Ratzel: A Biographical Memoir and Bibliography* (1961). Background is in Robert H. Lowie, *The History of Ethnological Theory* (1937), and Marvin Harris, *The Rise of Anthropological Theory* (1968).

RAUSCHENBERG / By Robert Reiff

The American painter and printmaker Robert Rauschenberg (born 1925) experimented freely with avant-garde concepts and techniques. His wild inventiveness and frank eclecticism were tempered by his almost unerring sense of color and design.

Monogram, a "combine" by Rauschenberg, constructed in 1959. (Leo Castelli Gallery, New York, Collection: Moderna Museet)

R obert Rauschenberg was born in Port Arthur, Tex., of German and Cherokee lineage. He attended the local public schools before becoming a naval corpsman. He began his formal art education at the Kansas City Art Institute in 1946. The following year he went to Paris to study at the Académie Julian.

In 1948 Rauschenberg returned to America to study with Josef Albers at Black Mountain College in North Carolina. Albers stressed design as a discipline, and Rauschenberg felt he needed such training. He later admitted that Albers was the teacher most important to his development. About 1950 Rauschenberg began to paint his all-white, then all-black, paintings. From these ascetic exercises in total minimalism he turned to making giant, richly textured and colored collage-assemblages, which he called "combines."

In 1952 Rauschenberg traveled in Italy and North Africa. The following year he was living in New York City and developing his concept of the combine. His best-known and most audacious combines are the *Bed* (1955), an upright bed, complete with a patchwork quilt and pillow, that has been spattered with paint; and the amazing *Monogram* (1959), a collagelike painting-platform resting flat on the floor, in the center of which stands a stuffed, horned ram with a rubber tire around its middle. About his art Rauschenberg explained: "Painting relates to both art and life. I try to act in the gap between the two." In the 1950s he participated in "happenings," an improvisational type of theater.

In 1958 Rauschenberg had an exhibition in New York City that catapulted him to prominence, and his paintings soon entered the collections of every large museum in America and abroad. Not satisfied with cultivating his career as a painter, in 1963 he toured with the Merce Cunningham Dance Theater as an active participant. In 1964 Rauschenberg received first prize at the Venice Biennale. In the late 1960s he concentrated on developing series of silk-screen prints and lithographs. *Current* (1970), a set of giant silk-screen prints, was politically inspired.

Robert Rauschenberg. (Leo Castelli Gallery, New York)

Further Reading

Robert Rauschenberg is listed in the Art study guide

(IV, G, 1). Jasper JOHNS also explored new subjects involving the everyday American image.

The most extensive monograph on Rauschenberg is Andrew Forge, *Rauschenberg* (1969), which offers a comprehensive collection of illustrations, 47 of them in color, biographical material, and a brief autobiography. An essay on Rauschenberg and background material are in Calvin Tomkins, *The Bride and the Bachelors: The Heretical Courtship in Modern Art* (1965).

RAUSCHENBUSCH

/ By Robert Moats Miller

The American clergyman Walter Rauschenbusch (1861–1918) broke the complacency and conservatism of late-19th-century American Protestantism, propounding a Social Gospel capable of responding to the challenges of an industrial, urban era.

Walter Rauschenbusch was born on Oct. 4, 1861, in Rochester, N.Y., the son of a German missionary, and reared in a pietistic environment. Years of study in his youth in Germany provided him with scholarly intellectual equipment and introduced him to the then revolutionary ideas shattering traditional dogmas. On graduation from the Rochester Theological Seminary in 1886, he was ordained to the Baptist ministry.

Rauschenbusch's first pastorate was on the edge of New York City's infamous Hell's Kitchen area, and daily observance of the terrible poverty of his block led him to question both laissez-faire capitalism and the relevance of the old pietistic evangelism with its simple gospel. As he observed during the depression of 1893, "One could hear human virtue cracking and crumbling all around." In these New York years he edited a short-lived labor paper; founded the Brotherhood of the Kingdom, a band of prophetic ministers; and formulated a theology of Christian socialism. In 1897 he left parish work for a professorship at Rochester Seminary, partly because deafness was reducing his ministerial effectiveness.

A series of books now came from Rauschenbusch's pen, most notably *Christianity and the Social Crisis*, *Christianizing the Social Order*, *A Theology for the Social Gospel*, and *Prayers of the Social Awakening*. These volumes, widely translated, reached hundreds of thousands. Penetrating in his critique of society, solidly grounded in theology, he towered above all the other prophets of the Social Gospel in the Progressive era.

Rauschenbusch believed that men rarely sinned against God alone and that the Church must place under judgment institutional evils as well as individual immorality. He held that men are damned by inhuman social conditions and that the Church must end exploitation, poverty, greed, racial pride, and war. The Church must not betray, as it had done since Constantine, its true mission of redeeming nations as well as men. But he was no utopian. He recognized the demonic in man, understood the power of entrenched interest groups, and predicted no easy or early establishment of God's reign of love. Therefore his theology, unlike that of so many bland modernists of the Progressive era, continues to speak for contemporary tragic conditions. Rauschenbusch died on July 25, 1918, deeply saddened by World War I, by the failure of pacifism to check the holocaust, and by the hatred poured out on all things German.

Further Reading

Walter Rauschenbusch is listed in the Religion study guide (I, Q, 1, j). Men as diverse as Reinhold NIEBUHR, Harry Emerson FOSDICK, Norman THOMAS, and Martin Luther KING, Jr., acknowledged him as their inspiration.

Dores Robinson Sharpe, *Walter Rauschenbusch* (1942), is a satisfactory but not definitive biography. Vernon Parker Bodein, *The Social Gospel of Walter Rauschenbusch and Its Relation to Religious Education* (1944), covers its limited subject well. Three fine studies of the Social Gospel are Charles H. Hopkins, *The Rise of*

Walter Rauschenbusch. (Colgate Rochester-Bexley Hall-Crozer Development Office)

the Social Gospel in American Protestantism, 1865–1915 (1940); Henry F. May, *Protestant Churches and Industrial America* (1949); and Robert T. Handy, ed., *The Social Gospel in America, 1870–1920* (1966).

RAVEL / By Laurence D. Berman

The French composer Maurice Joseph Ravel (1875–1937) wrote works in an impressionistic idiom that are characterized by elegance and technical perfection.

Maurice Ravel (pronounced ra̍-vĕl′) was born on March 7, 1875, at Ciboure, Basses-Pyrénées. From his Swiss father, a gifted engineer and inventor of a petroleum engine and combustion machine, he seems to have inherited that feeling for precision which dominates his scores and which once prompted Igor Stravinsky to characterize them (not unsympathetically) as the products of a "Swiss watchmaker." From his Basque mother Ravel learned to love the Basque and Spanish cultures. In later life there would be the summers spent in Saint-Jean-de-Luz (twin city of Ciboure). There would also be, spanning his entire creative life, works on Spanish themes: *Habañera* (1895) for piano, later orchestrated and incorporated in the *Rapsodie espagnole* (1907); *Pavane pour une infante défunte* (1899); *Alborada del gracioso* (1905); the opera *L'Heure espagnole* (1907); and *Boléro* (1928), virtually synonymous with the composer's name.

Although Ravel was continually attracted to cultures outside his immediate sphere of acquaintance as sources of musical inspiration—Greece (*Mélodies populaires grecques*, 1907), the Near East (*Schéhérazade*, 1903), Palestine (*Mélodies hébraïques*, 1914), Vienna (*Valses nobles et sentimentales*, 1911; *La Valse*, 1920), and Africa (*Chansons madécasses*, 1925)—the imprint of

Spain in his work has special significance. The Spanish elements in his music, although they did not alter his natural style, are an inseparable part of it.

Ravel grew up in Paris, where his family moved 3 months after his birth. It was natural for a boy of his talents to enter the conservatory at age 14, less natural to emerge at age 30. That Ravel, already the author of *Jeux d'eau* (1901) and the String Quartet (1903), chose to remain in Gabriel Fauré's composition class is testimony to a certain humility. But there were political reasons as well: his enrollment at the conservatory qualified him for the coveted Prix de Rome. Ironically, the prize was never to be his. After three unsuccessful attempts (1901–1903) he was denied the right to compete in 1905.

In the next few years Ravel wrote many of the works for which he is best remembered: *Ma mère l'oye* (1908), *Gaspard de la nuit* (1908), *Daphnis et Chloë* (1912), and the Piano Trio (1914). During World War I he served as an ambulance driver at the front. The war, coupled with the loss of his mother in 1917, left him physically and spiritually debilitated.

In 1921, sensing the need for further isolation in the interests of his work, Ravel moved to the village of Montfort l'Amaury. At this point his music changed radically. Unlike Claude Debussy, for whom understatement was a natural language capable of expressing the most elemental thoughts, Ravel had been an impressionist in sound only, not in spirit. The seductive sonorities of impressionism were now abandoned for a sparer texture, of which the Duo for Violin and Cello (1922) and the Sonata for Violin and Piano (1927) are the most austere examples. In spite of their less appealing surface, these pieces continued to enhance Ravel's reputation in France and abroad. His American tour of 1928 was a triumph, and that year Oxford awarded him an honorary doctorate.

In 1932 Ravel suffered a concussion in an automobile collision. After the accident he never finished another piece. The first symptoms of brain damage manifested themselves in his handwriting and then in his speech; the intelligence, unimpaired, continued to produce beautiful ideas, but the concentration necessary to put

Maurice Ravel about 1914.
(Library of Congress)

them together could not be sustained. In 1937 he consented to a brain operation; it was not successful, and he died on December 28.

An Evaluation

The case of Ravel remains something of an enigma. His position as a composer of the first rank is unquestioned, yet his achievement, viewed historically, had little consequence. His formal procedures, however masterfully they were realized, were not very innovative.

From the esthetic standpoint, Ravel's work poses a number of paradoxes. In 1912 he stated, "My aim is technical perfection . . . in my view, the artist should have no other goal." But in other places he spoke of the dependence of invention on instinct and sensibility and stressed the importance of emotionality over intellectuality in the creative process. In 1928 he wrote, "A composer . . . should create musical beauty straight from the heart and feel intensely what he composes."

Furthermore, according to Ravel a work of art exists in and of itself; the composer must take care not to write himself into it. However sincerely meant, this is something of a fallacy; an artistic creation is necessarily a reflection of its creator, if only in the sense that it owes its existence to him and is imbued with his esthetic intention. Ironically, Ravel may be present in his music much more than he would have wished—in the form of that "reticence" which was a determining factor in his emotional makeup. "People are always talking about my having no heart. It's not true. But I am a Basque and the Basques feel very deeply but seldom show it, and then only to a very few."

Opinion has traditionally refrained from conferring the epithet "great" on Ravel's total accomplishment. However, of the 60 works he wrote, perhaps not one is lacking in distinction. The works must finally speak for themselves: they continue, even the less famous ones, to be played; their powers of attraction seem not to have diminished over the years.

Further Reading

Maurice Ravel is listed in the Music study guide (I, I, 9). He studied with Gabriel FAURÉ. Impressionism is represented chiefly by the music of Claude DEBUSSY.

Rollo H. Myers, *Ravel: Life and Works* (1960), and Hans Heinz Stuckenschmidt, *Maurice Ravel: Variations on His Life and Work* (trans. 1968), are not intended as scholarly works, but they are dependable and useful. Material on Ravel and general background information are in Joseph Machlis, *Introduction to Contemporary Music* (1961).

*　　*　　*

J. **RAY** / By Anthony D. Smith

The English naturalist John Ray (1627–1705) was an early botanical and zoological

systematist who divided plants into monocotyledons and dicotyledons.

John Ray was born on Nov. 29, 1627, at Black Notley, Essex, where his father was the village blacksmith. At the age of 16 he entered Catharine Hall at Cambridge. In 1646 he transferred to Trinity College, where he graduated and was elected a fellow in 1649.

Early Exploration and Writing

In 1650 Ray fell ill, and, as he himself recounted, this led to a deepening of his interest in botany: "I had been ill, physically and mentally, and had to rest from more serious study and so could ride or walk. There was leisure to contemplate by the way what lay constantly before the eyes and were so often trodden thoughtlessly underfoot, the various beauty of plants, the cunning craftsmanship of nature." For 6 years Ray studied the literature, explored the countryside around Cambridge, and grew plants in the garden by his room in college. Only then was he able to start on his book, which was finished in 1659 and called *Catalogus plantarum circa Cantabrigiam nascentium* (Cambridge Catalogue). This small, unpretentious pocketbook contained a great store of information and learning and was destined to initiate a new era in British botany.

During the writing of the *Cambridge Catalogue*, Ray had the encouragement of several friends at Cambridge, one of whom was Francis Willughby. In 1659, before the *Cambridge Catalogue* had been published, he had written to Willughby proposing a much more ambitious project: a complete British flora. However, life at Cambridge was becoming difficult for Ray because of religious controversies. In 1660 he was ordained as a priest, according to the requirements of the college statutes, but in 1662 he refused to accept the Act of Uniformity, resigned his offices in the college, and returned to his native village. Because of his integrity he was now unemployed, cut off forever from the resources of the university, and yet he was free; all he asked was that his friends should not desert him.

Earlier in 1662 Ray had visited Wales with Willughby, and the journey deepened their friendship. Both shared the conviction that, for the naturalist, museum studies and the literature must be subordinate to firsthand knowledge of the organism in its wild environment and that classification must take into account the way of life, the function as well as the structure.

For 3 years (1663–1666) Ray, Willughby, and two other friends traveled throughout Europe, studying and recording the flora and fauna. Ray's journeys gave him the data for his lifework and also introduced him to the centers of learning in Europe. The fruit of these researches was harvested at intervals during the next 30 years in the series of volumes which helped to lay the foundations of botany and zoology. His tours in Britain had a more immediate sequel, for in 1670 he published the *Catalogus plantarum Angliae et insularum adjacentium*, which was a flora of the British Isles, modeled on his earlier *Cam-*

John Ray, a painting by an unknown artist. (National Portrait Gallery, London)

adult.'' This is the division into dicotyledons and monocotyledons which all subsequent botanists have adopted.

Following the publication of the *Methodus*, Ray decided to apply the principles he had discovered to a large-scale study of all the plants of the world. This occupied him for the rest of his life and was published in three volumes: *Historia generalis plantarum* (1686, 1688, 1704), each of about 1,000 pages. The book described about 6,100 species which he knew himself, but it was handicapped in its general appeal by having been written in Latin and having no illustrations.

Still inspired by Willughby's interest in zoology, Ray wrote an important work on mammals and reptiles (*Synopsis animalium quadrupedum et serpentini generis*, 1693) in which he rejected Aristotle's classification and introduced the names ungulates (animals in which the toes are covered with horny hoofs) and unguiculates (animals in which the toes are bare but carry nails). In about 1690 Ray began to collect insects, mainly Lepidoptera. He recorded his observations on some 300 species in *Historia insectorum* (1710), which was never completed and was published posthumously.

One of Ray's most famous books, *The Wisdom of God Manifested in the Works of the Creation*, was first published in 1691. In it Ray turns from the preliminary task of identifying, describing, and classifying to that of interpreting the significance of physical and physiological processes and the relations between form and function. He not only drew attention to these fascinating subjects but argued that this was a proper exercise of man's faculties and a legitimate field for Christian inquiry. He died at Black Notley on Jan. 17, 1705.

Ray's greatness as a scientist lies in his refusal to concentrate upon the study of one part of an organism to the exclusion of the whole and in his refusal to supplement his observations by speculation. He not only saw the need for precise and ordered knowledge but was able to provide, by his personal observations, classifications which form the basis of much of modern botany and zoology.

Further Reading

John Ray is listed in the Science study guide (IV, F, 1). Observations similar to Ray's on the distinctions between plant seeds were made by his contemporary Marcello MALPIGHI in *Anatome plantarum*.

A biography of Ray is Charles E. Raven, *John Ray, Naturalist: His Life and Works* (1942). Ray is discussed in Charles Singer, *A History of Biology* (1931; 3d ed. 1959). See also Geoffrey Keynes, *John Ray: A Bibliography* (1951).

bridge Catalogue. It contained a long section on the medicinal use of plants, which denounces astrology, alchemy, and witchcraft and is ruthless in its demands for evidence. In 1671 Ray was elected a fellow of the Royal Society.

Willughby died in 1672, and for the next 10 years Ray concentrated on preparing books based on Willughby's material; these were *Ornithologia* (1676) and *Historia piscium* (1686). In *Ornithologia*, 230 species of birds personally observed by the authors are described and classified: the book laid the foundations of scientific ornithology.

Biotic Classification Schemes

In 1673 Ray married a girl of 20 who was to bear him four daughters. The following year Ray sent a paper to the Royal Society which laid the foundation for his classification of plants. The paper, ''A Discourse on the Seeds of Plants,'' distinguished between plants with a single seed leaf and those with two such leaves. A second paper by Ray, also sent to the Royal Society in 1674, laid down the definition of a species in terms of the structural qualities alone. This was a highly original approach which was to bear fruit later.

Ray's first serious essay in classification, the *Methodus plantarum nova* (1682), raises his observations on seed leaves (soon to be called cotyledons) to a principle of great importance. He states that ''from the difference in seeds can be derived a general distinction of plants, a distinction in my judgment the first and by far the best of all—that is into those which have a seed plant with two leaves, and those whose seed plant is analogous to the

M. RAY / By Abraham A. Davidson

Man Ray (born 1890), painter, photographer, and object maker, was the principal American artist in the Dada movement.

an Ray was born in Philadelphia, Pa. In 1908 he studied painting at the National Academy of Design in New York City. He made his first abstract painting in 1911 and held his first one-man show in 1912. Before meeting the Dadaist artist Marcel Duchamp in 1915, Ray worked in a quasi-cubist fashion. His oil painting *The Rope Dancer Accompanies Herself with Shadows* (1916) shows the influence of synthetic cubism in the way forms are put together; but the influence of Duchamp is evident in the concern with movement, as seen in the repetitive positions of the skirts of the dancer.

After 1917, the year that Ray became important in the New York Dada group, he gave up conventional methods of painting. He became an object maker and adopted various mechanical and photographic methods of image making. A 1918 version of the *Rope Dancer* combined a spray-gun technique with pen drawing. Among his "ready-mades" was the *Gift* (1921), a flatiron with metal tacks. His *Enigma of Isidore Ducasse* featured a mysterious object (a sewing machine) wrapped in a cloth tied with cord. At that time he was working, too, with airbrush on glass, as seen in the *Aerograph* (1919).

In 1920 Ray helped Duchamp make his first machine, the *Rotary Glass Plate*, which was composed of glass plates turned by a motor—one of the earliest examples of kinetic art. With Katherine Dreier and Duchamp in 1920 Ray was instrumental in founding the Société Anonyme, an itinerant collection which in effect was America's first museum of modern art. (The collection was given to the Yale University Art Gallery in 1941.) Before settling in Paris in 1921, Ray teamed up with Duchamp to publish the one issue of *New York Dada* (1921).

Ray was interested in obtaining unusual effects through certain photographic processes. In 1921 he created his Rayographs, which were made without the use of a camera, by directly exposing to light sensitized papers on which various objects were placed. Strangely abstract forms resulted. He published an album of 12 Rayographs entitled *Les Champs délicieux* (1923). Ray also exploited the photographic technique of solarization, a process of over- and underexposing negatives which resulted in prints with strange "bleached" effects. The photograph of André Breton (1931) is an example of this process.

By 1924 Ray was associating with many of the surrealists in Paris, and that year he contributed illustrations to the first issue of *La Révolution surréaliste*. In 1926 he had a retrospective exhibition of his paintings and objects at the Gallerie Surréaliste. In 1928 he made the film *L'Étoile de mer*, and, the following year, at the home of the Vicomte de Noailles, he filmed *Les Mystères du château de dés*. In 1933 Ray participated in the surrealist group show "Exposition Surréaliste." He participated in many major surrealist exhibitions, took up surrealist causes, and illustrated surrealist publications.

In 1940 Ray returned to America and settled in California, where he taught photography. He contributed to Hans Richter's film *Dreams That Money Can Buy* (1944). In 1947 Ray participated in the last major surrealist group show in Paris. After 1949 he maintained a studio in Paris, where he evolved new methods for printing color photographs.

Further Reading

Man Ray is listed in the Art study guide (IV, E, 7). Marcel DUCHAMP was the main creator of the New York wing of international Dada.

Ray's autobiography, *Self Portrait* (1963), is rich in personal and historical material. Los Angeles County Museum of Art, *Man Ray* (1966), contains texts by Ray and his associates. For Ray's early years see the chapter on him in George Wickes, *Americans in Paris* (1969), a vividly written study of the self-exiled American artists in Paris after World War I.

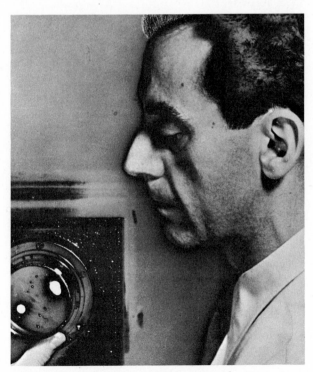

Man Ray, a self-portrait photograph, taken about 1940. (Library of Congress)

s. RAY / By Frederick R. Benson

The Indian film director Satyajit Ray (born 1921) was noted for his refined and subtly moving studies of native family life. His creations possess a humanistic warmth, crystalline purity, and mythic evocativeness which enable them to transcend the barriers of alien cultural sensibility.

atyajit Ray (pronounced rā) was born in Bengal into one of the nation's most prominent artistic families. His grandfather was a painter, a poet, and a scientist who edited the first children's magazine in Bengal. Ray's father was the author of, among other works, Bengal's classic *Book of Nonsense*. In 1940 Satyajit Ray graduated with a degree in economics from the University of Calcutta. With the encouragement of Rabindranath Tagore, the great Indian writer-philosopher and close friend of the Ray family, the youth undertook graduate courses in painting and graphics at the Santiniketan Institute. Ray was subsequently hired as an art director for the Calcutta branch of a British advertising agency in 1945. Sometime later he was transferred to the firm's London office, where, besides his regular assignments, he designed a new abridged edition of Bibhui Banerji's popular two-volume novel, *Pather Panchali*. With the cinematic version already germinating in his mind, Ray, a movie enthusiast from childhood, attended all the current films of John Ford and William Wyler; he was particularly impressed by Vittorio de Sica's *Bicycle Thief*; and, in addition, he studied the cinema theories of Sergei Eisenstein and Vsevolod Pudovkin.

When Ray returned to India in 1950, he met the French film maker Jean Renoir, who, while completing the location shooting of *The River*, gave Ray invaluable technical training. Stimulated by Renoir's personal interest, Ray began work on the scenario for the Banerji story. Produced on an extremely tight budget and employing such De Sica devices as the use of nonprofessional actors in their natural environs, Ray's sensitive visualization of the life of a poor Brahmin family, released in 1955, earned over 100 international film awards and fervent critical praise. Ray continued the events of Banerji's tale in his next production, *Aparajito*, a film as lyrical as the first, though more advanced technically and structurally. Before undertaking the concluding portion of the trilogy, the director shifted his focus from the physical hardships of the impoverished to the spiritual malaise of the declining aristocracy, creating *The Music Room* (1958). The final chapter in Ray's national epic, *The World of*

Apu (1960), contrasting the joys of married life and childbirth with the desolation of defeat and bereavement, provided an ideal ending for a work of art which functioned with equal intensity on the particular and mythical levels. "It is fascinating to note," wrote critic Stanley Kauffmann (1966) of the trilogy, "how in the most commonplace daily actions—gesturing, walking, carrying a jug—these people move beautifully, how in the poorest homes the bowls and platters, the windings of the ragged shawls, have some beauty ... not dainty aestheticism but an ingrained ethos."

With *Devi* (1960) Ray examined with intelligence and compassion the controversial problem of Hindu superstition, and in *Two Daughters* (1961) he explored the tension resulting from unyielding family ritual. *Kanchenjanga* (1962), the director's first color film, again dealt with domestic conflict.

Further Reading

Satyajit Ray is listed in the Asia study guide (II, A, 8, b). His contemporary Akira KUROSAWA was a leading Japanese director.

Ray gives his views in Hugh Gray's revealing interview with him, recorded in Andrew Sarris, ed., *Interviews with Film Directors* (1967). The most thorough and perceptive analysis of Ray's cinematography is in Erik Barnouw and S. Krishnaswamy, *Indian Film* (1963). See also sections of Pauline Kael, *I Lost It at the Movies* (1965); Eric Rhode, *The Tower of Babel* (1966); and Stanley Kauffmann, *A World on Film* (1966).

RAYBURN / By Charles Alexander

Samuel Taliaferro Rayburn (1882–1961) served as Speaker of the U.S. House of Representatives longer than any man in the nation's history.

Sam Rayburn was born in Roane County, Tenn., on Jan. 6, 1882, the eighth of 11 children. When he was 5 years old, his family moved to northern Texas. At the age of 16 he entered Mayo Normal School (now East Texas State University) and graduated in 1903.

Following a 3-year stint teaching in nearby rural schools, Rayburn won election to the Texas House of Representatives. While serving in the legislature, he attended the University of Texas law school and passed the state bar exam in 1908. Two years later he was elected Speaker of the Texas House of Representatives. In 1912 he led a field of eight candidates for U.S. representative in the Democratic party primary, thus assuring his election in overwhelmingly one-party Texas. He was renominated and reelected 23 times.

Rayburn was above all a devoutly loyal party man. Although the national platforms of an increasingly liberal Democratic party often conflicted with the social prejudices and economic conservatism of his Texas constitu-

Satyajit Ray. (Information Service of India, New York)

Sam Rayburn. (Library of Congress)

ents, he almost always fell into line behind his party's leaders. Yet over his many years in Washington, Rayburn himself introduced and worked to get through Congress a substantial amount of progressive legislation, including bills to police stock market transactions under the Securities and Exchange Commission, to provide Federal aid to rural power cooperatives under the Rural Electrification Administration, and to break up the pyramiding of public utilities companies. In 1937 he became Democratic majority leader in the House and, 3 years later, Speaker.

Except for 4 years, Rayburn held the speakership for the next 21 years. During the two 2-year intervals of Republican House majorities (1947–1949 and 1953–1955), he resumed his duties as Democratic minority leader. He also served as permanent chairman of the Democratic national conventions of 1948, 1952, and 1956, relinquishing his post in 1960 to manage Lyndon Johnson's unsuccessful bid for the presidential nomination. Rayburn died on Nov. 16, 1961, in Bonham, Tex.

Further Reading

Sam Rayburn is listed in the American History study guide (IX, A, 2). His friend and fellow Texan Lyndon JOHNSON was Senate majority leader from 1955 to 1960.

The only full-length biography of Rayburn is C. Dwight Dorough's laudatory *Mr. Sam* (1962). Rayburn's role in national politics and government is treated in Arthur S. Link, *Wilson* (5 vols., 1947–1965); Harry S. Truman, *Memoirs* (2 vols., 1955–1956); William E. Leuchtenburg, *Franklin D. Roosevelt and the New Deal, 1932–1940* (1963); Dwight D. Eisenhower, *Mandate for Change, 1953–1956: The White House Years* (1963) and *Waging Peace, 1956–1961: The White House Years* (1965); and Arthur M. Schlesinger, Jr., *A Thousand Days: John F. Kennedy in the White House* (1965).

✳   ✳   ✳

RAYLEIGH / By John N. Howard

The English physicist John William Strutt, 3d Baron Rayleigh (1842–1919), was one of the last of the great individual classical physicists whose interests spanned all disciplines.

John William Strutt was born in Maldon, Essex, on Nov. 12, 1842, the eldest son of the 2d Baron Rayleigh, a prosperous Essex farmer and land-owner. His talent in mathematics was recognized early, and in 1861 he entered Trinity College, Cambridge. Under the tutelage of a great teacher, E. J. Routh, he captured in 1865 the coveted position of senior wrangler and also won the Smith's Prize. At Terling Place, the family seat in Essex, he converted the stables into a laboratory. There he commenced experimental studies in photography, optics, electricity, and acoustics, working alone for the next 50 years. He remained active in his laboratory until a few days before his death on June 30, 1919.

In 1870 Strutt derived theoretically, and verified experimentally, the mechanism of the scattering of light by small particles (Rayleigh scattering), thus explaining the blue of the sky and red of the sunset. In 1872 he spent 3 months in Egypt convalescing from an attack of rheumatic fever; and although far from any library, he occupied his mind by writing a large part of his book *The Theory of Sound* (1879), which is still considered the bible of

Lord Rayleigh.

acoustics. On the death of his father in 1873, Strutt became the 3d Baron Rayleigh. After the death of James Clerk Maxwell in 1879, Lord Rayleigh served as the second Cavendish professor of physics at Cambridge, from 1880 to 1885. There he commenced a series of experimental investigations in electricity which led to new standard definitions of the volt, the ohm, and the ampere.

In 1891 Rayleigh succeeded John Tyndall as professor of physics at the Royal Institution in London. In studying carefully the densities of several common atmospheric gases, including hydrogen, oxygen, and nitrogen, he observed that nitrogen separated from the atmosphere was very slightly (1 part in 2,000) heavier than "chemical" nitrogen obtained by the dissociation of ammonia. He suspected the presence of an impurity and cooperated with the chemist William Ramsay, though both worked separately and in great secrecy. They astonished the scientific world in January 1895 by announcing that they had isolated a new element which they named argon (because of its inert chemical nature). They even proposed a new zeroth column for such elements in the periodic table. For this Rayleigh received the Nobel Prize in physics in 1904.

By his marriage to Evelyn Balfour, Rayleigh was brought close to high government circles: her uncle, the Marquis of Salisbury, was prime minister from 1885 to 1901, and her brother, Arthur Balfour, was also prime minister. Consequently, Rayleigh was influential in many government policies relative to science.

Rayleigh's honors are almost too numerous to mention. He was one of the original members of the Order of Merit and was secretary and later president of the Royal Society.

Further Reading

Lord Rayleigh is listed in the Science study guide (VI, C, 1). His successful collaboration with William RAMSAY resulted in Ramsay's discovering other rare gases and receiving the Nobel Prize in chemistry in 1904.

Robert John Strutt, 4th Baron Rayleigh, wrote *John William Strutt, Third Baron Rayleigh* (1924; rev. ed., 1968, entitled *Life of John William Strutt, Third Baron Rayleigh*). Biographical information on Rayleigh can be found in Nobel Foundation, *Physics* (3 vols., 1964–1967), a collection of Nobel laureates' lectures and biographies. Rayleigh's life and contribution to science are discussed in James Gerald Crowther, *Scientific Types* (1970).

AL-RAZI / By Ynez Viole O'Neill

> The Persian physician al-Razi (ca. 865–925), also known as Rhazes, prepared compilations that were influential in Western medicine for centuries. His monograph on smallpox and measles is still considered a medical classic.

Abu Bakr Muhammad ibn Zakariya al-Razi (pronounced al-ră-zē′) was born at Ray, a city not far from modern Teheran in northeastern Iran. He is believed to have devoted his early years to the study of music and philosophy. An accomplished lute player and singer, he enjoyed music throughout his life and even compiled an encyclopedia on the subject. According to one Islamic biographer, however, he never truly grasped the purpose of metaphysics and finally abandoned philosophy for more practical pursuits. He may even have earned his living for a time as a banker or money changer.

Authorities differ on precisely when al-Razi began to study medicine. Some maintain that he first left Ray and journeyed to Baghdad as a mature man, and others that he was still a youth when he arrived in the capital city of the Abbasid empire. As Baghdad at that time was the cultural and intellectual center of the Islamic world, there seems to be little doubt that he learned much about the healing art in Baghdad's well-equipped hospitals and remarkable libraries and in the research institutes that the Abbasid caliphs had richly endowed.

Returning to Ray, al-Razi was appointed chief administrator of the municipal hospital. He was soon summoned again to Baghdad, having been offered the post of chief physician and director of a great hospital in the capital. His appointment occurred during the caliphate of al-Muktafi, who reigned at Baghdad from 902 to 907.

His Practice

Al-Razi's success as chief physician of Baghdad is indisputable, and his services were in constant demand. Much of the remainder of his life was spent in traveling from city to city attending rulers and nobles as well as the poor, to whom he bestowed alms and ministered without charge.

Diet was a fundamental therapeutic procedure in al-Razi's medical methodology. He emphasized the importance of consulting the wishes of the patient concerning food, especially during the period of convalescence. Theoretically, no single factor in the treatment of the sick was more important to al-Razi than was the doctor-patient relationship. He stressed that a physician by a cheerful countenance and encouraging words should instill hopes of recovery in his patient even when the practitioner doubted that the case could terminate successfully. He also advised patients always to choose a physician in whom they had confidence and then to abide by his instructions exclusively. In practice, however, al-Razi's relations with his own patients were scarcely ever as placid as these calm injunctions would seem to indicate.

His Works

Al-Razi's writings, according to one authority, number over 230 and range in subject matter from medicine and surgery to mathematics, chess, and music. During the Middle Ages his most esteemed composition in the West was the concise handbook of medical science that he wrote for a ruler named Mansur, generally believed to

A medieval Persian physician prepares a medicine. Al-Razi was the greatest Islamic clinician of his day. Like most doctors of his time, he must have made much of the medicine he dispensed. (The Metropolitan Museum of Art, Rogers Rund, 1913)

be Mansur ibn Ishaq, who was appointed governor of Ray in 903. Called by al-Razi the *Kitab al Mansuri*, the Latin translation was known in Europe as the *Liber de medicina ad Almansorem* or *Liber Almansoris*, and its ninth book in particular formed part of the medical curriculum of almost every European university through the 16th century.

Al-Razi's most important medical work, the *Kitab al-Hawi*, is a compilation of the notes on his thoughts, reading, and practice that he amassed throughout his entire medical life. Perhaps never intended to appear as a single book, it was assembled posthumously by al-Razi's friends and students. In consequence, though the complete title of *al-Hawi* in Arabic means "System of Medicine," the book lacks the unity of design that only its author could have given it. Because of its immense size, copies of this medical encyclopedia were always rare, and even in the Islamic world it was not until modern times that a complete Arabic text was compiled for publication.

Since it is composed of extracts drawn from the writings of Greek, Islamic, and Hindu physicians enriched by al-Razi's own observations and comments, the book's utility was recognized early in the West, where a Latin version, entitled *Continens*, was prepared for Charles of Anjou, King of Sicily, in 1279 by the Jewish scholar Farj ibn Salim, who was known also by his Latin name, Farragut. The first Latin edition of the *Continens*, published at Brescia in 1486, is the largest and heaviest book printed before 1501. The *Continens* has been termed one of the most valuable and interesting medical books of antiquity, and al-Razi's reputation as the greatest Islamic clinician rests in large part on the case histories recorded in this work.

The most highly esteemed of al-Razi's works today is the monograph on smallpox and measles. Although smallpox had been described earlier, his account is astonishingly original and seems almost modern. Composed late in his life, the small work was translated from Arabic first into Syriac and Greek. The earliest Latin edition of the work, printed at Venice in 1498, was a transla-

tion from the imperfect Greek text, but in 1747 a more accurate version was prepared on which the first translation into English was based.

In his declining years, al-Razi was hindered by the slow deterioration of his sight. An anecdote relates that when urged to have the films removed from his eyes surgically, the old man rejected the proposal, replying that he had already seen enough of the world. Though the place and date of his death are uncertain, one rather reliable Islamic chronologer places it at Ray on Oct. 26, 925.

Further Reading

Al-Razi is listed in the Science study guide (II, B, 2). Unlike his successor AVICENNA, al-Razi was concerned with particular cases, not general systems.

Biographical material on al-Razi is in Edward G. Browne, *Arabian Medicine* (1921), and Cyril Elgood, *A Medical History of Persia and the Eastern Caliphate* (1951). See also Donald Campbell, *Arabian Medicine and Its Influence on the Middle Ages* (2 vols., 1926); George Sarton, *Introduction to the History of Science*, vol. 1 (1927); and Henry E. Sigerist, *History of Medicine*, vol. 2 (1961).

READING / By James D. Startt

The English lawyer and statesman Rufus Daniel Isaacs, 1st Marquess of Reading (1860–1935), known for his brilliant legal career, was an international figure during and immediately after World War I.

Rufus Isaacs, the fourth child and second son of Joseph and Sarah Davis Isaacs, was born on Oct. 10, 1860, in London. At 13 he entered the University College School and completed a year there.

At 15 years of age Rufus left school and entered the family business. His parents, however, desiring to instill a sense of discipline into his life, arranged to have him go to sea for several years. In 1876 he sailed as a shipboy on board the *Blair Athole*. He returned home 2 years later, having decided against a career at sea.

In the years following his adventure at sea, Isaacs returned to his father's business for a while and then spent 4 years at the stock exchange. Then in 1884 he unexpectedly decided to study law in order to pay off debts he had incurred during the financial slump of that year. Isaacs entered the Middle Temple in 1885, and 2 years later he was admitted to the bar. As a lawyer and later as a justice, he gained great repute for his tact, hard work, and suavity. He was attorney general from 1910 to 1913 and in 1913 was appointed lord chief justice. During these years Isaacs also actively engaged in politics and rose to prominence in the Liberal party. He was the first person to be knighted by George V when he became king; in December 1914 he was created a baron, Lord Reading of Erleigh.

Before and during World War I, Reading's counsel was sought frequently on financial questions; during the war he led several missions to the United States, and in January 1918 he became ambassador to Washington. Although he served as ambassador for just a little over a year, he quickly won the respect of high-ranking officials of both the United States and England and was a great champion of Anglo-American goodwill.

After the war Reading reached the pinnacle of his career when, in 1921, he was appointed viceroy of India. In the 1920s confusion and ill feeling were widespread in India. Mohandas Gandhi was advocating passive resistance, there was agitation against the dyarchy system, and the populace was aroused by the massacre of Indian nationalists in Amritsar in 1919. Throughout these troubled years Reading continued to display the dignity, sagacity, and sense of duty for which he had gained international fame. In 1926 he returned to England and was made a marquess; he became the first commoner since the Duke of Wellington to be so honored. He played a leading role in the Round Table Conferences of 1930 and 1931, which attempted to resolve the Indian problem. In 1931 he served briefly as foreign secretary, and in 1934 he was appointed lord warden of the Cinque Ports. Reading died in London on Dec. 30, 1935.

Further Reading

Lord Reading is listed in the Asia study guide (II, A, 6,

Lord Reading. (Radio Times Hulton Picture Library)

c). While in India, he authorized the imprisonment of Mohandas GANDHI.

The best biography of Reading is that by his son, Gerald Rufus Isaacs Reading, 2d Marquess of Reading, *Rufus Isaacs, First Marquess of Reading* (2 vols., 1942–1945). It is a detailed study of all phases of Reading's life; the chapters on his viceroyalty of India are of particular value. An older study is Stanley Jackson, *Rufus Isaacs, First Marquess of Reading* (1936). H. Montgomery Hyde, *Lord Reading* (1967), is a well-written and sympathetic recent biography. For his legal career see Derek Walker-Smith, *Lord Reading and His Cases: The Study of a Great Career* (1934). W. B. Fowler, *British-American Relations, 1917–1918* (1969), is also useful.

RECORDE / By Robert F. Erickson

Robert Recorde (1510–1558), the founder of the English school of mathematics, introduced algebra into England; he is also given credit for the introduction of the equals sign.

Robert Recorde was born in Wales. For a time, he taught mathematics at Cambridge and Oxford universities. He had first attended Oxford but received the medical degree from Cambridge in 1545. He then went to London, where he was court physician to Edward VI and Mary Tudor. The fact that Recorde graduated in medicine and was a practicing physician did not detract him from studies in mathematics; he published four books on that subject and only one on medicine.

Recorde's first book, *The Ground of Artes* (1540), was very popular. At the time of its publication, England had not made nearly the progress in mathematical books that was typical of the Continent, and his book served, in part, to close the gap. It was intended to be a basic arithmetic but has been described as a book of commercial arithmetic. It went through 18 editions in the 16th century and 12 in the 17th. In the preface Recorde introduces a dialogue between the teacher and the scholar in which the teacher explains the usefulness of arithmetic, mentioning, among other subjects, how much music, physics, and law depend on numbers and proportions. He also lists the number of occupations, such as those of merchant, steward, bailiff, army officer, and treasurer, in which, the master claims, a knowledge of arithmetic is an absolute necessity.

Recorde's other books included *The Castle of Knowledge* (1551), a work on astronomy which served to bring the Copernican hypothesis to the attention of the English reading public. *The Pathewaie to Knowledge* (1551) contains an abridgment of Euclid's *Elements of Geometry*. Of more importance was *The Whetstone of Witte* (1557), where the modern equals sign first appeared in print. The work also showed methods for extracting roots, the Cossike practice (algebra), the rule of

The definitions of the principles of
GEOMETRY.

GEOMETRY TEA-
cheth the drawyng, Meafuring
and proporcion of figures . but
in as muche as no figure can bee
drawen, but it mufte haue cer-
tayne boūdes and inclofures of
lines:and euery lyne alfo is be-
gon and ended at fome certaine
prycke, fyrft it fhal be meete to
know thefe fmaller partes of e-
uery figure, that therby the whole figures may the better bee
iudged, and diftincte in fonder.

A Poynt or a Prycke, is named of Geometricians that × poincto.
fmall and vnfenfible fhape, whiche hath in it no partes , that
is to fay : nother length,breadth nor depth. But as this exact-
nes of definition is more meeter for onlye Theorike fpecula-
cion, then for practife and outwarde woorke (confideringe
that myne intente is to applye all thefe whole principles to
woorke) j thynke meeter for this purpofe, to call a poynt
or prycke, that fmall printe of penne , pencyle , or other
inftrumente, whiche is not moued , nor drawen from his fyrft
touche,and therfore hath no notable length nor bredthe : as
this example doeth declare.

Where 3 haue fet . iij. prickes, eche of them hauyng both
lēgth and bredth,thogh it be but fmal,and therfore not notable
Nowe of a great numbre of thefe prickes,is made a Lyne,
as you may perceiue by this forme enfuyng.
where as 3 haue fet a numbre of prickes. fo if you with your
pen will fet in more other prickes betweene euerye two of
thefe,then wil it be a lyne, as here you may fee ———— and × lyne.
this lyne, is called of Geometricians , Lengthe withoute
breadth.

But as they in theyr theorikes (which ar only mind workes)
A   GO

A page from the 1551 edition of Robert Recorde's
The Pathwaie to Knowledge, *with Recorde himself
pictured in the initial G.*

equation, and "the woorkes of Surde [irrational] Nom-
bers."

The *Ground of Artes*, Recorde's most important book,
appeared at a time when commerce and finance were
flourishing as never before. The England of Elizabeth I
welcomed a book which told its merchants and investors
how to compute with both Arabic numerals and with
counting machines, how to establish proportions, the
methods of fractions, and many other commercial forms
and topics which had been established in Renaissance
Italy well before Recorde's time.

For a time Recorde held the post of comptroller of
mints and monies in Ireland, but his life ended in King's
Bench Prison, Southwark, London. It is said that he was
in prison for debt, but some evidence indicated that he
was involved in a scandal concerning Irish mines.

Further Reading

Robert Recorde is listed in the Science study guide (III,
A). Other Renaissance mathematicians were Niccolo
TARTAGLIA and Geronimo CARDANO.

A biographical sketch of Recorde, as well as a selection
from *The Ground of Artes*, is in James R. Newman, ed.,
The World of Mathematics, vol. 1 (1956). The older
work of David Eugene Smith, *History of Mathematics*,
vol. 1 (1923), gives a concise discussion of English mathematics in the early modern period.

* * *

RECTO / By Epifanio San Juan, Jr.

**Claro M. Recto (1890–1960) was a Philippine
nationalist leader and president of the 1934
constitutional convention. He was one of the
most vocal advocates of Philippine political and
social autonomy.**

Claro M. Recto (pronounced rĕk′tō) was born in
Tiaong, Tayabas, on Feb. 8, 1890. He worked for a
bachelor of arts at the Ateneo de Manila and finished a master of laws degree at the University of Santo
Tomas in 1914. From 1916 to 1919 he served as legal
adviser to the Philippine Senate. In 1919 he was elected
as representative of the third district of Batangas and
served as House minority floor leader. He was reelected
in 1922 and 1925.

Framing of the Constitution

In 1924 Recto went to the United States as a member
of a parliamentary independence mission. In the same
year he was admitted to the U.S. bar by the Supreme
Court. In 1934 a constitutional convention was held in
accordance with the provisions of the Tydings-McDuffie
Act, which required the drafting of a constitution as part
of the steps leading to Philippine independence. Recto
was elected president of the convention. It was due
mainly to Recto's sagacity and intellectual acumen that
the convention succeeded in framing and approving on
Feb. 8, 1935, a constitution which would truly reflect the
Filipinos' capacity to frame laws and principles that
would govern their lives as free, responsible citizens in a
democracy.

In 1931 Recto was elected to the Senate on the platform of the Democrata party. He acted as minority floor
leader for 3 years. In 1934 he became majority floor leader and president pro tempore of the Senate. He subsequently resigned his Senate seat when President Franklin
Roosevelt appointed him as associate justice of the Supreme Court. Recto left the Supreme Court in 1941 and
was elected anew as senator. In 1949 he was reelected
on the Nacionalista party ticket. In 1957 he ran for president but was defeated.

Apart from his numerous legal treatises and literary
works in Spanish, Recto is noted for his staunch nationalist stand on questions regarding political sovereignty and
economic independence.

World War II and Rehabilitation

Recto served in the wartime Cabinet of José Laurel
during the Japanese occupation and was subsequently
arrested and tried for collaboration. He wrote a defense
and explanation of his position in *Three Years of Enemy*

Claro M. Recto in 1957. (United Press
International Photo)

In perspective, Recto revived the tradition of the
radical dissenter fighting against feudal backwardness,
clericofascist authoritarianism, and neocolonial mentality
and imperialism. He strove to reawaken the consciousness of the Filipinos to the greatness of their revolutionary heritage and emphasized the need to transform the
character of the national life by reaffirming their solidarity as a sovereign, free people.

Recto was preparing to launch his Filipinist crusade in
the tradition of the Propaganda Movement of the 1880s
when he died of a heart ailment in Rome, Italy, on Oct. 2,
1960.

Further Reading

Claro M. Recto is listed in the Asia study guide (IV, C,
4). Philippine wartime leaders included Elpidio QUIRINO
and Ramon MAGSAYSAY.

For Recto's ideas and attitudes see his own books,
*Three Years of Enemy Occupation: The Issue of Politi-
cal Collaboration in the Philippines* (1946); *My Crusade* (1955); and *Recto Reader*, edited by Renato Constantino (1965). The best biographical account from a
nationalistic sociocultural point of view is Constantino's
*The Making of a Filipino: Story of Philippine Colonial
Politics* (1969). For other information about Recto's career consult Hernando J. Abaya, *The Untold Philippine
Story* (1967). For a thoughtful appraisal of Recto's
progressive tendencies by a young intellectual see José
Maria Sison, *Recto and the National Democratic Struggle* (1969).

Occupation (1946), which convincingly presented the
case of the "patriotic" conduct of the Filipino elite during World War II. Recto fought his legal battle in court
and was acquitted.

On April 9, 1949, Recto opened his attack against the
unfair impositions of the U.S. government as expressed
in the Military Bases Agreement of March 14, 1947, and
later in the Mutual Defense Treaty of Aug. 30, 1951, and
especially the Tydings Rehabilitation Act, which required
the enactment of the controversial parity-rights amendment to the constitution.

A Radical Gadfly

Recto's wit, irony, and sharp analytic powers exposed
the duplicity of the diplomatic agreements with the
United States and revealed the subservience of Filipino
opportunists to the dictates of American policy makers.
Recto opposed President Ramon Magsaysay on a number
of fundamental issues, among them the Philippine relations with the Chiang Kai-shek regime in Taiwan, the
Ohno-Garcia reparations deal, the grant of more bases to
the United States, the American claim of ownership over
these bases, the question of expanded parity rights for
Americans under the Laurel-Langley Agreement, and the
premature recognition of Ngo Dinh Diem's South Vietnam government. In all those issues, Recto's consistent
stand in favor of Philippine sovereignty and security was
proved right by the turn of events.

RED CLOUD / By Odie B. Faulk

*Chief of the proud Oglala Sioux Indians, Red
Cloud (1822–1909) saw his people defeated
and forced onto United States reservations.*

Born on a tributary of the North Platte River in Nebraska, Red Cloud early distinguished himself as a
warrior. By the 1860s Makhpiyaluta (his Indian
name) was leading his own band of warriors and had
gained an important reputation. In the Sioux War of
1865–1868 he was war chief of all the Oglala. In 1866 he
learned of the U.S. government's intention to build the
Bozeman Trail and to construct three forts along it; this
road would run through land guaranteed by treaty to the
Sioux. Red Cloud gathered 1,500 to 2,000 warriors and in
December lured Capt. W. J. Fetterman and 80 soldiers
into a trap and massacred them. Only the severe cold of
winter prevented his overrunning the post itself.

Though at the famous Wagon Box Fight of August
1867 Red Cloud saw the deadly accuracy of the U.S.
Army's new rifles, the government conceded defeat in
1868. The Bozeman Trail was closed and the forts abandoned. The Sioux happily set fire to these forts while
Red Cloud went to Ft. Laramie, Wyo. Here on Nov. 6,

Red Cloud (seated, second from left) at a gathering of Indian chiefs. (Library of Congress, Brady-Handy Collection)

1868, he signed a treaty that, unknown to him, provided for reservations and the cession of certain Indian lands. Finding out the terms of the treaty, angry young warriors turned more and more to the militant leader Crazy Horse. In 1870 Red Cloud journeyed to New York and Washington, D.C., to clarify the treaty and to speak in defense of the Sioux. His speeches aroused public opinion to the extent that the government revised the treaty. A special agency for the Oglala Sioux was created on the North Platte River.

Thereafter Red Cloud counseled his people to remain peaceful. He frequently charged the Indian agents with fraud, graft, and corruption, but he advised the Oglala to be loyal to the U.S. government. During the final Sioux War, of 1875–1876, though he opposed the war faction led by Crazy Horse, he refused to cede the Black Hills. In 1881 Red Cloud was removed as chief. Thereafter he declined in prestige and importance. His tribe was moved to the Pine Ridge Agency in South Dakota following the final Sioux War. He became blind in old age and died at the Pine Ridge Agency on Dec. 10, 1909.

Further Reading

Red Cloud is listed in the American History study guide (VII, C, 2). He was superseded as the Sioux war leader by CRAZY HORSE.

The best account of Red Cloud is James C. Olson, *Red Cloud and the Sioux Problem* (1965). Still excellent is Earl A. Brininstool, *Fighting Indian Warriors* (rev. ed. 1953; original title, *Fighting Red Cloud's Warriors*, 1926). An assessment by a contemporary of Red Cloud is James H. Cook, *Fifty Years on the Old Frontier as Cowboy, Hunter, Guide, Scout, and Ranchman* (1923; new ed. 1957).

REDFIELD / By Regna Darnell

The American anthropologist Robert Redfield (1897–1958) specialized in Meso-American folk cultures. He was concerned with socially relevant applications of social-science skills and researches.

Robert Redfield was born on Dec. 4, 1897, in Chicago, Ill., the son of an attorney. In 1915 he entered the University of Chicago to study law. During World War I he served as a volunteer ambulance driver, returning to the university to receive his bachelor's degree in 1920 and his law degree in 1921. Although he then joined a Chicago law firm, he had already been drawn toward social science by Robert Park (whose daughter he had married in 1920) of the sociology department of the University of Chicago. A 1923 trip to Mexico confirmed Redfield's interest in primitive cultures. He became an instructor in sociology at the University of Colorado in 1925 and the following year received a fellowship for his first Mexican fieldwork.

In 1927 Redfield returned to Chicago to an anthropology department which had just attained independence from sociology. After receiving his doctorate in

Robert Redfield. (The Department of Special Collections, The University of Chicago Library)

1928, he became an assistant professor. He was promoted to associate professor in 1930 and full professor in 1934, simultaneously becoming university dean of social sciences. The position as dean reinforced his broad conception of the integrated nature of the social sciences. Ties of the Chicago anthropology department to sociology encouraged him to concentrate on social anthropology, effectively excluding the archeology and linguistics which Franz Boas and his students considered integrally related to it. Redfield became chairman of the anthropology department in 1948 and Robert Maynard Hutchins distinguished service professor in 1953.

Redfield's fieldwork produced *Tepoztlan* (1930) and *Chan Kom: A Maya Village* (1934), the latter in collaboration with the village schoolteacher, Alfonso Villa. *Folk Culture of Yucatan* (1941) compared the effects of civilization on four Yucatan communities that shared a Mayan heritage but differed in amount of external communication. *Chan Kom: A Village That Chose Progress* (1950) dealt with the effort of Mexican peasants to adjust to the modern world.

Redfield's prevailing concern was with the effect of technological change on primitive peoples and the consequent responsibility of the social scientist for defining the resulting disruption of life-styles. He defined, within an established sociological tradition, two ideal types—"folk" and "urban" culture. *The Primitive World and Its Transformations* (1953) attempted to describe conflicts of the "moral order" accompanying the spread of civilization. Redfield's ideal types have been criticized primarily by students of Boas, who prefer to work with descriptions of particular culture histories rather than to find ways of comparing types of community.

The last book by Redfield, *The Little Community* (1955), drew on studies of Indian civilization. Although his own fieldwork in India was cut short by illness, he defined and contrasted a "great tradition" of urban intellectual life and a persistent "little tradition" of the villages. As in Mexico, communication rather than geography was crucial.

Redfield shared with Boas and many of his students a concern for social problems, maintaining that man and anthropologist were necessarily inseparable. During World War II he advised the War Relocation Authority; he participated in the initial UNESCO conferences in Europe; he became director of the American Council on Race Relations in 1948; and he served as president of the board of the American Broadcasting Company. He died on Oct. 16, 1958.

Further Reading

Robert Redfield is listed in the Social Sciences study guide (VII, E, 3). He was associated with many well-known anthropologists, including Franz BOAS, Ralph LINTON, Robert H. LOWIE, and Margaret MEAD.

Although articles have appeared criticizing various aspects of Redfield's theoretical formulations, there is no significant biographical study of him. Some background is in Don Martindale, *The Nature and Types of Sociological Theory* (1960).

REDON / By J. P. Hodin

The French painter and graphic artist Odilon Redon (1840–1916) was a leading symbolist and a forerunner of surrealism.

Odilon Redon (pronounced rə-dôN′) was born on April 20, 1840, in Bordeaux. His father was a rich French colonist in the southern United States; his mother, of French descent, was from New Orleans. Odilon lived on his uncle's estate in Peyrelebade until 1851, and he spent summers there from 1874 to 1897.

Redon began to study drawing in 1855 with Stanislas Gorin in Bordeaux. At his father's wish Redon started to study architecture in 1860. Four years later he was accepted in the painting class of the École des Beaux-Arts in Paris. He exhibited some prints in the Salon of 1867. During 1870–1871 he served in the Franco-Prussian War.

In 1878 Redon visited Belgium and the Netherlands, studied the works of Rembrandt, and learned from Henri Fantin-Latour the technique of lithography. He produced his first lithographic series, *In the Dream*, in 1879; his second, *For Edgar Allan Poe*, in 1882; and his third, *The Origins*, in 1883. In 1884 Redon became known in avant-garde literary circles through J. K. Huysman's symbolist novel *Against the Grain,* in which Huysman said Redon's drawings "were outside of any known category; most of them leap beyond the boundaries of painting, innovating a very special fantasy, a fantasy of sickness and delirium." That same year Redon exhibited in the first Salon des Indépendants, which he had helped to create.

Redon's next lithographic series were *Homage to Goya* in 1885 and *The Night* in 1886. He exhibited with the impressionists in Paris and with "The Twenty" in Brussels in 1886. He did three series of lithographs for Gustave Flaubert's *The Temptation of St. Anthony—* 1888, 1889, 1896—and a series for Charles Baudelaire's *Fleurs du mal* in 1890.

Not until 1890 did Redon produce his first pastels and oils. At this time he replaced Paul Gauguin as a mentor of the young Nabis. The lithographic series *Dreams* was produced in 1891, and his last series, the *Revelation of St. John,* in 1899. Redon also produced some fine portraits, decorative screens, and wall ornaments, and he executed designs for tapestries.

In 1900 Redon began a series of flower studies, turning away from the macabre subjects and nightmare visions of his black-and-white lithographs and drawings to paint in the most voluptuous colors, as in *Flowers in a Vase* (ca. 1905) and *Vase with Anemones* (1912–1914). He was more fully represented at the famous Armory Show of 1913 in New York City than any other artist. He died in Paris on July 6, 1916.

Odilon Redon, a self-portrait. (French Cultural Services of the French Embassy)

Further Reading

Odilon Redon is listed in the Art study guide (III, H, 1, g). Another symbolist painter was Pierre PUVIS DE CHAVANNES. Redon, James ENSOR, and Henri ROUSSEAU were pioneers in the transition from late-19th-century romanticism to early-20th-century fantasy.

The outstanding work on Redon in English is Klaus Berger, *Odilon Redon: Fantasy and Colour* (1964). An earlier work is Walter Pach, *Odilon Redon* (1913). The definitive book on Redon's graphics is André Mellerio, *Odilon Redon* (1913; repr. 1968), the text of which is in French. Redon is discussed in John Rewald, *Post-Impressionism: From Van Gogh to Gauguin* (2d ed. 1962).

J. **REED** / By Thomas W. Wood, Jr.

> John Silas Reed (1887–1920), American revolutionist, poet, and journalist, became a symbol in many American minds of the Communist revolution in Russia.

John Reed was born in the mansion of his maternal grandparents outside Portland, Ore., on Oct. 22, 1887. His father sold agricultural implements and insurance. Reed was a frail youngster and suffered with a kidney ailment. He attended Portland public schools and graduated from Harvard in 1910. Although he felt like an outsider, Reed had been active at the university.

Reed went to work for *American Magazine,* of muckraking fame, and *The Masses,* a radical publication. Journalists Ida Tarbell and Lincoln Steffens awakened his liberal feelings, but he soon bypassed them as a radical. In 1914 *Metropolitan Magazine* sent Reed to Mexico, where he boldly walked within the lines of Pancho Villa's army. Villa reportedly made Reed a staff officer and called the journalist "brigadier general." Reed next gave sympathetic coverage to striking coal miners in Colorado. He went to Europe for *Metropolitan Magazine* when World War I broke out in 1914. He covered the battle fronts in Germany, Russia, Serbia, Romania, and Bulgaria.

Reed and his wife, Louise Bryant, were in Russia during the October Revolution. In reporting the Bolshevik effort to gain control, Reed won V. I. Lenin's friendship. Here Reed gathered materials for his most noted work, *Ten Days That Shook the World* (1919). It is generally recognized that the book lacks factual accuracy, but Bertram Wolfe (1960) contends that "as literature Reed's book is the finest piece of eyewitness reporting the revolution produced."

In 1918 Reed was named Russian consul general at New York, a status never recognized by the United States. In 1919, after he had been expelled from the Na-

John Reed. (United Press International Photo)

Thomas B. Reed was born on Oct. 18, 1839, in Portland, Maine, an origin stamped in the nasal drawl in which he delivered the corrosive witticisms for which he became famous. Graduating from Bowdoin College in 1860, he studied law, traveled to California, and taught school briefly. In 1865 he joined the Maine bar and entered politics, becoming state legislator (1867–1868), state senator (1869–1870), and attorney general (1870–1873). Elected congressional representative in 1876, he served in the House until 1899.

Congressman Reed's first important assignment was to the "Potter Committee," appointed in 1878 to investigate alleged fraud in the Hayes-Tilden presidential election of 1876. Representing the Republican minority, Reed demonstrated that his party was not alone in fraud and even managed to implicate the nephew of Democratic candidate Samuel J. Tilden. During the 1880s Reed emerged as a leading party regular. As Speaker of the House (1889–1891, 1895–1899), he struggled to revise House rules, especially those that allowed the Democratic majority to avoid action through filibustering or absenteeism. His physical appearance, a towering height of 6 feet 3 inches and a weight of almost 300 pounds, contributed to his impressiveness. Although later congresses lessened his power, he helped establish the principle of party responsibility.

Reed was fiercely partisan. Democrats, he said, never spoke without diminishing the sum of human knowl-

tional Socialist Convention, he formed the Communist Labor party in the United States. He was arrested several times for incendiary speeches and finally, after printing articles in the *Voice of Labor*, was indicted for sedition. He fled to the Soviet Union on a forged passport. The thing usually unreported about Reed among the Muscovites was his unrelenting contention that decisions should be made democratically and his opposition to a monolithic society under dictatorial control. Twice he tried to return to the United States but was unsuccessful. Stricken by typhus, he died on Oct. 19, 1920, in Moscow. He was given a state funeral and buried in the Kremlin.

Further Reading

John Reed is listed in the American History study guide (VIII, F, 5). He was a friend of V. I. LENIN.

Bertram D. Wolfe's brilliant introduction to the 1960 Modern Library edition of *Ten Days That Shook the World* takes note of Reed's inconsistencies in the epic, which is more literary than historical. The best work on Reed is Granville Hicks, *John Reed: The Making of a Revolutionary* (1936). A portrait of Reed is in the anecdotal-historical collection of essays of Bertram D. Wolfe, *Strange Communists I Have Known* (1965).

T. B. **REED**/ By Robert C. Bannister

As Speaker of the U.S. House of Representatives, Thomas Brackett Reed

Thomas B. Reed. (Library of Congress)

edge. "A statesman," he noted in his most quoted epigram, "is a successful politician who is dead." Supporting the tariff, hard money, and internal improvements for national purposes, he believed business stability essential to progress. In advance of his time, he opposed capital punishment and advocated woman's suffrage.

In his later years neither party nor country entirely pleased Reed. "The convention could do worse," he said of his presidential ambitions in 1896, "and probably will." He resigned from the House in the aftermath of the Spanish-American War and then practiced law in New York. He died on Dec. 7, 1902, in Washington.

Considered an archconservative by those who opposed his economic views, Reed displayed a genuine humanity and broad learning in his speeches and articles. As a master of the parliamentary skills that make representative government effective, he has rarely been equaled.

Further Reading

Thomas B. Reed is listed in the American History study guide (VII, A, 3). The congressional committee created to decide the results of the election dispute between Rutherford B. HAYES and Samuel J. TILDEN awarded the election to Hayes.

Samuel W. McCall, *The Life of Thomas Brackett Reed* (1914), although weak on Reed's political career, is useful for personal detail. William A. Robinson, *Thomas B. Reed, Parliamentarian* (1930), details Reed's political skills. Arthur Wallace Dunn, *From Harrison to Harding* (2 vols., 1922), and H. Wayne Morgan, *From Hayes to McKinley: National Party Politics, 1877–1896* (1969), place Reed's career in the context of "gilded age" politics.

* * *

W. **REED** / By George H. Daniels

Walter Reed (1851–1902), American military surgeon and head of the U.S. Army Yellow Fever Commission, is widely known as the man who conquered yellow fever by tracing its origin to a particular mosquito species.

Walter Reed was born on Sept. 13, 1851, at Belroi, Va., the son of a Methodist minister. After attending private schools, Reed entered the University of Virginia, where he received his medical degree in 1869, after completing only 2 years. He then went to New York, where he received a second medical degree from the Bellevue Hospital Medical College in 1870. After working for the Board of Health of New York and of Brooklyn, Reed was commissioned an assistant surgeon in the U.S. Army with the rank of first lieutenant in June 1875. Then followed 11 years of frontier garrison duty, further study at Johns Hopkins Hospital while on duty in Baltimore, and an assignment as professor of bac-

Walter Reed. (National Library of Medicine, Bethesda, Md.)

teriology and clinical microscopy at the newly organized Army Medical School in Washington in 1893.

When yellow fever made its appearance among American troops in Havana, Cuba, in 1900, Reed was appointed head of the commission of U.S. Army medical officers to investigate the cause and mode of transmission. After some months of fruitless work in searching for the cause of the disease, Reed and his associates decided to concentrate upon determining the mode of transmission. Carlos Juan Finlay first advanced the theory that yellow fever was transmitted by mosquitoes (he blamed it on the *Stegomyia fasciata*, later known as the *Aedes aegypti*) and proved it by experiments, but physicians generally did not credit the possibility. Walter Reed confirmed Finlay's findings by using human subjects. In fact, there was no alternative to experimentation with humans; Reed and his associates argued persuasively that the results would justify the procedure. Mosquitoes that had been fed on yellow fever–infected blood were applied to several of Reed's associates, including Dr. James Carroll, who developed the first experimental case of the disease.

Then followed a series of controlled experiments with soldier volunteers. In all, 22 cases of experimental yellow fever were produced: 14 by mosquito bites, 6 by injections of blood, and 2 by injections of filtered blood serum. At the same time, in order to eliminate the possibility of transmission by contact, Dr. Robert P. Cook and a group of soldiers slept in a detached building in close contact with the clothing and bedding of yellow fever patients from the camp hospital. Since no case of illness resulted from any of these contacts, the theory was conclusively proved.

The value of the commission's work quickly became evident. In 1900 there had been 1,400 cases of yellow fever in Havana; by 1902, after the attack, mounted because of the commission's report, on the mosquito had been under way for over a year in Cuba and the Panama Canal Zone, there was not a single case. Now that its mode of transmission is known, there is no danger of yellow fever in any country with adequate control facilities.

Reed returned to Washington, D.C., in February 1901 and resumed his teaching duties at the Army Medical School. In 1902 Harvard University and the University of Michigan gave him honorary degrees. Only a few days before his death in Washington on Nov. 22, 1902, he was appointed librarian of the Army Medical Library. The Walter Reed Hospital in Washington was named in his honor.

Further Reading

Walter Reed is listed in the American History study guide (VII, F, 7, b). William C. GORGAS was the sanitation expert who put Reed's findings into effect by controlling mosquitoes in Cuba and the Panama Canal Zone.

Howard A. Kelly, *Walter Reed and Yellow Fever* (1906; 3d ed. rev. 1923), includes a bibliography of Reed's writings. See also Albert E. Truby, *Memoir of Walter Reed: The Yellow Fever Episode* (1943).

Tapping Reeve. (Litchfield Historical Society, Litchfield, Conn.)

REEVE / By James Axtell

Tapping Reeve (1744–1823), an American jurist and founder of the Litchfield Law School, helped bring order to the law through systematic and integrated instruction.

Tapping Reeve, the son of a Presbyterian minister, was born in Brookhaven, Long Island, in October 1744. He entered the College of New Jersey (now Princeton) at 15 and graduated first in his class in 1763. In 1771 Reeve left his post as tutor at Princeton to read law in the traditional way in a judge's office in Hartford, Conn. In a year he was admitted to the bar, and he moved to the remote village of Litchfield, Conn., to begin his practice.

As his reputation grew, young prospective lawyers began to seek Reeve out to supervise their legal preparation. But he soon went beyond the usual procedures (which gave the clerks little or no overview in their reading and only a perfunctory knowledge of established legal forms) to introduce them to the substantive principles and concepts of law. In the absence of accessible textbooks and reports, he inaugurated in 1782 a series of formal and connected lectures which embraced the whole field of jurisprudence. Two years later, with students overflowing home and office, he erected a small frame building near his home and assembled his law library there. In this school he met his classes of from 10 to 20 men. On Saturdays the students were examined on the week's lectures, and Monday evenings were reserved for moot court sessions.

For 14 years Reeve conducted the school alone, but when, in 1798, he was appointed a judge of the superior court, James Gould began to share the teaching duties. The notes from their lectures, as the school catalog noted in 1828, "constitute books of reference, the great advantage of which must be apparent to every one of the slightest acquaintance with the . . . Law."

Before the school closed in 1833 because of increased competition from New York, New Haven, and Boston, Reeve and Gould graduated more than 1,000 lawyers. The roster of names reads like a "Who's Who in Nineteenth-century America," including 2 U.S. vice presidents, 3 Supreme Court justices, 6 Cabinet members, and 116 congressmen.

After 16 years on the state supreme court Reeve was elevated in 1814 to chief justice. He retired the next year, at the age of 70. He published *The Law of Baron and Femme* (1816), a legal analysis of domestic relations that went into four editions. Financially straitened and flagging with age, he withdrew from his school partnership in September 1820 and died in Litchfield on Dec. 13, 1823.

Further Reading

Tapping Reeve is listed in the Social Sciences study guide (V, C, 3; VI, G, 3). Among his many students was the educator Horace MANN.

Samuel H. Fisher, *The Litchfield Law School, 1775–1833* (1933), contains a good description of the activities and alumni of Reeve's school and a sympathetic characterization of its teachers.

✳   ✳   ✳

REGIOMONTANUS

/ By Stanley L. Jaki

The German astronomer and mathematician Regiomontanus (1436–1476) constructed the first European observatory and established trigonometry as a separate area of study in mathematics.

Regiomontanus (pronounced rē-jē-ō-mŏn-tā′nəs), called after the Latinized form of his birthplace, Königsberg, in the duchy of Coburg, was born Johann Müller on June 6, 1436, the son of a miller. At the age of 12 he began the study of classical languages and mathematics at the University of Leipzig. In 1452 he moved to Vienna and became the favorite pupil of Georg Peurbach, astronomer and mathematician, who interested Regiomontanus in securing a truly reliable version of Ptolemy's *Almagest*.

A year after Peurbach's death in 1461, Regiomontanus went to Italy and established close contacts with Cardinal Bessarion, the leading Greek scholar of the time. Regiomontanus made quick progress in Greek and studied various Greek mathematical and astronomical texts in addition to Ptolemy's *Almagest*. The study of this latter work enabled him to complete Peurbach's *Epitome in Cl. Ptolemaei magnam compositionem*, but it saw print only in 1496.

The most important work of Regiomontanus, completed in 1464 but printed in 1533, was the first full-fledged monograph on trigonometry, *De triangulis omnimodis libri quinque* (Five Books on All Kinds of Triangles). The first two books dealt with plane trigonometry, while the rest were largely devoted to spherical trigonometry. Although Regiomontanus relied heavily on Arabic and Greek sources, such as al-Battani, Nasir al-Din al-Tusi, Menealos, Theodosius, and Ptolemy, his work was the starting point of a new development leading to modern trigonometry.

In 1468 Regiomontanus went to the court of King Matthias Corvinus of Hungary at Buda to serve as librarian of one of the richest collections of codices in existence in Europe. There he completed his *Tabulae directionum et projectionum*, the first European study of Diophantes' *Algebra*.

In 1471 Regiomontanus went to Nuremberg at the in-vitation of Bernhard Walther, a rich citizen who provided him with the means to set up the first observatory in Europe. It was equipped with instruments of Regiomontanus's own making, which he described in *Scripta de torqueto, astrolabio armillari*, first printed in 1544. His most important observations concerned the great comet of 1472 (probably Halley's comet). Walther also set up a printing press and published Regiomontanus's calendars and pamphlets. Regiomontanus published Peurbach's planetary theory, *Theoricae novae planetarum*, and his own ephemerides for 1474–1506, which contained a method of calculating longitudes at sea on the basis of the motion of the moon. The book was used by the leading navigators of the times.

At the summons of Pope Sixtus IV, Regiomontanus, a newly appointed titular bishop of Ratisbon, journeyed to Italy in the fall of 1475 to undertake the reform of the calendar. He died on July 6, 1476, probably the victim of an epidemic.

Further Reading

Regiomontanus is listed in the Science study guide (III, B). The geocentric viewpoint of the *Almagest* of PTOLE-

An illustration from a 1496 edition of Ptolemy's Almagest, showing Ptolemy (left) and Regiomontanus, who translated the work, seated beneath an armillary sphere.

MY was replaced in the 16th century by the heliocentric viewpoint of Nicolaus COPERNICUS.

There is a chapter on Regiomontanus in Lynn Thorndike, *Science and Thought in the Fifteenth Century* (1929). Also useful are J. L. E. Dreyer, *A History of Astronomy from Thales to Kepler* (1905; rev. ed. 1953); Lynn Thorndike, *A History of Magic and Experimental Science*, vols. 5 and 6 (1941); and A. C. Crombie, *Augustine to Galileo: The History of Science A.D. 400–1650* (1953).

*   *   *

REICHSTEIN / By E. Ashworth Underwood

The Polish-Swiss organic chemist Tadeus Reichstein (born 1897) shared the Nobel Prize in Physiology or Medicine for his discoveries relating to the hormones of the adrenal cortex.

The son of Isidor Reichstein, an engineer, Tadeus Reichstein (pronounced rīKH′shtīn) was born at Włocławek, Poland, on July 20, 1897. In 1914, shortly after his family moved to Zurich, he became a naturalized Swiss subject. He began the study of chemistry at the State Technical College at Zurich in 1916, qualified in 1920, and in 1922 graduated as a doctor of philosophy in chemistry. For some years thereafter he investigated the cause of the flavor of coffee. In 1929 he became lecturer in organic and pharmaceutical chemistry at the Zurich Technical College, where in 1934 he was appointed titular professor, and in 1937 associate professor, of organic chemistry. In 1933 he synthesized ascorbic acid, independently of (Sir) Norman Haworth and by a different process.

In 1938 Reichstein was appointed professor of pharmaceutical chemistry, and in 1946 also of organic chemistry, in the University of Basel. From 1948 to 1952 he supervised the design of the new Institute of Organic Chemistry at Basel, of which, having meanwhile relinquished the chair of pharmaceutical chemistry (1950), he was director until 1960.

Chemistry of the Adrenal Cortex

In 1929 a long-standing rheumatoid arthritic was, because of an acute attack of jaundice, referred to Philip Showalter Hench of the Mayo Clinic, Rochester, Minn. Within a few days most rheumatoid symptoms disappeared. During the next 5 years Hench saw 16 further cases, all of which were improved by the intercurrent jaundice. He concluded that the beneficial effect might be due to excess of a normal bile constituent or to an abnormal substance present in jaundice. He and his coworkers therefore administered bile and bile salts to rheumatoid arthritics, but no beneficial effects were observed. In 1931 Hench noted that female arthritics sometimes improved during pregnancy, and over several years

he and his coworkers confirmed this fact. Hench now assumed that the improvement was due to the presence of a substance X, which was the same in jaundiced cases as in pregnant women. About 1938 he concluded that substance X was probably not derived from the bile but was a hormone found in both males and females.

About 1929 scientists first prepared extracts of the adrenal cortex which checked the symptoms following removal of the adrenals in animals and also those of Addison's disease in human patients. These extracts were named "cortin," and it seemed desirable to elucidate its composition and to prepare it in a pure state.

In 1934 E. C. Kendall, of the University of Minnesota, found that an extract thought to be pure cortin was really a mixture. In 1934 also Reichstein entered this field, and he and Kendall soon isolated about 10 compounds from the adrenal cortex. Their detailed chemical investigation was mainly due to Reichstein. He soon proved that all such substances are steroids, and he continued to isolate new steroids from the cortex. By 1950, 29 were known.

The steroids are characterized by the presence of a complex nucleus, consisting of four rings bound together in a certain order to form a chain. This nucleus contains 17 carbon atoms, each bound to one or two hydrogen atoms. The nature of a particular steroid is determined by the nature of any substituent groups attached to carbon atoms in the nucleus. Of the 29 steroids isolated from the cortex by 1950, 6 were biologically active and not found in any other organ. They all contained 21 carbon atoms, that is, 4 additional to the 17 contained in the nucleus. The biological activity was dependent on the presence of a double bond. These cortical steroids were shown to influence the fluid balance of the body, the storage of sugar, and the metabolism of carbohydrates and proteins.

In 1934 both Reichstein and Kendall became interested in four of the active steroids, which Kendall called compounds A, B, E, and F. Compound E was isolated by Kendall in 1935 and about the same time by Reichstein. It was found to be 11-dehydro-17-hydroxycorticosterone. It was also found that it did not prolong the life of adrenalectomized animals but that it restored the power of their muscles to contract.

These substances were present in the adrenals in such minute amounts that to obtain enough for clinical purposes it was necessary to synthesize them. In 1937 Reichstein, starting with a bile acid, synthesized the simplest member of the group, deoxycorticosterone. Deoxycorticosterone acetate (DOCA) was soon available on an industrial scale and was satisfactorily used in treating Addison's disease.

For a long time other corticosteroids eluded synthesis. Manufacturers were not interested, as there were few patients with Addison's disease. In 1941 Hench and Kendall considered that Hench's substance X was probably Kendall's compound E, and they decided to administer compound E to rheumatoid patients as soon as a supply was available. In 1941 also the National Research Council of the United States, believing that the corticosteroids might be valuable in war, urged that attempts be made to

Tadeus Reichstein. (Swiss National Tourist Office, New York)

the salt balance of the body. He also worked on plant glycosides, especially the aglycones of the digitalis and strophanthus groups. His published work was entirely in the form of scientific papers.

In 1947 Reichstein became an Honorary Doctor of the University of Paris, and in 1951 he was awarded the Cameron Prize of the University of Edinburgh. In 1952 he was elected a Foreign Member of the Royal Society, and in 1968 he was awarded its highest honor, the Copley Medal.

Further Reading

Tadeus Reichstein is listed in the Science study guide (VII, G, 2). Study of the adrenal glands began with Thomas ADDISON in the mid-19th century and was continued in the 20th century by E. C. KENDALL and others.

There is a biography of Reichstein in *Nobel Lectures, Physiology or Medicine, 1942–1962* (1964), which also includes his Nobel Lecture, as well as those of Kendall and Hench. For an account of the earlier work see R. D. H. Heard, *The Hormones*, vol. 1 (1948). For related aspects of the corticosteroids see A. White, P. Handler, and E. L. Smith, *Principles of Biochemistry* (3d ed. 1964).

REID / By Raymond J. Langley

The Scottish philosopher, clergyman, and teacher Thomas Reid (1710–1796) originated the school of thought known as the philosophy of common sense.

Thomas Reid was the son of Lewis and Margaret Reid. He was born on April 26, 1710, at Strachan, Kincardineshire. Until he was 12 years old, he was educated at home and in the local parish school; he then entered Marischal College, from which he graduated in 1726. During the next decade he studied theology and read widely, and in 1737 he became a Presbyterian minister of the Church of Scotland. In 1740 Reid married his cousin Elizabeth Reid, and during their long life together they raised nine children. In 1752 he gave up his ministry at New Machar to become a professor of philosophy at King's College, Aberdeen. His best-known work, *An Inquiry into the Human Mind on the Principles of Common Sense* (1764), was derived essentially from material he had presented to the local philosophical society, which he had established.

Although David Hume claimed that his own major work, *A Treatise on Human Nature* (1739), "fell stillborn from the press," Reid seems to have been one of its few original readers. The two Scots, who were contemporaries, conducted an infrequent but complimentary correspondence, and Reid wrote, "I shall always avow myself as your disciple in metaphysics." In 1753 Reid succeeded Adam Smith, the famous economist, as

synthesize compound A preparatory to the synthesis of compound E.

In 1943 Reichstein synthesized compound A from deoxycholic acid. His method could not be applied on a large scale, but in 1944 Kendall synthesized it by a more practical method. In 1947 Lewis H. Sarett, of the Merck Laboratories, synthesized a very small quantity of compound E from compound A. In August 1948 Hench, still searching for the hypothetical substance X, reaffirmed his decision to try Kendall's compound E on arthritics, and on September 4 he formally asked the firm of Merck for a supply sufficient for clinical trials. The small amount prepared was sent to Hench, and on September 21 his coworker Charles H. Slocumb began to administer it to a rheumatoid arthritic. The excellent results led rapidly to the treatment of many other patients by Hench, Slocumb, and Howard F. Polley at the Mayo Clinic, and at the end of 1948 the name of compound E was changed to "cortisone." In February 1949 these workers obtained a small supply of the pituitary adrenocorticotropic hormone (ACTH), and this was also used successfully in treating rheumatoid arthritis, alone and in association with cortisone. Good results were also obtained in acute rheumatism, asthma, and the collagen diseases. The first report on the new treatment, by Hench, Kendall, Slocumb, and Polley, was presented on April 20, 1949. By the end of 1950 several thousand patients in many parts of the world had been successfully treated. In 1950 Reichstein shared with Kendall and Hench the Nobel Prize in Physiology or Medicine for their work in this field.

Later Life

After 1950 Reichstein discovered many other cortical steroids, including aldosterone, a hormone that regulates

professor of moral philosophy at Glasgow. He continued teaching until he retired at the age of 71. For the remaining 15 years of his life Reid published extensively. The two most important works of this period were *Essays on the Intellectual Powers of Man* (1785) and *Essays on the Active Powers of Man* (1788). Reid died on Oct. 7, 1796.

The philosophy of common sense took its point of departure from Hume's skepticism toward impressions and ideas. One of the chief tenets of modern classical philosophy is the representative theory of perception, which assumes that the immediate object of sensation is, in fact, a mental image that presents man with a world of material objects. Likewise, the relations between conceptual ideas are brought about by associations from past experience that are imaginatively projected into the future. Hume's skepticism led him to conclude that inferences on the basis of impressions and ideas are a matter of custom and belief rather than logical inference or demonstration. Reid's purpose was to reject such analysis as "shocking to common sense" and to rely on a description of the way in which perception, conception, and belief work together to produce an instinctive conviction of the validity of man's sensations of the external world and of other selves.

Further Reading

Thomas Reid is listed in the Philosophy study guide (V, A, 4) and the Social Sciences study guide (V, C, 1). He influenced Dugald STEWART.

Thomas Reid, a portrait by James Tassie dated 1789. (Scottish National Portrait Gallery)

Renewed interest in Reid's work is evident in Timothy Duggon's edition of Reid's *An Inquiry into the Human Mind* (1970). It partially supplements *The Works of Thomas Reid*, edited by Sir William Hamilton (2 vols., 1846–1863). This collection also contains Dugald Stewart's *Account of the Life and Writings of Thomas Reid* (1903). Studies of Reid include A. Campbell Fraser, *Thomas Reid* (1898), and Olin McKendree Jones, *Empiricism and Intuitionism in Reid's Common Sense Philosophy* (1927).

REMARQUE / By Mark Boulby

> The German author Erich Maria Remarque (1898–1970) was a popular novelist whose "All Quiet on the Western Front" was the most successful German best seller on the subject of the soldier's life in World War I.

Erich Maria Remarque (pronounced rə-märk′), whose real name was Erich Paul Remark, was born on July 22, 1898, in Osnabrück. He attended the Teachers' Training College there and afterward the University of Münster. Toward the end of World War I he served in the army. After the war he worked variously as a press reader, clerk, and racing driver. The immense success of *Im Westen nichts Neues* (1929; *All Quiet on the Western Front*) established him as an author. This novel falls into a clearly distinguishable class of antiwar and antimilitary fiction that grew rapidly in Germany in the later 1920s—Arnold Zweig's *Sergeant Grischa* is another famous example. These books belong in general to that school known as neorealism and are characterized by a matter-of-fact, unpretentious, often colloquial style approximating the newspaper or magazine report.

Although Remarque conceals little of the squalor and bloodiness of life in the trenches, at the same time there is in this book an undeniable sentimental vein which is maintained strongly right through to the pathetic last pages, in which, following the death of his friend, the hero himself falls 2 weeks before the armistice, on a day when all is reported quiet at the front. This novel was translated into some 25 languages and has sold over 30 million copies.

Remarque continued in a similar vein with another war novel, *Der Weg zurück* (1931; *The Road Back*). *Drei Kameraden* (1937; *Three Comrades*) deals with life in postwar Germany at the time of the inflation and is also a tragic love story. By 1929 Remarque had left Germany and from that time lived abroad. The pacifism implicit in his works and their strong sense of pathos and suffering could scarcely endear them to the Nazi government. In 1938, in fact, Remarque was deprived of his German citizenship. In 1939 he arrived in the United States and became an American citizen in 1947. His next novel,

Erich Maria Remarque in 1930. (National Archives, Washington, D.C.)

Liebe deinen Nächsten (1940), was published in America under the title *Flotsam*. After World War II Remarque's productivity increased, and he turned more and more to the study of personal relationships set against a topical background of war and social disintegration. *Arc de Triomphe* (1946), the story of a German refugee surgeon in Paris just before World War II, reestablished his name in the best-seller lists. His later works include *Zeit zu leben und Zeit zu sterben* (1954; *A Time to Love and a Time to Die*), *Der schwarze Obelisk* (1956; *The Black Obelisk*), *Der Funke Leben* (1957; *Spark of Life*), *Der Himmel kennt keine Günstlinge* (1961; *Heaven Has No Favorites*), and *Die Nacht von Lissabon* (1962; *The Night in Lisbon*). All these novels are competent and gripping narratives and are skillful stories of personal crisis, escape, adventure, and intrigue. Remarque also had one play produced, *Die letzte Station* (1956; *The Last Station*). He died in Locarno, Switzerland, on Sept. 25, 1970.

Further Reading

Erich Maria Remarque is listed in the Literature study guide (III, J, 2, a). Thomas MANN was a major German novelist of this period.

Despite his immense popularity there have been no general studies of Remarque in English or German. His career is briefly summarized in Harry T. Moore, *Twentieth-century German Literature* (1967). Useful for general background is Ernst Rose, *A History of German Literature* (1960).

*   *   *

REMBRANDT / By Madlyn Kahr

Rembrandt Harmensz van Rijn (1606–1669) was the paramount artist of the great age of Dutch painting. In range, originality, and expressive power his large production of paintings, drawings, and etchings has never been surpassed.

In the attempt to grasp the full measure of the achievement of Rembrandt (pronounced rĕm′brănt), the mistake has sometimes been made of interpreting his works as an autobiography. This they are not. His experiences are reflected in his works not directly, but transfigured into art. The events of art are different in nature from the events of life, and we understand very little about the relations between these two different realms of being. The few mundane facts we know about Rembrandt's life do not begin to explain his works or account for his extraordinary capacities.

Rembrandt was born in Leiden on July 15, 1606, next to the last of the nine or more children of the miller Harmen Gerritsz van Rijn and the baker's daughter Neeltgen Willemsd van Zuytbroeck. For 7 years Rembrandt was a student at the Latin school, and then, in 1620, he enrolled at the university. After only a few months, however, he left to become a painter. He was an apprentice for 3 years of the painter Jacob Isaacsz van Swanenburgh, who had studied in Italy.

In 1624 Rembrandt went to Amsterdam to work with Pieter Lastman, a painter of biblical, mythological, and historical scenes. In the 16th and 17th centuries art theory ranked "history painting" as superior to all other fields, and Lastman was one of the most respected specialists in this kind of subject matter in Holland at the time. Anecdotal painting like Lastman's came to be overshadowed in Rembrandt's time by other themes, such as landscape and still life. In fact, Rembrandt and his school were virtually the only painters of importance who continued to concern themselves with narrative subject matter, mainly based on biblical stories, through the second and third quarters of the century. Unlike Lastman, though, Rembrandt and his followers depicted a great variety of other subjects as well. Yet years later, even after Lastman's death in 1633, Rembrandt continued to borrow his teacher's subjects and motifs, for instance, in *Susanna Surprised by the Elders*. Rembrandt made a drawing in red chalk after Lastman's 1614 painting of the subject, and in 1647 he freely adapted this composition in a painting.

Works of the Leiden Years

It was Lastman's ability to tell a story visually that impressed his youthful pupil. The earliest works by Rembrandt that we know, beginning with the *Stoning of St. Stephen* (1625), show an only partially successful imitation of Lastman's style, applied to scenes in which a number of figures are involved in a dramatic action.

By 1625 Rembrandt was working independently in Leiden. He was closely associated at this time with Jan Lievens, also a student of Lastman's. The two young men worked so similarly that even in their own lifetime there was doubt as to which of them was responsible for a particular painting. They used the same models and even worked on each other's pictures. Rembrandt's paintings were small in size and scale in these years, however, while Lievens preferred a larger format with life-size figures.

In addition to his narrative subjects, Rembrandt was practicing with pen, brush, and etcher's needle the depiction of emotions conveyed by facial expressions. Throughout his career he was his own most frequent model. Other sitters have been identified as members of his family, but this is conjectural, except in the case of a drawing inscribed with his father's name in a contemporary hand. Rembrandt liked to have his models wear such embellishments as gold chains and plumed hats, testing his skill at depicting varied textures.

By 1631 Rembrandt was ready to compete with the accomplished portrait painters of Amsterdam. His portrait of the Amsterdam merchant Nicolaes Ruts (1631) is a dynamic likeness executed with a degree of assurance that makes it clear why its author was in demand as a portraitist. A major commission soon came to him: *Dr. Nicolaas Tulp Demonstrating the Anatomy of the Arm* (1632). For this large canvas Rembrandt devised a new unified composition for the traditional "anatomy lesson."

Early Amsterdam Years

In 1631 or 1632 Rembrandt moved to Amsterdam, where he had already achieved some recognition as a portraitist. Both his career and his personal life prospered. On a charming silverpoint drawing of a pensive young woman holding a flower, he wrote, "This was drawn after my wife when she was 21 years old, the third day after our engagement—June 8, 1633." After an engagement of more than a year, he married this well-to-do young woman, Saskia van Uijlenburgh. In 1639 the young couple set themselves up in a fine house in the Breestraat, now maintained as a museum, the Rembrandthuis.

Like many prosperous men of his time, Rembrandt soon began to collect works of art, armor, costumes, and curiosities from far places. He used some of these objects as props in his paintings and etchings. The vast collection of drawings and prints that he amassed in the course of time made him familiar with works by artists distant in time and place, as well as by contemporaries. It was, in a way, a substitute for travel; he was quoted as saying, at the age of 23, that he could learn about Italian art without leaving Holland. He had the opportunity to see some Italian paintings in the flourishing mercantile city of Amsterdam, but he would have had to rely mainly on prints to bring Italian art to him. His works reflect his responsiveness to art of the most diverse types, from monumental painting of the High Renaissance to Mogul miniatures.

Rembrandt's works of the middle 1630s were his most baroque; indeed he seemed to be deliberately challenging the enormous prestige of Peter Paul Rubens. This is most explicit in the scenes from the *Passion of Christ* (1633–1639) that Rembrandt painted for the stadholder Frederick Henry. The etching *Angel Appearing to the Shepherds* (1634) shows how the same drama and excitement, the combination of fine detail with a grandiose new sweep based largely on unification of the composition through light and shadow, and the choice of the crucial moment—all characteristic of Rembrandt's baroque style—permeated his graphic works as well as his paintings in this period. The mysterious landscape that adds so strikingly to the emotional communication of this great etching had its parallels in the landscape paintings that also occupied Rembrandt about this time, such as the *Landscape with an Obelisk*.

Middle Period

The *Visitation* (1640) serves well to sum up Rembrandt's style at this transitional point in his development. The rather fussy large-leaved plants and birds in the left foreground are still reminiscent of Lastman. The architecture is pure fantasy; Rembrandt usually represented, in both exterior and interior views, structures that were never seen in reality and, indeed, in many cases could not be built because they were not based on a rational ground plan. The landscape, too, has nothing to do with the innovative Dutch realistic landscape of the 17th century. Its function is to suggest the long distance that Mary has traveled to visit her cousin. Instead of a baroque thrust into depth, the figures are deployed parallel to the picture plane, and prominent horizontal and vertical elements stabilize the composition in the "classicizing" manner that was to predominate in the works of Rembrandt, as in Dutch painting in general, in the middle of the century. Most significant is the fact that the picture dwells on the meaning of the story in a human sense. It demonstrates Rembrandt's unique ability to communicate the inmost emotions of the participants in the scene. The arbitrary use of light is a major expressive resource; this was the hallmark of his genius throughout his career.

One of Rembrandt's largest and most famous paintings is the group portrait known since the mid-18th century as the *Night Watch*. This is, in fact, not a night scene at all, and it is correctly titled the *Militia Company of Captain Frans Banning Cocq*. For this important commission, completed in 1642 but probably begun in the late

---

(Opposite) Rembrandt's The Descent from the Cross, *dated 1653, in the Widener Collection, National Gallery, Washington, D.C. (Kodansha)*

Rembrandt, a self-portrait of 1658. (Copyright The Frick Collection, New York)

1630s, the artist devised an original, dynamic composition in the baroque style which he had already begun to abandon by this time. The painting was unfortunately cut down in the 18th century. Attempts have been made to relate this scene to an actual historical event, to a contemporary drama, and to emblematic ideas. These different interpretations reflect the persistent impression that this is something more than a group portrait.

There is no foundation at all for the legend that Captain Cocq and his company were dissatisfied with their painting and that this failure initiated a decline in Rembrandt's fortunes that persisted until the end of his life. On the contrary, there is considerable evidence that the picture was highly praised from the start. Such difficulties as Rembrandt had were not caused by any rejection of his work.

Having had three children who died in infancy, Saskia gave birth to a fourth child, Titus, in September 1641. In June 1642 Saskia died. Acrimony entered Rembrandt's household with the widow Geertge Dircx, who came to take care of Titus. Hendrickje Stoffels, who is first mentioned in connection with Rembrandt in 1649, remained with him until her death in 1663. She left a daughter, Cornelia, who had been born to them in 1654.

About 1640 Rembrandt developed a new interest in landscape which persisted through the next 2 decades. A series of drawings and etchings show keen observation of nature, great originality in composing, and marvelous economy. The etched *View of Amsterdam* (ca. 1640) was the forerunner of the splendid panoramic landscape paintings of Jacob van Ruisdael. The tiny painting *Winter Landscape* (1646) has all the earmarks of having been painted from life, on the spot. This would be a rare case in 17th-century Dutch landscape, which customarily was painted in the studio from sketches.

In contrast with Rembrandt's dramatic religious com-

The Night Watch *(Militia Company of Captain Frans Banning Cocq), a painting by Rembrandt, completed in 1642. (Rijksmuseum, Amsterdam)*

positions of the earlier period, those of the 1640s tend to be quiet, with exquisitely controlled light casting an almost palpable spiritual glow on scenes that might otherwise seem to depict humble everyday life. The painting *Holy Family* (1646) exemplifies this tender and compassionate quality, as does the *Hundred Guilder Print*, one of the most renowned of the master's etchings, on which he probably worked from about 1645 to 1648. Bust-length paintings of Christ, such as the one in Detroit, from the later 1640s, have a similar emotional tone. Richness of paint surface and warm, harmonious color add luster to the paintings of this period.

Later Years

The ruinous effect on commerce of the first Anglo-Dutch War (1652–1654) may have played a part in Rembrandt's financial difficulties, of which there is evidence from 1653 on. In 1656 he filed a petition of insolvency. In connection with this, an inventory was made listing all his possessions. This list of 363 items is an invaluable source of information as to the objects, and particularly the works of art, that Rembrandt had collected. It included numerous portfolios of drawings and prints. All these prized possessions were sold at auction, beginning in December 1657. In 1660 Rembrandt, Titus, and Hendrickje moved to a smaller house.

The idea that the formerly renowned artist was now friendless and neglected is a fiction. In fact the record shows that several prominent men who were his friends stood by Rembrandt through these misfortunes. Though it is true that fashionable taste in art began to favor a more highly finished and elegant type of painting at this time, nevertheless Rembrandt continued to receive commissions and to work productively.

In 1652 a Sicilian nobleman who was a discerning collector commissioned a painting from Rembrandt. If the painting was satisfactory, two more were to be ordered. *Aristotle Contemplating a Bust of Homer* was completed in 1653 and shipped off to Sicily, and the two additional pictures were sent in 1661. The meaning of the *Aristotle* is not yet fully understood, but its quality is unquestionable. The lavish impasto, the scintillating white and gold contrasted with velvety blacks, and the quality of inwardness and self-communion are characteristic features of Rembrandt's style at this time.

Even commissioned portraits, such as the one Rembrandt painted of his old friend, the Amsterdam patrician Jan Six (1654), were built up of the bold patches of paint that invite the eye of the beholder to see the solid form beneath the surface. Another important commission for a group portrait came to Rembrandt in 1656: the *Anatomy Lesson of Dr. Joan Deyman*, of which only a fragment has survived. A pen drawing, however, shows the symmetrical composition, with the surgeon standing in the center behind the cadaver, which is seen in sharp foreshortening, perpendicular to the picture plane. Other figures are grouped symmetrically on either side. The difference between this composition and the diagonal in depth that unified the *Dr. Tulp* (1632) is a measure of the change not only in Rembrandt but in the dominant style in Dutch painting between the 1630s and the 1650s.

Rembrandt's regal *Self-portrait* (1658; Frick Collection, New York) shows the aging artist seated squarely before us, meeting our eyes with forthright gaze, and wearing a fantastic costume whose sharp horizontals and verticals stress the composition based on right angles that epitomizes this period. A number of admirable etched portraits also date from this time, as well as etchings of religious subjects, such as the impressive *Ecce homo* (1655), which reflects an engraving made in 1510 by the great Dutch graphic artist Lucas van Leyden.

It is noteworthy that even in his full maturity Rembrandt adapted features from many sources. It may be that making the inventory and facing the loss of his collection caused him to give special attention to the prints and drawings in his portfolios. In 1658, for instance, he painted the small and sensitive *Jupiter and Mercury Visiting Philemon and Baucis*, which was based on a painting by Adam Elsheimer, whose work had greatly impressed Rembrandt's teacher, Lastman, when he was studying in Rome. Rembrandt could have known the Elsheimer painting through an engraving made after it by Goudt in 1612.

In 1660–1661 Rembrandt painted an enormous canvas commissioned for the splendid new town hall in Amsterdam. It was the *Conspiracy of the Batavians*, or the *Oath of Julius Civilis*, known to us through the remaining fragment and a pen-and-wash drawing of the entire composition. The 17th-century Dutch, who in 1648, after 80 years of war, had succeeded in finalizing their freedom from Spanish rule, considered themselves the descendants of the Batavians, who had rebelled against the Romans. The scene of the oath was painted broadly, to be viewed from a distance, and in the most luminous colors. For reasons not entirely understood, the painting was removed after hanging in the town hall for a time. Perhaps it was unacceptable because the style was too far from the traditional treatment of patriotic subjects for public places.

In any case, Rembrandt was even at this time held in high regard. In 1662 he painted the *Sampling Officials of the Drapers' Guild*, a group portrait whose vitality and psychological penetration certainly justified these dignified officials in their choice of a portraitist. The boldness of his brushstroke, the effulgence of his color, glowing like embers in a dark room, and the command of emotional content increased as he grew older. The beautiful pair of late portraits, *Man with a Magnifying Glass* and *Lady with a Pink*, have few peers in all the realm of art.

Hendrickje died in 1663. In February 1668 Titus married Magdalena van Loo; he died in September. The lonely Rembrandt continued to paint. His last *Self-portrait* (Mauritshuis, The Hague) is dated 1669. When he died, on Oct. 4, 1669, a painting, *Simeon with the Christ Child in the Temple*, was left unfinished on his easel.

Rembrandt the Teacher

Throughout his career Rembrandt was much sought after as a teacher, and the fees his pupils paid yielded considerable income. Even as early as the Leiden years students came to him; Gerard Dou was working in his studio by 1628, and it has been conjectured that it is Dou who is represented in Rembrandt's typical small painting of that year, the *Painter at His Easel*. Later pupils included Jacob Adriaansz Backer, Ferdinand Bol, Govaert Flinck, Phillips Koninck, Gerbrand van den Eeckhout, Samuel van Hoogstraten, Carel Fabritius, Abraham Furnerius, Lambert Doomer, Willem Drost, Abraham van Dyck, Heyman Dullaert, and Aert de Gelder.

It was common studio practice for the master to retouch or overpaint the drawings and paintings of his pupils and to sign works done in his studio even if they were not from his own hand. Rembrandt's students worked from life, but they also copied his works. These customs have added to the difficulties in attribution. Deliberate falsification has of course also contributed to the problems in determining the authenticity of Rembrandt's works.

Further Reading

Rembrandt is listed in the Art study guide (III, F, 1, b). The only 17th-century northern artist qualitatively comparable to him was Peter Paul RUBENS.

Concise introductions to Rembrandt and his work are Christopher White, *Rembrandt and His World* (1964); Joseph-Émile Muller, *Rembrandt* (1969); and Henry Bonnier, *Rembrandt* (1970). Bob Haak, *Rembrandt: His Life, His Work, His Time* (trans. 1969), has an excellent text and many reproductions. Scholarly studies of the artist include Jakob Rosenberg, *Rembrandt: Life and Work* (rev. ed. 1964), and Otto Benesch, *Rembrandt*, edited by Eva Benesch (1970).

The standard catalog of the paintings is Abraham Bredius, *Rembrandt: The Complete Edition of the Paintings*, revised by Horst Gerson (1969), although its reproductions leave much to be desired. Far more satisfactory are the plates in Horst Gerson, *Rembrandt Paint-*

ings (1968), which includes excellent essays on Rembrandt's life and his place in Dutch painting. The way in which our understanding of Rembrandt can best be increased, through the study in depth of individual works, is admirably demonstrated by Julius S. Held, *Rembrandt's "Aristotle" and Other Rembrandt Studies* (1969). Arthur M. Hind, *A Catalogue of Rembrandt's Etchings* (1923; 2d rev. ed. 1967), is the standard catalog of the prints; and Otto Benesch, *The Drawings of Rembrandt* (6 vols., 1954–1957), is the basic reference work on the drawings.

Recommended for general background are Paul Zumthor, *Daily Life in Rembrandt's Holland* (1959; trans. 1963); Pieter Geyl, *The Netherlands in the Seventeenth Century* (2 vols., 1961–1964); Jakob Rosenberg, Seymour Slive, and E. H. ter Kuile, *Dutch Art and Architecture, 1600–1800* (1966); and Johan H. Huizinga, *Dutch Civilization in the Seventeenth Century and Other Essays*, selected by Pieter Geyl (1968).

REMINGTON / By William Gerdts

Frederic Remington (1861–1909) was the leading American artist in portraying the West during the late 19th century.

Frederic Remington was born in October 1861 in Canton, N.Y. He grew up in Ogdensburg, and early came to love the outdoors. In 1878 he entered the newly formed Art School of Yale University. After 2 years at Yale, his father died, and Remington left school to go west. He worked as a clerk, cowboy, and rancher until 1885, when he went to New York City.

Remington made his reputation through his illustrations of scenes of the West that appeared in such magazines as *Century, Harper's Monthly, Harper's Weekly, Scribner's,* and *Collier's.* In 1895 he began to execute sculptures. His first sculpture, *The Bronco Buster,* was followed by such subjects as *The Wounded Bunkie, The Scalp, The Cheyenne, The Rattlesnake, The Outlaw,* and *Trooper of the Plain.* These popular bronzes, which appeared in fairly large editions and achieved a popularity equal to, or greater than, his illustrations and oil paintings, were unique in American art of the time.

It was only late in his life that Remington was considered a serious artist rather than an illustrator. Though his paintings have an immediate appeal as illustrations, he was not unaware of contemporary artistic trends, and his late oils reflect an interest in effects of sunlight and color which can be termed impressionistic.

Remington knew the subjects he illustrated, painted, and sculptured well. His Indians, cavalrymen, horses, and the way of life of settlers and Indian tribes were executed with utmost authenticity. He had full knowledge, too, of both human and animal anatomy. A major ingredient of his art was his concern with activity and his ability to

Frederic Remington. (Remington Art Memorial, Ogdensburg, N.Y.)

suggest motion, often of a violent nature. He died in Ridgefield, Conn., on Dec. 26, 1909.

Until recently Remington was considered primarily an illustrator, and though a successful one, he was not usually accorded the position of a true artist. This was partly because he often wrote the texts accompanying his illustrations and also because many of his finest works are monochromatic since they were intended to be reproduced in black and white. Now critical opinion has changed, particularly in regard to his sculpture.

Further Reading

Frederic Remington is listed in the Art study guide (IV, D, 3). His contemporary Charles Marion RUSSELL was also famous for his paintings of the West.

Frederic Remington's Own West (1960), composed of Remington's writings and illustrations, was edited by Harold McCracken. The standard biography is Harold McCracken, *Frederic Remington: Artist of the Old West* (1947). A recent examination of Remington is in G. Edward White, *The Eastern Establishment and the Western Experience: The West of Frederic Remington, Theodore Roosevelt, and Owen Wister* (1968). See also Oliver W. Larkin, *Art and Life in America* (1949; rev. ed. 1960).

REMOND / By C. Eric Lincoln

Charles Lennox Remond (1810–1873), American black leader, was one of the first black abolitionists and a delegate to the World Antislavery Convention held in London in 1840.

Charles Lennox Remond was born in Salem, Mass., on Feb. 1, 1810, the son of a free West Indian barber who had voluntarily emigrated to the United States. Remond was well educated and, like many of the free, middle-class black Americans of his day, was an ardent abolitionist and a major figure in the Antislavery Convention movement that served as a forum for black Americans after 1830.

Remond was one of the original 17 members of America's first Antislavery Society. The first black American to become a regular lecturer for the Massachusetts Antislavery Society, he was an ardent supporter of William Lloyd Garrison. In 1838 Remond was elected secretary of the American Antislavery Society and vice president of the New England Antislavery Society.

For several years Remond was the most distinguished black abolitionist in America. When his uniqueness was challenged by Frederick Douglass, Remond reacted bitterly. While he never got over his jealousy of Douglass, on several occasions the two found themselves allied. One occasion was the national antislavery convention at Buffalo, N.Y. (1843), at which Henry Highland Garnett challenged the slaves to liberate themselves by any means necessary. Remond and Douglass led the opposition that rejected the address as the sentiment of the convention. Neither man was at this time committed to violence, or even to political action, as a means of liberation.

As time passed, Remond grew increasingly frustrated over the injustice of color discrimination. He protested

Charles Lennox Remond and other abolitionists were united against the Federal Fugitive Slave Laws. This 1850 print by Hoff and Bloede favors the abolitionist cause and supports the position with two quotations. The first, from the Bible, begins "Thou shalt not deliver unto the master his servant which has escaped from his master unto thee. . . ."; the second, "We hold that all men are created equal . . .," is from the Declaration of Independence. (Library of Congress)

Charles Lennox Remond. (Library of Congress)

segregated travel in Massachusetts and was so incensed by the Dred Scott decision (1857) that he felt he could "owe no allegiance to a country . . . which treats us like dogs." For black people to persist in claiming citizenship under the U.S. Constitution seemed to him "mean-spirited and craven." Eventually he moved very close to the radical position of the fiery Garnett. Speaking at the State Convention of Massachusetts Negroes in New Bedford (1858), he urged that the convention promote an insurrection among the slaves, declaring that he would rather see his people die than live in bondage.

During the Civil War, Remond recruited for the Negro 54th Massachusetts Infantry. After the war he served as a clerk in the Boston customhouse until his death on Dec. 22, 1873.

Further Reading

Charles Lennox Remond is listed in the American History study guide (V, F, 3, e). Frederick DOUGLASS was America's most famous black abolitionist.

Useful information on Remond is offered by Herbert Aptheker, ed., *A Documentary History of the Negro People in the United States* (1951), and by August Meier and Elliot Rudwick, eds., *The Making of Black America: Essays in Negro Life and History* (2 vols., 1969). See also John Daniels, *In Freedom's Birthplace: A Study of the Boston Negroes* (1914; repr. 1968); Carter G. Woodson and Charles H. Wesley, *The Negro in Our History* (1922; 11th rev. ed. 1966); and Wilhelmena S. Robinson, *Historical Negro Biographies* (1967; 2d rev. ed. 1969).

RENAN / By B. F. Bart

A French author, philologist, archeologist, and founder of comparative religion, Ernest Renan (1823–1892) influenced European thought in the second half of the 19th century through his numerous writings.

Ernest Renan (pronounced rə-näN′) grew up in the mystical, Catholic French province of Brittany, where Celtic myths combined with his mother's deeply experienced Catholicism led this sensitive child to believe he was destined for the priesthood. He was educated at the ecclesiastical college at Tréguier, graduating in 1838, and then went to Paris, where he carried on the usual theological studies at St-Nicolas-du-Chardonnet and at St-Sulpice. In his *Recollections of Childhood and Youth* (1883) he recounted the spiritual crisis he went through as his growing interest in scientific studies of the Bible eventually made orthodoxy unacceptable; he was soon won over to the new "religion of science," a conversion fostered by his friendship with the chemist P. E. M. Berthelot.

Renan abandoned the seminary and earned his doctorate in philosophy. At this time (1848) he wrote *The Future of Science* but did not publish it till 1890. In this work he affirmed a faith in the wonders to be brought

Ernest Renan. (Library of Congress)

forth by a science not yet realized, but which he was sure would come.

Archeological expeditions to the Near East and further studies in Semitics led Renan to a concept of religious studies which would later be known as comparative religion. His was an anthropomorphic view, first publicized in his *Life of Jesus* (1863), in which he portrayed Christ as a historical phenomenon with historical roots and needing a rational, nonmystical explanation. With his characteristic suppleness of intellect, this deeply pious agnostic wrote a profoundly irreligious work which lost him his professorship in the dominantly Catholic atmosphere of the Second Empire in France.

The *Life of Jesus* was the opening volume of Renan's *History of the Origins of Christianity* (1863–1883), his most influential work. His fundamental thesis was that all religions are true and good, for all embody man's noblest aspirations: he invited each man to phrase these truths in his own way. For many, a reading of this work made religion for the first time living truth; for others, it made religious conviction impossible.

The defeat of France in the Franco-Prussian War of 1870–1871 was for Renan, as for many Frenchmen, a deeply disillusioning experience. If Germany, which he revered, could do this to France, which he loved, where did goodness, beauty, or truth lie? He became profoundly skeptical, but with painful honesty he refused to deny what seemed to lie before him, averring instead that "the truth is perhaps sad." He remained sympathetic to Christianity, perhaps expressing it most movingly in his *Prayer on the Acropolis of Athens* (1876), in which he reaffirmed his abiding faith in the Greek life of the mind but confessed that his was inevitably a larger world, with sorrows unknown to the goddess Athena; hence he could never be a true son of Greece, any more than any other modern.

Further Reading

Ernest Renan is listed in the Social Sciences study guide (VI, A, 2). Adolf von HARNACK also wrote about early Christianity.

Little has been written in English about Renan. The best studies are by Richard M. Chadbourne: *Ernest Renan as an Essayist* (1957) and *Ernest Renan* (1968).

RENI / By Robert Enggass

The Italian painter Guido Reni (1575–1642) is known for the gentle, highly decorative form of baroque classicism he developed.

Guido Reni (pronounced rā′nē) was born in Bologna on Nov. 4, 1575. He began his apprenticeship under the mannerist painter Denis Calvaert and then entered the new, more progressive art school run by the Carracci. Their influence was to prove deci-

Guido Reni, a self-portrait, in the Uffizi, Florence. (Alinari)

sive. The Carracci opposed mannerism and urged instead a return to the generalized realism of the great masters of the High Renaissance, above all to Raphael, Titian, and Veronese.

Reni's personal life is a delight to those who insist that artists must be peculiar. He was, according to contemporary reports, neither heterosexual nor homosexual but absolutely sexless. His obsessive fear of women reached the point where he believed their slightest touch might poison him. The discovery of a woman's blouse that had found its way into his laundry left him terrified. Even in his own day there was thought to be a relationship between the asceticism of his life and the subdued, withdrawn quality of his art.

During the first years of the 17th century Reni spent much time in Rome. At first the fame of Caravaggio overwhelmed him. In the *Crucifixion of St. Peter* (ca. 1603) Reni tried as best he could to imitate Caravaggio's rough peasant types and deep shadows. At the same time, through the rather formal poses of the figures and the careful symmetry of the composition, he attempted to maintain his native Bolognese classicism.

But Reni soon abandoned this uneasy compromise. By 1609 he had replaced Annibale Carracci as the leader of baroque classicism in Rome. The *Aurora* fresco that Reni painted in the Casino of the Pallavicini-Rospigliosi palace in Rome (1614) is justly famous for its crisp, Hellenistic elegance.

After Reni returned to Bologna in 1614, his formalism became still more accentuated. In *Atalanta and Hippomenes* (ca. 1625) the coldly impersonal nude figures, though shown in the act of running a race, are frozen like fragments of ancient marble statues that have been cemented into a wall so as to form abstract linear patterns.

Late in life Reni developed what 17th-century critics called his second manner. In paintings such as *Cleopatra* and *Girl with a Wreath* (ca. 1635) we no longer see elaborate arrangements of poses or garment folds. Their place is taken by a play not of line but of color, of paint laid on thinly in loose, open brushstrokes. The many pale, commingled hues are all grayed over, so that their color harmonies, at times almost painfully delicate, can be read only with intensive study. Reni died on Aug. 18, 1642, in Bologna.

Further Reading

Guido Reni is listed in the Art study guide (III, F, 1, a). He was greatly influenced by the CARRACCI.

The standard work on Reni is in Italian. In English, see the sections on him in Rudolf Wittkower, *Art and Architecture in Italy, 1600–1750* (1962; 2d ed. 1965), and in E. K. Waterhouse, *Italian Baroque Painting* (1962; 2d ed. 1969). The chapter on Reni in Robert Enggass and Jonathan Brown, *Sources and Documents in the History of Art: Italy and Spain, 1600–1750* (1970), gives an interesting picture of Reni's strange personality as seen through 17th-century eyes.

Karl Renner in 1934. (National Archives, Washington, D.C.)

RENNER / By Diethelm Prowe

The Austrian statesman and president Karl Renner (1870–1950) provided his nation with vigorous and able leadership after both world wars.

Karl Renner (pronounced rĕn′ər) was born on Dec. 14, 1870, the eighteenth and last child of impoverished peasants in the Moravian village of Unter-Tannowitz near the Austrian border. Forced to leave home at age 14, he eventually studied law at Vienna, where he first became active in the Social Democratic party. Upon receiving a doctor of laws degree in the spring of 1896, he secured a position in the library of the Austrian Parliament, where he remained until his election to Parliament as a Social Democrat in 1907. He established his political reputation primarily in the theoretical realm with the publication of numerous significant treatises on the crucial issues of nationalities and constitution plaguing the Austro-Hungarian Empire at that time. Combining Socialist thought with national sentiment, he envisioned a democratic Austria as the nucleus and model for a Central European confederation of autonomous nationalities.

Always a pragmatic Marxist, Renner devoted himself during World War I primarily to questions of food supply, social security payments, and tax burdens for the lower classes—beyond a continued and impassioned plea for peace and a solution of the nationalities question. He was selected provisional chancellor on Oct. 30, 1918, and then permanent chancellor in February 1919. In this position, which he held until June 11, 1920, he prepared for the abdication of the Emperor, presided over the establishment of the republic, defended the young republic against virulent attacks from extreme left and right, led the Austrian delegation to the peace negotiations of Saint-Germain (1919), and—as chancellor and as foreign minister until October 1920—struggled in vain for unification with Germany.

With the Socialists out of power, Renner, with the exception of his tenure as president of the National Assembly from April 1931 to March 1933, faded increasingly into the background and, during the fascist era of Engelbert Dollfuss, was branded a traitor and briefly imprisoned in 1934. Withdrawn in seclusion during the Nazi occupation and World War II, he was recalled as provisional chancellor by the Soviet occupation authorities on April 27, 1945. Beyond restoring governmental functions in Austria, he used this position with great skill to preserve the unity of Austria and secure free parliamentary elections through difficult negotiations with the Soviets and the Western Allied authorities. As the Second Republic's first president from Dec. 20, 1945, he secured vital respect and legitimacy for the republic both at home and abroad. He died in office in Vienna on Dec. 31, 1950.

Further Reading

Karl Renner is listed in the European History study guide (X, E, 1). His policies were opposed by Engelbert DOLLFUSS.

Neither Renner's memoirs nor the major biography of him has been translated into English. For background information on Renner and Austria see Richard Hiscocks, *The Rebirth of Austria* (1953); Friedrich Funder, *From Empire to Republic* (1956; trans. 1963); Wenzel Jaksch, *Europe's Road to Potsdam* (1958; trans. 1963); and Martin Gilbert, *The European Powers, 1900–45* (1965).

RENOIR / By Carl Belz

The French painter Pierre Auguste Renoir (1841–1919) was one of the central figures of the impressionist movement. His work is characterized by an extraordinary richness of feeling, a warmth of response to the world and to the people in it.

D uring the 1870s a revolution erupted in French painting. Encouraged by artists like Gustave Courbet and Édouard Manet, a number of young painters began to seek alternatives to the traditions of Western painting that had prevailed since the beginning of the Renaissance. These artists went directly to nature for their inspiration and into the actual society of which they were a part. As a result, their works revealed a look of freshness and immediacy that in many ways departed from the look of Old Master painting. The new art, for instance, displayed vibrant light and color instead of the somber browns and blacks that had dominated previous painting. These qualities, among others, signaled the beginning of modern art.

Pierre Auguste Renoir (pronounced rə-nwàr/) was a central figure of this development, particularly in its impressionist phase. Like the other impressionists, he struggled through periods of public ridicule during his early career. But as the new style gradually became accepted, during the 1880s and 1890s, Renoir began to enjoy extensive patronage and international recognition. The high esteem accorded his art at that time has generally continued into the present day.

Renoir was born in Limoges on Feb. 25, 1841. Shortly afterward, his family moved to Paris. Because he showed a remarkable talent for drawing, Renoir became an apprentice in a porcelain factory, where he painted plates. Later, after the factory had gone out of business, he worked for his older brother, decorating fans. Throughout these early years Renoir made frequent visits to the Louvre, where he studied the art of earlier French masters, particularly those of the 18th century—Antoine Watteau, François Boucher, and Jean Honoré Fragonard.

His deep respect for these artists informed his own painting throughout his career.

Early Career

In 1862 Renoir decided to study painting seriously and entered the Atelier Gleyre, where he met Claude Monet, Alfred Sisley, and Jean Frédéric Bazille. During the next 6 years Renoir's art showed the influence of Gustave Courbet and Édouard Manet, the two most innovative painters of the 1850s and 1860s. Courbet's influence is especially evident in the bold palette-knife technique of *Diane Chasseresse* (1867), while Manet's can be seen in the flat tones of *Alfred Sisley and His Wife* (1868). Still, both paintings reveal a sense of intimacy that is characteristic of Renoir's personal style.

The 1860s were difficult years for Renoir. At times he was too poor to buy paints or canvas, and the Salons of 1866 and 1867 rejected his works. The following year the Salon accepted his painting *Lise*. He continued to develop his work and to study the paintings of his contemporaries—not only Courbet and Manet, but Camille Corot and Eugène Delacroix as well. Renoir's indebtedness to Delacroix is apparent in the lush painterliness of the *Odalisque* (1870).

Pierre Auguste Renoir, a self-portrait. (French Cultural Services of the French Embassy)

Renoir and Impressionism

In 1869 Renoir and Monet worked together at La Grenouillère, a bathing spot on the Seine. Both artists became obsessed with painting light and water. According to Phoebe Pool (1967), this was a decisive moment in the development of impressionism, for "It was there that Renoir and Monet made their discovery that shadows are not brown or black but are coloured by their surroundings, and that the 'local colour' of an object is modified by the light in which it is seen, by reflections from other objects and by contrast with juxtaposed colours."

The styles of Renoir and Monet were virtually identical at this time, an indication of the dedication with which they pursued and shared their new discoveries. During the 1870s they still occasionally worked together, although their styles generally developed in more personal directions.

In 1874 Renoir participated in the first impressionist exhibition. His works included the *Opera Box* (1874), a painting which shows the artist's penchant for rich and freely handled figurative expression. Of all the impressionists, Renoir most consistently and thoroughly adapted the new style—in its inspiration, essentially a landscape style—to the great tradition of figure painting.

Although the impressionist exhibitions were the targets of much public ridicule during the 1870s, Renoir's patronage gradually increased during the decade. He became a friend of Caillebotte, one of the first patrons of the impressionists, and he was also backed by the art dealer Durand-Ruel and by collectors like Victor Choquet, the Charpentiers, and the Daidets. The artist's connection with these individuals is documented by a number of handsome portraits, for instance, *Madame Charpentier and Her Children* (1878).

In the 1870s Renoir also produced some of his most celebrated impressionist genre scenes, including the *Swing* and the *Moulin de la Galette* (both 1876). These works embody his most basic attitudes about art and life. They show men and women together, openly and casually enjoying a society diffused with warm, radiant sunlight. Figures blend softly into one another and into their surrounding space. Such worlds are pleasurable, sensuous, and generously endowed with human feeling.

Renoir's "Dry" Period

During the 1880s Renoir gradually separated himself from the impressionists, largely because he became dissatisfied with the direction the new style was taking in his own hands. In paintings like the *Luncheon of the Boating Party* (1880–1881), he felt that his style was becoming too loose, that forms were losing their distinctiveness and sense of mass. As a result, he looked to the past for a fresh inspiration. In 1881 he traveled to Italy and was particularly impressed by the art of Raphael.

During the next 6 years Renoir's paintings became increasingly dry: he began to draw in a tight, classical manner, carefully outlining his figures in an effort to give them plastic clarity. The works from this period, such as the *Umbrellas* (1883) and the *Grandes baigneuses* (1884–1887), are generally considered the least successful of Renoir's mature expressions. Their classicizing effort seems self-conscious, a contradiction to the warm sensuality that came naturally to him.

Late Career

By the end of the 1880s Renoir had passed through his dry period. His late work is truly extraordinary: a glorious outpouring of monumental nude figures, beautiful young girls, and lush landscapes. Examples of this style include the *Music Lesson* (1891), *Young Girl Reading* (1892), and *Sleeping Bather* (1897). In many ways, the generosity of feeling in these paintings expands upon the achievements of his great work in the 1870s.

Renoir's health declined severely in his later years. In 1903 he suffered his first attack of rheumatoid arthritis and settled for the winter at Cagnes-sur-Mer. By this time he faced no financial problems, but the arthritis made painting painful and often impossible. Nevertheless, he continued to work, at times with a brush tied to his crippled hand. Renoir died at Cagnes-sur-Mer on Dec. 3, 1919, but his death was preceded by an experience of supreme triumph: the state had purchased his portrait *Madame Georges Charpentier* (1877), and he traveled to Paris in August to see it hanging in the Louvre.

Further Reading

Pierre Auguste Renoir is listed in the Art study guide (III, H, 1, e). He was influenced by Eugène DELACROIX, Camille COROT, Gustave COURBET, and Édouard MANET. Renoir and Claude MONET were the main pillars of impressionism.

An intimate biography of Renoir is by his son, Jean Renoir, *Renoir: My Father* (trans. 1962). A standard monograph on the artist is Albert C. Barnes and Violette De Mazia, *The Art of Renoir* (1935). Renoir's drawings are richly represented in *Renoir Drawings*, edited by John Rewald (1946). For a complete survey of impressionism and Renoir's relation to the movement see Rewald's *The History of Impressionism* (1946; rev. ed. 1961). A more general survey, also of high quality, is Phoebe Pool, *Impressionism* (1967).

✳   ✳   ✳

RENWICK / By Paul F. Norton

The American architect James Renwick (1818–1895) designed churches, hotels, commercial buildings, and homes for the rich.

(Opposite) Renoir's Le Moulin de la Galette, *a detail of the 1876 painting, in the Louvre, Paris. (Kodansha)*

James Renwick was born on Nov. 1, 1818, in New York City. His father was a professor at Columbia College and an engineer. In 1836 James graduated from Columbia College. Following his father's example, he turned to engineering as a profession, taking a position with the Erie Railroad and then supervising construction for the Croton reservoir and aqueduct.

Renwick abruptly shifted to architecture by winning the competition for Grace Church (1843–1846) at Broadway and 10th Street in New York City. The design of the church, mainly late English Gothic in style, is remarkably coherent, except for the spire that was added later to replace the earlier wooden one. Following this success, he gained many commissions for churches in New York, such as Calvary Church (1846), Church of the Puritans (1846), Saint Bartholomew's (1872), and Saint Patrick's Cathedral (1853, dedicated 1879, completed 1887). Saint Patrick's is generally considered his finest church. Its west facade is as well composed as any Gothic revival building in America.

The Smithsonian Institution (1846–1855), Washington, D.C., though burned in 1865 and repaired by another architect, is as interesting a design as any conceived by Renwick. In its complete lack of harmony with the established classical style of the Mall, this building has an aura of romance, of a colorful fairyland of picturesque angles, turrets, towers, and gingerbread decorations. Also in

Washington, Renwick built the first Corcoran Gallery of Art (1859), which became the U.S. Court of Claims. Built of brick and brown stone, it is well proportioned and owes much to Jacques Lemercier's work on the Louvre in Paris. This is noticeable in the square dome, mansard roof, and imitative decoration.

Secure in his profession, Renwick was commissioned to build banks, hotels, and many private residences for well-to-do clients in New York, Staten Island, and Newport, R.I. In order to meet these obligations, he hired several young architects, among them John W. Root and Bertram Goodhue. (Both men were recognized as superior in the next generation.)

The Charity Hospital on Welfare Island in New York City (1858–1861), though esthetically unsuccessful, was considered otherwise by the Board of Governors, who commented that "Its truly magnificent structure presents the appearance of a stately palace." Renwick based this design on the Tuileries Palace in Paris. Its gray stone was quarried by prisoners on Welfare Island; its quoins and lintels were of a lighter shade, and purple slate covered the roof. He designed the first major building for Vassar College, Poughkeepsie, N.Y. (1860–1861). Built of red brick, with blue stone trim and a green and purple mansard roof, the structure is chiefly noted for its fireproofing, central heating from a separate building, cast-iron columns, and colorful, though awkward, appearance. Renwick died in New York City on June 23, 1895.

Further Reading

James Renwick is listed in the Art study guide (IV, C, 4). Richard UPJOHN was noted for his Gothic revival buildings.

There is no biography of Renwick, but some information on his life is in William R. Stewart, *Grace Church and Old New York* (1924).

✳   ✳   ✳

James Renwick, an engraved portrait by George S. Perine. (Courtesy of The New-York Historical Society, New York City)

RESPIGHI / By Peter S. Hansen

The rather conservative eclecticism of the music of the Italian composer Ottorino Respighi (1879–1936) made it immediately popular. His skill in writing for orchestra was unsurpassed.

The father of Ottorino Respighi (pronounced rĕ-spē′gē) was a professional musician and teacher at Bologna's Liceo Musicale, where Ottorino received his first musical training. He was a gifted violinist, and it was not until after his graduation from the conservatory that he definitely decided to be a composer rather than a violin virtuoso. Realizing that he needed a broader musical background than that supplied at home, he went to St. Petersburg to study with Nicolai Rimsky-Korsakov and later to Berlin to study with Max Bruch, a rather conservative German composer.

After his return to Italy, Respighi was appointed professor of composition at the prestigious Conservatory of Santa Cecilia in Rome, and in 1923 he became its director. Tours of Europe and the United States in 1925, 1928, and 1932, in which he conducted his compositions with leading orchestras, spread his fame.

Respighi is chiefly remembered as the composer of two tone poems, the *Fountains of Rome* (1916–1917) and the *Pines of Rome* (1924), brilliantly orchestrated evocations of the Eternal City. In a preface to the score of the former the composer wrote, "In this symphonic poem the composer has endeavored to give expression to the sentiments and visions suggested to him by four of Rome's fountains, contemplated at the hour in which their character is most in harmony with the surrounding landscape, or in which their beauty appears most impressive to the observer." The *Pines* also has four sections, depicting the Villa Borghese, a catacomb, the Janiculum, and the Appian Way. These are very effective programs because they allowed the composer to write music of contrasting moods and varying associations, both pictorial and historical.

These compositions show Respighi's complete mastery of modern orchestration. His use of solo woodwinds and brass reveals what he learned from Rimsky-Korsakov, but it is also apparent that he knew the scores of Claude Debussy, Maurice Ravel, Igor Stravinsky, and Richard Strauss as well. In the third section of the *Pines*, Respighi introduces a recording of an actual nightingale's song into the score.

Other compositions of Respighi are the operas *The Sunken Bell*, produced at the Metropolitan Opera in New York in 1928, *Maria Egiziaca* (1932), and *La Fiamma* (1934); a ballet commissioned by Sergei Diaghilev, *La Boutique fantasque* (1919), written on themes by Gioacchino Rossini; and a *Concerto Gregoriano* (1922) for violin and orchestra, based on Gregorian chant.

Further Reading

Ottorino Respighi is listed in the Music study guide (I, I, 8). He studied with Nicolai RIMSKY-KORSAKOV. Other composers of symphonic poems were Claude DEBUSSY, Richard STRAUSS, and Jean SIBELIUS.

There is no biography of Respighi in English, but his wife, Elsa Respighi, wrote a memoir, *Ottorino Respighi* (trans. 1962). He is discussed in Paul Collaer, *A History of Modern Music* (1955; trans. 1961), and David Ewen, *The World of Twentieth-century Music* (1968).

RETIEF / By A. P. J. van Rensburg

Pieter Retief (1780–1838) was a South African emigrant leader. Some historians call him the first "president" of the Dutch-speaking people of South Africa. He gave expression to the racial policies of his people and formulated their republican ideals.

P ieter Retief (pronounced rə-tēf′) was born on Nov. 12, 1780, at Wagenmakersvallei (modern Wellington, South Africa), strangely enough to pureblood French parents, although a century had elapsed since the Huguenot emigration. There was not much prospect of a livelihood for all 10 children on the family's wine farm, so Pieter became a clerk in a store. Later on, his employer entrusted him with a stock of goods, and he went trading eastward, reaching the border of the Cape Colony.

Retief's letters show him to have been an intelligent and refined person. He had an irrefutable record of moral integrity, honesty, and benevolence. He was a restless person, driven by an enterprising nature and boundless energy.

Life as a Frontiersman

In 1814 Retief married Lenie Greyling. He bought a farm on the Koega River but afterward moved to Grahamstown, where he became one of its wealthiest men. He eventually fell prey to his less scrupulous business partners and ended up bankrupt. Retief returned to farming—in the Great Winterberg. He soon regained solven-

Ottorino Respighi. (Italian Cultural Institute, New York)

cy and proved himself a brave, respected, and esteemed commandant, a favorite with the authorities and trusted leader of his fellow citizens.

Spokesman for His People

As mediator in all dealings between citizens and the government, Retief was the embodiment of cooperative force, a man who did his utmost to procure permanent peace and safety on the frontier. As time went by, these attempts proved futile, and he eventually despaired. He then planned and prepared the orderly emigration of the dissatisfied Boers northward to the country beyond the Orange and Vaal rivers.

Retief summarized the reasons for this Great Trek and formulated the ideals of the emigrant farmers. To check the frequent losses and disturbances experienced on the eastern frontier, he visualized a Voortrekker government in the interior that would be the embodiment of an orderly state, where there would be "prospects for peace and happiness for their children" and where "with resoluteness, the principle of true freedom will be esteemed" —a government with "proper laws," based upon the fundamental concept of "righteousness." He issued a manifesto on Jan. 22, 1837, which was the declaration of independence of the Voortrekker farmers.

Retief was elected governor of the Voortrekker community then assembled at Thabanchu in the interior. In September he undertook to explore Port Natal and to barter with the Zulu king Dingane. He arrived in November at the laager. His ambition to reside in the promised land between the Tugela and Umzimvubu rivers was almost fulfilled. Upon Dingane's request, Retief punished Sekonyela in January 1838 for the latter's theft of Zulu cattle. Then he proceeded to the Zulu capital to settle the ceding of the territory in Natal to the emigrant farmers.

But tragedy awaited the man who had done so much for the betterment of his fellow citizens. On February 6 Zulu warriors—acting upon Dingane's command "Kill the wizards!"—slaughtered Retief and his company in the hills of Umgungundlovu.

An Evaluation

The death of Retief deprived the Voortrekkers of a talented, far-seeing statesman. Two letters illustrate his genius. On July 18, 1837, Retief wrote to native captains in the neighborhood. This letter not only outlined the Voortrekker principles of segregation, that is, the still-held notion of separate development of European and non-European in South Africa, but also the all-important idea of the peaceful coexistence between nations. The racial policy of the Afrikaner had developed long before he wrote this letter, but Retief, as leader of the Voortrekkers, for the first time gave expression to these principles.

Three days later he wrote to the governor of the Cape Colony, declaring that the Voortrekker community desired to be acknowledged as "a free and independent people." This request was refused, but for the first time the republican notions of the Afrikaner were expressed at

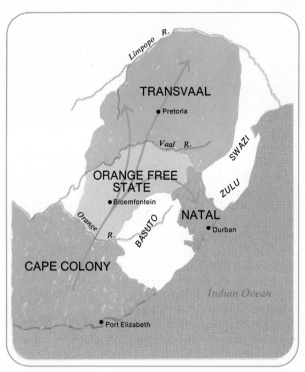

The Great Trek. To escape British rule in Cape Colony, Boer farmers in the 1830s migrated across the Orange and Vaal rivers and founded the Boer republics of Transvaal, Orange Free State, and Natal. Pieter Retief led the Voortrekkers whose destination was Natal, but he was slain by the Zulus before his plans could be accomplished.

the international level. Perhaps Preller did not exaggerate when he concluded his biography on Retief by saying, "[It is] Retief's greatest virtue that in his deeds and in his death, he compelled the Dutch-Afrikaans Emigrants to believe that they were not merely isolated, roaming individuals, but that everyone was a participant in a great national bond, with one concern and one destination."

Further Reading

Pieter Retief is listed in the Africa study guide (VII, F, 3, b). DINGANE and SHAKA were Zulu kings at the time of much of South Africa's colonization.

Major biographies of Retief are in Afrikaans. Recommended for general historical background are George M. Theal, *A History of South Africa* (1904); George E. Cory, *The Rise of South Africa* (1910); and Manfred Nathan, *The Voortrekkers of South Africa* (1937).

REUCHLIN / By Edward M. Peters

The German humanist and jurist Johann Reuchlin (1455–1522) was one of the greatest Hebraists of early modern Europe. He was involved in a great controversy concerning Hebrew literature that culminated in the famous "Letters of Obscure Men."

Johann Reuchlin (pronounced roiKH'lēn) was born at Pforzheim. He studied at Freiburg, Paris, Basel, and Rome; became a doctor of law; and began an impressive career as a public official and jurist. Reuchlin's studies in Italy had acquainted him with humanism, and his command of Greek and Latin was as accomplished as that of any scholar north of the Alps. A second journey to Italy, in 1492, caused Reuchlin to become interested in Hebrew, which he then studied intensely and described in a short book in 1494. Reuchlin soon became the most accomplished Gentile Hebraist of the Renaissance, and in 1506 he produced a grammar of Hebrew entitled *Rudimenta Hebraica*. His linguistic studies led Reuchlin to a genuine interest in Judaism and also into one of the most famous controversies in the history of anti-Semitism.

In 1506 a converted Jew named Johann Pfefferkorn began to produce a series of pamphlets in which he condemned Jewish "errors," ritual, and learning. He urged the forcible conversion of all Jews and obtained imperial permission to confiscate Jewish books. In 1509–1510 Pfefferkorn became more powerful, and Reuchlin's remarks in 1510 that Jewish books should not be burned but, indeed, chairs of Hebrew should be established in German universities made him a target not only of Pfefferkorn but also of the Dominican order at Cologne. In 1511, 1512, and 1513 Reuchlin issued pamphlets de-

fending his own position and the value to Christian scholars of Hebrew literature. Although Reuchlin by no means believed that Jewish literature did not contain errors dangerous to Christians, his spirited defense of Hebrew and of the Jews remains one of the earliest modern Christian attacks on anti-Semitism. In 1514 Reuchlin was acquitted of charges of heresy by the bishop of Speyer, but his enemies then managed to transfer the case to Rome.

In 1514 Reuchlin issued a collection of letters in his defense written by the greatest humanistic scholars in Europe, the *Letters of Eminent Men*. In 1515 another collection of letters, the *Epistolae obscurorum virorum* (*Letters of Obscure Men*), appeared. Ostensibly serious letters from monks supporting the persecution of Reuchlin, the collection was in fact a withering satire on Reuchlin's opponents. The *Letters of Obscure Men* caused a furor: it was a superb example of humanist scorn not only of bigotry and stupidity but also of the ecclesiastical circles in which these traits dominated. Both Sir Thomas More and Erasmus applauded this work, written by Crotus Rubianus and Ulrich von Hutten.

Reuchlin's enemies, however, attacked him with even greater savagery, finally securing a papal condemnation of his position in 1520. Reuchlin was severely hurt by the final condemnation. He spent the last few years of his life teaching and lecturing, honored by some of his contemporaries for his courage and learning and viciously condemned by others for his persistent defense of Hebrew literature and the Jews.

Further Reading

Johann Reuchlin is listed in the Religion study guide (I, G, 2) and the Social Sciences study guide (III, A, 1). He was praised by ERASMUS and Sir Thomas MORE.

Reuchlin's life and work are discussed in the historical introduction to Francis G. Stokes, trans. and ed., *Epistolae obscurorum virorum* (1909), and in Lewis W. Spitz, *The Religious Renaissance of the German Humanists* (1963). Particular aspects of Reuchlin's work are discussed in S. A. Hirsch, *A Book of Essays* (1905), and Joseph Leon Blau, *The Christian Interpretation of the Cabala in the Renaissance* (1944).

REUTHER / By A. H. Raskin

American labor leader Walter Philip Reuther (1907–1970) pioneered in unionizing the mass-production industries. In a movement traditionally preoccupied with bread-and-butter goals, he dedicated his career to broadening labor's political and social horizons.

Walter Reuther was born on Sept. 1, 1907. His father headed the central labor body in Wheeling, W.Va., and the five children spent their evenings earnestly debating social problems. Walter left

Johann Reuchlin. (Bildarchiv)

Walter Reuther (holding placard) joins members of his United Automobile Workers Union during a 1967 strike at the Ford plant in River Rouge, Mich. (Wide World Photos)

school at the age of 15 to work in a steel mill; 4 years later he moved to Detroit, resumed his schooling, and worked at night as a tool-and-die maker in automobile factories.

Reuther began preaching unionism before President Franklin D. Roosevelt's New Deal put a legal foundation under collective bargaining. The result was Reuther's dismissal from the Ford Company in 1933. On a trip around the world he worked for over a year in a Soviet auto plant. Returning to Detroit, he helped build the United Automobile Workers (UAW), the union that became the launching pad for his influence in national affairs.

The dynamic redheaded Reuther slithered through national guard lines in the 1937 sit-down strikes at General Motors; he was beaten by Ford Company guards in a strike later that year. Even after the UAW was well-established, thugs made him a target. In 1948 a shotgun blast fired through a window of his Detroit home left his right hand permanently crippled. Later his brother, Victor, the union's education director, lost an eye in an almost identical attack.

Under Reuther's leadership the UAW grew to 1.5 million members. It pushed collective bargaining into innovative fields that provided workers and their families with cradle-to-grave protection as an adjunct of their regular pay. Perhaps the most spectacular success was a 1955 employer-financed program that gave auto workers almost as much take-home pay when laid off as when at work.

Reuther consistently fought corruption, communism, and racist tendencies within labor. Convinced in 1955 that the American Federation of Labor (AFL), led by George Meany, had also become a foe of such influ-

ences, he renounced the presidency of the Congress of Industrial Organizations (CIO) to accept a secondary role in a merged labor movement. However, disenchanted by what he considered the AFL-CIO's standstill policies, he led his union out again in 1968.

The UAW joined the International Brotherhood of Teamsters, the biggest American union, in forming an Alliance for Labor Action. Its aim was to organize the working poor, especially in ghetto areas, and crusade for far-reaching social reforms. This venture reflected Reuther's social vision, but it died a year after his own death.

Reuther always looked forward to transforming the economy along lines of industrial democracy and social justice. He authored dozens of "Reuther plans" for the solution of problems ranging from housing and health to disarmament. Yet he found himself increasingly isolated from the general labor movement. He was killed in an airplane crash in Michigan on May 10, 1970.

Further Reading

Walter Reuther is listed in the American History study guide (X, D, 2). He was second in command under George MEANY in the AFL-CIO.

A well-balanced study of Reuther is William J. Eaton and Frank Cormier, *Reuther* (1970). More specialized is Alfred O. Hero, *Reuther-Meany Foreign Policy Dispute* (1970). Older studies are Irving Howe and B. J. Widick, *The UAW and Walter Reuther* (1949), and the section on Reuther in Paul Franklin Douglass, *Six upon the World: Toward an American Culture for an Industrial Age* (1954).

✳   ✳   ✳

REVELS / By Robert L. Southgate

Hiram Rhoades Revels (1822–1901), Afro-American clergyman and university administrator, was the first black American to sit in the U.S. Senate.

Hiram Revels was born of free parents on Sept. 27, 1822, in Fayetteville, N.C. His early education was limited, since it was illegal in North Carolina at that time to teach Afro-Americans, slave or free, to read or write. As soon as he was able, he moved to Union County, Ind., to further his education at a Quaker seminary. After completing his work there, he moved to Ohio to attend another seminary. Eventually he moved to Illinois and graduated from Knox College at Bloomington. In 1845 he was ordained a minister of the African Methodist Episcopal Church in Baltimore, Md.

As a minister, Revels served Afro-American churches in Ohio, Kentucky, Illinois, Indiana, and Tennessee. He finally settled in Baltimore, where he became minister of a church and principal of a school for Negroes. When the Civil War began in 1861, he helped organize the first two regiments of black soldiers from the state of Maryland.

In 1863 Revels moved to St. Louis, established a school for Afro-American freedmen, and recruited another regiment of black soldiers. In 1864 he joined the Federal forces in Mississippi as chaplain to an Afro-American regiment. For a short time he was provost marshal of Vicksburg. For 2 years he worked with the Freedmen's Bureau and established several schools and churches for Negroes near Jackson and Vicksburg.

In 1866 Revels settled in Natchez, Miss. He joined the Methodist Episcopal Church in 1868, the year he was elected alderman. In 1870 he was elected as a Republican to fill an unexpired term in the U.S. Senate, where he served until March 1871. As a senator, he was dignified and respected; his political views, however, were somewhat conservative.

After retiring from the Senate, Revels returned to Mississippi to serve as president of Alcorn College (1871–1874). He was removed from his post for political reasons but was appointed president of Alcorn again in 1876. Following this second term, he returned to church work in Holly Springs, Miss. While attending a church conference at Aberdeen, Miss., he died on Jan. 16, 1901.

Further Reading

Hiram Revels is listed in the American History study guide (VII, B, 1, d). Other black Reconstruction officials were Martin DELANY and Robert SMALLS.

Revels's unpublished papers are in the Library of Congress. There is no full-scale biography of him. Biographical sketches are in Wells Brown, *The Black Man: His Antecedents, His Genius, and His Achievements* (1863; new ed. 1968); Benjamin Brawley, *Negro Builders and Heroes* (1937); and William J. Simmons, *Men of Mark* (1968). The best book for general reading on the Afro-American in Congress is W. E. B. Du Bois, *Black Reconstruction* (1935). Other useful sources of information on this period are Samuel Denny Smith, *The Negro in Congress, 1870–1901* (1940); Lerone Bennett, *Black Power, 1867–1877* (1969); and Maurine Christopher, *America's Black Congressmen* (1971).

Hiram Revels. (Library of Congress, Brady Collection)

REVERE / By Joseph T. Butler

Paul Revere (1735–1818), American patriot, silversmith, and engraver, is remembered for his ride before the Revolutionary War to warn American patriots of a planned British attack. His silverware was among the finest produced in America in his day.

Paul Revere was born on Jan. 1, 1735, in Boston, Mass., the son of Apollos De Revoire, a French Huguenot who had come to Boston at the age of 13 to apprentice in the shop of a silversmith. Once Revoire had established his own business, he Anglicized his name. Paul, the third of 12 children, learned silversmithing from his father. On Aug. 17, 1757, he married Sarah Orne and eventually became the father of eight children.

As early as 1765, Revere began to experiment with engraving on copper and produced several portraits and a songbook. He was popular as a source for engraved seals, coats of arms, and bookplates, and he began to execute engravings which were anti-British. In 1768 Revere undertook dentistry and produced dental devices. The

Paul Revere, a portrait by John Singleton Copley. (Courtesy, Museum of Fine Arts, Boston, Gift of Joseph W., William B., and Edward H. R. Revere)

same year he made one of the most famous pieces of American colonial silver—the bowl commissioned by the Fifteen Sons of Liberty. It is engraved to honor the "glorious Ninety-two Members of the Honorable House of Representatives of the Massachusetts Bay, who, undaunted by the insolent Menores of Villains in Power . . . Voted not to rescind" a circular letter they had sent to the other colonies protesting the Townshend Acts. Revere's virtuosity as a craftsman extended to his carving picture frames for John Singleton Copley, who painted the famous portrait of Revere in shirt sleeves holding a silver teapot.

Paul Revere's Ride

Revere became a trusted messenger for the Massachusetts Committee of Safety. He foresaw an attempt by the British troops against the military stores which were centered in Concord, and he arranged a signal to warn the patriots in Charlestown. During the late evening of April 18, 1775, the chairman of the Committee of Safety told him that the British were going to march to Concord. Revere signaled by hanging two lanterns in the tower of the North Church (probably the present Christ Church). He crossed the river, borrowed a horse in Charlestown, and started for Concord. He arrived in Lexington at midnight and roused John Hancock and Samuel Adams from sleep; the two fled to safety. Revere was captured that night by the British, but he persuaded his captors that the whole countryside was aroused to fight, and they freed him. He returned to Lexington, where he

saw the first shot fired on the green. It is this ride and series of events which have been immortalized by Henry Wadsworth Longfellow in his poem "Paul Revere's Ride."

In the same year, 1775, the Massachusetts provincial congress sent Revere to Philadelphia to study the only working powder mill in the Colonies. Although he was only allowed to walk through the mill and not to take any notes about it, he remembered enough to establish a mill in Canton. During the Revolutionary War, he continued to play an active role. He was eventually promoted to the rank of lieutenant colonel.

After the war Revere became a pioneer in the process of copper plating, and he made copper spikes for ships. In 1795, as grand master of the Masonic fraternity, he laid the cornerstone of the new statehouse in Boston. Throughout the remainder of his life, he continued to experiment with metallurgy and to take a keen interest in contemporary events. He died in Boston on May 10, 1818.

The Silversmith

Revere is also remembered today as a craftsman. His work in silver spanned two major styles. His earliest work is in the rococo style, which is characterized by the use of asymmetric floral and scroll motifs and repoussé decoration; this was done before the Revolution. From this, he evolved a neoclassic style after the Revolution. This style, developed in England, was based on the straight lines and severe surfaces of Roman design. In 1792 Revere produced one of the acknowledged American masterpieces in this style—a complete tea set commissioned by John and Mehitabel Templeman of Boston. The type of ornamentation employed in this tea set was being used in Massachusetts architecture by Charles Bulfinch and Samuel McIntire.

Revere's silver is marked with the initials "P R" in a block. This was the usual type of marking on American

A silver tea service designed by Revere in 1792. (The Minneapolis Institute of Arts, Gift of Mr. and Mrs. James Ford Bell, 1960)

silver of the 18th century. Revere commanded a very distinguished Boston clientele and was called on to make a number of memorial and commemorative pieces. Like many silversmiths of the period, he also worked in brass.

Master Engraver

Revere was also a master of engraving. An on-the-spot reporter, he recorded the events leading up to and during the Revolution with great accuracy. These engravings were advertised in Boston newspapers and were eagerly purchased by the public. In 1770 the *Boston Gazette* advertised for sale Revere's engraving *A View of Part of the Town of Boston in New England and British Ships of War Landing Their Troops, 1768*. Revere added to the print a description of the troops, who paraded "Drums beating, Fifes playing . . . Each Soldier having received 16 rounds of Powder and Ball." Today, all his silver and engravings are eagerly sought by collectors.

Further Reading

Paul Revere is listed in the American History study guide (III, B, 1) and the Art study guide (IV, A, 3; IV, B, 4). It was Gen. Thomas GAGE who sent soldiers to seize the military stores at Concord. A famous American cabinetmaker of the time was Duncan PHYFE.

A full-length study of Revere is Esther Forbes, *Paul Revere and the World He Lived In* (1942). For information on his work see the publication of the Boston Museum of Fine Arts, *Colonial Silversmiths: Masters and Apprentices*, edited by Richard B. K. McLanathan (1956).

REVILLAGIGEDO / By Jaime Suchlicki

Juan Vicente Güemes Pacheco y Padilla, Conde de Revillagigedo (1740–1799), was viceroy of New Spain and one of its ablest and most efficient administrators.

Juan Vicente Güemes Pacheco was born in La Habana, Cuba. His father was viceroy of New Spain from 1746 until 1755. The young and ambitious Juan Vicente joined the Spanish military service, gaining renown during the Spanish siege of Gibraltar against England.

Viceroy of New Spain

As viceroy of New Spain (1789–1794), Revillagigedo (pronounced rā-vē′lyä-hē-hā′thō) gained the respect and admiration of its people. He strove to make effective José de Gálvez's reforms and inaugurated the intendant system. He improved the administration of finances and justice, enlarged the school system, and reorganized the colonial militia. He founded the General Archives and inaugurated in 1793 the Museum of National History. To keep himself informed of the desires and grievances of

the people, he placed a locked box in a public place for petitions and communications.

Perhaps one of Revillagigedo's most notable accomplishments was the transformation of Mexico from an unhealthy, filthy city into a modern metropolis. He ordered the principal streets paved, cleaned, and lighted. The great central plaza was cleared of street vendors, and new markets were set up in various parts of the city. He suppressed banditry, making Mexico a safer city. Concerned over the abuses being committed by some members of the clergy against the Indians, particularly in remote areas, he issued special instructions ordering that the Indians should not be compelled to perform personal services or to pay tribute to the clergy.

Administrative Reforms

Revillagigedo was particularly critical of the sale of public offices in New Spain and throughout the New World, for the system had led to corruption and inefficiency. Officials who came from Spain expected to recover at least a share of their investment, and many showed little interest in colonial affairs. Revillagigedo expressed his disapproval of the system, explaining that the greater efficiency of appointed officials would more than

"America" paints the portrait of the Conde de Revillagigedo in honor of his visit as viceroy of New Spain, a 1794 watercolor. (Bancroft Library, University of California, Photo by William Hawken)

compensate for the loss of the royal treasury. The system, however, was not officially abolished until 1812, and even then the sale of offices continued for several years.

Revillagigedo was also critical of the complicated and overlapping system of taxation; he increased the major taxes and abolished the minor ones. An efficient and honest official, he increased revenues, and New Spain enjoyed years of prosperity. The budget, which suffered a deficit during the previous administration, enjoyed a surplus during his tenure of office. He used some of the funds to encourage the planting and growing of cotton and other textile fibers.

Revillagigedo also encouraged explorations of the California and northern Pacific coast as far as the Bering Straits. However, under his administration Spain was forced to yield to England—as a result of the Nootka Sound controversy—territories on the northwest Pacific coast, thus acknowledging that Spain could not claim territories not effectively occupied.

At the end of his enlightened administration in 1794, Revillagigedo left a more modern and prosperous Mexico with an efficient and honest government. He returned to Spain, where he died on May 12, 1799.

Further Reading

The Conde de Revillagigedo is listed in the Latin America study guide (II, A, 1). Other colonial administrators were José de GÁLVEZ, Antonio de MENDOZA, and Pedro de la GASCA.

Valuable information on Revillagigedo's administration is in Donald E. Smith, *The Viceroy of New Spain* (1913), and C. H. Haring, *The Spanish Empire in America* (1947). Further background can be found in three works by Lillian E. Fisher: *Viceregal Administration in the Spanish American Colonies* (1926), *The Intendant System in Spanish America* (1929), and *The Background of the Revolution for Mexican Independence* (1934).

✳   ✳   ✳

A. **REYES** / By Malcolm D. McLean

Alfonso Reyes (1889–1959), one of Mexico's most distinguished men of letters, was especially well known as an essayist.

lfonso Reyes (pronounced rā′yās) was born on May 17, 1889, in Monterrey, Nuevo León. He attended the Escuela Nacional Preparatoria (National Preparatory School) and the Facultad de Derecho (Law School) in Mexico City. In 1909 he was one of the founders of the Ateneo de la Juventud (Athenaeum for Young People). He served as secretary of the Faculty for Advanced Studies, where he also taught the course on the history of the Spanish language and Spanish literature. His first book, *Cuestiones estéticas* (Esthetic Questions), appeared in 1911.

Reyes received his law degree in 1913, and that year

Alfonso Reyes in 1932. (Bibliothèque Nationale, Paris)

he was appointed second secretary of the Mexican legation in France. In 1914 he went to Spain, where he devoted himself to literature and journalism, working in the Centro de Estudios Históricos (Center for Historical Studies) in Madrid. His book *Visión de Anáhuac* was published in 1917.

In 1920 Reyes was named second secretary of the Mexican legation in Spain. From that time on he occupied various diplomatic posts: chargé d'affaires in Spain (1922–1924), minister to France (1924–1927), ambassador to Argentina (1927–1930), ambassador to Brazil (1930–1936), and again ambassador to Argentina (1936–1937).

When Reyes returned to Mexico in 1939, he became president of the Casa de España en México (Spanish House in Mexico), which later became the Colegio de México. He was one of the founders of the Colegio Nacional. In 1945 he won the National Prize in Literature, and he was a candidate for the Nobel Prize. He served as director of the Academia Mexicana de la Lengua (Mexican Academy of the Spanish Language) from 1957 to 1959.

The works by Reyes that have enjoyed the greatest success are *Simpatías y diferencias* (1921; Likes and Dislikes); *La experiencia literaria* (1942; Literary Experience); *El deslinde* (1944), a treatise on literary criticism which is considered his masterpiece; and *La X en la frente* (1952; X on the Forehead). His works have been more frequently translated into foreign languages than those of any other contemporary Mexican author.

Reyes symbolizes the humanist par excellence. To his immense intellectual curiosity and his vast culture he added a gift of style which made his prose creations peculiarly his own. He was a wise and penetrating critic, a short-story writer prodigal in surprises, and a poet of delicate sensitivity; educated in the school of Góngora and Mallarmé, he was learned in both classical and modern writers.

Reyes died in Mexico City on Dec. 27, 1959. He was buried in the Rotonda de Hombres Ilustres (Rotunda of Illustrious Men).

Further Reading

Alfonso Reyes is listed in the Latin America study guide (IV, K, 2, b). Other Mexican men of letters were José VASCONCELOS and Justo SIERRA.

Most biographical and critical work on Reyes is in Spanish. For English translations of his works see *The Position of America, and Other Essays* (1950) and *Mexico in a Nutshell and Other Essays* (1964), both translated by Charles Ramsdell with a foreword by Arturo Torres-Ríoseco. He is discussed in Carlos González Peña, *History of Mexican Literature* (3d ed., trans. 1968).

R. **REYES** / By John D. Martz

Colombian military and political leader Rafael Reyes (1850–1920) assumed the presidency following a disastrous civil war and established an absolutist regime which contributed to recovery from the excesses of the fighting.

Born in Santa Rosa, Rafael Reyes grew into a vigorous and robust youth addicted to outdoor life. At the age of 24, with two brothers, he undertook the exploration of the Putumayo River, which links Colombia with the upper Amazon Basin. For over a decade he charted jungle routes and located resources of rubber and quinine. One brother died of fever, and the other was killed by primitive Indians.

Reyes distinguished himself in the civil wars of both 1885 and 1895. During the 3 years' bloody fighting which commenced in 1899, however, he was outside Colombia. In 1904, with the support of the Conservatives, he ascended to the presidency.

Coming to power in the wake of disastrous bloodletting and Colombia's loss of its province of Panama, Reyes first attempted to institute a policy of compromise, dedicating himself to the resurrection and strengthening of national unity. Unable to secure cooperation from dissident political elements, he established a highly centralized and authoritarian government which was committed to material change and economic de-

Rafael Reyes. (Organization of American States)

velopment. Dissolving by executive decree an uncooperative Congress, he jailed many of its members, declared martial law, and assumed full dictatorial powers. Reyes sought the aura of legality by appointing a National Assembly whose task was to ratify his decisions. Impatient of dissent and uninterested in free elections or constitutional government, he turned to the improvement of material conditions.

Reyes adopted a series of stern measures. In 1905 he merged the finance and treasury ministries in order to tighten financial control and to reorganize the economy. The floating of foreign loans helped restore Colombian credit in world markets, and coffee production was encouraged. Public works included the building of highways and railroads, especially along the Magdalena River Basin.

In his early years in power Reyes encountered little opposition from a war-weary populace, but despite his efficiency the political situation grew stormy. He survived several attempts on his life, and the National Assembly voted to extend his term to 1914. In 1909 he negotiated treaties with Panama and the United States as final settlement of the independence movement in the former and was met by national protests and by student demonstrations. Although he withdrew the treaties, he was forced to resign in June 1909. After years of exile he returned home in 1919, where he died the following year.

Further Reading

Rafael Reyes is listed in the Latin America study guide (IV, F, 1, b). Other distinguished Colombian political leaders were Alberto LLERAS and Laureano GÓMEZ.

The best analysis of Reyes's career within the context of national history is Jesús María Henao and Gerardo Arrubla, *History of Colombia*, translated by J. Fred Rippy (1938). A North American historical survey which also places Reyes in historical perspective is Hubert Herring, *A History of Latin America* (1955; 3d ed. 1968).

REYNOLDS / By Joseph Burke

Sir Joshua Reynolds (1723–1792), the outstanding intellectual force among English artists of his age, virtually created a new type of portraiture by interpreting the humanity of his sitters in terms of the heroic tradition of Old Master history painting.

Joshua Reynolds was born on July 16, 1723, at Plympton, Devon, the third son and seventh child of the Reverend Samuel Reynolds, master of the Plympton Grammar School and sometime fellow of Balliol College, Oxford. Joshua was enabled by education, ability, and inclination to move all his adult life with ease and distinction in literary and learned circles. A vocation for art was confirmed by reading as a boy Jonathan Richardson's *Essay on the Theory of Painting* (1715), with its program for restoring portraiture to the dignity of high art, and at the age of 17 Joshua was apprenticed to Richardson's son-in-law, Thomas Hudson, in London.

Reynolds set up on his own in 1743 and practiced in Plympton and London. His work of this period shows the influence of Anthony Van Dyck and the innovations introduced by William Hogarth, then at the height of his powers.

In 1749 Reynolds sailed for Italy as the guest of Commodore Augustus Keppel. In Rome, Reynolds studied the Old Masters with a single-mindedness unmatched by any earlier English painter. His only diversion was a small number of caricature paintings in the manner of his fellow Devonian Thomas Patch. Raphael was Reynolds's hero, but on his way back to England he visited northern Italy and came under the spell of the Venetian painters and Correggio.

Reynolds settled in London in 1753 and established his reputation as the foremost portrait painter with *Captain the Hon. Augustus Keppel* (1753–1754), the first of a long series of portraits ennobled by a borrowed pose, here taken from the *Apollo Belvedere*. He used borrowed attitudes in two ways: as a mode of elevation and as a species of wit. As Horace Walpole noted, both usages are controlled by intellect and taste, manifested in the aptness of his application to the sitter's character, achievement, or role in society.

After his election as foundation president of the Royal Academy in 1768 until his death in London on Feb. 23, 1792, Reynolds's life was too closely intertwined with the artistic, literary, and social history of his time for a summary to be adequate. A small group of portraits of men of genius with whom he was intimate, headed by Dr. Johnson, is unique in European art in that each is accompanied by a written character sketch which is a masterpiece of psychological assessment.

Reynolds delivered 15 discourses to the members and students of the Royal Academy between 1769 and 1790. They upheld the ideal theory in art and constituted the classic formulation of academic doctrine after more than 2 centuries of debate.

Reynolds's main types of portraiture commemorate naval and military heroes, civil and ecclesiastical dignitaries, the English landowning oligarchy in both its public and private aspects, actors and actresses, and children in fanciful roles, related in their vein of sentiment to "fancy pictures" like the *Age of Innocence* (1788). His most ambitious translation of a subject picture into a portrait is the group of the daughters of Sir William Montgomery, the *Graces Adorning a Term of Hymen* (1774), a Miltonian bridal masque in which the rite of worship to the God of Wedlock is performed by three famous beauties, one recently married, another preparing for marriage, and the third still to be betrothed. Among the finest of his heroicized military portraits in a battle setting are

In his "heroic" portraits Joshua Reynolds often dramatized the sitter by depicting him with attributes symbolic of his position. Lord Heathfield, painted in 1788, was governor of Gibraltar and holds the key to the fortress, which in turn represents the key to the Mediterranean. (National Gallery, London)

Joshua Reynolds, a self-portrait painted in 1753. (National Portrait Gallery, London)

Colonel Banastre Tarleton (1782) and *George Augustus Eliott, Lord Heathfield* (1788).

A visit to Flanders and Holland in 1781 renewed Reynolds's enthusiasm for Peter Paul Rubens and was followed by a decade of prodigious creative energy. To this final phase belong most of Reynolds's history paintings, including those commissioned for John Boydell's Shakespeare Gallery and the *Infant Hercules* (1788), commissioned by the Empress of Russia. *Sarah Siddons as the Tragic Muse* (1784) shows the actress flanked by emblems of Open and Secret Murder and assembles motives borrowed from Michelangelo, with whose name he closed his last discourse.

As the foundation president of the Royal Academy, Reynolds guided its destinies in its momentous first phase, devoting his immense influence to the single goal of forming a national school of history painters choosing their exalted themes not only from the Bible and classical antiquity but also from Shakespeare and the national past. Courteous, affable, and open to new ideas, he steered a liberal and tactful course and stamped a character of devotion to high art on the institution that lasted into the age of J. M. W. Turner and even beyond.

Further Reading

Sir Joshua Reynolds is listed in the Art study guide (III, G, 1, c). The other outstanding portraitists of the day were Thomas GAINSBOROUGH and George ROMNEY.

The definitive edition of Reynolds's *Discourses on Art* was edited by Robert R. Wark (1959). Frederick Whiley Hilles edited *Letters of Sir Joshua Reynolds* (1929) and Reynolds's *Portraits* (1952), which contains written

character sketches of Oliver Goldsmith, Samuel Johnson, David Garrick, and others. The monumental study of Charles Robert Leslie and Tom Taylor, *Life and Times of Sir Joshua Reynolds* (2 vols., 1865), should be supplemented by Frederick Whiley Hilles, *The Literary Career of Sir Joshua Reynolds* (1936). See also Derek Hudson, *Sir Joshua Reynolds: A Personal Study* (1958). The best-illustrated and most critical study of Reynolds's art is Ellis K. Waterhouse, *Reynolds* (1941).

REZA SHAH PAHLAVI
/ By Yahya Armajani

Reza Shah Pahlavi (1878–1944) was the founder of the Pahlavi dynasty. He rose from the ranks to become minister of war, prime minister, and then shah of Iran. As a reformer-dictator, he laid the foundation of modern Iran.

Reza Khan, later Reza Shah Pahlavi (pronounced rĕ-zä′ shä pä′lə-vē), was born in the Caspian province of Mazandaran. He was orphaned in infancy, and at the age of 14 he chose the military career of his father and enlisted in the Persian Cossack Brigade, which was under the command of Russian officers. A tall and rugged young man, Reza Khan rose by sheer courage and ability. He was highly intelligent without any formal education, had vision without much information, and was a champion of Westernization without having seen any other country but Iran.

Reza Khan was also very sensitive, and from his youth he must have been disgusted with the despicable condition of the country and also of the army. As a soldier, he took part in many engagements, but what bothered him most was the fact that he was under the command of foreign officers. After the Russian Revolution, some of the Russian officers in the brigade left, but the White Russians, who could not go, remained in command. In 1920 Reza led his fellow Persian officers in ousting the Russians, and he himself became commander of the brigade.

Coup d'Etat

On Feb. 21, 1921, he, together with Sayyed Ziya al-Din Tabatabai, a brilliant journalist, overthrew the government in Tehran. Sayyed Ziya became prime minister and Reza Khan minister of war and commander in chief of the armed forces. During the next 3 months it became evident that the civilian and the soldier could not agree on specific goals or methods. Since Reza Khan was the stronger of the two, it was Sayyed Ziya who was forced to leave the country. From 1921 to 1925, as minister of war and later as prime minister, Reza Khan built a strong modern army, subdued the rebellious tribes, and brought about a peace and security which the country had not experienced for a century.

Ahmad Shah, the last of the Qajar kings, was so overshadowed by the popular Reza Khan that he left for an indefinite stay in Europe. The creation of a republic in Turkey influenced many Persians, including Reza Khan. For a time there was a movement to create a republic, but it soon became evident that, although Persians did not mind changing kings, they were reluctant to do away with the monarchical principle. So on Oct. 21, 1925, the Majles (Parliament) deposed the absent Ahmad Shah and in December of the same year proclaimed Reza Khan as the shahanshah (king of kings) of Iran.

The Persian Revolution, which had started in 1906, had at last produced a leader to implement its ideals, even though some of the early revolutionaries had not envisaged the methods used by Reza Shah. He was at first popular among the masses and peasants because he gave them security. He was also popular among the educated classes because he was for modernization and reform.

In the field of foreign affairs he ended the system of capitulation; created an autonomous customs; terminated the right of the British Bank to issue currency notes; and in 1931 negotiated a new oil agreement with the Anglo-Persian Oil Company which, he believed, was more advantageous to Iran.

Internal Reforms

Reza Shah's main activity, however, was in internal reforms, which he carried out with the help of the army, which remained the object of his special devotion. He built roads, established a wireless service, and took over the management of the telegraph service from the Brit-

ish. He was rightly proud of the trans-Iranian railway from the Persian Gulf to the Caspian, which he had built without a loan from any foreign government. He set up trade monopolies, thus limiting the freedom of the merchants, and established the National Bank of Iran.

Like his predecessors Shah Abbas I and Nader Shah, Reza Shah tried to break down the power and prestige of the clergy. Islamic law was partially discarded; Islamic education was abandoned; religious processions were forbidden; the Islamic calendar was replaced by the old Persian-Zoroastrian solar calendar; mosques were modernized, and some of them were equipped with pews; the call to prayer was frowned upon; and pilgrimage to Mecca was discouraged.

All titles were abolished, and people were asked to choose family names; Persian men were ordered to don European attire and headgear, and Persian women were encouraged to discard the veil. Reza Shah founded the University of Tehran in 1934 and established the Persian Academy, whose task was to rid the Persian language of borrowed Arabic and other foreign words.

These and many other far-reaching and essential reforms in a country ridden with illiteracy, superstition, and vested interests could not be accomplished without the use of force. So, in order to silence the critics of the reforms, all criticism was banned. In order to have internal security, the army had to be strengthened, but this very act made tyrants of a number of officers who suppressed the masses.

Reza Shah Pahlavi. (Harlingue-Viollet)

Reza Shah's greatest weakness was his desire to amass wealth, especially real estate. In the acquisition of property he had to depend upon others, who in the process acquired wealth for themselves. Being a self-made man, he was loathe to delegate power to others. Unlike other reformers, he had no ideology, no party, and no well-defined program. Being in complete control of every aspect of life, he improvised and made decisions on the spot as he saw fit. Perhaps his ideas of modernization were superficial, but undoubtedly he forced the country to face the necessity of change, without which modernization would not be possible.

At the outbreak of World War II, Iran declared its neutrality. When Germany attacked the Soviet Union, Iran, already important to the allies for its oil, became the best supply route to Russia. Reza Shah failed to comply with the Russo-British plan of using Iran as a supply route and with their demand to deal effectively with the German agents active in Iran. On Aug. 26, 1941, Russian and British troops entered Iran; the Persian army put up a token resistance which lasted less than a week. Reza Shah abdicated the throne in favor of his son, Mohammad Reza Shah Pahlavi. Reza Shah died in exile in South Africa.

Further Reading

Reza Shah Pahlavi is listed in the Asia study guide (I, D, 5). Like earlier founders of Persian dynasties such as AB-BAS I and NADER SHAH, Reza Shah rose from the military to kingship. He was succeeded by his son, MOHAM-MAD REZA SHAH PAHLAVI.

There is no adequate biography of Reza Shah. A sketch of his life is in his son's *Mission for My Country* (1961). Ramesh Sanghvi, *The Shah of Iran* (1969), is less a study than an enumeration of Reza Shah's political achievements. A brief, but probably the most sophisticated, treatment of him is in Richard Cottam, *Nationalism in Iran* (1964). The Shah is discussed in Peter Avery, *Modern Iran* (1965; 2d ed. 1967), and Yahya Armajani, *Middle East: Past and Present* (1970).

RHEE / By John Kie-chiang Oh

Syngman Rhee (1875–1965) was a leader in Korean independence movements. He was elected the first president of the Republic of Korea in 1948. His government was overthrown in 1960.

Yi Sŭng-man, who Westernized his name to Syngman Rhee (pronounced rē), was born on April 26, 1875, only son of Yi Kyŏng-sŏn, a member of the local gentry in the village of Pyŏng-san in Hwanghae Province. Rhee's boyhood name was Sŭng-yong. When he was very young, the family moved to Seoul, the capital city of a dynasty in rapid decline. He studied Chinese

Syngman Rhee in 1942. (United Press International Photo)

readers and classics before enrolling in the Paejae Hak-tang (academy), a Methodist mission school, in 1894. Upon graduation from Paejae, he was employed by the academy as an English instructor. He became interested in Western enlightenment ideas and joined reform movements which bitterly criticized the anachronistic and impotent Korean government. He was arrested and imprisoned in 1897. His conversion to Methodism came while he was a political prisoner. He was released from prison in 1904.

In the winter of the same year, Rhee traveled to the United States with a hope of appealing to President Theodore Roosevelt for assistance to Korea in its desperate efforts to maintain its independence from Japan. The appeal was futile, as the American-Korean treaty of 1882 had lost meaning and as the U.S. government was eager to cooperate with the Japan that was emerging victorious from the Russo-Japanese War. The Portsmouth Treaty led to the Japanese protectorate over Korea, and the United States promptly withdrew the American legation from Seoul.

Education in the United States

While Syngman Rhee was pursuing his elusive goal of attempting to save Korean independence through hopeless appeals, he also enrolled, in the spring of 1905, as a student in George Washington University. Upon graduation in 1907, he decided to do postgraduate work in the United States and was admitted to Harvard University.

He began to read extensively in international relations. When he received his master's degree in the spring of 1908, unstable conditions in his homeland prompted him to continue his education in the United States. He received his doctorate in political science from Princeton University in 1910, the year in which Japan formally annexed its Korean protectorate. The topic of his dissertation was "Neutrality as Influenced by the United States."

Rhee returned to Korea in 1910 as a YMCA organizer, teacher, and evangelist among the youth of Korea. When an international conference of Methodist delegates was held in Minneapolis in 1912, Rhee attended the meeting as the lay delegate of the Korean Methodists. After the conference, Rhee decided to stay in the United States and accepted the head position at the Korean Compound School—later the Korean Institute—in Honolulu in 1913.

President of Provisional Government

On March 1, 1919, a Korea-wide demonstration for the independence of the country took place as 33 leading Koreans signed a declaration of independence which was then read to crowds in the streets. The Japanese reaction to the massive "Mansei Uprising," which was partly inspired by the Wilsonian doctrine of self-determination, was swift and cruel. An outcome of the "Samil movement" was that a group of independence leaders, meeting in Seoul in April 1919, formed a Korean provisional government with Syngman Rhee—still in the United States—as the first president. The provisional government was subsequently located in Shanghai, and Rhee continued to lead the independence movement mostly from the United States, where he was best known. When Kim Ku became the president of the "government in exile," Rhee acted as its Washington representative.

In early 1933 Rhee was in Geneva attempting to make an appeal on behalf of Korea to the delegates attending the League of Nations, where Japan's military conquest of Manchuria was under discussion. His mission was once again frustrating, as major powers were then unwilling and unable to check the expansionist Japan. It was in Geneva that Rhee first became acquainted with Miss Francesca Donner, the eldest of three daughters of a well-to-do iron merchant in Vienna. She was in Geneva serving as a secretary to the Austrian delegation to the League. After Rhee's return to the United States via Moscow, Miss Donner entered the United States under the Austrian immigration quota. They were married in October 1933, saying the vows in both Korean and English. He was then almost 58. Francesca shared his life as a devoted wife. (After Rhee's death in 1965, she lived in Vienna.)

Return to Korea

When Korea was liberated from Japanese colonial domination in 1945 by the Allied Powers, Rhee was flown back to the country that he had not seen for some 33 years. He was given a hero's welcome by the American military government that was ruling the southern half of Korea and by the Korean people, who were overjoyed with the prospect of independence. Rhee quickly became the leader of conservative, right-wing political forces in South Korea, thanks to his background as a leader of the "exile government." Rhee's only potential rival in South Korea politics, Kim Ku, who had led the "exile government" in China, was assassinated.

When the first general elections in Korean history, to elect the members of the National Assembly, were held on May 10, 1948, under the supervision of the UN Temporary Commission on Korea, Rhee's Association for the Rapid Realization of Independence won a plurality of seats. When the National Assembly convened for the first time, on May 31, 1948, Rhee was elected as Assembly chairman—a first step to the presidency of the Republic of Korea.

President of the Republic

The National Assembly adopted the 1948 constitution of Korea, providing for an essentially democratic, presidential system of government. As one of its first official acts under the new constitution, the National Assembly elected Rhee as the republic's first president. The Republic of Korea was proclaimed on the third anniversary of VJ-day, thus ending the 3-year administration of South Korea by the U.S. military government.

In the first few months of the Rhee administration, what may be called a "personalism" of the strong-willed president, as opposed to "institutionalism," was established in the republic. The crisis conditions under which the Rhee government had to function in the southern half of the divided peninsula tended to accelerate the process. Communist-inspired mutinies in the Yŏsu-Sunchŏn areas, for instance, made normal operations of the government difficult already in October—barely 2 months after the inauguration of the government. When the Communist army of North Korea invaded the Republic of Korea on June 25, 1950, the Rhee administration quickly adjusted to the wartime situation, and Rhee became increasingly autocratic.

While UN action led by the United States was being resolutely taken to repulse the armed aggression, and while numerous South Korean troops were engaged in fierce combat against Communist troops, the Rhee administration initiated a "political crisis" in and around the wartime capital of Pusan, which was placed under martial law.

The executive thoroughly intimidated the legislature in the early summer of 1952 to adopt a series of constitutional amendments that Rhee desired. By now, Rhee was unlikely to be reelected as president by the National Assembly according to the Constitution of 1948. The 1952 amendments provided, among other things, for a direct popular election of the president and vice president. Rhee and his running mate, Ham T'ae-yŏng, were elected by an overwhelming majority of South Korean voters in the Aug. 5, 1952, elections. By the time the Korean truce agreement was signed in a wooden hut in P'anmunjŏm in July 1953, the political position of President Rhee and his Liberal party was supreme.

After the victory of the Liberal party in the May 20,

1954, Assembly election, the Rhee administration again proposed on September 6 a long series of constitutional amendments. The more important provisions of these amendments, which were adopted on November 27, eliminated the two-term restriction on presidential tenure and abolished the office of the prime minister. Rhee won his third presidential term in the May 15, 1956, election. Rhee had won this election with only 56 percent of the vote, however, compared to 72 percent in the wartime election of 1952. Furthermore, Korean voters had elected Chang Myŏn (John M. Chang) of the opposition party as the vice president. Many commentators observed that the 1956 election was a partial repudiation by the people of Rhee's administration and his Liberal party, which were becoming increasingly more oppressive.

Aware of the mounting discontent of the people, the administration and the Liberal party extensively "rigged" the March 15, 1960, presidential election, although the opposition candidate, Cho Pyŏng-ok, had died of complications resulting from an operation at the Walter Reed Hospital. When all the votes were "counted" after March 15, it was announced that there were, astoundingly, no recorded "posthumous" votes for Cho; it was claimed by the government that Rhee had "won" 92 percent of the vote; the remaining votes were simply termed "invalid." The opposition groups in the National Assembly, the only public gathering where a semblance of free speech still remained under the Rhee government, protested the elections vigorously. They charged that a number of votes, equal to 40 percent of the total electorate, had been fabricated and used to pad the Liberal party vote.

Student Uprising

Pent-up frustrations of the Korean people at these political manipulations exploded in the April 19, 1960, "Student Uprising." The Rhee administration attempted to blame "devilish hands of the Communists" for disturbances throughout South Korea. President Rhee himself asserted that the Masan riot, which had touched off the uprising, was the work of Communist agents. President Rhee declared martial law and made it retroactive to the moment when the police guarding his mansion fired against the demonstrators.

Heavily armed soldiers were moved into the capital. When bloody showdowns seemed imminent, the soldiers, under the martial law commander, Lt. Gen. Song Yo-ch'an, showed no intention of shooting at demonstrating students. In fact, the army seemed to maintain strict "neutrality" between the Rhee administration and the demonstrators. While the very life of the Rhee administration trembled in the balance, the coercive powers of the regime thus evaporated. President Rhee resigned on April 26, 1960. He flew to Hawaii in May to live out his life in exile. He died of illness on July 19, 1965.

Rhee's presidency for about 12 years was marked principally by his stern anti-communism, anti-Japanese policies, awesome "personalism," and paternalistic leadership. It was partly due to his prestige and leadership, however, that South Korea could maintain war efforts during the Korean conflict of 1950–1953. The first presidency of the Republic of Korea would have been an extremely difficult task for anyone; Rhee's evident obsession to prolong his regime turned it into a tragic one—for himself and for the country that he served so long.

Further Reading

Syngman Rhee is listed in the Asia study guide (III, C, 9). A short time after Rhee's resignation Chung Hee PARK founded Korea's Third Republic.

An exceptionally thorough, well-researched biography that is extremely favorable to Rhee is Robert T. Oliver, *Syngman Rhee: The Man behind the Myth* (1954), although it is now dated. A fairly objective and sometimes critical biography is Richard C. Allen, *Korea's Syngman Rhee: An Unauthorized Portrait* (1960). For an analysis of Rhee as president of the Republic of Korea see John Kie-chiang Oh, *Korea: Democracy on Trial* (1968).

✳ ✳ ✳

RHETT / By Horace Montgomery

> Robert Barnwell Rhett (1800–1876), American statesman, was a U.S. congressman and senator and the spokesman for Southern independence.

Robert Barnwell Rhett was born Robert Barnwell Smith on Dec. 21, 1800, in aristocratic Beaufort, S.C. His family had enjoyed a notable reputation in South Carolina history. At the age of 37 he changed his name from the plebeian Smith to the patrician Rhett. Although Rhett's schooling was irregular, at the age of 21 he was admitted to the South Carolina bar. He lived in the manner of the Carolina aristocracy throughout his life, owning two plantations and a succession of town residences.

In 1826 Rhett was elected to the state legislature, where he quickly became prominent in the protective tariff controversy. Initially he argued passionately for resistance, but he came to accept John C. Calhoun's theory of peaceful, constitutional nullification.

From 1837 to 1849 Rhett served in the U.S. House of Representatives. He worked closely with Calhoun, then senator from South Carolina, in propagating the notion that the Constitution, "rightly interpreted," protected the South. He also promoted Calhoun's plans for controlling the Democratic party. In 1844, when Calhoun failed to secure the presidential nomination, the Democrats deserted the South on the tariff issue; Rhett, defying Calhoun, led a movement for separate state action on the tariff.

When Calhoun died in 1850, Rhett was elected U.S. senator. By this time he had begun a campaign to promote South Carolina's secession from the Union. He was convinced that its withdrawal would encourage other

Robert Barnwell Rhett. (Library of Congress)

Southern states to secede. The next year, however, South Carolina rejected Rhett's leadership by accepting the Compromise of 1850.

Although in political retirement throughout the 1850s, Rhett remained in contact with Southerners of secessionist persuasion. In the aftermath of the critical 1860 election, he was so influential in spreading secession ideas in South Carolina that he was called the father of secession. His most effective forum was the *Charleston Mercury,* a newspaper owned by his son after 1857. In early 1861 Rhett attended the Southern Convention at Montgomery. While not a member of the convention, he did lobby to defeat measures he deemed too conciliatory toward the North, and he was chosen by the convention to compose an address to the people of the slaveholding states. He failed, however, to secure the presidency of the Confederacy and was ignored in the Cabinet appointments.

Rhett attacked the Confederate administration for its attempts at centralization. He was twice defeated for a seat in the Confederate lower house and spent his last energies defending Southern civilization against the Confederate proposals to arm, and free, the slaves. On Sept. 14, 1876, Rhett died in Louisiana.

Further Reading

Robert Barnwell Rhett is listed in the American History study guide (V, A, 4; VI, B, 2, b). John C. CALHOUN was a foremost Southern leader and a staunch defender of slavery.

The best study of Rhett is Laura Amanda White, *Robert Barnwell Rhett: Father of Secession* (1931), a significant contribution to Confederate history, especially in its

treatment of causative factors and immediate prewar events.

c. RHODES / By John E. Flint

The English imperialist, financier, and mining magnate Cecil John Rhodes (1853–1902) founded and controlled the British South Africa Company, which acquired Rhodesia and Zambia as British territories. He founded the Rhodes scholarships.

Cecil Rhodes was born on July 5, 1853, at Bishop's Stortford, Hertfordshire, one of nine sons of the parish vicar. After attending the local grammar school, his health broke down, and at 16 he was sent to South Africa. Arriving in October 1870, he grew cotton in Natal with his brother Herbert but in 1871 left for the newly developed diamond field at Kimberley.

In the 1870s Rhodes laid the foundation for his later massive fortune by speculating in diamond claims, beginning pumping techniques, and in 1880 forming the De Beers Mining Company. During this time he attended Oxford off and on, starting in 1873, and finally acquired the degree of bachelor of arts in 1881. His extraordinary imperialist ideas were revealed early, after his serious heart attack in 1877, when he made his first will, disposing of his as yet unearned fortune to found a secret society that would extend British rule over the whole world and colonize most parts of it with British settlers, leading to the "ultimate recovery of the United States of America" by the British Empire!

From 1880 to 1895 Rhodes's star rose steadily. Basic to this rise was his successful struggle to take control of the rival diamond interests of Barnie Barnato, with whom he amalgamated in 1888 to form De Beers Consolidated Mines, a company whose trust deed gave extraordinary powers to acquire lands and rule them and extend the British Empire. With his brother Frank he also formed Goldfields of South Africa, with substantial mines in the Transvaal. At the same time Rhodes built a career in politics; elected to the Cape Parliament in 1880, he succeeded in focusing alarm at Transvaal and German expansion so as to secure British control of Bechuanaland by 1885. In 1888 Rhodes agents secured mining concessions from Lobengula, King of the Ndebele, which by highly stretched interpretations gave Rhodes a claim to what became Rhodesia. In 1889 Rhodes persuaded the British government to grant a charter to form the British South Africa Company, which in 1890 put white settlers into Lobengula's territories and founded Salisbury and other towns. This provoked Ndebele hostility, but they were crushed in the war of 1893.

By this time Rhodes controlled the politics of Cape Colony; in July 1890 he became premier of the Cape with the support of the English-speaking white and non-white voters and the Afrikaners of the "Bond" (among whom 25,000 shares in the British South Africa Company had been distributed). His policy was to aim for the creation of a South African federation under the British flag, and he conciliated the Afrikaners by restricting the Africans' franchise with educational and property qualifications (1892) and setting up a new system of "native administration" (1894).

Later Career

At the end of 1895 Rhodes's fortunes took a disastrous turn. In poor health and anxious to hurry his dream of South African federation, he organized a conspiracy against the Boer government of the Transvaal. Through his mining company, arms and ammunition were smuggled into Johannesburg to be used for a revolution by "outlanders," mainly British. A strip of land on the borders of the Transvaal was ceded to the chartered company by Joseph Chamberlain, British colonial secretary; and Leander Jameson, administrator of Rhodesia, was stationed there with company troops. The Johannesburg conspirators did not rebel; Jameson, however, rode in on Dec. 27, 1895, and was ignominiously captured. As a result, Rhodes had to resign his premiership in January 1896. Thereafter he concentrated on developing Rhodesia and especially in extending the railway, which he dreamed would one day reach Cairo.

When the Anglo-Boer War broke out in October 1899, Rhodes hurried to Kimberley, which the Boers surround-

ed a few days later. It was not relieved until Feb. 16, 1900, during which time Rhodes had been active in organizing defense and sanitation. His health was worsened by the siege, and after traveling in Europe he returned to the Cape in February 1902, where he died at Muizenberg on March 26.

Rhodes left £6 million, most of which went to Oxford University to establish the Rhodes scholarships to provide places at Oxford for students from the United States, the British colonies, and Germany. Land was also left to provide eventually for a university in Rhodesia.

Further Reading

Cecil Rhodes is listed in the European History study guide (IX, A, 2) and the Africa study guide (VIII, A, 5). Lord KITCHENER was also active in the British Empire during this period.

Rhodes's letters and papers have not yet been edited and published, but Vindex (pseudonym for Rev. F. Verschoyle) published *Cecil Rhodes: His Political Life and Speeches, 1881–1900* (1900). There are a number of biographies: Sir Lewis Michell, *The Life of the Rt. Hon. Cecil John Rhodes, 1853–1902* (2 vols., 1910), comprehensive but eulogistic; Basil Williams, *Cecil Rhodes* (1921), which is still useful; Sarah Gertrude Millin, *Cecil Rhodes* (1933); and Felix Gross, *Rhodes of Africa* (1957), faulty in research, sometimes hostile, but suggesting interesting if often farfetched interpretations. J. G. Lockhart and C. M. Woodhouse, *Cecil Rhodes: The Colossus of Southern Africa* (1963), used the Rhodes papers and much new material, but the definitive biography remains to be written. A recent account of Rhodes's relationship to the Princess Radziwell and of the Jameson raid is Brian Roberts, *Cecil Rhodes and the Princess* (1969), an exciting piece of historical reconstruction.

Cecil Rhodes, a painting by George Frederick Watts. (National Portrait Gallery, London)

J. F. RHODES / By Thomas L. Hartshorne

James Ford Rhodes (1848–1927), American historian, wrote an influential multivolume political narrative of the Civil War and Reconstruction.

James Ford Rhodes was born on May 1, 1848, in Ohio City, Ohio, now a part of Cleveland. His father was a prosperous businessman. After a year of education beyond high school, Rhodes went into business. The business proved to be very successful, and Rhodes, who had literary interests, was able to retire in 1884 to pursue his desire to write history. He had in mind a general history of the United States from 1850 to 1888. After completing the first two volumes, covering the period from 1850 to 1860, in Cleveland, he moved to Cambridge, Mass., in 1891, hoping to find more congenial surroundings and a more intellectual atmosphere.

one of the last important amateurs in American historical writing. He died on Jan. 22, 1927.

Further Reading

James Ford Rhodes is listed in the American History study guide (VII, F, 3, a). Francis PARKMAN, a noted historian of the 19th century, wrote a multivolume history of the Anglo-French conflict in America.

The best book on Rhodes is Robert Cruden, *James Ford Rhodes: The Man, the Historian, and His Work* (1961), which contains biographical details and penetrating analyses of Rhodes's ideas and methods. Raymond Curtis Miller's essay on Rhodes in William T. Hutchinson, ed., *The Marcus W. Jernegan Essays in American Historiography* (1937), is brief but valuable. M. A. DeWolfe Howe, *James Ford Rhodes: American Historian* (1929), is adulatory and virtually ignores Rhodes's historical ideas but contains a large number of his letters.

RIBERA / By Eileen Lord

Jusepe de Ribera (1591–1652) was a Spanish painter and etcher who worked in Naples. Stylistically, his paintings show the progression from the early to the late baroque.

nformation concerning the life and personality of Jusepe de Ribera (pronounced rē-bā′rä) is sparse.

He was born the son of a shoemaker in Játiva, Valencia Province. He appears to have gone to the city of Valencia while still a boy, but nothing is known of his possible artistic training there. As an adolescent, he traveled to Italy and spent time in Lombardy. Next he was in Parma, from which, it is said, he was driven by the contentious jealousy of local artists. He located himself in Rome until an accumulation of debts forced him to flee. Finally he settled in Naples, where in 1616 he married Caterina Azzolino, the daughter of a painter, by whom he had seven children between the years 1627 and 1636.

The Academy of St. Luke in Rome elected Ribera to membership in 1625, and 6 years later the Pope conferred upon him the Order of Christ. It is understandably speculated that Ribera revisited Rome for these events. Being sought after in Naples by the Church and the various Spanish viceroys who ruled there in the name of the Spanish monarchy, he dismissed the idea of returning to his homeland. He was quoted as saying that he was honored and well paid in Naples and that Spain was a cruel stepmother to its own children and a compassionate mother to foreigners. Nevertheless, he generally added his nationality when he signed his works. This practice inspired the Italians to nickname him "the Little Spaniard" (Lo Spagnoletto).

The last decade of Ribera's life was one of personal struggle. He suffered from failing health, the taunts of other artists that his fame was "extinct," and difficulty in

James Ford Rhodes. (Library of Congress)

When the first two volumes appeared in 1892, they received almost universal acclaim. Rhodes, being a thoroughly middle-class American, found it easy and natural to say what middle-class America wanted to hear. According to Rhodes, the Civil War was a moral contest over slavery in which the North was entirely justified, although the South fought nobly to defend its views. Reconstruction was an unmitigated disaster, he believed, caused by the misguided attempt to elevate inferior Negroes to supremacy over superior whites.

Rhodes viewed history as a branch of literature, and he had an intensely personal view of the field. To Rhodes, the essence of history was the struggle between good people and bad people and not the result of conflicts between broad social forces. His historical views were attractive to the general reading public. As his subsequent volumes appeared, Rhodes came to be acknowledged as the leading authority on the Civil War and Reconstruction.

Despite declining health and his concern over World War I, Rhodes managed to publish the last two volumes of his history in the early 1920s, bringing his account up to the end of Theodore Roosevelt's first presidential administration. These books were not received as favorably as his earlier ones. Critics noted his exclusive preoccupation with political history, his failure to dig deeply into the forces causing historical change, his partiality for conservative business ideals, and his antipathy toward Negroes, immigrants, and workers.

Rhodes was one of the last men to write American history as a multivolume political narrative. He was also

Jusepe de Ribera. (MAS)

collecting payments due him. Nevertheless, he kept it from being a tragic defeat by continuing to paint until the very year of his death in Naples. Actually, he was the victim of the local politics and finances. Naples was in the throes of a severe economic depression for which the foreign rulers, the patrons of Ribera, were naturally blamed, and the desperate citizenry was rioting in the streets. It is significant that Ribera continued to receive commissions in such a time, even if there was a dearth of payments.

Ribera was inventive in subject matter, ranging through visionary spectacles, biblical themes, genre, portraits, mythological subjects, and portraits of ascetics and penitents. Three stylistic periods are pointed out by Elizabeth du Gué Trapier (1952): 1620–1635, dramatic chiaroscuro, dry and tight technique with the major influence from Caravaggio, as in the *Martyrdom of St. Andrew* (1628); 1635–1639, soft luminosity, sensitive line, and heavy impasto with influences from the Carracci, Guercino, Guido Reni, and Correggio, exemplified in the *Ecstasy of Mary Magdalene* (1636); and 1640–1652, looser brushstroke and less detail with a return to the Caravaggesque manner, for example, the *Communion of the Apostles* (1651). In etching he employed a painterly technique, refined and precise in the details.

Further Reading

Jusepe de Ribera is listed in the Art study guide (III, F, 1, f). He was influenced by the CARRACCI, CORREGGIO,

GUERCINO, Guido RENI, and, above all, CARAVAGGIO. In turn, Ribera influenced Bartolomé Esteban MURILLO, Diego VELÁZQUEZ, and Francisco de ZURBARÁN.

The definitive work on Ribera is Elizabeth du Gué Trapier, *Ribera* (1952). See also George Kubler and Martin Soria, *Art and Architecture in Spain and Portugal and Their American Dominion, 1500–1800* (1959).

RICARDO / By Reba N. Soffer

The English economist David Ricardo (1772–1823) was a founder of political economy. His economics armed reformers attacking the agricultural aristocracy's political, social, and economic privileges.

David Ricardo was born in London on April 19, 1772, the son of a Jewish merchant-banker émigré from Holland. Ricardo joined his father as a stockbroker at the age of 14. When he married a Quaker, his orthodox father cut him off. Ricardo became a Unitarian, and at 22, with a capital of £800 and support from the financial community, he became an independent stockbroker. At 42 he retired with a fortune of about £1 million and established himself as a landed proprietor.

Ricardo was an independent member of Parliament for the pocket borough of Portarlington from 1819 until his death. He supported a tax on capital to pay off the national debt; currency reform; abolition of the Corn Laws protecting British wheat; parliamentary, poor-law, legal, and military reform; a secret ballot; and Catholic emancipation; he also condemned political repression.

Ricardo's reputation rests upon *On the Principles of Political Economy and Taxation* (1817; rev. 3d ed. 1821), an analysis of the distribution of a fixed amount of wealth among three classes: the owner of land who receives rent, the owner of capital who earns profits, and the laborer who gets wages. Ricardo set out to "determine the laws which regulate this distribution" in relation to both the rate of capital growth and the yield of wheat per acre. Although the analysis is abstract, often ambiguous, and disorganized, seven related economic laws can be extracted.

First, prices are determined by the cost of production. Second, the value of any item is set by the quantity of labor used to produce it. In the revised edition of 1821, Ricardo suggested that value might also be influenced by the cost of production. A third law, a theory of rent, was based upon Malthus's prediction of increasing population. When population increases, more food is needed and less fertile land is planted. Rent is the difference in the price of wheat per acre between the most and least productive land. As population grows, rent increases at the expense of capital's profits and labor's wages. The interests of landlords were not only antithetical to the rest of the community, but landlords and capitalists were necessarily enemies.

The fourth and fifth laws deal with the wages fund and the natural price of labor. These laws assumed that the price of labor, like other market prices, fluctuated with supply and demand; but at any given time there was a fixed supply of money for the payment of wages. This wages fund was the amount of capital in circulation. As capital increased, population grew, less fertile land was planted, rent increased, capital profits decreased, and wages dropped. Ricardo held that population will tend constantly to rise above the wages fund, especially in old countries like England, causing the working man's standard of living to fall. Disaster was arrested only by population reduction, essentially through infant mortality. Ricardo, like Thomas Malthus, never anticipated either population control or technological increase of food supplies. If wages fell below subsistence level, population decreased; when wages neither increased nor decreased the labor supply, they reached their "natural" or subsistence level. Popularizers of Ricardo's general model interpreted this to mean that most people were doomed inexorably to bare subsistence.

The sixth law argues the "diminishing returns" of profits, the earnings of the most useful class. As increasingly inferior land is cultivated, rent and food prices rise, and profits fall since the higher wages required for subsistence wages come out of the existing amount of circulating capital. The final law, the quantity theory of money,

applies value theory to gold: the rise or fall in prices depends inversely upon the amount of money in circulation.

Ricardo's other important writings were *The High Price of Bullion* (1810); "An Essay on the Influence of a Low Price on Corn on the Profits of Stock" (1815); "Funding System" (1820), published posthumously in the *Encyclopaedia Britannica: Supplement* (1824); and the "Plan for the Establishment of a National Bank" (1824), also published posthumously. He died at Gatcombe Park, Gloucestershire, on Sept. 11, 1823.

Further Reading

David Ricardo is listed in the Social Sciences study guide (VI, C, 1). Cofounders of political economy with Ricardo were Thomas MALTHUS and Adam SMITH.

The definitive edition of Ricardo's *Works and Correspondence* is edited by P. Sraffa with the collaboration of M. H. Dobb (10 vols., 1951–1955). A helpful guide through the intricacies and inconsistencies of the Ricardian system is Oswald St. Clair, *A Key to Ricardo* (1957). Mark Blaug, *Ricardian Economics: A Historical Study* (1958), deals with Ricardo within the general context of his time. A chapter on Ricardo in Robert Lekachman, *A History of Economic Ideas* (1959), provides a lucid, less technical discussion of Ricardo's ideas.

RICCI / By Hok-lam Chan

Matteo Ricci (1552–1610) was an Italian Jesuit missionary who opened China to evangelization. He was the best-known Jesuit and European in China prior to the 20th century.

Born at Macerata on Oct. 6, 1552, Matteo Ricci (pronounced rēt′chē) went to Rome in 1568 to study law. In 1571 he entered the Society of Jesus. After studying mathematics and geography at a Roman college, he set out for Goa in 1577 and was ordained there in 1580. In 1582 he was dispatched to Macao and started to learn Chinese.

Soon after the Jesuits established themselves at Chaoch'ing west of Canton, Ricci and a fellow Jesuit, Michele Ruggieri, went there on Sept. 10, 1583. When the Chinese governor general ordered the expulsion of the Jesuits in 1589, Ricci managed to acquire a place in Shaochou, north of Kwangtung, where he soon established amicable relations with the officials and with members of the educated elite.

Ricci's ambition, however, was to go to Peking and establish himself in the imperial capital. Early in 1595 he set out to the north but was halted in Nanking, as all foreigners were held under suspicion following the Japanese invasion of Korea; hence he retreated to Nanchang, Kiangsi. In 1598 he found another opportunity to go

David Ricardo. (Trustees of The British Museum, Department of Prints and Drawings)

Matteo Ricci. (Radio Times Hulton Picture Library)

memory. The most famous of these are the *Mappamon-do* (World Map) and the *True Idea of God*.

Ricci owed his success, apart from his personality and learning, largely to his "accommodation method"—an attempt to harmonize the Christian doctrine with the Chinese tradition, which laid the foundation of the subsequent success of the Roman Catholic Church in China. Though the unhappy rites controversy (ca. 1635–1742) brought the mission to near ruin, the name of Ricci and his work left an indelible imprint on subsequent Chinese history.

Further Reading

Matteo Ricci is listed in the Religion study guide (I, M, 1, a). In the 16th century the Jesuit missionary St. FRANCIS XAVIER established missions in India and Japan.

Ricci's China journal was translated by Louis J. Gallagher as *China in the Sixteenth Century: The Journals of Matteo Ricci, 1583–1610* (1953), which unfortunately contains a number of errors. The standard biography of Ricci in English is Vincent Cronin, *The Wise Man from the West* (1955). For a scholarly estimation of Ricci's scientific contribution see Henri Bernard, *Matteo Ricci's Scientific Contribution to China* (trans. 1935). Recommended for general historical background are G. F. Hudson, *Europe and China* (1931), and George H. Dunne, *Generation of Giants* (1962).

north when the Nanking minister of rites, Wang Hung-hui, expressed willingness to escort him. They reached the gates of Peking but were again turned back due to the Sino-Japanese conflict. Ricci thereafter settled in Nanking, where he received warm welcome from the literati as a result of his broad knowledge of the Western sciences and deep understanding of the Chinese classics.

Ricci and his escort made another effort to go to Peking in 1600, but their entrance was delayed by the intrigue of the eunuch Ma T'ang, who had tried to take possession of the gifts brought for the Ming emperor. Eventually they arrived at the capital on Jan. 24, 1601, and subsequently received a warm welcome from the Emperor. This imperial favor provided Ricci with an opportunity to meet the leading officials and literati in Peking, some of whom later became Christian converts.

Finally, Ricci obtained a settlement with an allowance for subsistence in Peking, after which his reputation among the Chinese increased. Besides the missionary and scientific work, from 1596 on he was also superior of the missions, which in 1605 numbered 17. When he died on May 11, 1610, he was granted a place for burial in Peking. Some of the outstanding Chinese literati with whom Ricci had contact later became his converts, including the famous scholar-officials Hsü Kuang-ch'i, Li Chih-ts'ao, and Yang T'ing-yün. Ricci's writings include about 20 titles, mostly in Chinese, ranging from religious and scientific works to treatises on friendship and local

RICE / By William R. Reardon

Elmer Rice (1892–1967) was an American playwright and novelist. Often innovative in style, his plays reveal a concern with individual freedom confronted by the tyranny of impersonal institutions and destructive passions.

Elmer Rice was born Elmer Reizenstein on Sept. 28, 1892, in New York City. After 2 years of high school, he began working at the age of 14. He passed the regents' examinations and entered the New York Law School, from which he graduated *cum laude* in 1912. He passed the bar examinations but decided to try writing instead. His play *On Trial* (1914) was a resounding success. In 1915 he married Hazel Levy. Although not a member of any political party, Rice inclined toward socialism. After World War I he spent 2 years in Hollywood before moving to East Hampton, Conn.

Following *On Trial*, he had several plays produced in New York, but it was not until *The Adding Machine* (1923), an expressionistic tragic-comic portrait of dehydrated man, that he showed his true power. Two more plays, written in collaboration, were produced before he directed his powerful *Street Scene* (1929), a realistic presentation of environmental influences on character relationships. It won the Pulitzer Prize. *The Subway* (1929), a rather underrated play much on the order of *The Add-*

ing Machine, had a short run. In 1930 he published a novel, *A Voyage to Purilia*, and had an unsuccessful production of *See Naples and Die*. But in 1931 his *The Left Bank*, dealing with American expatriates, and *Counsellor-at-law* enlarged his reputation.

The impact of the Great Depression and Rice's trip to Russia and Europe in 1932 was manifested in the controversial *We, the People* (1933). After the production of *Judgment Day* and *Between Two Worlds* (1934), Rice excoriated New York critics and announced his retirement from the commercial theater. Nonetheless, between 1935 and 1938 he served with the Federal Theater Project, published a novel, helped organize The Playwrights' Company, and had his *American Landscape* produced.

After his divorce in 1942 Rice married Betty Field. During the war he worked for the U.S. Office of War Information, was active in the American Civil Liberties Union, and was president of the Dramatists' Guild. *Dream Girl* (1945), a psychoanalytical fantasy, was his final popular success. His novel *The Show Must Go On* appeared in 1949.

Rice's final work included essays, *The Living Theatre* (1959); an autobiography, *Minority Report* (1963); and additional plays. He received an honorary doctor's degree from the University of Michigan in 1961. Divorced

A scene from a 1923 production of The Adding Machine, a play written by Rice. The set design is by Lee Simonson. (Theatre Collection, The New York Public Library at Lincoln Center, Astor, Lenox and Tilden Foundations)

again, in 1966 he married Barbara Marshall. He died of a heart attack on May 8, 1967.

Further Reading

Elmer Rice is listed in the Literature study guide (I, E, 2, c). Thornton WILDER also experimented with new dramatic techniques.

Rice's *Minority Report* (1963) gives autobiographical details and personal accounts of his plays. The major critical work is Robert G. Hogan, *The Independence of Elmer Rice* (1965). Joseph Mersand, *The American Drama since 1930* (1949), and Allan Lewis, *American Plays and Playwrights of the Contemporary Theatre* (1965), provide additional criticism.

Elmer Rice in 1934. (Library of Congress, Carl Van Vechten Collection, Courtesy of Saul Mauriber)

RICHARD I / By Mary Cheney

Richard I (1157–1199), called the Lion-hearted, reigned as king of England from 1189 to 1199. He is famous for his exploits on the Third Crusade.

Born on Sept. 8, 1157, Richard I was the third son of Henry II of England and Eleanor of Aquitaine. From an early age he was regarded as his mother's heir and from 1168 lived with her in her duchy, chiefly at Poitiers. He was enthroned as duke in 1172; in the next year he and his brothers allied with the king of France against their father in a wide-ranging conspiracy. They were defeated, but Henry left Richard in Aquitaine, where he made his reputation as a soldier suppressing local risings. The death of his elder brother (1183) made Richard heir to the throne. He resisted by force his fa-

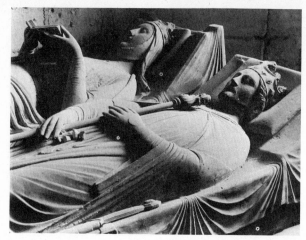

Richard I and his mother, Eleanor of Aquitaine, stone effigies in Fontevrault Abbey, France. (Archives Photographiques, Paris)

ther's proposed transfer of Aquitaine to his brother John, being determined to keep for himself all his father's French lands. In November 1188 he did homage for them to Philip II of France and campaigned with him against Henry II. Henry was defeated and had to grant all their demands before his death (July 6, 1189).

Richard succeeded his father without difficulty; he was installed as Duke of Normandy (July 20) and crowned king of England on September 3. His principal object was now to raise money for a crusade; everything was for sale, including offices and privileges, and Richard even released the king of Scots from vassalage for 10,000 marks.

Leaving England to a council of regency, Richard set out in 1190, traveling through Sicily. There he recognized Tancred as king, offending Emperor Henry VI, who was claiming the throne in the right of his wife. On his way east Richard seized Cyprus from its Greek ruler and there married Berengaria of Navarre. Richard twice defeated Saladin, at Arsuf (Sept. 7, 1191) and Jaffa (July 1192), and twice got within 12 miles of Jerusalem, but his military skill was offset by his quarrels with the other leaders. The crusade failed to reestablish the Latin kingdom, and Richard, deeply disappointed, left Palestine (September 1192) after concluding a truce that gave the Christians a narrow coastal strip and access as pilgrims to the holy places. On his way home he was captured and handed over to the Emperor, who demanded £100,000 as ransom and kept him a prisoner till February 1194, when a large part of the money was handed over.

The last years of Richard's life were spent in France, meeting the attacks of the King. Philip made no headway against Richard's superior generalship, but Richard's early death (April 6, 1199) in a minor foray opened the way for the conquest of Normandy and Anjou a few years later.

Further Reading

Richard I is listed in the European History study guide (II, C, 1, b; II, D, 1, c; II, M, 3) and the Asia study guide (I, B, 4, f). The son of HENRY II and ELEANOR OF AQUI-

TAINE, he defeated SALADIN and was succeeded by JOHN.

The standard biography of Richard I is Kate Norgate, *Richard the Lion Heart* (1924). A popular account is by Philip Henderson, *Richard Coeur de Lion* (1959). Steven Runciman, *A History of the Crusades*, vol. 2 (1952), describes Richard's crusade. A contemporary account is translated by Merton Jerome Hubert, *The Crusade of Richard Lion Heart, by Ambroise* (1941). A short account of Richard's activities in France by F. M. Powicke is in *The Cambridge Medieval History*, vol. 6 (1929); and Austin L. Poole, *From Domesday Book to Magna Carta* (1955), describes the government of England.

RICHARD II / By M. C. Rosenfield

Richard II (1367–1400) was king of England from 1377 to 1399. His reign, which ended in his abdication, saw the rise of strong baronial forces aiming to control the monarchy.

Richard II, known as Richard of Bordeaux from his birthplace, was born on Jan. 6, 1367, the younger son of Edward, Prince of Wales (the Black Prince), and Joan, daughter of Edmund, Earl of Kent. After his father's death, Richard became the heir apparent, was created Prince of Wales in the later part of 1376, and on June 22, 1377, succeeded Edward III, his grandfather, as king of England. While he was underage, the control of the government had been left to a regency that came increasingly under the influence of the Duke of Lancaster (John of Gaunt), one of his uncles. In 1381, during the revolt led by Wat Tyler, Richard showed his leadership potential by going out to meet the rebels and pacifying them after Tyler was killed.

After his marriage on Jan. 20, 1382, to Anne, the sister of King Wenceslaus and daughter of the emperor Charles IV, Richard attempted to end the regency's control of his minority and to take the leadership in national affairs, but Parliament was not eager to give up its powers. The following year, without consulting Parliament, Richard appointed Michael de la Pole as chancellor; and in 1384, hoping to check the opposition of his uncle Lancaster, he made his other uncles dukes of York and Gloucester.

As the barons under Gloucester's leadership hoped to rule Richard, he started to create a "new" nobility, raising Pole to Earl of Suffolk and Robert de Vare to Duke of Ireland, which resulted in Gloucester's forcing the King to accept a commission of 11 nobles with powers for reform in 1386. Using the law courts, Richard was able to have the commission declared unlawful in August 1387, but the barons were determined to retain the upper hand, and in the "Merciless" Parliament, which met that winter, those who supported the King were attacked, and some were executed.

Although he was able to regain ministers of his own choosing in the spring of 1389, Richard hoped to win over the barons by a policy of conciliation, but this failed partly because of his own weakness and partly because of the death of his first wife in June 1394 and his second marriage to Isabella, daughter of Charles VI of France, in November 1396. This marriage to the traditional enemy caused a loss of popular goodwill, and Gloucester called for the resumption of the French war. Fearing that a second attempt might be made by the barons to limit his royal powers, Richard was able to get the leaders of the opposition, Gloucester, Arundel, and Warwick, in his power by July 1397, and in the Parliament that met in the autumn of the following year these men were condemned to death. This Parliament, after moving from Westminster to Shrewsbury in 1398, undid the acts of the Merciless Parliament. Now Richard was in full control and started to act in an arbitrary manner, alienating both barons and lesser subjects.

In February 1399, on the death of the Duke of Lancaster, Richard refused the inheritance to Lancaster's son, the exiled Henry of Bolingbroke; 2 months later Richard went to Ireland to avenge the death of the Earl of March, who had been killed on royal service. As soon as Henry of Bolingbroke heard of the King's absence, he landed in Yorkshire and raised a force to try to replace the King. Richard returned but, failing in an effort to raise an army, went into hiding in the north and after several months surrendered to Henry on Aug. 19, 1399, in North Wales. Henry, already acting as Henry IV, forced Richard's abdication on September 29 and imprisoned him. Richard died on Feb. 14, 1400, while at Pontefract.

King Richard II of England, a painting by an unknown artist. (National Portrait Gallery, London)

Further Reading

Richard II is listed in the European History study guide (III, D, 1, a; III, E, 1, b). The son of EDWARD THE BLACK PRINCE, he succeeded EDWARD III and was succeeded by HENRY IV.

Of the many biographical studies of Richard II, the most important is Anthony Steel, *Richard II* (1941). See also Harold F. Hutchison, *The Hollow Crown: A Life of Richard II* (1961). Gervase Mathew, *The Court of Richard II* (1969), is a scholarly and interesting study of the court life, the social milieu, and the arts of the time; and Richard H. Jones, *The Royal Policy of Richard II: Absolutism in the Later Middle Ages* (1968), plays down Richard's personality and emphasizes the political imperatives of the time. For general historical background see Sir James H. Ramsay, *Genesis of Lancaster, 1307–1399* (2 vols., 1913); May McKisack, *The Fourteenth Century, 1307–1399* (1959); and the excellent work of Arthur Bryant, *The Atlantic Saga*, vol. 2: *The Age of Chivalry* (1964).

RICHARD III / By K. Fred Gillum

Richard III (1452–1485), last Yorkist king of England, reigned from 1483 to 1485 during the Wars of the Roses. He is generally considered a usurper and is suspected of the murder of Edward V and his brother.

Born on Oct. 2, 1452, at Fotheringhay Castle, Richard was the eleventh child and youngest son of Richard, Duke of York, and Cecily Neville. His father's 1454 and 1460 regencies for Henry VI caused Lancastrian opposition that brought York to his death in the Battle of Wakefield (Dec. 30, 1460). Richard and his brother George were fugitives until their 18-year old brother gained the throne as Edward IV in 1461. Thereafter George became a disloyal Duke of Clarence and Richard an able Duke of Gloucester. Richard shared command in the Yorkist victories at Barnet (April 14, 1471) and Tewkesbury (May 4).

Richard's 1472 marriage to 16-year-old Anne Neville caused disputes with Clarence, husband of Anne's older sister Isabella Neville, over the division of the estates of their late father, the Earl of Warwick. Clarence's treasonable habits led him to challenge the legitimacy of the King and his children, whereupon Edward's Parliament attainted Clarence as "incorrigible," resulting in his execution in 1478 and the disinheritance of his son, Edward of Warwick. This reduced the contention for influence to a rivalry between Richard and the Woodville relatives of Edward's queen.

His Regency

The April 9, 1483, deathbed will of Edward IV left his 12-year-old heir, Edward V, to the regency and protec-

King Richard III of England, a portrait by a contemporary painter. (National Portrait Gallery, London)

troops, and Queen Mother Elizabeth allowed 9-year-old Richard of York to join his brother in the Tower. Then commenced the "Richard for King" movement. From June 22 to 25, several meetings about London heard Buckingham and others claim the illegitimacy of Edward V and his brother and the need for the Protector to assume the crown. Richard was persuaded to occupy the throne on June 26, and on July 6 he was crowned with unusual ceremony as Richard III. Numerous pardons were given, although the June 25 execution of Lord Rivers, Lord Richard Grey, and Sir Thomas Vaughan showed little mercy for the Woodvilles. These deaths, the uncertain fate of the princes in the Tower, and the confinement of Clarence's son, Edward of Warwick, were evidence of at least some legal and moral confusion surrounding the new king.

In July, Richard commenced a royal progress through western and northern England, culminating in the September 8 ceremonies at York investing his only legitimate son, 10-year-old Edward, as Prince of Wales. At Lincoln on October 11, Richard learned that Buckingham was preparing a revolt in support of the exiled Henry Tudor on the claim that the princes in the Tower were dead by Richard's orders. Richard collected troops that dispersed Buckingham's forces and drove off Henry in October 1483. For this rebellion the duke was executed, but many of the rebels were pardoned.

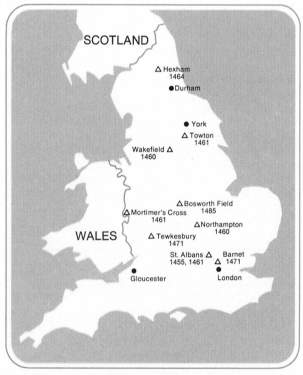

The Wars of the Roses. Civil war between the aristocratic houses of York and Lancaster from 1455 to 1485 culminated in the seizure of the throne by the Yorkist Richard III in 1483 and his defeat by the Lancastrian Henry Tudor 2 years later. The decimation of the old aristocracy in this struggle made possible the strong Tudor monarchy. (Triangular symbols indicate battle sites.)

torship of Richard; yet the late king's children, treasure, and ships were in Woodville custody. At Middleham Castle in Yorkshire, Richard learned from Lord Hastings of the queen mother's attempts to dominate the council and of the preparations of Anthony Woodville, Lord Rivers, for bringing the new king from Wales to London with an escort of 2,000 men. Richard added the Duke of Buckingham's troops to his own, confronted the King at Stony Stratford on April 30, and persuaded Edward V to accept the arrest of Rivers and other leaders of the royal escort. Richard and Buckingham accompanied Edward to London House, while the queen mother and her other children sought sanctuary at Westminster.

As protector, Richard retained most government officials but moved to gain control of Woodville-held ships and forts. Buckingham's council motion removed Edward V to the Tower on May 19, 1483, "until his coronation," and on June 10, Richard wrote to the city of York for armed help against adherents of the queen mother. At a June 13 council in the Tower, Richard had Hastings killed, John Morton and former Chancellor Rotherham imprisoned, and Lord Stanley confined to quarters. A royal herald explained this to Londoners as suppression of a plot against the Protector and denounced the immoral liaison of Hastings and Jane Shore.

Accession to the Throne

On June 16, 1483, Richard invested Westminster with

In April 1484 Edward, Prince of Wales, died, leaving Richard with no successor who would have a clear title and the ability to continue the compacts of feudal loyalty beyond the King's lifetime. Richard eventually selected as his heir the Earl of Lincoln, son of the Duke of Suffolk and Richard's sister Elizabeth.

As Queen Anne declined with tuberculosis in 1484, Richard seems to have considered the possibility of a second marriage, to his niece, Elizabeth of York, already the object of Henry Tudor's political affections. However, Anne's death on March 16, 1485, started the canard that Richard had poisoned her in order to be free to marry again. Richard publicly denied all intention of marriage to his niece and sent her from the court.

On Aug. 7, 1485, Henry Tudor landed at Milford Haven with 2,000 men and gained swift support from his fellow Welshmen. From Nottingham, Richard ordered an array of troops, and on August 22 the opposing forces met at Bosworth Field. Richard led a charge on Henry's bodyguard in the hope of slaying his rival but was himself killed by Lord Stanley's soldiers. The victor was proclaimed King Henry VII, and Richard's corpse was stripped and carried on horseback to exposure at Leicester and burial at the Grey Friars.

Further Reading

Richard III is listed in the European History study guide (III, D, 1, c). He was defeated by HENRY VII.

The biography by Paul Murray Kendall, *Richard the Third* (1955), provides a thoughtful interpretation and comprehensive bibliography. Also useful is Sir Clements Markham, *Richard III: His Life and Character* (1906; repr. 1968). James Gairdner, *Richard III* (1898), is a fair appraisal, accurate in its use of sources. The biography attributed to Sir Thomas More in 1513, *The History of King Richard III* (1963), inspired much of the Tudor propaganda on Richard as "royal monster." Recommended general political histories for the period are E. F. Jacob, *The Fifteenth Century* (1961); S. B. Chrimes, *Lancastrians, Yorkists and Henry VII* (1964); J. R. Lander, *The Wars of the Roses* (1966); and A. L. Rowse, *Bosworth Field* (1966).

I. A. **RICHARDS** / By Oscar Cargill

Ivor Armstrong Richards (born 1893), English-born American semanticist and literary critic, crusaded to have "Basic" English adopted as a fundamental English vocabulary.

On Feb. 26, 1893, I. A. Richards was born at Cheshire. He was educated at Clifton College in Bristol and Magdalen College in Cambridge. In 1922 he became a lecturer in English and moral science at Cambridge and 4 years later was made a fellow of Magdalen. He had collaborated with C. K. Ogden and Charles Woods, Cambridge psychologists, on the *Foun-*

I. A. Richards demonstrating the teaching of "Basic" English in 1942. (Wide World Photos)

dations of Aesthetics (1921). With Ogden he collaborated on *The Meaning of Meaning* (1923), a pioneer study in semantics, in which they established that what is known as "meaning" resides in the recipient as well as in the originator of the thought.

Richards's first independent book, *Principles of Literary Criticism* (1924), was revolutionary in the development of modern criticism. Deriding "bogus" esthetic terms, like "beauty" which has no "entity," Richards held that all value judgments reside in the communicant, not in the object or poem itself or in the communicator or poet. His principles of judgment are developed from this position. *Science and Poetry* (1925) treats, in terms of vocabulary, experiences that he terms "critical" and "technical." In 1926 he married Dorothy Eleanor Pilley.

In 1929 Richards published *Practical Criticism*, a report on the sad results of testing value judgments by presenting a class with specimens of writing whose authorship was not revealed. In 1929–1930 Richards was visiting professor at Tsing Hua University, Peking. He was a lecturer and later a professor at Harvard, retiring in 1963. During the 1930s he wrote *Mencius on the Mind* (1932) and *Coleridge on Imagination* (1935), careful examinations of the systems of these protean thinkers. He also completed *Interpretation in Teaching* and *How to Read a Page* (both 1934).

Richards joined his former collaborator C. K. Ogden in a crusade for the use of "Basic" English, which consisted of the 850 words most commonly used in the English vocabulary. To elaborate on his theories, Richards wrote three tracts: *Basic English and Its Uses* (1943), *Nations and Peace* (1943), and *So Much Nearer* (1968). His translations into "Basic" included *The Republic of Plato* (1942), *Tomorrow Morning, Faustus!* (1962), and *Why So, Socrates?* (1963). Two volumes of verse, *Good Bye, Earth* (1958) and *The Screens* (1960), won him the Loines Poetry Award in 1962.

Further Reading

I. A. Richards is listed in the Literature study guide (II, J,

1, a). Edmund WILSON was an important American critic of this era.

The best treatment of Richards is W. H. N. Hotopf, *Language, Thought, and Comprehension: A Case Study of the Writings of I. A. Richards* (1965); see also Stanley Edgar Hyman, *The Armed Vision: A Study in the Methods of Modern Literary Criticism* (1948). For the English reaction to Richards see D. W. Harding and F. R. Leavis in Eric Bentley, ed., *The Importance of Scrutiny* (1948).

* * *

T. W. **RICHARDS** / By Albert B. Costa

The American chemist Theodore William Richards (1868–1928) ushered in a new age of accuracy in chemistry by determining the atomic weights of many elements.

Theodore W. Richards. (Harvard University Library)

Theodore W. Richards was born on Jan. 31, 1868, in Germantown, Pa. His father, William Trost Richards, was a prominent landscape and marine artist; his mother, Anna Matlock Richards, was a poet and a woman of great cultivation. Until he entered college, his education was at home under his mother's direction. At age 14 he entered Haverford College as a sophomore, uncertain whether to become an astronomer or a chemist. He had defective eyesight, however, and by the time of his graduation he had decided on a career in chemistry.

In 1885 Richards entered Harvard as a senior and the following year was granted the bachelor's degree. Two years later he was awarded the doctorate with a dissertation on the atomic weights of hydrogen and oxygen. He won a Harvard grant for a year of travel and study in Europe. On his return to Harvard in 1889, he became an assistant and subsequently an instructor in analytical chemistry.

Atomic Weight Determinations

To Richards, atomic weights were the most fundamental constants in nature, and he associated them with deep questions about the universe. They offered more promise of contributing to the understanding of the universe than any other area of chemistry. By very thorough, painstaking work he published revised atomic weights for copper, zinc, barium, strontium, magnesium, and calcium.

In 1894 Richards introduced two new devices to overcome the two most prevalent sources of error in atomic weight work: the presence of moisture and the loss of traces of precipitate. His bottling apparatus enabled him to fuse, handle, and weigh solids under absolutely dry conditions. His nephelometer (cloud measurer) enabled him to determine traces of unrecovered precipitate by measuring the turbidity of the filtrate.

Along with his research Richards was teaching quan-

titative analysis. In 1894 he was promoted to assistant professor. Harvard sent him to Germany for a year of training in physical chemistry. On his return from Europe in 1896 he married Miriam Stuart Thayer.

Over the next few years Richards corrected the atomic weights of nickel, cobalt, iron, uranium, and cesium. In every instance his results became the official ones of the International Commission on Atomic Weights. His revision of the atomic weights of J. S. Stas involved correcting for errors in purification, drying, and weighing of materials, and it inaugurated a new era of accuracy. His papers published from 1905 to 1910 exceeded in accuracy any chemical research ever published.

In 1901 Richards was promoted to full professor, and in 1912 he became Erving professor of chemistry and director of the new Wolcott Gibbs Memorial Laboratory (1913), which was the finest chemical laboratory in the world.

By 1913 the study of radioactive decay led to the possibility that an element may have more than one atomic weight. Richards analyzed radioactive samples of lead, and all of his determinations were below the atomic weight of ordinary lead, the lowest being 206.08. He concluded that there was no doubt that uranium transmuted itself into a light variety of lead. Frederick Soddy announced the isotope concept in 1913, and Richards's experiments were the first confirmation of the new theory and the only conclusive evidence for isotopes until the development of the mass spectrograph.

Atomic weights have remained the most frequently required units by chemists in quantitative measurements of all kinds. Richards determined the atomic weights of 25 elements. His students, Gregory Baxter at Harvard and Otto Hönigschmidt at Munich, continued his work and were responsible for 30 additional elements.

Physical Chemistry

Of Richards's almost 300 papers, about one-half deal

with atomic weights, the remainder being concerned with several aspects of physical chemistry. He was a leader in introducing this new field into the United States, and his laboratory was a center which prepared a new generation of physical chemists. Richards made investigations in thermochemistry, electrochemistry, and the physicochemical study of the properties of matter. In physical chemistry, as in atomic weights, his work represented an advance in precision and accuracy.

One of Richards's most productive areas of research was thermochemistry. In 1905 he introduced the adiabatic calorimeter to prevent the loss or gain of heat to and from the surroundings. He published over 60 papers on thermochemistry and for many years was a pioneer in precision calorimetry.

In 1899 Richards began a study of the atomic volumes and compressibilities of the elements after noting that the constant b occurring in the Van der Waals equation $(p + a/V^2)(V - b) = RT$ was not a constant but varied with pressure and temperature. Since b was the space occupied by the molecule, Richards asserted that the concept of the atom as a hard, rigid particle was incorrect. He proposed that atoms were compressible, the forces of affinity and cohesion exerting a compressing effect on atoms resulting in enormous internal pressures. He devised methods to determine the compressibilities of the elements up to 500 atmospheres pressure and tried to correlate this property with the other fundamental properties of the elements in the hope of discovering important relationships. He never completed these studies; nevertheless, his experimental data proved to be invaluable to atomic physics.

His Character and Honors

Richards was primarily an experimentalist of exceptional ability. Yet his measurements were only a means to an end; with them he searched for an understanding of the material structure of the universe.

Richards received many honorary degrees and medals. A Harvard professorship was endowed in his name in 1925. He received the Nobel Prize in chemistry in 1914, the first American chemist to be so honored. He was a man of noble character who made a deep impression on those who met him. The guiding principles of his life he described as "kindliness and common sense." He died on April 2, 1928.

Further Reading

Theodore W. Richards is listed in the Science study guide (VII, D, 4). He was preceded in his work by Jöns Jacob BERZELIUS, the Swedish master of the art of atomic weight determination. Richards's work on the compressibility of atoms was continued by Percy BRIDGMAN at Harvard.

Richards presented his atomic weight research in *Determinations of Atomic Weights* (1910). In his Nobel Prize lecture, printed in Nobel Foundation, *Nobel Lectures: Chemistry, 1901–1921* (1966), he described both his research and his beliefs about the universe. Of the many biographical studies of Richards, the most informative are those in Benjamin Harrow, *Eminent Chemists of Our Time* (1927); Sir Harold Hartley, *Memorial Lectures Delivered before the Chemical Society* (3 vols., 1933); and Aaron J. Ihde, *Great Chemists* (1961).

✳   ✳   ✳

HENRY HANDEL **RICHARDSON**

/ By R. M. Younger

Henry Handel Richardson was the pen name of Ethel Florence Lindesay Richardson (1870–1946), an expatriate Australian novelist. She based a series of novels on characters and incidents taken mainly from her life.

Born in Melbourne on Jan. 3, 1870, Ethel Richardson was the daughter of an Irish doctor who emigrated in the 1850s, living at first on the Victorian goldfields and later practicing in Melbourne. During a generally unhappy childhood she attended the Presbyterian Ladies' College, and after her father's death she taught briefly as a governess. At 17, she went abroad with her mother and sister; she studied music at Leipzig and in 1895 married a Scottish student, John G. Robertson, meanwhile studying the masters of the European novel.

Henry Handel Richardson began her literary career as a

Henry Handel Richardson. (Australian News and Information Bureau, London)

translator of *Niels Lyhne* by Danish novelist Jens Jacobsen; this was published as *Siren Voices* (1896). Jacobsen's style—"romanticism imbued with the scientific spirit, and essentially based on realism," in her view—profoundly influenced all her writing; imagery in character construction and meticulous realism in the detail of settings became her guideposts. Her first novel, *Maurice Guest* (1908), was autobiographical to the extent that the central character is an Australian girl studying music in Germany. The novel, somber and naturalistic, was coolly received, being stigmatized variously as dull, verbose, morbid, and erotic. However, because of its revealing attention to detail, it had a considerable influence among writers and was a forerunner of novels presenting amoral behavior dispassionately.

The Getting of Wisdom (1910) was an engaging study of school life; it won only limited praise. Nevertheless, proceeds from it made it possible for Henry Handel Richardson to visit Australia briefly in 1912 "to test memories" and to gather material for the first volume of the *Fortunes of Richard Mahony* trilogy.

The Trilogy

Marking a major expansion in Henry Handel Richardson's creative range, *Australia Felix* (1917) re-creates the mental climate as well as the sights and sounds of the goldfields life. Richard Mahony is portrayed as an intellectual groping for the unknown through spiritualism (just as the author's father had done) but unable to find contentment. Irony supplies much of the tension. Mahony voices his displeasure with life in the colony, which seems to have brought curses rather than blessings; the end of the novel marks his departure for England full of expectations.

In *The Way Home* (1925) Mahony's temporary pleasure at being able to relive the familiar within a richly civilized society turns quickly to disillusionment when he and his colonial-born wife experience its provincial narrowness. In Europe he learns of financial losses, which make it necessary for him to return to Australia. Back in Melbourne, he finds his fortune restored; now he can build the mansion he has dreamed of so long—to be named Ultima Thule—but here his mental and physical deterioration begins.

In the final volume, *Ultima Thule* (1929), the author overlays her own psychological interpretations on the facts of her father's life and suggests that the emptiness and barrenness of the setting in which the fictional Mahony finds himself are powerful causes of his final mental disintegration. The trilogy has been described as an unusually thorough analysis of the "geographic disorientation" that sensitive immigrants suffered.

With the success of the *Richard Mahony* trilogy, the author's identity, previously concealed, was revealed. Her earlier novels were reprinted and reassessed. Her final work, *The Young Cosima* (1939), reconstructs the life of Franz Liszt's illegitimate daughter, Cosima. Fictionalizing the turbulent and massive influence of the life of Richard Wagner (whom Cosima married in 1870, after having left Hans von Bülow in 1865), this documentary novel is richly redolent with fact in its re-creation of the atmosphere of the period and its portraits of the great musicians.

In 1939 Henry Handel Richardson began writing her autobiography to 1903; she died before completing it, and it ends in 1895. It was published in 1948 as *Myself when Young*. She died at Hastings, Sussex, on March 20, 1946.

Further Reading

Henry Handel Richardson is listed in the Australia and New Zealand study guide (II, G). Other Australian writers were Marcus CLARKE, Miles FRANKLIN, and Henry LAWSON.

A comprehensive exposition, accompanied by some personal recollections and correspondence, is given in Nettie Palmer, *Henry Handel Richardson: A Study* (1950). An interesting review of Henry Handel Richardson's method is contained in Leonie J. Gibson, *Henry Handel Richardson and Some of Her Sources* (1954). Her writing style, as well as literary influences, is discussed in H. M. Green, *A History of Australian Literature* (2 vols., 1961). A telling analysis of the novels, with special attention to her aim of "scientific realism" in writing, is given by Leonie Kramer in Geoffrey Dutton, ed., *The Literature of Australia* (1964).

✳ ✳ ✳

HENRY HOBSON **RICHARDSON**
/ **By Lawrence Wodehouse**

Henry Hobson Richardson (1838–1886), American architect, helped set the standard for innovative design from which modern American architecture grew.

Henry Hobson Richardson was born in St. James parish, La., on Sept. 29, 1838. He studied engineering at Harvard College (1854–1859). During 1859 he traveled throughout the British Isles, and the following year he entered the École des Beaux-Arts in Paris, enrolling in the atelier of Jules Louis André. Later, lacking funds as a result of the blockade of New Orleans during the Civil War, Richardson went to work for Théodore Labrouste and probably worked on the Hospice d'Ivry near Paris, begun in 1862. Richardson was the second American to study at the École. Following the lead of his predecessor, Richard Morris Hunt, he avoided using the architectural idioms of the French Second Empire when he returned to practice in the United States in 1865.

Richardson's early designs were an outgrowth of the High Victorian Gothic style as developed by English architects William Butterfield, Edward Godwin, and William Burges. The High Victorian Gothic influence was spread throughout the United States by the circulation of such English periodicals as the *Builder*. Godwin's Town

Hall in Northampton, England (1861–1864), influenced Richardson's design for the Brookline, Mass., Town Hall (1870). It was also the basis for Richardson's American Merchants' Union Express Company Building, Chicago (1872), which introduced this style to the Midwest. Burges's entry in the competition for the London Law Courts (1866) influenced Richardson's Hampden County Courthouse, Springfield, Mass. (1871–1873). His Gothic style developed further in the Church of Unity, Springfield, Mass. (1866–1869); Grace Church, West Medford, Mass. (1867–1869); and the North Congregational Church, Springfield, Mass. (1868–1873). The English influence is also seen in his Cheney Building, Hartford, Conn. (1875–1876).

In 1870, when he won a design competition for the Brattle Square Church in Boston, Richardson introduced suggestions of a Romanesque revival style. The architectural historian Henry-Russell Hitchcock noted of the Brattle Square Church that Richardson "had now definitely chosen certain lines, no longer French or English, but his own." This originality developed through Trinity Church, Boston, for which he won the design competition in 1872 (built 1873–1877), and culminated in his design for the Marshall Field Wholesale Store, Chicago (1885–1887; demolished).

Trinity Church has the centralized Byzantine Greek-cross plan of St. Mark's in Venice, a church that Richardson considered the "most beautiful . . . in the world" when he saw it during his European trip in 1882. The silhouette is also Byzantine, but the lantern is influenced by Spain's Salamanca Cathedral. The apse is typical of the Romanesque churches of the French Auvergne, and the

Henry Hobson Richardson, photographed by George C. Cox. (History of Photography Collection, Smithsonian Institution, Washington, D.C.)

Henry Hobson Richardson's Marshall Field Wholesale Store, built in Chicago between 1885 and 1887 and demolished in 1930, was a definitive statement of his use of an arcaded front. (Chicago Architectural Photo Co.)

western entrance and the porch (which was added in the 1890s) were taken from the Provençal church at Saint-Gilles-du-Gard. In the interior the wooden roof trusses show Burges's influence. Britishers William Morris and Edward Burne-Jones were commissioned to design some of the stained-glass windows, and other windows and murals were executed by John La Farge of the United States.

Richardson's domestic architecture, after initial mid-Victorian derivatives, became an American extension of the English Arts and Crafts movement as expounded by the British architect Norman Shaw. The F. W. Andrews House (1872), with its open plan, and the William Watts Sherman House (1874), both in Newport, R.I., have the American "shingle" and "stick" qualities in addition to the Shaw influence. The M. F. Stoughton House at Cambridge, Mass. (1882–1883), goes beyond stylistic associations and is comparable in its simplicity to the Marshall Field Wholesale Store.

Richardson's Marshall Field store, described by architect Louis Sullivan as "massive, dignified, simple . . . foursquare and brown . . . a monument to trade," had an arcaded masonry skin over an iron skeleton frame. Richardson's work should be judged by this building, by the stark simplicity of the Allegheny County Jail, Pittsburgh (1884–1886), and by the J. J. Glessner House, Chicago (1885–1887). These were his ultimate architectural expressions at the height of his career. He died in Brookline, Mass., on April 27, 1886.

Richardson's influence spread far and wide. The work of the Burnham and Root architectural firm in the Monadnock Building in Chicago (1890–1891) and the whole span of Louis Sullivan's work captured the spirit of Richardson without copying his stylistic traits. Others who copied the "Richardson Romanesque" style designed buildings throughout the United States. His influence spread to Europe, where a host of architects took up his manner, adding local vernacular and sometimes historical traditions. From this great amalgam emerged modern architecture.

Further Reading

Henry Hobson Richardson is listed in the Art study guide (IV, D, 4, b). Louis SULLIVAN and Daniel H. BURNHAM, continuing the innovative phase in architectural design begun by Richardson, added newly refined engineering techniques. The sum of these was the skyscraper.

Mariana Van Rensselaer published a personal tribute to Richardson 2 years after his death, *Henry Hobson Richardson and His Works* (1888). Henry-Russell Hitchcock wrote *The Architecture of H. H. Richardson and His Times* (1936; rev. ed. 1961) and *Richardson as a Victorian Architect* (1966). See also Boston Museum of Fine Arts, *The Furniture of H. H. Richardson* (1962), an exhibition catalog of Richardson's furniture. Lewis Mumford revaluated Richardson in *Sticks and Stones* (1924; 2d rev. ed. 1955) and *The Brown Decades, 1865–1895* (1931; 2d rev. ed. 1955).

s. RICHARDSON / By Michael Shugrue

The English novelist Samuel Richardson (1689–1761) brought dramatic intensity and psychological insight to the epistolary novel.

F iction, including the novel told in letters, had become popular in England before Samuel Richardson's time, but he was the first English novelist to have the leisure to perfect the form in which he chose to work. Daniel Defoe's travel adventures and pseudobiographies contain gripping individual episodes and an astonishing realism, but they lack, finally, the structural unity and cohesiveness characteristic of Richardson's lengthy novels. Unlike his great contemporary Henry Fielding, who satirized every echelon of English society in such panoramic novels as *Tom Jones*, Richardson chose to focus his attention on the limited problems of marriage and of the heart, matters to be treated with seriousness. In so doing, however, he also provided his readers with an unparalleled study of the social and economic forces that were bringing the rising, wealthy English merchant class into conflict with the landed aristocracy.

Born in Derbyshire, Richardson was one of nine children of a joiner, or carpenter. He became an apprentice printer to John Wilde and learned his trade well from that hard master for 7 years. After serving as "Overseer

Samuel Richardson, painted in 1750 by Joseph Highmore. (National Portrait Gallery, London)

At the fashionable resort of Tunbridge Wells in 1748 Richardson mingled with Samuel Johnson, Colley Cibber, David Garrick, William Pitt the Elder, and other "remarkable characters." Beneath the drawing of the scene from which this engraving was derived, the celebrities are identified in Richardson's own hand. (Department of Prints and Drawings, Victoria and Albert Museum)

and Corrector" in a printing house, he set up shop for himself in Salisbury Court, Fleet Street, in 1720, where he married, lived for many years, and carried on his business. Within 20 years he had built up one of the largest and most lucrative printing businesses in London. Although he published a wide variety of books, including his own novels, he depended upon the official printing that he did for the House of Commons for an important source of income.

Richardson claimed to have written indexes, prefaces, and dedications early in his career, but his first known work, published in 1733, was *The Apprentice's Vade Mecum; or, Young Man's Pocket Companion*, a conduct book addressed to apprentices. *A Seasonable Examination* . . . (1735) was a pamphlet supporting a parliamentary bill to regulate the London theaters.

"Pamela"

In 1739, while at work on a book of model letters for social occasions proposed to him as a publishing venture by two booksellers, Richardson decided to put together a series of letters that would narrate the tribulations of a young servant girl in a country house. His first epistolary novel, *Pamela, or Virtue Rewarded*, was published in two volumes in November 1740 and became an instantaneous and enormous success. When its popularity led to the publication of a spurious sequel, Richardson countered by publishing a less interesting and, indeed, less popular continuation of his work in December 1741.

Richardson claimed in a letter to the Reverend Johannes Stinstra in 1753 that the idea for the story of *Pamela* had been suggested to him 15 years before, a claim he repeated to Aaron Hill. Regardless of the source for the story, however, Richardson's audience accepted and praised his simple tale of a pretty 15-year-old servant

girl, the victim of the extraordinarily clumsy attempts at seduction by her young master, Squire B— (later named Squire Booby in the novels of Henry Fielding), who sincerely, shrewdly, and successfully holds out for marriage.

Richardson's use of the epistolary form, which made it possible for him to have Pamela writing at the moment, enabled him to give a minutely particular account of his heroine's thoughts, actions, fears, and emotions. Pamela's letters give the reader a continuous and cumulative impression of living through the experience and create a new kind of sympathy with the character whose experiences are being shared. But Richardson's decision to have the entire story told through Pamela's letters to her parents also raised technical problems that he was not to overcome until his second novel. Because she alone must report compliments about her charms, testify to her virtue, and relate her successful attempts to repulse Squire B—'s advances, she often seems coy and self-centered rather than innocent.

Richardson's continuation of *Pamela*, which describes her attempts to succeed in "high life" after her marriage to Squire B—, is a less interesting story, more pretentiously told and far less moving.

He followed his triumph with *Pamela* in 1741 by publishing the delayed *Letters Written to and for Particular Friends, Directing the Requisite Style and Forms . . . in Writing Familiar Letters*, a collection of little interest to the modern reader.

"Clarissa"

By the summer of 1742 Richardson had evidently begun work on what was to become his masterpiece. *Clarissa Harlowe* was published in seven volumes in 1747–1748. Although he had finished the first version of the novel by 1744, he continued to revise it, to solicit the opinions of his friends (and disregard most of their advice), and to worry about its excessive length. The massive work, which runs to more than a million words and stands as one of the longest novels in the English language, contains 547 letters, most written by the heroine, Clarissa Harlowe, her friend, Anna Howe, the dashing villain, Lovelace, and his confidant, John Belford. Letters of enormous length and incredible intensity follow Clarissa's struggle with her family to avoid marriage to the odious Mr. Soames, her desperate flight from her unbending and despicable family into the arms of Lovelace, her drugged rape, her attempts to escape from Lovelace by soliciting the aid of her unforgiving family, and her dramatic death. Before the final volumes of the novel were published, many of Richardson's readers had pleaded with him to give the novel a happy ending by allowing Clarissa to live. Richardson, however, had set out to show that in losing her innocence a girl might be ennobled rather than degraded, but that no matter how much of a paragon of virtue and decorum she might be in this world, she would find true reward for her virtue only in the next. The novel shows clearly the influence of the Christian epic, the English stage, and the funereal literature popular in the period. With specific debts to Nicholas Rowe's *Fair Penitent* and John Milton's *Paradise Lost*, it explores the problem of humanity desperately, if futilely, seeking freedom in a society where duty and responsibility are constant limitations upon that search. Although its great length has earned for it the title of "one of the greatest of the unread novels," it maintains a commanding place in the corpus of major English fiction because of its exploration of property marriages in the shifting social milieu of mid-18th-century England, its dramatic and cumulative power, and its clear tie to such other great Western mythical stories as Romeo and Juliet and Tristan and Isolde.

"Sir Charles Grandison"

Richardson toiled for 5 years to depict the perfect Christian gentleman, especially in order to answer criticisms that he had allowed Lovelace to become too attractive a figure in *Clarissa*. His third and final novel, *Sir Charles Grandison*, was published in 1753–1754. Richardson's contemporaries, who had found Lovelace a fascinating and dramatic villain, thought Sir Charles chilly and priggish. Richardson's story of the earnest Christian gentleman who must choose between the English maiden, Harriet Byron, and the more attractive and more interesting Clementina della Porretta pleases few readers. Because Sir Charles is too faultless and too moral, he does not win the reader's sympathies.

After this Richardson wrote no more novels. He died in London on July 4, 1761.

Further Reading

Samuel Richardson is listed in the Literature study guide (II, F, 1, c). Other British novelists of this period were Henry FIELDING, Tobias SMOLLETT, and Laurence STERNE.

The major biography is T. C. Duncan Eaves and Ben D. Kimpel, *Samuel Richardson* (1971). Important studies of Richardson include Alan D. McKillop, *Samuel Richardson, Printer and Novelist* (1936); William M. Sale, *Samuel Richardson, Master Printer* (1950); Morris Golden, *Richardson's Characters* (1963); and Ira Konigsberg, *Samuel Richardson and the Dramatic Novel* (1968). Also useful are the chapters on Richardson in Alan D. McKillop, *The Early Masters of English Fiction* (1956); Ian P. Watt, *The Rise of the Novel: Studies in Defoe, Richardson, and Fielding* (1957); and Robert A. Donovan, *The Shaping Vision: Imagination in the English Novel from Defoe to Dickens* (1966). Recommended for general historical and social background are Louis Kronenberger, *Kings and Desperate Men: Life in Eighteenth-Century England* (1942); J. H. Plumb, *England in the Eighteenth Century* (1951); and A. R. Humphreys, *The Augustan World: Life and Letters in Eighteenth-Century England* (1954).

RICHELIEU / By Philip Dawson

The French statesman and cardinal Armand Jean du Plessis de Richelieu (1585–1642) devoted himself to securing French leadership in Europe and royal domination of the existing social order in France.

The policies and personal conduct of Richelieu (pronounced rē-shə-lyœ′) were distinguished by self-restraint, flexibility in response to changing opportunities, and alertness to remote consequences. His long-range intentions could be achieved only at the expense of Spain abroad and of the King's family and the great noblemen at home.

In the early 17th century a precarious balance existed between reasons of state and religious sectarianism as principles for international action. A similar balance existed in France between the rights of the King and the particular rights of provinces, localities, classes, and persons. Each balance was tipped toward the first alternative during Richelieu's career. The alignments of European states shifted and their relative power changed. The French political system began to define anew the relation of each social group to the monarchy and thus to other social groups. These historical developments eventually went far beyond Richelieu's plans, but he played a significant part in them.

Armand du Plessis was born on Sept. 9, 1585, in Paris, fourth of the five children of François du Plessis, the lord of Richelieu, and Suzanne de La Porte. His father was provost of the King's central administrative establishment and grand provost of France under Henry III and conducted the investigation of the King's murderer in 1589; he remained in the same post serving Henry IV but in 1590 died of a fever. His mother, the self-effacing daugh-

Cardinal Richelieu, a painting by Philippe de Champaigne, in the Louvre, Paris. (Alinari)

ter of a learned, vain lawyer prominent in the Paris bourgeoisie, was placed in severe financial difficulties by early widowhood. She moved to the old stone manor house of Richelieu, a few miles east of Loudun in Poitou, to reside with her mother-in-law, a proud noblewoman originally of the Rochechouart family. About 4 years later, Armand returned to Paris to study grammar and philosophy at the Collège de Navarre, from which he went on to a military academy.

The Du Plessis family's plans appeared to be settled. The eldest son, Henri, was seeking to become established in the entourage of the new queen, Maria de' Medici. The second son, Alphonse, was destined to be bishop of Luçon; the mother received the income of the benefice. But Alphonse declined the nomination and became a Carthusian monk. Armand was designated instead, and in 1603 he began serious study of theology. Younger than the canonical age to become a bishop, he went to Rome for a papal dispensation in 1607 and was consecrated there. He returned to Paris, obtained his degree in theology, and lingered to multiply his acquaintances among clergymen and among the associates of his brother Henri.

Career as Bishop

At the end of 1608 Richelieu arrived in Luçon, then little more than a village amid the marshes, a short distance from the Atlantic and north of La Rochelle. He

A patron of learning and the arts, founder of the French Academy, Richelieu in 1622 was made guardian of the Sorbonne. He rebuilt its buildings and endowed it with a chapel, in which he is buried. In this engraving the 13th-century founder of the university, Robert de Sorbon, bows in gratitude to Richelieu. (Bibliothèque Nationale, Paris)

found it "the most ignoble, mud-covered, unpleasant bishopric in France." He was an assiduous bishop, controlling his canons, carefully choosing parish priests, encouraging the preaching missions of the Capucin monks led by Father Joseph of Paris (François Le Clerc du Tremblay), and, while residing at his priory of Coussay between Loudun and Poitiers, cooperating with other active churchmen.

Richelieu's first important political opportunity came with the convocation of the Estates General in 1614. The clergy of Poitou elected him a deputy. At Maria de' Medici's suggestion he was chosen to speak for the clergy as a whole at the last session of the Estates (Feb. 23, 1615). He then went back to Poitou but a year later returned to Paris, served her in negotiations with the Prince of Condé, and was appointed secretary of state for foreign affairs and war. He held the post for only 5 months because Louis XIII seized power in April 1617 and dismissed his mother's councilors. Further steps against them followed, and in 1618 the bishop of Luçon was ordered into exile in the papal city of Avignon.

From Poitou, in 1617, Richelieu had joined in a pamphlet controversy between the King's Jesuit confessor and four Protestant ministers. In *Les Principaux points de la foi de l'église Catholique*, he employed moderate terms and rejected force as a means of conversion. He answered the Protestant ministers on several issues and told them, "You give to the people a power much greater than the one you deny to the pope, which is greatly disadvantageous to kings." In Avignon, in 1618, he finished a catechism he had been preparing in his diocese, *L'Instruction du Chrétien*, a calm, simple explanation of dogma and commandments which makes clear the sovereignty of God by comparing it to the sovereignty of the King.

Among Louis XIII's advisers, Father Joseph and others believed that Richelieu would be a moderating influence on the King's mother. Accordingly the King recalled him from Avignon in March 1619 and ordered him to resume serving her. Thereafter Richelieu's biography merges increasingly with the history of the monarchy. Representing the queen mother that spring, he negotiated an agreement with the King's commissioners that she would reside in Anjou. She designated his brother Henri de Richelieu as governor of the provincial capital; but 7 weeks later Henri was killed in a duel at Angoulême. This event, the personal sorrow of Armand de Richelieu's life, deprived him of a valued political ally.

The queen mother aspired to sit in the King's council. She also wanted the King to obtain Richelieu's nomination as a cardinal; for him this would mean undisputed political eminence, a voice in important decisions of state, and greater security than a bishop could expect. She hoped in the end to control royal policy through the influence Richelieu would exercise as a member of the King's council. These motives played an important part in the threat of an armed uprising in the summer of 1620 and in the tangle of duplicity and argument that ensued, with Richelieu in the role of mediator between the queen mother and her opponents. The resistance of the King and his ministers gradually crumbled. The queen mother was invited into the council at the beginning of 1622; in the following September, the Pope appointed Richelieu a cardinal; finally, the King called Richelieu to his council in April 1624 and designated him chief councilor 3 1/2 months later.

Position as Minister

Richelieu remained the King's principal minister until his death, and he was made a duke in 1631. He was never the only royal adviser, but he gradually built up in the council a group of men, his "creatures," loyal to him as well as to the King. He was never free from potential rivals. He relied on his family, which he extended by carefully arranging marriages of his nieces and cousins into great families. Thus he used intensively the kind of patron-client relation that had assisted his early career. He made clear that the King was his patron, and he made sure that Louis XIII knew that Richelieu was the King's creature.

From the first, Richelieu encountered a strong current of "devout" Catholic opinion that regarded Protestants everywhere as the enemy or as possible converts and insisted on reforms within France. The queen mother, Maria, the queen consort, Anne, and the keeper of the seals, Michel Marillac, shared that opinion. Richelieu partly satisfied it for a time, negotiating the marriage of the King's sister Henriette to Charles I of England, conducting the siege of the Huguenot city of La Rochelle, and cooperating with Marillac on a program of proposed reforms. But he firmly advised Louis XIII to intervene in northern Italy, against the Spanish king and the Emperor, in order to maintain a foothold on the route between Madrid and Vienna. Over this question the queen mother finally broke with Richelieu in 1630. The King eliminated her clientele and influence from his court.

Opposition to Richelieu and his policies arose also from ambitious, dissatisfied noblemen. This led to plots sanctioned by the King's brother Gaston (1626, 1632, 1636, and 1642), Queen Anne (1633), and a second cousin of the King, the Comte de Soissons (1636 and 1641). These all failed. Three scions of great families were beheaded (the Comte de Chalais in 1626, the Duc de Montmorency in 1632, and the Marquis de Cinq-Mars in 1642).

Foreign Policy

Richelieu gave first priority to foreign policy. He concluded, probably very early, that war against Spain in the long run would be unavoidable. He strove to delay it by encouraging German resistance to the Hapsburg emperor in Vienna, thereby diverting into central Europe the resources and attention of the Hapsburg king in Madrid. In his German policy, he relied heavily on Father Joseph. He subsidized the Dutch Republic and the Swedish warrior king Gustavus Adolphus (Gustavus II) and in 1634 was prepared to aid the Bohemian general A. E. W. von Wallenstein against the Emperor.

From 1635 until his death Richelieu was preoccupied by an overt war against Spain and by the diplomacy it entailed. The fighting occurred principally on the northern and eastern frontiers of France, secondarily on the Mediterranean coast and in the Pyrenees. It was complicated by armed revolts of the populace, especially in western provinces. Richelieu negotiated often with emissaries of Spain but insisted on French control of Lorraine and French garrisons in northern Italy. The negotiations broke down. The war was still going on when Richelieu died on Dec. 4, 1642.

Further Reading

Cardinal Richelieu is listed in the European History study guide (V, B, 1, a). He served LOUIS XIII and was succeeded by Cardinal MAZARIN.

The best brief study of Richelieu in English is a thoughtful essay by Dietrich Gerhard in Leonard Krieger and Fritz Stern, eds., *The Responsibility of Power: Historical Essays in Honor of Hajo Holborn* (1968). A narrative concentrating on international relations is Daniel Patrick O'Connell, *Richelieu* (1968), with a good bibliography. A more personal treatment is provided in Carl J. Burckhardt's trilogy, *Richelieu and His Age* (1934–1966), of which two volumes have appeared in English: *His Rise to Power*, translated by Edwin and Willa Muir, and *Assertion of Power and Cold War*, translated by Bernard Hoy. Valuable special studies include Orest A. Ranum, *Richelieu and the Councillors of Louis XIII* (1963), and Aleksandra D. Lublinskaya, *French Absolutism: The Crucial Phase, 1620–1629*, translated by Brian Pearce (1968).

* * *

RICHET / By E. Ashworth Underwood

The French physiologist Charles Robert Richet (1850–1935) was awarded the Nobel Prize in Physiology or Medicine for his discovery of the phenomenon of anaphylaxis.

Charles Richet (pronounced rē-shĕ′), the son of Alfred Richet, a professor in the University of Paris, was born in Paris on Aug. 25, 1850. He studied medicine in Paris and intended to become a surgeon, but he soon abandoned surgery for physiology. He graduated at Paris as a doctor of medicine in 1869 and as a doctor of science in 1878. He became a lecturer in physiology in 1879 and in 1887 professor of physiology in the Faculty of Medicine at Paris.

Discovery of Anaphylaxis

In 1890 the phenomenon of antitoxic immunity was discovered, and in 1891 diphtheria antitoxin was first used in treating diphtheria. It was soon found that the guinea pigs used for testing diphtheria antitoxin became acutely ill if long intervals separated the test injections. About 1900, while cruising in tropical waters, Richet studied the poison of the tropical jellyfish, the Portuguese man-of-war. Working with Paul Portier, he found that injection of a glycerol solution of the poison produced the symptoms of poisoning by the jellyfish. On their return to France they studied the toxins of local jellyfish. They determined the minimum dose that was

Charles Richet. (Library of Congress)

and antitoxin was used) that produced serious effects in guinea pigs injected with repeated small doses at long intervals, but the horse serum in which the toxin was contained. Further, the reaction depended not upon the dose but upon the time interval. It was soon shown that a guinea pig injected with horse serum showed no hypersensitivity to the serum of other animals, and also that specific reactions occurred after the injection of milk, egg, or muscle extract. It was thus conclusively demonstrated that Richet's anaphylaxis was due to the injection of any protein, whether or not it was toxic on the first injection.

In 1907 Richet showed that, if the serum of an anaphylactic dog was injected into a normal dog, the latter became anaphylactic. The anaphylactic state could therefore be passively transmitted, and it was an antigen-antibody reaction. He continued to study anaphylactic phenomena, and for his work he was awarded the Nobel Prize in 1913. Anaphylaxis is closely associated with serum sickness and allergy, and later investigations of allergic diseases stem from Richet.

Richet wrote numerous works on physiology and edited two journals. He retired from his chair in 1927 and died in Paris on Dec. 4, 1935.

Further Reading

Charles Richet is listed in the Science study guide (VII, F, 2). The phenomenon of antitoxic immunity was discovered by Emil Adolph von BEHRING and an associate while they were working in the laboratory of Robert KOCH.

There is a biography of Richet in *Nobel Lectures, Physiology or Medicine, 1901–1921* (1967), which also includes his Nobel Lecture. For his work in relation to the immunology of the period see C. Singer and E. A. Underwood, *A Short History of Medicine* (1962), and W. Bulloch, *The History of Bacteriology* (1938).

RICHIER / By William C. Lipke

The French sculptor Germaine Richier (1904–1959) explored the metamorphic dimensions of the insect-animal world. Technically, she exploited the deteriorating surface and the interior, felt structure of things.

Born in Grans near Arles, Germaine Richier (pronounced rē-shyā′) enrolled in the School of Fine Arts in Montpellier in 1922. After completing her studies in 1925, she left for Paris, where she became a private pupil of the sculptor Antoine Bourdelle for the next 4 years. Her work of the 1930s won several awards, including the Blumenthal Prize of 1936, yet the forms were essentially extensions of the more classical sculpture of her teacher.

In the 1940s Germaine Richier began creating the sculptural vocabulary for which she is best known, the

fatal for dogs several days after its injection. Smaller doses than this produced only transient effects. But if a dog that had been injected with a small dose received a similar small dose after an interval of several weeks, a violent reaction killed the dog.

By 1902 Richet had studied this phenomenon in different animals. Reactions produced by the injection of antitoxins or minute doses of toxins had already been called prophylactic, or protective. Richet realized that in this new phenomenon the first dose sensitized the animal, so that the second injection produced a violent reaction. The first dose was the opposite of prophylactic, and he therefore called the phenomenon anaphylaxis. He showed clearly that the first injection of an animal toxin sensitized the test animal to even a very small second injection, and that, with very small doses, the violent symptoms following the second injection were out of all proportion to the mild symptoms following the first. He also established that, to produce the violent reaction, there must be an interval of several weeks between the injections.

In 1903 Nicolas Maurice Arthus of Lausanne described the Arthus phenomenon. If a rabbit was injected subcutaneously with repeated doses of horse serum, no effect was produced by the subsequent injections at first, but as the interval from the first injection lengthened, the injection site became swollen, hardened, and ulcerous. In 1905 Richard Otto showed that it was not the toxin in the "diphtheria antitoxin" (at that time a mixture of toxin

classical rendering of the figure undergoing dramatic changes. *L'Eau* (*L'Amphore*, 1944) is partially a female form and partially a Greek vase. Similarly, the working of the piece changes from skeletal support in the lower portion of the piece to full female shape in the upper portion. This metamorphosis was carried further in the Insect series (*Spider* and *Small Grasshopper*, 1946) and found full expression in the *Bat Man* (1946), possibly the most powerful image of her career. Projecting from a central core are gauzelike wings, thinly threaded planes that suggest decay. This method of construction—an approach that defies both the material and gravitational limits—is one of many experimental techniques she used.

A more traditional freestanding figure conventionally modeled can be seen in the male *Thunderstorm* (1948) and the related female *Hurricane* (1949). These large metaphors of violent natural forces are now tamed, the expressive qualities being revealed in the expressionistic surface and dangling appendages. Another figurative treatment, closer to the eviscerated skeletal structures of Alberto Giacometti, can be seen in the *Large Don Quixote of the Forest* and the *Shepherd of the Landes* (both 1951).

Germaine Richier's formal language continued to enlarge and develop during the 1950s. She worked in stone, carving compact shapes with angular projections, as in the *Shadow of the Hurricane* (1956), seemingly an outgrowth of the more abstract "Bird Man" series of the early 1950s. Another set of problems, that of creating a context in the form of a perpendicular plane acting as a background or foil for smaller shapes played off against this plane, also found currency in her work at this time. She died in Montpellier.

Further Reading

Germaine Richier is listed in the Art study guide (III, L, 2). Her early work is in the tradition of Auguste RODIN. Her attenuated figures are reminiscent of those of Alberto GIACOMETTI.

Bat Man, a sculpture by Germaine Richier executed in 1946. (Courtesy Wadsworth Atheneum, Hartford, Gift of Susan Morse Hilles)

The most useful monograph on the sculptor, although narrow in scope, is Jean Cassou, *Germaine Richier* (1961). See also the catalog of the Arts Club of Chicago, *Germaine Richier* (1966). Further information is in Carola Giedion-Welcker, *Contemporary Sculpture: An Evolution in Volume and Space* (1956; rev. ed. 1961), and Michael Seuphor, *The Sculpture of This Century* (1960).

C. **RICHTER** / By Frederick R. Benson and Adele Kaminsky

Conrad Michael Richter (1890–1968), American novelist and short-story writer, depicted the nation's early frontier life and westward expansion. His works, based on his own adventures and research into American folklore, protest man's destruction of his environment.

Conrad Richter was born on Oct. 13, 1890, in Pine Grove, Pa. As a boy he traveled with his father throughout the farm settlements and was enchanted by the pioneer life-style and idiomatic speech. Graduating from high school, he determined to be a writer and began reporting for a local paper. After first working at random jobs—mechanics, coal breaking, farming—at the age of 19 he became editor of a country weekly. Following experience with the *Pittsburgh Dispatch* (1910) and the *Johnstown Leader* (1911) he moved to Ohio. His "Brothers of No Kin" was accepted by a magazine and selected by the *Boston Transcript* as the best short story of 1913. But discouraged by the low prices paid for fiction, Richter decided "to stick to business" and "write in my spare time only the type of story which would fetch a fair price, which I did."

After marrying Harvena M. Achenbach in 1915, Richter established a publishing firm. He started writing children's stories and then began his own juvenile periodical, *Junior Magazine Book*. During the next years his writing appeared under some 125 pseudonyms in various magazines. His short stories were collected in *Brothers of No Kin and Other Stories* (1924).

Richter was concerned with the vanishing frontier as well as the dubious benefits resulting from advancing technology. Desiring to escape encroaching industrial urbanization, he sold his business and moved his family to New Mexico in 1928. A collection of short stories, *Early Americana* (1936), structured with the minute details of daily living on the frontier, resulted from his painstaking search for diaries, journals, and artifacts of the Old Southwest. In *Sea of Grass* (1937), his first novel, he dramatized the cattleman-homesteader battle for the ranges of Texas and New Mexico at the turn of the century. It was later made into a motion picture.

A family migrating west from Pennsylvania is portrayed in *The Trees* (1940), the first of a trilogy. A saga of 18th-century pioneer heroics, this was a best seller. *The Fields* (1946) rather episodically traces the development of Ohio from its 18th-century wilds to the farms of the 19th century. Critic Orville Prescott noted that "seldom in fiction has the atmosphere of another age been so completely realized." *The Town* (1950) depicts the rise of industrialism in Ohio. The history is vivified in the simple and colloquial speech of the settlers.

Richter's novella *Tacey Cromwell* (1942), set in an Arizona mining town, effectively uses local color. *Always Young and Fair* (1947) is a sociopsychological exploration of a turn-of-the-century Pennsylvania town. Continuing the "wilderness" milieu, Richter produced nine novels in the next 17 years. *The Light in the Forest* (1953) and *A Country of Strangers* (1966) are critical of "civilized" man, contrasted with the "white child raised by Indians." *The Lady* (1957) returns to older tales of the Southwest. *The Waters of Kronos* (1960) portrays an Easterner who returns home after a satisfying stay in the West to find his residence under the waters of a hydroelectric plant. This novel takes a vigorous stand against man's heedless tampering with natural resources and, in effect, eternity.

Although afflicted with a serious heart ailment during his later years, Richter produced such novels as *A Simple Honorable Man* (1960), *The Grandfathers* (1964), *Individualists under the Shade Trees in a Vanishing America* (1964), and *Over the Blue Mountain* (1967). *The Aristocrat* was published a month before his death on Oct. 18, 1968. With his protest against man's ecological destruction, his work has assumed increasing significance.

Conrad Richter. (National Archives, Washington, D.C.)

Further Reading

Conrad Richter is listed in the Literature study guide (I, E, 3). His work recalled that of the earlier regional novelist Willa CATHER.

Richter's life and work are explored in Edwin W. Gaston, Jr., *Conrad Richter* (1965); Robert J. Barnes, *Conrad Richter* (1968); and the more specialized study by Clifford D. Edwards, *Conrad Richter's Ohio Trilogy: Its Ideas and Relationship to Literary Tradition* (1970).

J. P. RICHTER / By August Closs

The German humorist and prose writer Johann Paul Friedrich Richter (1763–1825), usually referred to as Jean Paul, achieved his greatest fame as a novelist.

On March 21, 1763, J. P. Richter (pronounced rĭKH′tər) was born at Wunsiedel, Fichtel Gebirge. As a boy, he went to school at the small town of Hof; then he moved to the University of Leipzig (1781–1784) to study theology. Financial difficulties forced him to become a tutor to various families. When he was 29, he called himself Jean Paul (after Jean Jacques Rousseau). Having given up the idea of entering the Church, he decided to become a writer. He was essentially a Platonist; Herder also had a profound influence on him, and they opposed Kant's speculative philosophy.

Jean Paul's early works were collections of satires about courtiers, society, and ladies: the *Grönländische Prozesse* (1783) and *Auswahl aus des Teufels Papieren* (1789). The first work that made him widely known and appreciated was *Die unsichtbare Loge* (1793), whose appendix contains the famous *Leben des vergnügten Schulmeisterleins Maria Wuz in Auenthal*. This story is a supreme example of an idyllic situation depicting happiness and complete contentment in a rustic existence. After that his great works followed in quick succession: *Hesperus* (1795), *Biographische Belustigungen unter der Gehirnschale einer Riesin* (1796), *Leben des Quintus Fixlein* (1796), *Blumen-, Frucht- und Dornenstücke, oder Ehestand, Tod und Hochzeit des Armenadvokaten Siebenkäs* (1796/1797), *Der Jubelsenior* (1797), and *Das Kampaner Thal* (1797).

After the death of his mother (1797), Jean Paul left Hof for Leipzig, Weimar, Berlin, Meiningen, and Coburg, and in 1804 he settled in Bayreuth. In the meantime (1801) he had married Karoline Mayer. From 1808 on, his financial situation improved considerably, as he received from the prince-primate Reichsfreiherr von Dalberg a yearly pension of 1,000 florins.

About the turn of the century Jean Paul had reached the height of his artistic achievements. He had developed an original poetic language. One of his favorite images is that of man's emerging from the chrysalis state into a new existence; another one is the (Platonic) image

J. P. Richter, painted in 1810 by Friedrich Meier. (Bildarchiv)

of shadows upon the wall, of the soul imprisoned in a shell, and the concept of *Hohe Menschen*, who are condemned to endure an earthly life but whose real home is a higher, unselfish world.

The theme of *Hohe Menschen* is the key problem in Jean Paul's masterpiece, *Titan* (1800/1803). According to him, this novel should bear the title *Anti-Titan*, as it proves that an artist's ruthless single-mindedness must destroy the ideal of harmony. In his self-centered vehemence, Roquairol spends all energy in a state of extravagant imagination and empties life of true human feeling. *Die Flegeljahre* (1804/1805), too, depicts a poetic Schwärmer who has to fulfill several practical tasks (as piano tuner, gardener, proofreader, and so on) and thus learn how to come to terms with life.

These two great works were followed by a number of novels in which the comic, satirical, and even grotesque elements are stressed: *Dr. Katzenbergers Badreise* (1809), *Des Feldpredigers Schmelzle Reise nach Flätz* (1809), *Das Leben Fibels* (1806–1811), and *Der Komet, oder Nikolaus Marggraf* (1820–1822). Moreover, there are the wealth and depth of his theoretical and critical writings on esthetics, education, society, and politics, which not until the 20th century received full appreciation: *Vorschule der Aesthetik* (1804), *Levana oder Erziehungslehre* (1807), *Friedenspredigt* (1808), and *Politische Fastenpredigten* (1817).

The last years were overshadowed by illness, misfortune, and disappointments. In 1821 his only son, Max, died of typhus. Lonely and almost blind, Jean Paul died in Bayreuth on Nov. 14, 1825.

Further Reading

J. P. Richter is listed in the Literature study guide (III, G, 2). He influenced Gustav FREYTAG, Gottfried KELLER, Hugo von HOFMANNSTHAL, and especially Stefan GEORGE.

An authoritative and readable study of Richter's visionary pieces is John William Smeed, *Jean Paul's Dreams* (1966), which also has a useful selective bibliography. For briefer discussions of Richter's work see George P. Gooch, *Germany and the French Revolution* (1920); Lawrence M. Price, *English Literature in Germany* (1953); and August Closs, ed., *Introductions to German Literature* (4 vols., 1967–1970; 3d vol. by E. L. Stahl and W. E. Yuill).

RICIMER / By Stephen L. Dyson

Flavius Ricimer (died 472) was a Romanized German political chief and the central power in the Western Roman Empire in the mid-5th century.

icimer (pronounced rĭs′ĭ-mər) came from royal Germanic stock on both sides of his family. His father was the king of the Suevians; his mother was the daughter of the Visigothic king Wallia. He was a Christian but, like most Goths, belonged to the heretical Arian sect of Christianity. Along with many other Germans, he decided to make his career in the service of Rome. Details of his early career are not preserved, but he must have been successful in both the political and military spheres. He formed important friendships such as that with Majorian, the future emperor, and he was selected in 456 by the emperor Avitus to stop a threatened attack of the Vandals on Sicily. He succeeded and was awarded the rank of *comes*. Shortly thereafter he was raised to the rank of master of soldiers.

His Political Force

At the same time, Ricimer began to display his political strength. In 456 he cooperated with Majorian to depose Avitus. After a short interval Majorian was recognized as emperor by the Eastern Roman Empire. Ricimer was raised to the rank of patrician in 457, and in 459 Majorian rewarded him with the consulship. However, Majorian and Ricimer began to draw apart, and when the former failed in his expedition against Gaiseric and the Vandals, Ricimer had him deposed and executed (461). In November 461 Ricimer made Livius Severus emperor, but the appointment failed to win approval either in the East or with Gaiseric, who had emerged as an independent political force. In 464 Ricimer defeated Beorger, the king of the Alans, who had invaded Italy. In 465 Severus died, and a political compromise was worked out. Leo, the Eastern Roman emperor, sent Anthemius to the West to become emperor. Ricimer agreed to the appointment when he received the hand of Anthemius's daughter in marriage.

Hostility soon developed, however, and by 470 the split was complete. Anthemius executed friends of Ricimer, and Ricimer in turn attacked Anthemius at Rome. In 472 Anthemius was defeated and killed by Ricimer. Ricimer's next candidate for the emperorship was Olybrius, who was satisfactory to Gaiseric. Olybrius was installed as emperor but soon lost the services of Ricimer, who died in 472.

Ricimer was the last strong man in the Western Roman Empire. His military skill kept Italy relatively free of invasion. Being both a barbarian and a heretical Arian, however, he was forced to act behind a screen of temporary emperors whose rapid succession added little to the strength and stability of the Western Empire.

Further Reading

Ricimer is listed in the Ancient History study guide (III, E, 1). Another barbarian strong man in Rome was STILICHO.

Some information on Ricimer appears in the poems of Sidonius Apollinaris. Colin Douglas Gordon, *The Age of Attila: Fifth-century Byzantium and the Barbarians* (1960), collects some of the fragments of the ancient historians on Ricimer. For the background of Ricimer's era see J. B. Bury, *History of the Later Roman Empire: From the Death of Theodosius I to the Death of Justinian, A.D. 395 to A.D. 565* (1923).

RIDGWAY / By Norman A. Graebner

Matthew Bunker Ridgway (born 1895), American Army officer, served as supreme Allied commander in Korea and immediately thereafter as supreme Allied commander in Europe.

Matthew B. Ridgway was born on March 3, 1895, at Fort Monroe, Va. He graduated from the U.S. Military Academy in 1917. Ridgway's early career took him to China, Nicaragua, and the Philippines, where in 1932–1933 he served as technical adviser to the governor general. In 1935 he attended the U.S. Command and General Staff School and in 1937 the Army War College.

When World War II broke out in 1939, Ridgway was in the War Department's War Plans Division. In 1942 he rose to commander of the 82d Infantry Division, which he converted into the 82d Airborne Division. He led the 82d in the invasions of Sicily and Italy and in 1944 parachuted with his troops into Normandy, France. Later that year he took command of the 18th Airborne Corps in Belgium, France, and Germany. In 1945 he became chief of the Luzon Area Command. Ridgway married Mary Anthony in 1947, and the couple had one son.

After the war Ridgway commanded the Mediterranean theater. From 1946 until 1948 he was chairman of the Inter-American Defense Board and from 1948 to 1949 chief of the Caribbean Command. In 1949 he returned to Washington as Army deputy chief of staff. Late in 1950, during the Communist Chinese offensive in South Korea, Ridgway assumed command of the U.S. 8th Army and organized the counteroffensive which drove the Chinese and North Koreans out of South Korea. In 1951 he succeeded Gen. Douglas MacArthur as supreme commander for the Allied Powers in Japan, as commander of United Nations forces in Korea, and as commander of all United States forces in the Far East.

Unlike the other generals who directed the Korean

Gen. Matthew B. Ridgway. (U.S. Army Photograph)

War, Ridgway rejected MacArthur's strategy for victory—an Allied advance to the Yalu River. Instead, he conducted a limited war until President Harry Truman transferred him to Europe to succeed Gen. Dwight Eisenhower as supreme commander of the Allied Powers in Europe in 1952. Ridgway served as chief of staff of the U.S. Army from 1953 until he retired in 1955.

Ridgway's many military decorations included the Distinguished Service Cross, the Distinguished Service Medal, the Legion of Merit, and the Silver Star. In civilian life, he became a business executive. He served as a member of the board of Colt Industries and as chairman of the board of trustees of the Mellon Institute of Industrial Research.

Further Reading

Matthew B. Ridgway is listed in the American History study guide (X, B, 2). President Harry TRUMAN removed Gen. Douglas MacARTHUR from his command when the general openly disagreed with government policy for a limited war in Korea.

Ridgway's accounts of his career are in his *Soldier: The Memoirs of Matthew B. Ridgway* (1956) and *The Korean War* (1967). His activity in World War II is assessed in John S. D. Eisenhower, *The Bitter Woods* (1969). His role in the Korean War is recounted in Harry J. Middleton, *The Compact History of the Korean War* (1965). An unsympathetic view of Ridgway is in Isidor F. Stone, *The Hidden History of the Korean War* (1952; with new appendix, 1969).

* * *

RIEL / By J. L. Granatstein

Louis Riel (1844–1885) was a Canadian rebel who led uprisings in the west in 1870 and 1884–1885 on behalf of the Métis people.

L ouis Riel (pronounced rē-ĕl′) was born at Saint-Boniface, Manitoba, on Oct. 23, 1844, of Métis parents. His quickness of mind was early recognized by the priests at Saint-Boniface, and Riel was sent east to study at the Seminaire de St-Sulpice in Montreal. Riel decided not to become a priest, however, and he returned to the Red River area. In 1869 he became the secretary of the Comité National des Métis, an organization created by the half-breed population of Assiniboia in an attempt to preserve their rights when the Canadian west was transferred from the Hudson's Bay Company to the Dominion.

As the brightest and best educated of the Métis, Riel soon became the unchallenged leader of his people, although he was only 25 years old. Proclaiming himself president of the provisional government of the Northwest Territories, he dispatched emissaries to Ottawa to negotiate with the Canadian government, and he was successful in securing the early grant of provincial status

Louis Riel. (The Public Archives of Canada)

for the territory, now named Manitoba, and promises of fair treatment for the Métis. Unfortunately Riel was somewhat overzealous in maintaining order in his domain, and he ordered the execution of Thomas Scott, a troublemaker from Ontario. The execution roused passions in Ontario, a military force was sent to Manitoba, and Riel was forced to flee.

For the next 14 years Riel was in limbo. Although he was three times elected to Parliament by Manitoba constituencies, he was never able to take his seat. In 1875, in fact, he was declared an outlaw. For part of the time he was in an insane asylum, and he was teaching school in the American West in 1884, when events again brought him to the fore.

Riel was approached by representatives of the Métis and other dissident groups in 1884 and asked to return to Canada. He leaped at the chance and was soon leading yet another rebellion against Ottawa. By this time he was clearly mad, believing himself the Messiah and certain that God was on his side. Unfortunately for his rebellion, the Canadian Pacific Railway was on the side of the government, and troops moved west with surprising speed. After a few skirmishes the second Riel rebellion was crushed, and Riel found himself a prisoner.

Soon the rebel was brought to trial by a completely English-speaking court and jury, and predictably Riel was found guilty of high treason. An insanity commission reported that he was sane, the Cabinet refused to commute the sentence, and Riel mounted the gibbet at Regina on Nov. 16, 1885. His death stirred animosity between French and English in Canada to fever pitch, and relations between the two peoples remained strained ever thereafter.

Further Reading

Louis Riel is listed in the Canada study guide (IV, B, 1). Albert LACOMBE did much to help the Métis population of Canada.

Of the numerous biographies of Riel the best is George F. G. Stanley, *Louis Riel* (1963). See also Joseph Kinsey Howard, *Strange Empire: A Narrative of the Northwest* (1952), and George F. G. Stanley, *The Birth of Western Canada* (1961).

* * *

RIEMANN / By John H. Wilson

The German mathematician Georg Friedrich Bernard Riemann (1826–1866) was one of the founders of algebraic geometry. His concept of geometric space cleared the way for the general theory of relativity.

On Sept. 17, 1826, Georg Riemann (pronounced rē′män) was born in Breselenz. Shortly afterward, the family moved to Quickborn, Holstein, where his father, a Lutheran minister, assumed the pastorate.

Georg Riemann, an 1863 engraving by August Weger. (Österreichische Nationalbibliothek, Vienna)

Riemann senior quickly recognized his younger son's mathematical talent. When Georg was 10 years old, he was placed under a mathematics tutor who soon found himself outdistanced by his pupil.

Riemann had planned on a career in the Church in accordance with his father's wishes. In 1846 he entered the University of Göttingen as a student of theology and philology. But mathematics called, and he had probably already decided to change his mind, should his father consent. He may have strengthened his argument by a grand attempt to prove Genesis mathematically. The proof was hardly valid, but Riemann senior appreciated the effort and gave his blessing to the mathematical career. In 1847 Georg transferred to the University of Berlin, where such vigorous innovators as K. G. J. Jacobi, P. G. Lejeune-Dirichlet, J. Steiner, and F. G. M. Eisenstein had created a livelier atmosphere for learning. In 1849 Riemann returned to Göttingen to prepare for his doctoral examinations under Wilhelm Weber, the famous electrodynamicist.

Riemann Surfaces

Riemann's doctoral dissertation was, in Karl Friedrich Gauss's words, the product of a "gloriously fertile originality." Its novel ideas were further developed in three papers published in 1857. Here is a crude explanation of the principal novelty:

A complex number may be represented by a point in a plane. A function (single-valued) of a complex variable is a rule which pairs each point in one plane with a *unique* point in another plane. Imagine a fly wandering about the surface of a plate-glass window. As the fly moves from point to point, its shadow moves from point to point on the floor of the room. Each point which the fly occupies on the window determines a *unique* point that its shadow occupies on the floor.

Now suppose that the floor is a highly reflective surface. The incoming light strikes the floor and is reflected to the wall, and we see a *second* image of our wandering fly. Now each position of the fly on the window determines *two* shadows—one on the floor and one on the wall.

But that is not quite right. There are some positions in which the fly still casts only one shadow. These are the points which throw the shadow on the line of intersection between floor and wall. Let us call these points branch points.

Now suppose that we replace the plate-glass window with *two* parallel sheets of plate glass (like a double window for insulation against cold). We endow the sheets with the following magical properties: any object on the outside sheet will cast a shadow only on the floor, and any object on the inside sheet will cast a shadow only on the wall. Furthermore, we join the two sheets along the line of branch points, so that they now form a single surface. Our fly may crawl from one sheet to the other, but to each point that he occupies on the glass surface, there once again corresponds one unique location of his shadow.

This is what Riemann did for multiple-valued functions

of a complex variable. His surfaces restore single-valuedness to functions and at the same time provide a method of representing these functions geometrically. Moreover, it turns out that the analytic properties of many functions are mirrored by the geometric (topological) properties of their associated Riemann surfaces.

His Göttingen Lecture

After successfully defending his dissertation, Riemann applied for an opening at the Göttingen Observatory but did not get the job. He next set his sights on becoming a privatdozent (unpaid lecturer) at the university. There were two hurdles to surmount before he could obtain the lectureship: a probationary essay and a trial lecture before the assembled faculty. The former, a paper on trigonometric series, included the definition of the "Riemann integral" in almost the form that it appears in current textbooks. The essay was submitted in 1853.

For his trial lecture Riemann submitted three possible titles, fully expecting Gauss to abide by tradition and assign one of the first two. But the third topic was one with which Gauss himself had struggled for many years. He was curious to hear what Riemann had to say "On the Hypotheses Which Lie at the Foundations of Geometry."

The lecture that Riemann delivered to the Göttingen faculty on June 10, 1854, is one of the great masterpieces of mathematical creation and exposition. Riemann wove together and generalized three crucial discoveries of the 19th century: the extension of Euclidean geometry to n dimensions; the logical consistency of geometries that are not Euclidean; and the intrinsic geometry of a surface, in terms of its metric and curvature in the neighborhood of a point. In his synthesis Riemann demonstrated the existence of an infinite number of different geometries, each of which could be characterized by its peculiar differential form. Finally, he pointed out that the choice of a particular geometry to represent the structure of real physical space was a matter for physics, not mathematics.

The impact of the lecture was enormous but delayed. Riemann worked out some of the analytical machinery in a memoir of 1861 on the conduction of heat, but the lecture itself was not published until 1868. Twenty years later a respected historian noted simply that the paper "had excited much interest and discussion." By 1908 the same historian was calling it a "celebrated memoir" which had attracted "general attention to the subject of non-Euclidean geometry."

"Riemann Hypothesis"

Riemann spent 3 years as a privatdozent. In 1857 he was appointed assistant professor, and 2 years later, when Dirichlet died, Riemann succeeded him in the chair of Gauss. After 1860 the honors, including international recognition, came thick and fast. He died on July 20, 1866, in Selasca, Italy.

Riemann's special genius was the penetrating vision that enabled him to see through a mass of obscuring detail and perceive the submerged foundations of a theory intuitively. This uncanny talent was most obvious in his geometric work, but the most remarkable instance occurs in analytic number theory. In an 1859 paper on prime numbers, Riemann proved several properties of what came to be called "Riemann's zeta function." Several other properties of the function he simply stated without proof. After his death a note was found, saying that he had *deduced* these properties "from the expression of it (the function) which, however, I did not succeed in simplifying enough to publish."

To this day no one has the slightest idea of what this "expression" might be. All but one of the properties have since been proved. The last one, now called the "Riemann hypothesis," still awaits its conqueror, despite the efforts of several generations of talented mathematicians.

Further Reading

Georg Riemann is listed in the Science study guide (VI, A, 2). His name is related to non-Euclidean geometry as is that of Karl Friedrich GAUSS. Riemann is considered by Bertrand RUSSELL to be the immediate predecessor of Albert EINSTEIN.

The best biography of Riemann in English is in Eric T. Bell, *Men of Mathematics* (1937). He is discussed in the first volume of Ganesh Prasad, *Some Great Mathematicians of the Nineteenth Century: Their Lives and Their Works* (1933). The place of Riemannian geometry in relativity theory is discussed in Jagjit Singh, *Great Ideas of Modern Mathematics: Their Nature and Use* (1959). For a nontechnical introduction to non-Euclidean geometries see Richard Courant and Herbert Robbins, *What Is Mathematics?* (1941).

* * *

RIEMENSCHNEIDER

By Robert A. Koch

Tilman Riemenschneider (1468–1531) was the most famous of all German late-Gothic sculptors. His style of carving is beautifully refined, with nervous, crackling drapery folds and superb surface finish of the alabaster, sandstone, or lindenwood with which he worked.

Tilman Riemenschneider (pronounced rē′mən-shnī-dər) was born in Osterode, Saxony. After traveling in the Rhineland and Swabia, he settled in the prince-bishopric of Würzburg in 1483. He became a citizen 2 years later and was mayor of the city in 1520–1521. As a Würzburg councilor, in 1525 he came into conflict with the Church authorities during the Peasants' War—an expression of the Reformation—and was imprisoned and tortured. He died in Würzburg on July 7, 1531.

Like his contemporaries at Nuremberg, notably Veit

Tilman Riemenschneider carved this lindenwood statue of St. Stephen about 1510. (The Cleveland Museum of Art, Purchase, Leonard C. Hanna, Jr., Bequest)

situ); the stone figures of Adam and Eve carved for the portal of the Marienkapelle in Würzburg (1491–1493), which are among the earliest known realistically treated nude figure sculptures in Germany; and a sandstone Virgin for the Marienkapelle (all three in the Mainfränkisches Museum, Würzburg), of which many variations, generally in wood, made Riemenschneider the most famous sculptor of his day.

Between 1500 and 1520 Riemenschneider carved the superb *Assumption of the Virgin* wooden altarpiece for the little country church at Creglingen, the stone tomb of Bishop Rudolph von Scherenberg in the Cathedral of Würzburg, and the wooden Altar of the Holy Blood in the Jakobskirche in Rothenburg ob der Tauber (1501–1505). In the center of the Rothenburg altar is the *Last Supper*; on the wings are the *Entry of Christ into Jerusalem* and *Christ in Gethsemane*, brilliantly executed in low relief. Sensing the beauty of the wood itself, Riemenschneider frequently did not polychrome his altarpieces, a novelty at this time.

Riemenschneider's masterpiece of funerary sculpture is the monumental memorial of the emperor Henry II and his wife, Kunigunde, in Bamberg Cathedral (1499–1513), executed in marble. Relief carvings on the sides of the tomb depict legendary events from their lives in a style that reveals a new human understanding.

Further Reading

Tilman Riemenschneider is listed in the Art study guide (III, C, 2). Other masters of late-Gothic sculpture were Michael PACHER and Veit STOSS.

There is no monograph on Riemenschneider in English. Bernd Lohse and others, eds., *Art Treasures of Germany* (1958), contains some biographical information on Riemenschneider and reproductions of his works. See also Clara Waters, *Painters, Sculptors, Architects, Engravers and Their Works* (1899).

RIENZI / By Joseph N. Scionti

The Roman popular leader Cola di Rienzi (1313/1314–1354) was tribune of Rome during a period of the Avignonese papacy. He led a republican movement that restored for a time the dream, if not the reality, of Roman greatness.

Cola di Rienzo (incorrectly but popularly Rienzi; pronounced rē-ĕn′zē) was born Niccola di Lorenzo Gabrini in Rome. His father was a tavern keeper whose Christian name, Lorenzo, had been shortened to Rienzo. As a boy, living at Anagni, Cola di Rienzi read voraciously of the heroes and deeds of ancient Rome. The poets and historians who told of the glories of the ancient city filled him with a burning zeal to restore its former greatness.

Stoss, Riemenschneider combined realism with picturesqueness. The figure groups on his altarpieces are crowded and expressively posed, and the folds of their garments are deep-cut and crisp. He developed a highly individual style characterized by a high-pitched sensibility and an intense seriousness. His figures are carefully posed and often seem to affect ungainly attitudes; their expressions are somewhat more restrained than the figures by Stoss.

Riemenschneider's chief early works are the wooden altarpiece of the parish church of Münnerstadt (1490–1492; portions are in Berlin and Munich, the rest are *in*

As a very young man, Rienzi attracted attention in Rome when, with eloquence and aided by the presence of monuments of antiquity all around him, he reminded his fellow citizens of the might of the empire. Rome had once bestowed order and justice first upon itself and then upon the world, and Rienzi believed it could do so again.

Rienzi became a notary and in 1343 was sent on a public mission to Avignon. In Avignon he won the favor of Pope Clement VI, whom he exhorted to return to Rome and to put an end to the corruption that prevailed there under the disorderly rule of the nobles. Rienzi returned to Rome in April 1344, and he then made plans for a general uprising, gathering ever greater support with a series of brilliant speeches.

On May 20, 1347, Rienzi appeared at the Capitol with the bishop of Orvieto, the Pope's vicar, and proclaimed to the Roman people that from that moment the republic was restored. Shouts of approval met his promises of equal justice and fair taxation, and he found himself at once in the possession of complete authority in Rome. The nobles fled in dismay, and Rienzi was given the title of tribune of the people.

Rienzi's rule began well. He dispensed justice impartially, gave attention to the storage of surplus food, and systematically drained nearby marshlands for cultivation. For a brief time, security and peace made the hearts of Roman citizens glad that the vicious and arbitrary rule of the aristocrats was past.

On Aug. 1, 1347, representatives of the Italian cities, on Rienzi's invitation, met at Rome to consider the question of a united Italy. Many of the Italian communes, though not all, gave this plan and Rienzi's leadership their formal recognition. Dazzled by his own eloquence and apparent success, Rienzi then staged, on August 15, a ceremony of incredible pomp and ostentation in which he was installed and crowned tribune. Rienzi's extravagance led him to decree that all Italians were free and citizens of Rome and that only they had the authority to choose an emperor.

Pretensions such as these and the growing ostentation of Rienzi's habits soon caused popular enthusiasm to diminish, and the Roman barons, led by Stefano Colonna, made plans to overthrow him. Pope Clement VI, who had earlier supported Rienzi, was offended by his efforts to create a Roman empire based exclusively on the will of the people and was now most eager to be rid of him. On November 20 Rienzi set out boldly with a Roman militia and met and defeated the barons in a battle in which Colonna, his bitterest enemy, was killed.

This victory caused Rienzi to lose all moderation. He became more arrogant in behavior and more sumptuous in dress. He was deaf to all pleas of the papal vicar, with whom he supposedly shared authority. The exasperated pope issued a bull on December 3 branding Rienzi a criminal and calling upon the Roman people to drive him out. With opposition mounting, Rienzi lost his vaunted courage and abdicated on December 15. He then secluded himself for more than 2 years, appearing in Prague in July 1350. There he begged Emperor Charles IV to restore Italy to liberty, but Charles imprisoned him and then handed him over to the Pope in August 1352.

Clement VI died in December of that year, and his successor, Innocent VI, pardoned Rienzi, hoping to use him against the barons in Rome. The former tribune returned to Rome in August 1354 accompanied by the papal legate, Cardinal Gil Álvarez Carrillo de Albornoz. Rienzi was acclaimed and restored to power, but again he succumbed to the fatal weakness of failing to recognize the limits of his power. He grew insufferably tyrannical, and on Oct. 8, 1354, he was murdered by a Roman mob at the Capitol, and his body was then dragged through the streets.

Further Reading

Cola di Rienzi is listed in the European History study guide (III, G, 1, d). He was opposed by CHARLES IV of the Holy Roman Empire.

The best account of Rienzi's life is in Ferdinand Gregorovius, *History of the City of Rome in the Middle Ages*, translated by Annie Hamilton (8 vols., 1900–1909). For a lively recent treatment see Will Durant, *The Renaissance* (1953).

✳   ✳   ✳

Cola di Rienzi, "Last of the Romans." (New York Public Library, Picture Collection)

RIETVELD / By James F. O'Gorman

Gerrit Thomas Rietveld (1888–1964), architect and furniture designer, was a member of the group of Dutch artists and architects known as de Stijl. He was the first to give its esthetic program visible form.

Gerrit Rietveld (pronounced rēt′fĕlt) was born on June 24, 1888, in Utrecht and lived there most of his life. He was trained as a cabinetmaker by his father (1899–1906) and as a jewelry designer in the studio of C. J. Begeer (1906–1911). For the next 8 years he was self-employed as a cabinetmaker while studying and working with the architect P. J. Klaarhamer. Rietveld's career as an independent architect began in 1919.

A commission to copy from photographs furniture designed by the American architect Frank Lloyd Wright for a client of the Dutch architect Robert van't Hoff brought Rietveld into contact with de Stijl (the Style), founded in 1917. De Stijl advocated a "pure" artistic expression based upon the interrelationship in space of rectangles of primary colors. Rietveld was a member of this group from 1919 to 1931, but already in 1917–1918 he had designed the so-called Red-Blue chair. Composed of a modular grid of square or rectangular sticks painted black and with a sustaining seat and back of red and blue rectangular plywood planes, this design enabled each element to maintain its own absolute identity because of the color scheme and the joinery. It was the first execut-

The Schröder House in Utrecht, designed by Rietveld in 1924. (The Netherlands Information Service, New York)

ed object to exhibit the artistic principles of de Stijl.

Rietveld applied the same interplay of rectangles to an architectural design in his remodeling of the ground-floor shop front of the G. & Z. C. Jewelry Store, Amsterdam (1920; destroyed). In 1921 he began a period of collaboration with the designer Truus Schröder-Schräder, for and with whom he designed the paradigm of de Stijl architecture, the Schröder House, Utrecht (1924). The flexible design of the two-story house included an upper floor which could be made into one large room by sliding back the movable partitions. Its interior extended out into the surroundings through balconies, corner casement windows, projecting floor and roof planes, and large areas of glass. The exterior was a de Stijl composition of particolored, stuccoed brick planes and painted steel stanchions that suggested an inner volume dynamically defined by discrete lines and planes, but not actually enclosed. It set the standard for the progressive architecture of the 1920s in Europe.

De Stijl principles also formed the series of designs for shop fronts (1924–1929) which, with large-scale housing projects, comprised the bulk of Rietveld's work of the late 1920s. The only one exceptional design from this period was a garage and chauffeur's quarters in Utrecht (1927–1928; now altered). Here his concern was as much for technique as for form. He used precast concrete slabs held in place by a frame of steel I-sections expressed as a de Stijl grid on the exterior. In 1928 Rietveld was one of the cofounders of the CIAM (International Congress of Modern Architecture).

By the 1930s Rietveld's time seemed to have passed. Commissions became fewer, although he continued to design furniture (Zig-Zag chair, 1934) and buildings. Most of the latter were country houses displaying the canonical white stucco cubes, large areas of glass, and flexible, open planning of the mature International Style in Europe (Hillebrandt House, The Hague, 1935). With renewed interest in de Stijl following World War II, Riet-

Gerrit Rietveld. (Copyright by A. W. Bruna and Son)

veld continued to design private houses (Stoop House, Velp, 1951) and again received important commissions, including the Hoograven Housing complex, Utrecht (1954–1957), the Jaarbeurs, Utrecht (1956), and the De Ploeg textile factory, Bergeyk (1956). He died in Utrecht on June 25, 1964.

Further Reading

Gerrit Rietveld is listed in the Art study guide (III, K, 2, e). Other members of de Stijl were Theo van DOES-BURG, Piet MONDRIAN, and J. J. P. OUD.

The only monograph on Rietveld is Theodore M. Brown, *The Work of G. Rietveld* (1958), which includes an illustrated catalog of Rietveld's work, a bibliography, and translations of some of his writings. Hans Ludwig C. Jaffé, *De Stijl* (1960), discusses Rietveld's connection with the group.

Jacob Riis. (Courtesy of The New-York Historical Society, New York City)

RIIS / By Louis Filler

Jacob August Riis (1849–1914), Danish-born American journalist and slum reformer, created new standards in civic responsibility regarding the poor and homeless in his reporting of New York City slum conditions.

Jacob Riis was born May 3, 1849, in Ribe, Denmark, one of 14 children. His father was a schoolteacher. Young Riis early showed a sensitive disposition and a faith in people that would sustain him through difficult days. Trained in carpentry, he emigrated to New York in 1870. Riis never forgot the bitter experiences with poverty and ill-treatment that followed, but they did not mar his hopeful outlook. In 1874 he became editor of the *South Brooklyn News* and began developing his skills as a reporter. In 1877 he joined the *New York Tribune* and was assigned to the Police Department in the slums of the lower East Side.

Although Riis was in some respects sentimental in outlook, he was able to investigate and report conditions that made cynics of less hardy journalists. Riis turned his energy and keen eye for human-interest stories into a weapon for rousing New Yorkers to the evil state of their slums. His articles for the *Tribune*, the *Sun* (which he joined in 1890), and elsewhere probed every aspect of human circumstances: sanitary conditions, family life, the fate of women and children, and even treatment of dead victims of hunger and cold. Riis's articles and exposés turned light on dark tenements, vice centers, lax police administration, firetraps, and other areas of civic neglect. *How the Other Half Lives* (1890) brought him fame and introduced him to his lifelong friend and associate Theodore Roosevelt, who termed him the most useful citizen in New York.

Although Riis never saw beyond the conditions to the causes, those conditions were so in need of correction that his reports constituted major reform. *Out of Mulberry Street* (1898), *The Battle with the Slum* (1902), and *Children of the Tenement* (1903) continued to report investigations which resulted not only in cleansing the city of sore spots but made Riis influential as writer and lecturer in cities throughout the land. Thanks to his efforts, Mulberry Bend, notorious for its crime and decay, became a park; its Jacob A. Riis Neighborhood House is symbolic of his benign crusades in behalf of children.

Riis married his childhood sweetheart in 1876 and raised a family. She died in 1905, and 2 years later he married his young secretary. Riis's energy and earnest concern took him about the country and finally cost him his health, which rest cures could not renew. He died May 26, 1914, at his summer house in Barre, Mass.

Further Reading

Jacob Riis is listed in the American History study guide (VII, G, 4, b). About this time Jane ADDAMS originated the profession of social work at Hull House in a Chicago slum.

Riis's *The Making of an American* (1901; new ed. 1970) is a folk masterpiece. His childhood memoirs are in *The Old Town* (1909). A biography is Louise Ware, *Jacob A. Riis: Police Reporter, Reformer, Useful Citizen* (1938).

RILEY / By Richard M. Ludwig

American poet James Whitcomb Riley (1849–1916), often called the "People's Laureate" or the "Hoosier Poet," established a reputation for dialect poetry designed for recitation and easy reading.

James Whitcomb Riley was born on Oct. 7, 1849, in Greenfield, Ind. His father, a successful small-town lawyer, allowed him to shape his education by instinct rather than formal precedents. Oratory, drama, painting, and music took James's earliest attention. He idolized Charles Dickens. Poets Robert Burns, for dialect verse, and Henry Longfellow, for moral precepts, were his models. Young Riley wrote voluminously and saved every scrap, particularly the local-color sketches, incorporating anecdotes he heard from the countrypeople around the courthouse. His musical ear was good; he played the violin, guitar, and banjo. His verbal ear was even better.

At the age of 16 Riley left school to become a "house, sign, and ornamental painter," wandering around Indiana. He read law for a while but took to the road with a traveling medicine man from whose wagon he learned to entertain the public with recitations in dialect. When he returned to Greenfield, he started a career in journalism, beginning with the local paper and expanding his horizons gradually. At one time he was local editor of the *Anderson Democrat*.

James Whitcomb Riley about 1913. (Library of Congress)

The *Indianapolis Journal*'s invitation to join its staff was the door to success. Riley published his dialect poems under the name "Benjamin F. Johnson of Boone," and by 1883 the demand was enough to issue a pamphlet edition. Calling his first collection *The Old Swimmin' Hole and 'Leven More Poems*, he did not need a public-opinion poll to tell him he had found his métier. He sold more than half a million copies of this book, followed it with 40 more books before his death, and on platforms across the country entertained audiences with homely philosophy and dramatic monologues. *Old-Fashioned Roses* (London, 1888) captured an English audience. *Pipes o' Pan at Zekesbury* (1888), *Rhymes of Childhood* (1890), and *Here at Home* (1893) expanded his American reputation.

Riley's attractions were personal, not cerebral. His winsome nature was contagious in a public gathering, and he was determined to give his listener "simple sentiments that come from the heart." His poems were never burdened with ideas, complexities, ambiguities. He invented a whole gallery of Hoosiers; Riley was the first to admit that they spoke patent clichés in a dialect such as no real Hoosier ever spoke. At his best, he captured a tranquil America, wholesome, eccentric, sentimental, bucolic. "The Raggedy Man," "Little Orphant Annie," and "Nine Little Goblins" attest to his vitality within his limited range. He died on July 22, 1916.

Further Reading

James Whitcomb Riley is listed in the Literature study guide (I, D, 1, d). Joaquin MILLER was a contemporary local-color poet.

The Complete Works of James Whitcomb Riley (6 vols., 1913) was edited by Edmund H. Eitel, and *Letters of James Whitcomb Riley* (1930) by William Lyon Phelps. Two biographical studies incorporate criticism with reminiscence: Jeannette Covert Nolan, *James Whitcomb Riley* (1941), and Richard Crowder, *Those Innocent Years: The Legacy and Inheritance of a Hero of the Victorian Era, James Whitcomb Riley* (1957). See also Marcus Dickey, *The Youth of James Whitcomb Riley* (1919).

RILKE / By Klaus W. Jonas

Rainer Maria Rilke (1875–1926) is considered the greatest lyric poet of modern Germany. His work is marked by a mystical sense of God and death.

Born in Prague on Dec. 4, 1875, Rainer Maria Rilke (pronounced rĭl′kə) grew up in a middle-class milieu he called "petit bourgeois," of which he later felt ashamed. In spite of his sensitive, almost feminine nature, he was expected to become an army officer

Rainer Maria Rilke. (Culver Pictures, Inc.)

and was forced to spend 5 years (1886–1891) in the military academies of St. Pölten and Mährisch-Weisskirchen. After graduation from high school, he enrolled for a year as a student of literature at the German University of Prague (1895–1896) before moving away from his family. He continued his studies at the University of Munich for the next few years.

Early Works

At 19 Rilke began his literary career by publishing at his own expense a collection of indifferent love poems, *Leben und Lieder* (1894; *Life and Songs*), written in the conventional style of the Heine tradition. This was followed in 1895 by a collection of poems, *Larenopfer*, revealing a sentimental attachment to his native Prague. Both of these slim volumes as well as the next ones, *Traumgekrönt* (1896; *Dream-Crowned*), *Advent* (1897), and *Mir zur Feier* (1899; *Celebrating Myself*), fail to show the sharpness of observation that characterizes his later verse. His prose tales of this period, *Am Leben hin* (1898; *On the Rim of Life*), also contain little to foreshadow his later genius.

In his second, religious or mystic, period (1899–1903), Rilke, opposed to the naturalism of his time, became an esthetic symbolist and, above all, a religious prophet and humanitarian. In August 1900 he settled in the north German artist colony Worpswede near Bremen, met a young sculptress, Clara Westhoff, and married her. There he wrote a monograph, *Worpswede* (1902), about the painters whose work he observed, and contributed book reviews to the *Bremer Tageblatt*. His marriage, doomed almost from the start, remained a brief episode, although it was never formally dissolved. A few months after the birth (Dec. 12, 1901) of his daughter, Ruth, he departed for Paris, leaving behind his wife and child.

Two books of poetry, written for the most part during his time in the painters' colony, eventually brought Rilke fame. One was *Das Buch der Bilder* (1901, 1906; *The Book of Images*), a volume of individual poems without a common theme, marked by intense musicality and the ability to conjure up moods almost independent of the meaning of the words that are used. The other volume contains a cycle of religious poems, *Das Stundenbuch* (1905; *The Book of Hours*), consisting of three parts, each marking a stage in his development: *Das Buch vom mönchischen Leben* (1899), *Von der Pilgerschaft* (1901), and *Von der Armut und vom Tode* (1903). Its genesis was Rilke's two trips to Russia, undertaken in 1899 and 1900. His delightful, childlike stories, *Vom Lieben Gott* (1900; *Stories of God*), reveal a "circling around God," as he himself calls it, in which God and the believer are mutually interdependent. These early works are sincerely mystical, revealing his sense of humility and brotherhood, his simple faith and genuine compassion for the poor and exploited.

Life in Paris

Rilke's life in Paris (1902–1910) initiated a new phase, marked by the most significant turn in his poetic career: his new attitude toward objective reality and his attempt to apprehend the very essence of things, animate as well as inanimate. The commission to write a monograph on the great French sculptor Auguste Rodin had brought Rilke to Paris. He served Rodin for a while as secretary, and he admired him more than any other living artist. Rodin taught Rilke not to wait passively for inspiration but rather to go out and look for subjects, to observe and study tangible objects. Rilke now developed a new concept of the artist as the hardworking craftsman. This new attitude manifests itself in those poems that appeared under the title *Neue Gedichte* (1907, 1908; *New Poems*). Here one finds his famous *Ding-Gedichte* (thing-poems), poetic re-creations of things he had seen and observed and which to him become impersonal symbols: animals and flowers, landscapes, and, above all, works of art.

During a trip to Sweden in 1904, Rilke composed the first version of *Die Weise von Liebe und Tod des Cornet Christoph Rilke*, a romantic, even melodramatic, sentimental account of the last hours of a young aspiring cavalry officer. Later he tried to disassociate himself from this poem that became his most popular work. After the publication of his *Neue Gedichte*, Rilke set about completing an autobiographical novel begun in Rome 4 years before. In this, his only major narrative work, *Die Aufzeichnungen des Malte Laurids Brigge* (1910; *Notebook of Malte Laurids Brigge*), he tells the story of his own inner suffering during his lonely Paris years.

With the completion of *Malte Laurids Brigge* in the winter of 1909/1910, Rilke's Paris time came to an end; he spent only 18 months of the next 4 1/2 years in Paris. These were the years of an inner crisis, and in his utter restlessness and despair he moved from country to country. Anxious to explore new territories, he traveled in the winter 1910/1911 to North African countries, Algiers, Tunis, and Egypt, and from November 1912 to February 1913 he lived in Spain. Amid the profound hopelessness and frustration of these years, however, was one event which was to change Rilke's whole literary career: Princess Marie of Thurn and Taxis offered him the hospitality of her Castle Duino, near Trieste, on the Dalmatian coast. Here in 1912 he began to compose a series of elegies that were to become his ultimate poetic achievement. They were not, however, completed until 10 years later.

Later Years

When the war broke out in August 1914, Rilke was caught in Leipzig and was forced to remain in Germany. Most of the next 5 years he spent in and around Munich, except for 7 months' service in the Austrian army. In the first days of the war, Rilke passed through a brief period of exaltation and wrote his patriotic *Fünf Gesänge* (Five Songs). But this initial enthusiasm and solidarity with his patriotic countrymen soon gave way to indifference and, finally, to outright opposition to the German war effort.

In June 1919 Rilke accepted an invitation for a lecture tour in Switzerland, where he remained, except for a few sojourns in Italy and France, including a 7-month stay in Paris in 1925, until the end of his life. During the first year or two, he searched desperately for a refuge where he could take up the cycle of poems that he had left unfinished for so long. He discovered in the summer of 1921 Muzot, a deserted medieval tower, hardly habitable, near Sierre in the canton of Valais. Here in February 1922 he completed within a few days the cycle of poems he had begun in Duino in 1912. Dedicated to his hostess and benefactress, Princess Marie, he called them in gratitude *Duineser Elegien* (Duino Elegies). Their publication in 1923 marked the high point of his career, and even Rilke himself, critical of his own work, regarded them as his most important achievement. The great themes of the *Elegien* are man's loneliness, the perfection of the angels, life and death, love and lovers, and the task of the poet. They were followed by the *Sonette an Orpheus* (Sonnets to Orpheus), a total of 55 poems which represent the other aspect of Rilke's vision: his sense of joy, affirmation, and praise.

In his last years (1923–1926) Rilke turned more and more to French literature, not only translating André Gide and Paul Valéry, but also writing poems in French (*Poèmes français*). He died of leukemia on Dec. 29, 1926, in a sanatorium in Valmont above Montreux.

Further Reading

Rainer Maria Rilke is listed in the Literature study guide (III, I, 2; III, J, 2, a). His only peers in modern German literature are Stefan GEORGE and Hugo von HOFMANNSTHAL.

A truly satisfactory biographical study of Rilke cannot be undertaken until all his papers become available. A first serious attempt was made by Eliza M. Butler in her monograph, *Rainer Maria Rilke* (1941), and later by Jean Rodolphe de Salis in a book which covers only the last 7 years of Rilke's life, *Rainer Maria Rilke: The Years in Switzerland* (1964). For analysis of Rilke's writings, the works of two American scholars are recommended: Frank H. Wood, *Rainer Maria Rilke: The Ring of Forms* (1958), and Heinz F. Peters, *Rainer Maria Rilke: Masks and the Man* (1960). Useful background material is in Cecil M. Bowra, *Heritage of Symbolism* (1943), and particularly in the short work on German literature by Ronald Gray, *The German Tradition in Literature, 1871–1945* (1965), which includes an incisive interpretation of some of the key works of Rilke.

RIMBAUD / By Alfred Garvin Engstrom

Jean Nicolas Arthur Rimbaud (1854–1891), the marvelous boy-poet of French literature, established in a few short years his reputation for hallucinative verbal creation, only to give up poetry at the age of 19.

The tempestuous life of Arthur Rimbaud (pronounced răN-bō′), his relations with Paul Verlaine, his idea of the poet as seer and of the derangement of the senses are all part of the legend. His literary fame depends primarily upon the poem *Le Bateau ivre* and the remarkable volumes called *Les Illuminations* and *Une Saison en Enfer*. His abandonment of art and "the ancient parapets of Europe" has made Rimbaud a symptomatic and fascinating figure of alienation in the modern world.

A brilliant student in his native town of Charleville, Rimbaud published his first known French verses (*Les Étrennes des orphelins*) in *La Revue pour tous* for Jan. 2, 1870. Other early poems were *Sensation, Ophélie, Credo in Unam* (later called *Soleil et chair*), and *Le Dormeur du val. Les Chercheuses de poux* is a memorable example of beauty created from what seems at first a most unpromising subject; and *Voyelles*, with its coloring of the vowels ("A black, E white, I red, U green, O blue: vowels . . ."), aroused considerable interest in the aspect of synesthesia known as *audition colorée* (colored hearing).

On May 15, 1871, Rimbaud wrote his famous *Lettre du voyant* to a friend, Paul Demeny: "I say that one must be a *seer*, make himself a *seer*. The Poet makes himself a *seer* by a long, immense and reasoned *derangement* of *all the senses*. . . . He exhausts in himself all the poisons, to preserve only their quintessences. . . . For he arrives at the *unknown*. . . ."

In late September 1871 Rimbaud joined Verlaine in Paris, bringing with him the manuscript of *Le Bateau*

Arthur Rimbaud (right) with Paul Verlaine, detail of Un Coin de table, a painting, dated 1872, by Henri Fantin-Latour, in the Louvre, Paris. (Photo-Hachette)

ivre, one of the most remarkable poems of the century. It describes the adventures of a boat left free to drift down American rivers after its crew have been murdered by screaming Indians. The boat's progress is traced from its first exaltation at its freedom to its awakening on the stormy "poem of the sea," through a wild tumult of snows and tides and suns and hurricanes, amid vast imagery from the beginning of the world, until it becomes at last only a waterlogged plank, nostalgic for Europe and no longer worth salvaging. The poem is a marvel of hallucinative evocation and seems in a way to foreshadow Rimbaud's own strange life.

The turbulent relationship between Verlaine and Rimbaud ended finally with Verlaine in prison for shooting his friend in the wrist and with Rimbaud disoriented and restless. Rimbaud had *Une Saison en Enfer* printed in Belgium in 1873 and distributed a few copies, but he did not even claim the rest of the edition. *Les Illuminations* did not appear until Verlaine published the volume in 1886. Meanwhile, Rimbaud had given up poetry forever.

After years of wandering, Rimbaud lived as an African explorer, trader, and gunrunner. In 1888 he was at Harar working for an exporter of coffee, hides, and musk. A tumor of the knee forced his return to Marseilles in 1891, where his right leg was amputated. He died in the hospital there on Nov. 10, 1891, at the age of 37.

Critics have called Rimbaud one of the creators of free verse for such poems as *Marine* and *Mouvement* in *Les*

Illuminations. Rimbaud had written in *Une Saison en Enfer*: "I believed I could acquire supernatural powers. Well! I must bury my imagination and my memories!" He apparently wrote nothing more after his farewell to letters at the age of 19.

Further Reading

Arthur Rimbaud is listed in the Literature study guide (III, I, 1, b). He was closely associated with Paul VERLAINE.

Rimbaud's works have been extensively translated into English. Biographies in English are Enid Starkie, *Arthur Rimbaud* (1938; rev. ed. 1961), and Elisabeth M. Hanson, *My Poor Arthur: A Biography of Arthur Rimbaud* (1960). Useful critical studies of the poet include Cecil Arthur Hackett, *Rimbaud* (1957); Wilbur Merrill Frohock, *Rimbaud's Poetic Practice: Image and Theme in the Major Poems* (1963); John Porter Houston, *The Design of Rimbaud's Poetry* (1963); Gwendolyn Bays, *The Orphic Vision; Seer Poets from Novalis to Rimbaud* (1964); and Wallace Fowlie, *Rimbaud* (1966), a rewriting of his earlier *Rimbaud: The Myth of Childhood* (1946) and *Rimbaud's Illuminations* (1953).

RIMMER / By William Gerdts

William Rimmer (1816–1879) was probably the most individual and independent American sculptor in the 19th century. He was also a painter and a physician.

William Rimmer was born in Liverpool, England, on Feb. 20, 1816. At the age of 2 he was brought to Nova Scotia and at 10 to Boston, Mass., with which city he was primarily associated. In 1840 he began his artistic career as an itinerant portrait painter and also studied medicine, which he began to practice in the mid-1850s. At the same time he began carving directly in stone, producing such works as *St. Stephen*, a colossal granite head that is very personal in its display of fierce emotionalism and full of life. In his use of granite as a favored medium, he departed from the smooth, unbroken surfaces of the contemporary neoclassicists.

Falling Gladiator (1861), Rimmer's best-known sculpture, was done for his most important patron, Stephen Perkins. Although the work was classical in theme, the sense of strain and struggle in it was unlike any other sculpture done at the time, and here Rimmer's knowledge of anatomy was well utilized. The work, shown in the Paris Salon of 1863, appeared so lifelike that some thought it had been cast from a human model. In 1864 he received his one significant public commission, the statue of Alexander Hamilton for Commonwealth Avenue in Boston. Although rigorous and tense, this granite

William Rimmer. (Dictionary of American Portraits, Dover)

statue is more fussy and less vital than most of the artist's other works.

Rimmer lectured on art anatomy in Boston and conducted a school of drawing and modeling. From 1866 to 1870 he was director of the Cooper Union School of Design for Women in New York City. On his return to Boston, he taught at the school of the Boston Museum of Fine Arts. His last two surviving sculptures are *Fighting Lions* and the *Dying Centaur* (both 1871).

Rimmer has often been called the "American Michelangelo" because of his emphasis upon personal, tragic symbolism and his high standard of anatomical expressiveness. He had early come under the influence of the painter Washington Allston, whose personal, romantic classicism and sense of mystery undoubtedly contributed to the development of Rimmer's art. In the sensuous surfaces of his sculptures with their alternating patterns of light and dark, he anticipated the impressionistic sculpture of the French artist Auguste Rodin. Rimmer is considered primarily a sculptor, but his paintings are arousing interest today. He was also one of the greatest American draftsmen of the 19th century, and his book, *Art Anatomy* (1877), shows his ability as a draftsman and his anatomical knowledge. He died in South Milford, Mass., on Aug. 20, 1879.

Further Reading

William Rimmer is listed in the Art study guide (IV, C, 3; IV, D, 3). A well-known contemporary sculptor was Hiram POWERS.

Two studies of Rimmer are Truman H. Bartlett, *The Art Life of William Rimmer, Sculptor, Painter, and Physician* (1882), and Lincoln Kirstein, *William Rimmer, 1816–1879* (1946), published by the Whitney Museum of American Art.

RIMSKY-KORSAKOV

/ By Stanley D. Krebs

Nikolai Andreevich Rimsky-Korsakov (1844–1908), composer, conductor, and pedagogue, was a member of the Russian "Mighty Five." He was largely responsible for establishing the rigor and uncompromising professionalism of the Russian school of the turn of the century.

Nikolai Rimsky-Korsakov (pronounced rĭm′skē kôr′sə-kôf) was born in the town of Tikhvin near Novgorod on March 6, 1844. His father had served prominently in the provincial government, and, although the boy showed an early musical talent, he was duly entered in the St. Petersburg Naval Academy at the age of 12. While there he took violoncello lessons and later piano lessons from Feodor Kanille (Théodore Canillé), who encouraged his efforts at composition.

About 1861 Kanille introduced the young cadet to the circle of talented dilettantes who depended on Mili Balakirev for professional advice and guidance. This "Balakirev Circle" sought a Russian-based expression on the model of Mikhail Glinka. Its prominent members—Balakirev, Rimsky-Korsakov, Aleksandr Borodin, Modest Mussorgsky, and César Cui, became what the critic Vladimir Stasov much later called the "Mighty Handful" or "Mighty Five."

From 1862 through 1865 Rimsky-Korsakov cruised around the world with the Russian navy. His First Symphony, composed during this trip, was performed upon his return by Balakirev, who conducted the orchestra of the Free Music School, which he had founded.

Rimsky-Korsakov now devoted less time to navy affairs. He composed the symphonic poem *Sadko* (1867), returning to the theme much later for an opera, and the Second (*Antar*) Symphony (1868). In 1871 he became a professor at the St. Petersburg Conservatory, and in 1873 he resigned his naval commission. From 1874 to 1881 he directed the Free School, and he served as director of navy bands until 1884. He became convinced of the need for professional training, professional mastery, and a professional attitude. He embarked on a thorough study of harmony, counterpoint, and especially orchestration and urged a similar course on his colleagues. He published a harmony text in 1884 and an orchestration text in 1896. He displayed his orchestral expertise in his Third Symphony (1874) and in the delightful tone poems *Capriccio español* (1887), *Scheherazade* (1888), and *Dubinushka* (1905). But most of his energy went into his operas, the most important of which are *Snow Maiden* (1882), *Sadko* (1898), *The Invisible City of Kitezh* (1907), and *The Golden Cockerel* (1909). The sources for these and other works were fairy stories, Eastern tales, and Russian folk epics.

During the political unrest of 1905 Rimsky-Korsakov vigorously protested police repression of the students. The conservatory was closed down and he was dismissed. Others, including Alexander Glazunov, resigned in protest. The conservatory eventually reopened on a more autonomous basis with Glazunov as director and Rimsky-Korsakov as head of the department of orchestration.

The orchestral color and the beguiling, if not authentic, ''orientalisms'' of Rimsky-Korsakov's work brought him considerable fame and popularity. He was by far the most prolific of the Five, with a long list of orchestral works, 15 operas, and a substantial amount of chamber and vocal music. Moreover, his major works were divisible with no great musical loss into small sections which could be put to utility concert and ''background'' use. Perhaps no less a contribution was his effort on the behalf of others' music: he finished, rewrote, and orchestrated many works of other Russian composers, including Alexander Dargomyzhsky's *Stone Guest*, Mussorgsky's

Khovanshchina and *Boris Godunov*, and (with Glazunov) Borodin's *Prince Igor*.

Rimsky-Korsakov died on June 21, 1908. His establishment of professional mastery of technique as the exclusive route to musical legitimacy is a legacy still preserved in the Soviet Union.

Further Reading

Nikolai Rimsky-Korsakov is listed in the Music study guide (I, H, 4). Other members of the Mighty Five were Aleksandr BORODIN and Modest MUSSORGSKY.

Rimsky-Korsakov's own *My Musical Life* (1909; trans. 1924; new ed. 1942) is basic. M. D. Calvocoressi and Gerald Abraham devote a chapter to Rimsky-Korsakov in their *Masters of Russian Music* (1936). Essentially the same chapter was published by Abraham as *Rimsky-Korsakov: A Short Biography* (1945). Any music history, especially an account of the romantic era, will contain a section on Rimsky-Korsakov. The most recent reference is Mikhail Zetlin, *The Five*, translated and edited by George Panin (1959).

RIO BRANCO / By Michael M. Smith

José Maria da Silva Paranhos, Barão do Rio Branco (1845–1912), was a Brazilian political leader whose success in defining Brazil's frontiers during the early years of the republic added extensive territory to the Brazilian patrimony and eliminated numerous causes of international friction.

Born in Rio de Janeiro, the Barão do Rio Branco (pronounced rē'ō bräng'kō) is often confused with his equally famous father, the Viscount of Rio Branco, former minister of foreign relations and author of the ''Law of Free Birth.'' Rio Branco attended the law academies of São Paulo and Recife, graduating from the latter in 1866. He was a war correspondent for the Parisian paper *L'Illustration* during the Paraguayan War and from 1869 to 1875 served with little distinction as deputy from Mato Grosso.

After earning a reputation as a bohemian and playboy, Rio Branco underwent a severe change of character after being appointed consul to Liverpool in 1876. In 1884 he was named counselor of the empire. In recognition of his distinguished foreign service, he was given the title of Barão (Baron) do Rio Branco in 1888. In 1891 he became the director of the Brazilian immigration service in Paris.

A longtime member of the Brazilian Geographical and Historical Institute, Rio Branco took advantage of his trips throughout the Continent to visit libraries and museums and regularly submitted historical articles to Brazilian

Nikolai Rimsky-Korsakov. (Novosti)

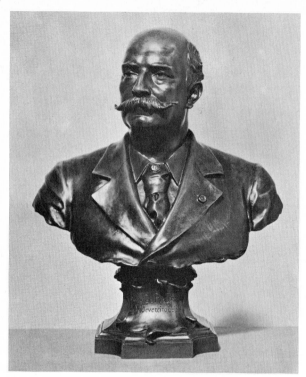

*The Barão do Rio Branco, a portrait bust dated
1895. (Organization of American States)*

journals. This experience was invaluable for later diplomatic work, for he developed language skills, social and official contacts, and an affinity for spending hours in study and research.

In March 1893 Rio Branco represented Brazil in an old boundary dispute with Argentina over the province of Misiones. On Feb. 6, 1895, the arbiter, U.S. president Grover Cleveland, awarded the 13,680-square-mile territory to Brazil. In December 1900, thanks to Rio Branco's meticulous research and presentation, Brazil was awarded the 101,000-square-mile Amapá territory on the Brazilian-French Guianese border. He was appointed minister to Germany on March 28, 1901, but his stay there was a short one, for President Francisco Rodrigues Alves invited him to become minister of foreign relations in July of the following year. Apprehensively accepting the position, Rio Branco returned to Brazil for the first time in 26 years.

Yet Rio Branco's years in the foreign service had singularly well prepared him for his new task, and he had a profound understanding of Brazil's traditional diplomacy. His immediate task in 1902 was the demarcation of Brazil's 9,000-mile, ill-defined frontier, which touched all South American countries except Chile and posed a constant threat of international conflict. His most pressing problem was the dispute between Brazil and Bolivia over the rubber-rich area of Acre, where fighting had broken out just as he came to office. Obtaining a cease-fire, on Nov. 17, 1903, he negotiated the Treaty of Petrópolis, which gave Brazil 73,000 square miles of the rich territory. Between 1904 and 1909 Rio Branco won favorable

decisions in boundary disputes with Ecuador, Venezuela, Surinam, Colombia, Uruguay, and Peru. In 15 years he had defined Brazilian boundaries, a cause of conflict for 4 centuries, and added almost 340,000 square miles to Brazilian national territory.

Besides his noted boundary successes, he jealously guarded Brazil's foreign coffee market and created numerous Brazilian diplomatic legations in all parts of the world. In 1905 he secured a cardinal for Brazil, which for 30 years was the only Latin American country that could boast of such a high Church official.

Rio Branco served four presidents and neither entered politics nor became involved in internal policies. He died in Rio on Feb. 10, 1912, after suffering a uremic attack.

Further Reading

The Barão do Rio Branco is listed in the Latin America study guide (IV, C, 1, a). He served under Manoel DEODORO DA FONSECA, Floriano PEIXOTO, and Candido RONDON.

The best work in English on Rio Branco is E. Bradford Burns, *The Unwritten Alliance: Rio Branco and Brazilian-American Relations* (1966), which includes more than the title suggests and gives a good biographical treatment.

RIPLEY / By Lewis C. Perry

George Ripley (1802–1880), American clergyman and journalist, was a leader of the transcendentalist movement and a founder of the famous utopian community Brook Farm. He later became an able literary critic for the "New York Tribune."

George Ripley was born of Puritan ancestry on Oct. 3, 1802, in Greenfield, Mass., the son of a prosperous merchant. New England Congregationalism was bitterly divided in the years of his youth, and the Ripley family joined the Unitarian side. George attended Harvard College, where liberal religious views prevailed, and graduated at the head of his class in 1823. For 3 years he taught mathematics at Harvard and studied at the divinity school. In 1826 he was ordained minister of a new Unitarian church in Boston. In 1827 he married Sophia Willard Dana.

Ripley's years at Harvard had been years of what would now be called student unrest. Students found the instruction dry and unrelated to new romantic currents in European scholarship. They wanted more attention to the needs of mankind and less to inherited theological dogmas. By the mid-1830s Ripley was a recognized leader of the younger dissident ministers, some of whom were called transcendentalists. He wrote a series of brilliant attacks on conservatism in the *Christian Register*. He helped edit the *Specimens of Foreign Standard Literature* (1838), a 14-volume work translating into English many important Continental authors. The transcendentalists moved steadily from religious to literary interests, and in 1840 Ripley began to help edit their magazine, the *Dial*. In 1841 he resigned from the ministry.

In April 1841 Ripley became president of the Brook Farm Association; he and his wife were devoted to establishing a utopian community. The community, outside Boston, sought to combine hard work with intellectual growth. In 1845 the community began issuing a journal, the *Harbinger*, edited by Ripley. But a bad fire in 1846 debilitated the struggling community, and in August 1847 it disbanded, with Ripley assuming the debts.

Ripley moved to New York City, where he continued publishing the *Harbinger* for 2 years. In 1849 he became literary critic for the *New York Tribune*, establishing himself as one of the most influential arbiters of American taste. He helped found and edited *Harper's New Monthly Magazine* (1850) and the *New American Cyclopaedia* (1858–1863). His wife died in 1861, and 4 years later he married Louisa Schlossberger. Ripley died on July 4, 1880, while writing an editorial for *Harper's*.

Further Reading

George Ripley is listed in the American History study guide (V, F, 4, b). His cousin Ralph Waldo EMERSON, famed essayist and poet, was an early transcendentalist spokesman.

George Ripley. (Library of Congress)

A good scholarly biography is Charles R. Crowe, *George Ripley: Transcendentalist and Utopian Socialist* (1967). Octavius B. Frothingham, *George Ripley* (1882), is an affectionate memoir, less detailed and accurate but containing many letters by Ripley. A brilliant introduction to transcendentalist writings is Perry Miller, ed., *The Transcendentalists* (1950), which describes Ripley's role in the movement. William R. Hutchison, *The Transcendentalist Ministers: Church Reform in the New England Renaissance* (1959), is useful on the controversies within Unitarianism. A good approach to Brook Farm is through the documents in Henry W. Sams, ed., *Autobiography of Brook Farm* (1958).

RITSCHL / By Daniel O'Connor

The German theologian Albrecht Benjamin Ritschl (1822–1889) was an influential interpreter of the New Testament whose views were, for a time, an effective counterweight to the dominant romantic tendency of 19th-century German theology.

Albrecht Ritschl (pronounced rĭch′əl) was born in Berlin on March 25, 1822, the son of a bishop and superintendent of the Evangelical Church in Pomerania. He studied philosophy and theology at Tübingen and other universities. His teaching career began at Bonn, where he was first lecturer (1846) and then professor (1852) of New Testament studies and patristics. In 1864 he accepted a call to Göttingen, where he remained as professor of theology until his death.

Early in his career, under the influence of Ferdinand Christian Baur, Ritschl subscribed to the speculative interpretation of the early Church introduced by G. W. F. Hegel and F. D. E. Schleiermacher. But he soon abandoned this in favor of an approach based solely on historical and theological interpretation of Scripture: no important Christian truth depends on metaphysical argument. At the same time, Ritschl firmly rejected all experiential approaches to religious truth as sheer sentimentalism: not what happens now in the subjective consciousness of the believer but what happened in history —this alone can be the starting point of theology. Ritschl therefore opposed all forms of mysticism, and in particular the Pietist movement, as being decadent relapses into pre-Reformation forms of piety.

Ritschl's historical work established, against the Baur interpretation, the important point that no sharp division exists between the account of St. Paul and the accounts of the other apostles. The tendency of Ritschl's constructive views, in spite of this emphasis on a historical basis, was toward regarding religion as a support, or a guarantee, for man's moral aspiration. Borrowing heavily from Immanuel Kant's moral philosophy, Ritschl asserts that

Albrecht Ritschl. (Bildarchiv)

"in every religion what is sought ... is a solution of the contradiction in which man finds himself as both a part of nature and a spiritual personality claiming to dominate nature."

This theme is argued forcefully in Ritschl's major work, *Justification and Reconciliation* (3 vols., 1870–1874). The effect of faith is to free us from guilt consciousness, to restore harmony between God and man, and to reinforce man's spiritual dominion over nature. Critics like Sebastian Brunner and Karl Barth argue that this emphasis on inner-worldly moral ends does not sufficiently bring out the "vertical," or transcendent, dimension of faith. Ritschl died in Göttingen on March 20, 1889.

Further Reading

Albrecht Ritschl is listed in the Religion study guide (I, P, 1, g). He was influenced by Ferdinand Christian BAUR.

Biographical studies of Ritschl are all in German. Interesting appraisals of him in English are in Hugh Ross Mackintosh, *Types of Modern Theology* (1937), and Karl Barth, *Protestant Thought: From Rousseau to Ritschl* (1959). A contemporary essay that draws heavily on themes from Ritschl is Philip J. Hefner, *Faith and the Vitalities of History* (1966).

*　　*　　*

RITTENHOUSE / By Monte A. Calvert

David Rittenhouse (1732–1796), American astronomer and instrument maker, was a noted

amateur scientist who constructed the finest orrery made at that time.

David Rittenhouse was born on April 8, 1732, near Germantown, Pa., into a poor farming family. He was stimulated by some books and tools of his uncle's and evidently educated himself in mathematics and astronomy. With help and encouragement from an Episcopal clergyman, he continued to advance his mathematical knowledge. In 1763 his boundary survey for Pennsylvania was so accurate that it was later accepted by the English surveyors Charles Mason and Jeremiah Dixon.

In 1767 Rittenhouse began his masterwork, the finest and most accurate orrery of that period. This mechanical representation of the movement of the planets through the universe was used widely in teaching and demonstration in the 18th century and also served as a demonstration of the reasonableness of nature. Rittenhouse's first orrery was capable of reproducing the relations of the planets forward or backward 5,000 years and emitted music when in operation.

Rittenhouse was in demand over the next few years by colleges that wanted him to make orreries, and the Commonwealth of Pennsylvania awarded him £300 as an honor and £300 more to make an orrery "for the use of the public." The fame derived from his orrery guaranteed him support for his observations in 1769 of the transit of Venus, which was an opportunity to measure the solar parallax. Rittenhouse's observations, made in a specially

David Rittenhouse, a painting by Charles Willson Peale. (Independence National Historical Park Collection, Philadelphia)

constructed laboratory, with instruments of his own design, were highly accurate and were favorably considered by European scientists working on the same problem.

In 1770 Rittenhouse moved to Philadelphia, where he was able to pursue a more active scientific career. He became a member of the informal scientific circle presided over by Thomas Jefferson. With his own improved telescopes he continued to make astronomical observations and to produce scientific and surveying instruments for himself and others, while making his living as a clockmaker. There is some uncertainty as to whether he independently developed a system of calculus, but he did become mathematically sophisticated and made some contributions in this area.

During the Revolutionary War, Rittenhouse was an avid patriot, serving on councils and committees of public safety, devising harbor defenses and methods of saltpeter production for gunpowder, and substituting iron weights in pendulum clocks to get lead for bullets. His last public service was as director of the U.S. Mint from 1792 to 1795. He died of cholera on June 26, 1796. He is often cited as an example of the untutored genius springing from American soil.

Further Reading

David Rittenhouse is listed in the American History study guide (II, D, 7). Benjamin FRANKLIN, another of Philadelphia's famed amateur scientists, conducted experiments in electricity.

The best biography is Brooke Hindle, *David Rittenhouse* (1964). Edward Ford, *David Rittenhouse: Astronomer-Patriot, 1732–1796* (1946), is also useful. For general background relating to Rittenhouse and the Jeffersonian circle see Daniel J. Boorstin, *The Lost World of Thomas Jefferson* (1948), and Brooke Hindle, *The Pursuit of Science in Revolutionary America, 1735–1789* (1956).

RITTER / By T. W. Freeman

Karl Ritter (1779–1859) was a German geographer of international fame and a founder of the modern school of German geography. His time is often called the "classical period" among geographers.

One of six children, Karl Ritter (pronounced rĭt′ər) was born at Quedlinburg on Aug. 7, 1779, into the much-respected family of F. W. Ritter, a medical doctor. Two years later his father died. Young Karl entered a school in which the pupils were taken out to study nature. Apparently inspired by the theories of Jean Jacques Rousseau, this school left a permanent mark on Ritter, who retained an interest in new ideas on education, including those of Johann Pestalozzi.

Much of Ritter's writing was based on Pestalozzi's

Karl Ritter, a portrait by Carl Begas. (New York Public Library, Picture Collection)

ideas of the three stages in teaching: the acquisition of the material, the general comparison of material, and the establishment of a general system. Ritter was largely concerned with comparison; some interesting general ideas emerged in his work, such as those of the water and land hemispheres, the contrast between the Northern and Southern Hemispheres, the contrast in form between the Old and the New World (the Old having great east-west length, and the New north-south), and the concept of the "space relations" of particular countries, meaning their position in relation to neighboring areas. Africa, he noted, had relatively the shortest and most regular coastline of all the continents, and the interior had little contact with the ocean. Asia was far better provided with sea inlets, but the interior was isolated from the margins. Europe was the most varied of all the continents, with a complex interpenetration of land and sea.

In 1796 Ritter went to Halle University for 2 years, and in 1798 he became a tutor for the Hollweg family, who were rich bankers in Frankfurt. He began to publish papers in 1802, and in 1804 and 1807 he published a two-volume work on Europe described as "geographical, historical [and] statistical." He traveled widely in Europe but only once went to Asia and then only to Smyrna. The first volume of his great *Erdkunde* (Geography), of some 10,-000 pages, dealt with Africa and appeared in 1817; the second edition, revised, of 1822, was the first of 19 volumes published at intervals to 1859.

Having married in 1819, Ritter became a history teacher in Frankfurt, but in 1820 he went to Berlin as professor of geography at the university and the Royal Military Academy. He was a founder member of the Berlin Geographical Society in 1828. Active almost to the last, Ritter died on Sept. 28, 1859, in Berlin.

Further Reading

Karl Ritter is listed in the Geography and Exploration study guide (VI, B). He was influenced by the theories of the Swiss educational reformer Johann PESTALOZZI. Ritter and Alexander von HUMBOLDT were the founders of the modern school of German geography.

An old biography is William L. Gage, *The Life of Carl Ritter* (1867). An appreciation of Ritter by H. Bögekamp is in Ritter's *Geographical Studies* (1863). Ritter's work is discussed in Richard Hartshoren, *The Nature of Geography* (1939); Gerald R. Crone, *Modern Geographers* (1955; rev. ed. 1970); and Thomas W. Freeman, *A Hundred Years of Geography* (1971).

✳   ✳   ✳

RIVADAVIA / By John L. Robinson

Bernardino Rivadavia (1780–1845) was a leader in Argentina's efforts to secure independence and after the break with Spain introduced a vast body of reforms to provide a sound basis for the newly independent country.

Bernardino Rivadavia (pronounced rē-vä-*th*ä′vyä) was born a citizen of Spain's colonial empire. Reared and educated in Buenos Aires, capital of the viceroyalty of the Río de la Plata, he was an early advocate of independence. In 1810 he joined the meeting of leading citizens which ousted the Spanish viceroy and secured virtual independence.

Newly independent Argentina was groping for stable government, and in 1811 a triumvirate replaced the revolutionary junta. Rivadavia served first as a secretary and then as a full member of the governing body. He was a zealous innovator, introducing all manner of reforms and institutions into the sociopolitical vacuum left by the disintegration of the colonial edifice.

With phenomenal breadth of interest, Rivadavia offered a staggering array of proposals for the developing nation. Greatly concerned with human rights, he supported decrees designed to guarantee civil liberties for all citizens, male and female. Logically, then, he sought to strip both the Roman Catholic Church and the military of the special privileges he felt inappropriate in the envisioned egalitarian society. He realized that a responsive and viable government would protect and encourage national growth, so he implemented electoral and structural reforms, making Buenos Aires a model for other provinces. The average citizen, he believed, needed education in order to operate the hoped-for democracy, so he pressed for educational improvements on all levels. He felt that happiness depended on at least a modicum of material prosperity and insisted on commercial reforms, ranging from freer commerce to the introduction of new mining and agricultural processes. These are but a sampling of the innovations, none of them an unqualified success, which leaped from Rivadavia's fertile mind.

Rivadavia also served his nation in the field of diplomacy, twice traveling to Europe on delicate missions and filling the office of foreign minister. His successes included persuading both Great Britain and the United States to recognize Argentina's independence from Spain. Further, his trips to Europe gave him the chance to savor the concepts of such thinkers as Bentham, Adam Smith, Jovellanos, and Campomanes.

In 1826 a constitutional congress named Rivadavia president of Argentina. Although that body's action was technically without legal sanction, Rivadavia carried out his duties to the fullest extent. But he soon ran into difficulties. An inconclusive war with Brazil drained the government's resources and stirred much resentment. His promulgation of a rather centralist constitution excited the wrath of jealous provincial chieftains. Faced with unrelenting opposition, he resigned in 1827.

Forced into exile by his enemies, Rivadavia wandered in Latin America and Europe for several years. He died in Cadiz, Spain. He left a rich heritage of reforms and institutions which, in more fortuitous times, Argentina would eagerly resurrect.

Bernardino Rivadavia. (Organization of American States)

Further Reading

Bernardino Rivadavia is listed in the Latin America study guide (IV, A, 1, a). Soon after his resignation Juan Manuel de ROSAS began a long reign as dictator.

Hubert Clinton Herring, *A History of Latin America: From the Beginnings to the Present* (1955; 3d rev. ed. 1968), gives an excellent short sketch of Rivadavia, putting him in proper historical perspective. A section on him is in George Washington University, *South American Dictators during the First Century of Independence*, edited by Alva Curtis Wilgus (1937). An outstanding account of Rivadavia's political work is in José Luis Romero, *A History of Argentine Political Thought* (1946; 3d ed. 1959; trans. 1963).

RIVAS / By Harriet S. Turner

The Spanish poet, dramatist, and statesman Angel de Saavedra, Duque de Rivas (1791–1865), is best known for his drama "Don Álvaro, or the Force of Destiny," which marked the triumph of romanticism in Spain.

The Duque de Rivas, a self-portrait. (MAS)

Angel de Saavedra, later the Duque de Rivas (pronounced rē′väs), was born on March 10, 1791, in Cordova, the second son of a family of grandees. In 1800 the family moved to Madrid, where Saavedra studied at the Seminario de Nobles. In 1808, at the outbreak of the War of Independence against Napoleon, he joined the Castilian army. Badly wounded in 1809, he went to Cadiz, where he met Quintana and Martinez de la Rosa, two major literary figures. Between 1814 and 1820 he wrote drama and poetry in the classical manner, publishing various poems with the title *Poesías* in 1814.

By 1823 Saavedra had joined the liberals against the despotic rule of Ferdinand VII. He became a deputy and secretary of the Cortes and was among those who imprisoned the King at Cadiz. When Ferdinand regained power, Saavedra was condemned to death but escaped, emigrating with other Spanish intellectuals to London in 1823. For the next 10 years he lived abroad in England, Italy, Malta, and France. In Malta in 1825 he met John Hookham Frere, a noted English Hispanist who introduced him to the British romantics and urged him to search for poetic themes in Spanish history. In 1828 Saavedra wrote his poem *El faro de Malta* and in 1829 began writing the first successful Spanish *leyenda*, *El moro expósito*, published in 1834. It is a long epic poem in 12 cantos that reworks the medieval story of the Siete Infantes de Lara and their Moorish half brother Mudarra. In keeping with the romantic spirit, Saavedra changed Mudarra into an exotic hero and sought to re-create the atmosphere of the days of chivalry.

In 1830 Saavedra witnessed in Paris the premiere of Victor Hugo's *Hernani*, which formally established romanticism in France. Saavedra was back in Spain when amnesty was granted in 1834, the year that his elder brother died without issue. Saavedra inherited the family fortune and title by which he is generally known. He adopted more conservative political views and in 1835 became minister of the interior.

The performance of Rivas's play *Don Álvaro, o la fuerza del sino* (*Don Álvaro, or the Force of Destiny*) in 1835 signaled the advent of romanticism in Spain. Don Álvaro is a typically romantic hero, and the play is charged with violent action and melodrama. Yet Rivas balanced these romantic elements with expertly designed stage settings and scenes of local color in which minor characters enact realistic, often comic, situations.

In 1837 Rivas was exiled again, this time for being a conservative. He returned in 1838 and in 1841 published *Los romances históricos*, poems inspired by Spanish ballad literature and ancient chronicles. During 1844–1860 Rivas served as ambassador in Naples, Paris, and Florence, and in Spain he was elected president of the Cortes and Consejo de Estado. After 1860 he withdrew from politics but continued as president of the Spanish Academy until his death on June 22, 1865, in Madrid.

Further Reading

The Duque de Rivas is listed in the Literature study guide (III, G, 4). Victor HUGO was a leading French romantic author.

The best book on Rivas's life and work is Edgar Allison

Peers, *Rivas and Romanticism in Spain* (1923). Rivas is discussed in two general background works: Gerald Brenan, *The Literature of the Spanish People* (1951; 2d ed. 1953), and Richard E. Chandler and Kessel Schwartz, *A New History of Spanish Literature* (1961).

* * *

D. RIVERA / By Malcolm D. McLean

Diego Rivera (1886–1957), Mexico's most famous painter, rebelled against the traditional school of painting and developed his own style, a combination of historical, social, and critical ideas depicting the cultural evolution of Mexico.

Diego Rivera (pronounced rē-vä′rä) was born in Guanajuato, Guanajuato State, on Dec. 8, 1886. He studied painting at the National School of Fine Arts, Mexico City, under Andrés Ríos (1897), Félix Para, Santiago Rebull, and José María Velasco (1899–1901).

In 1907 Rivera received a grant to study in Europe and

Diego Rivera at work on his controversial mural in the RCA Building in Rockefeller Center, New York, in 1933. Because the radical painter included a portrait of Lenin, the Rockefeller family had the work destroyed. (United Press International Photo)

lived there until 1921. He first worked in the studio of Eduardo Chicharro in Madrid and in 1909 settled in Paris. He was influenced by the impressionists, particularly Pierre Auguste Renoir. Rivera then worked in a postimpressionist style, inspired by Paul Cézanne, Paul Gauguin, Georges Seurat, Henri Matisse, Raoul Dufy, and Amedeo Modigliani.

The series of works Rivera produced between 1913 and 1917 are in the cubist idiom, for example, *Jacques Lipchitz (Portrait of a Young Man; 1914).* Some of them have Mexican themes, such as the *Guerrillero* (1915). By 1918 he was producing pencil sketches of the highest quality, exemplified in his self-portrait. Before returning to Mexico he traveled through Italy.

Rivera's first mural, the *Creation* (1922), in the Bolívar Amphitheater at the University of Mexico, painted in encaustic, was the first important mural of the century. From the beginning he sought for, and achieved, a free and modern expression which would be at the same time understandable. He had an enormous talent for structuring his works and a great hand for color, but his two most pronounced characteristics were intellectual inventiveness and refined sensuality. His first mural was an allegory in a philosophical sense. In his later works he developed various historical, social, and critical themes in which the history and the life of the Mexican people appear as an epic and as a specific example of universal ideas.

Rivera next executed frescoes in the Ministry of Education Building, Mexico City (1923–1926). The frescoes in the Auditorium of the National School of Agriculture, Chapingo (1927), are considered his masterpiece. The unity of the work and the quality of the component parts, particularly the feminine nudes, show him at the height of his creative power. The general theme is man's biological and social development and his conquest of nature in order to improve it. This idea, which sprang from positivist roots, is complicated by Rivera's sociohistorical criticism and by a revolutionary feeling under the symbol of the red star. The murals in the Palace of Cortés, Cuernavaca (1929–1930), depict the fight against the Spanish conquerors.

In 1930 Rivera went to the United States. In San Francisco he did the murals for the Stock Exchange Luncheon Club and the California School of Fine Arts. Two years later he had an exhibition at the Museum of Modern Art, New York City. One of his most important works is the fresco in the Detroit Institute of Arts (1933), which depicts industrial life in the United States. He returned to New York and painted part of a mural for Rockefeller Center (1933; destroyed) and a series of frescoes on movable panels depicting a portrait of America for the Independent Labor Institute.

When Rivera returned to Mexico City, he executed the mural for the Palace of Fine Arts (1934), a replica of the one he had started in Rockefeller Center, and completed the frescoes on the monumental stairway in the National Palace (1935), which interpret the history of Mexico from pre-Columbian times to the present and culminate in the symbolic image of Marx. Rivera later continued the fres-

Spaniards brand their Indian slaves in this detail of a mural by Diego Rivera depicting the conquest of Mexico. (National Palace, Mexico, D.F.)

coes along the corridors, but he never completed them. The four movable panels he executed for the Hotel Reforma (1936) were withdrawn from the building because of their controversial nature. During this period he did the portraits of Lupe Marín and of Ruth Rivera and two easel paintings, *Dancing Girl in Repose* and the *Dance of the Earth*.

In 1940 Rivera returned to San Francisco to do a mural for a junior college on the general theme of culture in the future, which he believed would consist of a fusion of the artistic genius of South America with the industrial genius of North America. His two murals in the National Institute of Cardiology, Mexico City (1944), portray the development of cardiology and include portraits of the outstanding physicians in that field. His mural for the Hotel del Prado, *A Dream in the Alameda* (1947), was based on a historical and critical theme.

In 1951 a great retrospective covering Rivera's 50 years of activity as an artist took place in the Palace of Fine Arts. His last works were the mosaics for the stadium of the National University and for the Insurgents' Theater and the fresco in the Social Security Hospital No. 1. In 1956 he made his second trip to Russia (his first was in 1927–1928). He died in Mexico City on Nov. 25, 1957.

Further Reading

Diego Rivera is listed in the Latin America study guide (IV, K, 2, b). One of his teachers was José María VELAS-CO. Ben SHAHN assisted Rivera on the Rockefeller Center mural.

Rivera's own writings include *Portrait of America*, written with Bertram D. Wolfe (1934), and *My Art, My*

Life, written with Gladys March (1960). Biographies are Wolfe's *Diego Rivera: His Life and Times* (1939) and *The Fabulous Life of Diego Rivera* (1963).

✳   ✳   ✳

F. **RIVERA** / By Philip B. Taylor, Jr.

Fructuoso Rivera (ca. 1788–1854) was the first president of Uruguay. Better known for his military spirit and leadership than for his statesmanship, he was a principal actor in the first 45 years of the country's history.

Fructuoso Rivera was a rancher in his youth. He volunteered for the army fighting for Uruguayan independence under José Gervasio Artigas in 1810. Rivera rose gradually to general, although he was not one of Artigas's principal lieutenants. When Artigas was forced into exile in 1820 by occupying Brazilian troops, Rivera fought on for a time. Brazil finally settled with him, however, recognizing his rank and granting him a pension.

In 1825 Juan Lavalleja and his "33 Immortals" landed in Uruguay from exile in Argentina. With Argentine support, including troops commanded by the Argentine general José Rondeau, they made the Brazilian claims to the region untenable. Rivera was closely associated with Lavalleja from the beginning, although there is disagree-

Fructuoso Rivera. (Organization of American States)

ment as to whether Rivera joined voluntarily. A skilled opportunist, Rivera was commander of troops at two important battles, Rincón and Sarandí. Disagreements forced him to leave the country for a year, and he was not present at the final battle of Ituzaingó in 1828.

As the newly independent government was being formed, Rivera returned and engaged Lavalleja in bitter feuding. Rondeau briefly became the compromise provisional president. Rivera was elected constitutional president for the term 1830–1835 but spent at least half this period leading troops against Lavalleja.

In 1835 Rivera designated Gen. Manuel Oribe as his choice for the presidency. Rivera stepped aside to become commander of the armed forces. Within a year, Oribe found it necessary to break with Rivera; although the two had joined in the field to defeat another uprising by Lavalleja, Rivera refused to recognize his subordinate role. The official excuse was Rivera's profligate habits with official funds, from 1830 onward. Civil war broke out, and Oribe was defeated in 1838 and forced to flee to Buenos Aires. It was at this time that Oribe's followers, wearing white identifying colors, became the so-called Blanco political party; similarly, Rivera's followers became Colorados, or reds.

Rivera regained the constitutional presidency for the term 1839–1843. In the meantime Oribe accepted a commission from the ambitious Argentine president-*caudillo* Juan Manuel de Rosas to invade and occupy Uruguay. Thus began the Guerra Grande, or Great War. Rivera spent most of his presidential term in the field, leading troops against Oribe and his allies. Finally, in December

1842, Oribe defeated Rivera in the battle of Arroyo Grande. Rivera fled to Montevideo; Oribe established a parallel government for the rest of Uruguay, just outside Montevideo's walls, at Cerrito. In effect Montevideo became "Colorado" and the rest of the country "Blanco."

Rivera remained de facto chief of government until 1847. His eccentric behavior made him many enemies, and he finally was forced into exile in Brazil, where he remained until 1853. In September the constitutional president of Uruguay, Juan Francisco Giró, was forced to resign after a troop mutiny. A triumvirate of officers—Lavalleja, Rivera, and Gen. Venancio Flores—was organized to take power. Lavalleja died almost immediately; Rivera died in northern Uruguay, en route to Montevideo, in January 1854.

Rivera's colorful personality, personal *machismo*, and popular support permitted him to indulge in many irregularities. Especially during the siege of Montevideo, he was virtually a law unto himself. On the other hand, his stubborn resistance to Rosas's ambitions preserved Uruguayan independence, and his leadership of the Colorado party gave stability to the political system at a period of national crisis.

Further Reading

Fructuoso Rivera is listed in the Latin America study guide (IV, N, 1, a). Other Uruguayan political leaders were Juan Antonio LAVALLEJA, José BATLLE, and Gabriel TERRA.

Works in English referring to Rivera are Philip Bates Taylor, *The Executive Power in Uruguay* (1951), and John Street, *Artigas and the Emancipation of Uruguay* (1959).

J. E. **RIVERA** / By John D. Martz

José Eustacio Rivera (1888–1928) was a Colombian novelist. He brought fresh vision to national literature and with "La vorágine" wrote perhaps the finest novel of the Latin American tropics.

Born in the southern Colombian town of Neiva, José Eustacio Rivera came from a provincial family of modest means. After becoming one of the first graduates of the recently organized teachers' college, he took a degree in law. For several years Rivera combined a law practice with modest literary activities and became a recognized member of Bogotá's urban intelligentsia. Named legal adviser and member of the Venezuela-Colombia Boundary Commission, he traveled first to the plains and then to the Amazon region. Exposed to these less well-known regions of the country, he lived with the Indians, for a time was lost in the jungle, and eventually contracted beriberi. During a period of convalescence he wrote *La vorágine* (*The Vortex*), one of the greatest Latin American novels. Its publication in 1924 assured Rivera lasting fame throughout the hemisphere and beyond, and it was translated into English, French, German, and Russian.

The Vortex, a kind of romantic allegory, was also a novel of protest. It was the first realistic description by a Colombian of the cowherders of the plains and the jungle rubber workers. Rivera attempted to arouse humanitarian feelings concerning the exploitation of these people, and he reflected a cultured urban gentleman's frightened vision of the barbarism foisted on them. The story is dominated by the magnificent yet savage setting, in which there is no law other than survival of the fittest.

Arturo Cova, the protagonist of the novel, is an urban man of letters who, forced to flee from Bogotá, encounters the brutal reality of life in the rural areas. Rivera's experience in the Amazonian jungle permits him to describe the tragedy of rubber exploitation. In publicizing the condition of the workers and their degradation at the hands of Colombian and European adventurers, Rivera provides an impassioned image of decay, death, and violence. *The Vortex*, a work romantic in spirit and poetic in style, strongly suggests that the veneer of civilization is thin. For Rivera, civilization should not be taken for granted.

Gaining swift recognition with his novel, Rivera was widely hailed both at home and abroad. While still enjoying his literary triumph during a trip to the United States, he died prematurely of pneumonia in New York City. He also authored one collection of poetry, *Tierra de promisión* (1921), and a volume of sonnets and at his death left an unpublished drama in verse.

Further Reading

José Eustacio Rivera is listed in the Latin America study guide (IV, F, 2). The Brazilian novelist Jorge AMADO took a similar interest in the life of the workingman, and the Brazilian sociologist Gilberto FREYRE studied the behavior of all classes.

The only extended critical treatments of Rivera are in Spanish. Literary surveys in English which include passages on Rivera are Arturo Torres-Ríoseco, *The Epic of Latin American Literature* (1942; rev. ed. 1946), and Jean Franco, *The Modern Culture of Latin America: Society and the Artist* (1967).

José Eustacio Rivera. (Bibliothèque Nationale, Paris)

RIZAL / By Epifanio San Juan, Jr.

José Rizal (1861–1896) was a national hero of the Philippines and the first Asian nationalist. He expressed the growing national consciousness of many Filipinos who opposed Spanish colonial tyranny and aspired to attain democratic rights.

José Rizal (pronounced rē-säl′) was born in Calamba, Laguna, on June 19, 1861, to a well-to-do family. He studied at the Jesuit Ateneo Municipal in Manila and won many literary honors and prizes. He obtained a bachelor of arts degree with highest honors in 1877. For a time he studied at the University of Santo Tomas, and in 1882 he left for Spain to enter the Central University of Madrid, where he completed his medical and humanistic studies.

Gadfly and Propagandist

In Spain, Rizal composed his sociohistorical novel *Noli me tangere* (1887), which reflected the sufferings of his countrymen under Spanish feudal despotism and their rebellion. His mother had been a victim of gross injustice at the hands of a vindictive Spanish official of the *guardia civil*. Because Rizal satirized the ruling friar caste and severely criticized the iniquitous social structure in the Philippines, his book was banned and its readers punished. He replied to his censors with searing lampoons and diatribes, such as *La vision de Fray Rodriguez* and *Por telefono*. Writing for the Filipino

José Rizal. (Library of Congress)

propaganda newspaper *La Solidaridad*, edited by Filipino intellectuals in Spain, Rizal fashioned perceptive historical critiques like *La indolencia de los Filipinos* (The Indolence of the Filipinos) and *Filipinas dentro de cien años* (The Philippines a Century Hence) and wrote numerous polemical pieces in response to current events.

Of decisive importance to the development of Rizal's political thought was the age-old agrarian trouble in his hometown in 1887–1892. The people of Calamba, including Rizal's family, who were tenants of an estate owned by the Dominican friars, submitted a "memorial" to the government on Jan. 8, 1888, listing their complaints and grievances about their exploitation by the religious corporation. After a long court litigation, the tenants lost their case, and Governor Valeriano Weyler, the "butcher of Cuba," ordered troops to expel the tenants from their ancestral farms at gunpoint and burn the houses. Among the victims were Rizal's father and three sisters, who were later deported.

Rizal arrived home on Aug. 5, 1887, but after 6 months he left for Europe in the belief that his presence in the Philippines was endangering his relatives. The crisis in Calamba together with the 1888 petition of many Filipinos against rampant abuses by the friars registered a collective impact in Rizal's sequel to his first book, *El filibusterismo* (1891).

Rizal's primary intention in both books is expressed in a letter to a friend (although this specifically refers to the first book): "I have endeavored to answer the calumnies which for centuries had been heaped on us and our country; I have described the social condition, the life,

our beliefs, our hopes, our desires, our grievances, our griefs; I have unmasked hypocrisy which, under the guise of religion, came to impoverish and to brutalize us. . . ." In *El filibusterismo*, Rizal predicted the outbreak of a mass peasant revolution by showing how the bourgeois individualist hero of both novels, who is the product of the decadent feudal system, works only for his personal and diabolic interests. Rizal perceived the internal contradictions of the system as the source of social development concretely manifested in the class struggle.

Prison and Exile

Anguished at the plight of his family, Rizal rushed to Hong Kong for the purpose of ultimately going back to Manila. Here he conceived the idea of establishing a Filipino colony in Borneo and drafted the constitution of the Liga Filipina (Philippine League), a reformist civic association designed to promote national unity and liberalism. The Liga, founded on July 3, 1892, did not survive, though it inspired Andres Bonifacio, a Manila worker, to organize the first Filipino revolutionary party, the Katipunan, which spearheaded the 1896 revolution against Spain. Rizal was arrested and deported to Dapitan, Mindanao, on July 7, 1892.

For 4 years Rizal remained in exile in Dapitan, where he practiced ophthalmology, built a school and waterworks, planned town improvements, wrote, and carried out scientific experiments. Then he successfully petitioned the Spanish government to join the Spanish army in Cuba as a surgeon; but on his way to Spain to enlist, the Philippine revolution broke out, and Rizal was returned from Spain, imprisoned, and tried for false charges of treason and complicity with the revolution. His enemies in the government and Church were operating behind the scenes, and he was convicted. The day before he was executed he wrote to a friend: "I am innocent of the crime of rebellion. So I am going to die with a tranquil conscience."

The day of Rizal's execution, Dec. 30, 1896, signifies for many Filipinos the turning point in the long history of Spanish domination and the rise of a revolutionary people desiring freedom, independence, and justice. Rizal still continues to inspire the people, especially the peasants, workers, and intellectuals, by his exemplary selflessness and intense patriotic devotion. His radical humanist outlook forms part of the ideology of national democracy which Filipino nationalists today consider the objective of their revolutionary struggle.

Further Reading

José Rizal is listed in the Asia study guide (IV, C, 2). Andres BONIFACIO was also a Philippine revolutionary.

Among the many books on Rizal, the following are reliable: Austin Craig, *Lineage, Life and Labors of José Rizal* (1913); Carlos Quirino, *The Great Malayan* (1940); Camilo Osias, *José Rizal: Life and Times* (1949); Rafael Palma, *The Pride of the Malay Race* (trans. 1949); Leon Maria Guerrero, *The First Filipino* (1963); Austin Coates, *Rizal* (1969); and Gregorio Zaide, *José Rizal* (1970).

Recommended for general background is Gregorio Zaide, *Philippine Political and Cultural History* (1949; rev. ed. 1957).

* * *

ROBBE-GRILLET

/ **By Frederick R. Benson
and Jane Rosenbaum**

The French novelist Alain Robbe-Grillet (born 1922) achieved fame for his innovative techniques in writing fiction. Influential in avant-garde Paris intellectual circles, his controversial critical theories regarding the concept of the modern novel were fulfilled in his own narratives.

Born in Brest, Alain Robbe-Grillet (pronounced rôb grē-yĕ′) was educated at the Lycées Buffon and St. Louis in Paris and at the Lycée de Brest. Having received his engineering degree from the National Agricultural Institute of France, he pursued a scientific career as an officer at the National Institute of Statistics in Paris from 1945 to 1948. Later, as an agronomist for the French Institute of Colonial Agriculture, he traveled extensively in the tropics, particularly Morocco, Martinique, and French Guinea, for 3 years. Robbe-Grillet joined the publishing house of Minuit as a literary director in 1955, married 2 years after, and was subsequently named a member of the High Committee for the Preservation and Expansion of the French Language.

Robbe-Grillet and his coterie—a select literary group composed of Nathalie Sarraute, Michel Butor, Bruce Morrissette, and Claude Simon—opposed the bourgeois, or Balzacian, novel of humanist tradition, preferring the geometrical precision and clinical exactitude of a scientific-literary approach. Robbe-Grillet, in particular, demonstrates a post-Sartrean sense of the alienated character and claims as the inspiration for his novels "the first fifty pages of Camus's *The Stranger* and the works of Raymond Rousset" (the latter is a little-known author who died in the 1930s). Critical analysis has also recognized the profound impact of the novels of Franz Kafka and Graham Greene on his work.

Known as the first "cubist" novelist and a "chosist," for his obsessive focus on inanimate objects, Robbe-Grillet initially described the *nouveau roman* and became the leading exponent of the New Wave in contemporary French literature. His revolutionary theories are based on the premise that man's perception of his milieu is distorted by his bourgeois background and its resulting emotionalism. Condemning the metaphorical phrasing of many existentialists, Robbe-Grillet attempts to illustrate in his fiction that all illusionary language falsely indicates a possible relationship between man and the material universe. The world is not man's domain, the novelist's essays and narratives insist, and objects exist independently of the transitory emotional content of human life. Characterized by an objective accuracy in its detailed descriptions, his writing is bare of intangible, inferential adjectives.

The Erasers (1953), Robbe-Grillet's first novel, appears to be a conventional detective thriller but thematically reworks Sophocles's *Oedipus Rex*. Intended as a comic parody, the narrative illustrates the chosist technique in its intense focus on the india rubber of the title as an antisymbol. *Le Voyeur* (1955) explores, without either conversation or interior monologue, the psychology of a rapist. The exaggerated realism of the physical descriptions imposes a dreamlike air of surrealism on this work.

The past, present, and future are juxtaposed in *Jealousy* (1957), an experiment with time and space elements, and humanity is characterized by mere behavior patterns, the identity of individuals being refined out of existence. The potential lushness of its tropical setting, based on Robbe-Grillet's equatorial travels, is deliberately reduced to a monochrome of color, measured distance, and tone and shape, with photographic precision. The antisymbol appears again, this time in the form of a centipede that to the nameless hero represents the image of jealousy itself. All indications of the subjective eye of the author are removed, resulting in a new literary mode. *In the Labyrinth* (1959) emphasizes the cinematic play of light and shadow over an endless expanse of snow. The Antonioni-like monotony of the landscape is reflected in the rhythm of language, and an unconventional attempt

Alain Robbe-Grillet. (French Cultural Services of the French Embassy)

is made to suggest inner reality through the external vision.

Robbe-Grillet's finest effort may be the film scenario *Last Year at Marienbad* (1961), which reads like a novel and is written in the "continuous present." The film, directed by Alain Resnais, created considerable critical controversy and captured the Golden Lion Award at the Venice Film Festival. In this scenario, the most objectively pictorial of Robbe-Grillet's fiction, space has been created as a function of psychological time, and the internal conscious reality exists in terms of external objects with endless repetitions of long, empty corridors, baroque ceilings, mirrored walls, and formal gardens. The suprising commercial success of the film permitted its author to undertake other cinema efforts, notably *The Immortal* (1963) and *Trans-Europe Express* (1967). He also published *Towards a New Novel* (1962), a widely acclaimed collection of essays in which he defends his literary thesis against those who say it lacks humanity.

Further Reading

Alain Robbe-Grillet is listed in the Literature study guide (III, J, 1, b). He was influenced by Albert CAMUS, Jean Paul SARTRE, Franz KAFKA, and Graham GREENE.

A full-length study of Robbe-Grillet in English is Ben F. Stoltzfus, *Alain Robbe-Grillet and the New French Novel* (1964). See also Bruce Morrissette, *Alain Robbe-Grillet* (1965). Robbe-Grillet is discussed in John Sturrock, *The French New Novel* (1969).

* * *

A Madonna and Child by Luca della Robbia, in the Museo Nazionale, Florence. (Alinari-Brogi)

ROBBIA / By Eleanor Dodge Barton

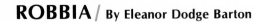

The Florentine sculptor Luca della Robbia (1399/1400–1482) is usually remembered for his singularly lovely images of the Madonna and Child in glazed terra-cotta.

Luca della Robbia (pronounced lōō′kä dĕl′lä rōb′byä) was praised by his compatriot Leon Battista Alberti for genius comparable to that of the sculptors Donatello and Lorenzo Ghiberti, the architect Filippo Brunelleschi, and the painter Masaccio. By ranking him with contemporary artists of this stature, Alberti reminds us of the interest and strength of Luca's work in marble and bronze, as well as in the terra-cottas always associated with his name.

There are no certain details of Luca della Robbia's youth, training, or early sculpture, and many of his most popular later works cannot be dated absolutely. He was born in Florence. His first documented commission, the marble *Singing Gallery* (1431–1438) for the Cathedral of Florence, proves that he must have been an accomplished artist long before joining the Sculptors' Guild in 1432. The *Singing Gallery* shows children singing, dancing, and making music to "praise the Lord" in the words

of Psalm 150. Their figures are at once lively, finely observed, and gracefully combined in groups designed to fit the 10 panels of the gallery.

In the next 2 decades Luca executed important commissions in marble and bronze: a series of marble reliefs (1437) for the bell tower of the Cathedral of Florence; a marble and enameled terra-cotta tabernacle (1443), now in S. Maria in Peretola; bronze angels to enrich the *Singing Gallery*; and, in collaboration with Michelozzo, the large project of bronze doors for the Sacristy of the Cathedral. These doors were not finished until 1469; their reliance on a few figures placed in simple, orderly compositions against a flat ground contrasts sharply with the elaborate pictorial effects of Ghiberti's more famous Baptistery doors.

Although the data of Luca's first work in colored, glazed terra-cotta is not known, his control of this medium was clearly enough recognized to justify two major commissions for the Cathedral of Florence: the large reliefs *Resurrection* (1445) and *Ascension of Christ* (1446). The pliant medium of baked clay covered with a "slip" of vitrified lead and refired permitted a lustrous, polished surface capable of reflecting light and using color that was beautifully appropriate for architectural sculpture. Whether animating the vast, somber space of the Cathedral or in the series *Twelve Apostles* gracing the pristine surfaces of the small Pazzi Chapel (1443–1450) in Florence, Luca's reliefs in this medium achieved a perfection never before or since attained.

Working with assistants, including members of his own family, Luca produced a number of decorative reliefs and altarpieces until the end of his life. One of the finest and richest examples is the enameled terra-cotta ceiling (1466) of the Chapel of the Cardinal of Portugal in S. Miniato, Florence. Luca della Robbia died in Florence in February 1482.

Further Reading

Luca della Robbia is listed in the Art study guide (III, B, 2). He collaborated on occasion with MICHELOZZO. Luca was influenced by Jacopo della QUERCIA and Lorenzo GHIBERTI but most importantly by DONATELLO.

Allan Marquand, *Luca della Robbia* (1914), remains the most important and readable monograph on the artist. The earliest account of Luca della Robbia, in Giorgio Vasari, *Lives of the Most Eminent Painters, Sculptors and Architects*, vol. 2, translated by Gaston De Vere (1914), is sympathetic but should be supplemented by Charles Seymour's more recent *Sculpture in Italy, 1400–1500* (1966).

ROBERT I / By Richard W. Pfaff

Robert I (1274–1329), or Robert Bruce, was king of Scotland from 1306 to 1329. Leader of the successful resistance to the threat of English domination of his country, Bruce is regarded as one of the great patriots of Scottish history.

R obert Bruce was the eighth male to bear that name in a direct line going back to the first Robert, who probably took part in the Norman conquest of England and died about 1094. The family subsequently gained considerable lands and prominence in Scotland. The fifth Robert Bruce (died 1245) married the niece of King William, "the Lion," thus establishing a possible claim, albeit a distant one, to the Scottish throne. This claim was advanced by the sixth Robert on the highly complicated succession quarrel that arose in Scotland in 1290. William the Lion's grandson, Alexander III, had died in 1286, leaving as direct heir only a 3-year old granddaughter, Margaret, the "Maid of Norway" (her father was king of Norway). The problems of how to manage the minority reign of a small girl were grave enough, but when she died suddenly in 1290, some 13 competitors claimed to be her rightful successor as monarch of Scotland.

In this situation the commanding nature of England's king, Edward I, was the decisive factor. Any choice opposed by Edward would most likely be untenable, and the question was submitted to him for arbitration. The claims of two competitors clearly stood out: John Balliol,

great-grandson of a brother of William the Lion by an eldest daughter; and Robert Bruce (VI), grandson by a younger daughter. Edward decided for Balliol; but before issuing his decision, he took oaths of allegiance from all the claimants, including Robert Bruce (VI) as well as his son Robert (VII).

This seventh Robert was the father of the patriotic leader and future king of Scotland; but, as has been seen, the position of the Bruces was originally that of appellants to, and sworn men of, the English king. Edward's decision had by no means settled the situation in Scotland. Balliol, suspected by the Scots of being an English puppet and by Edward of forswearing his oath, could not rule effectively, and the situation was complicated by the alliance of Scotland with France, an enemy of England. From 1296 Balliol was no longer a factor, and the only choices were direct English domination or Scottish independence, which meant war with England. William Wallace emerged as the leader of the Scottish resistance, winning a great victory at Stirling Bridge in 1297; but he was in turn defeated by Edward at Falkirk the following year, and though he kept up sporadic guerrilla warfare until his capture and execution in 1305, he was no longer a serious threat to the English. Besides, Wallace's movement was, nominally, to restore Balliol, a cause uncongenial to many of the leading Scots.

His Accession

Robert Bruce the eighth (hereafter called just Bruce) first emerged importantly as one of the "guardians" of the kingdom in December 1298, ostensibly on behalf of Edward I. The other principal guardian was John Comyn, nicknamed "The Red," whose affinity with the house of Balliol led to a lasting quarrel with Bruce from at least 1299. Bruce resigned as guardian in 1300, and though on the surface he was at peace with Edward, it is likely that he was thinking of the crown, especially after the death of his father (who had earlier transferred the Bruce claim to him) in 1304. He had apparently entered into a secret alliance with the patriotic Bishop Lamberton of St. Andrews, and perhaps through fear that his plans would be disclosed, he killed Comyn the Red in a church in Dumfries in February 1306. This violent and probably unpremeditated deed at once pushed Bruce to the head of the Scottish resistance. Within 6 weeks he was crowned as Robert I, King of Scotland.

In England, Edward I reacted strongly to the news and at the famous "Feast of Swans" swore to avenge Comyn's death and destroy Bruce (who had also been excommunicated by the Pope for profaning the church at Dumfries). Bruce was immediately in trouble from the well-led English forces, as well as from the adherents of Comyn, and soon found himself a king apparently without a following, hiding in the western highlands, or even in Ireland. But the long final illness and death of Edward I in 1307 marked a turning point. The new English king, Edward II, was from the first unpopular with his nobility and, as a military leader, was beneath comparison with his father. From spring 1307 Bruce's fortunes began to revive. Edward II was vacillating and indecisive in his ac-

Stirling Castle, near Bannockburn, Scotland, captured from the English in June 1314 by King Robert I of Scotland. (Radio Times Hulton Picture Library)

tions, and Bruce was able to make headway against both the English and his remaining Scottish enemies. In March 1309 a truce was made with England, whose holdings in Scotland were reduced to only a few castles.

In the next few years expeditions were made into the northern parts of England, and the last possession of the English in Scotland, Stirling Castle, was heavily besieged. In a concerted effort to remedy the situation, Edward II in 1314 led a large army to the relief of Stirling, but it was defeated by Bruce and his outnumbered Scots at the Battle of Bannockburn. The English fled in confusion, and Bruce was undisputed master of his country. Though tensions with England continued, there was no further major threat from the English in Bruce's lifetime; nor was there further serious dissension in Scotland.

From 1309 Bruce was holding parliaments and could attend in a systematic way to the government of the country. Parliament addressed itself to the succession problem in 1315, 1318 (when Bruce's brother and heir presumptive, Edward, was killed in Ireland), and 1326 (after the birth 2 years earlier of Bruce's first son and eventual successor, David). Bruce's relations with the papacy remained strained, until the papal refusal to recognize Bruce as king was reversed by John XXII in 1328. The Scottish hierarchy had consistently supported the King. In his later years Bruce suffered from what was called, and may have been, leprosy. He died at his country estate at Cardross in June 1329, just before the marriage of his son David to the sister of the new English king, Edward III, as the final provision of a peace treaty between the two countries.

Further Reading

Robert I is listed in the European History study guide (III, D, 1, a; III, E, 1, a). He was opposed by EDWARD I and EDWARD II.

John Barbour's long poem, *The Bruce* (ca. 1375; modern translation by Archibald A. H. Douglas, 1964), is the principal narrative source. The major modern work on Robert I is G. W. S. Barrow, *Robert Bruce and the Community of the Realm of Scotland* (1965). Older studies are Sir Herbert Maxwell, *Robert the Bruce and the Struggle for Scottish Independence* (1898), and Agnes Mure Mackenzie, *Robert Bruce: King of Scots* (1934). For historical background see William Croft Dickinson, *A New History of Scotland*, vol. 1 (1961; 2d ed. 1965).

ROBERT II / By Richard W. Pfaff

Robert II (1316–1390) was king of Scotland from 1371 to 1390. For many years heir presumptive to David II and frequently regent of the kingdom, Robert is important primarily for his role in Scottish affairs before he came to the throne.

Robert Steward (or Stewart) was the son of Walter Steward (the third of that name in a line stretching back to Walter "the Steward," ca. 1158) and Marjorie Bruce (daughter of Robert Bruce, who had become Robert I of Scotland in 1306). As early as 1318 the Scottish Parliament declared Robert Steward heir presumptive if the male line of Bruce should die out.

Robert first came to prominence at the battle of Halidon in 1333, where he was one of the commanders of the losing Scottish side and was in consequence dispossessed of his estates by Edward Balliol, the English-supported rival to Robert Bruce's son David II (born 1324; reigned 1329–1371). Robert Steward was among the leaders of the successful resistance to the puppet regime of Balliol and, as principal regent from 1338, paved the way for David's return 3 years later.

However, no love was lost between the two men (Robert being David's nephew and heir presumptive as well as being older and having controlled the regency), and contemporaries suspected that Robert treacherously fled the field at the crucial battle of Neville's Cross in 1346, at which David was taken prisoner by the English. Robert was again regent, for 11 years, but David's release in 1357 (obtained by a promise to pay a crushing ransom to the English) put him out of power, and in 1363 Steward joined a conspiracy against the King. This was unsuccessful, however, and David's attempt to get his ransom lowered by settling the Scottish crown on the English royal family (thus effectively disinheriting Robert) sealed the enmity between the two. Parliament rejected David's proposal, and on the King's death in 1371 Robert succeeded to the throne as Robert II.

The new king seems to have played very little part in the important events of his reign, being overshadowed by two of his many sons, first the Earl of Carrick (the future Robert III) and then the Earl of Fife. Robert was uninterested in, and powerless to stop, the renewed and increasingly bitter hostilities between the English and the Scots (the latter egged on by the French) culminating in the burning of Edinburgh in 1385 and the Scottish victory at Otterburn 3 years later. It is conjectured that Robert, now an old man, suffered physical, and perhaps mental, decline; and he had been put under a guardianship, tantamount to deposition, a few months before his death in

The seal of King Robert II of Scotland, showing the King astride a charger. (Trustees of The British Museum)

1390. He left a troubled succession, a quarrelsome and turbulent nobility, and a tradition of weak and largely ineffective kingship, all of which were to plague his country during the subsequent century.

Further Reading

Robert II is listed in the European History study guide (III, E, 1, b). He was succeeded by ROBERT III.

There is no work solely on Robert II or his reign. The standard histories of Scotland give background information about his times: P. Hume Brown, *History of Scotland*, vol. 1 (1899), and William Croft Dickinson, *A New History of Scotland*, vol. 1 (1961; 2d ed. 1965).

ROBERT III / By Richard W. Pfaff

> Robert III (ca. 1337–1406) was king of Scotland from 1390 to 1406. Notable as king primarily for the weakness of his reign, he played a larger part in the affairs of the kingdom before his accession than as monarch.

The future Robert III (actually christened John) was born some years before the marriage of his parents, Robert Steward (who was to become king as Robert II in 1371) and Elizabeth Mure. The children of this union were subsequently legitimized, by papal dispensation, in 1347, the young John being styled Lord of Kyle. He was made Earl of Atholl by the King in 1367 and Earl of Carrick (as he is usually referred to) in 1368.

On the accession of Robert II in 1371, the Scottish Parliament, to forestall any possible doubts about legitimacy, firmly established the succession on Carrick and his line and, failing that, on his brothers. Carrick seems to have played an important part in the early years of his father's reign, negotiating with John of Gaunt in 1380 and being directed to restore order in the Highlands in 1384. But a kick from a horse, apparently sometime after 1385 (though some historians place it earlier), resulted in a disability and perhaps even a lifelong weakness, for in 1388 Carrick was relieved of his responsibilities in favor of his next surviving brother, Robert, Earl of Fife.

Nonetheless, on the death of Robert II, Carrick succeeded, taking as his regnal name Robert. The Earl of Fife continued, however, as the chief power in the kingdom. The new king's reign was constantly troubled by the lawlessness of great lords and the quarrels of clans, especially the celebrated combat between 30 men each of the clans Kay and Quele. Apparently, Fife's influence waned after 1393, and in 1399 the King's elder son, David, was appointed by the General Council as "lieutenant" of the kingdom for 3 years.

This young man had been created Duke of Rothesay the previous year, his uncle, the Earl of Fife, becoming Duke of Albany at the same time (the first dukes in Scotland). The rivalry between these two was a prime factor in the fortunes of the country during the next 3 troubled

The seal of King Robert III of Scotland, showing the ruler enthroned. (Trustees of The British Museum)

famous of the Norman brothers, members of the Hauteville family, who entered the wars of southern Italy and carved out important principalities for themselves.

Of the early life in Normandy of Robert Guiscard (pronounced rô-bâr′ gēs-kár′), very little is known. In the 1030s his older brothers William, Drogo, and Humphrey went to southern Italy to serve as mercenary captains in the numerous wars between Lombards and Byzantine Greeks. Within 2 decades they had begun to establish themselves in castles and to carry great weight in the affairs of their adopted homeland. In 1046 Robert came to Italy to join them. Robert received no immediate benefits, and he, like other Norman knights ambitious for land and wealth in southern Italy, had to occupy himself in the many military campaigns and small battles that filled its 11th-century history. In 1049 Robert's brother Drogo offered him a castle in Calabria, and for the next 4 years Robert lived a life of brigandage and robbery, earning for himself the nickname Guiscard, the "Crafty One," which he was to retain throughout his life.

Robert came out of Calabria in 1053, when a papal army, backed by the forces of the German emperor, threatened the Norman possessions in the south. In the battle of Civitate in that year, the forces of Norman-controlled Apulia crushed the armies of Pope Leo IX and won papal recognition for their conquests in the south. Robert spent the next 2 years completing the conquest of the last Byzantine lands in Italy. In 1057 Robert's brother Humphrey, Count of Apulia, died, and Robert, by now the most renowned leader of the Normans, succeeded him. To his younger brother Roger, Robert gave the task of driving the Arabs out of Sicily and adding the island to his possessions.

In 1059 Pope Nicholas II formally confirmed Robert's titles: Duke of Apulia and Calabria and Duke of Sicily, although the island had not yet been conquered. Robert, in his turn, swore an oath of loyalty to the Pope and agreed to pay tribute. In the brief space of 6 years the Norman-papal relations had been reversed. Instead of thieves and usurpers, the Normans were now loyal and faithful papal vassals, servants and allies of the Church. By 1060 Robert and Roger had expelled the Greeks from all of southern Italy except Bari, and they now concentrated upon the conquest of Sicily. This task took 30 years, years that Robert spent in suppressing revolts in Apulia and Calabria and in pressing the remaining Byzantine stronghold at Bari. In 1071 Bari fell to Robert, and the last Byzantine enclave in the West was lost. In the same year Norman forces finally captured Palermo, the capital of Sicily, and in 1072 Robert entered his new domains in triumph.

After dealing with yet another rebellion and surviving a protracted illness, Robert renewed his attempts to crush pockets of resistance to his rule. In 1077 he conquered Salerno, and in 1080, after years of disputes, wrangling over rights, and personal insults, Robert renewed his

years. Resistance to the demands of the new English king, Henry IV, to have his overlordship of Scotland recognized was weakened by treachery and dissension among the leading magnates. Finally in 1402 Rothesay, whose profligacy had earned him many enemies, was arrested by order of his uncle and died in prison shortly afterward.

In all these events Robert III was virtually a cipher. Probably seeing, and fearing, the unbreakable ascendancy of Albany (lieutenant of the kingdom from 1402), the King sent his remaining son, James (born 1394), to France in 1406; but the young boy was intercepted by kidnapers and handed over to the English for a captivity that was to last 18 years. Robert's death followed quickly after the news reached him. He reportedly requested as his epitaph "Here lies the worst of kings and the most miserable of men."

Further Reading

Robert III is listed in the European History study guide (III, E, 1, b). He succeeded ROBERT II.

There is no work solely on Robert III or his reign. Background information on his times is given in standard histories of Scotland; recommended is William Croft Dickinson, *A New History of Scotland*, vol. 1 (1961; 2d ed. 1965).

ROBERT GUISCARD
/ By Edward M. Peters

The Norman adventurer Robert Guiscard, Count and Duke of Apulia (1016–1085), was the most

Norman horsemen in battle, a detail from the Bayeux Tapestry. Knights like these, who accompanied William the Conqueror to England in 1066, followed Robert Guiscard to Italy. The tapestry is in the Musee de l'Ancien Évêché, Bayeux, France. (Archives Photographiques, Paris)

oath of loyalty to the papacy in the person of Pope Gregory VII and was in return confirmed in the possession of his lands. From 1080 on, Robert began to form another plan, this time to attack the Byzantine Empire itself, across Greece and the northern Aegean Sea to the very capital city of Constantinople. Throughout 1081 Robert assembled a massive fleet and army at the ports of Brindisi and Bari. In May 1081 Robert's fleet crossed the Adriatic. In a furious battle at Durazzo, Robert defeated the army of the Byzantine emperor Alexius I Comnenus and forced him to retreat. Alexius, however, had instigated a revolt in Apulia, and this revolt, along with an appeal from Pope Gregory VII for aid against the army of the German emperor, Henry IV, recalled Robert to the Italian mainland, where he spent 1082 and 1083 in suppressing the revolt in Apulia and preparing an assault on Rome to rescue the embattled Pope Gregory.

In 1084 Robert attacked the city of Rome, the German defenders fled, and the Normans entered the city and sacked and burned it, taking Pope Gregory with them. Gregory was installed in a palace at Salerno, where he died in May 1085. Several months earlier Robert had returned to the campaign in Greece. He resumed the campaign, which had faltered during his absence, and captured the island of Corfu. After wintering on Corfu, the Norman army was suddenly struck by a ravaging epidemic, possibly typhoid fever, and on July 17, 1085, Robert himself succumbed to it. He was buried at Venosa in Apulia.

Further Reading

Robert Guiscard is listed in the European History study guide (I, J, 2, e; II, H, 1, d). He defeated ALEXIUS I. Robert's son BOHEMUND I was a leader in the First Crusade.

There is no better introduction to Robert Guiscard's life than John Julius Norwich, *The Normans in the South, 1016–1130* (1967), an excellent popular history of Norman expansion in southern Italy. See also David C. Douglas, *The Norman Achievement* (1969), the best survey of Norman activity in France, England, and southern Italy, and Denis Mack Smith, *Medieval Sicily* (1970).

✳ ✳ ✳

ROBERTS / By John E. Flint

The British soldier and field marshal Frederick Sleigh Roberts, 1st Earl Roberts of Kandahar, Pretoria, and Waterford (1832–1914), made his reputation in India and South Africa and then became the last commander in chief of the British army.

Frederick Roberts was born in Cawnpore, India, on Sept. 30, 1832, the son of Gen. Sir Abraham Roberts, a British soldier in Indian service. His family was Anglo-Irish, long settled in Waterford. Roberts was sent to Eton in 1845, entered Sandhurst in 1847, and then attended the East India Company's college at Addiscombe. In 1851 Roberts joined the Bengal Artillery.

Roberts began by serving with his father, who was ex-

Frederick (Lord) Roberts, painted in 1898 by George Frederick Watts. (National Portrait Gallery, London)

perienced in the affairs of the North-West Frontier. During the Indian mutiny, Roberts was at the siege of Delhi and at the second relief of Lucknow and won the Victoria Cross at Khudaganj in January 1858. During the years that followed, he rose steadily in rank, and he was involved in the 1860s and 1870s with the affairs of the North-West Frontier, although in 1868 he accompanied Sir Robert Napier on the British expedition to Ethiopia. During this time Roberts became an advocate of a "forward policy" toward Afghanistan, arguing for control of that country in order to check a supposed Russian threat to India.

In 1876 Lord Lytton became viceroy of India, and Roberts's influence increased. In 1878 he took command of the Punjab Frontier Force and in autumn headed one of the columns that invaded Afghanistan following the Emir's rejection of a British envoy while welcoming a Russian one. The Emir was deposed in 1878, and his successor signed a treaty with the British in 1879. In the previous year Roberts had been promoted to major general and knighted. In September 1879 Sir Louis Cavagnari

was murdered while on a mission to Kabul, and this led to the dispatch of Roberts and another British invasion of Afghanistan. Kabul was taken, and another Emir was installed on the throne. But the Afghans continued to resist, and in July 1880 they wiped out half a British brigade at Maiwand. Roberts force-marched his troops from Kabul and defeated the Afghans definitively at Kandahar in September, a victory that made him a popular hero in England, where he was feted after being given a baronetcy and made commander in chief of the Madras army (1881). Roberts tried unsuccessfully to persuade the government of William Gladstone to annex Kandahar.

In 1885 Roberts was named commander in chief in India. For the next 8 years he occupied himself with reorganizing military transport, increasing the training of troops, and developing obsessions about the Russian peril in the North-West Frontier. In 1892 he was created baron. From 1893 to 1895 Roberts held no official post, and he spent his time writing. In May 1895 he was given the rank of field marshal and appointed commander in chief in Ireland, where he served for the next 4 years.

In October 1899 the Boer War began, and the British soon suffered a series of disastrous defeats. Moreover, Roberts's son was killed at Colenso. In December, Roberts was appointed to command the British armies in the Boer War. He arrived in South Africa in January 1900 and immediately began reorganizing the poor transport, increasing the mounted troops, and planning a full-scale invasion of both Boer republics once reinforcements arrived. Roberts resisted pressures to scatter his troops in the relief of beleaguered garrisons, and the British advance began in February. Almost everywhere that the Boers stood to fight they were defeated, and by mid-March Bloemfontein had fallen. On May 31 Roberts's forces entered Johannesburg, and Pretoria fell on June 5. By September the British had occupied most of the towns in the northern Transvaal, and in October President Paul Kruger fled to Europe. The war seemed won, and Roberts returned to a hero's welcome as the man who had quickly reversed the tide and won the war. His reputation was enormous. Queen Victoria gave him an earldom in one of her last acts, and he was made commander in chief of the British army.

In this post, which he held until 1904, Roberts's reputation began to dim. It soon appeared that the Boer War was far from won, and Gen. Kitchener had to face 2 years of guerrilla warfare led by Christian De Wet and Louis Botha. Roberts was then criticized for having concentrated on capturing Boer towns rather than on destroying the Boer armies in the field. At the War Office, Roberts—with his experience drawn entirely from India and his brief stay in South Africa—was put in charge of the organization of the British army. The Esher Commission on the organization of the War Office recommended the abolition of the post of commander in chief in 1903, and Roberts left the post in 1904.

Roberts then devoted his activity to the championing of conscription for home defense, becoming president of the National Service League in 1905. When World War I broke out in 1914, Roberts, then 82 years old, was appointed to command the Indian troops fighting in France. He did not live to reach the Western front, dying of a chill at Saint-Omer on Nov. 14, 1914. He was buried in St. Paul's Cathedral, London, as a national hero.

Further Reading

Lord Roberts is listed in the Asia study guide (II, A, 6, b) and the Africa study guide (VIII, A, 5). Lord KITCHENER served under him in the Boer War.

Among Roberts's own writings, the most important are his *Forty-one Years in India* (2 vols., 1897) and *Speeches and Letters on Imperial Defence* (1906). The best biography, based on Roberts's official and private correspondence, is David James, *Lord Roberts* (1954).

ROBERTSON / By James A. Gherity

The English economist Sir Dennis Holme Robertson (1890–1963) was a major figure in the development of economic theory in the 20th century, particularly in the fields of monetary and business cycle theory and policy.

Dennis Robertson was born on May 23, 1890, the son of the Reverend James Robertson, clergyman and headmaster of Haileybury. Educated at Eton and at Trinity College, Cambridge, Robertson gained through his brilliance an abundance of medals, prizes, and honors. A large part of his first notable book, *A Study of Industrial Fluctuations* (1915), was written at the age of 22, when he was still in his third year of his economic studies. During World War I he served in Egypt and Palestine, winning the Military Cross and, according to rumor, narrowly missing the Victoria Cross.

Robertson was elected fellow of Trinity College in 1914 and reader in economics at Cambridge University in 1930; he remained at Cambridge until 1938. At that time he was named the Sir Ernest Cassel professor of economics at the University of London. He resigned this post in 1944 to return to Cambridge as professor of political economy, a position that he held until his retirement in 1957. He died of a heart attack at Cambridge on April 21, 1963.

A brief assessment of the contributions of any one of the Cambridge economists of the immediate post–World War I period is singularly difficult. The source of the difficulty is in large part in the close working relationship and in the free sharing of ideas among men like Robert-

Sir Dennis Robertson in 1957. (Wide World Photos)

son, A. C. Pigou, R. G. Hawtrey, and John Maynard Keynes. Keynes himself remarked at the difficulty of distinguishing his own original ideas from those of his coworkers. Nevertheless, in Robertson's *Banking Policy and the Price Level* (1926) and a number of articles, most of which are collected in *Economic Fragments* (1931), are to be found, partially concealed by clumsy mathematics and confusing terminology, attempts to work real factors (such as saving and investment) into a discussion that had been previously dominated by purely monetary variables (such as the quantity of money). Also to be found are the origins of period analysis, which became so useful to economists in the following decade.

With the publication of Keynes's *Treatise on Money* (1930) a rift developed between Robertson and Keynes for reasons that are not entirely clear. From this time on, Robertson was particularly critical of and unwilling to accept either Keynesian theory or Keynesian policies. Although it might be argued that his contributions would have been greater had he not approached Keynesian thought as he did, his criticisms did produce positive results. His work contributed to the clarification of the inconsistencies in Keynes's definitions of saving and investment as well as to a better statement of the liquidity preference theory of interest. During World War II Robertson handled financial relations between Great Britain and the United States and played an important role in the Bretton Woods Monetary Conference.

Further Reading

Sir Dennis Robertson is listed in the Social Sciences study guide (VII, C, 1). His theory of the cyclic nature of economics was shared by Joseph A. SCHUMPETER. A. C. PIGOU and John Maynard KEYNES were contemporary economists.

Ben B. Seligman, *Main Currents in Modern Economics: Economic Thought since 1870* (1962), devotes a chapter to Robertson's life and work. Also useful is Terence Wilmot Hutchinson, *A Review of Economic Doctrines, 1870–1929* (1953).

ROBESON / By Lamont H. Yeakey

Paul Leroy Robeson (born 1898) was an American singer, actor, and political activist. He crusaded for equality and justice for black people.

Paul Robeson made his career at a time when second-class citizenship was the norm for all Afro-Americans. Black people were either severely limited in, or totally excluded from, participation in the economic, political, and social institutions of America.

Robeson was born on April 9, 1898, in Princeton, N.J. His father was a runaway slave who fought for the North in the Civil War, put himself through Lincoln University, received a degree in divinity, and pastored a Presbyterian church in Princeton. Paul's mother was a member of the distinguished Bustill family of Philadelphia, which included patriots in the Revolutionary War, helped found the Free African Society, and maintained agents in the Underground Railroad.

At 17 Robeson won a scholarship to Rutgers University, where he was considered an athlete "without equal." He won an incomparable 12 major letters in 4 years. His academic record was also brilliant. He won first prize (for 4 consecutive years) in every speaking competition at college for which he was eligible, and he was elected to Phi Beta Kappa. He engaged in social work in the local black community. After he delivered the commencement class oration, Rutgers honored him as the "perfect type of college man."

Robeson graduated from the Columbia University Law School in 1923 and took a job with a New York law firm. In 1921 he married Eslanda Goode Cardozo; they had one child. Robeson's career as a lawyer ended abruptly

Paul Robeson. (New York Public Library, Schomburg Collection)

when racial hostility in the firm mounted against him. He turned to acting as a career, playing the lead in *All God's Chillun Got Wings* (1924) and *The Emperor Jones* (1925). He augmented his acting by singing spirituals. He was the first to give an entire program of exclusively Afro-American songs in concert, and he was one of the most popular concert singers of his time.

Robeson starred in such stage presentations as *Show Boat* (1928), *Othello*, in London (1930), *Toussaint L'Ouverture* (1934), and *Stevedore* (1935). His *Othello* (1943–1944) ran for 296 performances—a remarkable run for a Shakespearean play on Broadway. His most significant films were *Emperor Jones* (1933), *Show Boat, Song of Freedom* (both 1936), and *Proud Valley* (1939). Charles Gilpin and Robeson, as the first black men to play serious roles on the American stage, opened up this aspect of the theater for blacks. Robeson used his talents not only to entertain but to foster appreciation for the cultural differences among men.

During the 1930s Robeson entertained throughout Europe and America. In 1934 he made the first of several trips to Russia. He spoke out against the Nazis, sang to Loyalist troops during the Spanish Civil War, raised money to fight the Italian invasion of Ethiopia, supported the Committee to Aid China, and became chairman of the Council on African Affairs (which he helped establish in 1937). The most ardent spokesman for cultural black nationalism, and militant against colonialism in Africa, Robeson also continued to fight racial discrimination in America. While World War II raged, he supported the American effort by entertaining soldiers in camps and laborers in war industries.

After the war, Robeson devoted full time to campaigning for the rights of blacks around the world. In the period of anti-Communist hysteria, the American government and many citizens felt threatened by Robeson's crusade for peace and on behalf of exploited peoples. The fact that for over 15 years he was America's most popular black man did not prevent Robeson's being barred from American concert and meeting halls and being denied a passport to travel abroad. During the repressive 1950s Robeson performed in black churches and for trade unions. After 8 years of denial, he won his passport, gave a concert in Carnegie Hall, and published *Here I Stand* in 1958. He went abroad on concert, television, and theater engagements. He returned to America in 1963 in poor health and soon retired. He received numerous honors and awards: the NAACP's Spingarn Medal, several honorary degrees from colleges, the Diction Award from the American Academy of Arts and Letters, numerous citations from labor unions and civic organizations, and the Stalin Peace Prize.

Further Reading

Paul Robeson is listed in the American History study guide (IX, D, 6). Marcus GARVEY was a proponent of black nationalism before World War II.

Robeson's autobiography, *Here I Stand* (1958), remains the best statement explaining his political activism. All of the works on Robeson are somewhat inade-

quate. The best comprehensive account of his life is Marie Seton, *Paul Robeson* (1958). His wife, Eslanda Goode Robeson, wrote a short, colorful biography, *Paul Robeson, Negro* (1930), a personal account of Robeson's early years which strongly reflects her own biases and sentiments. An erroneous and distorted study is Edwin P. Hoyt, *Paul Robeson: The American Othello* (1967).

ROBESPIERRE / By Gordon H. McNeil

The French Revolutionary leader Maximilien François Marie Isidore de Robespierre (1758-1794) was the spokesman for the policies of the dictatorial government that ruled France during the crisis brought on by civil and foreign war.

Maximilien de Robespierre (pronounced rô-bəs-pyâr′) was an early proponent of political democracy. His advanced ideas concerning the application of the revolutionary principle of equality won for him the fervent support of the lower middle and working classes (the *sans-culottes*) and a firm place later in the 19th century in the pantheon of European radical and revolutionary heroes. These ideas and the repressive methods used to implement and defend them, which came to be called the Reign of Terror, and his role as

Maximilien de Robespierre, an ink drawing by F. A. Parseval-Grandmaison, in the Bibliothèque Nationale, Paris. The portrait was done at the meeting of the Convention on 9 Thermidor (July 27, 1794), during which Robespierre was attacked and arrested. (Photo-Hachette)

The execution of Robespierre and his accomplices "who conspired against liberty and equality," a color engraving in the Bibliothèque Nationale, Paris. (Photo-Hachette)

spokesman for this radical and violent phase of the French Revolution also won for him the opprobrium of conservative opponents of the Revolution ever since.

Career before the Revolution

Robespierre was born on May 6, 1758, in the French provincial city of Arras. He was educated first in that city and then at the Collège Louis-le-Grand in Paris. Upon completing his studies with distinction, he took up his father's profession of law in Arras and soon had a successful practice. But he had developed a sense of social justice, and as the Revolution of 1789 loomed, he assumed a public role as an advocate of political change, contributing to the pamphlet and *cahier* literature of the day, and being elected at the age of 30 a member of the Third Estate delegation from Arras to the Estates General, where he quickly associated himself with the Patriot party.

Role in Early Revolution

During the first period of the Revolution (1789–1791), in which the Estates General became the National (or Constituent) Assembly, Robespierre spoke frequently in that body. But his extremely democratic ideas, his emphasis on civil liberty and equality, his uncompromising rigidity in applying these ideas to the issues of the mo-

ment, and his hostility to all authority won him little support in this moderate legislature. He favored giving the vote to all men, not just property owners, and he opposed slavery in the colonies. On both of these issues he lost, being ahead of his time.

Robespierre found more receptive listeners at the Paris Jacobin Club, where throughout his career he had a devoted following that admired him not only for his radical political views but perhaps even more for his simple Spartan life and high sense of personal morality, which won for him the appellation of "the Incorruptible." His appearance was unprepossessing, and his old-fashioned, prerevolutionary style of dress seemed out of place. He lacked the warmth of personality usually associated with a popular political figure. Yet his carefully written and traditionally formal speeches, because of his utter sincerity and deep personal conviction, won him a wide following.

When his term as a legislator ended in September 1791, Robespierre remained in Paris, playing an influential role in the Jacobin Club and shortly founding a weekly political journal. During this period (1791–1792) he was an unremitting critic of the King and the moderates who hoped to make the experiment in limited, constitutional monarchy a success. Robespierre, profoundly and rightly suspicious of the King's intentions, spoke and wrote in opposition to the course of events, until August 1792, when events turned in his favor with the overthrow of the monarchy and the establishment of the First French Republic.

Period in Power

A Convention was quickly elected to perform the task of drafting a constitution, this time for a democratic republic, and to govern the country in the meantime. Robespierre was elected a member for Paris. As a spokesman for the Mountain, the radical Jacobin faction in the Convention, he played a prominent role in the successive controversies that developed. He was an uncompromising antagonist of the deposed king, who was finally placed on trial, convicted, and executed in January 1793.

The moderate Girondin faction had incurred the enmity of Robespierre and the leaders of the Mountain in the process, and for this and other reasons, both personal and political, there followed months of bitter controversy, climaxed by the victory of the Robespierrist faction, aided by the intervention of the Parisian *sans-culottes*, with the expulsion from the Convention and arrest of the Girondins (June 2, 1793) and the execution shortly thereafter of their leaders.

The dual crises of foreign war, in which most of Europe was now fighting against the Revolutionary government in France, and civil war, which threatened to overthrow that government, had led to the creation of the crisis machinery of government, the Reign of Terror. The central authority in this government was the Committee of Public Safety. For the crucial months from mid-1793 to mid-1794 Robespierre was one of the dominant members of and the spokesman for this dictatorial body. Under their energetic leadership the crisis was successfully surmounted, and by the spring of 1794 the threat of civil war had been ended and the French army was winning decisive victories.

Political controversy had continued, however, as Robespierre, having prevailed against the moderate Girondins, now faced new opposition on both the left and the right. The Hébertists, a radical faction that controlled the Paris city government and was particularly responsive to the grievances of the *sans-culottes* concerning wartime shortages and inflation, actively campaigned for rigorous economic controls, which Robespierre opposed. Nor could he support their vigorous anti-Christian campaign and atheistic Religion of Reason. Robespierre and his colleagues on the committee saw them as a threat, and in March 1794 the Hébertist leaders and their allies were tried and executed.

Two weeks later came the turn of the Indulgents, or Dantonists, the moderate Jacobins who, now that the military crisis was ended, felt that the Terror should be relaxed. Georges Jacques Danton, a leading Jacobin and once a close associate of Robespierre, was the most prominent of this group. Robespierre was inflexible, and Danton and those accused with him were convicted and guillotined.

Robespierre and his associates, who included his brother Augustin and his young disciple Louis de Saint-Just, were now in complete control of the national government and seemingly of public opinion. He thus could impose his own ideas concerning the ultimate aims of the Revolution. For him the proper government for France was not simply one based on sovereignty of the people with a democratic franchise, which had been achieved. The final goal was a government based on ethical principles, a Republic of Virtue. He and those of his associates who were truly virtuous would impose such a government, using the machinery of the Terror, which had been streamlined, at Robespierre's insistence, for the purpose. Coupled with this was to be an officially established religion of the Supreme Being, which Robespierre inaugurated in person.

Downfall and Execution

Opposition arose from a variety of sources. There were disaffected Jacobins who had no interest in such a program and had good reason to fear the imposition of such high ethical principles. More and more of the public, now that the military crisis was past, wanted a relaxation, not a heightening, of the Terror. The crisis came in late July 1794. Robespierre spoke in the Convention in vague but threatening terms of the need for another purge in pursuit of his utopian goals. His opponents responded by taking the offensive against him, and on July 27 (9 Thermidor by the Revolutionary calendar) they succeeded in voting his arrest. He and his colleagues were quickly released, however, and they gathered at the city hall to plan a rising of the Parisian *sans-culottes* against the Convention, such as had prevailed on previous occasions. But the opposition leaders rallied their forces and late that night captured Robespierre and his supporters. In the process Robespierre's jaw was fractured by a bullet, probably from his own hand. Having been declared outlaws, they were guillotined the next day. With this event began the period of the Thermidorian Reaction, during which the Terror was ended and France returned to a more moderate government.

Further Reading

Maximilien de Robespierre is listed in the European History study guide (VII, B, 1, b). Among his disciples was Louis de SAINT-JUST.

The best, and classic, work on Robespierre in English is the biography by James M. Thompson, *Robespierre* (2 vols., 1935; repr. 1968). A shorter and more popular study is Thompson's *Robespierre and the French Revolution* (1953). The imaginative fabrication by Henri Beraud, *My Friend Robespierre* (1938), provides a perceptive character analysis.

Robespierre's role as a member of the Committee of Public Safety is summarized in Robert R. Palmer, *Twelve Who Ruled* (1941). Excerpts from widely differing assessments of Robespierre which have been written since the Revolution are compiled by George Rudé in *Robespierre* (1967). The best advocate for Robespierre's cause was Albert Mathiez, who devoted his scholarly career to Robespierre's defense but who never wrote a biography; see, however, his *The Fall of Robespierre and Other Essays* (1927) and *The French Revolution* (1928). A more balanced but not unfriendly estimate of Robespierre's place in the history of the Revolution is in George Lefebvre, *The French Revolution* (2 vols., 1962–1964); and his place in the history of political thought is analyzed in two essays in Alfred Cobban, *Aspects of the French Revolution* (1968).

✳   ✳   ✳

E. A. ROBINSON / By Hyatt H. Waggoner

Edwin Arlington Robinson (1869–1935), American poet and playwright, was a leading literary figure of the early 20th century.

Edwin Arlington Robinson was born in Head Tide, Maine, on Dec. 22, 1869. He grew up in nearby Gardiner, which became the "Tilbury Town" of his poems. The story is told that for many months after his birth his parents called him "the baby" because they had not wanted a boy. The name "Edwin" was pulled from a hat by a stranger who happened to live in Arlington, Mass. Robinson hated his name, for it signified to him the accidental nature of man's fate. After studying at Harvard from 1891 to 1893, he returned to Gardiner.

Robinson published his first volume of poetry, *The Torrent and the Night Before* (1896), at his own expense. His early verse was largely ignored. In 1905 the struggling poet was presented with a way out of his oppressive poverty when President Theodore Roosevelt, who admired *Captain Craig* (1902), secured him a clerkship in the New York City Customs House. He resigned from this post in 1910 to devote himself to writing.

Eventually Robinson found a patron in Mrs. Edward MacDowell, who owned the MacDowell Colony in New

Edwin Arlington Robinson, photographed in 1929 by Pirie MacDonald. (Courtesy of The New-York Historical Society, New York City)

Hampshire; here, from 1911, Robinson spent his summers. His talent was finally recognized with *The Man against the Sky* (1916). His prose dramas, *Van Zorn* (1914) and *The Porcupine* (1915), which anticipate in many ways the plays of T. S. Eliot, are virtually unknown today, yet they are possibly more worthwhile than many of his celebrated long poetic narratives, such as *King Jasper* (1935).

Robinson's late poetry was both symbolic and experimental, but his reputation chiefly rests on the austere, ironic "Tilbury Town" portraits, which express his feeling that all men are "children of the night" who find no star to guide them and get no answers to their questions. "Luke Havergal," "Cliff Klingenhagen," "George Crabbe," "Miniver Cheevy," "Richard Cory," "Reuben Bright," "Bewick Finzer," "Eros Turannos," and "Mr. Flood's Party" remain incisive explorations of early-20th-century despair.

Robinson won the Pulitzer Prize for poetry three times. He died in New York City on April 5, 1935.

Further Reading

Edwin Arlington Robinson is listed in the Literature study guide (I, E, 1, b; I, E, 2, b). Another poet who depicted small-town American life was Edgar Lee MASTERS.

The standard edition of Robinson's verse is the *Collected Poems of Edwin Arlington Robinson* (1937). A shorter edition is *Selected Poems of E. A. Robinson* (1965). His letters are contained in *Selected Letters of Edwin Arlington Robinson* (1940); *Letters of Edwin Arlington Robinson to Howard George Schmitt* (1945); *Untriangulated Stars: Letters ... to Harry deForest Smith, 1890–1905* (1947); and *Edwin Arlington Robinson: Selected Early Poems and Letters* (1960).

Recommended studies of Robinson are Ellsworth Barnard, *Edwin Arlington Robinson: A Critical Study* (1952); Edwin S. Fussell, *Edwin Arlington Robinson: The Literary Background of a Traditional Poet* (1954); Wallace Anderson, *Edwin Arlington Robinson: A Critical Introduction* (1967); and Louis Coxe, *Edwin Arlington Robinson: The Life of Poetry* (1969). See also the section on Robinson in Hyatt H. Waggoner, *American Poets from the Puritans to the Present* (1968).

✳   ✳   ✳

J. ROBINSON / By David Voigt

Jack Roosevelt Robinson (1919–1972) was the first American Negro of the 20th century to play major league baseball.

Jackie Robinson was born on Jan. 31, 1919, in Cairo, Ga., the son of a sharecropper. After his father deserted his mother, the family moved in 1920 to Los Angeles. Robinson attended Muir Technical High School, where his athletic feats opened college

Jackie Robinson. (National Archives, Washington, D.C.)

doors. At Pasadena Junior College and at the University of California at Los Angeles, he won acclaim in basketball, football, and baseball. In 1941, when family financial problems forced him to leave the University of California without a degree, he played professional football. In 1942 he enlisted in the Army and in 1943 was commissioned a second lieutenant. He served as a morale officer, and his opposition to racial discrimination led to a court-martial for insubordination, but he was acquitted.

In 1944 Robinson began a professional baseball career, playing with the Kansas City Monarchs of the Negro Major League. His performance in the east-west championship games (1945) interested Branch Rickey, general manager of the Brooklyn Dodgers, who was scouting Negro players. A baseball innovator, Rickey knew that civil rights laws would soon end segregation in major league baseball, and he chose Robinson as a test case for integrating the sport. In 1946 Robinson signed a Dodger contract and was assigned to the Montreal team of the International League. Cautioned to prove himself worthy because other black players' futures depended on his success, Robinson maintained a subdued posture. He achieved stardom with the Dodgers, a team he joined in 1947, and in 1949 won the National League's batting championship and its Most Valuable Player Award.

With the admission of other black players to baseball, Robinson began to aggressively advocate more honest integration. His exposés of racial prejudice in baseball helped better the lot of black players but also branded him a troublemaker. He retired from the sport in 1956 and went into business. His lifetime batting average of .311 and his leadership prompted sportswriters in 1962 to vote him membership in Baseball's Hall of Fame.

As a businessman, Robinson fought for increased civil rights and economic opportunity for black Americans. For his civil rights work he received the Spingarn Medal from the National Association for the Advancement of Colored People in 1956. He died suddenly on Oct. 24, 1972, in Stamford, Conn.

Further Reading

Jackie Robinson is listed in the American History study guide (X, F, 4). Track star Jesse OWENS and boxing champion Joe LOUIS were prominent black athletes of the 20th century.

Five semiautobiographies deal with Robinson's career, of which Carl T. Rowan with Jackie Robinson, *Wait till Next Year: The Life Story of Jackie Robinson* (1960), is a candid portrayal. With other sportswriters Robinson coauthored *Jackie Robinson: My Own Story* (1948); *Jackie Robinson* (1950); *Baseball Has Done It*, edited by Charles Dexter (1964); and *Breakthrough to the Big League* (1965). Rickey's role in Robinson's breakthrough is described in Arthur Mann, *Branch Rickey: American in Action* (1957), and Branch Rickey, *The American Diamond* (1965). Richard Bardolph, *The Negro Vanguard* (1959), places Robinson's contribution in the context of the black civil rights movement, and David Q. Voigt, *American Baseball* (2 vols., 1966–1970), places him in the general history of baseball.

JAMES HARVEY **ROBINSON**
/ By Dwight W. Hoover

James Harvey Robinson (1863–1936), American historian, was the central figure in the New History movement, which attempted to use history to understand contemporary problems.

James Harvey Robinson was born on June 29, 1863, in Bloomington, Ill., the son of a local banker. He received his bachelor's and master's degrees from Harvard and did his doctoral work at the University of Freiburg. There he studied under Hermann von Holst, the constitutional historian, and wrote a dissertation on the Federal principle in the American constitution.

Robinson's first teaching position was in European history at the University of Pennsylvania, where the welfare economist Simon N. Patten, who had helped him secure the job, influenced him. After a year Robinson moved to Columbia University as an associate professor of European history and became active on the curriculum subcommittee of the National Education Association for history. In 1895 he became a full professor.

At Columbia, Robinson shared progressive, reformist views with colleagues like John Dewey and continued to develop his New History idea. This historiography movement believed in history as an instrument in helping solve contemporary problems, concentrated upon the life of the common man, and cooperated with other social sciences. Robinson's concepts appeared in his course, "The Intellectual History of Western Europe," which his students called "The Downfall of Christianity."

Robinson's first textbook, *An Introduction to the History of Western Europe* (1902), although quite popular, was more conventional than innovative. The ideas of the New History did not appear in significant text form until *The Development of Modern Europe* (1907), written in collaboration with his most famous student, Charles A. Beard. A group of Robinson's essays, all but one previously published, appeared in *The New History* (1912). This book brought together his ideas and remains the representative work in the movement.

In 1919 Robinson resigned from Columbia to help found the New School for Social Research. There he was chairman of the executive committee and taught one course. He continued to write, producing two popular polemical books—*The Mind in the Making* (1921), a best seller, and *The Humanizing of Knowledge* (1923). These books held that a just social order could be creat-

ed by applied intelligence. Robinson's ideas remained constant until his death on Feb. 16, 1936, in New York City; this is obvious in the collection of his essays edited by his student Harry Elmer Barnes and published posthumously as *The Human Comedy* (1937).

Further Reading

James Harvey Robinson is listed in the Social Sciences study guide (VII, A, 3). Another proponent of the New History was Charles A. BEARD.

Luther V. Hendricks, *James Harvey Robinson: Teacher of History* (1946), is short but good and includes a comprehensive bibliography of Robinson's writings. Harry Elmer Barnes's sketch of Robinson in Howard Odum, ed., *American Masters of Social Science: An Approach to the Study of the Social Studies through a Neglected Field of Biography* (1927), is the appraisal of an enthusiastic disciple. Harvey Wish's introduction to the paperback edition of Robinson's *The New History* (1965) is balanced and succinct.

JOHN BEVERLEY **ROBINSON**
/ **By Robert Hett**

Sir John Beverley Robinson (1791–1863) was a leading member of the Family Compact and of the Tory party of Upper Canada and chief justice of Upper Canada for 33 years.

John Beverley Robinson was born on July 26, 1791, at Berthier in Lower Canada. He was the second son of the American loyalist Christopher Robinson and was educated for some years at Kingston and Cornwall under the tutelage of John Strachan, the future bishop of Toronto. Beginning in October 1807, Robinson read law for 3 years in the office of D'Arcy Boulton, then the solicitor general of Upper Canada.

In 1812 Robinson received a commission under Gen. Sir Isaac Brock and was present at the capture of Ft. Detroit and at the battle at Queenston, where Brock lost his life. From late 1812 until the end of the war in 1815, Robinson was the acting attorney general of Upper Canada, and for much of this period he was the only crown officer in the province. On Feb. 6, 1815, he became the solicitor general, and in September he sailed for England to study law in Lincoln's Inn and to qualify for admission to the English bar.

Robinson returned to Canada late in 1817 and was appointed attorney general on Feb. 11, 1818. In 1821 he entered actively upon a political career, being elected to the Legislative Assembly for York. He was appointed to the Legislative Council as well and from 1828 to 1840 was its speaker. Robinson had, by the mid-1820s, become one of the leaders of the Tory party and a

James Harvey Robinson. (Brown Brothers)

Sir John Beverley Robinson, a portrait by George Theodore Berthon. (The Law Society of Upper Canada)

prominent member of the Family Compact, an early Canadian power elite. On July 13, 1829, he was appointed the chief justice of Upper Canada and held this office until 1862.

Robinson opposed the union of the two provinces of Upper and Lower Canada, and in 1840 he published a book on the issue entitled *Canada and the Canada Bill.* Nevertheless he continued to hold the office of chief justice in the new union until, in 1862, he was appointed the first president of the Court of Error and Appeal. In 1853 he was elected chancellor of the University of Trinity College in Toronto and in 1854 was made a baronet.

Though often given to defending the status quo in political and social matters, Robinson acted in most cases with logic and common sense. A man of presence and of marked ability, he served the people of the colony ably for many years. He died at his home, Beverley House, in Toronto on Jan. 31, 1863.

Further Reading

Sir John Beverley Robinson is listed in the Canada study guide (III, A, 2). John STRACHAN, Toronto's first Anglican bishop, also was a member of the power elite.

The major biography of Robinson was written by his son, Charles W. Robinson, *The Life of Sir John Beverley*

Robinson, Bart. (1904), which, although uncritical, contains valuable passages from many of Robinson's letters and journal entries. D. B. Read, *Lives of the Judges* (1888), is useful. For the earlier period of Robinson's life, Gerald M. Craig, *Upper Canada: The Formative Years, 1784–1841* (1966), offers a recent interpretation.

T. **ROBINSON** / By Mahonri Sharp Young

One of the leading American impressionist painters, Theodore Robinson (1852–1896) was instrumental in introducing impressionism into American painting.

Theodore Robinson was born in Irasburg, Vt., on June 3, 1852. He grew up in Evansville, Wis., where his father, a Methodist minister, ran a clothing store. At the age of 18 Robinson went to Chicago to study at the Art Institute. Chronically afflicted with asthma, he was sent to Denver for his health, after which he studied at the National Academy of Design in New York City. He was one of the founders of the Art Students League, whose name he suggested.

In 1877 Robinson went to Paris and studied with J. L. Gérôme and then with C. E. A. Carolus-Duran. In 1879 Robinson was in Venice, where James McNeill Whistler gave him a little picture and probably influenced his style. Robinson's stay in Venice was important in his artistic development. He returned to the United States in 1880.

Robinson was active in the Society of American Artists, which was formed in protest against the National Academy of Design. He taught, worked for 3 years for a decorating firm in Boston, and helped John La Farge on the decoration of the Vanderbilt house at Tarrytown.

In 1884 Robinson returned to his beloved France. In 1887 he went to Giverny to see Claude Monet, the decisive step of his career. Impressionism was on the way, and Monet drew Robinson to nature; for him and for a large part of American painting this marked the decisive shift from the Barbizon school to impressionism. From then on Giverny was the fixed point of his life, and he always passed through there on his trips back and forth to the United States. But he was in no sense a pupil of Monet's and did not receive criticism from him as did some other Americans. Despite his shyness and lack of self-confidence, Robinson was fiercely independent and it is most unlikely that he would have welcomed advice on his work.

A great traveler, Robinson would often disappear, and his numerous friends would not know where he was. He lived very frugally, almost secretively, and never married. He died in New York City on April 2, 1896.

A pioneer of impressionism in the United States, Robinson was one of the most brilliant and talented Ameri-

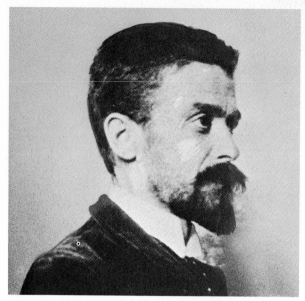

Theodore Robinson. (Courtesy Peter A. Juley & Son; Dictionary of American Portraits, Dover)

can artists of the period. It is a mistake to think of him merely as a follower of Monet, for he was a delicate and individual painter in his own right. Robinson said of himself that perhaps he was born to make sketches, but his fine and spirited little paintings have lasted far better than the monumental efforts of some of his contemporaries.

Further Reading

Theodore Robinson is listed in the Art study guide (IV, D, 1, e). Other pioneer American impressionist painters were John TWACHTMAN and Childe HASSAM.

The only modern treatment of Robinson is John I. H. Baur, *Theodore Robinson, 1852–1896* (1946), which was responsible for the current revival of interest in Robinson's work and has not been superseded. The best account by a contemporary is in Will H. Low, *A Chronicle of Friendships, 1873–1900* (1908).

ROCA / By Gilbert B. Becker

Julio Argentino Roca (1843–1914) was an Argentine general and the leader of the oligarchy that held political control of Argentina from 1880 to 1916. He was a typical 19th-century caudillo.

Julio Roca (pronounced rô′kä) was born of a prominent and wealthy Argentine family in Tucumán on July 17, 1843. He received a degree from the National College in Uruguay. When he was approxi-

mately 15, he volunteered to fight for the interior provinces in the struggle against the forces of Buenos Aires and was commissioned a sublieutenant; thereafter he remained on the military rolls for a period of 55 years of continuous service.

After graduation Roca took part in further fighting between the city and the provinces, this time on the side of the city. In the subsequent war against Paraguay he fought in several battles, and he achieved the rank of colonel in helping to put down the revolt of López Jordán in Entre Ríos. Roca finally reached the rank of general when he defeated and captured Gen. Aredondo, who had revolted in 1874.

Upon the death of the secretary of war, Adolfo Alsino, Roca undertook a successful campaign against the Indians in the south and added extensive land to the national domain, most of which fell into his and his friends' hands. Also, the Indian captives were to all intents and purposes forced into slavery under the application of old colonial laws. The results of the successful campaign made Roca popular in powerful circles, and he was elected president in 1880.

Rule by Oligarchy

Roca's administration ushered in a period of Argentine history known as the "era of the oligarchy," which lasted until 1916. Its core was made up of the great landowners, and it exerted its power through what has been called the most powerful farmers' organization in the Western Hemisphere, plus certain commercial elements with close ties with the British. On the credit side of the ledger, his government was powerful enough to end the many years of political chaos which had preceded his assumption of office.

Julio Roca. (Organization of American States)

Roca's platform proposed improvement in communications and a stronger army. Since the newly acquired Indian lands were useless without railroads, he spent vast sums during his administration to connect the area with the city of Buenos Aires. By diverting funds to the army he was able to count on its political support.

At the close of his administration, Roca left for Paris but soon returned to assist in the overthrow of his successor, Miguel Juárez Celmán. Roca was rewarded with the office of secretary of the interior, which enabled him to augment his personal fortune. He was once again elected president (1898–1904), having in the interim been president of the Senate. Roca's second administration is notable for the resumption of diplomatic relations with the Vatican, the settlement of the boundary dispute with Chile, and the pronouncement of the Drago Doctrine, an Argentine protest against intervention.

Roca retired from public life in 1904 until his appointment in 1913 as ambassador to Brazil. He was always a skillful politician and managed to cooperate better than most with leaders of both parties and was successful in smoothing over political quarrels. He was helped during both administrations by the universal prosperity resulting from the technological improvements of the time, and there is a great similarity between his administrations and those of President Ulysses S. Grant in the United States. Roca died in Buenos Aires on Oct. 19, 1914.

Further Reading

Julio Roca is listed in the Latin America study guide (IV, A, 1, a). During Roca's administration, Luis María DRAGO expounded his doctrine that forbade collection by force of arms of debts between nations.

There are no full-length biographies of Roca in English. Biographical material on Roca can be found in Ricardo Levene, *A History of Argentina* (trans. 1937); John W. White, *Argentina: The Life Story of a Nation* (1942); and Henry Stanley Ferns, *Argentina* (1969). See also Hubert Clinton Herring, *A History of Latin America: From the Beginnings to the Present* (1955; 3d rev. ed. 1968).

ROCHAMBEAU / By Martin Blumenson

The Frenchman Jean Baptiste Donatien de Vimeur, Comte de Rochambeau (1725–1807), commanded the French expeditionary force in the American Revolution. He was with Gen. George Washington at the Battle of Yorktown.

The Comte de Rochambeau (pronounced rō-shäN-bō′) was born at Vendôme on July 1, 1725. Educated for the Church, he entered the army at the age of 17 and fought with bravery and skill in the War of the Austrian Succession, serving in Bohemia, Bavaria, and along the Rhine. A colonel by 1747, he took part in the

The Comte de Rochambeau, painting by Charles Philippe Auguste de Larivière in the château of Versailles. (Courtesy of The New-York Historical Society, New York City)

Seven Years War as a brigadier general and achieved distinction in the expedition to Minorca and battles in Germany.

As a lieutenant general, Rochambeau was named commander of the French forces sent to America, and in July 1780 he landed at Newport, R.I., with about 5,500 troops. Although he was to launch combined operations with the Americans against New York, he was blockaded by a British fleet and was forced to spend a year entrenched while he awaited the arrival of French naval forces.

Rochambeau conferred with Washington in the spring of 1781, and they agreed that together they could overwhelm Henry Clinton at New York or Charles Cornwallis in Virginia, but not both. They decided to have Adm. de Grasse sail from the West Indies to Chesapeake Bay to cut the British communications and prevent mutual support between Clinton and Cornwallis; to avoid Clinton; and to strike Cornwallis.

The French forces under Rochambeau joined the Americans at White Plains, N.Y., in June and marched to Williamsburg, Va., where they met the Marquis de Lafayette's army in September. Reinforced by 4,000 troops brought by De Grasse from Haiti, Washington and Rochambeau besieged the British forces under Cornwallis at Yorktown on October 2. De Grasse's naval forces turned back Adm. Graves's ships coming to Cornwallis's rescue and thereby prevented Cornwallis's escape or his reinforcement. On October 19 Cornwallis surrendered. Rochambeau spent the winter in Virginia, returned to Rhode Island in the fall of 1782, and went back to France in 1783.

In 1790, during the revolutionary period in France, Rochambeau commanded the Army of the North. He was made a marshal of France in 1791. In the following year, disenchanted with governmental policy and the conduct near Lille of poorly trained troops sent to him, he resigned his command and was succeeded by Lafayette. He was arrested for treason but escaped the guillotine.

In 1804 Napoleon made him a grand officer of the Legion of Honor. His two volumes of *Mémoires, militaires, historiques, et politiques* were published in 1809, after his death at Thoré on May 10, 1807.

A striking figure, Rochambeau was simple in his tastes and dignified in his behavior. He eschewed ostentation and airs of self-importance. In America, he placed himself without reservation under Washington's orders and ensured the Franco-American cooperation that finally defeated the British in the American Revolution.

Further Reading

The Comte de Rochambeau is listed in the American History study guide (III, D, 3) and the European History study guide (VI, B, 1). He served under George WASHINGTON.

The latest work on Rochambeau is Arnold Whitridge, *Rochambeau* (1965). See also Allan Forbes, *Rochambeau* (1925), and Jean-Edmond Weelen, *Rochambeau: Father and Son* (1936).

ROCKEFELLER / By Peter d'A. Jones

John Davison Rockefeller (1839–1937), American industrialist and philanthropist, founded the Standard Oil Company, the University of Chicago, and the Rockefeller Foundation.

John D. Rockefeller was born on July 8, 1839, in Richford, N.Y. His father owned farm property and traded in many goods, including lumber and patent medicines. His mother, a straitlaced puritanical woman, brought up her large family very strictly. The family moved west by degrees, reaching Cleveland, Ohio, in 1853, when it was beginning to grow into a city. John graduated from high school there and after 3 months of commercial college found his first job at the age of 16 clerking in a produce commission house. In 1859, when he was 19, he started his first company with a young Englishman: Clark and Rockefeller. They grossed $450,000 in the first year of trading. Clark did the fieldwork; Rockefeller controlled office management, bookkeeping, and relationships with bankers.

John D. Rockefeller about 1913. (Library of Congress)

Early Businesses

From the start Rockefeller revealed a genius for organization and method. The firm prospered during the Civil War. With the Pennsylvania oil strike (1859) and the building of a railroad to Cleveland, they branched out into oil refining with Samuel Andrews, who had technical knowledge of the field. Within 2 years Rockefeller became senior partner; Clark was bought out, and the firm Rockefeller and Andrews became Cleveland's largest refinery. A second refinery, the Standard Works, was opened in 1865 by another firm established by Rockefeller in his brother William's name; and a sales office was opened in New York City in 1866.

With financial help from S. V. Harkness and from a new partner, H. M. Flagler, who also secured favorable railroad freight rebates, Rockefeller survived the bitter competition in the oil industry. The Standard Oil Company, chartered in Ohio in 1870 by Rockefeller, his brother, Flagler, Harkness, and Andrews, had a capital of $1 million and paid a dividend of 40 percent a year later. Standard Oil controlled one-tenth of American refining, but competitive chaos remained. The chief bottleneck was the transporting of the oil. Out of this situation came the controversial South Improvement Company scheme of 1872—a defensive alliance of Cleveland refiners to meet the bitter opposition of the oil producers of Pennsylvania. The sweeping freight rebate agreements in this scheme brought public opposition, and the plan was outlawed by the Pennsylvania Legislature. Meanwhile, a looser organization, a refiners' pool, also failed (1873).

Rockefeller still hoped to impose order on the oil industry. He bought out most of the Cleveland refineries, then acquired others in New York, Pittsburgh, and Philadelphia. He turned to new transportation methods, including the railroad tank car and the pipeline. By 1879 he was refining 90 percent of American oil, and Standard used its own tank car fleet, ships, docking facilities, barrel-making plants, draying services, depots, and warehouses. Strict economy and planning were enforced throughout. Rockefeller came through the Panic of 1873 still urging organization on the part of the refiners. As his control approached near-monopoly, he fought a war with the Pennsylvania Railroad in 1877, which created a refining company to try to break Rockefeller's control, but the bloody railroad strikes that year forced them to surrender to Standard Oil. Rockefeller's dream of order was near completion.

America's First Trust

By 1883, after winning control of the pipeline industry, Standard's monopoly was at a peak. Rockefeller created America's first great "trust" in 1882; since laws forbade one company's ownership of another's stock, ever since 1872 Standard had placed its acquisitions outside Ohio in the hands of Flagler as "trustee." All profits went to the Ohio company while the outside businesses remained nominally independent. In 1882 this was regularized. Nine trustees of the Standard Oil Trust received the stock of 40 businesses and gave the various shareholders trust certificates in return. The trust had a capital of about $70 million; it was the world's largest and richest industrial organization.

In the 1880s the nature of Rockefeller's business began to change; he moved beyond refining oil into producing crude oil itself and moved his wells westward with the new fields opening up. He pioneered in this by acquiring oil land in Ohio before it was certain that this sulfuric oil could be refined successfully; then he employed the scientist Herman Frasch, whose process (1886–1889) made these fields yield an enormous profit. Standard also expanded its marketing facilities and entered foreign markets in Europe, Asia, and Latin America. From 1885 a committee system of management was developed to control Standard Oil's enormous empire.

Attacking the Trust

Public opposition to Standard Oil grew with the emergence of the muckraking journalists; in particular, Henry Demarest Lloyd and Ida Tarbell published harsh exposés of the oil empire. Rockefeller was condemned for various alleged practices: railroad rebates (a system he did

A cartoon of Rockefeller by Horace Taylor: the trust giant Rockefeller, having transformed the Capitol and the Treasury Department into Standard Oil refineries, scrutinizes the White House and says, "What a funny little government." (The Verdict, Jan. 22, 1900; New York Public Library)

not invent and which many refiners used); price discrimination; industrial espionage and bribery; crushing smaller firms by unfair competition, such as cutting off their crude oil supplies or restricting their transport outlets. Standard Oil was investigated by the New York State Senate and by the U.S. House of Representatives in 1888. The rising tide of reform sentiment brought in the Sherman Antitrust Act (1890). Two years later the Ohio Supreme Court invalidated Standard's original trust agreement. Rockefeller formally disbanded the organization; though the trustees handed in their trust certificates, in practice the organization remained unified, and the four presidents of the state firms (John D. Rockefeller for Standard of Ohio, William Rockefeller for New York, Flagler for New Jersey, and J. A. Moffett for Indiana) still met regularly to fix overall policy. In 1899 Standard was re-created legally under a new form as a "holding company"; this merger was dissolved by the U.S. Supreme Court in 1911, long after Rockefeller himself had retired from active control in 1897.

Perhaps Rockefeller's most famous excursion outside the oil industry began in 1893, when he helped develop the Mesabi iron ore range of Minnesota. By 1896 his Consolidated Iron Mines owned a great fleet of ore boats and virtually controlled Great Lakes shipping. Rockefeller was now an iron ore magnate in his own right and had the power to dictate to the steel industry. He made an alliance with the steel king, Andrew Carnegie, in 1896: Rockefeller agreed not to enter steelmaking and Carnegie agreed not to touch transportation. In 1901 Rockefeller sold his ore holdings to the vast new merger created by Carnegie and J. P. Morgan, U.S. Steel. In that year his fortune passed the $200 million mark for the first time.

Philanthropic Endeavors

From his first employment as a clerk, Rockefeller sought to give away one-tenth of his earnings to charity. His benefactions grew with his income, and he also gave time and energy to philanthropic causes. At first he depended on the Baptist Church for advice; the Church wanted its own great university, and in 1892 the University of Chicago opened under the brilliant presidency of a man Rockefeller much admired, William Rainey Harper. The university was Rockefeller's first major philanthropic creation. He gave it over $80 million during his lifetime and left the university entirely independent under Harper. Rockefeller chose New York City for his Rockefeller Institute of Medical Research (now Rockefeller University), chartered in 1901. Among the institute's many achievements were yellow fever research, discovery of serums to combat pneumonia, advances in experimental physiology and surgery, and work on infantile paralysis. In 1902 he established the General Education Board.

The total of Rockefeller's lifetime philanthropies has been estimated at about $550 million. Eventually the amounts involved became so huge (his fortune reached $900 million by 1913) that he developed a staff of specialists to help him; out of this came the Rockefeller Foundation, chartered in 1913, "to promote the well-being of mankind throughout the world."

Rockefeller's personal life was fairly simple and frugal. He was a man of few passions who lived for his work, and his great talent was his organizing genius and drive for order, pursued with great single-mindedness and concentration. His life was absorbed by business and later by organized giving. In both areas he imposed order, efficiency, and planning with extraordinary success and sweeping vision. He died on May 23, 1937, in Ormond, Fla.

Further Reading

John D. Rockefeller is listed in the American History study guide (VII, E, 3; VIII, D, 2). At one point he made a deal with the other business titan of this period, Andrew CARNEGIE. His son, John D. ROCKEFELLER, Jr., took charge mainly of his father's philanthropies.

Rockefeller's *Random Reminiscences of Men and Events* (1909) remains interesting and important. The definitive life of Rockefeller is Allan Nevins, *Study in Power: John D. Rockefeller* (2 vols., 1940; rev. ed. 1953). A sympathetic account is Jules Abels, *The Rockefeller Billions* (1965).

For general economic history see the readings in Peter d'A. Jones, *The Robber Barons Revisited* (1968). The history of Standard Oil of New Jersey is treated in R. W. and M. E. Hidy, *History of Standard Oil Company: Pioneering in Big Business, 1882–1911*, vol. 1 (1955), and Standard is considered comparatively in Alfred D. Chandler, Jr., *Strategy and Structure: Chapters in the History of Industrial Enterprise* (1962). Standard's history in California to 1919 is described in Gerald T. White, *Formative Years in the Far West* (1962). For a broader history see Harold F. Williamson and Arnold R. Daum, *The American Petroleum Industry* (2 vols., 1959–1963).

ROCKEFELLER, JR.

/ By Elisha P. Douglass

John D. Rockefeller, Jr. (1874–1960), American philanthropist, utilized the family fortune to establish scores of philanthropic enterprises and participated actively in their management. He also became widely known as an expert in industrial relations.

Born to substantial wealth on Jan. 29, 1874, in Cleveland, John D. Rockefeller, Jr., was brought up in a rigorously puritanical atmosphere. The social life of the family centered in the Baptist Church, and young Rockefeller and his four sisters were taught to live upright, religious lives. Educated at Brown University, from which he graduated in 1897, he was shy and serious, determined to carry out what he felt were his duties to his God, his family, and society.

After graduation from college, young Rockefeller—largely to please his father, to whom he was devoted—

John D. Rockefeller, Jr. (Rockefeller Foundation)

Rockefeller from 1915 until his death were conservation and national park projects in the West, the Cloisters art museum in New York, and the Williamsburg restoration. He also planned and constructed Rockefeller Center in New York City and donated the land upon which the United Nations building now stands.

Somewhat below middle height, modest, unaffected, and unostentatious, Rockefeller did much to remove the ''robber baron'' stigma from big business and to awaken businessmen to social responsibilities. He died on May 11, 1960, in Tucson, Ariz.

Further Reading

John D. Rockefeller, Jr., is listed in the American History study guide (IX, B, 2). Son of the business titan John D. ROCKEFELLER, he was of the generation of businessman Thomas J. WATSON.

The best source of information on Rockefeller is the sympathetic biography by his friend and colleague Raymond B. Fosdick, *John D. Rockefeller, Jr.* (1956).

ROCKINGHAM/ By J. S. Cockburn

**The English statesman Charles
Watson-Wentworth, 2d Marquess of
Rockingham (1730–1782), as prime minister
and leader of the Whig opposition, advocated
leniency toward the American colonies.**

entered the offices of the family's Standard Oil Company in New York City to prepare himself to administer his father's vast business interests. But because of his retiring and extremely moralistic nature he disliked the bruising business world and occupied himself increasingly with managing his father's estates and philanthropic enterprises. The Rockefeller Institute for Medical Research, the General Education Board, and the Rockefeller Foundation were financed by the elder Rockefeller, but the son participated actively in management. The education board was concerned chiefly with improving Negro education in the South; the foundation became a vast holding company for hundreds of philanthropies.

From 1900 to 1908 John D. Rockefeller, Jr., became more closely involved with his father's business interests. But allegations of unfair competitive practices used by Standard Oil led him to separate himself from active policy making in his father's corporations in 1910. In 1913, however, because of a large family stockholding in the Colorado Fuel and Iron Company, he was implicated in a strike that not only shut down the company but threatened to balloon into a domestic insurrection. Although keenly hurt by accusations from liberals and labor leaders that he had helped intensify the strife by siding with an arbitrary and unsympathetic management, Rockefeller worked out a plan for worker representation in company affairs that became a model for industrial relations during the 1920s. Elaborating this scheme in speeches and periodical articles, he came to be considered a leading liberal in labor affairs.

Among the best-known philanthropies occupying

C harles Watson-Wentworth was born on May 13, 1730. He was educated at Westminster School and at Cambridge; in 1745, at the age of 15, he ran away without parental permission to join the Duke of Cumberland's army, which was fighting against the Young Pretender. Between 1748 and 1750, Watson-Wentworth completed the grand tour of Europe.

On the death of his father in 1750, Rockingham succeeded to the family estates in Yorkshire, Northamptonshire, and Ireland, and in 1752 he augmented his inheritance by marrying Mary Bright, a Yorkshire heiress. In 1751 Rockingham also succeeded to his father's offices of lord lieutenant of the North and East Ridings of Yorkshire, was appointed a lord of the bedchamber, and took his seat in the House of Lords. For the next 15 years Rockingham divided his time between the Lords and his consuming passion for horse racing. In general he entered little into political issues, but in 1762, in protest against the signing of the Peace of Paris, he resigned his place in the bedchamber. In consequence, he was dismissed from his lieutenancies.

During the regency crisis of 1765 Rockingham and the elder William Pitt were approached by the Duke of Cumberland with a view to forming a coalition; and on Pitt's refusal to serve, Rockingham became prime minister. Rockingham was among those ministers inclined to act

Lord Rockingham, a painting from the studio of Sir Joshua Reynolds. (National Portrait Gallery, London)

leniently on the American question. Nevertheless, it was not until the spring of 1766 that the government proposed and carried the repeal of the Stamp Act. The repeal was facilitated by a concurrent statutory declaration of the absolute supremacy of Parliament over the Colonies. George III, chagrined by the repeal of the Stamp Act, was further mortified by the coalition's refusal to grant an allowance to his brothers and by the passage of resolutions condemning general warrants. In July 1766 he dismissed Rockingham, and Pitt returned to power.

Disappointed, Rockingham took little part in public affairs until the conclusion of the Franco-American alliance. Then he bitterly attacked Lord North's American policy, and in March 1778 he declared for the immediate recognition of the independence of the Colonies. On the fall of North's administration in February 1782, Rockingham again became prime minister in a coalition government. This ministry conceded legislative independence to Ireland, and it considerably curtailed the political power of the Crown, chiefly by reducing the King's household. Rockingham's death on July 1, 1782, dissolved this short-lived administration. He was buried in York Minster.

Further Reading

Lord Rockingham is listed in the European History study guide (VI, A, 1, b). Unlike him, Lord NORTH advocated stern treatment of the rebellious American colonies.

Rockingham's relative unimportance in 18th-century politics is reflected by the absence of works devoted to his career. The only biographical study is short and deals with his life up to 1765: G. H. Guttridge, *The Early Career of Lord Rockingham, 1730–1765* (1952). A later study by Guttridge, *English Whiggism and the American Revolution* (1963), is important for the political philosophy of Rockingham and his associates. Recommended for general historical background is J. Steven Watson, *The Reign of George III, 1760–1815* (1960).

ROCKNE / By Arthur Daley

Knute Rockne (1888–1931), a genius in the sport of football, became an American folk hero and left his stamp of greatness on the entire sport.

Knute Rockne was born on March 4, 1888, in Voss, Norway. In 1891 his father came to America to exhibit his carriage-building art at the World's Columbian Exposition in Chicago, and 18 months later he sent for his family. Swiftly absorbed in the Chicago melting pot, Knute played football and baseball (and had his nose permanently flattened by a carelessly swung bat). In high school he also ran on the track team and pole-vaulted.

Lacking the finances to enroll at the University of Il-

Knute Rockne. (United Press International Photo)

linois, Rockne worked in a post office for 4 years. For exercise he ran or vaulted. Two foot-racing buddies begged him to matriculate at Notre Dame University; he reluctantly joined them. Before he impressed athletic coaches with his physical prowess, Rockne dazzled professors with his brilliant mind. (He graduated *summa cum laude*.) His roommate was Gus Dorais, quarterback on the Notre Dame football team. In 1913 the two experimented with forward-passing techniques, a stratagem that was legal but little used.

That autumn top-ranking West Point invited little-known Notre Dame to fill a schedule opening: the result stunned the football world. Dorais passed to Rockne for the first touchdown; Notre Dame took the game. The forward-passing show revolutionized football.

After graduation Knute married Bonnie Skiles. Notre Dame named him assistant football coach, head track coach, and chemistry professor. By 1918 he was head football coach; a season later he had his first unbeaten team. As a strategist, Rockne was imaginative and inventive. With his Notre Dame team, he became the top-ranking coach in the history of intercollegiate football, with a winning average of .897. He produced five unbeaten and untied teams. But it was Rockne's witty, dynamic personality that dominated every gathering. He was not only a spellbinding orator but a funny one as well.

Rockne had not even approached his peak when he died in a plane crash on March 31, 1931. The nation mourned. The President of the United States sent condolences to his widow; so did the king of Norway. Knute's death was front-page news in every paper in America, and editorials lavished praise on the immigrant boy who had become one of America's best-loved figures.

Further Reading

Knute Rockne is listed in the American History study guide (IX, D, 6). Jesse OWENS was a leading track star of this period.

Generally regarded as authoritative biographies are Arthur Daley, *Knute Rockne: Football Wizard of Notre Dame* (1960), and Francis Wallace, *Knute Rockne* (1960). A wealth of detail on Rockne is in Wallace's *The Notre Dame Story* (1949).

✳   ✳   ✳

RODGERS/ By Richard Jackson

Richard Charles Rodgers (born 1902), American composer, wrote the music for over 50 stage and film musicals and helped make the American musical a legitimate art form.

When Richard Rodgers, Lorenz Hart, and Dorothy Fields collaborated in 1925 on *Dearest Enemy*, "an American musical play" (as they called it), contributing respectively music, lyrics, and

Richard Rodgers. (USIS, Paris)

book, something new was added to the theatrical scene. Not only was the material original, charming, and witty, but the form and subject of the entertainment were distinctly unusual. Here was a play based on American history with unpredictable and pertinent musical sections. Rodgers and his lyricists, Hart and, later, Oscar Hammerstein II, were to repeat this sort of innovation on several occasions. Each occasion marked an important contribution to a more original, indigenous popular musical theater in the United States.

Richard Rodgers was born near Arverne, Long Island, N.Y., on June 28, 1902. His father was a successful physician and his mother, a well-trained amateur musician. Rodgers heard music in his home from earliest childhood and was regularly taken to the theater. He was especially delighted by the operettas of Victor Herbert and other popular composers. A little later he was inspired by the musicals of Jerome Kern, whose influence, Rodgers said, was "a deep and lasting one."

By the age of 6 Rodgers was playing the piano by ear and had begun receiving piano lessons. He attended secondary schools in New York. By the age of 14 he had written two songs in the popular vein (he was never interested in purely instrumental composition). His direction seemed fixed. Before he entered Columbia University in 1919, he had already written music for two amateur shows and had met Lorenz (Larry) Hart, a literate, amusing, somewhat driven creator of verse, with whom Rodgers would collaborate for the next 24 years. Their first published song was "Any Old Place with You" (1919), and hundreds followed. Rodgers left Columbia at the end of his second year to devote full time to musical studies at the Institute of Musical Art, where he spent another 2 years.

Collaboration with Hart

After working on amateur shows and on a few unsuccessful professional attempts, Rodgers and Hart won acclaim for their review *Garrick Gaieties* in 1925. *Dearest Enemy*, their second success, opened the same year. During the next decade they wrote three shows for the London stage and a number of Broadway musicals and Hollywood films. Though not all of them were successful, they were distinguished by a number of fine romantic ballads such as "My Heart Stood Still" (1927), "With a Song in My Heart" (1929), "Dancing on the Ceiling" (1930), and "Lover" (1932). Hart's lyrics always managed nicely to skirt sentimentality, and Rodgers matched them with tunes of grace and skill.

Among the nine stage shows written between 1935 and 1942 were several of Rodgers and Hart's most famous: *Jumbo* (1935); *On Your Toes* (1936), for which the distinguished Russian-born choreographer George Balanchine created the ballet *Slaughter on Tenth Avenue*; *Babes in Arms* (1937); *The Boys from Syracuse* (1938); and *Pal Joey* (1940). A number of the songs written during this time are among Rodgers and Hart's most durable: "There's a Small Hotel," "Where or When," "My Funny Valentine," "This Can't Be Love," and "The Lady Is a Tramp." These are sophisticated pieces which display a firm control of the medium.

Collaboration with Hammerstein

After Hart died in 1943, Rodgers entered a period of unprecedented success with lyricist Hammerstein. Of their 10 musicals, 5 were among the longest-running and biggest-grossing shows ever created for Broadway: *Oklahoma* (1943), *Carousel* (1945), *South Pacific* (1949), *The King and I* (1951), and *The Sound of Music* (1959).

If the best work of Rodgers and Hart was marked by a considerable measure of wit and sophistication, the style of the Rodgers and Hammerstein collaboration was dominated by a basic, almost folklike, simplicity. In many songs both music and words seem stripped to the barest essentials. Romantic sentiment is a major ingredient.

Through touring productions, film versions, and recordings, the Rodgers and Hammerstein shows have become known around the world. Songs that have become standards in the popular repertory include "Oh, What a Beautiful Morning," "People Will Say We're in Love," "If I Loved You," "You'll Never Walk Alone," "Some Enchanted Evening," "Hello, Young Lovers," and "Climb Every Mountain." After Hammerstein's death in 1960 Rodgers for the first time served as his own lyricist for the score of *No Strings* (1962).

Rodgers's long association with the popular musical theater was an important one. His best projects were aimed at giving the musical play an ever more natural American expression. *Oklahoma*, especially, brought an engaging simplicity and earthiness to the form. On many occasions his choice of subject matter was unconventional, involving certain characters, situations, and themes of a seriousness seldom encountered previously in musical comedy. His work enriched and broadened a genre once regarded as little more than frivolous entertainment and helped make it into an authentic American art form.

Further Reading

Richard Rodgers is listed in the Music study guide (II, D, 3; II, E). Cole PORTER and Irving BERLIN added a great number of famous melodies to the American musical theater.

David Ewen, *Richard Rodgers* (1957), a laudatory full-scale biography which contains lists of Rodgers's stage and film works, is quite comprehensive, although not without minor errors. Deems Taylor, *Some Enchanted Evenings* (1953), is a chatty, informal account of the Hammerstein collaboration and contains some musical analysis of Rodgers's songs and has numerous photographs. See also Stanley Green, *The Rodgers and Hammerstein Story* (1963).

* * *

RODIN / By Abraham A. Davidson

> The French sculptor Auguste Rodin (1840–1917) conceived of his sculpture largely as volumes existing in space, as materials to be manipulated for a variety of surface effects. Thus he anticipated the aims of many 20th-century sculptors.

Auguste Rodin (pronounced rō-dăN′), the son of a police inspector, was born in Paris on Nov. 12, 1840. He studied drawing under Horace Lecoq de Boisbaudran and modeling under the sculptor Jean Baptiste Carpeaux at the School of Decorative Arts in Paris (1854–1857). Simultaneously Rodin studied literature and history at the Collège de France. Rejected three times by the École des Beaux-Arts, he supported himself by doing decorative work for ornamentalists and set designers.

In 1862, as a result of the death of his sister Maria, who had joined a convent, Rodin attempted to join a Christian order, but he was dissuaded by the perceptive father superior. Rodin continued as a decorator by day and at night attended a class given by the animal sculptor Antoine Louis Barye.

In 1864 Rodin began to live with the young seamstress Rose Beuret, whom he finally married the last year of his life. Also in 1864 he completed his *Man with a Broken Nose*, a bust of an old street porter, which the Salon rejected. That year he entered the studio of Carrier-Belleuse, a sculptor who worked in the light rococo mode of the previous century. Rodin remained with Carrier-Belleuse for 6 years and always spoke warmly of him. In

1870 he and his teacher went to Brussels, where they began the sculptural decoration of the Bourse. The next year they quarreled, and Carrier-Belleuse returned to Paris, while Rodin completed the work under A. J. van Rasbourg.

The Human Figure

In 1875 Rodin went to Italy, where he was deeply inspired by the work of Donatello and of Michelangelo, whose sculpture he characterized as being marked by both "violence and constraint." Back in Paris in 1876, Rodin made a bronze statue of a standing man raising his arms toward his head in such a way as to project an air of uncertainty, a figure held in a pose of slight torsion suggestive of Michelangelo's *Dying Slave*. Rodin originally entitled the piece the *Vanquished*, then called it the *Age of Bronze*. When he submitted it to the Salon, it caused an immediate controversy, for it was so lifelike that it was believed to have been cast from the living model. The piece was unusual for the time in that it had no literary or historical connotations. After Rodin was exonerated by a committee of sculptors, the state purchased the *Age of Bronze*.

In 1878 Rodin began work on the *St. John the Baptist Preaching* and various related works, including the *Walking Man*. Lacking not only moral and sentimental overtones but a head and arms as well, the *Walking Man* was an electrifying image of forceful motion. Derived partially from some of Donatello's late works, it was based on numerous poses of the model in constant motion. Rodin raised the very act of walking into a subject worthy of concentrated study.

Rodin's interests continued to broaden. Between 1879 and 1882 he worked at ceramics, and between 1881 and 1886 he produced a number of engravings. By 1880 his fame had become international, and that year the minister of fine arts commissioned him to design a doorway for the proposed Museum of Decorative Arts. The project, called the *Gates of Hell* after Dante's *Inferno*, occupied Rodin for the rest of his life, and particularly in the next decade, but it was never finished. The *Gates* were cast in their incomplete state in the late 1920s.

For Rodin, the study of the human figure in a variety of poses indicative of many emotional states was a lifelong preoccupation. In the *St. John* the artist caught the prophet at the moment when he was moved deeply, gesturing automatically by the strength of the idea he was presenting. The gestures of Rodin's figures seem motivated by inner emotional states. In his bronze *Crouching Woman* (1880–1882) an almost incredibly contracted pose becomes something beyond a mere mannerism. The cramped posture of the woman suggests humility, perhaps a conviction of debasement.

One of Rodin's most ambitious conceptions was the group commissioned by the municipality of Calais as a civic monument. The *Burghers of Calais* (1884–1886), a group larger than life size, commemorates the episode during the Hundred Years War when a group of local citizens agreed to sacrifice their lives to save their city. The pathos and horror of the subject accord with the

Auguste Rodin. (French Embassy Press and Information Division, New York)

romantic sentiments of the time. One of the figures clutches his head, another exhorts his companion, an older man walks stoically ahead. Each of the burghers is individualized, even while they all move ahead to a common purpose. The psychological interactions of the figures were acutely observed, and a lifelike immediacy was achieved. The group was finally installed in 1895.

Portrait Busts

From the late 1880s Rodin received many commissions from private individuals for portrait busts and from the state for monuments commemorating renowned people. Most of the state commissions exist in the state of models, such as the monument to Victor Hugo (begun 1889), which was to have been placed in the Panthéon in Paris, and the monuments to James McNeill Whistler, Napoleon, and Pierre Puvis de Chavannes. Among Rodin's portrait busts are those of George Bernard Shaw, Henri Rochefort, Georges Clémenceau, and Charles Baudelaire.

In the *Head of Baudelaire* (1892), as in his other portraits, Rodin went beyond mere verisimilitude to catch the inner spirit. Baudelaire's face looks ahead with rapt attention, and the eyes seem to be transfixed upon something invisible. Remarkably, Rodin used as his model not Baudelaire, who had died in 1867, but a draftsman named Malteste, who, for the sculptor, had all the characteristics of the Baudelairean mask: "See the enormous forehead, swollen at the temples, dented, tormented, handsome nevertheless. . . ."

In 1891 the Société des Gens de Lettres commissioned

The Burghers of Calais, executed by Rodin during 1884–1886. The group sculpture was installed in Calais, an important seaport town of northern France, in 1895. (H. Roger-Viollet)

Rodin to do a statue of Honoré de Balzac, a work that was subsequently rejected. It was not until 1939 that this work was placed at the Raspail-Montparnasse intersection in Paris. Here, too, Rodin went beyond the external appearance of the subject to catch the inner spirit. As is seen in a bronze of 1897, Balzac, wrapped in his dressing gown, is in the throes of inspiration. Details and articulations of the body are not indicated, all the better to call attention to the haughty yet grandiloquent pose of the inspired writer.

Almost single-handedly Rodin inaugurated the modern spirit in sculpture by freeing it from its dependence upon direct representation and conceiving of sculptural masses as abstract volumes existing in space. To conceive of his aims as being analogous to those of the impressionist painters is not entirely correct, for while the roughness of the surfaces of his sculpture may be connected with the loose handling of the painters, Rodin's painfully slow, intense realizations of the inward spirit of his subjects are foreign to the surface effects of most of the impressionists.

Rodin matured slowly, and his first principal work, the *Age of Bronze*, was not made until he was past 35, yet he achieved fame in his lifetime. After 1900 he knew intimately many of the great men of his time, and his apprentices included Antoine Bourdelle and Charles

Despiau. In 1916 Rodin bequeathed his works to the state. He died in Meudon on Nov. 17, 1917.

"Gates of Hell" and Related Compositions

The *Gates of Hell* was conceived in the tradition of the great portals of Western art, such as Lorenzo Ghiberti's *Gates of Paradise* in Florence. Rodin was unable to plan the *Gates* as a total organized design, and they remained a loose federation of groups. Yet certain of the isolated figures or groups of figures, when enlarged and executed separately, became some of Rodin's finest pieces: *Three Shades* (1880), *Crouching Woman* (1885), the *Old Courtesan* (1885), the *Kiss* (1886), and the *Thinker* (1888).

The *Thinker* on the upper lintel of the *Gates* regards the debauchery and despair in the sections below. The *Thinker* was formally inspired by Michelangelo's *terribilità*, and the motif of the right elbow crossed over the left thigh derives from Michelangelo's Medici tombs. In this piece Rodin conceived of man as beset by intellectual frustrations and incapable of acting: the figure is self-enclosed, completely introverted.

The *Three Shades* on the top of the portal also derives from Michelangelo, especially from the figures of the *Slaves*, but instead of repeating the inner torment of Michelangelo's figures, they seem beset by languor and utter despair.

The *Kiss* was derived from one of the pairs of intertwined lovers on the *Gates*. The over-life-sized marble figures, sitting on a mass of roughhewn marble, seem to emerge out of the unfinished block in the manner of Michelangelo. But the surfaces of the bodies of the lovers are soft and fluid and suggest the warmth of living flesh. As seen in the *Kiss*, Rodin was capable of unabashed eroticism.

The *Old Courtesan*, based on a study of an aged Italian woman, may have been inspired by a poem of François Villon. Here Rodin showed through the sagging breasts, wrinkled skin, and phlegmatic gestures a completely different conception of the human female form, but the response of the observer is not one of revulsion. In this old, tottering body Rodin captured not ugliness but an uncommon sort of beauty.

Further Reading

Auguste Rodin is listed in the Art study guide (III, I, 1). He studied with Jean Baptiste CARPEAUX but was more greatly influenced by the Italian Renaissance sculptors DONATELLO and MICHELANGELO. Another pioneer of modern sculptor was Aristide MAILLOL.

Albert E. Elsen, *Rodin* (1963), is a well-documented study of Rodin as the great innovator in 19th-century sculpture, with particular emphasis on the *Gates of Hell*. Elsen's *Auguste Rodin: Readings on His Life and Works* (1965) contains writings about Rodin by the poet Rainer Maria Rilke, who was his secretary, and by Truman H. Bartlett and Henri Dujardin-Beaumetz. Other studies of Rodin include Rainer Maria Rilke, *Auguste Rodin* (1945), and Denys Sutton, *Triumphant Satyr: The World of Auguste Rodin* (1967). Sommerville Story, *Rodin and His*

Works (1951), and Robert Descharnes and Jean-François Chabrun, eds., *Auguste Rodin* (1967), are valuable for their illustrations. For background consult Louis W. Flaccus, *Artists and Thinkers* (1916), and Sheldon Cheney, *Sculpture of the World: A History* (1968).

RODNEY / By Martin Blumenson

The British admiral George Brydges Rodney, 1st Baron Rodney (1718–1792), by winning notable victories in Caribbean waters over French, Spanish, and Dutch forces, contributed substantially to British command of the seas in the late 18th century.

Born in February 1718, George Rodney attended Harrow before volunteering for naval service at the age of 14. Stationed in the Mediterranean, he became first a lieutenant and then a post captain. In October 1747, in command of the 60-gun *Eagle*, he took part in Adm. Edward Hawke's victory over the French off Ushant and was cited for gallantry. Two years later he was named governor and commander in chief of Newfoundland with the rank of commodore. In 1751 he was elected to Parliament.

Lord Rodney, after a painting by Sir Joshua Reynolds. (National Portrait Gallery, London)

During the Seven Years War, Rodney commanded the 74-gun *Dublin* and took part in the expedition against Rochefort in 1757; served under Adm. Edward Boscawen in 1758 at the siege and capture of Louisbourg, Nova Scotia; in 1759 and 1760 destroyed French transports collected along the Normandy coast for an invasion of Britain; was appointed commander in chief of the Lee-ward Islands station in 1761; and in 1762 reduced Martinique and forced the surrender of St. Lucia and Grenada.

Rodney was promoted to vice admiral of the blue and created a baronet. Governor of Greenwich Hospital from 1765 to 1770, he was appointed rear admiral in 1771. From then until 1774 he commanded the Jamaica station. Having fallen into debt, he lived in Paris for 3 years in order to escape his creditors.

Recalled to England in 1778, Rodney was promoted to admiral of the white. Late in 1779, named commander in chief of the Leeward Islands, Rodney was ordered to sail with 22 ships of the line and a large convoy of transports to the West Indies and on the way to relieve Gibraltar, which had been under Spanish siege since July 1779. In January 1780 he captured a Spanish convoy off Cape Finisterre and defeated Adm. Don Juan de Langara's 11 ships in the so-called Moonlight Battle, fought off Cape St. Vincent at night. These feats relieved Gibraltar and brought Rodney international fame.

In September 1780, leaving half of his fleet in West Indian waters, Rodney sailed to New York and foiled George Washington's designs for a Franco-American land and sea assault on the city. Returning to the Caribbean in February 1781, Rodney captured the Dutch islands of St. Eustatius and St. Martin and confiscated huge stocks belonging to British merchants trading illegally with American Revolutionists, thereby crippling a contraband trade on which the Americans depended. For the rest of his life he was involved in lawsuits with British merchants over this action.

In April 1782, after a running engagement with a fleet of 29 ships under Adm. François de Grasse, Rodney and his 34 ships defeated the French off Dominica by bursting in an unorthodox manner through the middle of the French formation and fragmenting it. Called the Battle of the Saints, this action was Rodney's greatest victory. Britain thereby won supremacy of the seas, but the action was too late to affect the outcome of the American Revolution.

When Rodney returned to England, he received a barony and a pension. A bold and irascible man who had been addicted to expensive tastes and to gambling, Rodney lived quietly in the country until he died in London on May 24, 1792. Dominating the waters of the West Indies during his periods of active service, Rodney personified the might of British naval power.

Further Reading

Lord Rodney is listed in the European History study guide (VI, A, 2). Sir Francis DRAKE was an earlier English naval hero.

The standard biography is Donald Macintyre, *Admiral Rodney* (1962). Francis Russel Hart, *Admirals of the Caribbean* (1922), contains a chapter on Rodney. See also Alfred T. Mahan, *The Influence of Seapower upon History, 1660–1783* (1890).

RODÓ / By Philip B. Taylor, Jr.

José Enrique Rodó (1872–1917) was a Uruguayan essayist and literary critic. A stylist and moralist, he aimed especially to maintain Latin American thought and society on a basis of respect for traditional European humanistic and ethical values.

José Enrique Rodó (pronounced rô-dō′) was born in Montevideo on July 15, 1872. The son of a Catalan father who died when José was 12, he was largely self-taught. He attended primary school but left secondary school for part-time employment. He read broadly in the good library left by his father and in the library of the Ateneo of Montevideo. An intellectual center in the arts and humanities, the Ateneo also provided the atmosphere that nourished Rodó's growth. He was greatly influenced by the works of French, Spanish, and British essayists and paid much attention to works on the United States.

Rodó's youth was a period of great, and occasionally violent, change in Uruguay. In March 1895, together with several other young men, Rodó founded the *Revista nacional de literatura y ciencias sociales*. Sixty issues appeared before its closing. Rodó had wanted to found an academy of literature and language, and this had been a compromise. Rodó's concerns for traditional values and proper use of the language were reflected in his publications. His work was unique to the extent that without signature it was recognized even in Spain for his control of ideas and of the *modernista* literary style.

The spiritual and intellectual unity of Latin America with Spain and Europe was Rodó's principal concern; he regarded even Brazil as a variation of this principle, and his main work, *Ariel* (1900), discussed his views in much detail. Latin America's peril lay in its enthusiasm for moral and intellectual change and the susceptibility to United States influence this produced.

Rodó admired some aspects of American life: its technology, spirit of personal liberty and open society, respect for useful labor, and rapid growth of political greatness. But these could entrap an uncritical society—and particularly the Latin masses. American materialism was an open challenge to Latin America.

Rodó praised the traditions of humanism and intellectual achievement of southern Europe's past and present. The "hallowed cultural tradition and respect for genius" should combine with the Latin Americans' sense of liberty and material progress but never to the disadvantage of

José Enrique Rodó. (Bibliothèque Nationale, Paris)

the superior minority which maintains its values alive. A leveling process should never occur through mass education or populist technical change.

In 1897 a revolution overthrew the President, and Rodó closed his journal in the interests of political peace and shortly after accepted a professorship in literature in the National University. Indicative of the open atmosphere was Rodó's recommendation by Samuel Blixen, publisher of an avowed anti-Catholic newspaper, for his own post.

In 1902 Rodó accepted election to the national Chamber of Representatives, where he served for 8 years. He opposed the government's open anti-Church position under José Batlle but made no headway. Rodó returned to intellectual work and supported himself by teaching and newspaper work. On July 14, 1916, he left for Europe as foreign correspondent for publications in Montevideo and Buenos Aires. He died in Palermo, Italy, on May 1, 1917.

Rodó's influence on the young intellectuals and idealists of his time, and Latin Americans up to the 1940s, was enormous. Since he never visited the United States, many of his ideas were less than accurate. But he stated strongly the principle of Latin uniqueness in contrast with the United States and set a standard that has retained importance.

Ariel was the third in a pamphlet series entitled *La vida nueva*. Other titles were *El que vendrá* (1897) and *Rubén Darío* (1899); the latter is a critical analysis of the

work of the famed Nicaraguan poet. In 1906, reflecting his political experience, Rodó wrote *Liberalismo y jacobinismo*, a pamphlet. In 1909 he published a book, *Motivos de Proteo*. A posthumous work is *El camino de Paros*, a collection of pieces written in 1916 and 1917.

Further Reading

José Enrique Rodó is listed in the Latin America study guide (IV, N, 2). Another Uruguayan writer was Juan ZORRILLA.

The most complete studies of Rodó in English are in Isaac Goldberg, *Studies in Spanish-American Literature* (1920); William Rex Crawford, *A Century of Latin-American Thought* (1944; rev. ed. 1961); and Arturo Torres-Rioseco, *New World Literature: Tradition and Revolt in Latin America* (1949) and *Aspects of Spanish American Literature* (1963).

J. **ROEBLING** / By Ralph D. Gray

John Augustus Roebling (1806–1869), German-born American engineer, was noted for introducing the manufacture of wire rope to America and for constructing magnificent suspension bridges.

J ohn Roebling was born in Mühlhausen, Thuringia, on June 12, 1806. He obtained an excellent formal education, graduating from the Royal Polytechnic Institute at Berlin in 1826 with a degree in civil engineering. After working for 3 years on government road-building projects, he became dissatisfied with his life and opportunities in Germany. In 1831 Roebling and

John Roebling. (The Smithsonian Institution)

Brooklyn Bridge, a photograph from the Wittemann Collection. (Library of Congress)

his brother, Karl, led a group of emigrants to the United States, where they established an agricultural community in western Pennsylvania.

Unsuccessful as a farmer, Roebling returned to engineering in 1837 and was employed by the state of Pennsylvania on various canal and railroad projects. He became interested in the Allegheny Portage Railroad linking the eastern and western sections of the Pennsylvania Canal, where he observed the difficulties involved in hauling bisected canal boats up and down the inclined planes of the railway. Roebling suggested using wire rope for hauling in place of the bulky and expensive fiber ropes which rapidly frayed and parted. He had read of experiments in Germany with ropes made of twisted wire but had not seen any. He made a number of experiments and eventually convinced the state Board of Public Works to test his idea; consequently, in 1841 Roebling manufactured the first wire cable in America. His small factory in Saxonburg, Pa., was equipped with machinery of his own design and fabrication. In the late 1840s the wire cable factory was relocated at Trenton, N.J., where Roebling subsequently made his home.

In 1844–1845 Roebling built his first structure utilizing his wire cables. He erected a wooden canal aqueduct across the Allegheny River. It consisted of seven spans, each 162 feet long, all supported by two 7-inch wire cables. Following this unprecedented achievement, Roebling built his first suspension bridge in 1845–1846; it was to carry a highway across the Monongahela River at Pittsburgh and consisted of eight spans of 188 feet each. Although he was anticipated in building wire suspension bridges by Charles Ellet, Jr., who in 1842 successfully introduced this type of design, Roebling achieved greater success and eminence in the field.

In many ways Roebling's most notable work was the pioneer railroad suspension bridge built at Niagara Falls between 1851 and 1855. This structure was begun in 1847 by Ellet, who withdrew from the job in 1849 after building a footbridge. Roebling built the railroad bridge, thus solidifying his reputation as the foremost suspension bridge builder in America. He subsequently built bridges over the Allegheny River at Pittsburgh (1860) and the Ohio River at Cincinnati (1867). Roebling's special building techniques included wrapping the numerous wires composing the cables. He also used special stiffening and bracing cables to protect against the weather and to add rigidity to the entire structure.

When plans for a bridge (the Brooklyn Bridge) over the East River connecting lower Manhattan and Brooklyn were revived in the 1860s, Roebling was appointed chief engineer of the mammoth project. His plans for the undertaking were approved in 1869, and work was about to begin when Roebling suffered the accident which cost him his life. On June 28, while he was working at the bridge site, a ferryboat rammed the piling on which Roebling was standing and crushed his foot. The injured toes were amputated, but tetanus set in and he died on July 22, 1869. The Brooklyn Bridge, completed 14 years later under the supervision of Roebling's son, Washington, remains an enduring monument to the Roeblings.

Further Reading

John Roebling is listed in the Science study guide (VI, H, 3). His son, Washington ROEBLING, worked with his father on several bridges before taking over supervision of the Brooklyn Bridge.

The best biography of Roebling is D. B. Steinman, *The Builders of the Bridge: The Story of John Roebling and*

His Son (1945), a comprehensive, well-researched study presented with a lively style but with a partisan flavor; it is based on a book by Hamilton Schuyler, *The Roeblings: A Century of Engineers, Bridge-builders and Industrialists* (1931), which quotes from primary sources. A dated but useful work is Charles B. Stuart, *Lives and Works of Civil and Military Engineers of America* (1871). See also Gene D. Lewis's scholarly biography of another pioneer suspension bridge builder, *Charles Ellet, Jr.: The Engineer as Individualist, 1810–1862* (1968), and Carl W. Condit, *American Building Art: The Nineteenth Century* (1960), for the excellent chapters on bridges.

*　　*　　*

w. ROEBLING / By Carroll Pursell

Washington Augustus Roebling (1837–1926), American engineer and manufacturer, was a noted bridge designer and builder.

Washington Roebling. (Library of Congress)

Washington Roebling was born on May 26, 1837, in Saxonburg, Pa., where his father, an engineer, had settled in 1831 with a group of German colonists. The boy was raised in a strict home; both German and English were spoken daily. At the age of 13 he moved with his family to Trenton, N.J., where his father set up a factory to manufacture wire rope. Roebling was educated by private tutor, at an academy, and finally at Rensselaer Polytechnic Institute in Troy, N.Y., then the leading civil engineering school in the United States. After graduating in 1857, he went to work at his father's factory. During this period he also helped his father build the Allegheny River Bridge at Pittsburgh.

At the outbreak of the Civil War, Roebling enlisted and saw considerable service, mostly as an army engineer. He built several suspension bridges for use by the Union forces and at one time rode in a captive balloon to observe Confederate movements. After the war he returned to civil engineering, working with his father on the construction of a bridge across the Ohio River at Cincinnati. When it was opened in 1867, this was the longest suspension bridge ever built. Roebling spent a year abroad learning about European bridge-building techniques but returned in time to assist his father's work on the Brooklyn Bridge.

Roebling's father, John Roebling, had pioneered the manufacture of wire rope in the United States and had originated the application of such cables to the building of suspension bridges. The Brooklyn Bridge, connecting Brooklyn to Manhattan, was to be John Roebling's greatest feat. Then, just as the actual construction was beginning, he died. His son carried on the work for 3 years, but in 1872, after an attack of the bends in one of the caissons, his health was broken. Within a few months he retired to a house on the Brooklyn side of the East River, and from there he observed the work through a telescope and directed construction.

After completion of the bridge in 1883, Roebling largely withdrew from active engineering work and from the family manufacturing business, of which he had become president in 1876. He spent his last years in Trenton, occupied with philanthropic and scientific pursuits. He died on July 21, 1926.

Further Reading

Washington Roebling is listed in the Art study guide (IV, D, 4, b). His father, John ROEBLING, built several of the finest and most spectacular suspension bridges in America.

The standard sources for Roebling's life and work are Hamilton Schuyler, *The Roeblings: A Century of Engineers, Bridge-builders and Industrialists* (1931), and D. B. Steinman, *The Builders of the Bridge: The Story of John Roebling and His Son* (1945). A good study of the Brooklyn Bridge, which traces its importance in art and literature, is Alan Trachtenberg, *Brooklyn Bridge: Fact and Symbol* (1965).

*　　*　　*

ROENTGEN / By Stanley L. Jaki

The German physicist Wilhelm Conrad Roentgen (1845–1923) discovered x-rays and

their use for obtaining pictures of the interior structure of animate and inanimate bodies.

Wilhelm Roentgen (pronounced rĕnt′gən) was born on March 27, 1845, in Lennep near Cologne. At the age of 17 he went to Utrecht to a technical school, and in late 1865 he began his studies at the Polytechnic (Eidgenössische Technische Hochschule), Zurich, in mechanical engineering. Roentgen's academic progress was so remarkable that he received the doctor's degree in physics from the Polytechnic's sister institute, the University of Zurich, on June 22, 1869.

That year found Roentgen as a laboratory assistant at the University of Würzburg. While still in Würzburg, in 1872 Roentgen married Anna Bertha Ludwig, whom he met during his student days in Zurich. In the same year Roentgen moved to the University of Strasbourg, where he obtained in 1874 the rank of privatdozent. His career in Strasbourg was interrupted by a year-long stay (1875–1876) as professor at the Academy of Agriculture of Hohenhelm in Württemberg.

Roentgen's second 3-year stay (1876–1879) in Strasbourg was marked by a steadily increasing interest in electrical discharges and the properties of crystals; but full professorship still eluded him. He accepted therefore with eagerness the invitation of the University of Giessen to the chair of physics. There Roentgen's presence soon produced impressive results. A year after his arrival, a new physics institute and several laboratories had been placed on the immediate building program of the university.

Roentgen's most important achievement in Giessen consisted in the discovery that when a dielectric body, such as a glass plate, is moved between the plates of a charged condenser, a magnetic field is created, exactly as is done by a current flowing in wire. The observed phenomenon provided powerful evidence on behalf of the hypothesis that electric current consisted of the motion of discrete charges. In 1889 Roentgen moved to the University of Würzburg. His research in Wüzburg showed him to be more and more preoccupied with the effect of changes of pressure on various phenomena. He investigated the change of the refractive indices of various fluids as a function of pressure and also devoted considerable attention to the compressibility of water. The most fascinating field of problems connected with the variation of pressure lay, of course, in the direction of very low pressures. Techniques of producing high vacuums began to improve rapidly during the second half of the 19th century. German technicians, like H. Geissler, and physicists, like J. Plücker and J. W. Hittorf, were chiefly responsible for the results. After the early 1870s when Hittorf's colleague, E. Goldstein, coined the name *Kathodenstrahlen* (cathode rays), experimentation with Geissler tubes and Hittorf tubes became an avidly pursued field of investigation. It certainly did not miss the attention of Roentgen, known for his thorough information on the latest developments in physics.

Discovery of X-Rays

Actually, Roentgen himself kept experimenting with Geissler tubes and cathode rays. On Nov. 8, 1895, he was busy determining the extent to which the glass wall of an 8-inch-long Hittorf tube was penetrated by cathode rays. As he activated the tube in his darkened laboratory, he noticed a fluorescent light about 3 feet away from the tube. The source of light was a 6- by 12-inch cardboard coated with fine barium cyanoplatinite crystals. Roentgen knew only too well that cathode rays could not travel more than an inch in air. Furthermore, the thin glass wall of the Hittorf tube almost completely stopped cathode rays as they made the glass glow in a greenish light at the point of impact. Could it be that in hitting the glass they produced some new form of energy, or radiation, that would travel much farther in air and make the coated cardboard fluoresce? To eliminate possible sources of external interference, he put a black paper cover around the tube, but the strange light did not disappear even when he turned off the Hittorf tube.

After a late dinner Roentgen excitedly went on with the experiment. He noticed that the fluorescent light on the coated cardboard changed in intensity as its distance from the glowing spot on the tube was increased or diminished. Various objects, books, metal plates, when interposed between the tube and the cardboard, produced a similar change in the intensity of the cardbourd's fluorescence. Then suddenly the silhouette of his finger bones appeared on the cardboard as he was holding a metal plate. His immediate idea was to record the phe-

Wilhelm Roentgen. (Culver Pictures, Inc.)

Roentgen's laboratory at the University of Würzburg. The photograph dates from about 1895, the year in which the German physicist discovered x-rays. (National Library of Medicine, Bethesda, Md.)

nomenon by putting in the cardboard's position a photographic plate wrapped in black paper. The first known x-ray picture showed, however, the right hand of Roentgen's wife and was dated Dec. 22, 1895.

By then Roentgen had established all the essential features of x-rays, and it only remained for him to write up the results. The paper was entitled *Eine neue Art von Strahlen* (A New Kind of Rays). The first 16 points consisted in a careful description of the experimental evidence. The seventeenth contained Roentgen's own hypothesis about the nature of the new radiation. There he took the wrong tack as he firmly excluded the possibility that the new rays might have anything in common with infrared, visible, and ultraviolet rays. Instead of classifying the x-rays as part of the electromagnetic spectrum, Roentgen viewed them as longitudinal vibrations in the ether.

This mistake was insignificant, however, compared with the extraordinary importance of the discovery. In fact, hardly ever did scientific discovery create a more startled reaction. For months x-rays formed the most sensational material for newspapers all over the world. In 1896 alone, some 50 books and more than 1,000 papers were published on the new discovery. By February of the same year Antoine Henri Becquerel's experiments in Paris showed that, beyond the fascinating prospects for medicine, the x-rays showed entirely new avenues in physics as well. The new world was the realm of radioactivity, and atomic energy with all its magnificence and horror.

Roentgen's epoch-making discovery earned him the Nobel Prize in physics, of which he was the first recipient, in 1901. By then he was at the University of Munich, where he remained for the rest of his life. He died on Feb. 10, 1923.

Further Reading

Wilhelm Roentgen is listed in the Science study guide (VI, C, 2). Among his teachers was R. J. E. CLAUSIUS, a pioneer in thermodynamics. In 1896 Antoine Henri BECQUEREL showed that x-rays opened up new avenues in physics.

The standard scholarly biography of Roentgen is Otto Glasser, *Wilhelm Conrad Röntgen and the Early History of the Roentgen Rays* (trans. 1934), of which a shorter version was published under the title *Dr. W. C. Röntgen* (1949; 2d ed. 1958). Arnulf K. Esterer, *Discoverer of X-Ray: Wilhelm Conrad Röntgen* (1968), is both very entertaining and informative. Also useful is Bern Dibner, *Wilhelm Conrad Röntgen and the Discovery of X Rays* (1968). See also the biographical sketch of Roentgen in Nobel Foundation, *Physics, 1901–1921*, vol. 1 (1964).

ROETHKE / By Richard M. Ludwig

American poet and teacher Theodore Roethke (1908–1963) is considered a major poet of his generation. He demonstrated a wide range of styles and growing awareness of how to transform his love of nature into a vehicle for expressing his mystical visions.

Theodore Roethke was born in Saginaw, Mich., on May 25, 1908. The family owned the largest greenhouses in the state. He called his home "a wonderful place for a child to grow up in and around"—25 acres under glass in town and "the last stand of virgin timber in the Saginaw Valley" out in the country.

Roethke claimed to have hated high school; nevertheless, he continued his education, earning a bachelor of arts degree at the University of Michigan (1929) and spending 1930–1931 at Harvard. He began teaching at Lafayette College (1931), later taught at Pennsylvania State College, then moved to Bennington as assistant professor of English (1943). By 1947 he had settled at the University of Washington in Seattle. In 1962 he was appointed poet in residence in addition to being professor of English. Awards and honors were frequent during these years, including a Pulitzer Prize (1953), the Bollingen Prize, the National Book Award (1958), and even a posthumous National Book Award for his last poems, *The Far Field* (1964).

Roethke began writing prose in high school but switched to poetry in graduate school (encouraged by Robert Hillyer and I. A. Richards). His first book, *Open House*, appeared in 1941. These short, intense lyrics demonstrated superior craftsmanship as well as a generous, ebullient personality: "My heart keeps open house,/ My doors are widely swung./ . . . I'm naked to the bone,/ With nakedness my shield./ Myself is what I wear:/ I keep the spirit spare." Years later Roethke said: "In those first poems I had begun, like the child, with small things and had tried to make plain words do the

trick. Somewhat later, in 1945, I began a series of longer pieces which try, in their rhythms, to catch the movement of the mind itself, to trace the spiritual history of a protagonist (not 'I' personally but all haunted and harried men)."

The Lost Son and Other Poems (1948), a group of remarkable poems, traces Roethke's spiritual biography and celebrates growing up in the atmosphere of greenhouses. His moving elegy "Frau Bauman, Frau Schmidt, and Frau Schwartze" is almost equaled by "Big Wind," "Root Cellar," and "The Lost Son." *Praise to the End!* (1951) was followed by *The Waking* (1953) and *Words for the Wind* (1958). By this time Roethke's reputation was firmly established as a superb metaphysical poet. "I learn by going where I have to go," he wrote in an early poem, and in the last years of his life he was taking his verse into the province of his master, W. B. Yeats: visionary lyrics, interior monologues, projected *personae*, transmuted life. He died on Aug. 1, 1963, of a heart attack. Had Roethke lived longer, he might well have surpassed his masters.

Further Reading

Theodore Roethke is listed in the Literature study guide (I, E, 3). With Robert LOWELL he was considered a major poet of his period.

Roethke's *Collected Poems* appeared in 1966. Ralph J. Mills, Jr., edited *Selected Letters* (1968) and a volume of selected prose, *On the Poet and His Craft* (1965). The only biography of Roethke is Allan Seager, *The Glass House: The Life of Theodore Roethke* (1968). The major critical study is Karl Malkoff, *Theodore Roethke: An Introduction to the Poetry* (1966). Arnold Stein, ed., *Theodore Roethke: Essays on the Poetry* (1965), contains an introduction by the editor and essays by critics.

✳ ✳ ✳

ROGER II / By Edward M. Peters

Roger II (1095–1154), king of Sicily from 1130 to 1154, was the most able ruler in 12th-century Europe. He organized a multiracial, multinational kingdom in which Arabic, Byzantine, Lombard, Jewish, and Norman cultures produced a brilliant cosmopolitan state.

Theodore Roethke in 1956. (United Press International Photo)

Roger II was the son of the "Great Count" Roger of Sicily and Adelaide of Savona, and the nephew of Robert Guiscard, the greatest Norman ruler of Apulia and Sicily. In 1101 Roger's father, who had been 64 when Roger was born, died, leaving his widow and two small sons to rule his turbulent and rebellious county of Sicily. Countess Adelaide managed to retain power in the county, and in 1105 her elder son, Simon, died, leaving Roger as sole heir. By 1112, when Roger II was knighted, he and his mother had made Palermo their

Roger II crowned by Christ, a Byzantine mosaic in the church of S. Maria dell'Ammiraglio, known as the Martorana, in Palermo, Sicily. The mosaic was executed about 1148. (Alinari-Brogi)

social structures, a kingdom. It was a kingdom, however, unlike any other European kingdom.

The first years of Roger's reign were spent in suppressing baronial revolts, countering the propaganda of Bernard of Clairvaux and Pope Innocent II, and defending his kingdom against the invading armies of the emperor Lothair. By 1139, however, Roger had succeeded in fending off all three dangers. The Emperor was dead, Roger was reconciled to Innocent II, and the last of the rebellious barons had been crushed. During the first 2 decades of his reign, Roger had begun to sponsor the architectural projects which were to make Norman Sicily one of the wonders of the world. The Cathedral at Cefalù, the Palatine Chapel at Palermo, and many other religious and secular buildings began to take on that unique combination of Greek, Arabic, and Norman artistic style which still fascinates the beholder. In 1140 Roger II promulgated the Assizes of Ariano, the most remarkable royal code of laws of the 12th century.

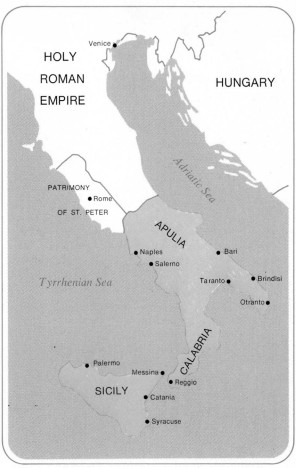

The kingdom of Sicily under Roger II. Land-hungry Norman adventurers first went to southern Italy early in the 11th century. At the time William the Conqueror was creating a Norman kingdom in England, Normans in Italy and Sicily were carving out principalities for themselves. The climax of the Norman adventure in the south was Roger II's creation of the kingdom of Sicily, the strongest and most brilliant of medieval monarchies.

capital. Roger, a member of the first generation of the Hauteville family to be born in their southern Italian domains, was raised in the cosmopolitan Arabic, Greek, and Norman culture of Sicily, and his subsequent character reflects that upbringing.

Adelaide died in 1118, and the 23-year-old Roger, his county somewhat pacified by the participation of many Norman knights in the First Crusade and in subsequent service in the Latin kingdom of Jerusalem, began to consider the exploitation of Sicily's strategic position along the Mediterranean trade routes. On the death of his cousin Duke William of Apulia in 1127, Roger claimed the mainland inheritance of his family as his own. In 1128 he was formally invested as Duke of Apulia by Pope Honorius II at Benevento. By 1129 Roger had imposed his rule over the turbulent Norman barons of the mainland and had extracted from them a closely binding oath of personal loyalty to himself.

Norman Sicily and southern Italy had always been a subject of dispute between Normans, Byzantines, the German emperors, and the papacy. In the disputed papal election of 1130, Roger sided with the antipope Anacletus II against Innocent II. Therefore on Christmas Day, 1130, Anacletus crowned Roger king of Sicily at Palermo. The Norman adventure of the 11th century had reached its apex. At one stroke the dubiously gotten lands had been transformed into that most sacred of all Christian

Not only did Roger and his officials patronize the arts and architecture, but they encouraged learning and literature. The great Arab geographer al-Idrisi dedicated his book to Roger, and Sicily, in continuous cultural contact with Byzantium, Islam, and Christian Europe, became not only a remarkable hybrid cultural meeting place but a center of Christian-Arab contacts from which much of Arabic and Greek learning would soon penetrate western Europe.

The old tensions among Sicily, Byzantium, and the German emperors were not, however, extinct. During the last years of his reign Roger had to counter a Byzantine-Western imperial alliance, and not until the death of the emperor Conrad III in 1152 was Roger able to cease his complex diplomatic efforts to neutralize this powerful threat to his independence. By 1153 Roger had once again vindicated his claims by his ability. In 1146 he had succeeded in establishing control of part of North Africa, and throughout his reign he succeeded in creating a stable political kingdom out of the most savagely opposed religious and racial factions which Christendom knew. His chancery issued documents in four languages: Arabic, Greek, Latin, and Hebrew, and his island and mainland kingdom knew a degree of racial and religious toleration and cross-cultural influence such as few societies have known before or since. Roger died on Feb. 26, 1154, leaving the kingdom to his son William; and his reputation as the most remarkable layman of the 12th century, to history.

Further Reading

Roger II is listed in the European History study guide (I, J, 2, e; II, H, 1, d). A nephew of ROBERT GUISCARD, he entered into conflict with St. BERNARD OF CLAIRVAUX.

The best work on Roger II in English is the two-volume study of John Julius Norwich, *The Normans in the South, 1016–1130* (1967) and *The Kingdom in the Sun, 1130–1194* (1970). David C. Douglas, *The Norman Achievement* (1969), surveys the entire Norman movement in France, England, and Sicily. Otto Demus, *The Mosaics of Norman Sicily* (1950), discusses the artistic style of Roger's period.

✳ ✳ ✳

J. ROGERS / By William Gerdts

John Rogers (1829–1904) was the most successful genre sculptor of mid-19th century America. His plaster groups sold by the thousands.

John Rogers was born in Salem, Mass., and spent his early life as a clerk in New England, New York, and the Midwest. He began to model sculpture before the middle of the century. In 1858 he went first to Paris and then to Rome for training. The ideals of contemporary neoclassicism, as practiced by both American

John Rogers about 1856. (Courtesy of The New-York Historical Society, New York City)

and European sculptors in Italy, did not inspire him, however, and he turned his back upon his sculptural pursuits when he returned to Chicago.

However, Rogers was persuaded to continue modeling small genre figures of a type he had done previously. Their success led him to open a studio in New York City in 1859. A combination of his sculptural ability and shrewd marketing practices quickly made that venture a success too. His work consisted of small, very detailed sculptures in plaster, built around a metal armature, and painted a neutral earth color. His grasp of anatomy and sharp observation of details of costumes and accessories were combined with an ability at compositional massing of figures and an appealing, sympathetic expressiveness. Some of his earliest works related to the Civil War, appealing to patriotism and to the popular sentiment against deprivation, the horrors of war, and slavery.

The majority of Rogers's sculptures featured scenes of everyday life—in the schoolhouse, at the parsonage, in the home, more often rural or small town. Among his more ambitious works were scenes taken from literature, including three sculptures from Washington Irving's *Rip Van Winkle*, some from Goethe's *Faust*, and a number of Shakespearean interpretations; even these stressed anecdotal rather than dramatic qualities. There were a few small portrait sculptures, too, of Abraham Lincoln, George Washington, and Henry Ward Beecher. As time went on, Rogers's compositions tended toward greater looseness, and he also depicted more scenes of action. In all, there were about 80 so-called Rogers Groups, of which about 80,000 plaster reproductions were made.

Rogers developed a mail-order business, and his works were often purchased as wedding presents. They cost about $10 or $15 each.

Rogers also executed a number of monumental sculptures, but these are far less significant than his plaster groups. They represent one phase of the reaction to the popular idealistic marbles, although in the 1850s some neoclassic sculptors were also producing genre works. Rogers had numerous imitators, but none achieved his renown.

Further Reading

John Rogers is listed in the Art study guide (IV, D, 3). His groups are the sculptural equivalents of the genre paintings of William Sidney MOUNT.

Two full-length studies of Rogers are Mr. and Mrs. Chetwood Smith, *Rogers Groups: Thought and Wrought by John Rogers* (1934), and David H. Wallace, *John Rogers: The People's Sculptor* (1967).

R. ROGERS / By John Bakeless

The colonial American Robert Rogers (1731–1795) was a frontiersman and army officer in the French and Indian War. Later he was extremely successful as a ranger, raider, and reconnaissance officer.

Robert Rogers was born in Methuen, Mass., on Nov. 18, 1731. He grew up in Dunbarton, N.H. Though formal education was slight in a frontier town like Dunbarton, his childhood in field and forest was ideal preparation for his career as a ranger officer.

Beginning service as a scout in King George's War (1744–1748), Rogers reentered service as a ranger officer when the French and Indian War (1755–1763) broke out, possibly because he was involved in alleged counterfeiting of the easily imitated colonial currency. Eventually, he commanded nine ranger companies and was promoted to major. He was in charge of reconnaissance, active in raiding around Lake Champlain, especially at Crown Point and Ticonderoga, and led the force that destroyed the St. Francis Indians, longtime terrors of the New England frontier. He was at the surrender of Montreal in 1760, which ended the French regime in Canada.

After the capitulation, Rogers led a party as far as Detroit to receive the surrender of the French garrison there and to persuade the Indians that they must henceforward look to the British as their "fathers." The popular hero was not completely successful. The Indians attacked in Pontiac's Conspiracy, and Rogers was with the British troops that moved to relieve Detroit, fighting in the defeat at Bloody Run and commanding the men who covered the British withdrawal to Detroit again.

After brief service in the South and a trip to England,

Rogers became commandant at the northwestern Mackinac post. Here he was accused of illegal trading with the Indians and other offenses, including treason; but a court-martial triumphantly acquitted him. Rogers had been unfortunate in business; the exact nature of his business is not clear, but it certainly included ventures in Indian trading. He also had difficulty with vouchers for expenses incurred during his Indian fighting, so that his debts eventually reached £13,000. When he returned to England in 1769, he was thrown into debtors' prison but was released with the aid of his brother James.

Returning to America in 1775 as a half-pay British lieutenant colonel, Rogers showed patriot sympathies, which may have been feigned. George Washington distrusted him, and Rogers eventually joined the service of the British with no great distinction. He died in poverty in London on May 18, 1795.

Further Reading

Robert Rogers is listed in the American History study guide (II, B, 4, d). Israel PUTNAM was among the officers under his command in the French and Indian War.

Rogers's *Journals* are the best source for his military exploits. Rogers's *Ponteach* (1914) contains a biography by the editor, Allan Nevins. An excellent biography is John R. Cuneo, *Robert Rogers of the Rangers* (1959). The second volume of the 1937 edition of Kenneth Roberts, *Northwest Passage*, contains documents and a lengthy bibliography.

ROJAS / By Thomas Blossom

Gustavo Rojas Pinilla (born 1900) was a Colombian general and dictator-president. Though he interrupted briefly Colombia's civil war, his rule ultimately became an oppressive regime of terror.

Gustavo Rojas (pronounced rô′häs) was born in ancient Tunja on March 12, 1900. After receiving his preuniversity education at Tunja Normal School, he began his military career in 1917, specializing in building airports. In 1927 he wrote a thesis at the Tri-State College of Engineering in Angola, Ind., on the building of airfields in Colombia. During the next 20 years, as he rose from lieutenant to general, Rojas was an engineer, building roads and airports. By 1945 he had become the director of civil aeronautics.

The *Bogotazo* riots of April 8, 1948, marked a turning point in Rojas's life and the start of his political career. He suppressed the Cali rioters with such efficiency and brutality that he won the hatred of the Liberals and the approval of the Conservative dictator, Laureano Gómez, who promoted him in 1950 to commander in chief of the armed forces and sent him in 1952 to Washington

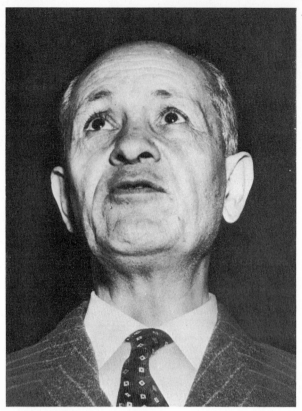

Gustavo Rojas in 1963. (United Press International Photo)

and Colombia, the Conservative and Liberal leaders jointly ousted Rojas and instituted their unique 16-year plan for "peace through alternation and parity." By this plan, Liberals and Conservatives alternated the presidency every 4 years after 1958, dividing the government jobs equally and giving Colombia years of comparative peace.

After a brief period of disgrace and exile, Rojas organized ANAPO, a rapidly growing party of left and right extremists who vowed to upset this "frozen democracy." In 1970 they claimed to have won a third of the votes and the presidency. When the Conservative Misael Pastrana was officially declared the winner, Rojas promised revolution and was held under house arrest. Bogotá was tense, but Pastrana became president.

Further Reading

Gustavo Rojas is listed in the Latin America study guide (IV, F, 1, b). Other Colombian presidents were Laureano GÓMEZ and Alberto LLERAS.

A chapter on Rojas appears in Tad Szulc, *Twilight of the Tyrants* (1959). For further information on his role in the context of Colombian politics see Vernon Lee Fluharty, *Dance of the Millions: Military Rule and the Social Revolution in Colombia 1930–1956* (1957); John D. Martz, *Colombia: A Contemporary Political Survey* (1962); and Robert H. Dix, *Colombia: The Political Dimensions of Change* (1967).

✳ ✳ ✳

to represent Colombia on the Inter-American Defense Board and to Korea to inspect Colombian troops there.

In 1953, threatened with demotion and removal by Gómez, Rojas led a plot of army officers in a successful coup against the dictator and brought a brief stop to the bloody civil war in Colombia. Colombians were so thankful to Rojas for peace that they elected him president, but by June 8, 1954, Rojas had started his own violence.

Rojas used the army and police against all opposition in Colombia. Hundreds of thousands of Colombians fled burning villages for the comparative safety of mushrooming city slums. By the end of the Rojas regime, in 1957, over 300,000 Colombians were dead, and Rojas, the peacemaker and builder, had acquired a different reputation. Hubert Herring described him as a "sadist . . . one of the most savage and venal and altogether incompetent administrators in the history of the nation." Other historians were not so harsh. Vernon Lee Fluharty considered him a much-maligned reformer trying to modernize a semifeudal society which had been run for centuries by two small elite oligarchies. Fluharty saw these oligarchies as unwilling to give up their privileges or to "cope with long-smoldering social revolution." Fluharty excused the violence but incorrectly predicted that the two rival oligarchies would never cooperate.

The new military coup against Rojas came suddenly on May 9, 1957. After months of secret negotiations in Spain

ROLFE / By Irwin H. Polishook

John Rolfe (1585–1622) was an English colonist who settled in Jamestown, Va., and pioneered in the cultivation of tobacco.

John Rolfe was born in the spring of 1585, the descendant of an old Norfolk family. His emigration to Virginia in 1609 was interrupted by a shipwreck on the newly discovered island of Bermuda. A child born to Rolfe's wife died while they were stranded in Bermuda. After almost a year the couple landed in Jamestown, Va.; the colony was in desperate condition. Apart from the danger of disease, which claimed Rolfe's wife shortly after their arrival, the province had no staple product, and there were constant threats of Indian attack.

Conceptions regarding colonization had proceeded no further in Rolfe's time than to think of plantations as trading ventures, places where quick returns might be won from a minimal investment. Finding neither precious metals nor other resources that could be exploited easily, the sponsors of Jamestown experienced continuing expense coupled with disappointment. The colony's settlers found the Indians growing and using tobacco, but its commercial possibilities seemed limited because the leaf tasted bitter.

Rolfe started to experiment with the cultivation of

tobacco. In 1612 he planted seeds of tobacco plants that had been found originally in the West Indies and Venezuela and that offered a milder smoke. He also developed new methods of curing the leaf, thereby further enhancing its flavor and facilitating its shipment to England. Rolfe's experiments were very successful, and his first shipments to London in 1614 were the foundation of the staple production that underlay the southern economy before 1800.

Given the importance of Rolfe's contribution in the cultivation of tobacco, it is unfortunate that his fame is largely associated with his marriage in 1614 to Pocahontas, daughter of the Indian chief Powhatan. Although Rolfe's marriage to Pocahontas grew out of mutual love, contemporaries also observed that it initiated an 8-year period of relative peace with the Indians. A triumphant tour of England by Pocahontas and her entourage in 1616, during which she was received as a visiting princess, ended sadly in her death from consumption.

Rolfe's last years were busy and fruitful. He served as secretary of Virginia and as a member of the council, writing important letters describing the problems of Virginia. He was killed during the Indian massacre of March 22, 1622. He left a third wife and daughter, as well as his son by Pocahontas, Thomas Rolfe.

Further Reading

John Rolfe is listed in the American History study guide (II, B, 3, a). John SMITH was also important in establishing the viability of the Jamestown colony.

In the absence of a biography, the best sources of information on Rolfe and the beginnings of Virginia are Richard L. Morton, *Colonial Virginia* (2 vols., 1960); Grace Steele Woodward, *Pocahontas* (1969); and Philip L. Barbour, *Pocahontas and Her World* (1970). Materials by contemporaries are in Lyon G. Tyler, ed., *Narratives of Early Virginia, 1606–1625* (1907). A short, authoritative account of Virginia's tobacco economy is G. Melvin Herndon, *Tobacco in Colonial Virginia* (1957).

who introduced him to the heroes of revolution and German romanticism; these various influences appear for the first time in his two unpublished dramas—*Empedocle* and *Orsino*.

Rolland returned to Paris in 1891, where he slowly turned toward the incipient socialism. In 1898, involved in the polemic aroused by the Dreyfus Affair, he wrote *Les Loups* (The Wolves), a play that transposed the case to 1793 and attempted to present objectively the arguments of both sides. The success of *Les Loups* encouraged him to write a whole cycle of plays on the French Revolution, whose spirit, he thought, must be carried into the future; among them were *Danton* (1900) and *Le Quatorze Juillet* (1902; The Fourteenth of July). Believing in the revolutionary role of culture, he wrote a series of essays in *Le Théâtre du peuple* (1903; The People's Theater).

In 1904 Rolland taught at the Sorbonne, inaugurating a course on the history of music. From 1904 to 1912 he wrote *Jean-Christophe*, a novel which shows the confrontation between an artist and a decadent society. Built like a symphony, *Jean-Christophe* is an affirmation of the German musical genius. *Colas Breugnon* (1914) is, on the contrary, a novel whose humor reminds one of François Rabelais. Meanwhile Rolland produced a series of biographies: *Beethoven* (1903), *Michel-Ange* (1906), and *Tolstoi* (1911).

Rolland spent the war years in Switzerland. He accused both France and Germany in a series of essays, *Au dessus de la melée* (Above the Battle). After the fall of Europe, only the Russian Revolution gave him some hope for the future. Opposing violence, he did not, however, join the Communist party. Throughout the 1920s he called for the unity of all truth-searching minds, regardless of political opinion, in *Déclaration d'indépendance de l'esprit* (1919; Declaration of the Independence of the Mind). His belief in nonviolence made him praise the Gandhian idea of revolution through his several books on Hindu thought.

Rolland meanwhile came back to his plays on the French Revolution; the last one was *Robespierre* (1939). In 1933 he published another novel, *L'Âme enchantée*

ROLLAND / By Antoinette Blum

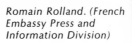

The French writer Romain Rolland (1866–1944) was the author of many works, all reflecting the conscience of a great humanist.

Romain Rolland (pronounced rô-läΝ′) was born on Jan. 29, 1866, in Clamecy (Burgundy). His family moved to Paris in 1880, where he graduated from the École Normale Supérieure in 1889 in history. During these years, disillusioned by the decadence of French society, having lost faith in Catholicism, but still looking for ideals, he turned toward the pantheism of Baruch Spinoza. In 1889 he arrived in Rome, where he discovered the Italian Renaissance and met Malvida von Meysenburg,

Romain Rolland. (French Embassy Press and Information Division)

(The Enchanted Soul), dealing with the problem of political action. Moved perhaps by the mounting fascism, he adhered more closely to communism; several essays show this evolution, in particular, *Quinze ans de combat* (Fifteen Years of Struggle).

In 1938 Rolland settled in Vézelay, where he composed his *Mémoires* and *Le Voyage intérieur* (Journey inside Himself), his spiritual autobiography. He died on Dec. 30, 1944.

Further Reading

Romain Rolland is listed in the Literature study guide (III, H, 1, b; III, J, 1, a). He was a contemporary of Anatole FRANCE.

Stefan Zweig, *Romain Rolland: The Man and His Work*, translated by Eden and Cedar Paul (1921), is one of the best studies but necessarily incomplete. William T. Starr, the specialist on Rolland who published the detailed and very useful *A Critical Bibliography of the Published Writings of Romain Rolland* (1950), also wrote *Romain Rolland: One against All—A Biography* (1971), based on Rolland's works, letters, notes, and diary.

✳   ✳   ✳

ROLLE OF HAMPOLE

/ **By Mary B. Lenhart**

The English prose and verse writer Richard Rolle of Hampole (ca. 1290–1349) gave the first formal expression to English mysticism and exerted a very important intellectual influence on the 14th century.

Richard Rolle of Hampole, from a 14th-century British manuscript. (Department of Manuscripts, The Trustees of the British Museum)

Richard Rolle of Hampole was neither a priest nor a monk but a simple layman. Born in the vicinity of Thornton-le-street, the son of William Rolle, a gentleman of Richmondshire, he was sent to Oxford by Thomas de Neville, who saw great intellectual promise in the boy. Richard progressed well in his studies until at the age of 19 he had a deeply moving mystical experience of love and union with God. He returned home intent on serving God by contemplation as a hermit. He borrowed two gowns from his sister and a rain hood from his father to make a habit and tried to set up a hermitage in the nearby woods. He had an unsatisfactory time of it until one day he was recognized by John de Dalton, son of his former benefactor, as he donned a surplice in the Dalton chapel and, with ecclesiastical permission, preached a moving sermon. The Nevilles set him up on the estate with shelter, food, and suitable clothing.

It was not long before Richard discovered that curious and intrusive friendship can destroy those essentials of a contemplative life, solitude and peace of mind. For a time he sought over the countryside for what he needed. At length he found a spot near the Cistercian convent of St. Mary's at Hampole. Here his freedom was unhampered, and he settled down for a course of contemplative prayer. His experiences could not be contained, and they overflowed in passionate writing. At first he wrote in Latin, the language of the learned. Little by little, as his reputation for holiness spread, he was asked for advice and guidance. Since many who appealed to him were simple people, he turned to English, the vigorous, malleable Northumbrian dialect. His manuscripts were widely distributed and highly prized, some of the more than 400 extant being passed down in wills as family heirlooms.

Richard died in Hampole in 1349, perhaps from the plague which was ravaging the country at the time. He had built an enduring reputation for holiness which encouraged the nuns at St. Mary's to write an office in view of a probable canonization. It is from this office that we learn most of the details of his life.

Richard Rolle's writing was a stupendous achievement. Of the English prose tracts, some running to 10,000 words, the following are outstanding: *The Form of Perfect Living, Ego dormio et cor meum vigilat, A Commandment of the Love of God,* and the *Commentary on the Psalter.* With these, his Latin works, his many shorter prose tracts, and his many versified themes, he influenced people as dissimilar as the great mystic Walter Hilton and that bumbling seeker for true sanctity Margery Kempe. His style is passionate and personal but controlled by moderation, reasonableness, and a sense of humor.

Further Reading

Richard Rolle of Hampole is listed in the Religion study guide (I, F, 5) and the Literature study guide (II, C, 2, b). Another noted English mystic was JULIAN OF NORWICH.

Two indispensable works on Rolle are George C. Heseltine, *Selected Works of Richard Rolle, Hermit* (1930), which contains both prose and verse, and Hope E. Allen, *English Writings of Richard Rolle, Hermit of Hampole* (1931), which includes good biographical notes. Much background information about mysticism as a Christian phenomenon is in Gerard Sitwell, *Spiritual Writers of the Middle Ages* (1961), and David Knowles, *The English Mystical Tradition* (1961).

that famous agreement, the Vikings received control of the territory at the mouth of the Seine in return for certain services to the King. Rollo himself was granted Upper Normandy (the territory between the Epte River and the sea), and he was converted to Christianity and baptized by the archbishop of Rouen. Rouen was the capital of the ecclesiastical province of Normandy, which Rollo's successors later added to their initial territory.

In 924 Rollo added the lands of Bessin and Maine to his holdings, and after his death his successor, William Longsword, completed the construction of the duchy by adding the lands of the Cotentin and the Avranchin to Rollo's acquisitions. Rollo's conversion to Christianity, however, and his gift of land from the king of France should not be misinterpreted. Very likely Rollo's Christianity was of a very limited character, and his supposed loyalty to the king of France could not be counted upon. Early Norman domination of the lower Seine Valley contributed to the disintegration of ecclesiastical and economic institutions in that area, but Rollo's able successors shaped a strong and flourishing duchy in the territory that their vigorous and bloodthirsty ancestor had conquered. Rollo was the great-great-great-grandfather of William the Conqueror (William I of England).

In 927 Rollo abdicated in favor of William Longsword.

Further Reading

Rollo is listed in the European History study guide (I, J, 2, c). Another Viking, CNUT, became king of England in

ROLLO / By Edward M. Peters

The Viking adventurer Rollo (ca. 860–ca. 932) founded the line of the dukes of Normandy. He established Viking control of the lands at the mouth of the Seine River and thus began what became the most powerful French dukedom.

Probably born in Norway, Rollo, or Rolf, was the son of Rögnvald, Earl of Möre. Chronicle sources, which are not always reliable, note that he was exiled from Norway because of lawlessness, probably about 900. Rollo became a Viking raider and for a time was successful. He went to Scotland, where he married a Christian woman by whom he had a daughter; and possibly from this marriage his son, later known as William Longsword, his successor in Normandy, also issued. Rollo then may have gone to Ireland, but with the waning of Norse power in Ireland he probably followed his compatriots who traveled to France, where raiding parties could find richer opportunities for looting.

Rollo probably arrived in Gaul between 905 and 911. During these years he became famous, and stories about him circulated in his homeland: "Rolf [Rollo] was a great Viking: he was so big that no steed could bear him, so that he was called Rolf 'the Ganger.' " Rollo's name figured prominently in the treaty between King Charles the Simple of France and the Seine Vikings in 911. By

Rollo, the 1st Duke of Normandy, detail of his tomb in Rouen Cathedral. (H. Roger-Viollet)

Viking raids and settlement areas in the 9th and 10th centuries. The eruption of the Vikings into European history had profound consequences. At first savagely destructive, the Vikings eventually settled in widely dispersed areas. The duchy of Normandy, awarded to the Viking leader Rollo in 911, became a great French principality and the progenitor of Norman kingdoms in England and Italy.

1016.

There is no biography of Rollo in English. A good recent survey of the Normans is David C. Douglas, *The Norman Achievement, 1050–1100* (1969), recommended as an introduction for the general reader. See also Richard W. A. Onslow, *The Dukes of Normandy and Their Origin* (1947).

RÖLVAAG / By Robert S. Gold

The Norwegian-American writer Ole Edvart Rölvaag (1876–1931) was a powerful, realistic chronicler of the lives of Norwegian immigrants on the farms of the midwestern United States. His work is grimly pessimistic.

Ole Edvart Rölvaag (pronounced rōl′väg) was born on April 22, 1876, on the island of Dönne, Norway; his family had been fishermen and seafaring people for generations. After a meager education Rölvaag worked for several years as a fisherman, but in 1896 he emigrated to the United States to work on his uncle's farm in Elk Point, S.Dak. He worked his way through Augustana College, S.Dak., from 1897 to 1901 and through St. Olaf's College, Minn., where he received a bachelor of arts degree in 1905. He then returned to Norway to spend a year at the University of Oslo.

Returning to America in 1906, Rölvaag joined the faculty of St. Olaf's College. In 1908 he became a United States citizen and married Jenny Berdahl; they had four children. In 1910 Rölvaag received his master of arts degree from St. Olaf's.

Rölvaag had begun writing during his early teaching years. His first book, written in Norwegian, appeared in 1912 under the title *Amerika-Breve* (Letters from America); with a succeeding volume, *På Glente Veie* (1914; On Forgotten Paths), it portrayed the life of the young immigrant in the Midwest. His next novel, *To Tullinger* (1920; Two Fools), is the study of a miser's temperament; it was translated into English a decade later under the title *Pure Gold* (1930). His most poetic and mystical work is *Laengselens Boat* (1921), which concerns a legendary vessel symbolic of the heartache caused by emigration. It was translated into English as *The Boat of Longing* (1933).

Rölvaag's artistic vision was doubtless shaped by the harshness of his life—the years of hard work and hard study and especially the tragic deaths of two of his chil-

ROMMEL / By Diethelm Prowe

The German field marshal Erwin Rommel (1891–1944), known as the "Desert Fox," achieved fame as a brilliant desert-warfare tactician in World War II.

Ole Edvart Rölvaag. (Brown Brothers)

dren. His novels are strong reminders of life's severity, and this is nowhere truer than in his masterpiece, *Giants in the Earth* (1927), written with the assistance of a friend, Lincoln Colcord, who helped Rölvaag translate idiomatically from the Norwegian. Rölvaag dedicated the book "To Those of My People Who Took Part in the Great Settling, To Them and Their Generation." The *Nation* called *Giants in the Earth* "the fullest, finest and most powerful novel that has been written about pioneer life in America."

The last book by Rölvaag, *Their Father's God* (1931), consists of intensely dramatic projections of the Minnesota–South Dakota prairie and of the whole westward movement in America. Toward the end of his life, he was appointed head of the Norwegian department at St. Olaf's, where he hoped to institute a center of Norwegian culture, a plan that was aborted by his death on Nov. 5, 1931, from a heart attack.

Further Reading

Ole Edvart Rölvaag is listed in the Literature study guide (I, E, 2, a). Another novelist who wrote about pioneering life in the Midwest was Willa CATHER.

Theodore Jorgenson and Nora O. Slocum, *Ole Edvart Rölvaag* (1939), is the standard biography.

Erwin Rommel (pronounced rŏm′əl) was born in Heidenheim near Ulm on Nov. 15, 1891, into an old Swabian middle-class family. After a traditional classical education, he joined the 124th Infantry Regiment as an officer cadet in 1910 and was commissioned as second lieutenant 2 years later. In World War I he served on the Western front in France and immediately distinguished himself as an outstanding soldier. In 1915 he was awarded the Iron Cross Class I. From autumn 1915 to 1918 he served in a mountain unit in Romania and on the Italian front, where, for unusual bravery in his capture of Monte Matajur, he was cited for the highest award offered in the German army, the Pour le Mérite, at the unprecedented age of 27.

After the war Rommel spent the 1920s as a captain with a regiment near Stuttgart. In the fall of 1929 he commenced his distinguished career as an infantry instructor at the infantry school in Dresden, where he stayed until

Field Marshal Erwin Rommel. (Süddeutscher Verlag)

1933. After a 2-year command of a mountain battalion, he continued his teaching career at the Potsdam War Academy in 1935 and finally—after the annexation of Austria in 1938—took over the command of the war academy in Wiener Neustadt as full colonel.

On the eve of the war Rommel was selected as commander of Hitler's bodyguard and served in that capacity in Hitler's first drives to the east into the Sudetenland, Prague, and finally Poland. His first field command in World War II was at the head of the 7th Tank Division, which swept toward the English Channel in May 1940.

Rommel's appointment in February 1941 as commander of the Afrikakorps with the rank of lieutenant general marked the beginning of his fame as a desert-war tactician. Initially he met with brilliant success. By June 1942 he had driven the British troops from his starting point in Libya all the way to El Alamein and was rewarded with a promotion to field marshal that same month—the youngest in the German armed forces. Because of lack of reinforcements he failed to take Alexandria and advance to the Suez Canal as hoped and was subsequently driven back by Field Marshal Bernard Montgomery's counterattack to Tunis, where he encountered fresh American troops under Gen. Dwight Eisenhower and lost the final, decisive battle at Médenine on March 5, 1943. Five days later he left for Germany on sick leave.

During the summer and fall of 1943 Rommel acted as a special adviser and troubleshooter for Hitler, a task which took him to Italy as commander of the newly formed Army Group B in a last effort to prop up the regime of Benito Mussolini. By December 1943 he was needed at the "Atlantic Wall," the coastal defenses along the coast from Norway to the Pyrenees, and in January 1944 he took over the command of all German armies from the Netherlands to the Loire River. He was unable to prevent the Allied landing in Normandy, however, and on July 17, 1944, was seriously wounded in an air raid, forcing him to return to his home in Herrlingen near Ulm.

Rommel had by this time become increasingly critical of Hitler and the Nazi party, of which he had never been a member. Although he disapproved of an assassination of Hitler, he maintained close contact with the officers who staged the unsuccessful coup of July 20, 1944, and he was to have succeeded Hitler as supreme commander in the event of success. Nazi investigators therefore sought him out at his home in Herrlingen on Oct. 14, 1944, and gave him the choice of taking poison or standing trial before the Nazi People's Court. Rommel chose the former. Hitler ordered national mourning and a state funeral with all honors.

Further Reading

Erwin Rommel is listed in the European History study guide (XI, P, 1, a). He was defeated by Bernard MONTGOMERY and Dwight EISENHOWER.

Rommel's own draft narrative of the African campaign was edited by Capt. B. H. Liddell Hart, together with pertinent letters and notes by Rommel, under the title *The Rommel Papers* (1953). The best-known biography of Rommel in English, and still the standard work, is Desmond Young, *Rommel, the Desert Fox* (1950), a compassionate yet carefully researched work of a British brigadier general with considerable experience in desert warfare. It has been supplemented and updated by Ronald Lewin's work, *Rommel as Military Commander* (1968), which concentrates almost entirely on Rommel's most active years in the field, from 1940 to 1944. Paul Carell's beautifully written, exciting, and meticulously researched account of the African campaign, *The Foxes of the Desert* (1960), was skillfully translated by Mervin Savill. See also Hans Speidel, *Invasion of 1944: Rommel and the Normandy Campaign* (1950), and Siegfried Westphal, *The German Army in the West* (1951).

* * *

ROMNEY / By Joseph Burke

George Romney (1734–1802) was one of the most sought-after portrait painters in England. His portrait style is free, swift, and bold.

The son of a cabinetmaker, George Romney was born in Dalton, Lancashire. He was apprenticed in 1755 to Christopher Steele, a provincial portrait painter, but was largely self-taught. Romney's ambition was to become a history painter. In 1762 he moved to London, where he studied the Duke of Richmond's collection of casts of antique sculpture and established himself as a portraitist. He went to Italy in 1773, and after his return in 1775 he became the favorite painter of high society.

Morbidly sensitive and retiring, Romney kept aloof from the social world of his sitters and from the Royal Academy. By 1782 he was under the spell of Emma Hart, later Lady Hamilton and the mistress of Nelson, who sat for him as Circe, a Bacchante, Cassandra, the Pythian Priestess, Joan of Arc, St. Cecilia, Mary Magdalene, and other impersonations he suggested. In the 1780s he executed a number of Eton leaving portraits, which established him as the supreme interpreter of aristocratic adolescence in his age.

For much of his life in London, Romney was under the wing of the poet William Hayley, who encouraged him in the choice of subjects from Milton and Shakespeare as well as the Bible and Greek tragedy. Romney's history paintings are today chiefly known from engravings, like the dramatic *Tempest* (1787–1790) commissioned for John Boydell's Shakespeare Gallery. A large number of drawings for these projects survive.

Romney had married early in life an uneducated woman whom he did not bring to London but to whom he returned when his health finally gave way. Ill health and the facility with which he converted his early realistic style into a fashionable sketchlike formula for idealizing his sitters probably account for an unevenness of execution that has partially justified his critics.

Unlike Joshua Reynolds, Romney did not enter into

RÓMULO / By Epifanio San Juan, Jr.

Carlos P. Rómulo (born 1899) was an author
and the foremost diplomat of the Philippines.
He was the only Filipino journalist who won the
Pulitzer Prize, and he gained prominence as
America's most trusted Asian spokesman.

Carlos Rómulo (pronounced rŏm′yoo͞-lō) was born
on Jan. 14, 1899, in Manila; but his well-to-do
parents lived in Camiling, Tarlac. His father, Gregorio, was a Filipino guerrilla fighter with the Philippine
revolutionary government of Emilio Aguinaldo during the
Filipino-American War. Rómulo claimed to have witnessed his grandfather tortured by the water cure administered by American soldiers. After early schooling in Tarlac, Rómulo entered the University of the Philippines,
where he received a bachelor's degree in 1918. After getting a master of arts from Columbia University in 1921,
he returned to work as professor of English and chairman
of the English department of the University of the Philippines (1923–1928).

Rómulo became editor in chief of TVT Publications in
1931 and publisher and editor of the *Philippines Herald*
(1933–1941). In 1929 he was appointed regent of the
University of the Philippines. Previously he had served as
secretary to Senate president Manuel Quezon (1922–1925) and as member of the Philippine Independence

*George Romney, a self-portrait painted in 1795.
(The Metropolitan Museum of Art, Bequest of
Marcia Dewitt Jessup, from the collection of her
husband, Morris K. Jessup, 1915)*

the character of his sitters, unless they possessed nervous
traits like his own, for example, the moving portrait *William Cowper.* But he was psychologically involved with
the generalized charms of youth, beauty, and breeding
that he admired in his aristocratic sitters, and by combining a neoclassic purity of line with free but masterly
brushwork he achieved a number of incomparable images which transcend the realism of portraiture. This is
exemplified in *Mrs. Lee Acton* (1791); with a faraway
gaze which borders on the apprehensive, her fingers
nervously clasped, she strays through a formless landscape menaced by storm clouds. In such paintings Romney is the "man of feeling" celebrated in Henry Mackenzie's novel (1771) with that title, just as the best of his
sketches earn him an honorable place in the neoclassic
avant-garde headed by William Blake and Henry Fuseli.
Romney died in Kendal, Westmorland.

Further Reading

George Romney is listed in the Art study guide (III, G,
1, c). He was the most fashionable portrait painter of the
late 18th century after Sir Joshua REYNOLDS and Thomas
GAINSBOROUGH.

The best biography of Romney is still Arthur B. Chamberlain, *George Romney* (1910), richly documented
from the memoirs of the time. For one of the rare appreciations of Romney's history paintings see W. Moelwyn Merchant, *Shakespeare and the Artist* (1959).

Carlos Rómulo. (Library of Congress)

Mission, headed by Quezon. Rómulo belonged to the elite, the oligarchic stratum of the Filipino ruling class, by virtue of his role as defender of the interests of the propertied minority.

In 1941 Rómulo received the coveted Pulitzer Prize for a series of pioneering articles on the Southeast Asian political situation in which he recorded his extensive travels in China, Burma, Thailand, Indochina, Indonesia, and elsewhere. Nonetheless, in spite of his candid reporting, he confessed in an interview, "I held back a lot because as a writer I knew hatred is created by incidents." This revealed Rómulo's gift for shrewd diplomacy and somewhat "opportunistic" manner of dealing with people and events.

With the outbreak of World War II in 1941, Rómulo joined the staff of Gen. Douglas MacArthur as press relations officer. He also served as secretary of information and public relations in Quezon's wartime Cabinet (1943–1944). He retreated with MacArthur from Bataan to Corregidor and then to Australia (1941–1942). While in Corregidor he broadcast for the Voice of Freedom. He served as aide-de-camp to MacArthur and rose from the rank of colonel (1942) to brigadier general (1944).

In 1945 Rómulo acted as Philippine delegate to the United Nations Organization Conference in San Francisco. He was Philippine ambassador to the United Nations from 1946 to 1954. He distinguished himself as the first Asian to become president of the UN General Assembly (Fourth Session, Sept. 20, 1949). In 1950–1951 Rómulo acted as secretary of foreign affairs of the Philippine Republic and, from 1952 on (with some interruptions), as Philippine ambassador to the United States.

After serving as president of the University of the Philippines and secretary of education (1963–1968), Rómulo was appointed by President Marcos to the post of secretary of foreign affairs. Rómulo was the recipient of more than a hundred honorary doctorates, awards, and medals, given by American and Asian universities, organizations, and foreign governments.

Rómulo's prolific pen is attested to by his books, such as *I Saw the Fall of the Philippines* (1942), *Mother America* (1943), *My Brother Americans* (1945), *I See the Philippines Rise* (1946), *Crusade in Asia* (1955), *The Magsaysay Story* (1956), *I Walk with Heroes* (1961), and *Identity and Change* (1965).

Further Reading

Carlos Rómulo is listed in the Asia study guide (IV, C, 6, a). Other influential Philippine leaders were Manuel QUEZON and Diosdado MACAPAGAL.

Rómulo's own books are informative, since most of them are autobiographical in some sense. A full-length work on him is Grace S. Youkey (pseudonym: Cornelia Spencer), *Rómulo: Voice of Freedom* (1953). Romulo figures prominently in Manuel Luis Quezon, *The Good Fight* (1946), and Teodoro A. Agoncillo, *The Fateful Years: Japan's Adventure in the Philippines, 1941–45* (2 vols., 1965).

RONDON / By Robert J. Alexander

Candido Mariano da Silva Rondon (1865–1958) was a Brazilian military man and Indianist. He explored much of the Brazilian interior and studied and helped the Indians of the region.

Candido Rondon (pronounced rôN-dôN´) was born in Cuiabá in the state of Mato Grosso on May 5, 1865. He entered the army in 1881 and by 1890 was substitute professor of mathematics in the Praia Vermelha Military School in Rio de Janeiro. That year he accepted a post with the Telegraphic Commission, which was extending telegraph lines into the deep interior of Brazil.

When Rondon began his career in the Amazonian region, the larger part of it had not been explored by civilized man, and Brazil's claim to sovereignty in the region was largely symbolic. He and his coworkers established the first contacts with the outside world for many parts of the Brazilian interior. During his long service with the Telegraphic Commission, he studied intensively the flora and fauna of the Amazon region. He became an expert on the vegetation and inhabitants of the Brazilian interior.

Rondon's work brought him into close contact with the Indian tribes who lived isolated in the forests and plains of the Amazon Valley. He became outraged at the way in which some were being exploited and degraded

Candido Rondon. (Organization of American States)

by outsiders and how contacts with the outside world were tending to destroy the culture and sometimes the very existence of these tribes.

Rondon convinced the Brazilian government to establish the Servico Nacional de Proteção aos Indios (National Service for Protection of the Indians) to help save the indigenous peoples from exploitation and disintegration. He headed this service until 1940, and during his tenure the service gained an international reputation for its struggle on behalf of the Indians and for its efforts to introduce the Indians peacefully and slowly into modern civilization. However, a decade after Rondon's death the service was wracked by scandals surrounding its mistreatment of those it was supposed to protect.

In 1913 Rondon accompanied former U.S. president Theodore Roosevelt on his expedition of exploration in the Amazon Valley. From 1927 to 1930 Rondon conducted an inspection trip that completely covered the land frontiers of his country. In 1934 he was the Brazilian representative on a commission which successfully settled a long-standing border dispute between Peru and Colombia which had led to open warfare in that year.

During his career in the Telegraphic Commission and the Indian Service, Rondon rose steadily in military rank. In 1955, on his ninetieth birthday, the Brazilian Congress passed a special law raising him to the rank of marshal, the highest in the nation's military service. He received many honors from his own and foreign governments. The new Amazonian territory and its capital city were named Rondonia in commemoration of his work there. Rondon died on Jan. 19, 1958.

Further Reading

Candido Rondon is listed in the Latin America study guide (IV, C, 1, b). Another Brazilian who contributed much to the knowledge and the acquisition of Brazilian territory was the Barão do RIO BRANCO.

There is a good discussion of Rondon's career in Donald Emmet Worcester, *Makers of Latin America* (1966). Theodore Roosevelt recounts an expedition with Rondon in his *Through the Brazilian Wilderness* (1914). Some of Rondon's explorations are discussed in Charles E. Key, *The Story of Twentieth-century Exploration* (1938).

RONSARD / By Donald Stone, Jr.

Pierre de Ronsard (1524–1585) was the greatest French poet of his day. His verse influenced French poetry well into the 17th century.

Pierre de Ronsard (pronounced rôN-sàr′) was born at La Poissonnière on Sept. 11, 1524. He was the son of Loys de Ronsard, an aristocrat whose nobility, if unquestionable, afforded him neither fame nor

Pierre de Ronsard, a portrait by an unknown artist, probably dating from the 17th century. (Photo-Hachette)

fortune. Pierre became a page in the royal house, where he attended briefly Francis I's eldest son and then the third son, Prince Charles. When James V of Scotland married Madeleine of France (1537), Charles gave the young page to his sister. Ronsard accompanied Scotland's new queen to her country but appears not to have stayed there more than a year. By 1540 he was acquainted with Lazare de Baïf, diplomat and humanist of distinction, who would help determine Ronsard's future. It began to take shape when an illness left the boy partially deaf and unsuited for a military career.

In 1543 Ronsard was tonsured. The act did not make the future poet a priest, but it did permit him to receive income from certain ecclesiastical posts—potentially an important source of revenue and one he would exploit. After his father died in 1544, Ronsard accepted an invitation from Lazare de Baïf to study in Paris with his son Jean Antoine under the direction of Jean Dorat. When Dorat became principal of the Collège de Coqueret in 1547, he took his pupils with him. Joined by Joachim du Bellay, the youths followed a strict but enlightened discipline that brought them into intimate contact with the languages, forms, and techniques of the ancient poets. In this way, the nucleus of that school of French poets known as the Pléiade was formed.

"Odes" and "Amours"

With the publication of *Les Quatre premiers livres*

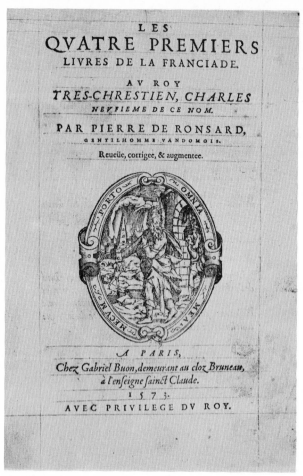

The title page from the 1573 edition of Ronsard's
Les Quatre premiers livres de la Franciade, *in the*
Bibliothèque Nationale, Paris. (Photo-Hachette)

des odes (1550), the story of Ronsard's life is inseparable from the chronology of his works. Ronsard determined to open his career with éclat and chose to imitate the long, difficult odes of Pindar written in praise of Olympic heroes. The subjects of Ronsard's odes are the royal family and court dignitaries, but the length and difficulty remain.

With the *Amours* of 1552, Ronsard attempted to prove his ability to rival yet another great poet, Petrarch. Indeed, the *Amours*, addressed to Cassandra (identified as a Cassandra Salviati), so seek to capture the traits of the Italian's famous love poems to Laura that the existence of a woman named Cassandra at that time must be considered as incidental. Poetry in the 16th century was an affair of imitation and skill but rarely biography. The sonnets, in decasyllabic verse, are highly conventional, and whereas some critics find an appealing "baroque" quality in certain of them, many poems are so obscure, poorly constructed, and basely derivative that even Ronsard's contemporaries found fault with them.

During the remainder of the 1550s, Ronsard published his licentious *Livret de folastries* (1553, unsigned), his philosophical *Hymnes* (1555–1556), and more love po-

etry, the *Continuations des Amours* (1555–1556). The love sonnets of the cycles, addressed primarily to a Marie, are often no different in style from those of 1552. The greatest innovation lies in Ronsard's experimentation—the use of the Alexandrine and the increased quantity of nonsonnet material, for example. Yet even here, especially in the songs in imitation of Marullus, mannered phrases betray the relative simplicity of Ronsard's *style bas*.

The Wars and an Epic

Ronsard had official as well as personal reasons for becoming involved in the tensions that in 1562 brought Catholics and Huguenots to war. That year he composed his most important works on France's troubles: the *Discours des misères de ce temps*, the *Continuation du Discours des misères de ce temps*, and the *Remonstrance au peuple de France*. With eloquent virulence Ronsard depicts the desperate situation created by a divided France. He begs Beza, John Calvin's lieutenant, to help restore peace.

With the *Remonstrance*, Ronsard's tone rises to the satiric as he scourges Calvinism. Adhering to the principle of one king, one law, and one faith, he maintained that disregard for the last of these elements was bringing in its wake disobedience for the first two. Moreover, whereas he admitted that the Church needed reform, nothing he saw assured him that Calvinism was a more Christian, charitable sect. His personal feud with the Protestants stemmed from an attack by them on Ronsard as a pagan and a mediocre poet. Ronsard replied in his *Réponse aux injures et calomnies de je ne sais quels prédicants et ministres de Genève* (1563) with a proud (and revealing) defense supported by devastating satire.

In 1572 Ronsard published *Les Quatre premiers livres de la Franciade*. The remaining books were never written; it was obvious even to Ronsard that the poem was a failure. Why did this versatile poet fail in the epic when he had been so successful in numerous other genres? Critics have pointed to the verse form (decasyllabic verse, not the Alexandrine) and to the subject (a learned myth tracing France's royal house back to Troy). No less revealing are Ronsard's own words about the epic genre he published in a preface to the *Franciade*. Here the poet makes clear that only an epic written on the pattern set by Homer and Virgil is acceptable and that this pattern is to be followed in the greatest detail. Ronsard is so true to his own principles that the *Franciade* is often little more than a sustained reproduction of a traditional form.

Final Years

Ronsard's failure in the *Franciade* is more than offset by a new collected edition of his works printed in 1578. It contains two of his best-known sonnets, *Comme on voit sur la branche* and *Quand vous serez bien vieille*. The former was inserted among the previously published Marie poems but was most certainly written at the death of the King's mistress, Marie de Clèves. *Quand vous serez bien vieille* belongs to an entirely new cycle of love poems, the *Sonnets pour Hélène*, inspired in part by Hélène de Surgères, a lady of the court. The cycle reproduces much of the Petrarchan material used in 1552 and 1555. Its remarkable qualities—to be found also in *Comme on voit sur la branche*—lie in the poet's ability to manipulate the tradition and the sonnet form. The best sonnets of 1578 abandon the nervous style of 1552 and achieve with the same Petrarchan commonplaces a simplicity that is not without richness of expression and emotion.

Ronsard died on Dec. 27, 1585, at the priory of St-Cosme near Tours. In his late works he was the forerunner of 17th-century French classicism.

Further Reading

Pierre de Ronsard is listed in the Literature study guide (III, E, 2). Joachim DU BELLAY was another member of the Pléiade.

Both the contemporary and modern biographies of Ronsard are unreliable mixtures of fact, fiction, and romance. Recent studies of his poetry include Isidore Silver, *Ronsard and the Hellenic Renaissance in France* (1961); Donald Stone, Jr., *Ronsard's Sonnet Cycles: A Study in Tone and Vision* (1966); and Elizabeth T. Armstrong, *Ronsard and the Age of Gold* (1968). Grahame Castor, *Pléiade Poetics: A Study in Sixteenth-century Thought and Terminology* (1964), discusses Ronsard's theoretical writings, and Richard A. Katz, *Ronsard's French Critics, 1585–1828* (1964), considers his influence.

Eleanor Roosevelt about 1961. (Dr. A. David Gurewitsch, New York City)

ELEANOR **ROOSEVELT**

/ By Charles Alexander

Anna Eleanor Roosevelt (1884–1962), wife of the thirty-second president of the United States, was a philanthropist, author, world diplomat, and resolute champion of liberal causes.

Eleanor Roosevelt was born in New York City on Oct. 11, 1884, into an economically comfortable but troubled family. Her father was Elliott Roosevelt, the younger brother of Theodore Roosevelt, himself a future president of the United States. Although handsome and charming, Elliott was plagued by frequent mental depressions and by alcoholism. Her mother, beautiful but neurotic, was preoccupied with the family's image in upper-class society and embarrassed by Eleanor's homeliness. Eleanor's father entered a sanitarium for alcoholics when she was a child. When Eleanor was 8 years old, her mother died, and she and two younger brothers went to live with their maternal grandmother in New York. Shortly thereafter the older brother died, and when Eleanor was not yet 10, she learned that her father

was dead. Her grandmother sheltered her from all outside contacts except for family acquaintances.

Eleanor Roosevelt began discovering a world beyond the family at Mademoiselle Souvestre's finishing school at South Fields, England, where she went at 15. Mademoiselle Souvestre taught a sense of social service and responsibility, which Eleanor began to act upon after her return to New York. Plain, gangly, and convinced that she would never marry, she plunged into social work. But soon her tall, handsome cousin, Franklin Delano Roosevelt, began courting her. They were married in March 1905. She now had to contend with a domineering mother-in-law and a gregarious husband who did not really understand his wife's struggle to overcome shyness and feelings of inadequacy.

Beginnings of a Public Career

Between 1906 and 1916 Eleanor Roosevelt bore six children, one of whom died in infancy. The family lived at their estate at Hyde Park, from which Franklin pursued his political ambitions in the Democratic party. He served a term in the New York State Senate before President Woodrow Wilson appointed him assistant secretary of the Navy in 1913. Although Mrs. Roosevelt did much Red Cross relief work during World War I and even toured the French battlefields shortly after the armistice, she remained obscure.

A major turning point in Eleanor Roosevelt's life came in 1921, when Franklin contracted polio and permanently lost the use of his legs. Finally asserting her will over

As First Lady of the United States, Eleanor Roosevelt broke with tradition by leading an active public life independent of that of the President. This 1935 photograph shows her touring a coal mine. (Wide World Photos)

her mother-in-law (who insisted that Franklin quietly accept invalidism), Eleanor Roosevelt nursed him back into activity. Within a few years he had regained his strength and political ambitions. Meanwhile, she entered more fully into public life. Speaking and working for the League of Women Voters, the National Consumers' League, the Women's Trade Union League, and the women's division of the New York State Democratic Committee, she not only acted as Franklin's "legs and ears" but began to acquire a certain notoriety of her own. During Franklin's New York governorship she saw the last of her children off to boarding school and kept busy inspecting state hospitals, homes, and prisons for her husband.

President's Wife

Roosevelt's election to the presidency in 1932 meant, as Mrs. Roosevelt later wrote, "the end of any personal life of my own." She quickly became the best-known (and also the most criticized) First Lady in American history. She evoked both intense admiration and intense hatred but almost never passivity or neutrality.

Besides undertaking a syndicated newspaper column and a series of radio broadcasts (the income from which she gave to charity), Mrs. Roosevelt traveled back and forth across the country on fact-finding trips for Franklin. She assumed the special role of advocate for those groups of Americans—working women, blacks, youth, tenant farmers—which Franklin Roosevelt's New Deal efforts to combat the Depression tended to neglect. Holding no official position, she felt she could speak more freely on issues than could Roosevelt, and she also

became a key contact within the administration for officials seeking the President's support. In short, Mrs. Roosevelt became an intermediary between, on the one hand, the individual citizen and his government and, on the other, the President and much of his administration.

Of particular concern to Mrs. Roosevelt were securing equal opportunities for women under the New Deal's work relief projects; ensuring that appropriate employment for writers, artists, musicians, and theater people became an integral part of the Works Progress Administration (WPA) program; promoting the cause of Arthurdale, a farming community built by the Federal government for unemployed miners in West Virginia; and providing work for jobless youth, both white and black (accomplished under the National Youth Administration, set up in 1935). Much more than her husband, Mrs. Roosevelt denounced racial oppression and tried to aid the struggle of black Americans toward full citizenship. Largely because of her efforts, Negroes, for the first time since the Reconstruction years, had reason to feel that the national government was interested in their plight.

World Figure

As the United States moved toward war in the late 1930s, Mrs. Roosevelt spoke out forcefully in favor of the administration's policy of aiding antifascist governments. She accepted an appointment as deputy director in the Office of Civilian Defense. She applied herself diligently to her new job but proved inefficient as an administrator and resigned in 1942 in the face of growing congressional criticism. That was her first and last official position under Roosevelt. Once the United States formally entered the war, she made numerous trips to England, Europe, and the Pacific area to boost troop morale and to inspect Red Cross facilities.

After Roosevelt's death in April 1945, Mrs. Roosevelt was expected to retire to a quiet, uneventful private life. By the end of the year, however, she was back in public life. President Harry S. Truman appointed her American delegate to the United Nations Commission on Human Rights. As chairman of the Commission, she worked the other delegates overtime to complete the Universal Declaration of Human Rights, adopted by the UN General Assembly in 1948. Mrs. Roosevelt remained in her post at the UN through 1952. She became the target for virulent right-wing attacks during the presidential campaign of that year. After the election of Republican Dwight D. Eisenhower, she gave up her UN post, but continued to work for international understanding and cooperation as a representative of the American Association for the United Nations.

During the last decade of her life Mrs. Roosevelt traveled to numerous foreign countries, including two trips to the Soviet Union, and authored several books. She continued to articulate a personal and social outlook which, while never profound and sometimes banal and obtuse, still inspired millions. But by the early 1960s, although she had accepted three new government appointments from President John F. Kennedy (delegate to the U.N., adviser to the Peace Corps, and chairman of the President's Commission on the Status of Women), her strength was waning. She died in New York City on Nov. 6, 1962.

Further Reading

Eleanor Roosevelt is listed in the American History study guide (IX, D, 4). She was the wife of President Franklin ROOSEVELT.

Mrs. Roosevelt's candid autobiographical writings are invaluable: *This Is My Story* (1937); *This I Remember* (1949); and *On My Own* (1958). These works are combined with an additional updated chapter in *Autobiography* (1961). An even more intimate view of Mrs. Roosevelt can be gained from Joseph P. Lash, *Eleanor and Franklin: The Story of their Relationship Based on Eleanor Roosevelt's Private Papers* (1971) and *Eleanor: The Years Alone* (1972). Also helpful is Tamara K. Hareven, *Eleanor Roosevelt: An American Conscience* (1968). James R. Kearney, *Anna Eleanor Roosevelt: The Evolution of a Reformer* (1968), is less a biography than a topically organized analysis of various facets of Mrs. Roosevelt's public life. Less critical though useful are Alfred Steinberg, *Mrs. R.* (1959); Joseph P. Lash, *Eleanor Roosevelt: A Friend's Memoir* (1965); and Archibald MacLeish, *The Eleanor Roosevelt Story* (1965). Information about Mrs. Roosevelt's role in relation to her husband's career is in Frank Freidel's uncompleted biography *Franklin D. Roosevelt* (3 vols., 1952–1956); Alfred B. Rollins, *Roosevelt and Howe* (1962); and James MacGregor Burns, *Roosevelt: The Lion and the Fox* (1963).

*   *   *

F. **ROOSEVELT** / By Rexford G. Tugwell

Franklin Delano Roosevelt (1882–1945), thirty-second president of the United States, led the nation out of the Great Depression and later into World War II. Before he died, he cleared the way for peace, including establishment of the United Nations.

Franklin Roosevelt was born on Jan. 30, 1882, of his father's second marriage, to Sara Delano, the daughter of a prominent family. The Roosevelts had been moderately wealthy for many generations. Merchants and financiers, they had often been prominent in the civic affairs of New York. When Franklin was born, his father was 51 years old and semiretired from a railroad presidency, and his mother was 28. Franklin was often in the care of governesses and tutors, until at the age of 14 he went to Groton School. Here he received a solid classical, historical, and mathematical training and was moderately good at his studies. His earnest attempts at athletics were mostly defeated because of his tall, ungainly frame.

Roosevelt wanted to go to Annapolis, but his parents insisted on preparation for the position natural for the scion of the Delano and Roosevelt families, so he entered Harvard University. He was a reasonably good student and found a substitute for athletics in reporting for the Harvard newspaper, of which he finally became editor. While seeming to be a Cambridge socialite, he spent an extra year studying public affairs. He also met and determined to marry his cousin, Eleanor, to his mother's annoyance. Eleanor was the daughter of Elliott

Franklin Roosevelt in 1937. (United Press International Photo)

Franklin Roosevelt (front, center) with British prime minister Winston Churchill (left) and Soviet premier Joseph Stalin at the Yalta Conference, February 1945. At this conference the Big Three laid plans for the final military defeat of Germany, the occupation of its territory, and the establishment of popular governments in the liberated countries. (U.S. Army Photograph)

Roosevelt, a weak member of the family who had died early. Raised by relatives, she received a lady's education but little affection. She was shy and retiring because she was tall, awkward, and homely; but Franklin found her warm, vibrant, and responsive.

Despite his mother's opposition, they were married in 1905, and Franklin entered Columbia University Law School. He prepared for the bar examinations and without taking a degree became a lawyer and entered a clerkship in the Wall Street firm of Carter, Ledyard and Milburn. He took his duties lightly, however, and it was later recalled that he had remarked to fellow clerks that he meant somehow to enter politics and finally to become president. There was never any doubt of his ambition.

Roosevelt's chance came in 1910. He accepted the Democratic nomination for the New York Senate and was elected. Opportunity for further notice came quickly. Although his backing had come from Democrats affiliated with New York City's notorious Tammany Hall, he joined a group of upstate legislators who were setting out to oppose the election of Tammany's choice for U.S. senator. The rebels were successful in forcing acceptance of another candidate.

Much of Roosevelt's wide publicity from this struggle was managed by Albany reporter Louis McHenry Howe, who had taken to the young politician and set out to further his career. (This dedication lasted until Roosevelt was safely in the White House.) The Tammany fight made Roosevelt famous in New York, but it also won him the enmity of Tammany. Still, he was reelected in 1912. That year Woodrow Wilson was elected president; Roosevelt had been a campaign worker, and his efforts had been noticed by prominent party elder Josephus Daniels. When Daniels became secretary of the Navy in Wilson's Cabinet, he persuaded Wilson to offer Roosevelt the assistant secretaryship.

Assistant Secretary of the Navy

As assistant secretary, Roosevelt began an experience that substituted for the naval career he had hoped for as a boy. Before long he became restless, however, and tried to capture the Democratic nomination for U.S. senator from New York. Wilson and Daniels were displeased. Daniels forgave him, but Wilson never afterward really trusted the brash young man. This distrust was heightened later by Roosevelt's departure from the administration's policy of neutrality in the years preceding World War I. Roosevelt openly favored intervention, agitated for naval expansion, and was known to be rather scornful of Daniels, who kept the Navy under close political discipline.

America soon entered the war, however, and Roosevelt could work for a cause he believed in. At that time there was only one assistant secretary, and he had extensive responsibilities. Howe had come to Washington with him and had become his indispensable guardian and helper. Together their management of the department was creditable.

Though Roosevelt tried several times to leave his civilian post to join the fighting forces, he was persuaded to remain. When the war came to an end and Wilson was stricken during his fight for ratification of the Versailles Treaty, there was an obvious revulsion throughout the United States from the disappointing settlements of the war. It seemed to many that the effort to make the world safe for democracy had resulted in making the world safe for the old empires.

The Allied leaders had given in to Wilson's insistence on the creation of the League of Nations only to serve their real interest in extending their territories and in imposing reparations on Germany. These reparations were so large that they could never be paid; consequently the enormous debts the Allies owed to the United States would never be paid either. The American armies had saved Europe and the Europeans were ungrateful. Resentment and disillusion were widespread.

The Republican party had the advantage of not having been responsible for these foreign entanglements. In 1920 they nominated Warren G. Harding, a conservative senator, as their presidential candidate. The Democrats nominated Governor James Cox of Ohio, who had had no visible part in the Wilson administration; the vice-presidential candidate was Roosevelt.

It was a despairing campaign; but in one respect it was a beginning rather than an ending for Roosevelt. He made a much more noticeable campaign effort than the presidential candidate. He covered the nation by special trains, speaking many times a day, often from back platforms, and getting acquainted with local leaders everywhere. He had learned the professional politician's breeziness, was able to absorb useful information, and had an infallible memory for names and faces. The defeat was decisive; but Roosevelt emerged as the most representative Democrat.

Victim of Poliomyelitis

Roosevelt retreated to a law connection in New York's financial district again and a position with a fidelity and deposit company. But in the summer of 1921, vacationing in Canada, he became mysteriously ill. His disease, poliomyelitis, was not immediately diagnosed. He was almost totally paralyzed, however, and had to be moved to New York for treatment. This was managed with such secrecy that for a long time the seriousness of his condition was not publicized. In fact, he would never recover the use of his legs, a disability that seemed to end his political career. His mother, typically, demanded that he return to Hyde Park and give up the political activities she had always deplored. He could now become a country gentleman. But Eleanor, joined by Howe, set out to renew his ambition.

Roosevelt's struggle during the convalescence of the next few years was agonizing and continually disappointing. Not much was known then about rehabilitation, and he resorted to exhausting courses of calisthenics to reactivate his atrophied muscles. In 1923 he tried the warm mineral waters of Warm Springs, Ga., where exercise was easier. He was so optimistic that he wrote friends that he had begun to feel movement in his toes. It was, of course, an illusion.

Roosevelt invested a good part of his remaining fortune in the place. It soon became a resort for all cripples. The facilities were overwhelmed, but gradually an institution was built up, and the medical staff began to have more realistic knowledge of aftereffects. There were no cures; but lives could be made much more tolerable. Meanwhile Roosevelt, realizing that cures were impossible, turned to the encouragement of prevention. (Ultimately, an effective vaccine was found.)

New York Governor

While at Warm Springs in 1928, Roosevelt was called to political duty again, this time by Al Smith, whom he had put in nomination at the Democratic conventions of 1924 and 1928. Almost at once, however, it became clear that Smith could not win the election. He felt, however, that Roosevelt, as candidate for governor, would help to win New York. Roosevelt resisted. He was now a likely presidential candidate in a later, more favorable year for the Democrats; and if he lost the race for the governorship, he would be finished. But the New Yorkers insisted, and he ran and was narrowly elected.

Roosevelt began the 4 years of his New York governorship that were preliminary to his presidency, and since he was reelected 2 years later, it was inevitable that he should be the candidate in 1932. Since 1929 the nation had been sunk in the worst depression of its history, and Herbert Hoover's Republican administration had failed to find a way to recovery. This made it a favorable year for the Democrats.

First Term as President

It would be more true to say that Hoover in 1932 lost than that Roosevelt won. At any rate, Roosevelt came to the presidency with a dangerous economic crisis at its height. Industry was paralyzed, and unemployment afflicted some 30 percent of the work force. Roosevelt had promised that something would be done, but what that would be he had not specified.

Roosevelt began providing relief on a large scale by giving work to the unemployed and by approving a device for bringing increased income to farmers, who were in even worse straits than city workers. Also, he devalued the currency and enabled debtors to discharge debts that had long been frozen. Closed banks all over the country were assisted to reopen, and gradually the crisis was overcome.

In 1934 Roosevelt proposed a comprehensive social security system that, he hoped, would make another such depression impossible. Citizens would never be without at least minimum incomes again. Incidentally, these citizens became devoted supporters of the President who had given them this hope. So in spite of the conservatives who opposed the measures he collectively called the New Deal, he became so popular that he won reelection in 1936 by an unprecedented majority.

Second and Third Terms

Roosevelt's second term began with a struggle between himself and the Supreme Court. The justices had held certain of his New Deal devices to be unconstitutional. In retaliation he proposed to add new justices who would be more amenable. Many even in his own party opposed him in this attempt to pack the Court, and Congress defeated it. After this there ensued the familiar stalemate between an innovative president and a reluctant Congress.

Nevertheless in 1940 Roosevelt determined to break with tradition and run for a third term. His reasons were partly that his reforms were far from finished, but more importantly that he was now certain of Adolf Hitler's intention to subdue Europe and go on to further conquests. The immense productivity and organizational ability of the Germans would be at his disposal. Europe would be defeated unless the United States came to its support.

The presidential campaign of 1940 was the climax of Roosevelt's plea that Americans set themselves against the Nazi threat. He had sought to prepare the way in numerous speeches but had had a most disappointing response. There was a vivid recollection of the disillusion after World War I, and a good many Americans were inclined to support the Germans rather than the Allied Powers. So strong was American reluctance to be involved in another world war that in the last speeches of this campaign Roosevelt practically promised that young Americans would never be sent abroad to fight. Luckily his opponent, Republican Wendell Willkie, also favored support for the Allies. The campaign, won by a narrow majority, gave Roosevelt no mandate for intervention.

Roosevelt was not far into his third term, however, when the decision to enter the war was made for him by the Japanese, whose attack on Pearl Harbor caused serious losses to American forces there. Almost at once the White House became headquarters for those who controlled the strategy of what was now World War II. Winston Churchill came immediately and practically took up residence, bringing a British staff. Together the leaders agreed that Germany and Italy must have first attention. Gen. Douglas MacArthur, commander in the Pacific, was ordered to retreat from the Philippines to Australia, something he was bitterly reluctant to do. But Roosevelt firmly believed that the first problem was to help the British, and then, when Hitler turned East, to somehow get arms to the Soviets. The Japanese could be taken care of when Europe was safe.

Hitler's grand strategy was to subdue the Soviet Union, conquer North Africa, and link up with the Japanese, who were advancing rapidly across the Eastern countries. Roosevelt wanted an early crossing of the English Channel to retake France and to force Hitler to fight on two fronts. Churchill, mindful of the fearful British losses in World War I, instead wanted to attack the underbelly of Europe, cut Hitler's lines to the East, and shut him off from Africa. The invasion of Europe was postponed because it became clear that elaborate preparation was necessary. But Allied troops were sent into Africa, with Gen. Dwight Eisenhower in command, to attack Field Marshal Erwin Rommel from the rear. Eventually an Allied crossing to Sicily and a slow, costly march up the Italian peninsula, correlated with the attack across the English Channel, forced the Italian collapse and the German surrender.

Meanwhile MacArthur was belatedly given the support he needed for a brilliant island-hopping campaign that drove the Japanese back, destroyed their fleet, and endangered their home island. After the German surrender, the Pacific war was brought to an end by the American atomic bomb explosion over the Japanese cities of Hiroshima and Nagasaki. By this time Roosevelt was dead. He had not participated in that doubtful decision; but he had been, with Churchill, in active command during the war until then.

Roosevelt had gone to Warm Springs early in 1945, completely exhausted. He had recently returned from a conference of Allied leaders at Yalta, where he had forced acceptance of his scheme for a United Nations and made arrangements for the Soviet Union to assist in the final subjugation of Japan. The strain was visible as he made his report to the nation.

At Warm Springs he prepared the address to be used at San Francisco, where the meeting to ratify agreements concerning the United Nations was to be held; but he found himself unable to enjoy the pine woods and the gushing waters. He sat wan and frail in his small cottage, getting through only such work as had to be done. He finished signing papers on the morning of April 12, 1945. Within hours, he suffered the massive cerebral hemorrhage that killed him.

A special train carried Roosevelt's body to Washington, and there he lay in the White House until he was taken to Hyde Park and buried in the hedged garden he himself had prepared. His grave is marked by a plain marble slab, and his wife is buried beside him. He had given the estate to the nation, and it is now a shrine much visited by those who recall or have heard how great a man he was for his time.

Further Reading

Franklin Roosevelt is listed in the American History study guide (IX, A, 2; IX, E, 1). Prominent members of his Cabinet were Harold L. ICKES and Cordell HULL. His wife, Eleanor ROOSEVELT, was important in her own right.

Samuel I. Rosenman, ed., *The Public Papers and Addresses of Franklin D. Roosevelt* (1938–1950), includes selected messages to Congress, speeches, executive orders, and transcripts from press conferences. There is also a collection of Roosevelt's letters edited by Elliott Roosevelt, *F. D. R.: His Personal Letters* (4 vols., 1947–1950). Eleanor Roosevelt, *This I Remember* (1949), is a frank account by Roosevelt's wife. Frances Perkins, *The Roosevelt I Knew* (1946), and Samuel I. Rosenman, *Working with Roosevelt* (1952), personal accounts, are helpful in assessing Roosevelt's character and work methods.

The only full biography of Roosevelt is Rexford G. Tugwell, *The Democratic Roosevelt* (1957). Frank B. Freidel's biography, *Franklin D. Roosevelt* (3 vols., 1952–1956), was never completed. Rexford G. Tugwell's brtfer *F. D. R.: Architect of an Era* (1967) studies the man and his work, and his *The Brains Trust* (1968) tells the part played in Roosevelt's presidency by a group of helpers, mostly from Columbia University. The presidential elections involving Roosevelt are covered in Arthur M. Schlesinger, Jr., ed., *History of American Presidential Elections* (4 vols., 1971). James MacGregor Burns, *Roosevelt: The Lion and the Fox* (1956), ranks Roosevelt among the great presidents. Basil Rauch, *Roosevelt: From Munich to Pearl Harbor, a Study in the Creation of a Foreign Policy* (1950), is a detailed, accurate history of events during this period. Written by an Albany newspaper correspondent when Roosevelt was governor, Ernest K. Lindley, *The Roosevelt Revolution: First Phase* (1933), helped establish Roosevelt as a progressive leader. An authoritative and readable history of Roosevelt's era is provided in the two volumes by Arthur M. Schlesinger, Jr., *The New Deal in Action, 1933–1939* (1940) and *The Crisis of the Old Order* (1957). Another account of the period is Basil Rauch, *The History of the New Deal, 1933–1938* (1944).

T. **ROOSEVELT** / By **William H. Harbaugh**

The first modern American president, Theodore Roosevelt (1858–1919) was also one of the most popular, important, and controversial. During his years in office he greatly expanded the power of the presidency.

A strong nationalist and a resourceful leader, Theodore Roosevelt gloried in the opportunities and responsibilities of world power. He especially enlarged the United States role in the Far East and Latin America. At home he increased regulation of business, encouraged the labor movement, and waged a long, dramatic battle for conservation of national resources. He also organized the Progressive party (1912) and advanced the rise of the welfare state with a forceful campaign for social justice.

Roosevelt was born in New York City on Oct. 27, 1858.

Theodore Roosevelt in 1912. (Brown Brothers)

His father was of an old Dutch mercantile family long prominent in the city's affairs. His mother came from an established Georgia family of Scotch-Irish and Huguenot ancestry. A buoyant, dominant figure, his father was the only man, young Roosevelt once said, he "ever feared." He imbued his son with an acute sense of civic responsibility and an attitude of noblesse oblige.

Partly because of a severe asthmatic condition, Theodore was educated by private tutors until 1876, when he entered Harvard College. Abandoning plans to become a naturalist, he developed political and historical interests, was elected to Phi Beta Kappa, and finished twenty-first in a class of 158. He also began writing *The Naval War of 1812* (1882), a work of limited range but high technical competence. Four months after his graduation in 1880, he married Alice Hathaway Lee, by whom he had a daughter.

Early Career

Bored by the study of law in the office of an uncle and at Columbia University, Roosevelt willingly gave it up in 1882 to serve the first of three terms in the New York State Assembly. He quickly distinguished himself for integrity, courage, and independence, and upon his retirement in 1884 he had become the leader of the Republican party's reform wing. Though his reputation was based on his attacks against corruption, he had shown some interest in social problems and had begun to break with laissez-faire economics. Among the many bills he drove through the Assembly was a measure, worked out with labor leader Samuel Gompers, to regulate tenement workshops.

Roosevelt's last term was marred by the sudden deaths of his mother and his wife within hours of each other in February 1884. After the legislative session ended, he established a ranch, Elkhorn, on the Little Missouri River in the Dakota Territory. Immersing himself in history, he completed *Thomas Hart Benton* (1886) and *Gouverneur Morris* (1887) and began to prepare his major work, the four-volume *Winning of the West* (1889–1896). A tour de force distinguished more for its narrative power and personality sketches than its social and economic analysis, it won the respect of the foremost academic historian of the West, Frederick Jackson Turner. It also gave Roosevelt considerable standing among professional historians and contributed to his election as president of the American Historical Association in 1912. Meanwhile, he published numerous hunting and nature books, some of high order.

Politics and a romantic interest in a childhood friend, Edith Carow, drew Roosevelt back east. Nominated for mayor of New York, he waged a characteristically vigorous campaign in 1886 but finished third. He then went to London to marry Miss Carow, who bore him four sons and a daughter.

In 1889 Roosevelt was rewarded for his earlier services to President Benjamin Harrison with appointment to the ineffectual Civil Service Commission. Plunging into his duties with extraordinary zeal, he soon became head of the Commission. He insisted that the laws be scrupulously enforced in order to open the government service to all who were qualified, and he alienated many politicians in his own party by refusing to submit to their demands. By the end of his 6 years in office Roosevelt had virtually institutionalized the civil service.

Roosevelt returned to New York City in 1895 to serve 2 tumultuous years as president of the police board. Enforcing the law with relentless efficiency and uncompromising honesty, he indulged once more in acrimonious controversy with the leaders of his party. He succeeded in modernizing the force, eliminating graft from the promotion system, and raising morale to unprecedented heights. "It's tough on the force, for he was dead square . . . and we needed him," said an unnamed policeman when Roosevelt resigned in the spring of 1897 to become President William McKinley's assistant secretary of the Navy.

As assistant secretary, Roosevelt instituted personnel reforms, arranged meaningful maneuvers for the fleet, and lobbied energetically for a two-ocean navy. He uncritically accepted imperialistic theories, and he worked closely with senators Henry Cabot Lodge and Alfred Beveridge for war against Spain in 1898. Although moved partly by humanitarian considerations, he was animated mainly by lust for empire and an exaggerated conception of the glories of war. "No qualities called out by a purely peaceful life," he wrote, "stand on a level with those stern and virile virtues which move the men of stout heart and strong hand who uphold the honor of their flag in battle."

Anxious to prove himself under fire, Roosevelt resigned as assistant secretary of the Navy in April to organize the 1st U.S. Volunteer Cavalry Regiment (the "Rough Riders"). He took command of the unit in Cuba and distinguished himself and his regiment in a bold charge up the hill next to San Juan. In late summer 1898 he returned to New York a war hero.

New York's Governor

Nominated for governor, Roosevelt won election in the fall of 1898 by a narrow margin. His 2-year administration was the most enlightened to that time. By deferring to the Republican machine on minor matters, by mobilizing public opinion behind his program, and by otherwise invoking the arts of the master politician, Roosevelt forced an impressive body of legislation through a recalcitrant Assembly and Senate. Most significant, perhaps, was a franchise tax on corporations. As the Democratic *New York World* concluded when he left office, "the controlling purpose and general course of his administration have been high and good."

Roosevelt accepted the vice-presidential nomination in 1900. A landslide victory for McKinley and Roosevelt ensued. Then, on Sept. 14, 1901, following McKinley's death by an assassin's bullet, Roosevelt was sworn in. Not quite 43, he was the youngest president in history.

First Presidential Administration

Roosevelt's first 3 years in office were inhibited by the conservatism of Republican congressional leaders and the accidental nature of his coming to power. He was able to sign the Newlands Reclamation Bill into law (1902) and the Elkins Antirebate Bill (1903); he also persuaded Congress to create a toothless Bureau of Corporations. But it was his sensational use of the dormant powers of his office that lifted his first partial term above the ordinary.

On Feb. 18, 1902, Roosevelt shook the financial community and took a first step toward bringing big business under Federal control by ordering antitrust proceedings against the Northern Securities Company, a railroad combine formed by J. P. Morgan and other magnates. Suits against the meat-packers and other trusts followed, and by the time Roosevelt left office 43 actions had been instituted. Yet he never regarded antitrust suits as a full solution to the corporation problem. During his second administration he strove, with limited success, to provide for continuous regulation rather than the dissolution of big businesses.

Hardly less dramatic than his attack on the Northern Securities Company was Roosevelt's intervention in a 5-month-long anthracite coal strike in 1902. By virtually forcing the operators to submit to arbitration, he won important gains for the striking miners. Never before had a president used his powers in a strike on labor's side.

Foreign Policy

Roosevelt's conduct of foreign policy was as dynamic and considerably more far-reaching in import. Believing that there could be no retreat from the power position which the Spanish-American War had dramatized but which the United States industrialism had forged, he stamped his imprint upon American policy with unusual force. He established a moderately enlightened govern-

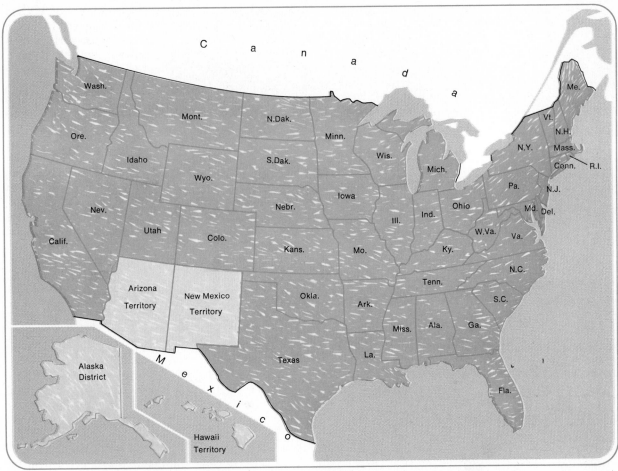

*The United States at the close of the Theodore Roosevelt administration (March 4, 1909).
During the presidency of Theodore Roosevelt, Oklahoma was admitted (1907) to the Union as
the forty-sixth state. By the Hay–Bunau-Varilla Treaty with Panama in 1903, the United States
acquired in perpetuity control of the Panama Canal Zone.*

ment in the Philippines, while persuading Congress to grant tariff concessions to Cuba. He settled an old Alaskan boundary dispute with Canada on terms favorable to the United States. And he capitalized on an externally financed revolution in Panama to acquire the Canal Zone under conditions that created a heritage of ill will.

At the instance of the president of Santo Domingo, Roosevelt also arranged for the United States to assume control of the customs of that misgoverned nation in order to avert intervention by European powers. He had about the same desire to annex Santo Domingo, he said, "as a gorged boa constrictor might have to swallow a porcupine wrong-end-to." But he had already forestalled German intervention in Venezuela in 1902 and was anxious to establish a firm policy against it. So on May 20, 1904, and again in December he set forth what became known as the Roosevelt Corollary to the Monroe Doctrine. The United States, he declared, assumed the right to intervene in the internal affairs of the Latin American nations in the event of "chronic wrongdoing" or "impotence."

Roosevelt's first administration was also marked by a revitalization of the bureaucracy. The quality of appoin-

tees was raised, capable members of minority groups were given government posts (in 1906 Roosevelt named the first Jew, Oscar Straus, to a Cabinet position), and the civil service lists were expanded. At the same time, however, the President ruthlessly manipulated patronage so as to wrest control of Republican party machinery from Senator Mark Hanna and secure his nomination to a full term in 1904. "In politics," he disarmingly explained, "we have to do a great many things we ought not to do." Overwhelming his conservative Democratic opponent by the greatest popular majority to that time, Roosevelt won the election and carried in a great host of congressional candidates on his coattails.

Second Administration

Although the resentment of the Republican party's Old Guard increased rather than diminished as his tenure lengthened, Roosevelt pushed through a much more progressive program in this second term. His "Square Deal" reached its finest legislative flower in 1906 with passage of the Hepburn Railroad Bill, the Pure Food and Drug Bill, an amendment providing Federal regulation of stockyards and packing houses, and an employers' liabili-

Theodore Roosevelt campaigning for the presidency in Philadelphia in 1912. (United Press International Photo)

ty measure. Yet he probably did even more to forward progressivism by using his office as a pulpit and by appointing study commissions such as those on country life and inland waterways. Several of his messages to Congress in 1907 and 1908 were the most radical to that time. In the face of the Old Guard's open repudiation of him, moreover, he profoundly stimulated the burgeoning progressive movement on all levels of government.

Conservation Program

In conservation Roosevelt's drive to control exploitation and increase development of natural resources was remarkable for sustained intellectual and administrative force. In no other cause did he fuse science and morality so effectively. Based on the propositions that nature's heritage belonged to the people, that "the fundamental idea of forestry is the perpetuation of forests by use," and that "every stream is a unit from its source to its mouth, and all its uses are interdependent," his conservation program provoked bitter conflict with Western states'-rightists and their allies, the electric power companies and large ranchers. In the end Roosevelt failed to marshal even a modicum of support in Congress for multipurpose river valley developments. But he did save what later became the heart of the Tennessee Valley Authority (TVA) by vetoing a bill that would have opened Muscle Shoals to haphazard private development.

By March 1909 Roosevelt's audacious use of executive power had resulted in the transfer of 125 million acres to the forest reserves. About half as many acres containing coal and mineral deposits had been subjected to public controls. Sixteen national monuments and 51 wildlife

refuges had been established. And the number of national parks had been doubled. As Roosevelt's bitter enemy Senator Robert M. La Follette wrote, "his greatest work was inspiring and actually beginning a world movement for . . . saving for the human race the things on which alone a peaceful, progressive, and happy life can be founded."

Foreign Policy

Roosevelt's pronounced impact on the international scene continued during his second term. He intervened decisively for peace in the Algeciras crisis of 1905–1906, and he supported the call for the Second Hague Conference of 1907. But it was in the Far East, where he gradually abandoned the imperialistic aspirations of his pre-presidential years, that he played the most significant role. Perceiving that Japan was destined to become a major Far Eastern power, he encouraged that country to serve as a stabilizing force in the area. To this end he used his good offices to close the Russo-Japanese War through a conference at Portsmouth, N.H., in 1905; for this service he received the Nobel Peace Prize. He also acquiesced at this time in Japan's extension of suzerainty over Korea (Taft-Katsura Memorandum).

By 1907 Roosevelt realized that the Philippines were the United States' "heel of Achilles." He had also come to realize that the China trade which the open-door policy was designed to foster was largely illusory. He consequently labored to maintain Japan's friendship without compromising American interests. He fostered a "gentleman's agreement" on immigration of Japanese to the United States. He implicitly recognized Japan's economic ascendancy in Manchuria through the Root-Takahira agreement of 1908. (Later he urged his successor, President William H. Taft, to give up commercial aspirations and the open-door policy in North China, though he was unsuccessful in this.)

Progressive Movement

Rejecting suggestions that he run for reelection, Roosevelt selected Taft as his successor. He then led a scientific and hunting expedition to Africa (1909) and made a triumphal tour of Europe. He returned to a strife-ridden Republican party in June 1910. Caught between the conservative supporters of Taft and the advanced progressive followers of himself and La Follette, he gave hope to La Follette by setting forth a radical program—the "new nationalism"—of social and economic reforms that summer. Thereafter pressure to declare himself a candidate for the nomination in 1912 mounted until he reluctantly did so.

Although Roosevelt outpolled Taft by more than 2 to 1 in the Republican primaries, Taft's control of the party organization won him the nomination in convention. Roosevelt's supporters then stormed out of the party and organized the Progressive, or "Bull Moose," party. During the three-cornered campaign that fall, Roosevelt called forcefully for Federal regulation of corporations, steeply graduated income and inheritance taxes, multipurpose river valley developments, and social justice for labor and other underprivileged groups. But the Democratic nominee, Woodrow Wilson, running on a more traditional reform platform, won the election.

World War I

Within 3 months of the outbreak of war in Europe in 1914, Roosevelt began his last crusade: an impassioned campaign to persuade the American people to join the Allies and prosecute the war with vigor. He believed that a German victory would be inimical to American economic, political, and cultural interests. But he was also influenced, as in 1898, by his romantic conception of war and ultranationalism. As a result, he distorted the real nature of his thought by trumpeting for war on the submarine, or American-rights, issue alone. More regrettable still, he virtually called for war against Mexico in 1916.

Following America's declaration of war in April 1917, Roosevelt relentlessly attacked the administration for failing to mobilize fast enough. Embittered by Wilson's refusal to let him raise a division, he also attacked the President personally. He was unenthusiastic about the League of Nations, believing that a military alliance of France, Great Britain, and the United States could best preserve peace. He was prepared to support Senator Henry Cabot Lodge's nationalistic reservations to the League Covenant, but he died in his home at Oyster Bay, Long Island, on Jan. 6, 1919, before he could be effective.

Roosevelt's reputation as a domestic reformer remains high and secure. He was the first president to concern himself with the judiciary's massive bias toward property rights (as opposed to human rights), with the maldistri-

bution of wealth, and with the subversion of the democratic process by spokesmen of economic interests in Congress, the pulpits, and the editorial offices. He was also the first to understand the conservation problem in its multiple facets, the first to evolve a regulatory program for capital, and the first to encourage the growth of labor unions. The best-liked man of his times, he has never been revered because his militarism and chauvinism affronted the human spirit.

Further Reading

Theodore Roosevelt is listed in the American History study guide (VII, D, 3, b; VIII, A, 1). His political enemies included Progressive Robert M. LA FOLLETTE and Mark HANNA. His distant cousin, Franklin ROOSEVELT, became the thirty-second president of the United States.

Roosevelt can be studied through his own writings. Especially valuable are his *Letters,* edited by Elting E. Morison and John M. Blum (8 vols., 1951–1954), and a collection of his essays, books, and speeches, *The Works of Theodore Roosevelt,* edited by Hermann Hagedorn (24 vols., 1923–1925). A general collection, *Writings,* was edited by William H. Harbaugh (1967). Roosevelt's *An Autobiography* (1913) is revealing despite the usual deficiencies of such works.

William H. Harbaugh, *Power and Responsibility: The Life and Times of Theodore Roosevelt* (1961; rev. ed., entitled *The Life and Times of Theodore Roosevelt,* 1963), is a full-length biography. The best study of Roosevelt's early career is Carleton Putnam, *Theodore Roosevelt,* vol. 1: *The Formative Years* (1958); the best treatment of his governorship is G. Wallace Chessman, *Governor Theodore Roosevelt* (1965). John M. Blum, *The Republican Roosevelt* (1954; new ed. 1962), is a penetrating essay. The roots of Roosevelt's imperialism are examined in David H. Burton, *Theodore Roosevelt: Confident Imperialist* (1968).

Howard K. Beale, *Theodore Roosevelt and the Rise of America to World Power* (1956), is a seminal study. Fine short accounts are George E. Mowry, *The Era of Theodore Roosevelt, 1900–1912* (1958), and G. Wallace Chessman, *Theodore Roosevelt and the Politics of Power,* edited by Oscar Handlin (1969).

ROOT / By William H. Harbaugh

Elihu Root (1845–1937), a U.S. secretary of war and secretary of state and a senator from New York, was the most constructive conservative of his times.

Elihu Root was born at Clinton, N.Y., on Feb. 15, 1845. His father was a college professor of old New England stock. Elihu attended Hamilton College during the Civil War, graduating as valedictorian in

Elihu Root. (Library of Congress)

1864. After taking a law degree at New York University in 1867, he went into private practice in New York City. He married Clara Frances Wales in 1878; they had two daughters and a son and were a devoted family.

Root was a junior counsel to William Tweed during the notorious boss's trial in 1873. A decade later Root served briefly as U.S. attorney for the district of southern New York. An astute and resourceful legal counselor, he afterward became one of the nation's preeminent corporation lawyers. He advised the Havemeyer Sugar Trust on the reorganization that enabled it to gain control of 98 percent of the market, and he represented the Whitney-Ryan traction interests and numerous other combines. "It is not a function of law," he explained, "to enforce the rules of morality."

Root opposed the encroachment of government upon individual rights, especially those involving property, but he never pursued the implications of corporate political and economic power. As he confessed in 1906, "The pure lawyer seldom concerns himself about the broad aspects of public policy. . . . Lawyers are almost always conservative. . . . Through insisting upon the maintenance of legal rule, they become instinctively opposed to change."

Secretary of War

Root accepted President William McKinley's urgent request in 1899 that he head the mismanaged War Department. His administration of the territories wrested from

Spain was at once realistic and enlightened. In Puerto Rico, where the illiteracy rate was 90 percent, he instituted a highly centralized administration virtually devoid of popular participation. At the same time, he pushed public health measures and persuaded McKinley to exempt the colony from American tariff restrictions. In Cuba, Root arranged for almost immediate civil government but insisted that the United States maintain control of its foreign relations. This was accomplished through the Platt Amendment, which he drafted.

In the Philippines, Root also pushed civil government, including extension of the Bill of Rights. He formed the army that suppressed Emilio Aguinaldo's independence movement and was so sensitive to the honor of American troops that he failed to act promptly against American atrocities. Satisfied with the Philippine government that President William Howard Taft created under his broad direction, Root was unsympathetic in later years to the Democrats' insistence that it be liberalized in order to prepare the Filipinos for full independence.

Meanwhile Root reorganized the general staff, created the Army War College, and established the Joint Army-Navy Board. President Theodore Roosevelt valued him for his calm, incisive, and eminently practical judgment, and when Root resigned in 1904, the President wrote, "I shall never have, and can never have, a more loyal friend, a more faithful and wiser adviser."

Secretary of State

In 1905 Root returned to government service as secretary of state under Roosevelt. Continuing to complement Roosevelt admirably, he pacified the Senate, promoted friendly relations with Latin America, kept a wary eye on Germany, and otherwise comported himself with patience, tact, and cordiality. He supported the Second Hague Conference and worked hard and skillfully to maintain amicable relations with Japan. His crowning achievement was the negotiation of 24 bilateral arbitration treaties. He was awarded the Nobel Peace Prize in 1912.

Senator from New York

Root seemed unable to understand the nature or aims of the Progressive movement, and his 6 years (1909–1915) as a U.S. senator were among the least productive of his life. He disapproved much of the reform legislation under President Taft, and all of it under Woodrow Wilson. His attacks on Wilson's Mexican policy were also unfair and simplistic. Concluding that World War I was a struggle for "Anglo-Saxon" liberty, he was a strong proponent of American entry. In 1917 he headed an ineffective and imperceptive mission to Russia designed to keep the provisional government in the war.

During the fight over the League of Nations, Root was caught between his general approval of the League, his strong nationalistic strain, and his own and his party's partisanship. He tried, but failed, to play a constructive role by advocating American entry with nationalistic reservations. Root came out of retirement in late 1921 to serve on the American delegation to the Washington

Conference. He also gave freely to the movement to adhere to the World Court and further invested himself in service to the Carnegie Endowment for International Peace and other Carnegie benefactions. He died on Feb. 7, 1937.

A charming, witty man in the company of intimates, Root lacked charisma in public. Aside from his obvious achievements in the War and State Departments, he is remembered for his embodiment of that which was wisest and most constructive in the conservative tradition.

Further Reading

Elihu Root is listed in the American History study guide (VIII, A, 1). He subscribed to the social Darwinism propounded by Herbert SPENCER and William Graham SUMNER.

Eight volumes of Root's writings and addresses up to 1923 were edited by Robert Bacon and James B. Scott and published between 1916 and 1925. The official biography is Philip C. Jessup, *Elihu Root* (2 vols., 1938), a full if somewhat adulatory account. It should be supplemented by Richard W. Leopold, *Elihu Root and the Conservative Tradition* (1954), a dispassionate work that benefits from recent scholarship. Considerable material on Root is contained in Julius W. Pratt, *America's Colonial Experiment: How the United States Gained, Governed, and in Part Gave Away a Colonial Empire* (1950), and in the biographies of Roosevelt, Taft, and other contemporaries.

ROSA / By Robert Enggass

The Italian painter and poet Salvator Rosa (1615–1673) was one of the innovators of romanticism. His best-known paintings represent scenes of wild, untrammeled nature, populated with small genre figures.

Salvator Rosa (pronounced rō′zä) was born in Naples on July 21, 1615. He first studied painting with his uncle, Domenico Greco, then with Jusepe de Ribera, and finally with Aniello Falcone. In 1640, after spending some time in Rome, Rosa moved to Florence, where he worked as a painter for the Medici court. In Florence he met Lucrezia, who became his mistress, and the poet Giovan Battista Ricciardi, who became his lifelong friend. Finding himself ill-adapted to court circles, in 1650 Rosa returned to Rome, this time permanently. There, on March 4, 1673, he married Lucrezia, with whom he had lived most of his adult life. Eleven days later he was dead.

Rosa emerges as a strangely touching figure, proud, melancholic, and fiercely independent. Alone among the major painters in the city, he had (by his own choice) no powerful patron. He rarely accepted commissions; instead, he tried to sell from his studio and to make himself known through public exhibitions, which were seldom and few. To a client who dared to suggest his own subject, Rosa said, "Go to a brickmaker, they work on order." In contrast, Pietro da Cortona, Rosa's enormously successful rival in Rome, boasted that he never chose the subject of any of his paintings and if asked would refuse to do so. In his stand for artistic independence Rosa was far ahead of his time.

Rosa's protest is still clearer in his satirical poetry. Here he ridiculed the official art of the papal court, especially the work of Cortona and Gian Lorenzo Bernini. Later Rosa's attacks extended to the papacy. His poetry won him a host of enemies, an entry in the Index of Forbidden Books that lasted for 2 centuries, and a place in the history of Italian literature, which, though small, appears to be permanent.

Grotto with Cascades is typical of Rosa's small landscapes, which his friends called "caprices." It is fully baroque in its painterly handling, open brushwork, dark shadows, and the silvery impasto that is used to suggest the sparkle of falling water. But it is also romantic. Above the tiny figures towers a gigantic natural bridge eroded by waterfalls. Man appears insignificant and irrelevant before the grandeur of nature.

L'umana fragilità is characteristic of the more serious current that imbues Rosa's later work. The young woman in the foreground wears a wreath of widely opened roses (which are fragile and impermanent). On her lap sits an

Salvator Rosa, a self-portrait that the artist gave to his friend Giovan Battista Ricciardi. (The Metropolitan Museum of Art, Bequest of Mary L. Harrison, 1921)

infant who, guided by a winged skeleton, writes the words, "conceived in sin, born to pain, a life of labor, and inevitable death." Other symbols of impermanence are infants blowing soap bubbles and burning tufts of flax. In sharp contrast to his wild, untamed landscapes, the mood of these late works is one of quietude and resignation in the face of destiny; they reflect the then current revival of the philosophy of stoicism.

Further Reading

Salvator Rosa is listed in the Art study guide (III, F, 1, a). In Naples he studied with the Spanish painter Jusepe de RIBERA. Baroque art in Rome was dominated by the painter Pietro da CORTONA and the sculptor Gian Lorenzo BERNINI.

Selections in English from Rosa's correspondence and poetry are in Robert Enggass and Jonathan Brown, *Sources and Documents in the History of Art: Italy and Spain, 1600–1750* (1970). The standard work on Rosa, by Luigi Salerno (1963), is in Italian. Ellis K. Waterhouse, *Italian Baroque Painting* (1962; 2d ed. 1969), contains a good essay on Rosa.

Juan Manuel de Rosas. (Organization of American States)

ROSAS / By Gilbert B. Becker

Juan Manuel de Rosas (1793–1877) was an Argentine dictator. He was the prototype of the caudillo dictators of South America and ruled supreme in the Argentine Confederation from 1829 to 1852.

Juan Manuel de Rosas (pronounced rô′säs) was born in Buenos Aires on March 30, 1793, and claimed descent from a noble Asturian family through Count Ortiz de Rosas. The first of his parents' 20 children, he detested school and spent most of his childhood on the family estancias, where he became one of the best horsemen in the Argentine and later excelled in all of the techniques of the gaucho frontiersman. His mediocre education led to his personal animosity toward his more highly educated contemporaries.

Rosas commenced his long military career at 15, when he volunteered in the Buenos Aires forces to combat the second English invasion of his homeland. This experience led him to mistrust the motives of any European powers dealing with his government.

He married Encarnación de Escurra despite the objection of his mother at a time when marriages were usually arranged by the parents. Under Juan Martín de Pueyrredon, he organized a cavalry troop to fight against the Indians and welded his men into a disciplined army completely subservient to his orders. He soon entered the power struggle between the urban commercial leaders of Buenos Aires (the *portenos*) and the landed aristocracy of the interior provinces on the side of the latter. When Rosas was victorious in battle, he seized control of the Buenos Aires government in 1829.

Supreme Dictator

At first Rosas was just a senior partner of the federalist leaders of the other provinces, but as these were overcome or liquidated, he became almost supreme in the Argentine. He then became the prototype of more recent 20th-century dictators. He destroyed the liberty of the press, dissolved Congress, organized a secret police (the Mazorca Club), and inaugurated a reign of terror which lasted until his final overthrow in 1852. He was a natural leader and a master of efficiency and ran the government like a well-organized estancia or a well-disciplined army.

Near the close of his first term Rosas turned over his office to Juan Ramón Balcarce and led an expedition to fight the Indians to the south. He was visited at his bivouac by Charles Darwin, who gives a flattering account of Rosas at this time. The campaign allowed Rosas to train and maintain a large armed force under his personal command.

Foreign Wars

During his absence, his wife and his former tutor, Dr. Maza, held the real reins of the government. Rosas resumed control of the government upon his return and became embroiled in constant warfare. In 1837 he was involved in a war with Andrés Santa Cruz of Bolivia. Victorious in this costly encounter, he was faced with the necessity of defending his government against an uprising by the *portenos*, under Juan Lavalle and aided by the French, who blockaded Buenos Aires. The French soon pulled out, and Rosas was once more victorious. When the defeated invaders took refuge in Uruguay, Rosas intervened in the political turmoil in that country and was drawn into a siege of Montevideo which lasted for 9 years. Britain and France intervened jointly, and once again the ports of the Argentine were blockaded. The Europeans were forced to give up their blockade, but Rosas was forced to withdraw from the Uruguayan venture.

Ouster and Exile

The blockade had curtailed commerce and caused a loss of customs revenues from which the Rosas government never recovered. The other provinces had been equally hurt, and Justo José Urquiza, governor of Entre-Ríos and a former Rosas lieutenant, turned against him and, in 1852, at the battle of Caseros, Rosas was overthrown and fled to England aboard the British ship *Locust*. He never returned to his native land and died in England in relative obscurity.

The new government tried Rosas in absentia and found him guilty of tyranny, violating natural law, and endangering the republic to satisfy his personal ambition. His immense fortune, consisting of lands and cattle, was confiscated, and most of his personal records were destroyed. Until the Juan Perón era no man's memory was more uniformly hated in Argentina, and to this day there are no monuments to his memory in his native land. Yet Rosas was the man who had done the most to keep Latin America free of European domination. Urquiza, who overthrew him, provided him with the necessary funds to enable him to sustain himself during his exile.

Rosas' life had been a series of contradictions. He had come to power as a federalist and had then centered the government in Buenos Aires and the power in his own hands. Lacking in imagination, he alienated all of the intelligentsia and instituted a reign of terror and bloodshed. Yet throughout, his love of country was unquestioned, and he served it in the only way he knew.

Further Reading

Juan Manuel de Rosas is listed in the Latin America study guide (IV, A, 1, a). He was succeeded by Justo José URQUIZA and Bartolomé MITRE.

Rosas was hated by all contemporary Argentine intellectuals, most of whom he had exiled. The outstanding example of such vituperation is D. F. Sarmiento, *Life in the Argentine Republic in the Days of the Tyrants: or, Civilization and Barbarism* (trans. 1868). An extensive biography is "Juan Manuel de Rosas, Greatest of Argentine Dictators" in George Washington University, Seminar Conference on Hispanic American Affairs, *South American Dictators during the First Century of Independence*, edited by A. Curtis Wilgus (1937). An excellent volume on the economic aspects of the Rosas administration is in Miron Burgin, *Economic Aspects of Argentine Federalism* (1946).

✳ ✳ ✳

ROSENWALD / By Saul Engelbourg

The American retailer and philanthropist Julius Rosenwald (1862–1932) held executive offices in Sears, Roebuck and Company, America's leading mail-order house.

Julius Rosenwald was born in Springfield, Ill., on Aug. 12, 1862. He was active in the wholesale clothing business from 1879 until he joined Sears, Roebuck in 1895, just as the modern history of the company began. Rosenwald became vice president and owner of one-third of the company's stock.

Rosenwald succeeded Richard Warren Sears as president of Sears, Roebuck in 1908. As chief executive, he emphasized administration, system, and order. He was a careful merchandiser concerned with merchandise selection and restrained selling. He had great faith in the mail-order business and looked for long-run advantages. The company expanded enormously and entered the retail chain-store business during the years Rosenwald was a dominant figure.

In 1916 Rosenwald testified on wage policy for sales clerks before the Illinois Senate Committee on Vice. A highly successful profit-sharing plan for Sears, Roebuck employees instituted in 1916 was partly his achievement.

However, the Panic of 1920–1921—when wholesale and retail prices declined precipitously—caught Sears, Roebuck with an excessive inventory bought at high prices during World War I. To bail the company out, Rosenwald advanced money to Sears, Roebuck in 1921, though he was under no legal or moral obligation to act in this fashion. He ended his term as president in 1924 and became chairman of the board of directors, a position he held until he died.

Rosenwald was active in public service between 1916 and 1919 and was absent from his company's affairs for about the same time. He was appointed a member of the Council of National Defense and chairman of its committee on supplies. Philanthropy became more important to him after the Panic of 1920–1921. Rosenwald's philanthropy aimed at social welfare, and his donations benefited the Young Men's Christian Association and the Young Women's Christian Association, among other

*Julius Rosenwald.
(Library of Congress)*

agencies. He was also active in a variety of Jewish organizations.

The most distinctive feature of Rosenwald's philanthropy was his interest in American Negroes; the breadth of his involvement was unmatched by any other contemporary philanthropist. The Julius Rosenwald Fund, organized in 1917, stressed education and aided all levels of education from grade school to the university. Rosenwald also aided the National Urban League. His gifts on behalf of the Negro served as a stimulant to other donors. He died in Chicago on Jan. 6, 1932.

Further Reading

Julius Rosenwald is listed in the American History study guide (VIII, D, 2). His contemporary F. W. WOOLWORTH pioneered in the chain-store business.

Morris R. Werner, *Julius Rosenwald: The Life of a Practical Humanitarian* (1939), a general biography, provides some material on Sears, Roebuck but focuses on Rosenwald's philanthropic interests. Boris Emmet and John E. Jeuck, *Catalogues and Counters: A History of Sears, Roebuck and Company* (1950), places Rosenwald in the context of his enterprise. An account of Rosenwald's foundation is Edwin R. Embree and Julia Waxman, *Investment in People: The Story of the Julius Rosenwald Fund* (1949). Henry Allen Bullock, *A History of Negro Education in the South* (1967), notes Rosenwald's philanthropic role in Negro education.

Franz Rosenzweig. (Margrit Rosenstock Huessy)

ROSENZWEIG / By Malachi B. Martin

The German-born Jewish philosopher and writer Franz Rosenzweig (1886–1929) was important for his formulations and definitions of Jewish-Christian relations.

Franz Rosenzweig (pronounced rō′zən-tsvīk) was born at Kassel on Dec. 25, 1886. Rosenzweig first took up medicine; but, not finding this to his liking and discovering also a certain dichotomy in his life, he turned to the study of history and philosophy. He followed this with law studies. His early upbringing and education inclined him more and more to conversion to Christianity. However, in 1913 he attended an Orthodox Day of Atonement service and suddenly decided to halt his drift to Christianity and to adopt seriously the religion of his Jewish forefathers. It was these three themes, Christianity, Judaism, and Atonement (redemption), that formed the kernel of his life achievement in religious research.

While serving in the German army during World War I, Rosenzweig initiated a lively correspondence with Eugen Rosenstock concerning the relationship of Jewish and Christian theology. This correspondence was published (1935) only after Rosenzweig's death. He also started at

this time one of his outstanding works—*Der Stern der Erlösung* (1921). In this he expressed his full thought on the nature of religion and the mutual relationship of Judaism and Christianity. Religion for Rosenzweig was a three-way relationship; he distinguished God, man, and the world as three distinct beings, none of which could be confused with the other. The point was important for Rosenzweig because on it he broke with the German idealism of his day and foreshadowed the position later taken up by the existentialist philosophers of the 20th century. He then proceeded to define the triple relationship: between God and the world, it is one of creator and created; between God and man, it is one of revelator to the recipient (man) of that revelation; and between man and the world, it is one of redemption. Man has a redemptive function for the world: he helps to save it.

Rosenzweig then proceeded to define Jewish-Christian relations. He spoke of two Covenants, one between God and the Jews, the other between God and other men (the Christian Covenant). He considered the two Covenants as complementary elements in God's overall plan of redemption for the world and for man. Yet, Rosenzweig held, the two Covenants were mutually exclusive. This was a bold step for a Jewish thinker; it involved an admission that some limitation had to be placed on the Jewish claim of being exclusively and uniquely the Chosen People. Consequently, it involved much protest and controversy.

Rosenzweig started off as an idealist philosopher; he broke, however, with this philosophic idealism because his religious beliefs and studies interfered. In 1920 he also established his Freies Jüdisches Lehrhaus, an adult study center, at Frankfurt am Main. Its academic excellence and religious commitment provided an example on which many such institutions were founded in Germany. Unfortunately, he was attacked by a progressive paralysis in 1921. In 2 years he lost his ability to speak, write, or move. With his wife's help, however, he turned out several important minor works published as his *Kleinere Schriften* in 1937 together with an annotated version of 92 poems of Judah Halevi. He undertook (1925) a German translation of the Bible with Martin Buber, but he did not see its completion and publication (1938). He died on Dec. 9, 1929, at Frankfurt.

Further Reading

Franz Rosenzweig is listed in the Religion study guide (II, F, 1, b). He worked with Martin BUBER.

A full-length work in English is Nahum Norbert Glatzer, ed., *Franz Rosenzweig: His Life and Thought* (1953; rev. ed. 1961). See also Bernard Martin, comp., *Great Twentieth Century Jewish Philosophers* (1969), and Eugen Rosenstock-Huessy, *Judaism despite Christianity* (1969).

ROSMINI-SERBATI
/ By Malachi B. Martin

The Italian philosopher and priest Antonio Rosmini-Serbati (1797–1855), who supported the Risorgimento, was one of the few churchmen of his day who endeavored to lay a philosophical and theological foundation for Roman Catholic involvement in national politics.

Antonio Rosmini-Serbati (pronounced rōz-mē′nē sär-bä′tē) was born at Rovereto on March 24, 1797. After the usual studies, he was ordained a priest in 1821. Up to his time and for some time after, the Church forbade Roman Catholics in Italy to take part in national politics. Rosmini's studies led him to consider in what way Catholics could actively engage in politics, social reform, and the study of science without having to renounce the principles of their faith. He perceived that the educational methods of the Roman Church and its presentation of doctrinal matters were not suited either to the minds or to the tempers of his contemporaries. He also saw great deficiencies in the training of the clergy.

In 1828 Rosmini-Serbati established his Institute of Charity (Rosminians) at Monte Calvario near Domodossola. He modeled it on the Jesuit order, whose devotion to the Church and multifaceted activities he admired; it was approved by Pope Gregory XVI in 1839. The institute was established in England by Father Luigi Gentili, and there it played a part in the revival of Catholicism.

At this time the two major forces with which the Roman Catholic Church contended were nationalism and philosophic idealism. Nationalism was to change the face of Europe within a hundred years. Philosophic idealism supplied Karl Marx and Friedrich Engels with the bases of their theories and influenced the scientific thought of men such as Charles Darwin and Sigmund Freud. To Rosmini's credit, he understood the importance of both movements. But in trying to change the minds of his contemporaries, he was like a man with his shoulder against a mountain.

The election of Pope Pius IX in 1848 seemed providential to Rosmini. The new pope was known as the "pope of progress" because of his liberal views. When war broke out between Italy and Austria in 1848, Pius declared the papacy to be neutral because of its universal significance for all men. By this time Rosmini was known for his views. The Piedmontese government empowered him to negotiate a settlement with Pius. Rosmini wrote an account of this mission called *Della missione a Roma . . . negli anni 1848–49* (1881). Pius soon changed from his earlier liberalism to a hard-core conservatism, and Rosmini fell into disfavor. He was attacked, his teachings were declared suspect, and he had to retire from all active participation in public life and teaching.

Antonio Rosmini-Serbati. (Österreichische Nationalbibliothek, Vienna)

Rosmini's philosophy and teaching were based on an adaptation of current idealism. He placed at the center of his system what he called "ideal being." This was a hybrid sharing traits of the Neoplatonist ideal of Renaissance thinkers and the abstract Kantian idea of the unknowable *Ding-an-Sich*. Rosmini held that the "ideal being" was a reflection of God to be found in every man. He rescued the Kantian idea from its unknowability by declaring that not only was it most knowable but that it was the foundation of all else: the rights of the individual and man's concepts of truth and logic, and of his political and legal system. He expounded his theories in a series of books: *Maxims of Christian Perfection* (1830); *New Essay on the Origin of Ideas* (3 vols., 1838); *Theodicy* (1845); and *Psychology* (1850). His political thought was expressed in his *Of the Five Wounds of the Holy Church* and *The Constitution according to Social Justice* (both 1848).

When Rosmini fell into disfavor, Pius IX had all his works examined for possible error. But on examination by the Roman Congregation of the Index, they were declared free from error. Rosmini died on July 1, 1855.

Further Reading

Antonio Rosmini-Serbati is listed in the Philosophy study guide (VI, E). His thought was opposed by PIUS IX.

Biographical studies of Rosmini-Serbati include Giovanni Battista Pagani, *The Life of Antonio Rosmini-Serbati* (Eng. trans. 1907), and Claude Richard Harbord Leetham, *Rosmini: Priest, Philosopher and Patriot* (1957).

Edward A. Ross. (The University of Wisconsin)

E. A. ROSS / By Julius Weinberg

Edward Alsworth Ross (1866–1951), one of the founders of American sociology, is best remembered for his "Social Control."

Edward A. Ross was born in Virden, Ill., on Dec. 12, 1866. His father was a farmer, and his mother a schoolteacher. At 20 Ross graduated from Coe College in Cedar Rapids, Iowa; at 22, after 2 years as a teacher at the Ford Dodge Commercial Institute, he left for graduate study at the University of Berlin; and at 24 he received his doctorate in political economy at Johns Hopkins University.

In 1893 Ross was appointed full professor at Leland Stanford University, where he remained until his celebrated dismissal, in 1900, over the question of his right to speak out as a reformer on public issues. After 5 years at the University of Nebraska, he left in 1906 for the University of Wisconsin, famed for its Progressive-minded faculty and teachings. He spent the rest of his career at Wisconsin, first as professor of sociology and then as department chairman. He retired in 1937 and died in Madison.

Ross achieved national fame as a writer and popular lecturer. He authored 27 books and over 300 articles. His work can best be understood as the creative response of a reform-minded sociologist to the problems produced by the rapid industrialization and urbanization of the nation. *Social Control* (1901), a classic in American sociology, surveyed the institutions and values that would be needed to maintain individual freedom and social stability in an industrial order. *Social Psychology* (1908), the first textbook published in that field in the United States, similarly delineated the role of public opinion, custom, ceremony, and convention in maintaining social stability. *The Principles of Sociology* (1920, 1930, 1937), for many years one of the most popular texts in the field, stressed the role that the social processes can play in ensuring human progress.

More explicitly reformist in outlook were Ross's many books for the layman. *Sin and Society* (1907) established Ross as a major figure in Progressive thought; other popular works advocating social reform include *Changing America* (1909) and *The Social Trend* (1922). He also published many books on social conditions in Europe, Asia, and Africa. In 1917 he went to Russia to report on the Bolshevik Revolution and for many years advocated recognition of the Soviet Union by the U.S.

government and an appreciation of the improvements the Soviets brought to the economic and social life of the Russian people.

For a time Ross was active as a nativist. In his early career he espoused the superiority of the Anglo-Saxon peoples and advocated immigration restriction to prevent a large-scale influx of southern and eastern Europeans to the United States. In the 1920s his nativism included a program of eugenics and the nationwide prohibition of liquor. By 1930 Ross shed these notions and spent the greater part of his efforts promoting the New Deal reform and the freedoms of the individual. He served as the national chairman of the American Civil Liberties Union (1940–1950).

As a popularizer of the notion that the purpose of sociology is the reform of society, Ross had no peer among American sociologists in his lifetime. An erudite scholar, inspiring lecturer, courageous reformer, and uncompromising champion of freedom for the individual, he fulfilled the role he established for himself admirably.

Further Reading

Edward A. Ross is listed in the Social Sciences study guide (VII, D, 3). One of his doctoral students at Wisconsin was C. Wright MILLS.

Ross's autobiography is *Seventy Years of It* (1936). For his biography see Julius Weinberg, *Edward Alsworth Ross and the Sociology of Progressivism* (1971). His sociological theories are best explained by William L. Kolb, "The Sociological Theories of Edward Alsworth Ross," in Harry Elmer Barnes, ed., *An Introduction to the History of Sociology* (1948). Other works which place Ross in the history of sociology are Charles Hunt Page, *Class and American Sociology: From Ward to Ross* (1940); Howard W. Odum, *American Sociology: The Story of Sociology in the United States through 1950* (1951); and Heinz Maus, *A Short History of Sociology* (1956; trans. 1962).

JAMES CLARK ROSS / By Barry M. Gough

The English admiral and polar explorer Sir James Clark Ross (1800–1862) is known for his discovery of the North magnetic pole and his magnetic surveys of the Antarctic.

James Clark Ross was born in London on April 15, 1800, the son of George Ross and a nephew of Rear Adm. John Ross. He entered the Royal Navy in 1812, serving with his uncle in four ships and accompanying him on his first Arctic voyage, in 1818. He was in William Edward Parry's four Arctic expeditions. The first was in 1819–1820 aboard the *Hecla*; the second was between 1821 and 1823 in H.M.S. *Fury*. Ross received a promotion on Dec. 26, 1822, and sailed as lieutenant of

the *Fury* on Parry's 1824–1825 Arctic expedition. He was also with Parry in 1827–1828 during the latter's unsuccessful attempt to reach the North Pole by sledge from West Spitsbergen.

Ross was promoted to commander on Nov. 8, 1827. From 1829 to 1833 he again served on one of his uncle's Arctic expeditions. On this trip James Clark Ross led a party across Boothia Isthmus, reaching the North magnetic pole on May 31, 1831. After his return home in 1833, Ross was promoted to captain and undertook the relief of whalers in Baffin Bay in 1836 and conducted a magnetic survey of Great Britain from 1835 until 1838.

In September 1838, with Ross as commander, H.M.S. *Erebus* and *Terror* sailed to the Antarctic to discover the South magnetic pole, examine Antarctica, and conduct numerous scientific tests according to directions of the Royal Society. They penetrated the ice belt as far south as latitude 78°9′30″ in January 1841, reaching open water and discovering the Ross Sea. They continued to sail south and discovered Victoria Land (now part of New Zealand's Ross Dependency). The Ross Shelf Ice barred their way further south, and they were forced to turn back. In November 1841 they sailed again, from New Zealand, to solve the "Great Barrier Mystery" and failed owing to bad weather conditions. This time they wintered in the Falkland Islands, but they were no more successful on their third attempt. Finally they sailed for home and reached England in September 1843.

This voyage gave Ross "a distinguished place amongst

Sir James Clark Ross. (By permission of the Trustees of the National Maritime Museum, Greenwich, England)

the most successful votaries of Science, and the brightest ornaments of the British Navy." He received gold medals from geographical societies in London and Paris; in 1844 he was knighted; and in 1848 he was elected a fellow of the Royal Society. He led the first naval expedition in 1848–1849 to search for Sir John Franklin, missing with H.M.S. *Enterprise* and *Investigator*, but this was unsuccessful. Until his death, Ross was frequently consulted as "the first authority on all matters relating to Arctic navigation." He died at Aylesbury, England, on April 3, 1862.

Further Reading

Sir James Clark Ross is listed in the Geography and Exploration study guide (VI, A, 3 and 4). Other polar explorers were Robert PEARY, Richard E. BYRD, and Sir John FRANKLIN.

Ross's account of his expedition is *A Voyage of Discovery and Research in the Southern and Antarctic Regions, 1839–43* (2 vols., 1847). Laurence P. Kirwan, *A History of Polar Exploration* (1960), devotes a chapter to the expedition, largely based on Ross's own account. Ross's discovery of the North magnetic pole is told in Sir John Ross, *Narrative of a Second Voyage in Search of a North-West Passage . . .* (1835).

JOHN ROSS / By Odie B. Faulk

John Ross (1790–1866), chief of the American Cherokee Indians, headed his tribe during the saddest era in its history, when it was removed from its ancestral lands to Oklahoma.

John Ross. (Library of Congress)

John Ross was born near Lookout Mountain, Tenn., on Oct. 3, 1790. His Indian name was Cooweescoowe. His father was a Scotsman; his mother was one-quarter Cherokee and three-quarters Scot. Ross was educated by private tutors and then at Kingston Academy in Tennessee.

Ross's rise to prominence began in 1817, when he was elected a member of the Cherokee national council. Two years later he became president of the council, a position he held until 1826. In 1827 he helped write the Cherokee constitution and was elected assistant chief. The following year he became principal chief of the tribe, and he remained in this position until 1839.

In 1829 the state of Georgia ordered the Cherokee Indians removed. Ross became a leader of the faction of the tribe that opposed removal, and he led in challenging the state ruling before the U.S. Supreme Court. His appeal was successful, but Georgia officials refused to obey the higher court's ruling.

In 1835 the U.S. government signed a treaty of removal with a small faction of the Cherokee tribe. Ross drafted an appeal against this treaty, saying that it was obtained by fraudulent means, and addressed it to President Andrew Jackson. Jackson approved the policy of removal,

however, as did Martin Van Buren, and when Gen. Winfield Scott arrived in Georgia with troops, Ross and the Cherokee were forced to acquiesce. In 1838–1839 Ross led his people in the removal westward (known as the "Trail of Tears") to the Indian Territory (Oklahoma).

Once there, Ross was instrumental in drafting a Cherokee constitution that united the eastern and western branches of the tribe. That year he was also chosen chief of the united tribe, an office he held until his death. He settled near Park Hill in Oklahoma, where he erected a mansion and farmed, using his many slaves to cultivate his fields. His first wife, a full-blooded Cherokee, Quatie, died in 1839. In 1845 he married a white woman who died in 1865.

Ross believed that the Cherokee Indians should not participate in the Civil War, and on May 17, 1861, he issued a proclamation of Cherokee neutrality. However, slave-owning Cherokee brought sufficient pressure to force a council resulting in a treaty of alliance with the Confederacy signed in October 1861. When Union troops invaded Oklahoma in 1862, Ross moved to Philadelphia and repudiated the Confederate alliance. This move caused some Confederate sympathizers in the tribe to dispute his right as chief. Ross lived in Philadelphia until the end of the Civil War. He died while negotiating a treaty for his tribe in Washington, D.C., on Aug. 1, 1866.

Further Reading

John Ross is listed in the American History study guide (V, C, 2). His contemporary SEQUOYAH created an alphabet for the Cherokee language.

The major study of Ross is Rachel Caroline Eaton, *John Ross and the Cherokee Indians* (1914). For Ross's political career see Morris L. Wardell, *A Political History of the Cherokee Nation, 1838–1907* (1938), and Henry T. Malone, *Cherokees of the Old South* (1956). An overall study of the tribe and an evaluation of Ross as a leader are in Grace S. Woodward, *The Cherokees* (1963).

* * *

CHRISTINA ROSSETTI / By Glen A. Omans

The English poet Christina Georgina Rossetti (1830–1894) wrote poems of love, fantasy, and nature, verses for children, and devotional poetry and prose. She may well be England's greatest woman poet.

Christina Rossetti was born on Dec. 5, 1830, in London, the youngest of the four remarkable Rossetti children. Educated entirely at home, she spoke English and Italian with ease and read French, Latin, and German. Her first verses were written to her mother on April 27, 1842. Her first published poems were the seven she contributed in 1850 to the Pre-Raphaelite magazine, the *Germ*, under the pseudonym Ellen Alleyne.

When her father died in 1854, Christina became the close companion of her mother and followed her older sister's example in becoming a devout Anglican. Though mild and virtuous, she was frequently anxious about her self-presumed sinfulness. She is said to have pasted strips of paper over the more blasphemous passages in Swinburne's poetry. Yet she remained devoted to her brother, Dante Gabriel, whose life was far from a model of conventional virtue. At 18 she fell in love with James Collinson, a minor Pre-Raphaelite painter, but broke off her engagement to him 2 years later, when he became a Roman Catholic. In 1862 she fell deeply in love with Charles Bagot Cayley. But she again refused to marry, this time because Cayley had no firm religious faith. These two broken love affairs are reflected in many of her poems, especially the sonnet sequence *Monna Innominata*. In other poems a melancholy regret for lost love is mixed with a disturbing obsession with death. Because she suffered long and frequent periods of poor health, Miss Rossetti came to regard life as physically and emotionally painful and to look forward to death both as a release and as the possible moment of joyful union with God and with those she had loved and lost.

Miss Rossetti's three major volumes of poetry were *Goblin Market and Other Poems* (1862), *The Prince's Progress and Other Poems* (1866), and *A Pageant and Other Poems* (1881). She also published *Commonplace* (1870), a book of short stories; *Sing-song: A Nursery Rhyme Book* (1872), beautifully illustrated by Arthur Hughes and a favorite of Victorian children; and *Speaking Likenesses* (1874), a book of tales for children. But her poetry alone has secured her fame. Her poems, like those of the later Victorian poet Gerard Manley Hopkins, reveal a dual, self-contradictory sensibility. They express a sensuous attraction to physical beauty fused with a mystical and saintly religious faith. They are sometimes highly sentimental in tone yet scrupulously austere in diction and form. And throughout many of them one may find a quiet sense of humor that controls the sentimentality and keeps contradictions in balance. "Goblin Market" is certainly her finest poem and her most disturbing in its presentation of the conflict between sisterly love and destructive passion.

From 1871 through 1873 Miss Rossetti was stricken by Graves' disease, which ruined her beauty and brought her close to death. When she recovered, she turned almost exclusively to religious writing, publishing a number of devotional books: *Annus Domini* (1874), *Seek and Find* (1879), *Called to Be Saints: The Minor Festivals* (1881), *Letter and Spirit* (1882), *Time Flies: A Reading Diary* (1885), *The Face of the Deep: A Commentary on the Revelation* (1892), and *Verses* (1893). In 1891 she began to suffer from cancer and died, after a long and painful illness, on Dec. 29, 1894, in London.

Further Reading

Christina Rossetti is listed in the Literature study guide (II, H, 2, b). Her poetry, like that of Gerard Manley HOP-

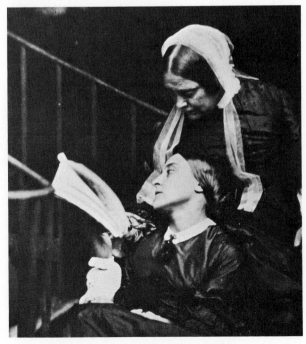

Christina Rossetti (seated) and her mother, photographed by Lewis Carroll. (Gernsheim Collection, University of Texas)

KINS, combined deep religious faith with strong physical sensibility.

A wealth of biographical detail is in *The Family Letters of Christina Georgina Rossetti*, edited by her brother William M. Rossetti (1908; repr. 1968); Marya Zaturenska, *Christina Rossetti: A Portrait with Background* (1949); and *The Rossetti-Macmillan Letters*, edited by Lona M. Packer (1963). The best biography is Lona Packer, *Christina Rossetti* (1963). An interesting study of her poetry is Thomas B. Swann, *Wonder and Whimsy: The Fantastic World of Christina Rossetti* (1960).

D. G. ROSSETTI / By Francis Ames-Lewis

> The English painter and poet Dante Gabriel Rossetti (1828–1882) was a cofounder of the Pre-Raphaelite Brotherhood. His works show an impassioned, mystic imagination in strong contrast to the banal sentimentality of contemporary Victorian art.

Dante Gabriel Rossetti, photographed by Lewis Carroll. (Gernsheim Collection, University of Texas)

Born on May 12, 1828, of Anglo-Italian parentage, Dante Gabriel Rossetti was steeped throughout childhood in the atmosphere of medieval Italy, which became a major source of his subject matter and artistic inspiration. After 2 years in the Royal Academy schools he worked briefly under Ford Madox Brown in 1848.

Shortly after Rossetti joined William Holman Hunt's studio later that year, the Pre-Raphaelite Brotherhood was formed, in Hunt's words, "to do battle against the frivolous art of the day." An association of artists so varied in artistic style, technique, and expressive spirit as the Pre-Raphaelites could not long survive, and it was principally owing to Rossetti's forceful, almost hypnotic personality that the Brotherhood held together long enough to achieve the critical and popular recognition necessary for the success of its crusade.

His Paintings

Rossetti did not have the natural technical proficiency that is evident in the minute detail and brilliant color of a typical Pre-Raphaelite painting, and his early oil paintings, the *Girlhood of Mary Virgin* (1849) and the *Ecce Ancilla Domini* (1850), were produced only at the expense of great technical effort. In the less demanding medium of watercolor, however, Rossetti clearly revealed his intense, compressed imaginative power. The series of small watercolors of the 1850s culminates in such masterpieces as *Dante's Dream* (1856) and the *Wedding of St. George and the Princess Sabra* (1857), characteristic products of Rossetti's inflamed sensibility, with typically irrational perspective and lighting, glowing color, and forceful figures.

In almost all his paintings of the 1850s Rossetti used

Elizabeth Siddal as his model. Discovered in a hatshop in 1850, she was adopted by the Brotherhood as their ideal of feminine beauty. In 1852 she became exclusively Rossetti's model, and in 1860 his wife. Beset by growing melancholy, she committed suicide 2 years later. Rossetti buried a manuscript of his poems in her coffin, a characteristically dramatic gesture which he later regretted. *Beata Beatrix* (1863), a posthumous portrait of Elizabeth Siddal, the Beatrice to his Dante, is one of Rossetti's most deeply felt paintings: it is his last masterpiece and the first in a series of symbolical female portraits, which declined gradually in quality as his interest in painting decreased.

His Poetry

Although early in his career poetry was for Rossetti simply a relaxation from painting, later on writing gradually became more important to him, and in 1871 he wrote to Ford Madox Brown, "I wish one could live by writing poetry. I think I'd see painting d——d if I could. . . ." In 1861 he published his translations from Dante and other early Italian poets, reflecting the medieval preoccupations of his finest paintings. In 1869 the manuscript of his early poems was recovered from his wife's coffin and published the next year.

Rossetti's early poems under strong Pre-Raphaelite influence, such as "The Blessed Damozel" (1850; subsequently revised) and "The Portrait," have a sensitive innocence and a strong mystical passion paralleled by his paintings of the 1850s. As his interest in painting declined, Rossetti's poetic craftsmanship improved, until in his latest works, such as "Rose Mary" and "The White Ship" (both included in *Ballads and Sonnets*, 1881), his use of richly colored word textures achieves a sumptuous grandeur of expression and sentiment.

At his death on April 9, 1882, Rossetti had reached a position of artistic prominence, and his spirit was a significant influence on the cultural developments of the late 19th century. Although his technique was not always the equal of his powerful feeling, his imaginative genius earned him a place in the ranks of English visionary artists.

Further Reading

Dante Gabriel Rossetti is listed in the Literature study guide (II, H, 2, b) and the Art study guide (III, H, 2, b). He, Sir John Everett MILLAIS, and William Holman HUNT founded the Pre-Raphaelite Brotherhood. Rossetti's sister, Christina ROSSETTI, was a poet.

The most recent work on Rossetti is G. H. Fleming, *Rossetti and the Pre-Raphaelite Brotherhood* (1967), a detailed study of his relations with the Brotherhood, which like Oswald Doughty's *A Victorian Romantic: Dante Gabriel Rossetti* (1949; 2d ed. 1960) is a general biography, not a specialized work on the paintings. Fundamental on the Pre-Raphaelites is William Holman Hunt's firsthand account, *Pre-Raphaelitism and the Pre-Raphaelite Brotherhood* (2 vols., 1905). Also important are Robin Ironside, *Pre-Raphaelite Painters* (1948); T. S. R. Boase, *English Art, 1800–1870* (1959); and John Dixon Hunt, *The Pre-Raphaelite Imagination, 1848–1900* (1968).

✳   ✳   ✳

ROSSI / By Gloria Rose

The Italian composer Luigi Rossi (ca. 1598–1653) wrote important works in the field of the chamber cantata.

Luigi Rossi (pronounced rōs′sē) was born in Torremaggiore. He studied in Naples with Jean de Macque and was subsequently employed by the Duke of Traetta. Quite early in his career Rossi moved to Rome, and this became his permanent residence. He was first employed in Rome by Marc'Antonio Borghese.

In 1627 Rossi married Costanza de Ponte, a harpist and an outstanding musician in her own right. When the Rossis visited the Florentine court in 1635, Costanza de Ponte was highly acclaimed for her performances.

In 1633 Rossi took on the additional post of organist at the church of S. Luigi dei Francesi. Although he retained this post for the rest of his life, it was secondary to his main interests and activities, for he was essentially a composer of secular music who was suited to court life.

Of Rossi's several aristocratic patrons, the most important was Cardinal Antonio Barberini. The Barberini family was famous for its patronage of the arts, and Cardinal Antonio was the most lavish of all in his support of music. When Rossi entered the service of the cardinal in 1641, he joined a sizable musical establishment of brilliant singers and instrumentalists. Not only chamber music but theatrical music was presented at the Palazzo Barberini. Operas, complete with star singers and splendid productions, had been given there since 1632.

Soon after his appointment to the Barberini establishment, Rossi began work on his first opera, *Il palazzo incantato*, with a libretto by Giulio Rospigliosi, after Ariosto's *Orlando furioso*. This was performed several times at the Palazzo Barberini in 1642. Rossi's second and only other opera, *Orfeo*, with a libretto by Francesco Buti, was performed not in Rome but in Paris in 1647. Rossi went to Paris himself to organize the performances of *Orfeo*. It was performed six times and had a marked success. One of the earliest operas given in France, it was highly influential on the subsequent development of French opera.

Rossi's chamber cantatas also proved to be very popular in French musical circles. Indeed, his success in France was so great that he was called to Paris again in 1648. He died in Rome on Feb. 19, 1653.

Rossi also wrote some Latin motets; probably some Italian oratorios (the authorship of these is uncertain); one harpsichord piece; and about 300 chamber cantatas, with Italian words, which represent his most important contribution. The great majority of the cantatas are composed for solo voice, usually soprano, accompanied by thorough-bass. Many others are written for two voices and thorough-bass. Some are for three or four voices and thorough-bass.

All sizes and varieties of the contemporary cantata appear in Rossi's output: short, simple pieces; long works in sophisticated forms; light airs; sorrowful laments; and pieces containing the most varied musical styles. His cantatas were copied and performed throughout Italy and abroad. They are outstanding examples of the Italian chamber cantata.

Further Reading

Luigi Rossi is listed in the Music study guide (I, D, 1). Other outstanding composers of chamber cantatas were Giacomo CARISSIMI and Pietro CESTI. When French national operas began to be composed, notably by Jean Baptiste LULLY, they were modeled on the Italian operas of Rossi and his Italian contemporaries.

Rossi's music is discussed by Manfred F. Bukofzer, *Music in the Baroque Era: From Monteverdi to Bach* (1947), and by Claude V. Palisca, *Baroque Music* (1968). A thematic catalog of Rossi's cantatas, with a detailed introduction by Eleanor Caluori, entitled *Luigi Rossi*, is fascicle 3 of *The Wellesley Edition Cantata Index Series* (2 vols., 1965).

✳   ✳   ✳

ROSSINI / By Charles Hamm

The operas of the Italian composer Gioacchino Rossini (1792–1868), particularly those in the comic genre, were among the most popular works of the entire 19th century. His best-known work is "The Barber of Seville."

Gioacchino Rossini (pronounced rô-sē′nē) was born in Pesaro on Feb. 29, 1792, into a musical family: his father was a trumpeter and horn player; his mother became a successful operatic singer. When he was 4 years old, Gioacchino's mother took him to Bologna, where she sought and found singing engagements and where the child received instruction in singing, theory, keyboard, and several other instruments. By the time he was in his early teens, he was an accomplished accompanist, sometimes played horn with his father in the orchestra at the opera, and had begun writing music.

During Rossini's formal musical training at the Liceo Comunale in Bologna (1807–1810) he composed prolifically. His first opera was *Demetrio e Polibio*, written in 1809, but his first work to be put on the stage was the comic opera *La cambiale di matrimonio*, composed in 1810 and performed successfully at the Teatro di S. Moisè in Venice that year.

Success came quickly to the young composer. He wrote rapidly and fluently, in a style pleasing to singers and audiences alike. *La pietra del paragone* was staged to great acclaim at La Scala in Milan in 1812; *Tancredi* became a genuine international hit following its premiere in Venice the following year. Operas flowed from his pen at the rate of three or four a year. In 1815 the San Carlo and Del Fondo theaters in Naples engaged him as musical director, and his duties included writing a new opera every year for each theater. *Elisabetta, regina d'Inghilterra*, his first work for Naples, enjoyed enormous success. This was the first opera, incidentally, in which he wrote out the ornamentation he expected from his singers rather than leaving this matter to them.

Rossini was in Naples until 1822; during this period he also composed works for such cities as Rome, Milan, Venice, and Lisbon. *Almaviva, ossia l'inutile precauzione*, based on Pierre Caron de Beaumarchais's *Le Barbier de Séville*, was poorly received on the occasion of its first performance in Rome in 1816, but soon (renamed *Il barbiere di Siviglia*) it enjoyed incredible success in Italy and all over the world, becoming one of the most widely sung works in the entire history of opera. *La Cenerentola*, based on the Cinderella story and premiered in Rome in 1817, was almost as successful; and these two comic operas established Rossini beyond question as the most successful operatic composer of the day.

The year 1822 was a critical one for Rossini in many ways. He went to Vienna for performances of several of his operas in German, married the famous singer Isabella Colbran, who had performed with great success in many of his operas, and worked with even greater care than usual on the new opera, *Semiramide*, for Venice. The poor reception of this work persuaded him that Italian audiences were no longer the proper ones for what he wanted to compose, and he resolved to write no more operas for performance in his native country. Later in the year he traveled—by way of Paris—to England, where he was royally received and realized a good profit from various performances of his works. He also sang some of his own vocal compositions.

In 1824 Rossini accepted an engagement as musical director of the Théâtre Italien in Paris. He revised a number of his earlier operas to suit the conventions of the French stage, presenting them to great acclaim. He wrote his last two operas for Paris: *Le Comte Ory* (1828) is one of the most brilliant and witty French comic operas of all time; and *Guillaume Tell* (1829), a spectacular five-act work integrating soloists, chorus, orchestra, dancers, and elaborate staging, became a model for an entire generation of French grand opera. He remained in Paris until 1836, when he returned to Bologna, where he served as honorary director of the Liceo Comunale. Political disturbances forced a move to Florence in 1847, the year after his marriage to his second wife, Olimpia Alessandrina Pélissier. In 1855 he returned to Paris, remaining there until his death on Nov. 13, 1868.

The most curious aspect of Rossini's later years is that he wrote no operas after 1829. He retained a lively interest in the musical scene, composed occasional cantatas, such religious works as the *Stabat Mater* and *Petite Messe solennelle* of 1864, and several hundred small "album" pieces for piano, voice and piano, and various

Gioacchino Rossini. (Photo Harlingue-Viollet)

A scene from a British production of Rossini's Barber of Seville. (Radio Times Hulton Picture Library)

instruments, but he never again attempted a work for the stage. He was a wealthy man, charming and witty, much in demand socially, and comfortable even with those men whose ideas about music were in conflict with his own. Much of his large estate went to the endowment of a conservatory of music in Pesaro. In 1887 he was reburied in the church of Sta Croce, Florence.

Rossini's 38 operas run the gamut from brief one-act comic works to the monumental and historic five-act *Guillaume Tell*. Some of his contemporaries and some historians, misled by the facility and speed of his writing, his habit of using portions of unsuccessful or forgotten works over again in new operas, and the easy charm of his solo arias and ensembles, have considered him a clever but superficial composer of no outstanding importance in the development of opera. But his works show remarkable craftsmanship, and in their brilliant integration of solo, ensemble, and orchestral writing and their sharp character delineation they are the most important link in the Italian operatic tradition between the late Italian works of Wolfgang Amadeus Mozart and the first works of Giuseppe Verdi. And Rossini's *Guillaume Tell* altered the entire course of French opera.

Further Reading

Gioacchino Rossini is listed in the Music study guide (I, G, 3). Another composer of grand opera in France was Giacomo MEYERBEER.

The standard work in English is Francis Toye, *Rossini: A Study in Tragi-comedy* (1934). An important contemporary study is Stendhal's *Life of Rossini* (2 vols., 1824; trans. 1869; new trans. 1957). A recent excellent study is Herbert Weinstock, *Rossini: A Biography* (1968). Rossini's life and career are discussed in Donald Jay Grout, *A Short History of Opera* (1947; 2d ed. 1965). Recom-

mended for general background is Kenneth B. Klaus, *The Romantic Period in Music* (1970).

IL ROSSO / By Robert Enggass

The Italian painter Il Rosso (1495–1540) was one of the leaders in the development of the mannerist style of painting, which he was the first to implant in France.

Giovanni Battista di Jacopo, known as Il Rosso (pronounced ēl rōs′sō) or Rosso Fiorentino, was born in Florence. He began studying art as a boy but had difficulty finding a teacher to his liking since, as Giorgio Vasari tells us, "He had an opinion of his own in opposition to their styles." About 1512 he entered the workshop of Andrea del Sarto, where he met Pontormo.

Il Rosso and Pontormo brought Florentine mannerism into being. This new style, which contrasts dramatically with the order and calm of High Renaissance art, is well illustrated by Il Rosso's *Deposition* (1521). In this painting, sharply angular, emaciated figures climbing up and down ladders surround the twisted body of Christ, which has turned green in death. His *Moses Defending the Daughters of Jethro* (ca. 1523) is even stronger. Great muscular nudes (derived from his studies of Michelangelo's cartoon for the *Battle of Cascina*) fill the crowded canvas. Wildly they lunge and twist, falling in a contorted heap that fills the foreground.

In 1523 Il Rosso moved to Rome, where he met Mi-

The Deposition, *a 1521 painting by Il Rosso, in the Cathedral of Volterra. (Alinari-Brogi)*

chelangelo and members of Raphael's circle. In 1527, when the city was sacked by troops under the emperor Charles V, Il Rosso was captured by the dreaded Germans. On his release he fled to Perugia. The next 3 years he spent wandering from town to town in search of commissions. Following a brawl with some priests in Borgo San Sepolcro he fled to Venice, where he was befriended by the writer Pietro Aretino.

Il Rosso "always hoped to end his days in France," wrote Vasari, "and thus to escape the misery and poverty to which, so he said, those who work in Tuscany are exposed." The call to France came in 1530, and he became a success overnight. The king, Francis I, granted him a generous pension, a town house in Paris, and commodious quarters at Fontainebleau (then the chief seat of the French court), "where he lived like a lord."

Il Rosso executed frescoes (1532–1535; destroyed) for the Pavilion of Pomona at Fontainebleau. For the Grand Gallery of Francis I at Fontainebleau he and his assistant and successor, Primaticcio, created an entirely new style of palace decoration that combined paintings set into the wall with complex stucco reliefs and intricately carved wooden panels (1534–1537). The influence of these two

major decorative projects on French art in the following centuries was enormous.

The painter died in Paris. Vasari tells us that, filled with remorse at having mistakenly accused a friend of theft, Il Rosso took his own life.

Further Reading

Il Rosso is listed in the Art study guide (III, E, 1, c). He and PONTORMO were briefly in the employ of ANDREA DEL SARTO. Il Rosso and PRIMATICCIO brought the mannerist style to France.

The only recent study of Il Rosso is in Italian: Paola Barocchi, *Il Rosso Fiorentino* (1950). By far the best account in English of his work at Fontainebleau is in Anthony Blunt, *Art and Architecture in France, 1500–1700* (1953). Giorgio Vasari, *Lives of the Most Eminent Painters, Sculptors and Architects* (many editions), contains a lively biography of Il Rosso.

ROSTOVTZEFF / By Dwight W. Hoover

Michael Ivanovich Rostovtzeff (1870–1952), Russian-born American historian and the foremost classical scholar of his day, specialized in the social and economic movements of Greece and Rome.

Michael Rostovtzeff (pronounced rô-stŏv′tsəf) was born on Nov. 10, 1870, in Kiev, where he went through the university, earning master and doctorate degrees in classical philology. From 1895 to 1898 he traveled throughout the classical lands. He then became professor of Latin at the University of St. Petersburg, a post he occupied until 1918.

Rostovtzeff and his wife left their country in 1918 because of the Russian Revolution and went to England. His *Proletarian Culture* (1919), published under the auspices of the Russian Liberation Committee, showed his revulsion against the principles of the Russian Revolution. In 1920 he became professor of ancient history at the University of Wisconsin, a position he held until 1925, when he went to Yale as Sterling professor of ancient history and archeology. In 1928 he directed Yale's archeological expedition to Dura-Europos on the Euphrates River in Syria. He continued as director and remained as editor of the excavation reports after he retired from teaching in 1944.

At the same time, Rostovtzeff was writing monographs and more general books. Two of his studies, *A Large Estate in Egypt in the Third Century B.C.* and *The Iranians and Greeks in South Russia* (both 1922), showed his interest in economic and cultural development. His *Social and Economic History of the Roman Empire* (1926) is considered one of the principal modern contributions to Roman historiography. In his popular text *A History of the Ancient World* (2 vols., 1926–1927) Ro-

expressionists who emerged in New York after World War II. His mature painting emphasized pure color.

Michael Rostovtzeff in 1931, a portrait in the Bibliothèque Nationale, Paris. (Giraudon)

stovtzeff devoted considerable space to art and literature, and he extended this interest to Chinese art in his next book, *Inlaid Bronzes of the Han Dynasty in the Collection of C. T. Loo* (1927). He continued to write on topics such as Italy, Seleucid Babylonia, the animal style in Russia and China, and the art of Dura-Europos. The *Social and Economic History of the Hellenistic World* (3 vols., 1941) is his most famous work. He died in New Haven on Oct. 20, 1952.

Rostovtzeff believed that the past had meaning for the present. He thought the ancient world displayed features similar to the modern and argued that the economic development of the ancient world roughly approximated that of the present, although it did not reach the full stage of industrial capitalism. He favored the open Greek economic system in contrast to the closed Egyptian one and the urban middle class over a rural aristocracy. He attacked the notions that the ancient world was a stage from which modern economic development evolved and that economic factors were the sole cause of cultural change.

Further Reading

Michael Rostovtzeff is listed in the Social Sciences study guide (VII, A, 3). The German historian Theodor MOMMSEN specialized in Roman society and culture.

Rostovtzeff presents his ideas about history in the preface to his *A History of the Ancient World* (2 vols., 1926–1927). Herman Ausubel, *Historians and Their Craft: A Study of the Presidential Addresses of the American Historical Association, 1884–1945* (1950), considers Rostovtzeff the greatest classicist since Mommsen.

ROTHKO / **By Carl Belz**

The American painter Mark Rothko (1903–1970) was one of the original abstract

Mark Rothko was born on Sept. 25, 1903, in Gvinsk, Russia, and emigrated to the United States in 1913. He attended Yale University (1921–1923), and he began painting in 1925, when he studied with Max Weber at the Art Students League in New York. He later traveled extensively in Europe.

In 1935 Rothko cofounded "The Ten," an organization of expressionist artists in New York. During 1936 and 1937 he worked on the government's Federal Arts Project. In 1948 he joined Robert Motherwell, Barnett Newman, and William Baziotes in founding a New York art school called "Subjects of the Artist." For extensive periods throughout his career Rothko taught at colleges and universities, including the Center Academy in Brooklyn (1929–1952), the California School of Fine Arts in San Francisco (summers of 1947 and 1949), Brooklyn College (1951–1954), the University of Colorado (1955), and Tulane University (1956).

Rothko's first important one-man show in 1945 at the Art of This Century Gallery in New York City established him as a leading figure in postwar American painting. During the 1940s and 1950s he exhibited regularly. In 1958 his work was included in the Venice Biennale, and in 1961 the Museum of Modern Art in New York City held a retrospective exhibition. Among Rothko's special

Mark Rothko, photographed by Robert E. Mates. (Courtesy Marlborough Gallery, New York)

awards were his election to the National Institute of Arts and Letters in 1968 and the honorary degree of doctor of fine arts from Yale University in 1969. Rothko committed suicide in New York on Feb. 25, 1970.

Like nearly all the advanced American painters who matured during the 1940s, Rothko's early work was founded on the tenets of both cubism and surrealism. This meant that his art leaned both toward the problems of formal abstraction and toward a more traditional notion of conceptualized subject matter. By the late 1940s, however, he gradually broke through to a style that rejected both cubism and surrealism, and his work became linked with the abstract expressionism of men like Jackson Pollock and Willem de Kooning. Rothko's best-known paintings of the 1950s and 1960s continued to be associated with this general style.

But Rothko's art reveals a distinct and personal interpretation of the abstract expressionist style. From his first emergence as a mature artist, he eschewed the gestural brushwork and the dense, painterly surfaces that became celebrated in the work of De Kooning, Franz Kline, and others. Instead, Rothko concentrated on expression through color alone, and to this end he radically simplified his imagery. In his best paintings, the imagery consists of two or three rectangles of color that float within an abstract space. Generally, the areas of color dissolve softly into one another, denying all traces of either hard or tactile edges. The softness is a function of the artist's delicate, feathery brushstrokes, and it results in an expanding pictorial space that seems to consist of pure color rather than colored objects. In many of Rothko's paintings his colors appear to generate their own magical or divine light.

Further Reading

Mark Rothko is listed in the Art study guide (IV, E, 9). Other abstract expressionists were Jackson POLLOCK and Willem DE KOONING.

The catalog of Rothko's Museum of Modern Art retrospective exhibition, *Mark Rothko,* by Peter Selz (1961) is especially rich with illustrations. Rothko's place within the abstract expressionist movement is presented in Barbara Rose, *American Art since 1900* (1967).

* * *

ROTTMAYR / By Edward A. Maser

Johann Michael Rottmayr (1654–1730) was the first native-born Austrian painter of the 18th century to achieve preeminence over the Italians, thus beginning the great century of Austrian baroque painting.

Johann Michael Rottmayr (pronounced rŏt′mī-ər), born in Laufen, a small town near Salzburg, on Dec. 10, 1654, probably learned the rudiments of his craft from his mother, who was a painter. About 1675

he went to Venice, entering the workshop of Karl Loth, an expatriate Bavarian, with whom he remained for 13 years. About 1688 he returned to Austria and soon entered the service of the prince-bishop of Salzburg, Johann Ernst Graf Thun, who favored German artists over the Italians, who still dominated art north of the Alps.

Rottmayr's lifelong friendship and collaboration with the architect Johann Bernhard Fischer von Erlach began in Salzburg. Rottmayr painted altarpieces and frescoes for most of Fischer's buildings in Salzburg—the Church of the Trinity (ca. 1702), the Church of the Hospital of St. John (1709), and the University Church (1721–1722)—as well as for the Residenz (1689, 1710–1714) and other secular and religious buildings in the city. The two men also collaborated at Frain Castle (Vranov) in Moravia (1695), creating, in the so-called Ancestral Hall, the first of their huge oval cupolas, where through painted illusionistic foreshortening and perspective the impression is given of seeing the open sky filled with mythological beings glorifying, in this case, the family of the owner. Rottmayr's early style, though very much like that of his master, Loth, is characterized by his own bright local color, massive forms, and strong movement.

Rottmayr moved to Vienna about 1699, where he continued to work with Fischer on such projects as Schönbrunn Palace (1700). But Rottmayr also began to receive other commissions, notably the fresco decoration of the Jesuit Church in Breslau (1704–1706) and of the Liechtenstein Summer Palace outside Vienna (1706–1707), as well as paintings for the Council Chamber of the Vienna City Hall (1712).

In Vienna, Rottmayr's style became more fluid, with subtler, more ingratiating color and more harmonious compositions, suggesting the influence of the works of Peter Paul Rubens and Anthony Van Dyck available to him there; yet it retained the strong plasticity and dynamic movement of his early years. During the first 2 decades of the 18th century he was the leading painter of Vienna and the Hapsburg domains. Although he continued to work intermittently elsewhere in the Holy Roman Empire—Salzburg, Franconia, and Bohemia—his work from this time on was largely in Vienna and its environs. He decorated the interior of the church of the monastery of Melk with frescoes and altarpieces (1716–1722), and in the Karlskirche in Vienna, Fischer von Erlach's most famous creation, Rottmayr painted the *Glorification of St. Charles Borromeo* in the dome as well as the entire fresco decoration of the church (1725–1729). One of his last important commissions was the frescoes for the church of the monastery of Klosterneuburg outside Vienna (1729).

A painter of great imagination, Rottmayr imbued his essentially idealized figures with a robust liveliness and naturalism of great appeal. His color, especially in his maturity, is often of enchanting beauty and refinement. The visionary effect of his ceiling paintings is sometimes reduced by the massiveness of his figures, but all are eminently effective in their swirling compositions.

Rottmayr was ennobled in 1704 with the title "von Rosenbrunn." He died in Vienna on Oct. 28, 1730, almost literally with his brush in his hand.

The Glorification of St. Benedict, *a fresco by Johann Michael Rottmayr on the nave ceiling of the monastery church of Melk, Austria. (Helmut Lackinger)*

Further Reading

Johann Michael Rottmayr is listed in the Art study guide (III, F, 1, e). He collaborated with Johann Bernhard FISCHER VON ERLACH. Other 18th-century Austrian painters were Franz Anton MAULBERTSCH and Paul TROGER.

There is no monograph on Rottmayr in English. He is discussed in Eberhard Hempel, *Baroque Art and Architecture in Central Europe* (1965). Edward A. Maser, *Disegni inediti di Johann Michael Rottmayer* (1971), in Italian, dealing with his drawings, is illustrated in color.

ROUAULT / By J. P. Hodin

Georges Rouault (1871–1958), a French painter and graphic artist, was the most outstanding religious painter of the modern movement.

Georges Rouault (pronounced rōō-ō′) was born on May 27, 1871, in Paris. His father was a cabinet-maker, and the family had artistic interests. Between 1885 and 1890 Rouault worked as an apprentice to stained-glass painters on the restoration of medieval windows and attended evening classes at the École des Arts Décoratifs. His predilection for luminous colors and black outlines had its origin in these early experiences.

In 1890 Rouault entered the École des Beaux-Arts, and the following year Gustave Moreau became his teacher. Henri Matisse and Albert Marquet were fellow students. Rouault became Moreau's favorite pupil, and his early works (mainly religious themes, with some portraits and somber landscapes) were painted in a traditional manner very like his teacher's. Rouault competed twice for the Prix de Rome (1893 and 1895), both times without success. In 1894, however, the artist won both a prize and a competition.

In 1901 Rouault spent some time in the Benedictine abbey at Ligugé, where the author J. K. Huysman tried to organize a brotherhood of artists. In 1903 Rouault became the first curator of the Moreau Museum and participated in the foundation of the Salon d'Automne with Matisse and Marquet. In 1904 Rouault met the Catholic writer Léon Bloy and, influenced by him, sought to depict the tragedy of the human condition. At that year's Salon d'Automne a large number of Rouault's watercolors appeared, depicting prostitutes, clowns, and acrobats painted in gloomy colors. Although he exhibited with the Fauves in 1905, he did not belong to this or any other group.

Rouault's *Prostitute before Her Mirror* (1906) is depicted with fierce loathing and revulsion. The series of judges and politicians, in which he attacked injustice and hypocrisy, began in 1908 and continued to about 1916.

The Old King, *painted by Rouault in 1937. (Museum of Art, Carnegie Institute, Pittsburgh, Patrons Art Fund)*

He also painted the poor and the humble. His indignation was expressed not only in subject matter but also in his brushwork.

In 1908 Rouault married Marthe Le Sidaner; they had four children. His first one-man show took place in Paris in 1910. In 1911 he moved to Versailles, where the philosopher Jacques Maritain and his wife were neighbors. In 1917 Ambroise Vollard became Rouault's dealer and set him up in a large studio in Paris. Between 1917 and 1927 Vollard commissioned illustrations for several books (*Père Ubu, The Circus, Les Fleurs du mal, Miserere,* and *Guerre*). Rouault developed a new and complex technique in his graphic work and worked in etching, wood engraving, and color lithography.

In 1918, when Rouault abandoned watercolor and gouache for oil, his palette became lighter and more jewellike. The artist's fury was replaced by compassion, as in his tender faces of Christ. His mature work has a vibrant luminosity, and heavy black outlines define the forms. Masterpieces of this style are the *Old King* (1937) and the *Head of Christ* (1937–1938).

Rouault wrote both prose and poetry. He also published autobiographical books, such as *Souvenirs intimes* (1926) and *Stella Vespertina* (1947). He produced designs for tapestries, stained-glass windows (church in

Georges Rouault. *(French Cultural Services of the French Embassy)*

Assy), and enamels. In 1929 he executed the sets and costumes for Sergei Diaghilev's ballet *The Prodigal Son*.

Between 1940 and 1956 large restrospective exhibitions of Rouault's work took place in many European and American museums and even in Japan. He died in Paris on Feb. 13, 1958, and was given a state funeral.

Further Reading

Georges Rouault is listed in the Art study guide (III, J, 1, b). An earlier French painter who was also known for his caricatures of politicians and judges was Honoré DAUMIER. The German expressionist Emil NOLDE, like Rouault, painted intensely religious paintings.

The most comprehensive study of Rouault is Pierre Courthion, *Georges Rouault* (1962), which contains a classified catalog, bibliography, list of exhibitions, and index. A useful survey of his life and work is Lionello Venturi, *Rouault: Biographical and Critical Study* (1959). For reproductions and commentary on his work see the two publications of the New York Museum of Modern Art: *Georges Rouault: Paintings and Prints*, by James Thrall Soby (1945; 3d ed. 1947), and *Georges Rouault, Miserere*, with a preface by Rouault and an introduction by M. Wheeler (1952).

ROUS / By Patsy A. Gerstner

The American pathologist and virologist Francis Peyton Rous (1879–1970) received the Nobel Prize in medicine for his pioneering work on the relation of viruses to cancer.

Peyton Rous was born in Baltimore, Md., on Oct. 5, 1879. He attended Johns Hopkins University in Baltimore, from which he received a bachelor's degree in 1900 and a medical degree in 1905. From 1905 to 1906 he served as resident house officer at the Johns Hopkins Hospital and from 1906 to 1908 was an instructor in pathology at the University of Michigan. In 1909 Rous went to the Rockefeller Institute for Medical Research in New York City, where he remained until his death on Feb. 16, 1970.

At the Rockefeller Institute, Rous began a series of studies of tumors in chickens. It was then widely believed that cancers were caused by chemical agents and that they could be transmitted from one animal to another only through the actual transplantation of cancerous cells. By 1911 Rous was able to show that tumors in chickens could be transferred from one chicken to another through a cell-free filtrate. The implication of this work was that the particular cancer being studied was caused by a virus. However, although Rous's observations were indicative of what would one day be a widely held belief, that is, that some cancers are virus-induced, his work was not well accepted in 1911.

Rous next attempted to show that a virus was present as a causative agent in mammalian tumors, but he failed, and it was not until the mid-1930s that he again turned to this line of research. In the interim he developed methods of cultivating cancer viruses in test tubes and in chick embryos, did research in liver and gallbladder physiology, and was a principal figure in the development of blood banks. The last-mentioned contribution was made during World War I, when, working with J. R. Turner, Rous found that whole blood could be preserved for many weeks under refrigeration when it was put in a citrate solution.

In the early 1930s Richard Shope, a member of the Rockefeller Institute and friend of Rous, demonstrated that a virus caused large warts in wild rabbits. Working with this fact, Rous and his laboratory associates were soon able to show that the virus causing these warts sometimes produced cancer. With this demonstration that viruses were associated with mammalian cancers, the virus theory made great progress. By the mid-1940s, that viruses were one cause of cancer was generally accepted; in 1966, at the age of 87, Rous was awarded the Nobel Prize in medicine. The prize was shared with Charles Brenton Huggins, a pioneer in the treatment of cancer.

Rous received many other awards and much public recognition. He was a member of the Board of Scientific Consultants of the Sloan Kettering Institute for Cancer Research and was coeditor of the *Journal of Experimental Medicine*.

Peyton Rous. (New York Academy of Medicine Library)

Further Reading

Peyton Rous is listed in the Science study guide (VII, G, 4). Other 20th-century virologists were F. Macfarlane BURNET, Jonas SALK, and John ENDERS.

Details on Rous's life and work are in George W. Corner, *A History of the Rockefeller Institute, 1901–1953* (1964). *McGraw-Hill Modern Men of Science*, vol. 1 (1966), includes an autobiographical sketch. Isaac Berenblum, *Men against Cancer* (1952), and Greer Williams, *Virus Hunters* (1959), are useful in placing Rous's work in an overall framework.

* * *

H. ROUSSEAU / By Abraham A. Davidson

The Frenchman Henri Rousseau (1844–1910) was the greatest modern European primitive painter. His works are infused with fantasy of a naively charming character.

Henri Rousseau (pronounced rōō-sō′) was born in Laval on May 21, 1844. At the age of 18 he enlisted in the army, where he played the saxophone in an infantry band. It is usually assumed by biographers, following Rousseau's own account, that he was stationed in Mexico from 1862 to 1866 as part of the French force supporting the emperor Maximilian.

Rousseau left the army in 1866, worked for a while as a clerk in a lawyer's office, and married in 1869. In 1871 he served as a corporal in the army in the Franco-Prussian War. Upon demobilization that year he took a minor position with the customs service (hence he is often called Rousseau le Douanier, "the Customs Officer"), where he remained until his early retirement in 1885.

Given a small pension, Rousseau settled in humble quarters and devoted himself to painting. In 1884 he had begun to copy in the Louvre. He studied briefly with the academic painter Jean Léon Gérôme at the École des Beaux-Arts. In 1886 Rousseau exhibited for the first time at the Salon des Indépendants, where he showed fairly regularly until his death. He helped support himself by giving lessons in painting, diction, and music—he was a skilled violinist. Though many ridiculed him, Paul Gauguin, Odilon Redon, Georges Seurat, Camille Pissarro, and Henri de Toulouse-Lautrec admired his work. Rousseau believed himself a great artist: in an autobiographical account of 1895 he wrote that he was becoming "one of France's best realist painters."

Of a generous and trusting nature, Rousseau was well liked by other artists, whom he invited to his soirées, but he was often made the object of practical jokes. In 1908 he was given a party by Pablo Picasso, whom he came to

Henri Rousseau's Sleeping Gypsy, painted in 1897. (Collection, The Museum of Modern Art, New York, Gift of Mrs. Simon Guggenheim)

Henri Rousseau, a self-portrait, in the Collection Serge Jastrebzoff, Paris. (Giraudon)

consider as one of the two greatest living painters, the other being himself. Rousseau died in Paris on Sept. 2, 1910, and Constantin Brancusi chiseled on his tombstone a eulogy composed by the poet Guillaume Apollinaire.

The power of Rousseau's paintings is derived from a remarkable combination of fantasy and actuality. His scenes are grounded in actuality, but even as he has tried to realize the concreteness of each event, they have been transformed into a quaint private world. Neither modeling nor atmospheric perspective, a technique in which objects are blurred to suggest distance from the observer, is used. He depicted weddings and family reunions of friends; cityscapes and landscapes of Paris and its suburbs, like the *Village Street* (1909); and, most remarkable of all, jungle scenes.

Rousseau's jungle pictures are an amalgamation of memory images of his Mexican trip (if, indeed, he ever was in Mexico), visual experiences from visits to botani-

cal gardens and zoos, and depictions of plants and wild animals he had seen on postcards and in photographs. In the *Sleeping Gypsy* (1897) a Negress, in a picturesque costume, lies asleep in the midst of a desert with a mandolin and a pitcher beside her. The moon is shining (it echoes in form the curved mandolin), and a lion sniffs curiously at her. The *Dream* (1910) may be connected with a youthful romance of Rousseau, who had been enamored of a Polish girl named Yadwigah (he wrote a poem to her in connection with this work). A nude woman lies on a couch in the middle of jungle. About her grows lush foliage in which fierce animals, surprisingly tame, lurk. His jungle scenes, though based on real objects and perhaps certain events, in their totality clearly existed only in his mind's eye.

Further Reading

Henri Rousseau is listed in the Art study guide (III, H, 1,

f). Other primitive painters were the Americans John KANE and Grandma MOSES.

A study that takes into account most previous research on Rousseau is Dora Vallier, *Henri Rousseau* (1964). Other works on him include Daniel Cotton Rich, *Henri Rousseau* (1942; rev. ed. 1946), and Jean Bouret, *Henri Rousseau* (1961). For Rousseau and his times see Roger Shattuck, *The Banquet Years: The Arts in France, 1885–1918* (1958; rev. ed. 1968).

✳   ✳   ✳

J. J. ROUSSEAU

/ **By James Dickoff and Patricia James**

The Swiss-born philosopher, author, political theorist, and composer Jean Jacques Rousseau (1712–1778) ranks as one of the greatest figures of the French Enlightenment.

Both Jean Jacques Rousseau the man and his writings constitute a problem for anyone who wants to grasp his thought and to understand his life. He claimed that his work presented a coherent outlook; yet many critics have found only contradictions and passionate outbursts of rhetoric. One interpreter has called

Jean Jacques Rousseau, a painting by Maurice Quentin de La Tour. (French Cultural Services of the French Embassy)

Rousseau "an irresponsible writer with a fatal gift for epigram." In the eyes of others Rousseau was not a "serious thinker" but only a mere feeler who occasionally had a great thought. Still others have found Rousseau a mere juggler of words and definitions. Even those who turn to him as an innovating genius have been at odds concerning what he advocated. Rousseau has been variously applauded or denounced as the founder of the romantic movement in literature, as the intellectual father of the French Revolution, as a passionate defender of individual freedom and private property, as a socialist, as a collectivist totalitarian, as a superb critic of the social order, and as a silly and pernicious utopian. Some few critics—notably Gustave Lanson and E. H. Wright—have taken Rousseau at his word and believe that he attempted to answer only one question: how can civilized man recapture the benefits of "natural man" and yet neither return to the state of nature nor renounce the advantages of the social state?

For Rousseau's biographers the man himself has been as puzzling as his work—a severe moralist who lived a dangerously "relaxed" life, a misanthrope who loved humanity, a cosmopolitan who prided himself on being a "citizen of Geneva," a writer for the stage who condemned the theater, and a man who became famous by writing essays that denounced culture. In addition to these anomalies, his biographers have had to consider his confessed sexual "peculiarities"—his lifelong habit of masturbation, his exhibitionism, his youthful pleasure in being beaten, his 33-year liaison with a virtual illiterate, and his numerous affairs—and, characteristic of his later years, his persecution suspicions that reached neurotic intensity.

Three major periods characterize Rousseau's life. The first (1712–1750) culminated in the succès de scandale of his *Discours sur les sciences et les arts*. The second (1750–1762) saw the publication of his closely related major works: *La Nouvelle Héloïse* (1761), *L'Émile* (1762), and *Du contrat social* (1762). The last period (1762–1778) found Rousseau an outcast, hounded from country to country, his books condemned and burned, and a *personnage*, respected and with influential friends. The *Confessions*, *Dialogues*, and *Les Rêveries du promeneur solitaire* date from this period.

Youth, 1712–1750

Rousseau was the second child of a strange marriage. His mother, Suzanne Bernard, had at the age of 33 married Isaac Rousseau, a man less wellborn than she. Isaac, exhausted perhaps by his frequent quarrels over money with his mother-in-law, left his wife in 1705 for Constantinople. He returned to Suzanne in September 1711. Jean Jacques was born on June 28, 1712, at Geneva, Switzerland. Nine days later his mother died.

At the age of 3, Jean Jacques was reading and weeping over French novels with his father. From Isaac's sister the boy acquired his passion for music. His father fled Geneva to avoid imprisonment when Jean Jacques was 10. By the time he was 13, his formal education had ended. Apprenticed to a notary public, he was soon dismissed as fit only for watchmaking. Apprenticed again, this time to an engraver, Rousseau spent 3 wretched years in hateful servitude, which he abandoned when he found himself unexpectedly locked out of the city by its closed gates. He faced the world with no visible assets and no obvious talents.

Rousseau found himself on Palm Sunday, 1728, in Annecy at the house of Louise Eleonore, Baronne de Warens. She sent him to a hospice for catechumens in Turin, where among "the biggest sluts and the most disgusting trollops who ever defiled the fold of the Lord," he embraced the Roman Catholic faith. His return to Madame de Warens in 1729 initiated a strange alliance between a 29-year-old woman of the world and a sensitive 17-year-old youth.

Rousseau lived under her roof off and on for 13 years and was dominated by her influence. He became her *Petit;* she was his *Maman.* Charming and clever, a born speculator, Madame de Warens was a woman who lived by her wits. She supported him; she found him jobs, most of which he regarded as uncongenial. A friend, after examining the lad, informed her that he might aspire to become a village curé but nothing more. Still Rousseau read, studied, and reflected. He pursued music and gave lessons. For a time he was a not too successful tutor.

First Publications and Operas

In 1733, disturbed by the advances made to Rousseau by the mother of one of his music pupils, Madame de Warens offered herself to him. Rousseau became her lover: "I felt as if I had been guilty of incest." The sojourn with Madame de Warens was over by 1742. Though she had taken other lovers and he had enjoyed other escapades, Rousseau was still devoted to her. He thought that the scheme of musical notation he had developed would make his fortune in Paris and thus enable him to save her from financial ruin. But his journey to Paris took Rousseau out of her life. He saw her only once again, in 1754. Reduced to begging and the charity of her neighbors, Madame de Warens died destitute in 1762.

Rousseau's scheme for musical notation, published in 1743 as *Dissertation sur la musique moderne,* brought him neither fame nor fortune—only a letter of commendation from the Académie des Sciences. But his interest in music spurred him to write two operas—*Les Muses galantes* (1742) and *Le Devin du village* (1752)—and permitted him to write articles on music for Denis Diderot's *Encyclopédie;* the *Lettre sur la musique française,* which embroiled him in a quarrel with the Paris Opéra (1753); and the *Dictionnaire de musique,* published in 1767.

From September 1743 until August 1744 Rousseau served as secretary to the French ambassador to Venice. He experienced at firsthand the stupidity of officialdom and began to see how institutions lend their authority to injustice and oppression in the name of peace and order. Rousseau spent the remaining years before his success with his first *Discours* in Paris, where he lived from hand to mouth the life of a struggling intellectual.

In March 1745 Rousseau began a liaison with Thérèse Le Vasseur. She was 24 years old, a maid at Rousseau's lodgings. She remained with him for the rest of his life—as mistress, housekeeper, bearer of his children, and finally in 1768 as his wife. He portrayed her as devoted and unselfish, although many of his friends saw her as a malevolent gossip and troublemaker who exercised a baleful influence on his suspicions and dislikes. Not an educated woman—Rousseau himself cataloged her malapropisms—she nonetheless possessed the uncommon quality of being able to offer stability to a man of volatile intensity. She bore Rousseau five children—though some biographers have questioned whether any of them were Rousseau's. Apparently he regarded them as his own even though he abandoned them to the foundling hospital. Rousseau had no means to educate them, and he reasoned that they would be better raised as workmen and peasants by the state.

By 1749 Diderot had become a sympathetic friend, and Rousseau regarded him as a kindred spirit. The publication of Diderot's *Lettre sur les aveugles* had resulted in his imprisonment at Vincennes. While walking to Vincennes to visit Diderot, Rousseau read an announcement of a prize being offered by the Dijon Academy for the best essay on the question: has progress of the arts and sciences contributed more to the corruption or to the purification of morals?

Years of Fruition, 1750–1762

Rousseau won the prize of the Dijon Academy with his *Discours sur les sciences et les arts* and became "l'homme du jour." His famous rhetorical "attack" on civilization called forth 68 articles defending the arts and sciences. Though he himself regarded this essay as "the weakest in argument and the poorest in harmony and proportion" of all his works, he nonetheless believed that it sounded one of his essential themes: the arts and sciences, instead of liberating men and increasing their happiness, have for the most part shackled men further. "Necessity erected thrones; the arts and sciences consolidated them," he wrote.

The *Discours sur l'origine de l'inégalité des hommes,* written in response to the essay competition proposed by the Dijon Academy in 1753 (but which did not win the prize), elaborated this theme still further. The social order of civilized society, wrote Rousseau, introduced inequality and unhappiness. This social order rests upon private property. The man who first enclosed a tract of land and called it his own was the true founder of civilized society. "Don't listen to that imposture; you are lost if you forget that the fruits of the earth belong to everyone and the earth to no one," he wrote. Man's greatest ills, said Rousseau, are not natural but made by man himself; the remedy lies also within man's power. Heretofore, man has used his wit and art not to alter his wretchedness but only to intensify it.

Three Major Works

Rousseau's novel *La Nouvelle Héloïse* (1761) attempted to portray in fiction the sufferings and tragedy that foolish education and arbitrary social conventions work among sensitive creatures. Rousseau's two other major treatises—*L'Émile ou de l'éducation* (1762) and *Du contrat social* (1762)—undertook the more difficult task

The "natural man" attempts to enlighten men who have been made unequal by the social institutions of agriculture, industry, property, and law; an illustration, engraved by Charles Eisen, from an early edition of Jean Jacques Rousseau's Discours sur l'origine de l'inégalité *in the Bibliothèque Nationale, Paris. (Photo-Hachette)*

seau was swept off his feet. Their relationship apparently was never consummated; Sophie pitied Rousseau and loved Saint-Lambert. But Madame d'Épinay and her paramour, Melchior Grimm, meddled in the affair; Diderot was drawn into the business. Rousseau felt that his reputation had been blackened, and a bitter estrangement resulted. Madame d'Épinay insulted Rousseau until he left the Hermitage in December 1757. However, he remained in Montmorency until 1762, when the condemnation of *L'Émile* forced him to flee from France.

La Nouvelle Héloïse appeared in Paris in January 1761. Originally entitled *Lettres de deux amants, habitants d'une petite ville au pied des Alpes*, the work was structurally a novel in letters, after the fashion of the English author Samuel Richardson. The originality of the novel won it hostile reviews, but its romantic eroticism made it immensely popular with the public. It remained a best seller until the French Revolution.

The notoriety of *La Nouvelle Héloïse* was nothing compared to the storm produced by *L'Émile* and *Du contrat social*. Even today the ideas promulgated in these works are revolutionary. Their expression, especially in *L'Émile*, in a style both readable and alluring made them dangerous. *L'Émile* was condemned by the Paris Parlement and denounced by the archbishop of Paris. Both of the books were burned by the authorities in Geneva.

"L'Émile" and "Du contrat social"

L'Émile ou de l'éducation remains one of the world's greatest speculative treatises on education. However, Rousseau wrote to a correspondent who tried to follow *L'Émile* literally, "so much the worse for you!" The work was intended as illustrative of an educational program rather than prescriptive of every practical detail of a proper education. Its overarching spirit is best sensed in opposition to John Locke's essay on education. Locke taught that man should be educated to the station for which he is intended. There should be one education for a prince, another for a physician, and still another for a farmer. Rousseau advocated one education for all. Man should be educated to be a man, not to be a doctor, lawyer, or priest. Nor is a child merely a little man; he is, rather, a developing creature, with passions and powers that vary according to his stage of development. What must be avoided at all costs is the master-slave mode of instruction, with the pupil as either master or slave, for the medium of instruction is far more influential than any doctrine taught through that medium. Hence, an education resting merely on a play of wills—as when the child learns only to please the instructor or when the teacher "teaches" by threatening the pupil with a future misfortune—produces creatures fit to be only masters or slaves, not free men. Only free men can realize a "natural social order," wherein men can live happily.

A few of the striking doctrines set forth in *L'Émile* are: the importance of training the body before the mind, learning first through "things" and later through words, teaching first only that for which a child feels a need so as to impress upon him that thought is a tool whereby he

of constructing an education and a social order that would enable men to be natural and free; that is, that would enable men to recognize no bondage except the bondage of natural necessity. To be free in this sense, said Rousseau, was to be happy.

Rousseau brought these three works to completion in somewhat trying circumstances. After having returned to the Protestant fold in 1755 and having regained his citizenship of Geneva that same year, Rousseau accepted the rather insistent offer of Madame Louise d'Épinay to install Thérèse and himself in the Hermitage, a small cottage on the D'Épinay estate at Montmorency. While Rousseau was working on his novel there, its heroine materialized in the person of Sophie, Comtesse d'Houdetot; and he fell passionately in love with her. He was 44 years old; Sophie was 27, married to a dullard, the mistress of the talented and dashing Marquis Saint-Lambert, and the sister-in-law of Rousseau's hostess. Rous-

can effectively manage things, motivating a child by catering to his ruling passion of greed, refraining from moral instruction until the awakening of the sexual urge, and raising the child outside the doctrines of any church until late adolescence and then instructing him in the religion of conscience. Although Rousseau's principles have never been fully put into practice, his influence on educational reformers has been tremendous.

L'Émile's companion master work, *Du contrat social*, attempted to spell out the social relation that a properly educated man—a free man—bears to other free men. This treatise is a difficult and subtle work of a penetrating intellect fired by a great passion for humanity. The liberating fervor of the work, however, is easily caught in the key notions of popular sovereignty and general will. Government is not to be confused with sovereignty of the people or with the social order that is created by the social contract. The government is an intermediary set up between the people as law followers and the people as law creators, the sovereignty. Furthermore, the government is an instrument created by the citizens through their collective action expressed in the general will. The purpose of this instrument is to serve the people by seeing to it that laws expressive of the general will of the citizens are in fact executed. In short, the government is the servant of the people, not their master. And further, the sovereignty of the people—the general will of the people—is to be found not merely in the will of the majority or in the will of all but rather in the will as enlightened by right judgment.

As with *L'Émile*, *Du contrat social* is a work best understood as elaborating the principles of the social order rather than schematizing the mechanism for those general principles. Rousseau's political writings more concerned with immediate application include his *Considérations sur le gouvernement de la Pologne* (1772) and his incomplete *Projet de constitution pour la Corse*, published posthumously in 1862.

Other writings from Rousseau's middle period include the *Encyclopédie* article *Économie politique* (1755); *Lettre sur la Providence* (1756), a reply to Voltaire's poem on the Lisbon earthquake; *Lettre à d'Alembert sur les spectacles* (1758); *Essai sur l'origine des langues* (1761); and four autobiographical *Lettres à Malesherbes* (1762).

Exile and Apologetics, 1762-1778

Forced to flee from France, Rousseau sought refuge at Yverdon in the territory of Bern. Expelled by the Bernese authorities, he found asylum in Môtiers, a village in the Prussian principality of Neuchâtel. Here in 1763 he renounced his Genevan citizenship. The publication of his *Lettres écrites de la montagne* (1764), in which he defended *L'Émile* and criticized "established" reformed churches, aroused the wrath of the Neuchâtel clergy. His house was stoned, and Rousseau fled to the isle of St. Pierre in the Lake of Biel, but he was again expelled by the Bernese. Finally, through the good offices of the British philosopher David Hume, he settled at Wotton, Derbyshire, England, in 1766. Hume managed to obtain from George III a yearly pension for Rousseau. But Rousseau, falsely believing Hume to be in league with his Parisian and Genevan enemies, not only refused the pension but also openly broke with the philosopher. Henceforth, Rousseau's sense of persecution became ever more intense, even at times hysterical.

Rousseau returned to France in June 1767 under the protection of the Prince de Conti. Wandering from place to place, he at last settled in 1770 in Paris. There he made a living, as he often had in the past, by copying music. By December 1770 the *Confessions*, upon which he had been working since 1766, was completed, and he gave readings from this work at various private homes. Madame d'Épinay, fearing an unflattering picture of herself and her friends, intervened; the readings were forbidden by the police. Disturbed by the reaction to his readings and determined to justify himself before the world, Rousseau wrote *Dialogues ou Rousseau, Juge de Jean-Jacques* (1772–1776). Fearful lest the manuscript fall into the hands of his enemies, he attempted to place it on the high altar of Notre Dame. Thwarted in this attempt, he left a copy with the philosopher Étienne Condillac and, not wholly trusting him, with an English acquaintance, Brooke Boothby. Finally, in 1778 Rousseau entrusted copies of both the *Confessions* and the *Dialogues* to his friend Paul Moultou. His last work, *Les Rêveries du promeneur solitaire*, begun in 1776 and unfinished at his death, records how Rousseau, an outcast from society, recaptured "serenity, tranquility, peace, even happiness."

In May 1778 Rousseau accepted Marquis de Giradin's hospitality at Ermenonville near Paris. There, with Thérèse at his bedside, he died on July 2, 1778, probably from uremia. From birth he had suffered from a bladder deformation. From 1748 onward his condition had grown worse. His adoption of the Armenian mode of dress was due to the embarrassment caused by this affliction, and it is not unlikely that much of his suspicious irritability can be traced to the same malady. Rousseau was buried on the Île des Peupliers at Ermenonville. In October 1794 his remains were transferred to the Panthéon in Paris. Thérèse, surviving him by 22 years, died in 1801 at the age of 80.

Further Reading

Jean Jacques Rousseau is listed in the Philosophy study guide (V, B, 2), the Literature study guide (III, F, 1; III, G, 1), and the Social Sciences study guide (V, B, 2; V, C, 2). Among his disciples were Immanuel KANT, Johann Wolfgang von GOETHE, Maximilien de ROBESPIERRE, Johann PESTALOZZI, and Leo TOLSTOY.

Rousseau himself is the best introduction to his own thought. Everyman's Library offers translations of *Emile* and a volume containing *The Social Contract* and the two *Discourses*. The *Confessions* is available in a Modern Library edition. The most accessible English version of Rousseau's novel is *Julie, or the New Eloise*, translated and abridged by J. H. McDowell (1968). A sampling of Rousseau's letters appears in *Citizen of Geneva: Selections from the Letters of J.-J. Rousseau*, edited by

C. W. Hendel (1937). Useful biographies include Matthew Josephson, *J. J. Rousseau* (1931); R. B. Mowat, *Jean-Jacques Rousseau* (1938); and Lester G. Crocker, *Jean-Jacques Rousseau: The Quest, 1712–1758* (1968).

The literature on Rousseau is vast. An excellent introduction to his thought as a whole is E. H. Wright, *The Meaning of Rousseau* (1929). A critical study of Rousseau's life and writings is Frederick C. Green, *Jean-Jacques Rousseau* (1955), valuable for his life but less illuminating on the works. Ronald Grimsley, *Jean-Jacques Rousseau: Study in Self-awareness* (1961), focuses on Rousseau's attempts to answer the riddle of his personal existence. See also Grimsley's *Rousseau and the Religious Quest* (1968). Ernst Cassirer, *The Question of Jean-Jacques Rousseau* (1932), presents Rousseau as offering a non-Christian interpretation of the universe; and in his *Kant, Rousseau, Goethe* (1945), Cassirer suggests that Rousseau was a profound influence on Kantian thought. Roger Masters, *Political Philosophy of Rousseau* (1967), examines an important aspect of Rousseau's work. Frederika Macdonald, *Jean-Jacques Rousseau: A New Criticism* (2 vols., 1906), presents Rousseau as a victim of Madame d'Épinay's vilification. For a helpful review of fairly recent Rousseau literature see Peter Gay's chapter on Rousseau in his *The Party of Humanity* (1964).

T. ROUSSEAU / By Francis E. Hyslop, Jr.

The French painter and draftsman Théodore Rousseau (1812–1867) was the most representative artist of the Barbizon school and an intermediary between the Dutch landscapists of the 17th century and the impressionist school.

Born in Paris, Théodore Rousseau seems to have been initially stimulated to paint landscape by a cousin. The example of Dutch painting supplemented the formal instruction that Rousseau received from minor artists of his own time. A precocious artist who was painting from nature at the age of 15, he combined an analytical eye with a romantic heart.

In the 1830s Rousseau established himself with a series of boldly painted and dramatic scenes from the Auvergne, such as the *Torrent* (ca. 1830). Among the pictures done in northern France, the *Forest of Fontainebleau, Bas-Bréau* (begun 1837–1839, completed 1867) is especially characteristic. The *Valley of Tiffauge* (1837–1841) is another outstanding illustration of an almost Flemish type of visual analysis.

Made controversial by his nonclassical bias, Rousseau was not able to exhibit at the Salon between 1837 and 1847. By that time he had settled at Barbizon, where he exploited the pictorial and "moral" qualities of oak trees

Théodore Rousseau, a portrait by Honoré Daumier, in the Louvre, Paris. (Photo N. D. Roger-Viollet)

and sunlight. At the same time, fine drawings such as *Country Road with Poplars* (1830–1840) reveal how sensitively he could interpret a flat, featureless plain like those of Berry, where he worked in the 1840s.

In spite of the fact that Rousseau did not show at the Salon for many years, he was widely acclaimed as a landscape artist. In the 1845 Salon the poet and critic Charles Baudelaire even went so far as to maintain that Rousseau was superior to Camille Corot. In 1864, however, Baudelaire modified his enthusiasm and remarked that the artist showed "too much love for detail, not enough for the architecture of nature."

Luminosity, which Rousseau considered the "great secret" of nature, is very much in evidence as early as 1842, when he painted the *Lowland Marsh* in surprisingly high-keyed, dramatically contrasted tones. The intensity of his response to nature is reflected repeatedly in active, dynamic scenes such as *Storm Effect, Road in the Forest of Fontainebleau* (1860–1865). But sometimes the painter of Barbizon, who, according to one critic, "never painted a stroke without thinking of Ruisdael," became dull in his "patient inventory of nature," heavy in his application of paint, and overripe in his use of color, as in *Sunset near Arbonne* (ca. 1865).

Rousseau's fundamentally romantic spirit is well expressed in one of his own statements: "I also heard the voices of the trees ... whose passions I uncovered. I wanted to talk with them ... and put my finger on the secret of their majesty."

Dependent though he was on Dutch and, to lesser degree, on English painting, Rousseau was also inspired directly by nature, as were his successors, the impressionists. Like them, he put a particular emphasis on light, but on a light that has a more symbolic and a less naturalistic character.

Further Reading

Théodore Rousseau is listed in the Art study guide (III, H, 1, b). Other members of the Barbizon school were Jean François MILLET and Charles DAUBIGNY.

Little has been written about Rousseau in English. David Croal Thomson, *The Barbizon School of Painters* (1890), gives a 19th-century view of this group of artists. See also Charles Sprague Smith, *Barbizon Days* (1903). The most outstanding recent study is Robert C. Herbert, *Barbizon Revisited* (1962).

✳   ✳   ✳

ROUSSEL / By Peter S. Hansen

Albert Roussel (1869–1937) was one of the most important French composers of his time. His early compositions reflect the main styles of the day; his later works were more advanced than those of his contemporaries.

Albert Roussel (pronounced rōō-sĕl´) was born in Tourcoing, a town close to the Belgian border, where his grandfather was mayor. Destined for a career in the navy, he studied at the Collège Stanislas in Paris and joined the service in 1887. After he was commissioned, he served several years at sea, mostly in the Far East.

Roussel started composing while on his long voyages, and when he received encouragement for his efforts, he resigned his commission in 1894 and went to Paris to study composition at the relatively advanced age of 25. He entered the newly established Schola Cantorum, where he studied with Vincent d'Indy, its founder. D'Indy was conservative in that he held out against Claude Debussy's impressionism and based his instruction on a thorough knowledge of earlier musical styles.

Roussel's first published composition, a piano piece, appeared in 1898. In 1902 he became a teacher of counterpoint at the Schola, a post he held until 1914, when he resigned to enter the French army during World War I. He served as a transportation officer and saw duty at Verdun and the Battle of the Marne. When his health broke down, he returned to Paris, where he spent the rest of his life.

The best known of Roussel's early works is the ballet *Le Festin de l'araignée* (1912; The Spider's Feast), a skillfully orchestrated tone poem, somewhat reminiscent of Camille Saint-Saëns's music in the transparency of the writing. This was followed by a large ballet-opera, *Padmavati* (1914–1918), based on an Indian legend and employing Indian melodies and scales, a result of Roussel's visits to the East as a naval officer. His ballet *Bacchus et Ariane* (1930) reflects the sumptuousness of Sergei Diaghilev's Ballets Russes that influenced so many composers of the time. This rich score shows Roussel's mastery of the impressionist idiom.

Roussel's later compositions reveal other ideals. Already in the Suite in F (1926) and in his Third and Fourth Symphonies (1930 and 1934) he wrote neoclassic pieces, shown in their avoidance of programs, economy of means, clarity of form, 18th-century textures, and driving rhythms. Igor Stravinsky was the chief exponent of neoclassicism, and Roussel was one of its principal exponents. In these compositions the astringent harmonies, wide-ranging melodies, strong rhythms, and bitonality bring Roussel close to the younger composers of the time.

It has been said that Roussel "possessed every quality but that of spontaneous invention." Even though he was not a pathbreaker, he was one of the most important French composers of the first half of the 20th century.

Further Reading

Albert Roussel is listed in the Music study guide (I, J,

Albert Roussel. (Photo Harlingue-Viollet)

2). His pupils at the Schola Cantorum included Erik SA-TIE, Edgard VARÈSE, and Bohuslav MARTINU. Neoclassicism began in the early 1920s with certain works by Igor STRAVINSKY.

Roussel is discussed in Aaron Copland, *The New Music, 1900–1960* (1941; rev. ed. 1968); Wilfrid Mellers, *Studies in Contemporary Music* (1947); and Joseph Machlis, *Introduction to Contemporary Music* (1961).

✳　　✳　　✳

ROWLAND / By George H. Daniels

The American physicist Henry Augustus Rowland (1848–1901) made fundamental contributions to magnetism and to celestial physics.

Henry Augustus Rowland was born on Nov. 27, 1848, in Honesdale, Pa., the descendant of a long line of clergymen. He studied at Phillips Academy, Andover, Mass., and then graduated from the Rensselaer Polytechnic Institute with a degree in civil engineering. During the next 2 years he did some work in his profession and taught natural science at Wooster University, Ohio. In the spring of 1872 he returned to Rensse-

Henry Augustus Rowland. (The Smithsonian Institution, Washington, D.C.)

laer as instructor in physics. While at Rensselaer he published an important paper on magnetism which brought him favorable attention from the English physicist James Clerk Maxwell and an appointment as professor of physics at the newly established Johns Hopkins University, designed to be the model of a graduate school. This early paper brought lasting fame to Rowland, for it proved to be the starting point for all calculations for the design of dynamos and transformers.

One of Rowland's first actions upon arrival at Johns Hopkins was the development of a workshop in which the apparatus for fundamental research could be produced; the machines that he himself devised were among his most valuable contributions to science. Becoming interested, for example, in the spectrum of the sun and the spectra of the elements, he designed a ruling machine to produce gratings for spectrum analysis more accurate than any previously known. Dissatisfied with the results obtained with the plane gratings of Joseph von Fraunhofer and Ernest Rutherford, he combined the principle of the grating with that of the concave mirror, eventually producing concave gratings of about 100,000 lines of 6 inches in length. With these superb diffraction gratings which split light into its components, he mapped the solar spectrum more thoroughly than anyone before him had done. Making possible the direct photography and higher resolution of spectra of the heavenly bodies, this work started a new era in spectroscopy.

In the field of measurements, in addition to his work on spectra, Rowland obtained long-accepted values for the mechanical equivalent of heat, the ohm, and the ratio of the electric units and the wavelengths of various spectra. In most cases, he designed his own measuring instruments.

Although Rowland had an engineer's training and always remained interested in practical applications—among his inventions was a printing telegraph and several other commercial instruments—he was primarily known as an ardent campaigner for the importance of basic research, and from his post at Johns Hopkins he trained many students who were imbued with this viewpoint. He was the first president of the American Physical Society. Rowland was married to Henrietta Troup Harrison of Baltimore in 1890. He died of diabetes on April 16, 1901.

Further Reading

Henry Augustus Rowland is listed in the Science study guide (VI, C, 3; VI, H, 3). Experiments in spectroscopy date from 1860, when Gustav KIRCHHOFF and Robert BUNSEN compared the sun's spectrum with flame spectra of various salts and metals. The Rowland grating was the most precise in its field until surpassed by the echelon grating of Albert MICHELSON.

The only biographical account of Rowland is Thomas C. Mendenhall's memoir, which appears in Mendenhall's edition of *The Physical Papers of Henry Augustus Rowland* (1902), in the *Biographical Memoirs* of the National Academy of Sciences, vol. 5 (1905), and is reprinted in

Bessie Zaban Jones, ed., *The Golden Age of Science: Thirty Portraits of the Giants of 19th-Century Science by Their Scientific Contemporaries* (1966). A profile of Rowland and an interesting selection of documents and letters are in Nathan Reingold, ed., *Science in Nineteenth-century America: A Documentary History* (1964).

✳   ✳   ✳

ROXAS / By Epifanio San Juan, Jr.

Manuel Roxas (1892–1948) was the last president of the Commonwealth and the first president of the Republic of the Philippines. His administration demonstrated decisively that political sovereignty without economic independence encourages reaction, perpetuation of social injustices, and exploitation.

Manuel Roxas in 1947. (Popperfoto)

Manuel Roxas (pronounced rô⁄häs) was born in Capiz, Capiz Province, on Jan. 1, 1892. In 1914 he graduated from the College of Law of the University of the Philippines. In 1916 he became provincial governor. In 1922 he was elected to Congress, becoming Speaker of the Philippine Assembly.

In December 1931 Roxas, together with Senate president pro tempore Sergio Osmeña, left for the United States to secure the Hare-Hawes-Cutting Act from the U.S. Congress, which would grant Philippine independence after a transition period of 10 years. This bill was rejected by the opposition forces led by Manuel Quezon. In 1934 Roxas was elected to the constitutional convention. In 1938 he was appointed secretary of finance by Commonwealth president Quezon and then became his trusted adviser. In 1941 Roxas ran for the Senate and won.

On Dec. 8, 1941, at the outbreak of the war, Roxas served as lieutenant colonel in the U.S. Army Forces in the Far East (USAFFE). He refused to join Quezon in fleeing to the United States because he wanted to preserve the morale of the Filipino soldiers fighting in Bataan and Corregidor. He was captured in 1942 by the Japanese forces in Malaybalay, Bukidnon, and was forced to serve in the puppet government of José Laurel. Roxas accepted the position of chairman of the Economic Planning Board in Laurel's wartime Cabinet. During the Japanese retreat he allegedly escaped from the Japanese high command in Baguio on April 15, 1945.

Because of Gen. Douglas MacArthur's unexplained intervention, Roxas was never tried as a collaborator, though he had served officially in Laurel's Japanese-sponsored administration. When the Philippine legislature convened during the liberation, Roxas was elected president of the Senate on June 9, 1945. He broke with President Osmeña and formed the Liberal party, which

he led to victory as presidential candidate on April 23, 1946. Roxas thus became the last president of the Commonwealth and the first president of the Republic of the Philippines when it was inaugurated on July 4, 1946.

Owing to the unfair demands of the Bell Trade Relations Act of 1945, which called for a revision of the Philippine constitution to give parity rights to Americans in exchange for rehabilitation money, Roxas found himself surrendering his country's freedom and its right to determine its own destiny. Faced by the unified opposition of workers and peasants, the majority of the people, Roxas sided with the oppressive landlord class and the colonialistic merchants to put down by force the legitimate aspirations of the electorate.

It is public knowledge that most of Roxas's policies were dictated by Gen. MacArthur and U.S. high commissioner Paul V. McNutt. Not only did Roxas lack the vision to foresee the causes that would strain Philippine-American relations later (for example, the Military Bases Agreement of March 14, 1947), but he also failed to sympathize with the plight of the majority of the poor.

Roxas was committing the Philippines to the side of the United States at the start of the cold war in a speech at the Clark Air Force Base when he suffered a heart attack on April 14, 1948. Loyal to the United States to the last, he died on American soil.

Further Reading

Manuel Roxas is listed in the Asia study guide (IV, C, 5). Other post–World War II Philippine leaders were Ramon MAGSAYSAY, Ferdinand MARCOS, and Carlos RÓMULO.

Two useful biographies of Roxas are Felixberto G. Bustos, *And Now Comes Roxas* (1945), and Marcial P. Lichauco, *Roxas* (1952). For Roxas's position in the collaboration issue see Hernando J. Abaya, *Betrayal in the Philippines* (1946), and David Joel Steinberg, *Philippine Collaboration in World War II* (1967).

✳   ✳   ✳

ROY / By David Kopf

> Ram Mohun Roy (1772–1833) was a Bengali social and religious reformer thoroughly identified with the cultural self-image of the people. He has been called the father of modern India.

Ram Mohun Roy (pronounced räm mō′hŭn roi) was born to a Kulin Brahmin family at Radhanagar, Hooghly District, West Bengal. According to early biographers, as a result of wanderings over Asia in search for religious truth, he became a gifted linguist in Persian, Arabic, Sanskrit, Hebrew, and Greek before he was 22. New evidence suggests that his father, a *zamindar* (landowner) of the traditional ruling class of Bengal, lost his property in 1800, went to jail, and died a ruined man in 1803.

It appears that between 1799 and 1802 Ram Mohun lent money to British civil servants in Calcutta as a livelihood. In 1804 he joined the East India Company as a subordinate official and was evidently employed in that fashion until 1814, when he retired from government service with a lucrative income from landed property.

After settling in Calcutta in 1815, Ram Mohun challenged the orthodox defenders of the contemporary religious and social systems. In the *Abridgement of the*

Ram Mohun Roy. (Radio Times Hulton Picture Library)

Vedanta (1815), *Translation of the Cena Upanishad* (1816), and the *Defense of the Monotheistical System of the Vedas* (1817) he condemned such common practices as caste distinction, idolatry, Kulin polygamy, and sati (or suttee; burning widows on the funeral pyres of their husbands) as excrescences upon the authentic Hindu tradition. Scripturally, that authentic tradition consisted of the *Vedas*, the *Upanishads*, and the *Vedanta Shastras*. Historiographically, his differentiation between a pure Hinduism of a remote past and the aberrational form in existence during his own time contributed to a new historical outlook among the intelligentsia, who increasingly divided the Indian past into a golden age and a subsequent dark age.

In the 1820s Ram Mohun's aim was to provide the means for awakening India and to guide it back again into the mainstreams of world progress. He sought an ideology of religious modernism which would be compatible with India's authentic tradition and equally in line with the dynamic and progressive forces shaping contemporary western Europe and America. He chose Christian Unitarianism for its rationalism and liberalism. With the assistance of a former Baptist named William Adam, Ram Mohun actually formed a Calcutta Unitarian Committee. In 1828 he and his followers founded the Brahmo Sabha, precursor of the Brahma Samaj (Society of God), which for most of the century was India's most effective indigenous agency for social and religious reform.

From 1830 Ram Mohun lived in England. In 1833 in Bristol a meeting was arranged of Unitarian leaders representing three continents: Ram Mohun of Asia, Joseph Tuckerman of the United States, and Lant Carpenter of Great Britain were the delegates. Ram Mohun died before the conference took place.

Further Reading

Ram Mohun Roy is listed in the Asia study guide (II, A, 6, a). Only Rabindranath TAGORE had a greater impact on the Bengalis' self-image.

Perhaps the best book on Ram Mohun Roy is the 1962 Sadharan Brahma Samaj edition of Sophia Dobson Collet's *The Life and Letters of Raja Rammohun Roy* (1962), originally published in 1900. Dilip Kumar Biswas and Prabhat Chandra Ganguli coedited the volume, updating it with extensive supplementary notes. The most useful collection of Ram Mohun's writings in English is *The English Works of Raja Rammohun Roy* (6 vols., 1945–1951), edited by Kalidas Nag and Debajyoti Burman. See also U. N. Ball, *Rammohun Roy: A Study of His Life* (1933), and Igbal Singh, *Rammohun Roy* (1958).

✳   ✳   ✳

ROYCE / By Gerald J. Goodwin

> The American philosopher Josiah Royce (1855–1916) was the last and the greatest spokesman for systematic philosophical idealism in the United States.

osiah Royce was born on Nov. 20, 1855, at Grass Valley, Calif. His forceful mother gave him his early education. He attended school in San Francisco, where the family moved when he was 11 years old. At the University of California the precocious youth's interests shifted from mining engineering to literature and philosophy.

When Royce graduated in 1875, his burgeoning intellectual powers won him a year of graduate study in Germany, where he immersed himself in philosophical idealism. On his return to the United States in 1876, he accepted a fellowship to Johns Hopkins University and took his doctorate in 1878. After teaching literature and composition at the University of California for 4 years, Royce was invited to teach philosophy at Harvard in 1882. The rest of his life as teacher and philosopher centered at Harvard.

His mother had impressed on Royce a concern for basic religious issues; his youth in California and his own solitary disposition had posed the problem of the relationship between the individual and the community. All of his philosophical writings revolved around these issues. His first major work, significantly entitled *The Religious Aspect of Philosophy* (1885), presented the central ideas that his later writings elaborated and refined. He developed this philosophy in a series of major works, the most important of which were *The Spirit of Modern Philosophy* (1892), *The Conception of God* (1897), *Studies of Good and Evil* (1898), *The World and the Individual* (2 vols., 1900–1902), and his summary statement, *The Problem of Christianity* (2 vols., 1913).

Royce's philosophy rested on the conviction that ultimate reality consisted of idea or spirit. "The world of dead facts is an illusion," he wrote. "The truth of it is a spiritual life." His central conception was the Absolute. The world exists in and for an all-embracing, all-knowing thought, Royce explained. This amounted to a philosophical conception of God, the Absolute which united all thought and all experience. Given this reality, the individual's task is to understand the meaning of the Absolute and to adopt its purposes freely.

Royce's ethical theory rested on his striking principle of loyalty, which he presented most effectively in *The Philosophy of Loyalty* (1908). He argued that loyalty was the cohesive principle of all ethical behavior and of all social practice. The moral law, he thought, could be reduced to the precept "Be loyal." Loyalty also linked the individual to the community. The loyal man was one who gave himself to a cause, but each individual must choose his cause so that it would advance the good of all. He should act to further loyalty to the very principle of loyalty.

In his later years Royce's increasing concern about the practical bearings of philosophy was reflected in his *War and Insurance* (1914) and *The Hope of the Great Community* (1916). By the time of his death on Sept. 14, 1916, Royce had become one of America's most important philosophers. His influence on his contemporaries was a tribute to his intellectual power and to his concern with fundamental religious issues.

Josiah Royce. (Fogg Art Museum, Harvard University, Given to Harvard College by Friends of Dr. Royce, 1923–1925)

Further Reading

Josiah Royce is listed in the Philosophy study guide (VI, A, 3). William JAMES helped secure Royce's first teaching position at Harvard.

The Letters of Josiah Royce, edited by John Glendenning (1970), is the companion volume of Royce's *Basic Writings* (2 vols., 1969). Stuart Gerry Brown edited two collections of Royce's writings and provided excellent introductory essays: *The Social Philosophy of Josiah Royce* (1950) and *The Religious Philosophy of Josiah Royce* (1952).

A fine presentation of Royce's complete ethical philosophy, using Royce's unpublished papers, is Peter Fuss, *The Moral Philosophy of Josiah Royce* (1965). Thomas F. Powell, in *Josiah Royce* (1967), argues that Royce's philosophy is relevant to contemporary religious thought. Vincent Buranelli, *Josiah Royce* (1964), gives considerable attention to Royce as a literary figure. For background see also Clifford Barrett, *Contemporary Idealism in America* (1932); and for a description of the rise of scientific methodology of inquiry during Royce's time at Harvard see Paul Buck, ed., *Social Sciences at Harvard, 1860–1902: From Inculcation to the Open Mind* (1965).

*   *   *

RUBENS / By John Rupert Martin

The Flemish painter and diplomat Peter Paul
Rubens (1577–1640) was not only the
unquestioned leader of the Flemish baroque
school but one of the supreme geniuses in the
history of painting.

During the last troubled decades of the 16th century the Flemish school of painting fell into a kind
of tepid and uninventive mannerism which gave
little promise of bringing forth a great master. Yet it was
in this school that Peter Paul Rubens (pronounced
rōō′bənz) received his first training as an artist and acquired that belief in the humanistic values of classical
antiquity that was to continue undiminished throughout
his career.

Within his own lifetime Rubens enjoyed a European
reputation which brought him commissions from Italy,
Spain, France, England, and Germany as well as from his
homeland, the southern Netherlands. His boundless
imagination, immense capacity for work, and sheer productivity were legendary. In 1621, when he was not yet
45 years old, an English visitor to Antwerp described him
as "the master workman of the world." And at almost the
same moment Rubens said of himself, without boasting,

"My talent is such that no enterprise, however vast in
number and in diversity of subjects, has surpassed my
courage." It reveals something of the many-sidedness of
this extraordinary man that, without interrupting his artistic activity, he was able to engage in a demanding career
of public service and also to conduct an extensive correspondence with learned men on scholarly and archeological matters.

Jan Rubens, the painter's father, was a lawyer of Antwerp who, because he was a Calvinist, fled to Germany
in 1568 to escape persecution at the hands of the Spaniards. In Cologne he entered into an adulterous relation
with the wife of William the Silent, Prince of Orange, as a
result of which he was thrown into prison. Released after
2 years owing to the devoted and untiring efforts of his
wife, Maria Pypelinckx, Jan Rubens was permitted to take
up residence at Siegen in Westphalia. It was there that
their second son, Peter Paul, was born on June 28, 1577.
The family, which had now become Catholic, lived for
some years in Cologne until Jan Rubens died in 1587, at
which time his widow returned to Antwerp, bringing her
three children with her.

After a period of schooling which included instruction
in Latin and Greek, the young Rubens became a page to a
noblewoman, Marguerite de Ligne, Countess of Lalaing.
This early experience of court life, though he was glad to
be released from it, was undoubtedly useful to the future
artist, much of whose time was to be passed in aristocratic and royal circles. Returning to his home in Antwerp,
he now decided to follow the profession of painter. He
studied under three masters—Tobias Verhaecht, Adam
van Noort, and Otto van Veen—and in 1598 was accepted as a master in the Antwerp Guild of St. Luke, the
painters' guild.

Italian Period, 1600–1608

In 1600 Rubens set out on a journey to Italy, where
within a short time he entered the service of Vincenzo
Gonzaga, Duke of Mantua, whose palace housed a notable art collection. Since Rubens was not expected to remain always at the ducal court in Mantua, he found time
to visit other cities in Italy, especially Rome, Florence,
and Genoa. In Rome, Rubens completed his education as
an artist, studying with unfailing enthusiasm the sculptures of antiquity and the paintings of the High Renaissance, especially those of Raphael and Michelangelo.
During his first sojourn in the papal city (1601–1602) he
painted three altarpieces for the Church of Sta Croce in
Gerusalemme (now in the Hospital at Grasse).

In 1603 Duke Vincenzo sent Rubens on a diplomatic
mission to Spain; here he made the impressive equestrian portrait of the Duke of Lerma and saw for the first
time the Spanish royal collection, with its wealth of
paintings by Titian.

Late in 1605 Rubens was again in Rome; he now contrived to remain there for almost 3 years. During this time
he was commissioned to decorate the high altar of S.
Maria in Vallicella—an extraordinary honor for a foreign-
er. His first solution, an altarpiece showing the Madonna
and Child with St. Gregory and other saints (now in the

Peter Paul Rubens, a self-portrait, in the Uffizi,
Florence. (Alinari)

Museum at Grenoble), did not make a good impression owing to unfavorable lighting conditions in the church, and he obligingly replaced it by a set of three pictures painted on slate. In October 1608, before this work had been unveiled, there came word that Rubens's mother was seriously ill, and the artist left at once for Antwerp. Though he did not know it at the time, he was never to see Italy again.

Antwerp Period, 1609–1621

Rubens arrived at his home to learn that his mother had died before he left Rome. Although it was surely his intention to return to Italy, he soon found reasons for remaining in Antwerp. The Archduke Albert and his consort, Isabella, the sovereigns of the Spanish Netherlands, appointed him court painter with special privileges. In October 1609 Rubens married Isabella Brant, and a year later he purchased a house in Antwerp. The charming painting *Rubens and His Wife in the Honeysuckle Arbor* was painted about this time.

The humanistic atmosphere of Antwerp that appealed so strongly to Rubens is epitomized in the so-called *Four Philosophers*. In reality this is a commemorative picture representing the late Justus Lipsius, the eminent classical scholar, with two of his pupils, one of whom is Rubens's brother Philip (also recently deceased); the artist himself stands a little to one side, an onlooker rather than a participant in the symposium.

The first big project to be undertaken after Rubens's return from Italy was the *Raising of the Cross*, a triptych (1609–1611) for the church of St. Walburga (now in the Cathedral of Antwerp). With this bold and intensely dramatic work Rubens at once established himself as the leading master of the city. It was followed by another triptych, equally large and no less successful, the *Descent from the Cross* (1611–1614) in the Cathedral. Rubens's baroque imagination found new outlets in subjects chosen from both the sacred and profane worlds: in the *Great Last Judgment* he conjured up an apocalyptic vision of the torments of the damned; the same tempestuous energy is encountered in the artist's hunting pieces, with their ferocious combats of men and wild beasts.

Rubens's workshop was now in full operation, and he was able, with the aid of his pupils and assistants, to achieve an astonishing output of pictures. The ablest and most brilliant of these assistants was Anthony Van Dyck, who entered his studio about 1617/1618 and who undoubtedly helped in the execution of a number of important commissions. Nevertheless it must not be concluded that the master took no responsibility for his paintings but was simply content to let them be carried out by his studio. The principal works exhibit no falling off in quality. Indeed the masterpieces crowd so closely upon one another at this time that it is difficult to select a few representative examples. Of the mythologies the *Rape of the Daughters of Leucippus* is one of the most dazzling. Among the finest of the ecclesiastical works are the two altarpieces glorifying the first saints of the Jesuit order, the *Miracles of St. Ignatius of Loyola* and the

Miracles of St. Francis Xavier, which fairly overwhelm the observer by their huge scale, richness of color, and depth of feeling.

In 1620 Rubens was commissioned to execute a series of 39 ceiling paintings for the Jesuit church in Antwerp. It was the largest decorative cycle that the artist had yet undertaken, and as such it called into play all his powers of invention and organization. The entire complex of ceiling paintings was destroyed by fire in 1718.

International Fame, 1621–1630

The Jesuit cycle was followed by an even larger commission from France. In 1622 Rubens was in Paris to sign a contract for the decoration of two great galleries in the Luxembourg Palace, the residence of the queen mother, Marie de Médicis. The first of these projects, the incomparable series of 21 large canvases illustrating the life of Marie (now in the Louvre, Paris), was finished in 1625. The subject matter was decidedly unpromising, but Rubens, undaunted as always, succeeded in transforming the dreary history of the Queen into one of the most brilliant and most spectacular of all baroque decorative programs. Work on the second cycle, which was to deal with the life of Marie's late husband, King Henry IV, was repeatedly delayed, and Rubens at length gave up the project in disgust.

There were other decorative schemes to occupy Rubens's attention during this period. For King Louis XIII of France he designed the tapestry series, the *History of Constantine the Great*, and several years later the Infanta Isabella commissioned him to design an even larger tapestry cycle, the *Triumph of the Eucharist*, for the Convent of the Descalzas Reales in Madrid.

Despite his being involved in these and other great undertakings, Rubens found time to paint important altarpieces for churches in Antwerp: the *Adoration of the Magi* (now in the Antwerp Museum) was made for St. Michael's Abbey in 1624; the *Assumption of the Virgin* for the high altar of the Cathedral in 1626; and—perhaps the most beautiful of all—the *Madonna and Saints* (sometimes called the *Mystic Marriage of St. Catherine*) for the church of the Augustinians in 1628. Some of his most memorable portraits also belong to these years. They range from the fresh and luminous *Susanna Fourment*, known as *Le Chapeau de paille*, to the stern and masterful *Thomas Howard, Earl of Arundel*.

In Windsor Castle is the famous *Self-portrait* (1623/1624) which Rubens painted at the request of the Prince of Wales, later King Charles I of England. It shows a strong and handsome face, with bold moustaches and curling hair and beard; the broadbrimmed hat not only lends animation by its sweeping oval shape but serves also to conceal the artist's baldness (about which he seems to have been rather sensitive).

Rubens's diplomatic activity, which had begun some time earlier, reached a peak in the years 1628–1630, when he was instrumental in bringing about peace between England and Spain. As the agent of the Infanta, he went first to Spain, where in addition to carrying out his political duties he found a new and enthusiastic art pa-

The Descent from the Cross, *painted in 1611–1614 by Rubens for the Cathedral in Antwerp. (Photo N. D. Roger-Viollet; Copyright A.C.L., Brussels)*

tron in King Philip IV and renewed his acquaintance with the works of Titian in the royal collection. His mission to England was equally successful. Charles I knighted the artist-diplomat, and the University of Cambridge awarded him an honorary master of arts degree. Rubens returned to Antwerp in March 1630.

Last Years, 1630–1640

Isabella Brant, Rubens's first wife, had died in 1626. In December 1630 he married Helena Fourment, a girl of 16. Though he had hoped, on returning to Antwerp, to withdraw from political life, he was obliged to act once more as confidential agent for the Infanta in the frustrating and unsuccessful negotiations with the Dutch. At

length he succeeded in being released from diplomatic employment. In 1635 he purchased a country estate, the Castle of Steen, situated some miles south of Antwerp, and henceforth divided his time between this rural retreat and his studio in town.

In the last decade of his life Rubens's art underwent a surprising expansion in variety and scope of subject matter. The enchanting *Garden of Love*, with its complex interweaving of the classical and the contemporary, may serve as an illustration. A new interest in nature, inspired perhaps by his residence in the country, found expression in a series of magnificent landscapes, among them the *Castle of Steen*. The portraits of this period, especially those of his wife, Helena, and their children, are characterized by informality and tender intimacy.

A lyrical quality pervades even the traditional Christian and classical subjects. In the *Ildefonso Altarpiece* the scene of the saint receiving a vestment from the Virgin Mary is transfigured by a silvery radiance. The secular counterpart to this work is the *Feast of Venus*, in which Rubens pays tribute both to the art of antiquity and to the paintings of Titian. The almost dreamlike poetry of the late mythologies is beautifully exemplified by the *Judgment of Paris* and the *Three Graces*, in which the opulent nudes seem to glow with light and color.

Rubens continued to carry out monumental commissions during his last decade. For Charles I he executed the ceiling paintings of the Banqueting House at Whitehall—the only large-scale decorative cycle by the artist that still remains in the place for which it was designed. In the Whitehall ceiling, which is a glorification of King James I and the Stuart monarchy, the artist profited from the experience gained in the decoration of the Jesuit church some years earlier. In 1635, when the new governor of the Netherlands, Cardinal Infante Ferdinand, made his "Joyous Entry" into Antwerp, Rubens was given the task of preparing the temporary street decorations. Swiftly mobilizing teams of artists and craftsmen to work from his designs, the master created a stupendous series of painted theaters and triumphal arches which surpassed all expectations by their magnificence. His last great project was the provision of a vast cycle of mythological paintings for the decoration of Philip IV's hunting lodge near Madrid, the Torre de la Parada.

Toward the end of his life Rubens was increasingly troubled by arthritis, which eventually compelled him to give up painting altogether. One of the most moving documents of the last years is the *Self-portrait* in Vienna, in which the master, though already touched by suffering, wears an air of calm and serenity. He died in Antwerp on May 30, 1640.

Further Reading

Peter Paul Rubens is listed in the Art study guide (III, F, 1, c). He was influenced by RAPHAEL, MICHELANGELO, and, particularly, TITIAN. Rubens's principal assistant was Anthony VAN DYCK. Rubens's influence was felt throughout Europe not only during his lifetime by such artists as REMBRANDT and Jacob JORDAENS but later, especially in France, by Antoine WATTEAU, Eugène DELACROIX, and Pierre Auguste RENOIR.

Rubens's letters are available in a first-rate translation by Ruth S. Magurn, *The Letters of Peter Paul Rubens* (1955). The standard biography is Max Rooses, *Rubens*, translated by H. Child (2 vols., 1904), which, although dated in some particulars, remains unsurpassed as a detailed, authoritative, and readable account of the artist and his times. Two shorter biographies, both handsomely illustrated and both taking account of recent research, are recommended: C. V. Wedgwood, *The World of Rubens, 1577–1640* (1967), and Christopher White, *Rubens and His World* (1968). Also enlightening is the lengthy essay by the 19th-century historian Jacob Burckhardt, *Recollections of Rubens*, translated by M. Hottinger,

with an introduction and additional notes by H. Gerson (1950).

On Rubens's drawings, abundant information is in J. S. Held, *Rubens: Selected Drawings* (1959), and Ludwig Burchard and R.-A. d'Hulst, *Rubens Drawings* (2 vols., 1963). A scholarly discussion of the influences on Rubens is Wolfgang Stechow, *Rubens and the Classical Tradition* (1968).

RUDOLF I / By Edward M. Peters

> Rudolf I (ca. 1218–1291), or Rudolf of Hapsburg, was Holy Roman emperor-elect from 1273 to 1291. He was the first of a long line of Hapsburg emperors.

The struggle between the emperor Frederick II and Pope Innocent IV had shattered the power of the imperial office in both Germany and Italy. The "emperors" who reigned between 1250 and 1273—William of Holland, Alfonso X of Castile, and Richard of Cornwall—were powerless because of their absenteeism and the lack of cooperation they had received in Germany. When an imperial election was called in 1273, the German princes whose responsibility it was to elect the new emperor wanted neither a powerful nor an ambitious ruler, and their choice fell on Rudolf, a wealthy but not potentially dangerous German noble.

However, not only did Rudolph's reign enhance the wealth and power of the minor Hapsburg house, but it also gave his dynasty a foothold in the imperial office, which was eventually secured in the 15th century and not relinquished until the 19th. In the face of considerable opposition, Rudolf managed to impose a temporary peace upon the warring German Estates and princes, to subdue the powerful Premysl dynasty of Bohemia, and to heal the rift between the imperial office and the papacy, which had destroyed imperial power 25 years before.

Rudolf was a compromise candidate for the imperial office. In 1273 the strongest prince in the empire was the Premysl line's Ottocar II, King of Bohemia. In order to block Bohemian power, the electoral princes turned to Rudolf. Rudolf's first task as emperor was to quell Bohemian power, which he accomplished in 1276 at Vienna and again at the battle of Marchfeld in 1278, thus permanently defeating the possibility of Bohemian domination of Germany and the imperial office. After these victories, Rudolf made Vienna the Hapsburg capital, which it remained until the 20th century.

The Emperor's second step was to heal the wounds of the Church, still smarting after its long bout with the imperial Hohenstaufen dynasty. In 1279 Rudolf renounced many of the imperial claims in Italy, gave the Romagna to the Pope, and thoroughly subordinated the powers of the imperial office and its incumbent to the authority of

Rudolf I of the Holy Roman Empire, an equestrian statue by Erwin de Steinbach, placed above the grand portal of Strasbourg Cathedral.

the Church in matters spiritual and temporal.

Rudolf's accomplished effectiveness as both diplomat and general gave Germany nearly 2 decades of peace. His next undertaking—and that of the Nassau, Wittelsbach, and Luxembourg dynasties, which each provided emperors in the century following Rudolf's death—was the extension and increase of his family power and wealth, for only by this method could any imperial dynasty sustain itself in the troubled 13th and 14th centuries. Ecclesiastical fear of the public resources of the imperial office had grown so great, and the imperial office had become so fragmented, that only the private family resources of individual emperors could sustain imperial power. From 1282 to 1286 Rudolf worked for the increase of the house of Hapsburg. His favor toward his son Albert of Bavaria, his lack of sufficient resources to quench the rivalry between German princes and cities, and his rivalry over Burgundy with the French king Philip IV troubled the last years of his reign. His eldest son, Rudolf, died at the age of 20, and Rudolf I then turned toward the advancement of the fortunes of his second son, Albert, later King Albert I.

Rudolf's reputation as a capable and intelligent ruler,

well aware of the limits of his real power, yet successful in the imposition of peace upon a torn Germany, stood him in good stead. Although his son did not succeed him directly, Rudolf worked for his succession up to the time of his own death. Rudolf died on July 15, 1291, at Speyer, attempting to the end to establish the house of Hapsburg on the throne, which it would, within 2 centuries, make a virtual family possession.

Further Reading

Rudolf I is listed in the European History study guide (III, C, 1, a and b). Hapsburg power reached its height under CHARLES V of the Holy Roman Empire.

There is no biography of Rudolf I in English. Adam Wandruska, *The House of Habsburg* (1964), is a history of the dynasty with several chapters on early Hapsburg history, including one on Rudolf. *The Cambridge Medieval History*, vol. 7 (1936), gives considerable information, as do Geoffrey Barraclough, *The Origins of Modern Germany* (1946; 2d rev. ed. 1966), James Bryce, *The Holy Roman Empire* (1956), and Friedrich Heer, *The Holy Roman Empire* (1969).

RUEF / By Gerald W. McFarland

An American political boss in San Francisco, Abraham Ruef (1864–1936) was convicted of bribery in a famous antigraft trial.

Abraham Ruef, the son of French-Jewish immigrants, was born in San Francisco, Calif., Sept. 2, 1864. A precocious young man, he graduated in 1883 from the University of California with high honors. He studied at Hastings College of Law in San Francisco and was admitted to the bar in 1886. Cultivated, moderately well-to-do, and dynamic, he was first attracted to politics as a reformer, but reform proved too uncertain an avenue to power.

About 1888 Ruef shifted his loyalties to San Francisco's corrupt Republican political machine. As "Boss Ruef," leader of a Latin Quarter (North Beach) district, he became an engaging campaign speaker and fully mastered the fine points of ward politics.

Ruef's desire for power and advancement led him to break with the Republican leadership in 1901. He first tried to defeat the organization in primary elections and, failing that, allied himself with the Union Labor party movement. San Francisco was a strong union town, but the party's leadership needed an experienced political "kingmaker." Ruef was adept at just such behind-the-scenes services. After selecting Eugene Schmitz, the handsome president of the musicians' union, as the party's candidate for mayor, Ruef masterminded Schmitz's successful campaign in 1901 and his reelection in 1903 and 1905. The 1905 election was an especially triumphant one, since not only Schmitz but Ruef's hand-picked board of supervisors were elected.

Abraham Ruef. (California Historical Society, San Francisco)

However, Ruef's triumph was also in large part the source of his downfall. Since Schmitz's first victory, large corporations had sought Ruef out as their "confidential attorney," paying him lucrative fees as a way of assuring the administration's friendship. Initially, these fees were retainers, not outright bribes. After 1905, however, Ruef's greedy allies sought direct payment for their votes on many measures: restaurant licenses, street railway franchises, utility rates, permits for boxing matches. Ruef became the middleman in an alliance between influential corporations and political grafters, demanding huge sums of money to distribute to the pliant supervisors.

In 1906 a small group led by Fremont Older of the *San Francisco Bulletin* brought legal indictments against Ruef. After a spectacular, and sometimes bizarre, trial Ruef was convicted of bribery in 1908. When his appeals were turned down, he entered San Quentin Penitentiary in 1911. Largely owing to the efforts of former enemies such as Older, Ruef was paroled in 1915 and pardoned in 1920. Avoiding politics, he tried his hand at real estate investments. He prospered in the 1920s but went bankrupt during the Depression years. He died in San Francisco on Feb. 29, 1936.

Further Reading

Abraham Ruef is listed in the American History study guide (VIII, A, 3). A contemporary "kingmaker" in New York City was Charles Francis MURPHY.

The colorful story of Ruef's career is told in vivid detail by Walton Bean, *Boss Ruef's San Francisco* (1952). See also Lately Thomas, *A Debonair Scoundrel* (1962).

*   *   *

RUFFIN / By David A. Williams

Edmund Ruffin (1794–1865), American editor and publisher, was a prominent scientific agriculturist as well as his period's most renowned advocate of establishing an independent Southern nation.

E dmund Ruffin was born in Prince George County, Va. Educated at home until he was 16, he attended the College of William and Mary for a year before he was dismissed. He saw brief military service in the War of 1812 and then began a life as a Southern planter. Agriculture in Virginia was in a depressed state, largely because of the dominant farming practices of the time. Ruffin developed methods of restoring the fertility of soils and described them in "An Essay on Calcareous Manures." This discovery and others, which Ruffin announced in his publication, the *Farmer's Register*, were adopted by large numbers of Virginia planters and led to an agricultural revival. Thereafter he contributed systematically to agricultural science—popularizing, distributing, writing, speaking, and informing Southern farmers of theoretical as well as practical, progressive agricultural methods.

In 1841 Ruffin was appointed a member of the Board of Agriculture of Virginia and became its secretary, and a year later he became agriculture surveyor of South Caroli-

Edmund Ruffin. (Library of Congress)

na. His detailed and clearly written *Report of the Commencement and Progress of the Agricultural Survey of South Carolina* became a landmark in the agricultural history of the state. On his estate, Malbourne, in Hanover County, Va., he applied his scientific farming ideas so successfully that the plantation became a showplace where record harvests were almost commonplace.

Ruffin is most widely known as a radical spokesman for Southern nationalism. Early in his career he became convinced that the Negro was inferior and that a slave system was necessary and generally superior. He was the first outspoken advocate of Southern secession, viewing the competition of the North and South for advantage in the Union as one which would inevitably end in Southern defeat. The South as an independent nation would enjoy great advantages: direct trade with Europe, the end of the hidden subsidy by the South of Northern industries in the form of tariffs on imports, and a general strengthening of the slave society.

Ruffin announced his views in assorted publications which he sometimes printed and distributed at his own expense. He advocated secession at the Democratic convention in Charleston in 1860; welcomed the election of Abraham Lincoln as a portent of the impending separation of the South from the Union; fired the first shot on Ft. Sumter to initiate the war; and fought in the Battle of Bull Run. He committed suicide when Confederate defeat became a fact.

Further Reading

Edmund Ruffin is listed in the American History study guide (VI, A, 2). William YANCEY and Barnwell RHETT were also radical secessionists.

The best biography of Ruffin is Avery O. Craven, *Edmund Ruffin, Southerner: A Study in Secession* (1932). His agricultural work is recounted in Albert Lowther Demaree, *The American Agricultural Press, 1819–1860* (1941).

* * *

RUISDAEL / By Madlyn Kahr

The Dutch landscape painter Jacob van Ruisdael (1628/1629–1682) raised to the highest level of quality and variety the painting of landscapes based on the observation of the visible world.

Jacob van Ruisdael (pronounced vän rois′däl) was born in Haarlem, the son of the painter Isaak van Ruisdael, whose works are unknown to us, and the nephew of the gifted landscape painter Salomon van Ruysdael. Jacob's youthful works reflect the influence of his uncle and other painters of the Haarlem school, which played a leading part in the development of Dutch realistic landscape painting from the early years of the 17th century. He was already an independent master by 1648, when he became a member of the Haarlem guild. Paintings dated as early as 1645 and 1646 confirm that he was an accomplished painter while still very young.

The flat countryside around his native town provided subject matter for Ruisdael's brush again and again. Within the area of a small canvas, the level fields, on which the linen cloth that was a major product of Haarlem was stretched out to bleach, appear to extend on both sides as far as the eye can see. Cloud formations dapple the fields with sunlight. On the distant horizon, the buildings of the town join earth to sky. Such a picture is based on nature, but with the elements selected, emphasized, and reorganized so that the natural scene is transformed into an esthetic unity. It is a poetic transfiguration of reality.

Shortly after 1650 Ruisdael became familiar with a different kind of landscape, hilly and wooded, through travels in the border areas of eastern Holland and western Germany. Reminiscences of this experience appear in many of his paintings. In the *Wooden Bridge* (1652) a new monumentality is incorporated into a rugged landscape, whose structural strength is characteristic of Dutch painting about 1650. Ruisdael enriched the basic framework of the composition with a remarkable counterpoint of gently undulating contours, in which the curves of the meandering river, the paths, hills, clouds, and branches and crowns of trees underline, echo, and complete one another. The oak tree that dominates the left side of the composition is full of vitality and individuality. The richness of color and plasticity of forms of his mature works are evident here.

About 1656 Ruisdael moved to Amsterdam, where he seems to have spent the rest of his life. His extraordinary

Jacob van Ruisdael. (Bildarchiv)

The Cemetery, *painted by Ruisdael about 1660. The other version of this work is in Dresden. (Courtesy of The Detroit Institute of Arts)*

gift for evoking a higher reality in nature was embodied in a series of masterpieces. The brooding, emotion-filled *Cemetery,* or *Jewish Cemetery at Ouderkerk* (ca. 1660; two versions), is unique in its explicitly allegorical intent. Death and the destruction of both natural and man-made objects is contrasted with the rainbow, symbol of resurrection. The preparatory drawings that he made for this painting show that the tombs were drawn from observation, the landscape background was imaginary, and the architecture was altered from a simple country church to a romantic ruin.

Paintings by his friend Allaert van Everdingen, who had traveled in Scandinavia, probably provided the vocabulary of rocky mountain streams and fir trees that began to appear in Ruisdael's paintings about 1660. These compositions tend to heroic grandeur, sometimes overstated. The *Waterfall with Castle* (mid-1660s) is an example of Ruisdael at his best in this type of theme, with an almost tangible differentiation of the textures of various materials, dramatic contrasts of light and dark, and intense local color, unified by firm compositional control.

Ruisdael painted as many as 50 seascapes, beginning in the mid-1660s. In these his energetic brushstroke and strongly contrasted values are particularly effective. This can be seen in *Stormy Sea* (ca. 1670), which might be called a portrait of the wind as it is reflected in sea and sky. He also painted forests, beaches, snow scenes, and town views. The figures in his paintings were often added by another artist. A number of drawings and some etchings by Ruisdael, mainly antedating 1650, have also come down to us.

By the mid-1670s Ruisdael's style had weakened. His most impressive pupil, Meindert Hobbema, carried on his tradition in a delightful but rather attenuated manner. Ruisdael's impact is seen in the great English landscapes of the 18th century, especially early works by Thomas Gainsborough, and in French landscapes of the 19th century, notably by Gustave Courbet.

Further Reading

Jacob van Ruisdael is listed in the Art study guide (III, F, 1, b). Other 17th-century landscape painters were Jan van GOYEN and Aelbert CUYP.

The best book in English for the study of Ruisdael is Wolfgang Stechow, *Dutch Landscape Painting of the Seventeenth Century* (1966). See also Neil MacLaren, *The Dutch School* (1960).

JOSÉ MARTÍNEZ RUÍZ / By Harriet S. Turner

The Spanish writer José Martínez Ruíz (1873–1967), who wrote under the name Azorín, was a spokesman for the Generation of 1898. He is famous for his impressionistic sketches and essays which evoke the essence of traditional and modern Spain.

José Martínez Ruíz (pronounced mär-tē′näth rōō-ēth′) was born on June 8, 1873, in Monóvar in Alicante Province. He spent his childhood in Yecla, later evoked in the autobiographical novel *Las*

José Martínez Ruíz. (MAS)

confesiones de un pequeño filósofo. He studied law in Valencia, Granada, and Salamanca but preferred literature and newspaper work. In 1896 he went to Madrid and wrote for several republican, anticlerical newspapers. He soon became known as an outspoken republican with anarchist sympathies, symbolically expressed by his persistent use of a red umbrella.

In 1900 Ruíz published his first important work, *El alma castellana 1600–1800,* in which he revealed the essence of Spain, symbolized in Castilian towns and landscapes. Three novels followed: *La voluntad* (1902), *Antonio Azorín* (1903), and *Las confesiones de un pequeño filósofo* (1904). Their protagonist is Antonio Azorín, whose name Ruíz adopted in a kind of personal identification with his fictional character. The novels, which lack plot or any significant action, portray in three separate stages the anxieties and reminiscences of a hypersensitive intellectual surrounded by the decadence of modern Spain.

But Ruíz's lyrical, fragmentary style was much more suited to short sketches than to the longer novel form. Books such as *Los pueblos* (1905), *La ruta de don Quijote* (1905), and *Castilla* (1912) manifest his art in its purest form. Preoccupied with the past, Ruíz evoked poetically the beauty and inner life of familiar scenes and things, ultimately revealing the recurrence of the past in present life. The paradox of time visualized as eternal repetition became one of his chief concerns.

Ruíz also wrote literary criticism. He offers in *Lecturas españolas* (1912), *Clásicos y modernos* (1913), and *Al márgen de los clásicos* (1915) original views of the classics and many forgotten authors. He is the spokesman for the Generation of 1898, having defined that group of writers in a famous essay.

Gradually Ruíz became politically more conservative. He was elected deputy to the Cortes (1907, 1914) and served as undersecretary of education (1917, 1919). In 1924 he was admitted to the Spanish Academy but renounced membership when Gabriel Miró Ferrer was refused entrance. During the 1920s Ruíz wrote three

more novels and a few unsuccessful plays, among them *Old Spain* (1926) and *Brandy, mucho Brandy* (1927). During the Civil War he lived in Paris, returning to Madrid in 1940. His subsequent works are inferior to his earlier works. He died on March 2, 1967, in Madrid.

Further Reading

José Martínez Ruíz is listed in the Literature study guide (III, H, 4; III, J, 4, a). Other members of the Generation of 1898 were Ramón del VALLE INCLÁN, Jacinto BENAVENTE, and Pío BAROJA.

The best work on Ruíz is Anna Krause, *Azorín, the Little Philosopher* (1948). His early novels are well analyzed in Katherine P. Reding, *The Generation of 1898 in Spain as Seen through Its Fictional Hero* (1936).

JUAN RUIZ / By Juan Bautista Avalle-Arce

The Spanish poet Juan Ruiz (1283?–1350?), the archpriest of Hita, was the author of the "Libro de buen amor," one of the most extraordinary poetic creations of the Middle Ages.

Practically nothing is known of the life of Juan Ruiz except for what can be reconstructed from his poem. However, since the history of literature repeatedly proves that such a biographical technique is dangerous, it is best to carefully weigh all such evidence. In his poem he says that he was born in Alcalá de Henares (V: 1,510), a fact that agrees with the knowledge of geography shown in the poem. He gives an alleged self-portrait in stanzas 1,485–1,489, but scholars have pointed out that before these lines can be accepted as a physical picture of Ruiz, the weight of rhetorical tradition in literary portraiture—the physical correlates that medieval medical sciences attributed to psychological characteristics—and the fact that the description is made by a go-between, Trotaconventos, must be taken into consideration.

Lastly, the colophon to one of the manuscripts in which Ruiz's poem has survived explains that the work was composed while its author was in prison by order of Gil Álvarez Carrillo de Albornoz, Archbishop of Toledo. Since the poet also mentions a prison at the beginning of the *Libro de buen amor* (The Book of Good Love), scholars have argued that the reference in the poem is to the symbolic prison of Christian man and that this reference was interpreted literally by the scribe. Documentary proof gives evidence that by 1351 Ruiz was no longer archpriest of Hita. It is assumed that he died sometime earlier.

The *Libro* has survived in three main manuscripts, each one incomplete at different points. Two of the manuscripts represent a version of the poem finished in

1330. The third one represents an amplification of that version finished in 1343. Some fragments are also extant, including one of a Portuguese translation. Leaving aside the prose introduction (the *Libro* contains four different preliminary pieces before it expounds its *propósito*, or purpose), the poem has 1,728 stanzas, mainly narrative and in *cuaderna vía* (a learned 14-syllable poetic form) but with frequent lyrical outbursts in a variety of meters. The poem is supposedly an erotic autobiography written with a moral purpose, more in the medieval Ovidian tradition (as evidenced in the *Pamphilus de amore*, and mainly in the still-unpublished *De vetula*) than in the tradition of the Arabic and Hebrew works that have been pointed out as possible models. Spiritually, the poem is a hybrid product, typical of 600 years of coexistence of Christians, Moors, and Jews on the Iberian Peninsula.

Ruiz's poetic imagination and individualism were such, however, that no poetic tradition or literary theme employed by him has remained the same after his treatment of it. He was "one of the greatest poets of the Middle Ages, the equal of Chaucer," according to one modern critic.

Further Reading

Juan Ruiz is listed in the Literature study guide (III, C, 5). Pedro LÓPEZ DE AYALA was another medieval Spanish poet.

E. K. Kane's notorious 1933 translation of *The Book of Good Love* was reissued in 1968. The *Libro* is analyzed at length in Anthony N. Zahareas, *The Art of Juan Ruiz, Archpriest of Hita* (1965). Américo Castro, *The Structure of Spanish History* (1948; trans. 1954), and María Rosa Lida de Malkiel, *Two Spanish Masterpieces* (1961), are good presentations of the case for Semitic influences; and Otis H. Green, *Spain and the Western Tradition*, vol. 1 (1963), presents the case for Occidental influences.

RUMFORD / By David W. Corson

The American-born British physicist Benjamin Thompson, Count Rumford (1753–1814), is best known for his attacks on the caloric theory of heat.

Benjamin Thompson was born on March 26, 1753, in Woburn, Mass. He received only 2 years of formal education and at 13 was apprenticed to a local merchant. At the age of 19, while teaching in Concord, N.H., he married a wealthy widow, 14 years his senior. He thus acquired not only an extensive estate but social and political influence as well.

Thompson's open support of the British crown, however, made his position increasingly precarious as political tensions mounted in the Colonies. As a result of his loyalist activities, he was forced in December 1774 to flee to Boston, abandoning his wife and infant daughter. He spent the next 15 months actively spying for the British government, supplying them with detailed reports on the condition and activities of the assembling colonial forces. When the British abandoned Boston in March 1776, Thompson departed for London.

Thompson arrived in London a confident, aggressive young man with a very useful knowledge of the colonial military situation; within 4 years he had risen to the position of undersecretary of state for colonial affairs. He also found time to pursue his scientific interests, and he soon gained a reputation as a productive natural philosopher as well. He undertook a series of studies on the explosive force of gunpowder, and his published report of these experiments was influential in his election as a fellow of the Royal Society in 1781. In that year he suddenly left London and returned to the Colonies, where he spent an undistinguished 2 years as a commanding officer in the British forces. He then returned to London and from there set out for the Continent.

Social Reform

In 1784 Thompson settled down in Munich as an aide-de-camp and confidential adviser to Elector Karl Theodor of Bavaria. Thompson did much to advance the stature of the Bavarian court by promoting scientific and technological advances and by instituting reform in the military, educational, and economic structure of the country. His standing was such as to guarantee him both the financial and technical support necessary for his varied, and often grandiose, projects, and in return for his activities he was

Count Rumford, engraved in 1797 by Joseph Rauschmayr after a drawing by Georg von Dillis. (Photo-Hachette)

Count Rumford demonstrating the production of heat. (The Science Museum, London)

in 1793 made a count of the Holy Roman Empire. He chose as his title Count Rumford, Rumford being the original name of Concord, N.H.

While in Munich one of Rumford's chief responsibilities was reorganizing the Bavarian army. In an effort to find more efficient and economical means of feeding and clothing the troops, he undertook an extensive study of the thermal conductivity of various types of cloth, in the process discovering the principle of heat transfer through what are today known as convection currents. Unable to persuade any commercial manufacturer to adopt the results of this research, Rumford set up what he called a "military workhouse" for producing the new military uniforms and in so doing became actively involved in social reform. Munich at the time was noted for its swarms of beggars, and on New Year's Day, 1790, Rumford had the Bavarian army arrest and jail every beggar in the city. These were then trained in his workhouse to manufacture the desired uniforms and in return for their labor received shelter, food, and education. The operation of this workhouse also involved Rumford in the associated practical problems of nutrition, heating, and lighting.

Theory of Heat

Rumford is best known today, however, for his contributions to the theory of heat. At the end of the 18th century the predominant theory of heat was the so-called caloric theory, according to which heat was a fluid substance that flowed into bodies when they were heated and flowed out of them as they cooled. The success of this theory in explaining then known phenomena is reflected in many terms, such as "heat flow" and "calorie," still used by physicists today. During his earlier gunpowder studies, however, Rumford had observed certain anomalies which the caloric theory seemed unable to explain, and for the remainder of his life he was constantly on the lookout for additional experimental evidence which might refute this theory.

Rumford's famous cannon-boring experiments present perhaps the most graphic evidence. One of his positions in Munich was inspector general of artillery for the Bavarian army, and, in the course of supervising work in the Munich arsenal, he was struck by the large amount of heat produced in boring a brass cannon. He devised an experiment in which, by utilizing a blunt borer to maximize the heat produced, he was able to boil large quantities of water with the resultant heat. The important aspect of this experiment, as Rumford himself noted, was the seemingly endless supply of heat that could be thus produced. According to the caloric theory, the boring tool produced heat by squeezing the caloric fluid out of the bodies rubbed together, but, as Rumford pointed out, anything which could be produced without limitation could not be a material substance such as caloric fluid. It should be emphasized, however, that although Rumford also produced numerous other experiments to refute the caloric theory, these experiments did not alone disprove the caloric theory, and not until much later in the 19th century was the concept of heat as a mode of motion generally adopted.

Royal Institution and Later Life

Rumford's position in Munich had always been somewhat precarious. His privileged status, the rapidity and success of his numerous innovations, and his ruthless disdain for his political opponents did nothing to silence the clamor of his enemies, and in 1798 the elector found it expedient to appoint him minister plenipotentiary to England, a position of honor which nonetheless effectively removed him from Munich politics. Arriving in London, he discovered that George III refused to accept a British subject (which Rumford still was) as minister from a foreign country.

Finding himself without a job, Rumford settled down in London to the task of establishing the Royal Institution. Justly renowned today for its research and popular lectures, the institution at its founding was part science museum and part technical school, reflecting Rumford's concern for the practical application of his researches. In 1801, after financial and personality difficulties, Rumford dissociated himself from the institution.

In 1804 Rumford moved to Paris and there, the following year, married Madame Lavoisier, the widow of the famous French chemist. A fashionable, though discordant, marriage, it lasted but 2 years, and in 1807 Rumford retired to the village of Auteuil near Paris. He became a member of the National Institute of France, as the Academy of Sciences was then called, and was a frequent contributor to its sessions and debates, as well as actively working to adapt his theoretical researches to practical applications. He died at Auteuil on Aug. 21, 1814.

Further Reading

Count Rumford is listed in the Science study guide (V, C, 1). Humphry DAVY was largely responsible for the Royal Institution's present prominence.

A new edition of Rumford's works is being edited by Sanborn C. Brown, *Collected Works of Count Rumford*, of which volume 1 is *The Nature of Heat* (1968). Of the full-length biographies the reader may most profitably consult W. J. Sparrow, *Knight of the White Eagle: A Biography of Sir Benjamin Thompson, Count Rumford* (1964). Sanborn C. Brown, *Count Rumford: Physicist Extraordinary* (1962), is an excellent, brief account. Other studies are James A. Thompson, *Count Rumford of Massachusetts* (1935), and Egon Larsen, *An American in Europe* (1953).

RUMI / By Robert N. Hill

The Persian poet and Sufi mystic Jalai ed-Din Rumi (1207–1273) was a brilliant lyrical poet who founded his own religious order, the Mevlevis. His poetry showed original religious and wonderfully esoteric forms of expression.

The unsurpassable peak of all Sufi thought was reached in the thought of Jalal ed-Din Rumi (pronounced rōo′mē), born in Balkh. He migrated to Konya in Asia Minor at a young age with his father, fleeing the Mongol invader of his day, Genghis Khan. On this trip in the city of Nishapur the young Rumi was presented to the famous old poet Attar, who, according to legend, predicted his future greatness and gave him his *Book of Secrets*. Then Rumi and his father traveled through Baghdad, Mecca, Damascus, and Erzincan, finally reaching Konya about 1226 or 1227, where he resided for most of his remaining life. His father was appointed to a high post in the empire of the Seljuks of Rum. Rumi inherited this post in 1231, when his father died. Thus Rumi was a man of means and could devote his efforts to more esoteric fields.

Two poets giving a reading; from a late-15th-century Persian manuscript of Rumi's Mathnawi. (The Metropolitan Museum of Art, Gift of Alexander Smith Cochran, 1913)

Religious Inspiration

The event which had the greatest influence on Rumi's intellectual and moral life was his meeting with the Sufi mystic Shams ed-Din Tabrizi. The latter, in the course of his wanderings, visited Konya and thoroughly inspired Rumi with religious fervor. As a result of this friendship, Rumi dedicated most of his writings to this wandering Sufi. Because of this also, Rumi founded the Mevlevi order of dervishes—the dancing dervishes. The unique trait of this order was that, contrary to general Moslem practice, Rumi gave a considerable place to music (the drum and reed) in the ceremonies.

The principal work of Rumi is his massive *Mathnawi*. This work is a compendium of poems, tales, anecdotes, and reflections—all meant to illustrate Sufi doctrine, the result of 40 years of work by Rumi. He also wrote a shorter *Diwan* and a prose treatise entitled *Fihi Ma Fihi* (What Is Within Is Within).

Rumi was a poet of the first rank. His style was simple and colloquial. His tales possessed diverse qualities: variety and originality, dignity and picturesqueness, learning and charm, depth of feeling and thought. The *Mathnawi* is no doubt very disjointed; the stories follow one another in no apparent order. But it is filled with lyrical inspiration. Each small tale may be read separately, and one cannot help but be impressed with its succinctness.

As a philosopher, Rumi is less original than as a poet. His subject is Sufism, expressed with glowing enthusiasm. But it is not systematically expounded, and lyrical fervor seems to run rampant. But it can be said that just as Ibn Arabi summed up and gathered into a single system all that had been said on mysticism in Arabic before him, so Rumi in his famous *Mathnawi* comes the closest to this in Persian.

As with other Sufi poets, many Neoplatonic ideas abound in Rumi's writing. Ties to Christian mysticism can also be found. But in the last analysis, Rumi was a Moslem of very special interest. He was philanthropic and strongly emotional, and his writings seem easily to fit in with the excitement of the dance of the whirling dervishes.

Further Reading

Rumi is listed in the Asia study guide (I, B, 3, e). Other 13th-century Persian literary figures were SADI and ATTAR.

A. J. Arberry's translation of Rumi's *Mathnawi* (2 vols., 1961–1963) contains short but useful introductions. Arberry also translated the *Discourses of Rumi* (1961) and *The Mystical Poems of Rumi* (1968), both with biographical introduction.

Biographical studies of Rumi are Afzal Iqbal, *The Life and Work of Muhammad Jalal-ud-Din* (1956; 2d rev. ed. 1964), and A. Reza Arasteh, *Rumi, the Persian: Rebirth in Creativity and Love* (1965), an interesting psychological study. Also reliable is Khalifal Abdul-Hakim, *The Metaphysics of Rumi* (1933), a critical sketch. A classic background work is Edward G. Browne, *A Literary History of Persia* (2 vols., 1902–1906). For a comprehensive discussion of the Sufi thought of Rumi see A. J. Arberry, *Sufism: An Account of the Mystics of Islam* (1950), and Idries Shah, *The Sufis* (1964).

RUNDSTEDT / By Diethelm Prowe

Field marshal Karl Rudolf Gerd von Rundstedt (1875–1953), the senior German field commander in World War II, directed the German war effort on the Western front from 1942 to 1945.

Gerd von Rundstedt (pronounced roŏnt′shtĕt) was born on Dec. 12, 1875, in Aschersleben near Magdeburg. His family was of old Prussian nobility with a long military tradition dating back to the Middle Ages. His father was a general, and his brother was a major. Rundstedt received all of his education in military schools, and in 1891 he entered the Prussian infantry. In 1906 he received his first general-staff assignment.

In World War I Rundstedt took part in the Battle of the Marne in the autumn of 1914, and then he alternately served on the Eastern and Western fronts in army corps chief of staff positions. By the end of the war he had become the chief of staff of the 15th Army Corps with the rank of major. From 1919 to 1932 Rundstedt held several staff and command positions related to the secret rearmament of Germany. During the time of troubles preceding the take-over of Adolf Hitler, he held, as a lieutenant colonel, the politically sensitive position of commander of the Berlin Military District. In this capacity in July 1932 he executed the eviction of the duly elected Social Democratic government of Prussia on the order of the German chancellor, Franz von Papen. A few weeks later Rundstedt advanced to commander in chief of the entire Army Group I (Berlin and central Germany).

During his term as Army Group I commander in chief, Rundstedt did much to improve and reform the infantry, most notably through the reequipment and reorganization of infantry commands into small, self-sufficient units, or *Einheiten*. By 1938 he had become increasingly alarmed at Hitler's policies toward the general staff and at the growing war preparations, and he expressed these concerns by signing an officers' petition circulated by the chief of the general staff, Gen. Ludwig Beck. In October 1938 Rundstedt asked for and obtained permission to retire.

Even before the outbreak of World War II, however, Rundstedt was recalled from retirement. In the invasion of Poland (1939), he commanded the group of German armies in the south that swept through Galicia toward Warsaw with brilliant precision. In the German attack on France in May 1940, Rundstedt led the vital drive of the centrally located Army Group A through the Ardennes and behind the French fortifications of the Maginot Line.

Gerd von Rundstedt, photographed in 1938. (National Archives, Washington, D.C.)

He was rewarded for his brilliant success with a promotion to the rank of field marshal on July 19, 1940. In the summer of 1941, Rundstedt commanded the southern group of German armies in their rapid advance into Russia. He overwhelmed the army of Marshal Semyon M. Budyenny on the southern flank of the Soviets and subsequently occupied the mineral-rich Ukraine. Once again, however, the field marshal expressed disagreement with Hitler's plans and demanded a general retreat of his forces to the Mius Line. In the ensuing quarrel, Rundstedt offered his resignation, which was accepted in December 1941.

Following the entry of the United States into the war in December 1941 and the consequent increase in the likelihood of an Allied invasion of the Continent, Hitler once again turned to Rundstedt, and on March 1, 1942, Hitler appointed him commander in chief West. After the sinking of the French navy in November, Hitler added military commander of France to Rundstedt's titles. In this capacity Rundstedt prepared French defenses against an Allied invasion, which, however, he was unable to prevent. After the landing on June 6, 1944, Rundstedt withdrew German troops to the Seine River, which brought his dismissal and replacement on July 6. After his successor failed to reverse the situation and committed suicide, Rundstedt once again returned to the position of commander in chief West in September. In the following months he oversaw the declining fortunes of the German defense and watched with great consternation as Hitler's last gamble, the Ardennes offensive (Battle of the Bulge), failed in December 1944.

Thoroughly disenchanted and quite ill, Rundstedt entered final retirement on March 13, 1945. He was captured by American troops in Bavaria on May 1 and was turned over to the British for trial. Because of Rundstedt's poor health, his trial never took place, and on May 26, 1946, he was released from a British military hospital. He died in Hanover on Feb. 24, 1953.

Further Reading

Gerd von Rundstedt is listed in the European History study guide (XI, P, 1, a). Erwin ROMMEL also served as a field marshal under Adolf HITLER.

The only major biographical source on the field marshal is the work of an admiring friend, Gen. Guenter von Blumentritt, *Von Rundstedt: The Soldier and the Man*, translated by Cuthbert Reavely (1952). A section on Rundstedt is in Siegfried Westphal, *The German Army in the West* (1951).

RURIK / By Josef Anderle

The legendary Norman warrior Rurik (died ca. 873) was the founder of the first Russian state and of the dynasty that ruled in Russia until the death of Feodor I in 1598.

According to the first Russian annals, the *Primary Chronicle*, Rurik (pronounced roo′rĭk) was a Scandinavian "from the tribe of the Rus" whom the people of Novgorod invited in 862 to assume rule over them, as they had been unable to govern themselves. Accompanied by his family and retinue, Rurik settled in Novgorod, and his brothers took control of adjacent regions. The area under their authority came to be called "the land of the Rus" and eventually Rus'. The descendants of Rurik continued to rule over this region following his death about 873.

Although this account of the origins of the first Russian state and dynasty enjoyed considerable credibility among older historians, modern scholars no longer accept it in its entirety and even question the actual existence of Rurik. The story of Rurik contains inconsistencies and information that cannot be confirmed from other sources. The origin of the name Rus' has never been satisfactorily explained. Scholars are certain only that the Scandinavians frequently invaded and migrated into Russia in the 9th century and that the origin of the names of early Russian princes, including the name Rurik, derives from the Normans. Though possibly reflecting earlier records or legends that have not been preserved, the *Primary Chronicle* has obviously used the story of Rurik to explain, justify, and antedate the rule of the Rurik dynasty, during which the chronicle was written and compiled (early 12th century).

The notion of Rurik's having been invited to rule in

An iron helmet found in the grave of a Viking warrior at Vendel in central Sweden. The helmet, which dates from about 200 years before the time of Rurik, is decorated with bronzework. (Antikvarisk-Topografiska Arkivet)

Russia seems in particular to be a product of such efforts. The original Rurik, if one existed at all, might have been one of the Norman chieftains who went to Russia from Scandinavia either as conquerors or as hirelings of local communities in which they often subsequently usurped power. At best, Rurik might have been invited to Novgorod as an auxiliary to one of several local parties competing for power. The establishment of his own power there under these circumstances was probably achieved through usurpation.

Further Reading

Rurik is listed in the European History study guide (I, J, 2, f; I, K, 1). VLADIMIR I, a member of the dynasty, was converted to Christianity about 988 and made it the state religion.

A standard translation of the *Primary Chronicle*, with a balanced commentary on its contents, is *The Russian Primary Chronicle: Laurentian Text*, edited and translated by Samuel Hazzard Cross and Olgerd P. Sherbowitz-Wetzor (1953). Compare with N. K. Chadwick, *The Beginnings of Russian History: An Enquiry into Sources* (1946). Varying interpretations of these events are reflected in a number of works on old Russia: Vilhelm Thomsen, *The Relations between Ancient Russia and Scandinavia and the Origin of the Russian State* (1877);

V. O. Kliuchevskii, *A Russian History*, vol. 1 (1911); George Vernadsky and Michael Karpovich, *A History of Russia*, vol. 1 (1943); and Boris D. Grekov, *Kiev Rus* (trans. 1959).

B. RUSH / By Monte A. Calvert

Benjamin Rush (1745–1813), physician, patriot, and humanitarian, represented the epitome of the versatile, wide-ranging physician in America. He insisted on a theoretical structure for medical practice.

Benjamin Rush was born on Dec. 24, 1745, on a plantation at Byberry near Philadelphia. He graduated in 1760 from the College of New Jersey (now Princeton) and then studied medicine in Philadelphia until 1766. He completed his medical education at the University of Edinburgh, Scotland. Here he studied under many of the greatest medical teachers of the time, most notably William Cullen, proponent of the concept of rational rather than empirical medical systems. Rush received his doctorate in 1768, then returned to Philadelphia.

Benjamin Rush. (National Library of Medicine, Bethesda, Md.)

Rush practiced medicine and was soon made the first professor of chemistry in America at the College of Philadelphia. He joined the American Philosophical Society and became a permanent part of Philadelphia's scientific and medical circle, though his outspoken views made as many enemies as friends. In 1774 he helped organize the Pennsylvania Society for Promoting the Abolition of Slavery and became an outspoken defender of American rights in the brewing quarrel with Great Britain. In 1775 Rush suggested that Thomas Paine write a tract in favor of American independence under the title *Common Sense*; Paine did and the pamphlet was very influential in turning public opinion toward independence. Rush continued to be active in the American independence movement, was a member of the Continental Congress, and signed the Declaration of Independence.

Appointed surgeon general of the armies of the Middle Department in 1777, Rush found the medical services disorganized and mounted an attack on William Shippen, the director general of medical services. When George Washington upheld Shippen, Rush resigned and resumed his medical practice. He began delivering lectures at the University of the State of Pennsylvania in 1780 and joined the staff of the Pennsylvania Hospital in 1783. By 1789 he was professor of theory and practice in the university. He became professor of the institutes of medicine and clinical practice in the University of Pennsylvania in 1792 and professor of theory and practice in 1796. From this base he developed a wide following.

Rush's great reputation as a teacher made him appear a more important innovator than he was. His major contribution was to introduce Cullen's concept of a rationally deduced medical system to replace empirical folk practice. He also supported the theory of John Brown of Edinburgh proposing a single cause for all disease—imbalance of the nervous energies. According to this theory, all illness was attributable to excesses or deficiencies in nervous energies; moderation in all things was the preventive medicine, but once illness occurred, either bleeding or purging was necessary. Rush was a zealot on bleeding and in extreme cases would remove as much as four-fifths of a patient's blood. His excesses in this brought much criticism, but his emphasis on moderation as a preventive was popular. He was thus led to advocate temperance, and he is sometimes regarded as the founder of the temperance movement in America.

Rush also became interested in the plight of the mentally ill and the poor, established the first free dispensary in the United States, and campaigned against public and capital punishment and for general penal reform. He also concerned himself with education, advocating education for women, less emphasis on classics and more on utilitarian subjects, and a national educational system capped by a national university. His ideas were behind the founding of Dickinson College in 1783.

The test of Rush's medical theories came during the yellow fever epidemic of 1793. His initial theory that the epidemic was partly caused by poor sanitation resulted in ostracism by fellow physicians. Rush bravely stayed in Philadelphia to treat yellow fever victims, while many other medical men fled. His treatment was bleeding, and he was charged with causing many more deaths than he prevented. Although Rush held to his theory, he was either unwilling or simply unable to keep records so that the theory could be checked against fact. However, his published accounts of the epidemic, especially his suggestion that poor sanitation was an ultimate cause, attracted attention in Europe.

Rush also did pioneering work relating dentistry to physiology and was influential in founding veterinary medicine in America. Both fields had been considered beneath the dignity of the professional. His observations on the mentally ill seem to presage modern developments in psychoanalytic theory, especially his *Medical Inquiries and Observations on the Diseases of the Mind* (1812).

Rush's insistence on a rational, systematic body of knowledge for the medical profession certainly helped set the stage for the later medical revolution in America. He died in Philadelphia on April 19, 1813.

Further Reading

Benjamin Rush is listed in the Science study guide (V, G, 3). Benjamin WATERHOUSE was the first American physician to establish inoculation as a general practice.

Primary sources on Rush include *The Autobiography of Benjamin Rush*, edited by George W. Corner (1948); Rush's *Letters*, edited by L. H. Butterfield (1951); and John A. Schutz and Douglass Adair, eds., *The Spur of Fame: Dialogues of John Adams and Benjamin Rush* (1966). Although several books have been written about Rush, there is no definitive study. The only fully documented scholarly work is Nathan G. Goodman, *Benjamin Rush: Physician and Citizen* (1934). Carl A. L. Binger, *Revolutionary Doctor: Benjamin Rush* (1966), is fairly sound. A popularized work is Sarah R. Riedman and Clarence C. Green, *Benjamin Rush* (1964). For general background see Daniel J. Boorstin, *The Lost World of Thomas Jefferson* (1948), and Brooke Hindle, *The Pursuit of Science in Revolutionary America, 1735–1789* (1956).

✳   ✳   ✳

W. **RUSH** / By William Gerdts

William Rush (1756–1833) was the most significant American sculptor to emerge from the folk-art and figurehead carving tradition of the early years of the republic.

William Rush was born in Philadelphia. His father was a ship carpenter, and as a boy William occupied himself by carving ship models. He was apprenticed to learn the trade of carving, probably before the Revolution; his earliest known commissions for figureheads date from about 1790. As time went on, Rush

William Rush, a life-size self-portrait bust.
(Pennsylvania Academy of Fine Arts, Philadelphia)

became famous as a carver, and he employed a number of apprentices. He was the only sculptor to become one of the founders, in 1794, of the short-lived Columbianum, the first art organization in America; and he was also one of the first directors of the Pennsylvania Academy of Fine Arts.

Probably because of his superior skill at figurehead carving, Rush was able to advance to a position beyond that of purely artisan work, and he received a number of significant commissions in the realm of "pure" sculpture. His first important works were the figures *Comedy* and *Tragedy* (1808) for the Chestnut Street Theater in Philadelphia. The following year he was commissioned to create what was probably his best-known sculpture, the *Water Nymph and Bittern.* In 1824, on the occasion of Lafayette's triumphal tour of the United States, Rush not only carved his portrait but also executed two monumental sculptures, *Wisdom* and *Justice,* which were placed atop a Philadelphia triumphal arch erected in Lafayette's honor. His last major works were two reclining figures, *Schuylkill River Chained* and *Schuylkill River Freed* (ca. 1828).

Rush executed a number of portraits. His subjects included Benjamin Rush, George Washington, Oliver Hazard Perry, Andrew Jackson, and Winfield Scott. Two of his finest works were portraits of himself and of his daughter, Elizabeth.

Rush was primarily a woodcarver, and the deep undercutting, broad planes, and general columnar form of many of his statues bear witness to his respect for his medium. He never worked in marble. Some of his portrait busts exist in plaster and some in terra-cotta, mediums in which he was also proficient. Stylistically, he was closer to the decorative rococo tradition of the 18th century than to the prevailing neoclassicism of his own time. Yet his allegories were not unlike those carved by European artists of his day, and his *Schuylkill River Chained* certainly relates to statues of classical river gods. While some critics have claimed that Rush was the first American sculptor, he really represents the apogee of the artisan tradition of woodcarving, for American sculpture would develop in the future along the lines of neoclassic marble carving.

Further Reading

William Rush is listed in the Art study guide (IV, B, 2). Hiram POWERS was the foremost American neoclassic sculptor of the next generation.

A biographical study of Rush is Henri Marceau, *William Rush, 1756–1833: The First Native American Sculptor* (1937).

RUSKIN / By William Coles

The English critic and social theorist John Ruskin (1819–1900) more than any other man shaped the esthetic values and tastes of Victorian England. His writings combine enormous sensitivity and human compassion with a burning zeal for moral value.

John Ruskin's principal insight was that art is an expression of the values of a society. Though he sometimes applied this insight in a narrow—even a bigoted—way, it nevertheless gave him an almost messianic sense of the significance of art to the spiritual well-being of a nation. Ruskin awakened an age of rapid change, uncertain taste, and frequently shoddy workmanship to the meaning of art. But because art was for Ruskin the evidence of society's underlying state of being, he gradually turned his attention, with a reformer's zeal, more and more from art to the transformation of society itself. Though his prose tracts were much abused, they were important and influential contributions to radical criticism of the dominant social and political philosophy of the age. Ruskin's art criticism found the most likely focus to interest a people whose leading concerns were more moral than esthetic.

Ruskin was born on Feb. 8, 1819, in London. His parents were of Scottish descent and were first cousins. His father was a well-to-do wine merchant with a fondness for art. His mother was stern and devout. Both parents lavished attention and supervision on their only child, recognizing his precociousness, but Ruskin's childhood was isolated and his education irregular. He was encouraged in reading, however, and received some instruction in art. In 1837 Ruskin matriculated at Christ Church, Oxford, but his studies were interrupted by ill health and consequent travel abroad so that he did not receive his degree until 1842.

"Modern Painters"

Ruskin had early begun to write both poetry and prose, and by the time he left Oxford he had already published articles on architecture and on other subjects. After leaving Oxford, he undertook his first major work, *Modern Painters*; it testified to his love of nature, especially of Alpine scenery, and to his reverence for J. M. W. Turner as the supreme modern interpreter of "truth" in landscape. The first volume of *Modern Painters*, published anonymously in 1843, was a success with the discerning public, but it was attacked by professionals, who spotted the author's tendency to dogmatize on an insufficient foundation of experience and technical study. Ruskin then set about to remedy his deficiencies through a first-hand study of the Italian painters, particularly those of the Florentine and Venetian schools. Ruskin's Italian tour of 1845 culminated in his discovery of Tintoretto, who, together with Fra Angelico, displaced Turner to become the heroes of volume 2 of *Modern Painters* (1846).

In 1848 Ruskin married Euphemia Chalmers Gray. The parents of the bridal couple were old friends, and the match was arranged without any bond of deep affection on either side. Ruskin and his bride honeymooned in Normandy, where he studied the Gothic cathedrals. The pair, unfortunately, were not suited to one another, and the marriage was annulled in 1854. Euphemia Ruskin had by then fallen in love with the painter John Everett Millais, whom she subsequently married.

Architectural Criticism

The weight of Ruskin's interest had now shifted to architecture as the most public of the arts. If, as Ruskin thought, all art expresses the spirit of its maker, architecture then most fully expresses the whole spirit of a people. His religious emphasis was implicit in the title of his next book, *The Seven Lamps of Architecture* (1849), as well as in his emphasis upon "truth of expression" in materials and in structure. This book and its successor, *The Stones of Venice* (1851–1853), a great Protestant prose epic of the decline and fall of the Venetian Republic, became the bibles of the Victorian Gothic revival. Ruskin's style in this period was powerfully evocative and readily expanded into sermonic flourishes that cloaked many historical inaccuracies. Once again professionals, though fascinated by his works, were moved to demur on many points where theory had replaced a concrete knowledge of the facts of architectural practice. Perhaps Ruskin's most enduring contribution to the development of modern style was his hostility to classicism. He himself was too devoted to ornament and too hostile both to the machine and to standardized construction ever to figure as a grandfather of functionalism. However, his celebrated chapter on the nature of Gothic in *The Stones of Venice* can be taken as the main testament of Victorian esthetic values.

Social Criticism

Ruskin had interrupted the composition of *Modern Painters* for his architectural studies. He now returned to the earlier work, completing it with volumes 3 and 4 in 1856 and volume 5 in 1860. He also lectured on art and defended the Pre-Raphaelites, but his concerns were inevitably drifting further toward social criticism as a way of transforming society. In reality, he had dropped the integument of art from his sermons, and following the lead of Thomas Carlyle, he began to inveigh directly against the values of the political economists. The year 1860 marks the official turning point in his interests, for Ruskin published a series of social essays in the *Cornhill Magazine* that he later collected as *Unto This Last*. Ruskin's attack on the dehumanized ethic of modern industrial capitalism drew a bitter response from readers, but it influenced the thinking of many reformers in the developing Labour movement.

Another series of articles on economic subjects, published in *Fraser's Magazine* (1862–1863) and collected as *Munera pulveris* (1872), drew a similar outcry from the public. Ruskin now began to lecture frequently, and he later published two collections derived from his lectures, *Sesame and Lilies* (1865) and *The Crown of Wild Olive* (1866). Both volumes circulated widely and brought him a popular following. In 1869 Ruskin was appointed the first Slade professor of art at Oxford, a post that he held with some interruption until 1885. These

Art Criticism, a cartoon depicting an esthetic John Ruskin extolling the virtues of "High Art." The flowers he is scattering bear the names of his books. (Radio Times Hulton Picture Library)

J. M. W. Turner's painting Grand Canal of Venice, *in the National Gallery, London, suggests two of Ruskin's most important critical writings:* Modern Painters *and* The Stones of Venice. *Ruskin began the first work as a defense of Turner's art, while in the second he discussed Venetian architecture. (Photo Anderson-Viollet)*

years, however, were turbulent and troublesome for Ruskin. His religious faith had been undermined, and he was tormented by frustrated love for Rose LaTouche, a girl 30 years his junior, whom he had first met when she was a child.

Last Years

On the death of his father Ruskin became independently wealthy. The variety and fever of his activities were an indication of his deeply disturbed condition. In 1871 he began to publish *Fors clavigera*, a periodical that lasted until 1884. An attack on James McNeill Whistler in *Fors* in 1887 occasioned a celebrated libel suit which was decided against Ruskin. He also endowed and led a variety of welfare and socialist schemes, thereby consuming most of his inheritance. In 1878 Ruskin suffered his first clear attack of mental illness. Seizures recurred until 1888, when he fell victim to a severe mental breakdown which confined him to his house at Brantwood in the Lake District until his death. In lucid intervals between 1885 and 1889 Ruskin worked on his unfinished autobiography, *Praeterita*, one of the most moving and revealing of his works. He died on Jan. 20, 1900.

Further Reading

John Ruskin is listed in the Literature study guide (II, H, 1, a) and the Social Sciences study guide (VI, A, 1; VI, B, 1). His contemporary Walter PATER was also a leading critic.

The standard biography of Ruskin is E. T. Cook, *The Life of John Ruskin* (2 vols., 1911). Important, more recent works are Derrick Leon, *Ruskin: The Great Victorian* (1949), and Joan Evans, *John Ruskin* (1954). The best introductions to Ruskin's thought and work are R. H. Wilenski, *John Ruskin: An Introduction to Further Study of His Life and Work* (1933), and John D. Rosenberg, *The Darkening Glass: A Portrait of Genius* (1961). The chapter on Ruskin in Graham Hough, *The Last Romantics* (1947), is very helpful. For intellectual and social background see G. M. Young, *Victorian England: Portrait of an Age* (1936; 2d ed. 1953), and Jerome Hamilton Buckley, *The Victorian Temper* (1951).

LORD RUSSELL / By Norbert J. Gossman

The English statesman John Russell, 1st Earl Russell of Kingston Russell (1792–1878), was the author of the Great Reform Bill of 1832 and one of the founders of the British Liberal party.

John Russell was born on Aug. 18, 1792, in London. He was the third son of the 6th Duke of Bedford. Russell was educated primarily by private tutors and at Edinburgh University.

Russell's parliamentary career began in 1813, when he was elected Whig member of Parliament for Tavistock. In poor health during his early parliamentary career, Russell rarely spoke in the Commons. His vanity was great, and he was easily disturbed by criticism. But he was a man of courage and conviction. In the 1820s he emerged as a champion of parliamentary reform and religious toleration. He worked for repeal of the Test and Corporation Acts and supported Catholic emancipation in 1829.

Russell was largely responsible for preparing the first Reform Bill and introduced it in the Commons in March 1831; the bill passed the Lords in June 1832. Russell was a member of the Whig Cabinets of Lords Grey and Melbourne in the 1830s, first as home secretary and then as secretary for war and the colonies (1839–1841). The Municipal Corporation Act of 1835, which expanded the electorate for town councils, was one of his contributions.

After the fall of Sir Robert Peel's second ministry in 1846 Russell became prime minister. He held this office for the next 6 years (1846–1852). During this period he faced the Great Famine in Ireland, but his relief measures were too cautious to succeed. The Ten Hours Act of 1847 was a turning point in the history of labor legislation. Russell sympathized with the popular outcry against the papal bull that restored a Roman Catholic hierarchy in

England in 1850, and he sponsored the Ecclesiastical Titles Bill (1851), which forbade the assumption by Roman Catholic clergy of titles within the United Kingdom. A more liberal attitude characterized his actions in imperial affairs. The Australian Colonies Act of 1850 extended self-government to New South Wales.

Lord Palmerston was the most controversial figure in the Russell Cabinet, and relations between the two were frequently strained. Palmerston was dismissed by Russell in December 1851 for having conveyed to the French ambassador Russell's approval of Louis Napoleon's coup d'etat. Two months later, however, Palmerston had his revenge when he successfully led the opposition in defeating the government's Militia Bill, and Russell resigned in 1852.

Russell served as foreign secretary for a few months in 1852–1853 in Lord Aberdeen's coalition and as colonial secretary for 5 months in Palmerston's Cabinet in 1855. He returned to the Foreign Office 4 years later in the second Palmerston ministry (1859–1865) and did much to preserve British neutrality during the American Civil War. Russell became prime minister for a second time in 1865, but he resigned the following year in a dispute over the specifics of a second Reform Bill. He then retired to a private life of writing, and he died on May 28, 1878.

Russell was known as "Finality Jack" to the British working classes, as one who opposed all further reform after 1832. This, however, was not true. He was active in the reform movement to the end of his life, and he helped to move the Whigs toward the new Liberal party under his immediate successor as party leader, William Gladstone.

Further Reading

Lord Russell is listed in the European History study guide (VIII, A, 1, b). He worked with Lord PALMERSTON. William GLADSTONE also played a large role in the Liberal party during this period.

The standard biography of Russell is Spencer Walpole, *Life of Lord John Russell* (2 vols., 1889; repr. 1968). A more recent, concise study is A. Wyatt Tilby, *Lord John Russell: A Study in Civil and Religious Liberty* (1930). Norman Gash, *Politics in the Age of Peel* (1953), is a penetrating study of the machinery of politics during the period of Russell's activities.

Lord Russell, a portrait by George Frederick Watts. (National Portrait Gallery, London)

B. **RUSSELL** / By Daniel O'Connor

The British mathematician, philosopher, and social reformer Bertrand Arthur William Russell, 3d Earl Russell (1872–1970), made original and decisive contributions to logic and mathematics and wrote with distinction in all fields of philosophy.

Bertrand Russell was born at Ravenscroft, Monmouthshire, Wales, on May 18, 1872, into an aristocratic family with many distinguished and some eccentric members. By the time he was 4 years old, his parents were dead, and his paternal grandparents, overturning his parents' will specifying that the child be reared by two atheist friends, became his guardians. Russell's grandfather, Lord John Russell, twice prime minister to Queen Victoria, died 3 years later, and young Bertrand was left in the care of his grandmother, a lady of strict puritanical moral views who nevertheless gave him great affection and "that feeling of safety that children need."

Early Life and Education

Russell's early education was provided at home by tutors, and in retrospect he found his childhood a happy one. In adolescence, however, he experienced intense loneliness, relieved by "one of the great events of my life, as dazzling as first love." His brother introduced him to the *Elements* of Euclid. "I had not imagined there was anything so delicious in the world. From that moment until [Alfred North] Whitehead and I finished *Principia Mathematica*, when I was 38, mathematics was my chief interest and my chief source of happiness."

At Trinity College

When he was 18 years old, Russell entered Trinity College, Cambridge. Alfred North Whitehead was the first to sense Russell's extraordinary talent, and he quickly un-

Bertrand Russell in 1951. (Radio Times Hulton Picture Library)

dertook to sponsor Russell among the Cambridge literati. In his second year at Cambridge Russell was elected to the Apostles, a weekly discussion group that since 1820 has included among its members many of the people of intellectual eminence at Cambridge. There he met and formed close friendships with, among others, G. Lowes Dickinson, G. E. Moore, and John McTaggart, and a little later with John Maynard Keynes and Lytton Strachey. Of his generation at Cambridge, Russell later wrote, "We believed in ordered progress by means of politics and free discussion."

After graduation Russell stayed on at Cambridge as a fellow of Trinity College and lecturer in philosophy. In 1916 he was dismissed because of a scandal over his conviction and fine for writing about the case of a conscientious objector in World War I. His association with Cambridge meant a great deal to Russell, and he was deeply wounded by its abrupt termination.

First Marriage and Mathematical Writings

In 1894, after overcoming the opposition of his family, Russell married an American girl, Alys Pearsall Smith. The first years of their marriage were largely spent traveling in Europe and in the United States, where Russell gave some lectures. From this period his first book, comprising a set of lectures on German socialism, and his fellowship dissertation, *An Essay on the Foundations of Geometry*, date. The latter work established Russell's reputation. The year 1900 was another turning point for Russell, for at the International Congress of Philosophy, he met Giuseppe Peano, the Italian mathematical theorist, and immediately saw the significance of Peano's work. Enormously stimulated, he began to rethink his own ideas about the fundamental notions of mathematics, and during the fall of 1900 he finished most of his first major work, *The Principles of Mathematics*. "Intellectually," he later wrote, "this was the highest point of my life."

A few years later Russell's views on mathematics deepened further, and he became "reluctantly convinced" that mathematics consists of tautologies. With Whitehead he undertook the enormous project of trying to show that mathematics—in particular, arithmetic, but in principle, all mathematics—was an extension of logic, that no underived concepts and no unproved assumptions need be introduced other than those of pure logic. The results were published as *Principia Mathematica* in three volumes (1910–1913). Russell and Whitehead each had to put up £50 toward publication costs. In spite of mistakes and later improvements, the work remains a landmark in the history of mathematics.

While serving a 6-month prison term in 1918 for writing an article about the British government and the American army that was judged libelous, Russell wrote his *Introduction to Mathematical Philosophy*. But Russell's interest was deflected from these abstract topics by the "vast suffering" caused by World War I; in the face of this tragedy his earlier work now seemed to him "thin and rather trivial." Increasingly thereafter, Russell's work showed a marked reformist bent. Seldom, indeed, has a

Bertrand Russell addressing a rally protesting the hydrogen bomb. The rally, in Trafalgar Square, climaxed a 1960 march of 100 ban-the-bomb demonstrators from Edinburgh to London. (United Press International Photo)

philosopher shown such a sense of social responsibility.

Theory of Knowledge and Metaphysics

Russell's views in epistemology and metaphysics, though influential, show less originality than his work on logic and on social questions. His views in these fields constitute, in effect, refinements or further developments in the tradition of British empiricism. Following a principle that he called the supreme maxim in scientific philosophy, "Wherever possible substitute constructions out of known entities for inferences to unknown entities," Russell argued that one's own private sense-data were the things most directly known. In *Our Knowledge of the External World* Russell tried to show that physical objects are logical constructions out of actual and possible sense-data. In his *Analysis of Mind* (1921) Russell went still further to argue that from sense-data, regarded as neutral elements, one can construct both mind and matter.

In his *Inquiry into Meaning and Truth* and *Human Knowledge: Its Scope and Limits*, Russell offered provocative opinions about the ways truth claims can be assessed, and he outlined a set of principles for use in defending the validity of inductive reasoning.

Travel and Controversy

After World War I Russell visited China and the Soviet Union. Initially sympathetic to the Bolshevik Revolution, he quickly saw its threat to the value he prized above all others—liberty—and he wrote a book, *The Practice and Theory of Bolshevism*, that proved prophetic regarding the developing course of the Russian Revolution. Russell also stood three times for election to Parliament, each time unsuccessfully.

In 1927, with his second wife, Dora, Russell founded a progressive school at Beacon Hill. There he tested the educational theories propounded in his books *Education Especially in Early Childhood* and *Education and the Social Order* (1932).

In the late 1930s Russell lectured frequently in the United States, and in 1940 he was appointed to teach at the College of the City of New York. Immediately he was subjected to a barrage of criticism in the American press by clergymen and city officials. These worthies had been offended by Russell's advocacy, in *Marriage and Morals* (1929), of temporary marriages for college students. A New York Supreme Court judge voided Russell's appointment on the grounds that he was an alien and an advocate of sexual immorality.

In the wake of this scandal Russell was offered a lectureship by the Barnes Foundation in Merion, Pa. The lectures prepared for this position formed the basis of Russell's *History of Western Philosophy* (1945), perhaps his most widely circulated book. However, in 1943 Russell was summarily dismissed from his Barnes post under circumstances that enabled him to bring a successful suit for redress of grievances.

Radical Sage

In 1944 Russell returned to England and was reelected a fellow of Trinity College, Cambridge. Honors began to pour in upon him. He was made an honorary fellow of the British Academy in 1949, and in the same year he received the Order of Merit. In 1950 Russell won the Nobel Prize for literature, being cited for "his many-sided and significant writings, in which he appeared as the champion of humanity and freedom of thought."

Russell had abandoned his pacifism at the outset of

World War II, but immediately thereafter he resumed his activities in the peace movement. He led the "Ban the Bomb" fight in England, taking part in a sit-down demonstration at the age of 89, for which he served a 7-day jail sentence. Russell tried to intervene in the Cuban missile crisis, and he vigorously opposed American involvement in Vietnam.

Russell was an essentially shy man, yet brilliant and witty in conversation. He had a remarkable capacity for friendship. Though unhappy in his first three marriages, he finally found, late in life, "ecstasy and peace" in his fourth marriage, to Edith Finch in 1952. Although frail in appearance, he was vigorous and active throughout most of his life, embroiled in social and political controversies to the very end. He died at Penrhyndendraeth, Wales, on Feb. 2, 1970.

Further Reading

Bertrand Russell is listed in the Philosophy study guide (VII, B; VII, F), the Science study guide (VII, A, 1), and the Literature study guide (II, J, 1, a). He collaborated with Alfred North WHITEHEAD and shared with G. E. MOORE and Ludwig WITTGENSTEIN an interest in logic and linguistic analysis.

Perhaps the most useful introduction to Russell's work is his *Basic Writings, 1903–1959*, edited by Robert E. Egner and Lester E. Dennon (1961), and his *My Philosophical Development* (1959). The most interesting accounts of his life are by Russell himself: a half-dozen earlier autobiographical essays were crowned by his *The Autobiography of Bertrand Russell* (3 vols., 1967–1969). Biographies include Alan T. Wood, *Bertrand Russell: The Passionate Sceptic* (1957), and Herbert Gottschalk, *Bertrand Russell: A Life* (1965). Russell published a great deal, and critical commentary on his work is considerable. An excellent bibliography is in Paul Schilpp, ed., *The Philosophy of Bertrand Russell* (1944; rev. ed., 2 vols., 1963), which also includes a large number of critical essays by eminent authors together with Russell's replies.

C. E. **RUSSELL** / By Louis Filler

Charles Edward Russell (1860–1941), American writer and reformer, was a leading Socialist and muckraker.

Charles Edward Russell was born in Davenport, Iowa, on Sept. 25, 1860, the son of the abolitionist editor of the *Davenport Gazette*. Charles learned newspaper skills and attended the St. Johnsbury (Vt.) Academy, from which he graduated in 1881. He then returned to become the *Gazette*'s managing editor. He later became an editor in Minneapolis and Detroit and then moved on to New York City. In 1894 he was

Charles Edward Russell. (Radio Times Hulton Picture Library)

city editor of Joseph Pulitzer's *World* and then a Hearst editor in New York and Chicago.

During his newspaper years Russell was interested in democratic politics; in Populist, single-tax, and other causes; and in music, theater, and poetry. In 1902 his health broke, and he left newspaper work. After traveling abroad, he returned to begin a literary career. His first book, *Such Stuff as Dreams* (1902), was a volume of verses. *Thomas Chatterton: The Marvelous Boy* (1908) retraced the writings and career of the English poet.

Meanwhile a literature of protest (muckraking) had appeared on the American scene, and Russell found himself part of it. *The Greatest Trust in the World* (1905) muckraked the beef trust in Chicago. In the popular magazines he effectively exposed a wide range of social evils, from New York church-owned slums to southern prison camps. *The Uprising of the Many* (1907) and *Lawless Wealth* (1908) summed up some of the reasons why he joined the Socialist party. His writings earned him a national reputation. He campaigned for governor, mayor, and U.S. senator in New York State. In 1916 he declined the Socialist party's presidential nomination.

Russell sided with the Allied Powers during World War I and was expelled from the Socialist party. An admirer of Woodrow Wilson, he became a member in 1917 of the American diplomatic mission to revolutionary Russia.

Unchained Russia (1918), *After the Whirlwind* (1919), and *Bolshevism and the United States* (1919) were earnest but perishable efforts to interpret the revolution. *The Story of the Non-partisan League* (1920) and *The Outlook for the Philippines* (1922) were Russell's efforts to rejoin the reform movement. As early as 1912, he had begun his memoirs in *The Passing Show. Julia Marlowe: Her Life and Art* (1926) was an outgrowth of his interest in the arts, as was *The American Orchestra and Theodore Thomas* (1927), for which he won the Pulitzer Prize.

Russell was eventually reconciled with the right wing of the Socialist party. He was a member of Clarence Darrow's National Recovery Administration Review Board and a staunch defender of oppressed people. He died in Washington, D.C., on April 23, 1941.

Further Reading

Charles Edward Russell is listed in the American History study guide (VIII, F, 4, e). Daniel DE LEON was a leading American Socialist at this time.

Russell's autobiography, *Bare Hands and Stone Walls: Some Recollections of a Sideline Reformer* (1933), throws light on his causes and attitudes. He figures significantly in Louis Filler, *Crusaders for American Liberalism* (1939; new ed. 1950).

C. M. **RUSSELL** / By Abraham A. Davidson

Charles Marion Russell (1864–1926), American painter, left one of the most extensive and accurate pictorial records of the Old West.

Charles Marion Russell was born on March 19, 1864, in St. Louis, Mo., to a comfortable family. As he was hard to control, his parents sent him to military school in Burlington, N.J. In 1880 he left for Montana and for the next 12 years worked as a sheepherder and cowpuncher. In 1888 he spent 6 months with the Blood Indians in the Northwest Territory. All the while, he drew and painted, seldom selling his work, more often giving it away.

Starting in 1890–1891 in Lewiston, Mont., Russell began to sell his paintings; he also executed a mural for a bank there for which he received $25—the most money he had ever earned for a single work. In 1891 a bartender in Great Falls, Mont., contracted for all of Russell's work. The following year he ceased riding the range.

In 1896 Russell married, and in 1903 he established his studio in Great Falls. That year he went to New York City to sell some of his paintings. As a result of the trip, his pictures were published in *McClure's, Leslie's Illustrated Weekly*, and other magazines. By 1906 he was known throughout Montana, and his work was featured in the Mint in Great Falls, an old-time saloon that functioned as a museum. Russell's first major show in New York was held in 1911. By the early 1920s he was so successful that a single small painting could fetch a price of over $10,000. He was also a gifted writer, and his *Rawhide Rawlins Stories* are among the finest sagas in western literature. He died in Great Falls on Oct. 24, 1926.

Russell vividly caught the blood-stirring action of the Old West in his paintings of Indian war parties, brawling cowboys, Indian buffalo hunts, and bucking broncos. *A Tight Dally and a Loose Lattice* (1920) depicts the movement called the dally: the half hitch a cowboy took around his saddle horn after lassoing a steer. *Loops and Swift Horses Are Surer than Lead* (1916) portrays cowboys lassoing a bear which was chasing a pack of horses. In the *Holdup* (1899) Russell memorialized the last crime of the notorious outlaw Big Nose George—the holdup of a stagecoach. *When Horse Flesh Comes High* (1909) pictures a posse charging two outlaws who fire while crouching behind their horses.

Russell also executed many small bronze sculptures of cowboys, Indians, and animals and modeled a few small groups in wax. One of these, the *Poker Game* (ca. 1893), depicts a Chinese, a cowboy, and an Indian sitting on the grass around a blanket on which the cards are placed.

Further Reading

Charles Marion Russell is listed in the Art study guide

Charles Marion Russell. (Library of Congress)

(IV, D, 1, g). Another painter who recorded the life of the American Indians was George CATLIN.

A readable, anecdotal biography of Russell was written by his nephew: Austin Russell, *C. M. R., Charles M. Russell: Cowboy Artist* (1957); it is rather short on the paintings themselves. Beautifully illustrated and copiously annotated is the catalog of the Amon G. Carter Museum of Western Art, *Charles M. Russell: Paintings, Drawings, and Sculptures* (1966), which also includes a biographical essay.

* * *

C. T. RUSSELL / By Charles Wetzel

Charles Taze Russell (1852–1916), American religious leader, founded a sect known as Russellites or Millennial Dawnists, which provided the nucleus for the Jehovah's Witnesses sect.

Charles Taze Russell. (Library of Congress)

Charles Taze Russell was born on Feb. 16, 1852, in Pittsburgh. His parents awed him at an early age with grim tales of hellfire and damnation. While helping his father build the family's chain of clothing stores, Russell began to question the validity of including the concept of eternal damnation in Christian dogma. Bible study, fascination with the Millerite, or Adventist, movement, and his own inability to reconcile hell with the Christian concept of mercy caused him to develop a personal theology which he began to teach others.

Unlike other Adventists, Russell believed that Christ's Second Coming might be invisible. When others were disappointed because Christ's much-predicted advent did not seem to occur in 1874, Russell, who believed it had happened invisibly, wrote *The Object and Manner of Our Lord's Returning*. He and a like-thinking Adventist, N. H. Barbour, published *Three Worlds or Plan of Redemption* (1877), which declared that a 40-year harvest of souls had begun which would end in 1914 with the termination of the time of the Gentiles and the coming of God's Kingdom. In 1879, having broken with Barbour, Russell started his magazine, *The Watch Tower and Herald of Christ's Presence*, destined to become a major voice in religion in the United States and abroad. In ensuing years he wrote his major theological work, the six-volume *Studies in the Scriptures*, which served as the dogma for Russellites during his lifetime.

After 1900 Russell encountered agonizing problems. His wife, Maria Frances Ackley, left him in 1897, after 18 years of childless marriage, amid tension over her role as associate editor of the *Watch Tower*. In 1903 she sued for divorce, and a scandalous case involving accusations of alleged affairs between Russell and women parishioners was dragged through the courts. In 1909 Russell moved his headquarters to Brooklyn, New York City. In 1911 the *Brooklyn Eagle* charged the ''Pastor'' with profiteering in the church's sale of ''miracle wheat'' to members, who were told it would produce fantastic yields. In 1914 the long-awaited end of the age of the Gentiles did not materialize, forcing Russell to revise his texts.

Russell was still popular in many quarters and was something of a hero to Zionists, whose cause he championed. He traveled widely to visit his many congregations and while in Texas on Oct. 31, 1916, died of a heart attack. His last request, to die in a toga, was adhered to by using Pullman sheets.

Further Reading

Charles Taze Russell is listed in the Religion study guide (I, Q, 1, i). Another religious leader of the period was Mary Baker EDDY, who founded the Church of Christ, Scientist.

There is no standard biography of Russell, but he is discussed in a number of studies of Jehovah's Witnesses, some laudatory, some denunciatory, few balanced. Some useful sources are Milton S. Czatt, *The International Bible Students: Jehovah's Witnesses* (1933); Herbert Stroup, *The Jehovah's Witnesses* (1945); and William J. Whalen, *Armageddon around the Corner* (1962).

* * *

RUSSWURM / By Edwin S. Redkey

John Brown Russwurm (1799–1851), Afro-American and Liberian journalist, educator, and governor, was coeditor of the first Afro-American newspaper. After he emigrated to Africa, he became governor of Maryland-in-Liberia.

John Russwurm was born on Oct. 1, 1799, in Jamaica, British West Indies, of a Creole woman and a white American father. When his father returned to the United States in 1807, the boy was sent to Canada for schooling. His father's new wife brought John to their Maine home and insisted that he be fully educated. He graduated from Bowdoin College in 1826, one of the first two Afro-Americans to graduate from any college.

Russwurm declined a position in Liberia and in 1827 joined Samuel Cornish, another free black, to edit *Freedom's Journal*, the first newspaper published by and for Afro-Americans. At first, following Cornish's lead and in line with the opinions of most articulate free blacks, the paper opposed the American Colonization Society (ACS), sponsor of Liberia as a home for Afro-Americans. When Cornish left, Russwurm began shifting editorial policy concerning emigration. In February 1829 he announced support for colonization; antagonistic black subscribers let the newspaper die and heaped verbal abuse on Russwurm. By the end of the year he had settled in Liberia.

In 1830 Russwurm became superintendent of schools, and he also edited the *Liberia Herald*. Elected to office by the Liberian settlers, he served as secretary of the colony until ACS officials in the United States dismissed him in 1836. Angered by this refusal to let black men govern themselves, he left Monrovia and became governor of Maryland-in-Liberia, the African settlement sponsored by the Maryland Colonization Society.

Russwurm governed the colony from 1836 until 1851, ruling wisely although with a strong hand. He enabled the colony to survive by keeping peace with surrounding Africans. He found remedies for problems of finance, trade, agriculture, justice, representative government, and relations with American supporters of the colony. After Liberia became an independent republic in 1847, Russwurm worked to unite the two settlements, but differences between the settlers and between their two supporting societies in the United States prevented unification until after his death.

Russwurm was a man of administrative ability and intellectual accomplishment. He had a proud sense of destiny for the African race, maintaining that Afro-Americans were equals of all men and should govern themselves. He left a clear mark on Afro-American history. Like other black nationalists, he despaired of gaining equality in the United States and rejected that nation for Africa. He died on June 17, 1851.

Further Reading

John Russwurm is listed in the American History study guide (V, F, 3, c). Paul CUFFE was another black American in favor of African colonization.

Mary Sagarin, *John Brown Russwurm* (1970), is a full, carefully researched biography. Accounts of Russwurm's Liberian career are in John H. B. Latrobe, *Maryland in Liberia* (1885), and Charles H. Huberich, *The Political and Legislative History of Liberia* (2 vols., 1947). His early life is briefly described in Nehemiah Cleaveland, *History of Bowdoin College*, edited by Alpheus Spring Packard (1882). Background on the attitudes of free blacks concerning emigration to Africa is in Howard Holman Bell, *A Survey of the Negro Convention Movement, 1830–1861* (1953; repr. 1969).

* * *

RUTH / By David Voigt

George Herman "Babe" Ruth, Jr. (1895–1948), American baseball player, was the sport's all-time champion, its greatest celebrity, and most enduring legend.

George Herman Ruth was born on Feb. 6, 1895, in Baltimore, one of eight children of a saloonkeeper. Judged as incorrigible at the age of 7, Ruth was committed to the St. Mary's Industrial School for Boys, where he learned baseball from a sympathetic monk. His left-handed pitching brilliance prompted Jack

Babe Ruth. (Library of Congress)

Dunn of the Baltimore Orioles to adopt him in 1914 to secure his release. That same year Dunn sold him to the American League Boston Red Sox. Ruth pitched on championship teams in 1915 and 1916, but his hitting soon marked him as an outfielder. In 1919 his 29 home runs set a new record and heralded a new playing style. Baseball had been dominated by pitching and offense; by 1920 Ruth's long hits inaugurated the "big bang" style.

In 1920 Babe Ruth was sold to the New York Yankees for $100,000 and a $350,000 loan. This electrifying event enhanced his popularity. His feats and personality made him a national celebrity. An undisciplined, brawling wastrel, he earned and spent thousands of dollars. By 1930 he was paid $80,000 for a season, and his endorsement income usually exceeded his annual income.

Ruth led the Yankees to seven championships, including four World Series titles. He was the game's perennial home run champion, and the 60 he hit in 1927 set a record for the 154-game season (Roger Maris hit 61 home runs in 1961, but on the extended game schedule). His lifetime total of 714 home runs is unsurpassed. With a .342 lifetime batting average for 22 seasons of play, many rate him the game's greatest player.

When his career ended in 1935, Ruth's reputation as being undisciplined frustrated his hopes of becoming a major league manager. In 1946 he became head of the Ford Motor Company's junior baseball program. He died in New York City on Aug. 16, 1948.

Further Reading

Babe Ruth is listed in the American History study guide (IX, D, 6). Another famous baseball player was Jackie ROBINSON.

So much has been written about Ruth, both in his lifetime and since his death, that it is surprising to find no adequate biography of him. A popular biography of his playing career is by sportswriter Thomas Meany, *Babe Ruth: The Big Moments of the Big Fellow* (1947). Also useful is Ruth's *The Babe Ruth Story as Told to Bob Considine* (1948). An intimate, iconoclastic account of Ruth's personal life was written by his wife, Claire M. Ruth (with Bill Slocum), *The Babe and I* (1959). A Pulitzer Prize–winning sketch of Ruth, written at the height of his career, is included in Laurence Greene, *The Era of Wonderful Nonsense: A Casebook of the Twenties* (1939). Ruth's impact on baseball history is assessed in David Q. Voigt, *American Baseball* (2 vols., 1966–1970).

RUTHERFORD / By Roger H. Stuewer

The British physicist Ernest Rutherford, 1st Baron Rutherford of Nelson (1871–1937), discovered transmutation of the elements, the nuclear atom, and a host of other phenomena to become the most prominent experimental physicist of his time.

I n searching for an experimental physicist to compare with Lord Rutherford, it is natural to think of Michael Faraday. Like Faraday, Rutherford instinctively knew what experiments would yield the most profound insights into the operations of nature; unlike Faraday, however, Rutherford established a school of followers by training a large number of research physicists. One of his colleagues observed that Rutherford always appeared to be on the "crest of the wave." Rutherford, with no sense of false modesty, replied, "Well! I made the wave, didn't I?" Then, after a moment's reflection, he added, "At least to some extent." Most physicists would agree that it was to a very large extent.

Ernest Rutherford was born on Aug. 30, 1871, in Spring Grove (Brightwater), near Nelson, New Zealand. His father, a Scot, was a wheelwright, farmer, timberman, and large-scale flax producer. Rutherford attended Nelson College, a secondary school (1886–1889), and then studied at Canterbury College in Christchurch, receiving his bachelor's degree in 1892. The following year he took his master's degree with honors in mathematics and physics.

First Research

Rutherford's interest in original research induced him to remain at Canterbury for an additional year. Using the rather primitive research facilities available to him, he proved that iron can be magnetized by the rapidly oscillating (and damped) electric field produced during the discharge of a Tesla coil. This indicated that electromagnetic (Maxwellian or Hertzian) waves might be detectable if they were allowed to demagnetize a magnetized wire, and by the end of 1894 he was sending and receiving these "wireless" signals in the laboratory.

Lord Rutherford. (Photo Harlingue-Viollet)

In 1895 Rutherford arrived in Cambridge, where he became the first research student to work under J. J. Thomson at the Cavendish Laboratory. He improved his earlier instrumentation and was soon transmitting and receiving electromagnetic signals up to 2 miles' distance, a great achievement in those days. Thomson asked Rutherford to assist him in his own researches on the x-ray–induced conduction of electricity through gases. Within a year these studies led Thomson to his discovery of the electron.

Rutherford then explored still another recent find, A. H. Becquerel's 1896 discovery of radioactivity. Rutherford soon determined that the uranium rays were capable of ionizing gases. He also discovered something new, namely, that uranium emits two different types of radiation, a highly ionizing radiation of low penetrating power, which he termed alpha radiation, and a much lower ionizing radiation of high penetrating power, which he termed beta radiation.

Rutherford remained with Thomson at the Cavendish Laboratory until 1898; he was therefore extremely fortunate in being at precisely the right place at precisely the right time. His scientific horizons broadened enormously during these years; and his confidence increased greatly owing to Thomson's open recognition of his exceptional ability.

Radioactive Transformations

Rutherford's first professorship was the Macdonald professorship of physics at McGill University in Montreal. In 1900 he married Mary Newton; the following year their only child, Eileen, was born.

Concerning research, Rutherford knew precisely the area he wished to study: radioactivity. On his suggestion, R. B. Owens, a young colleague in electrical engineering, had prepared a sample of thorium oxide to study the ionizing power of thorium's radiations. Owens found, oddly enough, that the ionization they produced apparently depended upon the presence or absence of air currents passing over the thorium oxide. Nothing similar had ever been observed with uranium. It was this mystery that Owens, going on vacation, left for Rutherford to solve.

Rutherford designed a series of masterful experiments from which he concluded that thorium somehow produces a gas, which he called "thorium emanation." It was this gas that Owens's air currents had transported, thereby influencing the recorded ionization. Rutherford also found that any thorium emanation produced soon disappeared before his very eyes! By passing some thorium emanation through a long tube at a constant rate, Rutherford discovered that half the amount present at any given time disappeared ("decayed") roughly every minute—its "half-life." He also found that, if thorium emanation came into contact with a metal plate, the plate would acquire an "active deposit" which also decayed but which had a half-life of roughly 11 hours. Further studies revealed that pressure or other external conditions did not influence these half-lives. In addition, the "activities" of the substances as a function of time

The Cavendish Laboratory at Cambridge University. Here in 1895 Rutherford began his studies under J. J. Thomson, whom he was to succeed as Cavendish Professor of Physics in 1919. (Radio Times Hulton Picture Library)

decayed exponentially, which Rutherford realized was possible only if the activity was directly proportional to the number of "ions" (atoms) present at any given time. In this way Rutherford discovered the first known radioactive gas, thorium emanation, and explored its behavior.

In 1900 Rutherford was joined by Frederick Soddy, a member of McGill's chemistry department. Together they resolved to isolate the sources of thorium's radioactivity by chemical separation techniques. By the end of 1901 their most important conclusions were, first, that thorium emanation is an inert gas like argon and, second, that thorium emanation is produced, not by thorium directly, but by some unknown, and apparently chemically different, element which they termed "thorium X." This was a key insight into the understanding of radioactivity, for it suggested that one element, thorium, can decay into a second element, thorium X, which in turn can decay into a third element, thorium emanation.

Item after item now fell into place. Soddy, turning from thorium to uranium, found that it decayed into a new radioactive element, "uranium X." Next, Rutherford came to understand the crucial fact that each radioactive transformation is accompanied by the *instantaneous* emission of a single alpha or beta particle. Rutherford also proved by a simple calculation that in radioactive transformations enormous quantities of energy are released, which, he argued could be derived only from an internal atomic source.

Although some links were still missing, Rutherford's revolutionary theory of radioactive transformations was essentially complete by early 1904. He summarized the results of all of his own researches, as well as those of the Curies and other physicists, in his Bakerian lecture, "The Succession of Changes in Radioactive Bodies," of May 19, 1904, which he delivered before the Royal Society of London. In this lecture, one of the classics in the literature of physics, he presented the complete mathematical formulation of his theory, identified the four radioactive series—uranium, thorium, actinium, and radium (neptunium)—and established the principle, albeit tacitly, that any radioactive element can be uniquely identified by its half-life.

Rutherford also delivered a lecture at the Royal Institution in which he dwelled at some length on an important consequence of his theory—its implications for the age of the earth. He realized that lead, a stable element, is the end product of each radioactive series. This meant that, by determining the relative amounts of, say, uranium and lead in a sample of rock, its age can be calculated—which is the basis of the radioactive dating method.

Rutherford's researches attracted a number of scientists to McGill. His activities there—teaching, experimenting, writing his famous book *Radioactivity*—were prodigious. Recognition came to Rutherford early: he was elected a Fellow of the Royal Society in 1902, was awarded the society's Rumford Medal in 1905, and delivered the Yale University Silliman Lectures and received his first honorary degree in 1906. In 1908 he received the Nobel Prize—in *chemistry*! Rutherford later remarked that he had in his day observed many transformations of varying periods of time, but the fastest he had ever observed was his own from physicist to chemist. He refused to disappoint the Nobel Committee, however, and titled his Nobel lecture "The Chemical Nature of the Alpha-Particles from Radioactive Substances."

Nuclear Atom and Artificial Transmutations

In 1907 Rutherford arrived at the University of Manchester to succeed Sir Arthur Schuster as Langworthy professor of physics. Rutherford seems to have enjoyed teaching at Manchester more than at McGill. As he later wrote to his friend B. B. Boltwood of Yale University: "I find the students here regard a full professor as little short of Lord God Almighty. . . . It is quite refreshing after the critical attitude of Canadian students."

By early 1908 Rutherford was ready to test some new ideas. One of the first questions he wanted to settle was the nature of alpha particles. He devised a very simple scheme for capturing alpha particles, from purified radium emanation, in a glass enclosure. There the alpha particles acquired free electrons and formed a gas which spectroscopic analysis proved to be helium. This work took on much broader significance as a result of another observation, namely, that alpha particles can be scattered by various substances. His coworkers, H. Geiger and E. Marsden, allowed alpha particles to strike various metal foils (for example, gold and platinum) and counted that between 3 and 67 alpha particles per minute—or about 1/8000 of those present in the incident beam—were scattered backward, that is, through more than a right angle.

Two years elapsed before Rutherford achieved the insights necessary for a satisfactory explanation of Geiger and Marsden's experiments. He had to realize that the alpha particle is not of atomic dimensions but that it can be considered to be a point charge in scattering theoretical calculations and that the number of electrons per atom is relatively small—on the same order of magnitude, numerically speaking, as the atom's atomic weight. He also had to realize the extreme improbability of obtaining Geiger and Marsden's results if the alpha particle was multiply scattered by presumably widely separated electrons in the atom, as a 1904 atomic model, as well as a 1910 scattering theory, of Thomson's suggested. In early 1911 Rutherford became convinced, through rather extensive calculations, that Geiger and Marsden's alpha particles were being scattered in hyperbolic orbits by the intense electric field surrounding a dense concentration of electric charge in the center of the atom—the nucleus. The nuclear atom had been born.

No one, however, noticed the new arrival. It was apparently not even mentioned, for example, at the famous 1911 Solvay Conference in Brussels, which Rutherford, Albert Einstein, Max Planck, and many other prominent physicists attended. Whatever novelty contemporary physicists attached to Rutherford's paper seems to have been to his scattering theory rather than to his model of the atom—which was only one of many models present in the literature. Only after Niels Bohr exploited the nucleus in developing his famous 1913 quantum theory of the hydrogen atom, and only after H. G. J. Moseley attached to the nucleus a unique atomic number through his well-known 1913–1914 x-ray experiments, was the full significance of Rutherford's nuclear model generally appreciated. Only then, for example, did the concept of isotopes become generally and clearly recognized.

The researches that Rutherford fostered at Manchester—partly for which he was knighted in 1914—were not confined to alpha scattering and atomic structure. For example, he and his coworkers studied the chemistry and modes of decay of the radioactive elements; the scattering, the wavelengths, and the spectra of gamma rays; and the relationship between the range of alpha particles and the lifetime of the elements from which they are emitted.

Most of this immense activity was brought to a halt at the outbreak of World War I. Rutherford became associated with the Admiralty Board of Invention and Research early in the war, and he carried out experiments relating to the detection of submarines, devising a variety of microphones, diaphragms, and underwater senders and receivers to study underwater sound propagation. He supplied American scientists with a vast amount of information when the United States entered the war in 1917.

In 1919 Rutherford and William Kay found, as the culmination of a long series of investigations, that when alpha particles strike hydrogen—or, in a more famous experiment, nitrogen—recoil "protons" (Rutherford's term) are produced. Rutherford realized at once that he had achieved the first artificial nuclear transmutation (alpha particle + nitrogen to proton + oxygen) known to man. He gave a full account of his and Kay's work in 1920 in his second Bakerian lecture, "Nuclear Constitution of Atoms." One surprising prediction he made in this lecture was that of a "kind of neutral doublet," perhaps a faint premonition of the neutron. Rutherford's discovery of artificial transmutation was, in general, a fitting capstone to his brilliant career at Manchester.

Cambridge and Honors

In 1919 Rutherford became Cavendish Professor of Physics and Director of the laboratory and, a bit later, Fellow of Trinity College, Cambridge. As the occupant of the most prestigious chair of physics in England, and, concurrently, as the holder of a Professorship of Natural Philosophy at the Royal Institution (1921), Rutherford was more and more called upon to deliver public lectures and serve in various professional offices. In 1923 he was elected President of the British Association for the Advancement of Science; in 1925, the same year in which he gained admittance into the coveted Order of Merit, he became President of the Royal Society for the customary 5-year term. In 1933 he accepted the presidency of the Academic Assistance Council, formed to aid Nazi-persecuted Jewish scholars. He died on Oct. 19, 1937, in Cambridge.

Portrait of the Man

C. P. Snow has provided the following portrait of Rutherford in mature life: "He was a big, rather clumsy man, with a substantial bay window that started in the middle of the chest. I should guess that he was less muscular than at first sight he looked. He had large staring blue eyes and a damp and pendulous lower lip. He didn't look in the least like an intellectual. Creative people of his abundant kind never do, of course, but all the talk of Rutherford looking like a farmer was unperceptive nonsense. His was really the kind of face and physique that often goes with great weight of character and gifts. It could easily have been the soma of a great writer. As he talked to his companions in the streets, his voice was three times as loud as any of theirs, and his accent was bizarre. . . . It was part of his nature that, stupendous as his work was, he should consider it 10 per cent more so. It was also part of his nature that, quite without acting, he should behave constantly as though he were 10 per cent larger than life. Worldly success? He loved every minute of it: flattery, titles, the company of the high official world."

Further Reading

Lord Rutherford is listed in the Science study guide (VII, C, 1). He was the founder of nuclear physics, and listed among his associates are some of the world's leading physicists, including J. J. THOMSON, Frederick SOD-DY, Peter KAPITSA, and James CHADWICK.

Rutherford's scientific papers, together with introductory notes by James Chadwick and other physicists, were assembled in *The Collected Papers of Lord Rutherford of Nelson* (3 vols., 1962–1965). Selections from his papers are in J. B. Birks, ed., *Rutherford at Manchester* (1962), and Alfred Romer, ed., *The Discovery of Radioactivity and Transmutation* (1964). Lawrence Badash edited *Rutherford and Boltwood: Letters on Radioactivity* (1969).

Arthur S. Eve, *Rutherford: Being the Life and Letters of the Rt. Hon. Lord Rutherford* (1939), is a full-length biography; Eve and James Chadwick wrote the obituary notice of Rutherford in the Royal Society of London, *Obituary Notices of Fellows of the Royal Society*, vol. 3 (1936–1938). Three other full-length biographies are Ivor B. N. Evans, *Man of Power: The Life Story of Baron Rutherford of Nelson* (1939); John Rowland, *Ernest Rutherford: Atom Pioneer* (1955); and Edward N. da C. Andrade, *Rutherford and the Nature of the Atom* (1964). A brief biography is C. M. Focken, *Lord Rutherford of Nelson* (1938). Extremely interesting recollections by H. R. Robinson, J. D. Cockcroft, M. L. Oliphant, E. Marsden, and A. S. Russell were published between 1943 and 1951 and separately reprinted in 1954 by the Physical Society of London under the title *Rutherford: By Those Who Knew Him* (1954). For help with questions on physics see W. E. Burcham, *Nuclear Physics: An Introduction* (1963).

RUTLEDGE / By Milton M. Klein

> John Rutledge (1739–1800), American jurist and statesman, was Revolutionary War governor of South Carolina. He exemplified the conservative views of the mercantile and planter aristocracy.

John Rutledge was born in Charleston, S.C., into an affluent and politically active family. He was tutored at home and then went to England at 18 to study law. After being admitted to the English bar in 1760, he returned to Charleston, where he developed a successful practice. He served as the province's attorney general (1764–1765), but as a member of the Commons House of Assembly (1761–1776), he was more often in vigorous opposition to the royal administration.

At the Stamp Act Congress, Rutledge vigorously defended American rights. In 1769 he fought for the Commons' appropriation of funds in support of the English radical John Wilkes. In the general quarrel with Britain, however, Rutledge was a moderate. At the First Continental Congress he approved the Galloway Plan for a constitutional accommodation with the mother country, although he joined the movement for independence; in

John Rutledge, a miniature portrait painted in 1791 by John Trumbull. (Yale University Art Gallery)

Further Reading

John Rutledge is listed in the American History study guide (III, C, 1 and 2; III, E, 2 and 4). John JAY negotiated the treaty which avoided a renewal of war with Great Britain.

The only full-length biography of Rutledge is Richard H. Barry, *Mr. Rutledge of South Carolina* (1942); it is based on extensive sources and is highly readable. His political career in South Carolina may be traced in Edward McCrady, *History of South Carolina* (4 vols., 1897–1902), and David D. Wallace, *History of South Carolina* (4 vols., 1934–1935; rev. ed., 1 vol., 1951). Rutledge's career on the Supreme Court in discussed in Charles Warren, *The Supreme Court in United States History* (3 vols., 1923; 2 vols., rev. ed. 1935), and in Leon Friedman and Fred L. Israel, eds., *The Justices of the United States Supreme Court, 1789–1969* (4 vols., 1969).

RUYSBROECK / By William J. Courtenay

The Flemish mystic Jan van Ruysbroeck (1293–1381) was the most important spiritual writer and mystic in the Low Countries in the 14th century.

the Second Congress he urged the establishment of new state governments. He helped to frame the South Carolina constitution of 1776 and was immediately chosen president (governor) of the state, but his innate conservatism caused him to resign 2 years later.

When South Carolina was confronted by a British invasion in 1779, the state again chose Rutledge as governor, and for the next 3 years he provided energetic leadership in the war effort, with such broad emergency powers that he was called "Dictator Rutledge." Resigning in 1782, he was elected to the state legislature and in 1784 was named to the state's chancery court. At the Constitutional Convention he resisted restrictions on the slave trade, urged property as a basis for representation, and sought election of the president by Congress, and of the Congress by state legislatures.

President George Washington named Rutledge to the Supreme Court when it was organized in 1789, but he resigned 2 years later, without ever having attended a single session of the Court, to become chief justice of South Carolina. In 1795 Washington appointed him chief justice of the United States, but Rutledge's violent speech against the Jay Treaty resulted in a Senate rejection of the nomination, even though he had presided at one term of the court. The ferocity of his tirade was symptomatic of a mental deterioration which had commenced a few years earlier upon the death of his wife. He died on July 18, 1800.

J
an van Ruysbroeck (pronounced rois′bröok) was born in the village of Ruysbroeck a few miles from Brussels. For his education and religious training he was sent to Brussels at the age of 11 to live with his uncle, John Hinckaert, a priest and canon of the Cathedral of St. Gudule. There he also came under the spiritual influence of another canon, Francis van Coudenberg, who was a friend of his uncle, and these two men had a strong effect on the young man's career and religious development.

Ruysbroeck's personal inclinations as well as his environment eventually persuaded him to adopt the religious life, and in 1317 he was ordained to the priesthood. For more than a quarter century he lived in the area of St. Gudule in Brussels and attained a reputation as a preacher and orthodox religious thinker. In order to recapture the quiet, contemplative life of his early years, in 1343 Ruysbroeck retired with his two aging spiritual advisers, Hinckaert and Coudenberg, to a hermitage in the forest of Soignes called Groenendael on the southeast edge of Brussels. With the disciples that joined them, they formed themselves into a community in 1349 according to the rule of Augustinian canons. In this place of solitude Ruysbroeck wrote the mystical treatises on which his reputation is based, and he remained there until his death in 1381, at the age of 88.

Most of Ruysbroeck's writings describe how the soul of man can be joined with God in mystical union. He was careful to avoid heresy. He rejected pantheistic doctrines that did not distinguish clearly enough between God and the creature; he rejected the overly optimistic evaluation that man could approach God apart from grace; and he rejected quietistic tendencies that obliterated human activity in the mystical union or seemingly prolonged the experience.

In one of his most important works, however, written early in his stay at Groenendael, *The Adornment of Spiritual Marriage*, Ruysbroeck suggested the possibility of an intuitive vision of the divine essence as well as the idea that part of the soul might be uncreated. Although stated more cautiously in his later writings, these ideas led to an attack on Ruysbroeck not long after his death. His writings, however, have been judged orthodox by most. He forms a link between the Rhenish mystics of the early 14th century, especially the Dominican mystics like Meister Eckhart, Heinrich Suso, and Johannes Tauler, and the Devotio Moderna, the major spiritual movement of the 15th century in the Low Countries, northern France, and the Rhine Valley.

Jan van Ruysbroeck. (Bibliothèque Nationale, Paris)

Further Reading

Jan van Ruysbroeck is listed in the Religion study guide (I, F, 5) and the Philosophy study guide (II, D, 2). Meister ECKHART was another leading mystic of this period.

Most of Ruysbroeck's writings have been translated into English. Biographical studies of Ruysbroeck in English are Vincent Scully, *A Medieval Mystic* (1911), and Alfred Wautier d'Aygalliers, *Ruysbroeck the Admirable* (1923; trans. 1969). Additional material on Ruysbroeck is in Stephanus Axters, *Spirituality of the Old Low Countries* (trans. 1954). Almost any survey of medieval thought or late medieval mysticism includes a description of Ruysbroeck's thought, such as the work by Etienne Henry Gilson, *History of Christian Philosophy in the Middle Ages* (1955).

RYDER / By Lloyd Goodrich

The painter Albert Pinkham Ryder (1847–1917) was the most original romantic artist of 19th-century America. His highly personal art, at the opposite extreme from the literal naturalism of his period, anticipated the expressionist and fantastic trends of modern art.

Albert P. Ryder was born on March 19, 1847, in New Bedford, Mass., then the world's busiest whaling port. His ancestors on both his father's and mother's sides were of old Cape Cod families. Many had been sailors, and his childhood was intimately associated with the sea. His education went no further than grammar school, as his eyes were oversensitive. Without professional training he began to paint landscape outdoors.

About 1870 Ryder moved with his family to New York, where he lived the rest of his life. At 23 (relatively late) he entered the National Academy of Design, where he studied for four seasons, mostly drawing from casts; but more important was the informal teaching he received from the portraitist and romantic painter William E. Marshall. This limited art education contrasted with the thorough academic training usual at the time.

Ryder's early paintings were landscapes, often including horses, cows, and sheep—memories of the country around New Bedford. Small in scale and relatively naturalistic in style, they were already marked by a dreamlike poetry and by extremely personal form and color. They were generally rejected by academy juries, and in 1877 Ryder was one of the founders of a new liberal organization, the Society of American Artists, with which he exhibited for the next decade.

By contrast with that of most American artists of his generation, Ryder's European experience was small. His

Albert P. Ryder. (Library of Congress)

first trip abroad was in 1877, when he spent a month in London. The next and longest trip was in the summer of 1882, when he visited France, Spain, Tangier, Italy, and Switzerland. In 1887 and 1896 he crossed and recrossed the Atlantic, for the sea voyages, spending only 2 weeks in London each time. These limited foreign contacts had little effect on his art.

About 1880, in his early 30s, Ryder embarked on the imaginative paintings which were his greatest achievements. They were based on the Bible, classical mythology, Chaucer, Shakespeare (his favorite poet), and 19th-century romantics such as Lord Byron, Thomas Campbell, Alfred Lord Tennyson, and Edgar Allan Poe. Two of his major paintings were based on Richard Wagner's operas. But Ryder's works were quite different from the "literary" pictures of the period. They were not illustrations but original works of art—great themes transformed by his imagination into highly personal visions. Nature always played an essential part. Youthful memories of the sea were embodied in his frequent image of a lone boat sailing the moonlit waters. But his major conceptions were more than simple nature poems; their central motif was the human being in relation to superhuman powers. Ryder's art was fundamentally religious; he was one of the few artists of his time to whom religion was not mere conformity but intense, profound belief.

Ryder's art was never bound by the literal naturalism of his time. For him painting was not mere representation but creation in the language of color, form, and rhythmic movement. As he said, "What avails a storm cloud accu-rate in form and color if the storm is not therein?" He used the elements of nature far more freely than any American contemporary painter, shaping them to his creative sense of design.

Ryder worked long over his pictures, building them in layer on layer of pigment, often keeping them for years, so that his total production numbers only about 165 paintings. Unfortunately he had no sound technical knowledge, and many of his pictures have deteriorated to some extent. Because of the small number of his works and their increasing value, forgeries began to appear in his last years; and after his death the production increased until there are now about five times as many fakes as genuine works.

As a person, Ryder was completely unworldly. He cared nothing for money or reputation. As he said, "The artist needs but a roof, a crust of bread and his easel, and all the rest God gives him in abundance. He must live to paint and not paint to live." He never married, and in later life he became a recluse except to a few old friends. He was utterly unable to cope with housekeeping, and the two rooms in which he lived were in a condition of incredible disorder, piled waist-high with all kinds of objects. After a serious illness in 1915, he lived with friends in Elmhurst, Long Island, where he died on March 28, 1917.

Though Ryder's art had little to do with the prevailing trends of his day, it had much to do with future trends. His freedom from literal naturalism, his relation to the subconscious mind, and the purity of his plastic creation were prophetic of much in modern art.

Further Reading

Albert P. Ryder is listed in the Art study guide (IV, D, 1, c). The other towering geniuses in native American painting of this period were Winslow HOMER and Thomas EAKINS.

Three monographs on Ryder have appeared. Frederic

Flying Dutchman by Ryder. (National Collection of Fine Arts, Smithsonian Institution)

Fairchild Sherman, *Albert Pinkham Ryder* (1920), is a sympathetic study, now outdated by recent research, especially as regards forgeries. Frederic Newlin Price, *Ryder* (1932), is unreliable, a considerable proportion of the works listed and illustrated being forgeries. Lloyd Goodrich, *Albert P. Ryder* (1959), gives the most complete biographical and critical account to date; all 81 works illustrated and referred to are unquestionably genuine.

✳   ✳   ✳

RYERSON / By Robert Hett

Adolphus Egerton Ryerson (1803–1882) was a Canadian Methodist clergyman and educator. One of the leading Methodists in Upper Canada, he opposed the pretensions of the Anglican Church.

Egerton Ryerson. (Radio Times Hulton Picture Library)

Egerton Ryerson was born on March 24, 1803, at Charlotteville, Norfolk County, Upper Canada. His father, Joseph, was a United Empire loyalist. Ryerson was educated at the district grammar school and then worked for a time on his father's farm. In 1821 he joined the Methodist Church and taught in the London district grammar school. In 1823 he returned to work on his father's farm once more, but in 1825 he was ordained a Methodist minister and assigned to the Niagara circuit. He was soon transferred to the Yonge Street circuit, which included York (Toronto), and he immediately entered into a strenuous campaign in opposition to the claims of the Church of England in Upper Canada to the income of the clergy reserves.

In 1829 he began to edit the *Christian Guardian* and remained its editor, with several interruptions, for the next decade. In 1833 he was sent as a delegate to the Wesleyan Methodist Conference in England and was a key figure in bringing about the uniting of the Wesleyans and the Methodist Episcopal Church in Canada. He returned to England in 1835 in search of financial support for a Methodist college in Upper Canada, and in 1841 Victoria College was incorporated, with Ryerson as its first president.

Ryerson at first favored the Reform cause in politics, but in the early 1830s he became disillusioned with many of the Reformers, and with William Lyon Mackenzie in particular, and increasingly gave his support to the governor's party. In the general election of 1844 he worked effectively on behalf of the administration of the new governor, Sir Charles Metcalfe.

In the same year he was appointed as the second superintendent of education for Upper Canada and thus began what, in effect, was the second of his careers. He studied schools and teaching methods in the United States, in England, and on the Continent and used his findings to remodel the educational system of Upper Canada.

In 1846 a school bill which incorporated many of Ryerson's ideas was passed by the legislature. After the Reformers obtained control of the government in 1848, they attempted to alter his system, but with the cooperation of Robert Baldwin, the attorney general for Canada West, Ryerson was able to maintain the basic structure intact.

Ryerson continued to administer the school system in the United Province of Canada and then, under confederation, the schools in the province of Ontario until he retired as superintendent in 1876. He died at Toronto on Feb. 19, 1882.

Further Reading

Egerton Ryerson is listed in the Canada study guide (III, A, 2). Another educator and prominent figure in the religious life of his time was John STRACHAN.

Ryerson's autobiography, *The Story of My Life*, was edited and published posthumously by J. George Hodgins (1883). The definitive biography of Ryerson is C. B. Sissons, *Egerton Ryerson: His Life and Letters* (2 vols., 1937–1947).

✳   ✳   ✳

RYLE / By Daniel O'Connor

The English philosopher Gilbert Ryle (born 1900) ranked among the leaders of the contemporary analytic movement in British philosophy. His most original work was his analysis of the concept of mind.

Gilbert Ryle was born on Aug. 19, 1900, in Brighton, the son of a prosperous doctor. He was educated at Brighton College and then entered Queen's College, Oxford, where he took first honors in two subjects: classical honor moderations and the school of philosophy, politics, and economics. He was also captain of the Queen's College Boating Club.

As a result of his brilliant academic work, Ryle was appointed lecturer in 1924 and a year later tutor in philosophy, both appointments at Christ Church, Oxford. In 1940 he was commissioned in the Welsh Guards, serving for the duration of World War II and ending his military career as a major.

Ryle then returned to Oxford to become Waynfleete professor of metaphysical philosophy, a post he held from 1945 to 1968. In 1947 he inherited from G. E. Moore the editorship of *Mind*, the most influential journal of English philosophy.

Early in his philosophical career, Ryle decided that the task of philosophy was "the detection of the sources in linguistic idioms of recurrent misconceptions and absurd theories." In his Tanner Lectures, published as *Dilemmas* (1954), he showed how certain philosophical impasses could be dissolved by a clearer understanding of the concepts employed by the apparently contradictory views.

In his major work, *The Concept of Mind* (1949), Ryle mounted a devastating attack on Cartesian dualism and, in particular, on the view of mind as a separate substance apart from the body. He caricatured this view as the "myth of the ghost in the machine." Ryle's own view of mental reality is that it consists in dispositions to behave in certain ways. He tried to show that mental concepts do not refer to private, unwitnessable events, maintaining against critics that his view was not identical with behaviorism.

In *Plato's Progress* (1966) Ryle exhibited an unexpected talent for ingenious speculation in an attempt to reconstruct the historical genesis of Plato's dialogues. Ryle, a bachelor, lived most of his life in college rooms. Friends said that "the Common Room atmosphere fits him like a glove." Quick and formidable in debate, Ryle was also the writer of clear and witty prose. He took particular delight in exploding pompous views and in inventing fresh metaphors and vivid aphorisms. Though

Gilbert Ryle in 1952. (Radio Times Hulton Picture Library)

professing to dislike erudition and intellectual matters, Ryle was both learned and highly intellectual. He was said to distrust imagination and its works, but he had a typically British love of gardening.

Further Reading

Gilbert Ryle is listed in the Philosophy study guide (VIII, F). He shared the concern of Ludwig WITTGENSTEIN with linguistic analysis.

Ryle's works are eminently readable even for the general reader. *The Concept of Mind* (1949) and *Dilemmas* (1954) are the most important. The only study of any length is the highly critical one by Laird Addis in *Moore and Ryle: Two Ontologies* (1965).

*　　*　　*

$$Sá \quad \mathbf{S} \quad Seymour$$

SÁ / By E. Bradford Burns

Mem de Sá (1504–1572) was a Portuguese jurist and a governor general of Brazil who served from 1558 to 1572 and helped to bring a new stability and prosperity to Portuguese America.

M em de Sá (pronounced sà) was born in Coimbra, Portugal. He studied law at the University of Salamanca. After receiving his law degree in 1528, he served as a judge in several of the highest courts of Portugal. A learned and able jurist, he enjoyed special favor with King João III. The Crown appointed him to be the third governor general of Brazil.

The cultured Sá brought peace and a certain degree of prosperity to Brazil after he assumed his duties in January 1558. Among others, the eminent Jesuit missionary Manuel da Nóbrega sang his praises: "As soon as Mem de Sá took the reins of government, he began to show his prudence, zeal, and virtue both in the good government of the Christians and the Indians by putting everything in order as Our Lord showed him." To increase the base of economic prosperity, Sá encouraged agriculture in general and sugar culture in particular. The number of sugar mills multiplied, particularly in the captaincies of São Vicente, Rio de Janeiro, Espírito Santo, Bahia, and Pernambuco, where the huge sugar plantations and their mills

quickly became powerful agricultural, industrial, and social organizations.

The Indians had proved to be an unsatisfactory answer to the labor shortage which plagued the colony, but they were pressed into service as the only available workers. The Church, most vocally the Jesuits, regarded the enslavement of the Indians as contrary to the Christian intentions of the King, and they intensified efforts to save them both physically and spiritually by gathering them into the Church-administered villages. The colonists loudly criticized the interference with their labor supply. Sá desired to bring the Indians within the pale of empire. On the one hand, he maintained close relations with the Jesuits and approved the continuation of the mission villages. On the other, he fought fiercely to pacify those Indians who had rebelled against Portuguese authority.

The perennial French threat demanded much of the governor's attention and resources. In 1555, Vice Admiral Durand de Villegaignon had founded France Antartique around Guanabara Bay. The French colony there threatened the Portuguese king's claims to the entire Brazilian coast. Sá attacked the French invaders on several occasions. On March 1, 1565, he established Rio de Janeiro as a base to fight against the stubborn French and after prolonged siege expelled them in 1567. After the defeat of the French, Rio de Janeiro grew rapidly in size and importance. The Crown manifested its delight with the accomplishments of Sá by retaining him as governor general long after his 4-year appointment expired. He stayed on until he died in office on March 12, 1572, in Salvador da Bahia.

Further Reading

Mem de Sá is listed in the Latin America study guide (II, B, 1). One of the founders of Jesuit missions in Brazil was José de ANCHIETA.

Sá is referred to in several useful background works on Latin America: Hubert Herring, *A History of Latin America* (1955; 3d rev. ed. 1968); Charles R. Boxer, *Four Centuries of Portuguese Expansion, 1415–1825: A Succinct Summary* (1961); and Helen M. Bailey and Abraham P. Nasatir, *Latin America: The Development of Its Civilization* (2d ed. 1968).

SAADIA BEN JOSEPH

/ **By Malachi B. Martin**

The Jewish scholar Saadia ben Joseph al-Fayumi (882–942) ranks as the most important medieval Jewish scholar of literature and history.

Little is known of the early life of Saadia ben Joseph (pronounced sä′dē-ä běn jō′zəf) except that he was born in Egypt, lived for sometime in Palestine, and finally settled in the Jewish communities of Babylonia. Saadia became affiliated with the academy at Sura, Babylonia, and became the *gaon* (head) of the academy in 928. Deposed in 930, he again became *gaon* in 936, holding this office until his death in 942. During this period the academy became the highest seat of learning among the Jews.

Saadia's numerous works were written for the most part in Arabic, which had become the vernacular and literary language of eastern Jews. When the Babylonian schools ceased to function in the middle of the 11th century and the Jews were expelled from Spain, Saadia's works ceased to be widely known until the late 19th and early 20th centuries. Their importance, however, cannot be exaggerated. In bulk, in range of interest, in breadth of knowledge, and in pioneer thinking, his works are a monument between the close of the Talmudic period in the 6th century and the rise of the Jewish Enlightenment in the 18th century.

At least 20 major works, apart from Saadia's translations and commentaries, exist. Saadia translated the Bible into Arabic and added a commentary. He composed a Midrashic work on the Decalogue, translated the five Megilloth (Song of Songs, Ruth, Lamentations, Ecclesiastes, and Esther), and also translated the Book of Daniel and added a commentary.

Saadia's major works divide into five categories: polemical tracts, exegetical writings, grammatical treatises, works on Talmudic subjects, and philosophic works. His polemical writings arose principally from his position in Sura. His *Book of the Festivals* was written against Ben Meir of Palestine in 922, when the latter attempted to make alterations in the Jewish calendar. Other writings were directed against the Karaite sect and against the skeptic Hivi of Balkh, David ben Zakkai, and others.

Of Saadia's grammatical works, only his treatise on the *hapax legomena* (words used once in the Bible) and a poem on the letters of the alphabet survive. His liturgical writings and poems survive in greater quantity. One poem, *Azharoth*, is a practical enunciation of the 613 Precepts. Saadia's philosophical works display his wide knowledge of Aristotle and of Christian, Moslem, and Brahmin teachings. In his *Kitab al-Amanat wal-Itiqadat* (933) Saadia expressed his views of religion and human destiny. He maintained that revealed religion and human reason do not clash but complement each other.

Saadia's health was broken by the continual controversies which surrounded his leadership of the Sura Academy, and he died in 942. His importance can be measured by the fact that without his extant works there would be no direct knowledge of the inner development of Judaism and Jewish literature between the 7th and the 10th century.

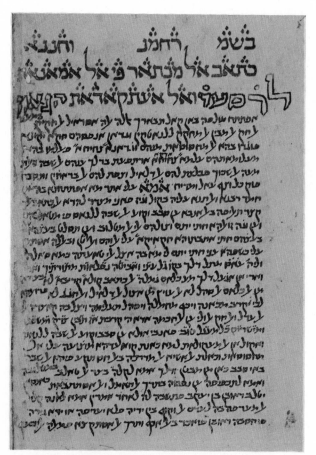

A 15th-century manuscript page from Saadia ben Joseph's Kitab al-Amanat. *The Arabic text is in Hebrew script. (Curators of the Bodleian Library, Oxford)*

Further Reading

Saadia ben Joseph is listed in the Religion study guide (II, C, 2). Joseph CARO was a Jewish scholar of the late Middle Ages.

David Druck, *Saadya Gaon: Scholar, Philosopher, Champion of Judaism* (trans. 1942), and Solomon Leon Skoss, *Saadia Gaon: The Earliest Hebrew Grammarian* (1955), are biographical studies. Various aspects of Saadia's life and career are discussed in two studies published on the thousandth anniversary of his death by the American Academy for Jewish Research, *Saadia Anniversary Volume*, edited by Boaz Cohen (1943), and by the Jewish Quarterly Review, *Saadia Studies*, edited by Abraham A. Neuman and Solomon Zeitlin (1943). Background information is in Heinrich H. Graetz, *History of the Jews* (trans. 1891–1898), and the highly technical work by Paul Ernst Kahle, *The Cairo Geniza* (1947; 2d ed. 1959).

Helsinki Central Railroad Station, in Finland, designed by Eliel Saarinen. The station, commissioned in 1904 and constructed in 1910–1914, was not used until after World War I. (Courtesy, The Museum of Finnish Architecture, Photo N. E. Wickberg)

SAARINEN / By Lawrence Wodehouse

Eliel (1873–1950) and Eero (1910–1961) Saarinen, father and son, were Finnish-American architects and industrial designers. Eliel had a profound interest in the total idea of the city. Eero developed new structural techniques for his eclectic works.

Eliel Saarinen (pronounced sär′ĭ-nĕn) was one of a small band of architects who rejected the architectural styles of the 19th century, stating, "Architecture has gone astray; something has to be done about it; now is the time to do things." His designs show a continuous progression, and all bear his unmistakable stamp. Eero Saarinen borrowed from a wide range of sources; he lacked the unifying philosophy of design which can be discerned in his father's architecture. Eero defined architecture as a "fine art" and the architect as a "form giver."

Eliel Saarinen

Eliel was born in Rantasalmi on Aug. 20, 1873. He studied painting and architecture at the University and the Polytechnic Institute of Helsinki, respectively, and in 1896, a year before graduating, he entered into partnership with two other institute graduates, Herman Gesellius, brother of Eliel's wife-to-be, Loja, and Armas Lindgren.

Finnish architecture at the turn of the century reflected national romanticism verging upon Art Nouveau. Eliel's design for the Finnish Pavilion at the 1900 Paris Exposition, with its bulging tower and Art Nouveau decorations, reflects this trend. The flowing line of Art Nouveau was replaced in Eliel's own home at Hvittrask (1902) by a more geometricized decor.

That Eliel was influenced by the later English architects of the Arts and Crafts movement there can be no doubt. His own house bespeaks the idioms, which lingered in his work until the 1920s. The handmade bricks and tiles, bay windows with leaded lights, lead rainwater pipes, wrought-iron decoration, and hand-carved woodwork and furniture are the trademarks of the Arts and Crafts movement.

The American Arts and Crafts developments, especially Henry Hobson Richardson's "Romanesque revival" and its outgrowth in the functionalism of Louis Sullivan, had also reached the Scandinavian countries. In 1904 Eliel won the competition for the Central Railroad Station, Helsinki (built 1910–1914). The building is antitraditional, with spacious interiors and monumental proportions, similar in character to the smaller buildings of Richardson and Sullivan.

In 1922 Eliel won the second prize in the Chicago Tribune Tower competition. His design, with a strong vertical emphasis and the upper portion set back, had the monumentality of a classical Mayan pyramid. That year he moved to the United States. He taught for a short while at the University of Michigan and then was invited to Bloomfield Hills, Mich., where he built the Cranbrook Academy of Art (1926–1943) in the Arts and Crafts tradition. He also headed the department of architecture and city planning there.

Eliel's later works, executed in collaboration with his son, include the Kleinhans Music Hall, Buffalo (1938–1940), the Tabernacle Church of Christ, Columbus, Ind. (1940–1942), the Christ Lutheran Church, Minneapolis (1949), and the projected Smithsonian Art Gallery, Washington (1939). All have a simple monumental dignity, with unadorned wall surfaces and a spacious light openness.

Eliel was always interested in city planning, and he

Trans World Airlines Flight Center at Kennedy Airport, N.Y., designed by Eero Saarinen and built between 1956 and 1962. (TWA by Ezra Stoller Assocs.)

became planning consultant to Budapest and to Estonia. He submitted an entry in the Canberra, Australia, competition and projected plans for Helsinki and other Finnish cities. Although his projects stressed organic informality, they usually included the mannerist and baroque motif of a long axis, terminated by a round point incorporating a monumental structure. Eliel abhorred skyscraper construction as the basis for increasing the value of the land, and he felt that low-cost housing was poorly constructed and thus expensive to maintain. He demanded social research, adequate and appropriate means and methods, and an architecture created to enhance the total environment.

Eliel's books, *The City: Its Growth, Its Decay, Its Future* (1943) and *Search for Form* (1948), as well as his "Proposal for Rebuilding Blighted Areas" and "Outline for a Legislative Program to Rebuild Our Cities," prepared for discussions at Cranbrook in 1942, contained concepts far ahead of their time. He died at Bloomfield Hills on July 1, 1950.

Eero Saarinen

Eero was born in Kirkkonummi on Aug. 20, 1910. He studied sculpture in Paris (1930–1931) and architecture at Yale, earning a bachelor of fine arts degree in 1934. He worked for, and in collaboration with, his father from 1936 to 1950. The leadership of Eliel seems to have been dominant. "As his partner," said Eero, "I often contributed technical solutions and plans, but only within the concept he created."

The two Saarinens designed the group of 25 buildings that make up the General Motors Technical Center, War-

ren, Mich. (1945–1956). Independently, in 1948, Eero won the competition for the Jefferson National Expansion Memorial, St. Louis (built 1962–1965). The memorial is a stainless-steel arch in the shape of an inverted weighted catenary curve. Eero designed the Kresge Auditorium and Chapel at the Massachusetts Institute of Technology, Cambridge (1953–1956); the auditorium was the first major shell construction in the United States.

In Eero's Trans World Airlines terminal at Kennedy Airport, N.Y. (1956–1962), the flow of space is dynamic. The quality of space is lost in the Dulles International Airport, Chantilly, Va. (1958–1962), where internal clutter negates the expression. The exterior of Dulles, however, has the splendor and grandeur of Versailles. At this airport Eero was attempting to solve the complex problem of passenger movement and access to aircraft by means of a mobile lounge system. His Morse and Stiles colleges at Yale University, New Haven, Conn. (1958–1962), are successfully integrated with the older buildings of the campus. Stylistically, the two colleges are dominated by the current trends.

Eero also designed the so-called womb chair (1948) and free-flowing plastic pedestal furniture (1958) capable of being mass-produced. He died in Bloomfield Hills on Sept. 1, 1961.

Further Reading

Eliel and Eero Saarinen are listed in the Art study guide (III, K, 2, g; IV, F, 2, b). Eliel's European work has much in common with that of Peter BEHRENS, Henry Hobson RICHARDSON, and Louis SULLIVAN. Eero's Dulles International Airport was inspired by the work of Erich MENDELSOHN. The severely rectangular buildings at the General Motors Technical Center are in the style of Ludwig MIES VAN DER ROHE.

Albert Christ-Janer, *Eliel Saarinen* (1948); Alan Temko, *Eero Saarinen* (1962); and Aline B. Saarinen, ed., *Eero Saarinen on His Work* (1962), are well-illustrated, comprehensive discussions of the total contribution to architecture of the two Saarinens.

SAAVEDRA LAMAS
/ By Victor C. Dahl

Carlos Saavedra Lamas (1878–1959) was an Argentine scholar, statesman, and diplomat who achieved world recognition for international reconciliation efforts during the 1930s.

Carlos Saavedra Lamas (pronounced sä-ä-vä′thrä lä′mäs) was born in Buenos Aires on Nov. 1, 1878, to a family of the *porteño* aristocracy. In 1903 he earned a doctorate of laws at the National University. His career in public service began with appointments as director of public credit (1906–1907) and as secretary of the Buenos Aires municipality (1907). He spent two terms in the National Congress, where he promoted the "Saavedra Lamas Law" of 1912, which protected domestic sugar producers from foreign competition. In 1915 he headed the Ministries of Justice and Public Education.

Saavedra Lamas presided over the International Labor Conference in Geneva in 1928. He served as minister of foreign affairs (1932–1938) and represented Argentina at several international conferences. He presided over the League of Nations Assembly in 1936, which Argentina had recently rejoined in an effort to engage in world affairs.

An ardent nationalist, Saavedra Lamas sought to increase his country's prestige by increasing ties with Europe and by assuming leadership of Spanish American nations. These policies intensified a long-standing United States–Argentina polarization in hemispheric affairs, countered the traditional United States Pan-American policies based upon the Monroe Doctrine, and hampered the Roosevelt administration's efforts to increase hemispheric solidarity by the new "good-neighbor" policy, which promised to treat all Latin American countries on a basis of equality. Nevertheless, Saavedra Lamas and U.S. Secretary of State Cordell Hull reconciled some

Carlos Saavedra Lamas. (Organization of American States)

of their countries' basic differences at the 1933 Inter-American Conference held in Montevideo.

A long-smoldering Bolivian-Paraguayan boundary dispute led to the Gran Chaco War (1932–1935), which defied the peacemaking efforts of Latin American nations and the United States and enabled Saavedra Lamas to assert Argentina's influence in hemispheric affairs. After failing to terminate the conflict by relying upon the League of Nations conciliation machinery, he engineered a permanent truce in 1935. Although the United States–Argentina rivalry probably prolonged the settlement, Saavedra Lamas, with Secretary Hull's support, received the Nobel Peace Prize for his efforts. Several European and Latin American governments also honored him for contributions to peace.

At the 1936 Inter-American Conference in Buenos Aires, Saavedra Lamas sought to safeguard hemispheric security through the League of Nations, thereby opposing the United States efforts to strengthen the inter-American system. Although President Franklin Roosevelt attended the conference and made many concessions in the interests of promoting inter-American cooperation, Foreign Minister Saavedra Lamas remained basically unmoved. Apparently he foresaw little danger to Argentina in the rise of European dictators, although later he became friendlier toward the United States and supported the Allies after the outbreak of World War II. Still, his policies helped to perpetuate the United States–Argentina estrangement.

After leaving the Foreign Ministry in 1938, Saavedra Lamas served at the National University as president (1941–1943) and as a professor of economics (1943–1946). He produced many books and articles on public education, economics, and international law. He died in Buenos Aires on May 5, 1959.

Further Reading

Carlos Saavedra Lamas is listed in the Latin America study guide (IV, A, 1, b). Another Argentinian well known in international affairs was Luis María DRAGO.

Saavedra Lamas's diplomatic involvement with the United States is thoroughly recounted by Harold F. Peterson in *Argentina and the United States, 1810–1960* (1964). For a briefer account see Arthur Preston Whitaker, *The United States and Argentina* (1954). The Chaco War settlement is described in David H. Zook, Jr., *The Conduct of the Chaco War* (1961); William R. Garner, *The Chaco Dispute: A Study of Prestige Diplomacy* (1966); and Leslie B. Rout, *Politics of the Chaco Peace Conference, 1935–1939* (1970).

✳   ✳   ✳

SABATIER / By Paul H. Emmett

The French chemist Paul Sabatier (1854–1941) is best known for his work in the field of catalyzed gas-phased reactions.

Paul Sabatier (pronounced så-bå-tyā′) was born in Carcassonne on Nov. 5, 1854. After graduating from the École Normale Supérieure in 1874 and teaching a year in the lycée at Nîmes, he became a laboratory assistant at the Collège de France in 1878. Two years later he received his doctoral degree with a thesis on the thermochemistry of sulfur and the metallic sulfides. After serving as *maître de conference* in physics in the faculty of sciences at Bordeaux for a year, he took charge of the course in physics in the faculty of sciences at Toulouse, the school at which he remained for the rest of his life. He became professor of chemistry in 1884 and went on to become one of the most brilliant representatives of the French chemical school.

After completing his thesis, Sabatier turned his attention to a host of inorganic and physical problems related to the thermochemistry of sulfides, chlorides, and chromates. A detailed study of the rate of transformation of metaphosphoric acid, studies on absorption spectra, and measurement of the partition coefficients of a base between two acids were included in the first 2 decades of his work.

Paul Sabatier. (French Embassy Press and Information Division)

Sabatier's efforts in the field of organic chemistry began about 1897 and led to the enunciation of a theory of catalytic hydrogenation over finely divided metals such as nickel, copper, cobalt, iron, and platinum. With the help of his colleagues he not only carried out a large number of experimental studies on catalytic hydrogenation but also proposed a theory of catalysis that is still useful and sound. He suggested that reactants combine with each other over catalysts as a result of forming unstable complexes or compounds with the catalyst surface. For this hypothesis and for his numerous experimental catalytic studies, science and industry will be eternally grateful.

The chemist received many honors. He was elected a member of the French Academy of Sciences, commander of the Légion d'Honneur, and an honorary member of the Royal Society of London, the Academy of Madrid, and the Royal Netherlands Academy of Sciences. He was awarded many prizes and medals as well, and "for his method of hydrogenating organic compounds in the presence of finely divided nickel" he received the Nobel Prize in chemistry in 1912.

Sabatier is described as being reserved and detached. He was fond of art and gardening. From his marriage to Mademoiselle Herail there were four daughters, one of whom married the Italian chemist Emile Pomilio. Sabatier died on Aug. 14, 1941.

Further Reading

Paul Sabatier is listed in the Science study guide (VII, D, 2). Other French chemists included Jean Baptiste DUMAS, Joseph GAY-LUSSAC, and Louis PASTEUR.

Biographical information on Sabatier is in Eduard Farber, *Nobel Prize Winners in Chemistry, 1901–1950* (1953); Eduard Farber, ed., *Great Chemists* (1961); and Nobel Foundation, *Chemistry: Nobel Lectures, Including Presentation Speeches and Laureates' Biographies* (3 vols., 1964–1966).

SÁBATO / By Philip B. Taylor, Jr.

The novelist and essayist Ernesto Sábato (born 1911) was one of Argentina's most challenging 20th-century intellectuals, concerned with both surrealist and real interpretations of phenomena, in real and imagined life.

Ernesto Sábato (pronounced sä′bä-tō) was born in Rojas, a provincial town of Buenos Aires Province, on June 24, 1911. One of 11 children of immigrant Italian parents, he received secondary and university training in La Plata, the provincial capital. Receiving a university degree in physics in 1937, he worked on a scholarship at the Joliot-Curie laboratory in Paris in 1938 and at the Massachusetts Institute of Technology in 1939. In 1939 he published a professional paper on his

Ernesto Sábato in 1969. (Wide World Photos)

specialty, cosmic radiation. From 1940 to 1945 he taught at the University of La Plata but was forced to resign by the Perón dictatorship as politically undesirable.

As a student, Sábato had been deeply involved in protest against the corrupting military manipulation of the country, and after discarding anarchism as a philosophy he became a leader of the Communist party's youth movement. In 1935 he attended the international Antifascist Congress in Brussels but refused to go to Moscow for indoctrination. After many months of traumatic self-examination in Paris, he broke with the party and returned to Argentina. To a degree, he remained a political iconoclast thereafter.

Simultaneously, Sábato became much interested in philosophy and literature. He credited Pedro Henríquez Ureña, the noted Mexican philosopher and writer, who was his teacher, with being the greatest early influence in his life. Sábato read with extraordinary breadth and increasingly skimped on his scientific work. By 1938 he already was doubted by his professional colleagues to some extent, and his expulsion from teaching in 1945 therefore was not a shock except to family income.

Sábato endured the Perón dictatorship through work for publishers and writing essays and articles. In 1955, when Perón fell, Sábato became director of *Mundo Argentino*, a reputable intellectual journal, but was removed when he took a dogmatic position against the torture of political opponents of the post-Perón military government of Pedro Aramburu. Sábato returned briefly to public life in 1958–1959, under Arturo Frondizi, but soon resigned.

Sábato's two novels are *El túnel* (1948) and *Sobre héroes y tumbas* (1961). His principal essays are *Uno y el universo* (1946), *Hombres y engranajes* (1951),

Heterodoxia (1953), *El otro rostro del peronismo* (1956), and *El escritor y sus fantasmas* (1963).

El túnel, a very short novel, is concerned with a figure unable to establish his own identity or effective relationships with others. Some autobiographical elements are suggested by the figure's anomie. Eventually the person resorts to violence against others, seeking a general understanding and awareness. *Sobre héroes y tumbas* is a longer and sweeping work and examines a variety of Argentine types, mores, and scenes. Critics find Sábato's novels influenced to some degree by the torment and anxiety of prerevolutionary Russian works. He employs imaginative metaphors and many asides in narration, in the style of romantic German novels. On the other hand, his scientific and epistemological training seems to have effected a precision and use of clarifying comparisons, especially in his novels.

Sábato's essays derive from his social and political concerns for the most part. At first he dealt with man's search for self and identity in a technocratic and indifferent society. His work of the Perón period was aphoristic, sarcastic, and critical of political abuses, but his later political essays show greater maturity of understanding and emphasize social morality and the need for consensual action to establish the responsibility and dignity of the society as well as of the individual.

In his later years, Sábato's work yielded to public appearances throughout the world and to popular television activity in Buenos Aires. He had married Matilde Kusminsky-Richter, a fellow student, and they had two children.

Further Reading

Ernesto Sábato is listed in the Latin America study guide (I, A, 2, b). Other Argentine intellectual leaders or writers were Carlos SAAVEDRA LAMAS, Luis María DRAGO, and Jorge Luis BORGES.

There is no full-length work on Sábato in English. For discussions of his work see Enrique Anderson-Imbert, *Spanish-American Literature: A History* (1954; trans. 1963; 2d ed., 2 vols., 1969), and Jean Franco, *The Modern Culture of Latin America: Society and the Artist* (1967).

SABBATAI ZEVI / By Malachi B. Martin

The Jewish mystic and pseudo-Messiah Sabbatai Zevi (1626–1676), or Sebi, was the founder of the Sabbatean sect.

Sabbatai Zevi (pronounced să-băt′ā-ī tsĕ-vē′) was born in Smyrna (modern Izmir), Turkey, of Spanish-Jewish parentage. At an early age he adopted the mysticism of Isaac ben Solomon Luria and began to lead an ascetic life. Sabbatai's continual prayer, prolonged ecstasies, and Messianic prophecies secured for him by the age of 22 a large and enthusiastic following.

Sabbatai's father was the local agent in Smyrna for an English firm. Perhaps through his father, Sabbatai heard excited talk about the English Fifth Monarch Men, a group that with Christian millennialists had fixed upon 1666 as the year of the Messiah and of millenarian fulfillment. The Jewish Cabalists had already proclaimed 1648 as the year of salvation. In that year Sabbatai announced himself as the coming Messiah, pointing to his birthday (the ninth day of the month Av) as the traditional birthday of the Messiah.

Sabbatai left Smyrna in 1651, lived at the Cabalist school of Salonika, and then proceeded to Constantino-

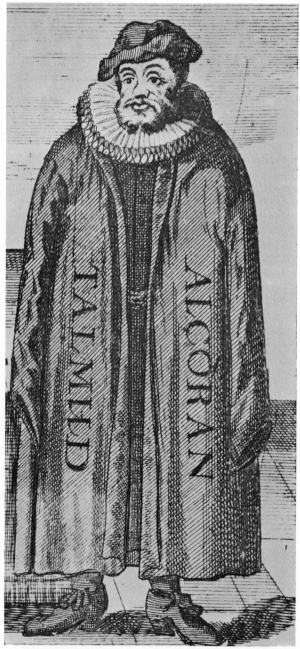

Sabbatai Zevi. (YIVO Institute for Jewish Research, New York City)

ple, where he met a man who claimed to have been told by angelic voices of Sabbatai's coming as the Redeemer. From Constantinople he traveled to Palestine and Cairo. The treasurer of the Turkish governor of Egypt, Raphael Halebi, gave Sabbatai moral support and funds. In Cairo he married a girl named Sarah who had survived the Chmielnicki massacre; he attributed a mystical value to his marriage, basing it as much on his wife's survival as on her name.

Sabbatai returned to Jerusalem to organize his movement. In the summer of 1665 Nathan of Gaza recognized Sabbatai as the Messiah, and he proclaimed that Sabbatai would win the longed-for Messianic victory "riding on a lion with a seven-headed dragon in his jaws."

The rabbis of Jerusalem, however, did not accept Sabbatai, and they also feared that his activities would arouse the anger of their Turkish overlords. Privately they threatened him with excommunication; publicly they could do nothing to stem the delirium of expectation that swept the Jewish communities of Egypt, Palestine, and Turkey and even those of Europe.

Sabbatai returned to Smyrna in the autumn of 1665, as the year of salvation approached. Jews in Venice, Amsterdam, London, Hamburg, southern Europe, and North Africa began to sell their belongings in expectation of being transported miraculously back to the restored Holy Land. At the beginning of 1666 Sabbatai went to Constantinople. Some reports say he was summoned by the Turkish authorities, who feared a popular uprising throughout their empire. He was arrested and imprisoned for 2 months in Constantinople and then transferred to the island of Abydos. Sabbatai's followers still believed in him, and in prison he held court, directed his movement, and lived like a king.

Denounced to the sultanate, Sabbatai was summoned to appear before the Sultan. To save his life he renounced Judaism and accepted Islam. Afterward, he was appointed doorkeeper to the Sultan. Later he was sent to Albania, where he died in complete obscurity. Long after his death many of his followers continued to believe in him. The influence of the Sabbatean movement survived into the 18th century.

Further Reading

Sabbatai Zevi is listed in the Religion study guide (II, E, 4). He was influenced by Isaac ben Solomon LURIA.

A study of Sabbatai is Julius Katzenstein (pseudonym: Josef Kastein), *The Messiah of Ismir: Sabbatai Zevi* (1930; trans. 1931). He is discussed in Israel Zangwill, *Dreamers of the Ghetto* (1898), and Solomon Schechter, *Studies in Judaism* (1958).

SACCO AND VANZETTI
/ By Charles Alexander

Nicola Sacco (1891–1927) and Bartolomeo Vanzetti (1888–1927), Italian-born anarchists, became the subject of one of America's most celebrated controversies and the focus for much of the liberal and radical protest of the 1920s in the United States.

The execution of Nicola Sacco and Bartolomeo Vanzetti in Boston in 1927 brought to an end a struggle of more than 6 years on the part of Americans and Europeans who had become convinced that they were innocent of the crimes of robbery and murder. For a sizable portion of the American intellectual community their case symbolized the fight for justice for ethnic minorities, the poor, and the politically unorthodox. The case had a catalytic influence on the subsequent development of leftist thought in America.

Sacco was born in Torremaggiore. When he was 17, he emigrated to the United States. He learned the trade of shoe edge-trimming and settled in Milford, Mass., working for a local shoe company. He married, fathered a son, and seemed to be building a stable and secure life.

Vanzetti, by contrast, was a bachelor and a wanderer. Born in Villafalletto, he went to the United States in early manhood. He worked as a kitchen helper in New York, then at various menial jobs in the Boston area. There Vanzetti, already committed to anarchist principles, met Sacco. When the United States entered World War I, they fled to Mexico to escape military conscription. Within a few months Sacco returned to his family; Vanzetti traveled around the American Midwest for a year.

Returning to New England, Vanzetti worked at a succession of jobs and renewed his friendship with Sacco, who was employed at a shoe factory. Vanzetti spent much time reading and reflecting on prospects for the revolutionary transformation of industrial society. Sacco, though little interested in books and ideas, also accepted the anarchist vision of brotherhood, peace, and plenty without government. The two moved in a circle of anarchists and sometimes distributed revolutionary literature.

Arrest, Trial, Conviction

Such were the ostensible circumstances of the two men's lives in May 1920, when they were arrested and charged with participating in the robbery of a shoe factory in South Braintree, Mass., on April 15 and murdering the plant's paymaster and payroll guard. They were arrested shortly after going to a garage to claim an automobile which had supposedly been seen near the South Braintree crime. Both were armed but protested they knew nothing of the crime and had planned to use the automobile to distribute anarchist literature.

Vanzetti, also charged with taking part in an attempted mail truck robbery the previous December, was speedily indicted, tried, convicted, and sentenced to 12 to 15 years' imprisonment. It was almost a year before Vanzetti and Sacco went on trial in Dedham for the South Braintree robbery and murders. Their trial turned into an extraordinarily vigorous and complicated legal struggle between the prosecutor and Fred H. Moore, who managed the Sacco and Vanzetti defense. After more than 6 weeks of listening to witnesses, to the presentation of ballistics evidence which supposedly matched a bullet from one of the victims with bullets from Sacco's pistol, and to grueling cross-examinations and closing speeches, the jury returned verdicts of guilty for both.

Posttrial Strategy

The Dedham trial received almost no publicity outside Boston while in progress; the anarchist issue was apparently of minor importance. But over the next 6 years

Nicola Sacco (left) and Bartolomeo Vanzetti (right), flanked by two plainclothesmen, entering Norfolk County Court House, Dedham, Mass., in 1921. (Library of Congress)

The Passion of Sacco and Vanzetti, *painted by Ben Shahn in 1931–1932. (Collection of Whitney Museum of American Art, New York, Gift of Mr. and Mrs. Milton Lowenthal in memory of Mrs. Force)*

Moore, William G. Thompson (who became chief defense counsel after Moore left), and the Sacco-Vanzetti Defense Committee (an array of anarchists, Boston free-thinkers from prestigious families, and middle-class liberals and radicals) reshaped the public image of the case into a political and ideological rather than a legal controversy. The thesis of the defense's campaign was that the trial had been conducted in an atmosphere of fear and repression and that the jury and especially Judge Webster Thayer had been prejudiced against the defendants. Therefore Sacco and Vanzetti stood convicted not because of the evidence but because of their radical political beliefs.

This strategy increasingly mobilized public sentiment as years passed and doubts multiplied regarding portions of the evidence. Some prosecution witnesses repudiated their identifications, then repudiated their repudiations. Another convicted murderer confessed that he had taken

part in the South Braintree crime and that Sacco and Vanzetti had not been in the gang, but his story was sketchy and inconsistent. The defense lawyers repeatedly but unsuccessfully presented motions for a new trial. On April 9, 1927, after the Massachusetts Supreme Judicial Court affirmed the convictions, Judge Thayer sentenced Sacco and Vanzetti to die in the electric chair.

Final Failure

The fight to save Sacco's and Vanzetti's lives continued. Governor Alvan T. Fuller, harassed on all sides, appointed a three-man panel to review the documents accumulated since 1920. The committee concluded that Sacco and Vanzetti should die. Desperate efforts to convince the U.S. Supreme Court to hear the case failed. On Aug. 22, 1927, as hundreds of heavily armed police faced crowds of demonstrators outside Boston's old Charlestown Prison, and as tens of thousands protested in the streets of New York and in many cities abroad, Sacco and Vanzetti were electrocuted.

The Sacco-Vanzetti case furnished a public cause around which American intellectuals of widely variant beliefs could unite. The case inspired a voluminous literary outpouring and seemed to dramatize the intolerance and injustice of American society. The movement to save Sacco and Vanzetti presaged the greater involvement of intellectuals with social issues that would mark the 1930s.

Further Reading

Nicola Sacco and Bartolomeo Vanzetti are listed in the American History study guide (IX, D, 4). The case inspired novels by Upton SINCLAIR and John DOS PASSOS and two plays by Maxwell ANDERSON.

Published material on the Sacco-Vanzetti case is voluminous. The classic brief for the defense is Felix Frankfurter, *The Case of Sacco and Vanzetti* (1927). G. Louis Joughin and Edmund M. Morgan, *The Legacy of Sacco and Vanzetti* (1948), an almost exhaustive résumé and analysis of the evidence, strongly upholds their innocence. Robert H. Montgomery, *Sacco-Vanzetti: The Murder and the Myth* (1960), concludes they were guilty, while Francis Russell, *Tragedy in Dedham* (1962), accepts the state's ballistics evidence and the guilty verdict for Sacco but exonerates Vanzetti. David Felix, *Protest: Sacco-Vanzetti and the Intellectuals* (1965), is more concerned with describing the development of the Sacco-Vanzetti "myth" and its impact on American intellectuals in the 1920s. Much of the atmosphere of the Sacco-Vanzetti protest movement can be gleaned from Upton Sinclair's novel *Boston* (1928) and John Dos Passos' *The Big Money* (1936) and *U.S.A.* (1937).

H. SACHS / By Edwin H. Zeydel

The German poet Hans Sachs (1494–1576) made Nuremberg famous in his time as a center of Meistergesang.

orn in Nuremberg, the son of a tailor of the upper middle class, Hans Sachs (pronounced zäks) was apprenticed to a shoemaker in 1508. As a journeyman, he traveled from one German town to another between 1511 and 1516 learning his trade. Simultaneously, he studied *Meistergesang* in the Singschulen, his principal teacher being Leonhard Nunnenbeck. *Meistergesang* is the German art of singing original poems to usually original tunes, according to the rules of the pedestrian craft of burgher poets; it was revived in the 19th century in parody form (as sung by Beckmesser in Richard Wagner's opera *Die Meistersinger*).

In Nuremberg in 1517 Sachs attained the rank of master in the shoemakers' guild and in *Meistergesang*. He declared himself in favor of Martin Luther in the poem *Die wittenbergisch Nachtigall* ("The Nightingale of Wittenberg") in 1523 and also in prose dialogues.

Sachs produced works in profusion: more than 4,000 *Meisterlieder*; 208 dramas, according to his own count; 85 Shrovetide plays; and many rhymed orations and other verses. During his lifetime three volumes of his verse appeared, and two more were issued posthumously. Other works remain unpublished in a collection in Zwickau, Saxony. His themes, derived from his reading in anecdotal and farcical literature of the time and from popularized and trivialized hero lore, cover a wide range from classical (Lucretia), biblical (Cain and Abel), and medieval (Siegfried) times to later periods. No matter what the subject or era, the time and locale are always those of Sachs's own Nuremberg; his characters talk like upright burghers of his age.

Sachs's so-called meistersinger dramas, a genre originating with his predecessor Rosenplüth, are merely dramatized dialogues, weak and heavy in the tragic mood, sprightly in the comic. Sachs excelled in the didactic-satiric manner. His best works are his later, exuberant Shrovetide plays, such as *Der fahrend schüler im Paradies* (1550; *The Itinerant Scholar in Paradise*) and *Das heiss Eisen* (1551; *The Hot Iron*), and such narrative skits as *St. Peter mit der Geis* (*St. Peter with the Goat*), all in rhymed doggerels.

Sachs's satire is good-natured, his humor never unduly coarse. He had a healthy moral instinct and a realistic bent, best employed on familiar ground. His comedies, performed in taverns and halls, though lacking dramatic quality, have influenced folk drama. Eclipsed after his death, Sachs's work was revived and popularized by Johann Wolfgang von Goethe in a poem of 1776; and in the opening scene of *Faust*, Goethe resuscitated Sachs's free doggerels. Sachs is the only German writer of his time whose short, witty, unsophisticated narrative poems and humble, jolly, dramatic Shrovetide skits can hold an audience today.

Further Reading

Hans Sachs is listed in the Literature study guide (III, D, 3). He continued the tradition of the minnesingers WALTHER VON DER VOGELWEIDE and GOTTFRIED VON STRASSBURG.

Some of Sachs's writings are in *Selections from Hans Sachs*, chosen by William M. Calder (1948). His work is discussed in Walter French, *Medieval Civilization as Illustrated by the Fastnachtsspiele of Hans Sachs* (1925).

NELLY **SACHS**

/ **By Frederick R. Benson and Monica Stoll**

The German-born Jewish poet and playwright Nelly Sachs (1891–1970), winner of the Nobel Prize, is noted for her austere but moving work, which constitutes a solemn monument to the hardships and sorrows of the Jewish people.

orn on Dec. 10, 1891, into a wealthy Jewish family, Nelly Sachs grew up in Berlin. After having studied dance and music with private tutors, she began at the age of 17 to write poetry. Her first collection of legends and sagas from the Middle Ages was published in 1921; this work reflected her fascination with the mystical elements of Christianity. Despite the influences of her own religious tradition, which can be traced throughout her poetry, in the years before the overt political persecution of the Jews accompanying Hitler's rise to power, she was not particularly concerned with her own religious origins. But with the advent of anti-Semitism, she turned to Orthodox Hasidism, where she discovered many of those occult aspects which had earlier attracted her to Christianity.

With the aid of Selma Lagerlöf, a well-known Scandinavian novelist, Miss Sachs and her mother fled Germany in 1940 and settled in Sweden. While still working on her own poetry, she acquired sufficient knowledge of

Hans Sachs in 1545. (Culver Pictures)

Nelly Sachs. (Süddeutscher Verlag)

Swedish to earn a living translating Swedish works into German. Her postwar anthology of Swedish verse, *Wave and Granite* (1947), brought some well-deserved acclaim to little-known writers. Her first collection of poetry was *But Even the Sun Has No Home* (1948). Both this volume and *Eclipse of the Stars* (1951), which were written during her flight from Germany, deal with the annihilation of 6 million Jews under the Third Reich; for diverse reasons they received little critical attention.

In 1950 a group of Swedish friends issued a private edition, 200 copies, of Miss Sachs's *Eli: A Miracle Play of the Suffering Israel*, which eventually found its way into Germany, where it became a widely acclaimed radio play. Like the other 11 plays written in this period, *Eli* was created in memory of those who had suffered and perished in Nazi concentration camps. Structurally the work has the simplicity of a medieval miracle play, but thematically it depicts a world devoid of trust and goodness, where innocence falls victim to evil.

Recognition of Nelly Sachs's gift as a lyric poet came in the late 1950s after the publication of *And No One Knows Where to Go* (1957) and *Flight and Metamorphosis* (1959). Once again the focus is on the black theme of the victims of the holocaust, as well as the author's personal loneliness. In the following decade she was the recipient of numerous honors, among which were the 1961 Nelly Sachs Prize, established by the city of Dortmund, and the Peace Prize of the German Book Trade at the Frankfurt Fair of 1965. In honor of her seventieth birthday, a Frankfurt publisher issued her collected works, containing a new series of poems, "Journey to the Beyond," which was dedicated by the author to "my dead brothers and sisters."

Despite the esteem in which she was held by many German-language readers, Nelly Sachs was little known to the rest of the European and American public when she received the Nobel Prize for literature in 1966. She died in Stockholm on May 12, 1970.

Further Reading

Nelly Sachs is listed in the Literature study guide (III, J, 2, b). She shared the 1966 Nobel Prize with the Israeli novelist S. Y. AGNON.

There is no substantial study of Nelly Sachs in English. A chapter in Paul Konrad Kurz, *On Modern German Literature*, vol. 1 (1967; trans. 1970), provides biographical information and comments on her work; and Harry T. Moore, *Twentieth-century German Literature* (1967), includes brief biographical data. A recent, important background study is Peter Demetz, *Postwar German Literature: A Critical Introduction* (1970)

SADE / By Paul G. Dobson

The French writer of psychological and philosophical works Donatien Alphonse François, Comte de Sade (1740–1814), was also a libertine, debaucher, pornographer, and sadist—a term derived from his name.

The Marquis de Sade (pronounced sàd) has been traditionally viewed as the greatest incarnation of evil that ever lived. Recently, however, new interpretations of his life and writings have begun to appear. It is now generally agreed that despite his reputation, his works, which were ignored for over a century, must be considered as of the first rank. Sade has been termed the "most absolute writer who has ever lived."

Born on June 2, 1740, to Marie Elénore de Maille de Carman, lady-in-waiting to and relative of the Princess de Condé, and Jean Baptiste Joseph François, Comte de Sade, who traced his ancestry to the chaste Laura of Petrarch's poems, the Marquis de Sade may be the most typical and the most unusual representative of the other side of the Enlightenment, the side at which the *philosophes* railed.

Very little is known of Sade's life. He graduated from the Collège de Louis le Grand, was commissioned as a coronet in the French army, and later sold his commission. He was forced to marry the eldest daughter of a leading magisterial family, Renée Pélagie de Montreuil, who bore him three children. Because of his libertinage, which included the seduction of and elopement with his wife's sister, Anne Prospère, he incurred the unending enmity of his mother-in-law, who eventually had him imprisoned in 1781. Sade had tasted imprisonment before for libertinage and indebtedness, and he spent half of his adult life in prisons and asylums. Only three public scandals can be proved against him, and none of these seems to merit the punishment meted out to him, reinforcing his claim that he was an unjust victim of his reputation and others' hatreds.

During the Revolution, Sade was released from prison, served as secretary and president of the Piques section of Paris, and represented it at least once before the National Convention, where he addressed a pamphlet calling for the abolition of capital punishment and the enfranchisement of women. His attitudes and actions gained the hatred of Maximilien de Robespierre, who had him imprisoned (1793). He was saved only by the death of the ''Incorruptible.'' Released in 1794, Sade was arrested in 1801 for being the supposed author of a scandalous pamphlet against Napoleon. He spent the rest of his life at Charenton insane asylum, where he died on Dec. 8, 1814. His best-known books include *Justine; ou, Les Malheurs de la vertu* (1791) and its sequel, *Histoire de Juliette; ou, Les Prospérités du vice* (1797).

Thus the life of the Marquis de Sade. Who was he? Why did he acquire the unique reputation he possesses? There are no simple answers regarding the life of any man. For Sade, there is possibly no answer at all. Recent works on his life have justly sought answers in his literary works, and because of this most commentators tend to psychoanalyze him. Although many of these works have offered brilliant insights into the character of the man, none of them is definitive and most treat him out of context, as though his life and aberrations were apart from life. Most Sadean scholars tend to agree that his hostility to religion, to the established social and political order, and to the despotism of existing law was similar in many ways to that of the *philosophes*. Some writers believe that he carried the beliefs of the *philosophes* to the rational conclusions, which in the end negated the conclusions and opened for succeeding generations a moral abyss. Others focus on what is termed a philosophy of destruction found in Sade's writings. Sade's atheism is viewed as the first element in a dialectic which destroys divinity through sacrilege and blasphemy and raises to preeminence an indifferent and unfolding nature which destroys to create and creates to destroy. Nature itself is then destroyed by being constantly outraged because it takes on the same sovereign character as God. What emerges is the ''Unique One,'' the man who rises above nature and arrogates to himself the creative and destructive capacities of nature in an extreme form, becoming solitary, alone, unique in the conscious awareness that he is the creative force and all others are but the material through which his energy is expressed.

Further Reading

The Marquis de Sade is listed in the Literature study guide (III, G, 1). Jean Jacques ROUSSEAU also opposed conventional morality.

Many of Sade's works are available in English. Biographies include Geoffrey Gorer, *The Life and Ideas of the Marquis de Sade* (1934; rev. ed. 1953), and Gilbert Lély, *The Marquis de Sade* (trans. 1962). Recommended for literary background is Mario Praz, *The Romantic Agony* (trans. 1933; 2d ed. 1956).

The Marquis de Sade. The engraver, H. Biberstein, surrounded the portrait with representations of the fantasies of Sade. (Photo-Hachette)

SADI / By Robert N. Hill

The Persian poet Shaikh Muslih-al-Din Sadi (ca. 1184–1291) is known in Iran today as its greatest ethical and worldly-wise poet. His works have a poignancy seldom equaled in world literature.

Born in Shiraz, Sadi (pronounced sä-dē′) was the son of a minor poet. His father's patron was Sad ben Zangi, from whom the younger poet took his *takhallus*, or poetical pseudonym, of Sadi.

Unfortunately, all our knowledge of Sadi must be derived from his own writings. Generally his life is broken into three main periods. First, he is thought to have studied in Shiraz, his birthplace, and in Baghdad until 1226, leaving these cities only to go on pilgrimages to different religious shrines. While in Baghdad, he studied under the well-known Sufi Shaikh Shihabud-Din Suhrawardi, of whose unselfish piety Sadi makes mention in his first major work, the *Bustan*. He proved to be a very fine student and soon gained fame as a wit and poet of short descriptive passages. His early poetry on the whole represented well the clever, half-pious, half-worldly side of the Persian character.

It was during the second period, from 1226 to 1256, that Sadi traveled widely and gained the experiences that were to be expressed so cogently later in his works. He left Shiraz largely because the old social and political infrastructure was breaking down. This was a period of warring and chaos in Persia. Sadi visited central Asia, India, Syria, Egypt, Arabia, Ethiopia, and Morocco.

Major Works

Sadi then returned home to his native town of Shiraz in 1256 to record his many experiences. This marks the third distinct period in his life. A year after his return he finished the *Bustan* (*Fruit Garden*). This is a collection of poems on ethical subjects always evidencing a practical train of thought. Then, in 1258, he finished the *Gulistan* (*Rose Garden*), which is a collection of moral stories in prose interspersed with verse. His last major work, the *Diwan*, was completed near the end of his life and is more biographical in nature.

Much has been said of the "ethical" nature of Sadi's writing, but this is so in a unique sense. The moral of the first story in the *Gulistan* is that "an expedient falsehood is preferable to a mischievous truth." The fourth story tries to show that the best education of a man is useless if he has inherited criminal tendencies. The eighth warns that a cornered cat will scratch out the eyes of a leopard. The ninth reiterates the sad truth that often a man's worst enemies are the inheritors of his wealth. And the fourteenth commends a soldier who deserted because his pay was in arrears.

As a moralist, Sadi gained much from the vicissitudes of life that he experienced on his travels. His knowledge of the world adds much to his cosmopolitan view. He seems to look upon the world with sympathetic humor and not harsh satire. And yet he is sometimes Machiavellian. Revenge is sometimes recommended in place of mercy, insincerity in place of veracity. Above all, man is encouraged to keep his independence from other people.

The different aspects of Sadi's morality make it difficult to believe in his sincerity. However, with a Persian poet it is often difficult to separate what belongs to the poet himself and what are concessions to his patrons. In any case, his popularity in the Eastern world should not be overlooked. Sadi has shown himself in all his humanity, and he has satisfied the predilections of the Persians for moralizing, a trait they have had since pre-Islamic times.

Finally, when speaking to the philosophy of his day—mysticism—there is no doubt that Sadi was a diligent student and believer. But when referring to the Sufis of his day, he is always more of a moralizer than a mystic. It was precisely the perishability of the world that made it of value for Sadi. He preached a this-worldliness with only a moderate fatalism, and he disapproved of extreme piety.

Further Reading

Sadi is listed in the Asia study guide (I, B, 3, e). Other famous Persian poets were FIRDAUSI and OMAR KHAYYAM.

Edward Rehatsek's translation *The Gulistan, or Rose Garden of Sa'di* (1964), includes an excellent biographical preface by W. G. Archer and a fine introduction by G. M. Wickens. There is no definitive full-length biography of Sadi. The best sources are Edward G. Browne, *A Literary History of Persia* (4 vols., 1906–1909), which discusses the full range of Persian literature and relates Sadi to many of his contemporaries, and Philip K. Hitti, *History of the Arabs* (1937; 10th ed. 1970). For good discussions of the Sufism of Sadi see A. J. Arberry, *Sufism: An Account of the Mystics of Islam* (1950), and Idries Shah, *The Sufis* (1964).

Sadi (center) at his home. (Bibliothèque Nationale, Paris)

SAICHO / By E. Dale Saunders

Saicho (767–822) was a Japanese Buddhist monk who bore the posthumous title Dengyo daishi. He was the founder in Japan of the

Tendai sect, which he imported after a period of study in China.

In 783 the emperor Kammu decided to remove his capital from the city of Nara, where it had been since 710. By training, Kammu was Confucian and generally anti-Buddhist. He was opposed to the great power that the six Nara sects had amassed. He had been particularly alarmed when, in 764, the monk Dokyo had almost succeeded in having himself declared ruler of Japan. Kammu's decision to move was based on his desire to preserve the prerogatives of the imperial court. To counterbalance the influence of the old, still powerful Nara sects on his new capital of Heian (Kyoto), which he founded in 794, he encouraged the founding of two new sects, which were to maintain a close relationship with the new government: Tendai, established by Saicho (pronounced sī-chō), and Shingon, by Kukai.

Of Chinese descent, Saicho was born in Shiga in the province of Omi, entered the priesthood at the age of 14, and was ordained in 785. He was, however, disenchanted with the worldliness of the Nara priesthood and was convinced of the need for a new location if there was to be a moral and ethical awakening. Thus, in 788, he founded a small temple, later called the Enryaku-ji, on Mt. Hiei. In 788 the area around Mt. Hiei was uncultivated marshland, but in 794 it was chosen as a site for the new capital of Heian. Perhaps Saicho was instrumental in the choice, for he enjoyed the patronage of the Emperor. He was asked to hold a ceremony for purification of the new emplacement, and in 797 the Emperor is said to have referred to Mt. Hiei as the true guardian of the empire.

Travel to China

In 804 Saicho was sent to China, forming part of the ambassadorial party of Fujiwara Kadonomaro. The Shingon master Kukai was a member of the group, but on a different ship, and it is not certain that the two men met. The purpose of this trip was most especially to obtain sanction for his temple on Mt. Hiei, Chinese approval being considered necessary for standing vis-à-vis the Nara sects. Saicho returned to Japan in 805.

It does not appear at first that Saicho wanted to found a new sect. His temple enshrined the Buddha of Medicine (Yakushi), as did many of the temples at Nara, but after a year abroad he was drawn to the universality of the T'ien-t'ai sect, which was flourishing at the time. The Tendai he introduced into Japan was essentially the same as the mother sect and was based on the Lotus Sutra. Nara sects, with the exception of Kegon, were all based on secondary sources—the commentaries—and Saicho considered Tendai superior to them, for it was based on the Buddha's own words, that is, a sutra. Tendai, for Saicho, was true Mahayana Buddhism.

Saicho's teaching was universal in that it claimed enlightenment for all. This universality stood against Hosso beliefs, for example, that some beings were excluded from Buddhahood by virtue of inborn defects. Tendai

Saicho, a 14th-century Japanese scroll painting from the Kamakura period. (Courtesy, Museum of Fine Arts, Boston, Gift of Mrs. Walter Scott Fitz)

claimed that all men had the innate possibility of enlightenment. It also stressed the basic unity of the Buddha and other beings; even the wicked man is Buddha. For Saicho, Buddhist perfection was a life of moral purity and contemplation, and he strongly stressed moral perfection over metaphysics. In 807 Saicho held an ordination ceremony on a *kaidan* (ordination platform) erected on Mt. Hiei. But such was the opposition of the Nara sects that further permission was denied until 827, five years after his death.

Tendai Sect

In contrast to Nara practice, Saicho demanded a severe discipline of the monks under him. In 818 he codified the rules for monks on Mt. Hiei. There they were obliged to remain 12 years, during which time they received the "training of a bodhisattva." This meant study of Mahayana sutras, most especially the Lotus, and a kind of mystic concentration called *shikan*. It was Saicho's intent that Mt. Hiei should supply the nation with teachers and leaders.

There were three classes of monks who received training. The first was the "Treasure of the Nation," those particularly gifted in actions and words. They would remain on Mt. Hiei and serve the country by religious practice. The less gifted would leave to serve the state: some would teach; others would engage in agricultural and engineering pursuits. Thus, unlike Nara Buddhism, the new sect was at the service of the court, and the Enryaku-ji was called the "Center for the Protection of the Nation."

Saicho's writing shows a streak of nationalism. His *Defense of the Country (Shugo kokkai sho)* considers Tendai teachings as a protection for Japan. He felt very strongly about the prestige of the court, and despite his Chinese origins he admired the "Country of great Japan" (*dai nippon koku*). Tendai monks were obliged to swear an oath which included acknowledgment of the sect's debt to the Emperor.

Kukai and Saicho

In 806 the emperor Kammu died, and Saicho and his sect were at once threatened, first by the Nara monks, who questioned his authority, and then by the return in the same year of Kukai, the Shingon ecclesiastic who gained the favor of Kammu's successor.

Relations between Kukai and Saicho were at first friendly. Saicho sincerely wanted to learn what Kukai had acquired and brought back with him from China. Indeed, Saicho was much impressed with Esoteric teachings. He went so far as to receive baptism from Kukai, and he borrowed works on Esotericism from him. Relations changed, however, when Saicho sent his favorite disciple, Taihan, to study with Kukai, for the latter refused to honor Saicho's request that his pupil return to Mt. Hiei. And when Saicho requested a loan of certain Esoteric sutras, Kukai's response was plainly impolite, if not insulting, and he suggested that if Saicho wished to learn he should become a regular student. Relations between the two men remained bitter until Saicho's death.

Saicho's contribution to Japanese Buddhism lies more in organization than in doctrine. His writing tends to be heavy and repetitious, lacking the distinction of Kukai's. His most winning feature, however, is his sincerity, his desire to know the truth, not only as it was propounded by his own sect but by others as well.

Further Reading

Saicho is listed in the Asia study guide (III, B, 3, c). Other travelers to China in his time were ENNIN and KUKAI.

Examples of Saicho's writings and an essay on his impact on Japanese Buddhism may be found in Ryusaku Tsunoda and others, eds., *Sources of the Japanese Tradition* (1958). There is no full-length biography of Saicho. However, Sir Charles Eliot, *Japanese Buddhism*

(1935), discusses Saicho and the Tendai sect. An excellent book depicting the times when Saicho lived is Ivan Morris, *The World of the Shining Prince: Court Life in Ancient Japan* (1964).

SAID / By Charles L. Geshekter

Seyyid Said (1790–1856) was the energetic and resourceful sultan of Oman who transferred his capital from Arabia to Zanzibar, where he initiated clove production and greatly expanded the East African slave trade.

Seyyid Said (pronounced sä-ēd′) became sultan of the Persian Gulf state of Oman in 1806. Although the area was neither rich nor easy to govern, Omani fortunes rose during the Napoleonic Wars, when European merchants relied heavily on Arab shipping throughout the northern and western Indian Ocean. This prosperity proved short-lived after Britain gained control of Indian Ocean ports, thereby enabling British companies to monopolize shipping in that "English lake"; simultaneously the British navy worked to eliminate piracy in the Persian Gulf. Said's prolonged struggles with the fierce Wahhabis from the desert marshes of Oman finally convinced him of the futility of attempting any expansion of his power within the Arabian peninsula. Oman quickly descended to the depths of poverty as unemployment rose and discontent spread.

A flexible and ambitious man, Said sought alternatives to improve the lot of his countrymen and agreed to a treaty with Britain in 1823 that forbade slave trading between his Moslem subjects and any Christian power, at least in the Persian Gulf. The British in return offered friendship and support for Said's commercial interests elsewhere, especially on the East African coast, where he tried to reassert dynastic claims to govern that region of long-standing Omani trading activity.

Move to Zanzibar

Devoting more energy to his African dominions in the 1830s, Said eventually relocated his capital from the city of Masqat to Zanzibar in 1840 and thus became an East African ruler with possessions in Arabia. Although Said never entirely abandoned Oman, it thereafter ranked as an unruly distant province rather than as the heart and soul of his realm. Said used military and naval expeditions, diplomatic scheming, and the personal appointment of governors to exploit local dynastic disputes among the East African Mazrui rulers; thus by 1841 the establishment of his authority over all main coastal towns made him the first ruler ever to control the coast from Mogadishu (Somalia) to southern Tanzania.

A merchant prince rather than a soldier, Said depended on mercantile and maritime resources for his power in

Seyyid Said. (The Peabody Museum of Salem)

both Oman and Zanzibar. Recognizing the suitability of Zanzibar climate and soil, he initiated large-scale cultivation of cloves—an essential meat preservative in Europe prior to the advent of refrigeration—and soon after sought slaves as cheap labor to plant and harvest the biennial crop. In order to reach potential slaving areas in the African interior, it was necessary to finance and equip caravans for this egregious activity; resident Indians long active in Indian Ocean business ventures were attracted by possible high returns on labor investments and not only extended credit to Arab-led caravans but henceforth supplied most loans for slave purchases at Zanzibar.

Said functioned as a skillful liaison, bringing together the available Indian capital for use by his Arab adventurers. He stood between these two disparate groups, preventing wasteful arguments and quarrels, protecting Arabs from arbitrary exactions by Indians, and requiring the moneylenders to make loans only to caravans and plantations controlled by men who had Said's personal approval. Despite Arab prestige and commercial power in the interior, Said never actually ruled over any sizable number of Africans there; and in fact, wherever Arabs offended powerful tribes such as the Nyamwezi and Shambaa of Tanzania, they were often expelled.

Said's creation of the Zanzibar sultanate brought renewed prosperity to his Omani followers, and by 1850 he reported an annual income exceeding £100,000. Zanzibar Town developed into an important international entrepôt exporting slaves and ivory from regions of present-day Mozambique and Tanzania, and the mainland north of the island witnessed the major development of grain and coconut plantations. This entire pattern of economic growth was continually underwritten

by Indian capitalists at Zanzibar and coordinated largely by Said's government at the coast. Seyyid Said ruled the East African coast in this way until his death in 1856; afterward the Arab-Indian alliance slowly collapsed because of British interference, succession disputes, and political squabbles.

What was Seyyid Said's contribution to East Africa? If the answer is based on what he left behind, then undoubtedly the increase in the Islamic faith and the spread of Swahili as the lingua franca of the coast and interior are the most enduring monuments of his rule. Although his economic revival helped launch the first sustained contact between the East African coast and interior, the Sultan must also be remembered for his part in at least a century-long pattern of domination and exploitation established, maintained, and encouraged by him and his successors.

Further Reading

Seyyid Said is listed in the Africa study guide (VII, E, 1). The pattern of exploitation he established was broken by the 1964 rebellion, which had among its leaders Sheikh Abeid KARUME.

Said's years in Oman and Masqat are thoroughly examined in J. B. Kelly, *Britain and the Persian Gulf, 1795–1880* (1968). Reginald Coupland, *East Africa and Its Invaders: From the Earliest Times to the Death of Seyyid Said in 1856* (1938), is an exhaustive historical survey of the East African coast, but many of its assumptions have been questioned and revised in Roland Oliver and others, eds., *History of East Africa*, vol. 1 (1963), and B. A. Ogot and J. A. Kieran, *Zamani: A Survey of East African History* (1968). A succinct statement on the slave trade is Edward A. Alpers, *The East African Slave Trade* (1967); and J. Spencer Trimingham, *Islam in East Africa* (1964), serves as a useful introduction to Moslem activity throughout the region.

SAIGO / By Peter Duus

> The Japanese rebel and statesman Takamori Saigo (1827–1877) was the military leader of the Meiji restoration. His eventual revolt against the Meiji government in 1877 represented the resistance of the old warrior class to the swift and often ruthless policy of Westernization of Japan.

Takamori Saigo (pronounced sī-gō) was born the eldest son of a lower-ranking samurai family on Feb. 7, 1827, in Kagoshima, the castle town of the Satsuma domain. As a youth, he showed much interest in both Wang Yang-ming Confucianism and Zen Buddhism, both of which stressed the importance of acting on individual conscience. After briefly attending the domain academy, he became a minor domain official. A huge

Takamori Saigo. (International Society for Educational Information, Tokyo, Inc.)

man, physically powerful with a dark penetrating gaze and a commanding presence, he attracted the attention of the lord of the domain, Nariakira Shimazu, who agreed with his views that major domestic reforms were necessary to meet the challenge of the West. He acted as courier and confidant to Nariakira until the latter's death in 1858.

After an abortive attempt at suicide in 1858, Saigo remained in retirement until 1864, when he reemerged as a military leader in the domain. He led Satsuma troops in skirmishes with Choshu forces at Kyoto in 1864 and later in the shogunate's expedition against Choshu. Gradually, however, he became convinced that it was in the interest of both his domain and the country that Satsuma act in concert with Choshu to bring an end to continued domination of the country by the Shogun. In 1868 Saigo served as field commander of the imperial forces in campaigns against the military resistance of the shogunate. As a result of this experience, he won a reputation as a great military hero and the universal respect of the samurai who served under him.

Discontent with Meiji

Once the Meiji restoration was accomplished, Saigo found himself in growing disagreement with the leaders of the new imperial government. Although he was appointed minister of war in 1871 and became a field marshal and court councilor in 1872, he opposed the growing centralization of the government, the trimming of the legal and social privileges of the samurai class, and the rapid pace of Westernization. In 1873 he finally broke with the government when some of its members, who had returned from an extended trip to Europe, rejected his plan for an invasion of Korea to provide military glory for former samurai and to enhance Japan's international position.

Saigo returned to his native province, where there was much samurai discontentment with the abolition of their privileges and the shift of power from the feudal domains to the central government. Saigo seems to have remained politically inactive and even resisted pressure by discontented elements in other domains to revolt. But in 1877, when an army of former Satsuma samurai rebelled against the central government's attempts to end Satsuma's semiautonomous administrative status, he agreed to lead them. On Sept. 24, 1877, he took his life in traditional samurai fashion during the final battle with government troops, which ended the rebellion.

Further Reading

Takamori Saigo is listed in the Asia study guide (III, B, 7, a). Another early supporter of Meiji who grew disenchanted with the government was Shigenobu OKUMA.

The only biography of Saigo in English is a translation of a work by a well-known novelist, Saneatsu Mushakoji, *Great Saigo: The Life of Takamori Saigo* (1942), which is romanticized and eulogistic. The story of Saigo's involvement in the rebellion of 1877 is treated in a contemporary journalistic account by Augustus H. Mounsey, *The Satsuma Rebellion: An Episode of Modern Japanese History* (1879).

ST. CLAIR / By Roger L. Nichols

Arthur St. Clair (1736–1818), Scottish-born American soldier and politician, was the first territorial governor in United States history.

Arthur St. Clair was born on March 23, 1736, in Thurso. He attended the University of Edinburgh and had some training with the prominent London anatomist William Hunter. St. Clair joined the British army as an ensign in 1757 and served with Col. Jeffery Amherst in Canada. Three years later he married Phoebe Bayard, who bore him seven children. In 1762 he resigned his army commission and bought 4,000 acres of land in western Pennsylvania, which made him the largest resident landholder in that area.

This distinction brought St. Clair local responsibilities. He served as the agent for Governor William Penn in 1771 and justice of the Westmoreland County Court 2 years later. For several years he represented Pennsylvania in its fight with Virginia over the territory at Pittsburgh, but he had little success.

In 1775 St. Clair became a colonel in the American army, and a year later he became a brigadier general, serving with George Washington's forces in the American Revolution. By the spring of 1777 St. Clair had been promoted to major general and received command of Ft. Ticonderoga. When he evacuated that post, Congress recalled him. Although a court-martial cleared him in 1778, he received no further army assignments.

Returning to civilian life, St. Clair reentered politics. He was a member of the Pennsylvania Council of Censors in 1783; in 1785 he was elected to the Continental Congress, becoming president of that body 2 years later. When Congress established the Northwest Territory in 1787, St. Clair was appointed territorial governor.

St. Clair's career as governor was stormy. His territorial militia was dealt disastrous defeats by the Indians in 1790 and 1791. Meanwhile, his efforts to govern the territory caused considerable difficulty. He used his authority to obstruct legislation designed to curtail his power and democratize the territorial government. He opposed the move for statehood and, to delay it, tried to split the territory into smaller political units. When he denounced the Ohio Enabling Act as null, President Thomas Jefferson removed him from office. St. Clair then retired to his home near Ligonier, Pa., where he died on Aug. 31, 1818.

Further Reading

Arthur St. Clair is listed in the American History study guide (IV, D, 2). After his defeat, Gen. Anthony WAYNE was authorized to act against the Ohio Indians.

Arthur St. Clair, a painting by Charles Willson Peale. (Independence National Historical Park Collection, Philadelphia)

The most recent and only book-length biography of St. Clair is Frazer Ellis Wilson, *Arthur St. Clair: Rugged Ruler of the Old Northwest* (1944), which presents a laudatory account of his checkered career. William Henry Smith, *The St. Clair Papers: The Life and Public Services of Arthur St. Clair* (2 vols., 1882), ignores St. Clair's weaknesses, presenting only his virtues. For general studies of the problems encountered in settling the Northwest Territory see Richard L. Power, *Planting Corn Belt Culture* (1953), and John D. Barnhart, *Valley of Democracy* (1953). Randolph C. Downes discusses frontier Indian affairs in *Council Fires on the Upper Ohio* (1940).

ST. DENIS / By Stuart Samuels

> Ruth St. Denis (1878?-1968), American dancer and choreographer, was one of the founders of modern dance. Her work was characterized by its religious and Far Eastern content.

Ruth St. Denis, whose name was originally Ruth Dennis, was born in Newark, N.J., on January 20, probably in 1878, the daughter of an inventor father and a physician mother. At the age of 10 Ruth started dancing and gave her first solo performance in 1893 in a play produced by her mother.

Professional dance at this time presented two equally uninspiring alternatives: the world of vaudeville and the moribund classical ballet of opera. Miss St. Denis was delivered from this dilemma when she discovered an advertising poster for Egyptian Deities cigarettes showing the goddess Isis sitting on a throne. Immediately she saw the possibility of developing a dance on an Egyptian theme. While doing research on the culture and dance of Egypt, she discovered the dances of India.

With the help of some Indian friends, Miss St. Denis danced the *radha*, a freestyle Indian dance. She was the first in the Western world to introduce to a legitimate audience Oriental and Eastern dancing. The dances were accompanied by European music performed on Western musical instruments. American audiences were hostile to her experiments, labeling her the "Jersey Hindoo" and comparing her with the belly dancers at the local burlesque houses.

Miss St. Denis toured in Europe from 1906 to 1909, and her dances proved a great success. Like the dancer Isadora Duncan, Ruth St. Denis was also preoccupied with mysticism and was not concerned with steps but with the expressive movement of the body. But her style was more exotic and more lavishly theatrical—combining lights, scenery, costumes, music, and story in one unified experience—and her dances were much more religious.

In 1910 Miss St. Denis became the first solo dancer to play a New York theater as the evening star attraction. She continued to experiment with new dance forms. In

1913 she presented her *Egypta* dances and gave the first performance of *O'Mika*, a Japanese ballet based on her study of Japanese No theater.

In 1914 Miss St. Denis married her dancing partner, Ted Shawn, and they set up the Denishawn School of Dancing, the first serious school of dance in America with a standard curriculum. From 1915 to 1931 it was *the* training ground for America's leading dancers and choreographers. Thirteen Denishawn tours of America helped create a basic audience for modern dance and establish dance in America as an accepted art form. The school's approach was eclectic and experimental. In 1925, for example, Miss St. Denis created *Tragica*, the first dance without music. In 1930 she and Shawn separated, and the school disbanded.

As a result of her study of Oriental systems of thought, Ruth St. Denis extended the religious implications of her dancing. In 1931 she founded the Society of Spiritual Arts to establish the dance as an instrument of worship. In 1947 she formed a Church of the Divine Dance in Hollywood, where she conducted dance masses and rituals. She continued to dance and experiment until her eighties. She died on July 21, 1968.

Further Reading

Ruth St. Denis is listed in the American History study guide (VIII, F, 6). Isadora DUNCAN was another pioneer of modern dance.

Ruth St. Denis's own account is *An Unfinished Life: An Autobiography* (1939). The authorized and most comprehensive biography is by a lifelong friend and

Ruth St. Denis. (Library of Congress)

dance critic, Walter Terry, *Miss Ruth: The "More Living Life" of Ruth St. Denis* (1969). An early appraisal was written by Ted Shawn, *Ruth St. Denis: Pioneer and Prophet* (1920). See also Walter Terry, *The Legacy of Isadora Duncan and Ruth St. Denis* (1959).

SAINT-EXUPÉRY / By Denis Boak

The French novelist and essayist Antoine de Saint-Exupéry (1900–1944), a pioneer commercial pilot, more than any other writer can be regarded as the poet of flight.

Antoine de Saint-Exupéry (pronounced săN-tĕg-zü-pā-rē′) was born in Lyons on June 29, 1900; he attended Jesuit schools in France and Switzerland. He was a poor and unruly student but took great interest in the rapidly developing science of flight. In 1921 he began military service and learned to fly, later being commissioned as an air force officer. After 3 years in business, Saint-Exupéry became a commercial pilot in 1926, flying first from France to Morocco and West Africa. From his experiences he drew the novel that launched his literary career in 1929, *Courrier Sud (Southern Mail)*. Here he portrays the pilot's solitary struggle against the elements and his sense of dedication to his vocation, stronger even than love.

In 1929 Saint-Exupéry was transferred to Buenos Aires, and he married in 1931. The same year he published his second book, *Vol de nuit (Night Flight)*. Again the theme is the pilot's devotion to duty, and although, as in *Courrier Sud*, it ends in his death, this is seen not as defeat but as victory, a step forward in man's conquest of his environment. For Saint-Exupéry there are higher values than human life, and the novel achieves an almost tragic intensity.

During the following years Saint-Exupéry pursued his flying career, despite several crashes, but published no more books until 1939, when he brought out *Terre des hommes (Wind, Sand and Stars)*. Less a novel than a series of essays containing the pilot's meditations, poetic in tone, on the spiritual aspects of the adventure of flight, it brought Saint-Exupéry to the height of literary fame.

In 1939 Saint-Exupéry rejoined the French air force and was decorated for bravery in 1940. After the French defeat, he went to the United States, where he wrote *Pilote de guerre (Flight to Arras)*, published in 1942. This is the record of a reconnaissance mission in May 1940, during the German invasion of France, and the author's almost miraculous survival against enormous odds. In 1943 he rejoined his unit in North Africa, fighting with the Free French; although now overage, he insisted on undertaking reconnaissance missions. On July 31, 1944, his aircraft disappeared near Corsica, probably shot down by a German fighter; no trace was ever discovered.

Antoine de Saint-Exupéry. (Harlingue-Viollet)

Other works of Saint-Exupéry include a children's story, *Le Petit prince* (1943; *The Little Prince*); a long philosophical work published posthumously, *Citadelle* (1948; *The Wisdom of the Sands*); and volumes of correspondence and notebook jottings.

Further Reading

Antoine de Saint-Exupéry is listed in the Literature study guide (III, J, 1, a). He was a contemporary of André MALRAUX.

Curtis Cate, *Antoine de Saint-Exupéry: His Life and Times* (1970), is an excellent biography. Other studies, biographical as much as literary, include Richard Rumbold and Lady Margaret Stewart, *The Winged Life* (1955); Maxwell A. Smith, *Knight of the Air: The Life and Works of Antoine de Saint-Exupéry* (1956); and Marcel Migeo, *Saint-Exupéry* (trans. 1961). A good short study of him is in Henri Peyre, *French Novelists of Today* (1967).

SAINT-GAUDENS / By William Gerdts

Augustus Saint-Gaudens (1848–1907), the leading American sculptor of the late 19th century, is best known for his bronze historical memorials.

Augustus Saint-Gaudens was born in Dublin, Ireland, on March 1, 1848, and taken to America as an infant. He grew up in New York City. At the age of 13 he was apprenticed to a cameo cutter, and he later attended classes at Cooper Union and the National Academy of Design. In 1867 he went to Paris, where he studied at the École des Beaux-Arts, and in 1870 he left for Rome. His marble *Hiawatha* and *Silence*, carved in Rome, were his only significant works in the still prevalent neoclassic style.

Shortly after Saint-Gaudens returned to the United States in 1875, he received the commission for the Adm. Farragut monument in Madison Square, New York City. This work, which was completed in 1881, is imbued with the spirit of the early Renaissance, and it established his reputation. It was the first of a number of memorials relating to the Civil War. In the Farragut monument he combines the idealistic sense of the heroic with vivid portraiture. The base is adorned with extremely delicate low-relief sculptures, a form which Saint-Gaudens revived from the Renaissance. He had already achieved success in low-relief portraits.

Saint-Gaudens next executed a sculpture of Abraham Lincoln standing in front of a Renaissance chair (1887) for Lincoln Park, Chicago. As in the Farragut, he was associated with the architect Sanford White in constructing the base. Saint-Gaudens's *Puritan* (1887), a memorial to Deacon Samuel Chapin in Springfield, Mass., is an eloquent embodiment of early New England Puritanism. His next major Civil War monument was the complex memorial to Robert Gould Shaw (1884–1897), who had led the first regiment of Negro troops from Massachusetts and died during the conflict in 1863. This monument, opposite the State House in Boston, has a high-relief equestrian statue and other figures in varying depths of relief.

Augustus Saint-Gaudens. (G. C. Cox Collection, History of Photography Collection, Smithsonian Institution, Washington, D.C.)

Probably Saint-Gaudens's best-known work is his memorial to Gen. Sherman (1892–1903) in Central Park, New York City, a work which blends realism and idealism. The figure of Victory is based on the ancient Victory of Samothrace, and the great equestrian statue is related to Donatello's 15th-century *Gattamelata. Diana* (1892; now in the Philadelphia Museum of Art) is Saint-Gaudens's one ideal nude. Perhaps his most moving and affecting sculpture is the figure sometimes entitled *Grief* (1891–1893), the monument to Mrs. Henry Adams in Rock Creek Cemetery, Washington, D.C. The inscrutable, enigmatic form is a touching embodiment of personal grief and tragedy, the greatest of all the allegories of death of the period.

Saint-Gaudens was eminently successful in his own time. He was the leader in the artistic community which grew up around his estate at Cornish, N.H. He died there on Aug. 3, 1907, and his house and studio have been preserved as the Saint-Gaudens Memorial.

Further Reading

Augustus Saint-Gaudens is listed in the Art study guide (IV, D, 3). He worked with Stanford WHITE. Another famous statue of Lincoln was executed by Daniel Chester FRENCH.

A definitive study of Saint-Gaudens by John Dryfhout was in preparation as of 1972. Useful works are Royal Cortissoz, *Augustus Saint-Gaudens* (1907), and *The Reminiscences of Augustus Saint-Gaudens*, edited by Homer Saint-Gaudens (2 vols., 1913).

SAINT-JUST / By Gordon H. McNeil

Louis Antoine Léon de Saint-Just (1767–1794), a radical political leader during the French Revolution, was a member of the ruling Jacobin group in Paris during the Reign of Terror.

Louis de Saint-Just (pronounced săN zhüst′) was born on Aug. 25, 1767, in Decize, the son of an army officer. After a period of schooling, he ran away from home to Paris, taking with him part of the family silver. He studied law for a time and also published a burlesque epic which was a mixture of the crudely erotic and of sharp criticism of the government and society of his day.

When the Revolution broke out in 1789, the youthful Saint-Just gave it his enthusiastic support, and he published in 1791 *The Spirit of the Revolution and of the Constitution of France*. He was too young to be elected to the Legislative Assembly that year, but in September 1792 he was elected a member of the Convention, whose task it was, now that the King had been deposed, to draft a new constitution and to govern France in the meantime. Saint-Just, handsome, proud, and self-possessed, spoke with the zeal of a dedicated revolutionist.

Louis de Saint-Just, a painting by Jacques Louis David. (French Cultural Services of the French Embassy)

He ruthlessly and brilliantly urged the trial and execution of the King; he participated actively in drafting the Constitution of 1793; and in the feverish atmosphere of foreign and civil war, he became the spokesman for the Jacobins in demanding the death of their moderate opponents, the Girondins.

In June 1793 Saint-Just became a member of the Committee of Public Safety, the executive body that ruled France in dictatorial fashion, using the so-called Reign of Terror as a means of repressing opposition. In October he was sent as a representative to the Army of the Rhine in Strasbourg, where the war was going badly and factionalism and opposition to the government in Paris were at their height. He was twice sent on similar missions to the Army of the North.

Back in Paris, Saint-Just defended the Terror in speeches and proposed a redistribution of the property of the disloyal rich, a plan that was never implemented. As spokesman for the Robespierrist faction, he denounced the extremist Hébertists; he also denounced Georges Jacques Danton and the Indulgents; and each time the objects of his scorn were sent to the guillotine.

Although a determined terrorist, Saint-Just was also an idealist. His unpublished *Fragments concerning Republican Institutions* reveals his Rousseauistic and Spartan utopianism. He and Robespierre were determined to fashion a new France, a "Republic of Virtue," and for that goal the continuation of the Terror was essential. But a moderate trend had begun, prompted in part by the military victory of Fleurus, to which Saint-Just had contributed during his last mission to the army. For this and other reasons, a fatal split took place.

Saint-Just prepared a report denouncing his and Robespierre's opponents, to be delivered to the Convention on July 27, 1794. But he was interrupted by the opposition, and he, Robespierre, and their colleagues were arrested. Released by their supporters, they gathered at the city hall, hoping to prevail over their enemies with the aid of the Parisian populace. But shortly after midnight they were captured and executed. Saint-Just's youthful beauty and his terrible virtue have earned him the sobriquet of "archangel of the Revolution."

Further Reading

Louis de Saint-Just is listed in the European History study guide (VIII, B, 1, b). He was a disciple and associate of Maximilien de ROBESPIERRE.

The most comprehensive and best biography, although sometimes unnecessarily detailed, is Eugene Newton Curtis, *Saint-Just: Colleague of Robespierre* (1935). A short and perceptive study is Geoffrey Bruun, *Saint-Just: Apostle of the Terror* (1932). Both studies are reasonably objective in their estimate of the man. Saint-Just's role as a member of the Committee of Public Safety is described in the excellent history of that organization by R. R. Palmer, *Twelve Who Ruled* (1941).

* * *

ST. LAURENT / By J. L. Granatstein

Louis Stephen St. Laurent (born 1882) was a Canadian statesman. He was prime minister and leader of the Liberal party of Canada, and during his efficient government Canada experienced an economic boom.

Louis St. Laurent (pronounced săN lō-räN′) was born in Compton, Quebec, on Feb. 1, 1882, of French- and Irish-Canadian parents. Completely bilingual, St. Laurent was educated at Laval University, where he did brilliantly in legal studies. Until 1941 he was content to be a lawyer, building a large practice and earning a reputation for integrity and honesty.

In 1941, however, World War II was under way, and Ernest Lapointe, the minister of justice and French Canada's spokesman in Ottawa, had just died. Prime Minister Mackenzie King selected St. Laurent to be Lapointe's successor, and after giving serious consideration to the request, St. Laurent decided to accept for war service only.

The relations between French Canadians and English Canadians had always been delicate, but in wartime they were more so. St. Laurent played a major role in reconciling Quebec to conscription, and he quickly established himself as the Prime Minister's right-hand man. With the end of the war, he was persuaded to remain in the Cabinet as secretary of state for external affairs, and in this post he became one of the architects of the North Atlantic Treaty.

When Mackenzie King retired in 1948, St. Laurent was selected as his successor at a leadership convention, and in the next year he led the Liberals to a sweeping victory in a general election. St. Laurent's administration was fortunate to be in office in boom times, and with C. D. Howe, his English-Canadian lieutenant, St. Laurent opened the doors to foreign investment. The results in the short term were astonishing: Canada's gross national product climbed; population increased; the standard of living rose; and resources development proceeded apace. In 1953 the government was again victorious in a general election.

Although the boom continued, charges of arrogance and contempt for Parliament soon were leveled against the St. Laurent government, particularly after the extraordinary measures employed in the House of Commons during the great "pipeline debate" of 1956. St. Laurent's angry attacks on the policies of Britain and France during the Suez crisis of 1956 did little to improve matters, and in the general election of 1957 the government was defeated. St. Laurent continued as leader of the Liberal party until January 1958, after which he entered retirement. St. Laurent was a manager rather than a leader, and although he and his government were undoubtedly efficient, there were few tears shed over the end of his regime.

Further Reading

Louis St. Laurent is listed in the Canada study guide

Louis St. Laurent. (National Film Board, Canada)

(IV, A, 3). Lester PEARSON later followed in his footsteps as a conciliatory prime minister.

There are few serious studies of St. Laurent or his administration. The only biography, Dale C. Thomson, *Louis St. Laurent, Canadian* (1967), is uncritical. William Kilbourn, *Pipeline: Transcanada and the Great Debate* (1970), sheds interesting light on the pipeline debate of 1956.

*   *   *

SAINT-PIERRE / By Patricia Zele Gossen

The French political and economic theorist Charles Irénée Castel, Abbé de Saint-Pierre (1658–1743), was an early philosophe of the Enlightenment. His pamphleteering expressed the intellectual unheaval and fascination with affairs of state which marked this era.

Of noble lineage, in 1680 Charles Irénée Castel, who is known as the Abbé Saint-Pierre (pronounced săN pyâr′), left his native Normandy and boyhood dreams of a monastic vocation for the ebullient intellectual atmosphere of Parisian university studies. For 5 years he followed every course available in the physical sciences, drifting further and further away from preoccupations with his ecclesiastical state as well as from what remained of his faith. After 1685 he experienced a brief return to the concerns of ethics and moral theology before abandoning the divine again for what would be the area of his real intellectual vocation— political theory. Henceforth his religion and his "consecration" to Holy Orders provided him with a comfortable living in sinecures which left him free to speculate on the art of government.

In 1712 Saint-Pierre composed his first important treatise, the *Project for an Everlasting Peace in Europe*, a text he would refine for years to come. He envisioned a confederation of European sovereigns who would renounce the use of arms and submit their differences to a council of arbitration. He was in fact simply modernizing a 1624 treatise of Henry IV's minister the Duc de Sully.

The basic political principle of Saint-Pierre's work was his refusal to accept as either inevitable or rational the divine right of kings. His treatise *La Polysynodie* (1718) represented, at the height of the regent's liberalization policies, an outright attack on individual sovereignty, suggesting rule by multiple councils and offering many unfavorable comparisons drawn from the recently ended rule of Louis XIV. The French Academy, to which he had been elected in 1694, was scandalized, and when Saint-Pierre refused to recant, he was summarily dismissed. His political influence was growing, however; the previous year he had issued *Mémoire sur la taille tarifiée*, suggesting tax reforms which amounted to the first version of proportional, declared revenue taxation. Historians consider this his most important contribution to governmental affairs, since some of its provisions actually found limited application after 1832.

In the ensuing years Saint-Pierre became a habitué of the salon of Madame de Tencin and a regular contributor to meetings of the Club de l'Entresol; it was here that the Baron de Montesquieu, who called Saint-Pierre his master, met him. The Abbé was very likely responsible for this progressive group's dissolution, however, when in 1731 A. H. de Fleury suggested that he and others like him should refrain from discussing politics. In the last years of his life Saint-Pierre continued to write assiduously on governmental practice and management while pursuing his *Annales politiques*, a comprehensive, chronological treatment of the affairs of France eventually covering the years from 1658 to 1739; critics have compared this last work favorably to the *Siècle de Louis XIV* of Voltaire.

Curiously, Voltaire and most of the later *philosophes*, including Jean Jacques Rousseau, disdained the Abbé, readily placing him with cranks and inventors and remembering his chimerical *Trémoussoir* (a therapeutic chair which jolted its user like a carriage) better than his insightful projects for public assistance to orphans and the aged and infirm, the maintenance of highways in winter (complete with statistical evidence of its economic advantage), and Parisian postal reform. But Saint-Pierre lacked the doctrinaire assurance of the next generation; avoiding grandiose plans for human betterment, he continued to the end refining his practical suggestions, a modest reformer who died in 1743, before the age of prerevolutionary visions.

The Abbé de Saint-Pierre in 1695, a portrait in the collection of the French Academy.
(Photo-Hachette)

Further Reading

The Abbé de Saint-Pierre is listed in the International

Law study guide (III, A, 1) and the Social Sciences study guide (V, B, 2). Jean Jacques ROUSSEAU later wrote on the philosophy of government.

In English, a recent treatment of Saint-Pierre is Merle L. Perkins, *The Moral and Political Philosophy of the Abbé de Saint-Pierre* (1959), which contains an extensive bibliography. Partial studies of him appear in E. V. Souleyman, *The Vision of World Peace in Seventeenth and Eighteenth-century France* (1941); Carl Joachim Friedrich, *Inevitable Peace* (1948); and Francis Harry Hinsley, *Power and the Pursuit of Peace: Theory and Practice in the History of Relations between States* (1963).

* * *

SAINT-SAËNS / By Philip Friedheim

The French composer Charles Camille Saint-Saëns (1835–1921) wrote music in almost every form and medium, characterized by polish and skill although lacking in ultimate depth or passion.

Camille Saint-Saëns. (Harlingue-Viollet)

Born in Paris into a moderately poor family, Camille Saint-Saëns (pronounced săN säNs′) began his musical education by studying piano with his grandaunt. As a child, he exhibited considerable talent in performance and composition. He made his official concert debut as a pianist at the age of 11 and 2 years later was admitted to the Paris Conservatory. He studied composition with Jacques Fromentin Halévy and won prizes in organ in 1849 and 1851. Saint-Saëns's dexterity at this instrument, coupled with his ability to improvise, led in 1853 to his appointment as organist at the church of St-Merry and 5 years later at the Madeleine. From 1861 to 1865 he taught piano at the École Niedermeyer.

In 1871 Saint-Saëns helped found the National Society of Music, an organization devoted to the encouragement of young French composers, but he withdrew 5 years later as his essentially conservative nature had come into conflict with the changing interests of the younger composers. He resigned from his position at the Madeleine in 1877 and spent the following years touring North and South America, England, Russia, and Austria, conducting and performing his own compositions. Highly honored in his lifetime, he was admitted into the French Legion of Honor in 1868, gaining its highest order, the Grand-Croix, in 1913. He was outspoken against the music of Claude Debussy and the French impressionist school.

The compositions of Saint-Saëns include five Piano Concertos, of which the Second (1868) and the Fourth (1875) hold a secure place in the repertoire today. His *Introduction and Rondo Capriccioso* for violin and orchestra (1870) is better known than his other concertos. Among his symphonic poems the *Danse macabre* (1874) is probably his most popular composition. Its charm lies not only in its melodic appeal but in the delightful way in which Saint-Saëns imitates Death playing his out-of-tune violin and the rattling of the bones as the skeletons dance. Another composition that reveals his sense of humor is the *Carnival of Animals* (1866); the lovely cello solo "The Swan" comes from this work. More impressive than these occasional compositions is the Third Symphony (1886), the orchestration of which includes an organ as well as piano. His only operatic success, *Samson et Dalila* (1877), contains the well-known aria "My heart at thy sweet voice" and a colorful bacchanale.

In addition to his activities as composer and performer, Saint-Saëns was also the general editor of the complete works of Jean Philippe Rameau. The English conductor Sir Thomas Beecham, in an oft-quoted statement, called Saint-Saëns the greatest second-rate composer who ever lived.

Further Reading

Camille Saint-Saëns is listed in the Music study guide (I, H, 5). César FRANCK was another composer who was also an outstanding organist. Gabriel FAURÉ studied with Saint-Saëns.

Considerable biographical information is in Saint-Saëns's autobiographical book, *Musical Memories* (1913; trans. 1919). James Harding, *Saint-Saëns and His Circle* (1965), is the most important study of the composer in English. Saint-Saëns is one of the subjects of Donald Brook, *Five Great French Composers* (1946).

* * *

DUC DE **SAINT-SIMON**
/ By Herbert De Ley

The French writer Louis de Rouvroy, Duc de Saint-Simon (1675–1755), provides in his classic "Memoirs" a major source of information on the court of the "Sun King," Louis XIV.

The Duc de Saint-Simon was born on Jan. 16, 1675, in Paris. As a young aristocrat, he studied horsemanship and fencing as much as letters and entered the elite King's Musketeers at the age of 16. Three years later, apparently inspired by the memoirs of Marshal Bassompierre and others, which he read in the field, he began making notes for memoirs of his own.

Passed over for promotion in 1702, Saint-Simon abandoned his military career and went to live at the court of Versailles. He apparently continued to make notes and read extensively in the works of other memorialists and historians, to the point that his fellow courtiers often consulted him on questions of history, genealogy, and court etiquette. However, both his resignation from the army and his sometimes unwelcome knowledge of court traditions irritated Louis XIV, who excluded him from any official post for the rest of his reign.

After the death of Louis XIV in 1715, Saint-Simon played an important role as public and private counselor to the regent, Philippe II d'Orléans, retiring upon the death of the latter in 1723. After spending several years on such other historical projects as his *Notes on the Dukedoms and Peerages* and his *Additions* to the Marquis of Dangeau's *Journal*, he began revising and writing out his *Memoirs* in 1739.

In the *Memoirs*, Saint-Simon's observations allowed him to describe vividly both the elegance and the corruption of the court of Versailles. Despite some errors of fact and interpretation, his knowledge of history made him aware of the breakdown of traditional checks and balances that underlay Louis XIV's royal absolutism and which was to lead, in the next century, to the French Revolution. Saint-Simon's intensely written accounts of court intrigues and such events as the deaths of the Grand Dauphin, the Duke of Burgundy, and Louis XIV himself—as well as his incisive word portraits of his fellow courtiers—make him perhaps the world's greatest writer on the prestige, the ambitions, the uncertainties, and the ironies of public life. He completed his *Memoirs* in 1752. Saint-Simon died on March 2, 1755, in Paris.

Further Reading

The Duc de Saint-Simon is listed in the Literature study guide (III, F, 1). He influenced STENDHAL, Honoré de BALZAC, and Marcel PROUST.

Saint-Simon's *Memoirs* have never been completely translated into English. The most recent partial translation is by Lucy Norton, *Historical Memoirs of the Duc de Saint-Simon* (2 vols., 1967–1968). The best study of Saint-Simon in English is Edwin Cannan, *The Duke of Saint Simon* (1885).

* * *

COMTE DE **SAINT-SIMON**
/ By Martin U. Martel

The French social philosopher and reformer Claude Henri de Rouvroy, Comte de Saint-Simon (1760–1825), was one of the founders of modern industrial socialism and evolutionary sociology.

The Comte de Saint-Simon (pronounced săN sē-môN′) was born in Paris to the poorer side of a prominent noble family. From childhood on he was filled with great ambitions that took him on many different paths. First commissioned into the army at 17, he served 4 years, during which he fought with some distinction in the American Revolution.

On his return to Europe, Saint-Simon tried a series of bold commercial ventures but had limited success before the French Revolution. During the Terror of 1793–1794 he was imprisoned for a year and barely escaped execution. This experience left him deeply opposed to revolutionary violence. After his release, for a short time he obtained a sizable fortune by speculating in confiscated properties, which he spent on a lavish Paris salon that

The Duc de Saint-Simon, an engraving after Van Loo in the Bibliothèque Nationale, Paris. (Bulloz)

attracted many intellectual and government leaders. But his funds were soon exhausted, and he lived his remaining years in constant financial difficulties.

In 1802 Saint-Simon turned to a new career as writer and reformer. In numerous essays and brochures written during the chaotic years of Napoleon's rule and the Bourbon restoration that followed, he developed a broad-ranging program for the reorganization of Europe. Although many of its ideas were commonplace, his program is distinctive for its blending of Enlightenment ideals, the more practical materialism of the rising bourgeoisie, and the emphasis on spiritual unity of restorationists.

All three strands are joined in Saint-Simon's evolutionary view of history—as a determined progression from one stable form of civilization to another—which gave his program a distinctive rationale. Each higher form was thought to be based on more advanced "spiritual" as well as "temporal" (that is, political-economic) principles, reflecting a more general process of cultural enlightenment. But each in turn also is destined to become obsolete as further cultural progress occurs.

Saint-Simon argued that all of Europe had been in a transitional crisis since the 15th century, when the established medieval order (based on feudalism and Catholicism) began to give way to a new system founded on industry and science. He wrote as the new system's advocate, urging influential leaders to hasten its inception as the only way to restore stability. In this he was one of the first ameliorators to argue for reform as an evolutionary necessity.

Saint-Simon's earlier writings, during Napoleon's reign (*Introduction aux travaux scientifiques du XIX siècle*, 1807–1808; and *Mémoire sur la science de l'homme*, 1813), stress the spiritual side of the transitional crisis. He argued that disorder was rampant because theistic Roman Catholicism, the spiritual basis of medieval society, was being undermined by the rise of science and secular philosophies. Although the trend was inevitable, Saint-Simon was highly critical of many scientists and intellectuals for their "negativism" in breaking down an established creed without providing a replacement. Instead, he called for the creation of an integrative social science, grounded in biology, to help establish a new "positive" credo for secular man in the emerging social order. This "positivistic" notion was developed by his one-time disciple Auguste Comte.

After Napoleon's downfall Saint-Simon shifted his attention from the ideology of the new system to its temporal structure and policies in a series of periodicals: *L'Industrie* (1816–1818); *La Politique* (1819); *L'Organisateur* (1819–1820); and *Du Système industriel* (1821–1822). These contain his main socialist writings, but his doctrines often are closer to venture capitalism and technocracy than to Marxism or primitive communalism. Saint-Simon's future society is above all one of productive achievement in which poverty and war are eliminated through large-scale "industrialization" (a word he coined) under planned scientific guidance. It is an open-class society in which caste privileges are abol-

The Comte de Saint-Simon, a print in the Bibliothèque Nationale, Paris. (Giraudon)

ished, work is provided for all, and rewards are based on merit. Government also changes from a haphazard system of class domination and national rivalries to a planned welfare state run by scientific managers in the public interest.

Saint-Simon's final work, *Le Nouveau Christianisme* (1825), inspired a Christian socialist movement called the Saint-Simonians, who were devoted to a secular gospel of economic progress and human brotherhood. After his death, his ideas were reworked by followers into the famous *Doctrine de Saint-Simon* (1829). This was the first systematic exposition of industrial socialism, and it had great influence on the Social Democratic movement, Catholic reforms, and Marxism.

Further Reading

The Comte de Saint-Simon is listed in the Social Sciences study guide (VI, B, 2). His program offered a blending of the rationalist faith of the Marquis de CONDORCET and the spiritual unity of restorationists such as Joseph de MAISTRE. In linking socialism to industrial progress, Saint-Simon abandoned the ideal of the small egalitarian commune upheld by Charles FOURIER.

F. M. H. Markham edited and translated *Selected Writings of Saint-Simon* (1952). The best account of Saint-Simon's life and work is Frank E. Manuel, *The New World of Henri Saint-Simon* (1956). Other accounts include Mathurin M. Dondo, *The French Faust: Henri de Saint-Simon* (1955), and the section on Saint-Simon in Manuel's *The Prophets of Paris* (1962). For his place in socialist thought see volume 1 of G. D. H. Cole, *A History of Socialist Thought* (1953).

* * *

SAINTE-BEUVE

/ **By Emmett J. Gossen, Jr.**

The French literary critic Charles Augustin Sainte-Beuve (1804–1869), who developed a very personal technique of literary criticism, remains the most important literary arbiter of his century.

Born in Boulogne-sur-Mer, Charles Augustin Sainte-Beuve (pronounced săNt bœv′) went to Paris in 1824 to study medicine. But by 1826 he was contributing actively to the *Globe*, where an article favorable to Victor Hugo won him the young poet's confidence and a place in his *Cénacle*, or coterie, among the most innovative literary talents of the time. Saint-Beuve's *Tableau historique et critique de la poésie française et du théâtre français au XVI siècle* (1828) not only rehabilitated the neglected Pléiade poets (Pierre Ronsard, Joachim du Bellay) but laid a claim to respectability for his contemporaries, "romantic" descendants of those forgotten giants of lyricism.

Saint-Beuve's own elegiac efforts in *Vie, poésies et pensées de Joseph Delorme* (1829) and *Consolations* (1830) enhanced a prestige among his peers that was not echoed by the public; his unhappy affair with Hugo's wife, Adèle (allusively chronicled in his novel *Volupté*, 1834), led to an open break with his most ardent supporters and initiated a period (mid-1830s) of spiritual upheaval during which he sought guidance in Saint-Simonism and even in the renewed Catholicism of Félicité Robert de Lamennais. His interest in the Jansenist community of Port Royal dates from these years, although he continued producing critical articles for the *Revue des deux mondes*, which would be collected in *Portraits littéraires*, *Portraits de femmes*, and *Portraits contemporains*. The *Histoire de Port-Royal* (3 vols., 1840–1848; originally a lecture series given in Lausanne in 1837–1838) remains his most important single contribution, however, and is often termed the most valuable and original work of literary criticism in the 19th century. Here his ideal role as "naturalist of human spirits," seeking to classify by "families" and "generations" those writers whose interior lives he deliberately pursues, is clearly expressed. Sainte-Beuve sought here, as he would throughout his career, that "relative truth of each thing" by which literature remained for him a domain of vital and infinite variety.

The second half of Sainte-Beuve's career (1849–1869), marked by a hasty and widely criticized rallying to the regime of Napoleon III, saw his elevation to a place in the French Academy and finally (1865) a seat in the Senate. These were his most productive years, during which the *Causeries du lundi* ("Monday Chats" in the *Moniteur*) regularly confirmed his official status as arbiter of national taste under the Second Empire. *Chateaubriand et son groupe littéraire* (1861; dating from a course given at Liège in 1848–1849) stands with *Port-Royal* as a major, unitary contribution. The *Lundis* and *Nouveaux Lundis*, however, best reveal that shifting, curious, always allusive talent with which he attempted to join "physiology" and "poetry" in an art of evocation and critical appraisal. Sainte-Beuve, by abandoning the dogmatic evaluations of his predecessors, made of criticism an inductive process based on detailed examination of the author's character, his life, and so his literary work. This historical, biographical method established Sainte-Beuve as the first "modern" literary critic.

Further Reading

Charles Augustin Sainte-Beuve is listed in the Literature study guide (III, H, 1, a). Nicholas BOILEAU was an earlier French critic.

There is no complete edition of Sainte-Beuve's works in either French or English, although many of his works

Charles Augustin Saint-Beuve, a portrait by Alfred de Musset. (French Cultural Services of the French Embassy)

have been translated. Two particularly useful critical biographies and appraisals are Harold Nicolson, *Sainte-Beuve* (1957), and Andrew George Lehmann, *Sainte-Beuve: A Portrait of the Critic, 1804–42* (1962).

*   *   *

SAIONJI / By George O. Totten

Kimmochi Saionji (1849–1940) was the last elder statesman, or genro, of Japan. Catapulted by birth into high position, he played a major role in the Japanese government both during and after the Meiji restoration of 1868. He made the final recommendations for premiers until his death.

Kimmochi Saionji. (International Society for Educational Information, Tokyo, Inc.)

Born on Oct. 23, 1849, the second son of Kinzumi Tokudaiji, Kimmochi was adopted at the age of 2 by the Saionji (pronounced sī-ôn-jē) family, who were court nobles (*kuge*) close to the imperial family. He served Emperor Komei as boy chamberlain and imperial guard and knew Mutsuhito as prince. When the latter became the Meiji emperor, Saionji at 19 was made a councilor (*sanyo*) and later was appointed a commander, assisted by Aritomo Yamagata, 10 years his senior.

After 10 years in France, imbibing liberal ideas, Saionji returned home in 1881 and was happy to find the Freedom and People's Rights movement in progress. He consented to head the *Toyo Jiyu Shimbun* (Oriental Liberal Newspaper) but was quickly ordered by the Emperor to step down.

Government Career

In 1882 Saionji accompanied Hirobumi Ito to Europe on his constitutional research mission and later spent 6 years as minister to Austria-Hungary, Germany, and Belgium. Returning home, Saionji became president of the Bureau of Decorations, then vice president of the House of Peers, and, when he was 46, during the Sino-Japanese War, minister of education in the second Ito Cabinet. It was thus natural for Saionji to assist Ito in founding the Seiyukai party in 1900 and later, after a turn at the presidency of the Privy Council, to follow Ito as party president. This in turn led to two premierships alternating with those of Taro Katsura, Yamagata's protégé. Yet on Yamagata's recommendation Saionji became *genro* in 1916 and was appointed chief delegate to the Paris Peace Conference in 1919, where he took part in founding the League of Nations. For this he was raised from marquis to prince.

With the death of Masayoshi Matsukata in 1924, Saionji became the only living *genro* and thus the ultimate "Cabinet maker." Although he was partial to the idea of a Cabinet based on a majority party, he could not find statesmen of real stature to choose from. This he blamed on the poor quality of the parties and the low level of the people's political understanding. As pressure from the military and support for aggression grew, Saionji lost confidence and considered resigning.

Fearing that civilians would be assassinated, Saionji recommended military men as premiers. In 1937 Saionji mistakenly thought that he had found an ideal premier in Prince Fumimaro Konoe, who could control the military. Saionji died on Nov. 24, 1940, still faintly hoping Japan could negotiate with Chiang Kai-shek and avoid war with the United States. Theoretically a bachelor, Saionji had three common-law wives and successive mistresses; he adopted a son who married his eldest daughter and became his heir, Hachiro Saionji. Saionji also distinguished himself as an author, a translator, and a musician on the biwa.

Further Reading

Kimmochi Saionji is listed in the Asia study guide (III, B, 7, b). He played a major role in the emergence of party politics in Japan together with Hirobumi ITO, Koi HARA, and Tsuyoshi INUKAI.

A scholarly study, *Prince Saionji* (trans. 1933), was written by Yosaburo Takekoshi, a noted Japanese historian. A fascinating fictionalized biography published before Saionji's death is Bunji Omura, *The Last Genro:*

Prince Saionji, the Man Who Westernized Japan (1938), which contains glossaries. Although generally accurate and offering much background and personal detail, Omura did not have available the great amount of material that has since been published in Japanese by persons who knew Saionji personally. They include Sakutaro Koizumi, who edited Saionji's autobiography in 1949, and Kumao Harada, his personal secretary and official spokesman, who published a nine-volume work on him between 1950 and 1956, volume 1 of which, *Fragile Victory: Prince Saionji and the 1930 London Treaty Issue* (trans. 1968), is introduced and annotated by the translator, Thomas Francis Mayer-Oakes.

*   *   *

SALADIN / By Everett U. Crosby

Saladin (1138–1193), a Kurdish ruler of Egypt and Syria, is known in the West for his opposition to the forces of the Third Crusade and for his capture of Jerusalem.

From about 1130 Zengi, the Turkish atabeg (regent) of Mosul and his son, Nur-ad-Din (Nureddin), who succeeded him in 1146, undertook a holy war to unify Syria. Saladin (pronounced săl′ə-dĭn; Arabic, Salah-ad-Din Yusuf ibn Aiyub) served with his uncle, Shirkuh, under Nur-ad-Din and was strongly impressed with the need to complete the unity of Islam under orthodox rule.

After several expeditions into Egypt, where the Fatimid dynasty remained the most important of the successor kingdoms established after the fall of the Abbasid em-

Saladin, a portrait executed during his lifetime. (Radio Times Hulton Picture Library)

pire, Saladin assumed full military power on the death of Shirkuh in 1168. He was successful in repulsing the combined French-Byzantine invasion of Amalric, King of Jerusalem, a victory which opened the way for him to move his armies up into the Transjordan area. The Fatimid caliphate was crushed by 1171, and on the death of Nur-ad-Din 3 years later, Saladin began the conquest of the Frankish lands and of the old Zengid empire. He shortly occupied Damascus and married the widow of Nur-ad-Din. He thus faced increased hostility from two sides: from the Zengid rulers at Mosul, who were in no way enthusiastic about his conception of the *jihad*, or holy war, and from the Latin forces under Baldwin IV, the Leper King. The complexities of operating on two fronts at the same time were reduced somewhat by diplomatic negotiations with Baldwin and Raymond of Tripoli as well as with the Byzantine emperor and certain of the Italian maritime cities. In the former case the result was essentially negative. A series of provisional treaties served to forestall an attack on the vulnerable western side, for Baldwin proved to be quite capable of containing Saladin, although he was unable to do him any damage. But in the latter case not only were assurances of nonintervention given, but material aid was obtained.

By the end of 1185 Saladin had imposed his authority in northern Syria and Mesopotamia, and he was ready to turn his full attention to the crusading kingdom. After the unfortunate betrayal of a peace treaty by a Western knight, the *jihad* was declared in the beginning of 1187. Drawing troops from Syria as well as from Egypt, Saladin brought his combined forces to face the Latin army at Hattin near Tiberias in July. The star-crossed monarchy in Jerusalem, born of the antagonisms among the leaders of the First Crusade, was never able to operate from a position of strength, and once again personal jealousies were responsible for the overwhelming defeat by the Moslem forces. Saladin set a trap for the crusaders; they marched into it and were annihilated. By any measure Hattin was a disaster for the West, and in rapid sequence most of the other important towns, Acre, Sidon, Jaffa, Caesarea, Ascalon, fell into Moslem hands. Finally, Jerusalem was occupied on October 2. Further campaigning reduced the extent of Frankish power in Syria to Tyre, Antioch, and Tripoli.

The kings of western Europe responded to the fall of Jerusalem by taking the cross and then by gathering their knights together in the expeditions known to history as the Third Crusade. Their chief victory was the successful siege and relief of Acre, which capitulated in July 1191. King Richard I of England defeated Saladin at Arsuf and then concluded an armistice in the fall of 1192 without having been able to retake Jerusalem. Nevertheless, Richard's presence in the East clearly prevented Saladin from capitalizing fully on his victory at Hattin. After 12 days of illness, Saladin died on March 4, 1193.

Saladin is described in the pages of his biographer, Baha ad-Din, as one who was entirely committed to the justice of the *jihad* against the unbelievers. Of medium height and gentle manners, courageous, even ruthless,

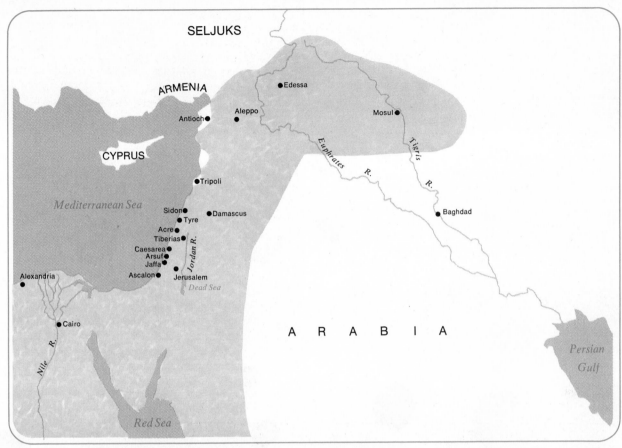

Saladin's empire in 1190. Sultan of Egypt, Saladin subdued Moslem Palestine and Syria and in 1187 destroyed the Latin kingdom of Jerusalem. The Third Crusade was launched in 1189 against a unified Moslem state under Saladin.

but generous and humane, he was respected by his followers and by his adversaries for the steadfast manner in which he kept his promises. Strong in his faith, he was orthodox to the point of intolerance, as in the summary murder of as-Suhrawardi, a heretical preacher of Aleppo. It should be remembered that it was Saladin who carried on the work of Nur-ad-Din and completed the unity of Islam, although his success did not long survive him.

Further Reading

Saladin is listed in the Asia study guide (I, B, 4, c and f; I, C, 1) and the Africa study guide (I, E, 3, b). The Third Crusade was led by PHILIP II of France, RICHARD I, and FREDERICK I.

The fundamental full-length treatment of Saladin is S. Lane-Poole, *Saladin and the Fall of the Kingdom of Jerusalem* (1898; rev. ed. by H. W. C. Davis, 1926). Other works on him are Charles J. Rosebault, *Saladin, Prince of Chivalry* (1930), and G. E. T. Slaughter, *Saladin, 1138–1193* (1955). An important chapter on his early career by Sir H. A. R. Gibb is in Kenneth M. Setton, *A History of the Crusades*, vol. 1 (1969).

SALAZAR / By Robert W. Kern

The government of the Portuguese statesman António de Oliveira Salazar (1889–1970) once was considered to be the very model of a modern authoritarian political system.

António de Oliveira Salazar (pronounced sä-lə-zär′) was born on April 28, 1889, in Vimieiro near Santa Comba Dão in the province of Beira Alta. His parents, owners of several small estates, as well as innkeepers, were António de Oliveira and María de Resgate Salazar, who, despite financial problems, saw to it that Salazar was well educated. He entered the seminary of Viseu in 1900, but after 8 years of religious training he decided to teach. In 1910 he began to study economics at the University of Coimbra, spending 4 years there as a student and another 7 as an economics professor. He obtained a chair of political economy in 1918. A knowledge of economics was valuable in underdeveloped Portugal, and soon Salazar was well known by the government for his monetary skills.

The emergence of Salazar as a national figure came at a

difficult moment in Portuguese history. After more than a century of economic difficulties tied to imperial decline, political life had degenerated badly. The double assassination of Carlos I and the crown prince in February 1908 and the overthrow of Manuel II in October 1910 had led to creation of a republic which in the 16 years of its existence went from crisis to crisis. The University of Coimbra furnished many republican leaders in the first phase of the period, but spread of a deeper radicalism engendered a conservative reaction led by António Sardinha. He sought an "organic monarchy" that would be traditionalist and antiparliamentary, but chaos prevented any success.

Economic Policies

In the stalemate after 1918 Salazar's star rose. His economic thought was strongly influenced by Catholic corporatism and Leo XIII's *Rerum novarum*. He favored joint labor-management industrial commissions, compulsory arbitration, and Catholic trade unions. In January 1921 Salazar was one of three Catholic deputies elected to the Parliament, but turmoil was still so great that he attended only a few sessions before returning to the university. However, in May 1926, when a military dictator-

António de Oliveira Salazar. (Cifra Grafica, Madrid)

ship overthrew the republic, Salazar was offered the Ministry of Economic Affairs. He refused the position until 1928, when he received great powers which made him the most important figure in the government.

Salazar's reforms brought some national stability by prohibiting the import of foreign goods, cutting the state budget, and developing a new tax system. Soon he turned to a revision of the structure of government itself. "In an administrative system in which lack of sincerity and clarity were evident," he said, "the first requirement is a policy of truth. In a social order in which rights were competitive and unaccompanied by equivalent duties, the crying need is for a policy of sacrifice. And in a nation divided against itself by groups and clashing interests which threatened its unity, the main need is a national policy."

Ruler of Portugal

The national policy emerged during 1929 in the wake of Portugal's newfound stability, when Salazar's reforms stood the test of the Depression. The military leaders of the dictatorship no longer had as much prestige or interest in ruling, and Salazar informally became the strongest man in the regime. He immediately began to write a new constitution which was approved by plebiscite on March 19, 1933. It created a corporative state divided by levels into *sindicatos* (government unions by industry), *gremios* (guilds of employers), and *ordens* (white-collar organizations). Each of these handled welfare arrangements, employment of their members, and vocational training and negotiated national wage agreements. Each was also guided by special government secretariats that dictated policy. A fourth level was made up by the armed forces, although here there was more autonomy in honor of the role played by the services in establishing the new regime. All four levels elected representatives who then chose deputies for the national Parliament, giving the franchise to the corporative institutions rather than to the national electorate—a variation of the indirect franchise. Salazar's motto was "control by stability," which was facilitated further by the provision that only his National Union party had official status. The president of the party became president of the republic with enormous executive powers, not the least being control of the newly established secret police, the PIDE.

Much of this structure had been modeled on Mussolini's Italy, and Salazar remained diplomatically close to Mussolini in the 1930s. He intrigued several times against the Spanish Republic, and when the Civil War broke out in Spain, he recognized Franco's Nationalists in December 1937. Portugal supplied funds and arms to the Burgos government until the end of the war, and on March 17, 1939, a pact of friendship and nonaggression was signed between the two countries which pledged eternal opposition to communism and created an "Iberian bloc" linking them together against outside attack. For Portugal it was the first time since 1640 that it had cooperated directly with Spain, but even so Salazar was restrained by long-standing treaties with Great Britain, which kept him from closer cooperation with either Franco or Mussolini.

Portugal, as a result, remained correctly neutral during World War II until 1943, when Salazar granted the Allies bases in Portuguese territory. His anticommunism brought Portugal into NATO in 1949 and won him backing to join the United Nations at the same time.

Postwar Period

The postwar period, despite these successes, was troubled, first because of domestic economic difficulties and then because of colonial unrest in Angola and Mozambique. Government mismanagement of both problems led to renewal of opposition to Salazar's dictatorship in 1956. Two years later, an opposition candidate, Humberto Delgado, polled a quarter million votes for the presidency, which Salazar had occupied since 1951. The PIDE became more active, but the opposition continued to grow until 1965, when Delgado was assassinated in Spain. By that time Draconian measures in the colonies diminished the drive for independence to the point where there was less unrest in metropolitan Portugal, although vestiges of opposition continued to manifest themselves spasmodically until September 1968, when Salazar was incapacitated by a massive brain hemorrhage. His 36-year rule thus came to an end on September 27, when Marcelo Caetano of the National Union replaced him in the premiership. Salazar died on July 27, 1970, in Lisbon.

Further Reading

António de Oliveira Salazar is listed in the European History study guide (XI, K; XII, E, 1). His authoritarian policies were similar to those of Benito MUSSOLINI and Francisco FRANCO.

A biography of Salazar is Christine Garnier, *Salazar: An Intimate Portrait* (1952; trans. 1954). See also Gowan Pinheiro, *Oldest Ally: A Portrait of Salazar's Portugal* (1961).

SALISBURY / By Anne Fremantle

The English statesman and diplomat Robert Arthur Talbot Gascoyne-Cecil, 3d Marquess of Salisbury (1830–1903), was prime minister of Great Britain in 1885–1886, 1886–1892, and 1895–1902. His life spanned the period of England's greatest affluence and power.

Lord Robert Cecil was born at Hatfield on Feb. 3, 1830, the second son of James Brownlow William Gascoyne-Cecil, 2d Marquess of Salisbury, Lord Privy Seal and Lord President of the Council, and of his wife, Frances Gascoyne, an heiress. Educated at Eton and at Christ Church, Oxford, where he received a fourth-class in mathematics, he was elected in 1853 to a fellowship at All Souls College, Oxford, and in the same year

Lord Salisbury. (Popperfoto)

was elected unopposed to the House of Commons for Stamford.

In July 1857 Cecil married Georgina Alderson, a woman of great ability. His father, however, objected to the marriage and cut off funds, so Cecil became partly dependent on his pen. He wrote for the *Standard* and the *Saturday Review*, but his most famous articles, such as "The Conservative Surrender," were published in the *Quarterly*. Cecil revealed in these articles his deep distrust of democracy, considering the poor as subject to more temptations. Cecil reached a wide public with his articles, and his style was "a rare model of restrained, pungent, and vigorous English."

On the death of his elder brother in 1865, Cecil became Lord Cranborne, and in July 1866 he was appointed secretary of state for India. On the death of his father in 1868, he entered the House of Lords as Marquess of Salisbury and in 1869 became chancellor of Oxford University. In 1874 the Conservatives were back in office, and Lord Salisbury was again at the India Office, where he was censured for refusing to check the export of wheat during a famine in Bengal.

After Lord Derby resigned from the Foreign Office in April 1878, Salisbury was appointed in his stead. Twenty-four hours later he issued the "Salisbury Circular," requiring all articles of the Treaty of San Stefano to be submitted to the proposed Berlin Conference. This speech did not prevent Salisbury from concluding a secret negotiation with the Russian ambassador to London by which the Balkans were to be divided. This secret convention was balanced by the Cyprus convention with Turkey, which secured for Britain the semblance of a diplomatic success at the Congress of Berlin (June 13–July 13, 1878). By the treaty provisions, Austria was to administer Bosnia and Herzegovina; the idea of a big Bulgaria was abandoned; and Russia received Kars, Ardahan, and Batum on condition it make Batum a free port.

In 1880 the Conservatives were defeated, and Salisbury became their leader in the Lords. In 1881 Benjamin Disraeli died, and on June 12, 1885, the Liberals fell. Salisbury became prime minister and foreign secretary. He made the protocol of Sept. 18, 1885, securing the Zulfikar Pass to the emir of Afghanistan, and he secured the eastern frontier of India against the French by the annexation of Burma. In Parliament he promoted a bill for the housing of the working classes that penalized landlords for renting unsanitary tenements.

In December 1885 the general election left the Irish members in command, and the government was defeated. Later that year Gladstone was defeated on home rule. Salisbury said in a speech that some races, such as the Hottentots and the Hindus, were unfit for self-government. A month later he became prime minister again, making Lord Randolph Churchill his chancellor of the Exchequer. In December, Churchill left the government, thinking thereby to force Salisbury's hand on the army estimates, but the latter appointed George Goschen in Churchill's place. In 1887 Salisbury initiated the first colonial conference, and in 1888 he granted a royal charter to the British East Africa Company by which England recovered its hold over the upper sources of the Nile.

In 1890 Germany acknowledged a British protectorate of Zanzibar; in exchange Salisbury gave up Helgoland. In 1899 he encouraged the British South Africa Company under Cecil Rhodes to colonize Rhodesia. The Portuguese claimed Matabeleland, but Salisbury sent an ultimatum to Lisbon, and Portugal yielded. In 1888 Salisbury introduced the Life Peerage Bill, which was withdrawn, and in 1891 he got the Free Education Act passed. In 1895 a coalition of Salisbury and Joseph Chamberlain won a majority. In 1897 the Working Men's Compensation Act was passed.

From 1895 to 1900 Salisbury pursued a policy of brinkmanship with each of the four Great Powers. In the United States, President Grover Cleveland declared that the British refusal of arbitration between British Guiana and Venezuela was a violation of the Monroe Doctrine, but the U.S. Commission decided in favor of Britain. Salisbury allowed the United States a free hand in Cuba, surrendered British rights in Samoa to the United States, and abrogated the Clayton-Bulwer Treaty of 1850 by allowing the United States to build the Panama Canal under American control. He had to deal with the Germans in 1896 over the Kaiser's telegram to Paul Kruger congratulating him on suppressing the Jameson Raid, and with the French from 1897, when Gen. Horatio Kitchener dislodged the French flag from Fashoda after his victory at Omdurman, until 1899, when they abandoned all de-signs on the Sudan. In 1899 the Czar's rescript led to the Hague Conference.

In 1900, after Salisbury had refused foreign mediation, the largest army ever assembled by England set off to fight the Boers. In 1902 Salisbury negotiated the Anglo-Japanese Treaty, and on May 31 peace was signed with the Boers. In July, Salisbury resigned, and he died on Aug. 22, 1903.

Further Reading

Lord Salisbury is listed in the European History study guide (IX, A, 1, a) and the Africa study guide (VIII, A, 1). Benjamin DISRAELI and William GLADSTONE also served as prime ministers under VICTORIA.

Salisbury's life is recounted in Samuel Henry Jeyes, *Life and Times of the Marquis of Salisbury* (4 vols., 1895–1896), and in Aubrey Leo Kennedy, *Salisbury, 1830–1903: Portrait of a Statesman* (1953). Aspects of his career are covered in Rose L. Greaves, *Persia and the Defense of India, 1884–1892: A Study in the Foreign Policy of the Third Marquis of Salisbury* (1959); J. A. S. Grenville, *Lord Salisbury and Foreign Policy: The Close of the Nineteenth Century* (1964); Cedric J. Lowe, *Salisbury and the Mediterranean, 1886–1896* (1965); and Michael Pinto-Duschinsky, *The Political Thought of Lord Salisbury, 1854–1868* (1967).

✳   ✳   ✳

SALK / By Patsy A. Gerstner

The American physician, virologist, and immunologist Jonas Edward Salk (born 1914) developed the first effective poliomyelitis vaccine.

Jonas Salk was born in New York City on Oct. 28, 1914. At the age of 16 he entered the College of the City of New York with the thought of studying law. He decided instead to study medicine and in 1934 enrolled in the College of Medicine of New York University, from which he graduated in 1939. He interned at New York's Mount Sinai Hospital from 1940 to 1942, when he went to the University of Michigan, where he helped develop an influenza vaccine. In 1944 he was appointed research associate in epidemiology, and in 1946 he was made assistant professor.

In 1947 Salk accepted a position at the University of Pittsburgh as associate professor of bacteriology, where he carried out his researches on a polio vaccine. Polio vaccines had been attempted before but without success because, as was apparent by 1949, there were three distinct types of polio viruses. This provided a starting point for Salk, who, working under a grant from the National Foundation for Infantile Paralysis, prepared a killed-virus vaccine effective against all three types. Testing began in 1950, and the preliminary report on the vaccine's effec-

Jonas Salk. (National Library of Medicine, Bethesda, Md.)

tiveness was published in the *Journal of the American Medical Association* for 1953. National field trials were held in 1954, and in 1955 the vaccine was determined safe for general use.

Acceptance of the vaccine was not without problems for Salk. Fear, skepticism, opposition from medical colleagues who favored a live-virus vaccine, improper production of the vaccine by some pharmaceutical companies, and a glaring Hollywood-like promotion for the vaccine caused much scientific criticism of Salk. Many also felt that the National Foundation had improperly favored him. Although the Salk vaccine was effective, it was replaced largely by the Sabin oral vaccine, a live-virus vaccine which, unlike the Salk vaccine, provides permanent protection.

During his polio researches Salk was made research professor of bacteriology at Pittsburgh (1949–1954) and professor of preventive medicine (1954–1957). In 1957 he was named Commonwealth professor of experimental medicine. In 1963 he opened the Salk Institute for Biological Studies in San Diego, where he and his colleagues studied problems relating to the body's autoimmunization reaction, that is, why the body rejects foreign material, for example, an organ transplant.

Further Reading

Jonas Salk is listed in the Science study guide (VII, G, 4). The problem of immunological response to tissue grafts and organ transplants was investigated by Peter MEDAWAR and F. Macfarlane BURNET.

Richard Carter, *Breakthrough: The Saga of Jonas Salk* (1966), details the development of the vaccine and emphasizes Salk's dedication to humanity. A harsher view of Salk's role in developing the vaccine is John R. Wilson, *Margin of Safety* (1963). Several books contain well-balanced sections on Salk, such as Greer Williams, *Virus Hunters* (1959), and H. J. Parish, *A History of Immunization* (1965).

SALLUST / By Robert W. Carrubba

Sallust (86–ca. 35 B.C.), or Gaius Sallustius Crispus, was a Roman statesman and historian. Rejecting the annalistic method of writing history, he concentrated with improved accuracy and narrative technique on critical stages in the decline of the Roman Republic.

S allust (pronounced săl′əst) was born of plebeian stock in the small Sabine town of Amiternum. Joining the Popular faction, he was elected tribune of the people in 52 B.C. When Clodius was murdered by Milo, Sallust was instrumental in arousing public outrage against Milo. Sallust's motives probably went beyond loyalty to Clodius and certainty of Milo's guilt to revenge arising from the whipping Sallust endured for an adulterous relationship with Milo's wife. In 50 his immoral life and factionalism caused Sallust's name to be stricken from the senatorial roll.

With the outbreak of civil war in 49, Sallust joined Julius Caesar, who secured for him a quaestorship and command of a legion in the unsuccessful campaign against Pompey in Illyricum. Sallust continued to serve Caesar as praetor in Africa and was rewarded with a proconsular governorship of Numidia. Sallust plundered the province to amass his great wealth, but he either was not brought to trial or was acquitted. In 44 Sallust retired to Rome and the splendor of his residence, situated amid the famous Gardens of Sallust (Horti Sallustiani). The estate later was the residence of several Roman emperors. His last years were devoted to elegant leisure and the writing of history. He died in 35 or 34 B.C.

Sallust's first historical monograph, *The Conspiracy of Catiline* (*De Catilinae coniuratione*), was apparently published in 43. The work begins with a grave account of the moral decline of the Romans and narrates the career of Catiline with emphasis on the detection and suppression of the conspiracy. Despite Sallust's knowledge of the facts from personal experience and contemporary records, the work is more notable for brilliant speeches and character sketches.

The Jugurthine War (*Bellum Iugurthinum*) was published about 41. After a philosophical introduction and an account of the career of Jugurtha, Sallust narrates the war of the Romans against the Numidian king (111–106 B.C.). Sallust drew upon his own knowledge of Africa and

Sallust, a portrait on a Roman medallion of the 4th century A.D. *(From* The Birth of Western Civilization, *published by Thames & Hudson, London, and McGraw-Hill, New York)*

literary sources which included translations of Punic documents, but he does falter on chronology and topography.

Probably after 39 Sallust composed his *Histories (Historiae),* in five books, devoted to the critical period from the death of Sulla in 78 B.C. to Pompey's rise to power in 67 B.C. Unfortunately, only fragments, including two letters and four speeches, survive.

Sallust was judged by Quintilian to rival Thucydides, and Martial ranked him as Rome's foremost historian. Some critics allege that Sallust's works are politically inspired in favor of Caesar. Whatever his biases may be, Sallust's avowed ambition was an impartial and trustworthy narrative. Rather than writing general or annalistic history, he deliberately selected subjects and portions of history on the basis of their interest and value. Like Thucydides, he fathoms character and motivation; thus his works are never dreary or monotonous but are dramatic, colorful, and concentrated. Sallust's polished, vigorous, and varied style shows a fondness for concise expression, neatly turned phrases, figurative language, archaisms, and colloquialisms.

Further Reading

Sallust is listed in the Ancient History study guide (III, B, 4). He emulated the terse diction of CATO THE ELDER and THUCYDIDES in his writing.

Sallust, translated by John Carew Rolfe (1921), contains the major works. An excellent, incisive critique of Sallust, his work, and his cultural milieu is Ronald Syme's scholarly *Sallust* (1964). Also useful is D. C. Earl, *The Political Thought of Sallust* (1961). A brief but clear account of Sallust for the general reader is in Stephen Usher, *The Historians of Greece and Rome* (1970), which, since it reports the conclusions of modern scholarship, is more useful than the older works by J. B. Bury, *The Ancient Greek Historians* (1909), and Max Ludwig Wolfram Laistner, *The Greater Roman Historians* (1947).

SALVEMINI / By Fredric Cheyette

The Italian historian and journalist Gaetano Salvemini (1873–1957) introduced economic and social analysis into Italian historiography. He spent his later years combating the Fascist dictatorship.

Gaetano Salvemini (pronounced säl-vä′mē-nē) was born in Molfetta on Sept. 8, 1873, the second of nine children in a poor peasant family. As a child, he had little to read but the Bible and the novels of Alexander Dumas and Eugène Sue. But his success on his school examinations led him to try for a scholarship at the Institute for Higher Studies at Florence, which he barely won.

In Florence he was soon caught up in the Socialist movement. His thesis on the Florentine knighthood in the Renaissance was followed by *Magnati e popolani nelle commune di Firenze 1280–1295* (1899), in which he described the origins of the Florentine Republic as the product of class conflict. Salvemini saw the history of this period as one of conflict between the aristocracy and the great merchants, in which economic change brought institutional change in its wake. Though the book sold very few copies, it was considered the manifesto of the new Italian historiography. The work won Salvemini a professorial chair in 1901 and a prize from the Accademia dei Lincei that allowed him to marry Maria Minervini, whose acquaintance he had made as a student.

In 1897 Salvemini had begun to contribute to the Socialist journal *Critica sociale.* After his professorial appointment he helped organize secondary school teachers and joined a campaign to promote universal suffrage and universal education. At the same time he wrote *La Rivoluzione francese* (1905; *The French Revolution*), introducing to the Italian reading public the work of the French historian Alphonse Aulard, and a study *Mazzini* (1905), the first major analysis of this Italian statesman's ideas in the European context. These productive years were brought to a sudden end when an earthquake at Messina killed Salvemini's entire family in 1908, a tragedy from which he only slowly recovered.

In 1910 and 1913 Salvemini stood for election to Parliament but was defeated by government-instigated electoral fraud. Meanwhile he founded a new socialist journal, *L'unità,* on whose pages he fought the exacerbated nationalism of the war and immediate postwar years. In 1919 he was elected to Parliament by a large majority. But parliamentary government was already in deep trouble; in 1921, after the Fascists had gained power, he withdrew from politics. Though this move probably saved him from an assassin's bullet, it deprived the opposition of one of its most courageous leaders.

In 1925, after being arrested for clandestine anti-Fascist activities, Salvemini managed to escape and flee the country. He went first to France and England, then in

Gaetano Salvemini. (Egone Photo, Boston)

1933 to the United States to teach the history of Italian civilization at Harvard. He worked to awaken the English and American world to the dangers of fascism. He returned to Florence in 1947 and died there on Sept. 6, 1957.

Further Reading

Gaetano Salvemini is listed in the Social Sciences study guide (VII, A, 2). As a leader of the anti-Fascist movement in Parliament, he denounced the activities of Gabriele D'ANNUNZIO and Benito MUSSOLINI.

Salvemini's own works, which give considerable insight into his character, include *The Fascist Dictatorship in Italy* (1927) and, in collaboration with George LaPiana, *What To Do with Italy* (1943). Also of interest is his *Under the Axe of Fascism* (1936). For background see Charles F. Delzell, *Mussolini's Enemies: The Italian Anti-Fascist Resistance* (1961).

SAMUDRAGUPTA

/ By Brijen K. Gupta

Samudragupta (reigned 350–375) was the second emperor of the Gupta dynasty of India. His reign ushered in the Golden Age of India, and he is remembered both as a benevolent imperial conqueror and as a patron of the arts and letters.

A detailed record of the reign of Samudragupta (pronounced sə-mŏo′drə-gōop′tə) is preserved in the shape of an inscription—a *prasasti*, or panegyric, composed by the poet Harisena and engraved on the same pillar on which Emperor Asoka, centuries before, had had an edict carved. The two inscriptions make a contrasting reading: Asoka's, written in simple Pali, speaks of peace and righteousness; Samudragupta's, written in elegant and classical Sanskrit, glorifies war.

At the time of his accession, Samudragupta's territories comprised present-day north Bihar and north and west Bengal. Acting on his father's dying behest, the young ruler embarked upon *digvijaya*, a lofty Hindu political ideal to conquer the four quarters of the Aryan universe. The *prasasti* divides Samudragupta's opponents into four categories: rulers slain, whose dominions Samudragupta annexed outrightly; rulers defeated, but reinstated as tributaries; "frontier" kings, who were forced to pay homage; and "distant" kings, who acknowledged Samudragupta as an emperor by sending him embassies. Among the first were independent potentates of the Gangetic Basin; their extermination made Samudragupta the ruler of all territories from the Ravi in the west to the Brahmaputra in the east, and from the Himalayan foothills in the north to the Narbada in the south. In the second category were 12 potentates with territories between the Mahanadi and the Godavari. In the third category came more than a dozen tribal leaders of Assam, Malwa, Gujarat, and western Punjab and Rajputana. Lastly, Saka satraps of western India and Kushan rulers of northwest India and Afghanistan seem to have paid him homage. The ruler of Ceylon sent an embassy to secure privileges for Sinhalese monks at Bodhgaya. About 365 Samudragupta offered the horse sacrifice, the traditional symbol of lordship over Aryan India.

Samudragupta issued gold dinars: they weigh as much as 123 grains and have a gold content of 87 percent. One shows him performing the horse sacrifice; another shows him playing a harp. He was a gifted musician, a poet, and a person who took part in religious discussions. None of the many buildings he appears to have erected has survived. Though personally a Hindu, he extended his patronage to other religions, and one of his chief courtiers appears to have been the great Buddhist philosopher Vasubandhu. Not much is known of his administrative system, but he must have been an ideal ruler as is evidenced by the introductory portion of a late Javanese text, the *Tantri Kamandaka*, which refers to him in eloquent terms.

Further Reading

Samudragupta is listed in the Asia study guide (II, A, 2, a). ASOKA and CHANDRAGUPTA were Indian kings of the Maurya period, which preceded Samudragupta's Gupta period.

The best biography is Balkrishna Govind Gokhale, *Samudra Gupta: Life and Times* (1962). Information is also in John F. Fleet, ed., *Inscriptions of the Early Gupta Kings and Their Successors* (1888; rev. ed. 1963).

SAMUEL / **By Nathan H. Winter**

The prophet Samuel (ca. 1056–1004 B.C.) was the last judge of Israel and the first of the prophets after Moses. He inaugurated the monarchy by choosing and anointing Saul and David as kings of Israel.

S amuel was the son of Elkanah and Hannah, and he was born at Ramathaim-zophim in the hill country of Ephraim. Brought to the Temple at Shiloh as a young child to serve God in fulfillment of a vow made by his mother, he succeeded Eli as the high priest and judge of Israel. Because the Philistines had destroyed Shiloh, Israel's religious center, Samuel returned to Ramah, making it the center of his activity.

Samuel made annual circuits through the cities of Bethel, Gilgal, and Mizpah, judging the people, exhorting them to stop worshiping idols, and using his influence to hold the tribes together. He seemed able to penetrate the future, and the people looked upon him as a prophet.

Israel at this time was subjected to Philistine domination, constant threats from the Ammonites, and disunion among its own tribes. The people lacked respect for Samuel's corrupt sons, Joel and Abijah, whom he appointed to judge Israel in his stead. The elders urged Samuel to seek a forceful national leader to become king. Samuel acceded and chose Saul, son of Kish of the tribe of Benjamin, and he took an active role in Saul's coronation.

Samuel later broke with Saul because Saul twice disobeyed him. Samuel then proclaimed that Saul was rejected as king of Israel and that his dynasty would not continue on the throne. The prophet transferred his support to David, selecting him and secretly anointing him king of Israel. Samuel's last days are obscured by the conflict between Saul and David. The Bible makes a brief reference to his death and to his burial at Ramah.

Samuel, though counted among the greatest of the judges, like Moses, is also numbered among the prophets. He was not a warrior but, like Moses, was a hero who rallied the spirit of his people in the midst of oppression, keeping alive their hope and faith.

Further Reading

Samuel is listed in the Religion study guide (II, A, 4). He disagreed with SAUL and supported DAVID.

Although there is no single authoritative biography of Samuel, there are numerous volumes of fiction, making it difficult to distinguish between the historical and the legendary. The best short essays are in Rudolph Kittel, *Great Men and Movements in Israel* (trans. 1929), and James Fleming, *Personalities of the Old Testament* (1939). The best treatment of Samuel is, of course, in the Holy Scriptures, with commentaries published by each of the major religious groups. Recommended for the historical background are Max I. Margolis and Alexander Marx, *A History of the Jewish People* (1944); William Foxwell Albright, *From the Stone Age to Christianity* (1940; 2d ed. with new introduction, 1957); Salo Wittmayer Baron, *A Social and Religious History of the Jews*, vol. 1 (2d ed. 1952; 2d rev. ed. 1969); and Martin Noth, *The History of Israel* (trans. 1958; 2d ed. 1960).

✳   ✳   ✳

Samuel anoints David in this scene on an early-7th-century Byzantine silver dish. (The Metropolitan Museum of Art, Gift of J. Pierpont Morgan, 1917)

SAMUELSON / By Jesse W. Markham

The American economist Paul Anthony Samuelson (born 1915) was the most distinguished of the economists who entered the profession during and after the mid-1930s—the "Keynesian generation." He is frequently referred to as the last of the generalists.

P aul Samuelson was born on May 15, 1915, in Gary, Ind. He graduated from the University of Chicago in 1935 and pursued graduate study in economics at Harvard University, where he received the master's degree in 1936 and the doctorate in 1941 and was made a member of the prestigious Harvard Society of Junior Fellows. In 1940 he joined the faculty of the Massachusetts Institute of Technology.

Samuelson's *Foundations of Economic Analysis* and numerous pioneering articles on economic theory, statistics, mathematical economics, and the important postwar policy issues had placed him among the select few of the world's leading economists by 1947, the year he was awarded the John Bates Clark Medal, which ac-

Paul Samuelson. (United Press International Photo)

Councils of Economic Advisers, government agencies, and other public and private institutions; his frequent appearances on television and radio and in the printed media made Samuelson's name, and his economic views on vital economic issues, widely familiar. The economics profession became accustomed, over 3 decades, to hearing MIT students proclaim, with justifiable pride, that they were taught by Professor Samuelson. In a much broader sense, he taught more economics to more of the world's citizenry than any other economist of the 20th century.

Further Reading

Paul Samuelson is listed in the Social Sciences study guide (VII, C, 3). John Maynard KEYNES developed a system of economics called Keynesian economics, or the new economics. Other 20th-century American economists were Joseph A. SCHUMPETER and Edwin R. A. SELIGMAN.

Information on Samuelson is in Ben B. Seligman, *Main Currents in Modern Economics: Economic Thought since 1870* (1962), and in Robert Lekachman, *The Age of Keynes* (1966).

SAN MARTÍN / By Robert W. Delaney

The South American soldier and statesman José de San Martín (1778–1850) played an important role in winning the independence of several South American countries from Spain.

knowledged him as the outstanding American economic scholar under the age of 40.

A continuing steady stream of scientific books and articles and the appearance of Samuelson's textbook, *Economics: An Introductory Analysis* (1948), made him not only the most respected but also the best-known economist of his time. His *Economics* has been the standard textbook in the United States and throughout the world for more than 2 decades. Its unprecedented success is of course attributable to its overall greatness, but high on the list of specific reasons are Samuelson's concern with the big, vital economic issues, his changing of these issues as appropriate with each new edition, and his sparkling and lucid writing style, which makes these issues come alive to both teacher and student.

Samuelson was president of the Econometric Society (1951), the American Economic Association (1961), and the International Economic Association (1965–1968). In 1970 he was awarded the Nobel Memorial Prize in Economics, the first American economist to be so honored. He received honorary degrees from a host of colleges and universities. He delivered, among many other prestigious lectures, the Stamp Memorial Lecture (London, 1961), the Wicksell Lectures (Stockholm, 1962), and the Franklin Lecture (Detroit, 1962).

Samuelson was a leading figure in the new, more activist intelligentsia: he advised U.S. presidents and their

José de San Martín (pronounced sän mär-tēn′) was born at Yapeyú, a village on the northern frontier of Argentina, where his father was an official of the Spanish colonial government. At the age of 7, San Martín returned to Spain with his parents. He entered the Royal Academy as a cadet and was educated there with sons of the nobility of Spain. As a member of the Spanish army, he fought in some of the campaigns against French forces in the Peninsular War and by 1811 had acquired the rank of lieutenant colonel.

Hearing of the revolt against Spain in his native Argentina, San Martín resigned from the Spanish army in 1812 and sailed for Buenos Aires to join the patriot forces. He took a prominent part in organizing Argentine troops and soon became military governor of the north to organize defense against Spanish troops in Upper Peru. In 1814 he secured the governorship of the province of Cuyo at the foot of the Andes. Here for 3 years he recruited and trained his Army of the Andes, since he believed that Argentina could not be safely independent unless Spanish forces were dislodged from Chile, Peru, and Bolivia.

In January 1817 San Martín led his army of Argentines and fugitives from Chile over the Andes and surprised the Spanish army in Chile. After having captured and oc-

José de San Martín. (Organization of American States)

cupied Santiago on February 15, San Martín was offered the supreme dictatorship of Chile but declined in favor of his friend and colleague Bernardo O'Higgins. He made Chile completely free of Spanish troops by May 15, 1818, and began planning for an invasion of Peru.

San Martín was 2 years assembling a fleet which, under the able command of Lord Cochrane, swept Spanish shipping from the west coast of South America. In August 1820 the army of San Martín was transported toward Peru, convoyed by warships under Lord Cochrane. Within a year San Martín was able to occupy the capital, and on July 28, 1821, he proclaimed the independence of Peru from Spain. On August 3 he accepted the position of supreme protector of Peru.

However, considerable fighting was still needed before Peruvian independence was assured, since the bulk of the Spanish army had merely withdrawn into the mountains and was still a viable fighting force and a threat. San Martín considered that he did not have enough force to meet the Spaniards and would need the aid of the armies of Simón Bolívar, who had just liberated the areas of Venezuela, Colombia, and Ecuador. For that purpose, San Martín and Bolívar met at Guayaquil; that conference is one of the most disputed points in South American history.

Possibly they disputed over Guayaquil, which Bolívar had just occupied and which San Martín wanted to be a part of Peru. Possibly they disagreed on the type of government to be instituted in South America. San Martín did not believe that the South Americans were ready for

democracy, and he probably preferred a constitutional monarchy, whereas Bolívar believed, at that time, in complete democracy. Possibly they disagreed on the terms by which the armies of Bolívar would be brought into Peru. At any rate, San Martín left the conference in a precipitous manner, returned immediately to Peru, resigned his power and positions to the Congress, and left Bolívar in undisputed leadership.

San Martín made his way to Argentina and then to Europe, where he spent the rest of his life. He died on Aug. 17, 1850, at Boulogne-sur-Mer.

Further Reading

José de San Martín is listed in the Latin America study guide (III, B, 3). Simón BOLÍVAR, Antonio NARIÑO, and Francisco de Paula SANTANDER occupied important positions after successful military commands.

The standard biography of San Martín is Bartolome Mitre, *The Emancipation of South America* (trans. 1893; new introduction, 1969), a good starting place for understanding the liberation of Chile and Peru. A popular short biography by an Englishman is John C. J. Metford, *San Martín: The Liberator* (1950). Other biographies include Anna Schoellkopf, *Don José de San Martín, 1778–1850: A Study of His Career* (1924); Margaret H. Harrison, *Captain of the Andes* (1943); and Ricardo Rojas, *San Martín: Knight of the Andes* (trans. 1945).

SANCTORIUS / By Audrey B. Davis

The Italian physician and physiologist Sanctorius (1561–1636) is noted for his application of quantitative methods to the study of human physiology and pathology.

S anctorius (pronounced săngk-tō′rĭ-əs), the Latin name of Santorio Santorio, was born on March 29, 1561, at Capo d'Istria. The University of Padua, the leading medical institution of the period, provided his medical education between 1575 and 1582. After receiving his medical degree, he practiced as a physician up to 1599 in Croatia (Yugoslavia), where he had been invited by some Croatian nobility. In 1611 he assumed the chair of theoretical medicine at Padua and held this distinguished post until 1624, when he went to Venice. He died in Venice on Feb. 22, 1636. He endowed an annual lectureship at Padua, which is still continued.

As is typical of many pioneers, Sanctorius, without realizing the full value of his ideas, recognized the necessity of measurement in medicine. Therefore he directed all his energies toward one goal: the development of instruments and appliances which would permit the physician investigator to quantify all known facts about the body.

Sanctorius's classic experiment was carried out over a period of 30 years, during which he spent as much time as possible seated in a chair rigged up to a balance so that he could weigh himself frequently. He also weighed all the food he ingested and all the excreta that he passed. These measurements provided convincing evidence for the existence of the then controversial "insensible perspiration," by which volatile substances were supposed to leave the body. He published his results in *De medicina statica aphorismi* (1614), of which there were 32 editions up to 1784 and many translations into modern languages. Sanctorius's constant endeavors to conduct systematic measurements entitle him to rank among the founders of experimental medicine.

Sanctorius gave impetus to the iatrophysical school of medicine, that is, the school which explained all body processes and diseases and their treatments within a numerical and geometrical context. However, iatrophysics began to flourish outside of Italy only in the early 18th century, three-quarters of a century after Sanctorius's death.

Among the instruments Sanctorius invented or perfected for use in physiology and pathology are the balance, the thermometer, the hygrometer, the trocar (for removing excess water from the abdomen and the chest), and a catheter for removing kidney stones. The best-known of these instruments is the thermometer described by Sanctorius in his commentary on Arab medicine. He also developed an apparatus for measuring pulse rates by comparing them to the swings of a pendulum on strings of different lengths. Then, by comparing the string lengths, the pulse rates were calibrated as a function of time. Thus, medieval medicine and Renaissance physics were combined in the imaginative mind of Sanctorius to develop this important instrument.

Further Reading

Sanctorius is listed in the Science study guide (IV, G, 2). He worked within the framework of the ancient medical theory of GALEN.

There are no books on Sanctorius in English. Most biographical accounts are in Italian. The closest to a definitive biography is in Serbian by Mirko Drazen, *Santorio Santorio* (Zagreb, 1952); it includes a few pages of summary in English. For background see Henry E. Sigerist, *The Great Doctors: A Biographical History of Medicine* (trans. 1933); Ralph H. Major, *A History of Medicine*, vol. 1 (1954); and Katherine B. Shippen, *Men of Medicine* (1957).

SAND / By Neal Oxenhandler

The French novelist George Sand (1804–1876) was the most successful woman writer of her century. Her novels present a large fresco of romantic sentiment and 19th-century life, especially in its more pastoral aspects.

George Sand (pronounced säNd) was born Armandine Aurore Lucille Dupin in Paris on July 1, 1804. On her father's side she was related to a line of kings and to the Maréchal de Saxe; her mother was the daughter of a professional bird fancier. Aurore's father, Maurice Dupin, was a soldier of the Empire. He died when Aurore was still a child.

At the age of 14, tired of being the "apple of discord" between her mother and grandmother, Aurore went to the convent of the Dames Augustines Anglaises in Paris. Though she did her best to disrupt the convent's peaceful life, she felt drawn to quiet contemplation and direct communication with God.

To save Aurore from mysticism, her grandmother called her to her home in Nohant. Here Aurore studied nature, practiced medicine on the peasants, read from the philosophers of all ages, and developed a passion for the works of François René Chateaubriand. Her eccentric tutor encouraged her to wear men's clothing while horseback riding, and she galloped through the countryside in trousers and loose shirt, free, wild, and in love with nature.

Marriage and Lovers

When her grandmother died, Aurore became mistress

Sanctorius. (University of Pennsylvania Library)

George Sand about 1835, a portrait by Alfred de Musset. (Bulloz)

of the estate at Nohant. At 19 she married Casimir Dudevant, the son of a baron and a servant girl. He was good-hearted but coarse and sensual, and he offended her lofty and mystical ideal of love. Aurore soon began to seek her idealized love object elsewhere. For a time she maintained a platonic relationship with Aurélien de Sèze, but eventually this affair languished. She had begun to realize that it was impossible to sustain love without physical passion.

At the age of 27 Aurore moved to Paris in search of independence and love, leaving husband and children behind. She began writing articles to earn her living and met a coterie of writers. Henri de Latouche and Charles Sainte-Beuve became her mentors.

Aurore fell in love with Jules Sandeau, a charming young writer. They collaborated on articles and signed them collectively "J. Sand." When she published her first novel, *Indiana* (1832), she took as her pen name "George Sand."

George Sand made a home for Sandeau and for her daughter, Solange, but eventually she wearied of his jealousy and idle disposition. He, in turn, realized that he could never overcome her essential frigidity. She felt as though she had failed in marriage as well as in adultery. Several novels of disillusioned love were the fruit of this period of her life. Then she met the young poet Alfred de Musset, and they became lovers.

George Sand legally separated from her husband; she gained custody over Solange, while her husband kept the other child, Maurice. She now came to enjoy great renown in Paris both as a writer and as a bold and brilliant woman. She had many admirers and chose new lovers from among them. Her lovers included the Polish composer Frédéric Chopin and the doctor who attended Musset in Venice. Perhaps it was her inability to be aroused to physical passion that drove her from one lover to another. She compensated for this deficiency by the spiritual intensity of her love.

Political Views

George Sand was a democrat; she felt close to the people by birth, and she often praised the humble virtues of the urban and country poor in her novels. She was a Christian of sorts and advocated a socially conscious religion. Like Jean Jacques Rosseau, she believed that inherently good man was corrupted by civilization and faulty institutions.

Despite her own feminist leanings, George Sand never advocated political equality for women. It was in love that she demanded equality, in the free choice of the love object; the inequality of men and women before the law seemed to her a scandal.

Last Years

As she grew older, George Sand spent more and more time at her beloved Nohant and gave herself up to the intoxications of pastoral life, the entertainment of friends, the staging of puppet shows, and most of all to her grandchildren. Though she had lost none of her vital energy and enthusiasm, she grew less concerned with politics. Her quest for the absolute in love had led her through years of stormy affairs to the attainment of a tolerant and universal love—of God, of nature, of children. She died in Nohant on June 9, 1876.

Early Novels

Every night from midnight until dawn, George Sand covered her daily quota of 20 pages with her large, tranquil writing, never crossing out a line. All her novels are love stories in which her romantic idealism unfolds in a realistic setting. The characters are people she knew, although their sentiments are idealized.

The early works by George Sand are novels of passion, written to alleviate the pain of her first love affairs. *Indiana* (1832) has as its central theme woman's search for the absolute in love. *Valentine* (1832) depicts an aristocratic woman, unhappily married, who finds that a farmer's son loves her. *Lélia* (1854) is a lyrical but searching confession of the author's own physical coldness. Lélia is a beautiful woman loved by a young poet, but she can show him only maternal affection.

Socialist Novels

During the 1840s George Sand wrote a number of novels in which she exposed her socialist doctrine joined with a humanitarian religion. *Le Compagnon du tour de France* (1840), *Consuelo* (1842–1843), and *Le Péché de Monsieur Antoine* (1847) are typical novels of this period. Her socialism was of an optimistic, idealistic nature. She sympathized in these novels with the plight of the worker and the farmer. She also wrote a number of novels devoted to country life, most produced during her retreat to Nohant at the time of the 1848 uprising. *La Mare au diable* (1846), *La Petite Fadette* (1849), and *Les Maîtres sonneurs* (1852) are typical novels of this genre. They celebrate the humble virtues of a simple life and offer idealized portraits of the peasants of Berry.

George Sand's last works show a tendency to moralize; in these novels the characters become incarnated theories rather than human beings.

Further Reading

George Sand is listed in the Literature study guide (III, G, 1). Her friends included the novelists Victor HUGO and Gustave FLAUBERT.

George Sand's appeal to biographers has inspired a number of good works. Elizabeth W. Schermerhorn, *The Seven Strings of the Lyre: The Romantic Life of George Sand, 1804–1876* (1927), is authoritative and carefully compiled. Felizia Seyd, *Romantic Rebel: The Life and Times of George Sand* (1940), is a straightforward account. André Maurois, *Lélia: The Life of George Sand* (1952; trans. 1953), is readable and emotionally compelling. Two books that emphasize George Sand's love life are Marie J. Howe, *George Sand: The Search for Love* (1927), and Frances Winwar, *The Life of the Heart: George Sand and Her Times* (1945).

SANDBURG / By Hyatt H. Waggoner

An American poet, anthologist, singer of folk songs and ballads, and biographer, Carl Sandburg (1878–1967) is best known for his magnificent biography of Abraham Lincoln and his early "realistic" verse celebrations of Chicago.

The legend of Carl Sandburg as a raw, folksy poet of midwestern democracy has overshadowed his later development. From the time he wrote his moving elegy on the death of Franklin D. Roosevelt, "When Death Came April Twelve 1945," until his final volume of poetry, *Honey and Salt* (1963), he exhibited a newly achieved depth and originality that far surpassed his earlier work. His youthful career as an impassioned revolutionary socialist has largely been forgotten, and he died one of America's best-known and best-loved poets.

Sandburg was born in Galesburg, Ill., on Jan. 6, 1878, of a poor Swedish immigrant family. At the age of 13 he quit school to work as a day laborer. He traveled extensively through the West, where he began developing a lifelong devotion to his country and its people. Following Army service during the Spanish-American War, he entered Lombard (now Knox) College in Galesburg. Here he wrote his first poetry.

After graduation Sandburg worked as a newspaperman in Milwaukee, Wis. In 1907 and 1908 he was district organizer for the Social Democratic party in Wisconsin and served as secretary to Milwaukee's Socialist mayor (1910–1912). Later he moved to Chicago, becoming an editorial writer for the *Daily News* in 1917. Meanwhile his verse began appearing in the avant-garde *Poetry* magazine; his first volume, *Chicago Poems*, was published in 1916. His reputation as vital poet of the American scene was solidified with *Cornhuskers* (1918), *Smoke and Steel* (1920), and *Slabs of the Sunburnt West* (1922).

Early Writings

Sandburg's early poetry was as close to being "subliterary" as the work of any American poet of comparable stature. Meant to illustrate his humanitarian socialist ideology, his early verse is scarcely above the level of political oratory. "I Am the People, the Mob" from the *Chicago Poems* is characteristic. The ending of the poem is reminiscent of Walt Whitman at his most prosaic: "When I, the People, learn to remember, when I, the People, use the lessons of yesterday and no longer forget

Carl Sandburg in 1963. (United Press International Photo)

who robbed me last year, who played me for a fool—then there will be no speaker in all the world say the name: 'The People,' with any fleck of a sneer in his voice or any far-off smile of derision. The mob—the crowd—the mass—will arrive then.''

Neither in use of language nor in metrics does this qualify even as free verse; in style it is closer to John Dos Passos' contemporary experiments in prose than to poetry. The revolutionary naturalistic esthetic of the time called for a poetry of direct imitation; but Sandburg's ''imitations'' exhibited little artistry.

Sandburg's early poetry not only tended toward excessively unshaped imitation of reality but also copied other poets as well. T. S. Eliot's ''The Love Song of J. Alfred Prufrock'' had appeared the year before Sandburg's ''Fog'' was published. Eliot's image of the fog as a cat has profound implications in the context of the rest of his poem; ''Fog,'' which was hailed as a fine example of an imagist poem, has no context whatsoever and hence no meaning. In terms of imagist poetics, ''Fog'' might be considered successful, but Sandburg had never counted himself a member of that movement; nor had he ever seriously considered its esthetic.

Similarly, Sandburg's ''Happiness'' compares unfavorably with Ezra Pound's ''Salutation,'' and his ''Buffalo Bill'' expresses mere nostalgia in relation to E. E. Cummings's more penetrating ''Buffalo Bill's.'' Some of the poems in *Cornhuskers* are more original and fully realized than those discussed here, but none meets the standards of the best of his contemporaries.

Later Work

From 1926 to 1939 Sandburg devoted himself primarily to writing the six-volume biography of Abraham Lincoln, presenting Lincoln as the embodiment of the American spirit; he received a Pulitzer Prize in history for this work (1939). He also was collecting the folk songs that made up *The American Songbook* (1927).

Honey and Salt (1963), a remarkable achievement for a ''part-time'' poet in his 80s, contains much of Sandburg's best poetry. Here the mellowness and wisdom of age are evident; the sound of an American idiom echoes through these poems more effectively than in the earlier ''realistic'' verse. By this time Sandburg had moved from his dependence on ideology to a deeply felt sympathy and concern for actual people. Tenderness replaces sentimentality; emotional control replaces defensive ''toughness.'' There is an explicitly religious consciousness in these last poems, only implicit in the earlier work, where it was often submerged in political ideology and naturalistic poetics.

Sandburg also published a collection of children's stories, *Rootabaga Stories* (1922). Other volumes of poetry are *Good Morning, America* (1928); *The People, Yes* (1936); *Collected Poems* (1950), which won a Pulitzer Prize; and *Harvest Poems, 1910–1960* (1960). *Remembrance Rock* (1948), an epic panorama of American history, was his only novel. He died in Flat Rock, N.C., on July 22, 1967.

Further Reading

Carl Sandburg is listed in the Literature study guide (I,

E, 1, b). He was inspired by the poetry of Walt WHITMAN.

Sandburg's autobiography is *Always the Young Strangers* (1953). A biography is Harry L. Golden, *Carl Sandburg* (1961). Good critical commentary includes ''Carl Sandburg's Complete Poems'' in William Carlos Williams, *Selected Essays* (1954); Newton Arvin's ''Carl Sandburg'' in Malcolm Cowley, ed., *After the Genteel Tradition: American Writers since 1910* (1959); Roy Harvey Pearce, *The Continuity of American Poetry* (1961); and Hyatt H. Waggoner, *American Poets: From the Puritans to the Present* (1968).

SANDYS / By Carl E. Prince

Sir Edwin Sandys (1561–1629), a great figure in the British Parliament during the turbulent first quarter of the 17th century, was important in the English colonization of America.

Born on Dec. 9, 1561, in Worcestershire, Edwin Sandys was the son of an archbishop of the Church of England and thus a member of the English nobility. He was educated at Oxford University and the Middle Temple.

Sandys entered Parliament in 1586 and distinguished himself as an energetic legislator. He also traveled much and found time to write about religious matters, early displaying his liberalism. He was among James I's first supporters; under his patronage Sandys emerged as a prime mover in parliamentary circles.

Within a decade, however, Sandys deserted the Crown and took leadership of the opposition. He had come to believe that a king ruled *under* law and this imposed limitations on the rights of both the Crown and its subjects, and that if the former trespassed the latter's rights, he could legally be overthrown. Thus it was that Sandys contributed immensely to the active leadership of the budding Whig (parliamentary) cause and to the dogma opposing the king's prerogative that grew out of it.

When the Crown suspended Parliament in 1613 (a suspension lasting 6 years), Sandys turned his attention to the growing colonial empire. He appeared first as a power in the East India Company, but the contributions for which he is remembered were to the Virginia Company. For several years treasurer of that overseas joint stock company, Sandys was in a position to influence policies both in London and the New World.

One historian has noted that Sandys ''was virtually managing'' the company from 1617 on. The Virginia Company's operations, then, became a natural source of enmity between the Crown and the Whigs during the 1620s, for the King ''cherished a grudge against Sandys'' and in 1624 dissolved the company. By that time, however, the Virginia Colony had been successfully estab-

Sir Edwin Sandys, a portrait by an unknown artist.
(National Portrait Gallery, London)

lished; Sandys had been instrumental during the colony's crucial years in settling large numbers to repopulate Virginia after the "starving time." Sandys also gained a monopoly in England for Virginia's tobacco and tried to introduce manufactures into the colony.

However, with Virginia's economic well-being and population restored, Sandys became dispensable to the Crown; over the protests of the shareholders he was removed from the company's management by James I. "It was the manipulations of Sandys," a historian has written, that played a crucial part in establishing the "supremacy of Parliament [that] was embodied in the unwritten constitution" of England. He was one of the few Englishmen who contributed significantly both to the establishment of the rule of law in the British Isles and to the expansion of England's overseas empire. He died in October 1629.

Further Reading

Sir Edwin Sandys is listed in the European History study guide (V, A, 2) and the American History study guide (II, B, 3, a). One of the investors in the Virginia Company, John SMITH, was president of the governing council of the Jamestown settlement in Virginia.

There is no modern acceptable biography of Sandys. For the period as a whole and for insights into Sandys's career see Wallace Notestein, *The English People on the Eve of Colonization, 1603–1630* (1954).

SANGALLO / By David R. Coffin

The Sangallo family (active late 15th–mid-16th century) was a large and important clan of Florentine artists. The three most prominent figures were architects amd military engineers.

Descended from the woodworker Francesco Giamberti, the family received the name Sangallo (pronounced säng-gäl′lō) from its residence near the Porta S. Gallo in Florence. The chief members were Francesco's sons, Giuliano (ca. 1443–1516) and Antonio the Elder (ca. 1453–1534), and their nephew, Antonio the Younger (1483–1546). Giuliano, as leader of the second generation of Florentine Renaissance architects, refined the architectural style of Filippo Brunelleschi to suit the less heroic and more sensuous age of Lorenzo de' Medici. His brother, Antonio the Elder, who often assisted him, was more concerned with military engineering, but his late church at Montepulciano reflects the High Renaissance architectural style inaugurated by Donato Bramante.

Giuliano da Sangallo

Giuliano was trained as a woodcarver in the shop of Il Francione, a local woodworker and military engineer. Giuliano probably accompanied his master to Rome and was certainly there in 1465, as he notes on the title page of his large sketchbook of antiquities (in the Vatican Library). Although there has been some uncertainty about his identification in Roman documents, he was probably active in several of the papal building projects, such as the Palace of S. Marco (1469–1470), St. Peter's (1470–1472), and the benedictional loggia (1470) which once stood in front of old St. Peter's.

After Giuliano returned to Florence, he aided Il Francione with the fortification of Colle Val d'Elsa (1479) and prepared a model for the church of the Servi (1480). With Antonio the Elder, he completed a model for the church and monastery of the Badia (1482) and carved a crucifix for SS. Annunziata (1481–1483).

By the mid-1480s Giuliano was the most prominent architect in Florence and in favor with Lorenzo de' Medici. Nearby at Prato he designed the Church of the Madonna delle Carceri (1485–1491) on a Greek-cross plan of four equal arms with an interior melon-shaped dome over the crossing. The interior with its contrast of dark architectural moldings against the light wall surface is a reflection of the influence of Brunelleschi. The green-and-white marble revetment of the exterior conveys that element of elegance so characteristic of Giuliano. At the same time he built the villa at Poggio a Caiano (ca. 1485) for Lorenzo de' Medici. Organized with separate apartments at the corners of the large central salon, the living quarters of the villa are set in two stories above a great arcaded podium which serves as a terrace around the building. The rectangular mass of the villa is relieved by an entrance loggia designed as a temple front set into the center of the first floor. In 1488 Lorenzo de' Medici sent Giuliano to Naples to deliver to

The Church of the Madonna di S. Biagio at Montepulciano, designed by Antonio da Sangallo the Elder. The church is one of the best examples of High Renaissance architecture. (Alinari)

been discovered, in anticipation of the Pope's acquisition of it for his collection in the Vatican Palace.

By November 1507 Giuliano was again in his native city of Florence, where he was principally active with fortifications at Pisa and Leghorn. When Leo X of the Medici family became pope in 1513, Giuliano immediately returned to Rome. In July he designed for the new pope a tremendous palace near the Piazza Navona which was never executed. On Jan. 1, 1514, Giuliano was appointed supervisor of work for the new St. Peter's, which the architect Bramante was building, and in April he continued in that position with Raphael, who succeeded Bramante.

Giuliano returned to Florence in July 1515. He prepared several unexecuted designs, preserved among his drawings, for the completion of the facade of Brunelleschi's S. Lorenzo. He died on Oct. 20, 1516. His son, Francisco (1494–1576), was a sculptor who was particularly known for his tomb monuments.

Antonio da Sangallo the Elder

Antonio the Elder was active with fortifications in and near Rome in the early 1490s. He worked on the Castel Sant'Angelo in Rome (1492–1493) and designed the citadel of Civita Castellana (1494). In 1517 he collaborated with Baccio d'Agnolo on the design of the loggia on the Piazza dell'Annunziata in Florence, matching that of Brunelleschi's Ospedale degli Innocenti.

Antonio's most important independent commission was the Church of the Madonna di S. Biagio at Montepulciano (1518–1529). The centralized Greek-cross plan of the church with independent towers in the reentrant angles of the facade and the tall dome on a drum over the crossing obviously reflect Bramante's ideas for St. Peter's.

Antonio da Sangallo the Younger

Antonio the Younger, whose real name was Cordini,

King Ferdinando I the model of a palace, whose plan is in the Vatican sketchbook.

On his return to Florence in 1489 Giuliano prepared the model for the Sacristy of Sto Spirito, and from September 1489 to February 1490 he was paid for the model of the Strozzi Palace. This massive palace was begun in 1490 by Benedetto da Maiano with some minor changes, particularly in the rustication of the stone, from Giuliano's model (preserved in the palace). The Gondi Palace, begun in 1490 after his designs, is a very refined descendant of Michelozzo's Medici Palace in Florence. In 1492 Giuliano traveled to Milan with the model of a palace for Duke Lodovico Sforzo, and the same year he designed the church of S. Maria dell'Umiltà at Pistoia.

Giuliano followed Cardinal Giuliano della Rovere to Lyons, France, in June 1494. By August, Giuliano had returned to Italy, probably to the cardinal's native city of Savona, where he designed a palace for the cardinal. With his appointment in 1497 as military engineer of Florence, Giuliano's activity was primarily in Tuscany.

The election in 1503 of his patron, Cardinal della Rovere, as Pope Julius II soon attracted Giuliano to Rome, where he remained until 1507. During this second residence in Rome he was involved in expanding the papal hunting lodge at La Magliana. In 1506 the Pope sent him and the great Florentine sculptor Michelangelo to view the ancient sculpture Laocoon, which had just

The villa at Poggio a Caiano near Florence, commissioned by Lorenzo de' Medici, was designed by Giuliano da Sangallo. (Alinari-Brogi)

was the son of a sister of Giuliano and Antonio the Elder. Accompanying Giuliano to Rome in 1504, Antonio the Younger soon assisted Bramante and served as master carpenter on the work of St. Peter's. In 1516 Antonio was appointed chief assistant to Raphael at St. Peter's. Antonio designed the Farnese Palace in Rome for Cardinal Alessandro Farnese. Work on the palace began in 1517 but was interrupted about 1520, when Antonio succeeded Raphael as chief architect of the new St. Peter's.

For the next decade Antonio undertook numerous papal commissions, although little was executed because of the political and religious upheavals of the period. The Mint, or Zecca, in Rome (1523–1524; now the Banco di Sto Spirito) was designed with a slightly concave facade modeled on a triumphal arch motif above a rusticated ground floor. In 1525 Antonio was concerned with fortifications for Parma and in the following year for Piacenza. At Orvieto he built an amazing public well, the Pozzo di S. Patrizio (1528–1535), with double spiral ramps penetrating to the base of the well around an open core.

The election in 1534 of Cardinal Farnese as Pope Paul III brought renewed architectural activity for Antonio. He redesigned and enlarged the Farnese Palace, resulting in a tremendous three-story building arranged around a square central court. The palace was completed by Michelangelo after Antonio's death. Antonio practically rebuilt the Farnese town of Castro with fortifications, a ducal palace, and the Zecca (all destroyed in 1649). For the entry into Rome of the emperor Charles V in 1536, Antonio organized the artists of Rome to prepare the festival decorations, including temporary triumphal arches near the palace of S. Marco and at the entrance to the Vatican Borgo. Under the threat of Turkish attacks Antonio began in 1537 to prepare new fortifications for Rome, which work continued until his death, including the unfinished Porta di Sto Spirito near the Vatican.

Although Antonio had continued since 1520 to be the architect of the new St. Peter's, assisted by Baldassare Peruzzi, it was only with the Farnese pope that extensive work was accomplished. Antonio built a great wooden model (1539–1546) for a new design for the church (preserved in St. Peter's). The design is of a tremendous Greek-cross plan with a large additional entrance vestibule and twin-towered facade with a benedictional loggia. His actual work on the church was principally concentrated on the southern arm, but he also raised the floor level, changing the interior spatial proportions. In the Vatican Palace from 1539 Antonio was architect for the Sala Regia, where the Pope received royalty, and the adjacent Pauline Chapel. Antonio died at Terni on Aug. 3, 1546.

Further Reading

The Sangallo family is listed in the Art study guide (III, D, 3). Giuliano was influenced by Filippo BRUNELLESCHI and MICHELOZZO, and Antonio the Elder by Donato BRAMANTE. Antonio the Younger worked with RAPHAEL. MICHELANGELO completed most of the Farnese Palace immediately after Antonio the Younger's death.

There are no monographs in English on the Sangallos.

The Farnese Palace in Rome, designed by Antonio da Sangallo the Younger. It was completed by Michelangelo. (Alinari)

Biographical information on them is in Giorgio Vasari, *Lives of the Most Eminent Painters, Sculptors and Architects* (many editions), and in André Chastel, *The Studios and Styles of the Renaissance, Italy 1460–1500* (1966).

F. SANGER / By E. Ashworth Underwood

The English biochemist Frederick Sanger (born 1918) was awarded the Nobel Prize in Chemistry for his discovery of the chemical structure of insulin.

Frederick Sanger, son of Frederick Sanger, a medical practitioner, was born at Rendcombe, Gloucestershire, on Aug. 13, 1918. Entering St. John's College, Cambridge, in 1936, he graduated with the degree of bachelor of arts (in natural sciences) in 1939. In 1943 he received his doctorate of philosophy (in chemistry) with a thesis on lysine. He held a Beit Memorial Fellowship from 1944 to 1951 and then joined the staff of the Medical Research Council. He later became director of the Division of Protein Chemistry in the Council's Laboratory for Molecular Biology at Cambridge.

Sanger worked entirely on the chemical structure of the proteins, especially insulin. About 1900 Emil Fisher had succeeded in breaking down proteins into polypeptides, consisting of their ultimate constituents, amino acids. About 25 different amino acids occur in nature, and of these 20 are found in most mammalian proteins.

By 1943 it was known that proteins consisted of long chains of amino acid residues bound together by peptide linkages. A. C. Chibnall and others knew the 51 amino acid residues that composed insulin; they also knew that phenylalanine was at the end of one of the chains. The insulin molecule appeared to consist of a large number of polypeptide chains, and it was held that what was important biologically was the sequence in which the amino acids followed each other in the chains. This sequence was unknown for any protein.

Sanger introduced the reagent fluorodinitrobenzene (FDNB), which reacted with the free amino acid at the end of a chain to form a dinitrophenyl derivative (DNP) combined with that amino acid. The DNP acids are bright yellow. If the chains were then split by hydrolysis, the colored terminal acid of each link could be identified by chromatographic and electrophoretic methods. Sanger at first thought that the insulin molecule contained four long chains; but he later concluded that it consisted of only two chains containing 21 and 30 amino acids respectively. He then split the bridges joining the chains by oxidation with performic acid and dealt with each chain individually. The chain was separated into successively shorter links, and in each link the terminal amino acid was identified. He was able to determine the exact sequence of amino acids in each chain.

Sanger then determined that the two chains were linked by two disulfide bridges of cystine residues, with a third bridge linking two parts of the short chain. The determination of the exact positions of these bridges enabled Sanger, after over 12 years of research, to give a diagram for the structure of insulin. For this work he was awarded the Nobel Prize in Chemistry in 1958.

In 1951 Sanger was awarded the Corday-Morgan Medal of the Chemical Society. In 1954 he was elected a Fel-

low of the Royal Society and a Fellow of King's College, Cambridge; and in 1958 he was elected a Foreign Honorary Member of the American Academy of Arts and Sciences.

Further Reading

Frederick Sanger is listed in the Science study guide (VII, D, 1). Others who worked on related biochemical problems were E. C. KENDALL, Tadeus REICHSTEIN, Albert von SZENT-GYÖRGYI, and Arne TISELIUS.

There is a biography of Sanger in *Nobel Lectures, Chemistry, 1942–1962* (1964). This work also includes his Nobel Lecture, which gives an admirable summary of his work. For the chemical background see P. Karrer, *Organic Chemistry* (4th ed. 1950).

MARGARET SANGER / By Charles Alexander

The pioneering work of Margaret Higgins Sanger (1884–1966), American crusader for scientific contraception, family planning, and population control, made her a world-renowned figure.

Margaret Higgins was born on Sept. 14, 1884, in Corning, N.Y. Her father was a thoroughgoing freethinker. Her mother was a devout Roman Catholic who bore 11 children before dying of tuberculosis. Although Margaret was greatly influenced by her father, her mother's death left her with a deep sense of dissatisfaction concerning her own and society's medical ignorance. After graduating from the local high school and from Claverack College at Hudson, N.Y., she took nurse's training. She moved to New York City and served in the poverty-stricken slums of its East Side. In 1902 she married William Sanger. Although plagued by tuberculosis, she had her first child, a son, the next year. She had another son by Sanger, as well as a daughter who died in childhood.

Margaret Sanger's experiences with slum mothers who begged for information about how to avoid more pregnancies transformed her into a social radical. She joined the Socialist party, began attending radical rallies, and read everything she could about birth control practices. She became convinced that oversized families were the basic cause of poverty. In 1913 she began publishing a monthly newspaper, the *Woman Rebel*, in which she passionately urged family limitation and first used the term "birth control." After only six issues, she was arrested and indicted for distributing "obscene" literature through the mails. She fled to Europe, where she continued her birth control studies, visiting clinics and talking with medical researchers.

Mrs. Sanger returned to the United States in 1916 and, after dismissal of the indictment against her, began nationwide lecturing. In New York City she and her associ-

Frederick Sanger in 1958. (Keystone)

Margaret Sanger. (Library of Congress)

ates opened a birth control clinic in a slum area to give out contraceptive information and materials. This time she was arrested under state law. She spent a month in prison, as did her sister. Leaving prison in 1917, Mrs. Sanger intensified her activities, lecturing, raising money from a group of wealthy patrons in New York, and launching the *Birth Control Review*, which became the organ of her movement for 23 years. Encouraged by a state court decision that liberalized New York's anticontraceptive statute, she shifted her movement's emphasis from direct action and open resistance to efforts to secure more permissive state and Federal laws. Although regularly in trouble with New York City authorities, she continued lecturing to large crowds and keeping in touch with European contraceptive research. Her brilliantly successful visit to Japan in 1922 was the first of several Asian trips. A year later she and her friends opened clinical research bureaus to gather medical histories and dispense birth control information in New York City and Chicago. By 1930 there were 55 clinics across the United States. Meanwhile Mrs. Sanger obtained a divorce and married J. Noah H. Slee.

Margaret Sanger's fame became worldwide in 1927, when she helped organize and spoke before the first World Population Conference at Geneva, Switzerland. She and her followers continued to lobby for freer state and Federal laws on contraception and for the dissemination of birth control knowledge through welfare programs. By 1940 the American birth control movement was operating a thriving clinic program and enjoying general acceptance by the medical profession and an increasingly favorable public attitude.

For most Americans, Margaret Sanger *was* the birth control movement. During World War II her popularity continued to grow, despite her opposition to United States participation in the war based on her conviction that wars were the result of excess national population growth. In 1946 she helped found the International Planned Parenthood Federation. This was one of her last great moments. She was troubled by a weak heart during her last 20 years, although she continued traveling, lecturing, and issuing frequent statements. She died in Tucson, Ariz., on Sept. 6, 1966.

Further Reading

Margaret Sanger is listed in the American History study guide (IX, D, 4). During this period Eleanor ROOSEVELT became prominent in a number of social causes.

Margaret Sanger: An Autobiography (1938) incorporates much of Mrs. Sanger's earlier *My Fight for Birth Control* (1931). The most recent biography is Emily Taft Douglas, *Margaret Sanger* (1969), a carefully researched and sympathetic account. See also Lawrence Lader, *The Margaret Sanger Story and the Fight for Birth Control* (1955). David M. Kennedy, *Birth Control in America: The Career of Margaret Sanger* (1970), focuses on her public career and examines the whole controversy over birth control. Less solid but of possible interest is the fictionalized biography by Noel B. Gerson, *The Crusader* (1969). Brief treatments of her are in Mary R. Beard, *Woman as a Force in History* (1946); Mark H. Haller, *Eugenics: Hereditarian Attitudes in American Thought* (1963); and Donald K. Pickens, *Eugenics and the Progressives* (1968).

SANMICHELI / By David R. Coffin

The Italian architect and military engineer Michele Sanmicheli (ca. 1484–1559) introduced to north Italy the Roman High Renaissance style of architecture. His work is generally characterized by a boldness and strength inspired by his military interests.

Born in Verona, Michele Sanmicheli (pronounced säm-mē-kâ′lē) went to Rome about 1500. With the counsel of the architect Antonio da Sangallo the Elder, Sanmicheli served from 1509 as supervisor of the completion of the facade of the Cathedral at Orvieto. His first involvement with military architecture was in 1526, when he inspected the papal fortifications in the Romagna with Antonio da Sangallo the Younger.

Returning to Verona about 1527, Sanmicheli began the Pellegrini Chapel (ca. 1528) attached to S. Bernardino. The interior of this circular, domed chapel is very richly decorated with relief sculpture and elegant Corinthian

Michele Sanmicheli, an engraving by Giovanni Battista Cecchi, in the Civica Raccolta Stampe Bertarelli, Milan. (Editorial Photocolor Archives, Inc.)

columns, some with spiral fluting. In 1529 he commenced work on the nearby fortifications of Legnago and was soon charged with the fortifications of many of the cities controlled by Venice, such as Verona (from 1530), Chioggia (from 1541), and Udine (from 1543). In 1535 he was appointed engineer of the state for lagoons and fortifications by the Venetian Senate, and from 1537 to 1539 he traveled to Corfu, Crete, and Dalmatia to design fortifications. Incorporated in these fortifications were powerful gates combining heavily rusticated stonework with massive Doric columns and prominent keystones, as in the Porta Nuova, Verona (1533–1550), the Forte di S. Andrea a Lido, Venice (1543–1549), and the Porta Palio, Verona (1548–1557).

The chronology of Sanmicheli's architecture in Verona is controversial. The spiral fluting of the half columns and the relief sculpture on the upper story of the Bevilacqua Palace resemble the interior of the Pellegrini Chapel, suggesting a date of about 1530 for the palace. The Canossa Palace (ca. 1530–1537) is much more planar and reveals the influence of Giulio Romano's work in Mantua. In the 18th century the roof was raised, drastically changing the character of the facade. The Pompei Palace (ca. 1550; now the Museo Civico) marks a return to the severe classicism of Donato Bramante, but the robust Doric order and large keystones resemble Sanmicheli's Porta Palio.

Sanmicheli designed two imposing palaces in Venice:

the Cornaro a S. Polo Palace (after 1545–1564) and the Grimani Palace (ca. 1556–ca. 1567). On the mainland near Castelfranco Veneto he built the Villa La Soranza (ca. 1545–1550), of which only a portion of the service buildings is preserved. Originally the villa consisted of a casino flanked by separate one-story, arcaded service buildings. Built of brick covered with stucco lined in imitation of stone, it had a rustic character emphasized by the simplicity of architectural detail and omission of the classical orders.

The Lazzaretto, or pesthouse, outside Verona (1549–1603), attributed to Sanmicheli, was a large, rectangular, arcaded court lined with cells. In the center of the court was a circular chapel with dome on a high drum. At his death in August 1559 he had just begun another circular, domed church, the Madonna di Campagna (1559–1561) near Verona.

Further Reading

Michele Sanmicheli is listed in the Art study guide (III, D, 3). He and Jacopo SANSOVINO disseminated the architectural ideas of Donato BRAMANTE in the Veneto.

The only monograph in English on Sanmicheli is Eric J. Langenskiöld, *Michele Sanmicheli, the Architect of Verona: His Life and Works* (1938). Piero Gazzola edited *Michele Sanmicheli* (1960), a fully illustrated catalog for an exhibition of Sanmicheli's architectural work which contains a complete bibliography to 1960. Sanmicheli is discussed in Peter Murray, *The Architecture of the Italian Renaissance* (1963), and T. A. West, *History of Architecture in Italy* (1968).

SANSOVINO / By Eleanor Dodge Barton

The Italian artist Jacopo Sansovino (1486–1570) executed sculpture and architecture in Venice whose quality and extent create much of the effect of the city today.

Trained in Florence and active in Rome and Florence in the crucial early decades of the 16th century, Jacopo Sansovino (pronounced sän-sō-vē′nō) became the man of destiny for Venetian architecture and trained so many young sculptors that Giorgio Vasari credited him with virtually running an academy. In his 40 years of service as principal architect to the city of Venice, Sansovino profited by his early Florentine training in his skillful use of sculpture to enrich and animate buildings distinguished by a breadth, grandeur, and structural harmony surely based on his close study and understanding of ancient and current Roman architecture.

Jacopo Tatti was born in Florence, the son of Antonio Tatti. In 1502 Jacopo entered the workshop of the sculptor and architect Andrea Sansovino and adopted his master's name. Jacopo followed Andrea to Rome in 1505; he may have assisted his teacher in the Rosso and Sforza tombs in S. Maria del Popolo, but he also worked independently restoring antiques and making one of the first copies of the newly excavated *Laocoon*.

Sansovino's earliest major commissions came shortly after he returned to Florence in 1511: the large statue *St. James* for the Cathedral of Florence and the nearly life-size statue *Bacchus*. Both works reveal his technical facility; the ease in handling drapery invests the spare figure of St. James with a needed surface enrichment, and the graceful, swinging movement and dextrous carving makes the Bacchus instantly attractive.

After collaborating on the decorations for Pope Leo X's triumphal entry into Florence, Sansovino was disappointed in hopes for a share in the project to complete the facade of the Medici church of S. Lorenzo. He returned to Rome in 1518 and executed such varied works as the idealized *Madonna* in S. Agostino, the more taut and complex *St. James* in S. Maria del Monserrato, and the elaborate tomb of Cardinal St. Angelo in S. Marcello. He was also consulted on the preliminary designs for the Florentine church in Rome, S. Giovanni dei Fiorentini.

The violent disaster of the sack of Rome in 1527 proved ultimately a blessing for Sansovino, who, fleeing Rome for France, found in Venice a city that stimulated his full development as an artist and provided a totally congenial atmosphere. His first work there was the utilitarian but crucial problem of strengthening the dangerously weakened fabric of S. Marco. This led to his appointment as protomagister to S. Marco in 1529 and his decision to stay in Venice. While he soon became a leading figure in Venice, the friend of such men as Titian, Tintoretto, and Pietro Aretino and the easy associate of noble patrons, Sansovino never felt himself above a concern for the countless practical details that together affected the appearance of his adopted city.

Appointed principal architect of Venice in 1529, Sansovino also continued to execute sculpture, creating works ranging from the fluent precision and richness of his bronze sculpture for S. Marco (tribune reliefs, 1530s; statues of the Evangelists, 1553; doors, 1563) to the harsh colossal figures *Mars* and *Neptune* on the Scala dei Giganti of the Ducal Palaco (1550s). A more chilly and disciplined classicism characterizes his marble reliefs for the church of S. Antonio in Padua (1562).

Sansovino's most formidable assignments as an architect were centered in and near the Piazza di S. Marco. The Library, designed to provide handsomely for the collection left to the city of Venice by Cardinal Bessarion, the Mint, and the Loggetta involved different functions, but all demanded a careful adjustment to the preexisting buildings. The memorable impression of all these buildings in their relation to each other and to the one large open space in Venice, the Piazza di S. Marco, demonstrates Sansovino's brilliance and originality as an architect. The Mint (1537–1554) is deliberately compact in its use of the severe Doric order and heavy rustication to emphasize its function as a secure treasury. The Library (1536–1554; completed by Vincenzo Scamozzi in 1588), with its long, horizontal facade kept low to harmonize with the Ducal Palace on the opposite side of the Piazzetta, is far richer in its architectural and sculptural detail and strong contrasts of light and shadow. The small Loggetta received the greatest amount of sculptural adornment in the form of a triumphal arch to act as a firm base for the soaring bell tower.

In addition to his major public buildings, Sansovino also regulated the markets, improved the city, and executed countless designs for churches, private dwellings, and mainland villas. While some of his designs were never executed or were completed by other architects, Sansovino's presence and the ideas expressed in his drawings and buildings exerted a strong and lasting influence on contemporary and later Venetian architects. His grand Corner Palace (begun 1537), for example, was decisive in its transformation of the lighter arcades and ornamental patterns of the persistent Venetian Gothic into the measured balance of the larger, simpler forms of Donato Bramante and current Roman architecture, adapted to Venetian requirements.

Sansovino died in Venice; one son was a distinguished writer. The quality of Sansovino's life is touchingly conveyed by Vasari, who wrote that he was "very dear both to the great and to the small and to his friends" and that "his death was a grief to all Venice."

Further Reading

Jacopo Sansovino is listed in the Art study guide (III, D, 2 and 3). He and his contemporary Michele SANMICHELI brought the classicism of Donato BRAMANTE to the Veneto.

The fullest and most important study of Sansovino re-

Jacopo Sansovino, a portrait by Tintoretto in the Uffizi, Florence. (Alinari)

The Library, designed by Sansovino, on the Piazza di S. Marco, Venice. (Alinari-Anderson)

mains that by Giorgio Vasari in *Lives of the Most Eminent Painters, Sculptors, and Architects*, edited by Gaston du C. de Vere, vol. 9 (1915; abr. ed. 1959). There is no modern biography in English, but John Pope-Hennessy, *Italian High Renaissance and Baroque Sculpture*, vol. 2 (1963), includes a discerning presentation of Sansovino's work as a sculptor. For a discussion of his architecture see Peter Murray, *The Architecture of the Italian Renaissance* (1963), and T. A. West, *A History of Architecture in Italy* (1968).

SANTA ANA / By Albert L. Michaels

The Mexican general and statesman Antonio López de Santa Ana (1794–1876) was often called the "man who was Mexico." An unprincipled adventurer, he dominated Mexico for some 25 years, during which he served as president six times, switching parties and ideologies at will.

The Mexican struggle for independence was as bloody and destructive as any in the Western Hemisphere. The struggle, a bitter civil war, destroyed trade, farming, communications, and commerce. The ultimate victors, conservative churchman and soldiers, had no intention of sharing their power or wealth with their millions of poor countrymen, of either Indian or mixed blood.

The three decades following independence (1821) saw a continuation of civil war as the small ranchers and farmers of the north and west tried to break the economic, political, and social stranglehold of the colonial elites. Virtually the only beneficiary of this struggle was the United States, which violently seized over 50 percent of Mexico's territory. Gen. Antonio López de Santa Ana (pronounced sän′tä ä′nä) did not cause this tragic situation or Mexico's varied problems. A vain, pompous man with great leadership qualities, he only used the contemporary chaos to personal advantage. His very character epitomized one of the most unfortunate periods in Mexican history.

Early Career

Antonio López de Santa Ana was born in Jalapa, Veracruz. His family was Spanish and Caucasian. His father, a well-to-do Veracruz mortgage broker, had estates in Jalapa. When Santa Ana was 16, the family sent him to the military academy, from which he graduated in time to serve in the royalist army against the forces of independence. He fought against Miguel Hidalgo, the priest and original leader of the independence movement, in Texas and distinguished himself in battle. Apparently a gambling scandal delayed his promotion, and by 1821, despite a distinguished record in the Spanish army, Santa Ana had reached only the rank of captain. In that year he defected to the conservative but proindependence army of Gen. Agustín de Iturbide. The grateful rebels made him first a colonel and later a brigadier general.

Santa Ana did not remain loyal for long; he was one of the first to pronounce against Iturbide's empire, seizing the port of Veracruz in the name of the 1823 revolt which ended Iturbide's short-lived imperial experiment. In 1823 Santa Ana endorsed a republic but later admitted that a Jalapa lawyer had only briefly explained to him all that he knew about republicanism. He remained a political illiterate all his life, one year a rabid Jacobin liberal, the next a monarchist.

In the late 1820s the "republican" general Santa Ana served various Mexican governments as an officer first in Yucatán and later in Veracruz. In 1827 he was one of the principal supporters of the presidential bid of independence hero Vicente Guerrero. The same year at Tampico he took the surrender of a small yellow fever–ridden Spanish force from Cuba which had attempted to invade Mexico. Now the "hero of Tampico," he became an important figure in the chaotic world of Mexican politics. The liberal Congress elected him president, and he took office in 1833 with the determined anticlerical Valentín Gómez Farías as his vice president.

Presidential Career

Santa Ana's first presidency never even got started. The newly elected president pleaded sick and remained on his hacienda, Magna de Clavo, in Veracruz, leaving Gómez Farías as provisional president. The latter attacked Church and military legal privileges and attempted to reduce the army's size. Santa Ana then posed as the champion of traditional interests and overthrew Gómez Farías. Calling himself "liberator of Mexico," he assumed a dictatorship, dismissed Congress, restored military and ecclesiastical prerogatives, and exiled the leading liberals.

The result was a period of confusion: revolts and counterrevolts, with Santa Ana resigning and again taking office. In 1836 he led a Mexican army into Texas, and

Antonio López de Santa Ana, a painting by Paul L'Ouvrier. (Courtesy of The New-York Historical Society, New York City)

after some initial successes his forces were annihilated by Sam Houston at San Jacinto on April 21, 1836. Santa Ana, a prisoner of the Texans, signed the Treaty of Velasco, granting the withdrawal of Mexican troops and the "independence" of Texas. During a short sojourn as a prisoner in Washington, he conferred with President Andrew Jackson and returned to Mexico in February 1837.

While imprisoned in the United States, Santa Ana had been deposed by the conservative Congress, which had abrogated his agreement with the Texans and recalled former president Anastasio Bustamante. Still somehow a national hero, Santa Ana retired to Magna de Clavo for 18 months. In November 1838 he emerged to lead a Mexican force against a French squadron bombarding San Juan de Ulúa in the "pastry war." Caught in a cannonade, he lost a leg to the invaders, a sacrifice which apparently greatly increased his political appeal. He was now the "hero of Veracruz."

In 1839, faced with a liberal revolt, President Bustamante named Santa Ana interim president, a post which he held from March to July. In a period of further confusion and fiscal bankruptcy, Santa Ana doggedly maneuvered through various alliances. By October 1841 he had returned to Mexico City, where he was once again president of Mexico by virtue of a conservative junta. This time his government lasted until 1842. He raised revenue by taxation but spent lavishly on festivals and a private army. In March 1843 he again resumed the executive and ruled until July 1844. He apparently began to see the possibilities of a monarchy as the solution to Mexico's problems.

Overthrown in 1844, Santa Ana again retreated to Veracruz. In 1845 the government captured him and exiled him to Cuba. He solicited aid from the United States, promising to amicably settle the Texas boundary dispute if he returned to power. Permitted to pass through the American blockade of the Mexican coast, he broke his promise and began to prepare Mexico for war. In December 1846 he became Mexico's president. In 1847 he once more led Mexican troops against American forces. The Mexicans, badly beaten owing in part to Santa Ana's incompetence and in part to internal quarrels, lost much valuable territory. In 1847, fleeing both his Yankee and Mexican enemies, the general took refuge on the British Island of Jamaica, but his incredible career had not yet closed. He spent 2 years in Venezuela, devoting his time to farming while Mexico sank further into chaos.

In 1853 the conservatives again seized power. Their leader, Lucas Alamán, sponsored Santa Ana as an interim president until a suitable monarch could be found. In April 1853 Santa Ana again returned as president of Mexico. But Alamán's constructive influence ended with his death in June, and Santa Ana continued to dissipate government funds. In April 1854 he signed the Gadsden Treaty, selling Arizona to the United States for $10 million. In August 1855 the liberals, led by Juan Álvarez, revolted against the increasingly corrupt regime. Santa Ana again fled. A decade later he attempted to stage yet another comeback during the European intervention, but he no longer had any following. He again went into exile but was allowed to return in 1873 to Mexico. No longer a danger, he lived out his last days in semipoverty, dying in Mexico City in June 1876.

Further Reading

Antonio López de Santa Ana is listed in the Latin America study guide (IV, K, 1, a). Other hopefuls for Mexico's leadership were Agustín de ITURBIDE and MAXIMILIAN.

Santa Ana's own account is *The Eagle: The Autobiography of Santa Ana*, edited by Ann Fears Crawford (trans. 1967). There is no definitive work on Santa Ana. The basic biography, although dated, is Wilfrid Hardy Callcott, *Santa Ana* (1936; repr. 1964); also useful is Callcott's general study *Church and State in Mexico, 1822–1857* (1926). Oakah L. Jones, *Santa Anna* (1968), scholarly and well written, is not distinctly different from Callcott's account. Useful for a flavor of the times are the memoirs of Frances Erskine Calderón de la Barca, *Life in Mexico* (1843; new ed. 1966). The war with the United States and Santa Ana's role are best related in George Lockhart Rives, *The United States and Mexico, 1821–1848* (2 vols., 1913; repr. 1969), and Justin H. Smith, *The War with Mexico* (2 vols., 1919). For life in Mexico during the war see José Fernando Ramírez, *Mexico during the War with the United States*, edited by Walter V. Scholes (trans. 1950).

Andrés de Santa Cruz, a lithograph by A. Sirouy, in the Bibliothèque Nationale, Paris. (Bulloz)

SANTA CRUZ / By C. Norman Guice

The Bolivian military leader Andrés de Santa Cruz (1792–1865) was a supporter of a united Peru-Bolivia and was president of a short-lived confederation of the two.

A ndrés de Santa Cruz (pronounced sän′tə krōōz) was born on Dec. 5, 1792, in La Paz, the mestizo son of a Peruvian Creole and a Bolivian Indian heiress. After receiving a Church-directed education in La Paz and Cuzco, he elected to follow his father's army career. He was commissioned in a militia unit in 1809 and began active duty a year later, with the onset of the Wars of Independence. His royalist service lasted until early 1821 and included military action in Bolivia (then Upper Peru) and Peru, as well as an interval as a prisoner of war in Argentina. In January 1821, when once again a captive, he volunteered for the patriot army and served the cause of liberation through the remaining 3 years of fighting.

Santa Cruz commanded units under both José de San Martín and Simón Bolívar, became chief of staff for the Peruvian units under the latter, and then was given a series of administrative assignments, first military and then, with the end of fighting, civilian ones.

In July 1825 Santa Cruz became prefect of Chuquisaca (now Sucre), the capital of the newly created Bolivia. He had opposed this Bolívar-designed transformation of Upper Peru, favoring a continued union with Peru. He nevertheless accepted a series of assignments, both in Bolivia and in Peru, given him by Bolívar. Santa Cruz was, in fact, serving in Lima as president of the Peruvian Council of State when, in September 1826, Bolívar left Peru to return to Colombia. In June 1827 Santa Cruz surrendered that office to an elected successor but, after a brief period in Chile, became the chief executive of Bolivia in early 1829. Until 1835 he gave his full attention to governing that country. Under his stern authority, order was restored and some economic gains were achieved.

Meanwhile, Peru was nearly torn apart by the rivalries of political and military factions. In 1835 Santa Cruz was invited to intervene and, with the help of Peruvian allies, established the Confederation of Peru and Bolivia. The new nation was to have three states, each with a large measure of autonomy but with overall control exercised by Santa Cruz, now named to the office of supreme protector.

The union was maintained, although shakily, until early 1839, when it was brought to an end by the united efforts of Argentina, Chile, and its Peruvian opponents. Santa Cruz, forced out of both Peru and Bolivia, spent the next 6 years, mostly in Ecuador, plotting a return to power. In 1845, when it was clear that Chile and the other nations would not allow this, he left for Europe, where he remained for the rest of his life.

Further Reading

Andrés de Santa Cruz is listed in the Latin America study guide (IV, B, 1). José BALLIVIÁN succeeded him as ruler of Bolivia.

There is no biography of Santa Cruz in English, although his career is partially discussed in several general histories of Peru and Bolivia, most notably Frederick B. Pike, *The Modern History of Peru* (1967), and Robert Barton, *A Short History of the Republic of Bolivia* (1968). For an understanding of Chile's opposition to the confederation see Robert N. Burr, *By Reason or Force: Chile and the Balancing of Power in South America, 1830–1905* (1965). See also Charles W. Arnade, *The Emergence of the Republic of Bolivia* (1957).

Bartholomew Santamaria in 1961. (Australian News & Information Bureau)

SANTAMARIA / By Trevor R. Reese

Bartholomew Augustine Santamaria (born 1915), a Roman Catholic publicist and organizer in Australia, founded the Catholic Social Movement.

Bartholomew Santamaria was born in Brunswick, Victoria, on Aug. 14, 1915, the son of Italian immigrants. He was educated at the University of Melbourne and soon became prominent as a Roman Catholic ideologist and organizer in Victoria. In 1937 he became assistant director and, in 1947, director of the National Secretariat of Catholic Action, which had been founded to enlist the support of the laity in the pastoral work of the Roman Catholic Church and existed in all parts of the world under the patronage of the Pope. In 1943 Santamaria created, and became president of, the Catholic Social Movement, which was organized and largely recruited by the members of Catholic Action.

By the 1940s Santamaria's principal concern was the advance of communism in the Australian Labour party, and to counter it he sought to organize the Catholics in the trade union movement. He and his followers in the Labour party in Victoria regarded communism rather than capitalism as the enemy, and they attempted to secure the elimination of communists from the leadership of the trade unions.

The Catholic Social Movement supported efforts of the non-Labour federal government of Robert Gordon Menzies to proscribe communism and, fearing socialism as a potential menace to the property of the Catholic Church, was vigorously antagonistic to some of the more radical and dogmatic ideas of the Labour party. Santamaria's influence within the ranks of the Victoria Labour party steadily increased, causing much sectarian bitterness, and in October 1954 the federal leader of the Australian Labour party, Herbert Vere Evatt, publicly de-

nounced what he called "a small minority of Labour members located particularly in the state of Victoria" who, he said, had become "increasingly disloyal to the Labour movement and the Labour leadership."

This public accusation split the Labour party in Victoria; the supporters of Santamaria resigned from the party and formed themselves into what was termed the Anti-Communist Labour party and, later, the Democratic Labour party. In the elections in Victoria in May 1955, these dissident elements campaigned and voted independently of the Australian Labour party and contributed to the defeat of the state's Labour government. Similarly, in Queensland the split in the party resulted in the defeat of a state Labour government.

In the federal sphere, the Democratic Labour party, though never in a position to secure a substantial number of seats in Parliament, helped to destroy the Australian Labour party's chances of regaining office for the next decade and more. Santamaria himself, however, tended to drop out of public prominence, but he remained an important contributor to public debate on political problems facing Australia.

Further Reading

Bartholomew Santamaria is listed in the Australia and New Zealand study guide (II, F). One of his staunch supporters was Daniel MANNIX.

Santamaria's own account of the Catholic Social Movement is in his *The Price of Freedom* (1968) and in his contribution to Henry Mayer, *Catholics and the Free Society* (1961). *Point of View* (1969) is a collection of his commentaries on Australian foreign policy and domestic affairs. Tom Truman, *Catholic Action and Politics* (1960), is a detailed discussion of the entire subject.

SANTANA / By Bleecker Dee

The Dominican Republic military leader and president Pedro Santana (1801–1864) inflicted several decisive defeats on Haitian forces, at one time or another quarreled with all sectors of his country's society, and finally led the Dominican Republic into annexation by Spain.

Born in Hincha, Pedro Santana (pronounced sän-tä′nä) appears, from his portraits, to have been of mixed Caucasian, Negro, and Indian ancestry. Unlike his contemporary Buenaventura Baez, he was uneducated, rough, and uncouth; but like Baez, he did not lack for personal courage.

Fresh from military triumphs over the Haitians, on July 12, 1844, only 5 months after the Dominican declaration of independence, Santana and his troops deposed his country's provisional government. He called a convention which drafted the Dominican Republic's first constitution. It was promulgated on Nov. 6, 1844, and according to one of its provisions, that the convention select the president for the first two terms, Santana became his country's first constitutional president.

Baez acceded to the presidency after Santana's handpicked successor refused to serve. Beset by financial problems and the ever present possibility of revolt, Baez resigned on Aug. 4, 1848, but was recalled to inflict still another defeat on the Haitians, who were trying to reconquer the Dominican Republic. Santana then again deposed a president and was given the title of "Liberator."

From the ensuing electoral confusion, on Dec. 24, 1849, Baez was chosen president. At the end of his term, on Feb. 15, 1853, he passed the power back to Santana. This was one of the rare occasions when a Dominican president served out his term and constitutionally and personally delivered up the office to his successor. However, Santana and Baez soon fell out, and the next decade of Dominican history revolved around their quarrels.

By July 1853 Santana had exiled Baez, accusing him of treason. Baez countered with accusations of despotism, which appeared to be accurate as Santana constantly fought with his Congress, banishing or shooting his opponents. In 1854 Santana called another constitutional convention, extended his own term to 6 years, and established the office of vice president.

Under Santana's second presidency, on Dec. 22, 1855, the final Haitian invasion was defeated. Nevertheless, by March 26, 1856, he had again resigned. This paved the way for the return of Baez, who promptly exiled Santana. But by mid-1857 he was back, and after prolonged strife he was instrumental in toppling the Baez government on June 12, 1858. Using the 1854 Constitution, Santana had himself declared president on Jan. 31, 1859, repudiated many outstanding European debts, and appealed to Spain to annex the Dominican Republic. This was arranged, and on March 18, 1861, while the United States

Pedro Santana, a lithograph in the Civica Raccolta Stampe Bertarelli, Milan. (Editorial Photocolor Archives, Inc.)

was distracted by its Civil War, the Dominican Republic again became a Spanish colony. Santana was named governor and captain general, with the rank of lieutenant general in the Spanish army.

True to form, Santana soon quarreled with his Spanish subordinates, who opposed his increasingly harsh methods of rule. He resigned on Jan. 7, 1862, and was granted a title and a lifetime pension.

By August 1863 the Dominicans revolted against the Spaniards. To help crush the revolt, Santana was given command of a Spanish force but because of insubordination was removed from this command. On the verge of being shipped off in disgrace to Cuba, Santana died in the capital, Santo Domingo, on June 14, 1864. The revolt, known as the War of the Restoration, culminated in the final retreat of all Spanish forces on July 11, 1865, and the Dominican Republic was once again independent.

Further Reading

Pedro Santana is listed in the Latin America study guide (IV, H, 1). Buenaventura BAEZ dominated Dominican affairs when Santana was out of power.

Probably the classic work on the Dominican Republic is Sumner Welles, *Naboth's Vineyard* (2 vols., 1928; new foreword, 1966), which explains and interprets the history, culture, and society of that nation. Another valuable work is Otto Schoenrich, *Santo Domingo* (1918). Current useful studies include Robert D. Crassweller,

Trujillo (1966), and John Bartlow Martin, *Overtaken by Events* (1966).

* * *

SANTANDER / By David Bushnell

Francisco de Paula Santander (1792–1840), a Colombian general and statesman, was one of the leaders of Spanish American independence. He later served as first constitutional president of the Republic of New Granada.

Francisco de Paula Santander (pronounced sän-tän-děr′) was born on April 12, 1792, at Rosario de Cúcuta near the Venezuelan border. His family were cacao planters, members of the local gentry. When the independence movement began in 1810, he was a law student at Bogotá, but he soon left his books to join the patriot forces. Although the first independent government was crushed in 1816, Santander escaped to the eastern plains, or *llanos*, and there helped organize a base of continuing patriot resistance.

Accepting the leadership of the Venezuelan Simón Bolívar, Santander took part in the expedition that climbed the Colombian Andes, won the decisive victory of Boyacá (Aug. 7, 1819), and finally expelled the Spaniards from Bogotá. Bolívar placed him in charge of administering the liberated provinces, and 2 years later he was chosen vice president of the new nation of Gran Colombia, which included present-day Venezuela, Colombia, Panama, and Ecuador. Since Bolívar, as president, preferred to continue fighting at the head of his armies, Vice President Santander became acting chief executive.

Administrator of Gran Colombia

Though he held the rank of general, Santander is chiefly remembered as a vigorous civil administrator. He lacked Bolívar's magnetism but was a man of impressive personal bearing and dignity. Highly conscious of his own prerogatives, he nevertheless generally respected legal formalities: Bolívar dubbed him the "Man of Laws." As ruler, furthermore, he promoted a series of liberal reforms designed to curb clerical influence, aid economic development along lines of free enterprise, and extend public education.

Conflict with Bolívar

The stability of Gran Colombia was shaken in 1826 by the outbreak of a revolt in Venezuela under José Antonio Páez. Even more serious was a growing conflict between Santander and Bolívar, who later that year returned from Peru. Santander suspected Bolívar of seeking to change the constitution by illegal means and also resented his leniency toward Páez in finally settling the Venezuelan revolt. When Bolívar reassumed full control of the government in 1827, Santander drifted into open opposition, and in 1828 he was exiled on the charge, never really proved, of complicity in a plot against Bolívar's life.

After the dissolution of Gran Colombia in 1830, Santander's supporters gained control of the new Republic of New Granada, corresponding to modern Colombia plus Panama. Santander returned to serve as president from 1832 to 1837. He now showed greater caution in pressing liberal reforms, but he energetically repressed would-be conspirators, and he succeeded in organizing the national administration on a sound basis.

Santander retired briefly from public life on leaving the presidency, but he soon emerged to win a seat in the lower house of Congress. There he joined the opposi-

The dissolution of Gran Colombia. Created by Simón Bolívar and effectively administered by Santander, Gran Colombia soon fell victim to separatist movements and the growing rivalry between Bolívar and his former lieutenants.

Francisco de Paula Santander. (Bibliothèque Nationale, Paris)

tion to his successor, the moderate liberal J. I. Márquez, whose election he had opposed. He was still serving in Congress at the time of his death in Bogotá on May 5, 1840.

Further Reading

Francisco de Paula Santander is listed in the Latin America study guide (III, B, 2). He was one of a number of northern South American independence fighters that included José Antonio PÁEZ and Simón BOLÍVAR.

Santander's political and administrative career, roughly from 1819 to 1827, is related in detail in David Bushnell, *The Santander Regime in Gran Colombia* (1954). He is also discussed in Jesús María Henao and Gerardo Arrubla, *History of Colombia* (1938).

SANTAYANA / By Gerald J. Goodwin

George Santayana (1863–1952), Spanish and American philosopher, developed a personal form of critical realism that was skeptical, materialistic, and humanistic.

George Santayana (sän-tə-yä′nä) was unique among American and European philosophers during his long lifetime. While others strove to make philosophy "scientific" and to apply philosophy and science to society, Santayana proclaimed, "My philosophy neither is nor wishes to be scientific." He rejected the inherited genteel tradition in American thought as well as his contemporaries' pragmatism,

idealism, and positivism. He openly disliked the liberal and democratic drift of Western civilization. In his philosophy he strove to combine philosophical materialism and a deep concern for spiritual values. A prolific writer with a graceful style, he also published several volumes of poetry, and his most popular book was a novel, *The Last Puritan* (1936). He is singular among American philosophers for the special flavor of his thought and for his treatment of religion and art.

Life, Career, and Personality

As a girl Santayana's mother was taken to the Philippines, where she met and married George Sturgis, a Bostonian. Santayana later observed that this "set the background for my whole life." After being widowed, she tried to settle in Boston with her children but soon returned to Spain and remarried. The only child of this marriage was born in Madrid on Dec. 16, 1863, and christened Jorge Agustin de Santayana. He lived until the age of 9 in Ávila with his father, a lawyer and student of painting, then joined his mother, who was raising the children of her first marriage in Boston. Although he visited his father in Ávila and traveled in Europe frequently, Santayana lived and wrote in America for the next 40 years. As a boy he was quiet, studious, and lonely.

In spite of his connection to the Boston Sturgises and his American education, Santayana never felt fully at home in the United States. Indeed, he never felt fully at home anywhere. Dark-eyed, gentle, unobtrusive, witty, and very detached, he described himself as "a stranger at heart." His philosophy is clearly marked by a sense of detachment. "I have been involuntarily uprooted," he explained without regret. "I accept the intellectual advantages of that position, with its social and moral disqualifications."

Santayana's years at Harvard College, which he attended after Boston Latin School, were generally happy and satisfying. After graduating from Harvard in 1886, he studied philosophy in Germany. He returned to America in 1888 and completed the work for his doctorate in philosophy under the direction of Josiah Royce at Harvard. In 1889 Santayana joined Harvard's department of philosophy, with the apparent intention of retiring as soon as it was financially possible. When he inherited a modest legacy, he resigned his professorship in 1912.

Santayana lived the remainder of his life in Europe, traveling extensively and eventually settling in Italy. He spent his final years in Calvary Hospital, Rome, under the care of the Sisters of the Little Company of Mary. He died on Sept. 26, 1952.

His Philosophy

Santayana's true life was intellectual. "My career was not my life," he wrote. "Mine has been a life of reflection." His philosophy reflected the diversity of his own experience. Spanish Catholic by cultural inheritance and personal inclination, Protestant American by education and environment, disengaged by circumstances and temperament, he regarded his philosophy as a synthesis of these traditions. It is not surprising that his philosophy is full of ironies and ambiguities. At the same time, he was consistent in his concerns, if not in his opinions, and in the mood and tone of his philosophy. His primary orientation was spiritual, although not in the conventional sense, and his primary interest was moral, in the broadest sense.

The philosophy of Santayana is characterized by its skepticism, materialism, and humanism. His skepticism is evident throughout his writings: "My matured conclusion has been that no system is to be trusted, not even that of science in any literal or pictorial sense; but all systems may be used and, up to a certain point, trusted as symbols." His materialism or naturalism was "the foundation for all further serious opinions." Unlike that of so many contemporaries, Santayana's materialism depended not on science but on his own experiences and observations, for which he found philosophical confirmation in the works of Democritus, Lucretius, and Spinoza. In addition, in Greek ethics he found a vindication of order and beauty in human institutions and ideas. His systematic reading and thought culminated in the writing of his masterwork, *The Life of Reason* (5 vols., 1905–1906), which he intended as a critical history of the human imagination. He developed his philosophy further in *Scepticism and Animal Faith* (1923), which served as an introduction to his philosophical consummation, *Realms of Being* (4 vols., 1927–1940).

Santayana's materialism, the foundation of his philosophy, was the conviction that matter is the source of everything; he held that there are purely natural or materialistic causes of all the phenomena of existence. Consequently, thought is the product of material organization and process. Throughout *The Life of Reason* he assumed that the whole life of reason was generated and controlled by the animal life of man in the bosom of nature. One critic has described him as a nondeterministic fatalist who believed that dark, irrational, impersonal powers determined events. The human mind could not affect nature. Santayana wrote, "We are creatures and not creators." This important feature of his thought is clear in his conception of essences, which he defined as the obvious features that distinguish facts from each other. Apart from the events they may figure in, essences have no existence. Ironically, the mind cannot know existence; it can know only essences. This means that there is no necessary relation between what is perceived (or thought) and what exists. Consequently, "The whole life of imagination and knowledge comes from within." It is no wonder that Santayana was thoroughly skeptical about the possibility of attaining genuine knowledge.

It is also no wonder that Santayana believed that the works of the imagination "alone are good; and [that] the rest—the whole real world—is ashes in its mouth." Religion, science, art, philosophy were all works of the imagination. But religion he regarded as "the head and front of everything." In spite of his sympathies, Santayana was not a practicing Catholic and did not believe in the existence of God. He considered religion a work of the imagination: "Religion is valid poetry infused into common life." The truth of religion was irrelevant, for all religions were imaginative, poetic interpretations of experience and ideals, not descriptions of existing things. The value of religion was moral, as was the value of art.

Beauty, to Santayana, was a moral good. He valued the arts precisely because they are illusory. Like religion, he explained, genuine art expresses ideals that are relevant to human conditions. "Of all reason's embodiments," Santayana exulted, "art is . . . the most splendid and complete." "This is all my message," he wrote by way of summary, "that morality and religion are expressions of human nature; that human nature is a biological growth; and finally that spirit, fascinated and tortured, is involved in the process, and asks to be saved."

His Influence

Santayana had few disciples, but his philosophy has attracted considerable critical attention since his death. The grace and beauty of his prose and the strength of his intellect partly account for this interest. In addition, in the intellectual climate of the years following World War II his philosophy of disillusion struck a sympathetic chord. Santayana, like others of his generation, found himself confronted with a choice between Catholicism and complete disillusion. He did not hesitate or complain: "I was never afraid of disillusion, and I have chosen it."

Further Reading

George Santayana is listed in the Philosophy study guide (VII, B). The philosophers Josiah ROYCE and Wil-

George Santayana. (National Archives, Washington, D.C.)

liam JAMES also taught at Harvard when Santayana did.

Santayana's autobiography, *Persons and Places* (3 vols., 1944–1953), reveals his personality, character, and some of his key ideas. It is supplemented by his *Letters*, edited by Daniel Cory (1955). An excellent anthology is Irwin Edman, ed., *The Philosophy of Santayana: Selections from All the Works of George Santayana* (1936; rev. ed. 1953).

Valuable critical and descriptive essays on his philosophy and Santayana's replies are in Paul Arthur Schilpp, ed., *The Philosophy of George Santayana* (1940; 2d ed. 1951). Although there is no full intellectual biography of Santayana, Mossie M. Kirkwood, *Santayana: Saint of the Imagination* (1961), is a pleasant introduction. Willard E. Arnett, *George Santayana* (1968), compares Santayana's philosophy with that of his contemporaries.

SANTOS-DUMONT

/ By Richard Graham

Alberto Santos-Dumont (1873–1932) was a Brazilian inventor of dirigibles and airplanes. He was the first man to successfully combine the internal combustion engine with ballooning, and Europeans long believed him to be also the first to fly a heavier-than-air motorized plane.

Alberto Santos-Dumont in the basket of a balloon. (National Air Museum, Smithsonian Institution)

Alberto Santos-Dumont (pronounced săN′tōōzh dōō-môN′), the grandson of a French emigrant to Brazil, was born in the state of Minas Gerais. His father was an engineer, entrepreneur, and coffee planter, married to the daughter of a distinguished Brazilian family. In 1891 Alberto was sent to Paris to study mechanics and other sciences, more or less on his own. His father's death the next year left Alberto a fairly wealthy young man. After 4 years of desultory studies, the alternately dreamy and practical Brazilian began to devote all his money and energy to his inventions.

The idea of flight had long exerted a strange fascination for the boy; and as a wealthy and daring young man, he was also one of the first Parisians to invest in a gasoline-driven automobile. He made his first balloon flight in the spring of 1898, blown by the wind and depending for ascent and descent on the careful balancing of ballast and gas-produced lift. Like many others at the time, he was struck by the possibility of attaching a gasoline motor with propeller to a balloon and thus being able to drive against the wind as well as to change altitude by pointing the craft upward or downward. He was the first to succeed in doing so (fall 1898), 2 years before the successful flight of the rigid dirigibles later known as Zeppelins. In 1901, after several setbacks, he won the Deutsch de la Meurthe Prize of 100,000 francs and much acclaim for the first airship to complete a specified circuit around the Eiffel Tower and back within a half hour.

A few years later Santos-Dumont turned his attention to manned flight in craft that were heavier than air. In September 1906 he flew the "14-bis," an awkward machine resembling a box kite, for a few feet, and within the next 2 months he won prizes for the first aircraft to fly 25 meters and the first to do 100. Three years earlier the Wright brothers had flown in the United States, but their feat had been at first ignored and then systematically denied by most of the American press, so that Europeans hailed Santos-Dumont as the first man to fly. As often happens with inventors, others were fast on his heels, and his own achievement hastened their work. A few months later he himself flew all over Paris in a new and graceful instrument of his design that resembled a modern airplane.

In 1910 Santos-Dumont retired from aviation, apparently because of the onset of multiple sclerosis. He then entered a period of slow physical and mental decline ending in his suicide in Brazil at the age of 59.

Further Reading

Alberto Santos-Dumont is listed in the Latin America study guide (IV, C, 2, b). The Americans Wilbur and Orville WRIGHT made the first successful flight in a motor-driven craft.

Santos-Dumont's autobiography is *My Airships: The Story of My Life* (1904). Peter Wykeham, *Santos-Dumont: A Study in Obsession* (1963), is a balanced, fair account that avoids both adulation and deprecation, but it is inadequately documented. An older account is Henrique Dumont Villares, *Santos-Dumont: The Father of Aviation* (trans. 1956).

SAPIR / By J. David Sapir

Edward Sapir (1884–1939) was a distinguished American linguist and anthropologist who developed a basic statement on the genetic relationship of American Indian languages and pioneered in modern theoretical linguistics.

Edward Sapir was born in Lauenburg, Germany, on Jan. 26, 1884, and emigrated in his early childhood to the United States, first living in Richmond, Va., and then moving to New York City, where he spent the greater part of his youth. As a student at Columbia University, he first studied Germanics, but under the influence of Franz Boas, the founder of modern American anthropology, Sapir switched to anthropology and linguistics. His main contributions concerned American Indian, Indo-European, and general linguistics; American Indian and general anthropology; and what has come to be called culture and personality, or psychological anthropology. Beyond these scientific pursuits Sapir also made numerous contributions to American letters by publishing reviews and poems in such journals as *Poetry*, the *Dial*, *Freeman*, and the *Nation*.

Study of Indian Languages

Upon receiving a doctorate at Columbia, Sapir obtained his first important position, as head of the division of anthropology at the Canadian National Museum in Ottawa, in 1910. During the 15 years spent in Canada, Sapir studied the American Indian languages of western Canada. This work, coupled with previous studies in the United States of Takelma, Chinook, Yana, and Paiute, permitted Sapir, in collaboration with his colleagues, to simplify and considerably clarify the earlier genetic classification of American languages.

Two important works were published during the Canadian years. The first, *Time Perspective in Aboriginal American Culture: A Study in Method* (1916), was a succinct account of the techniques available to ethnographers for the reconstruction, in the absence of written sources, of culture history. This short monograph represented a position paper, one of a number produced in those years by Franz Boas and his students, in counterstatement to the rather facile historiography promulgated by the various schools of evolutionary determinism that had been current from the 19th century until well into the first decades of the 20th.

The second work, Sapir's only full-length book, was an introduction to scientific linguistics—*Language* (1921)—in which with great brilliance he delineated the full range of what the study of language, both structure and history, entails. *Language* included a discussion of phonetics as it was practiced at that time and a particularly subtle grammatical typology that took into account the great diversity of natural languages. In this book he also introduced the concept of linguistic drift, a theory arguing that grammatical change in language is never random but, rather, the result of certain systematic trends followed through in the course of a language or language family's history. He took as his main example the drift apparent in many Indo-European languages away from complex case systems in favor of syntactic position; that is, the grammatical function of a word tends to be indicated less by inflection than by its position in the overall sentence.

Linguistic and Cultural Theory

In 1925 Sapir accepted a teaching position in the newly created department of anthropology at the University of Chicago. During this period Sapir began publishing his most important papers in linguistic and cultural theory. The ideas and viewpoints set out in these papers had a deep and lasting influence on the subsequent development of linguistics and anthropology.

In "Sound Patterns in Language" (1925) Sapir demonstrated that the sounds of language are not merely physical but also mental or psychological phenomena, in that for all languages any sound is part of a system of discrete contrasts that are altered and combined in ways determined by shared linguistic conventions rather than physical necessity. That the systematic and conventional nature of sounds is available to the intuitions of a native speaker was set out in a paper published a number of years later ("The Psychological Reality of the Phoneme," 1933).

These two papers, especially the first, laid the groundwork for much that was to follow in the field of phonemics (the study of conventionally relevant sounds) and in large measure converged with, and to a certain extent anticipated, similar discoveries made by European lin-

Edward Sapir. (Yale University Library)

guists who had been working under the inspiration and influence of the Swiss linguist Ferdinand de Saussure.

Recognizing the unconscious reality of both the phonological and grammatical aspects of language led Sapir to argue that culture should be considered as patterns of individually learned conventions (both conscious and unconscious) rather than external facts ("The Unconscious Patterning of Behavior in Society," 1927). That is, in more current phrasing, culture is best defined as learned rules for behaving rather than the results of conventional behavior.

Two other important ideas already implicit in earlier work were succinctly formulated by Sapir during his Chicago years in his short paper "The Status of Linguistics as a Science" (1929). First, language, because of its central place in culture, acts as a "guide to 'social reality'" and to a large extent shapes, if not completely determines, an individual's and a culture's understanding and perception of the "external world," or reality. Second, language, which yields to systematic analysis, can in its study provide tools for the systematic investigation of other, more elusive aspects of culture.

Last Years

In 1931 Sapir was offered and accepted a position at Yale University as Sterling professor of anthropology and linguistics. At Yale he continued refining aspects of his theoretical positions, writing a series of papers on language and various aspects of culture for the *Encyclopaedia of Social Sciences*. He also, more than previously, devoted time and interest to the relationship between culture and the individual personality, always arguing that both must be taken into account if meaningful statements about one or the other are to be made. The exploratory papers written as a result of these interests had great influence in defining the general subject of culture and personality.

During these last years of his life, Sapir continued to find time for detailed work on particular languages, though at this time his interest shifted (though never completely) away from American Indian languages to problems of Indo-European and Semitic linguistics. He died on Feb. 4, 1939.

Further Reading

Edward Sapir is listed in the Social Sciences study guide (VII, E, 3). He was a student of Franz BOAS.

A chapter-length portrait of Sapir is in Thomas A. Sebeok, ed., *Portraits of Linguists*, vol. 2 (1966). For general background see Hoffman R. Hays, *From Ape to Angel: An Informal History of Social Anthropology* (1958).

SAPPHO / By Walter Donlan

Sappho (ca. 625–570 B.C.), a Greek lyric poet, was the greatest female poet of antiquity. Her vivid, emotional manner of writing influenced poets through the ages, and her special quality of intimacy has great appeal to modern poetic tastes.

The poetry of Sappho (pronounced săf′ō) epitomizes a style of writing evolved during the 7th and 6th centuries B.C. At that time the main thrust of Greek poetry turned away from the epic form, which was concerned mainly with telling the stories of heroes and gods, utilizing the traditional and highly formulaic dactylic hexameter. The poets of the 7th and 6th centuries wrote choral songs, which were sung and danced by a choir, and solo songs, in which the poet was accompanied by a lyre or flutelike instrument. Doubtless these types of composition had existed side by side with the epic tradition, but after 700 B.C. poets refined the techniques of the choral and solo song, employing a variety of meters and a wide range of subject matter. Among the most prominent features of this kind of poetry were the infusion of the poet's personality and a concentration on his own inner feelings and motivations. No poet of this

Sappho (right) and Alkaios, as depicted on an Attic hydra dating from about 500 B.C. Alkaios, a contemporary of Sappho whose poems are also known only from fragments, was from Lesbos and, according to tradition, was her associate. He is singing and accompanying himself on a barbiton (a Greek form of lyre), which instrument Sappho also holds. (Staatliche Antikensammlungen, Munich)

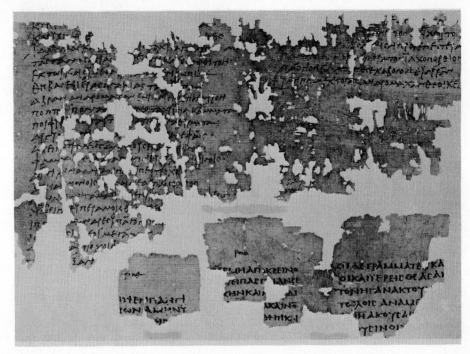

These fragments of a papyrus dating from the 3d century A.D. bear the only extant text of Sappho's poem The Wedding of Andromache. *(From Grenfell and Hunt,* The Oxyrinchus Papyri)

period displays the personal element more than Sappho.

Her Life

Despite the highly personal tone of her poetry, Sappho gives very few details of her life. She was born either in the town of Eresus or in Mytilene on the island of Lesbos in the northern Aegean Sea and lived her life in Mytilene. She is said to have married a wealthy man named Cercylas, and she herself mentions a daughter, Cleis. Apparently Sappho came from one of the leading noble families in Mytilene, and, although she herself never mentions politics, tradition has it that her family was briefly exiled to Sicily shortly after 600.

Sappho had three brothers: Larichus, who served as a wine bearer in the town hall of Mytilene (an honor reserved for youths of good family); Charaxus, a merchant, whom Sappho scolds in her poetry for loving a prostitute in Egypt; and Eurygyus. There is some evidence that she lived to a fairly old age. Tradition relates that she was not beautiful but "small and dark." A more charming description is a one-line fragment from another Aeolian poet, Alcaeus: "Violet-haired, pure, honey-smiling Sappho." The legend that she killed herself by leaping from the Leucadian Rock out of love for a young man named Phaon is one of many fictitious stories about her.

Her Works

We can only estimate how much Sappho actually wrote, but her output must have been large because her works were collected in nine books (arranged according to meter) in the 3d century B.C. Although she enjoyed great popularity in antiquity, changes in literary fashion, the general decline of knowledge in the early Middle Ages, and Christian distaste for a poet who was considered vile resulted in the loss of most of her poetry. Book

1 alone contained 1,320 lines; yet a total of fewer than 1,000 lines survive, many of them preserved by ancient grammarians citing peculiarities of the Aeolian dialect. Since the late 19th century many new fragments have been recovered from papyrus finds in Egypt.

Except for a few wedding songs and some narrative poems, most of what remains of Sappho's poetry may be termed "occasional pieces," addressed to some person or to herself, very personal in content and manner. The subject is nearly always love and the attendant emotions —affection, passion, hatred, and jealousy—which Sappho felt toward the young girls who made up her "circle" or her rivals in love. Much scholarly controversy rages over the relationship between Sappho and the women about whom she wrote. On the one hand, it has been maintained that she was a corrupter of girls and instructed them in homosexual practices; on the other hand, it is said that she headed a kind of polite "finishing school" which prepared young ladies for marriage or that she was the leader of a *thiasos* (religious association), sacred to Aphrodite, in which girls were taught singing and other fine arts, with no hint of sexual irregularity. The precise nature of this circle of young women remains unclear. From the poems themselves it is clear that Sappho associated with girls, some of whom came from long distances, to whom and about whom she wrote poems detailing her frankly erotic feelings toward them.

Sappho's poetry is characterized by its depth of feeling and delicacy and grace of style. She wrote in her native Aeolian dialect, using ordinary vocabulary; her thoughts are expressed simply and unrhetorically but with exquisite care. Her grace and charm together with her technical skill in handling language and meter are most fully realized in the several longer fragments which have survived. One poem, "He appears to me like a god," a masterpiece of erotic lyric poetry, was closely imitated by the Roman poet Catullus over 500 years later and suggests the esteem in which the ancients held Sappho. Plato called her "the tenth Muse."

Further Reading

Sappho is listed in the Literature study guide (III, A, 1, a). She influenced many later poets, among them CATULLUS, OVID, and Algernon Charles SWINBURNE.

An excellent modern translation of Sappho with Greek text and notes is Willis Barnstone, *Sappho* (1965). The best general account in English of Sappho's life and poetry is Sir Cecil M. Bowra, *Greek Lyric Poetry from Alcam to Simonides* (1936; rev. ed. 1961). A more detailed analysis of Sappho's works is Denys L. Page, *Sappho and Alcaeus: An Introduction to the Study of Ancient Lesbian Poetry* (1955; rev. ed. 1959).

*   *   *

SAPRU / By Joyce Lebra

Sir Tej Bahadur Sapru (1875–1949) was an Indian lawyer and statesman. His career aptly illustrates the significance of the legal profession in the political and constitutional development of India.

Tej Bahadur Sapru (pronounced să′prōo) was born in Aligarh into an aristocratic Kashmiri Brahmin family living in Delhi. He attended high school in Aligarh and matriculated at Agra College, where he took his law degree. After an apprenticeship at Moradabad he joined the Allahabad High Court in 1898. He was knighted in 1923 for outstanding legal contributions. He set impeccable standards in his personal and professional life and possessed a scholarly knowledge of Persian and Urdu as well as English.

Sapru was appointed a member of the governor general's executive council and served on the Round Table Conferences in London and on the Joint Parliamentary Committee. As a liberal favoring moderate change within the constitutional and legal framework, Sapru worked untiringly in the role of mediator between the British authority and Indian nationalists and between Hindu and Moslem leaders. He sought, for example, to mediate between the Congress and the British in the Round Table Conferences but was unable to exact concessions from either side. In other instances he was successful, as with the Gandhi-Irwin Pact in 1931. He objected equally to Congress tactics of civil disobedience as prejudicial to compromise and to government imprisonment of Congress leaders.

Most notably he was chairman of the Sapru Committee, appointed in November 1944 by the Standing Committee of the Non-party Conference. The committee was charged with examining the whole communal question in a judicial framework following the breakdown of the Gandhi-Jinnah talks on communal problems. Sir Tej selected 29 committee members representative of all communal groups. The committee submitted proposals to the viceroy, Lord Wavell, in an attempt to break the political deadlock ensuing on the collapse of the Gandhi-Jinnah talks.

The committee's report contained a detailed historical analysis of proposals and claims of each community and a rationale for its constitutional recommendations. On the critical question of partition, the Sapru Committee made a final but fruitless plea to avert the creation of Pakistan. Sapru was also a member of the defense committee in the 1945 trials of Indian National Army officers for treason. The defenses argued that as the INA was an independent army representing an independent government-in-exile, its officers could not be prosecuted for treason.

Throughout the constitutional debates Sapru played a key moderating role, appealing at each stage to Hindu and Moslem and to Englishman and Hindu to conciliate their differences. He sought in the process to safeguard the rights of each communal group. He died on Jan. 20, 1949.

Further Reading

Sir Tej Bahadur Sapru is listed in the Asia study guide (II, A, 7). Mohammad Ali JINNAH was the foremost proponant of the creation of a separate Moslem state on the Indian subcontinent.

An excellent source of information on Sapru's career is an article about him by Donald Anthony Low in *Soundings in Modern South Asian History*, edited by Low (1968). Aspects of his career are also discussed in Cyril Henry Philips and Mary Doreen Wainwright, eds., *The Partition of India: Policies and Perspectives, 1935–1947* (1970). For general historical background see Romesh Chandra Majumdar and others, *An Advanced History of India* (1946; 3d ed. 1967).

*   *   *

SARGENT / By Frederick A. Sweet

John Singer Sargent (1856–1925) was America's most technically brilliant portrait painter. His work profoundly influenced his generation.

Born on Jan. 20, 1856, in Florence, Italy, of American parents, John Singer Sargent spent the greater part of his life in Europe but made frequent short visits to the United States. His father was a doctor from Gloucester, Mass.; his mother, who came from Philadelphia, preferred Continental life and persuaded her husband to give up his medical practice. Sargent was a

sionist phase, as seen in the two versions of *Luxembourg Gardens at Twilight* (1879). His most brilliant early portrait was of Mrs. Charles Gifford Dyer (1880). The tragic beauty of the face shows the artist's intuitive faculties. The *Pailleron Children* (1880) shows great sophistication and an almost Jamesian sinisterness. His great early success, more liked by fellow artists than by critics, was the *Daughters of Edward Darley Boit*, shown at the Salon of 1883. Four little girls are placed asymmetrically in a composition as remarkable for its subtle balances as for its luminous effect.

Sargent's most daring and brilliant portrait, known as *Madame X*, was of Madame Gautreau, one of the most elegant and fashion-conscious beauties of Parisian society. He painted her standing, wearing an extremely low-cut evening gown, and he made effective use of the contrast of her white skin with the black dress. When the picture was shown at the Salon of 1884, the public as well as her family were shocked, and Sargent was forced to withdraw it. Largely because of this, he left Paris and established himself in London, where he remained for the rest of his life.

In the mid-1880s Sargent painted two portraits of Robert Louis Stevenson, both brilliant, spontaneous, and sensitive portrayals of this frail and talented man. In 1887 Sargent went to America to paint the Marquands and a stark and commanding portrait of the austere matriarch Mrs. Adrian Iselin. By 1890 he was so firmly established that all the peeresses and notables of England clamored for the privilege of having him do their portraits. In 1898 Asher Wertheimer, a famous London art dealer, commissioned him to paint all the members of his family. One of the finest of this group is the portrait of Mrs. Wertheimer, which is elegant and impervious but facile and penetrating. His portrait of the great beauty Lady Sassoon, dressed in the highest fashion, is sparkling and vivacious and a technical tour de force. Although he painted men less often than women, one of his most dashing achievements was of Lord Ribblesdale in riding costume. The Duchess of Devonshire, the Duchess of Sutherland, the Countess of Warwick, and dozens of others were all painted with the same facile elegance. He also did groups such as the Marlborough family, the Sitwell family, and the Wyndham sisters.

Some of Sargent's greatest accomplishments were in watercolor, which he undertook mostly during summer trips to the Tirol, Italy, and Spain. These works are transparent, luminous, and brilliantly executed. In 1890 he was commissioned to do murals for the Boston Public Library (completed in 1916), the finest of which is the series of prophets. In 1916 he executed murals for the rotunda of the Museum of Fine Arts, Boston. He died in London on April 15, 1925.

Further Reading

John Singer Sargent is listed in the Art study guide (IV, D, 1, d). His watercolors are considered the equal of those of his American contemporary Winslow HOMER.

Biographies of Sargent include W. H. Downes, *John S.*

Madame X, a painting executed by John Singer Sargent in 1884. (The Metropolitan Museum of Art, Arthur H. Hearn Fund, 1916)

born artist, very precocious, and fortunate in having his mother's encouragement. At the age of 9 he was sketching animals at the Paris Zoo. In 1868–1869 he worked in the studio of Carl Welsch in Rome, then attended school in Florence and took courses at the Accademia delle Belle Arti.

In 1874 the family settled in Paris, and Sargent worked at the École des Beaux-Arts, but in October he entered the studio of Carolus-Duran, a skillful portrait painter. In 1876 Sargent made his first trip to America, to establish his American citizenship. In 1877 he exhibited a portrait of Miss Watts, his first appearance at the Paris Salon. After an early period of realism he went through an impres-

John Singer Sargent in 1903. (Library of Congress)

Sargent (1925); Frederick A. Sweet, *Sargent, Whistler and Mary Cassatt* (1954); and Charles Merrill Mount, *John Singer Sargent* (1955). See also David McKibbin, *Sargent's Boston* (1956).

✳   ✳   ✳

SARGON / By Margaret S. Drower

Sargon of Agade (reigned ca. 2340–2284 B.C.) was the first Semitic king of Mesopotamia. He founded the Akkadian dynasty and was the first ruler in history to win and hold an empire. He became a heroic figure of literature.

S argon (pronounced sär′gŏn) was born, according to legend, in the city of Saffron on the banks of the Euphrates. His father was a nomad, his mother a temple votary who set him, like Moses, afloat in a basket. He was found by a peasant who adopted him and brought him up. He became cupbearer to the king of Kish, and later he himself became king. He founded Agade, or Akkad (the site of which is not known), as his new capital and, by defeating the paramount ruler of the Sumerian city-states, became master of all Mesopotamia. In 34 battles he conquered "as far as the shore of the sea."

In the first year of his rule Sargon marched northwest up the Euphrates to conquer Hit and Mari (near Deir-ez-Zor), and in the eleventh year he reached the Mediterranean coast, claiming dominion over the Cedar Forest (Lebanon or Amanus, the latter now called Alma Dag) and the Silver Mountain (perhaps the eastern Taurus). Legends credit him with the conquest of the land of Tin and the island of Crete and also with a successful expedition to central Anatolia. The text relating this incident, called the "King of Battle," may be based on stories handed down by trading colonies established by the Akkadians in this rich mining area. Whether or not Sargon went as far as the Salt Lake (Tuz Lake, or Tuz Gölü), he undoubtedly reached the Mediterranean and could with right claim territories "from the Lower Sea [the Persian Gulf] to the Upper Sea" and from the rising to the setting sun.

In other remarkable campaigns, Sargon went east to conquer the lands of Elam and Barakhshe, in the Plain of Khuzistan and the Zagros Mountains, and north to Assyria. The king lists say that he reigned for 56 years. In later ages his name was synonymous with success, and his adventures became legend. An itinerary which sur-

King Sargon of Agade, a bronze head from Nineveh dating from the second half of the 3d millennium B.C. (Directorate General of Antiquities, Baghdad)

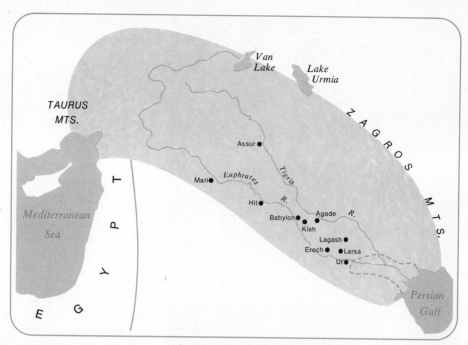

Sargon's Akkadian empire, 2300 B.C. Sargon welded history's first empire out of the city-states of Mesopotamia. It extended from the Persian Gulf to the Mediterranean. (The site of Agade is speculative.)

vives in a late Assyrian version credits him with further conquests, including the lands around the Persian Gulf and Bahrein and, perhaps, the coast of Makran.

Further Reading

Sargon is listed in the Ancient History study guide (I, B, 1). Later conqueror-kings were CYRUS THE GREAT and ALEXANDER THE GREAT.

For a recent study of the Akkadian period, with an ample bibliography, see C. J. Gadd's "The Dynasty of Agade" (1921) in the revised edition of volume 1 of the *Cambridge Ancient History* (12 vols., 1967). The contemporary inscriptions are translated by George A. Barton in *Royal Inscriptions of Sumer and Akkad* (1929); and the later legends are discussed in Sidney Smith, *Early History of Assyria* (1928).

SARGON II / By Margaret S. Drower

The Assyrian king Sargon II (reigned 722–705 B.C.) was one of the chief architects of the late Assyrian Empire and the founder of its greatest line of kings.

Sargon II, upon his accession, took the name Sharrukin (Sargon is the biblical form), after the illustrious founder of the Akkadian dynasty, who had died 1,600 years before. This name and the fact that his predecessor, Shalmaneser V, reigned very briefly suggest that Sargon may have been a usurper. His first task was to restore order and overcome opposition at home; he then turned to the problems facing his army on the frontiers of the empire. He captured Samaria, the Israelite capital, and deported its inhabitants; next he defeated the rebel Syrian vassels at Qarqar. In the northeast, the turbulent Iranian tribes had been stirred into revolt by Assyria's old enemy, the Kingdom of Urartu. Punitive campaigns between 719 and 717 B.C. restored order, but trouble broke out again, and in 715 Sargon, in a demonstration of strength, marched round Lake Urmia to Van, Urartu's capital. Van held out, however, creating a stalemate on Assyria's northern frontier.

In 717 Sargon was faced with a revolt in the west encouraged by King Midas of Phrygia. Sargon's army overran northern Syria and the Taurus region, and by 710 all Syria and Palestine had submitted to Assyrian rule with the exception of Judah; Egypt was friendly. Only the Babylonians enjoyed virtual independence under their Chaldean leader, Merodach-baladan; but when Sargon marched south in 708, Merodach-baladan fled to Elam, and Sargon was crowned king of Babylon. The king of Bahrein sent gifts, and so did seven kings of Cyprus. Like his ancient namesake, Sargon could claim sway from the Upper Sea (the Mediterranean) to the Lower Sea (the Persian Gulf).

Sargon lived in Calah (modern Nimrud), the military capital, which he fortified and embellished. He also created a new residence city, Sargonsburg, 15 miles northeast of Nineveh, near modern Khorsabad. The city, which was inaugurated in 706, took 10 years to build. It was laid out in a rectangle, and its walls were pierced by eight gates. The great palace and temple, which stood on a 50-foot-high citadel platform, contained spacious halls decorated with stone reliefs. Colossal figures of man-headed bulls stood at the doorways. Early in 705 Sargon was called to the northwest, where he fell in battle against the nomadic Cimmerians.

King Sargon II of Assyria, a relief sculpture of the 8th century B.C., from the Palace of Sargon at Khorsabad (Sargonsburg) and now in the Louvre, Paris. (Alinari)

Further Reading

Sargon II is listed in the Ancient History study guide (I, B, 3). He was succeeded by his son, SENNACHERIB.

Contemporary sources are collected in *The Inscriptions of Sargon II, King of Assyria*, translated and edited by A. G. Lie (1929). For the University of Chicago's excavation of Sargonsburg consult Gordon Loud, *Khorsabad*, vol. 1 (1936), in which references are given to the publications of the 19th-century French excavators. Many of the sculptures from Khorsabad are now in the Louvre in Paris. Volume 3 of *The Cambridge Ancient History* (12 vols., 1925) contains a reliable general account of Sargon's reign by Sidney Smith. A. T. Olmstead, *Western Asia in the Days of Sargon of Assyria* (1908), is still of use.

SARIT / By David K. Wyatt

The Thai army officer and prime minister Sarit Thanarat (1908–1963) overthrew the government of Phibun Songkhram in 1957 and was responsible for initiating major programs of economic development and social welfare.

The son of Maj. Luang Rüangdetanan (Thongdi Thanarat), an army officer whose career was spent mainly on the eastern frontier and who is remembered for his translations from Cambodian, Sarit (pronounced sä′rĭt) was born in Bangkok on June 16, 1908. His youth was spent with maternal relatives in the remote frontier district of Mukdahan in Nakhon Phanom Province, an experience which gave him a lifelong interest in and affinity for the Lao provinces of northeast Thailand. He attended a monastery school in Bangkok and entered the royal military academy in 1919. Completing his studies there only in 1928, he was commissioned a second lieutenant in 1929.

Sarit at first rose slowly in the army ranks. The first decade of his military career was spent in infantry regiments and training schools in Bangkok and nearby Lopburi. A major at the outbreak of war in 1940, he saw service in northern Thailand and at the conclusion of the war was in command of Thai occupation troops in the Federated Shan States of northeast Burma.

Political Career

Unlike many of his fellow officers, Sarit did not take a prominent role in politics until 1947, when, as a colonel commanding an infantry battalion in Bangkok, he assumed a leading role in the military coup which overthrew civilian parliamentary government. This was the turning point in his public life. He was jumped in rank to major general and placed in command of the troops of the Bangkok military region and in 1949 was primarily responsible for crushing a navy and marine rebellion on behalf of Pridi Phanomyong. He then took charge of the 1st Army in Bangkok, which after 1932 always retained particular political significance. In that position he was responsible for suppressing a further attempted coup by the navy and marines in 1951.

Sarit's promotion in rank to lieutenant general in 1950 and general in 1952 served to confirm power he already had. The restoration of Phibun by the 1947 coup was in effect the assumption of power by a generation of army officers which, unlike Phibun and the leaders of prewar governments, had not had foreign training. They were slow in developing their own political leadership, and the coups and countercoups of the late 1940s and early 1950s saw a jockeying for power which by 1951 had resulted in a rivalry centering on two figures: Sarit—who became deputy commander of the army and deputy minister of defense in 1951 and commander in chief of the army in 1954—and Police Gen. Phao Siyanon, who became director general of the paramilitary police department in 1951 and acted as the strong arm of the regime.

Leader of a Coup

Phibun's power slipped rapidly in the 1950s as economic conditions worsened after the Korean War boom;

official corruption became more blatant; and Phao's ruthless attacks on political rivals, the Chinese business community, and civilian political figures got out of hand. Sarit, having become a field marshal in 1956, was increasingly aloof from the regime, although he kept the loyalty of the armed forces and gained some popular support. When Phibun, in a bid for popular support to counterbalance his rivals, attempted a return to parliamentary government in 1957, Phao blatantly managed the elections in Phibun's favor. Sarit capitalized on the publicly displayed royal displeasure with Phibun, public outrage, and student demonstrations to call out his troops and overthrow the Phibun government in September 1957.

Leaving the government in the hands of a newly elected parliamentary regime under his deputy, Gen. Thanom Kittikachorn, Sarit flew hurriedly to the United States for urgently needed medical treatment. In his absence, representative government almost ground to a halt for lack of consensus and leadership, and economic conditions worsened. Returning quietly to Bangkok, Sarit staged a second coup in October 1958 and, with Thanom's consent, seized power.

The revolutionary government Sarit established then, legitimized by a new constitution styled on those of Gaullist France and the United Arab Republic, moved quickly and with great force to execute positive policies of economic development and social reform and services. A commanding executive, he early gained a reputation for getting things done, as when he personally wielded an ax to smash opium dens and arrested arsonists. He encouraged King Bhumibol Aduldej to travel, and he revived neglected royal ceremonies to bolster national identity.

Sarit traveled widely himself, often swooping down on remote villages in an army helicopter to chat with peasants. He attempted to restore some of the authority of specialist bureaucrats in the important ministries, though, through his army, he retained control of the Ministry of Interior. He promised an eventual return to parliamentary democracy but moved only slowly to implement this intention.

Economic Reformer

Sarit will be remembered for his effective policies of economic development, which brought the country rapidly to an annual growth rate of 8 percent in the gross national product, for his strong promotion of education, especially in rural areas, and for the special attention he devoted to the impoverished northeast, which had long been neglected by Bangkok governments. The statistics were only beginning to show the success of these policies when he died suddenly on Dec. 8, 1963.

An unusually tall, heavyset, and dark-complexioned man, with a booming, growling voice, Sarit is said to have been genuinely concerned that he be remembered in Thai history as one who revived the kingdom and gave it a clear direction. The successful continuance of his policies, and the beginning of a return to parliamentary democracy in the late 1960s, reflected favorably on his intentions and hopes.

Further Reading

Sarit Thanarat is listed in the Asia study guide (IV, A, 2, d). He shared the spotlight of 20th-century Thai politics with PRIDI Phanomyong and PHIBUN Songkhram.

There is no full biography of Sarit in any Western language, although numerous popular accounts of his life appear in Thai. The important events of his time are recounted in David A. Wilson, *Politics in Thailand* (1962), and Frank C. Darling, *Thailand and the United States* (1965).

SARMIENTO / By Irving A. Leonard

The Argentine statesman, educator, and gifted journalist Domingo Faustino Sarmiento (1811–1888) was known as the "Teacher President" for his unremitting efforts to foster education in his country. He was also an intuitive writer with a prophetic gift who created a classic of Argentine literature.

Domingo Sarmiento (pronounced sär-myän′tō) was born on Feb. 15, 1811, in San Juan, an old and primitive town of western Argentina near the Andes, of humble, hardworking parents living in near poverty. His formal education was scanty, and he was largely self-taught, reading whatever came within his

Domingo Sarmiento. *(Organization of American States)*

reach. Benjamin Franklin's *Autobiography* exercised a powerful influence on his young mind, and in later life he wrote, "No other book has done me more good than that one." At the age of 15 Sarmiento taught in a country school; later he clerked briefly in a general store with little success, tried his hand at surveying, and entered politics at a youthful age, thus emulating Abraham Lincoln's early life. Sarmiento's features, about which he often joked, were also rugged and homely. Indeed, these statesmen from opposite ends of the Western Hemisphere had a certain affinity, and in the last decades of his life, Sarmiento always kept near him plaster busts of his "household divinities"—Lincoln and the New England educator Horace Mann.

Sarmiento turned to politics with passionate dedication. The independent provinces of Argentina had lapsed into general anarchy, from which emerged the classic Latin American dictatorship of the cruel and despotic Juan Manuel de Rosas. Liberal and constructive elements of society fled into exile, and Sarmiento's opposition soon obliged him to seek asylum in Chile. In that hospitable land he promoted public schools and, with equal passion, assailed the dictator of Argentina with fiery pamphlets and newspaper articles. In the heat of this fray he wrote the classic *Civilization and Barbarism; or, The Life of Juan Facundo Quiroga* (1845), more succinctly known as *Facundo*.

This anomalous work in three parts is neither history, biography, a novel, nor sociology, yet it partakes of the characteristics of all of these. The first part is a geographical and social description of the vast pampas, or plains, of Argentina. Isolated cities are oases of civilization in the empty wilderness, over which wild gauchos roam in semibarbarism. The influence of James Fenimore Cooper, particularly his novel *The Prairie*, is apparent in these pages, and it is of interest to note that neither writer at the time of composition had actually seen the region that he described with intuitive genius. The second part is a melodramatic biography of the *caudillo* Facundo, who symbolizes the barbarism of the pampas and the tyranny of the despot Rosas. The third part is a program of social and political reorganization after the overthrow of the dictator.

From 1845 to 1848, while Sarmiento was still an expatriate, the Chilean government enabled him to travel in Europe and the United States to study educational systems, and these journeys inspired some of his finest descriptive writing, in *Travels in Europe, Africa, and the United States* (1849–1851). On returning to Chile he wrote his nostalgic *Hometown Memories* (1850) to defend himself from political slander, and this work, describing his childhood and early home life, contains some of his most moving pages.

The comments on North American life and ways in his travel book are both humorous and penetrating. They clearly reveal his profound and unfailing admiration for all things American, particularly public education. His veneration for Horace Mann approached adoration and later extended to the Massachusetts educator's widow, Mary Tyler Mann, who became Sarmiento's confidante and correspondent for the remainder of his days.

With the fall of the Rosas dictatorship in 1852, Sarmiento returned from exile to devote his energies with ceaseless intensity to bringing unity and a sense of nationality to his people. From 1865 to 1868 he was again in the United States as minister plenipotentiary of Argentina, during which time he met Emerson, Longfellow, Ticknor, and many other North American notables. The most prized distinction that he received was an honorary doctorate from the University of Michigan in June 1868, on the eve of his return to Argentina to assume the presidency.

Sarmiento's term as chief executive, from 1868 to 1874, was one of frustration owing to the exhausting war with Paraguay and to other circumstances unfavorable for a cherished program of reform. Nevertheless, he did much to advance learning and to promote public schools, including arrangements for American women schoolteachers to go to Argentina under contract to give instruction in the newly established teacher-training institutions and in the primary schools of provincial towns and cities.

Despite a strong reluctance to step down from his high office at the end of his term, Sarmiento patriotically turned over the presidency to an elected successor. Then, in minor positions, he continued to work to unify his countrymen and to prepare them for civic participation. Deafness and ill health saddened his last years. compelling him to spend his winters in the milder climate of Paraguay, where he died on Sept. 11, 1888. Shortly before his death he wrote to a friend: "I must soon start on one last journey. But I am ready ... for I carry the only acceptable passport, because it is written in every language. It says: Serve mankind!"

Further Reading

Domingo Sarmiento is listed in the Latin America study guide (IV, A, 2, a). Other Argentine writers were Ernesto SABATO and Ricardo GÜIRÁLDEZ.

A good selection of Sarmiento's writings is in Allison Williams Bunkley, ed., *A Sarmiento Anthology*, translated by Stuart Edgar Grummon (1948). Bunkley is also author of a full-length biography, *The Life of Sarmiento* (1952). Mary Tyler Mann provided a biographical sketch in the translation of Sarmiento's *Life in the Argentine Republic in the Days of the Tyrants; or, Civilization and Barbarism* (1868; repr. 1960).

✳   ✳   ✳

SARNOFF / By Thomas B. Brewer

The American pioneer in radio and televison David Sarnoff (1891–1971) was chairman of the board of the Radio Corporation of America.

David Sarnoff was born on Feb. 27, 1891, in the Russian-Jewish community of Uzilan close to Minsk. In 1895 his father left to try his luck in the United States; 5 years later he sent for his family. When

David Sarnoff in 1961. (RCA News)

pushed its development to commercial feasibility. As president of RCA (since 1930), he appeared on the first public demonstration of television, in April 1939. Although NBC launched commercial telecasting in 1941, World War II retarded its growth. Sarnoff served as communications consultant to Gen. Dwight D. Eisenhower and emerged as a brigadier general.

In 1947 Sarnoff became chairman of the board of RCA, which grew into one of the world's largest corporations, its activities including leadership in black-and-white and color television and many other associated industries. He received honorary degrees from over 26 universities and numerous awards from foreign governments and technical institutes. He died on Dec. 12, 1971, in New York City.

Further Reading

David Sarnoff is listed in the American History study guide (VIII, F, 2; IX, B, 2; X, D, 1). Other leaders of commerce and industry in America were John D. ROCKEFELLER, Henry FORD, and Henry J. KAISER.

For the serious student of communications, Sarnoff's own *Looking Ahead: The Papers of David Sarnoff* (1968) is valuable for its predictive glances into the future of electronics and masterful coverage of the history of broadcasting. A biography is Eugene Lyons, *David Sarnoff* (1966).

the father died in 1906, David, as the eldest son, became the family provider. He started as a messenger boy for the Commercial Cable Company. Six months later he became an office boy for the Marconi Wireless Telegraph Company of America.

Studying in his spare time, Sarnoff finally was promoted to wireless operator. While working at Sea Gage, N.Y., he completed a course in electrical engineering at Pratt Institute and later acquired practical experience as a marine radio operator on various ships. He then became the operator for John Wanamaker's New York station, where he was the first to pick up the distress call of the S.S. *Titanic* on April 12, 1912. This unfortunate incident proved rewarding for Sarnoff, for his dedicated work in the disaster won him an appointment as a radio inspector and instructor at the Marconi Institute. By 1914 he had risen to contract manager, and in 1919, when Owen D. Young's Radio Corporation of America (RCA) absorbed American Marconi, Sarnoff was commercial manager. In 1917 he married Lizette Hermant, who bore him three sons.

By 1921 Sarnoff was general manager of RCA and had revived an earlier idea to send music over the air. RCA's directors were reluctant to invest much money, but after Sarnoff broadcast the 1921 Dempsey-Cartier fight, they quickly changed their minds. Sarnoff became a vice president in 1922 as RCA began the manufacture of radio sets. He also was responsible for the creation of the National Broadcasting Company (NBC) in 1926.

Sarnoff is known as the father of American television. From the initial experiments in the early 1920s, he

SAROYAN / By William R. Reardon

The skill of William Saroyan (born 1908), American short-story writer, dramatist, and novelist, in evoking mood and atmosphere is noteworthy, and his imaginary world, peopled with common men, is warm and compelling.

William Saroyan was born in Fresno, Calif., on Aug. 31, 1908, the son of Armenian immigrants. After his father's death in 1911, William spent 4 years in an orphanage. Selling newspapers at the age of 8, he attended public schools in Fresno until, as he said, "I had been kicked out of school so many times that I finally left for good when I was fifteen."

In 1928 Saroyan decided to become a writer, but it was 1934 before his short stories began appearing consistently in major magazines. His first book was *The Daring Young Man on the Flying Trapeze and Other Stories* (1934). At this time he concentrated on short stories. Seven collections appeared, from *Inhale and Exhale* (1936) to *My Name Is Aram* (1940). The works centered on memories of San Francisco and Fresno and show his joy in living. *My Name Is Aram* is particularly lyrical.

From 1939 through 1943 Saroyan was among America's most active playwrights. In *My Heart's in the Highlands* (1939) he departed from the current dramatic practice, for he believed that "it is folly for emotionality to be

William Saroyan in 1962. (Wide World Photos)

prolonged as a means by which to achieve drama." Completely episodic, bonded by a tenuous mood deriving from free spirits, the play is distinctive. He created a similar piece in *The Time of Your Life* (1939). Awarded the Pulitzer Prize and the Drama Critics' Circle Award for this play, Saroyan rejected the former. *Love's Old Sweet Song* (1940) was less effective, but his firm grip was evident again in *The Beautiful People* (1941). *Hello Out There* (1942), atypical of Saroyan, is an effective realistic one-act play of human isolation. Another dark play, *Get Away Old Man* (1943), failed, but his film *The Human Comedy* (1943) won an Academy Award.

During World War II Saroyan served in the Army. In 1943 he married Carol Marcus. Divorced in 1949, they remarried in 1951 and were again divorced in 1952. Although he continued to write plays, his work was mainly novels, autobiographies, film and television scripts, short stories, and even songs. His most praised novels are *The Human Comedy* (1943), *The Assyrian* (1950), *Tracy's Tiger* (1951), *The Laughing Matter* (1953), and *Mama I Love You* (1956).

Further Reading

William Saroyan is listed in the Literature study guide (I, E, 2, c). Thornton WILDER experimented with new dramatic forms during this period.

Saroyan's autobiographies are *The Bicycle Rider in Beverly Hills* (1952), *Here Comes: There Goes: You Know Who* (1961), and *Not Dying* (1963). The major critical work on him is Howard R. Floan, *William Saro-*

yan (1966). A major bibliographical work is David Kherdian, *A Bibliography of William Saroyan, 1934–1964* (1965). Useful insights are in John Mason Brown, *Broadway in Review* (1940); Brooks Atkinson, *Broadway Scrapbook* (1947); and George Jean Nathan, *The Magic Mirror: Selected Writings on the Theatre* (1960).

SARPI / By Edward M. Peters

The Italian prelate and statesman Paolo Sarpi (1552–1623) was one of the greatest historians of early modern Europe and a founder of the modern historical method.

Paolo Sarpi (pronounced sär⁄pē) was born in Venice, the son of a merchant. His early education was supervised by a family friend, a member of the Servite order of friars. In 1565 Sarpi himself joined the Servites, and in 1574 he was ordained a priest. His intellectual gifts brought him into contact with some of the most important people and cities in Italy. He spent 3 years as court theologian in Mantua and then traveled to Milan. He returned to Venice, where he taught philosophy while studying at the nearby University of Padua, the

A portrait of a friar believed to be Paolo Sarpi. The painting, by Volterrano, is in the Uffizi, Florence. (Alinari)

intellectual center of Italy in this period. In 1579 he became provincial of the Venetian province of the Servites, and in 1584, at the age of 32, he moved to Rome as procurator general of the whole order.

Between 1588 and 1606 Sarpi lived in studious retirement in Venice, participating in the vigorous scientific life of Venice and Padua and making friends with such men as Galileo. In 1606 he was called out of retirement and made theologian and canon lawyer of the Republic of Venice. It was a critical moment in Venetian history: the republic had been laid under an interdict by Pope Paul V, and Sarpi's duties entailed the defense of the Venetian cause against the weight and authority of the Counter Reformation papacy. His role in the defense of Venice led him directly to the most important phase of his career, that of skilled and penetrating historian of the medieval and Renaissance Church.

Sarpi's first historical work was a long memorandum, intended for private circulation, of the events in Venice between 1605 and 1607. His second work was the great *History of Benefices* (1609), in which he relied upon his access to the secret archives of Venice and expressed his conviction that individuals and circumstances, political as well as economic, influenced this important chapter of ecclesiastical history. By 1616 Sarpi had completed his greatest work, *History of the Council of Trent*, which was published in Italian in London in 1619.

In these original historical works, Sarpi deals with limited topics, opens his analysis of causality to economic and political influences, and tries wherever possible to base his conclusions upon documentary evidence. His perception of complex human background made his *History of the Council of Trent* a landmark in the technique of ecclesiastical and institutional history.

During his lifetime Sarpi was honored and protected by the Republic of Venice, a popular and well-known figure. After his death, he became a revered civic hero, not only of the republic but of all Europe.

Further Reading

Paolo Sarpi is listed in the Social Sciences study guide (IV, A, 2). In the 17th century Jean MABILLON used critical methods in writing history.

The introductory remarks that preface the selections from Sarpi's writings in translation by Peter Burke, *Sarpi: History of Benefices and Selections from the History of the Council of Trent* (1967), provide an excellent introduction to Sarpi's method. The best study of his life and ideas is William Bouwsma, *Venice and the Defense of Republican Liberty* (1968).

* * *

SARTON / By Dwight W. Hoover

The Belgian-born American historian of science George Sarton (1884–1956) founded the history of science in America.

George Sarton was born in Ghent on Aug. 31, 1884, the son of one of the directors and chief engineers of the Belgian national railroad system. Sarton studied philosophy at the University of Ghent and then turned to science, winning his doctorate in mathematics in 1911. He had, however, already become known as an author and scientist for his published novels and poems and his award-winning essay on chemistry (1908). Sarton emerged from his training with admiration for the insights of Auguste Comte and Henri Poincaré and a conviction that the basis of scientific philosophy was the history of science.

Sarton married an English artist, Eleanor Noble Elives, in 1911. In March 1913 he published the first issue of *Isis*, a journal of the history of science. At the beginning of World War I he fled to Holland, then to England, and, finally, to the United States. He arrived in 1915 and lectured at Harvard from 1916 to 1918, the first academic year in philosophy and the second in history of science. The appointment was not a regular one, and he was supported in the main by friends. The Lowell Lectures at Harvard in 1916 started Sarton on his lifetime project of tracing the history of science to Leonardo da Vinci.

The Carnegie Institution in Washington appointed Sarton a research associate in 1918, thus making him economically secure. He remained at Cambridge and, beginning in 1920, gave a course on the history of science in exchange for library space at Harvard. Meanwhile, he had published the second issue of *Isis* in September 1919. Sarton became an American citizen in 1924 and

George Sarton. (Harvard University News Office)

helped found the History of Science group the same year.

Sarton's major work, *Introduction to the History of Science*, consists of *From Homer to Omar Khayyam* (1927), *From Rabbi Ben Ezra to Roger Bacon* (1931), and *Science and Learning in the 14th Century* (1947–1948). During this time he went to North Africa and the Near East (1931–1932) to study Arabic and Islam; founded *Osiris* (1936), a journal designed for articles longer than those in *Isis*; and wrote and lectured.

In his writings Sarton used the model of a map maker. He combined biography and science, using secondary sources. As a result, he slighted Egyptian and Babylonian sources and relied heavily on Greek and medieval Arabic ones, which were more available to him. All of his works emphasized the continuity of science and its close affinity with magic.

Sarton officially became professor of the history of science at Harvard in 1940 and retired in 1951. He continued to lecture and write until his death on March 22, 1956.

Further Reading

George Sarton is listed in the Social Sciences study guide (VII, A, 3). He was influenced by the theories of Auguste COMTE. Another science historian was Pierre DUHEM.

Sarton's most important theoretical essays were collected in *Sarton on the History of Science*, edited by Dorothy Stimson (1962). May Sarton in *I Knew a Phoenix: Sketches for an Autobiography* (1959) treats her father sympathetically and poetically. His contributions to the history of science are critically analyzed in Joseph Agassi, *Towards an Historiography of Science* (1963).

SARTRE / By Daniel O'Connor

The French philosopher and man of letters Jean Paul Sartre (born 1905) ranks as the most versatile writer and as the dominant influence in 3 decades of French intellectual life.

Jean Paul Sartre (pronounced sàr′tr′) was born in Paris on June 21, 1905. His father, a naval officer, died while on a tour of duty in Indochina before Sartre was 2 years old. His mother belonged to the Alsatian Schweitzer family and was a first cousin to Albert Schweitzer. The young widow returned to her parents' house, where she and her son were treated as "the children." In the first volume of his autobiography, *The Words* (1964), Sartre describes his unnatural childhood as a spoiled and precocious boy. Lacking any companions his own age, the child found "friends" exclusively in books. Reading and writing thus became his twin passions. "It was in books that I encountered the universe."

Sartre entered the École Normale Supérieure in 1924

Jean Paul Sartre with Simone de Beauvoir. (French Cultural Services of the French Embassy)

and after one failure received first place in the *agrégation* of philosophy in 1929. The novelist Simone de Beauvoir finished second that year, and the two formed an intimate bond that endured thereafter. After completing compulsory military service, Sartre took a teaching job at a lycée in Le Havre. There he wrote his first novel, *Nausea* (1938), which some critics have called the century's most influential French novel.

From 1933 to 1935 Sartre was a research student at the Institut Français in Berlin and in Freiburg. He discovered the works of Edmund Husserl and Martin Heidegger and began to philosophize in the phenomenological vein. A series of works on the modalities of consciousness poured from Sartre's pen: two works on imagination, one on self-consciousness, and one on emotions. He also produced a first-rate volume of short stories, *The Wall* (1939).

Sartre returned to Paris to teach in a lycée and to continue his writing, but World War II intervened. Called up by the army, he served briefly on the Eastern front and was taken prisoner. After 9 months he secured his release and returned to teaching in Paris, where he became active in the Resistance. During this period he wrote his first major work in philosophy, *Being and Nothingness: An Essay in Phenomenological Ontology* (1943).

After the war Sartre abandoned teaching, determined to support himself by writing. He was also determined that his writing and thinking should be *engagé*. Intellectuals, he thought, must take a public stand on every great question of their day. He thus became fundamentally a moralist, both in his philosophical and literary works.

Sartre had turned to playwriting and eventually produced a series of theatrical successes which are essentially dramatizations of ideas, although they contain some finely drawn characters and lively plots. The first two, *The Flies* and *No Exit*, were produced in occupied Paris. They were followed by *Dirty Hands* (1948), usually called his best play; *The Devil and the Good Lord* (1957), a blasphemous, anti-Christian tirade; and *The Prisoners of Altona* (1960), which combines convincing character portrayal with telling social criticism. Sartre also wrote a number of comedies: *The Respectful Prostitute* (1946), *Kean* (1954), and *Nekrassov* (1956), which the critic Henry Peyre claims "reveals him as the best comic talent of our times."

During this same period Sartre also wrote a three-volume novel, *The Roads to Freedom* (1945–1949); a treatise on committed literature; lengthy studies of Charles Baudelaire and Jean Genet; and a prodigious number of reviews and criticisms. He also edited *Les Temps modernes.*

Though never a member of the Communist party, Sartre usually sympathized with the political views of the far left. Whatever the political issue, he was quick to publish his opinions, often combining them with public acts of protest.

In 1960 Sartre returned to philosophy, publishing the first volume of his *Critique of Dialectical Reason.* It represented essentially a modification of his existentialism by Marxist ideas. The drift of Sartre's earlier work was toward a sense of the futility of life. In *Being and Nothingness* he declared man to be "a useless passion," condemned to exercise a meaningless freedom. But after World War II his new interest in social and political questions and his rapprochement with Marxist thought led him to more optimistic and activist views.

Further Reading

Jean Paul Sartre is listed in the Literature study guide (III, J, 1, b) and the Philosophy study guide (VII, H, 2). He was influenced by the writings of Edmund HUSSERL and Martin HEIDEGGER. Albert CAMUS also wrote existential novels.

Sartre's *The Words* (trans. 1964) gives a highly unusual account of his childhood, subjecting his early years to the same "existential psychoanalysis" that he applied to Baudelaire and Genet. The autobiography of Simone de Beauvoir, *The Prime of Life* (trans. 1962), contains a detailed and intimate account of Sartre. Mary Warnock, *The Philosophy of Sartre* (1965), is a readable account of the philosophical writings. Philip Thody, *Jean-Paul Sartre: A Literary and Political Study* (1960), gives a thoughtful appraisal of the literary works.

SASSETTA / By Edmund Eglinski

The Italian artist Sassetta (ca. 1400–1450), the greatest painter of the Sienese school in the 15th century, is noted for the gentle piety of his art.

The place and date of birth of Stefano di Giovanni, known as Sassetta (pronounced sä-sě′tä), are unknown. He may have been born in Cortona, the home of his father, Giovanni di Consolo. A baptismal record preserved in Siena dated Dec. 31, 1392, for one Stefano di Giovanni is widely accepted as evidence that he was born in Siena that year. Some scholars, however, would suggest a birth date not before 1400 on the basis of Sassetta's earliest dated work of 1423.

Sassetta's style was wholly Sienese in character, suggesting that he was trained in the shop of some Sienese master. Whether or not that master was Paolo di Giovanni Fei, as suggested by some critics, is unknown. In 1440 Sassetta married Gabriella di Buccio di Biancardo. The eldest of their three children was the sculptor Giovanni di Stefano. Sassetta died in April 1450, after contracting pneumonia the previous month while frescoing the Porta Romana, Siena.

On July 1, 1423, the wool guild (Arte della Lana) com-

Sassetta's large altarpiece for the church of S. Francesco in Borgo San Sepolcro, painted between 1437 and 1441, has been split up among various museums. The Mystic Marriage of St. Francis, *one of eight panels with scenes from the life of St. Francis that flanked the back of the altarpiece, is now in the Musée Condé, Chantilly. (Giraudon)*

missioned an altarpiece (now disassembled) from Sassetta for its chapel next to the church of S. Pellegrino, Siena. From 1426 to 1431 he was associated with the Cathedral Works, Siena. Among the documents from this period are records of payment dated December 1427 for a drawing of the baptismal font "in the shape that it ought to take." This suggests that he may have collaborated with Jacopo della Quercia, the sculptor who built the font.

On March 25, 1430, Sassetta was commissioned to paint an altarpiece of the Madonna with Saints with the legend of the founding of S. Maria Maggiore, Rome, in the predella. The *Madonna of the Snow*, as it is called, was finished by mid-October 1432. His style in this work betrays the influence of Masaccio, especially in the broad modeling of the Virgin and Child and in the arrangement of figures in the predella. Little is known of Sassetta's activities between 1433 and 1436, though this is the period when he probably painted the *Crucifixion* for S. Martino (of which fragments remain) and the altarpiece for S. Domenico, Cortona.

The altarpiece of the Madonna with Saints Jerome and Ambrose, dated 1436, in the Church of the Osservanza, Siena, formerly attributed to Sassetta, is now generally attributed to another artist, the so-called Osservanza Master. Some critics would extend the oeuvre of the Osservanza Master to include the *Birth of the Virgin* in Asciano and the group of panels with the life of St. Anthony Abbot from an altarpiece dedicated to the saint. These panels still have advocates who attribute them to Sassetta.

Two small panels, the *Journey of the Magi* and the *Adoration of the Magi*, were probably once part of a single composition. The most important extant later work by Sassetta is the altarpiece (now dismembered) commissioned on Sept. 5, 1437, and completed by June 5, 1441, for the church of S. Francesco, Borgo San Sepolcro. His style in these panels is somewhat flatter and more decorative than in the *Madonna of the Snow*. When Sassetta died, he left at least two major works unfinished: the fresco decoration of the Porta Romana, Siena, and the *Assumption of the Virgin*.

Further Reading

Sassetta is listed in the Art study guide (III, B, 1, b). He was influenced by MASACCIO. Sassetta may have worked with the Sienese sculptor Jacopo della QUERCIA.

John Pope-Hennessy's monograph *Sassetta* (1939) gives the facts of the artist's life. See also Bernhard Berenson, *A Sienese Painter of the Franciscan Legend* (1909).

SASSOON / By Robert J. Kingston

The English poet Siegfried Sassoon (1886–1967) wrote a group of dramatic, intense lyrics in reaction to the horrors of World War I. His six volumes of partly fictionalized memoirs are a detailed record of the sensibilities of his age.

Siegfried Sasson was born in Brenchley, Kent, on Sept. 8, 1886, and spent his childhood at the family home in Weirleigh, in the protected and somewhat rarefied atmosphere of a family near the center of the late Victorian and Edwardian literary and artistic world. He was formally educated at Marlborough School and at Clare College, Cambridge, and began publishing poems privately in 1906. However, Sassoon's distinctive voice was not heard until the publication of his war poems—in *The Old Huntsman* (1917) and *Counter-attack* (1918). He was the first of the younger Georgian poets to react violently against sentimentally patriotic notions of the glories of war; these poems have an extraordinary vigor—a stridency of tone, in fact—expressing with unconcealed irony and in colloquial terms a passionate hatred of the horrors of war. Some of Sassoon's contemporaries produced poems that addressed more seriously the confusion of values that World War I revealed; but none responded with such passion or with such hatred of the ignorance and folly that permitted such pain.

Sassoon's poems of the 1920s—represented in *Satirical Poems* (1926 and 1933) and in *The Road to Ruin* (1933—although they set out to satirize the corruptions and the pretensions of a disintegrating and confused materialistic society, were more controlled, artificial, less intense—and vastly less effective than the war poems.

Perhaps Sassoon's reputation will ultimately rest on his

Siegfried Sassoon, photographed in 1920 by Pirie MacDonald. (Library of Congress)

prose works. *The Memoirs of George Sherston* (1937), his three-volume fictional autobiography, describes, on one level at least, the way of life and the decline in influence of the educated, cultivated, English country gentry during the first quarter of the 20th century. More significantly, it delineates the decay of a culture and the character of an age. It is composed of *Memoirs of a Foxhunting Man* (1928), *Memoirs of an Infantry Officer* (1930), and *Sherston's Progress* (1936).

Sassoon later wrote three volumes of direct autobiography to complement his Sherston trilogy. They are brilliant evocations of characters and patterns of life in one period, but they remain fundamentally the explorations of a man whose own experience, whose own alienation, is by no means representative. These volumes are *The Old Century and Seven More Years* (1938), *The Weald of Youth* (1942), and *Siegfried's Journey* (1945).

The latter half of Sassoon's life was lived in semiretirement from the world of pressing public issues and changing literary values. His critical biography of George Meredith, published in 1948, valued Meredith largely for his "freedom of spirit" and for his unimpaired, instinctive love of nature. Sassoon died in Warminster, Wiltshire, on Sept. 1, 1967.

Further Reading

Siegfried Sassoon is listed in the Literature study guide (II, J, 2). Rupert BROOKE also wrote poetry deploring World War I.

The absence of any full-scale biography of Sassoon is offset, to a degree, by his memoirs. Much incidental criticism of his work is available in periodicals, and his war poetry is evaluated in the many studies of Georgian and war poetry. Early evaluations are in Frank Swinnerton, *The Georgian Literary Scene* (1934; rev. ed. 1951), and Edmund Blunden, *The Mind's Eye: Essays* (1934), reprinted in *Edmund Blunden: A Selection of His Poetry and Prose*, edited by Kenneth Hopkins (1950). Joseph Cohen, in a sound and comprehensive critical essay, *The Three Roles of Siegfried Sassoon* (1957), distinguished three phases of Sassoon's poetry, but the only book-length study is Michael Thorpe, *Siegfried Sasson: A Critical Study* (1966). Geoffrey Keynes prepared *A Bibliography of Siegfried Sassoon* (1962).

SATIE / By Peter S. Hansen

Erik Satie (1866–1925) was an eccentric but important French composer. His works and his attitude toward music anticipated developments of the next generation of composers.

Erik Satie (pronounced sà-tē′) was born in Honfleur to a French father and a Scottish mother. Because he showed musical talent, he was sent to the conservatory, but his real interest lay in the cafés of

Erik Satie. (H. Roger-Viollet)

Montmartre, where he played the piano and for which he composed sentimental ballads.

From the beginning Satie had a flair for novel musical ideas, and his first serious compositions reveal this originality. The *Gymnopédies* for piano (1888) avoid all the clichés of the time and strike a note of chasteness, quite different from the feverish and sentimental music of the day. His *Three Sarabandes* for piano (1887) include some very interesting parallel ninth chords that later became an important feature of the styles of Claude Debussy and Maurice Ravel. In some of his compositions of the next few years Satie used Gregorian modes as well as chords built in fourths, again anticipating musical idioms that would be extensively developed in the next 25 years.

In 1898 Satie "withdrew" to Arcueil, a suburb of Paris, where he spent the rest of his life. He lived quietly, spending a day each week with Debussy, writing café music, and studying counterpoint. He gave the piano pieces he wrote at this time ridiculous, almost surrealistically humorous titles, such as *Three Pieces in the Shape of a Pear*, *Three Flabby Preludes for a Dog*, and *Desiccated Embryos*—perhaps parodying the elaborately evocative titles Debussy sometimes gave his compositions. Satie also included in his scores such puzzling directions as "play like a nightingale with a toothache," "with astonishment," "from the top of the teeth," and "sheepishly."

Satie's tendency to underplay the importance of his compositions reached its climax in the music he wrote in 1920 for the opening of an art gallery. The score, for piano, three clarinets, and a trombone, consists of fragments of well-known tunes and isolated phrases repeated over and over, like the pattern of wallpaper. In the program he stated, "We beg you to take no notice of the music and behave as if it did not exist. This music . . . claims to make its contribution to life in the same way as a private conversation, a picture, or the chair on which you may or may not be seated."

This violently antiromantic attitude toward music attracted the attention of the group of young French composers who were to become known as "Les Six" and of Jean Cocteau, their poet–artist–publicity agent. Another group acclaimed Satie as the leader of the "School of Arcueil." Serge Diaghilev commissioned Satie to write the music for a surrealist ballet, *Parade* (1917). Cocteau wrote the libretto, and Pablo Picasso designed the cubist sets and costumes. Satie's *Mercure* (1924) and *Relâche* (1924), again with the collaboration of Picasso, anticipated surrealism with their noticeable lack of connection between the action on the stage and the mood of the music. A surrealist movie, part of the ballet, is accompanied by music that alternates between two neutral, "wallpaper" compositions.

Socrate (1919), for four solo sopranos and chamber orchestra, is a serious work. The words are fragments from three Platonic dialogues, one having to do with the death of Socrates. *Socrate* is distinguished by its atmosphere of calm and gentle repose. It is completely nondramatic, for one of the sopranos sings Socrates's words. The music consists of simple melodic lines and repetitive accompaniment figures. It is this simplicity, this avoidance of the big gesture that made Satie's music important and prophetic of an important branch of 20th-century musical developments.

Further Reading

Erik Satie is listed in the Music study guide (I, J, 2). He influenced Claude DEBUSSY and Maurice RAVEL. Members of Les Six included Arthur HONEGGER, Darius MILHAUD, and Francis POULENC.

Two studies of Satie's life and music are Pierre-Daniel Templier, *Eric Satie* (1932; trans. 1969), which contains many photographs of Satie's friends and family, and Rollo H. Myers, *Eric Satie* (1948). Roger Shattuck, *The Banquet Years* (1958), contains an interesting chapter on Satie in the context of Paris in the early years of the century.

✳ ✳ ✳

SATO / By Kenneth B. Pyle

Eisaku Sato (born 1901) was a Japanese political leader who served as prime minister longer than anyone else in Japanese history. Under his leadership Japan gradually began to translate its immense economic strength into enhanced political power in the international environment.

Eisaku Sato (pronounced sä′tō) was born on March 27, 1901, in Yamaguchi Prefecture into a family of samurai descent. His home province, Choshu, provided much of the leadership (including Sato's great-grandfather) in the movement that overthrew the Tokugawa shogunate in 1868 and established the new imperial government. During the first century after the Meiji restoration, Yamaguchi provided more premiers than any other prefecture.

Sato therefore grew up in an atmosphere highly charged with political concerns; and his mother is reported to have impressed upon her sons a sense of obligation to serve the state. Sato's eldest brother, Ichiro, became a rear admiral, retiring just prior to World War II. Another older brother, Nobusuke Kishi, served in the Hideki Tojo Cabinet as minister of commerce and industry during the war and subsequently, after serving 3 years in prison as a Class A war criminal, became a leader of the Liberal Democratic party and served as Japanese prime minister from 1957 to 1960.

Career in the Bureaucracy

Like Kishi, Sato attended Tokyo Imperial University, a ladder to success in Japanese society, and graduated in 1924 after studying German law. For a time he was interested in working for the N.Y.K. steamship line or the Ministry of Finance, but neither yielded him an opportunity, and he eventually ended up in the Transportation Ministry. His rise in the bureaucracy was not meteoric in the way Kishi's was in the Ministry of Commerce and Industry. Starting in a minor provincial post, he slowly rose through the ministerial hierarchy to become director of the Automobile Bureau. He was reportedly demoted after an argument with the deputy minister and sent to Osaka. The fact that he was not at ministerial headquarters saved him from the postwar purge.

Immediately after the war Sato was named general director of the Railway Administration and was soon promoted to deputy minister of transportation, the highest rank a civil servant could aspire to. At this juncture he made a decisive departure from his bureaucratic career.

Career in Politics

The Occupation's purge of large numbers of the prewar political elite left room for new people to enter parliamentary politics. Shigeru Yoshida, the prime minister, was in the midst of building up a strong personal following in the Diet, composed mainly of former bureaucrats. One who came to his attention was Sato. It is said that Sato's handling of troublesome new labor unions caught the attention of Yoshida. However that may be, Yoshida asked Sato, in 1948, to become his chief Cabinet secretary, a position of considerable importance in running the affairs of the Cabinet and supervising relations with the party. Sato accepted and soon after won a seat in the Diet.

Sato's association with Yoshida lasted for several years, and he was intensely loyal to the old man. Yoshida suffered public criticism in the spring of 1954, when he rescued Sato from legal charges growing out of a scandal that involved shipping interests and many top leaders of

Eisaku Sato, considered an outstanding student of calligraphy, practices with brush and ink. (Japan Information Center, London)

Yoshida's Liberal party. Sato, who was serving as secretary general of the party, was accused of having received political bribes from shipbuilding executives. Yoshida employed the powers of his office to intervene and prevent the arrest of Sato, who thereafter always maintained his innocence.

Rise to Prime Minister

In late 1954 Yoshida, whose position had been weakened by the scandal and more basically by increasing factionalism among the conservatives, was unseated by Ichiro Hatoyama. The following year Yoshida's Liberal party merged with Hatoyama's conservatives to form the Liberal-Democratic party. Behind the thin facade of party unity, factional strife continued unabated. Sato had by this time built up a strong personal following which he threw behind his brother Nobusuke Kishi, who with Sato's help became prime minister from 1957 to 1960. Sato entered the Cabinet as minister of finance. The immense popular disturbances that attended the Security Treaty crisis in 1960 toppled Kishi, who was succeeded by Hayato Ikeda.

Sato himself gradually built up his own claims to the premiership. Ikeda defeated him in a bitter struggle for the party presidency in 1964; but later in the year Ikeda, dying of cancer, was forced to retire, and Sato succeeded to the party presidency and the premiership by acclamation.

The crisis in the universities and continuing problems of Japanese-American relations were two of the major challenges confronting Sato during his term as prime minister. To deal with campus disorders, which wracked nearly all the universities in Japan, Sato's response was a bill that would allow the Ministry of Education to take over a school if the disruption persisted more than 9 months. It was evident in elections that Sato's party benefited from a hard line on student disorders.

In November 1969 Sato flew to Washington seeking to conclude negotiations for the reversion of Okinawa to Japanese sovereignty by 1972. Upon returning to Japan, he dissolved the House of Representatives, and in the

general elections held on December 27 his party won a resounding victory. In June 1971 the United States and Japan signed a treaty to restore Okinawa and the other Ryukyu Islands to Japanese sovereignty in 1972; the accord was ratified by both countries in March 1972. In July the 71-year-old premier resigned.

Further Reading

Eisaku Sato is listed in the Asia study guide (III, B, 7, d). After World War II, he, Nobusuke KISHI, and Shigeru YOSHIDA dominated Japan's political life.

There is no reliable biography of Sato. For a perceptive analysis of the workings of Japanese politics see Donald C. Hellmann, *Japanese Foreign Policy and Domestic Politics* (1969). Another useful book for understanding the intricacies of the politics in Sato's party is Nathaniel B. Thayer, *How the Conservatives Rule Japan* (1969).

* * *

SAUER / By T. W. Freeman

Carl Ortwin Sauer (born 1889) was an American geographer and anthropologist with a strong interest in historical fieldwork and other forms of geographical research.

On Dec. 24, 1889, Carl Sauer was born in Warrenton, Mo. His father taught in the Central Wesleyan College, a German Methodist enterprise, since closed. His parents sent young Sauer to a school at Calur, Württemberg, and he gained his first degree from Central Western College before his nineteenth birthday. In 1915 he earned a doctorate of philosophy from the University of Chicago, and from 1915 to 1922 he served on the staff at the University of Michigan. In 1923 he went to the University of California, Berkeley, where he remained to his retirement in 1957.

Sauer's first paper was an "outline for fieldwork" in geography, published in 1915 and developed further in 1919 and 1921 in the *Geographical Review* and the *Annals of American Geographers*. Physical geographers in America already had a long and distinguished record of field survey, but Sauer, with a few other vigorous young men in the University of Chicago, saw the potential of land-use mapping, possibly with a view to evaluation of the most suitable use. In time he saw the fascination of human settlements and other patterns in relation to the culture of the people who established them.

Sauer recognized the difficulty of reconstructing past landscapes, even in America, where some areas had been settled only for a very few generations, and he turned with admiration to such studies as the 10-volume *Corridors of Time* series (1927–1956) of H. J. E. Peake and H. J. Fleure. Perpetually concerned with the human imprint on the landscape, he said in 1956 that the geographer need not fear the expression of a value judgment, for the use of resources will influence the lives of future generations for good or evil. He also organized the international Symposium on Man's Role in Changing the Face of the Earth, held at Princeton, N.J., in 1955.

Agricultural dispersals, the origins of various cultures, the destruction of plant and animal life, the strivings of man for life under adverse conditions, and the effects of climatic change all attracted the scholarly attention of Carl Sauer. Apart from a school text, *Man in Nature: America before the Days of the White Man* (1939); the Bowman Memorial Lectures, published as *Agricultural Origins and Dispersals* (1952); and *The Early Spanish Main* (1967), virtually all his writing was in the form of articles, scholarly, fascinating, persuasive, and well documented, if at times arousing the opposition of readers.

Further Reading

Carl Sauer is listed in the Geography and Exploration study guide (VII, B). Another American geographer was Isaiah BOWMAN.

Sauer's *Land and Life*, edited by John Leighly (1963), is a selection of his papers with an introduction by Leighly. Sauer's work is briefly discussed in Richard J. Chorley and Peter Haggett, eds., *Models in Geography* (1967), and Robert E. Dickinson, *The Makers of Modern Geography* (1969).

SAUL / By Nathan H. Winter

The first king of Israel, Saul (reigned ca. 1020–1000 B.C.) was a man of valor who brought the virtues of modesty and generosity to his office.

The youngest son of Kish of the tribe of Benjamin, Saul was a modest shepherd boy, a resident of Gibeah, when the prophet Samuel, after a chance meeting, secretly chose and anointed him king of Israel. It was a period of national humiliation, for the Philistines had defeated the Israelites at Shiloh and captured the Ark of the Covenant, which symbolized the presence of God in their midst. This calamity convinced the Israelites that they must either strive for national unity with a king as leader or face complete and permanent subjugation.

Saul succeeded in freeing Israel of its enemies and extending its boundaries. He fought successfully against the Philistines, Ammonites, Moabites, Edomites, Arameans, and Amalekites. He also succeeded in drawing the tribes of Israel into a closer unity.

Saul's initial conflict with Samuel occurred after Saul offered a sacrifice to God, thereby assuming Samuel's office. Samuel rebuked Saul and proclaimed that Saul's dynasty would not be continued on the throne of Israel. Their second disagreement took place after Saul retained the war booty of the defeated Amalekites, Israel's traditional enemy, and spared the life of their king, Agag. Samuel publicly pronounced Saul's deposition from the throne. Saul fell into a state of melancholia that developed into an emotional disorder.

Saul's fits of depression and his moody, suspicious temperament caused him to attack the lad David, who had been brought into his household to soothe him by

David Playing the Harp before Saul, *a painting by Rembrandt. (Mauritshuis, The Hague; Foto A. Dingjan)*

playing music. Jealous of David, Saul persecuted him, attacked him, sent him on perilous expeditions, and finally made him into an outlaw.

The Philistines then renewed their attack on Israel. Without David's support and depressed by the feeling that God had deserted him, Saul consulted a witch of Endor, seeking to recall the spirit of the dead Samuel. He was reproached and advised of his impending doom. In a battle against the Philistines Saul fought valiantly but vainly. His forces routed and his three sons slain, Saul died by his own hand. The tragic tale is told by David in an exquisite elegy lamenting the death of Saul and Jonathan. It is one of the most beautiful poems in the Bible.

The affection in which Saul was held is reflected in the action of the men of Yabesh-gilead, whose city he had saved in his first act as monarch. They risked their lives to rescue his body from the Philistines and gave it an honorable burial.

Further Reading

Saul is listed in the Religion study guide (II, A, 5). He disagreed with SAMUEL and was succeeded by DAVID.

Although there is no single authoritative biography of Saul, there are numerous volumes of fiction, making it difficult to distinguish between historical and legendary accounts. An excellent short essay on him is in Rudolph Kittel, *Great Men and Movements in Israel* (trans. 1929). For historical background the following works are recommended: William Foxwell Albright, *From the Stone Age to Christianity* (1940; 2d ed. with new introduction, 1957); Max I. Magolis and Alexander Marx, *A History of the Jewish People* (1944); Salo Wittmayer Baron, *A Social and Religious History of the Jews*, vol. 1 (2d ed. 1952; 2d rev. ed. 1969); and Martin Noth, *The History of Israel* (trans. 1958; 2d ed. 1960).

* * *

SAUNDERS / By John H. Archer

Sir Charles Edward Saunders (1867–1937) was a Canadian cerealist who developed early-maturing hard spring wheat—in particular, Marquis wheat, an early high-protein variety.

Charles Edward Saunders was born in London, Ontario, on Feb. 2, 1867, son of William and Sarah Agnes Robinson Saunders. He received his early education in the elementary and collegiate system in London and his university education at the University of Toronto, Johns Hopkins University, and the Sorbonne. He married Mary Blackwell of Toronto in 1892.

Saunders began an academic career as professor of chemistry and geology at Central University, Ky., in 1893. Within 2 years, however, he turned to a musical career in Toronto, where, in addition to acting as an agent, he gave lessons in singing and flute playing and wrote as

Sir Charles Edward Saunders. (Radio Times Hulton Picture Library)

music critic in a newspaper. His musical career was not a financial success, however, and in 1903 he accepted appointment as Dominion cerealist at the Experimental Farm in Ottawa. The new work was not a break with family tradition, for Saunders's father had founded the system of experimental farms established in Canada, and his brother, Percy, had done considerable work in cross-breeding strains of wheat.

Saunders turned enthusiastically to his new tasks. Following up his brother's research, he developed Marquis wheat in 1904, a variety which showed marked superiority in milling quality for bread flour over other varieties popular in western Canada. Marquis had the advantage of maturing 10 days earlier than its competitors—a factor of great importance in the Canadian wheat belt. The Indian Head Experimental Farm in Saskatchewan raised Marquis wheat for seed, and by 1909 its use was widespread. By 1920 90 percent of the wheat grown in western Canada was Marquis. However, Marquis was not resistant to stem rust. In seeking newer and better varieties Saunders developed three other strains of wheat—Ruby, Garnet, and Reward—specifically adapted to prairie conditions. He was also responsible for improved varieties of oats and barley.

In 1922 Saunders retired and turned to the study of French, a subject which had always attracted him. He spent the years 1922–1925 at the Sorbonne, returning to Canada to write a book, *Essais et vers*, in 1928. In recognition of his work in the French language he was decorated by the French government and was presented with the Medaille de l'Académie Française.

Saunders won honor in his own country also. He was elected a fellow of the Royal Society of Canada in 1921 and won the society's Flavelle Medal in 1925. He was knighted in 1933. He died on July 25, 1937.

Further Reading

Sir Charles Edward Saunders is listed in the Canada study guide (IV, B, 2). Henry A. WALLACE developed several strains of hybrid corn that were as important to American farmers as Marquis wheat was to Canadians.

The best book on Saunders and his family is Elsie M. Pomeroy, *William Saunders and His Five Sons* (1956).

* * *

SAVAGE / By J. J. Eddy

Michael Joseph Savage (1872–1940) was a prime minister of New Zealand and a labor leader. He won a high place in his nation's esteem for the social and political leadership he offered in a time of depression and economic insecurity.

Michael Joseph Savage. (New Zealand House, London)

Michael Joseph Savage was born on March 23, 1872, near Benalla in Victoria, Australia. His parents were among the first Irish settlers of the colony. Educated up to the age of 14 at the local state school, Savage worked as a store hand for some years, during which he and his family experienced the full weight of the depression of the 1890s. After a period of unemployment and farm laboring in New South Wales, Savage returned in 1900 to Victoria, where he took up gold mining for a living. Already known as a fine debater, he helped establish and manage a cooperative and a local labor league.

In 1907 Savage emigrated to New Zealand in order to join friends who had moved there from Victoria. Instead of going to the mining areas on the west coast, he stayed on in the North Island working as a miller and later as a cellarman. He never married.

Union Leader

Savage represented Auckland at the National Conference of Trades and Labour Councils of 1910 and in the next year stood as a parliamentary candidate of the New Zealand Socialist party for the seat of Auckland Central. He was unsuccessful, and he again failed as a candidate for the Social Democratic party in 1914. Despite the splintering of the unionist groups, the burly Savage was emerging as a popular figure.

When the New Zealand Labour party was formed in 1916, he became a member and was eventually elected national secretary in 1919. In the general election of December 1919 he won the seat of Auckland West and kept this seat for the rest of his life. In 1923 he was voted deputy leader of the parliamentary Labour party.

Prominent for his championing of the working man, Savage concentrated during his political career on social questions. When Harry Holland died in October 1933, Savage had become sufficiently trusted by his colleagues to be elected leader of the Labour party, and in the depression years from 1933 to 1935 he made a great impression on the New Zealand public with his sympathetic manner, humane sincerity, and common sense.

His Government

The election of 1935 was a spectacular victory for Labour, which under Savage's leadership had gained a moderate, or middle-of-the road, reputation with the electorate. As prime minister, Savage bore responsibility also for external affairs, native affairs, and broadcasting. He had a flair for publicity and in 1936 introduced the broadcasting of parliamentary proceedings.

In 1937 Savage went to London to attend the Imperial Conference and sought guarantees from the British for defense against possible Japanese attack. On his failure to obtain specific agreements he initiated a defense conference with Britain and Australia at Wellington in April 1939. Reluctantly he became concerned that New Zealand should rearm heavily, and he threw his considerable influence behind the recruiting campaign which preceded the outbreak of war in September.

During Savage's time as prime minister the foundations were laid for a very comprehensive social security scheme. He was not by any means a doctrinaire socialist, and he referred to his Social Security Bill as "applied Christianity." In 1938 his popularity assured the Labour party of an even more significant electoral victory than that of 1935.

In 1938 Savage's health deteriorated, however, and divisions within the party further sapped his strength and taxed his considerable skill in public relations. By August 1939 he was forced to hand over his duties to Peter Fraser, who became acting prime minister. Savage died in Wellington on March 27, 1940.

Not as well read or as able as Holland or Fraser, Savage was nevertheless an affable, popular, and shrewd father figure for a small democracy which seemed intent on giving high priority to personal and social security. His simplicity appealed to the plain man in the street and gave New Zealand government a human touch.

Further Reading

Michael Joseph Savage is listed in the Australia and New Zealand study guide (III, B). His successor, Peter FRASER, became one of the founding fathers of the United Nations.

John A. Lee, *Simple on a Soap-box* (1964), is an autobiography by a former colleague of Savage and contains extensive material on him. His career is well covered in Bruce M. Brown, *The Rise of New Zealand Labour* (1962). For background material see Frederick L. W. Wood, *The New Zealand People at War* (1958), and Keith Sinclair, *A History of New Zealand* (1959; rev. ed. 1969).

SAVIGNY / By Lothar L. Tresp

The German jurist Friedrich Karl von Savigny (1779–1861) advocated the doctrine of historical continuity, according to which historical rather than natural rights and actual historical facts rather than legal theory were the bases for legal systems.

Friedrich Karl von Savigny (pronounced säv′ĭn-yē) was born on Feb. 21, 1779, in Frankfurt am Main, one of 13 children. By the time he reached the age of 13, he had lost all his brothers and sisters and his parents.

In 1795 Savigny entered the University of Marburg, and in 1800 he received his doctor of laws degree. He began a teaching career as privatdozent (unpaid lecturer) the same year. His first major work, *Das Recht des Besitzes* (1803; *The Law of Possession*), was well received by other jurists.

In 1804 Savigny married Kunigunde Brentano, the sister of Clemens Brentano, the poet, and the young couple set out on an extended study tour through France and southern Germany to collect legal materials for Savigny's

planned work on the history of medieval law. Upon their return in 1808, he accepted a professorship in Roman law at the University of Landshut in Bavaria. Two years later, at the instigation of Wilhelm von Humboldt, who was assembling a faculty at the new University of Berlin, Savigny moved to the Prussian capital as professor of Roman law. He joined the commission for the establishment of the university and organized the law faculty and a *Spruch-Collegium* as an extraordinary tribunal for the purpose of delivering opinions on cases submitted by lower courts.

In 1814 Savigny issued a protest pamphlet, *Vom Beruf unserer Zeit für Gesetzgebung und Rechtswissenschaft* (On the Vocation of Our Age for Legislation and Jurisprudence), where he spoke out against the pamphlet by the famous Heidelberg jurist A. F. J. Thibaut entitled *On the Necessity of a General Code for Germany* (1814). Thibaut had advocated the establishment of a completely new civil and criminal code of German law, pointing out that the presently used chief sources were based on Roman law, "the work of a nation which was very unlike us, and from the period of the lowest decline of the same." Savigny maintained that "law comes into being through custom and popular acceptance, through internal, silently working forces and not through the arbitrariness of a law giver." The historical continuity prevalent in the sources of Roman law was a better foundation for a legal system than the arrogance and shallow philosophy of the so-called "natural law."

In 1815 Savigny, Karl Friedrich Eichhorn, the author of

Friedrich Karl von Savigny, an engraving by Carl Mayer, in the Civica Raccolta Stampe Bertarelli, Milan. (Editorial Photocolor Archives, Inc.)

the multivolume *History of German Law and Institutions*, and the publisher Johann Friedrich Ludwig Göschen founded the *Zeitschrift für geschichtliche Rechtswissenschaft*, which became the organ of the new historical school of jurisprudence. The same year Savigny published the first volume of his monumental *Geschichte des römischen Rechts im Mittelalter* (6 vols., 1815–1831; *History of Roman Law in the Middle Ages*). He described the survival of Roman law in western Europe and stimulated at the same time historical writing based on actual source materials.

Between 1817 and 1822 Savigny served on various legal boards. Because of a serious nervous illness he sought relief and recuperation in travel, spending more than a year in Italy, where he completed a number of smaller writings while continuing work on his *History of Roman Law*. In the late 1830s he undertook another major research project which culminated in the publication of *Das System des heutigen römischen Rechts* (8 vols., 1840–1849; *The System of Contemporary Usage of Roman Law*).

In 1842 Savigny's teaching career came to an end when he was appointed *Grosskanzler* (high chancellor), a position which put him in charge of the Prussian Ministry of Legislation, which was being separated from the administration of justice. The main legal concerns during his tenure dealt with bills of exchange, divorce regulations, and questions of civil and criminal court procedures. He retired from office in 1848. In 1853 he added to his earlier writings on contemporary Roman law with the treatise *Das Obligationenrecht* (*The Law of Obligations*). He died on Oct. 25, 1861, in Berlin.

Although Savigny was not the founder of the historical school of jurisprudence, he was its most famous representative. Many of his interpretations were challenged during his lifetime and later, but by reintroducing the juridical methods of Roman law he provided an important impetus for the study of modern law.

Further Reading

Friedrich Karl von Savigny is listed in the Social Sciences study guide (VI, A, 2). Another admirer of Roman institutions, though from a historical viewpoint, was Barthold Georg NIEBUHR.

There is no full-length biography of Savigny in English. A short but useful introduction to Savigny's work is in G. P. Gooch, *History and Historians in the Nineteenth Century* (1913). The Thibaut-Savigny controversy is described in A. W. Small, *Origins of Sociology* (1924), which also deals with other German historians and writers and their impact on the social sciences.

SAVONAROLA / By Joseph N. Scionti

The Italian religious reformer Girolamo Savonarola (1452–1498) became dictator of Florence in the 1490s and instituted there, in the middle of the Renaissance, a reign of purity and asceticism.

Girolamo Savonarola (pronounced sä-vō-nä-rō′lä) was born in Ferrara on Sept. 21, 1452. He was the third of seven children of Niccolo Savonarola, a physician, and Elena Bonacossi. His father groomed Girolamo for the medical profession, but even as a youth he took more interest in the writings of the Schoolmen, particularly Thomas Aquinas. Savonarola had time for neither the comfortable, courtly life of his father's household nor youthful sports and exercises, so absorbed was he in the subtleties of the scholastics and their spiritual father, Aristotle.

Repelled by the corruption of the world around him, Savonarola withdrew ever further into solitude, meditation, and prayer. In 1475 he entered a Dominican monastery at Bologna. After living quietly there for 6 years, Savonarola transferred to the convent of S. Marco in Florence and began preaching in the church of S. Lorenzo. His style, laden with scholastic didacticism, was not appealing, and few came to hear him. In 1486, however, while preaching in Lombardy, he shed all syllogisms and circumlocutions and began to speak directly, simply, and passionately of the wrath of God. His popularity as a

Girolamo Savonarola, a portrait by his disciple Fra Bartolommeo, in the Museo di S. Marco, Florence. (Courtesy of The New-York Historical Society, New York)

The execution of Savonarola in the Piazza della Signoria, Florence, a painting by a contemporaneous artist, in the Museo di S. Marco, Florence. Savonarola was led to the stake from the Palazzo Vecchio, in which he had been imprisoned. (Museo San Marco, Florence)

preacher grew immensely.

Savonarola's fame spread to Florence as he prophesied the doom of all tyrants who then prevailed in the world. In 1490, through the influence of Pico della Mirandola, he was called back to Florence and in July 1491 became prior of S. Marco. All the while he thundered against the vanity of the humanists and the viciousness of the clergy. Because he spared no one, Lorenzo de' Medici, the ruler of Florence, urged him to bridle his tongue. He would not yield, and in April 1492 Savonarola refused to grant Lorenzo absolution because the ruler would not give liberty to the Florentines.

Lorenzo's son and successor, Piero, was weak, and the 2-year period of his rule witnessed Savonarola's rise to the most powerful authority in the city. He acquired with difficulty the consent of the new pope, Alexander VI, to sever his convent from the Lombard Congregation of the Dominican order. Then, as leader of an independent monastic house, Savonarola instituted reforms that inspired respect and swelled the ranks of recruits. Admiration and wonder filled Florentine hearts when the prophecies that accompanied his fiery denunciations proved frighteningly accurate. He had predicted the deaths of Lorenzo and Pope Innocent VIII in 1492. Now Savonarola foretold the terrible fate about to descend upon Italy as punishment for the sins of its tyrants and priests. Early in 1494 he told his congregation that Charles VIII, King of France, would invade Italy and that this would be divine retribution. In September the prophecy was fulfilled.

Savonarola as Dictator

When Charles arrived in Florentine territory, Piero surrendered to the invader. When the Florentine Signory heard of this, they angrily deposed Piero and revived the republic. A delegation including Savonarola met Charles at Pisa and attempted to persuade him to moderate his demands. The King showed that he was not so disposed. After he entered Florence on Nov. 17, 1494, Charles insisted on exorbitant indemnities, yielding only to the eloquence of Savonarola, who persuaded him to reduce his demands and leave the city. Upon Charles's departure Florence's grateful citizens placed themselves in the hands of the monk.

Like the Medici before him, Savonarola held no public office, but under his guidance a new constitution was promulgated, establishing a new republic on June 10, 1495. He initiated the abrogation of arbitrary taxation and its replacement with a 10 percent tax on all real property. He undertook the immediate relief of the poor and the strict administration of justice. He also instituted a regime of austerity that seemed out of place in the Florence of the High Renaissance. Hymns supplanted profane songs, art objects and luxuries were cast aside or burned, and somber unadorned clothing was worn by all.

Fall from Power

At the height of his power, Savonarola made bitter

enemies both at home and abroad. The Arrabiati, or Medicean adherents in Florence, and Pope Alexander VI were eager to rid Florence of the troublesome monk. Alexander's motives were mainly political, for he was angered by Savonarola's alliance with France. He was also displeased at the public criticism leveled by Savonarola against his scandalous pontificate. Twice in 1495 the Pope summoned Savonarola to Rome and ordered him to stop preaching, but the monk refused to obey. On May 5, 1497, encouraged by the Arrabiati, Alexander excommunicated him. Savonarola remained rebellious and continued to celebrate Mass. Alexander then warned the Signory that unless Savonarola was silenced he would place an interdict upon the city. On March 17, 1498, the Signory ordered Savonarola to stop preaching, and he obeyed.

By this time the Florentines had grown weary of puritanic life. Maddened by disappointment when an ordeal by fire to which Savonarola had been challenged did not take place because of rain, they joined the Arrabiati. With unexampled fickleness, the Florentines demanded Savonarola's arrest. A mob attacked the monastery of S. Marco, and peace was restored only when Savonarola himself begged all men to lay down their arms. Savonarola was tortured until he confessed many crimes, and on May 23, 1498, convicted falsely of heresy, he was burned at the stake in the Piazza della Signoria.

Further Reading

Girolamo Savonarola is listed in the Religion study guide (I, F, 4; I, G, 1). ALEXANDER VI regarded Savonarola as a political threat because of the monk's support of France.

The definitive work on Savonarola is Pasquale Villari, *The Life and Times of Girolamo Savonarola*, translated by Linda Villari (1889). Donald Weinstein, *Savonarola and Florence: Prophesy and Patriotism in the Renaissance* (1971), emphasizes the impact of Florence on the reformer. Also useful is Ralph Roeder, *The Man of the Renaissance* (1933). Still excellent is Ludwig Pastor, *History of the Popes*, vol. 3 (1898).

✳ ✳ ✳

SAXE / By Martin Blumenson

Hermann Maurice, Comte de Saxe (1696–1750), was a marshal of France. His active campaigns, methods of organizing and training troops, and general principles of warfare influenced both his own and later times.

Maurice de Saxe (pronounced săks), who is known as Marshal Saxe, was born in Dresden on Oct. 28, 1696, the first of the 354 acknowledged illegitimate children of Augustus II, Elector of Saxony and King of Poland. His mother was the Countess

Maurice de Saxe, a painting by Maurice Quentin de La Tour, in the Louvre, Paris. (Alinari)

Aurora von Konigsmark. Like his father in "his fabulous strength, the immensity of his appetites, and his limitless lust," Saxe also possessed a high intelligence.

When he was 12 years old, Saxe entered the Saxon army. He fought in the battle of Malplaquet under the Duke of Marlborough and Eugene of Savoy. By the time of the Peace of Utrecht, he had participated in four campaigns in Flanders and Pomerania and had commanded a cavalry regiment. He served under Eugene in the war against the Turks, and in 1717 he took part in the capture of Belgrade.

In 1720 Saxe went to Paris, becoming a camp marshal to the Duc d'Orléans. When his father died, he was offered the command of the Saxon army, but he preferred to remain in France. Saxe fought in the War of the Polish Succession (1733–1738) as a lieutenant general. In the War of the Austrian Succession (1740–1748), after leading his troops in a successful surprise attack on Prague in 1741, he restrained them from pillaging the city.

In 1743, made marshal of France, Saxe was placed in command of an army assembling at Dunkirk for a proposed invasion of England. When France declared war on England in 1744, he took operational command of the main army in Flanders, led personally by Louis XV. Later Saxe took full control.

In May 1745 Saxe led his army of about 70,000 men to Tournai and invested the city, which was defended by 50,000 English troops. On May 10 he moved 52,000 troops to Fontenay to block an allied relief force, which he defeated. Then he took Tournai, Ghent, Bruges, Audenarde, Ostende, and Brussels. These battles, plus Rascoux in 1746 and the capture of Maastricht in 1748, firmly established Saxe's reputation. In gratitude for his services, Louis XV gave him life tenure of the château of Chambord.

There Saxe wrote *Mes rêveries* (*My Reveries*), his reflections on the art of war. His descriptions of how to raise and train recruits and how to establish garrison and field camps soon became standard procedure. Saxe stimulated acceptance of breech-loading muskets and cannon and invented a gun capable of accompanying the infantry. He rediscovered and initiated the practice of marching in cadence, lost since the Romans. He also modified the normal linear battle formations and tactics of his day by using an embryonic form of attack column that required less training and became the usual assault method a hundred years later.

A fearless man in battle, Saxe led a dissolute life of debauchery between campaigns. He died at Chambord on Nov. 30, 1750.

Further Reading

Maurice de Saxe is listed in the European History study guide (VI, B, 1). EUGENE OF SAVOY and the Duke of MARLBOROUGH were other noted military leaders of this period.

The standard works for information on Saxe are Leslie H. Thornton, *Campaigners Grave and Gay* (1925), and Jon Manship White, *Marshal of France: The Life and Times of Maurice, Comte de Saxe* (1962). See also Basil Henry Liddell Hart, *Great Captains Unveiled* (1927); Edmund B. D'Auvergne, *The Prodigious Marshal* (1931); and Thomas R. Phillips, ed., *Roots of Strategy* (1940).

SAY / By William Jaffé

The French economist Jean Baptiste Say (1767–1832), one of the founders of the classical school, is best known for his law of markets. He was the first academic teacher of economics in France.

Jean Baptiste Say (pronounced sā) was born on Jan. 5, 1767, in Lyons of a Protestant merchant family. Though he became a deist, he retained the deep-rooted sense of moral earnestness he inherited from the martyrs of the revocation of the Edict of Nantes. His outlook was no less affected by his mercantile upbringing and education. After serving two business apprenticeships in England, he entered an insurance firm in Paris, and at the suggestion of his employer he read Adam Smith's *Wealth of Nations*. Thereupon he decided to become an economist, abandoning business to write economic articles for a republican periodical, *La Décade philosophique*, of which he was editor.

During the French Revolution, Say espoused its principles and in 1792 fought in defense of the republic. Under the Consulate, he was made a member of the Tribunate, but when he refused on principle to acquiesce to Napoleon's financial policies, he was shorn of his high official position and became a successful textile manufacturer in the north of France, where he introduced the new cotton-spinning methods copied from England. After Napoleon's fall, Say returned to Paris and instituted a series of public lectures on political economy at the Athénée. In 1819 he was appointed the first incumbent of the chair in industrial economy at the Museum of Arts and Crafts, and in 1830 he became the first professor of political economy at the Collège de France.

In his major work, *A Treatise on Political Economy* (1803), Say improved upon Smith's *Wealth of Nations* in form and content. His tripartite division of the classical doctrine into production, distribution, and consumption set a precedent which was followed in standard treatises for more than a century. He gave precision to the concept of the entrepreneur, whom Smith had failed to distinguish from the capitalist investor. Viewing the entrepreneur as buyer and coordinator of the services of land, labor, and capital, Say envisaged production essentially as a market phenomenon. This led him to his famous "law of markets," according to which production, by generating income flows without any leakage into monetary hoards, automatically assured effective demand for aggregate output. Siding with James Mill and David Ricardo, but against Thomas Malthus, he held that general gluts were impossible. Controversy over "Say's law" continues to this day, especially since it was attacked by John Maynard Keynes. Moreover, Say repudiated the labor-cost theory of value and stressed utility as the cause of value. The subsequent development of general equilibrium economics owes much to Say's contribution.

Say's introduction to economics, the ideological flavor he imparted to it, and the social purpose he hoped it

Jean Baptiste Say, a print in the Bibliothèque Nationale, Paris. (Bulloz)

would fulfill are all reflections of his life and times. In his teaching, as in his voluminous writings, which include a *Catechism of Political Economy* (1817) and *A Complete Course in Practical Political Economy* (1828–1829), his aim was to lay a new moral foundation of society by revealing economics as a science of laws of nature which cannot be violated without bad effect. Say was thus an apostle of economic liberalism, utterly opposed to government intervention in business and to all socialistic schemes. For him, moral legitimacy attaches to a social order in which individual self-interest is the only guiding rule. After his death on Nov. 15, 1832, his son Horace and his grandson Léon, who were also economists, helped propagate this ultraliberal doctrine, which dominated French economics throughout the 19th century.

Further Reading

Jean Baptiste Say is listed in the Social Sciences study guide (VI, C, 2). He, Adam SMITH, David RICARDO, and Thomas MALTHUS founded the classical school of economics.

Although there is no book in English on the life and writings of Say, useful appreciations of his contributions and historical background are in J. A. Schumpeter, *History of Economic Analysis* (1954), and Leo Rogin, *The Meaning and Validity of Economic Theory* (1956).

* * *

SAYRE / By David K. Wyatt

Francis Bowes Sayre (1885–1972) was an American law teacher and public official. He was responsible for negotiating the treaties with European powers which ended extraterritoriality in Thailand.

Francis Sayre was born on April 30, 1885, in South Bethlehem, Pa., the son of Robert Heysham Sayre (1824–1907), a civil engineer and official of the Lehigh Valley Railroad. He graduated from Williams College in 1909 and from the Harvard Law School in 1912. Theodore Roosevelt assisted in obtaining his first job, as a deputy assistant to the district attorney of New York County. He married Jessie Woodrow Wilson, daughter of President Woodrow Wilson, in a White House ceremony in 1913.

Offered a position as instructor in government and assistant to the president of Williams College, Sayre returned there in 1914 and then went back to the Harvard Law School in 1917 to study for the doctorate in jurisprudence, which he received in 1918. He remained on the Harvard faculty until 1934, teaching international, maritime, and criminal law, and taught the first course on labor law offered in any law school.

When Eldon James, third in a series of Harvard law professors to serve as adviser in foreign affairs to the government of Siam, returned to Cambridge in 1923,

Francis Sayre in 1947. (National Archives, Washington, D.C.)

Sayre was chosen to succeed him and went to Bangkok intending to serve only a year. He went at a time when decades-long negotiations to end the unequal treaties of the previous century were stalled. Sayre gave new direction to discussions with the French in Bangkok and, on suggesting that more rapid progress could be made by negotiating with the European powers directly, he took charge of treaty negotiations in Europe in 1924–1925.

Against considerable obstacles, treaties with 10 nations were concluded which ended extraterritoriality and lifted restrictions on Thai import duties. A superbly effective and principled negotiator, Sayre was entitled *Phya Kalyan Maitri* and appointed permanent minister plenipotentiary and Siam's representative on the Permanent Court of Arbitration at The Hague.

Returning to Harvard as a full professor, Sayre again entered public service as Massachusetts state commissioner of correction in 1932 and then, in 1933, as an assistant secretary of state in charge of the negotiation of trade agreements in the first Roosevelt administration. Serving also as chairman of the interdepartmental commission on the Philippines, he was appointed U.S. high commissioner to the Philippines in 1939 and was evacuated by submarine in 1942.

Sayre became diplomatic adviser to the United Nations Relief and Rehabilitation Administration (1944–1947) and then U.S. representative on the Trusteeship Council of the UN (1947–1952), of which he was the first president. In 1952–1954 he was the personal representative in Japan of the presiding bishop of the Protestant Episcopal Church, service in which his high Christian ideals were more explicitly but no less strongly expressed than in his more public appointments. Sayre died in Washington, D.C., on March 29, 1972.

Further Reading

Francis Sayre is listed in the Asia study guide (IV, A, 2, d). Both Frank MURPHY and Leonard WOOD were also governors general in the Philippines. PRIDI Phanomyong was an important Thai political leader shortly after Sayre's departure.

Sayre's autobiography, *Glad Adventure* (1957), is an unusually lively and expressive self-portrait. His views on international trade are in his *The Way Forward: The American Trade Agreements Program* (1939). For background information on Sayre as assistant secretary of state see Samuel Flagg Bemis, ed., *The American Secretaries of State and Their Diplomacy*, vols. 12 and 13 by Julius W. Pratt (1964).

✳ ✳ ✳

A. SCARLATTI / By R. Alec Harman

Pietro Alessandro Gaspare Scarlatti (1660–1725) was an Italian composer. Over 600 of his chamber cantatas survive; they represent the peak of the genre. The most outstanding and influential operatic writer of his day, he founded the so-called Neapolitan opera school.

The operas by Alessandro Scarlatti (pronounced skär-lät′ē) that primarily influenced his younger contemporaries were written during his first sojourn in Naples, when he felt obliged to cater to Neapolitan taste—one that preferred simple, immediately attractive melodies, embellished with coloratura, and that elevated the importance of the solo singer, especially the castrato, to unprecedented heights, and, as a result, severely limited the number of ensembles and the role of the orchestra. Three other important features of this period are the increasing use of the da capo form of aria, which by the turn of the century virtually ousted all other forms; the establishing of the so-called Italian overture, or sinfonia, as a tripartite form—quick, slow, quick—first introduced in the 1696 revival of Scarlatti's *Tutto il mal ...* (1681); and the inclusion in most of the operas of two comic characters who are an integral part of the plot.

Scarlatti's greatest operas are those he wrote after he left Naples in 1702. In them the orchestra is more important and colorful, the melodies are more subtly expressive and phrased, the harmony is clearer and more varied, and the texture ranges from simple homophony to rich polyphony. It was these operas that influenced, in varying degrees and in different ways, such composers as George Frederick Handel, Johann Adolf Hasse, and Scarlatti's son Domenico, the last two being among the most significant figures in the transition period between the baroque and the Viennese school of the late 18th century.

Scarlatti was born in Palermo on May 2, 1660, the eldest son of Pietro and Eleonora d'Amato Scarlata. Details of his early life are sketchy; he probably went to relatives in Rome in 1672 in company with his two sisters, Anna Maria and Melchiorra, and, tradition has it, became a pupil of Giacomo Carissimi. This tradition is supported by the earliest record of Scarlatti as a musician, namely, a commission, dated Jan. 27, 1679, to compose an oratorio for the Arciconfraternità del SS. Crocifisso, for which Carissimi had written several similar works.

In April of the previous year Scarlatti married Antonia Anzalone; they had 10 children, of whom by far the most distinguished was Domenico. The first of Scarlatti's op-

Alessandro Scarlatti, a portrait by an unknown painter, in the Conservatorio di Bologna. (Editorial Photocolor Archives, Inc.)

eras to bring him fame, *Gli equivoci nel sembiante* (1679), also brought him an appointment, for the libretto of his next opera, *L'honestà negli amori* (1680), describes him as chapelmaster (*maestro di cappella*) to Queen Christina of Sweden, who spent most of her life in Rome after her abdication.

In 1683 Scarlatti was put in charge of the entire opera season at Naples, producing in December his first original work for the city, *Psiche*. The following year he became chapelmaster to the royal chapel in Naples, an appointment that was largely, if not wholly, due to an influential official whose mistress was Scarlatti's sister Melchiorra. In the ensuing scandal the highly esteemed second chapelmaster, Provenzale, who had expected to be promoted, resigned, the official was fired, and Melchiorra was ordered to leave the city or enter a convent!

During the next 18 years Scarlatti composed at least 38 operas, in addition to serenatas, cantatas, and church music; all but six of the operas were performed initially in Naples, and many of them received performances elsewhere. But although his fame was spreading, Scarlatti was becoming increasingly frustrated by the kind of music he was expected to produce. In 1702 he was granted 4 months' leave of absence, but once out of Naples it is clear he had no intention of returning, and for the next 7 years he looked in vain for a position that would satisfy his needs and wishes.

At first Scarlatti enjoyed the patronage of Prince Ferdinand de' Medici in Florence, for whose private theater he wrote several operas; no permanent position transpired, however, and in 1703 he accepted a very inferior post as assistant chapelmaster at the church of S. Maria

Maggiore, Rome. In 1707 he became principal chapel-master, but this did nothing to lessen his frustration, for in Rome at this time opera was virtually nonexistent, owing to strong papal disapproval. But he continued to write operas for Prince Ferdinand, most of which have not survived, and composed his first opera for Venice (1707), where he spent some months.

Although Scarlatti's operatic production had waned during this period, his reputation had not, and in 1709 he returned to his old post at Naples, with an increase in salary and free to compose as he wished. Here he remained until 1717, producing some of his best operas, notably *Tigrane* (1715), and receiving a knighthood from the Pope the following year. But Rome still held a great fascination for him, and in 1717, encouraged by a change in the papal attitude toward opera, he settled there. In the ensuing 5 years or so he composed his last works for the stage, including his one comic essay in the genre, *I trionfo dell'onore* (1718), and, according to the libretto, his 114th opera—*Griselda* (1721). (This is the last of 35 complete extant operas from a known total of 115.)

In 1722 or 1723 Scarlatti returned to Naples, where he lived in complete retirement, composing very little, and virtually ignored. In 1724 Hasse, then aged 25, became his pupil and close friend. Scarlatti died on Oct. 24, 1725.

Further Reading

Alessandro Scarlatti is listed in the Music study guide (I, D, 1). He may have studied with a leading master of the oratorio, Giacomo CARISSIMI. Scarlatti's late operas influenced his son, Domenico SCARLATTI, and George Frederick HANDEL. Giovanni Battista PERGOLESI and Domenico CIMAROSA were opera composers of the Neapolitan school.

An old but still useful biography of Scarlatti is Edward J. Dent, *Alessandro Scarlatti* (1905; rev. ed. 1960). He is discussed in Manfred F. Bukofzer, *Music in the Baroque Era* (1947), and Donald J. Grout, *A Short History of Opera* (1947; 2d ed. 1965).

* * *

D. SCARLATTI / By Gloria Rose

Domenico Scarlatti (1685–1757) was an Italian harpsichordist and composer. His harpsichord sonatas are highly distinctive and original.

Domenico Scarlatti was born in Naples on Oct. 26, 1685, the son of Alessandro Scarlatti, the most famous composer in Italy in the early 18th century. Other members of the Scarlatti family were active as professional musicians. This background may have helped Domenico, for it encouraged his musical gifts and provided contacts in the musical profession. On the other hand, it gave him the problem of developing in his own way while under the influence of his father. Alessandro was not only a composer of genius, but a man of strong personality who did not get along well with some of his pupils and colleagues.

It is natural to assume, though there is no actual proof, that Domenico studied first with his father. As early as 1701, Domenico was appointed organist in the royal chapel at Naples. The following year he went to Florence with his father and stayed there for 4 months. Domenico then returned to Naples, where several operas of his were produced in 1703 and 1704.

A more important trip for Domenico occurred in 1708, when he went to Venice. There he became acquainted with Francesco Gasparini, a leading composer and the author of an excellent treatise on thorough-bass. It has been assumed, though again not proved, that Domenico studied with Gasparini in Venice. Also while he was in Venice, Domenico met and struck up a friendship with a young man, his exact contemporary, who was to become even more celebrated a composer: George Frederick Handel. It is from this period in Venice that we have our first report of Domenico's harpsichord playing. It describes how he played at a private musical gathering and astonished his audience by his brilliant virtuoso performance.

For the next 10 years Scarlatti worked in Rome. From 1709 to 1714 he was in the service of Maria Casimira, Queen of Poland, and for her private theater he wrote a number of operas. When Maria Casimira left Rome in 1714, Scarlatti became chapelmaster of the Portuguese ambassador. Then, from 1715 to 1719, he served as chapelmaster of the Cappella Giulia in the Vatican.

In 1720, or shortly before, Scarlatti left Italy; although he later returned to his native country, it seems that he never again took up a permanent post there. Probably in 1720 he was appointed chapelmaster of the royal chapel in Lisbon. This proved to be a most consequential appointment for Scarlatti. One of his duties was to teach members of the royal Portuguese family, and one of these members, the Infanta Maria Barbara, was a gifted and enthusiastic pupil. Her devotion to music was no passing fancy: she practiced and played the harpsichord apparently all her life. She also remained devoted to her teacher.

After Maria Barbara married Fernando, Prince of Asturias, in 1729, she moved to the Spanish court at Ma-

Domenico Scarlatti. (Library of Congress)

drid, and Scarlatti went with her. He remained in her service for the rest of his life. He was knighted in Madrid in 1738; he married a Spanish woman, after the death of his first (Italian) wife; and he died in Madrid on July 23, 1757.

Scarlatti wrote 12 operas (2 of which were written in collaboration with other composers), chamber cantatas, sacred music, and over 550 sonatas for harpsichord. He composed much of his vocal music, both sacred and secular, before he settled in Spain. Most of it is characteristic music of the period: well composed but not particularly individual. A few of his vocal works are outstanding. But by and large Scarlatti was not at his best in writing for the voice. His true genius is revealed rather in his sonatas for harpsichord.

These sonatas are so individual, so varied in their forms and styles, that it is difficult to give a general description of them. One can say that the majority of the sonatas are built of two sections: they move from the tonic to the dominant key or to the relative major or minor and then back again to the tonic key. But within this basic form there are numerous substructures. And some of the sonatas are composed in forms altogether different.

The chronology of Scarlatti's sonatas has been much discussed and is still problematic. Most of his sonatas are preserved in copies made late in his life; but this does not necessarily mean that they were composed so late. Probably Scarlatti improvised his pieces, and perhaps wrote them down partially, during the course of his life. Then, at a later date, he had them written down in fair copies.

It seems that the earliest harpsichord pieces by Scarlatti are those in dance forms, or in forms similar to the toccatas of his father. Somewhat later Scarlatti began to compose those sonatas on which his fame rests: the brilliant virtuoso pieces with striking harmonies, bold dissonances, and sudden contrasts of texture. His sonatas are remarkable for the way they exploit the resources of the harpsichord—to musical advantage. They call for a large, two-manual harpsichord and for a highly proficient harpsichordist.

But brilliance and virtuosity do not account for the greatness of Scarlatti's sonatas. The best ones are perfectly realized works of art. Each one carries through its own, distinctive musical ideas, and each one is different from the others. This individuality is a central feature of Scarlatti's sonatas.

The characteristic, unique style of the sonatas seems to be original with Scarlatti himself. Although elements of his style can be traced to earlier keyboard music in Italy, Portugal, or Spain, there is nothing quite like the total effect. On the basis of his harpsichord sonatas, Scarlatti must rank as one of the most original creative minds in the history of music.

Further Reading

Domenico Scarlatti is listed in the Music study guide (I, D, 1; I, E, 2). His father was Alessandro SCARLATTI. Other baroque composers of harpsichord music were Girolamo FRESCOBALDI, Johann Jakob FROBERGER, Johann Sebastian BACH, François COUPERIN, and Jean Philippe RAMEAU.

The standard work on the life and works of Scarlatti is Ralph Kirkpatrick, *Domenico Scarlatti* (1953). Scarlatti's sonatas are discussed by Manfred F. Bukofzer, *Music in the Baroque Era* (1947), and William S. Newman, *The Sonata in the Classic Era* (1963).

SCHACHT / By Diethelm Prowe

The German economist and banker Hjalmar Horace Greeley Schacht (1877–1970), widely admired and hated as Germany's "financial wizard," played a vital role in his country's economic recoveries after the inflation of 1923 and in the Hitler years.

Hjalmar Schacht (pronounced shäKHt) was born in the small border town of Trigleff in German Schleswig on Jan. 22, 1877, shortly after his parents had returned from their emigration to America. After earning his doctorate in economics at the University of Kiel in 1900, he entered one of Germany's great Industrial "D"-banks, the Dresdener Bank, in 1903, where he remained for 13 years. During World War I he set up a new central bank in occupied Belgium to print and regulate the Occupation currency. At the end of the war—now director of the smaller National bank—Schacht participated in the founding of the new progressive liberal party, the Democratic party, to which he belonged until 1926.

Schacht first gained a national reputation when he

Hjalmar Schacht.
(Süddeutscher Verlag)

became currency commissioner in 1923 and in that position played a vital role in the stabilization of the currency after the runaway inflation of 1922–1923 by the creation of the new Rentenmark. In December 1923 his fame as the "savior of mark" brought him an appointment to the presidency of the Central Bank, which he held until 1930. During this time he actively fought foreign credits, and in 1929 he took part in the negotiations for a new plan of reparations, the Young Plan. On his return from the conference, however, he immediately disowned the plan in the face of opposition by fellow nationalists. After the Hague Conference of March 1930 he resigned his position and openly blamed the German Republican government for the continuation of reparations in a pamphlet entitled *End of Reparations* (1931) and other writings. In October 1931 he was instrumental in the formation of the Harzburg Front, a loose coalition of industrialists, national conservatives, and Hitler, and in November 1932 he recommended to the old president of the republic, Paul von Hindenburg, that Hitler be appointed chancellor.

After the Nazi take-over, the grateful Hitler immediately reappointed Schacht to the Central Bank. From that position and from the office of minister of economics from 1934 to 1937, Schacht presided over Germany's second interwar recovery until, by 1938, mounting armament costs began to threaten his concept of a sound, balanced economy and brought on serious disagreement with Hitler. A blunt memorandum of warning in January 1939 brought his downfall and subsequent contacts with the Resistance. After the unsuccessful coup of July 1944 he was arrested but survived the end of the war and was found not guilty at the Nuremberg Trials. After the war he lived in retirement and was called upon for economic advice by several developing nations, most prominently by Indonesia and the Philippines. He died on June 4, 1970, in Munich.

Further Reading

Hjalmar Schacht is listed in the European History study guide (XI, D, 1, a and b). The KRUPP family was also an important force in German economic life during this period.

Schacht's autobiography was published in the United States as *Confessions of "The Old Wizard"* (trans. 1956). His self-defense against implication with Nazi crimes is set down in his *Account Settled* (trans. 1949). He wrote once more about his life experiences and his general views on finance in *The Magic of Money* (trans. 1967). The best general biography in English is Edward N. Peterson, *Hjalmar Schacht: For and against Hitler* (1954), a fair-minded, well-documented account. Norbert Mühlen, *Schact: Hitler's Magician* (trans. 1938), is a bitterly critical portrayal of Schacht as a ruthless economic dictator by a prominent journalist. The most recent biographical study in English is Earl R. Beck, *Verdict on Schacht* (1956), which deals with the question of Schacht's guilt as Hitler's chief economist.

SCHAFF / By Charles Wetzel

Philip Schaff (1819–1893) was a Swiss-born American religious scholar and a great historian of religion. His evolutionary view of Christian development led him to support ecumenical efforts in religion.

Philip Schaff (originally Schaf) was born on Jan. 1, 1819, in Chur, Switzerland. He studied in German schools. At the University of Berlin he came under the influence of the famous theologian August Neander, who impressed upon him the importance of historical insight to Christian understanding. Following his graduation in 1841, Schaff traveled in southern Europe as a private tutor, during which time he observed appreciatively the Christian heritage embodied in Roman Catholic culture.

On his return to Berlin Schaff joined the university faculty but soon accepted a post at the German Reformed Seminary in Mercersburg, Pa.; this post was apparently created to save German-Americans from religious error in the New World. He arrived in the United States in 1844. He was soon married and rapidly embarked upon an exceedingly fruitful collaboration with his brilliant Mercersburg colleague John Williamson Nevin. Schaff and Nevin, cosponsoring the "Mercersburg theology," challenged several popular Protestant attitudes in the United States, particularly hatred of Roman Catholicism, belief that the Reformation marked a radical break from the Christian past, and fondness for revivalistic enthusiasm over organic growth. Shocked churchmen brought Schaff before the Pennsylvania Synod for heresy in 1845, but that body exonerated him.

Schaff's reputation as historian and theological critic

Philip Schaff. (Library of Congress)

reached a new plane with publication abroad and in the United States of his *America: A Sketch of Its Political, Social, and Religious Character* (1854). In a series of lectures given during a visit in Germany, which were the basis for the book, Schaff criticized Puritanical, antihistorical, and denominational facets of American religion. But he also told his German audiences they might well admire the religious vitality of Americans, which he attributed to the voluntarism of churchly life in the United States.

Schaff moved to New York City in 1863, and in 1869 he accepted a professorship at Union Theological Seminary. He now produced many of his most important works, among them a 25-volume *Commentary of the Holy Scriptures* (1865–1880) and a 3-volume *Religious Encyclopaedia* (1882–1884), still a major reference source. He edited a 13-volume *American Church History Series* (1893–1897), a project of the American Society of Church History, which he founded in 1888. Schaff also participated in national and international ecumenical movements. He retired in 1893, and on October 20 he died. His dedication to religious history inspired succeeding generations of scholars.

Further Reading

Philip Schaff is listed in the Religion study guide (I, Q, 1, h). He collaborated with John Williamson NEVIN in creating the "Mercersburg theology."

Probably the best book on Schaff is by his son, David Schley Schaff, *The Life of Philip Schaff* (1897). James Hastings Nichols discusses Schaff's years with Nevin in *Romanticism in American Theology: Nevin and Schaff at Mercersburg* (1961). Also revealing is Perry Miller's introduction to the edition of Schaff's *America* which Miller edited (1961).

SCHARNHORST / By Paul P. Bernard

The Prussian general Gerhard Johann David von Scharnhorst (1755–1813) rebuilt the Prussian army after its collapse at Jena in 1806.

On Nov. 12, 1755, G. J. D. von Scharnhorst (pronounced shärn′hôrst) was born in Bordenau, the son of a former sergeant. In the Prussia of Frederick the Great his origins debarred him from an officer's career, so he took service as an artillery officer in the Hanoverian army, distinguishing himself by considerable valor in the war against revolutionary France. In 1801 he was able to transfer to the Prussian army, being appointed director of the military academy in Berlin. Two years later he was made a member of the general staff. In the campaign of 1806–1807 he served as a staff officer. He did so well in that capacity that, after the collapse, he was appointed minister of war, chief of the general staff, and head of the Military Reconstruction Commission.

G. J. D. von Scharnhorst, a painting by Gebauer. (German Information Center, New York)

Scharnhorst was convinced that only thorough reform, closely tied to the proposed reform of the civil establishment under Baron Stein and Prince Hardenberg, could restore Prussia's army. Every vestige of the brutalized peasant-soldier of Frederick the Great, living in terror of the corporal's stick, would have to go. He insisted on the introduction of universal military service to replace the practice of pressing the sons of peasants and whatever foreigners could be rounded up—and won his point. As it was not possible to keep all those liable for service under the colors at any one time, this meant organizing a reserve, the Landwehr, which consisted of men who had returned to civilian life but were subject to immediate recall and were given occasional training to keep them in trim. This enabled him to keep within the limits that Napoleon allowed the Prussian army but to have a vast reserve on hand. This new citizen army differed radically from that of the 18th century. Beatings, formerly the universal means of enforcing discipline, were abolished. There were no more automatic commissions for the sons of the Prussian nobility. Instead of tedious and endless marching drills, the infantry was schooled in the use of its weapons, techniques of rapid firing, and deployment.

As soon as his reforms had begun to take effect, Scharnhorst urged on his government a war of revenge against Napoleon. This resulted in his dismissal as minister of war on French insistence, but he retained his other positions. In the campaign of 1813 he served as chief of Field Marshal Blücher's staff, was wounded in the battle

of Grossgörschen, and died of his wounds in Prague on
June 28, 1813.

Further Reading

G. J. D. von Scharnhorst is listed in the European History
study guide (VIII, C, 1, a). He tied his reforms to
those of Baron STEIN and Prince HARDENBERG and later
served under Gebhard von BLÜCHER.

Scharnhorst figures in a number of general works on
German history: William Oswald Shanahan, *Prussian
Military Reforms, 1786–1813* (1945); Koppel Shub Pinson,
Modern Germany (1954); and Hajo Holborn, *A History
of Modern Germany* (3 vols., 1959–1964).

SCHECHTER / By Charles Berlin

Solomon Schechter (1849–1915),
Romanian-American Jewish scholar and
religious leader, laid the foundation for the
development of Conservative Judaism in the
United States in his capacity as president of the
Jewish Theological Seminary of America.

*Solomon Schechter. (Jewish Theological Seminary,
New York)*

S olomon Schechter was born into a family of Hasidic background in Focsani, Romania, in December 1849. After a traditional education in Jewish
schools in Romania and Poland, Schechter studied at the
rabbinical seminary of Vienna and at the universities of
Vienna and Berlin. In 1882 he settled in London as a tutor. In 1887 he married Matilda Roth. In 1890 he was
appointed reader in rabbinics at Cambridge University.
During the next 12 years he held several academic posts,
including curator of Hebrew manuscripts in the Cambridge Library and professor of Hebrew at University College in London.

During this period, in addition to numerous journal
articles on Jewish history and theology—later published
in book form as *Studies in Judaism* (1896, 1908, 1924)
and *Some Aspects of Rabbinic Theology* (1909—
Schechter published critical editions of rabbinic texts: the
Talmudic tractate *Aboth de Rabbi Nathan* (1887) and
two Midrashic texts, one on the "Song of Songs" (1896)
and one on Genesis (1902).

Schechter's most notable achievement, however, was
bringing to England much of the archive of an ancient
Cairo synagogue, including thousands of fragments of
manuscripts and documents shedding light on a millennium of Jewish history. Schechter's scholarly work
henceforth centered on this material. His chief works
were *The Wisdom of Ben Sira* (with C. Taylor, 1899),
portions of the Hebrew original of the Apocryphal Book
of Ecclesiasticus; *Saadyana* (1903), new material on the
9th-century Jewish scholar Saadia Gaon; and *Documents
of Jewish Sectaries* (1910), dealing with the 1st-century
Zadokites and the Karaites, a medieval sect.

In 1902 Schechter assumed the presidency of the Jewish Theological Seminary of America in New York and
devoted the rest of his life to developing this institution
and its constituency. In England, Schechter had been
mainly a scholar; he now became the spiritual leader of
Conservative Judaism and, to a certain extent, a leader of
American Judaism. He advocated the concept of the unity and solidarity of Jews throughout the world. He
viewed "the collective conscience of Catholic Israel as
embodied in the Universal Synagogue ... as the sole
true guide for the present and future" development of
Judaism.

In 1913, attempting to unify American Jewry, he established, and served as first president of, the United Synagogue of America, an organization of Conservative Jewish congregations in America. Viewing the rebirth of
Jewish nationalism as embodied in the Zionist movement as integral to the revival of Judaism, he was active
in American Zionism. His other contributions included
service as chairman of the committee that prepared the
new English translation of the Bible later published by
the Jewish Publication Society of America; editor of the
department of Talmud for several volumes of the *Jewish
Encyclopedia*; and coeditor of the new series of the
Jewish Quarterly Review. He died on Nov. 20, 1915.

Further Reading

Solomon Schechter is listed in the Religion study
guide (II, F, 1, c and d). Isaac M. WISE was a founder of
Reform Judaism in America.

A collection of papers from Schechter's American period is in his *Seminary Addresses and Other Papers* (1915; repr. 1969). The best study of Schechter is Norman Bentwich, *Solomon Schechter* (1938).

* * *

SCHEELE / By Owen Hannaway

The Swedish pharmacist and chemist Karl Wilhelm Scheele (1742–1786) discovered chlorine and oxygen and isolated and characterized a variety of organic acids.

K arl Wilhelm Scheele (pronounced shā′lə) was born on Dec. 9, 1742, at Stralsund in Swedish Pomerania. His formal education ended at age 14, when he was apprenticed to a pharmacist in Gothenburg. In this shop Scheele's scientific education began. Here was at hand a treasury of chemical materials and apparatus which excited the curiosity and latent talents of the young apprentice. In addition, he had access to his master's library, which included many of the most noteworthy chemical works of the 18th century.

Following 8 years' apprenticeship in Gothenburg, Scheele moved to Malmö as an apothecary clerk. Again he was fortunate in his master, who allowed him facilities and time for research. In Malmö, Scheele's talents received their first recognition in the person of Anders Johan Retzius, who was later to become professor of chemistry and natural history at the University of Lund. Retzius encouraged Scheele to keep a systematic record of his researches and brought his name to public attention in a paper on tartaric acid published in 1770 in the memoirs of the Royal Swedish Academy of Sciences.

Spurred by Retzius's encouragement, Scheele decided to seek employment closer to the intellectual and scientific centers of Sweden. From 1768 to 1770 he was an apothecary clerk in Stockholm and from 1770 to 1775 held a similar position in a pharmacy in Uppsala. He earned a leading position among the savants and university professors who formed the very notable elite of Swedish science at this time.

Chemical Researches

The bulk of Scheele's scientific work was published between 1770 and 1786 in the memoirs of the Swedish Academy of Sciences. He was also the author of one book, the famous *Chemical Treatise on Air and Fire* (1777). His researches cover such a broad range of topics that one can pinpoint only the highlights.

In the realm of inorganic chemistry Scheele's first important discoveries were made in 1774 in connection with a study of pyrolusite (manganese dioxide). He also discovered a new earth (baryta, or barium oxide) associated with pyrolusite. But the most important outcome of his researches on pyrolusite was his discovery of chlorine. This he prepared by heating a solution of pyrolusite in acid of salt (hydrochloric acid). He collected the greenish-yellow gas in a bladder and studied its highly reactive properties and noted its bleaching action. He thought this gas was acid of salt deprived of its phlogiston, and hence he called it dephlogisticated acid of salt.

In the realm of organic chemistry Scheele is noted for his isolation of a large number of organic acids derived from a variety of vegetables, fruits, and other sources. These included citric acid (from lemons), oxalic acid (from sorrel and rhubarb), malic acid (from apples and other fruits), gallic acid (from nut galls), lactic acid (from milk), and uric acid (from urine). These were among the first organic substances obtained in a chemically pure and well-identified form. Scheele has thus good claim to be considered the founder of modern organic chemistry.

Scheele's greatest claim to fame, however, rests on his discovery of oxygen. He performed his experiments on oxygen sometime between 1770 and 1773, but they were not published until 1777 in his *Chemical Treatise on Air and Fire*, by which time Joseph Priestley had published his independent discovery of the gas (1775). In this book Scheele first proved that common air was composed of two components: "spoiled," or "foul," air and "fire" air (oxygen). The latter was named fire air because only it will support combustion and it is therefore necessary for the production of fire. He prepared this fire air by heating a mixture of nitric and sulfuric acid in a retort and collecting the gas in a bladder attached to the neck. He also prepared the fire air by heating mercuric oxide

Karl Wilhelm Scheele. (The New York Public Library, Picture Collection)

The interior of Scheele's pharmacy at Köping, as it has been restored. (American Institute of the History of Pharmacy)

(Priestley's method) and mixtures of manganese dioxide and sulfuric and phosphoric acids.

Later Career

In 1775 Scheele was admitted to the Royal Swedish Academy of Sciences—perhaps the only apothecary's assistant to be so honored. This same year he also achieved his lifelong ambition: his own pharmacy in the small town of Köping. Although the time he could devote to his scientific research was reduced, he continued to work in a makeshift wooden laboratory behind the shop, and he produced some of the researches described above. By 1782 he had prospered sufficiently to build himself a new house and laboratory. He did not enjoy this newfound prosperity for long, however, for he died on May 26, 1786.

Further Reading

Karl Wilhelm Scheele is listed in the Science study guide (V, D, 2). Other 18th-century chemists were Joseph PRIESTLEY and Antoine Laurent LAVOISIER.

A selection of Scheele's works is *The Collected Papers of Carl Wilhelm Scheele*, translated by Leonard Dobbin (1931). See also J. Murray, *The Chemical Essays of Karl Wilhelm Scheele* (1901). Uno Boklund, distinguished Swedish historian of chemistry, is currently preparing a definitive biography together with editions of all Scheele's works. A very readable account of his life is in Sir Edward Thorpe, *Essays in Historical Chemistry* (1894). A well-illustrated account is in Georg Urdang, *Pictorial Life History of the Apothecary Chemist Carl Wilhelm Scheele* (1942).

SCHELLING/ By Arleen B. Dallery

The German idealist and romantic philosopher
Friedrich Wilhelm Joseph von Schelling

(1775–1854) developed a metaphysical system based on the philosophy of nature.

Born in Württemberg on Jan. 27, 1775, the son of a learned Lutheran pastor, F. W. J. von Schelling (pronounced shĕl′ĭng) was educated at the theological seminary at Tübingen. He became friends with two older classmates, G. W. F. Hegel and Friedrich Hölderlin, and shared their ardent support of the French Revolution. Schelling read widely in the philosophies of Baruch Spinoza, Immanuel Kant, and Johann Gottlieb Fichte. His first two treatises, *Über die Möglichkeit einer Philosophie überhaupt* (1795; *On the Possibility of a Form of Philosophy in General*) and *Vom Ich als Prinzip der Philosophie . . .* (1795; *On the Ego as Principle of Philosophy*), were influenced by Fichte's philosophy of the Absolute Ego. Indeed Fichte's critics mockingly referred to Schelling as the "street peddler of the Ego."

Philosophy of Nature

In the second phase of his thought Schelling turned against Fichte's conception of nature. He then claimed that nature was not a mere obstacle to be overcome through the moral striving of the subject. Nature rather was a form of spiritual activity, an "unconscious intelligence." This organistic, vitalistic conception of nature was developed in *Ideen zu einer Philosophie der Natur* (1797; *Ideas toward a Philosophy of Nature*), in *Von der Weltseele* (1798; *On the World Soul*), and in several works on the physical sciences published between 1797 and 1803. Schelling's brilliance was quickly recognized; owing to J. W. von Goethe's influence, he gave up his position as private tutor and assumed the rank of full professor at Jena. He was only 23 years old.

Jena was the center of German romanticism. This prestigious circle included Ludwig Tieck, the folklorist; Novalis, the poet; Friedrich and August von Schlegel, the translators of Shakespeare; Caroline, August's wife; and in nearby Weimar, Goethe and Friedrich von Schiller. Schelling was briefly engaged to Caroline's daughter by her first marriage, but she died under mysterious circumstances. His affection quickly turned to Caroline, a woman of tremendous wit and intelligence. In 1803, after divorcing Schlegel, Caroline married Schelling.

In 1800 Schelling published the most systematic statement of his philosophy, *System des Transzendentalen Idealismus* (*System of Transcendental Idealism*). In this work and in *Darstellung meine Systems der Philosophie* (1801; *An Exposition of My System*), Schelling argued for the absolute identity of nature and mind in the form of reason. Although this third turn in Schelling's thought was probably influenced by Hegel's philosophy, it earned him only Hegel's scorn.

Munich Period

From 1803 to 1806 Schelling taught at the University of Würzburg. In 1806 he was appointed secretary to the Academy of Arts at Munich, a post that allowed him to complete his most interesting work and to lecture at

Stuttgart. During this period his most important work was the *Philosophische Untersuchungen über das Wesen der Menschlichen Freiheit* (1809; *Of Human Freedom*). Schelling's emphasis on human freedom—"the beginning and end of all philosophy is freedom"—anticipates the major concerns of contemporary existentialism.

In just 14 years Schelling's kaleidoscopic philosophy had undergone several shifts. Hegel uncharitably remarked that Schelling "carried on his philosophical education in public." Schelling was, however, a rigorous thinker, although he never constructed a complete metaphysical system. Schelling wrote eloquent and impassioned prose, liberating German philosophy from its turgid, jargonistic style.

Later Period

Schelling's wife died in 1809, and that same year marked the rising prominence of Hegel. These two events dampened Schelling's philosophical enthusiasm and self-confidence. Schelling was remarried in 1812—to Pauline Gotter, a friend of Caroline's—but did not publish another book in the remaining 42 years of his life. From 1820 to 1827 he lectured at Erlangen, and in 1827 Schelling became a professor at Munich. Extremely bitter about the success of Hegel, he accepted a post as Prussian privy councilor and member of the Berlin Academy in order to quell the popularity of Hegel's disciples, the so-called Young Hegelians.

To combat further the influence of Hegel, Schelling

F. W. J. von Schelling, a drawing by Franz Kruger. (Bildarchiv Staatsbibliothek, Berlin)

lectured at Berlin for 5 years. His lectures on mythology and religion signaled the last stage in his thought, the opposition of negative and positive philosophy. God cannot be known through reason (negative philosophy), but He can be experienced through myth and revelation (positive philosophy). This relatively neglected aspect of Schelling's philosophy has aroused considerable interest among today's Protestant theologians. Never regaining his early prominence, Schelling died on Aug. 20, 1854, at Bad Ragaz, Switzerland.

Schelling was called the "prince of the romantics." With his immense charm, wit, and radiant spirit, he endeared himself to the coterie of intellectuals known as the German romantics. With them he celebrated, in both word and deed, the vision of artistic genius and the principles of organicism and vitalism in nature.

Further Reading

F. W. J. von Schelling is listed in the Philosophy study guide (VI, A, 1). A close friend of Friedrich HÖLDERLIN, he influenced Samuel Taylor COLERIDGE. Once regarded as merely the precursor of G. W. F. HEGEL, Schelling is now considered a forerunner of existentialism.

A short critical biography is in James Gutman's introduction to his translation of Schelling's *Of Human Freedom* (1936). Frederick Copleston, *A History of Philosophy* (7 vols., 1946; rev. ed., 7 vols. in 13, 1962), provides a thorough exposition of Schelling's thought. Other accounts of the development of Schelling's later philosophy are in the introduction to Schelling's *The Ages of the World* (a fragment of *Die Weltalter*), translated by Frederick de Wolfe Bolman (1942), and in Paul Collins Hayner, *Reason and Existence: Schelling's Philosophy of History* (1967). Recommended for the background of idealism and romanticism are Josiah Royce, *The Spirit of Modern Philosophy* (1892), and Eric D. Hirsch, *Wordsworth and Schelling* (1960).

SCHIFF / By Louis M. Hacker

Jacob Henry Schiff (1847–1920) was the outstanding member of the American-German Jewish banking group that became important after the Civil War. He played a major role in railroads and in industrial mergers at the turn of the century.

Jacob Schiff was born in Frankfurt am Main, Germany, on Jan. 10, 1847, of a middle-class family and a long line of rabbis and bankers. At the age of 14 he was apprenticed to a business firm. In 1865 he emigrated to New York and soon set up his own brokerage office. In 1872 Schiff went to Germany to go into banking.

When Schiff returned to New York in 1875, he was invited to join the private banking firm of Kuhn, Loeb and Company. He soon became a leading member of the house and in 1885 its senior partner. Interested in railroad financing, Schiff found his big chance when he and E. H. Harriman (America's greatest railroad man) took over the Union Pacific Railroad in 1897.

Schiff and Harriman set out to acquire the Northern Pacific Railroad from J. P. Morgan and James J. Hill by stock-exchange maneuvers. The result was a financial panic in 1901. The titans settled on a holding company, the Northern Securities Company, which owned the stock of the Northern Pacific, the Great Northern, and the Burlington railroads, with the Schiff-Harriman interests fully recognized. Thanks to Schiff and J. P. Morgan, this was the golden age of American railroading; and Schiff was recognized as Morgan's peer.

Also between 1895 and 1910 Schiff's firm headed banking syndicates (using European money markets for funds and as outlets for the new securities) that formed several important American industrial mergers. From 1897 to 1906 Kuhn, Loeb and Company cooperated with other firms to market over $800 million in securities; during 1907–1912 it alone underwrote $530 million worth, and with other houses an additional $821 million. Schiff was imaginative enough to see that an American capital market had developed, and he floated dollar bonds to finance Mexican railroads and to raise money for Japan's war against Russia. Unlike Morgan, Schiff was not interested in voting trusts or in sitting on the boards of the companies he organized or reorganized, and he did not seek to become their depositories. His company did not control a group of banks or dominate credit agencies; to this extent, therefore, he did not earn the censure of the Pujo Committee's Money Trust Investigation of 1913.

As a devout Jew, Schiff became a spokesman for those Jews who believed in assimilation into American culture. He helped establish Jewish philanthropic agencies—hospitals, family- and child-care societies, recreation and settlement house centers—to help less fortunate coreligionists adjust to American life. Schiff also helped put the Jewish Theological Seminary on a sound footing, created the Semitic Museum at Harvard, and financed the departments of Semitic literature at the New York Public Library and the Library of Congress. He died in New York on Sept. 25, 1920.

Further Reading

Jacob Schiff is listed in the American History study guide (VII, E, 1). He and J. P. MORGAN were America's most important early industrial financiers.

Although *Jacob H. Schiff: His Life and Letters*, edited by Cyrus Adler (2 vols., 1928), is useful, more exciting and informative about Schiff's business life is Stephen Birmingham, *Our Crowd* (1967). Fritz Redlich, *The Molding of American Banking* (1968), is very good on Schiff and is the best discussion of investment banking extant.

SCHILLER / By August Closs

The German dramatist, poet, and historian Johann Christoph Friedrich von Schiller (1759–1805) ranks as one of the greatest of German literary figures. He was a founder of modern German literature.

F riedrich von Schiller (pronounced shĭl′ər) was born at Marbach, Württemberg, on Nov. 10, 1759. His father, Johann Kaspar Schiller, was an army captain in the service of Duke Karl Eugen of Württemberg. His mother, Elisabeth Dorothea, the daughter of a Marbach innkeeper, was a gentle and religious person. Schiller had four sisters, one older and three younger.

As a boy, Schiller, under the influence of Philipp Ulrich Moser, a parson, wanted to become a preacher. He attended the duke's military academy, the Karlsschule, near Stuttgart for 2 years. After the academy was moved to Stuttgart, Schiller endured 5 more years of harsh discipline there. He studied medicine because that was the domineering duke's will. In spite of frequent illnesses, fevers, stomach upsets, and headaches, he wrote his final dissertation on the interrelationship between man's spiritual and physical natures. At the same time he was writing his first play, *Die Räuber*, which was published in 1781. It ranks as one of the literary monuments of the German *Sturm und Drang* period.

Early Works

In December 1780 Schiller was appointed medical of-

Jacob Schiff. (Library of Congress)

Friedrich von Schiller. (Collection Viollet)

ficer to a regiment stationed in Stuttgart at a pitiably low salary. A loan toward the publication of *Die Räuber* marked the beginning of a succession of agonizing debts that characterized Schiller's early career. In 1782 *Die Räuber* received its first stage performance, in Mannheim. It brought him both public acclaim and the wrath of the duke, who forbade him to write anything except medical treatises. That same year Schiller published the *Laura-Oden* in his *Anthologie auf das Jahr 1782*. The inspiration for these poems was a 30-year-old widow, Dorothea Vischer, who had three children. She had rented a simple ground-floor room to Schiller and another lieutenant.

Meantime, Schiller's conflict with the Duke of Württemberg forced him to flee Stuttgart in September 1782. A period of great deprivation and uncertainty followed until Schiller became dramatist at the Mannheim theater in September 1783. During this time he composed *Die Verschwörung des Fiesko zu Genua* (1783) and *Kabale und Liebe* (1784). He also began work on *Don Carlos, Infant von Spanien*, which appeared in 1785 and in its revised form in 1787.

In 1784 Schiller completed *Die Schaubühne als moralische Anstalt betrachtet*, which appeared in his *Rheinische Thalia*, a literary journal, in 1785. The second issue of *Thalia* contained Schiller's hymn *An die Freude*, which later inspired Ludwig van Beethoven to create his magnificent Ninth Symphony in D Minor. In the third issue of *Thalia* Schiller published part of *Don Carlos*. During this period Christian Gottfried Körner generously offered Schiller financial help and hospitality, becoming his patron and friend.

Don Carlos was important in Schiller's dramatic development not only for its use of a historical setting but also for its employment of blank verse. For the first time, too, Schiller accomplished the presentation of a perfectly

drawn and perfectly convincing noblewoman. The character of Queen Elisabeth of Valois was to some extent based on that of Charlotte von Kalb, an intimate friend.

Schiller occupied himself for many years afterward with the themes he employed in this drama. In *Don Carlos* the conflict between love and the demands of the state was exalted into the idea of the dignity and freedom of man. The struggle against love is a struggle for a high goal, and it is not the love of Don Carlos for the Queen or his friendship for the Marquis of Posa that forms the crux of the play but the ideal of spiritual and national freedom.

In all of Schiller's earliest tragedies—*Die Räuber, Die Verschwörung des Fiesko*, and *Kabale und Liebe*—he presents either a great criminal, a great adventurer, or a great enthusiast. All of his characters speak in the grand style. Schiller captures the secret of great passion even in his earliest dramas. The robber chieftain Karl Moor of *Die Räuber* judges himself when he admits that two men like him would destroy the organic structure of the civilized world. Fiesko contemplates the idea that it is great to win a crown but that it is divine to be able to cast it off.

In 1787 Schiller paid a visit to his friend Frau von Kalb in Weimar, the residence of Johann Wolfgang von Goethe, who at that time was traveling in Italy. The two great German poets met the following year in the house of Frau von Lengefeld (later to be Schiller's mother-in-law) in Rudolstadt. They had met once before, in December 1779, when Duke Karl August of Weimar and Goethe had come to the Karlsschule in Stuttgart to award the annual student prizes. Schiller had received three silver medals.

In 1788 Schiller's poems *Die Götter Griechenlands* and *Die Künstler* appeared, and that same year he published *Geschichte des Abfalls der vereinigten Niederlande*, a history of the revolt of the Netherlands against Spain. These works assured Schiller's fame and social position. Together with Goethe's support they gained him a professorship of history at the University of Jena in 1789. He held this position for 10 years. Schiller's inaugural, *Was heisst und zu welchem Ende studiert man Universalgeschichte*, caused a sensation. Afterward more than 500 students paid homage to the poet, but at later lectures the number of students in attendance dwindled considerably. Early in 1790 Schiller married Charlotte von Lengefeld, a gifted writer. In February 1803 he was created a nobleman.

Esthetic Theory

After 1790 Schiller became intensely interested in the philosophy and esthetics of Immanuel Kant. His *Geschichte des Dreissigjährigen Krieges*, a history of the Thirty Years War, appeared in 1791–1792. His studies in esthetics accompanied his historical researches. Schiller strove to capture the essence of "freedom and art." He determined not to read the works of any modern writer for 2 years. In his poem *Die Götter Griechenlands* Schiller had looked upon Greece with the eyes of Johann Joachim Winckelmann, the classical archeologist and historian of ancient art. Under the influence of Winckelmann's conception of the "schöne Antike," Schiller became convinced that only art can ennoble the barbarian and bring him culture. Art became, for Schiller, in the Platonic sense a basis of education. In 1795 he wrote in his *Über die aesthetische Erziehung des Menschen*, "There is no other way to make the sensuous man rational and reasonable than by first making him esthetic." The iron necessity of man's daily existence degraded him, said Schiller, and utility became the idol of the masses. But by means of the esthetic form man can "annihilate" the material aspects of life and triumph over transient matter. Man thus becomes the creator of a pure and permanent world.

In his grandiose philosophic poem *Die Künstler*, Schiller venerated art as the ennobling power that can create a higher culture and disclose a world harmony. In the opening strophe of this work, man, standing on the threshold of a new century, is depicted as the master of nature. He is shown as free, enlightened, strong through laws, great in his gentleness, matured through time, proud, and manly. Art, said Schiller, teaches man how to overcome his desires. Art is the first step away from the bondage of the flesh into a realm where the nobility of the soul reigns. The artist frees form from material in the same manner that waves separate a reflection from its source. In nature the artist discovers the laws of beauty. For example, in a tree he perceives the form of a pillar, and in the crescent moon the artist becomes aware of the mystery of the universe. For Schiller reality was merely illusion; only in the higher, spiritual realm was truth to be found. Just as the stage had changed into a tribunal in his famous poem *Die Kraniche des Ibykus*, so to him true art changes into higher reality.

Schiller wrote his important essay in esthetics, *Über naive und sentimentalische Dichtung*, in 1795–1796. It forms the basis of modern poetry criticism. In it Schiller points out that the "naive" poet has an advantage over other poets in his powerful, sensitive, and inherent clarity, while the "sentimentalische" poet has an advantage in his power of moral enthusiasm. By now Schiller had reached an artistic maturity incompatible with moralizing. In his philosophic poem *Das Ideal und das Leben* (1795) the poet presents no clumsy didactic lesson. No mention of reward or recompense for the sufferer, or of moral striving after inner freedom, is made. The subject of this poem is purely the growth of a powerful personality beyond the confines of the self into a higher world.

Later Dramas

In 1798–1799 Schiller completed his great trilogy on Albrecht von Wallenstein, the condottiere of the Thirty Years War. These three plays—*Wallensteins Lager*, *Piccolomini*, and *Wallensteins Tod*—represent Schiller's most powerful tragedy. In them he comes nearest to the tragic grandeur of William Shakespeare and Heinrich von Kleist. The *Wallenstein* plays stress Schiller's view of man as a creative force, and they exhibit his concept of historical inevitability. Schiller ennobles Wallenstein as a great creative statesman who bows before inexorable fate. Wallenstein recognizes his guilt and acknowledges

the justice of his end because he realizes that every evil deed brings with it its angel of revenge.

The famous literary friendship between Goethe and Schiller began in earnest in 1794. On July 20, 1794, after a meeting in Jena of a nature society of which both were honorary members, Goethe went to Schiller's house to continue a discussion on the interpretation of natural phenomena, the metamorphosis of plants, and the interrelationship or separation between idea and experience. Goethe believed he had "observed with his own eyes" tangible truths of nature that Schiller, however, called "ideas." An important correspondence between the two poets followed. Schiller enjoyed the friendship of Goethe, with whom he began editing the literary journals *Horen* (1795–1797) and *Musenalmanach* (1796–1800). Goethe's residence in Weimar was a main reason for Schiller's move there, from Jena with his family, in 1799. During his Weimar years Schiller created many of his finest plays and poems.

Schiller wrote his most popular play, *Maria Stuart*, in 1800. He employed tragic irony as an artistic means in the memorable scene between the two queens in which Mary speaks daggers to Elizabeth but is hoist with her own petard. Mary remains a noble and tragic character right up to the scaffold. As with Elizabeth, the decisive factor in her fate lies in her personality and not in politics. Mary's death is subject not to "poetic justice" but to the justice of human conscience. By her death she atones for a previous guilt.

Schiller's next play, *Die Jungfrau von Orleans* (1801), is his poetically richest drama. Its theme is again guilt and redemption. Compared to *Maria Stuart*, it is loosely constructed, diffuse, and romantic not only in regard to the material itself but also in regard to the poetic character of the heroine. On the other hand, *Die Braut von Messina* (1803) is compact and stylized. Artistry dominates it at the cost of poetry. This play reflects Schiller's interest in classical antiquity. Its chorus has passages of lyrical and rhetorical magnificence.

In the preface to the first edition of this play, Schiller explained his views on the function of the chorus. The chorus, he wrote, should not be an accompaniment to the drama as in some ancient plays. Rather it should bring out the poetry of the play, thereby converting the modern world into a poetic one. The chorus should express the depth of mankind, and it should be a judging and clarifying witness of the actions in that it reflects them and endows them with spiritual power.

Schiller revealed his technical mastery at its most supreme in *Wilhelm Tell* (1804). Although this play is stylized, its artistry is less obvious than that of *Die Braut von Messina*. Schiller created the character of Wilhelm Tell as a manly hero without making him into a leader. When Gessler, the governor, brutally interferes with life and nature, the Swiss, and with them Wilhelm Tell, fight for family and freedom. In this play Schiller for once placed history and hero in favorable conjunction.

In the fragmentary drama *Demetrius*, Schiller unfolds a mysterious fate, revealing through his analytical dramatic technique a past crime more terrible to contemplate than

A modern performance of Schiller's Maria Stuart in Berlin. (Library of Congress)

any dread of the future. Whereas Oedipus in the hands of Sophocles subjects himself to divine command, Schiller's Demetrius defies his fate in order to perish.

Schiller's final tragedies are concerned with man's profoundest experience, the assertion and attainment of free will despite bodily claims or passion. After months of intermittent illness, Schiller died in Weimar on May 9, 1805.

Further Reading

Friedrich von Schiller is listed in the Literature study guide (III, G, 2). He was an intimate of Johann Wolfgang von GOETHE.

An early biography of Schiller is Thomas Carlyle, *The Life of Friedrich Schiller* (1825; 2d ed. 1845). Of the many critical biographies see William Witte, *Schiller* (1949) and *Schiller and Burns* (1959). Other useful studies include Henry B. Garland's three works, *Schiller* (1949), *Schiller Revisited* (1959), and *Schiller: The Dramatic Writer* (1969); Ernst L. Stahl, *Friedrich Schiller's Drama: Theory and Practice* (1954); William F. Mainland, *Schiller and the Changing Past* (1957); and the essay on Schiller in Thomas Mann, *Last Essays* (trans. 1959). Other useful studies are Stanley S. Kerry, *Schiller's Writings on Aesthetics* (1961); Elizabeth M. Wilkinson and L. A. Willoughby, eds., *Schiller: On the Aesthetic Education of Man, in a Series of Letters* (trans. 1967), which has an extensive introduction about Schiller along with some of his works; and John Martin Ellis, *Schiller's Kalliasbriefe and the Study of His Aesthetic Theory* (1969). For a discussion of *Sturm and Drang* and Weimar classicism see the relevant chapters in Ernst L. Stahl and W. E. Yuill, *Introductions to German Literature*, vol. 3: *German Literature of the 18th and 19th Centuries*, edited by August Closs (1970).

SCHINDLER / By Louis Filler

Solomon Schindler (1842–1915), German-American rabbi and social theorist, contributed to the reform movement in Judaism and to the religious socialism of his era.

Solomon Schindler was born in Neisse, Germany, on April 24, 1842, the son of a rabbi. Although he was prepared for the rabbinate, his liberal religious tendencies caused him to enter the Royal Teachers' Seminary at Büren, from which he graduated in 1870. He had married Henrietta Schutz. His unusual conduct and ideas closed certain opportunities, and his openly antipatriotic stand during the Franco-Prussian War made it desirable for him to leave the country.

Schindler and his family arrived in America without resources. Reluctantly, because of financial need, he accepted a post as rabbi in Hoboken, N.J. In 1874 he became reader, teacher, and preacher of a temple in Boston. He proceeded to transform this temple into the Jewish church of his dreams, dispensing with many orthodox rituals and Americanizing the institution in every way possible. Although this lost him some of his congregation, he gained many more. In 1885 a new temple was dedicated with such liberal Protestant ministers as Phillips Brooks and Edward Everett Hale attending.

Schindler expanded his social concerns in ways that made him popular among Bostonians of various religions. He was a friend of the Catholic editor and poet John Boyle O'Reilly. His sermons collected as *Messianic Expectations and Modern Judaism* (1885)—critical of what he deemed outmoded and unwarranted illusions—were circulated by the *Boston Globe*. His hope for the world was social reform, particularly as expounded by Edward Bellamy in his novel *Looking Backward*, which

Solomon Schindler. (Courtesy, Temple Israel, Boston, Mass.; Dictionary of American Portraits, Dover)

Schindler translated into German. Schindler also wrote a sequel, *Young West* (1894).

Schindler's approach to religion and social reform brought him local popularity, so that from 1888 to 1894 he was elected to the Boston School Board by all factions. Nevertheless he lost his appeal for his congregation, which sought a native pastor and dismissed Schindler in 1893. He went on to found the pioneer Federation of Jewish Charities of Boston and was its superintendent until 1899. Thereafter until his retirement in 1909, he headed the Leopold Morse Home for Infirm Hebrews at Mattapan, Mass. Schindler in later years offered a sermon, "Mistakes I Have Made," which modified the sweeping nature of his criticism of traditional Judaism. He died on May 5, 1915.

Further Reading

Solomon Schindler is listed in the Religion study guide (II, F, 1, d). The founder of Reform Judaism in the United States was Isaac M. WISE.

Schindler's reputation has been lost in the uncertain currents of the Christian Socialism of his time. The one treatment of him in modern times, an incomplete analysis, is in Arthur Mann, *Yankee Reformers in the Urban Age* (1954). See also B. O. Flower, *Progressive Men, Women and Movements of the Past Twenty-five Years*

(1914), and Arthur E. Morgan, *Edward Bellamy* (1944). David Philipson, *The Reform Movement in Judaism* (1907; new and rev. ed. 1931), does not include Schindler but develops some of the principles that influenced his thought.

SCHINKEL / By James F. O'Gorman

The German architect, painter, and designer Karl Friedrich Schinkel (1781–1841) was one of the most important and influential architects of his time. He was equally at home with the medieval and the classical tradition.

Karl Friedrich Schinkel (pronounced shǐng′kəl) was born on March 13, 1781, in Neuruppin west of Berlin; the family moved to the Prussian capital in 1794. Inspired by Friedrich Gilly's 1796 project for a monument to Frederick II (Frederick the Great), Schinkel turned to architecture and studied with Gilly (1798–1800). Schinkel traveled in Italy and France (1803–1804). He became a painter of romantic landscapes and panoramas (*Medieval City by the Water*, 1813) and stage sets (*Magic Flute*, 1815). In 1813 he designed the Iron Cross, Germany's highest military award. In 1815 Frederick William III appointed him Prussian state architect.

Although Schinkel designed important buildings for cities other than Berlin, such as the church of St. Nicholas in Potsdam (1826–1837) and the Guard House in

Karl Friedrich Schinkel, a portrait medallion by David d'Angers, in the Berlin Museum. (Photo Albin-Guillot-Viollet)

Dresden (1833), his major works were erected in the capital. In fact, he reshaped the monumental center of the city (now in the Eastern Zone), and before the holocaust of 1945 it was said that he who knew Berlin knew Schinkel. His first building was the Royal Guard House (Neue Wacht-Gebäude) on the Unter den Linden (1816). A stone block with Doric portico, it established Schinkel as a master of Neo-Greek forms.

The reshaping of the Lustgarten (now Marx-Engels-Platz), a square at the eastern end of the Unter den Linden in front of the Royal Palace (now demolished), occupied the architect's attention during the 1820s. He remodeled the Cathedral to the east, but his major work was a new museum (now the Altes Museum) opposite the palace (designed 1822; finished 1830). A low block with a central rotunda for sculpture flanked by courts and surrounded by galleries for paintings, the museum closed the north side of the square with a majestic row of 18 Ionic columns framed by a podium below, entablature above, and pilasters to either side. The museum was Schinkel's masterpiece, one of the principal monuments of European neoclassicism and a continuing source of inspiration for classically oriented architects of the 20th century, such as Ludwig Mies van der Rohe and Philip Johnson.

Schinkel's other notable buildings in Berlin show the variety of his work. The Theater (Schauspielhaus) on the Gendarmenmarkt (1818; gutted 1945) sat on a podium with its Ionic portico contrasting with the low, flat, pilastered wings. The whole was capped by sculpture-enriched pediments. It was meant to form a unit with the porticoed and domed French and German churches that flank it. The monument to Napoleon's defeat that still crowns the Kreuzberg is a cast-iron Gothic pinnacle designed in 1818 (finished 1821; site later altered). For the Friedrich Werder Church near the Lustgarten, Schinkel submitted alternative designs, one classical and one medieval; the existing church (finished 1831) is Neo-Gothic.

The School of Architecture (Bauakademie) on the Spree River near the Lustgarten (1831–1835; destroyed) was characteristic of Schinkel's later work. A simple red-brick block enriched on the exterior by shallow pilasters and restrained decoration, it was a direct statement of structure and enclosure without overt historical details. Schinkel was appointed professor of architecture at the academy in 1820, and through his students his influence continued long after his death. He died in Berlin on Oct. 9, 1841.

Further Reading

Karl Friedrich Schinkel is listed in the Art study guide (III, I, 2, c). The leading practitioners of the neoclassic style in England at this time were John NASH and Sir John SOANE.

The basic works on Schinkel are in German. A brief discussion of Schinkel's buildings in the context of the architecture of the early 19th century is in Henry-Russell Hitchcock, *Architecture: Nineteenth and Twentieth*

Altes Museum, Berlin, designed by Schinkel and completed in 1830. (Library of Congress)

Centuries (1958). Schinkel as city planner of Berlin is discussed in Hermann G. Pundt, *Schinkel's Berlin: A Study in Environmental Planning* (1972).

SCHLEGEL / By Richard Unger

> The critic and author Friedrich von Schlegel (1772–1829) was one of the chief founders of the German romantic movement. He is best known for his writings in literary theory and cultural history.

Friedrich von Schlegel (pronounced shlā′gəl) was born in Hanover on March 10, 1772. He studied philosophy and literature at Göttingen University and later at Leipzig. Between 1794 and 1796 he lived in Dresden, later moving to Jena, making acquaintances in the literary circles of both cities. In Jena, Schlegel was especially influenced by the philosophy of Johann Gottlieb Fichte, whose teachings he later applied to literary theory.

In 1797 Schlegel moved to Berlin, where he associated with such romantic writers as Ludwig Tieck. In 1798 Schlegel published two essays, *Vom Studium der griechischen Poesie* (On the Study of Greek Poetry) and *Geschichte der Poesie der Griechen und Römer* (History of the Poetry of the Greeks and Romans), in which he expounded the thesis that the Greeks had achieved perfect harmony in their civilization and art. With other

Friedrich von Schlegel. (German Information Center, New York)

members of the romantic movement he edited the literary quarterly *Athenaeum* (1798–1800). In its pages he developed his literary theories—he considered romantic poetry to be a "progressively universal poetry," expanding its subject matter to include all aspects of life. An example of such "poetry" was Schlegel's experimental novel, *Lucinde* (1799), in which he analyzed the psychological details of his relationship with Dorothea Veit, the daughter of the Jewish intellectual Moses Mendelssohn. Friedrich and Dorothea were married in 1804.

After teaching briefly at the University of Jena, Schlegel moved to Paris in 1802, where he studied Oriental literature and culture. In 1808 he went to Cologne, converted to Roman Catholicism, and published a study of Indian culture, *Über die Sprache und Weisheit der Indier* (On the Language and Wisdom of the Indians).

Although Schlegel had previously taught absolute freedom in thought and action and preached free love in his novel, in later years he tended toward increasing intellectual and political conservatism. He became affiliated with the Austrian government, at that time a reactionary force in European politics. In 1809 he became court secretary in Vienna, although he continued his literary activities. Between 1810 and 1812 he gave lectures in Vienna on medieval poets as forerunners of romanticism, and he perfected his philosophy of history, which viewed national cultures as organic developments. Among his translated lectures are *The Philosophy of History, The*

Philosophy of Life and the Philosophy of Language, and *The History of Literature.*

In 1815 Schlegel assisted the Austrian delegation at the Congress of Vienna. In his later years he served as editor of the ultraconservative journal *Concordia*. He died in Dresden on Jan. 12, 1829.

Further Reading

Friedrich von Schlegel is listed in the Literature study guide (III, G, 2). He, NOVALIS, and Ludwig TIECK helped to found the *Athenaeum*, the critical organ of the romantic group.

The best extensive treatment of Schlegel, especially his theoretical writings, is in Oskar Walzel, *German Romanticism* (1932). Walzel demonstrates Schlegel's central importance as a romantic theorist. More general discussions of Schlegel's life and work are in Walter Silz, *Early German Romanticism* (1929), and Ralph Tymms, *German Romantic Literature* (1955).

SCHLEIERMACHER

/ **By Malachi B. Martin**

The German theologian and philosopher Friedrich Ernst Daniel Schleiermacher (1768–1834) held that man's consciousness of being springs from the presence of God within him. He believed that all morality is an attempt to unite man's physical nature with his mind.

Born on Nov. 21, 1768, Friedrich Schleiermacher (pronounced shlī′ər-mä-KHər) was educated at Moravian Church schools and destined to be a pastor. Doubting religion, he studied at the University of Halle, becoming absorbed first in Kantian philosophy and then in Plato, Baruch Spinoza, and Johann Gottlieb Fichte. He became one of the early Berlin romantics and associated particularly with Friedrich von Schlegel. In 1799 he published his famous *Reden über die Religion,* in which he claimed that religion was separate and apart from morality and knowledge. His *Monologen* (1800) outlined his ethical system. His *Grundlinien einer Kritik der bisherigen Sittenlehre* (1803) was a philosophical work, and his *Die Weihnachtsfeier* (1806) outlined his views on Jesus. He was pastor at Stolp from 1802 to 1804 and then became a professor at Halle until 1809, when he moved to Berlin, where he remained until his death on Feb. 12, 1834.

Schleiermacher was the most influential thinker of 19th-century Protestantism. In philosophy, however, he was overshadowed by G. W. F. Hegel. Schleiermacher was an idealist, holding that human knowledge was at best a mere approximation to reality and that man arrives at this knowledge by a conflict (the *Dialektik*). All German idealism was somehow saddled with the a priori conviction that reality was either very difficult to reach or totally unreachable in itself. Schleiermacher labored with this a priori in his attempt to establish his religious beliefs on a solid foundation. In this he was a child of the Enlightenment and a victim of the romantic illusion that in the final analysis it was only the ego or the individual who counted. This illusion cohered with his Protestant persuasion that the individual conscience was the ultimate criterion of what was correct in belief and good in morality.

Religion, Schleiermacher held, results from the feeling man has that he is absolutely dependent. He derived the structure of his theology from this basic notion. He considered Christianity to be the highest stage of the monotheistic urge in man. To Christ, Schleiermacher assigned a role of mediator, thereby leaving great doubts as to the divinity of Jesus and his identity with God. He reinterpreted the traditional Christian doctrines of sin, justification, Christology, Last Judgment, hell, and heaven.

Schleiermacher foreshadowed the later religious thought of the 19th and early 20th centuries. His doctrine concerning the rise of natural and supernatural religions is a foretaste of the later evolutionary theories. His attempt to bridge rationalism and supernaturalism invoked the theories and the principles which animated Ethical Culture movements of the 20th century.

Further Reading

Friedrich Schleiermacher is listed in the Religion study

Friedrich Schleiermacher. (German Information Center, New York)

guide (I, Q, 1, g). His rejection of much of the historicity of the Bible anticipated the thought of Rudolf BULT-MANN.

Terence N. Tice, *Schleiermacher Bibliography* (1966), is highly recommended as an extensive guide to the literature by and about Schleiermacher. Aspects of his life and thought are discussed in Richard B. Brandt, *Philosophy of Schleiermacher* (1941), and Jerry F. Dawson, *Friedrich Schleiermacher: The Evolution of a Nationalist* (1966).

SCHLESINGER / By Dwight W. Hoover

> The American historian Arthur Meier Schlesinger (1888–1965) was one of the pioneers in the study of the social aspects of American history.

Arthur M. Schlesinger was born in Xenia, Ohio, on Feb. 27, 1888, the son of a first-generation immigrant. Schlesinger graduated in 1910 from Ohio State University. As a graduate student at Columbia, he was influenced by Herbert Levi Osgood, James Harvey Robinson, and Charles A. Beard. His dissertation, finished in 1917, was *The Colonial Merchants and the American Revolution* (1918), which Sir Denis Brogan called "perhaps the most remarkable Ph.D. dissertation in modern American historiography." Schlesinger had used Osgood's methods and Beard's insights.

While finishing his dissertation, Schlesinger taught at Ohio State, beginning in 1912. He became a full professor in 1917, the same year he received his doctorate. During his stay at Ohio State, he married Elizabeth Bancroft. In 1919 he moved to the State University of Iowa as chairman of the history department. In 1922 he inaugurated a course entitled "Social and Cultural History of the United States," the first of its kind in the country. His *New Viewpoints in American History* (1922) presents his ideas on the craft and content of history. He joined Harvard in 1924 as a visiting professor of history and became Francis Lee Higginson professor of history in 1939. He was a charter member of the Social Science Research Council, an organization he later chaired (1930–1933).

The first four volumes of *A History of American Life*, under the joint editorship of Schlesinger and Dixon Ryan Fox, appeared in 1927. Schlesinger's own contribution was volume 10, *The Rise of the City, 1878–1898* (1933), an outstanding pioneer effort in social and urban history. The 13-volume series was completed in 1948 and was an original attempt to portray the everyday life of ordinary people, touching on health, public welfare, and recreation. Schlesinger also wrote college texts during this period. His interest in immigration led him to finish two books by Marcus Lee Hansen: *The Atlantic Migration,*

Arthur M. Schlesinger. (Harvard University Archives)

1607–1860 (1940), which won a Pulitzer Prize, and *The Immigrant in American History* (1940). His presidential address to the American Historical Association in 1942, reprinted in his *Paths to the Present* (1949), again called attention to the study of American character.

Schlesinger retired from Harvard in 1953. He died on Oct. 30, 1965. His son, Arthur M. Schlesinger, Jr., became famous as a historian and also as part of President John F. Kennedy's intellectual group.

Further Reading

Arthur M. Schlesinger is listed in the Social Sciences study guide (VII, A, 3). He had many famous students, including Pulitzer Prize–winner Oscar HANDLIN.

The best account of Schlesinger's professional life is his autobiography, *In Retrospect: The History of a Historian* (1963). His ideas are set forth in his *New Viewpoints in American History* (1922) and *Paths to the Present* (1949; rev. ed. 1964), as well as in John Higham, Leonard Kreiger, and Felix Gilbert, *History* (1965).

SCHLICK / By Daniel O'Connor

The German physicist and philosopher Friedrich Albert Moritz Schlick (1882–1936) revived positivism as a leading force in 20th-century thought and was the founding spirit of the Vienna Circle.

Moritz Schlick (pronounced shlĭk) was born in Berlin on Feb. 28, 1833, and educated there. His secondary school training was largely focused on mathematics and physics, and he pursued these subjects further in his university studies at Heidelberg, Lausanne, and Berlin. His doctoral thesis at Berlin, written under Max Planck, was *Reflection of Light* (1904).

By 1910 Schlick's interests had shifted from physics proper to epistemology and the philosophy of science. With his inaugural dissertation, "The Nature of Truth in the Light of Modern Physics," he began his teaching career at Rostock. There he continued to follow developments in physics, partly through his friendship with Planck and Albert Einstein; and he wrote the first interpretation of the latter's relativity theory in 1917. Also during this period, Schlick worked out his fundamental ideas on scientific knowing and published them as *The General Theory of Knowledge* (1918). This earned him wide attention and a call to a professorship, first at Kiel in 1921 and a year later at Vienna.

At Vienna, Schlick quickly became the center of a

Moritz Schlick. (Österreichische Nationalbibliothek, Vienna, Photo Theo Bauer)

group of men interested in scientific philosophy, logic, and mathematics. The group included among others Otto Neurath, Rudolf Carnap, Herbert Feigl, Friedrich Waismann, and Kurt Gödel and later the English philosophers Alfred Ayer and Susan Stebbing and an American, Charles Morris. There were weekly meetings to discuss fundamental questions in logic and the philosophy of science. Setting very exact (critics would say "narrow") criteria for knowledge, the group rejected metaphysical propositions as meaningless and severely limited the range of significant speech in ethics and esthetics. In 1929, on the occasion of Schlick's return from a guest lectureship at Stanford, Calif., he was presented with a pamphlet describing the history, membership, orientation, and goals of the group. It was called "The Scientific View of the World: The Vienna Circle."

The reading of Ludwig Wittgenstein's *Tractatus* in 1921 fundamentally altered Schlick's conception of the task of philosophy. He now held that philosophy's task was the analysis of the concepts used in science and the language spoken in everyday life. Widely propagated by members of the Vienna Circle, this is the dominant view in English and American philosophy today.

Schlick was shot by a deranged former student while on his way to lecture at the University of Vienna on June 22, 1936. Owing to his death and to the hostility of the Nazi regime after the Anschluss, the members of the Circle were widely dispersed to Scandinavia, England, and the United States.

Further Reading

Moritz Schlick is listed in the Philosophy study guide (VII, F). The Vienna Circle was strongly influenced by Ludwig WITTGENSTEIN and G. E. MOORE and to a lesser extent by Ernst MACH, Gottlob FREGE, and Bertrand RUSSELL.

There is no major work on Schlick. Victor Kraft, *The Vienna Circle: The Origin of Neo-positivism* (1953), gives an account of the history and central doctrines of the group.

SCHLIEMANN / By Lothar L. Tresp

> Heinrich Schliemann (1822–1890) was a German merchant, world traveler, and archeologist. A man of enormous linguistic ability and personal determination, he combined a romantic enthusiasm and the calculating abilities of a practical realist in his search for the historical sites of Homeric Greece.

Heinrich Schliemann (pronounced shlē′män) was born on Jan. 6, 1822, at Neubukow in Mecklenburg. The early death of his mother and the financially straitened circumstances of his poor pastor father

Heinrich Schliemann. (The Bettmann Archive)

made it necessary for the family to separate when Schliemann was 9 years old. He was brought up by an uncle, but further family misfortunes forced him to leave high school and to attend a commercial school, from which he graduated in 1836.

Apprenticed to a small grocer, Schliemann labored in unhappiness and desolation for 5 years until a working accident forced him to give up this life. Determined to seek a new situation, he embarked upon a voyage to Venezuela, where he hoped to find more congenial employment. Shipwrecked off the coast of Holland, he found a position with a commercial firm in Amsterdam and engaged in intensive language study during his spare time. He devised his own method and learned English and French in 6 months each, adding Dutch, Spanish, Italian, and Portuguese in even shorter periods of study.

In 1844 Schliemann became corresponding clerk and bookkeeper with B. H. Schröder and Company. This firm's Russian connections induced him to add that language to his linguistic accomplishments, and in 1846 his employers sent him to St. Petersburg as their commercial agent. Although he continued to represent the Dutch firm for 11 years, Schliemann founded a mercantile house of his own in 1847 to which he added a Moscow branch in 1852. His enterprises flourished, aided by the demand for war materials during the Crimean War, and he accumulated a huge fortune.

Travels of Leisure

In 1863 Schliemann gave up his Russian enterprises to devote his time and wealth to the pursuit of his childhood dream, the discovery of historical Troy and Homer's Greece. He set out in 1864 on a world tour which took him to Carthage, India, China, Japan, and America, where he received citizenship, for which he had applied during an earlier visit. He settled in Paris, published his first book, *La Chine et le Japon* (1865; *China and Japan*), and engaged in studies in preparation for his archeological search. In 1868 he proceeded to Greece, where he visited various Homeric sites. From these experiences he published the book *Ithaka, der Peloponnes und Troja* (1869), in which he advanced two theories (later to be tested and borne out) that Hissarlik, not Bunarbashi, was the true site of Troy and that the Atreid graves at Mycenae were situated inside the walls of the citadel. This work earned him a doctorate from the University of Rostock.

Excavation of Troy

In 1870 Schliemann's excavations at Troy began in earnest. He discovered a great treasure of gold jewelry and other objects and published his findings in *Antiquités troyennes* (1874). Largely because of poor illustrations and organizational shortcomings, the book was not well received. In addition, he encountered difficulties from the Turkish government regarding permission to continue his excavations. He went to Mycenae, where he began to dig near the Lion Gate, eventually unearthing the famous Dome Tombs, the burial place of the Mycenaean kings. The finds of gold, silver, bronze, stone, and ivory objects were enormous, perhaps the greatest treasure trove ever discovered, and eventually led to Schliemann's book *Mycenae* (1877).

In 1878 Schliemann returned to Troy to resume the excavations. His finds were published in *Ilios, City and Country of the Trojans* (1880). In 1881 he presented his Homeric treasures to the German people to be housed in specially designated Schliemann Halls in the State Museum of Berlin.

Having meanwhile worked at another Homeric site, Orchomenos, Schliemann returned to Troy in 1882, accompanied by Wilhelm Dörpfeld, whose archeological and architectural knowledge introduced much-needed professional methodology into the excavations. The resulting evaluations were published as *Troja* (1884) and were a much-improved sequel to Schliemann's *Ilios* of 1880.

The last 6 years of Schliemann's life were spent with further excavations at the citadel of Tiryns (1884) and at Orchomenos (1886), with plans for work in Egypt and Crete and with actual excavation starts on Cythera and in Pylos. On Dec. 25, 1890, while Dörpfeld was leading another dig at Troy, Schliemann died in Naples. He had had a life of great accomplishments, rushing impatiently and with insurmountable energy from project to project. Although his findings frequently lacked a correct final interpretation, his drive and enthusiasm subjected the world of Homer and the profession of archeology to a fresh breeze which blew away the cobwebs of established assumptions and ushered in a new era of archeological scholarship.

Further Reading

Heinrich Schliemann is listed in the Social Sciences study guide (VI, A, 2). Another archeologist working in the Middle East was Sir Flinders PETRIE.

Schliemann's own account remains important as a basic source: *Mycenae: A Narrative of Researches and Discoveries at Mycenae and Tiryns* (1880; repr. 1967), which includes over 700 engravings and drawings. A sympathetic biography that contains many quotations from Schliemann's writings and letters is Emil Ludwig, *Schliemann of Troy: The Story of a Gold-seeker* (1931). Lynn and Gray Poole, *One Passion, Two Loves* (1966), describes Schliemann's life after 1869 and focuses on his close relationship with his second wife, Sophia. The most scholarly work on his excavations is Karl Schuchhardt, *Schliemann's Excavations: An Archaeological and Historical Study* (trans. 1891), which includes many sketches, pictures, and diagrams of the sites. Pierre S. R. Payne, *The Gold of Troy* (1959), with a chapter on Schliemann scholarship and a select bibliography, is useful for the general reader.

SCHLÜTER / By Edward A. Maser

Andreas Schlüter (ca. 1660–1714), German sculptor and architect, was the greatest exponent of the baroque style in northern Germany. His works are characterized by powerful, dynamic forms and great dignity.

Andreas Schlüter (pronounced shlü′tər), whose exact birth date is uncertain but which must have been in the early 1660s, came from the north of Germany, probably Hamburg or Danzig. Little is known of his early training. He worked in Warsaw as a sculptor (1689–1693). In 1694 he was working in Berlin as a sculptor, apparently called there by the prince-elector of Brandenburg, Frederick III, who later became King Frederick I of Prussia. In 1695 Schlüter was sent on a brief study trip to France and, in 1696, on one to Italy at the expense of the elector. Later that year Schlüter produced statues for the Long Bridge leading to the palace in Berlin, as well as over 100 decorative heads of warriors for the keystones of the arches of the Arsenal in Berlin. These heads were largely produced by his assistants after his models.

Monument to the Great Elector

In 1696 Schlüter began his designs for the bronze equestrian monument to the King's father, the Great Elector, his most famous work in sculpture. This over-life-size statue was executed between 1698 and 1700, and the four enchained warriors, symbolizing the four temperaments, at its base were completed in 1708. The monument was originally on the Long Bridge, but after

Andreas Schlüter. (Österreichische Nationalbibliothek, Vienna)

World War II it was placed in front of the Charlottenburg Palace. Inspired by such monuments as the Marcus Aurelius on the Capitol in Rome and François Girardon's equestrian statue of Louis XIV, the monument of the Great Elector is noteworthy for its great vitality and movement. Yet the dynamism of its large forms is more reminiscent of Gian Lorenzo Bernini than the aforementioned classical or classicizing examples.

Berlin Schloss

In 1699 Schlüter was appointed surveyor general of works for the elector, in charge of all buildings, and began work on a new palace on the island in the Spree, the famous Berlin Schloss. For it he designed not only the massive block of the structure itself but also all decorative details and the interiors. His organizational abilities were as important as his architectural talents in this enterprise, for he held the same sort of position in Berlin during the first decade of the 18th century that Bernini had earlier held in Rome, controlling all aspects of every architectural undertaking.

The construction of the Schloss was under Schlüter's direction until 1707, after which work continued under his successors, such as Eosander von Göthe. Those parts that were after Schlüter's designs were the Great Court, the Great Portal, and the main rooms of the first floor. All

revealed Schlüter's basically sculptural approach to architectural problems: his tendency to enliven large areas through the dramatic use of strongly projecting articulating elements. The sculptural decoration of the stairway and the ceiling of the Hall of the Knights (Rittersaal), representing the four continents, were also his. The Schloss, although less damaged during World War II than many other buildings in Berlin, was the victim of political considerations and was demolished by the East German authorities in 1950. Only the sculpture is preserved (Bode Museum, Berlin).

In Berlin, Schlüter also designed and executed such works as the pulpit in St. Mary's Church (1703), the Alte Post (1701–1704; destroyed in the late 19th century), and the Münzturm (1706), a water tower attached to the Mint. The imminent collapse of this tower, and the discovery of structural problems in his other buildings, notably the Arsenal, led to the downfall of the architect. Although he demolished the water tower himself and sought to justify his errors, his enemies at court thoroughly discredited him. He lost one office after another and became seriously ill. By 1710 he was in disgrace at court and was permitted to work only as a sculptor. The sarcophagus of the elector (1713) was his last important work in Berlin.

In 1714 Schlüter left for St. Petersburg, where he had been offered employment. He died there the same year shortly after his arrival.

Further Reading

Andreas Schlüter is listed in the Art study guide (III, F, 2; III, F, 3, d; III, G, 3, c). His statue of the Great Elector was influenced by works of François GIRARDON and Gian Lorenzo BERNINI.

The standard monographs on Schlüter are in German. In English only Eberhard Hempel, *Baroque Art and Architecture in Central Europe* (1965), deals with the artist to any degree.

SCHMOLLER / By Franklin Parker

The German economist Gustav Friedrich von Schmoller (1838–1917) broadened the study of economics by insisting that it be studied dynamically in the context of history and sociology.

Gustav Schmoller (pronounced shmōl′ər) was born on June 24, 1838, in Württemberg-Baden. He was from a family of civil servants and continued in that tradition. His studies in civic administration at the University of Tübingen included public finance, statistics, economics, administration, history, and sociology. He served as professor of civic administration at the universities of Halle (1864–1872), Strassburg (1872–1882), and

Berlin (1882–1913). He was also a member of academies in Berlin, Munich, St. Petersburg, Copenhagen, Vienna, and Rome.

In the early 1860s Schmoller defended the commercial treaty between France and the German Customs Union, negotiated with Prussian leadership. This defense curtailed his career in Württemberg but gained favor for him with Prussian authorities, and he was appointed official historian of Brandenburg and Prussia in 1887. He became a member of the Prussian state council in 1884 and representative of the University of Berlin in the Prussian upper house in 1889. He died at Bad Harzburg on June 27, 1917.

Schmoller was the founder and leader of the Association of German Academic Economists. He was also editor of several publications series, one of which was later known as *Schmoller's Yearbook* (from 1881). One of the first great organizers of research in the social sciences, he dominated for several decades the development of economics and of related social sciences. During this time hardly a chair of economics in German universities was filled without his approval.

In political activities Schmoller was a royalist, favored strong government, and had high regard for the Prussian civil service. He was a conservative social reformer who wanted to improve working-class conditions by means of better education, government regulations, cooperatives, and other reforms.

Schmoller's contribution to economics was to reject its study in a narrow analytical view and to place it in the context of the other social sciences. Opposing a theoretical approach, he preferred to include in economics relevant aspects of history, statistics, sociology, social psychology, social anthropology, geography, and even ethics and philosophy. He was eclectic in assembling these aspects into a panorama of the social sciences. He was challenged as superficial by theoretical economist Carl Menger of Vienna in an 1883 pamphlet, by historian Georg von Below in 1904, and by others. Modern critics view Schmoller's long dominance of German social scientists as unfortunate because its effect was to retard development of economic theory in Germany. Outside Germany his influence in economics was small, although he did influence American institutional economics.

Further Reading

Gustav von Schmoller is listed in the Social Sciences study guide (VI, C, 2). Other economists of this time were Karl MARX and Friedrich ENGELS.

For evaluations of Schmoller's place in economics and the social sciences see Charles Gide and Charles Rist, *A History of Economic Doctrines from the Time of the Physiocrats to the Present Day* (trans. 1915; 2d ed. 1948); Karl Menger, *Problems of Economics and Sociology*, edited with an introduction by Louis Schneider (1963); and Jurgen Herbst, *The German Historical School in American Scholarship: A Study in the Transfer of Culture* (1965).

Gustav von Schmoller, a painting by Kirin Chevalier. (New York Public Library, Picture Collection)

SCHNITZLER / By Klaus W. Jonas

The Austrian dramatist and novelist Arthur Schnitzler (1862–1931) is at his best in one-act plays and novellas that often deal with extreme situations—death, sexual conflicts, and neurotic and even psychotic states.

Born of Jewish parents in Vienna, where he spent almost his entire life as a physician, Arthur Schnitzler (pronounced shnĭts′lər) looked upon himself primarily as a scientist and never gave up his medical practice. His first creative period (1893–1900) saw the publication of numerous poems and sketches, largely centered on themes of infidelity and jealousy, and two major works, his first novella, *Sterben* (1894; *Dying*), and his first successful play, *Anatol* (1893).

In the mid-1890s Schnitzler was associated for a short time with a literary movement of impressionist writers, including Hugo von Hofmannsthal, who were violently

Arthur Schnitzler. (Süddeutscher Verlag)

ness technique to reveal a psychotic young girl's motives for disrobing in a hotel lobby.

Schnitzler's third and last period, from 1912 to the time of his death, has often been referred to as "retrospective." To this phase belong such masterpieces as *Frau Beate und ihr Sohn* (1913; *Beatrice*) and *Casanovas Heimfahrt* (1918; *Casanova's Homecoming*) and the novella *Traumgekrönt* (1925; *Rhapsody*). In two important works, his long autobiographical novel, *Der Weg ins Freie* (1908; *The Road to the Open*), and the play *Professor Bernhardi* (1913), Schnitzler deals with racial and religious prejudice, specifically with anti-Semitism, which he sees as a problem of general human concern. He chooses many of his characters from the medical profession and assigns to them the role of the *raisonneur* who expresses his own tolerant views on life and love.

Further Reading

Arthur Schnitzler is listed in the Literature study guide (III, H, 2, b). Frank WEDEKIND was another dramatist of this period.

Schnitzler's *My Youth in Vienna*, translated by Catherine Hutter (1970), is his diary of his early years, through the 1870s. The most complete study of him in English is Solomon Liptzin, *Arthur Schnitzler* (1932). A good sampling of critical investigations is the eight papers delivered at the University of Kentucky in 1962: *Studies in Arthur Schnitzler: Centennial Commemorative Volume*, edited by Herbert W. Reichert and Herman Salinger (1963). The most comprehensive and reliable guide to the literature by and about Schnitzler is Richard H. Allen, *An Annotated Arthur Schnitzler Bibliography, 1879–1965* (1966).

SCHOENBERG / By Dika Newlin

Arnold Schoenberg (1874–1951) was an Austrian composer whose discovery of the "method of composition with twelve tones" radically transformed 20th-century music.

opposed to the naturalism then in vogue in Berlin. But soon he broke away from café society—the Jung-Wien group, which gathered in Vienna's famous Café Griensteidl—and he never again joined any literary circle.

The highlight of Schnitzler's second phase (1900–1912) was his famous play *Reigen* (1900; *La Ronde*), which Eric Bentley has called "a great 'comedy' of sexual promiscuity." Banned, attacked, censored on its first appearance, and later withdrawn by Schnitzler himself, it has gradually won the reputation of a masterpiece of modern drama. *La Ronde*, in 10 brief dialogues between a man and a woman, reveals the attitudes of partners from all social classes before and after the act of love. Modern critics no longer see this play as pornographic but rather as a bitter, witty, and yet tender and melancholy examination of the human condition expressed through the metaphor of man's endless "round dance" of sexuality and desire.

As a writer of fiction, Schnitzler developed early in his career the technique known as stream of consciousness and later made famous by James Joyce. The best examples are two of his stories, *Leutnant Gustl* (1900; *None but the Brave*) and *Fräulein Else* (1925). The former is a long interior monologue describing an unpleasant young lieutenant who, insulted by a baker, broods until he reaches the decision to commit suicide in order to preserve his honor, only to be saved accidentally by the knowledge that the baker has died of a heart attack. In *Fräulein Else* Schnitzler used the stream-of-conscious-

The early music of Arnold Schoenberg (pronounced shœn'bûrg) represents the culmination of romantic musical ideals. His gigantic cantata *Gurre-Lieder* is, together with Gustav Mahler's Eighth Symphony, one of the last great works in the monumental style. It seemed impossible for music to develop any further in this direction. Thus, Schoenberg became one of the first 20th-century composers to write for small, specialized chamber ensembles. He transcended traditional tonal limitations and began to write "atonal" or "pantonal" music without a key center. This new style offered much freedom, but there was need of a system to control the new harmonic material thus made available.

After a period of experimentation, Schoenberg developed such a system: the method of composition with twelve tones. So far-reaching were the results of this discovery that Schoenberg's theories became, for a time, more famous than his compositions. However, since his death, his music has received more of the recognition that it deserves. Most important musical developments of the second half of the 20th century owe their impetus directly or indirectly to him.

Schoenberg was born in Vienna on Sept. 13, 1874. His interest in music began early. When he was 8 years old, he started to learn the violin, and he soon began composing violin duets. His parents were not musicians—his father, Samuel, owned a shoe store—but they enjoyed music and were sympathetic to his musical development.

Early Works

In the amateur orchestra Polyhymnia, Schoenberg met Alexander von Zemlinsky. They became close friends, and Zemlinsky began to give Schoenberg instruction in composition, the only formal teaching of this sort that he ever had. The String Quartet in D Major (1897, published 1966) is a good example of the immediate results. This was Schoenberg's first work to be played publicly in Vienna. As its Brahmsian style was quite accessible to the conservative taste of the audience, it was well received.

Quite different is Schoenberg's *Verklärte Nacht* (Transfigured Night), a string sextet inspired by Richard Dehmel's poem of the same name. While the orchestral tone poem, or symphonic poem (a composition telling a story in music), was common in the 19th century, Schoenberg's work represents the first attempt to transfer this form to chamber music. It was written in the summer of 1899. Zemlinsky tried to have it performed that fall, but its Wagnerian style was rejected by the conservative program committee of the Tonkünstlerverein. It was finally premiered in 1903. At that time it was still considered controversial, and audience reaction was hostile. Since then it has become one of Schoenberg's most popular works, especially in its versions for string orchestra.

From 1901 to 1903 Schoenberg lived in Berlin, where he conducted at the Überbrettl cabaret and later taught composition at the Stern Conservatory. He became friendly with Richard Strauss, who suggested Maurice Maeterlinck's *Pelléas et Mélisande* to him as a good subject for an opera. Without knowing of Claude Debussy's opera based on this play, Schoenberg began to write a symphonic poem on the same subject; he completed it in 1902. It is his only orchestral tone poem in the tradition of Franz Liszt and Richard Strauss.

Development of Atonality

Back in Vienna, Schoenberg began to teach privately. He attracted talented pupils: Alban Berg and Anton Webern came to him at this time. A stylistic change was beginning to occur in Schoenberg's work. Tonality, which had been more and more freely treated in such pieces as his Second String Quartet, was finally aban-

Arnold Schoenberg in 1944. (Wide World Photos)

doned. The date of completion of the piano piece Opus 11, no. 1 (Feb. 19, 1909), is an important one in the history of music, for this is the first composition to dispense completely with traditional tonality. In this new style any chord combination can be freely used, and there is no differentiation in the treatment of consonances and dissonances.

Writing about his new music in connection with a concert on Jan. 14, 1910, at which the piano pieces Opus 11 were premiered, Schoenberg said: "I have succeeded for the first time in approaching an ideal of expression and form that had hovered before me for some years. Hitherto I had not sufficient strength and sureness to realize that ideal. Now, however, that I have definitely started on my journey, I may confess to having broken the bonds of a bygone esthetic; and if I am striving toward a goal that seems to me to be certain, nevertheless I already feel the opposition that I shall have to overcome. I feel also with what heat even those of the feeblest temperament will reject my works, and I suspect that even those who have hitherto believed in me will not be willing to perceive the necessity of this new development."

Twelve-tone System

Schoenberg was right in his fears that he would be misunderstood. Even more misunderstood was his next stylistic change, which was gradually being prepared between 1916 and 1920. During those years he completed no major compositions; instead, he worked toward a solution of the structural problems of nontonal music. One day in July 1921 Schoenberg told his pupil Josef Rufer, "Today I have discovered something which will assure the supremacy of German music for the next hundred years." It was the method of composition with twelve tones. The Prelude of Schoenberg's Piano Suite, Opus 25 (completed July 29, 1921), is probably the first twelve-tone composition.

In the twelve-tone method each composition is based on a row, or series, using all twelve notes of the chromatic scale in an order chosen by the composer. Besides being presented in its original form, the row may be inverted, played backward, played backward in inversion, or transposed to any scale step. All harmonies and melodies in a composition are derived from its special row; thus, unity is assured. While some critics feared that music written in this way might become mechanical and inexpressive, Schoenberg continued to write highly personal and expressive compositions, using the expanded resources made available by the new method. From time to time he would return to traditional tonality in one or more works. However, it really made no difference to him whether his compositions were tonal, atonal, or twelve-tonal. As he said once, "I like them all, because I liked them when I wrote them."

In the 1920s Schoenberg seemed to have reached a peak in his career. His appointment as director of a composition class at the Prussian Academy of Arts, Berlin, took effect in 1926. Four years later he began his great biblical opera, *Moses und Aron.* (He never finished this work, but in its incomplete, two-act form it became, after his death, one of his greatest popular successes.) Under normal circumstances he might well have spent the rest of his life in Berlin. However, when the Nazis assumed power in Germany, Schoenberg, a Jew, was unwelcome. In September 1933 he was dismissed from the academy. The next month he sailed for America.

American Works

Schoenberg's first American teaching post was at the Malkin Conservatory in Boston (1933–1934). His health suffered from the climate, and he decided to move to Los Angeles. There, he taught first at the University of Southern California and then at the University of California, until age forced his retirement in 1944. He wrote some of his finest instrumental music in California: the Fourth String Quartet (1936), the Violin Concerto (1934–1936), the Piano Concerto (1942), and the String Trio (1946).

After his retirement, Schoenberg had hoped to find time to complete *Moses und Aron* and the oratorio *Die Jakobsleiter* (Jacob's Ladder), which he had begun in 1917. However, his poor health and the necessity of earning a living by private teaching made this impossible. During the last year of his life, he wrote a series of texts called *Modern Psalms,* which he described as "conversations with and about God." He was still able to compose part of the first psalm; the last words he set to music are "und trotzdem bete ich" (and yet I pray). On July 13, 1951, he died in Los Angeles.

Further Reading

Arnold Schoenberg is listed in the Music study guide (I, J, 1; II, D, 1). The romantic movement came to a close

with Schoenberg's early works and the late symphonies of Gustav MAHLER. Schoenberg's principal disciples were Alban BERG and Anton WEBERN. Other composers who used the twelve-tone system were Ernst KŘENEK, Luigi DALLAPICCOLA, and Milton BABBITT.

A representative collection of Schoenberg's correspondence is in *Letters,* edited by Erwin Stein (trans. 1964). Of Schoenberg's other writings, the collection of essays *Style and Idea,* edited by Dika Newlin (trans. 1950), has the greatest general interest. A useful preliminary biography, though not a definitive study, is H. H. Stuckenschmidt, *Arnold Schoenberg* (trans. 1959). Harold C. Schonberg, *The Lives of the Great Composers* (1968), briefly discusses Schoenberg.

Dika Newlin, *Bruckner-Mahler-Schoenberg* (1947; rev. ed. in preparation), presents Schoenberg's work as the culmination of a historical development that can be traced back to the 18th-century classical Viennese School. René Leibowitz, *Schoenberg and His School* (trans. 1949), takes a similar viewpoint but carries the line of development to Berg and Webern. A helpful general discussion of twelve-tone music is George Perle, *Serial Composition and Atonality: An Introduction to the Music of Schoenberg, Berg and Webern* (1962; 2d rev. ed. 1968). K. H. Wörner, *Schoenberg's Moses and Aaron* (trans. 1963), offers a detailed musical and textual analysis of what is probably Schoenberg's most important work.

SCHOLEM / By Malachi B. Martin

The Jewish scholar Gershom Scholem (born 1897) was a noted authority on Jewish mysticism. He examined the origins and influence of the Cabalist movement.

Born in Berlin, Germany, on Dec. 5, 1897, Gershom Scholem (pronounced shô′ləm) was educated at Berlin, Jena, Bern, and Munich universities. In 1923 he emigrated to Palestine, which became his permanent residence. In 1925 he became professor of Jewish mysticism at the Hebrew University, a post he retained until 1965. He was dean of the university from 1941 to 1943. In 1946 he was assigned the task of salvaging Jewish cultural treasures in the aftermath of World War II. He was a visiting professor and lecturer at many American universities, including Brown University (1956–1957).

Scholem's scholarly achievements are enormous in the field of Jewish mysticism. No other contemporary writer and, indeed, no former student of this field equaled him in breadth of knowledge, depth of perception, and power of synthesis. His publications are numerous, and they include *Das Buch Bahir* (1923), *Bibliografia Kabbalistica* (1927), *Major Trends of Jewish Mysticism* (1946), *The Beginnings of Kabbalism* (1949), *Sabbatai Zvi and*

Gershom Scholem. (American Friends of the Hebrew University, New York)

the *Sabbataian Movement* (2 vols., 1957), *Jewish Gnosticism and Talmudic Tradition* (1960), *Zur Kabbala und ihrer Symbolik* (1960), *Von der mystischen Gestalt der Gottheit* (1962), and *Judaica* (1963).

Before Scholem's time academic study of Jewish mysticism was not well developed. Scholem set out to master the manuscriptal tradition and thus to provide himself with an indispensable and superb instrument for analyzing the origin, the nature, and the history of Jewish mysticism. His work emphasized the Cabalist movement, since this is the only genuine form of mysticism developed by Judaism. Scholem examined the 12th-century rise of Cabalism in Provence, France. He concentrated on the *Book of Bahir,* the oldest Cabalist text known in the 12th century, and the Cabalist works composed in Provence during the 12th century. His analysis of the *Bahir* led him back to the early Jewish Gnosticism of the Middle East. He showed that even in the early Middle Ages and in strictly rabbanate circles, Gnostic doctrines and ideas flourished. This was probably because of the proximity of Syrian Gnostic and Mandaean sects. Sometime about the end of the 11th and the beginning of the 12th century, this Gnostic tradition met with a very vibrant Neoplatonism in southern France. A century later a fresh school of Cabalist mysticism sprang up in Spain around the town of Gerona in Catalonia.

Scholem established relationships between the Kathari movement, the teaching of John Scotus Erigena, and these traditions, besides elucidating the lines and teaching of many renowned Cabalists. He also demonstrated the influence of Cabalism on the Haskalah and Hasidic movements of the 18th and 19th centuries and noted its impact on the Zionist movement.

Further Reading

Gershom Scholem is listed in the Religion study guide (II, F, 1, e). Moses de LEON was a noted Cabalist.

There is no biography of Scholem. His work is often cited in Alexander Altmann, *Studies in Religious Philosophy and Mysticism* (1969).

SCHONGAUER / By Robert A. Koch

The German engraver and painter Martin Schongauer (ca. 1435–1491) was the first identifiable maker of fine prints in Germany and the finest master of this medium before Dürer.

Martin Schongauer (pronounced shōn′gou-ər) was the son of Caspar Schongauer, a goldsmith who moved from Augsburg to Colmar, on the upper Rhine, where he became a citizen in 1445. The earliest paintings of Martin have not been identified with certainty, but he apparently worked near Ulm about 1462. He is documented in 1465 as matriculating for a semester at the University of Leipzig, either to study or else to undertake some artistic commission; between that year and his reappearance in the records of Colmar in 1469, art historians have assumed a trip to the Netherlands.

The records show that Schongauer owned a house in Colmar in 1477. After 1488 he was working on the *Last Judgment* fresco, traces of which were uncovered in 1932, in the church at Breisach, where he died in 1491.

His Paintings

Schongauer's one certain extant panel painting is the magnificent *Madonna in the Rose Garden* (1473), a life-sized image commissioned by the church of St. Martin in Colmar. Monumental yet intimate, Mary bends her head in humility as two angels hover above with a golden crown, her attribute as Queen of Heaven. The figure style is based on that of the Dutch painter Dirk Bouts, but the dense and minutely described trellis of rose vines and birds which enclose her betray the hand of an engraver.

Two other paintings, both small, reveal Schongauer's characteristic style and, because of their high quality, are probably by his own hand: a *Nativity* and a *Holy Family.* Both seem to reflect the mature style of his engravings from the late 1470s.

Late Gothic Master

It is as engraver that Schongauer's importance in the development of European art justly lies. Since original prints may exist in many "originals" and are highly mobile, the master's fame quickly spread in his own lifetime. The young Albrecht Dürer journeyed to Colmar to meet him—in vain, as it turned out, for the master had recently died.

Schongauer forms a link between the early engravers, as represented by Master E. S., and the Renaissance ideals first forcibly expressed by Dürer. In both subject matter and style his prints manifest the quintessence of the late Gothic spirit in a special way, as do the sculptures of Tilman Riemenschneider and the paintings of Rogier van der Weyden.

All of Schongauer's 115 engravings bear his monogram, but none is dated, so that time sequence is based on stylistic grounds. There is, however, a distinction between early and late in the rendering of the "M" of the monogram: in the earlier the lines of the "M" are vertical, and in the later they are flared. The first period dates from about 1465 to 1475, the second from about 1475 until his death.

Quite a number of Schongauer's religious compositions were derived from paintings by the Flemish masters Jan van Eyck, Hugo van der Goes, Bouts, and especially Van der Weyden. Schongauer never slavishly copied but re-created their world of concrete forms, based on realistic observation, into a wonderfully spiritualized, late Gothic form world that is abstracted in the pure terms of black and white lines.

His Engravings

The *Virgin and Child with a Parrot*, one of his earliest engravings and dating possibly about 1465, with a half-

Gabriel, one of the pair of engravings forming the Annunciation *by Schongauer. (Musée d'Unterlinden, Colmar)*

Martin Schongauer, a portrait by Hans Burgkmair, dated 1483, in the Alte Pinakothek, Munich. (Bildarchiv Staatsbibliothek, Berlin)

length Madonna and nude Child in an abstracted architectural setting, is related to a painting by Bouts. Schongauer's progress in the technique of engraving over his predecessor, Master E. S., is evidenced by the use of modeling lines that follow the forms and reveal their shapes and of cast shadows and reflected lights. Whereas the background in this print is merely a filler, Schongauer soon developed this space so that it is filled with exciting and varied passages, as in the early *Nativity*, the figures of which are inspired by Van der Weyden's *Bladelin Triptych*. Schongauer's *Death of the Virgin* presents a dramatic perspective rendering which has a parallel in design and emotion in the painting by Van der Goes, dating about 1480. Finally, a lost painting by Jan van Eyck, the *Road to Calvary*, was the inspiration for Schongauer's largest and most famous print. The composition teems with caricatured figures in a dramatically pictorial landscape setting.

Strictly Schongauer's own invention is the famous *Temptation of St. Anthony* print, in which the resolute man of God is shown airborne, being assaulted by wildly imaginative zoomorphic creatures. Also original and unprecedented is the greatly detailed rendering of the *Censer*, a reminiscence in the artist's later years of his earliest years in his father's goldsmith shop.

Schongauer made series of prints unified in theme and

size. In his late style are the 10 exquisite figures of the *Wise* and *Foolish Virgins*, silhouetted against the pure whiteness of the paper sheet. In his own day, and down to the present, the most famous series is the *Passion of Christ*, a set of 12 plates. Innumerable copies of these designs were made throughout Europe, and they achieved almost canonical importance in the art of the time.

Among other prints in Schongauer's mature style is the stunning pair of the *Annunciation*, with Gabriel and Mary on separate sheets. These decoratively abstracted figures possess a refined metallic brilliance and subtle tone expressive of the particular nature of engraving that can only be called classic. Schongauer's art, especially his prints, marks a milestone in the history of draftsmanship.

Further Reading

Martin Schongauer is listed in the Art study guide (III, C, 2). He was influenced by Dirk BOUTS, Jan van EYCK, Hugo van der GOES, and Rogier van der WEYDEN. Another late Gothic master was the sculptor Tilman RIEMENSCHNEIDER. Albrecht DÜRER introduced Italian Renaissance ideas to the north.

There is no book-length study of Schongauer in English. The paintings and engravings are most conveniently reproduced in the German edition by Julius Baum, *Martin Schongauer* (1948). For the engravings alone, and for a fine text in English, see Alan Shestack, *The Complete Engravings of Martin Schongauer* (1969).

SCHOOLCRAFT
/ **By Charles and Joyce Crowe**

The American explorer and ethnologist Henry Rowe Schoolcraft (1793–1864) was one of the earliest writers on American Indian culture and history.

Henry Schoolcraft was born on March 28, 1793, in Albany County, N.Y. His father was a glassmaker. After attending local schools, Schoolcraft took up glassmaking, which he combined with private study and lectures at Middlebury College.

Between 1810 and 1817 Schoolcraft managed factories in New York, Vermont, and New Hampshire and wrote a treatise on glassmaking. In 1818 he traveled westward to pursue his geological interests. *A View of the Lead Mines of Missouri* (1819) established his scientific reputation and won him a place with an expedition to the copper mines around Lake Superior. He wrote of this adventure in *Narrative Journal of Travels through the Northwestern Regions of the United States . . . to the Mississippi River* (1821).

By 1821 Schoolcraft was a well-known geologist, but he had become acquainted with the northern Indians, and in 1822 he was appointed Indian agent in Sault Ste.

Henry Schoolcraft. (Library of Congress)

Marie, Mich. In 1823 he married Jane Johnston. He pursued Indian studies, carried on negotiations between the Indians and the government, and was promoted to superintendent of Indian affairs for Michigan. As Indian superintendent, he negotiated several important Indian treaties transferring land to the state.

Although as Indian agent Schoolcraft deprived the Indians of vast tracts of land, he demonstrated a sympathetic, if somewhat paternalistic, concern for their welfare. His treaty of 1836 provided for a system of annuities to be paid individually to the Indians rather than in lump sums to tribal chiefs. He supported government schools and mission schools as well, in the belief that it was necessary to "Christianize" Indians in order to educate them. He urged the teaching of agriculture to compensate for the loss of their hunting grounds and took a strong stand against alcohol.

Schoolcraft is best remembered as a scholar of Indian ethnology. Among his numerous volumes containing descriptions of Indian life and culture are *Algic Researches* (2 vols., 1839); *Oneóta* (8 vols., 1844–1845); *Notes on the Iroquois* (1847); *Personal Memories . . . of Thirty Years with the Indian Tribes* (1851); and *Historical and Statistical Information Respecting the History, Condition, and Prospects of the Indian Tribes of the United States* (6 vols., 1851–1857). These accounts of Indian life and folklore contributed greatly to anthropological science. Schoolcraft died on Dec. 10, 1864.

Further Reading

Henry Schoolcraft is listed in the American History

study guide (VI, C, 3). His ethnographic works provided source material for poets Henry Wadsworth LONGFEL-LOW and James Russell LOWELL.

Schoolcraft is a neglected figure, but Chase S. and Stellanova Osborn have a long, appreciative account in *Schoolcraft, Longfellow, Hiawatha* (1942). See also Edmund W. Gilbert, *The Exploration of Western America, 1800–1850* (1933), and Rufus W. Griswold, *Henry Rowe Schoolcraft* (1849).

* * *

SCHOPENHAUER / By Carleton Dallery

The German philosopher Arthur Schopenhauer (1788–1860), whose pessimistic philosophy was widely known in the late 19th century in Europe and the United States, held that ultimate reality was nothing but senseless striving or will, having no divine origin and no historical end.

Arthur Schopenhauer (pronounced shō′pən-hou-ər) was born in Danzig on Feb. 22, 1788. His father, a successful Dutch businessman, had a taste for urbane living, travel, and bourgeois culture, while his mother aspired to the more exotic culture of writers and nonconformists. When Schopenhauer was 5, Danzig, formerly a free mercantile city, was annexed by Poland. As a consequence, his family moved to Hamburg, Germany, in search of a more congenial setting for his father's business. In 1797 Schopenhauer was sent to stay with a family in France, returning to Hamburg after 2 years to enter a private school. Later he became interested in literature, earning the disapproval of his father, who nonetheless gave him the choice of pursuing serious literary studies or traveling with the family for 2 years. Schopenhauer chose to travel.

His voyages over, Schopenhauer took a job as a clerk in a Hamburg merchant's office. That year, 1805, his father died, apparently a suicide. The mercantile world held only drudgery for young Schopenhauer, whose ambitions and desires were both unfocused and frustrated. Feeling constrained by a promise to his father, Schopenhauer remained at work until 1807, when he joyfully resigned in order to study Greek and Latin in a school at Gotha. Having enraged an unsympathetic instructor, he transferred to a school in Weimar, where his mother had already established herself as mistress of a literary salon frequented by Goethe and other notables. But Schopenhauer had earlier quarreled with his mother, whom he thought too free with her ideas and her favors. He therefore resided with his mentor, the philologist Franz Passow, who paid his tuition. Schopenhauer's studies went well, and in 1809, on acquiring a handsome legacy, he enrolled at the University of Göttingen. He studied mostly the sciences and medicine but eventually turned to philosophy.

Philosophical Studies

Schopenhauer's new passion for philosophy led him to the University of Berlin, where he hoped to cull the wisdom of Johann Gottlieb Fichte, then the foremost philosopher in Germany. He was disappointed in Fichte but remained at the university until 1813, when Prussia mobilized to expel the French after Napoleon's defeat. Seeing the dangers of staying in Berlin and having no heart for nationalistic fervor, Schopenhauer sought refuge in Rudolstadt. There he completed his doctoral dissertation, which he submitted successfully to the University of Jena. He published the dissertation at his own expense and then returned to Weimar. He met Goethe, who seemed sympathetic to his thinking. One fruit of their conversations was Schopenhauer's brief study *Über das Sehn und die Farben* (1816; *On Vision and Colors*).

"The World as Will and Idea"

Schopenhauer's unhappy relations with his mother finally terminated in open hostility, and he moved to Dresden. By this time the central and simple idea of his philosophy had taken hold in his mind. The principal source of this idea was his own experience and moods, but the expression of it owed much to the philosophies of Plato and Immanuel Kant and the mystical literature of India. He foresaw that his reflections would eventually lift him above the absurd stresses and conflicts of his life, and he thought that ultimately his writings would usher in a new era not only in philosophy but also in human history. Whereas former philosophies had been parceled

Arthur Schopenhauer in 1854. (New York Public Library, Picture Collection)

into schools and special problems, his own, as he envisaged it, would be a single, simple fabric. The simplest expression of this potent idea is probably the very title of the book he wrote at Dresden, *Die Welt als Wille und Vorstellung (The World as Will and Idea)*. The world is necessarily present to a subject that perceives it; thus the world is "idea" or "representation." Yet the world is not created or constructed by the subject or the mind; its own nature is will, or blind striving. "My body and my will are one," and in the final analysis one person's will is indistinguishable from every other form of willing.

The book was printed by a reluctant publisher in 1818 and failed to gain a public. Nevertheless, with two books to his credit, Schopenhauer was given a lectureship in philosophy at the University of Berlin. At that time G. W. F. Hegel was the center of attention, and Schopenhauer decided to compete with him by lecturing at the same hour. But he addressed an empty room, and shortly his academic career was over.

Other Writings

In 1831 cholera was epidemic in Berlin, and Schopenhauer fled to Frankfurt, where he stayed for the rest of his life. In 1836 he published a study of contemporary science, *Über den Willen in der Natur (On the Will in Nature)*, showing that his philosophy was consistent with the sciences. In 1839 he won a prize from the Norwegian Scientific Society for an essay on freedom of the will. To this essay he added another, publishing them in 1841 as *Die Beiden Grundprobleme der Ethik (The Two Fundamental Problems of Ethics)*. During these years he revised and augmented the text of *The World as Will and Idea*, which was republished in 1844 with 50 new chapters. In 1847 he republished his dissertation, *Über die vierfache Wurzel des Satzes vom zureichenden Grunde (On the Fourfold Root of the Principle of Sufficient Reason)*. By now he was attracting some notice, but the fame he had predicted for himself was still only a dream.

Schopenhauer's style of life in his Frankfurt years has always both fascinated and puzzled his admirers. Though he wrote about the ultimate value of negating the will, he displayed unusual willfulness; though he extolled tranquility, he was always energetic; though he wrote savage diatribes against women, he could not forgo female company.

"Parerga und Paralipomena"

At last, in 1851, Schopenhauer published the book that brought him fame and followers. Titled *Parerga und Paralipomena*, it was a collection of highly polished, insightful essays and aphorisms. Its style was probably the chief reason for the book's immediate success. Yet the ideas were important too, particularly the notion that will was primary over intellect. The pessimism that follows from such a notion was already in vogue, and Schopenhauer became its voice. Another reason for his fame was surely his appeal to the inner experience of moods and feelings, in contrast to the more traditional appeals to history, reason, authority, and objective evidence. His philosophy takes its source in "the selfsame unchangeable being which is before us." Life is all suffering, he said, but it can be reflected upon, and then it will be seen to be "nothing." Schopenhauer died on Sept. 21, 1860. By then he had countless followers, and he was idolized as a kind of savior.

Further Reading

Arthur Schopenhauer is listed in the Philosophy study guide (VI, A, 1). He influenced Leo TOLSTOY, Marcel PROUST, Thomas MANN, and Ludwig WITTGENSTEIN.

Schopenhauer's own writings are readily available in translation. Particularly noteworthy is a selection of the essays and aphorisms from *Parerga and Paralipomena*, edited and translated by R. J. Hollingdale (1970), which includes an introduction containing biographical information. Patrick Gardiner, *Schopenhauer* (1963), is a study of the philosopher's life and works. Schopenhauer's life is presented in detail in Helen Zimmern, *Arthur Schopenhauer: His Life and Philosophy* (1876), and in William Wallace, *Life of Schopenhauer* (1890). A more critical assessment of Schopenhauer's work is in Frederick Copleston, *Arthur Schopenhauer: Philosopher of Pessimism* (1946).

SCHOUTEN / By Brian H. Fletcher

William Cornelius Schouten (ca. 1580–1625) was a Dutch explorer and navigator. In 1616 he discovered a new route to the Pacific via Cape Horn.

The exact birth date of William Schouten (pronounced sKHou′tən) is unknown, but the year was probably 1580 and the place Hoorn in what is now Holland. He became a seafarer and made three trips to the East Indies between 1601 and 1603. His reputation as a navigator and interest in exploring distant parts attracted the attention of Isaac Le Maire, a wealthy Amsterdam merchant who in 1615 appointed him to command the *Eendracht* on a voyage to the Pacific.

One object was to search for the great south land about whose existence and riches rumors abounded. Another was to find a route into the Pacific other than those then known to exist via the Strait of Magellan and the Cape of Good Hope. The Dutch East India Company alone was permitted to use these routes; thus it had a monopoly over trade in the Pacific. Le Maire, who had formed a rival trading company, believed that another entrance lay south of the Strait of Magellan. If it could be found, the trade of the Pacific would be open to his company.

The *Eendracht*, accompanied by the *Hoorn*, later destroyed by fire in Patagonia, sailed for South America on June 14, 1615. Schouten's official position was that of master mariner, and Le Maire's son Jacob accompanied

*Dutch sailing ships from the time of William Schouten. The vessel on the right is a merchant
ship of the Dutch East India Company, the company whose trade restrictions Schouten tried to
evade.*

the voyage as merchant and president. In January 1616
their first goal was attained when a new entrance to the
Pacific around Cape Horn was discovered and named after their hometown.

From there they sailed across the Pacific, passing
through some of the islands of the Tuamoto and Tonga
groups. They moved on to New Ireland and to other islands of the Bismarck Archipelago and later spent some
time examining the northern coastline of New Guinea.
From there they sailed among more of the Pacific islands,
arriving at Ternate on Sept. 17, 1616, where they encountered a large Dutch fleet under Adm. van Spilber-
gen.

Their efforts were favorably received, but at Batavia,
their last port of call, the Dutch governor general, Jan
Pietersz Coen, refused to believe that they had discovered a third route into the Pacific. Viewing them as tres-
passers who had broken the East India Company's charter, he confiscated their ship and sent them back to
Holland under arrest. Eventually Le Maire succeeded in
clearing their name and securing recompense for their
treatment.

Following his release Schouten published a narrative of
the voyage under his own name, thereby precipitating a
clash with Jacob Le Maire, who objected to being given
no credit. A later edition of the same work was issued by
Le Maire, and some historians believe that he was justified in claiming most of the credit. Schouten in Septem-

ber 1619 captained a vessel of the Dutch East India Company and made several voyages to the East Indies. In
1625 bad weather forced him into Antongil Bay, on the
east coast of Madagascar, where he died.

Further Reading

William Schouten is listed in the Geography and Exploration study guide (IV, A, 3). An explorer in the service of the Dutch East India Company was Abel TAS-
MAN.

Biographical details about Schouten are scarce and
mainly found scattered in Dutch sources. Accounts of
Schouten's voyage are in Alexander Dalrymple, *Historical Collection of the Several Voyages and Discoveries
in the South Pacific Ocean* (1770–1771; repr. 1967),
and John C. Beaglehole, *The Exploration of the Pacific*
(1934; 3d ed. 1966). See also Peter H. Buck, *Explorers of
the Pacific* (1953).

SCHRÖDINGER / By Roger H. Stuewer

**The Austrian physicist Erwin Schrödinger
(1887–1961) was the founder of wave
mechanics and described the quantum behavior
of electrons.**

For nearly 5 decades, Erwin Schrödinger (pronounced shrœ'dĭng-ər), one of the most creative theoretical physicists of the 20th century, contributed papers to the scientific literature. Yet, from the start, his intellectual life was broadly based. He illustrated the breadth of his interests when he described how he intended to fulfill the duties of a professorship he expected to receive in 1918 at Czernowitz, Austria: "I was prepared to do a good job lecturing on theoretical physics ... but for the rest, to devote myself to philosophy, being deeply imbued at the time with the writings of Spinoza, Schopenhauer, Mach, Richard Semon and Richard Avenarius." This professorship did not materialize. Nevertheless, throughout his life his philosophical concerns came to the surface, principally because he recognized that physics alone cannot provide an answer to Plotinus's ancient question, "And we, who are we, anyway?" Schrödinger's life was unified by his search for an answer to that simple but profound question.

Schrödinger was born on Aug. 12, 1887, in Vienna, the son of a successful and cultured businessman. In 1906 he entered the University of Vienna, where he was most stimulated by the experimental physicist Franz Exner and the theoretical physicist Fritz Hasenöhrl. After Schrödinger completed his doctoral degree in 1910, he remained as an assistant to Exner. In that capacity he explored various problems, many in solid-state physics.

In 1914 Schrödinger became privatdozent at Vienna but almost immediately found himself serving as an artillery officer in Italy. Shortly after he married Annamaria Bertel in 1920, he went to the University of Jena as an assistant to Max Wien. Within the next year he was called, first as associate professor to the Technische Hochschule in Stuttgart, then as full professor to the University of Breslau, and finally as full professor to the University of Zurich. His years at Zurich (1921–1927) were, scientifically speaking, the most productive in his career.

Discovery of Wave Mechanics

In the immediate post–World War I years, Schrödinger worked on a variety of problems in different areas of physics: general relativity, statistical mechanics, radiation theory, the theory of colors, solid-state physics, and atomic spectroscopy. Some of his results are of great historical interest but have been superseded by new insights; others have remained of permanent interest. All of this work was but a prelude to those famous 2 months in 1925/1926, when, in an outburst of genius, he discovered wave mechanics.

When Schrödinger learned of Louis de Broglie's "matter-wave" hypothesis, he immediately tried to use it to explain the bright line spectrum emitted by the hydrogen atom; that is, he tried to apply it to the case of a single electron electrically "bound" to a proton. The results of his investigations—the wave equation he postulated and to which he applied the appropriate "boundary conditions"—were not in agreement with experiment. Discouraged, he put the work aside for some months—until one day in late 1925 the thought struck him that perhaps he should go against his instincts and not take account of

Erwin Schrödinger. (Suddeutscher Verlag, Munich)

the relativistic mass increase of the electron. The results were in striking agreement with experiment! Interestingly, it is now known that even Schrödinger's first, relativistic treatment of the problem is essentially correct—earlier, he had simply not taken account of the "spin" of the electron, a concept unknown to him at the time.

The nonrelativistic wave equation that Schrödinger assumed to govern the behavior of the electron in the hydrogen atom was of course the equation now universally known as the Schrödinger wave equation, the fundamental equation of wave mechanics. In less than 2 months he discovered his equation and began applying his elegant and beautiful theory to enough physical situations to carry complete conviction of its correctness. The capstone of his achievements was his proof of the logical equivalence of wave mechanics and "matrix mechanics," the latter discovered almost simultaneously by Werner Heisenberg in 1926.

Later Scientific Work

In 1927 Schrödinger became Max Planck's successor at the University of Berlin, where he remained until the political events of 1933 and the accompanying anti-Semitic attacks on many of his colleagues forced him, as a matter of conscience, to resign his position. That year he received the Nobel Prize in physics, sharing it with Paul Dirac.

Schrödinger was a fellow at Oxford University from 1933 to 1936, when he accepted a professorship at the University of Graz. After Hitler annexed Austria in 1938, Schrödinger's outspoken anti-Nazism forced him to flee to Italy. As a member of the Pontifical Academy in Rome, he was reasonably safe and began to explore an idea communicated to him earlier by Eamon De Valera, a mathematician who at the time was also president of the Irish Republic, to establish a research institute in Dublin modeled after the Institute for Advanced Study in Princeton. Schrödinger went to Dublin in 1939 as director of the institute's School of Theoretical Physics. By the time he left Dublin in 1956 for Vienna (where a special chair in theoretical physics was created for him), his health was badly damaged and his productive life in physics was over.

During the preceding 3 decades, however, Schrödinger had continued to contribute to the development of quantum theory. He explored the theory of the Compton effect and potential barrier-penetration problems, and he developed the elegant factorization ("ladder operator") technique for generating solutions to the Schrödinger equation for some particular problems. In 1930 he demonstrated that a Dirac electron traveling in free space has superimposed on its motion a very small oscillatory motion, or *Zitterbewegung*, an insight which was subsequently of considerable theoretical importance for certain studies. Schrödinger carried out studies on relativity, cosmology, the unified field theory, meson physics, counter (detector) statistics, and statistical mechanics. He rarely worked with a colleague or student. Like Albert Einstein, he was a "horse for single harness" whose influence was disseminated and perpetuated not by a band of devoted followers but, rather, by his extensive writings.

Humanistic Concerns

Schrödinger was always deeply concerned with philosophical questions—not only those that pertain to scientific issues but also those that pertain to essentially humanistic issues. The fundamental reason for his concern with these issues was his full recognition of the limitations of science. He was convinced, for example, that Heisenberg's uncertainty principle has nothing whatsoever to do with the age-old question of human free will. He believed that to illuminate questions such as these—to obtain a complete world picture—one requires the union of all knowledge, the insights achieved in all disciplines.

Schrödinger's quest to understand the nature of science and self led him to the study of history, particularly ancient history. He regarded Thales of Miletus as the first scientist because of Thales's profound insight that nature is understandable or comprehensible and not characterized by a capricious interplay of superstitions and uncontrollable forces. A century later Heraclitus concluded that this comprehensibility is possible only if the world is so constructed as to appear the same to all sane, waking, persons—only if there exists a "world in common."

According to Schrödinger, this world in common is discovered through observation in combination with insights of a metaphysical nature—hunches, spontaneous creative thought, and the like—that guide the interpretation of the observations. He believed that this world in common, to be comprehensible, had to be to a large degree a deterministic, causal world. Chance elements could enter only through the "intersection of causal chains"; these chance elements are precisely the sort of events that scientists prefer not to talk about, but that theologians and philosophers are profoundly interested in. Thus, once again, Schrödinger was led to conclude that the only way to achieve a complete world picture is to take account of nonscientific as well as scientific

knowledge. He felt this to be particularly true when discussing questions like the origin and nature of life, as well as the profoundly interesting role that chance played in Darwinian evolution.

Schrödinger died in Vienna on Jan. 4, 1961.

Further Reading

Erwin Schrödinger is listed in the Science study guide (VII, C, 2). His wave mechanics and the matrix mechanics of Werner HEISENBERG, supplemented by the work of Paul DIRAC, Max BORN, and others, are collectively known as "quantum mechanics," which revolutionized knowledge of atomic structure.

Schrödinger discussed his work in his Nobel lecture, reprinted in *Nobel Lectures in Physics*, vol. 2 (1965). A collection of letters exchanged by Schrödinger, Einstein, Planck, and Hendrik Lorentz is *Letters on Wave Mechanics*, edited by K. Przibram and translated by M. J. Klein (1967). The most complete source of information on Schrödinger and his work is William T. Scott, *Erwin Schrödinger: An Introduction to His Writings* (1967), which includes a bibliography. An obituary by Walter Heitler is in the *Biographical Memoirs of Fellows of the Royal Society of London*, vol. 7 (1961). For the historical significance of Schrödinger's work see Max Jammer, *The Conceptual Development of Quantum Mechanics* (1966).

SCHUBERT / By Elaine Brody

Franz Peter Schubert (1797–1828), an early romantic Austrian composer, is best known for his lieder, German art songs for voice and piano.

The lieder of Franz Schubert (pronounced shoo´bərt) assumed great importance during the 19th century as a result of several concomitant cultural and sociological developments in Germany, which included the new profusion of lyric poetry, particularly in the works of Goethe, and the evolution of the piano into a highly complex mechanism. As a composer, Schubert possessed an astonishing lyric gift and at times turned out several songs in a day.

In musical history Schubert stands with others at the beginning of the romantic movement, anticipating the subjective approach to composition of later composers but lacking Beethoven's forcefulness and inventive treatment of instrumental music. Despite his more conservative tendencies, however, Schubert's contributions include the introduction of cyclical form in his *Wanderer Fantasy* for piano, the use of long-line melodies—instead of motto-type themes—in his piano sonatas and chamber music, and the increased emphasis on the role of the piano accompaniments in his lieder. Many of his large-scale instrumental pieces were unknown until after

Franz Schubert in 1825, a wash drawing by Wilhelm August Rieder. Schubert's friends considered this drawing to be the most accurate likeness of the composer. (Bildarchiv)

the middle of the 19th century. (The *Unfinished* Symphony, for example, did not receive its first public performance until 1865, 43 years after it was written!) Furthermore, unlike many of the other romantic composers, such as Carl Maria von Weber, Hector Berlioz, Franz Liszt, and Richard Wagner, Schubert did not engage in a literary career; nor was he a conductor or virtuoso performer. Consequently he did not achieve considerable public recognition during his lifetime.

Childhood and Training

Schubert was born in Vienna on Jan. 31, 1797, the fourth son of Franz Theodor Schubert, a schoolmaster, and Elizabeth Vietz, in domestic service in Vienna. Franz received instruction in the violin from his father, his older brother Ignaz, and Michael Holzer, the organist at the Liechtenthal parish church. In 1808, through a competitive examination, Franz was accepted into the choir of the Imperial Court Chapel as well as the Stadtkonvikt (Royal Seminary), where he received a fine education and his talents were encouraged by the principal. A 20-year-old law student, Joseph Spaun, who founded an orchestra among these students, formed a lifelong friendship with Schubert.

In 1814 the genius of Schubert was first manifest in *Gretchen am Spinnrade*, inspired by his reading of Goethe's *Faust*. His first Mass, which included solos for a young woman friend, Therese Grob, and his first symphony appeared about this time and showed the influence of Franz Joseph Haydn. Schubert modeled his earliest songs, particularly the ballads, for example, *Hage's Klage* (1811), after those by Johann Rudolf Zumsteeg. Besides *Gretchen*, Schubert wrote five other Goethe songs that year. Before he died, he had set approximately 57 poems by the poet, at times exceeding in his music the high attainment of Goethe in the poetry.

Early Period, 1814–1820

By the end of 1814 Schubert was an assistant in his father's school and had begun to make the acquaintance of numerous poets, lawyers, singers, and actors, who soon would be the principal performers of his works at private concerts in their homes or in those of their more affluent friends. Spaun, now a student at the University of Vienna, introduced Schubert to his colleagues at the school, Johann Mayrhofer and Franz von Schober, the latter a dilettante in law, acting, writing, and publishing, who in turn introduced Schubert to the renowned singer Michael Vogl.

In 1816 Spaun sent a volume of Schubert's songs to Goethe for his consideration. All the songs were to texts by Goethe, and some, *Gretchen*, *Wandrers Nachtlied*, *Heidenröslein*, and *Erlkönig*, are among Schubert's most celebrated songs. Eventually Goethe returned the album, but he was unimpressed. Other 18th-century lyric poets whose works Schubert set include J. G. von Herder, the collector and translator of folk songs, and F. G. Klopstock. Friedrich von Schiller's poems account for 31 settings. None can compare, however, with the remarkable Goethe lieder. Even the uninitiated must respond to the excitement of the *Erlkönig,* where by means of changing accompaniment figures, sharp dissonance, and effective modulations Schubert differentiates the four characters of the ballad—narrator, father, son, and Erlking—and creates one of the masterpieces of romantic music.

The significance of Schubert's lieder tends to eclipse his equally fine choral writing in his six Masses. Unfortunately we cannot say the same of his approximately 11 completed works for the stage. Schubert's lyrical gift did not extend to large-scale dramatic works; his talents showed themselves most effectively in the more precise miniatures.

While still a schoolmaster, Schubert composed Symphonies No. 2 through No. 5, the outer two works being in the key of B-flat, a tonality he seems to have favored. At this time he also wrote many of the delightful dances, waltzes, and *Ländler* for which he was known during his lifetime. By 1817 Schubert was installed in the home of his friend Schober, where the presence of an excellent instrument may have inspired him to write several piano sonatas. In his father's house there had been no piano. Examination of the sonatas will prove Schubert to have been rather daring in his juxtaposition of keys, particularly in development sections.

In addition to instrumental compositions of 1817, lieder still flowed from Schubert's pen (50 that year). Among the best are Schiller's *Gruppe aus dem Tartarus;* the delightful *Die Forelle,* which later provided the theme for the variation movement of the so-called *Trout Quintet; An die Musik,* Schubert's hymn to music which was inspired by Schober's poem; and *Der Tod und das Mädchen* to words by the minor poet Claudius. This last song appears again as the theme of the variations in the second movement of the String Quartet *Death and the Maiden.* In July 1817 Schubert was appointed to the ménage of Count Esterhazy, who, with his wife and children, spent winters in an estate slightly north of Schönbrunn and summers at Zseliz in Hungary. There Schubert composed many of his four-hand works.

Middle Period, 1820–1825

Between 1820 and 1823 Schubert achieved his musical maturity. Two of his operettas and several of his songs were performed in public; amateurs and professional quartets sang his part-songs for male voices; and some of his works began to be published. Private concerts at the Sonnleithners and other middle-class residences soon brought Schubert a degree of renown. Sonnleithner has left us the following description of the composer (as repeated in O. E. Deutsch's *Memoirs,* 1958): "Schubert was below average height, with a round fat face, short neck, a not very high forehead, and thick, brown, naturally curly hair; back and shoulders rounded, arms and hands fleshy, short fingers, his eyes . . . gray blue, eye-

brows bushy, nose stubby and broad, lips thick; the face somewhat negroid. . . . His head sat somewhat squeezed between his shoulders, inclining rather forward—Schubert always wore spectacles. In repose his expression appeared rather dull rather than vivacious; sullen rather than cheerful; one could have taken him for an Austrian or more likely a Bavarian peasant."

In September 1821 Schubert and Schober left Vienna for the country with the intention of writing *Alfonso und Estrella,* his only grand opera. Shortly after his return to the city, he met Edward Bauernfeld, who introduced him to Shakespeare's works. In the fall of 1822, having completed his Mass in A-flat, Schubert began work on the Symphony in B Minor, which became known as the *Unfinished.* Three movements were sketched; two were completed. The reasons for the work being left incomplete are open to conjecture.

Schubert's health deteriorated, and in May he spent time in the Vienna General Hospital. Soon afterward, while working on the third act of another opera, *Fierabras,* he began his remarkable song cycle *Die schöne Müllerin* to the poetry of Wilhelm Müller. *Rosamunde,* a play for which Schubert had written incidental music— only the overture and ballet music are heard today— failed in 1823 and brought to a close his extended efforts to achieve a successful opera.

Schubert now turned to chamber music. At the Sonnleithners he had met Ferdinand Bogner, a flutist, and Count Troyer, a clarinetist. The latter commissioned Schubert's Octet for woodwinds and strings, which in style and number of movements closely resembles Beethoven's Septet, Opus 20. The A Minor and D Minor (*Death and the Maiden*) Quartets stem from 1824, the G Major from 1826. In 1825 Schubert moved again, this time next door to the artist Moritz Schwind. There, with Bauernfeld and Spaun, they formed the mainstay of the Schubertiads, evenings at which Vogl and others sang Schubert's songs. Schwind's illustrations of these evening musicales are among the best contemporary descriptions left to us.

Final Years, 1826–1828

In 1826 and 1827, despite a recurrence of his illness, Schubert wrote four masterpieces, each of which has remained a staple in the repertory: the String Quartet in G, the Piano Sonata in G, the Piano Trio in B-flat (all 1826), and the second Piano Trio in E-flat (1827). In his final years his style changed considerably. On March 26, 1827, Beethoven died, and Schubert, who, with the Hüttenbrenners, had supposedly visited the dying man on March 18, was one of the torchbearers at the funeral. Toward the end of that year Schubert completed his two series of piano pieces that he himself entitled *Impromptus,* thus enabling us to disregard Robert Schumann's suggestion that D. 935 (Opus 142) was conceived as a sonata.

In 1828, the last year of his life, Schubert composed several first-rate works: the magnificent F-Minor Fantasy for piano duet dedicated to Esterhazy, the C-Major Symphony, the E-flat Mass, and nine songs to Ludwig Rell-

Schubert's birthplace in Vienna. The house is now a museum. (Bildarchiv der Österreichischen Nationalbibliothek, Vienna)

stab's poems, which Schubert may have intended as a cycle. Seven of these songs, six Heinrich Heine songs, and one setting of a poem by J. G. Seidl appeared as *Schwanengesang* (Swansong), a title given them by the publisher. On March 26, 1828, Schubert participated in the only full-scale public concert devoted solely to his own works.

On November 11, suffering from nausea and headache, he took to his bed in the house of his brother Ferdinand. Five days later the doctors diagnosed typhoid fever. One of the two doctors was a specialist in venereal disease; thus the suspicion that Schubert had syphilis is well founded. He was correcting the proofs of the second set of his song cycle *Die Winterreise* when he became delirious and died 2 days later on Nov. 19, 1828. Schubert's meager estate and all his manuscripts were left by default to his brother Ferdinand, who, fortunately for posterity, worked ceaselessly to enlist the aid of publishers, editors, and conductors in having them published.

In 1830 a subscription fund helped to raise money for a memorial stone over Schubert's grave. The dramatist Franz Grillparzer wrote this much-criticized epitaph: "The Art of Music here entombed a rich possession but even far fairer hopes." Schubert's closest friends were unaware of his achievement. A wealth of scholarly material has been devoted to the composer in recent years. Nobody, however, has done as much to correct the record as the great scholar O. E. Deutsch, whose initial is now inextricably linked to each Schubert work in his catalog.

Further Reading

Franz Schubert is listed in the Music study guide (I, F, 1). The romantic movement was foreshadowed in the late works of Ludwig van BEETHOVEN and was first championed by Schubert and Carl Maria von WEBER. Outstanding composers of German lieder were Robert SCHUMANN and Johannes BRAHMS.

On Schubert's life, the two works edited by Otto E.

Deutsch are definitive, *The Schubert Reader: A Life of Franz Schubert in Letters and Documents* (trans. 1947), with commentary designed to bring the documents into sharper focus, and *Schubert: Memoirs by His Friends* (1958). Two books by Maurice J. E. Brown, *Essays on Schubert* (1954) and *Schubert: A Critical Biography* (1958), are reliable. Marcel Brion, *Daily Life in the Vienna of Mozart and Schubert* (trans. 1962), describes the milieu in which Schubert lived and worked.

Alfred E. Einstein, *Schubert: A Musical Portrait* (1951), and Gerald Abraham, ed., *The Music of Schubert* (1947), offer valuable insights into the man and his music. Martin Chusid, ed., *Schubert's Unfinished Symphony* (1968), a critical edition of the score, treats a particular piece to a stylistic analysis, offering a historical essay, analytical notes, and a section on contemporary views and comments. Richard Capell, *Schubert's Songs* (2d ed. rev. 1957), is worth consulting. Ernest Porter, *Schubert's Song Technique* (1960), is easy to read. Particularly important is Otto E. Deutsch, *Schubert Thematic Catalogue* (1950), a list of all the works in chronological order.

SCHULLER / By Peter S. Hansen

The versatility of the American musician Gunther Schuller (born 1925) was recognized when he received the Alice M. Ditson Award from Columbia University in 1970: "You have already achieved distinction in six careers, as conductor, as composer, as horn virtuoso and orchestral musician, and as author and educator."

Gunther Schuller was born in New York City, the son of a New York Philharmonic Orchestra violinist. He sang as a boy soprano in the St. Thomas Church choir, studied flute and French horn privately, and studied music theory at the Manhattan School of Music. Before he was 20, he was a professional hornist, playing in the Ballet Theater Orchestra and later with the Cincinnati Symphony. From 1945 to 1959 he played with the Metropolitan Opera Orchestra.

Schuller's first published compositions date from 1950, but it was his *Seven Studies on Themes of Paul Klee* (1959) that brought him wide attention through performances by many orchestras and through recordings. In this piece Schuller revealed himself as a masterful orchestrator in complete control of a serialism inspired by Anton Webern. The piece has wit and charm, unusual components of serial compositions. In some of the *Studies* Schuller matches the color of the pictures with orchestral color, and in others, such as "The Twittering Machine," and the "Arab Village," he reflects the mood and atmosphere of the pictures in the music.

There is a strong jazz influence in all of Schuller's compositions. The composer called the combination of jazz

Gunther Schuller. (The
New England Conservatory
of Music)

elements with serial practices "third stream" music, a term which has been generally adopted to describe this typically American musical development. During the 1960s Schuller received a number of grants that allowed him to devote himself entirely to composition.

In 1965, as composer-in-residence in Berlin, Schuller completed his opera *The Visitation*, first produced in Hamburg in 1966. For his libretto the composer adapted Franz Kafka's story *The Trial*, changing the setting to the American South and the characters to Negroes. Thus altered, it became a powerful and timely statement of the plight of black Americans. The music was in Schuller's "third stream" manner with much jazz. *The Visitation*, a sensational success in its first European productions, was less successful when produced in the United States.

In 1968 Schuller published the first volume of his monumental history of jazz, proving himself to be the outstanding authority in this field. After teaching at Yale, he became president of the New England Conservatory in 1966, and a few years later, director of the Berkshire Music Center in Tanglewood as well. He was unrivaled among American musicians of his generation for the versatility and quality of his accomplishments.

Further Reading

Gunther Schuller is listed in the Music study guide (II, E). Contemporary composers working in experimental areas included Luciano BERIO, Milton BABBITT, and John CAGE.

David Ewen, *The World of Twentieth-century Music* (1968), provides biographical information and a discussion of Schuller's works. A short biography of him is in Gilbert Chase, ed., *The American Composer Speaks* (1966).

*　　*　　*

SCHUMAN / By Jack E. Reece

The French statesman Robert Schuman (1886–1963) was the public author of the plan that pooled the French and German coal and steel industries into the European Coal and Steel Community.

Born in Luxembourg on June 29, 1886, into a prosperous family from Lorraine, Robert Schuman (pronounced shoo-mäN') was educated in Germany as a lawyer. Of military age during World War I, he did not serve in the German army, although later his political opponents often made that accusation. After the Treaty of Versailles restored Lorraine to France in 1919, Schuman was elected to the French Parliament, a deputy of the Catholic Popular Democratic party.

Exerting a generally conservative influence, Schuman was a member of the parliamentary finance commission for 17 years and its president in 1940. Undersecretary of state for refugees in the Paul Reynaud government after March 1940, he was arrested by the Gestapo in September and confined at Neustadt. Schuman escaped in 1942 and immediately joined the resistance movement. During this time he played an important role in the creation of the Popular Republican Movement (MRP), which after 1945 replaced his former party as the major organ of French Christian democracy.

Elected to the Constituent Assembly in 1945, Schuman was appointed its finance chairman. Minister of finance under Georges Bidault and Paul Ramadier during 1946–1947, Schuman favored a program of austerity. Becoming prime minister in late 1947 amid widespread Communist-inspired strikes and disorders, Schuman and his interior minister, Jules Moch, stood firm, facing down the Communist challenge and enabling the Fourth Republic to survive its first great crisis. Forced to resign after only 7 months in office, Schuman held the post again for a few days in September 1948.

Robert Schuman. (German Information Center, New York)

Schuman earned his greatest fame as foreign minister in 10 successive governments from July 1948 to December 1952. He stood as the foremost advocate of Franco-German reconciliation and European unity. He was the enthusiastic sponsor in 1950 of Jean Monnet's plan for combining French and German coal and steel production, which was later realized with the formation of the European Coal and Steel Community in June 1952. In 1950 Schuman also launched a plan for an integrated European army, but that project was defeated in the French Chamber in 1954.

In 1958 Schuman was elected first president of the European Parliamentary Assembly, the consultative body of the Common Market, in which position he served for 2 years. For his efforts in the cause of European unity he was awarded the Charlemagne Prize by the city of Aachen in 1958 and the Erasmus Prize by the European Cultural Foundation in 1959. Schuman died near Metz on Sept. 4, 1963, after a long illness.

Further Reading

Robert Schuman is listed in the European History study guide (XII, B, 1) and the International Law study guide (V, A, 3, a). His views were similar to those of Jean MONNET.

There is no biography of Schuman in English. His role in the Fourth Republic is extensively discussed in Alexander Werth, *France, 1940–1955* (1956). Useful works for historical background are Herbert Luethy, *France against Herself* (trans. 1955); John T. Marcus, *Neutralism and Nationalism in France* (1958); and Frederick F. Ritsch, *The French Left and the European Idea, 1947–1949* (1966).

SCHUMANN / By Henry W. Kaufmann

The music of the German composer and critic Robert Alexander Schumann (1810–1856) made a significant impact on the burgeoning romantic movement in its rhythmic novelty and harmonic and lyrical expressiveness.

Robert Schumann (pronounced shoō′män) created no intrinsically new forms, but he infused them with a personal subjectivity and emotional intensity that transformed an inherited classical tradition into the quintessence of romantic experience. Much of his music is characterized by literary allusions and autobiographical references, which are "nothing more than delicate directions for performance and understanding" added to the music to indicate the composer's poetic intent. Yet he was not averse to experimenting with the contrapuntal devices of a J. S. Bach or the symphonic structures of a Beethoven. He thus stands midway between the conservatives and ultraprogressives of the 19th century.

Robert Schumann. (Bulloz)

Schumann was born at Zwickau on June 8, 1810, the youngest of the five children of Friedrich Schumann, a bookseller and publisher, and Johanna Schumann. Robert spent hours in his father's bookshop and developed a lifelong interest in German literature, especially the works of Jean Paul (Richter), Heinrich Heine, and Joseph von Eichendorff. At 7 Robert went to a private school and studied piano with the local church organist, who introduced him to the works of C. P. E. Bach, Franz Joseph Haydn, and Wolfgang Amadeus Mozart. By the time Robert was 9, he had begun his first efforts at composition.

During his years in secondary school (1820–1828) Schumann continued to practice the piano, often participating in concerts at the school and in the salons of eminent patrons. By 1825 he had made such progress in improvisation and composition that his father tried to interest Carl Maria von Weber in becoming Robert's teacher, but Weber was on his way to England and nothing came of the attempt. The following year Schumann's sister, Emilie, committed suicide as the result of a mental disorder, and his father, also suffering from a nervous illness, died a few months later.

In 1828 Schumann began to study law at his mother's request at the University of Leipzig. After a short visit to Munich, where he met Heine, Schumann returned to his law studies in earnest. He continued his musical studies with Friedrich Wieck, an eminent piano teacher. At his teacher's home Schumann met Wieck's daughter Clara, already a remarkable pianist at the age of 9. In 1829 Schumann moved to Heidelberg, ostensibly to continue his law studies but essentially to study composition and piano. He frequented the home of the law professor Anton Thibaut, a musical amateur who was instrumental in reviving an interest in the choral music of the Renaissance and the baroque. That summer Schumann went on holiday to Switzerland and Italy and wrote the first part of his *Papillons* for piano.

A concert by Niccolo Paganini in 1830 in Frankfurt was the decisive factor that turned Schumann permanently to music. After some stormy correspondence with his mother, she finally agreed to let him continue his studies with Wieck. He took up residence in the Wieck home and concentrated on developing into a virtuoso pianist. In his anxiety to make rapid progress he experimented with a sling device to strengthen his fingers; by irrevocably straining his right hand he ruined all chance of becoming a virtuoso. He therefore decided to concentrate on his composition studies and worked with Heinrich Dorn, choirmaster at the Leipzig opera, under whom Schumann completed the second part of the *Papillons* and an Allegro for piano. He also embarked on an intensive study of the music of J. S. Bach.

In 1834 the first issue of the *Neue Zeitschrift für Musik* (New Journal for Music) appeared. It was the organ of the Davidsbündler, a group of musicians, named for the Old Testament King David, who concentrated their struggle against the musical Philistines of their own day. Schumann edited this reforming journal until 1844, and it became a model for music criticism. In order to observe music from all points of view, Schumann invented three artistic characters: the stormy, impetuous Florestan; the gentle, lyrical Eusebius; and the arbiter between the two, Master Raro. In later years Schumann signed many of his own compositions with these appellations.

Schumann's *Twelve Symphonic Études* appeared in 1834, and the next year saw the completion of *Carnaval* and the Piano Sonata, Opus 11. His mother died in 1836. He stayed on in Leipzig with the Wiecks, fell in love with Clara, and, over the strong objections of her father, became engaged to her in 1837. Through the success of his journal, Schumann became an eminent voice in cultural matters and an artistic critic of European rank, more famous for his writings than for his compositions, which most musicians found too difficult to play. Nevertheless, he kept on composing and produced such pianistic masterpieces as the *Études symphoniques*, the *Scenes from Childhood*, the *Kreisleriana*, and the *Fantasy*. On a visit to Vienna in 1838 to further the aims and influence of his journal, he made the sensational discovery of Franz Schubert's C-Major Symphony, which Mendelssohn eventually performed.

In February 1840 Schumann was honored by a doctorate from the University of Jena. A month later he met Franz Liszt, who played part of Schumann's *Carnaval* at a recital in Leipzig. Schumann married Clara, against her father's will, in September. Seven children were born of this union.

The ensuing years were a high point in Schumann's compositional activity. During 1840 he wrote a veritable outpouring of songs, including the cycles *Myrthen* (Myrtles), *Frauenliebe und Leben* (Women's Love and Life), and *Dichterliebe* (Poet's Love). The next year he composed his Symphony No. 1, the *Spring* Symphony, and in 1842 he wrote many of his finest pieces of chamber music, including three String Quartets dedicated to Mendelssohn and the Quintet in E-flat for piano and strings. The Piano Concerto in A Minor and the Symphony No. 2 were also well under way.

A crisis of mental exhaustion followed on these productive years. A visit from Hector Berlioz in 1843, however, inspired Schumann to new activity, and he began his *Paradise and the Peri* for solo voices, chorus, and orchestra. That same year Mendelssohn called him to teach composition at the newly founded Leipzig Conservatory. In 1844, after a reconciliation with Wieck, the Schumanns embarked on a successful concert tour of Russia. On their return to Leipzig, Schumann suffered a serious nervous breakdown which caused him to resign as editor of the *Neue Zeitschrift*. The Schumanns moved to Dresden in December 1844, where they became acquainted with Richard Wagner, whose stage technique Schumann admired more than his music. In Leipzig, Schumann founded the Society for Choral Singing and taught privately for a living. Here he finished his Piano Concerto in A Minor, which was premiered by Clara in 1846, and the Symphony No. 2. He completed his opera *Genoveva* early in 1848.

In 1849 Schumann's health improved dramatically, and he composed more than 20 works that year, including the *Album for the Young*, the incidental music to Lord Byron's *Manfred*, and a group of short works for various instruments.

In 1850 Schumann became civic music director in Düsseldorf. The Düsseldorf years were not happy ones. Times of great inspiration in composition alternated with profound periods of melancholy and despondency, often lasting weeks or even months. His overall creativity began to lag so that one critic dared to write of him, "Schumann has worked his way down from genius to talent." Nonetheless these years witnessed the completion of the *Scenes from Goethe's "Faust,"* the *Waldscenen* (Woodland Scenes) for piano, innumerable songs, and Symphony No. 3, the *Rhenish*.

Wagner had once remarked on Schumann's "strange lack of skill in conducting," and this unsuitability for the conductor's post led to constant bickering with the authorities in Düsseldorf. His choir also began to grow more and more recalcitrant. Eventually Schumann was left to conduct his own works only, and all the other conducting was entrusted to the concertmaster.

In 1853 Schumann's Symphony No. 4 was performed successfully at the Lower Rhine Festival, but his mental condition continued to deteriorate. The only bright spot in his life that year was a visit from Johannes Brahms, whom Schumann greatly admired and in whose behalf he wrote a laudatory article, "New Paths," for the *Neue Zeitschrift*. There was also a brief concert tour of Holland with his wife and a visit to Hanover, where Joseph

Joachim conducted Schumann's Symphony No. 4 and played the *Fantasy* for violin and orchestra.

Schumann went completely berserk on Feb. 27, 1854, when he threw himself into the Rhine in a suicide attempt. He was rescued by some passing fishermen, and at his own request he was taken to an asylum in Endenich. Clara, aided by their loyal friend Brahms, did all that was possible to bolster Schumann's spirits but to no avail. He died on July 29, 1856.

Further Reading

Robert Schumann is listed in the Music study guide (I, G, 1). Contributors to his *Neue Zeitschrift* included Felix MENDELSSOHN and Richard WAGNER. Among the new composers the journal introduced were Frédéric CHOPIN and Johannes BRAHMS.

There is unfortunately no really good work on Schumann in English. Even the monumental German study, *Robert Schumann* by Wolfgang Boetticher (1941), is marred by Nazi overtones. Very useful are Joan Chissell, *Schumann* (1948), and Gerald Abraham, ed., *Schumann: A Symposium* (1952). Percy M. Young, *Tragic Muse: The Life and Works of Robert Schumann* (1957), is also worth examining. For general historical background Donald Jay Grout, *A History of Western Music* (1960), is recommended.

SCHUMPETER / By James A. Gherity

Joseph Alois Schumpeter (1883–1950) was an Austrian economist who advocated the view that business cycles are an integral part of the process of economic development in a capitalist economy.

Joseph Schumpeter (pronounced shŏŏm′pā-tər) was born in Triesch in Moravia (now Czechoslovakia) on Feb. 8, 1883, the only son of Alois Schumpeter, a clothing manufacturer who died when Joseph was 4 years old. Because of his mother's remarriage 7 years later to the commanding general of all Austrian troops in Vienna, Schumpeter was raised in the manner traditional to the Austrian aristocracy. In 1901 he graduated with high honors from the Theresianum, a school distinguished for its classical education.

From 1901 to 1906 he studied law and economics at the University of Vienna, where he attended the seminars of Eugen Philippović, Friedrich von Wieser, and Eugen Böhm-Bawerk. He received the degree of doctor of law in 1906 and spent a brief period visiting England and practicing law in Egypt. In 1909 he returned to Austria, where he accepted a professorship in economics at the University of Chernovtsy. In 1911 he joined the faculty at the University of Graz, where, except for the academic year 1913/1914, he remained until 1918. During this peri-

Joseph Schumpeter in 1932. (Wide World Photos)

od he had written his first major article and three important books and had established his preeminence in economic theory.

During World War I Schumpeter took part in the intrigues to negotiate a separate peace for Austria and in putting forward proposals for economic reconstruction. In 1919 he became finance minister in the coalition government of the Austrian Republic but was forced to resign before even presenting his financial proposals to Parliament.

Next, Schumpeter became president of a private bank in Vienna which, because of economic conditions and the dishonesty of some of his associates, failed in 1924. He returned to academic life, accepting a professorship at the University of Bonn in 1925. He visited Harvard in the following year and again in 1930 and, in 1932, moved there permanently. During his years at Harvard he produced several more major books, the last of which was in rough manuscript at his death and was edited and published by his wife, Elizabeth Boody Schumpeter. Schumpeter died in his sleep, of a cerebral hemorrhage, on Jan. 8, 1950.

Schumpeter's work, published in 15 books and pamphlets, over 200 articles, book reviews, and review articles, defies classification by school of thought or by methodology. Although his *Theory of Economic Development* (1912) is a classic in the abstract-deductive tradition of Léon Walras and Böhm-Bawerk, many of his articles and his *Business Cycles* (1939) demonstrate his interest in and capacity for statistical and econometric research. Finally, his writings on socialism, *Imperialism and Social Classes* (1951) and *Capitalism, Socialism and Democracy* (1942), and on the history of economic theory, *Economic Doctrine and Method* (1914) and *History of Economic Analysis* (1954), reveal an insight into the broad sweep of sociological and historical forces on economic ideas and events that can be compared only to that of Marx.

Further Reading

Joseph Schumpeter is listed in the Social Sciences study guide (VII, C, 2). Contemporary economists, though with divergent views, were Ludwig von MISES and Werner SOMBART.

Seymour E. Harris, ed., *Schumpeter, Social Scientist* (1951), contains a number of excellent essays about Schumpeter's life and work. Richard V. Clemence and Francis S. Doddy, *The Schumpeterian System* (1950), is a study of his system of economic analysis. His career is discussed briefly in Joseph Dorfman, *The Economic Mind in American Civilization* (5 vols., 1946–1959), and Ben B. Seligman, *Main Currents in Modern Economics: Economic Thought since 1870* (1962).

SCHURZ / By James M. McPherson

The most prominent foreign-born American in 19th-century public life, Carl Schurz (1829–1906) was soldier, statesman, and journalist. He was at the center of many political reform movements.

Carl Schurz was the foremost of a remarkable group of emigrés who went to the United States after the failure of the 1848–1849 revolution in Germany. In his adopted land Schurz crusaded against slavery, campaigned for his friend Abraham Lincoln, fought for the North in the Civil War, helped shape a Reconstruction policy that enfranchised the freed slaves, championed civil service reform, founded the Liberal Republican movement, was a leader of the "Mugwump" exodus from the Republican party, and denounced American imperialism in the Spanish-American War.

Carl Schurz was born on March 2, 1829, in Liblar near Cologne, Germany. He graduated from the gymnasium at Cologne and entered the University of Bonn in 1847 as a candidate for the doctorate in history. At the age of 19 he was a leader of the student movement that became the spearhead of democratic revolutionary ferment in many parts of Germany. In 1849 Schurz was commissioned a lieutenant in the revolutionary army, which was finally defeated by the Prussians. Knowing he would be shot if captured, he fled the country. He later returned under a false passport to rescue a professor from Spandau prison and spirit him out of Germany in the most daring exploit of the entire revolution.

American Civil War Record

After short residences in France and England, in 1852 Schurz went to the United States. He joined the antislavery movement and helped build the Republican party in Wisconsin, where he settled in 1856. An excellent orator, Schurz made speeches for John C. Frémont in the 1856 presidential election and for Lincoln against Stephen Douglas in the 1858 Illinois senatorial campaign. He was chairman of the Wisconsin delegation to the 1860 Republican convention. He campaigned tirelessly in the 1860 election and was gratified by a letter from Lincoln

declaring that "to the extent of our limited acquaintance, no man stands nearer my heart than yourself." Rewarded by appointment as minister to Spain, Schurz resigned that post in 1862 and returned to the United States to work for Union victory and emancipation.

Schurz's military experience was limited to a few weeks of fighting in Germany 13 years earlier, but he worked hard at mastering military strategy and was finally promoted to major general of volunteers in 1863. He was popular with his troops, but his battle record was mixed. After limited success as a division commander at Chancellorsville and a corps commander at Gettysburg, he was given charge of an instruction corps at Nashville. This was not to his liking, and in 1864 he obtained release from command to campaign for Lincoln's re-election. Schurz finished out the war as a chief of staff in William T. Sherman's army.

Postwar Political Career

In the summer of 1865 Schurz began investigating Southern conditions for President Andrew Johnson and a Boston newspaper. He found that many Southerners were defiant and recalcitrant, determined to keep Negroes subordinate. Schurz's long report contradicted the premises of Johnson's Reconstruction policy, and the President did not acknowledge the report. But congressional Republicans secured its publication and wide distribution. This document was of great influence in molding a radical Reconstruction policy based on Negro suffrage.

Schurz was Washington correspondent of the *New York Tribune*, then editor of the *Detroit Post*, and in 1867 he became part owner and editor of the German-language *St. Louis Westliche Post*. Schurz made the keynote address at the Republican national convention

Carl Schurz. (Library of Congress)

in 1868 and the next year was elected to the U.S. Senate from Missouri. His views on Reconstruction had become less radical; he advocated the removal of all political disabilities from former Confederates and was increasingly critical of Federal intervention in behalf of what he considered corrupt and oppressive Republican regimes in Southern states.

A proponent of civil service reform, Schurz was also repelled by the corrupt political atmosphere of Ulysses S. Grant's administration. In 1872 he led reformers out of the regular Republican party and organized the Liberal Republican party, which nominated Horace Greeley to run against Grant. Schurz's actions split the Republican party in Missouri and allowed the Democrats to capture the legislature, so he was not reelected to the U.S. Senate in 1875. In 1876 he returned to the regular Republican party and supported the presidential reform candidacy of Rutherford B. Hayes. Schurz was rewarded with appointment as secretary of the interior, and he made considerable progress in reform of Indian affairs and introduction of the merit system into the department.

Journalism and Reform

In 1881 Schurz returned to journalism, serving for 2 years as an editor of the *New York Evening Post* and of the *Nation*. For several years thereafter he free-lanced, and from 1892 to 1898 he was chief editorial writer for *Harper's Weekly*. In 1884 he joined the revolt of the "Mugwumps" (reform Republicans) against the party's presidential nominee, James G. Blaine, and supported Grover Cleveland. Schurz was president of the National Civil Service Reform League (1892–1900) and of the Civil Service Reform Association of New York (1893–1906). Opposing the Spanish-American War in 1898, he became a leading anti-imperialist, urging independence for the Philippines rather than American colonialism there. Schurz died in New York City on May 14, 1906. His wife had died some years before; he was survived by three of his five children.

Further Reading

Carl Schurz is listed in the American History study guide (VII, A, 1; VII, G, 4, a). Another governmental reformer at this time was Dorman EATON.

The basic source for Schurz's life is *The Reminiscences of Carl Schurz* (3 vols., 1907–1908). Also of value are Frederic Bancroft, ed., *Speeches, Correspondence and Political Papers of Carl Schurz* (6 vols., 1913), and Joseph Schafer, ed., *Intimate Letters of Carl Schurz, 1841–1869* (1928). There is no biography of Schurz incorporating modern scholarship. The best account is Claude M. Fuess, *Carl Schurz, Reformer* (1932).

SCHUSCHNIGG

/ By Wayne S. Vucinich

The Austrian statesman Kurt von Schuschnigg (born 1897) served as chancellor of Austria from 1934 to 1938. He succeeded in preventing German absorption of Austria until he lost the support of Mussolini in 1937.

Kurt von Schuschnigg (pronounced shŏŏsh′nĭk) was born on Dec. 14, 1897, at Riva on Lake Garda (now a part of Italy). He was the son of an Austrian army officer. Educated in a Jesuit gymnasium at Feldkirch, Schuschnigg served in the Austro-Hungarian army on the Italian front in World War I. He was decorated for bravery and was a prisoner of war during 1918–1919. In 1922 he received a doctorate in law from the University of Innsbruck.

After practicing law in Innsbruck, Schuschnigg became a candidate of the Christian Socialist party for Parliament and, through the backing of the influential Christian Socialist leader Ignaz Seipel, was elected to Parliament in 1927. In 1932 Schuschnigg was named Austrian minister of justice, and in 1933 he assumed the portfolio of the Ministry of Education in addition to his earlier post. After the assassination of the Christian Socialist chancellor Engelbert Dollfuss during the abortive Nazi putsch of July 25, 1934, Schuschnigg became Austrian chancellor, pledged to defend Austria's independence from Nazi Germany.

Schuschnigg's political views were characteristic of Austrian clerical conservatism. He was a zealous Catholic, staunch antileftist, vehement anti-Nazi, and fervent legitimist. He would have preferred to solve Austria's po-

Kurt von Schuschnigg (right) in 1936. (New York Public Library, Picture Collection)

litical problems through the restoration of the Hapsburg dynasty. Schuschnigg had no recourse but to follow Dollfuss's reliance on Italian premier Benito Mussolini's protection against Nazi Germany's desire for Anschluss. The imposition by the League of Nations of sanctions against Italy for its aggression against Ethiopia in 1935 drove Italy into the arms of Germany and rendered Mussolini unable further to defend Austrian independence from German encroachment.

On Feb. 12, 1938, Adolf Hitler summoned Schuschnigg to Berchtesgaden, where he demanded that Schuschnigg order the amnesty of jailed Austrian Nazis and that he include Nazis in his Cabinet, particularly Artur Seyss-Inquart. Schuschnigg agreed to Hitler's demands, but on his return to Vienna he restated his vow to preserve Austria's independence. Hitler then ordered the Austrian Nazis to foment disorder throughout the country. When Schuschnigg ordered a plebiscite to ascertain the country's opinion of his determination to maintain Austria's independence, Hitler demanded the plebiscite's delay and he ordered troops to Austria's border on Schuschnigg's refusal. Schuschnigg then resigned, and he was succeeded by Seyss-Inquart, who called German troops into the country in March 1938.

After the German Anschluss, Schuschnigg was imprisoned by the Germans until 1945, when he was liberated by American troops. He then emigrated to the United States and became professor of political science at St. Louis University, Mo.

Further Reading

Kurt von Schuschnigg is listed in the European History study guide (XI, E, 1). He succeeded Engelbert DOLLFUSS as Austrian chancellor.

There are few sources in English for a study of Schuschnigg. His own works, such as *Farewell Austria* (1937; trans. 1938) and *Austrian Requiem* (1946), contain valuable information but must be used cautiously. Perhaps the best discussion of Schuschnigg's career as Austrian chancellor is in John A. Lukacs, *The Great Powers and Eastern Europe* (1953). See also Dieter Wagner and Gerhard Tompowitz, *Anschluss: The Week That Hitler Siezed Vienna* (trans. 1972).

SCHÜTZ / By Edward R. Lerner

The German composer Heinrich Schütz (1585–1672) is credited with an important role in bringing the Italian baroque style to Germany.

Born in Köstritz, Saxony, to prosperous, middle-class parents, Heinrich Schütz (pronounced shüts) learned the rudiments of music in the chapel choir of Moritz, Landgrave of Hesse-Cassel. In 1608 Schütz entered the University of Marburg to study law, but when the landgrave, who recognized his ex-

Heinrich Schütz. (German Information Center, New York)

traordinary musical gift, offered to support him, Schütz was able to leave for Venice in 1609 to study with Giovanni Gabrieli. Schütz returned in 1613 after his teacher's death.

While in Italy, Schütz published his first collection, *Il primo libro de madrigali* (1611), dedicated to Landgrave Moritz. These 19 chromatic madrigals reveal the close attention Schütz was always to give both the syntax and content of his texts. Even more Italianate are the *Psalmen Davids* (1619), published after the composer became kapellmeister to Johann Georg, Elector of Saxony, in Dresden. In these 26 works, composed for multiple groups of vocal and instrumental soloists, reinforced by two or more choruses, Schütz brought to northern Europe the colorful, polychoral methods of his beloved master, Gabrieli. The music, of overwhelming grandeur, was written for the enhancement of the Protestant liturgy and the edification of the court.

Schütz's *Historia der Auferstehung Jesu Christi* (1623), the Easter Story, was his first oratorio in the Italian style. While the Evangelist performs solos to the accompaniment of four viols, the roles of Jesus and Mary Magdalene are sung as duets over the basso continuo. In his next important work, the *Cantiones sacrae* (1625), Schütz seemed to return to the older polyphonic style. But their chromaticism, "madrigalisms" illustrating the text, and intensely subjective qualities relate these sacred songs more closely to the madrigals of 1611.

To fulfill his task of transforming church music through

the southern concerted style, Schütz made a second pilgrimage to Italy in 1628. Now he studied the techniques of Claudio Monteverdi as he observed them in the vocal and instrumental writing of the great Italian. The first fruits of the visit appeared the following year as part 1 of Schütz's *Symphoniae sacrae.* Solo singing with obbligato instruments over the continuo—such was the new style exemplified by the masterpiece of this first collection, *Fili mi, Absalon.*

A short while after Schütz returned to Germany, he found musical activity severely curtailed because of the religious wars raging throughout Saxony. During the 1630s and early 1640s he stayed only intermittently at Dresden, obtaining permission from the elector to work in Copenhagen, Wolfenbüttel, Hanover, and Weimar. Because of limited resources, the master now wrote shorter compositions for one to five parts with continuo. Two such collections were issued in 1636 and 1639 with the title *Kleine Geistliche Konzerte.*

By 1647 conditions at the Saxon court had improved somewhat, and Schütz released part 2 of his *Symphoniae sacrae.* Unlike part 1, which had Latin settings for voices and various obbligato instruments, part 2 was set to German words and used only the strings and continuo. In part 3 of the *Symphoniae sacrae* (1650) Schütz joined the polychoral writing of his early *Psalmen Davids* with the soloistic style he learned from Monteverdi. The masterpiece *Saul, Saul, was verfolgst du mich?* is scored for a six-voice ensemble, two four-voice choruses, and two obbligato instrumental parts. In few of his later pieces did he go beyond the resources of these compositions, which are truly cantatas.

Although Schütz was the foremost German protagonist of the new baroque style, he did not foresee that his apparent deemphasis of counterpoint would persuade younger compatriots to abandon it. By 1648 this danger had become so manifest that Schütz was persuaded to publish his *Geistliche Chormusik,* a collection of 29 motets in the older style, to show young composers "before they proceed to concertizing music to crack this hard nut (wherein the true kernel and the right foundation of good counterpoint is to be sought) and to pass their first tests in this category." Schütz obviously viewed his artistic mission as a union of counterpoint and *stile recitativo, a cappella* and *concertato,* rather than as a rejection of the older Flemish style.

In 1665 Schütz completed three Passions according to Luke, John, and Matthew. What first impresses us in these works is their external austerity. Gone are the instrumentally accompanied recitative of the Easter Story and the polychoral writing with instruments in part 3 of the *Symphoniae sacrae.* Here the Bible narrative is sung *a cappella* with solo portions chanted in a "Germanized" plainsong.

Even though these works seem archaic, it would be incorrect to believe that Schütz rejected his entire mission of a concerted, soloistic church music. Only a year or two before, he had composed the *Historia der Freuden- und Gnaden-reichen Geburt Gottes und Marien Sohnes Jesu Christi,* the Christmas Story, in the richly

concerted style he had espoused for over 50 years. In the Passions he abandoned the luxuriant apparatus for pure chant and polyphony, in part as an object lesson to younger composers and in part to demonstrate that his own era could still use the *a cappella* style of the past.

Schütz passed the last of his 55 years of service to the elector of Saxony in Weissenfels and in Dresden, where he died. Through his efforts German church music took on features we easily recognize as baroque. In the way he put polyphony on an equal footing with the new concerted style, Schütz resembles Monteverdi, who also brought the past into the present and subjected it to a new esthetic.

Further Reading

Heinrich Schütz is listed in the Music study guide (I, D, 4). His mentors were Giovanni GABRIELI and Claudio MONTEVERDI. Other baroque German composers were Johann Jakob FROBERGER, Dietrich BUXTEHUDE, and Johann PACHELBEL.

Hans J. Moser, *Heinrich Schütz: His Life and Work* (1936; trans. 1959), is the most complete study of the master. The music of Schütz in relation to his contemporaries is treated in Manfred E. Bukofzer, *Music in the Baroque Era: From Monteverdi to Bach* (1947), and in Claude V. Palisca, *Baroque Music* (1968).

SCHUYLER / By Armin Rappaport

The American Revolutionary War general Philip John Schuyler (1733–1804) was a leader in the political and commercial life of his state and nation.

Philip Schuyler was born in Albany, N.Y., on Nov. 11, 1733, into an old, aristocratic Dutch family, one of the colony's largest landholders. He received an excellent education. After commanding a company of New York militia in the French and Indian War, he managed the large estate left him by his father in the Mohawk and Hudson River valleys.

At the same time, Schuyler was active in supporting the colonial cause in the controversy with Great Britain. He argued the colonial position in the provincial Assembly in 1768 and went to the Second Continental Congress in May 1775 as delegate from New York. There he served with George Washington on a committee to make rules and regulations for the army. In June 1775, shortly after the Revolution began, Congress appointed him a major general, one of four to serve under Washington.

Schuyler's assignment was to command the Northern Department (consisting of New York) and to prepare an attack on Canada. After raising and supplying an army and strengthening Ticonderoga and Crown Point on the

Philip Schuyler, a painting by Pieter Vanderlyn. (Courtesy of The New-York Historical Society, New York City)

route north, he was forced by ill health to turn over command of the troops to Gen. Richard Montgomery. The attack failed, and Schuyler was given much of the blame. He had, actually, delayed too long in ordering the army to get under way and had been too slow and deliberate in executing his plan, but the true cause of the defeat lay in factors beyond his control. He also made some bad decisions during the course of the campaign of British general John Burgoyne in northern New York in 1777; one of these contributed to the loss of Ft. Ticonderoga, an American stronghold. Accusations of incompetence were leveled against him, along with a rumor of intrigue with the enemy. In 1778 Schuyler demanded a court-martial to air the charges. He was acquitted that October but felt it best to resign his commission.

After leaving the army, Schuyler was active in politics, holding office continually until 1798, when illness forced his permanent retirement. He served as state senator for 13 years and for 3 years as U.S. senator from New York under the new Federal Constitution, in whose creation he had played a leading role with his son-in-law, Alexander Hamilton. Schuyler died in Albany on Nov. 18, 1804.

Further Reading

Philip Schuyler is listed in the American History study guide (III, D, 1, a). He and Rufus KING were the first U.S. senators from New York.

The best biography of Schuyler is Benson J. Lossing,

The Life and Times of Philip Schuyler (2 vols., 1872–1873). Bayard Tuckerman, *Life of General Philip Schuyler* (1903), is good for Schuyler's military phase. For special aspects of Schuyler's life see George W. Schuyler, *Colonial New York: Philip Schuyler and His Family* (2 vols., 1885), and Don R. Gerlach, *Philip Schuyler and the American Revolution in New York, 1733–1777* (1964).

SCHWAB / By Saul Engelbourg

> Charles Michael Schwab (1862–1939), American industrialist, became a multimillionaire in the steel industry but died bankrupt.

Charles M. Schwab was born on Feb. 18, 1862, in Williamsburg, Pa. He graduated from high school in 1880 and 2 years later joined the steel enterprise of Andrew Carnegie as an unskilled manual laborer. In 6 months he was an assistant manager. He was appointed superintendent of Carnegie's Homestead Works in 1887. No wonder Carnegie declared about Schwab, "I have never met his equal."

The steel industry at the turn of the 20th century was in the throes of a competitive struggle in which Carnegie was the ruthless competitor and other firms attempted to achieve stability. Schwab served as the intermediary between Carnegie and banker J. P. Morgan, and the sale of Carnegie's company became the main step in organizing the U.S. Steel Corporation in 1901. Morgan chose Schwab as president of the new giant corporation. In 1903 Schwab left because of internal disagreements with his associates.

Schwab acquired control of the Bethlehem Steel Company in 1901. When the concern was merged into the United States Shipbuilding Company, Schwab's stock was exchanged for bonds. When this company failed owing to an improper financial policy, Schwab as the prime creditor became the owner. Bethlehem Steel Corporation, organized in 1904, was his own creation, and he made it a major steel producer and a worthy competitor of U.S. Steel. During World War I Bethlehem Steel became an important producer of materiel for the Allied war effort. He also spurred the American shipbuilding program to new heights after he was appointed director of the Emergency Fleet Corporation in April 1918.

After the war Schwab entered into semiretirement. He continued as the chairman of the board of directors of Bethlehem Steel until his death but delegated the responsibility to the president. During the 1930s Bethlehem was accused of having earned extortionate profits during the war, but the courts upheld the company's actions. Schwab died in London, England, on Sept. 18, 1939.

Charles M. Schwab. (Library of Congress)

Further Reading

Charles M. Schwab is listed in the American History study guide (VIII, D, 2). Working for Andrew CARNEGIE brought Schwab into contact with financier J. P. MORGAN.

There is no biography of Schwab. Information on various phases of his career must be pieced together from works which have another emphasis: James H. Bridge, *The Inside History of the Carnegie Steel Company* (1903); Ida M. Tarbell, *The Life of Elbert H. Gary* (1925); Arundel Cotter, *The Story of Bethlehem Steel* (1916) and *United States Steel: A Corporation with a Soul* (1921); Burton J. Hendrick, *The Life of Andrew Carnegie* (2 vols., 1932; new introduction, 1969); Stewart H. Holbrook, *Age of the Moguls* (1953); Joseph Frazier Wall, *Andrew Carnegie* (1970); and Louis M. Hacker, *The World of Andrew Carnegie* (1968). Both Arthur S. Dewing, *Corporate Promotion and Reorganizations* (1914), and Henry R. Seager and Charles A. Gulick, Jr., *Trust and Corporation* (1929), contain a chapter on the U.S. Shipbuilding Company.

SCHWANN / By Oscar T. Walle

The German biologist Theodor Schwann (1810–1882) is considered a founder of the cell theory. He also discovered pepsin, the first digestive enzyme prepared from animal tissue, and experimented to disprove spontaneous generation.

Theodor Schwann (pronounced shvän) was born at Neuss near Düsseldorf on Dec. 7, 1810. At the University of Bonn, which he entered in 1829, he met Johannes Müller, the physiologist, whom he assisted in his experiments. Schwann continued his medical studies at the University of Würzburg and later at the University of Berlin, from which he graduated in 1834. His doctoral dissertation dealt with the respiration of the chick embryo.

Contributions to Physiology and Anatomy

At Berlin, Schwann again came into contact with Müller, who convinced him that he should follow a scientific career. Very soon after he began to work under Müller, he had his first success. From extracts which he made of stomach lining, Schwann demonstrated that a factor other than hydrochloric acid was operating in digestion. Two years later, in 1836, he succeeded in isolating the active principle, which he named pepsin.

Between 1834 and 1838 Schwann undertook a series of experiments designed to settle the question of the truth or falsity of the concept of spontaneous generation. His method was to expose sterilized (boiled) broth only to heated air in a glass tube, the result being that no microorganisms were detectable and no chemical change (putrefaction) occurred in the broth. He was convinced that the idea of spontaneous generation was false. His sugar fermentation studies of 1836 also led to his discovery that yeast originated the chemical process of fermentation.

At Müller's suggestion, Schwann also began research on muscle contraction and discovered striated muscles in the upper portion of the esophagus. He also identified the delicate sheath of cells surrounding peripheral nerve fibers, which is now named the sheath of Schwann.

Cell Theory

In 1838 Schwann became familiar with Matthias Schleiden's microscopic research on plants. Schleiden described plant cells and proposed a cell theory which he was certain was the key to plant anatomy and growth. Pursuing this line of research on animal tissues, Schwann not only verified the existence of cells, but he traced the development of many adult tissues from early embryo stages. This research and the cell theory which followed were summarized in *Mikroskopische Untersuchungen ueber die Uebereinstimmung in der Struktur und dem Wachstum der Thiere und Pflanzen* (1839; *Microscopical Researches on the Similarity in the Structure and the Growth of Animals and Plants*, 1847). This work, which in Schwann's own words demonstrated that "the great barrier between the animal and vegetable kingdoms, viz. the diversity of ultimate structure, thus vanishes," established the cell theory to the satisfaction of his contemporaries.

Schwann proposed three generalizations concerning the nature of cells: First, animals and plants consist of cells plus the secretions of cells. Second, these cells have independent lives, which, third, are subject to the organism's life. Furthermore, he realized that the phenomena of individual cells can be placed into two classes: "those which relate to the combination of the molecules to form a cell. These may be called plastic phenomena," and "those which result from chemical changes either in the component particles of the cell itself, or in the surrounding cytoblastema [the modern cytoplasm]. These may be called metabolic phenomena." Thus Schwann coined the term "metabolism," which became generally adopted for the sum total of chemical processes by which energy changes occur in living things.

Contributions to Histology

Schwann also contributed to the understanding and classification of adult animal tissues. He classified tissues into five groups: separate independent cells, such as blood; compacted independent cells, such as skin; cells whose walls have coalesced, such as cartilage, bones, and teeth; elongated cells which have formed fibers, such as tendons and ligaments; and finally, cells formed by the fusion of walls and cavities, such as muscles and tendons. His conclusions were also basic to the modern concept of embryology, for he described embryonic development as a succession of cell divisions.

This generalization of the essential structural kinship of all living things had been denied for centuries by the old Aristotelian doctrine of vegetable and animal souls. Perhaps Schwann's findings were more disturbing than he liked to admit, since he realized that they supported an ultimate physical rather than a theological explanation. Schwann saw the implications of his discovery, and the idea of the world of life being nothing more than a machine appalled him. He found refuge in the Roman Catholic faith, choosing, as he said, a God "more sensitive to the heart than to reason."

In 1839 Schwann was appointed professor of anatomy at the University of Louvain, Belgium, where he remained until 1848, when he accepted a professorship at the University of Liège. He remained there until his retirement in 1880. After leaving the influence of Müller, Schwann's productivity practically ceased; in Belgium he published only one paper, on the use of bile. He was an excellent, conscientious teacher, loved and appreciated by his students.

Schwann's work was ultimately recognized by scientists in other countries, and in 1879 he was made a member of the Royal Society and also of the French Academy of Science. In 1845 he had received the Copley Medal. Death came to Schwann on Jan. 11, 1882, 2 years after his retirement, in Cologne.

Further Reading

Theodor Schwann is listed in the Science study guide (VI, F, 2; VI, G, 2). He was the first student of Johannes MÜLLER to break with vitalistic philosophy and to lead toward a chemical-physical explanation of the ultimate nature of life.

Excerpts in English translation from *Mikroskopische Untersuchungen* are found in the following works: Forest Ray Moulton and Justus J. Schifferes, eds., *The Autobiography of Science* (1945; rev. ed. 1960); Augusto Pi Suñer, *Classics of Biology* (1955); Friedrich S. Bodenheimer, *The History of Biology: An Introduction* (1958); and George Schwartz and Philip W. Bishop, eds., *Moments of Discovery* (2 vols., 1958). There is no biography of Schwann. Gilbert Causey in *The Cell of Schwann* (1960) devotes the first chapter to a sparse recital of the essential details of Schwann's life. Erik Nordenskiöld, *The History of Biology* (1928; new ed. 1935), gives a brief biographic account, as does Gordon R. Taylor, *The Science of Life* (1963). A good treatment of the cell theory and Schwann's part in it is in William A. Locy, *Biology and Its Makers* (1908; rev. ed. 1915).

Theodor Schwann. (The Smithsonian Institution, Washington, D.C.)

SCHWEITZER / By Norman Cousins

Albert Schweitzer (1875–1965) was an Alsatian-German religious philosopher, musicologist, and medical missionary in Africa.

He was known especially for founding the Schweitzer Hospital, which provided unprecedented medical care for the natives of Lambaréné in Gabon.

Albert Schweitzer (pronounced shwīt′sər), the son of an Evangelical Lutheran minister, was born on Jan. 14, 1875, in Kaysersberg, Alsace, which was then under German rule. Albert's early life was both comfortable and happy. One Sunday morning, when he was about 8, he had an experience that helped to shape his life. At the strong urging of another lad, he reluctantly aimed his slingshot at several birds which, as he later wrote, "sang sweetly into the morning sunshine." Moved, he "made a silent vow to miss. At that moment, the sound of church bells began to mingle with the sunshine and the singing of the birds. . . . For me, it was a voice from heaven. I threw aside my slingshot, shooed the birds away to protect them from my friend's slingshot, and fled home."

When Albert was 10 years old, he went to live with his granduncle and grandaunt in Mulhouse so that he could attend the excellent local school. He graduated from secondary school at the age of 18. During these 8 years he learned directly from his elderly relatives the demanding ethical code and rigorous scholarly outlook of their early-1800s generation.

In 1893 Schweitzer enrolled at the University of Strasbourg, where, until 1913, he enjoyed a brilliant career as student, teacher, and administrator. His main field was theology and philosophy, and in 1899 he won a doctorate in philosophy with a thesis on Immanuel Kant.

Schweitzer also made a profound study of Nietzsche and Tolstoy, recoiling from Nietzsche's adulation of the all-conquering "superman" and being greatly attracted to Tolstoy's doctrine of love and compassion. The definitive influence, however, on Schweitzer was the life of Jesus, to whose message and messiahship he devoted years of research and reflection. His classic work *The Quest of the Historical Jesus* (1906) deals with major scholarly writings on Jesus from the 17th century onward; the volume was well received and quickly became a standard source book.

Renunciation and Dedication

Meanwhile, Schweitzer's biography of J. S. Bach, written in 1905, had also proved an immediate success. At 30 years of age Schweitzer was tall, broad-shouldered, darkly handsome, and a witty, charismatic writer, preacher, and lecturer: clearly, a bright future lay before him. However, one spring morning in 1905, he experienced a stunning religious revelation: it came to him that at some point in the years just ahead he must renounce facile success and devote himself unsparingly to the betterment of mankind's condition.

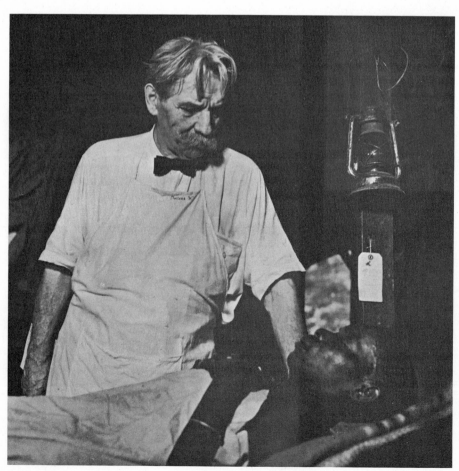

Albert Schweitzer with a patient in his hospital at Lambaréné, Gabon. (Culver Pictures, Inc.)

Patients waiting in front of Schweitzer's dispensary at Lambaréné. This photograph was taken in 1963. (Wide World Photos)

Accordingly, several years later, Schweitzer threw over his several careers as author, lecturer, and organ recitalist and plunged into the study of medicine—his aim being to go to Africa as a medical missionary. He won his medical degree in 1912. The year before, he had married Helene Bresslau, a professor's daughter who had studied nursing in order to work at his side in Africa; in 1919 the couple had a daughter, Rhena.

Establishment in Africa

In 1913 the Schweitzers journeyed to what was then French Equatorial Africa. There, after various setbacks, they founded the Albert Schweitzer Hospital at Lambaréné, on the Ogooué River, "at the edge of the primeval forest." This area now lies within the independent West African republic of Gabon. Funds were scarce and equipment primitive, but native Africans thronged to the site, and in the decades that followed, many thousands were treated.

Reverence for Life

One hot afternoon in 1915, as he sat on the deck of an ancient steamboat chugging its way up the Ogooué, Schweitzer noticed on a sandbank nearby four hippopotamuses with their young. Instantly, "the phrase Reverence for Life struck me like a flash." He had anticipated this phrase more than 3 decades earlier in his refusal to shoot his slingshot at the sweetly singing birds; now, it became the coping stone of his philosophical system and of his everyday life at the hospital.

Somewhat to Schweitzer's chagrin, the news of his lonely, heroic witness at Lambaréné spread abroad, and he became a world-famous exemplary figure. An American named Larimer Mellon, a member of the wealthy Mellon family, was one of the many whose lives were affected by Schweitzer. Inspired by Schweitzer's example, Mellon, then in his late 30s, returned to college, obtained his medical degree, and with his wife, Gwen, set up the Albert Schweitzer Hospital deep in a primitive rural area of Haiti. Many hundreds of lives were similarly changed by Schweitzer's charismatic witness.

Despite his demanding schedule at Lambaréné, Schweitzer found time to lecture in the United States in 1949, received the Nobel Peace Prize in 1952, and published in 1957 and 1958 notable appeals to the superpowers in the name of humanity, urging them to renounce nuclear-weapons testing. He died at Lambaréné on Sept. 4, 1965; at the time, he was still working vigorously on the third volume of his monumental *Philosophy of Civilization.* On his death his medical associates and his daughter, Mrs. Rhena Eckert-Schweitzer, took over direction of the hospital with the aim of carrying out Schweitzer's wish that its facilities be drastically modernized.

Further Reading

Albert Schweitzer is listed in the Africa study guide (IX, H, 2). Another missionary to Africa was Cardinal LAVIGERIE.

The best introduction to Schweitzer's thought and personality is through his own engagingly written autobiographical works: *At the Edge of the Primeval Forest* (1922), *Memoirs of Childhood and Youth* (1925), and *Out of My Life and Thought* (1933). One of the best studies of Schweitzer is George Seaver, *Albert Schweitzer: The Man and His Mind* (1947). Also valuable are

Norman Cousins, *Dr. Schweitzer of Lambaréné* (1960), and Henry Clark, *The Philosophy of Albert Schweitzer* (1964).

Lively personal and pictorial introductions to Schweitzer are Erica Anderson, *Albert Schweitzer's Gift of Friendship* (1964) and *The Schweitzer Album: A Portrait in Words and Pictures* (1965). Two general, readable studies of Schweitzer are Dr. Joseph F. Montague, *The Why of Albert Schweitzer* (1965), which includes a bibliography of Schweitzer's writings, and Magnus Ratter, *Schweitzer—Ninety Years Wise* (1964). Also consult Hermann Hagedorn, *The Prophet in the Wilderness* (1947; rev. ed. 1962); Erica Anderson, *The World of Albert Schweitzer* (1955); Robert Payne, *The Three Worlds of Albert Schweitzer* (1957); and Werner Picht, *The Life and Thought of Albert Schweitzer* (trans. 1964).

✳   ✳   ✳

Kaspar von Schwenkfeld, a woodcut, dated 1565, by Balthasar Jenichen. (Bildarchiv)

SCHWENCKFELD
By Edward M. Peters

The Silesian nobleman and theologian Kaspar von Schwenckfeld (1489/1490–1561) formulated doctrines concerning the nature of Christ and the Eucharist that caused him to break with Luther and spend much of his life in exile as a religious outlaw.

Kaspar von Schwenckfeld (pronounced shvĕngk′fĕlt) was born in the town of Ossig in Silesia. After university training he became sympathetic to the principles of the early Lutheran Reformation, and his influence at the court of the Duke of Liegnitz was instrumental in bringing the Reformation to Silesia. Schwenckfeld, however, did not agree with Martin Luther on all points, and he disagreed particularly on the questions of "real presence" (that is, whether or not Christ is present in the Eucharist) and on the nature of Christ.

In 1525 Schwenckfeld went to Wittenberg to discuss his differences with Luther, but the two failed to agree. Another opponent of Luther, Ulrich Zwingli, then published a treatise by Schwenckfeld, and the ensuing difficulties in Silesia forced Schwenckfeld to leave his home in 1529, the first of many such journeys. From 1529 to 1533 Schwenckfeld lived in Strasbourg, the home of many Reformation exiles. In 1533, however, Schwenckfeld's doctrines came under heavy criticism from Martin Bucer, and their condemnation at the Synod of Strasbourg in 1533 caused Schwenckfeld to leave that city. From 1533 to 1538 Schwenckfeld lived in Ulm, but eventually another controversy arose over his Christological doctrines, and he left Ulm in 1538. Schwenckfeld's doctrines were again formally condemned at Schmalkalden in 1540.

At this time Schwenckfeld wrote his most important treatises on theology: *Vom Fleische Christi* (1540; *On the Body of Christ*) and *Grosse Confession* (1541; *The Great Confession*). From 1540 until his death, Schwenckfeld produced many letters and treatises, so many that Philip Melancthon referred to Schwenckfeld as a "hundred-hander,"—a man who wrote so much that he must have had a hundred hands. Schwenckfeld's chief influence lay in his Christological doctrines. He was particularly concerned with the process of human salvation and saw this process as an indwelling of Christ in the saved man. Besides this concern, however, there lay also his opposition to religious persecution and his persistent defense of freedom of conscience and religious liberty.

Schwenckfeld's place in the Reformation has long been obscured because of the many condemnations heaped upon him and his followers in their own time both by Protestant sects and by Catholics. Schwenckfeld's harried later years drew more opposition down upon him, and when he died, he was buried under the house of friends in Ulm so that his body could not be exhumed and burned as that of a heretic. After his death his followers published his works and lived in Silesia until the arrival of the Jesuits in 1719. They then emigrated to Saxony, to England, and finally to North America, where they settled in eastern Pennsylvania in 1734.

Further Reading

Kaspar von Schwenckfeld is listed in the Religion study guide (I, H, 1). He and Ulrich ZWINGLI opposed some of the teachings of Martin LUTHER.

The best biography of Schwenckfeld in English is Selina Gerhard Schultz, *Caspar Schwenckfeld von Ossig* (1946). Schwenckfeld's place in the Reformation is examined in George H. Williams, *The Radical Reformation* (1962). His theology is discussed in the good study by Paul L. Maier, *Caspar Schwenckfeld on the Person and Work of Christ* (1959), which also contains further bibliographical references to Schwenckfeld's life and thought.

SCIPIO AFRICANUS MAJOR
/ By Ursula Heibges

Publius Cornelius Scipio Africanus Major (236–184/183 B.C.) was a Roman official during the Second Punic War. He defeated Hannibal in the Battle of Zama and was a champion of both Roman imperialism and the enlightened pro-Hellenic spirit of a new age.

Scipio (pronounced skĭp′ē-ō) was married to Aemilia, sister of Lucius Aemilius Paullus (victor of Pydna in 168 B.C.), and became the father of Cornelia, mother of the Gracchus brothers.

As a youth of about 18, Scipio was credited with having saved his father's life at the Battle of the Ticinus (Ticino) in 218, and as military tribune in 216, he rallied the survivors after the disastrous defeat of Cannae. The young Scipio held the office of curule aedile in 213. When, in 211, Lucius and Gnaeus Scipio, his father and uncle, fell in Spain, he was appointed by vote of the Roman people to their proconsular command, the first *privatus* (private citizen) in Roman history to obtain this privilege.

Punic Wars

In Spain, Scipio seized New Carthage, the enemy's headquarters, but won great sympathy by his humane treatment of his Spanish captives. In 208 he defeated Hasdrubal Barca at Baecula but was unable to prevent the enemy's escape and march across the Pyrenees. After defeating two other enemy armies at Ilipa, he captured Gades (Cadiz), the last stronghold of the Carthaginians in Spain. In 206 he left for Rome to stand for the consulship.

As consul in 205, Scipio was assigned the province of Sicily and, after strong senatorial opposition, also the province of Africa. In 204 he crossed to Africa with 35,-000 men. He besieged Utica for 40 days until the beginning of winter forced him to encamp on a nearby headland. Early in the following year he defeated the Carthaginians at Campi Magni, overran their territory, and captured Tunis. Scipio granted the enemy an armistice to seek peace terms in Rome, but late in 203 Hannibal returned to Africa to renew the war. Landing his troops at Leptis, Scipio headed for Zama, a 5 days' march west of Carthage. Here the decisive battle took place, ending in a complete victory for Scipio and King Masinissa, his Numidian ally. Scipio concluded the peace and returned to Rome, where he celebrated his triumph. Henceforth he carried the honorary cognomen Africanus.

Elected censor in 199, Scipio became *princeps sena-*

tus (leader of the Senate) till the end of his life. Consul for the second time in 194, he was thwarted by the Senate in his desire to obtain the province of Macedonia, where he hoped to pursue his pro-Hellenic policy against the threat of the Syrian king Antiochus III. In the following year he was sent to Africa to arbitrate in a border conflict between Carthage and King Masinissa. In 190 Scipio was instrumental in obtaining for his brother Lucius, consul of the year, the command against Antiochus by offering to accompany him as legate on his campaign.

Seriously ill in Asia Minor, Scipio Africanus took no part in the decisive victory of Magnesia in 189 but was active again during the peace negotiations at Sardis. When the two brothers returned to Rome, they were immediately attacked by the party of Cato the Elder, a vigorous opponent of the pro-Hellenic policy of the Scipios.

Lucius was accused of embezzling the money paid by Antiochus as a war indemnity to the Roman people. Asked to produce the account books, Scipio Africanus tore them up before the eyes of the senators. When, according to one tradition, he was himself accused of accepting bribery from Antiochus, he invited the people to follow him up to the Capitol in order to give thanks to Jupiter for the victory of Zama. His power broken, Scip-

Scipio Africanus Major. (Museo Nazionale, Naples)

io left Rome as a private citizen, disillusioned and ill, to retire on his estate at Liternum in Campania.

Further Reading

Scipio Africanus Major is listed in the Ancient History study guide (III, B, 2). His adoptive grandson, SCIPIO AFRICANUS MINOR, finally subdued the Carthaginians.

The definitive biography is Howard Hayes Scullard, *Scipio Africanus: Soldier and Politician* (1970). Extremely valuable are Scullard's *Scipio Africanus in the Second Punic War* (1930) and Richard M. Haywood, *Studies on Scipio Africanus* (1933). Designed for the general reader are Basil Henry Liddell Hart, A *"Greater than Napoleon": Scipio Africanus* (1926), and the fictional account by Friedrich Donauer, *Swords against Carthage*, translated by F. T. Cooper (1932). Recommended for general historical background are J. B. Bury and others, eds., *The Cambridge Ancient History*, vol. 8 (1930), and Howard H. Scullard, *A History of the Roman World from 753–146 B.C.* (1935; rev. ed. 1951) and *Roman Politics 220–150 B.C.* (1951).

SCIPIO AFRICANUS MINOR

/ **By Ursula Heibges**

Publius Cornelius Aemilianus Scipio Africanus Minor (185/184–129 B.C.) was a Roman official and general in Africa and Spain. He was also the brilliant leader of the so-called Scipionic Circle, a group of pro-Hellenic philosophers, poets, and politicians.

The second son of Lucius Aemilius Paullus, Scipio was adopted by Publius Cornelius Scipio, son of Scipio Africanus Major, and married Sempronia, sister of the Gracchus brothers. As a youth of 18 years, Scipio accompanied his father to Greece in 168 B.C., fought in the Battle of Pydna, and participated in his father's triumph. Among the Achaean hostages was the historian Polybios, who remained in the house of Paullus and won the friendship of young Scipio. In 151, although assigned to the province of Macedonia, Scipio volunteered to serve as military tribune with Lucullus in Spain. Scipio distinguished himself in single combat with a Spanish horseman, won the mural crown, and negotiated the surrender of the city of Intercatia.

War against Carthage

Sent by Lucullus to Africa to procure elephants for the Celtiberian War, Scipio mediated peace between the Carthaginians and the Numidian king, Masinissa. Back in Rome he aided in the release of Polybios and the other Achaean hostages. In 149 Scipio served as military tribune under Manilius in Africa, where he won the crown of siege by saving a beleaguered force against the attack of Hasdrubal.

After the death of King Masinissa in 148, Scipio settled the succession to the Numidian kingdom by dividing it among the King's sons. Returning to Rome to stand for the aedileship, Scipio was elected consul instead. The vote of the people exempted him from the laws on legal age and granted him the command against Carthage without the lot.

Crossing over to Utica, Scipio blockaded Carthage and in 146 captured and destroyed the city. Tradition reports that Scipio, while gazing at the city in flames and meditating on the uncertainties of human events, feared for his own city and wept. At any rate, he cursed the site, sold the remaining population into slavery, organized the new province of Africa, and returned to Rome to celebrate a brilliant triumph, accepting his inherited cognomen, Africanus, for his own merits.

During his censorship in 142, which gained him a reputation for severity, Scipio completed the building of the Aemilian Bridge. As head of an embassy to the East in 140, he observed and settled Roman relations with the Eastern allies. In 134 a special dispensation exempted him from the law on reelection to the consulship, and, again, he was granted a military command by popular vote, this time in Hither Spain (Tarraconensis). After restoring discipline in the army, he blockaded and destroyed the Spanish stronghold of Numantia in 133.

Civil War in Rome

While still in Spain, Scipio received the news of the stormy tribunate and death of Tiberius Sempronius Grac-

Scipio Africanus Minor, ancient bronze portrait bust in the Louvre, Paris. (Giraudon)

Ruins of an ancient Roman villa in Carthage. (H. Roger-Viollet)

chus and expressed his undisguised hostility to Gracchus's agrarian program and unconstitutionality. After celebrating his second triumph Scipio continued to oppose the pro-Gracchan party by rejecting the proposal of the tribune Carbo to legalize repetition of the tribunate and by sponsoring a measure which deprived the Gracchan land commission of its judicial function.

Tension rose to a climax during the Latin Festival of 129, when Scipio faced the populace in a public address which ended in hostile altercations. Escorted home by an impressive throng, he withdrew to his bedroom to compose another speech for the next day. In the morning he was found dead. Carbo, Gaius Gracchus, Scipio's wife Sempronia, and his mother-in-law Cornelia were all suspected of responsibility for his death. However, the eulogy written by his friend Gaius Laelius made no mention of a violent death.

Scipio, though liberal in culture and a great admirer of Greek literature and learning, was basically a political conservative who vigorously supported senatorial control of the constitution and Roman dominion in the provinces. Emerging as the ideal statesman during the century of revolution, Cicero chose Scipio as the central figure for his dialogue *On the Commonwealth* and celebrated Scipio's lifelong friendship with Laelius in his essay *On Friendship*.

Further Reading

Scipio Africanus Minor is listed in the Ancient History study guide (III, B, 2). He opposed the reforms of Tiberius Sempronius and Gaius Sempronius GRACCHUS.

Ancient sources on Scipio's life are Livy, Polybios, and Cicero. The definitive modern biography is A. E. Astin, *Scipio Aemilianus* (1967). For an understanding of Scipio and his friends see Ruth M. Brown, *A Study of the Scipionic Circle* (1934). Recommended for general historical background are Tenney Frank, *Roman Imperialism* (1914); J. B. Bury and others, eds., *The Cambridge Ancient History*, vol. 8 (1930); and Howard H. Scullard, *Roman Politics 220–150 B.C.* (1951).

D. SCOTT

/ By Lamont H. Yeakey

The American Negro slave Dred Scott (1795–1858), in an effort to gain his freedom, waged one of the most important legal battles in the history of the United States.

Dred Scott was born a slave in Southampton County, Va. Industrious and intelligent, he was employed as a farmhand, stevedore, craftsman, and general handyman. In 1819 his original owner moved to Huntsville, Ala., and later to St. Louis, Mo. In 1832 he died, and Scott was sold for $500 to a surgeon in the U.S. Army who took Scott to the free state of Illinois in 1834 and on to Wisconsin Territory. Later the doctor returned with Scott to Missouri.

When the surgeon died, Scott passed to John Sanford. During these years he had married and had two daughters. Scott had tried unsuccessfully to escape from slavery and later to buy his freedom. In 1846 he filed suit in the Missouri state courts for his freedom on the grounds that residence in a free territory had liberated him.

Scott's suit finally came before the U.S. Supreme Court. On March 6, 1857, in *Dred Scott v. John Sanford*, after much debate the Supreme Court ruled against Scott 7 to 2, with Chief Justice Roger B. Taney giving the majority opinion. According to Taney, Scott could not sue Sanford because he was not a U.S. citizen. The justice argued that Scott was not a citizen because he was both a Negro and a slave. Taney's remarks that black men "had no rights which the white man was bound to respect" came as a severe blow to black people and outraged white abolitionists.

This crucial decision electrified the country, for Taney had ruled that black people were not citizens of the United States and that an act of Congress (the Missouri Compromise of 1820) was unconstitutional. He also had redefined the relationship between the states and the Federal government, making possible the expansion of slavery into the territories. Southerners rejoiced at the verdict; abolitionists denounced it and even went as far as discrediting the legitimacy of the Court itself.

A few months after the decision, on May 26, 1857, Scott's owner freed him. Scott continued to live in St. Louis until his death on Sept. 17, 1858. Although black men would not become citizens of the United States until the ratification of the 14th Amendment (1868), Scott's bid for freedom remained the most momentous judicial event of the century.

Further Reading

Dred Scott is listed in the American History study guide (VI, A, 3). Henry M. TURNER was a black leader during the Civil War period.

The best account of Scott and his case is Vincent C. Hopkin, *Dred Scott's Case* (1951). Alfred H. Kelly and Winfred A. Harbison, *The American Constitution: Its Origins and Development* (4th ed. 1970), is a useful text in examining the constitutional questions. Stanley I. Kutler, *The Dred Scott Decision: Law or Politics?* (1967), provides a critical assessment of the controversial issues and implications surrounding the case. Another invaluable aid in understanding the case and its ramifications is Loren Miller, *The Petitioners: The Story of the Supreme Court of the United States and the Negro* (1966). An excellent background study is John Hope Franklin, *From Slavery to Freedom: A History of American Negroes* (1947).

R. F. SCOTT / By Barry M. Gough

The English naval officer and polar explorer Robert Falcon Scott (1868–1912) made monumental scientific findings in Antarctica, and his geographical discoveries were extensive. He failed in his attempt to be the first to reach the South Pole.

Robert F. Scott was born on June 6, 1868, at Devonport. In 1880 he entered the naval college, H.M.S. *Britannia*, and 2 years later became a midshipman. He was promoted to first lieutenant in 1897. As early as 1887 Scott had come to the attention of Sir Clements Markham, the principal promoter of British exploration in the late 19th century. In 1899, after Markham had won partial government backing for the intended dash to the pole, Scott was chosen to head the National Antarctic Expedition.

Leaving England in August 1901, the *Discovery*, with Scott as commander, sailed south and reached the Ross Sea in January 1902. For 2 years the ship remained off

Dred Scott (left) with an unidentified man. (Courtesy of The New-York Historical Society, New York City)

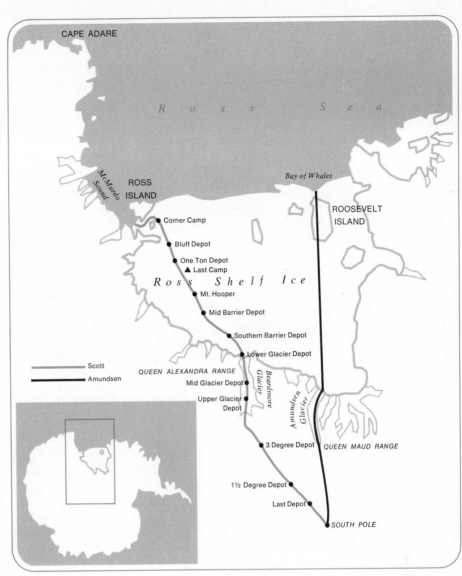

CAPE ADARE

Ross Sea

McMurdo Sound

ROSS
ISLAND

Bay of Whales

ROOSEVELT
ISLAND

● Corner Camp

● Bluff Depot

● One Ton Depot
▲ Last Camp

Ross Shelf Ice

● Mt. Hooper

● Mid Barrier Depot

● Southern Barrier Depot

● Lower Glacier Depot

———— Scott
———— Amundsen

QUEEN ALEXANDRA RANGE

Beardmore Glacier

Mid Glacier Depot

Upper Glacier
Depot

Amundsen Glacier

● 3 Degree Depot   QUEEN MAUD RANGE

● 1½ Degree Depot

● Last Depot

● SOUTH POLE

Robert F. Scott's and Roald Amundsen's routes to the South Pole. Scott reached the pole on Jan. 18, 1912, only to discover that the Norwegian explorer had been there 35 days before.

Hut Point, Ross Island, in McMurdo Sound, and it was from here that many sledge journeys, including two led by Scott himself, began. On Dec. 30, 1902, Scott and two of his associates reached latitude 82°16′33″S over the Antarctic Plateau; this was then the southern record. A year later Scott reached latitude 77°59′S, longitude 146°33′E. A general reconnaissance of the area around South Victoria Land and the Ross Sea and Ross Shelf Ice was undertaken, and the findings added much to man's knowledge of Antarctica. The expedition ended when the *Discovery*, with the relief ships *Morning* and *Terra Nova*, reached New Zealand in April 1904. Promoted to captain on his return to England in 1904, Scott commanded, in turn, three warships and in 1909 became a naval assistant at the Admiralty. Scott recorded his impressions of his first expedition in *The Voyage of the "Discovery"* (1905).

Enthusiasm for Antarctic explorations had waned after 1904, but in 1909 Scott announced plans to reach the South Pole. British and Dominion governments gave financial support, and the *Terra Nova* sailed in June 1910. While at sea, Scott learned that Roald Amundsen and his Norwegian party were also attempting to reach the pole. The race was on. From winter headquarters at Cape Evans (latitude 77°38′24″S), Scott began his sledge journey on Nov. 1, 1911. He had placed much faith, too much as events were to prove, on motor sledges and ponies. The former broke down; the latter either died in crevasses or were shot for food. Consequently, the strength of Scott and his men was taxed even before they left the last supporting party at latitude 86°32′S on Jan. 4, 1912, for the attempt on the pole. On January 18 the party, composed of Scott and four others, reached the South Pole and found there the Norwegian flag, a tent, and a note left for Scott by Amundsen, who with his excellent knowledge and use of dogs, had reached the goal on December 14, 1911.

Heartbroken and weary, the party now turned for base

Robert F. Scott. (Library of Congress)

second expedition are Leonard Huxley, *Scott's Last Expedition* (1913), and Edward Ratcliffe Garth Russell Evans, *South with Scott* (1921). The scientific findings of this voyage were published in *British Antarctic Expedition ("Terra Nova"), 1910–13: Scientific Results* (1914).

WALTER SCOTT / By Avrom Fleishman

The Scottish novelist and poet Sir Walter Scott (1771–1832) is the acknowledged master of the historical novel. He was one of the most influential authors of modern times.

Walter Scott was born in Edinburgh on Aug. 15, 1771, the son of a lawyer with a long family tradition in law. By birth Scott was connected with both the rising middle class of Britain and the aristocratic Scottish heritage then passing into history. He was educated at Edinburgh University and prepared for a career in law, but his avocations were history and literature. He read widely in English and Continental literatures, particularly medieval and Renaissance chivalric romances, German romantic poetry and fiction, and the narrative folk poems known as ballads.

Translations and Poetry

From these intense interests Scott's earliest publications derived: a translation of J. W. von Goethe's play *Götz von Berlichingen* (1799) and other translations from German; *Minstrelsy of the Scottish Border* (1802–1803), a collection of ballads that generated great interest in folk poetry; and a succession of narrative poems, mainly of chivalric or historical action. These poems—including *The Lay of the Last Minstrel* (1805), *Marmion* (1808), and *The Lady of the Lake* (1810)—became best sellers, and Scott established his first literary reputation as a poet of the romantic school.

During these years Scott also pursued a legal career, rising to the official position of clerk of the Court of Session. His enormous energies allowed him to engage in scholarly and journalistic activities. His edition and biography of John Dryden, the English poet and dramatist, published in 1808, remains of value. His politically motivated founding of the *Quarterly Review*, a literary journal, helped make Edinburgh the most influential center of British intellectual life outside London. In these years Scott also began to create an estate, Abbotsford, to reflect his antiquarian interests. He modeled its furnishings and architecture on the traditions of the medieval era.

Waverley Novels

When sales of his verse narrative *Rokeby* (1813) declined and a new poet, Lord Byron, appeared on the literary scene, Scott began to develop another of his many capacities. Picking up the fragment of a novel he had begun in 1805, he tried his hand at fiction, and his most

camp. But weakened by the strain and lack of warm food, which brought on frostbite, the men became involved in a "race against time to reach one depot after another" before their strength gave out. At latitude 79°40'S, 11 miles from One Ton Depot, the remaining three members of the party made camp for the last time. On March 29 Scott made his last journal entry. Eight months later a relief expedition found the tent, bodies, journals, and records. In 1964 an account of this expedition was published as *Scott's Last Expedition: From the Personal Journals of Captain R. F. Scott.*

When news of the tragic and heroic end reached London and Europe, admiration was forthcoming from many quarters. A lasting action was the opening of a fund to commemorate the explorers which enabled publication of their scientific results and the opening of the great Scott Polar Research Institute in Cambridge, England.

Further Reading

Robert F. Scott is listed in the Geography and Exploration study guide (VII, A, 3). Other polar explorers were Sir James Clark ROSS, Robert PEARY, Sir John FRANKLIN, and Roald AMUNDSEN.

Biographies of Scott are Stephen Gwynn, *Captain Scott* (1930); Martin Lindsay, *The Epic of Captain Scott* (1934); George Seaver, *Scott of the Antarctic: A Study in Character* (1940); and Maude Carter, *Captain Scott: Explorer and Scientist* (1950). Illuminating works on his

fully characteristic novel, *Waverley* (1814), resulted. As its subtitle, *'Tis Sixty Years Since*, established, *Waverley* was a historical novel about the 1745 rebellion to restore the Stuart line to the British throne. By leading a young and naive Englishman through a wide range of Scottish classes, political factions, and cultural modes, Scott built up a substantial picture of an entire nation's life at a dramatic historical juncture.

The success of *Waverley* established Scott in the career of a novelist, but it did not establish his name in that role. Unwilling to stake too much on his venture into fiction, he had published *Waverley* anonymously. Finding that the mask of anonymity had stimulated public interest, Scott signed his subsequent novels "by the Author of Waverley." This signature became his trademark, the novels bearing it being called the "Waverley" novels. The Waverley novels exercised enormous fascination not only for Scots and Englishmen but also throughout the Continent. These novels provided the characters and plots for innumerable stories, plays, and operas, the most famous of which is Gaetano Donizetti's opera *Lucia di Lammermoor*.

Scott's achievement as a novelist can best be summarized by grouping his novels according to their themes and settings. His first successes were largely in the realm of Scottish history. In the order of their chronological setting, the Scottish novels are *Castle Dangerous* (1832) and *The Fair Maid of Perth* (1828), both set in the 14th century; *The Monastery* and *The Abbot* (both 1820), its sequel, set during the 16th century's religious upheavals;

Abbotsford, Sir Walter Scott's home near Melrose, Roxburghshire, Scotland. The Neo-Gothic mansion—begun in 1816 on an estate Scott had purchased in 1812—was the work of two architects: Edward Blore, who designed the original house, and William Atkinson, who was responsible for the 1822–1823 additions. (The British Tourist Authority, London)

Sir Walter Scott, an 1824 portrait by Sir Edwin Landseer. (National Portrait Gallery, London)

A Legend of Montrose (1819) and *Old Mortality* (1816), which deal with the campaigns of the 17th-century civil wars; and a series of novels of the Jacobite (Stuart) rebellions of the 18th century—*Rob Roy* (1817), *Waverley*, and *Redgauntlet* (1824). Other Scottish novels indirectly related to historical themes are *The Black Dwarf* (1816), *The Heart of Midlothian* (1818), *The Bride of Lammermoor* (1819), and *The Pirate* (1822). Scott also wrote a group of novels set in nearly contemporary times: *Guy Mannering* (1815), *The Antiquary* (1816), and *St. Ronan's Well* (1824).

English Novels

At a critical point of his career, Scott turned to English history for his subject matter. Critics are generally agreed that the English (and Continental) novels, mainly set in medieval times, are inferior in social and psychological realism, but they include Scott's most enduringly popular works. He began with *Ivanhoe* (1820) and then wrote three other novels set in the period of the Crusades: *The Talisman* (1825), *The Betrothed* (1825), and *Count Rob-*

ert of Paris (1832). *Quentin Durward* (1823) and *Anne of Geierstein* (1829) deal with the later Middle Ages, and the Renaissance is represented by *Kenilworth* (1821) and *The Fortunes of Nigel* (1822). The English phases of the civil-war and Restoration periods were rendered in *Woodstock* (1826) and *Peveril of the Peak* (1822), respectively.

So massive a literary corpus cannot be reduced to broad generalizations. Most critics and readers seem to prefer Scott's early novels. On the whole, Scott's work is flawed by sentimentality and rhetoric, but his novels command the power to put modern readers in touch with men of the past.

Scott's later years were clouded by illness, throughout which he continued to write. He spent the energies of his last years trying to write enough to recover honorably from the bankruptcy of a publishing firm in which he had invested heavily. He died at Abbotsford on Sept. 21, 1832.

Further Reading

Sir Walter Scott is listed in the Literature study guide (II, G, 2, a). He and Charles DICKENS were the most popular novelists of the 19th century. An earlier Scottish poet was Robert BURNS.

The authorized biography by Scott's son-in-law, John Gibson Lockhart, *Memoirs of the Life of Sir Walter Scott* (3 vols., 1837–1838), has been supplemented by the definitive, scholarly work of Edgar Johnson, *Sir Walter Scott: The Great Unknown* (2 vols., 1970), which combines biography and criticism. The most thorough critical examination of the novels is Francis R. Hart, *Scott's Novels: The Plotting of Historical Survival* (1966). Another approach is presented in Alexander Welsh, *The Hero of the Waverley Novels* (1963). The most influential recent interpretation is that of George Lukács, *The Historical Novel* (1962).

✳ ✳ ✳

WINFIELD SCOTT / By Odie B. Faulk

The American Winfield Scott (1786–1866) was the leading general of the Mexican War and a superb tactician. He was the Whig nominee for president in 1852.

Winfield Scott became a soldier at a time when the U.S. Army was very ineffective. By study and hard work, he made himself the best military man in the country, wrote the standard manuals on tactics and infantry, and upgraded the Army into an effective unit. Moreover, he was a negotiator who avoided war on several occasions. Yet the presidency, which he coveted, eluded him.

Scott was born near Petersburg, Va., on June 13, 1786. Failing to inherit the family wealth through legal technicalities, he attended William and Mary College but quit

The Mexican War, 1846–1848. United States columns under generals Zachary Taylor, Alexander Doniphan, and John E. Wool had crossed the Rio Grande into northern Mexico before Winfield Scott, in March 1847, boldly landed an army at Veracruz and launched the decisive campaign against Mexico City.

because he disapproved the irreligious attitude of the students. After reading law, he was admitted to the Virginia bar in 1806 and practiced until appointed a captain in the military in 1808. Sent to New Orleans, he was soon in trouble. He declared that the commanding general of the department, James Wilkinson, was as great a traitor as Aaron Burr; Scott was court-martialed and suspended from the Army for a year (1810).

War of 1812

A lieutenant colonel at the outbreak of war, Scott distinguished himself in a number of battles. Several times wounded, the 6-foot 5-inch, 230-pound officer showed such judgment and courage that he was promoted to brigadier general, was breveted a major general, and was voted the thanks of Congress and a gold medal. He declined the offered position of secretary of war in James Madison's administration.

Scott went to Europe in 1815 and in 1829 to study foreign military tactics, and he wrote military manuals for the Army that remained standard for half a century. He married Maria D. Mayo of Richmond, Va., in 1817. He also conducted military institutes for the officers of his command, the Eastern Division, which was headquartered at New York City.

In 1828 Scott participated in the Black Hawk War. Four years later President Andrew Jackson sent him to South Carolina during the nullification controversy, and his tact prevented civil war at that time. In 1835 Jackson sent him to fight the Seminole and Creek Indians in Florida, but he was deprived of materials and moved slowly. Jackson removed him from command to face a board of inquiry. The board promptly exonerated him with praise for his "energy, steadiness and ability."

Following the abortive Canadian revolt of 1837, President Martin Van Buren sent Scott to bring peace to the troubled Niagara region. Later in 1838 Scott convinced 16,000 outraged Cherokee that they should move peacefully from Tennessee and South Carolina to the Indian Territory; he also persuaded them to be vaccinated. His tact and skill as a negotiator in 1839 brought peace in the "Lumberjack War" over the boundary between Maine and New Brunswick. In reward for these activities, he was named general in chief of the Army in 1841, a position he held for 20 years.

Mexican War

Scott's name had been mentioned prominently for the Whig nomination for president in 1840 and 1844; thus, at the outbreak of the Mexican War, President James K. Polk did not want Scott to achieve the prominence that would earn him the presidential nomination. When Zachary Taylor's campaign in northern Mexico failed to achieve victory, however, Polk had to turn to Scott. Scott's strategy proved effective: landing at Veracruz in March 1847, he was in Mexico City within 6 months after brilliant victories at Cerro Gordo, Molino del Rey, and Chapultepec. His force then became an army of occupation, restoring order so effectively that a delegation of Mexicans asked him to become dictator of the nation. Polk wanted to court-martial Scott and thereby discredit him as a rival, but Congress voted Scott a second gold medal and thanks for his conduct of the war. Polk's charges were withdrawn.

Winfield Scott reviewing troops in Mexico City during the Mexican War, a painting by W. H. Powell. (Alexander McCook Craighead Collection, Dayton, Ohio)

Presidential Nominee

In 1848 the Whig party elected Zachary Taylor to the White House. In 1852 the Whig presidential nomination went to Scott, but he was defeated easily in a pompous and lackluster campaign. Congress 3 years later recognized his accomplishments by naming him a lieutenant general, the first American to hold that rank since George Washington.

In 1857 Scott argued against the "Mormon War" in favor of negotiation. Though President James Buchanan sent him to negotiate a dispute with England over the San Juan Islands in the Pacific Northwest in 1859, he refused Scott's advice to strengthen Southern forts and posts to avoid their capture should civil war break out.

In 1861, at the beginning of the Civil War, Scott stayed in the Union Army despite his Virginia heritage. He recommended the policy of dividing and containing the South to President Abraham Lincoln, a policy later followed successfully. On Nov. 1, 1861, Scott retired at his own request. Lincoln summarized the nation's sentiment when he said, "We are . . . his debtors." Scott died on May 29, 1866, at West Point, N.Y., and was buried in Arlington National Cemetery.

Scott's insistence on maintaining strict standards of dress and discipline in the Army caused the troops to refer to him as "Old Fuss and Feathers." Opposed to the use of strong alcoholic beverages, he once ordered that any soldier found intoxicated had to dig a grave for his own size and then contemplate it, for soon he would fill it if he persisted in drinking. His arguments against alcoholic beverages led to the founding of the first temperance societies in the United States.

Further Reading

Winfield Scott is listed in the American History study guide (IV, C, 3; V, B, 1). Zachary TAYLOR also served in the Mexican War under President James K. POLK.

Memoirs of Lieut.-General Scott, LL.D., Written by Himself (2 vols., 1864), filled with rhetorical flourishes, contains Scott's own version of his life and times. Two standard biographies are Charles W. Elliott, *Winfield Scott: The Soldier and the Man* (1937), and Arthur D. H. Smith, *Old Fuss and Feathers: The Life and Exploits of Lt.-General Winfield Scott* (1937). Justin H. Smith, *The War with Mexico* (2 vols., 1919), traces Scott's activities in that conflict.

SCRIABIN / By Stanley D. Krebs

The composer and pianist Alexander Nikolayevich Scriabin (1871–1915) was a striking representative of the early modern school of Russian music. The romantic symbolism of his late work often obscures his genuine innovations.

Alexander Scriabin (pronounced skryä′bĭn) was born in Moscow on Dec. 25, 1871. His musical talent was discerned at an early age. He studied piano and, at the age of 14, took theory and composition instruction from Alexander Taneev. Scriabin entered the Moscow Conservatory in 1888; one of his classmates was Sergei Rachmaninov. Scriabin graduated with the Gold Medal in 1892. His accomplishment as a pianist outweighed the value of his early, Chopin-like compositions for piano, and it was as a performer that he began appearing abroad. Except for a 6-year term (1897–1903) as a piano teacher at the Moscow Conservatory, he spent most of his mature years in the West, years in which his zest for living brought him almost as much attention as his art.

From about the turn of the century Scriabin began to cast away both his tonal and formal moorings: he is often lauded for the former and criticized for the latter, but the phenomena are inseparable. The steady progression is seen in his numerous short piano pieces—nocturnes, mazurkas, études, and preludes—and becomes focused in the last sonatas (Nos. 6–10, 1912–1913) and the re-

Alexander Scriabin, a portrait in the Glinka Museum of Musical Culture, Moscow. (Novosti from Sovfoto)

markable orchestral works: the Third Symphony (*Divine Poem*; 1905), the Fourth Symphony (*Poem of Ecstasy*; 1907), and the Fifth Symphony (*Poem of Fire* or *Prometheus*; 1910).

In pushing away from tonality Scriabin developed chords from superimposed fourths, including the "mystic chord." He handled form in erratic time segments; some of his études are only seconds long. Overlaying this technical and expressive development was a highly personal, egocentric, verbose, quasi-devout mysticism which has led some biographers to judge Scriabin insane. Indeed, sketches for a final, unfinished work, *Mystery*, seem musically senseless; it was to be performed as a "multimedia" event on a Tibetan mountain by thousands of supplicants and, in Scriabin's imagination, was to bring the world to a close.

On April 14, 1915, Scriabin died in Moscow. His family, whom he legitimized at the end, was left with little money, and Rachmaninov, among others, came to their aid. Scriabin's son, Julian, seemed a prodigious copy of the father; he, too, died early and tragically in 1919.

Scriabin stands somewhat aside from the mainstream of musical development and seems unclassifiable in either Russian or Western terms. His contribution may best be seen in his small piano pieces. He wrote no chamber music, no opera, and very little vocal music, so his influence is uniquely limited. The innovative sophistication and mysticism of his later works were not appreciated by the ideologists of the young Soviet Union, and this, too, was a limiting factor. Like many of his generation, he moves in and out of vogue. But his legacy, though limited, is of lasting value.

Further Reading

Alexander Scriabin is listed in the Music study guide (I, I, 6). Sergei RACHMANINOV was also a piano virtuoso and composer.

Biographers either fight shy of or linger dotingly on some of the extramusical sensations in Scriabin's life. The soberer accounts are those of Arthur E. Hull (1916) and Alfred Swan (1923). The works by Leonid Sabaneev (1923) and Faubion Bowers (2 vols., 1969) are less restrained; the Bowers book is unusually entertaining though not altogether accurate. Chapters on Scriabin appear in M. Montagu-Nathan, *Contemporary Russian Composers* (1917); M. D. Calvocoressi and Gerald Abraham, *Masters of Russian Music* (1936); David Brook, *Six Great Russian Composers* (1946); and William Austin, *Music in the Twentieth Century* (1966).

SCRIPPS / By Louis Filler

The confidence of Edward Wyllis Scripps
(1854–1926) in free enterprise and democracy
enabled him to create the first newspaper chain
in the United States and to contribute
significantly to the new journalism of his era.

Born in Rushville, Ill., on June 18, 1854, E. W. Scripps came from a publishing family. His grandfather had issued the *London Literary Gazette*, and relatives in America were associated with newspapers. Scripps was raised on the family farm in Winchester, Ohio. At 18 he became an office boy on the *Detroit Advertiser and Tribune*, managed and owned by his half brother James Scripps. Later he served in business and editorial capacities for James. Borrowing money from relatives, notably his half sister Ellen, who would be his close associate for 40 years, Scripps founded the *Cleveland Penny Press* in 1877.

Scripps was a philosopher of journalism as well as a businessman. He believed that the psychology of people had to be studied if they were to be satisfied. He reached controversial conclusions over the years, as when he held that "one mature white American is a better prospect [as a newspaper purchaser] than two or three Negroes or comparatively recent immigrants. . . ." On the other hand, he thought that the differences between people were the products of accident and environment. He fought boldly and under stress for the right to print news independently, and he was conspicuous in battles against municipal corruption.

In 1880 Scripps again joined relatives to take on the *St. Louis Evening Chronicle* and then the paper that became the *Cincinnati Post*. With the Detroit and Cleveland papers, they constituted the first newspaper chain in the country. Disagreements in policy, particularly Scripps's liberal, prolabor views, caused Scripps to

E. W. Scripps. (Courtesy Scripps-Howard Newspapers)

leave the group with only the *Cincinnati Post*. He began a drive which multiplied his newspaper holdings in the Midwest and South, retaining 51 percent of stock in all papers. In 1889 he and Milton A. McRae founded the Scripps-McRae League of Newspapers. Dissatisfied with telegraphic news from the Associated Press and opposing its monopolistic features, in 1897 Scripps organized the Scripps-McRae Press Association, later the United Press Association. Scripps later developed a feature service, the Newspaper Enterprise Association.

Although Scripps maintained rigid control of his properties, he sought to spread responsibility for them among associates, and by the time of his death on March 12, 1926, he owned only 40 percent of the stock. Scripps's interest in science expressed itself in his organization (1920) of the journalistic Science Service. With his sister he also endowed what became the Scripps Institution of Oceanography at La Jolla, Calif.

Further Reading

E. W. Scripps is listed in the American History study guide (VII, G, 5). Contemporary newspaper publisher Joseph PULITZER fought political corruption.

Scripps speaks for himself in two books: one arranged by his family and edited by Charles R. McCabe, *Damned Old Crank* (1951), the other edited by Oliver Knight, *I Protest* (1966), a volume of "selected disquisitions." Biographical accounts written by associates are Gilson Gardner, *Lusty Scripps: The Life of E. W. Scripps* (1932), and Negley O. Cochran, *E. W. Scripps* (1933). Scripps figures also in Milton A. McRae, *Forty Years in Newspaperdom* (1924).

SCULLIN / By Trevor R. Reese

James Henry Scullin (1876–1953) was an Australian politician and the first native-born Labour prime minister of Australia.

James Scullin was born the son of a railway worker near Ballarat, Victoria. He was brought up a Roman Catholic and formally educated only at primary school, but he later attended evening classes. He became a small grocer and editor of a newspaper in Ballarat before turning his attention to politics.

Scullin joined the Labour party in 1903 and was organizer for the Australian Workers Union for 4 years until, in 1910, he was elected to the federal Parliament. He lost his seat in 1913 and became editor of the *Ballarat Echo*, an evening daily. He returned to Parliament in 1923 and became deputy leader of the Labour party in 1927 and leader the following year. In the election of October 1929 he decisively defeated the governing Liberal and Country parties, and the Labour party gained its largest parliamentary majority since the federation in 1901.

Scullin lacked ministerial experience when he became

James Scullin in 1930. (National Archives, Washington, D.C.)

prime minister, and though he was a man of moderate views and was respected on all sides for his integrity, his modesty and gentleness ill matched the heavy burdens that were to fall on his shoulders. As the effects of the worldwide economic depression spread to Australia, his ministry was torn by internal dissension. His task was made more difficult by a hostile upper house, where, in contrast to its large majority in the lower house, the Labour party held only 7 of the 36 seats and was thus powerless to put several of its proposals into effect.

Because of the economic crisis, Scullin's government was obliged to repudiate election pledges and to assume responsibility for deflation, retrenchment, reduction in wages and the standard of living, and, at the end of 1931, a devaluation of the Australian pound in terms of sterling. Throughout his tenure of office Scullin was harassed by political difficulties arising out of his government's management of the economic crisis.

In August 1930 Scullin left to attend the imperial conference in London, where one of his duties was to advise the King that, in accordance with Labour party views in Australia, the next governor general should be an Australian. In his absence, his parliamentary following split on economic policy, and when he returned, there was outright defection. Five members from New South Wales left the federal Labour party and formed themselves into a group attached to the policies of John Thomas Lang, the controversial Labour premier in their state; and Joseph Lyons, the postmaster general, resigned from the ministry and joined the opposition. In the election of

December 1931 the opposition was led by Lyons and supported by some other erstwhile members of the Labour party.

The crippled Labour government was swept from office, and Scullin was replaced as prime minister by his former lieutenant. He continued as leader of the Labour party until 1935, when he resigned on account of ill health. He remained in Parliament until 1949 and died on Jan. 28, 1953.

Further Reading

James Scullin is listed in the Australia and New Zealand study guide (II, E). Joseph LYONS and William Morris HUGHES were other Australian Labour leaders.

W. E. Denning, *Caucus Crisis* (1937), is an account of the rise and fall of Scullin's government. Edward R. Walker, *Australia in the World Depression* (1933), and D. B. Copland, *Australia in the World Crisis, 1929–1933* (1934), cover the economic problems of the period. See also William R. McLaurin, *Economic Planning in Australia, 1929–36* (1937).

SEABURY / By Henry L. Swint

> The American theologian Samuel Seabury (1729–1796) was an important figure in the establishment of the Episcopal Church in the United States.

S amuel Seabury was born in Groton, Conn., on Nov. 30, 1729, a son of Samuel Seabury, a minister of the Congregational Church who became a convert to the Church of England and was ordained in its ministry in 1730. Young Seabury graduated from Yale College in 1748, went to England in 1751, studied medicine in Edinburgh, and was ordained in 1753. A year later he returned to America under the auspices of the Society for the Propagation of the Gospel and became rector of Christ Church, New Brunswick, N.J. Later he served churches in Jamaica and Westchester, N.Y.

Conflict characterized Seabury's life. He was a High Churchman and a royalist. He believed that the establishment of a strong episcopate in America should take precedence over the organization of a national church. An early controversy left a mark on him. Dissenters, who were in the majority in the Jamaica vestry, opposed the governor's action in making Seabury, rather than the man they had chosen, the town minister. Later, in Westchester, using a pseudonym, he wrote pamphlets in defense of the Church of England and of British rule in America. In November 1775 he was arrested but was permitted to return to Westchester 2 months later. He sought refuge behind the British lines in September 1776 and in 1778 was appointed chaplain to a British regiment. After the war he received a pension from the British government.

Samuel Seabury. (Courtesy of The New-York Historical Society, New York City)

In 1783 Seabury was chosen by the Connecticut clergy to obtain consecration as a bishop. The lack of bishops in America had been an obstacle to the growth of the Church, for ordination could be effected only in England. But the English authorities would not agree to Seabury's candidacy, and he was consecrated in the Episcopal Church of Scotland in November 1784. The following year he returned to America as rector of St. James Church, New London, Conn., and bishop of Connecticut, the first bishop of the Episcopal Church in the country.

Efforts to establish a national Episcopal Church had begun during Seabury's absence. His position as bishop caused some opposition to unification; some clergymen condemned him because of his actions in support of the British; others doubted the validity of his consecration. He was strongly supported by most of the New England clergy, however, and Church unity was achieved at the General Convention of 1789 in Philadelphia. Seabury died on Feb. 25, 1796, in New London.

Further Reading

Samuel Seabury is listed in the Religion study guide (I, O, 1, q). Timothy DWIGHT was also active in reorganizing American churches after the Revolution.

James Thayer Addison, *The Episcopal Church in the United States, 1789–1931* (1951), gives an account of Seabury's activities. Raymond W. Albright, *A History of the Protestant Episcopal Church* (1964), contains more detail and documentation. The classic biographical sketch of Seabury is in *The Episcopate in America* by William Stevens Perry (1895).

* * *

SEDDON / By Trevor R. Reese

Richard John Seddon (1845–1906) was a New Zealand political leader and Liberal prime minister who instituted liberal reforms and advocated imperial solidarity and expansion.

Richard John Seddon was born at St. Helens, Lancashire, England, on June 22, 1845, the son of a schoolmaster. He left school at the age of 12 and at 18 emigrated to Australia, where he worked on the goldfields in Victoria. He moved on to New Zealand in 1866 and established himself as a hotelkeeper. He entered local politics in 1869 and 10 years later transferred to the House of Representatives as a Liberal.

Seddon soon showed himself to be an astute party manager, a hard worker, and a loud, forceful, and verbose speaker who had little time for experts and possessed a strong faith in the virtues of the common man. In 1891 he became minister of public works, defense, and mines in the Liberal government, and in 1892, when John Ballance, the prime minister, became ill, Seddon acted as leader of the House. When Ballance died in 1893, Seddon was invited to form a government.

Richard John Seddon. (Brown Brothers)

Seddon was prime minister for 13 years, and his administration pursued an energetic social program. Graduated land and income taxes were introduced, large holdings were broken up by means of taxes on unimproved property and estates with absentee owners, and attempts were made to encourage the small farmers. In 1894 industrial conciliation and arbitration boards were set up for what was the first compulsory system of state arbitration in the world. An 8-hour working day was established by law in 1897, old-age pensions were introduced in 1898, the free place system in secondary schools was established in 1903, and, somewhat by chance, female suffrage was adopted in 1893.

In external affairs Seddon was the most prominent colonial advocate of imperial preference. He favored a policy of imperial solidarity and expansion: the Cook Islands were annexed to New Zealand in 1900, and a contingent of New Zealand troops was dispatched to support the British Empire in the Boer War.

The social reforms were not necessarily Seddon's own handiwork, of course, but his support was always an essential factor in getting legislation passed. Personally, he was gross, vulgar, domineering, and probably dishonest, but he was well liked and gained a firm hold on the affections of the general public. He centralized the administration too much, and he held too many ministerial portfolios himself, but his personal style became the model for later leaders in New Zealand politics. He died in office on June 10, 1906.

Further Reading

Richard John Seddon is listed in the Australia and New Zealand study guide (III, A). An earlier New Zealand premier was Sir Julius VOGEL.

The best biography is Randal M. Burdon, *King Dick: A Biography of Richard John Seddon* (1955). An earlier but still useful work is James Drummond, *The Life and Work of Richard John Seddon* (1907).

* * *

SEDGWICK / By John Challinor

The English geologist Adam Sedgwick (1785–1873) was the founder of the Cambrian system, the first period of the Paleozoic geologic era.

Adam Sedgwick was born on March 22, 1785, at Dent in his ancestral region of the Yorkshire Dales. In 1804 he entered Trinity College, Cambridge, which became his chief home for the rest of his life. After being made a fellow in 1810, he was ordained; he later became a canon of Norwich. In 1818 he was elected to the professorship of geology, not because he knew anything about geology but on his general merits. However, he began enthusiastically to study the subject, giving lectures and making geological tours, but he con-

Adam Sedgwick, painted in 1832 by Thomas Phillips. (Courtesy of the Sedgwick Museum, Cambridge)

stantly allowed himself to be diverted by business irrelevant to his geological work.

During 1821–1824 Sedgwick carried out researches in the north of England—on the Magnesian Limestone and New Red Sandstone and in the Lake District—but he delayed in the announcement and publication of his findings. Nevertheless, his standing in the world of science at that time and his general popularity were recognized by his being elected president of the Geological Society of London in 1829 and president of the British Association for the Advancement of Science in 1833.

In 1831 Sedgwick began the work which will always be associated with his name: the establishing of a rock-succession, the revealing of a grand structure among the mountains of North Wales, and the consequent founding of the Cambrian system. He did not put his researches into writing, and this was the chief cause of the regrettable controversy which eventually developed with Roderick Murchison over priorities of discovery and nomenclature among these Lower Paleozoic rocks (as they soon came to be called). However, Sedgwick did compose a few important treatises on the structure of rock-masses. In 1839 he and Murchison reported the results of their joint work which founded the Devonian system.

Thereafter Sedgwick's duties at his college and university caused his geological work, other than his lectures and the augmentation of his collections, to be almost entirely laid aside. Sedgwick never married. He died at

Cambridge on Jan. 27, 1873. His lasting memorial is the Sedgwick Museum at Cambridge, opened in 1904, one of the most famous geological schools.

Sedgwick's reputation as a geologist and as a man rests almost entirely on his personality, which was conspicuous for its integrity, vigor, and charm, though he could be bitter in controversy. The influence of his presence and the power of his spoken word are not to be gathered from contemporary written records.

Further Reading

Adam Sedgwick is listed in the Science study guide (VI, E, 1). Some of his geological explorations were carried out jointly with Roderick MURCHISON.

Sedgwick's *A Discourse on the Studies of the University* was recently reprinted with an introduction by Eric Ashby and Mary Anderson (1969), which focuses on Sedgwick's personality, his career as a teacher, and his efforts at educational reform. The standard biography is John Willis Clark and Thomas McKenny Hughes, *The Life and Letters of the Reverend Adam Sedgwick* (2 vols., 1890). Additional light is thrown on Sedgwick and his work in Sir Archibald Geikie, *The Founders of Geology* (1897; 2d ed. 1905), and Horace B. Woodward, *The History of the Geological Society of London* (1907). A good profile of Sedgwick is in Carroll Lane Fenton and Mildred Adams Fenton, *Giants of Geology* (1945; rev. ed. 1952).

SEFERIS / By Patricia Zele Gossen

The Greek poet and statesman George Seferis (1900–1971) combined a diplomatic career with the creation of a body of poetic works unique for their synthesis of modern man's anguished estrangement and the redemptive promise of an ancient artistic heritage.

The son of a law professor who was a poet in his own right, George Seferis (pronounced sə-fĕr′ĭs), or Georgios Seferiadis, spent the first 14 years of his life at his birthplace, Smyrna (Izmir), Turkey. The Seferiadis family fled Asia Minor with the outbreak of World War I, taking up residence first in Athens, where George completed secondary school, then in 1918 moving to Paris, where his father pursued a law practice. Richly endowed from childhood with the poetic experience of a living, oral literature and encouraged by the example of his father, Seferis found himself very early divided between the exigencies of a practical and a literary career. While studying law in Paris, he began writing poetry, and his first titled composition (1924, published later), "Fog," dates from a stay in London, where Seferis had gone to perfect his English prior to taking the Greek Foreign Service examination. Seferis returned to Athens and to the Foreign Ministry in 1925, continuing to write

George Seferis in 1963. (United Press International Photo)

verse and to produce translations and literary criticism until, in 1931, his first collection of poems, *Strophe* (*Turning Point*), appeared.

Diplomacy summoned Seferis to London, where he served as vice-consul until 1934, all the while continuing to publish works (notably "The Cistern," 1932) in magazines and reviews. His next major collection—*Mythistorema* (*Mythical Story*, 1935)—represented an evolution away from the rigidly "pure," stylistically self-conscious early works toward the sober, almost denuded manner that marked the best of his mature poetry, keeping it attuned to real patterns of speech.

Modern desolation for Seferis expressed itself amid particular ruins—the broken statues and columns of an immensely rich Greek heritage. The enduring materiality of these past creations weighed heavily on Seferis, living on for the poet as proof of human continuity, of a glorious but evolving Hellenism.

In *Kichle* ("The Thrush," written during World War II), Seferis faced the ravaged modern world defiantly: "the fragments/ Are not the statues./ You are yourself the remains." But new ruins were being made of Greece. The poet-diplomat continued his dual service, fleeing with the Free Greek government during the Nazi occupation. His published works swelled by five volumes during the war: *Himerologion katastromatos* (*Log Book*) *I, II,* and *III*; *Tetradio gymnasmaton* (*Exercise Book*); and *Poïmata* (*Poems*). Married in 1941, Seferis had journeyed with his wife Maria in official exile from Ankara to South Africa, to Cairo, and to Italy; he wrote all the while

—including a group of *Dokimes* (*Essays*) in 1944—becoming more and more a recognized poet of his unsettled times. In 1947 Seferis received the Palamas Prize from the Athens Academy, and during the postwar years he held diplomatic assignments of ever-increasing responsibility. By the time he returned to Great Britain as Greek ambassador in 1957, his official stature in public service and in letters was already internationally recognized. Seferis retired from the Foreign Service in 1962. He won the Nobel Prize for literature in 1963. Seferis died in Athens on Sept. 20, 1971.

Further Reading

George Seferis is listed in the Literature study guide (III, J, 6). Another modern Greek poet was Kostes PALAMAS.

Recent translations of Seferis's works include those of Rex Warner, *Poems* (1960) and *On the Greek Style* (*Dokimes*) (1966), and Edmund Keeley and Philip Sherrard, *George Seferis: Collected Poems, 1924–1955* (1967), annotated with bibliography. No complete translation or definitive critical presentation has been undertaken to date. Background may be found in Edmund Keeley and Philip Sherrard, trans. and eds., *Six Poets of Modern Greece* (1961), and Philip Sherrard, *The Marble Threshing Floor: Studies in Modern Greek Poetry* (1970). A brief biography and Nobel Prize presentation and acceptance speech appear in Horst Frenz, ed., *Nobel Lectures: Literature, 1901–1967* (1969).

SEJO / By Gari Ledyard

The Korean king Sejo (1417–1468) was an effective yet cruel ruler. In his attempt to maintain royal prerogative against the pressures of the Confucianist gentry-officials, his ruthlessness nurtured a reaction which in time led to a net loss of power for his successors.

Sejo (pronounced sā-jō), formally named Yi Yu, and known as Prince Suyang before taking the throne, was born Nov. 7, 1417, the second son of the great king Sejong. Among eight royal heirs Sejo was perhaps the most capable, but since the designation as crown prince had gone to his elder brother (Yi Hyang, who reigned as Munjong, 1450–1452), Sejo was from the beginning cut off from the succession. Throughout Sejong's reign the royal brothers worked well together, directed by an even-handed father who kept them busy. Sejo was well informed on military affairs, having observed frontier operations against the Jürchen and participated in the development of munitions and ordnance during the early 1440s. He made a major contribution as director of his father's land-survey commission; the formulas developed by this body for measuring crop yields and assessing taxes became a fundamental part of Yi-dynasty fiscal structure. Sejo as a prince also wrote in the vernacular an account of the Buddha's life, which provided the inspiration for his father's Buddhist poetry.

Sejo's brother Munjong succeeded Sejong in 1450 and was competent enough as king; but his health was poor, and he quickly became a target for bureaucrats and officials. Sejo and his younger brother, Prince Anp'yŏng (1418–1453), helped their weaker brother by seeing that the throne's interests were asserted. But when on the King's premature death, in 1452, Munjong's 10-year-old son, Tanjong (Yi Hongwi, also known as Prince Nosan), succeeded, a rift grew between the two brothers over the exercise of power during Tanjong's minority.

Finally, in November 1453, Sejo, charging Prince Anp'yŏng and his followers with plotting to overthrow the young king, banished his brother to an island, where he was forced to commit suicide, and murdered the principal men of his faction. With Sejo now in complete control, Tanjong grew increasingly edgy. Convinced that Sejo's coups were not yet over, he abdicated on July 25, 1455. Sejo took the throne the same day, while Tanjong moved to a lonely exile in remote Kangwŏn Province.

Sejo justified his usurpation on the grounds that unless a strong king sat on the throne the royal power would steadily be eroded. But many men of his day felt he had gone too far, and inevitably a movement grew to restore Tanjong. A group of loyalists planned a coup for July 1456 but were betrayed by an informer. Sejo personally carried out their interrogation, subjecting the six plotters to unspeakable torture and mutilation. The historical accounts of this confrontation show the six men composing defiant poetry and lecturing Sejo to silence before finally breathing their last. Soon afterward Sejo ordered Tanjong's suicide.

These murders echoed through the centuries that followed, with the overwhelming opinion falling on the side of the boy king and the "Six Dead Ministers," as they came to be called. (Six sympathetic officials who went into lifetime retirement to protest Sejo's action are called the "Six Live Ministers.") Tanjong and all loyalists were posthumously rehabilitated during the 17th cen-

tury, but long before that the reverberations of the affair had precipitated factional struggles and purges (notably in 1498, when defense of the loyalists was adjudged *lèse-majesté*).

From 1456 on, Sejo's power was not again questioned. He had his way in virtually everything, and it can be said in his favor that, once established, he was a remarkably effective king. Among his achievements were lavish support of Buddhist writings and their publication, effective frontier defense, suppression of a major rebellion, and institution of the "secret censor" system, by which royal spies circulated covertly through the provinces ferreting out and summarily punishing corruption. In time these posts became themselves major focuses of graft, but the original idea of incorruptible censors had a long life in popular fiction.

Sejo abdicated in favor of his son Yejong on Sept. 22, 1468, and died the next day of an incurable disease.

Further Reading

Sejo is listed in the Asia study guide (III, C, 6). His father was King SEJONG.

There is no biography of Sejo in English. Some details of his reign appear in such standard survey histories as Takashi Hatada, *A History of Korea*, translated and edited by Warren W. Smith, Jr., and Benjamin H. Hazard (1969); and Woo-keun Han, *The History of Korea*, edited by Grafton Mintz (trans. 1970).

SEJONG / By Gari Ledyard

Sejong (1397–1450) was a Korean king and inventor of the Korean alphabet. His long reign, 1418–1450, is generally acknowledged to have been the most brilliant period of the Yi dynasty.

Sejong (pronounced sā-jŏng), formally named Yi To, and known as Prince Ch'ungnyŏng before taking the throne, was born on May 7, 1397. Since his eldest brother, Prince Yangnyŏng, had been designated crown prince in 1404, Sejong in early life did not anticipate the throne. But Yangnyŏng's erratic behavior led to his deposition and Sejong's elevation in July 1418. (An unofficial tradition holds that Prince Yangnyŏng feigned instability so that Sejong might rule.) Sejong became king, following his father's abdication, on Sept. 7, 1418.

During his reign Sejong introduced improved administrative procedures, new census laws, penal reforms, and some civil rights for slaves and outcast groups. He maintained proper relations with China and a firm stance with Japan. His devastating attack on the island of Tsushima in 1419, in retaliation for the coastal raids of Japanese pirates, eliminated the immediate peril and ultimately led to a treaty (1443) which established a long-lasting, peaceful relationship with Japan. To the north he incor-

Sejo's tomb near Seoul, Korea. (From E. McCune, The Arts of Korea, published by Charles E. Tuttle, Inc.)

Sejong Memorial. (Courtesy of King Seijong Memorial Society, Seoul, Korea)

porated new territory south of the Yalu and Tumen rivers, which until then had been occupied or threatened by the Jürchen barbarians. Korea's modern borders are thus one of his legacies.

In the cultural field, Sejong ordered the compilation of outstanding historical works, and his system of branch depositories for historical records ensured the survival of many valuable books through the destructive Japanese invasions of 1592–1598. He reformed the court music. Voluminous encyclopedias of agriculture, medicine, military science, and public administration were compiled. He sponsored the compilation of gazeteers, instituted standardized weights and measures, and installed rain gauges throughout the country, all of which contributed to his rationalization of tax-assessing procedures. His researchers designed clepsydras, armillary spheres, and other scientific instruments.

Sejong's greatest achievement was the alphabet. It was first announced late in 1443 and formally proclaimed in 1446. Sejong was not merely the patron of this alphabet but its actual theoretician and inventor. It reflects in its structure and graphic symbolism a very sophisticated understanding of linguistics. Although the script was coolly received by his officials and did not for many years completely replace the classical Chinese in which they wrote, it was a long-run success and is today the writing system of all Koreans.

Sejong was quick to promote those who showed promise; especially intelligent young men received his "reading vacations," paid leaves for untrammeled study.

The most promising scholars were appointed to the famous "College of Assembled Worthies" (organized 1420), where the research for his cultural and technical projects was done. Many of their publications survive today and reveal a uniformly high standard of scholarship. Sejong's friendship with his scholars was legendary. In political life too he got on well with his highest officers.

But beginning in the late 1430s, Sejong's relations with his officials became strained over two issues. The first was his attempt to delegate certain royal duties to the crown prince in order to conserve his own health. From about 1437, Sejong suffered from rheumatism and diabetes, and about 1442 his eyesight also began to fail. He repeatedly asked his ministers' assent to his plans for the crown prince; just as regularly this assent was withheld. (Korean kings, while theoretically all-powerful, were by tradition and practice required to obtain a consensus of support for their actions.) The debate was resolved only in 1445, when the crown prince finally took over limited duties, but the ill feeling remained.

A second issue was Sejong's belief in Buddhism. The Yi dynasty had come to power partly as a reaction against the previous dynasty's excessive patronage of Buddhism, and from the beginning it had enforced strict limitations on the numbers of monks and monasteries and on tenable church property. As king, Sejong enforced these public policies, but personally he was a devout believer, especially after the death of his wife, Queen Sohŏn, in 1446. For this he suffered constant abuse from his Confucianist officials. Some of the opposition to his alphabet was doubtless a result of this antagonistic atmosphere.

Because of these struggles and his increasingly poor health, Sejong after 1446 began to turn from his official duties to his private pursuits. In addition to the assistance of the crown prince (later reigned as Munjong, 1450–1452), Sejong was helped by two other capable sons, Princes Anp'yŏng and Suyang (Sejo). Sejong spent his last years writing Buddhist devotional poetry, much of which still survives. Early in 1450, he left the palace and retired to the Seoul residence of his youngest son, where he died of a massive stroke on March 30.

Further Reading

Sejong is listed in the Asia study guide (III, C, 6). The Confucian scholar SŎL Ch'ong contributed an earlier system for writing Korean.

No biography of Sejong appears in English. His reign is discussed in Takashi Hatada, *A History of Korea*, translated and edited by Warren W. Smith, Jr., and Benjamin H. Hazard (1969); and Woo-keun Han, *The History of Korea*, edited by Grafton Mintz (trans. 1970).

SELEUCUS I / By Jack M. Balcer

Seleucus I Nikator (ca. 358–281 B.C.), a Macedonian general, was a Companion of Alexander the Great, king of Babylonia and

Syria, and founder of the Seleucid empire and dynasty.

The son of a Macedonian nobleman, Seleucus (pronounced sə-lōō′kəs) was born between 358 and 354 B.C. in Macedon, then ruled by Philip II. He grew up with the king's son, Alexander, and became Alexander's close associate during his expedition through Persia. Seleucus was present with Alexander at Susa in 324, and according to Alexander's bidding, Seleucus married the Bactrian princess Apama. Unlike many of the Macedonians, Seleucus never repudiated this political marriage.

Scramble for the Throne

When Alexander died in 323, Seleucus ranked well below the leading "successors." The kingship went jointly to Alexander's epileptic and half-witted half brother, Philip Arrhidaeios, and the unborn child carried by Alexander's Bactrian wife, Rhoxana. Perdikkas, the leading general and Macedonian nobleman in Babylon, became their regent. Of the other prominent generals, Ptolemy sought the satrapy of Egypt; Antipater remained in Greece as governor and, allied with Craterus, crushed the Athenian rebellion; Lysimachus obtained Thrace; and Antigonus "the One-eyed" gained the powerful satrapy of Phrygia.

Opposition arose to Perdikkas, and in 321 war erupted. Caught between the northern powers and Ptolemy to the south, Perdikkas divided his forces. Seleucus, who had received no lands or personal power other than a generalship under Perdikkas, supported the regent. Perdikkas and Seleucus marched against Ptolemy and three times failed to cross the Nile Delta.

Seleucus, wishing to overthrow his perpetual subordination, turned on Perdikkas and joined in his assassination. Consequently, Seleucus gained the satrapy of Babylonia and the power he sought. Although the satrapy of Babylonia remained the heart of Alexander's empire, Seleucus found the borders difficult to maintain. In Asia Minor, Antigonus rapidly gained more power, and leaders in Media and Susiana also sought to overthrow Seleucus.

When Antipater, the new royal regent, died in 319, Antigonus sought greater power and larger realms. In 321 Antipater had appointed Antigonus commander of the royal armies in Asia, and Antigonus desired to reunite Alexander's empire. When royalist uprisings in Asia threatened Seleucus's insecure power, out of necessity he summoned Antigonus's assistance. Once in Babylonia, Antigonus assumed supreme command and reduced the royalists, and in 316 Seleucus fled to Egypt and Ptolemy's protection. Together, Ptolemy, Cassander (the son of Antipater), and Lysimachus opposed Antigonus and demanded that Seleucus be restored to Babylonia. By 311,

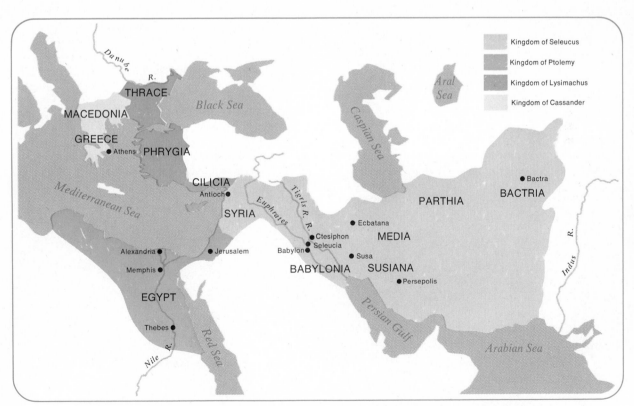

The kingdoms of the Diadochi in 301 B.C. After the death of Alexander the Great, his generals fought among themselves for portions of his empire. In 301, after the Battle of Ipsus, four of these "successors" (Diadochi)—Seleucus, Ptolemy, Lysimachus, and Cassander—reigned as kings over large parts of the Hellenistic world.

with Antigonus back in Asia Minor, Seleucus and Ptolemy entered Palestine. The victorious Seleucus headed for Babylon, gaining the support of the people, the armies, and minor officials. From 311 on, Seleucus retained Babylonia. Pushing eastward Seleucus rapidly conquered the once rebellious Media and Susiana. Antigonus, however, remained a threat and regained Palestine.

Securing a Power Base

In 311 Seleucus founded Seleucia on the Tigris as his new capital. It replaced ancient Babylon and became an eastern outpost of Greek civilization–a major entrepôt blending Greeks, Babylonians, and Jews. With the Chaldean Magi, Seleucus also founded the eastern city of Ctesiphon across the Tigris from Seleucia.

During the next 9 years Seleucus strengthened his eastern borders and crossed the Indus River and invaded India. In the west Antigonus still dominated and in 305 assumed the royal title. In Babylonia, Seleucus ruled a tight, efficient government modeled upon the earlier Persian absolutism. He developed his army and the bureaucracy and built new cities during a humane and able kingship.

In 302 Seleucus marched against Antigonus and entered Phrygia. In the following spring he allied once again with the "separatist generals" Ptolemy, Cassander, and Lysimachus, and at Ipsus in a heated battle he defeated and killed Antigonus. As booty, Seleucus obtained Syria. Seleucus thus gained the chief military and political position among the kings, which caused an estrangement with them. In Syria he built Antioch-on-the-Orontes in 300. Seleucus's son by Apama, Antiochus (I), ruled as viceroy of the dominions east of the Euphrates. Seleucus's love for Antiochus was such that he divorced his second wife, Stratonice, in 293 to allow his son to marry her.

In 293 Seleucus occupied Cilicia in eastern Asia Minor and began to plot against Demetrius (his former father-in-law), who had seized the Macedonian throne. Seleucus once again allied himself with Ptolemy and Lysimachus. Lysimachus, however, took Macedonia for himself, and Seleucus turned against him. In the spring of 281 Seleucus set out to conquer Asia Minor and to defeat Lysimachus. With him was the eldest son of Ptolemy I, Ptolemy Keraunos, who continually intrigued against his father and against Seleucus. The aged Ptolemy I failed to aid Lysimachus, who fell to a traitor's spear. But when Seleucus advanced on Macedonia that summer, Ptolemy Keraunos stabbed him to death in a vain attempt to claim the Macedonian throne.

Further Reading

Seleucus I is listed in the Ancient History study guide (I, D, 2). He shared the empire of ALEXANDER THE GREAT with ANTIGONUS I and PTOLEMY I.

Edwyn Bevan, *The House of Seleucus* (2 vols., 1902), remains the major study of Seleucus and the Seleucid dynasty. General studies of the Hellenistic era are W. W. Tarn and G. T. Griffith, *Hellenistic Civilization* (1927; 3d rev. ed. 1952), and Pierre Grimal and others, *Hellenism and the Rise of Rome* (1968).

SELIGMAN / By Richard C. Clark

The American economist and editor Edwin Robert Anderson Seligman (1861–1939) was known as editor in chief of the "Encyclopaedia of the Social Sciences" and for editing the "Columbia University Studies in History, Economics, and Public Law."

On April 25, 1861, Edwin R. A. Seligman was born in New York City, where his father was a banker of some prominence in both national and international financial circles. For his early education (until the age of 11) he was tutored at home. He then entered the innovative Columbia Grammar School, and at the age of 14 he entered Columbia College, where he received his bachelor's degree in 1879. He then went abroad to study at universities in Berlin, Paris, and Heidelberg.

In 1882 Seligman returned to Columbia to pursue simultaneously graduate studies in economics and in law; he received his master's in economics and was admitted to the New York State bar in 1884. In the same year, he received an appointment as lecturer in economics in the faculty of political science at Columbia. This discipline had been newly established under the aegis of John W. Burgess and was a truly pioneering development in the history of American education. In 1888 Seligman was promoted to adjunct professor of political economy and in 1891 received the rank of professor of

King Seleucus I of Syria, an antique portrait cameo in the Bibliothèque Nationale, Paris. (Giraudon)

Edwin R. A. Seligman. (Wide World Photos)

His works on taxation were quite influential when written, but unlike his treatments of the development of economic doctrine, they are less frequently cited today. Many of the tax reforms that he advocated were adopted, such as the progressive income tax.

Perhaps Seligman's chief contribution to modern education, however, was his editorship (1927–1935) of the influential and highly esteemed *Encyclopaedia of the Social Sciences*, the most important and comprehensive reference work in the social sciences. In the original edition, Seligman himself wrote several articles reflecting his own wide interests, including an introductory essay, "What Are the Social Sciences?"

Further Reading

Edwin R. A. Seligman is listed in the Social Sciences study guide (VII, C, 3). With Frank KNIGHT he founded the American Economic Association.

There is no definitive biography of Seligman. Some information on his life is in *Edwin R. A. Seligman, 1861–1959: Addresses Delivered at the Memorial Meeting Held on December the Thirteenth, 1939* (1942), and his career is discussed in Joseph Dorfman, *The Economic Mind in American Civilization* (5 vols., 1946–1959), and Ralph G. Hoxie and others, *A History of the Faculty of Political Science, Columbia University* (1955). His position in the history of economic thought is assessed in Ben B. Seligman, *Main Currents in Modern Economics: Economic Thought since 1870* (1962). A list of Seligman's works is included in Columbia University, Faculty of Political Science, *A Bibliography . . . 1880–1930* (1931).

political economy and finance, which he retained until his death.

Seligman's efforts through his life were dispersed over a wide range of activities. Not only was he energetically engaged in academic, professional, and editorial areas, but he worked in governmental and civic spheres, especially with groups concerned with promoting various social reforms. He was a cofounder of the American Economic Association and served as its president (1902–1904). He was president of the National Tax Association (1913–1915) and was one of the moving forces behind the founding of the American Association of University Professors in 1915, serving as its president (1919–1920). He was also a frequent adviser to New York State and New York City tax commissions, this being the area of his special competency. In the same capacity he acted as consultant to the League of Nations (1922–1923) and the reform-minded government of Cuba in 1931.

At Columbia, Seligman taught mainly in the field of political economy and the history of economic doctrines, originally a subfield of political philosophy, which attained an independent status in the 20th century. Recent thought on this matter, however, has reverted to the ancient view that economics cannot be really considered or understood apart from political philosophy, which sets the goals for economic activities. Seligman was one of a small group of scholars who worked actively to establish economics as an independent discipline. His own works on the history of economic doctrines and on economic terminology exercised an important influence in the United States and Europe; several of them were translated and are still cited today in professional works.

SELIM I / By Janet E. Ragatz

> Selim I (ca. 1470–1520), the ninth Ottoman sultan, was the instigator of large-scale conquest and administrative consolidation in Asia that left the Ottomans dominant in the Middle East.

The son of Bayezid II (Bajazet), Selim (pronounced sĕ-lēm′) gained administrative experience as governor of Trebizond and Semendra. In contention for the succession with his older brothers, Selim won with the support of the Janissaries, who forced Bayezid to abdicate on April 25, 1512.

For a year the new sultan was preoccupied with eliminating his brothers and nephews. Then he turned to consolidating Ottoman power in Anatolia, which was threatened by religious attractions from Persia. In the fall of 1513 lists were prepared of Shiite heretics. Some 40,000 died, and others were imprisoned or deported in the persecution that followed.

Selim's declaration of war on Iran the following spring initiated a famous correspondence between himself and

Shah Ismael. The Sultan, later remembered as a poet, wrote in an elegant style—the message, however, proving provocative and insulting. On Aug. 23, 1514, Turkish artillery routed the Persians at Chaldiran.

To quiet Janissary opposition to the war, Selim executed several leaders, a procedure for which his reign is noted. He later appointed men from his own household as generals in order to increase control over the Janissary group. Selim is called "Yavuz" ("the Grim"), connoting both respect and fear. Essentially a stern ruler, he nevertheless survives in Ottoman history as a hero.

Selim campaigned in eastern Anatolia again in 1515 and resumed the attack on Persia the following year. In August, however, the Turks encountered the Mamluk ruler of Egypt, a supporter of Ismael, and defeated him in a brief battle north of Aleppo. Egyptian forces were unpaid, undisciplined, and dissentious, the state weakened by the recent loss of Eastern trade to the Portuguese.

The Levantine cities surrendered peacefully, and Ottoman administrators took over but with remarkably few changes. When the new Egyptian sultan executed Selim's ambassadors, who were bearing offers of peace in exchange for acceptance of Turkish sovereignty, the Ottomans moved on Cairo, which fell in January 1517. En route to Egypt, Selim made a pilgrimage to Jerusalem.

During his months in Cairo, Selim accepted the voluntary submission of the sharif of Mecca, thus bringing the holy places under Ottoman control. Tradition has it that one consequence of this campaign was the official surrendering to the Ottomans of the paraphernalia of the Caliph (the Prophet's standard, mantle, and sword) by the last "Abbasid" caliph, al-Mutawwakil, captured from the Egyptians at Aleppo. This alleged transference of authority was the later legal justification for Osmanli use of the title, although Selim had earlier referred to himself as caliph.

Selim returned to Istanbul in July 1518. As skilled at administration as in military affairs, he subsequently devoted himself to government. On Sept. 20, 1520, he suddenly died, apparently of cancer.

Further Reading

Selim I is listed in the Asia study guide (I, E, 1). His son, SULEIMAN I, the Magnificent, succeeded him.

General works on Selim's period include G. W. F. Stripling, *The Ottoman Turks and the Arabs, 1511–1574* (1942), and A. D. Alderson, *Structure of the Ottoman Dynasty* (1956).

SELIM III / By Janet E. Ragatz

> Selim III (1761–1808), the twenty-eighth Ottoman sultan, was a late-18th-century reformer who sought to end the stagnation and decay weakening the empire.

Born on Dec. 24, 1761, Selim was the son of Mustafa III and successor to his uncle Abdul Hamid I, who died April 7, 1789. As a youth, the new sultan had benefited from a moderately free existence in contrast to the century-old custom of caging Osmanli princes. He was better educated then most of his recent predecessors.

Selim initially devoted himself to prosecuting the 2-year-old Austro-Russian War, an outgrowth of the first detailed plan to divide the Ottoman Empire, drawn up by Austria and Russia in 1782. The Peace of Sistova, in August 1791, involved no territorial changes with Austria, but the Peace of Jassy (Iaşi), in January 1792, advanced the Russian border to the Dniester.

Internal Reforms

Profiting from unrest in Europe which preoccupied his enemies, Selim introduced domestic reforms to strengthen his government. He solicited suggestions throughout the governing institutions. As a basis for change, he created a new treasury, filled, in large part, from confiscatory punishment leveled at fief holders who had ceased to respect their military obligations.

Among the changes was an attempt to curtail the

Ottoman sultan Selim I. (Turkish Tourism and Information Office, New York)

Ottoman sultan Selim III. (Turkish Tourism and Information Office, New York)

grand vizier's power by enlargement of the Divan and insistence that important issues be brought before it. Schools were opened, attention was given to printing and to the circulation of Western translations, and young Turks were sent to Europe for further study. The most significant reforms, however, involved the military. The navy was strengthened, and a navigation school was opened. The army commissariat was changed, officer training was improved, the Bosporus forts were strengthened, the artillery was revitalized, and the new engineering school was reorganized. Foreign advisers, largely French, assisted.

The major innovation was the founding of a new body of regular troops known as *nizam-i-jedid* (new regulation), a term also applied to the reforms as a whole. The first of these new units, uniformed, well disciplined and drilled, was formed in 1792 by a former Turkish lieutenant in the Russian army. Other units followed, involving, in some instances, extensive barracks building with related town facilities, such as the mosques and baths of Scutari. Such buildings constitute Selim's major architectural legacy.

Foreign Relations

On the international scene all remained peaceful until 1798, although foreign affairs received considerable at-

tention. New resident embassies were established in Britain, France, Prussia, and Austria. Selim, a cultured poet and musician, carried on an extended correspondence with Louis XVI. Although distressed by the establishment of the republic in France, the Porte (Ottoman government) was soothed by French representatives in Istanbul who maintained the goodwill of various influential personages, including the later Swedish minister, Mouradgea d'Ohsson, whose *Tableau de l'Empire Othoman* (1820) provides a good overview of this period.

On July 1, 1798, however, French forces landed in Egypt, and Selim declared war on France on September 4. In alliance with Russia and Britain, the Turks were in periodic conflict with the French on both land and sea until March 1801. Peace came in June 1802.

The following year brought trouble in the Balkans. For decades a sultan's word had had no power in outlying provinces, prompting Selim's reforms of the military in order to reimpose central control. This desire was not fulfilled. One rebellious leader was Austrian-backed Osman Pasvanoglu, whose invasion of Wallachia in 1801 inspired Russian intervention, resulting in greater autonomy for the Dunubian provinces.

Serbian conditions also deteriorated. They took a fateful turn with the return, in 1799, of the hated Janissaries, ousted 8 years before. These forces murdered Selim's enlightened governor, ending the best rule this province had had in the last 100 years. Their defiant, outrageous actions prompted the anti-Janissary revolt of 1804. Neither arms nor diplomacy could restore Ottoman authority.

French influence with the Porte did not revive until 1806, but it then led the Sultan into defying both St. Petersburg and London, and Turkey joined Napoleon's Continental System. War was declared on Russia on December 27 and on Britain in March 1807. Meanwhile, reform efforts had continued, but in March 1805 a general levy for new troops had led the Janissaries to revolt. These events culminated in the murder of reform leaders and, on May 29, 1807, the deposition of Selim. He was charged with childlessness and the use of military innovations to incite revolt.

Incarcerated in the *saray*, or palace, by his cousin, the new sultan Mustafa IV, Selim occupied himself instructing Mustafa's brother Mahmud in the art of government. On July 28, 1808, he was executed, as supporters, demanding his reinstatement, broke down the palace gates. Mustafa gained nothing, however; he was replaced by Mahmud II.

Further Reading

Selim III is listed in the Asia study guide (I, E, 2). MAHMUD II could not halt the decay of the Ottoman Empire but broke the power of the Janissaries.

For general biographical information on Selim III see A. D. Alderson, *Structure of the Ottoman Dynasty* (1956). V. J. Puryear, *Napoleon and the Dardanelles* (1951), considers diplomacy.

SELKIRK / By J. E. Rea

Thomas Douglas, 5th Earl of Selkirk (1771–1820), was a Scottish colonizer in Canada. Concerned about the depressed state of the Highlands of Scotland and Ireland, he devoted much of his fortune, and his health, to establishing new communities in North America.

Thomas Douglas was born in Kirkcudbrightshire on June 20, 1771, the seventh son of the 4th Earl of Selkirk. With little prospect of family support, he went to the University of Edinburgh to study law and there developed an interest in social and political affairs. In 1792, a tour of the Highlands convinced him that the lot of its people could never be improved and their only hope lay in emigration.

The breakdown of the clan system and the conversion of large areas of the Highlands into sheep walks had reduced the crofters to a life of marginal existence. Douglas was even more shocked by the condition of the Irish peasantry. His concern led to the passion of his life, the colonization of these people in North America, where their economic prospects would be improved and the British Empire strengthened. He was able to do something about it when the last of his brothers died in 1797, and he succeeded to the family estate 2 years later.

Selkirk besieged the Colonial Office with his emigra-

tion schemes and was finally granted permission in 1803 to undertake his first ventures. Lands in Prince Edward Island and in Upper Canada were granted, and his first two colonies were planted. Selkirk spent most of 1803 and 1804 in British North America supervising his experiments. The former colony prospered, but the second, at Baldoon, was less successful and collapsed.

Settlement of the Red River

Selkirk returned to England in 1804 and then devoted several years to politics as a Whig. He was married in 1807 to Jean Wedderburn-Colville, whose family was involved in the Hudson's Bay Company. The following year Selkirk began to acquire stock in the company. His old interest in colonization rekindled. His attention shifted westward to the Red River valley, and he began to plan the migration for which he is best remembered. In 1811 he received from the company a grant of 116,000 square miles in what is now Manitoba, Minnesota, and North Dakota. In July the first of a stream of Selkirk settlers set out for their new home.

They had to contend not only with natural hazards but also with the hostility of the North West Company, which felt settlement threatened the fur trade, a business that Selkirk "hated from the bottom of his heart." In 1815, and again the following year, the colony was attacked by the traders, with considerable loss of life on the second occasion. Selkirk arrived at Red River in 1817 and began the task of reconstruction, establishing a school and a church. His arrest of some of the traders resulted in a drawn-out trial which eventually exonerated the Nor'westers.

Selkirk returned home in 1818. He died at Pau, France, on April 8, 1820. His humanitarian impulse had broken his health and consumed his fortune, but it left a warm and cherished memory in the Canadian west.

Further Reading

Lord Selkirk is listed in the Canada study guide (III, B). The earliest Canadian settlements were in the east, established by Charles de Menou CHARNISAY and the Sieur de MAISONEUVE.

The best and probably definitive study of Selkirk is John M. Gray, *Lord Selkirk of Red River* (1963). Older but still useful are George Bryce, *Mackenzie, Selkirk, Simpson* (1905) and *The Life of Lord Selkirk: Coloniser of Western Canada* (1912), and Chester Martin, *Lord Selkirk's Work in Canada* (1916).

Lord Selkirk. (The Public Archives of Canada)

SEMENOV / By Maxim W. Mikulak

The Soviet physicist and physical chemist Nikolai Nikolaevich Semenov (born 1896) is famous for his experiments explaining chemical reactions by means of the mechanism of chain reactions.

Nikolai Semenov (pronounced sĭ-myŭn′əf) was born on April 15, 1896, in Saratov. He displayed a keen interest in the physical sciences by the time he was 16 and in 1913 entered the physics and mathematics department of the University of St. Petersburg (later Petrograd and now Leningrad). At the age of 20 he published his first paper on the collision of molecules and electrons. In 1917 he ended his studies at the University of Petrograd, obtained a position as physicist in the Siberian University of Tomsk and later, in 1920, returned to work for the next 11 years at the Petrograd (in 1924 Leningrad) Institute of Physics and Technology.

In 1928 Semenov became a professor at the Leningrad Polytechnical Institute and organized its physics and mathematics department. Three years later he was appointed scientific chief of the Institute of Physical Chemistry of the Soviet Academy of Sciences. In 1932 he was elected to full membership in the academy, and from 1957 to 1963 he was the academy's secretary of the division of the chemical sciences. In 1944 he was assigned to the University of Moscow, heading the department of chemical kinematics. He also was instrumental in launching scientific journals and organizing Soviet conferences on physical chemistry.

Semenov's scientific investigations dealt primarily with molecular physics and electronic phenomena, the mechanism of chemical transformations, and the propagation of explosive waves. He published in "The Oxidation of Phosphorus Vapor at Low Pressures" (1927) his discovery of branching reaction chains in chemical transformations having the character of an explosion. Semenov intensively continued his researches in chemical reactions involving the chain theory and published his results in *Chemical Kinetics and Chain Reactions* (1935) and in the exhaustive two-volume study *Some Problems in Chemical Kinetics and Reactivity* (1958–1959). For his contributions to reaction kinetics, Semenov was awarded the Nobel Prize in 1956, the first resident Soviet citizen to achieve this distinction.

Semenov also played an active role in his country's affairs. He first joined the Communist party of the Soviet Union in 1947, served as a deputy in the Supreme Soviet in 1958, 1962, and 1966, and in 1961 was elected an alternate member of the party's Central Committee. In the Soviet Union he fought for the liberty of experimentation for the scientist, freedom of expression for the artist, and "chain reactions of success" for humanity as a consequence of international scientific exchanges.

Further Reading

Nikolai Semenov is listed in the Science study guide (VII, D, 2). He shared the Nobel Prize with the English physical chemist Cyril HINSHELWOOD, noted for contributions to reaction kinetics.

Only scattered articles on Semenov have thus far appeared in English and Russian newspapers and journals. A brief biographical sketch of Semenov by Albert Parry is in George W. Simmonds, ed., *Soviet Leaders* (1967). Semenov's scientific contributions receive mention in the comprehensive work of V. N. Kondratev, *Chemical*

Nikolai Semenov. (Sovfoto)

Kinetics of Gas Reactions, translated by J. M. Crabtree and S. N. Carruthers (1964), and in Keith J. Laidler, *Reaction Kinetics* (1966).

SEMMELWEIS / By Chester R. Burns

The Hungarian physician Ignaz Philipp Semmelweis (1818–1865) was a pioneer of antisepsis in obstetrics and demonstrated that many cases of puerperal fever could be prevented.

Ignaz Philipp Semmelweis (pronounced zĕm′əl-vīs), the son of a prosperous shopkeeper, was born on July 1, 1818, at Buda, a city united with Pest in 1873 to form Budapest. After 2 years at the University of Pest, 19-year-old Ignaz matriculated at the University of Vienna as a law student. Unhappy, he returned to the University of Pest and studied medicine (1838–1840). After completing further studies at the University of Vienna, he received a medical degree in April 1844. Following 4 months of special instruction in midwifery, Semmelweis became a provisional assistant at the First Obstetric Clinic in the large Vienna Lying-In Hospital. Two years later he became a regular assistant to the director of this clinic.

Semmelweis was especially distressed by the horrors of puerperal fever. Within a few hours after delivery, numerous mothers would be afflicted with high fever, rapid pulse, distended abdomen, and excruciating pain. One out of 10 would die as a result of this infection. One observation haunted Semmelweis. The hospital was divided into two clinics: the first for the instruction of medical students, the second for the training of midwives. The mortality due to puerperal fever was significantly greater in the first clinic. Traditional ideas ascribed puerperal fever to epidemic influences; if this were true, both clinics should be equally affected. Overcrowding was suggested; yet the second clinic was ordinarily more crowded than the first. Semmelweis incessantly searched for a better understanding of his puzzling observations.

In 1847 Semmelweis's colleague J. Kolletschka unexpectedly died of an overwhelming infection following a wound he sustained while performing an autopsy. Semmelweis realized that the course of the disease in his friend was remarkably similar to the sequence of events in puerperal fever. Here was an explanation of the difference in mortality between the two clinics: the medical students and teachers dissected corpses, whereas the midwives did no autopsies. The teachers and pupils could thus carry infectious particles from the cadavers to the natural wounds of a woman in childbirth. Accordingly, teachers and students who had been dissecting were requested to wash their hands with a solution of chlorinated lime before examining the laboring patients. As a result, during 1848 the mortality of the first clinic was less than that of the second clinic.

Surprisingly, opposition to Semmelweis's observations was intense, for the paradox of being healer and murder-

A view of a 19th-century obstetric ward in a hospital in Prague. (Österreichische Nationalbibliothek, Vienna)

er was intolerable for most. When confronted with Semmelweis's explanations, conscientious obstetricians pleaded "not guilty." Semmelweis could not understand these reactions. A few outstanding doctors supported him; nevertheless, the tide of controversy grew to such an extent that Semmelweis was "retired" from his position as assistant at the first clinic. In 1850 he left Vienna and returned to Budapest.

At the St. Rochus Hospital in Budapest, Semmelweis was allowed to introduce disinfection in the obstetrical division. In 1855 he became professor of theoretical and practical midwifery at the University of Pest. In 1857 he married. But the deaths of two children during the next few years added personal grief to professional suffering, a suffering that intensified as opposition to his ideas spread throughout Europe.

With much reluctance Semmelweis organized his observations and published his great work on puerperal fever, *The Etiology, Concept, and Prophylaxis of Childbed Fever* (1861). Even this did not silence his opponents, and Semmelweis, unable to accept this resistance, was committed to an insane asylum in 1865, where he died of blood poisoning. Not until 1883 did the Boston Lying-In Hospital introduce methods of antisepsis, methods similar to those used several decades earlier by Semmelweis.

Further Reading

Ignaz Philipp Semmelweis is listed in the Science study guide (VI, G, 2). Widespread acceptance of antisepsis by the medical profession was accomplished after years of work by Joseph LISTER, Louis PASTEUR, and Robert KOCH, men who also encountered resistance to their discoveries about microbes and disease.

The most readable biography of Semmelweis is Frank G. Slaughter, *Immortal Magyar: Semmelweis, Conqueror of Childbed Fever* (1950). For greater detail, especially about the opposition to Semmelweis's views, see Sir William J. Sinclair, *Semmelweis: His Life and His Doctrine* (1909).

Ignaz Philipp Semmelweis. (National Library of Medicine, Bethesda, Md.)

SEMMES / By Ludwell H. Johnson

Raphael Semmes (1809–1877), American naval officer of the Confederacy, commanded the "Sumter" and "Alabama" in their daring raids on Northern shipping during the Civil War.

Raphael Semmes was born in Charles County, Md. Appointed a midshipman in the U.S. Navy at 16, in 1837 he was promoted to lieutenant. During the long periods of inactivity that characterized naval service in those days, Semmes had the opportunity to study and then to practice law.

During the Mexican War, Semmes commanded the brig *Somers* and then served with distinction in the campaign against Mexico City. He recounted these experiences in *Service Afloat and Ashore during the Mexican War* (1851).

Soon after Alabama seceded from the Union, Semmes resigned his commission and accepted an appointment as commander in the Confederate Navy. In April 1861 he was assigned to command the C.S.S. *Sumter* at New Orleans. The *Sumter* ran the Federal blockade in June and, during a long voyage that culminated at Gibraltar, took 18 prizes. Semmes left the worn-out *Sumter* at Gibraltar and started back to the Confederate States. At Nassau he was intercepted by orders to take command of the English-built steam bark *Enrica*, which he armed and on Aug. 24, 1862, commissioned off the Azores islands as the C.S.S. *Alabama*.

During almost 2 years on the high seas commanding the *Alabama*, Semmes burned, sank, or captured and sold 55 Union vessels. But on June 19, 1864, the *Alabama*'s career abruptly ended at Cherbourg, France, where the U.S.S. *Kearsarge* had blockaded it. In an ill-advised burst of chivalric resolve, Semmes had chal-

Raphael Semmes. (Cook Collection, Valentine Museum, Richmond, Va.)

lenged the better-equipped *Kearsarge* to combat. Superficially the antagonists were evenly matched; in reality the odds heavily favored the *Kearsarge*. After an engagement of about half an hour, the *Alabama* struck its colors and then sank. Semmes was rescued by an English yacht,

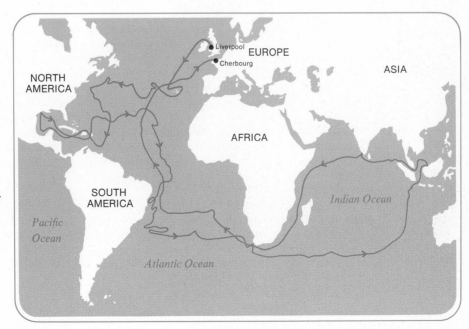

The cruise of the Alabama. In 22 months at sea, the Alabama covered more than 30,000 miles and destroyed or captured 55 Union ships. The raider was built in England, and most of its crew were English.

one of many that had come to witness the engagement.

Returning to the Confederacy, Semmes was promoted to rear admiral and assigned to command the James River squadron. When Richmond fell, he destroyed his gunboats and retreated south with his sailors. He and his men were included in the surrender of Gen. Joseph E. Johnston's army on April 26, 1865.

After the war Semmes (like many Confederates) spent several months in Federal prison. Afterward he was occupied variously as a teacher, editor, and lawyer. He also wrote his famous *Memoirs of Service Afloat* (1869), a vivid account of the voyages of the *Sumter* and the *Alabama* in which he took literary revenge on the enemy. In 1877 he died at his home in Mobile after a brief illness.

Further Reading

Raphael Semmes is listed in the American History study guide (VI, B, 2, e). Union naval officer David G. FARRAGUT made daring and successful raids against the Confederacy.

Semmes's *Memoirs of Service Afloat, during the War between the States* (1869) is available in an abridged version, *The Confederate Raider Alabama*, edited with an introduction by Philip Van Doren Stern (1962). Biographies of Semmes include Colyer Meriwether, *Raphael Semmes* (1913); Walter Adolphe Roberts, *Semmes of the Alabama* (1938); and Edward Carrington Boykin, *Ghost Ship of the Confederacy: The Story of the Alabama and Her Captain* (1957).

* * *

SEN / By David Kopf

> Ram Camul Sen (1783–1844) was a Bengali intellectual and entrepreneur. Part of a group that inaugurated the Bengal renaissance, he proved less a prolific writer and scholar and more a gifted organizer and administrator.

A Kashatriya by caste and, according to his own account, a descendant of the medieval Bengali king Ballal Sena, Ram Camul Sen (pronounced räm kä-mōōl′ sĕn) left a Hooghly village for Calcutta in 1790, at the age of 7. His father was proficient in Persian and secured clerical positions, and Ram Camul himself learned English, Sanskrit, and Persian in the manner of the sons of the Calcutta elite.

Ram Camul found his first job in 1803, as a subordinate clerk's assistant in the Calcutta chief magistrate's office. The chief magistrate was evidently impressed with Ram Camul's industrious work habits. In 1804 two scholars associated with the Asiatic Society of Bengal invited Sen to work for the Hindoostanee Press as a compositor.

Despite a very low salary of 8 rupees a month, Ram Camul always performed far more than was expected of him, profited from his knowledge of English, and extended his range of contacts. In 1810, after he met the eminent Orientalist Horace H. Wilson at the Press, Ram Camul's fortunes took a rapid upward swing. The two men developed a warm friendship that lasted until Sen's death. Under Wilson's sponsorship, and utilizing the skills and techniques acquired during his employment at the Hindoostanee Press, Ram Camul began his extraordinary rise as an intellectual entrepreneur. By 1814 he had been appointed the "native" manager of the Hindoostanee Press.

In 1829 Wilson, then secretary of the Asiatic Society, proposed that members of the Bengali intelligentsia, including Ram Camul Sen, be admitted to membership in that association. In December 1833, shortly before Wilson's departure for England to be Oxford University's first Sanskritist, Sen reviewed his "29 years with the Society" in a letter accepting the post of native secretary.

A year later Ram Camul completed a project by publishing the second volume of his *Dictionary of the English and Bengalee Languages*, one of the best efforts of its kind in the 19th century and the earliest accurate and comprehensive dictionary of the Bengali language compiled by a Bengali. The introduction to the second volume is important not only for a linguistic analysis of Bengali but for its history of modern Bengali prose from 1800, when the missionary William Carey was hired to teach that language to civil service trainees at the College of Fort William.

Ram Camul, however, was best known during his own time as an efficient, activist intellectual whom the British frequently employed to help manage their newly introduced institutions, especially educational facilities. During the last 20 years of his life, he became the most influential Asian in associations as diverse as the Hindu College and the Calcutta Mint. Largely as a result of such administrative endeavors, when Sen died in August 1844, he left an estate estimated at 1 million rupees.

Further Reading

Ram Camul Sen is listed in the Asia study guide (II, A, 6, a). He was a contemporary of Ram Mohun ROY and Radhakant DEB.

There is only one full-length biography of Ram Camul Sen in English, Peary Chand Mitra, *Life of Dewan Ram Camul Sen* (1880). As with most figures of the 19th-century Bengali intelligentsia, aspects of Sen's life and career are continually referred to in numerous books on modern Indian history, but he has not been the subject of a serious scholarly monograph. Some attempt to update Sen's role in the light of modern scholarship is made in David Kopf, *British Orientalism and the Bengal Renaissance* (1969).

* * *

SENECA / By Robert Dale Sweeney

> Lucius Annaeus Seneca the Younger (ca. 4 B.C.–A.D. 65) was a Roman philosopher

The philosophical works of Seneca (pronounced sĕn′ĭ-kə), although not especially original, show such nobility of sentiment that Christian writers on morality and ethical conduct have drawn on him over the centuries; he seems to have invented a highly rhetorical type of tragedy, the influence of which was especially widespread in the Renaissance; and his literary style, terse, epigrammatic, and full of intermittent brilliance, provided a respectable rhetorical alternative to the long, periodic sentences of Cicero and had some influence on the development of the normal literary prose style of English, French, and other languages.

Seneca was born in Cordova, Spain, about 5 or 4 B.C., the son of the famous writer on rhetoric known as Seneca Rhetor. Seneca's elder brother was proconsul of Achaea in A.D. 51–52 and was the "Gallio" before whose tribunal Paul was brought. His younger brother was the father of the poet Lucan. His mother was Helvia, a cultivated woman deeply interested in philosophy, and one of her sisters was the wife of a man who was later prefect of Egypt. This sister brought Seneca to Rome as a small child.

Seneca's schooling had a great influence on his later life. He disliked his studies under teachers who insisted on verbal criticism and on detailed learning, but his rhetorical studies, under the leading men of his day, including his own father, left a deep impression on his style. He was, however, most deeply involved in the study of philosophy. His teachers, disciples of the eclectic but basically Stoic Roman philosopher Quintus Sextius, filled him with an enthusiasm for philosophy which he never lost and never wholly lived up to, and the rigorous asceticism into which he plunged so weakened his already poor constitution that his health began to decline. He thought of suicide, but was stopped by his regard for his father, who also pointed out that he might be mistaken for a devotee of certain foreign superstitions which the emperor Tiberius was attempting to stamp out. Instead, Seneca was sent to visit his aunt in Egypt.

After his return from Egypt, Seneca secured election (ca. A.D. 31) to the quaestorship as a result of his aunt's influence and began his legal career. His oratory (all of it lost) rapidly gained him renown, which became dangerous after the accession in 37 of Emperor Caligula, who wanted no rivals in this field. Seneca would probably have been murdered if Caligula had not been informed that Seneca was very sick and could not live long. Seneca then betook himself to other literary fields, to alternating periods of retreat and meditation with his public work, and to building his private fortune.

Trial and Exile

After the accession of Claudius as emperor in 41, Seneca was for a while prominent in the court as a member of the party of Agrippina and Julia Livilla, Claudius's nieces. The empress Messalina, however, whose influ-

Seneca, an ancient portrait sculpture, in the Uffizi, Florence. (Alinari)

ence over Claudius was all-powerful, saw the two princesses as dangerous rivals and secured the banishment of Julia Livilla in 41 on charges of immorality. Seneca was accused of being her lover and condemned to death by the Senate, but his punishment was changed to banishment to Corsica by the Emperor.

Seneca spent the next 8 years in exile on Corsica. He was miserable. He was a literary man, without access to learned men; a man who loved human society, removed from his friends; a man of acquisitive instincts, deprived of his property; and a man who enjoyed power and influence, reduced to impotence and apparent friendlessness. Cringing flattery of the Emperor and of the Emperor's powerful freedman Polybius proved useless, but in 49 he was recalled at the behest of Agrippina, who had survived Messalina and married her uncle Claudius. Seneca was to be tutor to Nero, her son and the adopted son of Claudius, and he was appointed praetor for the year 50.

Life under Nero

Claudius was murdered by Agrippina in 54, and Nero acceded to the throne. The next 5 years, while Nero was under the influence of Seneca and Sextus Afranius Bur-

Scenes from the story of Hippolytus and Phaedra, a relief from a sarcophagus of the 2d century B.C. In his tragedy Phaedra, *Seneca reworked the Greek myth, which had earlier been handled by Euripides in his* Hippolytus. *(Alinari)*

rus, became famous for their good government and general happiness. The court was also aware of crimes and intrigues, most notably the murder of Britannicus, Claudius's son, and thus Nero's most dangerous rival, in 55. In 55 or 56 Seneca was appointed to a suffect consulship.

In 59 Agrippina, who had been Seneca's patroness, was murdered by her son—quite possibly, as Nero explained to the Senate in a statement written by Seneca, as the result of the discovery of plots on her part against the throne. In 62 Burrus died, and one of his successors, Ofonius Tigellinus, soon came to exercise an evil influence over his master. Realizing that his major support was gone and that Tigellinus was working for his removal, Seneca, who must have been sick of being compromised by the necessities of state, asked to be allowed to retire and offered to put at Nero's disposal the vast fortune he had acquired in his service; Nero permitted his retirement but refused the proferred wealth.

Seneca devoted the next 3 years of his retirement to his studies and writings, but in 65 he was implicated (along with, among others, his nephew Lucan) in Piso's conspiracy, and his death became inevitable. He was ordered to commit suicide by Nero, according to Tacitus.

Much of the shabbiness of Seneca's life was made up for by the manner of his death, calm and philosophical, which showed true Stoic nobility. Tacitus related that Seneca's body had become so thin from fasting that he had difficulty in getting the blood to flow from his opened veins. His second wife, Pompeia Paulina, wanted to commit suicide with him but was prevented from doing so.

Philosophical Works

Seneca's philosophical works are marked by neither originality of thought nor depth of speculation, but rather by enthusiasm of presentation and an understanding of the practical limitations of life and the weaknesses of

human nature. The chronological arrangement of these works is uncertain, but it is generally agreed that very few of them predate his exile.

Ten works, in 12 books, have been handed down to us under the name *Dialogues*, although only one of them could be considered an actual dialogue. Three of these are *consolationes*, treatises, partly philosophical, partly rhetorical, attempting to cure grief. In addition, there are three books composing *On Anger*. *On the Happy Life* develops the standard Stoic view that happiness is to live in accordance with nature and to practice virtue, and it contains an interesting defense of the wise man's possession and good use of wealth. There are three works addressed to Annaeus Serenus, *On the Constancy of a Wise Man*, *On Tranquility of Mind*, and the fragmentary *On Leisure*.

Some other philosophical works of Seneca are seven books called *Natural Questions*, written in 62–63, a loosely arranged compilation of information on natural science, which formed the standard work on cosmology for the Middle Ages until the rediscovery of Aristotle. The 124 *Epistles* to Lucilius contain innumerable digressions which give a fascinating picture of Roman life.

His Tragedies

Ten plays are ascribed to Seneca. One of these, the *Octavia*, the only extant Roman historical drama, is almost universally rejected as being written by Seneca. The *Hercules Oetaeus* has also been generally rejected, but the consensus of scholarship favors Senecan authorship for the *Hercules Furens*, *Troades*, *Medea*, *Phaedra*, *Phoenissae*, *Oedipus*, *Agamemnon*, and the *Thyestes*, the only play whose Greek model has not been preserved. Nothing is known about the time of composition of these plays.

Seneca's major inspiration was Euripides, the source of half of his dramas. He took from Euripides an interest in psychological analysis, especially of abnormal types, in philosophical speculation, and in rhetorical effect and developed each of these to what often seems an excessive degree. The Stoic doctrine which proclaimed that a good man is totally good and a bad man totally evil makes his characters less humanly alive than the Greek characters. In these plays Seneca's rhetoric is almost unrestrained: overelaboration of realistic detail until it becomes ludicrous, mythological pedantry, and unending verbal cleverness and epigrammatic morality are but part of an overall exaggeration and declamatory urgency which soon wearies the reader.

Seneca's tragedies were not written for actual performance but for dramatic reading. Some actions, such as the murder of Medea's children, could hardly have been presented on an ancient stage, and many speeches and choruses, while too long to be tolerable in the theater, would have been especially pleasing as readings to literary circles trained to appreciate ingenious rhetoric and description. Seneca wrote a very cruel and witty satire on the deification of Claudius, the *Apocolocyntosis* ("Pumpkinification"). The Emperor's habits, such as his fondness for acting as a judge and playing dice, speech mannerisms, and physical infirmities are mercilessly parodied. The work is, in form, a Menippean satire, composed of mingled prose and verse, and is amusing for its use of legal language and parodies of Claudius's and Augustus's prose styles.

Further Reading

Seneca is listed in the Ancient History study guide (III, C, 5). He influenced Pierre CORNEILLE, LOPE DE VEGA, and Christopher MARLOWE with his rhetoric and stock characters.

The best biography of Seneca in English is Francis C. Holland, *Seneca* (1920); the best brief account appears in J. Wight Duff, *A Literary History of Rome in the Silver Age from Tiberius to Hadrian* (1927; 3d ed., edited by A. M. Duff, 1964). Seneca's philosophical works are discussed in E. Vernon Arnold, *Roman Stoicism* (1911); Richard Mott Gummere, *Seneca the Philosopher and His Modern Message* (1922); and T. P. Hardeman, *The Philosophy of Lucius Annaeus Seneca* (1956). The best account of Seneca's *Apocolocyntosis* is in Allen Perley Ball, *The Satire of Seneca on the Apotheosis of Claudius* (1902), but see also J. Wight Duff, *Roman Satire: Its Outlook on Social Life* (1936).

Almost all of the numerous studies of Seneca's tragedies concentrate either on the use he made of his Greek models or on his influence on later tragedy. Among these studies are John William Cunliffe, *The Influence of Seneca on Elizabethan Tragedy* (1893; repr. 1925); Frank Laurence Lucas, *Seneca and Elizabethan Tragedy* (1922); Howard Vernon Canter, *Rhetorical Elements in the Tragedy of Seneca* (1925); Norman T. Pratt, *Dramatic Suspense in Seneca and in His Greek Precursors* (1939); and Charles W. Mendell, *Our Seneca* (1941).

SENFL / By Edward R. Lerner

Ludwig Senfl (ca. 1486–ca. 1543) was a German composer of Swiss birth. His Masses, motets, and vernacular lieder mark the adoption by 16th-century German masters of Franco-Flemish imitative polyphony emanating from the Low Countries.

Ludwig Senfl (pronounced zĕn′fəl) was born in Basel. As a young boy, he sang first at Augsburg and later at Vienna in the imperial choir of Maximilian I of Austria. During this period he studied with Heinrich Isaac, official court composer of the Hapsburgs, and subsequently succeeded to the same post. In later years Senfl offered homage to Isaac by completing the older master's unfinished cycle of Mass Propers, printed in 1550 as the *Choralis Constantinus*, and by apotheosizing him in an original poem set to music.

After the death of Emperor Maximilian in 1519 and the dissolution of the imperial chapel choir the following year, Senfl traveled to Augsburg to supervise the publication of a motet collection, *Liber selectarum cantionum*, as a memorial to the late monarch. By 1523 he found a new position with William IV of Bavaria, at whose court in Munich he remained for the rest of his life.

Like many artists and musicians of the time, Senfl was drawn into the vortex of religious strife attending the Reformation. Although he served only Catholic rulers and never formally abandoned the older faith, he corresponded with and occasionally sent compositions to Martin Luther, with whom he seems to have been on

Ludwig Senfl, as represented on a medallion. (Bildarchiv)

friendly terms. For the most part, however, Senfl's service music was composed for Catholic worship. A self-effacing, lovable, and versatile composer, he was widely respected by his contemporaries and honored by his employer.

Senfl's extant works number 7 Masses, 240 motets, 262 lieder, and a few pieces for instruments. His beautifully chiseled imitative polyphony discloses the unmistakable influence of his two great predecessors, Josquin des Prez and Isaac. Two of the Masses are "parodies," or reworkings, of earlier polyphonic pieces. This new technique stamps him as the first German master to abandon the older *cantus firmus* Mass. Among the motets are many Mass Propers composed for divine services at the Bavarian court. Although Senfl generally wrote for four voice parts, some ceremonial pieces were for as many as eight. Throughout his works is a profound understanding of both the declamation and meaning of the text.

In Senfl's lifetime more of his lieder were published than either the Masses or motets. Like earlier masters, he set the old "court" tunes in polyphonic garb, but he devoted far more attention to arranging "folk" and "popular" songs. His melodic inventiveness, smooth linear writing, and polished counterpoint made them universal favorites.

Further Reading

Ludwig Senfl is listed in the Music study guide (I, C, 3). He was influenced by JOSQUIN DES PREZ and Heinrich ISAAC. Senfl's contemporary Paul HOFHAIMER also wrote lieder.

Some of Senfl's works are analyzed in Gustave Reese, *Music in the Renaissance* (1959). For background on the music of the period see Paul Henry Lang, *Music in Western Civilization* (1941).

SENGHOR / By Irving Leonard Markovitz

Léopold Sédar Senghor (born 1906) was an African poet, philosopher, and president of Senegal. He was one of the originators of "Negritude," a "black is beautiful" doctrine begun in Paris during the 1930s.

The map of Africa as it exists today owes something to the efforts of Léopold Senghor (pronounced săN-gôr'), who took a leading role in the negotiations that led to independence of France's sub-Saharan colonies. He established relations with the former mother country that endure to this day. While asserting the uniqueness and greatness of black culture, the equal in every respect to that of the Greeks and the French, he held out the promise of an eventual synthesis of diverse peoples' contributions to a coming great "civilization of the universal."

Léopold Senghor. (Embassy of Senegal, Washington, D.C.)

Senghor was born on Oct. 9, 1906, at Joal, the son of a wealthy Catholic trader who descended from a Serer royal family. Raised as a Catholic among an overwhelmingly Moslem population, Senghor in 1914 attended the school of the Fathers of the Holy Ghost at N'Gazobil and went on to pursue his studies in Dakar until 1928, when he left for France. In Paris he was the first African to be awarded an *agrégation* certificate, in 1935, qualifying him to teach at a lycée, which he did from 1936 to the outbreak of the war, first in Tours and then in Paris. Captured while fighting against the Germans in 1940, he organized a resistance among his fellow prisoners.

Political Career

After the war, Africa's representation in the French National Assembly was greatly increased, and opportunities for indigenous political activity were expanded. In 1945 Senghor joined with Lamine Gueye in cofounding a new political party affiliated with the French Socialist party, the Bloc Africain, which appealed to newly enfranchised people in the rural areas. In the same year, and again in 1946, the people of Senegal elected Senghor as deputy to the French National Assembly. In 1946 he was also selected the official grammarian for the new constitution of the Fourth Republic.

Senghor's alliance with Lamine Gueye soon grew thin, as Senghor turned more to cultivate his rural following and as he rejected Gueye's assimilation politics. In 1948

Senghor formed his own political party and rejected affiliation with all metropolitan organizations. In 1951 his organization won both seats to the National Assembly. Senghor's proposal in 1953 that the French government divide French West Africa into two federations, one with its capital at Dakar in Senegal and the other at Abidjan in the Ivory Coast, was defeated. This defeat, as Senghor predicted, meant the "Balkanization" of West Africa, the creation of many small, not really economically viable, political units.

Senghor served as a minister in the Edgar Faure government in 1955; the following year Senghor's group for the final time won the elections to the National Assembly and then won 47 out of 60 seats in the newly established territorial council of Senegal. A division occurred among African leaders over the value of these councils, for some saw them as a positive step toward self-government, but others (Senghor foremost among them) argued that what counted was the unity of the region as a whole and that "territorialization" would only make this task more difficult.

Unlike the modernizing Africans in the British colonies, Senghor also argued that "mere political independence" could be a sham and therefore was not necessarily the highest goal African peoples should seek. Economic and technological realities in his day meant that even the "super powers" could not go it alone; what chance then for Senegal by itself? Not surprisingly, in 1958, when the new De Gaulle government offered the territories of West Africa the chance to "opt for independence" in a referendum—on the understanding that all financial and technical aid would be immediately withdrawn—Senghor, in spite of much domestic opposition, campaigned against this type of "self-government." Senegal joined the Sudanese Republic in 1959 to form the short-lived Mali Federation. Finally, on Aug. 20, 1960, Senegal became independent but remained part of a reconstituted "French community."

Thereafter Senghor survived several attempted coups d'etat, the most serious occurring in 1962, at least one assassination effort (1967), and widespread riots and demonstrations against rising prices and government financial policies (1968 and 1969). Nevertheless, throughout all these developments, he maintained his position as president of the republic and head of the governing political party while absorbing the major organized opposition groups and appeasing the central elements of his own coalition.

Negritude and Socialism

The evolution of Senghor's doctrine occurred in three distinct periods—the era preceding World War II, the period of achieving independence, and the epoch following independence. Senghor argued that the work of the black has distinction not in substance or subject matter but, rather, in a special approach, method, and style. In the pre–World War II period, Senghor particularly argued that one must look for the Negro's uniqueness in the Negro himself. "Negritude" arises first, then, from the singular racial characteristics of the black. Later, after the war, Senghor became caught up in the problem of reorganizing societies—in Europe after fascism, in Africa after colonialism.

Revolted by Nazism, he placed increasing emphasis in his theory of Negritude on the historical context of the black evolution as an explanation for the rise of unique civilizations. Socialism he viewed as a way toward a renewed humanism through the ending of exploitation. Revolutionary change in France and the West as well as in the developing areas would allow a new type of community to be created. After independence in 1960, Senghor turned increasingly to the day-to-day problems of building a viable economy.

Significantly, Senghor used the term Senegalese socialism for the first time early in 1962. His ideas and ideology became increasingly pragmatic and technocratic as he attempted to maximize the effectiveness of modern agricultural methods, capital, industry, and social engineering.

His Writings

The year 1945 marked not only Senghor's entry into political life but also the publication of his first collection of poems, *Chants d'ombre*. In 1948 he published another volume of poetry, *Hosties noires*, and edited an anthology of new Negro and Malagasy poetry. Later poetic offerings were *Chants pour Naëtt* (1949), *Éthiopiques* (1956), and *Nocturnes* (1961).

Senghor's major prose works were *Nation et voie africaine du socialisme* (1961), *Pierre Teilhard de Chardin et la politique africaine* (1962), *Liberté I: Négritude et humanisme* (1964), *Les Fondements de l'Africanité ou Négritude et Arabité* (1967), and *Politique, nation et developpement moderne* (1968).

Further Reading

Léopold Senghor is listed in the Africa study guide (IX, C, 5). A contemporary Senegalese statesman was Lamine GUEYE.

A substantial collection of Senghor's poetry is in *Selected Poems*, translated and introduced by John Reed and Clive Wake (1964). Several of Senghor's major political writings were translated by Mercer Cook in *On African Socialism* (1964). Irving Leonard Markovitz, *Léopold Sédar Senghor and the Politics of Negritude* (1969), which has an exhaustive bibliography, traces the development of Senghor's ideas from 1931 and views them within the changing social, political, and historical scene of French colonialism and African development. See also Michael Crowder, *Senegal: A Study in French Assimilation Policy* (1962), for a good general treatment of the historical background.

SENNACHERIB / By Margaret S. Drower

Sennacherib (reigned 705–681 B.C.), a king of Assyria, was one of the four great kings of the

Late Assyrian Empire. He rebuilt Nineveh and destroyed Babylon.

Sennacherib (pronounced sĭ-năk′ər-ĭb) is the biblical form of the name Sin-akhe-eriba. Though a younger son, he was chosen as heir by his father, Sargon II. As crown prince, he gained experience fighting on the northern frontier. On hearing of Sargon's death, he hastened back to Nineveh, but rebellion broke out. In Babylonia, a Chaldean, Merodach-Baladan, seized the throne, supported by the Elamites, but he was put to flight and the Chaldean tribes surrendered. The city-states and kingdoms of Syria and Palestine, encouraged by Egypt, refused tribute. In 701 B.C. Sennacherib marched to the coast and occupied Ascalon and Sidon; Judah was next invaded, Lachish captured by assault, and Jerusalem invested. Hezekiah, King of Judah, defied the Assyrians and was forced to pay a heavy indemnity. Sennacherib then attempted to invade Egypt, but disaster, perhaps plague, struck his army and he was forced to turn back.

A second rebellion in Babylonia was foiled, and Sennacherib made his son, Assur-nadin-shum, king of Babylon. Merodach-Baladan took refuge in the marshes of southern Elam. Seven years later, after repeated provocation, Sennacherib decided to seek him out; building a fleet at Nineveh, he sailed the ships downriver to Opis, then dragged them overland to the Euphrates, and thence to the Persian Gulf. After a sea battle, Elamite coastal towns were destroyed. Meanwhile, Assur-nadin-shum was murdered and replaced by an Elamite nominee. In 689 Sennacherib avenged his son. Marching to Babylon, he took the city by storm and mercilessly destroyed it, deporting the inhabitants and flooding the ruins. This sacrilege to a holy city shocked the ancient world but effectively discouraged further rebellion.

The war annals of Sennacherib depict him as a ruthless destroyer, "the flame that consumes those who will not submit." In his building inscriptions, however, he appears as "he who cares for the welfare of Assyria." His greatest achievement was the rebuilding of Nineveh, the ancient capital. He strengthened the walls, cut new streets, and replanned the water system. Water was brought from the hills 50 miles away and carried over a valley on a stone aqueduct—one of the engineering feats of antiquity. His palace, built on an artificial platform, covered 8 acres and was surrounded by parks and orchards stocked with exotic plants and animals. In January 681, while at prayer, Sennacherib was murdered by his own sons.

Further Reading

Sennacherib is listed in the Ancient History study guide (I, B, 3). His father, SARGON II, was one of the most powerful Assyrian kings.

The events of Sennacherib's reign are recounted in volume 3 of the *Cambridge Ancient History* (1925), as well as in A. T. Olmstead, *History of Assyria* (1923), and H. Saggs, *The Greatness That Was Babylon* (1962). Daniel D. Luckenbill collected the inscriptions in *Ancient Records of Assyria and Babylonia*, vol. 2 (1927). For Sennacherib's rebuilding of Nineveh see R. Campbell Thompson, *A Century of Exploration at Nineveh*

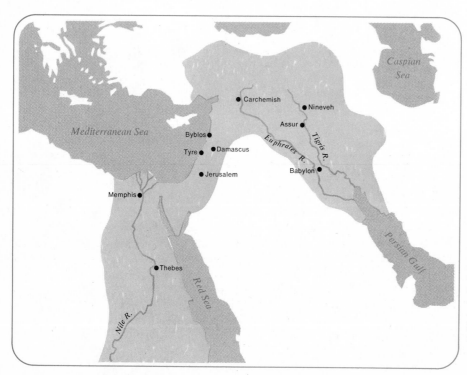

The Assyrian Empire in the 7th century B.C. Four great kings—Tiglath-pileser III, Sargon II, Sennacherib, and Ashurbanipal—made Assyria the dominant power in the Near East for more than a century.

Sennacherib, enthroned, receives the surrender of the city of Lachish on this stone wall slab excavated at Kuyunjik (ancient Nineveh) in modern Iraq. (Trustees of the British Museum)

(1929). On the reliefs from his palace, most of which are in the British Museum, consult C. J. Gadd, *The Stones of Assyria* (1936) and *Assyrian Sculptures in the British Museum, from Shalmaneser III to Sennacherib* (1938). See also Th. Jacobsen and S. Lloyd, *Sennacherib's Aqueduct at Jerwan* (1935).

SENNETT / By Frederick R. Benson and David Lissandrello

The American silent-screen producer and director Mack Sennett (1884–1960) is frequently considered the originator of film comedy. He perfected the art of silent-screen slapstick in his "Keystone" series.

Mack Sennett was born Michael Sinnott on Jan. 17, 1884, in Quebec, Canada. He emigrated to New York at the beginning of the 20th century to act in films by D. W. Griffith. Not very successful, Sennett turned to movie direction, and his first two efforts, *Comrade* (1911) and *One-round O'Brien* (1912), were so popular that sequels were immediately demanded. Assured of financial backing, he formed his own organization, the Keystone Company, and moved to Hollywood, Calif.

During the first year Sennett produced 140 "Keystone Comedies," the most famous of which were *Uncle Tom without the Cabin* and *Salome vs. Shenandoah*. Unable to direct every comedy personally, Sennett supplied himself with a talented crew of gag writers, comedians, cameramen, and stunt men. At the completion of each film, he would attend the final screening and perfect the structure and timing through careful editing. All of these films were made so that, in projection, the action was faster than life.

Sennett's comic philosophy is perhaps best expressed in his comments on the Italian folk form commedia dell'arte: "The round, fat girls in nothing much doing their bumps and grinds, the German-dialect comedians, and especially the cops and tramps with their bed-slats and ladders appealed to me as being funny people. Their approach to life was earthy and understandable. They made fun of themselves and of the human race. They reduced convention, dogma, stuffed shirts ... to nonsense, and then blossomed into pandemonium. . . . I especially enjoyed the reduction of authority to absurdity, the notion that sex could be funny, and the bold insults that were hurled at pretension."

The Sennett films defied logic and gravity in their epic chases and wild pie-throwing contests. In a Sennett comedy it was not unusual for a bandit to rob a bank with a vacuum cleaner or for a flood to carry a man out of his house in a bathtub. The Sennett Bathing Beauties, which featured such curvaceous creatures as Louise Fazenda and Gloria Swanson, added a touch of sexual delight to the then puritanical American film. Sennett's comedies, when they are at their best, are a combination of impudent satire, vulgar burlesque, and exhilarated madness.

The tragedy of Sennett's career was the arrival of sound in movies in the late 1920s; he was unable and unwilling to adjust to its demands. In 1928 Sennett permanently closed his studio. That same year the Academy of Motion Picture Arts and Sciences awarded the classic innovator a special award, "for his lasting contribution to the comedy technique of the screen." He died on Nov. 6, 1960, in Woodland Hills, Calif.

Further Reading

Mack Sennett is listed in the American History study

Mack Sennett. (Library of Congress)

Crippled for life in a hunting accident, Sequoyah became an excellent silversmith. As an adult, he had contacts with whites which piqued his curiosity about "talking leaves," as he called books. In 1809 he determined to master this secret and to apply it to his own people. After a dozen years of ridicule and insults, he invented a Cherokee alphabet of 85 or 86 characters that allowed every sound in Cherokee to be written.

In 1821 Sequoyah demonstrated his invention before the Cherokee council, which approved his work. Within 2 years thousands of Cherokee had mastered the syllabary, an advance which stimulated the printing of books in the Cherokee language as well as some newspapers printed partly in Cherokee.

In 1823 Sequoyah went to Arkansas to teach his syllabary to the Cherokee who already had migrated westward, and he moved with them to Oklahoma in 1828. He became somewhat active in tribal politics and was a Cherokee delegate to Washington, D.C., in 1828. With his syllabary a success, Sequoyah devoted much of his time to studying other tribal languages in a search for common elements. His tribe recognized the importance of his contribution when, in 1841, it voted him an allowance, which became an annuity of $300.

Early in 1843 Sequoyah became interested in a tribal tradition that said that part of the Cherokee nation had migrated west of the Mississippi River prior to the American Revolution. He set out to find this group, a trek that led him westward and southward, and he died in

guide (VIII, F, 6). He nurtured the talents of gifted screen clowns such as Charlie CHAPLIN.

The standard biography of Sennett is Cameron Shipp, *King of Comedy* (1954). Excellent critical studies of the film maker's work are in Gilbert Seldes, *The Seven Lively Arts* (1924); James Agee, *Agee on Film* (1958); Edward C. Wagenknecht, *The Movies in the Age of Innocence* (1962); and Kenneth McGowan, *Behind the Screen* (1965).

SEQUOYAH / By Odie B. Faulk

Sequoyah (ca. 1770–1843), Cherokee scholar, is the only known American Indian to have formulated an alphabet for his tribe. This advance enabled thousands of Cherokee to become literate.

Sequoyah (pronounced sĭ-kwoi′ə) was born at the Cherokee village of Taskigi in Tennessee. His father probably was Nathaniel Gist, a trader. His mother was part Cherokee and was abandoned by her husband before the birth of Sequoyah. He used his Indian name until he approached manhood, when he assumed the name George Guess (as he understood his father's last name to be).

Sequoyah demonstrating his Cherokee syllabary. (Library of Congress)

August 1843, possibly in the state of Tamaulipas in Mexico.

Sequoyah is commemorated by the state of Oklahoma, which placed a statue of him in the nation's capital. Also, a redwood tree, the Sequoia, was named in his honor, as was the Sequoia National Park.

Further Reading

Sequoyah is listed in the American History study guide (V, C, 2). While he was working to make his people literate, BLACK HAWK and OSCEOLA were struggling to prevent the government from moving their tribes from their homelands.

The standard biography of this great Indian is Grant Foreman, *Sequoyah* (1938). Brief but useful is Kate Dickinson Sweetser, *Book of Indian Braves* (1913). Grace S. Woodward, *The Cherokees* (1963), assesses the impact of Sequoyah's syllabary.

SERRA / By Sandra L. Myres

A Franciscan missionary and founder of the Spanish missions of California, Junípero Serra (1713–1784) was one of the most respected and best-known figures in California history.

Junípero Serra (pronounced sĕr′ə), whose sobriquets "Apostle of California" and "Father of the Missions" typify the love and esteem with which he is still regarded, was born Miguel José Serra at Petra on the island of Majorca just off the eastern coast of Spain. Educated by the Franciscan fathers at Palma, Serra joined the order in 1730 and took the name Junípero in memory of a companion of St. Francis of Assisi. For several years following his ordination, Serra remained at Palma as both student and teacher. He received a doctorate in theology in 1742 and served as professor of theology at the Franciscan university in Palma from 1744 to 1749.

Then, at the age of 36, Serra joined a group of missionaries setting out for Mexico. In company with his pupil and friend Fray Francisco Palóu, Serra arrived in Mexico City in December 1749. Shortly thereafter he volunteered to go to the mission field of Sierra Gorda in northeastern Mexico, where for 8 years he served as preacher and teacher. He learned the Otomí language of the natives, built several churches which are still in use today, and established a successful and thriving mission system.

In 1758 Serra prepared for a new assignment at Mission San Sabá on the Texas frontier, but before he could go north, hostile Comanches attacked and burned the mission. The Church then ordered Serra to the Franciscan college of San Fernando in Mexico City, and from 1758 to 1767 he served as home missionary, preached throughout Mexico, and served as a commissioner of the

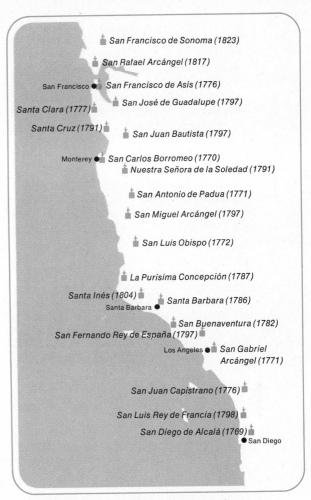

The California missions. In the late 18th century Junípero Serra and other Franciscans founded a string of missions extending from San Diego to San Francisco. Intended to bring Christianity to the Indians, they served also as centers of Spanish settlement in old California.

Holy Office, or Inquisition.

California Missions

In 1767, when the Spaniards expelled the Jesuit order from New Spain, Serra became president of the former Jesuit missions in Baja California. He arrived at Loreto in April 1768 and immediately set about the task of improving and enlarging the mission establishments. In 1769 he volunteered to go to Alta California to establish the first missions there. During the march north Serra suffered from painful bleeding ulcers on his legs and feet, but he refused to turn back. He arrived at San Diego in late June 1769 and immediately began construction of the first mission plant.

During the next 15 years Serra devoted his time and energy to the Franciscan establishment in California. When others despaired, Serra persevered. By 1782 the indefatigable priest had founded nine missions: San Diego, San Carlos Borromeo de Monterey (Carmel), San Antonio, San Gabriel, San Luis Obispo, San Francisco, San

Juan Capistrano, Santa Clara, and San Buenaventura. Slowly he overcame the fear and hostility of the natives and converted them to the Christian religion. Serra was as concerned with the Amerinds' physical well-being as with their spiritual life. He introduced domestic animals and new agricultural methods and trades to the neophytes at his missions and did everything possible to help the natives adjust to a different way of life. Under his care the California missions became the most successful and prosperous in all of New Spain.

Not only did Serra have responsibility for the missions, but after the founding of the pueblos of San José and Los Angeles he also administered the churches there as well as those at the presidios of San Diego, Monterey, San Francisco, and Santa Barbara. His devotion and constancy were in large part responsible for the growth and development of Spanish California.

Serra died in August 1784 at Mission San Carlos Borromeo and was buried in the mission church (at present-day Carmel), which has become a shrine to his memory. Monuments to Serra dot the map from Majorca to San Francisco, and several societies, including Serra International, have been established in his honor.

Further Reading

Junípero Serra is listed in the Latin America study guide (I, B, 3). Juan de OÑATE tried to colonize New Mexico.

Junípero Serra. (Courtesy of the Bancroft Library, University of California)

Although adulatory, the work by Serra's friend and companion Francisco Palóu, *Life of Fray Junípero Serra* (1787; trans. 1955), is the best known of the Serra biographies, available in several editions and translations. The best of the modern works is Maynard J. Geiger, *The Life and Times of Fray Junípero Serra* (2 vols., 1959). The study by Katherine and Edward Maddin Ainsworth, *In the Shade of the Juniper Tree: A Life of Fray Junípero Serra* (1970), is thoroughly researched, but the wealth of factual material tends to obscure Serra's personal qualities. Most histories of California devote at least part of a chapter to Serra's career. Particularly recommended is the discussion in Charles E. Chapman, *A History of California: The Spanish Period* (1928).

SERVETUS / By Joseph N. Scionti

The Spanish religious philosopher Michael Servetus (ca. 1511–1553), often called the first Unitarian, denied the divinity of Christ and the doctrine of the Trinity. His views made him abhorrent to both Catholics and Protestants.

Michael Servetus (pronounced sər-vē′təs) was born at Villanueva. The son of a notary, he became a law student in Toulouse, where he developed an avid interest in the Bible. A Franciscan named Juan de Quintana befriended him in 1525. Quintana became confessor to Emperor Charles V in 1530, and that year Servetus accompanied Quintana to Bologna for Charles's coronation. There the pomp surrounding the Pope repelled him and tended to alienate him from the Roman Catholic Church. This journey was decisive in shaping Servetus's thought, for he also visited Augsburg, where he came into immediate contact with Protestantism, which impressed him favorably. He soon became acquainted with the leading spirit of Rhenish Protestantism, Martin Bucer.

Servetus then published a book that separated him philosophically not only from Catholicism but also from all the current reforming movements: *De Trinitatis erroribus* (1531; On the Errors of the Trinity). Its erudition was astonishing in light of the fact that its author was so young. But its thesis horrified Servetus's contemporaries, making him in their eyes a heretic. Servetus viewed Jesus as a man upon whom God had bestowed divine wisdom. Jesus came forth as a prophet bearing God's precious gift, but he did not partake of God's immortality. If Servetus denied Jesus' equality to the godhead, he yielded to none in his praise of Jesus, calling him the Light of the World. Servetus insisted that those who believed in the Trinity were tritheists who could not escape the logic that they denied the One True God.

Because of these views Servetus was forced to take flight, moving in 1532 from Switzerland to France. There he lived for a time unmolested, traveling in 1536 to Paris to study medicine. He met John Calvin briefly, but Ser-

Michael Servetus. (New York Academy of Medicine Library)

vetus concentrated for a time on medicine rather than on religious reform. He became assistant to the physician Johann Günther and continued to study avidly, taking up theology and Hebrew as well as medicine.

In 1546 Servetus wrote to Calvin, sending him elaborate manuscripts on his theological views. Calvin answered without warmth, letting Servetus know he would not be welcome in Geneva. The reformer very probably, through correspondence, was partially responsible for Servetus's arrest by the inquisitor general of Lyons on April 4, 1553. On April 7 Servetus escaped, turning up 4 months later in Geneva. He was seized, tried, and on Oct. 27, 1553, burned alive with the acquiescence of Calvin.

Further Reading

Michael Servetus is listed in the Religion study guide (I, I, 1 and 4). John CALVIN condemned Servetus's anti-Trinitarian views.

A scholarly biography of Servetus is Roland H. Bainton, *Hunted Heretic: The Life and Death of Michael Servetus* (1953; new foreword, 1960). Also useful is John F. Fulton, *Michael Servetus: Humanist and Martyr* (1953). A good account of Servetus's theology is in Louis Israel Newman, *Jewish Influence on Christian Reform Movements* (1925).

SESSHU / By Hugo Munsterberg

The Japanese painter and Zen priest Toyo Sesshu (1420–1506) is generally regarded as Japan's greatest painter. His Zen-inspired paintings are credited with establishing a truly Japanese style of ink painting which had a great influence on all later Japanese painting.

The Muromachi, or Ashikaga, period during which Sesshu (pronounced sĕs-shoo) lived was profoundly influenced by Zen Buddhism, which had been introduced from China during the Kamakura period. Under its impact the Chinese-style ink paintings of the great masters of the Southern Sung period, especially the landscape painters Ma Yüan and Hsia Kuei and the Ch'an painters Mu Ch'i and Yu-chien, served as models for the Japanese painters. Not only did these artists derive their style from China, but the landscape they represented was also that of South China in spite of the fact that many of them had never been there.

Sesshu was born in Bitchu Province in western Honshu. As a youth, he became a Buddhist novice at the Shokoku-ji, a well-known Zen temple in Kyoto which was not only a famous Buddhist sanctuary but a celebrated cultural center as well. At the monastery young Sesshu came under the influence of the famous painter Shubun, who was a fellow monk, and the Zen master Shunrin Suto, who became his spiritual adviser.

Little is known about Sesshu's early artistic work prior to his journey to China (1467–1469), during which he visited Buddhist monasteries and traveled as far as Peking. Although the artist was well received and also much impressed by the grandiose landscape, he was disappointed with the state of painting in Ming China, which to his way of thinking compared unfavorably to the painting of the Sung period some 2 centuries earlier.

Returning to Japan in 1469, Sesshu moved from place to place in northern Kyushu to avoid the civil war which was raging in Kyoto and finally settled in Oita, where he enjoyed the patronage of the Otomo family. His friend, the monk Bofu Ryushin, in commenting upon Sesshu's position at this time, reported that everyone from the nobility to the common people of Oita admired his painting and asked for examples of his work. Between 1481 and 1484 the artist made a long journey through Japan, visiting many parts of the country and making numerous sketches of the landscape.

After Sesshu returned to western Japan, he settled at Yamaguchi in Suho Province, where he set up the Ten-kai-toga-ro studio and enjoyed the patronage of the Mori family. He spent the remainder of his life at Yamaguchi, enjoying ever-growing fame as Japan's leading artist.

Landscape Paintings

Of all the various subjects treated by Sesshu, landscapes form by far the largest and most important category. The earliest of these is a set of hanging scrolls depicting the four seasons (National Museum, Tokyo). Painted either in China or shortly after his return, they reflect the rather dry and academic style of the Chinese Che school of the time. His mature style is best seen in a pair of landscape scrolls depicting fall and winter, which originally belonged to the Manju-in in Kyoto (now in the National Museum, Tokyo). Painted in ink on paper in a vigorous and expressive manner, they show the artist at his very best. The style and the subject are derived from Chinese models, but Sesshu's paintings show far greater contrasts between solid blacks and lighter tones, more emphasis on heavy lines, and a flatter space than would be found in Chinese Sung painting.

While these pictures are in the form of hanging scrolls, called kakemono, other landscapes by Sesshu are in the form of horizontal hand scrolls known as makimono. The most famous of these, and perhaps Sesshu's most outstanding work, is the long scroll landscape (collection of

A detail from Sesshu's haboku sansui scroll.
(National Museum, Tokyo)

the Mori family, Yamaguchi). Measuring more than 50 feet in length and painted in 1486, when the artist was at the peak of his power, it represents suiboku ink painting at its best, combining magnificent brushwork with a profound interpretation of the moods and aspects of nature. Starting with a spring landscape, it ends with winter scenes depicting mountains, gnarled pines, picturesque rocks, tiny figures, fishing boats, village huts, and town houses.

Two other celebrated Sesshu landscapes are the *haboku sansui* scroll (National Museum, Tokyo) of 1495 and the *Ama-no-hashidate*, or Bridge of Heaven scroll (National Museum, Kyoto), a work from the very end of Sesshu's life, about 1502 to 1506. The *haboku sansui* is painted in the so-called spilled-ink style, a free and very spontaneous manner derived from the Zen tradition. The *Ama-no-hashidate*, which is a kind of topographical painting of a celebrated beauty spot located on the Japanese sea coast, is executed in a very meticulous style. Several other landscapes can with more or less certainty be attributed to Sesshu, but none of them is equal in quality to these masterpieces. Among the landscapes in American collections which are attributed to Sesshu, the spilled-ink-style picture in the Cleveland Museum is the most authentic as well as the finest esthetically.

Zen Subjects

Although Sesshu remained a Buddhist monk all his life and his landscape painting was religious in inspiration, several of his other works are Zen paintings in a more specific sense. Among these is a large scroll painted in 1496 (collection of the Sainen-ji, Aichi prefecture). It depicts Hui-ko cutting off his arm to demonstrate his will power to the founder of Zen, Bodhidarma, or Daruma, as he is called in Japan. Both the bold, inspired brushwork of the picture and the choice of the subject matter are typical of Zen Buddhist thought. The portrait of Daruma, with bushy eyebrows and a fierce expression, reveals his spiritual power in a masterful way.

Bird and Flower Paintings

The third main category of Sesshu's work consists of decorative screen paintings depicting birds and flowers as well as monkeys and all sorts of trees and plants. This type of painting, which was particularly popular in Ming China, is very different from Sesshu's other work owing to its greater attention to realistic detail and emphasis on decorative design rather than religious feeling. The format too tends to differ from most of his other works, for these paintings tend to be folding screens instead of scroll paintings. Among the screens of this type, the finest is a pair showing birds and flowers rendered in a very decorative and detailed manner (Kosaka Collection, Tokyo).

The best such painting in America is the monkey screen (Museum of Fine Arts, Boston), which, although signed and dated 1491, is no longer believed to be by Sesshu. However, since he had many followers working in his style, the question of which works are actually by the master and which are by his workshop or his follow-

Monkeys and Birds, a
screen attributed to
Sesshu. (Courtesy,
Museum of Fine Arts,
Boston, Fenollosa-Weld
Collection)

ers is very difficult to determine.

Further Reading

Sesshu is listed in the Asia study guide (III, B, 5, b). His style was formed by studying the landscapes of the Chinese painters HSIA Kuei and MA Yüan.

The most complete work on Sesshu in English is still Jon Carter Covell, *Under the Seal of Sesshu* (1941). A more recent work is Tanio Nakamura, *Sesshu Toyo, 1420–1506*, with an English text by Elise Grilli (1957). There is a brief introduction to Sesshu's life and work in the Tokyo National Museum's edition of *The Masterpieces of Sesshu* (1956).

* * *

SESSIONS / By Laurence Berman

The works of the American composer Roger Huntington Sessions (born 1896) are characterized by a dense chromaticism of an expressive and individual character. He was also an influential teacher.

Roger Sessions was born in Brooklyn, N.Y., on Dec. 28, 1896. He entered Harvard at the age of 14. Later he studied music under Horatio Parker at Yale and Ernest Bloch at the Cleveland Institute of Music (1919–1922) and then stayed on at the institute as Bloch's assistant. Sessions' his first major orchestral work, *The Black Maskers* (1923), is usually heard today in its form as a suite. It remains the best introduction to his music by virtue of its accessibility: the warmth and color of the orchestral writing and the rhythmic ingenuity create an immediacy of excitement not characteristic of his later style; at the same time, he is in command of every compositional detail.

In following Sessions' development, one realizes that his music, though unmistakably "progressive" in style,

was independent of the current trend at any given moment. Thus his First Piano Sonata (1930) opens in an atmosphere reminiscent of César Franck or Gabriel Fauré; and Sessions' music of the 1930s, in general, bears only the most superficial imprint of neoclassicism. The "pandiatonicism" of the Violin Concerto (1935) is perhaps the closest he ever approached to Aaron Copland's manner, while the four piano pieces known as *From My Diary* (1937–1940) far surpass in harmonic and gestural complexity anything to be found in American neoclassic works of the period.

The 1930s were a time of compositional struggle for Sessions and of readjustment to America after 8 years spent in Europe. Returning in 1933, he immediately began teaching at Princeton, moving to Berkeley in 1945, then back to Princeton in 1953. After he retired from Princeton in 1964, he taught at the Juilliard School in New York.

The later years brought noticeable changes in Sessions' music. While the pieces of the 1930s and 1940s were produced slowly and sporadically, the works of the 1950s and 1960s came in fair profusion. Six Symphonies, two Piano Concertos, and a Mass were written between 1957 and 1968. The harmonic complexity of the middle years proceeds quite inevitably through the "diatonic atonality" of the Second String Quartet (1951) to a chromaticism reminiscent of Arnold Schoenberg, beginning with the *Idyll of Theocritus* (1956) and the Third Symphony (1957). The affinity with Schoenberg is seen especially in the later orchestral works, with their motivic elaboration, contrapuntal density, long-breathed lines, and kaleidoscopic play of instrumental color.

Sessions' music has been called difficult, but for those familiar with the more advanced 20th-century works it poses no problems. It is consistently serious in tone; even the most gently lyrical moments are internally too complex to be considered "light" or "charming." But the complexity has expressive force and is entirely appropriate to the scope and grandeur of design typical of his large-scale works.

Sessions was held in high regard by his contemporaries and students. He received countless honors and

Roger Sessions. (Princeton University)

many commissions. Of his several books and articles *Harmonic Practice* (1951) and two collections of lecture-essays, *The Musical Experience of Composer, Performer, Listener* (1950) and *Questions about Music* (1970), are the most significant.

Further Reading

Roger Sessions is listed in the Music study guide (II, D, 1; II, E). Among the many composers who studied with him was Milton BABBITT.

There is no biography of Sessions, but considerable information is in several background works: Gerald Abraham, *A Hundred Years of Music* (1938; 3d ed. 1964); David Ewen, *World of 20th Century Music* (1968); and H. H. Stuckenschmidt, *Twentieth Century Music* (1969).

SETON / By Henry L. Swint

Elizabeth Ann Bayley Seton (1774–1821), the first American woman to be beatified, founded the first American order of nuns, initiated the parochial school system, and established the first Catholic orphanage in the United States.

lizabeth Bayley was born in New York City on Aug. 28, 1774, a daughter of Richard Bayley, health officer for the port of New York and professor of anatomy at King's College. The Bayley family were members of the Episcopal Church. Elizabeth grew up in fashionable New York society. In 1794 she married William Magee Seton, a prosperous New York banker and merchant. They had five children. Mrs. Seton was so active in her aid to the sick, the poor, and the unfortunate that she became known as the "Protestant Sister of Charity."

In the fall of 1803 the Setons went to Italy to visit friends, the Filicchi family, who were prominent bankers and shippers. Mr. Seton, already ill, was seriously affected by the voyage and died in December. The Filicchis introduced Mrs. Seton to Catholicism, and Antonio Filicchi accompanied her when she returned to America in 1804. Despite the opposition of her close friend, the Episcopal minister John Henry Hobart, she joined the Catholic Church in March 1805.

For her conversion Mrs. Seton was ostracized by New York society. She had difficulty in supporting her family, although Antonio Filicchi was generous in giving her aid. She considered going into a convent but followed the advice of Bishop John Carroll of Baltimore and did not do so. Father William Dubourg of Baltimore told Mrs. Seton that he wanted to establish a school in that city, and in September 1808 she opened a boarding school for girls. She and her small group of assistants adopted the name Sisters of Charity of St. Joseph. The rules of the order were similar to those of a French order, the Daugh-

Elizabeth Seton. (College of Mount Saint Vincent)

ters of Charity of St. Vincent de Paul. In 1809 the sisters moved to Emmitsburg, Md., to property which had been given the Church for use in the education of the poor.

The first winter in the new location was harsh. The house was incomplete and the food inadequate, but within a few months the school was thriving. Members of the group took over an orphanage in Philadelphia in 1814 and established orphanages and schools in New York and Philadelphia.

Mother Seton died on Jan. 4, 1821, in Emmitsburg. She was declared venerable on Dec. 18, 1959, and was beatified on March 17, 1963.

Further Reading

Elizabeth Seton is listed in the Religion study guide (I, Q, 2, c). She was advised on her course by Bishop John CARROLL of Baltimore.

Joseph I. Dirvin, *Mrs. Seton: Foundress of the American Sisters of Charity* (1962), is a detailed, scholarly biography, based on an impressive bibliography, including many primary materials. Leonard Feeney, *Mother Seton: An American Woman* (1947), is written in a somewhat popular style, but it contains excerpts from some of Mrs. Seton's letters.

SEURAT / By Carl Belz

The French painter Georges Pierre Seurat (1859–1891) was the leading figure in the neoimpressionist movement of the 1880s and in the development of the technique of pointillism.

The impressionist style, which marked a radical shift in the course of Western painting, blossomed for the most part in the 1870s. During the next 2 decades a number of young painters sought to work out the tenets of impressionism in terms of their personal styles. These artists are generally separated into two groups: the postimpressionists, which included Vincent Van Gogh, Paul Gauguin, and Paul Cézanne, and the neoimpressionists, which included Georges Seurat (pronounced sœ-rä′) and Paul Signac. In particular, Seurat wished to carry the theories of impressionism to their logical conclusions and to establish an art with a truly scientific base.

Seurat was born in Paris on Dec. 2, 1859. As a student, he worked in the school of the sculptor Justin Lequien, and, for less than a year during 1878–1879, he studied at the École des Beaux-Arts. During these years Seurat developed a deep respect for antique sculpture and Renaissance painting. In terms of his own century, he particularly admired the painting of J. A. D. Ingres, and he made a careful study of the new landscape tradition that had begun with the Barbizon school and culminated in impressionism.

Georges Seurat, a self-portrait drawn in crayon about 1884 and entitled the Artist in His Studio. *(Philadelphia Museum of Art, A. E. Gallatin Collection)*

Development of Pointillism

But Seurat was interested in science as well as art, especially in scientific color theory. During the late 1870s and the early 1880s he read numerous treatises on this subject, including those by M. E. Chevreul, H. von Helmholtz, and O. N. Rood; he also studied Eugène Delacroix's writings on color.

Essentially, Seurat's aim was to separate each color into its component parts (this process is known as divisionism) and to apply each of the component colors individually on the canvas surface. In order to have the colors blend optically, each one had to be applied in the form of a small dot of pigment. The phenomenon whereby colors were allowed to blend optically instead of being mixed on the palette had been the discovery of the impressionists, but Seurat carried the process further. He analyzed it scientifically and developed a theory to explain it. The term "pointillism" refers to the actual application of these theories to painting.

His Paintings

Seurat's first major demonstration of pointillism was *A Sunday Afternoon on the Island of La Grande Jatte* (1884–1886). This is also his most celebrated painting. A large work, it is extremely complicated, consisting of numerous figures scattered both across and into pictorial space. The scene itself is typically impressionist in presenting an outdoor world. Yet the work departs radically from impressionism: it was painted entirely in the studio with each of its many elements being carefully calculated in terms of color, light, and composition. *La Grande Jatte* is thus a tour de force in revealing Seurat's painstaking method: like his academic predecessors, he made careful studies for each figure. As a result, each seems frozen in its position, but each scintillates because it is composed of a myriad of individual color spots. As a whole, the painting is at once both classical and modern.

Seurat, Signac, and Odilon Redon were instrumental in organizing the Société des Artistes Indépendants, which had its first exhibition in 1884. Like the impressionists before them, these artists originated their own shows because their radical art had been rejected by the juries of the official Salon. And although these shows contained a wide variety of individual styles, Seurat's ambitious demonstrations of pointillism clearly established him as the major figure of neoimpressionism. Between 1886 and 1890 his influence thus spread to numerous other painters, including Gauguin, Camille Pissarro, Van Gogh, and Henri de Toulouse-Lautrec, all of whom went through pointillist periods in their own work.

After completing *La Grande Jatte*, Seurat consciously sought to expand the expressive range of his work. He became interested in motion and in the emotional quality of linear rhythms. Seurat's friend, the esthetician Charles Henry, encouraged and shared these interests, which are reflected in *La Parade* (1887–1888), *La Chahut* (1889–1890), and the *Circus* (unfinished). In contrast to the formality of *La Grande Jatte*, these works contain moving figures, sparkling lights, and a generally lyric atmosphere. In spite of this expanded content, however, Seurat did not relinquish his methodical, scientific technique. He continued to work slowly, carefully developing his theories and producing numerous drawings and oil studies for each painting.

His Drawings

Because of his painstaking working process, Seurat completed relatively few major paintings. Throughout his life, however, he was a tireless and consummate draftsman. As a student, he made drawings of classical sculpture, architectural motifs, and the human figure. Many of these are reminiscent of the touch and style of Ingres. But by the early 1880s Seurat began to evolve a more personal style, generally employing Conté crayon and an unusually high-grain paper. The range of feeling in these drawings is extraordinary—and occasionally surprising in comparison to the rather cool tenor of his paintings. The master delicately used his materials to suggest figures, spaces, and atmosphere; frequently he

Seurat's A Sunday Afternoon on the Island at La Grande Jatte, *painted 1884–1886. (Courtesy of The Art Institute of Chicago, Helen Birch Bartlett Memorial Collection)*

allowed the grain of the paper to show through the Conté crayon and achieved a sense of quiet intimacy that has few parallels in the history of the medium.

Early in 1891 Seurat contracted infectious angina. He died on March 29 at the height of his artistic powers.

Further Reading

Georges Seurat is listed in the Art study guide (III, H, 1, f). Camille PISSARRO, Paul GAUGUIN, Vincent VAN GOGH, and Henri de TOULOUSE-LAUTREC went through a neoimpressionist phase. Seurat greatly influenced Gino SEVERINI.

The most authoritative treatment of Seurat's techniques and color theories is William Innes Homer, *Seurat and the Science of Painting* (1964). Monographs on the artist include Daniel Catton Rich, ed., *Seurat: Paintings and Drawings* (1958), and John Russell, *Seurat* (1965). For Seurat's drawings see Robert L. Herbert, *Seurat's Drawings* (1962). For a general survey see John Rewald, *Post-Impressionism, from Van Gogh to Gauguin* (1956; 2d ed. 1962).

* * *

SEVERINI / By J. P. Hodin

> Gino Severini (1883–1966) was one of the leading painters of the Italian futurist movement, which proposed a radical renovation of artistic activity in keeping with the dynamism of modern mechanized life.

Gino Severini (pronounced sā-vā-rē′nē) was born on April 7, 1883, in Cortona. In Rome in 1901 he met Umberto Boccioni, and the following year he became acquainted with Giacomo Balla, who had studied in Paris. Severini and Boccioni became Balla's pupils. Thus Severini was acquainted with the theories of divisionism when he himself arrived in Paris in 1906. There it was Georges Seurat, above all, who impressed Severini.

In his studio at the Impass Guelma, Severini created his most famous futurist pictures, such as *Le Boulevard* (1909) and *Danse du Pan Pan au Monico* (1911). He was particularly attracted by subject matter connected with cabarets and night clubs, and his paintings represent hectic rhythms with dissected and multiplied forms, as in the *Dynamic Hieroglyphic of the Bal Tabarin* (1912). He was one of the five artists who signed the Futurist Manifesto in 1910, and he took part in the historic exhibitions of the futurist group in Paris, London, and Berlin.

Severini's pictures, painted in Seurat's clear colors, influenced the cubists to lighten their palette, and his personal contribution was to combine the futurist program with the analytical and geometrical spirit of cubism.

In 1915 Severini joined the artists of the Effort Moderne. The experimental work produced in the style of the Section d'Or group led Severini into a transitional period, which he described in his book *Du Cubisme au*

Gino Severini. (Presidenza del Consiglio, Rome)

classicisme (1921). In the 1920s he was drawn more to murals than to easel painting, creating a series of harlequins and frescoes, based on the commedia dell'arte, at the Castle of Montefugoni near Florence (1922). He also executed frescoes in Switzerland for churches at Semsales and La Roche (1926–1927), the Capuchin church at Sion, and Notre Dame du Valentin in Lausanne (1935). Severini designed mosaics for the University of Fribourg, Switzerland (ca. 1925), and for the Palace of Art (1933) and the Palace of Justice (1939) in Milan.

Severini's development from a cubist to a neoclassicist style occurred under the influence of Pablo Picasso and the Valori Plastici group. About 1930, however, Severini returned to a sort of decorative cubism. His late work showed a tendency toward concrete art.

In 1950 Severini won a prize at the Venice Biennale. He died in Paris on Feb. 26, 1966.

Further Reading

Gino Severini is listed in the Art study guide (III, J, 4). Other futurist artists were Giacomo BALLA and Umberto BOCCIONI. Severini's early work was influenced by Georges SEURAT and his later paintings by Pablo PICASSO.

Severini is discussed in Alfred H. Barr, Jr., *Cubism and Abstract Art* (1936). Raffaele Carrieri, *Avant-garde Painting and Sculpture in Italy, 1890–1955* (1955), gives a panorama of the development of modern Italian art with detailed studies of the leading artists. See also James Thrall Soby and Alfred H. Barr, Jr., *Twentieth Century Italian Art* (1949), and Guido Ballo, *Modern Italian Painting from Futurism to the Present Day* (1958).

* * *

SEVERUS / By Frank C. Bourne

> Lucius Septimius Severus (146–211) was a Roman emperor. His reign is notable for the militarization of the government, growing

Oriental influences in society, and high
development of civil law.

Severus (pronounced sə-vēr′əs) was an African from Leptis Magna. He rose through the regular course of Roman offices, was consul in 190, and was serving as governor of Upper Pannonia in 193, when Emperor Pertinax was murdered by the praetorian guard. Severus's command of 12 legions and proximity to Rome made him a favored contender for the throne. He appeared in Rome as the dead emperor's avenger and won the senators' approval by promising them respectful treatment, by disbanding the praetorian guard, which he replaced with elite from the legions, and by naming his Western rival, Albinus, his caesar (successor-designate).

After defeating his more formidable rival, Pescennius Niger, in 194, Severus started a successful campaign against the Parthians. But fear of the activities of Albinus in the West led Severus to break off his campaign and hurry back to Gaul to meet and defeat his rival at Lyons in early 197.

Now firmly established, Septimius began to show more candidly his sentiments toward Roman traditions. He had 29 senators executed on suspicion of favoring Albinus, and their property was confiscated. Famous cities, such as Byzantium, Antioch, and Lyons, were humiliated or destroyed. And his elder son, Bassianus (Caracalla), was renamed Marcus Aurelius Antoninus, in pretense that Septimius had been adopted into the prestigious Antonine family of emperors.

A Parthian attack in 197 brought the Emperor back to the East. He captured the Parthian capital at Ctesiphon and reestablished a province of Mesopotamia. From 199 to 202 the Emperor visited various Eastern provinces, where he established frontier outposts and improved the living conditions of the soldiers.

For the next 6 years Septimius remained chiefly in Rome. His administrative activities included pay raises for the troops, whom he also allowed for the first time to marry while in service. Veterans were given rapid advancement in the civil service, and the bureaucracy became militarized. Italy's formerly preferred status in the empire was lessened, while favored status was given to many places in his native Africa and his wife's homeland in Syria. Severus appointed prominent jurists to high administrative posts; and the appearance of a number of Rome's greatest legal names on the Emperor's council brought a humane approach and increased protection for the humble in the legislation of the Emperor.

From 208 to his death at York in 211 Septimius was in Britain fighting the Caledonians. Whether or not he really advised his sons on his deathbed to enrich the soldiers and disregard all others, the anecdote is a just estimate of the direction he gave the Roman world.

Further Reading

Severus is listed in the Ancient History study guide (III, C, 4). The Roman emperors MARCUS AURELIUS and TRAJAN also conducted major wars against the Parthians.

An ancient life of Severus in *Scriptores historiae Augustae* was translated by David Magie for the Loeb Classical Library (3 vols., 1921–1932). The standard life is Maurice Platnauer, *The Life and Reign of the Emperor Lucius Septimius Severus* (1918). A more recent work is Gerard J. Murphy, *The Reign of the Emperor L. Septimius Severus* (1945).

SEVIER / By Roger L. Nichols

John Sevier (1745–1815), American frontiersman, soldier, and politician, was a leading figure during the frontier period in the Old Southwest and became the first governor of Tennessee.

John Sevier was born on Sept. 23, 1745, in the Shenandoah Valley of Virginia. The eldest of seven children, he worked for his father, who had a farm, kept a tavern, traded for furs, and speculated in real estate. At the age of 16 John married Sarah Hawkins and began a similar career.

By his late 20s Sevier had decided to go west, and in 1771 he purchased land on the Holston River in eastern Tennessee. Two years later he moved his wife and seven

Severus, an ancient Roman portrait bust in the Capitoline Museum, Rome. (Alinari)

Migration routes to the West, 1790–1830. In the 1770s John Sevier was a pioneer in the trans-Appalachian West. By the time of his death, migrants were streaming westward in ever growing numbers along several well-marked routes.

children there. Sevier gained his new neighbors' respect, and soon they elected him to positions of leadership which included membership on the local Committee of Public Safety and one term in the North Carolina Provincial Congress. Although a lieutenant colonel in the militia, he took little part in the War for Independence until 1780, when he led several hundred frontiersmen east to help defeat the British at Kings Mountain. Shortly after this, he led a punitive expedition against the Cherokee Indians in Tennessee, the first of many such campaigns.

In 1784 North Carolina ceded its western lands to the Confederation Congress to reduce the state war debt and tax burden. This cession stimulated a movement for statehood among the frontiersmen living beyond the Appalachians. In August 1784 they held a convention and decided to petition Congress for statehood, but before they acted, North Carolina rescinded its land cession. The settlers met again in spite of this, adopted the North Carolina statutes temporarily, and elected John Sevier as governor of the state of Franklin. Opposition from the United States, North Carolina, the Indians, and some settlers defeated the statehood movement by 1788.

*John Sevier, a painting by Charles Willson Peale.
(Tennessee Historical Society)*

The next year Sevier began a single term in the U.S. House of Representatives, and in 1791 he became a brigadier general in the territorial militia. Three years later he was elected as the first governor of the new state of Tennessee, an office he held for the constitutional limit of three consecutive terms. Then, after he had been out of office for 2 years, the voters chose him for still another three terms. Following that, Sevier served in the Tennessee Senate and in 1811 was elected to the U.S. House of Representatives, where he served until his death in 1815.

Further Reading

John Sevier is listed in the American History study guide (IV, D, 3). Andrew JACKSON, later U.S. president, tried to curb Sevier's power in Tennessee.

The best study of Sevier is Carl S. Driver, *John Sevier: Pioneer of the Old Southwest* (1932), which gives an accurate discussion of his activities as land speculator, militiaman, and politician, although it fails to present much personal material. Samuel C. Williams, *History of the Lost State of Franklin* (1924; rev. ed. 1933), offers the most complete account of Sevier's role in the movement for statehood.

* * * * * *

SEWALL / By Everett H. Emerson

The voluminous diary of Samuel Sewall (1652–1730), American jurist, provides a vivid picture of the Boston of his day as well as of himself.

Samuel Sewall was born on March 28, 1652, in North Baddesley, Hampshire, England. His father was an occasional minister and cattle raiser who had spent from 1634 to 1646 in Massachusetts, where he had met his wife. After study at a grammar school, Samuel went to Newbury, Mass., where his father had returned 2 years earlier. Samuel's education continued under the local minister. In 1667 he entered Harvard; he graduated in 1671 and became master of arts in 1674. Unlike most of his classmates, he did not become a minister.

In 1676 Sewall married the daughter of a prosperous merchant. The story that his wife's dowry was her weight in the pine-tree shillings her father minted may not be apocryphal. Sewall went to work for his father-in-law. He became a constable in 1679, and in 1681 he was appointed to the Massachusetts General Court. His wife's inheritance after her father's death in 1683 was substantial, and it permitted Sewall to shift from business to civic service.

Sewall's diary records his daily life, with few opinions and no introspection. He was mainly conservative, conventionally religious, worldly but charitable, a Puritan and a Yankee. His diary indirectly reveals contemporary attitudes. It covers a business trip he made to England in 1688–1689. It is less detailed than one might wish on the Salem witch trials of 1692, when he served as one of seven judges. Eventually he saw the evil of which he had

*Samuel Sewall, a painting by John Smibert.
(Courtesy, Museum of Fine Arts, Boston)*

been guilty by his condemnation of "witches," and in 1697 he publicly acknowledged his error.

Following the witch trials, Sewall was appointed a judge of the Superior Court of Massachusetts, a post he held for 25 years. Then for 11 years he was chief justice. He was devoted to the cause of Christianizing the Indians and freeing Negro slaves. To the latter cause he devoted a pamphlet, *The Selling of Joseph* (1700). Another pamphlet, *Phaenomena quadem Apocalyptica ad aspectum Novi Orbis configurata* (1687), argued that New England was a suitable site for the new Jerusalem.

Sewall's wife died in 1717. Of their 14 children, only 5 survived her. Sewall married two more times. One failed courtship attempt is described in one of the diary's most attractive episodes. Sewall died in Boston on Jan. 1, 1730.

Further Reading

Samuel Sewall is listed in the American History study guide (II, B, 1, b) and the Literature study guide (I, A, 2, a). His diary and that kept by William BYRD II are the most valuable diaries of the colonial period.

Sewall's diary was published by the Massachusetts Historical Society in three volumes (1878–1882); abridged versions were edited by Mark Van Doren (1963) and Harvey Wish (1967). An attractive biography is Ola E. Winslow, *Samuel Sewall of Boston* (1964). The Salem witchcraft trials are treated in Chadwick Hansen, *Witchcraft at Salem* (1969).

William H. Seward, photographed about 1848. (Library of Congress)

SEWARD / By Avery Craven

William Henry Seward (1801–1872), American statesman, is noted for his staunch opposition to the spread of slavery and for his handling of foreign affairs as a member of Abraham Lincoln's Cabinet during the Civil War.

William H. Seward was born on May 16, 1801, in Florida, N.Y. He attended school there and at the age of 15 entered Union College. In 1818, after a disagreement with his father over money matters, Seward ran away to Georgia, where he taught school and learned something of the South and Negro slavery. He returned and in 1820 graduated from Union.

Seward then studied law and was admitted to the bar in 1822. He began practice as a junior partner of Judge Elijah Miller in "the bustling village of Auburn." He married the judge's capable daughter, Frances, and success came at once. The rise of the Anti-Masonic party lured him into politics, where he came into contact with master politician Thurlow Weed, who became his political mentor and shrewd guide into public office. Seward was elected state senator in the fall of 1830 as the advocate of internal improvements, sound banking, and social re-

forms. Following defeat in 1833, he cast his lot with the Whigs.

New York Governor

With Weed's help, Seward became the Whig candidate for governor of New York, and in 1837, when the poor economic situation made those in office look bad, he was elected. As governor for two terms, he attracted wide attention for his battle with Southern governors over the return of fugitive slaves and his efforts to secure equal opportunity for the education of Catholic children in New York. In 1842 he returned home to resume his law practice and to restore his depleted finances.

Seward was not, however, out of the public eye. His position against slavery had given him a leading place in the formation of the new Liberty party. His own idea was to take a firm but moderate course. "Let the world have assurance that we neither risk nor sympathize with convulsive, revolutionary or sanguine measures." He was for compensation to the slaveholder with "regard for his feelings" and for equal compassion "to the slave."

In 1846 two Negroes, both clearly insane, were brought to trial in Auburn on the charge of murder. Seward's eloquent defense of these two "spread his fame far and wide and his *Argument in Defense of William Freeman . . .* went into four editions the same year." William Gladstone called his summation "the finest forensic effort in the English language."

Seward was elected to the U.S. Senate in 1849. Sectional feelings had meantime become intense, and the Mexican War had raised again the issue of slavery in the territories. Seward supported a proviso barring slavery from any territory acquired from Mexico but sharply opposed Henry Clay's compromise bill, which left the slavery issue unsettled. Seward was reelected in 1854, the year Stephen A. Douglas introduced his Kansas-Nebraska Bill and the Republican party was created. He spoke against Douglas's bill but only gradually shifted to the new party.

In Lincoln's Cabinet

With the Republican victory in November 1860, Lincoln quickly chose Seward as secretary of state. Seward accepted with the assumption that responsibility for conducting the administration rested on his shoulders. He would assume the role of "prime minister" for a president who was inferior in experience and abilities to himself. Though he soon learned better, only the modesty and wisdom of a Lincoln would have endured Seward's unsolicited advice and his independent course in dealing with Southern matters. When he finally discovered that a conciliatory attitude and a willingness to leave slavery to each state was not enough to preserve the Union, Seward became one of Lincoln's most loyal defenders and, in the end, one of the nation's greatest secretaries of state.

Although Seward's conduct during the period that the Southern states began seceding from the Union is open to serious criticism, his handling of foreign affairs deserves the highest praise. While the North rejoiced at the seizure of two Confederate agents on board the British ship *Trent*, Seward wisely accepted England's protest and returned the men. He handled the matter of English and French recognition of the Confederacy with such dignity and firmness that neither took official action. His pressure, coupled with a veiled threat of dangerous consequences, caused British officials to "take due precautions" in outfitting Confederate privateers.

Seward urged Lincoln to run again in 1864. Seward was connected so closely with all that Lincoln represented that an attempt was made on his life the same night the President was assassinated. Seward remained in the Cabinet after Lincoln's death and supported President Andrew Johnson's efforts to bring the Southern states back into the Union. He remained loyal even when impeachment proceedings were brought against the President.

Seward rounded out his diplomatic career by crowding France and Maximilian out of Mexico, settling the Alabama Claims, and purchasing Alaska from Russia. He spent his last days traveling, ending with a trip around the world. He died at his home in Auburn, N.Y., on Oct. 10, 1872.

Further Reading

William H. Seward is listed in the American History study guide (VI, B, 1, a). In the Cabinet of Abraham LINCOLN, he was often in conflict with Secretary of the Treasury Salmon P. CHASE.

Seward's writings and speeches are gathered in *The Works of William H. Seward*, edited by George E. Baker (5 vols., 1884–1889). An indispensable biography is Glyndon G. Van Deusen, *William Henry Seward* (1967). The older, once standard life by Frederic Bancroft, *The Life of William H. Seward* (2 vols., 1900; repr. 1967), which devotes less space to Seward's personal life, remains useful for reference. Other biographies are T. K. Lothrop, *William Henry Seward* (1896), and Edward E. Hale, Jr., *William H. Seward* (1910). Seward figures prominently in James G. Randall, *Lincoln the President* (4 vols., 1946–1965).

SEYMOUR / By Harry Ammon

Horatio Seymour (1810–1886), a governor of New York, was a leading figure in the Democratic party. He owed his influence to his absolute integrity and his ability to bring conflicting factions together.

Horatio Seymour was born of a well-to-do family (his father was a banker) in the frontier village of Pompey Hill, N.Y., on May 31, 1810. He was admitted to the bar but practiced only briefly. From 1833 to 1839 he served as military secretary to New York governor William M. Marcy, his lifelong friend.

In 1841 Seymour entered the lower house of the New York Legislature. Although the conflict between two party factions endured for nearly 2 decades, Seymour was one of the few leaders capable of reconciling them even temporarily. Since he never sought to create a personal following through the use of patronage and generally followed a moderate course, he was able to command wide respect. He served as Speaker from 1845 to 1847 and in 1850 was elected governor, serving for two terms.

In national politics Seymour used his influence to preserve Democratic party harmony by supporting candidates, such as James Buchanan, who took the position that the Federal government lacked the power to regulate slavery. At the outbreak of the Civil War, he supported the Union cause but only in the expectation that a peaceful settlement would be arranged.

In 1862 Seymour was again elected governor, defeating a Radical Republican. Although he criticized Abraham Lincoln's excessive use of executive power and condemned the Emancipation Proclamation (which he ascribed to abolitionist influence), he worked diligently to fill New York's troop quotas for fighting the Civil War. Erroneous reports (propagated by Radical Republicans) that he had failed to take strong measures to repress the

Horatio Seymour, photographed by Mathew Brady about 1865. (Courtesy of The New-York Historical Society, New York City)

draft riots of 1863 in New York City because he wished to aid the Southern cause led to his defeat when he sought reelection in 1864.

In 1868 Seymour was nominated as the Democratic candidate to run against Ulysses S. Grant in the presidential election. A compromise candidate, he repudiated the party's written platform during his campaign. In spite of this action, he lost the election by a margin of only 300,000 votes. Refusing further offices, he continued to be a major influence in party politics. He aided Samuel J. Tilden in breaking the Tweed ring and backed efforts to reform Tammany Hall. He died in Albany on Feb. 12, 1886.

Further Reading

Horatio Seymour is listed in the American History study guide (VI, A, 2; VI, B, 1, c). He helped destroy the power of political boss William TWEED.

Stewart Mitchell, *Horatio Seymour of New York* (1938), is an excellent biography. See also De Alva S. Alexander, *A Political History of the State of New York* (4 vols., 1906–1923), and New York State Historical Association, *History of the State of New York*, edited by Alexander C. Flick (10 vols., 1933–1937; new ed., 5 vols., 1962).